DICTIONARY OF
CONTEMPORARY
AMERICAN
ARTISTS

DICTIONARY OF CONTEMPORARY AMERICAN ARTISTS

FIFTH EDITION

PAUL CUMMINGS

St. Martin's Press   New York

Library of Congress Cataloging in Publication Data

Cummings, Paul.
   Dictionary of contemporary American artists.

   Bibliography: p.
   Includes index.
   1. Artists—United States—Biography. 2. Art,
Modern—20th century—United States. I. Title.
N6536.C8   1982   709'.2'2 [B]   82-7337
ISBN 0-312-00232-7 (pbk.)

Design by Tim McKeen

Fifth Edition
10 9 8 7 6 5 4 3 2 1

Contents

Acknowledgments

To all the artists who graciously took time to complete the questionnaires I should again like to express my gratitude. Without their assistance this fifth revised edition could not have been completed.

In addition I wish to thank the many art dealers and their gallery staffs for so generously providing information and photographs for this and so many other projects. The following people and institutions deserve a particular word of gratitude: May Castleberry, librarian, Whitney Museum of American Art; the librarians and staff of The Museum of Modern Art, The New York Public Library, the Frick Art Reference Library, and the Metropolitan Museum of Art Library.

I should also like to acknowledge the significant editorial work of Deborah Felstehausen whose quick mind saved us from egregious fault in multiple instances in her checking of the manuscript in draft and its proofing. Many thanks to Shelley Leizman for fact checking and Janet Pietsch for typing the manuscript.

To the artists, collectors, museum and art dealers for permission to illustrate works of art in their possession, my sincere appreciation.

PC

June, 1987
New York City

How to Use This Book

This edition of the Dictionary, first published in 1966, has been extensively revised. 127 artists have been deleted; 87 have been added. The annotated bibliography has been expanded by over 100 titles. It serves as a ready reference for additional research and reading on these artists and on American art of the past half century. There is a new selection of illustrations.

Questionnaires, personal interviews, and intensive research have brought together significant data regarding the careers of these 900 artists, chosen essentially on the basis of the following criteria: representation in museum, public, and private collections; representation in major American and international exhibitions; influence as teachers; recognition received from fellow artists, dealers, critics, and others with a professional interest in the fine arts. May 1987 was chosen as the terminal date for all data, except for obituary notices which are accurate through July 1, 1987.

The artists' entries are organized on the following plan: where they studied art, and with whom; teaching experience; participation in the Federal Art Project; commissions executed; scholarships and/or awards won (P.P. in this category denotes "purchase prize" or "purchase award"); spouse (if prominent in art); address and dealer(s) of record; important one-man retrospectives, and group exhibitions (circ. in this category indicates that the exhibition circulated among various institutions); and bibliography. Archives, appearing at the end of some of the entries, indicates that the artist's papers and/or taped, in-depth interviews with the artist are available at the Archives of American Art, Smithsonian Institution. The Archives maintains complete mircofilm files in their Boston, New York, Washington, D.C., Detroit, and San Francisco offices.

Naturally many artists have won the same awards, been represented in the same exhibitions and collections, and are mentioned in the same books. Repetition of the complete data in each case would have made this volume far too large. Therefore the data have been compressed into a series of keys, found in the front of the book; the keyed, annotated bibliography is located at the back. Abbreviations used in the body of the book are explained in the keys. The often long and complex names of museums and public collections have generally been abbreviated and codified in the Key to Museums and Institutions. Commonsense methods have been used, most often acronyms (MOMA for The Museum of Modern Art) and reductions, either to the name of the city (Mons, for the Musée des Beaux-Arts, Mons,

Belgium), to a combination of city and key word (Albany/Institute for the Albany Institute of History and Art), or to city and acronym (Akron/AM for the Akron Art Museum).

In the listing entitled Galleries, addresses are given for those dealers representing the artists listed in this volume; other galleries cited in the Exhibitions portions of the entries are identified therein by city.

The use of boldface type in the Bibliography sections of the entries distinguishes the writings of the artist himself, comprehensive exhibition catalogues, or monographs.

The Index of Artists in the front of this volume offers both a pronunciation guide and breakdown of the types of work for which each artist is best known.

Example:
. . . **One-man Exhibitions:** (first) The Babcock Gallery, 1946; Blank Gallery, Washington, D.C., 1949. **Group:** Toledo/MA; Corcoran, 1950; NAD, 1951; Venice Biennials. **Collections:** Springfield, Mass./MFA; Montclair/AM. **Bibliography:** Baur 1, 5, **6, 7**.

Explanation:
Because it functions as a dealer, the address of The Babcock Gallery is given in the Gallery list at the front of this book; the Blank Gallery was located in Washington, D.C., at the time of this exhibition and may still be there, but it does not represent any of the artists listed. Toledo/MA stands for the Toledo Museum of Art, and its full name may be found under T in the Key to Museums; the names of all coded institutions are listed alphabetically in the Key. The bibliographic notation indicates that this artist, among others, is referred to in the four similarly numbered books among the seven by Baur listed in the Bibliography, with boldface number 6 being a monograph.

Illustrations

Pat Adams
Burst Round. 1985
10 × 11 in. mixed media on paper
Collection of Pamela Dickson
Courtesy Zabriskie Gallery
Photograph by D. James Dee

Gregory Amenoff
Avalon. 1987
92 × 56 in. oil on canvas
Courtesy Hirschl & Adler Modern
Photograph by Steven Sloman

Carl Andre
Sphinges. 1985
12 × 12 × 36 in. each; 36 × 132
× 132 in. overall. 16 Eastern
pine timbers
Courtesy Paula Cooper Gallery
Photograph by Geoffrey Clements

Richard Anuszkiewicz
Temple of Golden Orange. 1983
84 × 72 in. acrylic on canvas
Courtesy Graham Gallery
Photograph by Otto E. Nelson

Robert Arneson
Doggie Bob. 1982
36 × 33 × 21 in. glazed ceramic
Courtesy Allan Frumkin Gallery
Photograph by M. Lee Fatherree

Charles Arnoldi
Untitled. 1984
58½ × 96 × 4 in. oil on wood
Courtesy Charles Cowles Gallery,
Inc.

Richard Artschwager
Low Overhead. 1984-85
96 × 94 × 20 in. formica,
polychrome on wood
Courtesy Leo Castelli Gallery
Photograph by Dorothy Zeidman

Milton Avery
Artist's Wife. 1962
35 × 23 in. oil on paper
Courtesy Grace Borgenicht Gallery,
Inc.
Photograph by Walter Rosenblum

John Baeder
Moran Sq. Diner. 1986
42 × 66 in. oil on canvas
Courtesy O.K. Harris Works of Art
Photograph by D. James Dee

William Bailey
Still Life-Noto. 1986
40 × 50 in. oil on canvas
Courtesy Robert Schoelkopf Gallery

Robert Barnes
Secrets Revealed by the North Sea.
1984
55 × 60 in. oil on canvas
Courtesy Allan Frumkin Gallery
Photograph by eeva-inkeri

Will Barnet
Swing. 1986
45¼ × 48 in. oil on canvas
Courtesy Kennedy Galleries, Inc.

Leonard Baskin
Prodigal Son. 1922
55 in. bronze
Courtesy Kennedy Galleries, Inc.
Photograph by Taylor & Dull, Inc.

William Baziotes
Phantom. 1953
30⅛ × 37¾ in. oil on canvas
Courtesy BlumHelman Gallery Inc.
Photograph by Jerry L. Thompson

Jack Beal
Still-Life with Self Portrait. 1982
24 × 36 in. oil on canvas

Courtesy Allan Frumkin Gallery
Photograph by eeva-inkeri

Robert Bechtle
Sunset Stroller. 1985
48 × 69 in. oil on canvas
Courtesy O.K. Harris Works of Art
Photograph by D. James Dee

William Beckman
Diana, No. 6. 1983-85
84½ × 51 in. oil on panel
Courtesy Allan Frumkin Gallery
Photograph by eeva-inkeri

Tony Berlant
Untitled Romance, #61-1985. 1985
102 × 84 in. found metal collage
    on plywood with steelbrads and
    found painting
Courtesy Xavier Fourcade, Inc.

George Biddle
*King Street Movie, Charleston, South
    Carolina.* 1931
40 × 30 in. oil on canvas
Courtesy Deedee Wigmore Gallery

Charles Biederman
#34, Aix. 1972-74
42½ × 30 × 6¾ in. painted
    aluminum
Courtesy Grace Borgenicht Gallery

Robert Birmelin
Noticing Separate Things. 1985
48 × 96 in. acrylic on canvas
Courtesy Sherry French Gallery
Photograph by Adam Reich

Ronald Bladen
Harmon. 1985
35 × 20 × 18 in. aluminum and
    wood
Courtesy of Washburn Gallery

Hyman Bloom
Seascape I-85. 1985
56½ × 43¼ in. oil on canvas
Courtesy Kennedy Galleries, Inc.

Mel Bochner
Palisade. 1984

106½ × 78 in. oil on sized canvas
Courtesy Sonnabend Gallery
Photograph by Jon Abbott

Ilya Bolotowsky
Blue Diamond. 1940-41
29½ × 29½ in. oil on canvas
Courtesy of Washburn Gallery

William Brice
Untitled. 1984
50 × 58 in. oil on canvas
Courtesy of Robert Miller Gallery

Jonathan Borofsky
Head in the Trees at 2,942,771. 1985
828¹⁵⁄₁₆ × 480 × 84 in. enamel on
    aluminum
Courtesy Paula Cooper Gallery
Photograph by D. James Dee

Louise Bourgeois
Nature Study. 1986
35 × 61 × 29 in. marble
Courtesy Robert Miller Gallery
Photograph by Peter Bellamy

Roger Brown
Corporate Farms. 1985
72 × 48 in. oil on canvas
Courtesy Phyllis Kind Gallery

Deborah Butterfield
Blue Roan. 1985-86
30½ × 12 × 41 in. copper
    sheeting, patinaed steel
Courtesy Edward Thorp Gallery
Photograph by Zindman/Fremont

John Chamberlain
Iceberg. 1986
116½ × 42½ × 24 in. painted and
    chromium-plated steel
Courtesy Xavier Fourcade, Inc.
Photograph by Ivan Dalla Tana

Carmen Cicero
Running Scared. 1984
60 × 40 in. acrylic on canvas
Courtesy Graham Modern Gallery
Photograph by Ellen Page Wilson

William Copley
It's Raining in Chicago. 1985-86
77 × 60 in. oil on canvas
Courtesy Phyllis Kind Gallery

Ralston Crawford
H.M.S. Queen Mary. 1952
24 × 16 in. oil on canvas
Courtesy Robert Miller Gallery
Photograph by Steven Sloman

Ronald Davis
Star Drips Near Malibu. 1981
110 × 236 in. acrylic on canvas
Courtesy BlumHelman Gallery, Inc.

Stuart Davis
Town Square. 1924
26 × 34 in. oil on canvas
Courtesy Grace Borgenicht Gallery,
Inc.

George Deem
School of Caravaggio. 1984
34 × 42 in. oil on canvas
Courtesy of the artist

Willem de Kooning
Untitled III. 1984
80 × 70 in. oil on canvas
Courtesy Xavier Fourcade, Inc.

Walter De Maria
Large Rod Series: Circle/Rectangle 9.
1986
Circle diameter: 149⅜ in. nine-
sided stainless steel rods
Courtesy Xavier Fourcade, Inc.
Photograph by David Lubarsky

José de Rivera
Maquette for Hilton Hotel
Commission, Dallas, Texas. 1955
5¼ × 13 × 8½ in. stainless steel
painted yellow
Courtesy Grace Borgenicht Gallery,
Inc.
Photograph by Sarah Wells

David Deutsch
Curved Garden. 1983
18 × 18 in. acrylic, gouache and

pumice on paper mounted on
canvas
Courtesy BlumHelman Gallery, Inc.
Photograph by Bill Jacobson Studio

Rackstraw Downes
Portland Water District Wastewater
Treatment Plant. 1984
10 × 44 in. oil on canvas
Courtesy Hirschl & Adler Modern
Photograph by Zindman/Fremont

Martha Mayer Erlebacher
Girl on Cushions. 1983
16 × 20 in. pencil
Courtesy Robert Schoelkopf Gallery
Photograph by eeva-inkeri

Alan Feltus
Another Summer. 1984
48 × 36 in. oil on linen
Courtesy Forum Gallery

Joel Fisher
Family. 1987
11 × 6 × 6 in. bronze
Courtesy Diane Brown Gallery
Photography by Bill Jacobson
Studio

Eric Fischl
Salad Days (from "The Rooms of the
House"). 1985
84 × 168 in. oil on linen
Courtesy Mary Boone Gallery
Photography by Zindman/Fremont

Janet Fish
Flying Kites. 1986
95 × 80 in. oil on canvas
Courtesy Robert Miller Gallery

Llyn Foulkes
That Old Black Magic. 1985
67 × 57 in. mixed media
Courtesy Kent Fine Art

Mary Frank
Flowers: Auras and Reflections. 1984
35 × 28 in. monotype
Courtesy Zabriskie Gallery

Sondra Freckelton
Cut Flowers. 1979
44¼ × 45 in. watercolor
Courtesy Robert Schoelkopf Gallery
Photography by Nancy K. Lloyd

Paul Georges
Goodbye Sagaponack. 1983-84
113 × 192 in. oil on canvas
Courtesy Anne Plumb Gallery

Gregory Gillespie
Self Portrait. 1985
60 × 43 in. mixed panel
Courtesy Forum Gallery

Juan Gonzalez
New York, Year 1986. 1986
49 × 29 × 3 in. watercolor and
     gouache
Courtesy of Nancy Hoffman
     Gallery
Photography by Zindman/Fremont

Arshile Gorky
Fireplace in Virginia. 1946
21¾ × 29½ in. pencil and crayon
     on paper
Courtesy of Xavier Fourcade, Inc.
Photograph by Ivan Dalla Tana

Art Green
Common Knowledge. 1985
49½ × 30¼ in. oil on canvas
Courtesy of Phyllis Kind Gallery
Photograph by William H.
     Bengtson

Robert Grosvenor
Untitled. 1981-83
36 × 96 × 84 in. steel, vinyl
     coated steel and undercoating
Courtesy of Paula Cooper Gallery
Photography by Andrew Moore

Roy Gussow
Stelae 10-24-84. 1984
11½ × 8¾ × 8¾ in. stainless steel
Courtesy of Grace Borgenicht
     Gallery
Photograph by Sarah Wells

Duane Hanson
Working Cowboy. 1987
Lifesize. bronze
Courtesy of O.K. Harris Works of
     Art
Photograph by D. James Dee

Philip Hanson
Tantric Jacket. 1983
44¹¹⁄₁₆ × 36¾ in. oil on canvas
Courtesy of Phyllis Kind Gallery

Eva Hesse
Accession II. 1967
36 × 36 × 36 in.
Courtesy Xavier Fourcade Gallery

Tom Holland
Pine. 1981
72½ × 50 × 4¾ in. epoxy on
     aluminum
Courtesy Charles Cowles Gallery
Photograph by M. Lee Fatherree

Robert Hudson
Gaze. 1985-86
31⅛ × 18¾ × 16 in. unique
     polychrome bronze
Courtesy Allan Frumkin Gallery
Photograph by M. Lee Fatherree

John Hultberg
Habitable Void. 1979
48 × 66 in. oil on canvas
Courtesy Anita Shapolsky Gallery

Bryan Hunt
Dancers. 1985
92¼ × 27⅝ × 24 in. overall. cast
     bronze on limestone base
Courtesy BlumHelman Gallery
Photograph by Jerry L. Thompson

John Stuart Ingle
Still Life with Daguerrotypes. 1985
21½ × 16 in. watercolor on paper
Courtesy of Tatistcheff Gallery, Inc.

Angelo Ippolito
August Landscape. 1973
50 × 55 in. oil on canvas
Courtesy Grace Borgenicht Gallery

Valerie Jaudon
File. 1986
94 × 94 in. oil on linen
Courtesy Sidney Janis Gallery
Photograph by Allan Finkelman

Paul Jenkins
Phenomena White Shadow. 1984
58 × 77 in. acrylic on canvas
Courtesy Gimpel & Weitzenhoffer
Ltd.
Photograph by Margaret Dwyer
Becker

Bill Jensen
Denial. 1983-86
40 × 31 in. oil on linen
Courtesy Washburn Gallery
Photograph by Geoffrey Clements

Jasper Johns
Untitled. 1984
75 × 50 in. oil on canvas
Courtesy Leo Castelli Gallery
Photograph by Dorothy Zeidman

Lester Johnson
Untitled. 1983
40 × 50 in. oil on canvas
Courtesy Zabriskie Gallery
Photograph by Joseph Szaszfai

Donald Judd
Untitled. 1986
39⅜ × 39⅜ × 19⅝ in. cor-ten
steel and purple plexiglass
Courtesy Paula Cooper Gallery
Photograph by D. James Dee

John Kacere
Lauren. 1984
40 × 80 in. oil on canvas
Courtesy O.K. Harris Works of Art
Photograph by D. James Dee

Wolf Kahn
Barn in a Warm Tonality. 1982
36 × 52 in. oil on canvas
Courtesy of Grace Borgenicht
Gallery
Photograph by Larry Bercow

Alex Katz
Rudy. 1980
71 × 10 in. oil on aluminum
Courtesy Robert Miller Gallery
Photograph by eeva-inkeri

Ellsworth Kelly
Dark Blue. 1986
109½ × 108 in. oil on canvas
Courtesy of BlumHelman Gallery,
Inc.
Photograph by Jerry L. Thompson

Frederick Kiesler
Arch as Triumph of Man. 1964
78 × 102 × 40 in. bronze,
aluminum and gold plate
Courtesy Jason McCoy, Inc.

Barry LeVa
Sculptured Activities: Silver Green.
1986-87
60 × 60 in. spray-paint, ink,
collage on paper
Courtesy Sonabend Gallery

Les Levine
Breathe, Move, Mind. 1985
108 × 96 in. oilstick on canvas
Courtesy Ted Greenwald Gallery
Photograph by Les Levine

Roy Lichtenstein
Mountain Village. 1985
9 × 14 in. oil and magna on
canvas
Courtesy Leo Castelli Gallery
Photograph by Dorothy Zeidman

Frank Lobdell
Winter 1979. 1979
96 × 78 in. oil on canvas
Courtesy of Oscarsson Siegeltuch
Gallery
Photograph by Ellen Page Wilson

David Lund
Coral Bluff. 1980
58 × 44 in. oil on canvas
Courtesy of Grace Borgenicht
Gallery

Robert Mangold
*Four Color Frame Painting #15
(Variant)*. 1985
42 × 31 in. acrylic, pencil on 4
sheets of paper
Courtesy of Paula Cooper Gallery
Photograph by Geoffrey Clements

Brice Marden
Untitled 3. 1986-87
72 × 58 in. oil on linen
Courtesy of Mary Boone Gallery
Photograph by Zindman/Fremont

Marisol
Portrait of William Burroughs. 1981
57¾ × 27¾ × 29 in. charcoal and
acrylic on wood, plaster and
electric lights
Courtesy of Sidney Janis Gallery
Photograph by Allan Finkelman

Robert Morris
Untitled. 1955-83
55¾ × 65½ in. cast hydrocal,
graphite on paper
Courtesy of Sonnabend Gallery
Photograph by Jon Abbott

Catherine Murphy
Cellar Light. 1985
35½ × 46 in. oil on canvas
Courtesy of Xavier Fourcade, Inc.
Photograph by Ivan Dalla Tana

Elizabeth Murray
Slip Away. 1986
129½ × 101½ × 9 in. oil on
canvas
Courtesy of Paula Cooper Gallery
Photograph by D. James Dee

Robert Natkin
Hitchcock Series. 1984
48 × 44 in. acrylic on canvas
Courtesy of Gimpel &
Weitzenhoffer Gallery

Manuel Neri
Mujer Pegada Series No. 3. 1985
75½ × 55½ × 10½ in. bronze
Courtesy of Charles Cowles Gallery
Photograph by M. Lee Fatherree

Gladys Nilsson
Forewarned. 1986
60 × 40 in. watercolor on paper
Courtesy of Phyllis Kind Gallery

Jim Nutt
What I've Got Is Much Worse! 1984
30⅞ × 30⁵⁄₁₆ in. acrylic on
masonite and wood
Courtesy of Phyllis Kind Gallery
Photograph by William H.
Bengtson

Doug Ohlson
Lady X. 1985
62 × 60 in. acrylic on canvas
Courtesy of Ruth Siegel Ltd.

Claes Oldenburg
*Proposal for a Monument to the
Survival of the University of El
Salvador: Blasted Pencil (Which
Still Writes)*. model, 1983
11 × 24 × 84 in. cardboard,
wood, urethane foam, resin, etc.
Courtesy of Leo Castelli Gallery
Photograph by Dorothy Zeidman

John Opper
Color Series 8-72. 1972
56 × 80 in. acrylic
Courtesy of Grace Borgenicht
Gallery
Photograph by Walter Rosenblum

Alfonso Ossorio
Sunt Lacrimae Rerum. 1982
96 × 48 in. mixed media
Courtesy of Oscarsson Siegeltuch
Gallery
Photography by Noel Rowe

Ed Paschke
Joeski. 1986
68 × 80 in. oil on linen
Courtesy of Phyllis Kind Gallery
Photograph by William H.
Bengtson

Philip Pearlstein
Two Nudes on Bedouin Carpet. 1987
41½ × 30 in. watercolor on paper

Courtesy of Hirschl & Adler
Modern
Photograph by Zindman/Fremont

Gabor Peterdi
Werland Gold. 1978-79
40 × 64 in. oil on canvas
Courtesy of Grace Borgenicht
Gallery

Irving Petlin
*On the Beach . . . in the Spirit of
Evaporation*. 1985
84 × 96 in. oil on canvas
Courtesy of Kent Fine Art, Inc.

Jackson Pollock
Untitled Drawing. 1944
9½ × 7¾ in. pen and crayon on
paper
Courtesy of Jason McCoy Inc.

Joseph Raffael
Haven. 1986
77 × 57 in. oil on canvas
Courtesy of Nancy Hoffman Gallery
Photograph by Zindman/Fremont

Robert Rauschenberg
Tatoo (Spread). 1981
73½ × 96½ × 17 in. solvent
transfer on cloth, objects
mounted on paper
Courtesy of Sonnabend Gallery
Photograph by Jon Abbott

Edda Renouf
Gongs. 1985
59 × 93 in. oil and acrylic on linen
Courtesy of BlumHelman Gallery,
Inc.
Photograph by Andrew Moore

Paul Resika
Horseleech Pond, Grey. 1984
27½ × 40 in. oil on canvas
Courtesy of Graham Modern
Gallery
Photograph by Ellen Page Wilson

Milton Resnick
Straws in the Wind #1. 1981

80 × 60 in. oil on linen
Courtesy of Robert Miller Gallery

George Rickey
Two Open Triangles Up. 1983
52 × 44 × 6 in. stainless steel
Courtesy of Zabriskie Gallery
Photograph by Eric Pollitzer

Dorothea Rockburne
Narcissus. 1984
Three panels 97 × 123 × 6⅜ in.;
93 × 123 × 6⅜ in. oil on
gessoed linen
Courtesy of Xavier Fourcade, Inc.

Robert Rohm
Untitled (Post). 1986
70 × 24 × 55 in. wood, steel, with
paint and encaustic
Courtesy of O.K. Harris Works of
Art
Photograph by D. James Dee

James Rosenquist
Mute Transformations II. 1985-86
Two panels, each 120 × 60 in. oil
on canvas
Courtesy of Leo Castelli Gallery
Photograph by Dorothy Zeldman

Barbara Rossi
Day for Divers. 1982
31⅝ × 41⅝ in. acrylic on masonite
Courtesy of Phyllis Kind Gallery
Photograph by William Bengtson

Theodore Roszak
White and Steel Polars. 1945
106 in. steel and wood
Courtesy of Zabriskie Gallery
Photograph by J. Ferrari

David Salle
Maid of Germany. 1986
108 × 148 (2) in. acrylic, fabric, oil,
wood on canvas
Courtesy of Mary Boone Gallery
Photograph by Zindman/Fremont

Peter Saul
Self Portrait: Splithead ($10). 1986
40 × 59½ in. acrylic on paper

Courtesy of Allan Frumkin Gallery
Photograph by eeva-inkeri

Wade Saunders
Breathe. 1986
36 × 36 × 12 in. bronze and gold
Courtesy of Diane Brown Gallery
Photograph by Bill Jacobson

Salvatore Scarpitta
Trolley Stop. 1979
21 × 30 × 7 in. enamel and
plasticized canvas
Courtesy of Leo Castelli Gallery
Photograph by Zindman/Fremont

George Segal
Nude on Coach (On Her Stomach).
1985
43 × 68 × 39 in. plaster and
mixed media
Courtesy of Sidney Janis Gallery
Photograph by Allan Finkelman

Joel Shapiro
Untitled. 1986
50½ × 35¾ × 30¼ in. bronze
Courtesy of Paula Cooper Gallery
Photograph by D. James Dee

Kenneth Snelson
Model for Virlane Tower. 1980
129 × 23½ × 26½ in. aluminum
and stainless steel
Courtesy of Zabriskie Gallery

Raphael Soyer
Elissa
40 × 30 in. oil on canvas
Courtesy of Forum Gallery
Photograph by eeva-inkeri

Richard Stankiewicz
1972-1. 1972
28 × 22 × 21 in. steel
Courtesy of Zabriskie Gallery
Photograph by Strong-Meyer

Gary Stephan
Madame As Recamier. 1986
13½ × 32 × 10 in. bronze
Courtesy of Mary Boone Gallery
Photograph by Zindman/Fremont

George Sugarman
For Watteau. 1984
58 × 64 × 42 in. painted
aluminum
Courtesy Robert Miller Gallery, Inc.
Photograph by Steven Sloman

Donald Sultan
*Five Lemons and Tangerine, April 21,
1986.* 1986
12⅜ × 12½ in. oil, spackle and tar
on tile over wood
Courtesy of BlumHelman Gallery,
Inc.
Photograph by Bill Jacobson

Michael Todd
Shiva's Dance IV. 1986
39½ × 39 × 15 in. stainless steel
Courtesy of Charles Cowles Gallery

Joyce Treiman
Sailing Away. 1985-86
48 × 30 in. oil on canvas
Courtesy of Schmidt Bingham
Gallery

David True
Promises Kept. 1986
60 × 72 in. acrylic on canvas
Courtesy of BlumHelman Gallery,
Inc.

Richard Tuttle
Blue Over. 1986
16½ × 12 × 5 in. foam core,
cardboard, styrofoam, wire, hot
glue, acrylic with powdered
pigments, enamel
Courtesy of BlumHelman Gallery
Inc.
Photograph by Bill Jacobson

Jack Tworkov
Q3-82-OP#10. 1981
15 × 22 in. oil on paper
Courtesy of Nancy Hoffman
Gallery
Photograph by Alan Zindman

James Valerio
Spring Mambo. 1986
96 × 110 in. oil on canvas

Courtesy of Allan Frumkin Gallery
Photograph by eeva-inkeri

Peter Voulkos
Untitled. 1982
39¼ × 24 in. ceramic
Courtesy of Charles Cowles Gallery
Photograph by eeva-inkeri

Andy Warhol
Self Portrait. 1979
40 × 40 in. acrylic and silkscreen
on canvas
Courtesy of Leo Castelli Gallery
Photograph by Dorothy Zeidman

Idelle Weber
The Saugerties Vase I. 1986
24 × 20¼ in. oil on linen
Courtesy of Ruth Siegel Ltd.

James Weeks
Towards the Japanese Gardens.
1983–84
84 × 66 in. acrylic on canvas
Courtesy of Hirschl & Adler
Modern
Photograph by Koplin Gallery

Tom Wesselmann
Amy in the Bedroom. 1986
55 × 95 in. enamel on laser-cut
steel
Courtesy of Sidney Janis Gallery

H. C. Westermann
Death Ship Out of San Pedro, Adrift.
1980
6 × 7 × 24 in. gaboon ebony and
brass
Courtesy of Xavier Fourcade, Inc.
Photograph by Bruce C. Jones

Margaret Wharton
Chastity. 1985
32½ × 18 × 3 in. wood
construction
Courtesy of Phyllis Kind Gallery

Paul Wiesenfeld
Still Life with Oranges. 1974
38¼ × 39½ in. oil on canvas

Courtesy Robert Schoelkopf Gallery
Photograph by eeva-inkeri

John Wilde
*Myself Lecturing on the Divine
Physiognomy of Rock.* 1983
8 × 11 in. oil on wood panel
Courtesy of Schmidt Bingham
Gallery

William T. Wiley
For Guitar Players Forsoothe Sayers.
1985
110 × 91 in. acrylic and graphite
on canvas
Courtesy of Allan Frumkin Gallery
Photograph by eeva-inkeri

Christopher Wilmarth
Delancey Backs. 1983-86
96 × 26 × 30 in. glass, steel,
bronze
Courtesy of Hirschl & Adler
Modern
Photograph by Jerry L. Thompson

Thornton Willis
Split End. 1984
84 × 84 in. cardboard and acrylic
on canvas
Courtesy of Oscarsson Siegeltuch
Gallery
Photograph by Allan Finkelman

Karl Wirsum
*Martian Arts Made with Pre-War
Rubber.* 1984
58½ × 42⅜ in. acrylic on canvas
Courtesy of Phyllis Kind Gallery

Isaac Witkin
Waife's Anchor. 1985
28½ × 26 × 8 in. bronze
Courtesy of Hirschl & Adler
Modern
Photograph by Pelka/Noble

Jerome Witkin
Tit for Tat. 1983-84
62 × 73 in. oil on canvas
Courtesy of Sherry French Gallery
Photograph by Geoffrey Clements

Philip Wofford
   Child's Prayer Wheel. 1985
   31¾ × 37 in. oil and acrylic on
   canvas
   Courtesy of Nancy Hoffman
   Gallery
   Photograph by Zindman/Fremont

Paul Wonner
   The Five Senses. 1984
   72 × 72 in. acrylic on canvas
   Courtesy of Hirschl & Adler
   Modern
   Photograph by Zindman/Fremont

Jack Youngerman
   Untitled. 1986
   30 × 22¼ in. charcoal and pastel
   on paper
   Courtesy of Washburn Gallery
   Photograph by Geoffrey Clements

Ray Yoshida
   Mindless Mimic. 1985
   38 × 50 in. acrylic on canvas
   Courtesy of Phyllis Kind Gallery
   Photograph by William H.
   Bengtson

Index of Artists
and Pronunciation Guide

(A) Painter; (A¹) Watercolorist; (B) Sculptor; (C) Printmaker; (D) Assemblagist; (E) Teacher; (F) Happenings; (G) Mosaicist; (H) Draftsman; (I) Conceptualist.

A

Aach, Herb (A)
Acconci, Vito (B)
  Ah con she
Acton, Arlo C. (B)
Adams, Clinton (A, C)
Adams, Pat (A)
Adler, Samuel M.
Agostini, Peter (B)
Albers, Josef (A, C, E)
Albert, Calvin (B)
Albright, Ivan Le Lorraine (A)
Alcalay, Albert (A)
Alexander, John (A)
Alexander, Peter (A)
Allan, William B. (A)
Altman, Harold (C, A)
Altoon, John (A)
Amen, Irving (C)
Amenoff, Gregory (A)
Anderson, Guy Irving (A)
Anderson, Jeremy (B)
Anderson, John S. (B)
Anderson, Lennart (A)
Andre, Carl (B)
Andrejevic, Milet (A)
  An **dre** avic
Andrews, Oliver (B)
Antonakos, Stephen (B)
Antresian, Garo (C)
  An **tray** sian
Anuskiewicz, Richard (A)
  Anu **skay** vitch
Arakawa, Shusaku (A, C)
Archipenko, Alexander (B, E)
Armajani, Siah (B)
  See ah
Arman (B, D)
Arneson, Robert (B)
Arnold, Anne (B)
Arnoldi, Charles (B)

Aronson, David (A)
Artschwager, Richard (A, B)
Ault, George (A)
Avedisian, Edward (A)
Avery, Milton (A)
Aycock, Alice (B)
Azuma, Norio (C)

B

Baber, Alice (A)
Baeder, John (A)
  Bay der
Baer, Jo (A)
  Bear
Bailey, William (A, E)
Baizerman, Saul (B)
Baldessari, John (I)
Bannard, Walter Darby (A)
Barnes, Robert (A)
Barnet, Will (A, C, E)
Barry, Robert (B, I)
Barth, Frances (A)
Bartlett, Jennifer (A)
Baskin, Leonard (B, C, E)
Bayer, Herbert (A)
Baynard, Edward (A, C)
Baziotes, William A. (A, E)
Beal, Gifford (A)
Beal, Jack (A)
Bearden, Romare (A)
  Roh **mayr**
Beasley, Bruce (B)
Beauchamp, Robert (A)
  Beechem
Bechtle, Robert (A)
  Beck tl
Beck, Rosemarie (A)
Beckman, William G. (A)
Behl, Wolfgang (B)

Bell, Charles (A)
Bell, Larry (B)
Benglis, Lynda (B)
Bengston, Billy Al (A)
Benjamin, Karl (A)
Benton, Fletcher (B)
Benton, Thomas Hart (A, B)
Ben-Zion (A)
Berger, Jason (A)
Berlant, Tony (B)
Berman, Eugene (A)
Berthot, Jake (A)
    Bear toe
Bertoia, Harry (B)
    Ber **toy** a
Bess, Forrest Clemenger (A)
Biddle, George (A, C)
Biederman, Charles (Karel) Joseph
    (B)
    Bee derman
Bireline, George (A)
    Beer e line
Birmelin, A. Robert (A, E)
Bischoff, Elmer (A)
    Bish off
Bishop, Isabel (A)
Bishop, James (A)
Blackwell, Tom (A)
Bladen, Ronald (B)
Blaine, Nell (A)
Blanch, Arnold (A)
Blaustein, Al (A)
Bleifeld, Stanley (A)
Bloom, Hyman (A)
Bluemner, Oscar (A)
    Bloom ner
Bluhm, Norman (A)
    Bloom
Blume, Peter (A)
Boardman, Seymour (A)
Bochner, Mel (B, I)
Boghosian, Varujan (B, D)
    Ba **go** sian
Bohrod, Aaron (A)
Boice, Bruce (A)
Bollinger, William (B)
Bolomey, Roger (B)
    Bolo **may**
Bolotowsky, Ilya (A, B, E)
Bonevardi, Marcelo (A)
Bontecou, Lee (B)
Borofsky, Jonathan (A, B)
Bosa, Louis (A)

Bourgeois, Louise (B)
    Boor **jwah**
Bowman, Richard (A)
Boxer, Stanley (A, B)
Boyce, Richard (B, E)
Boyle, Keith (A)
Boynton, James W. (A)
Brach, Paul (A)
    Brock
Brackman, Robert (A)
Brady, Carolyn (A[1])
Brainard, Joe (A)
Brandt, Warren (A)
Brauntuch, Troy (A)
Brecht, George (A, B, D, F)
Breer, Robert (B)
Brice, William (A)
Briggs, Ernest (A)
Broderson, Morris (Gaylord) (A)
Broner, Robert (A, C)
    Brauner
Brook, Alexander (A)
Brooks, James (A)
Brown, Joan (A)
Brown, Roger (A)
Brown, William Theo (A)
Browne, Byron (A, E)
Browning, Colleen (A)
Bruce, Patrick Henry (A)
Buchwald, Howard (A)
Buck, John (A)
Bultman, Fritz (A, B)
Bunce, Louis (A)
Burchfield, Charles (A[1])
Burden, Chris (B, F, I)
Burkhardt, H. G. (A)
Burlin, Paul (A)
Burliuk, Paul (A)
Burton, Scott (B)
Butterfield, Deborah (B)
Button, John (A)

C

Cadmus, Paul (A)
Caesar, Doris (B)
Cajori, Charles (A)
Calcagno, Lawrence (A)
    Cal **cahn** yo
Calder, Alexander (B)
Callahan, Kenneth (A)
Callery, Mary (B)

Caparn, Rhys (A, B)
  Ca parn, Reese
Carles, Arthur B. (A, B)
  Carls
Casarella, Edmond (C)
Castellon, Federico (C, A)
Cavallon, Giorgio (A)
Celmins, Vija (A)
  Sell mins, **Vee** yah
Chaet, Bernard (A)
  Chate
Chamberlain, John (A, B)
Chinni, Peter (B)
  Keeny
Christensen, Dan (A)
Christo (B, D)
Chryssa (B)
  Kree sa
Cicero, Carmen Louis (A)
Clarke, John Clem (A)
Clerk, Pierre (A, C)
Cloar, Carroll (A)
  Clore
Close, Chuck (A)
Clutz, William (A)
Coates, Ross (A)
Congdon, William (A)
Conlon, William (A)
Conncr, Bruce (D, A)
Conover, Robert (A)
Cook, Howard (A)
Copley, William N. (CPLY) (A)
Corbett, Edward (A)
Cornell, Joseph (D)
Cornell, Thomas (A, C)
Cottingham, Robert (A)
Covert, John (A)
Cramer, Konrad (A)
  Craw mer
Crawford, Ralston (A)
Cremean, Robert (A)
  Cre **mee** an
Crile, Susan (A)
  Cry il
Criss, Francis H. (A)
Cronbach, Robert M. (B)
Cronin, Robert (B)
Curry, John Steuart (A)

D

Dallman, Daniel (A)

Daphnis, Nassos (A, B)
D'Arcangelo, Allan (A)
Darrow, Paul Gardner (A)
Dasburg, Andrew (A)
Dash, Robert (A)
Davis, Gene (A)
Davis, Jerrold (A)
Davis, Ronald (A)
Davis, Stuart (A)
DeAndrea, John (B)
de Creeft, Jose (B)
Deem, George (A)
De Forest, Roy Dean (A)
Dehn, Adolf Arthur (A, C)
Dehner, Dorothy (B)
De Knight, Avel (A, A[1])
de Kooning, Elaine (A)
de Kooning, Willem (A)
DeLap, Tony (B)
Della-Volpe, Ralph (A)
De Maria, Walter (B)
Demuth, Charles (A)
Denby, Jillian (A)
De Niro, Robert (A)
de Rivera, Jose (B)
Deshaies, Arthur (C)
  De **shay**
Deutsch, David (A)
Dickinson, Edwin (A, E)
Diebenkorn, Richard (A)
  Dee ben korn
Dill, Laddie John (A)
Diller, Burgoyne (A, E)
Dine, Jim (A, F)
di Suvero, Mark (B)
Dobkin, Alexander (A)
Dodd, Lamar (A, E)
Dodd, Lois (A)
Dole, William (A)
Donati, Enrico (A)
Dove, Arthur (A)
Downes, Rackstraw (A)
Doyle, Tom (B)
Drewes, Werner (A, E)
  Dray vess
Drummond, Sally Hazelet (A)
Du Bois, Guy Pene (A)
  Du **Bwah**
Duchamp, Marcel (A)
Duff, John (B)
Dugmore, Edward (A)
Duran, Robert (A)
Dzubas, Friedel (A)

E

Eddy, Don (A)
Edmondson, Leonard (A)
Engman, Robert (B)
Erlebacher, Martha Meyer (A, G)
Ernst, Jimmy (A)
Estes, Richard (A)
Etting, Emlen (A)
Evergood, Philip Howard Francis
    Dixon (A)

F

Fahlstrom, Oyvind (A, F)
Faulkner, Frank (A)
Feeley, Paul (A, E)
Feininger, Lyonel (A)
Feitelson, Lorser (A)
Feltus, Alan (A)
Ferber, Herbert (B)
Ferrara, Jackie (B)
Ferren, John (A, E)
Fiene, Ernst (A)
Fischl, Eric (A)
Fish, Janet (A)
Fisher, Joel (B)
Flack, Audrey (A)
Flannagan, John (B)
Flavin, Dan (B)
Fleischner, Richard (B, I)
Forakis, Peter (A, B)
Forst, Miles (A)
Foulkes, Llyn (A)
    Folks
Francis, Sam (A, C)
Frank, Mary (B)
Frankenthaler, Helen (A)
Frasconi, Antonio (C)
Freckelton, Sondra (A[1])
Freilicher, Jane (A)
    Fry likker
French, Jared (A)
Friedensohn, Elias (A, B)
Fuller, Sue (B)

G

Gablik, Suzi (A, E)
Gabo, Naum Neemia Pevsner (B)
Gallatin, Albert E. (A)
    Gal atin
Gallo, Frank (B)

Ganso, Emil (A)
Garet, Jedd (A)
Gatch, Lee (A)
Gechtoff, Sonia (A)
    Getch off
George, Thomas (A)
Georges, Paul (A)
    George's
Gibran, Kahlil (A)
Gikow, Ruth (A)
    Geeko
Gillespie, Gregory (A)
Gilliam, Sam (A)
Ginnever, Charles (B)
Giobbi, Edward (A)
Glackens, William (A)
Glarner, Fritz (A)
Glasco, Josephy (A)
Goings, Ralph (A)
Goldberg, Michael (A)
Goldin, Leon (A)
Golub, Leon (A)
Gonzalez, Juan J. (A)
Gonzalez, Xavier (A)
Goode, Joe (A)
Goodman, Sidney (A)
Goodnough, Robert (A)
    Good know
Goodyear, John (B)
Gorchov, Ron (A)
Gordin, Sidney (B)
Gordy, Robert (A)
Gorky, Arshile (A)
Goto, Joseph (B)
Gottlieb, Adolph (A)
Goulet, Lorrie (B)
    Goo **lay**
Graham, John D. (A)
Graham, Robert (B)
Granlund, Paul (B)
Graves, Morris Cole (A)
Graves, Nancy Stevenson (A, B)
Gray, Cleve (A)
Green, Art (A)
Green, George D. (A)
Greene, Balcomb (A, E)
Greene, Stephen (A)
Greenly, Colin (B)
Gregor, Harold Laurence (A)
Griefen, John Adams (A)
Grillo, John (A)
Grippe, Peter (B)
    Grippy

LeWitt, Sol (B)
Liberman, Alexander (A, B)
Lichtenstein, Roy (A)
   Lick ten stine
Ligare, David (A)
Lindner, Richard (A)
Lipchitz, Jacques (B)
Lippold, Richard (B)
Lipton, Seymour (B)
Lobdell, Frank (A)
Loberg, Robert W. (A)
Loew, Michael (A)
   Lowe
Longo, Robert (A)
Longo, Vincent (A, C, E)
Loran, Erle (A, E)
Lorber, Stephen (A)
Lostutter, Robert (A, A[1])
Louis, Morris (A)
   Lewis
Lozowick, Louis (A)
Lucchesi, Bruno (B)
Lund, David (A)
Lundeberg, Helen (A)
Lye, Len (B)
Lytle, Richard (A)
   Littell

M
MacConnel, Kim (A)
Macdonald-Wright, Stanton (A)
MacIver, Loren (A)
   Mac **Eye** ver
Madsen, Loren (B)
Mallary, Robert (B)
Mangold, Robert (A)
Mangold, Sylvia Plimack (A)
Man Ray (A)
Manship, Paul (B)
Manso, Leo (A)
Marca-Relli, Conrad (A)
Marcus, Marsha (A)
Marden, Brice (A)
Margo, Boris (A, C)
Marin, John (A[1])
Marisol (Escobar) (B)
Markman, Ronald (A)
Marsh, Reginald (A, E)
Marsicano, Nicholas (A)
Martin, Agnes (A)
Martin, Fred (A, H)

Martin, Knox (A)
Martinelli, Ezio (B)
Maryan (A, C)
Mason, Alice Trumbull (A)
Matulka, Jan (A, E)
Mayhew, Richard (A)
Mazur, Michael B. (A)
McChesney, Robert P. (A)
McCracken, John (B)
McFee, Henry Lee (A)
McGarrell, James (A)
McLaughlin, John (A)
McLean, Richard (A)
McNeil, George (A)
Meeker, Dean Jackson (C)
Meigs, Walter (A)
   Megs
Menkes, Sigmund (A)
   Menkeys
Mesibov, Hugh (B)
Middaugh, Robert (A, A[1])
   Mid dah
Miller, Kenneth Hayes (A, E)
Miller, Richard (A)
Miller, Richard McDermott (A)
Mitchell, Fred (A)
Mitchell, Joan (A)
Maholy-Nagy, Laszlo (B)
   Ma **holy**-Nazh
Moller, Hans (A)
Moore, John (A)
Morley, Malcomb (A)
Morris, Carl (A)
Morris, George L. K. (A)
Morris, Robert (A, B, F)
Moskowitz, Robert (A)
Motherwell, Robert (A)
Moy, Seong (A)
Moyer, Roy (I)
Muller, Jan (A)
Mullican, Lee (A)
Murch, Walter Tandy (A)
Murphy, Catherine (A)
Murray, Elizabeth (A)
Murray, Robert (B)

N
Nadelman, Elie (B)
Nakian, Reuben (B)
Natkin, Robert (A)
Nauman, Bruce (B, I)

Neal, Reginald (A, C)
Nepote, Alexander (A)
    Ne **po** ty
Neri, Manuel (B)
Nesbitt, Lowell (A)
Neuman, Robert S. (A)
    Newman
Nevelson, Louise (B)
Nevelson, Mike (B)
Newman, Barnett (A)
Nice, Don (A)
Nick, George (A)
Nilsson, Gladys (A)
Nivola, Constantino (B)
Noguchi, Isamu (B)
Noland, Kenneth (A)
Novros, David (A)
Nowack, Wayne K. (A)
Nutt, Jim (A)

O
Ohlson, Doug (A)
Okada, Kenzo (A)
Okamura, Arthur (A)
O'Keeffe, Georgia (A)
Okulick, John (B)
Oldenburg, Claes Thure (A, B, F)
    Klaus
Olitski, Jules (A)
Oliveira, Nathan (A)
Onslow-Ford, Gordon (A)
Oppenheim, Dennis (I)
Opper, John (A, E)
Ortman, George (A)
Ossorio, Alfonso (A)
Osver, Arthur (A)
Ott, Jerry (A)

P
Pace, Stephen (A)
Padovano, Anthony (B)
Paik, Nam June (D, I)
    Pike
Palmer, William C. (A)
Paone, Peter (A, C)
    Pay **oh** ni
Paris, Howard P. (B)
Park, David (A)
Parker, Raymond (A)

Parker, Robert Andrew (A)
Parrish, David (A)
Paschke, Ed (A)
Pearlstein, Philip (A)
Pearson, Henry Charles (A)
Peirce, Waldo (A)
Penney, James (A)
Pepper, Beverly (B)
Pereira, I. Rice (A)
    Per **err** a
Perlin, Bernard (A)
Perlman, Joel (A)
Peterdi, Gabor (C, A)
    Pet er di
Petersen, Roland Conrad (A)
Petlin, Irving (A)
Pettet, William (A)
Pfriem, Bernard (A)
    Freem
Phillips, Matt (A, C)
Pineda, Marianna (B)
    Peen **yay** da
Pinto, Jody (A, B)
Plagens, Peter (A, E)
Pollack, Reginald (A)
Pollock, Jackson (A)
Ponce de Leon, Michael (C)
Pond, Clayton (A, C)
Poons, Lawrence M. (A, C)
Poor, Henry Varnum (A)
Porter, David (A)
Porter, Fairfield (A)
Porter, Katherine (A)
Porter, Liliana (A, C)
Portnow, Marjorie (A)
Posen, Stephen (A)
Pousette-Dart, Richard (A)
Pozzatti, Rudy (C)
Prestopino, Gregorio (A)
Price, Kenneth (B, C)

Q
Quaytman, Harvey (A)
Quisgard, Liz Whitney (A)

R
Rabkin, Leo (A)
Racz, Andre (A, C)
    Racks

Key to Museums and Institutions and Their Schools
that own works of art by the artists in this book

A

AAIAL. American Academy and Institute of Arts and Letters, NYC; formerly **AAAL**, American Academy of Arts and Letters, NYC

A.F.A. American Federation of Arts, NYC

ASL. Art Students League, NYC

AT&T. American Telephone and Telegraph Co.

Aachen. Museen der Stadt Aachen, West Germany

Aachen/Kunstverein. Kunstverein, Aachen, West Germany

Aachen/Ludwig. Neue Galerie-Sammlung Ludwig, Aachen, West Germany

Aachen/NG. Neue Galerie in der Stadt Aachen, Aachen, West Germany

Aachen/S-L. Suermondt-Ludwig Museum, Aachen, West Germany

Abbott Academy, Andover, Mass.

Abbott Laboratories

Abilene Christian College

Academy of Fine Arts, Warsaw—*see* Warsaw

Academy of Natural Sciences, Philadelphia—*see* PMA

Achenbach Foundation for Graphic Arts, San Francisco

Ackland. William Hays Ackland Memorial Art Center, Chapel Hill, N.C.

Addison Gallery of Art—*see* Andover/Phillips

Adelaide. The Art Gallery of South Australia, Adelaide

Adelphi U.

Aetna Oil Co.

Agricultural and Mechanical College of Texas

Ain Harod. Michkan Le'omanuth Museum of Art, Ain Harod, Israel

Akademie der Kunste, Berlin, West Germany

Akron/AM. Akron Art Museum, Akron, Ohio; formerly **Akron/AI**, Akron Art Institute

Alabama Institute of Technology

Alabama Polytechnic Institute, Auburn, N.Y.

U. of Alabama

Albany/Institute. Albany Institute of History and Art, Albany, N.Y.

Albany Mall—*see* South Mall, Albany

Albany/SUNY. State University of New York at Albany

Josef Albers Museum, Bottrop, West Germany—*see* Bottrop/Albers

U. of Alberta, Edmonton, Canada

Albertina (Vienna)—*see* Graphische Sammlung Albertina

Albion College

Albrecht Gallery Museum of Art—*see* St. Joseph/Albrecht

Albright-Knox Art Gallery—*see* Buffalo/Albright

Albuquerque Museum, Albuquerque, N.M.

Alcoa. Aluminum Company of America

Larry Aldrich Museum—*see* Ridgefield/Aldrich

Alfred/SUNY. State University of New York at Alfred

Allegheny College

Allen-Bradley Co., Inc.

Allen Memorial Art Museum—*see* Oberlin College

Allentown/AM. Allentown Art Museum, Allentown, Pa.

Lyman Allyn Museum—*see* New London

Alverthorpe Gallery, Jenkintown, Pa.

Amarillo Art Center, Amarillo, Tex.

Amerada Hess Corp., Inc.

American Academy, Rome

American Academy and Institute of Arts and Letters—*see* AAIAL

American Airlines

American Association of University Women

American Broadcasting Co.

American Can Corp.

American Car and Foundry Co.

American Export Isbrandtsen Lines, Inc.

American Federation of Arts—*see* A.F.A.

American Foundation for the Arts, Miami, Fla.

American Life and Casualty Insurance Co.

American Locomotive Co.

American Museum of Immigration, NYC

American National Fire Insurance Co. Collection

American Republic Insurance Co.

American Swedish Historical Museum, Philadelphia, Pa.

American Swedish Institute, Minneapolis, Minn.

American Telephone & Telegraph Co.—*see* AT&T

American Tobacco Co.

American U.

Amherst College

Amsterdam/Stedelijk. Stedelijk Museum, Amsterdam, Holland

Amstar Corp.

Anchorage. Anchorage Historical and Fine Arts Museum, Anchorage, Alaska

Arthur Anderson & Co.

Anderson Clayton Company

Andover/Phillips. Phillips Academy, Addison Gallery of American Art, Andover, Mass.

The M.L. Annenberg Foundation, Philadelphia, Pa.

Anthology Film Archives

Antwerp. Musée Royal des Beaux-Arts, Antwerp, Belgium

Antwerp/ICC. International Cultural Center, Antwerp, Belgium

Antwerp/Middelheim. Musée de Sculpture en pleine air, Middelheim, Antwerp, Belgium

Argentina/Nacional. Museo Nacional de Bellas Artes, Buenos Aires, Argentina

Arizona State College

Arizona State U.

U. of Arizona

U. of Arkansas (incl. Arkansas Arts Center)

Arnhem. Gemeentemuseum, Arnhem, Holland

Thurman Arnold Building, Washington, D.C.

Arnot Art Museum, Elmira, N.Y.

Art Academy of Cincinnati, Cincinnati, Ohio

Art Gallery of Ontario, Toronto, Canada

Art Council of Pakistan—*see* Karachi

Art Gallery of New South Wales—*see* Sydney/AG

Art Gallery of South Australia—*see* Adelaide

Art Gallery of Western Australia, Perth

Art Museum of South Texas, Corpus Christi

Art Students League—*see* ASL

Art of This Century (Peggy Guggenheim), Venice, Italy

Arts Club of Chicago, Illinois

Arts Council of Great Britain, London

Asheville Art Museum, Asheville, N.C.

Ashland Oil Inc.

Aspen Institute for Humanistic Studies, Aspen, Col.

Associated Coin Amusement Company

Astor Place, NYC

Atlanta/AA. Atlanta Art Association, Atlanta, Ga.

Atlanta U.

Atlantic Richfield Co.

Atwater Kent Museum, Philadelphia, Pa.

Auburn U.

Aubusson. College de la Manufacture d'Aubusson, Aubusson, France

Auckland. Auckland City Art Gallery, Auckland, New Zealand

Augusta, Me./State. Maine State Museum, Augusta, Me.

Austin. Texas Fine Arts Association, Austin

Australian National Gallery, Canberra—*see* Canberra/National

Avco Corp.

Avon Products, NYC

L.S. Ayres & Co.

B
Baker U.
Ball State U. (formerly Teachers College) Muncie, Ind.
Baltimore/MA. Baltimore Museum of Art, Baltimore, Md.
U. of Balitmore
Baltimore/Walters. Walters Art Gallery, Baltimore, Md.
Bangor Public Library, Bangor, Me.
Bank of America
Bank of California
The Bank of California N.A., Portland, Ore.
Bank of Chicago
The Bank of New York, NYC
Bank of Omaha
Bankers Trust Company, NYC
Banque Lambert, Brussels, Belgium
Barat College of the Sacred Heart
Barcelona. Museo de Arte Moderno, Barcelona, Spain
Barnard College
Barnes Foundation, Merion, Pa.
Baruch College of the City U. of New York, NYC
Baseball Museum, Baltimore, Md.
Basel. Kunstmuseum Basel, Basel, Switzerland
Basel/Kunsthalle. Kunsthalle Basel, Switzerland
Basel/Offentliche. Offentliche Kunstsammlung, Basel, Switzerland
Basler Denkmalpflege, Basel, Switzerland
Bass Museum of Art—see Miami/Bass
Bat-Yam Museum—see Rybak
Baton-Rouge. State of Louisiana Art Commission, Baton Rouge, La.
Bauhaus-Archiv, Darmstadt, Germany
Beach Public School, Portland, Ore.
Beaumont Art Museum, Beaumont, Texas
Belgian Ministry of National Education, Brussels, Belgium
Belgrade/National. Narodni Muzej (National Museum), Belgrade, Yugoslavia
Bellevue Hospital, NYC
Bellevue, Wash. Bellevue Arts & Crafts Association, Bellevue, Wash.
Beloit College (incl. Wright Art Center)
Belvedere. Osterreichische Galerie im

Belvedere in Wein, Vienna, Austria
Bennington College
Berea College
Bergen Community College, Paramus, N.J.
John Nelson Bergstrom Art Center and Museum—see Neenah/Bergstrom
Berkshire/Atheneum—see Pittsfield/Berkshire
Berlin. Staatliche Museen, Berlin, West Germany
Berlin/National. Nationalgalerie, Berlin, West Germany
Berne. Kunsthalle Berne, Berne, Switzerland
Best Products Corp.
Betcar Corp.
Bethlehem Steel Corp.
Bezalel Museum and Bezalel Art School—see Israel Museum
Bibliothèque Royale de Belgique, Brussels, Belgium
Bielefeld. Stadtisches Kunsthaus, Bielefeld, Germany
Birla Academy of Art and Culture—see Calcutta
Birmingham, Ala./MA. Birmingham Museum of Art, Birmingham, Ala.
Black Mountain College, Beria, N.C.
Blanden Memorial Art Gallery—see Fort Dodge/Blanden
Block Drug Co., Jersey City, N.J.
Boca Raton Museum of Art, Boca Raton, Fla.
Bochum. Museum Bochum, Bochum, Germany
Boise-Cascade Corp.
Bonn. Rheinisches Landesmuseum, Bonn, West Germany
Bordeaux/Contemporain. Musée d'Art Contemporain, Bordeaux, France
Bordighera. Galleria d'Arte Moderna, Bordighera, Italy
Borgon Associates
Borg-Warner International Corporation
Boston/MFA. Museum of Fine Arts, Boston, Mass.; **Boston Museum School**
Boston Public Library, Boston, Mass.
Boston U.
Bottrop/Albers. The Josef Albers Museum, Bottrop, West Germany
Boulogne. Musée des Beaux-Arts,

Boulogne, France
Bowdoin College
Bowling Green State U., Bowling Green, Ohio
Bradford Junior College, Bradford, Mass.
Bradley U.
Brandeis U. (incl. Rose Art Museum)
Archie Bray Foundation, Helena, Mont.
Bremen. Kunsthalle Bremen, Bremen, Germany
Brenton Bank, Des Moines, Ia.
Bridgeport. Museum of Art, Science and Industry, Bridgeport, Conn.
Bridgestone Museum, Tokyo
Brigham Young U.
Bristol (R.I.) Art Museum
Bristol-Myers Co.
Britannica. Encyclopaedia Britannica
U. of British Columbia, Vancouver, Canada
British Museum, London
Brockton/Fuller. Fuller Memorial Art Center, Brockton, Mass.
Bronx Museum of the Arts, Bronx, N.Y.
Brookgreen Gardens, Georgetown, S.C.
Brookings Institute, Washington, D.C.
Brooklyn College of the City U. of New York
Brooklyn Museum, Brooklyn, N.Y.; **Brooklyn Museum School**
Bobbie Brooks Inc.
Brooks Memorial Art Gallery—*see* Memphis/Brooks
Brown U.
Bruce Museum, Greenwich, Conn.
Brunswick. Stadtisches Museum, Braunschweig, Germany
Brunswick Corp.
Brussels/Beaux-Arts. Musées Royaux des Beaux-Arts de Belgique, Brussels, Belgium
Brussels/Moderne. Musée d'Art Moderne, Brussels, Belgium
Bryn Mawr College
Buckingham Palace, London
Budapest/National. Hungarian National Gallery, Budapest, Hungary
The Budd Co.
Buenos Aires/Moderno. Museo de Arte Moderno, Buenos Aires, Argentina
Buenos Aires/Municipal. Museo Municipal de Bellas Artes y Arte Nacional, Buenos Aires, Argentina
Buffalo/Albright. Albright-Knox Art Gallery, Buffalo, N.Y.; **Albright Art School** (prior to 1962)
Bundy Art Gallery—*see* Waitsfield/Bundy
Burlington Industries
Burlington Mills Collection
Harry and Della Burpee Gallery—*see* Rockford/Burpee
Burroughs Wellcome Co., Raleigh, N.C.
Busch-Reisinger Museum, Cambridge, Mass.
Business Card, Inc.
The Butler Institute of American Art—*see* Youngstown/Butler
Byers Museum of the Arts—*see* Evanston/Byers

C
CIA. Central Intelligence Agency, Washington, D.C.
CIT Corp.
CNAC. Centre National d'Art Contemporain, Paris (*see also* Paris/Beaubourg)
CSFA (California School of Fine Arts)—*see* SFAI
Calcutta. Birla Academy of Art and Culture, Calcutta, India
U. of Calgary, Alberta, Canada
California Academy of Science, Museum and Library, San Francisco
California College of Arts and Crafts
California Federal Savings and Loan Association, Los Angeles
California Palace of the Legion of Honor, San Francisco
California School of Fine Arts—*see* SFAI
California State Fair
California State Library
California State U.
California Watercolor Society
U. of California (*see also* UCLA)
The Cambridge School, Weston, Mass.
Cambridge. U. of Cambridge, England

The Canada Council, Ottawa
Canadian Industries Ltd., Montreal
Canadian Society of Graphic Art
Canajoharie Library and Art Gallery, Canajoharie, N.Y.
Canberra/National. Australian National Gallery, Canberra
Canton Art Institute, Canton, Ohio
Capehart Corp.
Cape Town. South African National Gallery, Cape Town
Capitol Records, Inc.
Capitol Research Co., Los Angeles
Caracas. Museo de Bellas Artes de Caracas, Venezuela
Caracas/Contemporaneo. Museo de Arte Contemporaneo, Caracas, Venezuela
Carborundum Company
Cardiff—see National Museum of Wales
Carleton College
Carnegie Institute of Technology, Pittsburgh, Pa.
Carnegie-Mellon U.
Carolina Art Association—see Charleston/Carolina
Amon Carter Museum of Western Art, Fort Worth, Texas
La Casa del Libro, San Juan, Puerto Rico
Case Institute of Technology
Case Western Reserve U.
The Catholic U. of America
Cedar Rapids/AA. Cedar Rapids Art Association, Cedar Rapids, Iowa
Cedars-Sinai Medical Center, Los Angeles
Center for Inter-American Relations, NYC
Central Florida Museum—see Orlando
Centraal Museum—see Utrecht
Central Research Corp., NYC
Centre National d'Art Contemporain—see CNAC
Centro Artistico de Barranquilla, Barranquilla, Colombia
Centro Cultural de los Estados Unidos, Madrid
Century Association, NYC
Ceret. Musée d'Art Moderne, Ceret, France
Chaffey College

Charleston/Carolina. Carolina Art Association, Charleston, S.C.
Charleston, W.Va. Charleston Art Gallery, Charleston, W.Va.
Charlotte/Mint. Mint Museum of Art, Charlotte, N.C.
Chase Manhattan Bank
Chase Park Plaza Hotel, St. Louis, Mo.
Château de Rohan, Strasbourg, France
Chattanooga/AA. Chattanooga Art Association, Chattanooga, Tenn.
Chattanooga/Hunter. Hunter Museum of Art, Chattanooga, Tenn.
Chautauqua Institute, Chautauqua, N.Y.
Cheekwood. The Tennessee Botanical Gardens and Fine Arts Center, Nashville, Tenn.
Cheney Cowles Memorial Museum, Spokane, Wash.
Chicao/AI. The Art Institute of Chicago; Chicago Art Institute School (and Junior School)
Chicago Arts Club—see Arts Club of Chicago
Chicago/Contemporary. Museum of Contemporary Art, Chicago, Ill.
Chicago Public Schools, Chicago, Ill.
Chicago/Terra. Terra Museum of American Art, Chicago; formerly in Evanston, Ill.
U. of Chicago (incl. Renaissance Society; Smart Gallery)
Chico State College (incl. Chico Art Center)
Choate-Rosemary Hall School, Wallingford, Conn.
Chouinard Art Institute, Los Angeles
Christian Theological Seminary, Indianapolis, Ind.
Chrysler Corp.
Walter P. Chrysler Museum of Art—see Norfolk/Chrysler
Ciba-Geigy Corp., Ardsley, N.Y.
Cincinnati/AM. The Cincinnati Art Museum, Cincinnati, Ohio; Cincinnati Museum School
Cincinnati/Contemporary. Contemporary Arts Center, Cincinnati, Ohio
U. of Cincinnati
Cinémathèque de Belgique, Brussels, Belgium
Cinémathèque Française, Paris
Citicorp, NYC

Citizens Fidelity Bank, Louisville, Ky.
City of Chalon-sur-Sâone, France
City of Claremont, Calif.
City College of the City U. of New York
City of Fresno, Calif.
City of Hamburg, Germany
City of Hannover, Germany
City Investing Corp., NYC
City of Mill Valley, Calif.
City of Oakland, Calif.
City of Portland, Ore.
City of San Francisco
City of Tilburg, Holland
City of Toronto, Canada
Civic Center Synagogue, NYC
Clairol Inc.
Claremont College
Clearwater/Gulf Coast. Florida Gulf Coast Art Center, Inc., Clearwater
Cleveland/MA. The Cleveland Museum of Art, Cleveland, Ohio
Cleveland Trust Co.
The Coca-Cola Co.
Cochran Memorial Park, St. Paul, Minn.
Coe College
Colby College
Colgate U.
Collection de l'Etat, Paris
College des Musées Nationaux de France, Paris
College of St. Benedict
Cologne. Wallraf-Richartz-Museum, Cologne, West Germany
Cologne/Kunstverein. Kolnischer Kunstverein, Cologne, West Germany
Cologne/Ludwig. Museum Ludwig, Cologne, West Germany
Cologne/NG. Neue Galerie im Alten Kulturhaus, Cologne, West Germany
Cologne/Stadt. Museen der Stadt Köln, Cologne, West Germany
Colonial Bank & Trust Co., Waterbury, Conn.
Colonial Williamsburg, Williamsburg, Va.
Colorado College
Colorado Springs/FA. Colorado Springs Fine Arts Center, Colorado Springs, Col.

Colorado State U.
U. of Colorado
Columbia, Mo. State Historical Society of Missouri, Columbia, Mo.
Columbia, S.C./MA. Columbia Museum of Art, Columbia, S.C.
Columbia Banking, Savings and Loan Association, Rochester, N.Y.
Columbia Broadcasting System
Columbia U.
Columbus. Columbus Gallery of Fine Arts, Columbus, Ohio
Columbus, Ga. Columbus Museum of Arts and Crafts, Columbus, Ga.
Commerce Bank (or Bancshares) of Kansas City, Mo.
Commerce Bank of St. Louis
Commerce Trust Co., Kansas City, Mo.
Community Arts Foundation, Los Angeles
Concordia Teachers College (Ill.)
Concordia Teachers College (Neb.)
Connecticut College
Connecticut Community College
Connecticut General Life Insurance Company
U. of Connecticut
Conover-Mast Publications Inc.
Container Corp. of America
Continental Grain Company
Cooperative Insurance Society, Manchester, England
Cooper Union. The Cooper Union Museum and Art School, NYC
Coos Bay Art Museum, Coos Bay, Ore.
Copenhagen. Statens Museum für Kunst, Copenhagen, Denmark
Corcoran. The Corcoran Gallery of Art, Washington, D.C.; The Corcoran Gallery School of Art
Cordoba/Municipal. Museo Municipal de Cordoba, Argentina
Cordoba/Provincial. Museo Provincial de Bellas Artes, Cordoba, Argentina
Cornell College, Mt. Vernon, Iowa
Cornell U. (incl. Herbert F. Johnson Museum of Art)
Cortland/SUNY. State University of New York at Cortland
Corvallis (Ore.) First Federal Savings and Loan
Courtauld Institute, London
Cranbrook. Cranbrook Academy of

Art, Bloomfield Hills, Mich.

E.B. Crocker Art Gallery—*see* Sacramento/Crocker

Crown Zellerbach Foundation, San Francisco

Cuenca. Museo Municipal de Arte, Cuenca, Spain

Cummer Gallery of Art—*see* Jacksonville/Cummer

Currier. Currier Gallery of Art, Manchester, N.H.; **Currier Gallery School**

D

Dallas Museum for Contemporary Arts—*see* Dallas/MFA

Dallas/MFA. Dallas Museum of Fine Arts, Dallas, Texas; **Dallas Museum School**

Dallas Public Library, Dallas, Texas

Dalton School, NYC

Danforth Museum, Framingham, Mass.

Darmstadt/Hessisches. Hessisches Landesmuseum, Darmstadt, Germany

Darmstadt/Kunsthalle. Kunsthalle, Darmstadt, Germany

Dartmouth College (incl. Hopkins Art Center)

Davenport/Municipal. Davenport Municipal Art Gallery, Davenport, Iowa

Davidson, N.C. Davidson Art Center, Davidson, N.C.

Davison Art Center—*see* Wesleyan U. (Conn.)

Dayton/AI. Dayton Art Institute, Dayton, Ohio; **Dayton Art Institute School**

De Beers Collection, Johannesburg, South Africa

Debevoise, Plimpton, Lyons and Gates, NYC

Decatur Art Center, Decatur, Ill.

De Cordova and Dana Museum—*see* Lincoln, Mass./De Cordova

De Kalb—*see* Northern Illinois U.

Delaware Art Center—*see* Wilmington

Delaware Art Museum, Wilmington, Del.

U. of Delaware

Isaac Delgado Museum of Art—*see* New Orleans/Delgado

Denison U.

Denver/AM. Denver Art Museum, Denver, Col.

De Pauw U.

Des Moines. The Des Moines Art Center, Des Moines, Iowa

Des Moines Register & Tribune, Des Moines, Iowa

Detroit/Institute. The Detroit Institute of Arts, Detroit, Mich.

de Young. M.H. de Young Memorial Museum, San Francisco

Diablo Valley College

Didrichsen Foundation, Helsinki, Finland

Dillard U.

Djakarta Museum, Djakarta, Indonesia

Doane College

Donaldson, Lufkin & Jenrette, Inc.

Dord Fitz School of Art

Jay Dorf, Inc.

Downey Museum of Art, Downey, Calif.

Downtown Community School, NYC

Drake U.

Dresdener Bank, Los Angeles

Dublin/Municipal. Municipal Gallery of Modern Art, Dublin, Ireland

Dublin/National. National Gallery, Dublin, Ireland

U. of Dublin, Dublin, Ireland

Dubuque/AA. Dubuque Art Association, Dubuque, Iowa

Duisburg. Wilhelm-Lehmbruck-Museum der Stadt Duisburg, Germany

Duke U.

Dulin Gallery of Art, Knoxville, Tenn.

Dunkin' Donuts Inc.

Düsseldorf. Kunstmuseum der Stadt, Düsseldorf, West Germany

Düsseldorf/KN-W. Kunstsammlung Nordrhein-Westfalen, Düsseldorf, West Germany

Düsseldorf/Kunsthalle. Stadtische Kunsthalle, Düsseldorf, West Germany

E

Earlham College

U. of East Anglia, Norwich, England

East Tennessee State College Museum of Art, Johnson City, Tenn.

Eastern Michigan U.

Eastern Oregon College

Eastland Shopping Center, Detroit, Mich.

Eaton Paper Corp.

Edinburgh/Modern. Scottish National Gallery of Modern Art, Edinburgh, Scotland

Edinburgh/National. National Gallery of Scotland, Edinburgh, Scotland

Edmonton Art Gallery, Edmonton, Canada

Eilat. Museum of Modern Art, Eilat, Israel

Eindhoven. Stedelijk van Abbe-Museum, Eindhoven, Holland

Ellerby Associates

Elmira College (N.Y.)

El Paso Museum of Art, El Paso, Texas

Craig Elwood Associates

Emory U., Atlanta, Ga.

Equitable Life Assurance Society of the U.S.

Escuela Nacional de Artes Plasticas, Mexico City, Mexico

Essen. Museum Folkwang, Essen, Germany

Essen/NG. Neue Galerie, Essen, Germany

Esslingen. Stadtische Museum, Esslingen, Germany

Evanston/Byer. Byer Museum of the Arts, Evanston, Ill.

Evansville. Evansville Museum of Arts and Sciences, Evansville, Ind.; Evansville Museum School

Everett Junior College, Everett, Wash.

Everhart Museum—*see* Scranton/Everhart

Everson Museum of Art—*see* Syracuse/Everson

Exchange National Bank, Chicago, Ill.

Exeter. Phillips Exeter Academy, The Lamont Art Gallery, Exeter, N.H.

F

F.T.D. Association. Florists Transworld Delivery Association

Fabick Tractor Co.

Fairleigh Dickinson U.

Fairmont Park Association, Philadelphia, Pa.

Farmers Elevator Insurance Co.

William A. Farnsworth Library and Art Museum—*see* Rockland/Farnsworth

Father Judge Mission Seminary, Lynchburg, Va.

Fayetteville Museum of Art, Fayetteville, N.C.

Federal Deposit Insurance Corporation

Fidelity Bank, Philadelphia, Pa.

Hamilton Easter Field Foundation, Portland, Me.

57th Madison Corp., NYC

Fine Arts Museum of the South—*see* Mobile/FAMS

First City National Bank of Boston

First City National Bank of Chicago

First National Bank of Dallas

First National Bank of Iowa City, Iowa

First National Bank, Madison, Wisc.

First National Bank of Memphis, Tenn.

First National Bank, Minneapolis, Minn.

First National Bank of Nevada, Reno

First National Bank of Ohio, Columbus

First National Bank of Oregon

First National Bank of Seattle, Wash.

First National Bank, Tampa, Fla.

First National Bank of Tulsa, Ok.

First National City Bank

Fisk U.

Fitchburg/AM. Fitchburg Art Museum, Fitchburg, Mass.

525 William Penn Plaza, Philadelphia, Pa.

Robert Hull Fleming Museum—*see* U. of Vermont

Flint/Institute. Flint Institute of Arts, Flint, Mich.

Florence, Italy. Galleria dell'Accademia, Florence, Italy

Florence (Italy)/Modern. Galleria d'Arte Moderna, Florence, Italy

Florence, S.C. Museum. Florence Museum, Florence, S.C.

Florida Gulf Coast Art Center, Inc.—*see* Clearwater/Gulf Coast

Florida Southern College

Florida State U.

U. of Florida

Florsheim Foundation, Chicago, Ill.
Fogg Art Museum—*see* Harvard U.
Fondation Maeght, St. Paul-de-Vence, France
Fontana-Hollywood Corp.
Ford Foundation
Fordham U.
Ford Motor Company
Fort Dodge/Blanden. Blanden Memorial Art Gallery, Fort Dodge, Iowa
Fort Lauderdale. Fort Lauderdale Museum of Art, Fort Lauderdale, Fla.
Fort Wayne/AM. Fort Wayne Art Museum, Fort Wayne, Ind.
Fort Worth. Fort Worth Art Center, Fort Worth, Tex.
Fort Wright College, Spokane, Wash.
405 Park Avenue, NYC
Four Seasons Restaurant, NYC
Fourth National Bank and Trust, Wichita, Kan.
France/National. Musée National d'Art Moderne, Paris, France (*see also* Paris/Moderne)
Franchard Corp.
Frank Construction Company
Frankfurt am Main. Stadelsches Kunstinstitut, Frankfurt am Main, West Germany
Frankfurt/Moderne. Museum für Moderne Kunst, Frankfurt, West Germany
Franklin Institute, Philadelphia, Pa.
Simon Frazer U.
Fredonia/SUNY. State University of New York at Fredonia
Free Library of Philadelphia, Pa.
French Ministry of National Education, Paris, France
Fresno State College
Friends of Art, Uniontown, Pa.
Friuli, Italy/MOMA. Museum of Modern Art, Friuli, Italy
Fukuoda. Fukuoda Art Museum, Fukuoda, Japan
Fuller Memorial Art Center—*see* Brockton/Fuller
Fullerton Junior College, Calif.
Fundacion Juan March, Madrid

G
GSA. General Services Administration

Galerie des 20. Jahrhunderts, Berlin, West Germany
Galleria Communale d'Arte Contemporanea, Arezzo, Italy
Gallery of Modern Art, NYC—*see* New York Cultural Center
Gallery of Modern Art, Washington, DC—*see* WGMA
Galveston. Galveston Historical Foundation Inc., Galveston, Tex.
Garcia Corp.
Garnett Public Library, Garnett, Kan.
Geigy Chemical Corp.—*see* Ciba-Geigy Corp.
Gelsenkirchen. Stadtische Kunstsammlung, Gelsenkirchen, Germany
General Electric Corp.
General Mills Inc.
General Motors Corp.
General Reinsurance Corp.
Geneseo/SUNY. State University of New York at Geneseo
George Washington U.
George Washington Carver Junior College, Rockville, Md.
Georgia Institute of Technology
Georgia State U.
U. of Georgia (incl. Georgia Museum of Art)
Gettysburg College
Ghent. Musée des Beaux-Arts, Ghent, Belgium
Ghent/Contemporary. Het Museum van Hedendaagse Kunst te Gent, Ghent, Belgium
Ghent/Moderne. Musée d'Art Moderne, Ghent, Belgium
Gibraltar Savings & Loan Association
Gimbel Bros.
Glasgow/AGM. Glasgow Art Gallery and Museum, Glasgow, Scotland
U. of Glasgow, Scotland
Glen Alden Corp.
Goddard Art Center, Ardmore, Ok.
Goddard College
Golden Gateway Center, San Francisco
Golden State Mutual Life Insurance Co.
Goldman Sachs, & Co., NYC
Goldring International
Gothenburg—*see* Sweden/Goteborgs
Goucher College
Govett-Brewster Art Gallery, New

Plymouth, New Zealand
The Grace Line
Grand Rapids. Grand Rapids Art Gallery, Grand Rapids, Mich.
Graphische Sammlung Albertina, Vienna, Austria
Graphische Sammlung der E.T.H. (Eidg. Technischen Hochschule), Zurich, Switzerland
Great Southwest Industrial Park, Atlanta, Ga.
Great Western Savings and Loan Association of South California, Los Angeles
Greece/National. National Picture Gallery, Athens, Greece
Greenville County Museum of Art, S.C.
Grenchen. Sammlungen der Museumgesellschaft, Grenchen, Switzerland
Grenoble. Musee des Beaux-Arts de Grenoble, France
Griffiths Art Center—*see* St. Lawrence U.
Grinnell College
Grolier Club, NYC
Grunewald Foundation for Graphic Arts, Los Angeles
Guadalajara. Museo de Bellas Artes, Guadalajara, Mexico
Solomon R. Guggenheim Museum—*see* SRGM
Guild Hall, East Hampton, N.Y.
Guild Plastics Co.
Gulf Coast Art Center—*see* Clearwater/Gulf Coast
Gulf Life Insurance Co., Jacksonville, Fla.
Gulf Oil Corp.
Gulf and Western Industries Inc.
A.V. Gumuchian, Inc.

H
Hackley Art Center—*see* Muskegon/Hackley
Hagen. Karl-Ernst-Osthaus-Museum, Hagen, Germany
Hagerstown/County MFA. Washington County Museum of Fine Arts, Hagerstown, Md.

The Hague. Haags Gemeentemuseum, The Hague, Netherlands
Haifa. Museum of Modern Art, Haifa, Israel
Haifa/National. National Maritime Museum, Haifa, Israel
Hall of Justice, San Francisco
Hallmark Collection
Hamburg. Hamburger Kunsthalle, Hamburg, Germany
Hamburg/Kunstverein. Kunstverein in Hamburg, Germany
Hamilton College
Hamline U.
Hampton Institute
Hampton School, Townsend, Md.
Hannover. Stadtische Galerie, Hannover, Germany
Hannover/K-G. Kestner-Gesellschaft, Hannover, Germany *(see also* Kestner-Museum, Hannover)
Hannover/Kunstverein. Kunstverein Hannover, Hannover, Germany
Harcourt Brace Jovanovich Inc.
Harlem Hospital, NYC
Hamron Foundation Inc., NYC
Harrisburg, Pa./State Museum. Pennsylvania State Museum, Harrisburg, Pa. (incl. William Penn Memorial Museum)
Hartford (Conn.) State Library
Hartford/Wadsworth. The Wadsworth Atheneum, Hartford, Conn.
U. of Hartford
Harvard U. (incl. Fogg Art Museum)
Havana/Nacional. Museo Nacional, Havana, Cuba
Hayden Stone Inc.
Le Havre/Municipal. Musée Municipal, Le Havre, France *(see also* Musée du Havre)
Hawaii State Foundation
U. of Hawaii
Health and Hospital Corp., NYC
Hebron Academy, Hebron, Me.
Heckscher Museum—*see* Huntington, N.Y./Heckscher
H.J. Heinz Co., Pittsburgh, Pa.
Hellerup Commune, Copenhagen, Denmark
Helsinki. Ateneumin Taidemuseo, Helsinki, Finland
Hemisphere Club, NYC

Hempstead Bank, Hempstead, N.Y.
Henies-Onstadts Stiftelser, Hovikodden, Norway
John Herron Art Institute—*see* Indianapolis/Herron
Hershey Foods Corp.
Christian Herter Center, Boston, Mass.
Hessisches Landesmuseum, Darmstadt—*see* Darmstadt/Hessisches
The Hertz Corp.
Het Museum van Hedendaagse Kunst te Gent, Ghent—*see* Ghent/Contemporary
Hickory, N.C. Hickory Museum of Art, Hickory, N.C.
High Museum of Art, Atlanta, Ga.
Hiroshima State Museum of Art, Japan
Hirshhorn. The Hirshhorn Museum and Sculpture Garden, Smithsonian Institution, Washington, D.C.
Historical Society of Montana, Helena
Hoffman-La Roche Inc.
Hofstra U.
Hokkaido Prefectural Museum of Modern Art—*see* Sapporo
Hollins College
Holyoke Public Library, Holyoke, Mass.
Home Savings and Loan Association, Los Angeles, Calif.
Honolulu Academy of Arts, Honolulu, Hawaii; **Honolulu Academy School**
Hope College, Holland, Mich.
Hopkins Art Center—*see* Dartmouth College
Hospital Corp. of America
Hotel Corp. of America, NYC
Housatonic Community College, Stratford, Conn.
Houston/Contemporary. Contemporary Arts Museum, Houston, Tex.
Houston/MFA. Museum of Fine Arts, Houston, Tex.; **Houston Museum School**
U. of Houston
Howard College
Howard U.
J.L. Hudson Co.
Hudson River Museum, Yonkers, N.Y.
Humlebaek/Louisiana. Louisiana Museum of Art, Humlebaek, Denmark
Hunt Foods & Industries

Hunter College of the City U. of New York
Hunter Museum of Art—*see* Chattanooga/Hunter
Huntington, N.Y./Heckscher. Heckscher Museum, Huntington, N.Y.
Huntington, W. Va. Huntington Galleries, Huntington, W. Va.
Huntsville Museum of Art, Huntsville, Ala.
Hyde Collection, Glens Falls, N.Y.

I

IBM. International Business Machines Corp.
ICA, Boston. Institute of Contemporary Art, Boston, Mass.
ICA, Los Angeles. Institute of Contemporary Art, Los Angeles
ICA, U. of Pennsylvania. Institute of Contemporary Art, U. of Pennsylvania, Philadelphia
ICA, Washington, D.C. Institute of Contemporary Arts, Washington, D.C.
ICP. International Center of Photography, NYC
IEF. International Exhibitions Foundation, Washington, D.C.
IIE. International Institute of Education
ILGWU. International Ladies' Garment Workers Union
College of Idaho
Idemitsu Museum, Tokyo, Japan
Illinois Bell Telephone Company
Illinois State Museum of Natural History and Art—*see* Springfield, Ill./State
Illinois State Normal U.
U. of Illinois (incl. Krannert Art Museum)
Illinois Wesleyan U.
Immaculate Heart College, Los Angeles
Imperial Household, Tokyo, Japan
Indian Head Mills, Inc.
Indiana National Bank, Indianapolis, Ind.
Indiana State U. (formerly Indiana State College), Terre Haute
Indiana (Pa.) State Teachers College

Indiana U.

Indianapolis Museum of Art, Indianapolis, Ind.

Indianapolis/Herron. John Herron Art Institute, Indianapolis, Ind.

Industrial Electronics Engineers, Inc.

Industrial Museum, Barcelona, Spain

Inland Steel Co.

Inmont Corp.

Institut für Moderne Kunst, Nurnberg, Germany

Institute of Contemporary Art—see ICA, various cities

Institute for Policy Studies, Washington, D.C.

Interchemical Corp.

Interchurch Center, NYC

International Center of Photography—see ICP

International Cultural Center, Antwerp—see Antwerp/ICC

International Exhibitions Foundation—see IEF

International Institute for Aesthetic Research, Turin, Italy

International Institute of Education—see IIE

International Minerals & Chemicals Corp.

International Monetary Fund, Washington, D.C.

International Nickel Co.

International Museum of Photography at George Eastman House, Rochester, N.Y.

Iowa Arts Council, Des Moines

Iowa State Teachers College

Iowa State U. of Science and Technology

U. of Iowa

Iowa Wesleyan College

Israel Museum, Jerusalem (incl. Bezalel National Art Museum)

Ithaca College

Ivest-Wellington Corp.

J

Jackson/MMA. Mississippi Museum of Art, Jackson

Jacksonville/AM. Jacksonville Art Museum, Jacksonville, Fla.

Jacksonville/Cummer. Cummer Gallery of Art, Jacksonville, Fla.

Jacksonville U.

Jamestown/Prendergast. James Prendergast Free Library Art Gallery, Jamestown, N.Y.

Japanese Craft Museum, Tokyo, Japan

Jay Mfg. Co.

Jersey City Museum, Jersey City, N.J.

Jerusalem/Modern—see Israel Museum

Jerusalem/National—see Israel Museum

Jesus College of Cambridge U., Cambridge, England

Jewish Museum, NYC

Jewish Theological Seminary of America

Johannesburg/Municipal. Municipal Art Gallery, Johannesburg, South Africa

Johns Hopkins U.

Johnson College

Herbert F. Johnson Museum—see Cornell U.

Lyndon B. Johnson Library, Austin, Tex.

Johnson Publishing Co., Chicago, Ill.

S.C. Johnson & Son, Inc.—see NCFA

Johnson Wax Co.

J. Turner Jones, Inc.

Jones & Laughlin Steel Corp.

Joslyn Art Museum—see Omaha/Joslyn

James Joyce Museum, Dublin, Ireland

Julliard School, NYC

K

Kaiserslautern Museum, Kaiserslautern, Germany

Kalamazoo College

Kalamazoo/Institute. The Kalamazoo Institute of Arts, Kalamazoo, Mich. (incl. Kalamazoo Art Center)

Kamakura. Modern Art Museum of Kanagawa Prefecture, Kamakura, Japan

U. of Kansas

Kansas City/AI. Kansas City Art Institute and School of Design, Kansas City, Mo.

Kansas City/Nelson. Nelson-Atkins Art Gallery, Kansas City, Mo. (for-

merly William Rockhill Nelson Gallery of Art)
U. of Kansas City
Kansas State College
Karachi. Art Council of Pakistan, Karachi
Karamu House, Cleveland, Ohio
Karlsruhe. Staatliche Kunsthalle, Karlsruhe, Germany
Kassel. Stadtische Kunstsammlungen, Kassel, Germany
Kemper Insurance Co.
John F. Kennedy Library, Cambridge, Mass.
Kent State U.
Kentucky Southern College, Louisville
U. of Kentucky
Kenyon College
Kestner-Museum, Hannover, Germany (*see also* Hannover/K-G)
Kingsborough Community College
Kirkaldy Museum and Art Gallery, Kirkaldy, Scotland
Kirkland College, Clinton, N.Y.
Kitakyushu Museum, Kyushu, Japan
Knox College, Galesburg, Ill.
Kolnisher Kunstverein—*see* Cologne/Kunstverein
Krakow/National. National Museum, Krakow, Poland
Krannert Art Museum—*see* U. of Illinois
Krefeld/Haus Lange. Museum Haus Lange Wilhelmshofallee, Krefeld, Germany
Krefeld/Kaiser Wilhelm. Kaiser Wilhelm Museum, Krefeld, Germany
Kresge Art Center—*see* Michigan State U.
Kulturministerium, Hannover, Germany
Kulturministerium Baden-Wurttemberg, Stuttgart, West Germany
Kunsthalle Basel—*see* Basel/Kunsthalle
KunstgewerbeMuseum der Stadt—*see* Zurich/KS
Kunstkredit, Basel, Switzerland
Kunstverein in Hamburg—*see* Hamburg/Kunstverein
Kunstverein Hannover—*see* Hannover/Kunstverein
Kupferstichkabinett, Berlin, Germany

Kutztown State College
Kyoto National Museum of Modern Art, Kyoto, Japan

L
La France Art Institute, Philadelphia, Pa.
Laguna Beach Museum of Art, Laguna Beach, Calif.
Laguna Gloria Art Museum, Austin, Tex.
La Jolla. Museum of Contemporary Art, La Jolla, Calif.; formerly Museum of Art; also formerly Art Center in La Jolla
Lakeview Center for Arts and Science, Peoria, Ill.
The Lamont Art Gallery—*see* Exeter
Lane Foundation, Leominster, Mass.
Lannan Foundation, NYC/Palm Beach, Fla./Chicago
Lansing Sound Corp.
La Plata. Museo de La Plata, Argentina
H.E. Laufer Co.
Laumeier Sculpture Park, St. Louis, Mo.
Lawrence College
Layton School of Art, Milwaukee, Wisc.
League of Nations, Geneva, Switzerland
Lehigh U.
Lehman Bros., NYC
Leicester Education Committee, London
Leipzig Museum der Bildenden Kunste, Leipzig, Germany
Lembke Construction Co.
Lenox School, Lenox, Mass.
Leverkusen. Stadtisches Museum, Leverkusen, Germany
Levin Townsend Computer Corp.
Lewiston (Me.) Public Library
Liaison Films, Inc.
Library of Congress, Washington, D.C.
Liège. Musée des Beaux-Arts, Liège, Belgium
Lille. Palais des Beaux-Arts, Lille, France
Eli Lilly & Co.

Lima, Peru. Instituto de Arte Contemporaneo, Lima, Peru

Abraham Lincoln High School, Brooklyn, N.Y.

Lincoln, Mass./De Cordova. De Cordova and Dana Museum, Lincoln, Mass.

Lincoln Center for the Performing Arts, NYC

Lincoln Life Insurance Co.

Lindenwood College

Linz. Oberösterreichisches Landesmuseum, Linz, Austria

Lipschultz Foundation

Little Rock/MFA. Museum of Fine Arts, Little Rock, Ark.

Litton Industries

Liverpool/Walker. Walker Art Gallery, Liverpool, England

Loch Haven Art Center, Orlando, Fla. (see also Orlando)

Lodz. Museum Sztuki w Lodzi, Lodz, Poland

London Film Society

Long Beach/MA. Long Beach Museum of Art, Long Beach, Calif.

Long Beach State College

Long Island U.

Longview Foundation

Longwood College

Los Angeles County Fair Association, Los Angeles

Los Angeles/County MA. Los Angeles County Museum of Art, Los Angeles

Los Angeles/MOCA. Museum of Contemporary Art, Los Angeles

Los Angeles Public Library, Los Angeles

Los Angeles State College, Los Angeles

Lotus Club, NYC

Louisiana Museum of Art—see Humlebaek/Louisiana

Louisiana State U. and Agricultural and Mechanical College

Louisville/Speed. J.B. Speed Art Museum, Louisville, Ky.

U. of Louisville

The Joe and Emily Lowe Art Gallery—see U. of Miami

The Joe and Emily Lowe Foundation, NYC

Lucerne. Kunstmuseum Luzern, Lucerne, Switzerland

Lugano. Museo Civico di Belle Arti, Lugano, Switzerland

Lummis Tower Building, Houston, Tex.

Luther College

Lynchburg Art Gallery—see Randolph-Macon Woman's College

Lytton Savings and Loan Association

M

MIT. Massachusetts Institute of Technology, Cambridge

MMA. The Metropolitan Museum of Art, NYC

MOMA. The Museum of Modern Art, NYC; MOMA School

Norman MacKenzie Art Gallery—see Regina/MacKenzie

MacMurray College

MacNider Museum, Mason City, Iowa

Macomb County Community College, Warren, Mich.

R.H. Macy & Co.

Madison Art Center, Madison, Wisc.

Madison College

Madison Square Garden, NYC

Madrid/Nacional. Museo Nacional de Arte Contemporaneo, Madrid

Maeght—see Fondation Maeght

Maine State Museum—see Augusta, Me./State

U. of Maine

Malmo Museum, Malmo, Sweden

Manchester, England. City of Manchester Art Galleries, Manchester, England

Manila. Ateneo de Manila, Philippines

Mannheim. Stadtische Kunsthalle, Mannheim, Germany

Mansfield State College

Mansion House Project, St. Louis, Mo.

Manufacturers Hanover Trust Co.

Manufacturers and Traders Trust Co., Buffalo, N.Y.

Marbach Galerie, Berne, Switzerland

Marin Art and Garden Center, Ross, Calif.

Marine Midland Bank and Trust Co.

Marist College, Poughkeepsie, N.Y.
Mark Twain Bankshares, St. Louis, Mo.
Marquette U.
Marseilles/Cantini. Musée Cantini, Marseilles, France
Marshall Field & Co.
Marshall U.
Martha Washington U.
Maryland Institute, Baltimore; Maryland Institute School of Art
U. of Maryland
Mary Washington College of the U. of Virginia
U. of Massachusetts
Massillon Museum, Massillon, Ohio
Mattatuck Museum, Waterbury, Conn.
McCormick Place-on-the-Lake, Chicago, Ill.
McCann-Erickson, Inc.
McCrory Corp.
McDonald & Company
McDonnell & Co., Inc.
Marion Koogler McNay Art Institute—see San Antonio/McNay
Mead Corporation
Mechanics National Bank, Worcester, Mass.
Melbourne/National. National Gallery of Victoria, Melbourne, Australia
Memphis/Brooks. Brooks Memorial Art Gallery, Memphis, Tenn.
Memphis State U.
Mendoza. Museo de Historia Natural, Mendoza, Argentina
Mestrovic Gallery, Split, Yugoslavia
Mestrovic Museum, Zagreb, Yugoslavia
Metalcraft Corp.
Meta-Mold Aluminum Co.
Metropolitan Museum and Art Center, Coral Gables, Fla.
The Metropolitan Museum of Art, NYC—see MMA
Mexico City/Moderno. Museo de Arte Moderno, Mexico City, Mexico
Mexico City/Nacional—see Mexico City/Moderno
Mexico City/Tamayo. Museo de Arte Contemporaneo Rufino Tamayo, Mexico City, Mexico
Miami/Bass. Bass Museum of Art, Miami, Fla.

Miami-Dade Junior College
Miami/Modern. Miami Museum of Modern Art, Miami, Fla.
U. of Miami (incl. The Joe and Emily Lowe Art Gallery)
Miami U., Oxford, Ohio
James A. Michener Foundation—see U. of Texas
Michigan Consolidated Gas Co.
Michigan State U. (incl. Kresge Art Center)
U. of Michigan
Middlebury College
Middle Tennessee State U.
Milan. Galleria Civica d'Arte Moderna, Milan, Italy
Miles College, Birmingham, Ala.
Miles Laboratories Inc.
Miles Metal Corp., NYC
The Miller Co.
Millikin U.
Mills College
Mills College of Education
Milton Academy, Milton, Mass.
Milwaukee Art Center, Milwaukee, Wisc.
Milwaukee-Downer College
Milwaukee Journal
Minneapolis College of Art & Design, Minneapolis, Minn.
Minneapolis/Institute. Minneapolis Institute of Arts, Minneapolis, Minn.; Minneapolis Institute School
Minnesota/MA. Minnesota Museum of Art, St. Paul
U. of Minnesota (incl. Tweed Gallery, Duluth)
Mint Museum of Art—see Charlotte/Mint
Mississippi Museum of Art—see Jackson/MMA
Missoula/MA. Missoula Museum of the Arts, Missoula, Mont.
U. of Missouri
Mitsui Bank of Japan
Mobil Oil Co.
Mobile/FAMS. Fine Arts Museum of the South, Mobile, Ala.
Moderna Museet—see Stockholm/National
Monchengladbach. Stadtisches Museum, Monchengladbach, Germany

Mons. Musée des Beaux-Arts, Mons, Belgium
Montana State College
Montana State U.
U. of Montana
Montclair/AM. Montclair Art Museum, Montclair, N.J.
Montclair State College
Montevideo/Municipal. Museo Municipal de Bellas Artes, Montevideo, Uruguay
Montgomery Museum of Fine Art, Montgomery, Ala.
Montpelier/Wood. Thomas W. Wood Art Gallery, Montpelier, Vt.
Montréal/Contemporain. Musée d'Art Contemporain, Montréal, Canada
Montreal/MFA. Montréal Museum of Fine Arts, Montréal, Canada
Montréal Trust Co.
Moorpark College, Moorpark, Calif.
Moravian College, Bethlehem, Pa.
The Morgan Library. The Pierpont Morgan Library, NYC
Morgan State College
Moriarty Brothers, Manchester, Conn.
Morristown/Junior. Morris Junior Museum, Morristown, N.J.
Moscow/Western. Museum of Western Art, Moscow, USSR
Mount Holyoke College
Mt. Vernon High School, Mt. Vernon, Wash.
Muckenthaler Cultural Center, Fullerton, Calif.
Muhlenberg College
Mulvane Art Museum—see Washburn U. of Topeka
Munich/Modern. Modern Art Museum, Munich, West Germany
Munich/NP. Neue Pinakotek, Munich, West Germany
Munich/SG. Stadtische Galerie, Munich, West Germany
Munich/State. Munchner Stadtmuseum, Munich, West Germany
Municipal U. of Omaha
Munson-Williams-Proctor Institute—see Utica
Munster. Landesmuseum für Kunst und Kulturgeschichte, Munster, Germany
Munster/WK. Westfalischer Kunstverein, Munster, Germany

Murray State U., Murray, Ky.
Musée d'Art, Toulon—see Toulon
Musée d'Art Contemporain, Bordeaux—see Bordeaux/Contemporain
Musée d'Art Contemporain, Montreal—see Montreal/Contemporain
Musée des Arts Décoratifs, Paris, France
Musée des Beaux Arts, Nice—see Nice
Musée Cantini— see Marseilles/Cantini
Musée Cantonal des Beaux-Arts, Lausanne, Switzerland
Musée Guimet, Paris, France
Musée du Havre, Le Havre, France (see also Le Havre/Municipal)
Musée du Jeu de Paume, Paris, France
Musée Municipal, Brest, France
Musée de Quebec—see Quebec
Musée St. Pierre, Lyon, France
Musée de Verviers, Verviers, Belgium
Musée du Vin, Pauillac (Gironde), France
Museen der Stadt Köln—see Cologne/Stadt
Museo de Arte Contemporaneo, Caracas—see Caracas/Contemporaneo
Museo de Arte Contemporaneo "La Tertulia," Cali, Colombia
Museo de Arte Contemporaneo Rufino Tamayo—see Mexico City/Contemporaneo
Museo de Arte Moderno, Barcelona—see Barcelona
Museo de Arte Moderno, Bogota, Colombia
Museo de Arte Moderno, Buenos Aires—see Buenos Aires/Moderno
Museo de Arte Moderno, Mexico City—see Mexico City/Moderno
Museo Dr. Genaro Perez, Cordoba, Argentina
Museo Emilio A. Caraffa, Cordoba, Argentina
Museo Juan B. Castagnino, Rosario, Argentina
Museo Municipal de Bellas Artes, Montevideo—see Montevideo/Municipal
Museo Nacional de Bellas Artes, Buenos Aires—see Argentina/Nacional
Museo Nacional de Bellas Artes, Montevideo—see Uruguay/Nacional
Museo Nacional de Historia, Mexico City, Mexico

Museo Provincial de Bellas Artes, Bilbao, Spain

Museo Provincial de Bellas Artes, Vitoria, Spain

Museo Rosario, Santa Fe, Argentina

Museu de Arte Contemporanea, Sao Paolo—*see* Sao Paolo/Contemporanea

Museum of African American Art, Santa Monica—*see* Santa Monica/MAAA

Museum of the City of New York

Museum of Contemporary Art, La Jolla—*see* La Jolla

Museum of Contemporary Art, Los Angeles—*see* Los Angeles/MOCA

Museum of Contemporary Art, Utrecht—*see* Utrecht/Contemporary

Museum of Contemporary Crafts, NYC

Museum Klingspor, Offenbach—*see* Offenbac/Klingspor

Museum of Living Art—*see* PMA

Museum Ludwig, Cologne—*see* Cologne/Ludwig

Museum of Military History, Washington, D.C.

Museum of Modern Art, Haifa—*see* Ilaifa

Museum of Modern Art, NYC—*see* MOMA

Musem of Modern Art, Saitama—*see* Saitama/Modern

Museum of Modern Art, Skopje—*see* Skopje/Modern

Museum für Moderne Kunst, Frankfurt—*see* Frankfurt/Moderne

Museum für Moderner Kunst, Vienna—*see* Vienna/Moderner

Museum of New Mexico Art Gallery—*see* Santa Fe, N.M.

Museum Schloss Marburg, Leverkusen, Germany

Museum of Science and Industry, Chicago, Ill.

Museum der Stadt Leoben, Leoben, Austria

Museum des 20. Jahrhunderts, Vienna, Austria

Muskegon/Hackley. Hackley Art Center, Muskegon, Mich.

Mutual Life Insurance Building, Chicago, Ill.

N

NAACP. National Association for the Advancement of Colored People

NAD. The National Academy of Design, NYC

NCFA. National Collection of Fine Arts, Washington, D.C.

NIAL. National Institute of Arts and Letters, NYC

NMAA. National Museum of American Art, Washington, D.C.

NMWA. National Museum of Women in the Arts, Washington, D.C.

NPG. National Portrait Gallery, Washington, D.C.

NYPL. The New York Public Library, NYC

NYU. New York University (incl. Grey Art Gallery)

Nagaoka City Hall, Nagaoka, Japan

Nagaoka, Japan. Museum of Contemporary Art, Nagaoka, Japan

Nantucket. Artists' Association of Nantucket, Mass.

The Naropa Institute, Boulder, Col.

Nashville. Tennessee Fine Arts Center, Nashville, Tenn.

Nassau County Museum of Fine Art, Syosset, N.Y.

The National Academy of Design—*see* NAD

National Academy of Sciences, Washington, D.C.

National Arts Foundation,, NYC

National Bank of Des Moines

National Economics Research Association

National Gallery of Canada—*see* Ottawa/National

National Gallery, Dublin—*see* Dublin/National

National Gallery, Reykjavik—*see* Reykjavik

National Gallery of Scotland—*see* Edinburgh/National

National Gallery of Art, Washington, D.C.

National Institute of Arts and Letters—*see* NIAL

National Life Insurance Co.

National Museum, Athens—*see* Greece/National

National Museum, Jerusalem—*see* Israel Museum

National Museum, Sofia—*see* Sofia

National Museum of Art, Osaka—*see* Osaka/National

National Museum of American Art, Washington, D.C.—*see* NMAA

National Museum of Wales, Cardiff, Wales

National Museum of Western Art, Tokyo, Japan

National Museum of Women in the Arts—*see* NMWA

National Orange Show, San Bernadino, Calif.

National Portrait Gallery—*see* NPG

National U.—*see* George Washington U.

Nebraska State Teachers College

U. of Nebraska (incl. Sheldon Memorial Art Gallery)

Needham Harper & Steers Inc.

Neenah/Bergstrom. John Nelson Bergstrom Art Center and Museum, Neenah, Wisc.

Neiman-Marcus Co.

William Rockhill Nelson Gallery of Art—*see* Kansas City/Nelson

Nelson-Atkins Art Gallery—*see* Kansas City/Nelson

Netherlands Film Museum, Amsterdam, Holland

Neue Galerie, Essen—*see* Essen/NG

Neue Galerie-Sammlung Ludwig, Aachen—*see* Aachen/Ludwig

Neue Pinakotek, Munich—*see* Munich/NP

U. of Nevada

Newark Museum, Newark, N.J.

Newark Public Library, Newark, N.J.

Newberry Library, Chicago, Ill.

New Britain/American. New Britain Museum of American Art, New Britain, Conn.

New Brunswick Museum—*see* St. John, N.B.

New College, Sarasota, Fla.

New England Merchants National Bank, Boston

U. of New Hampshire (incl. Paul Creative Arts Center)

The New Harmony Gallery of Contemporary Art, New Harmony, Ind.

New Haven Public Library, New Haven, Conn.

New Jersey State Cultural Center, Trenton, N.J.

New Jersey State Museum—*see* Trenton/State

New London. Lyman Allyn Museum, New London, Conn.

New Mexico State U.

U. of New Mexico (incl. University Art Museum, Albuquerque)

New Museum of Contemporary Art, NYC

New Orleans/Delgado. Isaac Delgado Museum of Art, New Orleans, La.

New Orleans Museum of Art, New Orleands, La.

New Paltz/SUNY. State University of New York at New Paltz

Newport Harbor Art Museum, Newport Beach, Calif.

New School for Social Research, NYC

Newsweek Magazine

New Trier High School, Winnetka, Ill.

The New York Bank for Savings, NYC

New York Coliseum, NYC

New York Cultural Center (formerly Gallery of Modern Art, NYC)

New York Hilton Hotel

New York Hospital, NYC

The New York Public Library—*see* NYPL

New York School of Interior Design

New York State Art Commission, Albany

New York, State University of—*see* individual campuses

The New York Times

New York University—*see* NYU

Nice. Musée des Beaux Arts, Nice, France

Niigata Museum, Japan

Norfolk. Norfolk Museum of Arts and Sciences, Norfolk, Va.

Norfolk/Chrysler. Walter P. Chrysler Museum of Art, Norfolk, Va.

North Carolina Museum of Art—*see* Raleigh/NCMA

North Carolina National Bank

North Carolina/State. North Carolina State Museum, Raleigh (*see also* Raleigh/NCMA)

North Carolina State U.

U. of North Carolina (incl. Weatherspoon Art Gallery of The Women's

College at Greensboro)
North Central Bronx Hospital, Bronx, N.Y.
U. of North Dakota
Northeast Missouri State Teachers College
Northern Illinois U., De Kalb
U. of Northern Iowa
Northern Trust Co., Chicago, Ill.
Northland College
North Shore State Bank, Milwaukee, Wisc.
North Texas State U.
Northwest Missouri State College
Northwestern National Life Insurance Co.
Northwestern U.
Northwood Institute, Dallas, Tex.
Norton Gallery and School of Art—*see* West Palm/Norton
U. of Notre Dame
Nurnberg. Stadtische Kunstsammlung, Nurnberg, Germany

O

OBD—*see* Basler Denkmalpflege
Oak Cliff Savings and Loan, Dallas, Tex.
Oakland Museum, Oakland, Calif.; formerly **Oakland/AM,** Oakland Art Museum
Oakland Public Library, Oakland, Calif.
Oberlin College (incl. Allen Memorial Art Museum)
Offenbach/Klingspor. Museum Klingspor, Offenbach, West Germany
Offentliche Kunstsammlung, Basel— *see* Basel/Offentliche
Ogunquit. Museum of Art of Ogunquit, Me.
Ohara Art Museum, Kurashiki, Japan
The Ohio Company, Columbus, Ohio
The Ohio State U.
Ohio Wesleyan U.
Ohio U.
Oklahoma. Oklahoma Art Center, Oklahoma City, Ok.
Oklahoma State Art Collection
U. of Oklahoma
Oldenburg. Oldenburger Stadtmuseum, Oldenburg, Germany
Olivet College
The Olsen Foundation Inc., New Haven, Conn.
Olympia/Washington State Capital Museum, Olympia, Wash.
Omaha/Joslyn. Joslyn Art Museum, Omaha, Neb.
The 180 Beacon Collection of Contemporary Art, Boston, Mass.
Oran. Musée Demaeght, Oran, Algiers
Orange Coast College, Costa Mesa, Calif.
Oregon State U.
U. of Oregon
Orlando. Central Florida Museum, Orlando, Fla. (*see also* Loch Haven Art Center)
Osaka/Municipal. Osaka Municipal Art Museum, Osaka, Japan
Osaka/National. National Museum of Art, Osaka, Japan
Oslo/National. Nasjonalgalleriet, Oslo, Norway
Oswego/SUNY. State University of New York at Oswego
Otis Art Institute, Los Angeles, Calif.
Ottawa/National. National Gallery of Canada, Ottawa
Otterbein College
Outre-Mer—*see* Paris/Outre-Mer
Owens-Corning Fiberglass Corp.
Oxford. U. of Oxford, England
Oxford/MOMA. Museum of Modern Art, Oxford, England

P

PAFA. The Pennsylvania Academy of the Fine Arts, Philadelphia
PCA. Print Council of America, NYC
PMA. Philadelphia Museum of Art, Philadelphia, Pa. (incl. Museum of Living Art, Academy of Natural Sciences, and Rodin Museum)
P.S. 144, NYC
U. of the Pacific
Pacific Indemnity Co.
Palais des Beaux-Arts, Brussels—*see* Brussels/Beaux-Arts
Palm Beach Company, NYC
Palm Springs Desert Museum, Palm Springs, Calif.

Palomar College, San Marcos, Calif.

Palos Verdes Art Gallery, Palos Verdes, Calif.

Palos Verdes Community Arts Association

Paris/Beaubourg. Centre National d'Art et de Culture Georges Pompidou, Centre Beaubourg, Paris

Paris/Moderne. Musée d'Art Moderne de la Ville de Paris, France (*see also* France/National)

Paris/Outre-Mer. Musée de la France d'Outre-Mer, Paris

Park College

Parkersburg Art Center, Parkersburg, W.Va.

The Parrish Museum—*see* Southampton/Parrish

Pasadena/AM. The Pasadena Art Museum, Pasadena, Calif.; **Pasadena Museum School**

Paul Creative Arts Center—*see* U. of New Hampshire

Peabody College, Memphis, Tenn.

Peabody Institute of the City of Baltimore

Peabody Museum, Salem, Mass.

Pecos Art Museum, Marfa, Tex.

Pendleton High School, Pendleton, Ore.

William Penn Memorial Museum—*see* Harrisburg, Pa./State Museum

The Pennsylvania Academy of the Fine Arts—*see* PAFA

The Pennsylvania State U.

U. of Pennsylvania

J.C. Penney Corp.

Pensacola Art Center, Pensacola, Fla.

The Pentagon, Washington, D.C.

Pepperdine U.

Pepsi-Cola Co.

Philadelphia Art Alliance, Philadelphia, Pa.

Philadelphia College of Art (formerly Philadelphia Museum School)

The Philadelphia Museum of Art—*see* PMA

Philadelphia Zoological Gardens

Philbrook Art Center—*see* Tulsa/Philbrook

Philip Morris Collection, NYC

Phillipines/MA. Phillipines Museum of Art, Manila

Phillips. The Phillips Gallery, Washington, D.C.; **The Phillips Gallery School**

Phillips Academy, Addison Gallery of American Art—*see* Andover/Phillips

Phillips Exeter Academy, The Lamont Art Gallery—*see* Exeter

Phoenix Art Museum, Phoenix, Az.

Pinacotheca Museum, Osaka, Japan

Pinacothèque National Museum, Athens, Greece—*see* Greece/National

Pinakothiki, Athens, Greece—*see* Greece/National

Pioneer Aerodynamic Systems

Pittsfield/Berkshire. Bershire Atheneum, Pittsfield, Mass.

Pitzer College

Plattsburgh/SUNY. State University of New York at Plattsburgh

Pomona College

Ponce Museum of Art, Ponce, Puerto Rico

Poole Technical College, Dorset, England

Port Authority of New York & New Jersey

Port Washington, L.I. Library Gallery, Port Washington, Long Island, N.Y.

Portland, Me./MA. Portland Museum of Art, Portland, Me.

Portland, Ore./AM. Portland Art Museum, Portland, Ore.; **Portland (Ore.) Museum School**

Portland (Ore.) State College

Potsdam/SUNY. State University of New York at Potsdam

Power Gallery of Contemporary Art—*see* U. of Sydney

Prague/National. Norodni (National) Galerie, Prague, Czechoslovakia

Pratt Institute

Prendergast Free Library Art Gallery—*see* Jamestown/Prendergast

Prentice-Hall Inc.

Princeton Print Club, Princeton, N.J.

Princeton U.

The Print Club, Philadelphia, Pa.

Print Club of Rochester, N.Y.

Print Council of America—*see* PCA

Pro-Civitate-Christiana, Assisi, Italy

Provincetown/Chrysler—*see* Norfolk/Chrysler

Prudential Insurance Co. of America, Newark, N.J.
Prudential Lines Inc.
Publishers Printing Co.
U. of Puerto Rico
Purchase/SUNY. State University of New York at Purchase (incl. Neuberger Museum)
Purdue U.
The Pure Oil Co.

Q

Quaker Oats Co.
Quaker Ridge School, Scarsdale, N.Y.
Quebec. Musée de Quebec, Canada
Queens Museum, Flushing, N.Y.
Queens College of the City U. of New York
Queens U., Kingston, Ontario, Canada
Quimica Argentia, Buenos Aires, Argentina

R

RAC. Richmond Art Center, Richmond, Calif.
RISD. Rhode Island School of Design
Radcliffe College, Cambridge, Mass.
Radio Corporation of America
Rahr-West Museum, Manitowoc, Wisc.
Raleigh/NCMA. North Carolina Museum of Art, Raleigh (see also North Carolina/State)
Randolph-Macon College
Randolph-Macon Woman's College (incl. Lynchburg Art Gallery)
Ration Mfg. Co.
Raycom Industries
Reader's Digest
Reading/Public. Reading Public Museum and Art Gallery, Reading, Pa.
Recklinghausen. Stadtische Kunsthalle, Recklinghausen, Germany
U. of the Redlands
Red Wing. Interstate Clinic, Red Wing, Minn.
Reed College
Regina/MacKenzie. Norman MacKenzie Art Gallery, Regina, Canada
Remington-Rand Corp.
Renaissance Society—see U. of Chicago

Renault & Cie, Paris, France
Rennes. Musée des Beaux-Arts of the Musée de Rennes, France
Rensselaer Polytechnic Institute
Revere Copper & Brass, Inc.
Revlon Inc.
Reykjavik. National Gallery, Reykjavik, Iceland
Reynolds Metals Co.
Rhode Island School of Design—see RISD
U. of Rhode Island
Rice U., Houston, Tex.
Rich-Lan Corp.
Richmond (Calif.) Art Center—see RAC
U. of Richmond (incl. Marsh Gallery)
Ridgefield/Aldrich. Larry Aldrich Museum of Contemporary Art, Ridgefield, Conn.
Rijksmuseum Amsterdam, Holland
Rijksmuseum Kröller-Müller, Otterlo, Holland
Ringling. John and Mable Ringling Museum of Art, Sarasota, Fla. Ringling School of Art
Rio Cuarto. Museo Municipal de Bellas Artes, Rio Cuarto, Argentina
Rio Hondo College, Whittier, Calif.
Rio de Janeiro Museu de Arte Moderna, Rio de Janeiro, Brazil
Ripon College
Riverside Museum, NYC—see Brandeis U.
Roanoke Fine Arts Center, Roanoke, Va.
Sara Roby Foundation, NYC
Rochester Institute of Technology, Rochester, N.Y.
U. of Rochester (incl. Rochester Memorial Art Gallery)
Rockefeller Brothers Fund, NYC
Rockefeller Center, NYC
Rockefeller Institute—see Rockefeller U.
Rockefeller U., NYC
Rockford/Burpee. Harry and Della Burpee Gallery, Rockford, Ill.
Rockland/Farnsworth. William A. Farnsworth Library and Art Museum, Rockland, Me.
Rock River (Wyo.) High School
Rodin Museum, Philadelphia—see PMA

Nicholas Roerich Museum, NYC

Will Rogers Shrine, Colorado Springs, Col.

Rome/Nazionale. Galleria Nazionale d'Arte Moderna, Rome, Italy

U. of Rome, Italy

Edward Root Collection—*see* Utica

Rose Art Museum—*see* Brandeis U.

Rosenthal China Co.

Rosenwald Collection—*see* National Gallery of Art, Washington, D.C.

Roswell Museum and Art Center, Roswell, N.M.

Rotterdam. Museum Boymans-van Beuningen, Rotterdam, Holland

Rouen. Musée des Beaux-Arts et de Céramique, Rouen, France

Rumsey Hall School, Washington, Conn.

Russell Sage College

Rutgers U.

Rybak. Rybak Art Museum, Bat Yam, Israel

S

SAGA. The Society of American Graphic Artists, NYC.

SFAI. San Francisco Art Institute, San Francisco, Calif.

SFMA. San Francisco Museum of Modern Art, San Francisco, Calif.; formerly San Francisco Museum of Art

SFPL. San Francisco Public Library, San Francisco, Calif.

SRGM. The Solomon R. Guggenheim Museum, NYC

Saarlandmuseum, Saarbrucken, Germany

Sacramento/Crocker. E.B. Crocker Art Gallery, Sacramento, Calif.

Sacramento State U. (formerly Sacramento State College)

Sacred Heart Seminary, Detroit, Mich.

Safad. Glicenstein Museum, Safad, Israel

Safeco Building

Saginaw Art Museum, Saginaw, Mich.

St. Albans School, Washington, D.C.

St. Anthony's College of Oxford U., Oxford, England

St. Bernard's Church, Hazardville, Conn.

St. Cloud State College

St.-Etienne Musée Municipal d'Art et d'Industrie, St.-Etienne, France

St. George's Episcopal Church, NYC

St. John, N.B. New Brunswick Museum, St. John, Canada

St. John's Abbey, Collegeville, Minn.

St. Joseph/Albrecht. Albrecht Gallery Museum of Art, St. Joseph, Mo.

St. Lawrence U. (incl. Griffiths Art Center)

St. Louis/City. The City Art Museum of St. Louis, Mo.

St. Mary's College, Indiana

St. Patrick's, Menasha, Wisc.

St. Paul Gallery and School of Art—*see* Minnesota/MA

St. Petersburg, Fla. Art Club of St. Petersburg, Fla.

U. of St. Thomas, Tex.

Saitama/Modern. Museum of Modern Art, Saitama, Japan

Salem (Ore.) Art Museum

Salk Institute, La Jolla, Calif.

Salt Lake City Public Library, Salt Lake City, Utah

Salzburg. Salzburger Museum Carolino Augusteum, Salzburg, Austria

San Antonio/MA. San Antonio Museum of Art, San Antonio, Tex.

San Antonio/McNay. Marion Koogler McNay Art Institute, San Antonio, Tex.

Carl Sandburg Memorial Library

San Diego. The Fine Arts Gallery of San Diego, Calif.; **San Diego Fine Arts School**

San Diego State U. (formerly San Diego State College)

San Fernando Valley State U.

San Francisco Art Association—*see* SFAI

San Francisco Municipal Art Commission, San Francisco, Calif.

San Francisco Museum of Modern Art—*see* SFMA

San Francisco Public Library—*see* SFPL

San Francisco State College

San Joaquin Pioneer Museum and Haggin Art Galleries—*see* Stockton

San Jose Library, San Jose, Calif.

San Jose Museum of Art, San Jose, Calif.

San Jose State U. (formerly San Jose State College)

San Salvador Museo Nacional, San Salvador, El Salvador

Santa Barbara/MA. Santa Barbara Museum of Art, Santa Barbara, Calif.; Santa Barbara Museum School

Santa Fe, N.M. Museum of New Mexico Art Gallery, Santa Fe, N.M.

Santa Monica/MAAA. Museum of African American Art, Santa Monica, Calif.

Santiago, Chile. Museo Nacional de Bellas Artes, Santiago, Chile

Sao Paolo. Museu de Arte Moderna, Sao Paolo, Brazil

Sao Paolo/Contemporanea. Museu de Arte Contemporanea, Sao Paolo, Brazil

Sapporo. Hokkaido Prefectural Museum of Modern Art, Sapporo, Japan

Sarah Lawrence College

U. of Saskatchewan, Saskatoon, Canada

Satakumman Museo, Pori, Finland

Savannah/Telfair. Telfair Academy of Arts and Sciences, Inc., Savannah, Ga.

Savings Bank Association of New York State

Schaeffer School of Design, San Francisco, Calif.

The Schenectady Museum, Schenectady, N.Y.

Michael Schiavone & Sons Inc., North Haven, Conn.

Scheidam/Stedelijk. Stedelijk Museum, Scheidam, Holland

J. Henry Schroder Banking Corp.

Schwebber Electronics

Scientific American Inc.

Scottish National Gallery of Modern Art—see Edinburgh/Modern

Scovill Mfg. Co.

Scranton/Everhart. Everhart Museum, Scranton, Pa.

Scripps College

Seagram Collection

Seaton Hall Inc., NYC

Seattle/AM. Seattle Art Museum, Seattle, Wash.

Seattle Civic Center, Seattle, Wash.

Seattle Public Library, Seattle, Wash.

Seattle U.

Security Pacific National Bank, Los Angeles, Calif.

Seibu Museum of Art, Tokyo, Japan

Shasta College, Redding, Calif.

Shelburne Museum Inc., Shelburne, Vt.

Sheldon Memorial Art Gallery—see U. of Nebraska

Shell Oil Co.

E. Sherry Truck Company

Shuttleworth Carton Co.

Sierra Nevada Museum of Art, Reno, Nev.

Silvermine Guild of Arts, New Canaan, Conn.; Silvermine Guild School of Art

Simmons College

Norton Simon Museum, Pasadena, Calif.

The Singer Company Inc.

Sioux City Art Center, Sioux City, Iowa

Skidmore College

Skidmore, Owings & Merrill

Skopje/Modern. Museum of Modern Art, Skopje, Yugoslavia

Skowhegan School of Painting and Sculpture, Skowhegan, Me.

Slater Memorial Museum, Norwich, Conn.

W. & J. Sloane, Inc.

Smith College

Smithsonian Institution, Washington, D.C. (see also Hirshhorn; NCFA; NPG)

Société National des Arts Contemporains, Paris, France

The Society of American Graphic Artists—see SAGA

Society of the Four Arts, Palm Beach, Fla.

Society of New York Hospitals

Sofia. National Museum, Sofia, Bulgaria

Sofu School of Flower Arrangement, Tokyo, Japan

Southampton/Parrish. The Parrish Museum, Southampton, N.Y.

South County Bank, St. Louis, Mo.

Southeast Banking Corp., Miami, Fla.

U. of Southern California

Southern Idaho College, Twins Falls

Southern Illinois U.

Southern Methodist U.

Southern Oregon College

Southern Vermont Art Center, Manchester

U. of South Florida

South Mall, Albany, N.Y.

Southwestern College, Chula Vista, Calif.

Southwestern (College) at Memphis

Southwest Missouri State College

J.B. Speed Art Museum—see Louisville/Speed

Spelman College

Spokane Coliseum, Spokane, Wash.

Sports Museum, NYC

Springfield Art Center, Springfield, Ohio

Springfield College, Springfield, Mass. (incl. Dana Art Center)

Springfield, Ill./State. Illinois State Museum of Natural History and Art, Springfield, Ill.

Springfield, Mass./MFA. Museum of Fine Arts, Springfield, Mass.

Springfield, Mo./AM. Springfield Art Museum, Springfield, Mo.

Staatliche Graphische Sammlung Munchen, Munich, West Germany

Stadtische Galerie im Lehbachhaus, Munich, West Germany

Stadtische Galerie, Munich—see Munich/SG

Stadtische Kunsthalle, Düsseldorf—see Düsseldorf/Kunsthalle

Stamford Museum, Stamford, Conn.

Standard Oil Co. of California

Standard Oil Co. of New Jersey

Stanford U.

Starr King School for the Ministry, Berkeley, Calif.

State Art Collection, Oklahoma City, Ok.

State of California

State of Hawaii

State of Iowa

State of Louisiana Art Commission—see Baton Rouge

State College of Iowa

State College at Salem, Mass.

State Historical Society of Missouri—see Columbia, Mo.

State Street Bank and Trust Co., Boston, Mass.

State U. of Iowa

State U. of New York—see individual campuses

Staten Island Institute of Arts and Sciences, St. George, S.I., N.Y.

Steel Service Institute, Cleveland, Oh.

Stephens College

Steuben Glass

Stockholm/National. Moderna Museet (Nationalmuseum), Stockholm, Sweden

Stockholm/SFK. Svenska-Franska-Konstgalleriet, Stockholm, Sweden

Stockton. San Joaquin Pioneer Museum and Haggin Art Galleries, Stockton, Calif.

Stony Brook/SUNY. State University of New York at Stony Brook

Storm King Art Center, Mountainville, N.Y.

Stratford College, Danville, Va.

Studio Museum. The Studio Museum of Harlem, NYC

Stuttgart. Staatsgalerie Stuttgart, West Germany

Stuttgart/WK. Wurttembergischer Kunstverein, Stuttgart, West Germany

Peter Stuyvesant Collection, Amsterdam, Holland

Suermondt-Ludwig Museum—see Aachen/S-L

Suffolk County National Bank, Riverhead, N.Y.

Sunflower Corp.

Svenska Handelsbanken, Stockholm, Sweden

Svenska-Franska Konstgalleriet—see Stockholm/SFK

Svest, Germany

Swarthmore College (incl. Wilcox Gallery)

Sweden/Goteborgs. Goteborgs Konstmuseum, Gothenburg, Sweden

Sweet Briar College

Swiss Bank Corp.

Sheldon Swope Art Gallery—see Terre Haute/Swope

Sydney/AG. The Art Gallery of New South Wales, Sydney, Australia

U. of Sydney (incl. Power Gallery of

Contemporary Art)

Syracuse/Everson. Everson Museum of Art, Syracuse, N.Y.; **Syracuse Museum School**

Syracuse U.

T

Tacoma Art Museum, Tacoma, Wash.

Taconic Foundation, Inc., NYC

Taft Museum, Cincinnati, Ohio

Talavara. Museo Talavara, Ciudad Bolivar, Venezuela

Tampa/AI. Tampa Art Institute Gallery, Tampa, Fla.

Taos (N.M.) County Court House

Tate Gallery, London, England

Taubman Corp., Ann Arbor, Mich.

Technimetrics, NYC

Tel Aviv Museum of Art, Tel Aviv, Israel

Telfair Academy of Arts and Sciences, Inc.—*see* Savannah/Telfair

Temple Beth El, Detroit, Mich.

Temple Israel, St. Louis, Mo.

Temple U.

Tennessee Fine Arts Center—*see* Nashville

Tennessee State Museum, Nashville

U. of Tennessee

Terra Museum of American Art, Chicago—*see* Chicago/Terra

Terre Haute/Swope. Sheldon Swope Art Gallery, Terre Haute, Ind.

Terry Art Institute, Miami, Fla.

Texas Fine Arts Association—*see* Austin

Texas Technological College, Lubbock

Texas Tech U., Lubbock

Texas Wesleyan College

Texas Western College

U. of Texas (incl. James A. Michener Foundation)

3M Company, St. Paul, Minn.

Louis Comfort Tiffany Foundation, NYC

Time Inc.

Tishman Realty & Construction Co., Inc., NYC

Tokyo/Central. Tokyo Central Museum, Tokyo, Japan

Tokyo Folk Art Museum, Tokyo, Japan

Tokyo/Modern. National Museum of Modern Art, Tokyo, Japan (see also National Museum of Western Art, Tokyo)

Tokyo U. of Arts, Tokyo, Japan

Toledo/MA. Toledo Museum of Art, Toldeo, Ohio

Topeka Public Library, Topeka, Kan.

Topeka U.—*see* Washburn U. of Topeka

Toronto. Art Gallery of Toronto, Canada

Torrington Mfg. Corp.

Tougaloo College

Toulon. Musée d'Art, Toulon, France

Tourcoing. Musée Municipal, Tourcoing, France

Towner Art Gallery, Eastbourne, England

Towson State College, Baltimore, Md.

Trade Bank and Trust Company, NYC

Trade Building, Moscow, USSR

Traders National Bank, Kansas City, Mo.

Transamerica Corp.

Travenol Laboratories, Deerfield, Ill.

Treadwell Corp., NYC

Trenton/State. New Jersey State Museum, Trenton

Tretyakov Art Gallery, Moscow, USSR

Trinity College, Dublin, Ireland

Harry S. Truman Library, Independence, Mo.

Tucson Art Center, Tucson, Az.

U. of Tucson

Tufts Dental College, Boston, Mass.

Tulane U. of Louisiana

Tulsa/Philbrook. Philbrook Art Center, Tulsa, Ok.

Tupperware Museum, Orlando, Fla.

Turin/Civico. Museo Civico di Torino, Turin, Italy (incl. Galleria Civica d'Arte Moderna)

Turku Museum, Finland

Tusculum College, Greenville, Tenn.

Tweed Gallery—*see* U. of Minnesota

Twentieth Century-Fox Film Corp.

Two Trees, NYC

U

UCLA. U. of California, Los Angeles

USIA. United States Information Agency
US Coast Guard
US Department of the Interior
US Labor Department
US Maritime Commission
US Military Academy, West Point, N.Y.
US Navy
U.S. Rubber Co.
US State Department
U.S. Steel Corp.
US Treasury Department
Uffizi Gallery, Florence, Italy
Ulster Museum, Belfast, Northern Ireland
Underwood-Neuhaus Corp.
Union Camp Corp.
Union Carbide Corp.
Union College (N.Y.)
Union of Plastic Artists, Bucharest, Romania
Unitarian Church, Princeton, N.J.
United Aircraft Corp.
United Mutual Savings Bank
United Nations
United Tanker Ltd.
Upjohn Co.
Uris Buildings Corp.
Uris-Hilton Hotels
Uruguay/Nacional. Museo Nacional de Bellas Artes, Montevideo, Uruguay—*see* *also* Montevideo/Municipal
Utah Museum of Fine Arts, Salt Lake City
Utah State U.
U. of Utah
Utica. Munson-Williams-Proctor Institute, Utica, N.Y. (incl. Edward Root Collection)
Utica Public Library, Utica, N.Y.
Utrecht. Centraal Museum, Utrecht, Holland
Utrecht/Contemporary. Museum of Contemporary Art, Utrecht, Holland

V
VMFA. Virginia Museum of Fine Arts, Richmond
Valley Bank of Springfield, Mass.

Valparaiso U. (Ind.)
Vancouver Art Gallery, Vancouver, Canada
Vanderbilt U.
Vassar College, Poughkeepsie, N.Y.
Venice/Contemporaneo. Museo dell'Arte Contemporaneo, Venice, Italy
U. of Vermont (incl. Robert Hull Fleming Museum)
Victoria (B.C.). Art Gallery of Greater Victoria, B.C., Canada
Victoria and Albert Museum, London, England
Vienna/Moderner. Museen für Moderner Kunst, Vienna, Austria
Virginia Commonwealth U.
Virginia Museum of Fine Arts—*see* VMFA
Virginia National Bank, Norfolk
Virginia State College
U. of Virginia (incl. Bayly Museum, Charlottesville)

W
WDAY, Fargo, N.D.
WGMA. Washington Gallery of Modern Art, Washington, D.C.
WMAA. Whitney Museum of American Art, NYC
Wadsworth Atheneum—*see* Hartford/Wadsworth
Wagner College
Waitsfield/Bundy. Bundy Art Gallery, Waitsfield, Vt.
Wake Forest U. (formerly Wake Forest College)
Wales—*see* National Museum of Wales
Walker. The Walker Art Center, Minneapolis, Minn.
Walker Art Gallery, Liverpool, England—*see* Liverpool/Walker
Wallraf-Richartz-Museum—*see* Cologne
Walnut Creek Municipal Collection, Walnut Creek, Calif.
Walters Art Gallery—*see* Baltimore/Walters
Warner Bros.
Warsaw. Academy of Fine Arts, Warsaw, Poland
Warsaw/National. Muzeum Narodwe

(National Museum), Warsaw, Poland

Washburn U. of Topeka (incl. Mulvane Art Museum)

Washington County Museum of Fine Arts—*see* Hagerstown/County MFA

Washington Federal Bank, Miami, Fla.

Washington Gallery of Modern Art—*see* WGMA

Washington Post

Washington State U. (incl. Spokane Art Center)

Washington U., St. Louis, Mo.

U. of Washington

Wasserman Development Corp.

Waterloo Municipal Galleries, Waterloo, Iowa

U. of Waterloo

Wayne State U., Detroit, Mich.

Weatherspoon Art Gallery—*see* U. of North Carolina

Wellesley College, Wellesely, Mass.

Wellington Management Co.

Wells College

Wells, Rich, Greene, Inc., NYC

Wesleyan College (Ga.)

Wesleyan U. (Conn.) (incl. Davison Art Center)

Western Art Museum, Tokyo—*see* National Museum of Western Art, Tokyo

Western Art Museum, USSR—*see* Moscow/Western

Western Michigan U.

Western New Mexico U.

Western Washington State College

Westfalischer Kunstverein, Munster—*see* Munster/WK

Westfield. State College at Westfield, Mass.

Westinghouse Electric Corp.

Westminster Academy, Salisbury, Conn.

Westminster Foundation, Iowa City, Ia.

Westmoreland County/MA. Westmoreland County Museum of Art, Greensburg, Pa.

West Palm Beach/Norton. Norton Gallery and School of Art, West Palm Beach, Fla.

West Point—*see* US Military Academy

Westport Art Education Society, Westport, Conn.

Westport Savings Bank, Westport, Conn.

West Virginia State College

Whatcom Museum of History and Art, Bellingham, Wash.

Wheaton College

The White House, Washington, D.C.

Whitman College, Walla Walla, Wash.

Whitney Communications Corp., NYC

Whitney Museum of American Art—*see* WMAA

Whitworth Art Gallery, U. of Manchester, England

Wichita/AM. The Wichita Art Museum, Wichita, Kan.

Wichita State U.

Wiesbaden. Stadtisches Museum Wiesbaden, Wiesbaden, Germany

Wilberfeld. Stadtisches Museum, Wilberfeld, Germany

Wilcox Gallery—*see* Swarthmore College

College of William and Mary, Williamsburg, Va.

Williams College (incl. Williams College Art Museum), Williamstown, Mass.

Williamstown/Clark. Sterling and Francine Clark Art Institute, Williamstown, Mass.

Willowbrook High School, Villa Park, Ill.

Wilmington. Delaware Art Museum, Wilmington, Del.

Windsor Art Museum, Windsor, Canada

Winston-Salem Public Library, Winston-Salem, N.C.

Wisconsin State U.

U. of Wisconsin (incl. Elvehjem Museum of Art)

Witte Memorial Museum, San Antonio, Tex.

Thomas W. Wood Art Gallery—*see* Montpelier/Wood

Woodward Foundation, Washington, D.C.

College of Wooster, Wooster, Ohio

Worcester/AM. Worcester Art Museum, Worcester, Mass.; Worcester Museum School

Wrexham Foundation, New Haven, Conn.

Wright Art Center—*see* Beloit College
Wright State U., Dayton, Ohio
Wuppertal. Stadtisches Museum, Wuppertal, Germany
Wuppertal/von der Heydt. Von der Heydt-Museum der Stadt Wuppertal, Wuppertal, Germany
Wurttembergischer Kunstverein, Stuttgart—*see* Stuttgart/WK
Wylain Corp., Fort Worth, Tex.
U. of Wyoming

X
Xerox Corp.

Y
Yaddo, Saratoga Springs, N.Y.
Yale U., New Haven, Conn.
Yellowstone Art Center, Billings, Mont.
York U., Toronto, Canada
Youngstown/Butler. Butler Institute of American Art, Youngstown, Ohio
Youngstown U.

Z
Zanesville/AI. Art Institute of Zanesville, Ohio
Zurich. Kunsthaus Zurich, Switzerland
Zurich/KS. KunstgewerbeMuseum der Stadt, Zurich, Switzerland

Galleries Representing the Artists in This Book

ACA Galleries
41 East 57th Street
New York, NY 10022

Abante Gallery
124 Southwest Yamhill
Portland, OR 97204

Adams-Middleton Gallery
3000 Maple Avenue
Dallas, TX 75201

Adelle M. Gallery & Art Service
3317 McKinnley Avenue
Dallas, TX 75204

Brooke Alexander, Inc.
59 Wooster Street
New York, NY 10012

Allrich Gallery
251 Post Street
San Francisco, CA 94108

Alpha Gallery
121 Newbury Street
Boston, MA 02116

Gallery Paule Anglim
14 Geary Street
San Francisco, CA 94108

Anhalt/Barnes Gallery
750 North La Cienega Boulevard
Los Angeles, CA 90069

Ankrum Gallery
657 North La Cienega Boulevard
Los Angeles, CA 90069

Armstrong Gallery
50 West 57th Street
New York, NY 10019

Arras Gallery
24 West 57th Street
New York, NY 10019

Asher/Faure
612 North Almont Drive
Los Angeles, CA 90069

Ruth Bachofner Gallery
804 North La Cienega Boulevard
Los Angeles, CA 90069

Galerie Beaubourg
23, rue du Renard
Paris, France 75004

Galerie Jacques Benador
7, rue de l'Hôtel-de-Ville
Geneva, Switzerland

John Berggruen Gallery
228 Grant Avenue
San Francisco, CA 94108

Galerie Claude Bernard
5-9, rue des Beaux Arts
Paris, France 75006

Galleria Blu
via Senato 18
Milan, Italy 20121

Blum Helman Gallery Inc.
20 West 57th Street
New York, NY 10019

Bluxome Gallery
173 Bluxome Street
San Francisco, CA 94107

Bologna-Landi Gallery
49 Sag Harbor Road
East Hampton, NY 11937

Mary Boone Gallery
417 West Broadway
New York, NY 10012

Grace Borgenicht Gallery
724 Fifth Avenue
New York, NY 10019

Braunstein Gallery
254 Sutter Street
San Francisco, CA 94108

Hal Bromm Gallery
90 West Broadway
New York, NY 10013

Diane Brown Gallery
560 Broadway
New York, NY 10012

Suzanne Brown Gallery
7160 Main Street
Scottsdale, AZ 85251

Marilyn Butler Fine Art
4160 North Craftsman Court
Scottsdale, AZ 85251

Susan Caldwell Inc.
383 West Broadway
New York, NY 10012

Gallery Camino Real
399 Camino Gardens Boulevard
Boca Raton, FL 33432

Campanile Gallery
200 South Michigan Avenue
Chicago, IL 60604

Charles Campbell Gallery
647 Chestnut Street
San Francisco, CA 94133

Leo Castelli Inc.
420 West Broadway
New York, NY 10012

Cherry Stone Gallery
Wellfleet, MA 02667

Christie's Contemporary Art
799 Madison Avenue
New York, NY 10021

Jeanne-Claude Christo
48 Howard Street
New York, NY 10013

Jan Cicero Gallery
221 West Erie
Chicago, IL 60610

Circle Gallery Ltd.
435 West Broadway
New York, NY 10012

Coe Kerr Gallery
49 East 82nd Street
New York, NY 10028

Sylvan Cole
200 West 57th Street
New York, NY 10019

Condeso/Lawler Gallery
76 Greene Street
New York, NY 10012

Paula Cooper Gallery
155 Wooster Street
New York, NY 10012

James Corcoran Gallery
8223 Santa Monica Boulevard
Los Angeles, CA 90046

Cordier & Ekstrom, Inc.
417 East 75th Street
New York, NY 10021

Charles Cowles Gallery
420 West Broadway
New York, NY 10012

Crown Point Press
568 Broadway
New York, NY 10012

Dart Gallery, Inc.
155 East Ohio Street
Chicago, IL 60611

Peter M. David Gallery
400 First Avenue North
Minneapolis, MN 55401

Maxwell Davidson Gallery
415 West Broadway
New York, NY 10012

Davis & Langdale Co., Inc.
231 East 60th Street
New York, NY 10022

Galerie Michel Delormé
9, rue Linné
Paris, France 75005

Marisa del Re
41 East 57th Street
New York, NY 10022

Tibor de Nagy
41 West 57th Street
New York, NY 10019

Sid Deutsch Gallery
20 West 57th Street
New York, NY 10019

DiLaurenti Gallery
383 West Broadway
New York, NY 10012

Terry Dintenfass, Inc.
50 West 57th Street
New York, NY 10019

Dolan/Maxwell Gallery
1701 Walnut Street
Philadelphia, PA 19103

Exhibit A Gallery
361 West Superior Street
Chicago, IL 60610

G.W. Einstein Co.
591 Broadway
New York, NY 10012

The Elkon Gallery
18 East 81st Street
New York, NY 10028

Andre Emmerich Gallery
41 East 57th Street
New York, NY 10022

R.C. Erpf Gallery
568 Broadway
New York, NY 10012

Fairweather-Hardin Gallery
101 East Ontario Street
Chicago, IL 60611

Joe Fawbush Editions
578 Broadway
New York, NY 10012

Ronald Feldman Fine Arts Inc.
31 Mercer Street
New York, NY 10013

Fendrick Gallery
3059 M Street, NW
Washington, DC 20007

Filmmakers Cooperative
175 Lexington Avenue
New York, NY 10016

Fischbach Gallery
24 West 57th Street
New York, NY 10019

James Fisher Gallery
1440 Blake Street, Suite 250
Denver, CO 80202

The Forum Gallery
1018 Madison Avenue
New York, NY 10021

Foster-White Gallery
311½ Occidental South
Seattle, WA 98104

Fountain Gallery
115 SW Fourth Avenue
Portland, OR 97200

Fraenkel Gallery
55 Grant Avenue
San Francisco, CA 94108

Sherry French Gallery
41 West 57th Street
New York, NY 10019

Nina Freudenheim Gallery
560 Franklin Street
Buffalo, NY 14202

Allan Frumkin Gallery
50 West 57th Street
New York, NY 10019

Fuller Goldeen
228 Grant Avenue
San Francisco, CA 94108

Galleria Il Gabbiano
via delle Frezza 51
Rome, Italy

Gimpel & Weitzenhoffer Ltd.
724 Fifth Avenue
New York, NY 10019

Barbara Gladstone Gallery
99 Greene Street
New York, NY 10012

Marian Goodman Gallery (Multiples,
Inc.)
24 West 57th Street
New York, NY 10019

The Graham Gallery
1014 Madison Avenue
New York, NY 10021

Richard Gray Gallery
620 North Michigan Avenue
Chicago, IL 60611

Ted Greenwald Gallery
181 Mott Street
New York, NY 10012

Gruenebaum Gallery
415 West Broadway
New York, NY 10012

Gump's Gallery
250 Post Street
San Francisco, CA 94108

Stephen Haller Fine Art
415 West Broadway
New York, NY 10012

Harcus Gallery
7 Newbury Street
Boston, MA 02116

Harmon-Meek Gallery
1258 Third Street
Naples, FL 33940

OK Harris Works of Art
383 West Broadway
New York, NY 10012

Haslem Fine Arts, Inc.
2121 P Street NW
Washington, DC 20037

Heath Gallery
416 East Paces Ferry Road NE
Atlanta, GA 30305

Henri Gallery
1500 21st Street NW
Washington, DC 20036

Hirschl & Adler Galleries
21 East 70th Street
New York, NY 10021

Hirschl and Adler Modern
851 Madison Avenue
New York, NY 10021

Hodges/Banks Gallery
319 First Avenue South
Seattle, WA 98104

Nancy Hoffman Gallery
429 West Broadway
New York, NY 10012

Hooks-Epstein Gallery, Inc.
1200 Bisonnet
Houston, TX 77005

Elaine Horwitch Gallery
4211 North Marshall Way
Scottsdale, AZ 85251

Hoshour Gallery
417 Second Street SW
Albuquerque, NM 87102

Max Hutchinson Gallery
127 Greene Street
New York, NY 10012

Ingber Art Gallery
415 West Broadway
New York, NY 10021

Irving Galleries
332 Worth Avenue
Palm Beach, FL 33480

Sidney Janis Gallery
110 West 57th Street
New York, NY 10019

The Jones Gallery
1264 Prospect Street
La Jolla, CA 92037

Katonah Gallery
28 Bedford Road
Katonah, NY 10536

Kauffman Galleries
2702 West Alabama
Houston, TX 77089

Kennedy Galleries
40 West 57th Street
New York, NY 10019

Kent Fine Art, Inc.
41 East 57th Street
New York, NY 10022

Phyllis Kind Gallery
313 West Superior Street
Chicago, IL 60610

Patrick King Contemporary Art
427 Massachusetts Avenue
Indianapolis, IN 46204

M. Knoedler & Co., Inc.
19 East 70th Street
New York, NY 10021

B.R. Kornblatt Gallery
406 Seventh Street NW
Washington, DC 20004

Kouros Gallery
23 East 73rd Street
New York, NY 10021

Barbara Krakow Gallery
10 Newbury Street
Boston, MA 02116

Kraushaar Galleries
724 Fifth Avenue
New York, NY 10021

Carlo Lamagna Gallery
50 West 57th Street
New York, NY 10019

Yvon Lambert
5, rue du Grenier-St. Lazare
Paris, France 75003

Margo Leavin Gallery
812 North Robertson Boulevard
Los Angeles, CA 90069

Janie C. Lee
1209 Berthea
Houston, TX 77006

Leedy-Voulkos Gallery
1919 Wyandotte
Kansas City, MO 64108

Jon Leon Gallery
31 Desbrosses Street
New York, NY 10013

Lisson Gallery
66-68 Bell Street
London, England NW1 6SR

Marion Locks Gallery
1524 Walnut Street
Philadelphia, PA 19102

Meredith Long Gallery
2323 San Felipe Road
Houston, TX 77019

Long Point Gallery
492 Commercial Street
Provincetown, MA 02657

Galleria Lorenzelli
via Sant'Andrea 19
Milan, Italy 20124

L.A. Louver Gallery
55 North Venice Boulevard
Venice, CA 90291

Galerie Lelong
20 West 57th Street
New York, NY 10019

Paul Maenz Gallery
Bismarckstrasse 50
Cologne, West Germany

Curt Marcus Gallery
578 Broadway
New York, NY 10012

Marden Fine Arts
41 Union Square
New York, NY 10003

Marlborough Gallery, Inc.
40 West 57th Street
New York, NY 10019

Marlborough Fine Art Ltd.
6 Albemarle Street
London, England W1X 4BY

Barbara Mathes Gallery
851 Madison Avenue
New York, NY 10021

Pierre Matisse Gallery
41 East 57th Street
New York, NY 10022

McIntosh/Drysdale
406 Seventh Street NW
Washington, DC 20004

David McKee Gallery
41 East 57th Street
New York, NY 10021

Louis K. Meisel Gallery
141 Prince Street
New York, NY 10012

Mekler Gallery
651 North La Cienega Boulevard
Los Angeles, CA 90069

Metro Pictures
150 Greene Street
New York, NY 10012

Middendorf Gallery
2009 Columbia Road NW
Washington, DC 20009

The Midtown Galleries
11 East 57th Street
New York, NY 10022

Robert Miller Gallery
41 East 57th Street
New York, NY 10019

Alexander F. Milliken
98 Prince Street
New York, NY 10012

Miname Gallery
3-3 Chome, Nihonbashitori, Chuo-ku
Tokyo, Japan

David Mirvish Gallery
596 Markham Street
Toronto, Canada

Modernism Gallery
236 Eighth Street
San Francisco, CA 94103

Moody Gallery
2815 Colquitt
Houston, TX 77098

Galleria Juan Mordo
Villanueva 7
Madrid, Spain 28001

Donald Morris Gallery
105 Townsend
Birmingham, MI 48011

Tobey C. Moss Gallery
7321 Beverly Boulevard
Los Angeles, CA 90036

Munson Gallery
33 Whitney Avenue
New Haven, CT 06511

Mussavi Arts Center
623 Broadway
New York, NY 10012

Newmark Gallery
1194 Third Avenue
New York, NY 10021

Newspace
5241 Melrose Avenue
Los Angeles, CA 90038

John Nichols Printmakers & Publishers
83 Grand Street
New York, NY 10013

Nielsen Gallery
179 Newbury Street
Boston, MA 02116

Odyssia Gallery
775 Park Avenue
New York, NY 10021

Frank Oehlschlaeger Gallery
28 Boulevard of the Presidents
St. Armands Key
Sarasota, FL 33578

Oil & Steel Gallery
30-40 Vernon Boulevard
Long Island City, NY 11102

Oscarsson Siegeltuch & Co.
568 Broadway
New York, NY 10012

Osuna Gallery
406 Seventh Street NW
Washington, DC 20004

The Pace Gallery
32 West 57th Street
New York, NY 10019

Herbert B. Palmer Gallery
802 North La Cienega Boulevard
Los Angeles, CA 90069

Marilyn Pearl Gallery
420 West Broadway
New York, NY 10021

Perimeter Gallery
356 Huron Street
Chicago, IL 60610

Katherine Rich Perlow Gallery
980 Madison Avenue
New York, NY 10021

Marilyn Pink Gallery
760 North La Cienega Boulevard
Los Angeles, CA 90069

Anne Plumb Gallery
81 Greene Street
New York, NY 10012

Galleria Ponce
Belgrado 5 ZP 6
Mexico City, Mexico

Princeton Gallery of Fine Art
8 Chambers Street
Princeton, NJ 08540

Max Protetch Gallery
37 West 57th Street
New York, NY 10021

Pucker-Safrai Gallery
171-73 Newbury Street
Boston, MA 02116

Yvonne Rapp Matchmaker Arts Space
2007 Frankfort Avenue
Louisville, KY 40206

Margarete Roeder Gallery
545 Broadway
New York, NY 10012

Rorick Gallery
637 Mason
San Francisco, CA 94108

Rosenfeld Gallery
113 Arch Street
Philadelphia, PA 19106

Mary Ryan Gallery
425 Columbus Avenue
New York, NY 10024

Alex Rosenberg Gallery
20 West 57th Street
New York, NY 10019

Saidenberg Gallery
1018 Madison Avenue
New York, NY 10021

Salander-O'Reilly Galleries
22 East 80th Street
New York, NY 10021

William Sawyer Gallery
3045 Clay Street
San Francisco, CA 94115

Gallery Schlesinger-Boisanté
822 Madison Avenue
New York, NY 10021

Schmidt-Bingham Gallery
41 West 57th Street
New York, NY 10019

Robert Schoelkopf Gallery
50 West 57th Street
New York, NY 10019

Galerie Schreiner
115½ East 62nd Street
New York, NY 10022

Schutz & Co.
205 West 57th Street
New York, NY 10019

Joyce Pomeroy Schwartz
Works of Art for Public Spaces
17 West 54th Street
New York, NY 10019

Galleria Schwarz
via Gesu 17
Milan, Italy

Francine Seders Gallery
6701 Greenwood Avenue North
Seattle, WA 98103

Tony Shafrazi Gallery
163 Mercer Street
New York, NY 10012

Jack Shainman Gallery
500 East 11th Street
New York, NY 10009

Anita Shapolsky Gallery
99 Spring Street
New York, NY 10012

Ruth Siegel, Ltd.
24 West 57th Street
New York, NY 10019

Smith-Andersen Gallery
200 Homer Avenue
Palo Alto, CA 94301

Soghor, Leonard & Associates
419 Broome Street
New York, NY 10013

Holly Solomon Gallery
724 Fifth Avenue
New York, NY 10019

Carl Solway Gallery
314 West Fourth Street
Cincinnati, OH 45202

Sonnabend Gallery
420 West Broadway
New York, NY 10012

Space Gallery
6015 North La Cienega Boulevard
Los Angeles, CA 90038

Sperone Westwater Inc.
142 Greene Street
New York, NY 10012

Darthea Speyer Gallery
6, rue Jacques Callot
Paris, France 75006

Staempfli Gallery
47 East 77th Street
New York, NY 10021

Elaine Starkman Gallery
465 West Broadway
New York, NY 10012

Bernice Steinbaum Gallery
132 Greene Street
New York, NY 10012

John Stoller & Co.
400 Marquette Avenue
Minneapolis, MN 55401

Allan Stone Gallery
48 East 86th Street
New York, NY 10028

Stremmel Galleries
1400 South Virginia Street
Reno, NV 89502

Gallery Takagi
Takagi-Komura Building
1-17-71 Nishiki, Naka-ku
Nagoya, Japan 460

Tatistcheff & Co.
50 West 57th Street
New York, NY 10019

Barbara Toll Fine Arts
146 Greene Street
New York, NY 10012

Tortue Gallery
2917 Santa Monica Boulevard
Los Angeles, CA 90404

Triangle Gallery
95 Minna Street
San Francisco, CA 94105

Jan Turner Gallery
8000 Melrose Avenue
Los Angeles, CA 90046

Twining Gallery
568 Broadway
New York, NY 10012

Valley House Gallery
6616 Spring Valley Road
Dallas, TX 75240

Galerie Annemarie Verna
Scheuchzerstrasse 35
Zurich, Switzerland 8006

Washburn Gallery Inc.
41 East 57th Street
New York, NY 10021

Watson Gallery
3510 Lake Street
Houston, TX 77098

John Weber Gallery
142 Greene Street
New York, NY 10012

Daniel Weinberg Gallery
619 North Almont Drive
Los Angeles, CA 90069

Wellfleet Art Gallery
Route 6
Wellfleet, MA 02667

Weyhe Gallery
794 Lexington Avenue
New York, NY 10021

Stephen Wirtz Gallery
345 Sutter Street
San Francisco, CA 94108

Woodside-Braseth Gallery
1101 Howell Street
Seattle, WA 98101

Worthington Gallery Inc.
620 North Michigan Avenue
Chicago, IL 60611

Yares Gallery
3625 Bishop Lane
Scottsdale, AZ 85251

The Zabriskie Gallery
724 Fifth Avenue
New York, NY 10019

Galerie Zabriskie
37, rue Quincampoix
Paris, France 75004

Zaks Gallery
620 North Michigan Avenue
Chicago, IL 60611

Andre Zarre Gallery
379 West Broadway
New York, NY 10012

Zolla/Lieberman Gallery
356 West Huron Street
Chicago, IL 60610

AACH, HERB. b. March 24, 1923, Co-
logne, Germany. d. October 13, 1985,
NYC. **Studied:** Stanford U.; Brooklyn
Museum School; Pratt Institute; School
of Fine Arts, Cologne; Escuela de Pin-
tura y Escultura, Mexico City (with
John Ferren, Rufino Tamayo, Max
Beckmann, Edwin Dickinson, Arthur
Osver, Xavier Gonzalez). Traveled Eu-
rope, USA, Central America, Middle
East. **Taught:** Brooklyn Museum
School, 1947-51; Hazleton Art League;
Kingsbridge Community Center,
Bronx, N.Y.; Pratt Institute, 1966-69;
Queens College, 1966-85. **Member:**
College Art Association; National Art
Education Association. Technical con-
sultant on colors. **Awards:** Hazleton
Art League, First Prize, 1956, 63. **One-
man Exhibitions:** (first) Creative Gal-
lery, NYC, 1952; Stroudsberg Gallery;
Hazleton Art League; The Pennsyl-
vania State U.; Scranton/Everhart; Al-
bert Landry, NYC; J. Seligmann and
Co., 1964; Martha Jackson Gallery,
1974; Buffalo/Albright, 1975; Aaron
Berman Gallery, NYC, 1977. **Retrospective:** Queens College, NYC, 1986.
Group: WMAA; PAFA; U. Of Illinois,
1961; ART: USA, NYC; Scran-
ton/Everhart; Riverside Museum, NYC;
Lehigh U., 1965, 67; Cranbrook, 5th
Biennial; National Religious Art Exhibition, 1966; U. of Texas, Color Forum,
1972. **Collections:** Boston/MFA; Calcutta; Harrisburg, Pa./State Museum;
Scranton/Everhart. **Bibliography:** Archives.

ACCONCI, VITO. b. January 24, 1940,
Bronx, N.Y. **Studied:** College of the
Holy Cross, Worcester, Mass., 1958-62,
BA; U. of Iowa, Iowa City, 1962-64,
MFA. Traveled Europe. **Taught:** School
of Visual Arts, NYC, 1968-71; UCLA,
1981; SFAI, 1983; Chicago Art Institute
School, 1983; Minneapolis College of
Art, 1984; Yale U., 1985; Cooper Union,
1986. **Commissions:** The Coca-Cola
Co., 1986. **Awards:** Guggenheim Foun-
dation Fellowship, 1979; National En-
dowment for the Arts, 1983. **Address:**
39 Pearl Street, Brooklyn, N.Y. 11201.
Dealer: Rhona Hoffman Gallery, Chicago. **One-man Exhibitions:** John Gibson Gallery, 1971; Ileana Sonnabend
Gallery, Paris, 1972, NYC, 1972, 73, 75,
76, 79; Galleria l'Attico, Rome, 1972;
Modern Art Agency, Naples, Italy,
1973-77; Galerie D., Brussels, 1973-77;
Galleria Schema, Florence, 1973; Gal-
leria Forma, Genoa, 1974; Galleria A.
Castelli, Milan, 1974, 75; Portland
(Ore.) Center for the Visual Arts, 1975;
Museum of Conceptual Art, San Fran-
cisco, 1975; James Mayor Gallery,
London, 1975; The Kitchen, New York,
1976, 77; Anthology Film Archives,
NYC, 1976; Minnesota College of Art,
Minneapolis, 1978; Akron/AI, 1978;
SFMA, 1978; Lucerne, 1978; Amster-
dam/Stedelijk, 1978; Young-Hoffman
Gallery, Chicago, 1979; UCLA, 1981;
Padiglione d'Arte Contemporanea,
Milan, 1981; Protetch Gallery, NYC,
1981; The Kitchen, NYC, 1981; Portland
(Ore.) Center for the Visual Arts, 1982;
VMFA, 1982; San Diego State U., 1982;
U. of Massachusetts, 1982; Miami-Dade
College, 1983; Williams College, 1983;
Nature Morte, NYC, 1984; U. of
Nebraska, 1984; Carpenter +
Hochman Gallery, NYC, 1985; U. of
North Carolina, 1985; Hart-
ford/Wadsworth, 1985; Brooklyn Mu-

seum, 1985; The Palladium, NYC, 1986. **Retrospective:** Anthology Film Archives, 1977; Chicago/Contemporary, 1980; La Jolla, 1987. **Group:** Jewish Museum, Software, 1970; MOMA, Information, 1971; Dusseldorf/Kunsthalle, Prospect '71, 1971; VII Paris Biennial, 1971; Documenta V, Kassel, 1972; MOMA, Some Recent American Art, circ., 1973; Parcheggio di Villa Borghese, Rome, Contemporanea, 1974; MOMA, Eight Contemporary Artists, 1974; Cologne, Project '74, 1974; Chicago/AI, Idea and Image in Recent Art, 1974; MOMA, Video Art, 1975, Chicago/Contemporary, Body Art, 1975; Venice Biennale, 1976; ICA, U. of Pennsylvania, Improbable Furniture 1977; WMAA Biennial, 1981; Chicago/Contemporary, Art of the '70s, 1977; ICA, U. of Pennsylvania, Machine Works, 1981; Hirshhorn, Metaphor, 1981; Documenta VII, Kassel, 1982; Pratt Institute, NYC, Bridges, 1983; Amsterdam/Stedelijk, The Luminous Image, 1984; C. W. Post College, Long Island Garden Estates, 1985. **Collections:** Los Angeles/County MA; MOMA; Chicago/AI; Middlebury College; New Museum; Ohio State U.; Paris/Beaubourg; WMAA; Williams College. **Bibliography:** *Contemporanea; Drawings: The Pluralist Decade;* Hunter, ed.; Lippard 3; Lucie-Smith; Meyer; Pincus-Witten; De Wilde 2.

ACTON, ARLO. b. May 11, 1933, Knoxville, Iowa. **Studied:** Washington State U., 1958, BA; California Institute of Arts, 1959, MFA. US Army Medical Corps, 1955-57. Traveled France, Italy. **Taught:** U. of California, Berkeley, 1963, 67, 68. **Awards:** SFMA, Edgar Walter Memorial Prize, 1961; California State Fair, 1961; Richmond (Calif.) Art Association Annual, Second Prize, 1961; San Francisco Art Association, cash award, 1964. **Address:** P.O. Box 75, North San Juan, Calif. 95960. **One-man Exhibitions:** (first) Bolles Gallery, San Francisco, 1962; The Lanyon Gallery, 1965; Nicholas Wilder Gallery,

1965, 66; Esther Robles Gallery, 1969. **Group:** SFMA Annuals, 1960, 61, 62, 63, 64, 65; RAC, 1961, 62; Los Angeles/County MA, Cross-section LASF, 1961; Oakland/AM, 1960, 61; SFMA, Arts of San Francisco, 1962; Stanford U., Some Points of View for '62, 1962; Fort Worth, The Artist's Environment: The West Coast, 1962; WMAA, Fifty California Artists, 1962-63; Kaiser Center, Oakland, California Sculpture, 1963; III Paris Biennial, 1963; U. of Arkansas, Contemporary Americans, 1966; U. of California, Berkeley, Funk, 1967; Los Angeles/County MA, American Sculpture of the Sixties, circ., 1967; Portland, Ore./AM, The West Coast Now, 1968. **Collections:** U. of Nevada; Oakland/AM; SFMA; SFPL. **Bibliography:** Selz, P., 2; Tuchman 1.

ADAMS, CLINTON. b. December 11, 1918, Glendale, Calif. **Studied:** UCLA, 1940, BA, 1942, MFA. US Army, World War II. Traveled USA and Europe extensively. **Taught:** UCLA, 1946-54; U. of Kentucky, 1954-57; U. of Florida, 1957-60; U. of New Mexico, 1961. Associate Director, Tamarind Lithography Workshop, 1960-61; Director, Tamarind Institute, 1970-85. Editor, *The Tamarind Papers,* 1974- **Awards:** Governors Award, New Mexico, 1985. **Address:** 1917 Morningside Drive, N.E., Albuquerque, NM 87110. **One-man Exhibitions:** (first) UCLA, 1950; Felix Landau Gallery, 1952, 56, 58, 61, 63, 65; Pasadena/AM, 1954; Louisville/Speed, 1956; U. of Texas, 1957; U. of Florida, 1957; Galleria Mazzuchelli, Florence, Italy; Jonson Gallery, Albuquerque, N.M., 1961, 63, 68; Roswell, 1972; U. of New Mexico, 1985. **Retrospective:** U. of New Mexico, 1973; U. of Iowa; U. of Georgia. **Group:** MOMA; MMA; Brooklyn Museum; Library of Congress; Carnegie; PAFA; Cincinnati/AM; Ringling; Oakland/AM; De Kalb, National Print and Drawing Exhibition, 1968; MOMA, Tamarind: Homage to Lithography, 1969; Honolulu Academy, First Hawaiian National Print Exhibition, 1971; Albuquerque Museum, Here and Now, 1980; U. of New Mexico, Tamarind: 25 years, 1960-1985, circ., 1985. **Collections:** Achenbach Foundation; Amon Carter Museum; Bibliotheque Nationale; Bradley U.; Brooklyn Museum; Chicago/AI; Dallas/MFA; De Kalb; De Pauw U.; Florida State U.; Grunwald Foundation; U. of Illinois; La Jolla; Los Angeles/County MA; MOMA; U. of New Mexico; NYPL; Otis Art Institute; Pasadena/AM; San Diego; Santa Fe, N.M.; Seattle/AM; UCLA; Victoria and Albert Museum; Canberra/National; Portland, Ore./AM. **Bibliography:** Archives.

ADAMS, PAT. b. July 8, 1928, Stockton, Calif. **Studied:** U. of California (with Glenn Wessels, John Haley, Margaret O'Hagan, Erle Loran), 1949, BA, PBK; Brooklyn Museum School (with Max Beckmann, Reuben Tam, John Ferren). Traveled Europe, Middle East. **Taught:** Bennington College, 1964-; Yale U., 1971-72, 76, 79; Queens College, 1972; U. of Iowa, 1976; U. of New Mexico, 1978. **Awards:** PBK; Yaddo Fellowship, 1954, 64, 69, 70; Fulbright Fellowship (France), 1956; National Council on the Arts, $5,000 Award, 1968; MacDowell Colony Fellowship, 1968, 72; National Endowment for the Arts;

Pat Adams *Burst Round* 1985

Distinguished Teaching of Art Award, College Art Association, 1984; AAIAL, 1986. **Address:** 370 Elm Street, Bennington, VT 05201. **Dealer:** The Zabriskie Gallery. **One-man Exhibitions:** (first) Stockton, 1950; Korman Gallery, NYC, 1954; The Zabriskie Gallery, 1954, 56, 57, 60, 62, 64, 70, 72, 74, 76, 78, 79, 80, 82, 84, 86; Wheaton College, 1959; Bennett College, 1959; Green Mountain College, 1962; Arts and Crafts Gallery, Wellfleet, Mass., 1963; Hotchkiss School, Lakeville, Conn., 1960; Windham College; Williams College, 1972; Yale in Norfolk, 1977; U. of Vermont, 1977; Cincinnati/Contemporary, 1978; Rutgers U., 1978; Fiedler Gallery, Washington, D.C., 1980; Galerie Zabriskie, Paris, 1980; Artemisia Gallery, Chicago, 1982; Columbia, S.C./MA, 1982; Virginia Commonwealth U., 1982; Image Gallery, Stockbridge, Mass., 1983; Stockton, 86. **Retrospective:** Cincinnati/Contemporary, 1979. **Group:** Bordighera, Americans in Europe, 1952; WMAA Annuals, 1956, 58, 61; A.F.A., Collage in America, circ., 1957–58; MOMA, 41 Watercolorists, circ., Europe, 1957; U. of Nebraska, 1958; A.F.A., The New Landscape in Art and Science, circ., 1958–59; WMAA, Fulbright Artists, 1958; Hirschl & Adler Galleries, Inc., NYC, Experiences in Art I & II, 1959, 60; Tanager Gallery, NYC, The Private Myth, 1961; A.F.A., Lyricism in Abstract Art, circ., 1962-63; PAFA, Watercolor Annual, 1959; U. of Michigan, One Hundred Contemporary American Drawings, 1965; U. of Texas, Color Forum, 1972; GEDOK, Kunsthaus, Hamburg, American Women Artists, 1972; New York Cultural Center, Women Choose Women, 1973; Hirshhorn, Inaugural Exhibitions, 1974; IIE, 20 American Fulbright Artists, 1975; U. of Texas, Austin, New in the Seventies, 1977; Chicago/AI, 100 Artists, 100 Years, *Alumni of the SAIC*, 1979; Houston/MFA, Miró in America, 1982. **Collections:** Bordighera; Hirshhorn; U. of Michigan; U. of North Carolina; Williams College; WMAA; Brooklyn Museum; U. of California, Berkeley; Kent State U.; Montclair/AM; PMA; Rutgers U.; U. of Vermont; Yale U. **Bibliography:** *Art: A Woman's Sensibility*; Chaet; *New in the Seventies*; Archives.

ADLER, SAMUEL M. b. July 30, 1898, NYC; **d.** November 12, 1979, NYC. **Studied:** NAD, 1911. Traveled North and Central America, Europe, Africa. A professional violinist through student years. **Taught:** Privately, 1934-48; NYU, 1948-72; U. of Illinois, 1959-60; Associate Member, Institute of Advanced Study, U. of Illinois, 1964; U. of Notre Dame, 1965; U. of Georgia, 1967-69. **Ex-member:** Artists Equity, formerly vice-president and president of the New York chapter. **Awards:** PAFA, J. Henry Schiedt Memorial Prize, 1951; U. of Illinois, **P.P.,** 1952; WMAA, **P.P.,** 1952, 63; Audubon Artists, 1956, First Hon. Men., 1957, 59, Gold Medal of Honor, 1960; Staten Island, **P.P.,** 1962; Ford Foundation Artist-in-Residence, 1965; American Society of Contemporary Artists, Second Prize, 1967, First Prize, 1968. **One-man Exhibitions:** (first) Joseph Luyber Galleries, NYC, 1948; Indiana U., 1950; Louisville Art Center Association, 1950; Charlotte/Mint, 1951; Grace Borgenicht Gallery, Inc., 1952, 54; Philadelphia Art Alliance, 1954; U. of Illinois, 1959, 60, 64; Grand Central Moderns, NYC, 1960; The Babcock Gallery, 1962; U. of Notre Dame, 1965; Rose Fried Gallery, 1965 (2); U. of Iowa, 1966; U. of Georgia, 1967, 68; Ripon College, 1968; Rehn Galleries, 1971, 72, 76; Andover/Phillips, 1972; Wichita State U., 1976; Terry Dintenfass Inc., 1981. **Group:** AAAL; Chicago/AI; ART: USA, NYC; Atlanta/AA; Audubon Artists; Birmingham, Ala./MA; Youngstown/Butler; California Palace; Cincinnati/AM; St. Louis/City; Columbia, S.C./MA; Columbus; Corcoran; Dallas/MFA; Dayton/AI; Lincoln, Mass./De Cordova; Denver/AM; Honolulu Academy; Howard U.; Jewish Museum; Omaha/Joslyn; Los Angeles/County MA; MMA; Milwaukee; Cranbrook; Boston/MFA; Santa Barbara/MA; NAD; PAFA; Stanford U.; WMAA; Royal Academy, London. **Collections:** Brooklyn Museum; Clearwater/Gulf Coast; Cornell U., Fourth National Bank and Trust, Wichita; U. of Georgia; Hirshhorn; Illinois Wesleyan U.; Michigan State U.; NCFA; NYU; U. of Nebraska; Norfolk; U. of Notre Dame; Safad; St. Lawrence U.; Slater; Staten Island; Utica; WMAA; Wichita State U.; Youngstown/Butler. **Bibliography:** Biddle 4; Nordness, ed.; Pearson 2; Pousette-Dart, ed.; Weller. Archives.

AGOSTINI, PETER. b. 1913, NYC. **Studied:** Leonardo da Vinci Art School, NYC. **Taught:** U. of North Carolina, Greensboro, 1967-84; New York Studio School. **Commissions:** New York World's Fair, 1964-65. **Awards:** Longview Foundation Grant, 1960, 61, 62; Brandeis U., Creative Arts Award, 1964; Guggenheim Foundation Fellowship, 1964; National Endowment on the Arts, 1969. **Address:** 47 Greene Street, NYC 10013. **Dealer:** Bernice Steinbaum Gallery, Ltd., NYC. **One-man Exhibitions:** Galerie Grimaud, NYC, 1959; Stephen Radich Gallery, 1960, 62-65, 67, 68; Richard Gray Gallery, 1965; U. of North Carolina, 1969; The Zabriskie Gallery, NYC, 1971, 73, 76; Artist's Choice Museum, NYC, 1977; New York Studio School, 1981, 83; Bernice Steinbaum Gallery, Ltd., 1985. **Group:** New School for Social Research; Jewish Museum, Recent American Sculpture, 1964; WMAA; MOMA; Claude Bernard, Paris, 1960; Chicago/AI, 1962; Hartford/Wadsworth, 1962; Battersea Park, London, International Sculpture Exhibition, 1963; Sao Paulo Biennial, VII, 1963; WMAA Annuals, 1964, 66, 68, 70; Los Angeles/County MA, American Sculpture of the 60's, 1967; Fondation Maeght, L'Art Vivant aux Etats-Unis, 1970; U. of North Carolina, Art on Paper, 1981;

WMAA, The Third Dimension, 1984. **Collections:** Brandeis U.; Hartford/Wadsworth; ILGWU; Kalamazoo/Institute; MIT; MOMA; U. of Southern California; U. of Texas; Union Carbide Corp.; Walter; Cleveland/MA; Hirshhorn; MMA; U. of North Carolina; SRGM; U. of Texas; WMAA. **Bibliography:** Hunter, ed.; Lippard 5; Read 3; Rose, B., 1. Archives. Phillips, Lisa.

ALBERS, JOSEF. b. March 19, 1888, Bottrop, Westphalia, Germany; **d.** March 26, 1976, New Haven, Conn. **Studied:** Royal Art School, Berlin, 1913-15; School of Applied Art, Essen, 1916-19; Academy of Fine Arts, Munich, 1919-20; Bauhaus, Weimar, 1920-23, where he became an instructor (Weimar-Dessau-Berlin), 1923-33. To USA, 1933, to teach and head art department at Black Mountain College, to 1949. US citizen, 1939. Headed Department of Design at Yale U., 1950-58; Visiting Critic, 1958-60; The **Josef Albers Museum,** Bottrop, West Germany, opened in 1983. **Taught:** Design, drawing, color and painting. Presented courses, seminars, lecture series in many European and North and South American universities, until his retirement, 1960. **Member:** American Abstract Artists; PCA. **Commissions** (murals): Harvard U.; Corning Glass Building, NYC. **Awards:** German Federal Republic, Officers Cross First Class of the Order of Merit; Corcoran, William A. Clark Prize, 1954; Chicago/AI, Ada S. Garrett Prize, 1954; Hon. DFA, U. of Hartford, 1957; Ford Foundation Fellowship, 1959; PMA, Citation, 1962; Hon. DFA, Yale U., 1962; American Institute of Graphic Art, Medal of the Year, 1964; Carnegie, 1967; Hon. DFA, California College of Arts and Crafts, 1964; Bridgeport U., 1966; U. of North Carolina, 1967; U. of Illinois, 1969; Kenyon College, 1969; Minnesota College of Art and Design, 1969. AAAL, Award, 1970; Royal Society, 1971; Maryland Institute, 1972; York U., 1973;

Pratt Institute, 1975. **One-man Exhibitions:** (first) Goltz Gallery, Munich, 1919; Sidney Janis Gallery, NYC, 1949, 52, 55, 58, 59, 61, 64, 68, 70, 76, 84; Cincinnati/AM, 1949; Yale U., 1956, 78; Galerie Denise Rene, Paris, 1957, 58; Kunstverein Freiburg im Breisgau, 1959; Zurich, 1960; Amsterdam/Stedelijk, 1961; Raleigh/NCMA, 1962; MOMA, Josef Albers, circ., Latin America, 1964; WGMA, 1965; Gimpel & Hanover Galerie, Zurich, 1965; Hannover/K-G, 1968; Landesmuseum fur Kunst und Kulturgeschichte, Munster, 1968; Bielefeld, 1968; Dusseldorf/Kunsthalle, 1970; MMA, 1971; Princeton U., 1971; Pollock Gallery, Toronto, 1972; Galerie Gmurzymska & Bargera, Cologne, 1973; Galerie Melki, Paris, 1973; and some 100 others; Bottrop/Albers, 1983; Margo Leavin Gallery, 1985. **Retrospective:** Yale U., 1956; WGMA, Josef Albers, The American Years, 1965; Josef Albers, circ., Germany and Switzerland. **Group:** American Abstract Artists, 1939; Herbert Hermann Gallery, Brooklyn, 1949; Galerie Stuttgart, 1948; U. of Illinois, 1951, 52, 53; Hartford/Wadsworth, Josef and Annie Albers, 1953; Zurich, 1956; WMAA, Geometric Abstraction in America, circ., 1962; SRGM, Cezanne and Structure in Modern Painting, 1963; SRGM, Abstract Expressionists and Imagists, 1961; Smithsonian, Paintings from the Museum of Modern Art, New York, 1963; MOMA, The Responsive Eye, 1965; MOMA, Two Decades of American Painting, circ., Japan, India, Australia, 1967; and some 500 others. **Collections:** Amsterdam/Stedelijk; Baltimore/MA; Basel; Bennington College; Berea College; Brown U.; Buffalo/Albright; Carnegie; Chicago/AI; Corcoran; Currier; Denver/AM; Detroit/Institute; Duke U.; Essen; Hagen; Hartford/Wadsworth; Harvard U.; Hollins College; Leverkusen; Los Angeles/County MA; U. of Louisville; MIT; MMA; MOMA; Mills College; U. of Minnesota; Morgan State College; Muhlenberg College; Munster; New London; U. of New Mexico; North Texas State U.; Park College; Portland, Ore./AM; Rio de Janeiro; SFMA; SRGM; Smith College; Smithsonian; Springfield, Mass./MFA; Stockholm/National; Svest; Toronto; Utica; VMFA; WMAA; Wesleyan U.; U. of Wisconsin; Yale U.; Zurich. **Bibliography:** *Abstraction Creation 1931-1936*; Downes, ed.; *From Foreign Shores*; Gablik; Honisch and Jensen, eds.; Sandler; Tomkins 2; MOMA, The Albers Archive: 1. "Documentation in Manuscript" (photocopy, artist's personal record of his professional chronology); 2. Writings on art (photocopies of typescripts); 3. Scrapbooks, clippings, catalogues, photographs, etc. Additional and overlapping data may be found at the Bauhaus-Archiv, Darmstadt, Germany, the Busch-Reisinger Museum, Cambridge, Mass., and the Yale U. Library, New Haven, Conn.; Lane and Larsen; Murken-Altrogge; Weber, Nicholas Fox 1; Weber, Nicholas Fox 2. **Albers 1, 2, 3, 4, 5, 6, 7;** American Abstract Artists, ed.; Battcock, ed.; Baur 7; Bihalji-Merin; Blanchard; Blesh 1; Calas, N. and E.; Chaet; Cheney; Christensen; Coplans 3; Davis, D.; Dorner; Eliot; Frost; Gaunt; Gerstner; Gomringer; Goodrich and Baur 1; Haftman; **Hamilton, G.H.;** Henning; Hess, T.B., 1; Hunter, ed.; Janis and Blesh 1; Janis, S.; Kepes, ed.; Kuh 2; Lynton; MacAgy 2; McCurdy, ed.; Mendelowitz; *Metro*; Morris; Motherwell 1; Neumeyer; Nordness, ed.; Pearson 2; Ponente; Pousette-Dart, ed.; Read 2, 3; Rickey; Ritchie 1; Rodman 2, 3; Rose, B., 1, 4; Roters; Seuphor 1; Tomkins; Trier 1; Tyler, K. E.; Weller; Wingler, ed. Archives.

ALBERT, CALVIN. b. November 19, 1918, Grand Rapids, Mich. **Studied:** Institute of Design, Chicago, with Lazlo Moholy-Nagy, Gyorgy Kepes, Alexander Archipenko. Traveled Europe. **Taught:** Institute of Design, Chicago, 1941-1946; NYU, 1950; Brooklyn College, 1951-52; Pratt Institute, 1949-. Federal A.P.; Painting, sculpture, design exhibitions; Pratt Institute, 1949-85. **Member:** College Art Association; AAUP (1969, president, Pratt chapter); Sculptors Guild; Artists Equity. **Commissions:** St. Paul's Episcopal Church, Peoria, Ill.; Temple Israel, Bridgeport, Conn.; Temple Israel, Tulsa, Okla.; Park Avenue Synagogue, NYC; Temple Emmanuel, Grand Rapids, Mich., 1973, 74. **Awards:** Detroit/Institute, The Haass Prize, 1944; ICA, London/Tate, International Unknown Political Prisoner Competition, Hon. Men., 1953; Audubon Artists, First Prize, 1954; Fulbright Fellowship, 1961; L. C. Tiffany Grant, 1963, 65; Guggenheim Foundation Fellowship, 1966; NIAL, **P.P.**, 1975; NIAL, grant, 1975. **Address:** 114 Three Mile Harbor/HC, East Hampton, N.Y. 11937. **Dealer:** Ingber Art Gallery, NYC. **One-man Exhibitions:** Paul Theobald Gallery, Chicago, 1941; Puma Gallery, NYC, 1944; Chicago/AI, 1945; California Palace, 1947; Grand Rapids, 1948; Laurel Gallery, NYC, 1950; Grace Borgenicht Gallery, Inc., 1952, 54, 56, 57; MMA, 1952; Walker, 1954; U. of Nebraska, 1955; The Stable Gallery, NYC, 1959, 64; U. of Georgia, 1970; Free Public Library, Fair Lawn, N.J., 1973; Landmark Gallery, Inc., NYC, 1974, 77; Benson Gallery, 1975; Guild Hall, East Hampton, N.Y., 1979; Ingber Art Gallery, 1983, 85; Light Gallery, Southampton, N.Y., 1981; Phoenix Gallery, Washington, D.C., 1982; Bologna-Landi Gallery, East Hampton, N.Y., 1983. **Retrospective:** Jewish Museum, 1960. **Group:** Andover/Phillips, The American Line—100 Years of Drawing, 1959; Chicago/AI, Contemporary Drawings from 12 Countries, 1952; MMA, American Watercolors, Drawings, and Prints, 1952; A.F.A., The Embellished Surface, circ., 1953-54; Contemporary Drawing from the United States, circ. France, 1954; MOMA, Recent Drawings, USA, 1956; U. of Illinois, 1957, 65; WMAA Annuals, 1954, 55, 56, 58, 60, 62, 66, 68; A.F.A., God and Man in Art, circ., 1958-59; Brooklyn Museum, Golden Year of American Drawing, 1956, Chicago/AI, 1962; PAFA, 1949, 53, 64; Flint/Institute, American Sculpture, 1900-1965, 1965; PAFA Annual, 1967; U. of Nebraska, American Sculpture, 1970; AAL, 1975. **Collections:** Brooklyn Museum; Chicago/AI; Colby College; Detroit/Institute; Guild Hall; Jewish Museum; Kansas City/Nelson; MMA; U. of Nebraska; Norfolk/Chrysler; U. of North Carolina. **Bibliography:** Weller. Archives.

ALBRIGHT, IVAN LE LORRAINE. b. February 20, 1897, North Harvey, Ill. **d.** November 18, 1983, Woodstock, Vt. **Studied:** Chicago Art Institute School, 1920-23; PAFA, 1923; NAD, 1924; Northwestern U., 1915-16; Illinois School of Architecture, 1916-17; Ecole Regionale des Beaux-Arts, Nantes, 1919. US Army, 1918-19. Traveled Venezuela, USA, Europe. **Member:** NAD; Chicago Society of Arts, Inc. **Commissions** (paintings): *The Portrait of Dorian Gray* for the film, 1943; *The Temptation of St. Anthony* for the film, 1943. **Awards:** Chicago/AI, Faculty Hon. Men., 1923; Chicago/AI, Hon. Men., 1926; Chicago/AI, John C. Shaffer Prize, 1928; Chicago/AI, Norman Wait Harris Medal, 1941, 43; Society for Contemporary American Art, Silver Medal, 1930, Gold Medal, 1931; Chicago/AI, First Prize, 1948; PAFA, Joseph E. Temple Gold Medal, 1942; MMA, Artists for Victory, First Prize, 1942; NAD, Benjamin Altman Prize, 1961; Corcoran, Silver Medal, 1955; Northwestern U., Centennial Award, 1951; Tate, $5,000 Dunn International Prize, 1963; NIAL, 1957. **One-man Exhibitions:** Walden Book Shop, Chicago, 1930; Chicago/AI, 1931; A.A.A. Gallery, NYC (two-man), 1945, Chicago (two-man), 1946; Kennedy Gallery; Sylvan Cole Gallery, NYC, 1986. **Retrospective:** Chicago/AI, 1964. **Group:** Chicago/AI, 1918, 23, 26, 28, 41, 43, 48; PAFA, 1924, 42; Brussels World's Fair, 1958; WMAA; Corcoran, 1955; NAD. **Collections:** Brooklyn Museum; Carnegie;

Chicago/AI; Dallas/MFA; Hartford/Wadsworth; Library of Congress; MMA; MOMA; PMA; Phoenix; US Labor Department. **Bibliography:** Barker 1; Baur 7; Blesh 1; Canaday; Cheney; Cummings 1; Eliot; Flanagan; Flexner; Haftman; Hall; Jacobson, ed.; Kuh 1, 2, 3; McCurdy, ed.; Mendelowitz; Newmeyer; Pearson 1, 2; Pousette-Dart, ed.; Reese; Richardson, E. P.; Rose, B., 1, 4, **Croydon; Sweet;** Weller. Archives.

ALCALAY, ALBERT. b. August 11, 1917, Paris, France. To USA 1951. Traveled France, England, Italy, Yugoslavia, Israel, 1970-71. **Studied:** School of Architecture, Belgrade. **Taught:** Harvard U. 1959-; U. of Maryland, 1971; Harvard U. 1959-82. **Awards:** Guggenheim Foundation Fellowship, 1959; Boston Arts Festival, First Prize, 1960. **Address:** 66 Powell Street, Brookline, MA 02146. **One-man Exhibitions:** Cortile Gallery, Rome, 1947; Gaetano Chiurazzi, Rome, 1950; Boston Museum School, 1951; Lincoln, Mass./De Cordova, 1954; Philadelphia Arts Club, 1951; The Krasner Gallery, 1959, 61, 62, 64, 66; The Swetzoff Gallery, Boston, 1952-54, 56, 58; Wittenborn Gallery, NYC, 1958; The Pace Gallery, Boston, 1961, 62; Mickelson's Gallery, Washington, D.C., 1964, 67; Ward-Nasse Gallery, Boston, 1965, 67; Pucker-Safrai Gallery, 1971, 73; Smith-Andersen Gallery, Palo Alto, 1973; Elca London Gallery, Montreal, 1975; Barbara Battin Fiedler, Washington, D.C., 1976; Baak Gallery, Cambridge, Mass., 1976; Clark Gallery, Lincoln, Mass., 1979; Visconti Gallery, Boston, 1983. **Retrospective:** Lincoln, Mass./De Cordova, 1968; Harvard U., 1982. **Group:** Rome National Art Quadriennial, 1947; U. of Illinois, 1955, 57, 59; WMAA, 1956, 58, 60; ICA, Boston, View, 1960; PAFA, 1960; MOMA, 1955; AAAL. **Collections:** Andover/Phillips; Boston/MFA; Brandeis U.; Colby College; First National Bank of Boston; Harvard U.; Lincoln, Mass./De Cordova; MOMA;

Rome/Nazionale; U. of Rome; Simmons College; State Street Bank and Trust Co., Boston; Wellesley College; Smith College. **Bibliography:** Archives.

ALEXANDER, JOHN. b. 1945, Beaumont, Tx. **Studied:** Lamar U., 1968, BFA; Southern Methodist U., 1970, MFA. **Taught:** U. of Houston, 1972-. **Address:** 482 Broadway, NYC 10012. **Dealer:** Marlborough Gallery, NYC; Zolla/Lieberman Gallery, Chicago. **One-man Exhibitions:** Meredith Long Gallery, Houston, 1975, 76; Houston/Contemporary, 1975; Kornblatt Gallery, Baltimore, 1976, 77; New Mexico State U., 1976; Delahunty Gallery, Dallas, 1977; Long Beach/MA, 1977; Max Hutchinson Gallery, NYC, 1978; Max Hutchinson Gallery, Houston, 1978; Corcoran, 1980; Dobrick Gallery, Chicago, 1981; Janie C. Lee Gallery, Houston, 1982, 84; Diane Brown Gallery, Washington, D.C., 1982; ICA, Boston, 1983; Marlborough Gallery, 1983, 85; Lawrence Oliver Gallery, Philadelphia, 1983, 84; Houston/MFA, 1984; Janus Gallery, Venice, Calif., 1984; Zolla/Lieberman Gallery, 1985; Jan Turner Gallery, Los Angeles, 1986. **Group:** ICA, U. of Pennsylvania, Philadelphia-Houston Exchange, 1976; Corcoran Biennial, 1977; New Orleans Museum, Biennial, 1977; Florida State U., Four Houston Artists, 1978; Indianapolis, 1978; U. of Texas, Austin, Made in Texas, 1979; Houston/MFA, Fresh Paint, 1985; Houston/MFA, The Texas Landscape, 1986. **Collections:** Beaumont Art Museum; Birmingham, Ala./MA; Chicago/Contemporary; Corcoran; Houston/MFA; Long Beach/MA; Louisville/Speed; MMA; Southern Methodist U.; U. of Texas, Austin.

ALEXANDER, PETER. b. 1939, Los Angeles. **Studied:** U. of Pennsylvania, 1957-60; Architectural Association, London, 1960-62; U. of California,

Berkeley, 1962-63; U. of Southern California, 1963-64; UCLA, 1964-65, BA, 1965-68, MFA. **Taught:** California Institute of Technology, 1970-71; California State U., Long Beach, 1976; U. of Colorado, 1981; Centrum Foundation, Washington, D.C., 1982. **Awards:** National Endowment for the Arts, 1980. **Address:** 9½ Wavecrest, Venice, Calif. 90291. **Dealer:** Fuller Goldeen Gallery, San Francisco; Charles Cowles Gallery, NYC. **One-man Exhibitions:** Robert Elkon Gallery, NYC, 1968, 69; Janie C. Lee Gallery, Dallas, 1969; Locksley-Shea Gallery, Los Angeles, 1969; Nicholas Wilder Gallery, Los Angeles, 1970; Michael Walls Gallery, San Francisco, 1971; Jack Glenn Gallery, Corona del Mar, Calif., 1972, 74; Akron/AI, 1972; Galerie Art in Progress, Munich, 1973; Morgan Gallery, Kansas City, 1973; U. of California, Irvine, 1975; Comsky Gallery, Beverly Hills, 1975; California State U., Long Beach, 1976; Fullerton College, 1976; ICA, Los Angeles, 1980; Mizuna Gallery, Los Angeles, 1980; James Corcoran Gallery, Los Angeles, 1981, 85; U. of Colorado, 1981; Thomas Babeur Gallery, La Jolla, Calif., 1982, 83; Cirrus Gallery, Los Angeles, 1982, 83; Charles Cowles Gallery, NYC, 1982, 84, 85; ARCO Center, Los Angeles, 1983; Municipal Art Gallery, Los Angeles, 1983; Stephen Wirtz Gallery, San Francisco, 1984; Van Straaten Gallery, Chicago, 1984; Fuller Goldeen Gallery, 1984. **Group:** Portland, Ore./AM, The West Coast Now, 1968; MOMA, New Media: New Methods, circ., 1969; Walker, 14 Sculptors: The Industrial Edge, 1969; WMAA Annual, 1969; Milwaukee, A Plastic Presence, circ., 1969; Omaha/Joslyn, Looking West, 1970; Chicago/AI, 1969, 72; Documenta V, Kassel, 1972; SFMA, California Painting and Sculpture: The Modern Era, 1976; California State U., Fullerton, California Perceptions: Light and Space, 1979; La Jolla, Artists Quilts: Quilts by Ten Artists, 1981; College of Design, Pasadena, Decade: Los Angeles Painting in the Seventies, 1981; Corcoran Biennial, 1983; Brooklyn Museum, The American Artist as Printmaker, 1983; MOMA, International Survey of Recent Painting and Sculpture, 1984; NYU, Precious, 1985. **Collections:** Akron/AM; Brooklyn Museum; California State U., Los Angeles; U. of California, Berkeley; Corcoran; Des Moines; Federal Reserve Bank, Los Angeles; Fort Worth; Harvard U.; La Jolla; Los Angeles/County MA; MMA; MOMA; Minneapolis/Institute; Newport Harbor; Oberlin College; Pasadena/AM; U. of Rochester; SFMA; SRGM; Stanford U.; Vancouver; Walker.

ALLAN, WILLIAM. b. March 28, 1936, Everett, Washington. **Studied:** San Francisco Art Institute, BFA, 1958. **Taught:** U. of California, Davis, 1965-67; U. of California, Berkeley, 1969; San Francisco Art Institute, 1967-69; Sacramento State College, Sacramento, 1968-. Has made several 16mm films. **Awards:** National Endowment for the Arts, grant, 1972. **Address:** 327 Melrose Avenue, Mill Valley, CA 94941. **Dealer:** Odyssia Gallery, NYC; Fuller Goldeen Gallery, San Francisco. **One-man Exhibitions:** Scott Galleries, Seattle, 1964, 65; Berkeley Gallery, San Francisco, 1968; SFMA, 1970; Reese Palley, San Francisco, 1971; Hansen-Fuller Gallery, San Francisco, 1973, 76, 80; WMAA, 1973; Western Association of Art Museums, circ., 1974-75; Palace of the Legion of Honor, San Francisco, 1974; Nancy Hoffman Gallery, NYC, 1977; ICA, Boston, 1977; Odyssia Gallery, NYC, 1979, 81; Arts Club of Chicago, 1978; Baltimore/MA, 1979; Chan Elliot Gallery, Sacramento, 1983. **Group:** Carnegie, 1957; PAFA Annual, 1957; Art USA, 1958; WMAA Annuals, 1969, 72, 73; La Jolla, Continuing Surrealism, 1972; Chicago/AI, 70th American Exhibition, 1972, 74; WMAA, American Drawings, 1973; U. of Illinois, Krannert, 1974; US Department of the Interior, America 1976, circ., 1976; Springfield, Mo./AM, Watercolor USA, 1976; SFMA, California

Painting and Sculpture: The Modern Era, 1976; Akron/AI, Contemporary Images in Watercolor, 1976; Buffalo/Albright, American Painting of the 1970s, 1978; U. of Nebraska, Realists, 1978; Creighton U., A Century of Master Drawings, 1978; New Museum, The 1970's New American Painting, 1979; U. of California, Santa Clara, Northern California Art of the Sixties, 1982; Laguna Beach Museum of Art, West Coast Realism, circ., 1983. **Collections:** Berkeley; U. of California; Charlotte/Mint; Chicago/AI; Dallas/MFA; Detroit/Institute; Fort Worth; Gulf Oil and Chemical Corp.; U. of Iowa; MOMA; PMA; RISD; Rutgers U.; Sacramento/Crocker; Santa Barbara/MA; SFMA; WMAA; Oakland Museum; PMA. **Bibliography:** *America 1976*; Arthur 2.

ALTMAN, HAROLD. b. April 20, 1924, NYC. **Studied:** ASL (with George Bridgeman, Stefan Hirsch), 1941-42; Cooper Union (with Morris Kantor, Byron Thomas, Will Barnet), 1941-43, 1946-47; New School for Social Research (with Abraham Rattner), 1947-49; Black Mountain College (with Josef Albers), 1946; Academie de la Grande Chaumiere (with McAvoy), 1949-52; US Army, 1943-46. Traveled Europe, Mexico. **Taught:** N.Y. State College of Ceramics; U. of North Carolina; Indiana U.; U. of Wisconsin, 1956-62; The Pennsylvania State U., 1962-. **Member:** SAGA; California Society of Printmakers; PCA. **Commissions** (print editions): MOMA; Jewish Museum; New York Hilton Hotel; SAGA; Container Corp. of America, "Great Ideas of Western Man" advertising series. **Awards:** Guggenheim Foundation Fellowship, 1961, 63; NIAL Grant, 1963; Chicago/AI, John Taylor Arms Medal; SAGA; PAFA; Tamarind Fellowship; Silvermine Guild; Fulbright-Hayes Research Scholar to France, 1964-65; The Pennsylvania State U., 1968, 69; Oklahoma, 1969; and some 200 others. **Address:** P.O.

Box 57, Lemont, PA 16851. **Dealers:** Newmark Gallery, NYC. **One-man Exhibitions:** (first) Galerie Huit, Paris, 1951; Martha Jackson Gallery, 1958; Philadelphia Art Alliance, 1959, 63; Peter H. Deitsch Gallery, 1960; Chicago/AI, 1961; SFMA, 1961; Santa Barbara/MA, 1961; Escuela Nacional de Artes Plasticas, Mexico City, 1961; The Goodman Gallery, Buffalo, 1961; Kasha Heman, Chicago, 1961, 63; Felix Landau Gallery, 1962; Gump's Gallery, 1962, 64; Irving Galleries, Inc., Milwaukee, 1962, 64, 66; Kenmore Galleries, Inc., Philadelphia, 1963; The Pennsylvania State U., 1963; Kovler Gallery, 1963, 66; A. B. Closson Gallery, Cincinnati, 1965; Weyhe Gallery, 1966; Oklahoma, 1966; Ohio State U., 1966; Franklin Siden Gallery, Detroit, 1966; Sagot-Le Garrec Gallery, Paris, 1968, 74; Graphics Gallery, NYC, 1969, 71; Haslem Fine Arts, Inc., 1970, 71; David Barnett Gallery, Milwaukee, 1972; Gloria Luria Gallery, 1973; Gallery 1640, 1973; Marjorie Kauffman Gallery, Houston, 1973, 74; Wustum Museum of Art, 1974; Impressions Workshop, Inc., 1975. **Group:** WMAA Annuals; I Paris Biennial, 1959; PCA, American Prints Today, circ., 1959-62; SAGA, 1960-74; MOMA, Recent Painting USA: The Figure, circ., 1962-63; Festival of Two Worlds, Spoleto; St. Paul Gallery, Drawing USA, 1962, 64, 66, 71; PAFA Annuals, 1963, 66, 67, 69; MMA, Walter C. Baker Master Drawings Collection; Basel, Five American Printmakers, 1965; Santiago, Chile, II Interamerican Biennial of Printmaking, 1965; WMAA, A Decade of American Drawings, 1965. **Collections:** Achenbach Foundation; Amsterdam/Stedelijk; Auburn U.; Basel; Bibliotheque Nationale; Bibliotheque Royale de Belgique Nationale; Bibliotheque Royale de Belgique; Boston Public Library; Boston U.; Buffalo/Albright; Chicago/AI; Clairol, Inc.; Cleveland/MA; The Coca-Cola Co.; Container Corp. of America; Copenhagen; Detroit/Institute; Escuela Nacional de Artes Plasticas, Mexico City; First National

Bank of Dallas; First National Bank, Minneapolis; U. of Georgia; U. of Glasgow; Grinnell College; Grunwald Foundation; Haifa; Hartford/ Wadsworth; Hershey Foods Corp.; IBM; U. of Illinois; U. of Kentucky; Library of Congress; Lincoln Mass./De Cordova; Los Angeles/County MA; Lytton Savings and Loan Association; MMA; MOMA; Malmo; Milwaukee; Milwaukee Journal; NYPL; NYU; National Gallery; Newark Museum; New York Hilton Hotel; Norfolk; PAFA; PMA; The Pennsylvania State U.; Philip Morris Collection; Princeton U.; Raleigh/NCMA; SFAI; Smithsonian; Syracuse U.; Victoria (B.C.); WMAA; Walker; Woodward Foundation; Yale U.; Youngstown/Butler.

ALTOON, JOHN. b. 1925, Los Angeles, Calif.; **d.** February 8, 1969, Los Angeles, Calif. **Studied:** Otis Art Institute; Art Center School, Los Angeles; Chouinard Art Institute. US Navy, World War II. Traveled France, Spain. **Taught:** Otis Art Institute, 1951-62; Art Center School, Los Angeles, 1956-60; UCLA, 1962-63; Chouinard Art Institute, 1962-63; La Jolla, summer, 1962; Pasadena/AM, 1965-68. **Awards:** SFMA, Stacy Award, 1950; Joe and Emily Lowe Foundation Award, 1955; Pasadena/AM, **P.P.,** 1959; SFMA, James D. Phelan Award, 1961; Los Angeles/County MA, **P.P.,** 1962; William and Noma Copley Foundation Grant, 1964. **One-man Exhibitions:** (first) Santa Barbara/MA, 1951, also 1965; Artists' Gallery, NYC, 1953; Ganso Gallery, NYC, 1954; Ferus Gallery, Los Angeles, 1958-62; La Jolla, 1960; de Young, 1963; David Stuart Gallery, 1964, 65; Phoenix, Hack-Light, 1965; Quay Gallery, 1966, 68, 73; Fischbach Gallery, 1967; SFMA, 1967; Stanford U., 1967; Tibor de Nagy Gallery, NYC (three-man) 1970, 71, 73, 79; WMAA, 1971; Galerie Hans R. Neuendorf, Cologne, 1972; Felicity Samuel Gallery, London, 1973; Nicholas Wilder Gallery,

1973, 75; Seder/Creigh Gallery, Coronado, 1975; Braunstein/Quay Gallery, NYC, 1977; Tortue Gallery, Santa Monica, 1979; Edward Thorpe Gallery, NYC, 1979, 82, 84; Braunstein-Quay Gallery, San Francisco, 1981; California State U., Fullerton, 1981; Faith and Charity in Hope Gallery, Hope, Id., 1982; Riverside Art Center, 1982; Tortue Gallery, 1982; U. of Nevada, Las Vegas, 1983; Arts Club of Chicago, 1984; California Institute of Technology, Pasadena, 1984. **Group:** Carnegie, 1959; Santa Barbara Invitational, 1962; WMAA, Fifty California Artists, 1962-63; SRGM, American Drawings, 1964; SFMA, 1964, 65; U. of Texas, 1966; WMAA, 1967; NCFA, Eight from California, 1974; California Painting and Sculpture: The Modern Era, 1976. **Collections:** La Jolla; Los Angeles/County MA; MOMA; Pasadena/AM; SFMA; Stanford U.; WMAA. **Bibliography: John Altoon;** Lippard 5; *The State of California Painting.*

AMEN, IRVING. b. July 25, 1918, NYC. **Studied:** ASL with Vaclav Vytlacil, William Zorach, John Hovannes; Pratt Institute; Leonardo da Vinci Art School, NYC; Academie de la Grande Chaumiere, 1950; Florence and Rome, Italy. US Air Force, 1942-45. Traveled Europe extensively, Russia, Mexico. **Taught:** Pratt Institute, 1961; U. of Notre Dame, 1962. **Commissions:** A peace medal to commemorate the end of the Vietnam War. **Member:** Artists Equity; Audubon Artists; Boston Printmakers; SAGA; Fellow of the International Institute of Arts and Letters, 1960. **Address:** 90 S.W. 12th Terrace, Boca Raton, Fla. 33432. **One-man Exhibitons:** (first) New School for Social Research, 1948; Smithsonian, 1949; The Krasner Gallery, 1948; Nebraska Wesleyan U., Lincoln, 1969. **Group:** USIA, Contemporary American Prints, circ. France, 1954; USIA, 20th Century American Graphics, circ.,

1959-61; MOMA, Master Prints from the Museum Collection, 1949; MOMA, Young American Printmakers, 1953; MMA; Graphic Arts, 1955; U. of Illinois, 50 Contemporary American Printmakers, 1956; ART: USA: 59, NYC, 1959; Library of Congress; Brooklyn Museum; IV Bordighera Biennial, 1957; PAFA; NAD; Silvermine Guild; Audubon Artists; SAGA; American Color Print Society. **Collections:** Bezalel Museum; Bibliotheque Nationale; Bibliotheque Royale de Belgique; Boston/MFA; Cincinnati/AM; Graphische Sammlung Albertina; Harvard U.; Library of Congress; MMA; MOMA; NYPL; PMA; Smithsonian; Victoria and Albert Museum; Wilberfeld. **Bibliography:** Archives.

AMENOFF, GREGORY. b. 1948, St. Charles, Ill. **Studied:** Beloit College, 1970, BA. **Awards:** Massachusetts Bicentennial Painting Award, 1976; The Artists Foundation (Mass.) 1979; Tiffany Foundation Grant, 1980; National Endowment for the Arts, 1980, 81; CAPS, 1981. **Address:** 533 Canal Street, NYC 10013. **Dealer:** Hirschl & Adler Modern, NYC. **One-man Exhibitions:** Brockton/Fuller, 1972; MIT, 1976; Nielsen Gallery, Boston, 1977, 78, 80; Robert Miller Gallery, NYC, 1981, 83, 85; U. of Virginia, 1983; Stephen Wirtz Gallery, San Francisco, 1983; Texas Gallery, Houston, 1984; Middendorf Gallery, Washington, D.C., 1984; Betsy Rosenfield Gallery, Chicago, 1985; Galerie Montenay-Delsol, Paris, 1985. **Group:** ICA, U. of Pennsylvania, Eight Abstract Painters, 1978; WMAA Biennials, 1981, 85; Kunsthalle, Nurnberg, Internationale Jugendtriennale, 1982; U. of North Carolina, Art on Paper, 1983; MMA, New Narrative Painting, 1984; MOMA, International Survey of Recent Painting and Sculpture, 1984; Fort Lauderdale, An American Renaissance: Painting and Sculpture Since 1940, 1986. **Collections:** Atlantic Richfield Co.; Bank of Boston; Boston/MFA; Brandeis U.; Buf-

Gregory Amenoff *Avalon* 1987

falo/Albright; Chemical Bank; First Bank of Minneapolis; Goldman Sachs, & Co.; MMA; PaineWebber Inc.; Purchase/SUNY; WMAA.

ANDERSON, GUY IRVING. b. November 20, 1906, Edmonds, Wash. Traveled USA, Mexico, Canada, Europe. Federal A.P.: Spokane (Wash.) Art Center, 1938-39; staff member, Seattle/AM, 1944; Helen Bush School, Seattle, 1954-55; Fidalgo Allied Arts, La Conner, Wash., 1957-59. **Commissions:** Tacoma Art League, 1960; murals for: Hilton Inn, Seattle-Tacoma International Airport; Seattle Opera House; Bank of California, Seattle, 1973; stone mosaic for First National Bank of Seattle; Seattle World's Fair, 1962; Washington Mutual Savings

Bank, Seattle; Bothell Public Library, Washington, 1981. **Awards:** L. C. Tiffany Grant, 1929; Seattle/AM, Art Award; Seattle/AM, Margaret E. Fuller, **P.P.;** State of Washington Governor's Award, Man of the Year, 1969; Guggenheim Foundation Fellowship, 1975; Governor's Arts Award, Washington, 1983. **Address:** Box 217, La Conner, WA 98257. **Dealer:** Francine Seders Gallery. **One-man Exhibitions:** (first) Seattle/AM, 1936, also 1945, 1953 (four-man), 1960; Zoe Dusanne Gallery, 1954, 59, 63, 65; College of Puget Sound, 1954; Tacoma, 1960; Smolin Gallery, NYC, 1962; Michel Thomas Gallery, Beverly Hills, Calif., 1962; Orris Gallery, San Diego, 1962; Kenmore Galleries, Inc., Philadelphia, 1963; Francine Seders Gallery, 1970, 73, 75, 77, 78, 79, 80, 82, 84; George Belcher Gallery, San Francisco, 1979. **Retrospective:** Seattle/AM, 1977; Henry Art Gallery, U. of Washington, Seattle, 1977. **Group:** Seattle/AM, Northwest Annual, 1929-68, with four exceptions; MMA, American Watercolors, Drawings and Prints, 1952; USIA, Eight American Artists, circ., Europe and Asia, 1957-58; Seattle World's Fair, 1962; Olympia, Wash., I Governor's Invitational, 1963; A.F.A., Drawing Society National Exhibition, 1970; NCFA, Art of the Pacific Northwest, 1974; Olympia, Two Centuries of Art in Washington, 1976; Seattle/AM, Northwest Traditions, 1977; Kobe, Japan, Portopia '81, 1981; U. of Washington, Spiritualism in Northwest Art, 1982; Osaka/National, Pacific Northwest Artists and Japan, circ., 1982. **Collections:** Brooklyn Museum; Dublin/Municipal; Long Beach/MA; Melbourne/National; Mt. Vernon High School; NCFA; U. of Oregon; Santa Barbara/MA; Seattle/AM; Seattle Public Library; Tacoma; Utah; U. of Washington, Seattle; Utica; Victoria (B.C.); Washington State U.; Whatcom; Wichita/AM; Brooklyn Museum; Rotterdam. **Bibliography:** *Art of the Pacific Northwest; Northwest Traditions;* Clark and Cowles.

ANDERSON, JEREMY R. b. October 28, 1921, Palo Alto, Calif. **d.** June 18, 1982, Mill Valley, Calif. **Studied:** San Francisco Art Institute (with David Park, Clyfford Still, Robert Howard, Mark Rothko, S. W. Hayter, Clay Spohn), 1946-50. US Navy, 1941-45. Traveled France. **Taught:** U. of California, Berkeley, 1955-56; SFAI, 1958-74; U. of California, Davis, 1974-75. **Awards:** SFAI, I. N. Walter Memorial Sculpture Prize, 1948; Abraham Rosenberg Foundation Traveling Fellowship, 1950; San Francisco Art Association, Sculpture Prize, 1959. **One-man Exhibitions:** (first) Metart Gallery, San Francisco, 1949; Allan Frumkin Gallery, Chicago, 1954; The Stable Gallery, 1954; Dilexi Gallery, San Francisco, 1960-62, 1964, 66; Dilexi Gallery, Los Angeles, 1962; SFMA, 1966; Quay Gallery, 1970, 75, 78; Braunstein Gallery, 85; U. of California, Davis, 1984. **Retrospectives:** SFMA and Pasadena/AM, 1966-67. **Group:** SFMA Annual, 1948, 49, 51-53, 58, 59, 63; U. of Illinois, 1955, 57; WMAA Annuals, 1956, 62, 64; Stanford U., Some Points of View for '62, 1962; WMAA, Fifty California Artists, 1962-63; Kaiser Center, Oakland, California Sculpture, 1963; Musée Cantonal des Beaux-Arts, Lausanne, II Salon International de Galeries Pilotes, 1966; U. of California, Berkeley, Funk, 1967; Los Angeles/County MA, American Sculpture of the Sixties, 1967; Portland, Ore./AM, 1968; Expo '70, Osaka, 1970; Oakland/AM, 1973; Newport Harbor, drawing exhibition, 1975; JPL Fine Arts, London, Sculptors as Draughtsmen, 1975; SFMA, California Painting and Sculpture: The Modern Era, 1976. **Collections:** U. of California; MOMA; Oakland/AM; Pasadena/AM; SFMA; Dallas/MFA. **Bibliography: Jeremy Anderson;** McChesney; **Nordland 3;** Selz, P., 2; Seuphor 3; Tuchman 1.

ANDERSON, JOHN S. b. April 29, 1928, Seattle, Wash. **Studied:** Art Center School, Los Angeles, 1953-54; Pratt

Institute, 1954-57, with Calvin Albert. US Army, 1951-53. Traveled Europe, Mexico, USA. **Taught:** Pratt Institute, 1959-62; School of Visual Arts, NYC, 1968-69; U. of New Mexico, 1969; Cooper Union, 1971-75. **Awards:** Guggenheim Foundation Fellowship, 1966, 67; New Jersey State Council on the Arts Grant, 1972. **Address:** Box 59, School Street, Asbury, NJ 08802. **Dealer:** Allan Stone Gallery. **One-man Exhibitions:** (first) Allan Stone Gallery, 1962, also 1964, 65, 67, 69, 71, 75, 77; Allan Stone Gallery, 1981. **Group:** Waitsfield/Bundy, 1963; United States Plywood Corp., 1964; WMAA, 1964, Sculpture Annuals, 1965, 67, 69; World House Galleries, NYC, 1965. **Collections:** MOMA; WMAA. **Bibliography:** Atkinson.

ANDERSON, LENNART. b. August 22, 1928, Detroit, Mich. **Studied:** Chicago Art Institute School, 1946-50, BFA; Cranbrook Academy of Art, 1950-52, MFA; ASL, 1954, with Edwin Dickinson. Traveled Europe; resided Rome, 1958-61. **Taught:** Chatham College, 1961-62; Pratt Institute, 1962-64; Swain School, New Bedford, Mass., summers, 1963, 64; ASL; Yale U., 1967; Skowhegan School, 1968; Finch College, NYC; Brooklyn College. **Member:** AAIAL, 1976; NAD, 1979. **Awards:** L. C. Tiffany Grant, 1957, 61; Prix de Rome, 1958-60; Silvermine Guild, Quinto Maganini Award, 1963; Ingram Merrill Foundation Grant, 1965; PAFA, Raymond A. Speiser Memorial Prize, 1966; National Council on the Arts, 1966; National Endowment for the Arts, grant 1966; Guggenheim Foundation Fellowship, 1983. **Address:** 877 Union Street, Brooklyn, NY 11215. **Dealer:** Davis & Langdale Co., Inc., NYC. **One-man Exhibitions:** (first) Tanager Gallery, NYC, 1962; The Graham Gallery, 1963, 67; Kansas City/Nelson (two-man, with Edwin Dickinson), 1964; Davis & Long Co., NYC, 1976; Meredith Long and Co., Houston, 1974; Davis & Long Com-

pany, NYC, 1976; Davis & Langdale Co., Inc., 1981, 84, 85; Suffolk Community College, 1976; Swain School of Design, New Bedford, Mass., 1982; Darien (Conn.) Library, 1984. **Group:** American Academy, Rome, 1958-60; Kansas City/Nelson, 1962, 64; IBM Gallery of Arts and Sciences, NYC; American Heritage, 1963; Silvermine Guild, 1963; WMAA Annuals, 1963, 64; Gallery of Modern Art, NYC, 1964; Boston U., 9 Realist Painters, 1964; Corcoran, 1964, and Biennial, 1965; Carnegie, 1964, 67; Norfolk, Contemporary Art USA, 1966; Vassar College, 1968; Ravinia Festival, Highland Park, Ill. 1968; Boston U., The American Landscape, 1972; The Pennsylvania State U., Contemporary Artists and the Figure, 1974; Boston/MFA, Trends in Contemporary Realist Painting, 1974; US Department of the Interior, America, circ., 1976; PAFA, Contemporary American Realism Since 1960, 1981; NAD, 1983; Hudson River Museum, Form or Formula: Drawing and Drawings, 1986. **Collections:** Bowdoin College; Brooklyn Museum; Hirshhorn; Minneapolis/Institute; U. of North Carolina; WMAA; Boston/MFA; Cleveland/MA; Hobart and William Smith College; PAFA; The Pennsylvania State U.; U. of Virginia. **Bibliography:** *America 1976*; Strand, ed.

ANDRE, CARL. b. September 16, 1935, Quincy, Mass. **Studied:** with Patrick Morgan, 1953, Frank Stella, 1958. US Army Intelligence Analyst. Employed by the Pennsylvania Railroad, 1960-64. Traveled England, France, Germany, Holland, Belgium. **Awards:** National Council on the Arts, 1968. **Address:** P.O. Box 1001 Cooper Station, NYC 10003. **Dealer:** Paula Cooper Gallery, NYC. **One-man Exhibitions:** (first) Tibor de Nagy Gallery, NYC, 1965, 66; Dwan Gallery, Los Angeles, 1967; Dwan Gallery, NYC, 1967, 69, 71; Konrad Fischer Gallery, Dusseldorf, 1967, 69, 71, 72, 73, 74, 76, 80, 82, 84; Monchengladbach, 1968; Galerie

Carl Andre *Sphinges* 1985

Heiner Friedrich, Munich, 1968, 71; Cologne, 73; Irving Blum Gallery, Los Angeles, 1969; Wide White Space Gallery, Antwerp, 1969, 71, 74; Galleria Sperone, Turin, 1969, 73; The Hague, 1969; ACE Gallery, Los Angeles, 1970, 76, 78; St. Louis/City, 1971; Yvon Lambert, Paris, 1971; Lisson Gallery, London, 1972; Janie C. Lee Gallery, Dallas, 1972; Galerie Annemarie Verna, Zurich, 1972; Max Protetch Gallery, Washington, D.C., 1973; Portland (Ore.) Center for the Visual Arts, 1973; Andover/Phillips, 1973; MOMA, 1973; Wide White Space Gallery, Brussels, 1974; John Weber Gallery, NYC, 1974, 75, 76; ACE Gallery, Vancouver, 1974, 75, 78; Cusack Gallery, Houston, 1975; Wesleyan U., Conn., 1976; The Clocktower, NYC, 1976; Kabinett fur Aktuelle Kunst, Bremerhaven, 1976; Minneapolis College of Art and Design, 1976; Otis Art Institute, 1977; Laguna Gloria Art Museum, Austin, 1978; Cincinnati/Contemporary, 1978; Buffalo/Albright, 1978; Chicago/AI, 1978; Newcastle Region Art Gallery, Australia, 1978; Art Gallery of South Australia, Adelaide, 1978; Van Abbemuseum, Eindhoven, 1978; Art Agency Co. Ltd., Tokyo, 1978; Pinacotheca, Melbourne, 1978; U. of California, Berkeley, 1979; Dallas/MFA, 1979; Musée d'Art Contemporain, Montreal, 1979; Palais des Beaux Arts, Brussels, 1979; Paris/Moderne, 1979; ICA, Boston, 1980; Lisson Gallery, London, 1975; Gran Enzo Sperone, Rome, 1975; Sperone Westwater Fischer, NYC, 1975, 77, 78; Weinberg Gallery, San Francisco, 1975; Cusack Gallery, Houston, 1976; ACE Gallery, Venice, 1976, 78; Galerie Lambert, Paris, 1976; Hartford (Conn.) Art School, 1977; Humboldt State U., 1979; ACA Gallery, Calgary, 1979; Paula Cooper Gallery, 80, 81, 83, 85; David Bellman Gallery, Toronto, 1980; Ottawa/National, 1980; Portland State U., 1980; Susan Caldwell Gallery, NYC, 1981, 82; Stuttgart/WK, 1981; Anthony d'Offay Gallery, London, 1981; Krefeld/Haus Lange, 1981; Alberta College of Art, 1982; U. of New Mexico, 1982; Colorado State U., 1982; U. of Wyoming, 1982; Hans Mayer Gallery, Basel, 1982; U. of Miami, 1982; Konrad Fischer Gallery, Zurich, 1983; Heath Gallery, Atlanta, 1983; Galerie Daniel Templon, Paris, 1983, 85; Nouveau Musee, Villeurbanne/Lyon, 1983; Le Coin du Miroir, Dijon, 1983; The

Clocktower, NYC, 1983; Flow Ace Gallery, Venice, Calif., 1983; Plus-Kern, Brussels, 1983, 84; Broward Community College, 1984; Richland College, 1984; Munster/WK, 1984; Galleria Primo Piano, Rome, 1984; Galerie im Kornerpark, Berlin, 1984; Stony Brook/SUNY, 1984; Galerie Andre, Berlin, 1984. **Retrospective:** SRGM, 1970. **Group:** Jewish Museum, Primary Structure Sculptures, 1966; Los Angeles/County MA, American Sculpture of the Sixties, 1967; Documenta IV, Kassel, 1968; The Hague, Minimal Art, 1968; MOMA, The Art of the Real, 1968; Amsterdam/Stedelijk, Op Losse Schroeven, 1969; Berne, When Attitudes Become Form, 1969; WMAA, Anti-Illusion: Procedures/Materials, 1969; Chicago/AI, 69th American Exhibition, 1970; Tokyo Biennial, 1970; Foundation Maeght, 1970; SFMA, Unitary Forms: Minimal Sculptures, 1970; Seattle/AM, 557, 087, 1969; WMAA Sculpture Annuals, 1970, 73; MOMA, Information, 1970; SRGM, Guggenheim International, 1971; Arnhem, Sonsbeek '71, 1971; ICA, U. of Pennsylvania, Grids, 1972; New York Cultural Center, 3D into 2D, 1973; Basel Diagrams and Drawings, 1973; MOMA, Some Recent American Art, circ., 1973; Cologne/Kunstverein, Kunst uber Kunst, 1974; Indianapolis, 1974; Hayward Gallery, London, The Condition of Sculpture, 1975; NCFA, Sculpture: American Directions 1945-1975, 1975; Rijksmuseum Kroller-Muller, Functions of Drawing, 1975; MOMA, Drawing Now, 1976; WMAA, 200 Years of American Sculpture, 1976; Akademie der Kunst, Berlin, SoHo, 1976; Corcoran, Andre, Long, Le Va, 1976; Paris/Moderne, Paris-New York, 1977; WMAA, 20th Century American Drawings, 1978; Venice Biennale; Lincoln, Mass./De Cordova, Born in Boston, 1979; Humlebaek/Louisiana, Andre, Dibbets, Long and Ryman, 1980; Hayward Gallery, London, Pier + Ocean, 1980; Dublin/Municipal, International Quadriennal (ROSC), 1980, 84; Cologne/Stadt, Westkunst, 1981;

Stedelijk/Amsterdam, '60, '80-Attitudes/Concepts/Images, 1982; Documenta VII, Kassel, 1982; SRGM, The New York School: Four Decades, 1982; WMAA, The Sculptor as Draftsman, circ., 1983; Bruglingerpark, Basel, Skulptur im 20. Jahrhundert, 1984; Seattle/AM, American Sculpture: Three Decades, 1984; MOMA, Contrasts of Form: Geometric Abstract Art 1910-1980, 1985. **Collections:** Basel; Brandeis U.; Buffalo/Albright; Chicago/Contemporary; Cologne; Columbus; Darmstadt/Hessisches; Dayton/AI; Krefeld/Haus Lange; La Jolla; MOMA; Milwaukee; Monchengladbach; Ottawa/National; Pasadena/AM; Ridgefield/Aldrich; Stuttgart; Tate; Toronto; Walker; WMAA. **Bibliography:** Alloway 4; *Art Now 74*; Battcock, ed.,; Calas, N. and E.; De Wilde 2; Haskell 5; Rowell. **Carl Andre Sculpture;** Celant; *Contemporanea*; Cummings 1; De Vries, ed.; Gablik; Goossen 1; Honnef; Honisch and Jensen, eds.; Johnson, Ellen H.; Krauss 2; Lippard 3; Lippard 4; Lippard ed.; Monte and Tucker; Muller; Tuchman 1; **Waldman 1;** *When Attitudes Become Form.* Archives.

ANDREJEVIC, MILET. b. September 25, 1925, Zrenjanin, Yugoslavia. **Studied:** School of Applied Arts, Belgrade, 1939-42; Academy of Fine Arts, Belgrade, 1942-47, BA; Academy of Fine Arts, 1951, MFA. Traveled Europe; resided Paris, 1953-58. To USA, 1958. **Taught:** NYU, 1955-56; Brooklyn College, 1973-76. **Awards:** National Endowment for the Arts, grant; National Endowment for the Arts, 1985; New York Foundation for the Arts, grant, 1985. **Address:** 133 West 72nd Street, NYC 10023. **Dealer:** Robert Schoelkopf Gallery, NYC. **One-man Exhibitions:** (first) Belgrade/National, 1948; Green Gallery, NYC, 1961, 63; Noah Goldowsky, 1970, 72, 76; Robert Schoelkopf Gallery, 1980. **Group:** Galerie Creuze, Paris, 1956-57; Dallas/MFA, 1962; Corcoran, 1963; WGMA, The Formalists,

1963; WMAA Annuals, 1963, 65; Chicago/AI, 1964; New York Cultural Center, Realism Now, 1972; Hofstra U., Green Gallery Revisited, 1972; MOMA, 76 Jefferson St, 1975; PAFA, Contemporary American Realism Since 1960, 1981; The Pennsylvania State U., Realistic Directions, 1983; IEF, Twentieth Century American Drawings: The Figure in Context, circ., 1984. **Collections:** Allentown/AM; WMAA; Hirshhorn; U. of Texas, Austin; U. of Virginia; Charlottesville; RISD; Chemical Bank; Lehman Bros.; MMA. **Bibliography:** Lippard 4.

ANDREWS, OLIVER. b. June 21, 1925, Berkeley, Calif. **d.** 1978, Santa Monica, Calif. **Studied:** U. of Southern California, 1942; Stanford U., 1942-43, 1946-48, BA; U. of California, Santa Barbara, 1950-51; with Jean Helion, Paris, 1948-49. US Army, 1943-46. Traveled Europe, the Orient. Designed stage sets, 1951-52; began public events utilizing helium-filled balloons, 1969-. **Taught:** UCLA, 1957-; San Fernando Valley State College, 1962-63. **Commissions:** sculptural lighting fixtures for Yale U.; the David S. Ingalis Rink, 1958; Stiles and Morse Colleges, 1962; fountain for West Valley Professional Center, San Jose, Calif., 1963; I. Magnin Co., Los Angeles, 1965; UCLA, 1965; U. of California, Riverside, 1967; Metromedia Television Co., Los Angeles, 1969; Los Angeles Times-Mirror Co., 1970; Federal Reserve Bank of Cleveland, 1972. **Awards:** Los Angeles/County MA, Junior Art Council **P.P.,** for Sculpture, 1957, 61; U. of California Institute for Creative Work in the Arts, Travel Fellowship, 1963. **One-man Exhibitions:** Santa Barbara/MA, 1950, 56, 63; Stanford U., 1952, 60 (three-man); The Alan Gallery, NYC, 1955, 59, 61, 66; Frank Perls Gallery, Beverly Hills, 1960, 61; Gallery Eight, Santa Barbara, 1961; Los Angeles Municipal Art Gallery (two-man), 1963; David Stuart Gallery, 1967, 70; Palomar College, 1967; UCLA, 1970; Nordness

Galleries, 1971; A.B. Closson Co., Cincinnati, 1971; California State U., Fullertton, 1971; U. of Rochester, 1971; Northwest Craft Center, Seattle, 1974; Leslie Wenger Gallery, San Francisco, 1974. **Group:** Los Angeles/County MA, 1953, 56, 57, 59, 61; U. of Minnesota, Contemporary American Sculpture, 1955; WMAA Annual, 1956; Chicago/AI Annual, 1957; U. of California, Riverside, Four Sculptors, 1958; MOMA, Recent Sculpture USA, 1959; UCLA, 1959; Hartford/Wadsworth, Smallscale Sculpture, 1960; La Jolla, 1960, 61; SFMA Annual, 1960, 61, 63, 66; SRGM, The Joseph H. Hirshhorn Collection, 1962; WMAA, Fifty California Artists, 1962-63; Long Beach State College, 1963; Buffalo/Albright, Contemporary Sculpture, 1963; Municipal Art Gallery, Los Angeles, 1965; U. of Hawaii, 1965; Southern Sculpture '67, circ., 1967; Century City Sculpture Park, Los Angeles, Sculpture in the City, 1968; UCLA, Electric Art, 1969; Columbus, Art in Public Places, 1973. **Collections:** U. of California, Riverside; Hirshhorn; Johnson Wax Co.; Los Angeles/County MA; SFMA; Santa Barbara/MA; Storm King Art Center; UCLA. **Bibliography:** Archives.

ANTONAKOS, STEPHEN. b. Agios Nikolaos, Militinis, Gythion, November 1, 1926, Greece. To USA, 1930. **Studied:** Brooklyn (N.Y.) Community College. Traveled Europe. **Taught:** Brooklyn Museum School; U. of North Carolina, Greensboro, 1967, 69; U. of Wisconsin, Madison, 1968; U. of California, Fresno, 1970. **Commissions:** Dayton, Ohio, Federal Building (GSA), 1978; Hampshire College, Amherst, Mass., 1978; Atlanta International Airport, 1980; Baltimore, Md., subway, 1983; Cambridge, Mass., subway line and commuter terminal, 1984; Seattle Center Resident Theatre, 1981. Made a film of "package" projects, 1970-75; Neon for Bagley Wright Theatre, Seattle, 1983; U. of Dijon, 1984; South Campus Station, Buffalo, 1984; Southwestern Bell, Dallas, 1984; Tacoma (Wash.) Dome, 1984; Transit Center, Davenport, Iowa, 1985; Brandeis U., 1986; Columbus Museum of Art, 1986; 14th District Police Station, Chicago, 1986; La Jolla, 1986. **Awards:** CAPS, 1972; National Endowment for the Arts, 1973; DAAD, West Berlin, 1980. **Address:** 435 West Broadway, NYC 10012. **One-man Exhibitions:** Avant Garde Gallery, NYC, 1958; The Byron Gallery, 1964; Miami Modern, 1964; Schramm Galleries, Fort Lauderdale, Fla., 1964; Fischbach Gallery, 1967-69, 1970, 71, 72; Madison Art Center, 1971; Wisconsin State U., Oshkosh, 1971; Houston/Contemporary, 1971; Fresno State College, 1972; CAPS, 1973; Rosa Esman Gallery, 1974; John Weber Gallery, 1974, 75, 76, 77; Buffalo/Albright, 1974; The Clocktower, NYC, 1974; Cusack Gallery, Houston, 1974; Fort Worth, 1974; Galleria Marilena Bonomo, Bari, Italy, 1975; Galerie 27, Paris, 1975; Wright State U., 1975; Art & Project, Amsterdam, 1976; Galerie Bonnier, 1976; Nancy Lurie Gallery, Chicago, 1976; Galerie Aronowitsch, Stockholm, 1977; Bernier Gallery, Athens, 1977; U. of Massachusetts, Amherst, 1978; Young-Hoffman, Chicago, 1978; Galerie Nancy Gillespie/Elizabeth de Laage, Paris, 1979; Galerie Tanit, Munich, 1980; U. of Miami, 1980; Nassau County Museum, 1982; Jean Bernier Gallery, Athens, 1983; Bonnier Gallery, New York, 1983; Le Coin du Miroir, Dijon, France, 1983; Maison de Culture de Nevers, France, 1983; La Jolla, 1984; Davenport/Municipal, 1985; Sandpiper Gallery, Tacoma, 1985; Brandeis U., 1986. **Group:** Martha Jackson Gallery, New Media—New Forms, I & II, 1960, 61; Van Bovenkamp Gallery, NYC, 1965; Eindhoven, Kunst-Licht-Kunst, 1966; Kansas City/Nelson, Sound, Light, Science, 1966; WMAA, 1966, 68-69; Carnegie, 1967; Worcester/AM, 1967; Los Angeles/County MA and PMA, American Sculpture of the Sixties, 1967; Trenton/State, Focus on Light, 1967; Milwaukee, Light Motion Space, 1967;

A.F.A., 1968; Kansas City/Nelson, The Magic Theatre, 1968; WMAA, Light: Object and Image, 1968; UCLA, Electric Art, 1969; Newark Museum, Light in Contemporary Art, 1969; WMAA, Human Concern/Personal Torment, 1969, Annual, 1970; Jacksonville/Cummer, Light Art, 1970; Hayward Gallery, London, Kinetics, 1970; Portland, Me./MA, Light, 1971; U. of North Carolina, Works on Paper, 1971, 72; U. of Maryland, What's Happening in Soho, 1971; U. of Nebraska, Light and Motion, 1972; Katonah (N.Y.) Art Gallery, Drawing in Space, 1972; WMAA, American Drawings: 1963-1973, 1973; SFMA, Works in Spaces, 1973; Indianapolis, 1974; Webster College, Webster Groves, Mo., 4 Dimensions in 2, 1975; Ackland, Light/Sculpture, 1975; Leverkusen, USA Zeichnungen 3, 1975; Berlin/Akademie der Kunst, SoHo, 1976; Kassel, Documenta 6, 1977; SFMA, A Shade of Light, 1978; Ridgefield/Aldrich, The Minimal Tradition, 1979; ICA, U. of Pennsylvania, Urban Encounters, 1980; Wellesley College, Aspects of the Seventies: Sitework, 1980; American Center, Paris, Murs/Tensions/Lumiere, 1981; Washington Project of the Arts, Washington, D.C., Neon Fronts, 1981; Antwerp/ICC, Europalia 82 Greece: Emerging Images, 1982; Paris/Moderne, Elektra, 1983; Brooklyn Museum, Public and Private: American Prints today, 1986. **Collections:** Brandeis U.; Chase Manhattan Bank; Ciba-Geigy Corp.; Dayton, Ohio, Federal Building; SRGM; Hampshire College; Hartford/Wadsworth; La Jolla; MOMA; U. of Maine; Miami/Modern; Milwaukee; Newark Museum; U. of Massachusetts; U. of North Carolina; Phoenix; Ridgefield/Aldrich; U. of Utah; WMAA. **Bibliography:** Battock, ed.; *Report*; Tuchman 1. Archives.

ANTREASIAN, GARO. b. February 16, 1922, Indianapolis, Ind. **Studied:** John Herron Art Institute, B.F.A. **Taught:** John Herron Art Institute,

1948-59, 1961-64; U. of New Mexico, 1964-. Technical director, Tamarind Lithography Workshop, 1960-61; Technical director, Tamarind Institute, 1970-72; U. of New Mexico, 1981-84. **Member:** Board of Trustees, Albuquerque Museum, 1981. **Commissions:** (murals) Butler U.; Indiana National Bank, Indianapolis; Indiana U., Bloomington. **Awards:** Hoosier Salon, 1944, 49; MOMA, 1953; The Print Club, Philadelphia, 1958, 61; Albion College, 1968; Northern Illinois U., 1968; Hon. DFA, Purdue U., 1972; National Endowment for the Arts, 1982. **Address:** 421 Jefferson Street NE, Albuquerque, N.M. 87108. **One-man Exhibitions:** Tulane U.; U. of Notre Dame; Stephens College; Wabash College; Kalamazoo/Institute; Martha Jackson Gallery, 1969; Maluina Miller Gallery, San Francisco; Marjorie Kauffman Gallery, Houston, 1984; Cottonwood Gallery, Albuquerque; Lantern Gallery, Ann Arbor; Marjorie Kauffman Gallery, Houston, 1979; Elaine Horwitch Gallery, Santa Fe, 1977-78; Alice Simsar, Inc., Ann Arbor, 1979; Utah State U., 1970; The Pennsylvania State U., 1981; Foundation Gallery, NYC, 1982; Lyman-Snodgrass Gallery, Indianapolis, 1982; Wildine Gallery, Albuquerque, 1982, 83; Iowa State U., 1983; Robishon Gallery, Denver, 1984; U. of New Mexico, 1985. **Retrospective:** Ohio State U.; Washburn U.; U. of Nebraska; Miami U., Oxford, Ohio; Kansas State U.; U. of Georgia; U. of New Mexico. **Group:** SFMA, 1942; NAD, 1943; Library of Congress, 1949, 66, 68; MMA, 1950; Boston/MFA; PMA; NYPL; USIA; ART; USA:59, NYC, 1959; PCA, 1959; Brooklyn Museum Print Biennials; SAGA, 1964; Florida State U., 1965, 67, 69; Seattle/AM, 1966, 68; Smithsonian, 1968; Potsdam/SUNY, 1968; Albany/SUNY, 1968; Tokyo Print Biennial, 1972; U. of Kentucky, Graphics Now; USA, 1972; Bradford, England, III British Print Biennial, 1972; Honolulu Academy Print Biennial, 1973; California State U., Sacramento, Print Invitational,

1974; Dulin Gallery, 17th National Works on Paper Exhibition, 1985; U. of Minnesota, Artists in the Trenches, 1985; U. of New Mexico, Albuquerque, Tamarind: 25 years, 1960-1985, 1985. **Collections:** Albion College; L. S. Ayres & Co.; Boston/MFA; Bradley U.; Brooklyn Museum; Chicago/AI; Cleveland/MA; Coos Bay; Dallas/MFA; Drake U.; Grand Rapids; Indiana National Bank; Indiana U.; Indianapolis; Los Angeles/County MA; MMA; MOMA; U. of Michigan; U. of Minnesota; NCFA; National Gallery; U. of Notre Dame, Olivet College; PMA; The Print Club, Philadelphia; Reed College; Roswell; SRGM; San Jose State College; Santa Fe, N.M.; Seattle/AM; Smith College; Southern Illinois U.; Stephens College; Terre Haute/Swope; USIA; US Coast Guard; U. of Wisconsin. **Bibliography:** Archives.

ANUSZKIEWICZ, RICHARD. b. May 23, 1930, Erie, Pa. **Studied:** Cleveland Institute of Art, 1948-53; Kent State U., 1955-56, BS.Ed.; Yale U., 1953-55, MFA. Traveled Western Europe, North Africa. **Taught:** Dartmouth College, Artist-in-Residence, 1967; U. of Wisconsin, 1968; Cornell U., 1968; Kent State U., 1968. **Awards:** Silvermine Guild, Philosophers Stone Prize, 1963, First Prize, 1964; Flint/Institute, **P.P.**, 1966. **Address:** 76 Chestnut Street, Englewood, NJ 07631. **Dealer:** Alex Rosenberg Gallery, NYC; The Graham Gallery, NYC. **One-man Exhibitions:** Youngstown/Butler, 1955; The Contemporaries, NYC, 1960, 61, 63; Sidney Janis Gallery, 1965, 67, 69, 71, 73; Cleveland/MA, 1966; Dartmouth College, 1967; U. of Wisconsin, 1968; Kent State U., 1968; J.L. Hudson Art Gallery, Detroit, 1968; Free Public Library, Fair Lawn, N.J., 1969; Trenton/State (two-man), 1971; A.A.A. Gallery, 1973; Andrew Crispo Gallery, NYC, 1974, 75, 76; La Jolla, 1976; Pine Free Public Library, Fairlawn, N.J., 1976; U. of California, Berkeley, 1977; Columbus, 1977; Reed College, 1977; Graphics Gal-

Richard Anuszkiewicz *Temple of Golden Orange* 1983

lery, Toronto, 1977; Montclair State College, 1977; Galerie 99, Bay Harbor Islands, 1978; Ringling, 1978; Allentown/AM, 1978; Terre Haute/Swope, 1978; Wichita/AM, 1978; Alex Rosenberg Gallery, NYC, 1979; Williamstown/Clark, 1979; Brooklyn Museum, 1980; Carnegie, 1980; U. of Miami, 1981; Hokin Gallery, Bay Harbor Islands, Fla., 1981; Fort Lauderdale, 1982; Charles Foley Gallery, Columbus, Ohio, 1982; Atlantic Center for the Arts, New Smyrna Beach, Fla., 1983; Pembroke Gallery, Houston, 1984; Youngstown/Butler, 1984; Huntington/Heckscher, 1984; The Graham Gallery, NYC, 1984, 86; Schweyer Galdo Gallery, Birmingham, Mich., 1985; Hokin/Kaufman Gallery, Chicago, 1985; Canton Art Institute, 1985. **Retrospective:** Brooklyn Museum, 1980. **Group:** U. of Illinois, 1961, 63; NYU, 1961; PAFA, 1962, 67; WMAA, Geometric Abstraction in America, circ., 1962; U. of Minnesota, 1962; Silvermine Guild, 1962, 63; Allentown/AM, 1963; Lincoln, Mass./De Cordova, New Experiments in Art, 1963; MOMA, Americans 1963, circ., 1963-64; WGMA, The Formalists, 1963; WMAA Annual, 1963, 67; Chicago/AI,

1964; Tate, Painting and Sculpture of a Decade, 1954-64, 1964; Carnegie, 1964, 67; MOMA, The Responsive Eye, 1965; Corcoran Biennial, 1965, WMAA, A Decade of American Drawings, 1965; Buffalo/Albright, Plus by Minus, 1968; Flint/Institute, I Flint Invitational, 1966; WMAA, Art of the U.S. 1670-1966, 1966; Detroit/Institute, Color, Image and Form, 1967; Trenton/State, Focus on Light, 1967; Expo '67, Montreal, 1967; Documenta IV, Kassel, 1968; WMAA, Artists under 40, 1968; Corcoran Biennial, 1975; Indianapolis, 1976; Brooklyn Museum, Thirty Years of American Printmaking, 1976; MOMA, Printed Art: A View of Two Decades, 1980; Yale U., 20 Artists: Yale School of Art, 1950-1970, 1981; Montclair/AM, Inside/Out, 1984. **Collections:** Akron/AI; Allentown/AM; Amherst College; Buffalo/Albright; Carnegie; Charlotte/Mint; Chicago/AI; Cleveland/MA; Corcoran; Dartmouth College; Detroit/Institute; Flint/Institute; Harvard U.; Hirshhorn; Honolulu/Academy; Milwaukee; MIT; Norfolk/Chrysler; MOMA; PMA; Princeton U.; Ridgefield/Aldrich; RISD; Rutgers U.; SFMA; U. of Texas; Trenton/State; VMFA; U. of Wisconsin; WMAA; Yale U.; Youngstown/Butler; Birmingham, Ala./MA; Brooklyn Museum; U. of California, Berkeley; Columbus; Cornell U.; Denver/AM; Indianapolis; MMA; Norfolk/Chrysler; PAFA; Ringling; SRGM; St. Louis/City; VMFA; Wichita; U. of Wisconsin. **Bibliography:** Battcock, ed.; Hunter, ed.; MacAgy 2; Rickey; Weller. Archives.

ARAKAWA, SHUSAKU. b. 1936, Nagoya City, Japan. **Studied:** U. of Tokyo, 1954-58; Massachusetts College of Art, Boston. To USA, 1961. Traveled Germany, France. **Awards:** DAAD Grant, 1972; Chevalier des Arts et des Lettres, France, 1986. **Address:** 124 West Houston Street, NYC 10012. **Dealer:** Ronald Feldman Fine Arts, Inc.; Galleria Blu, Milan; Gallery Takagi, Nagoya. **One-man Exhibitions:** Mudo Gallery, Tokyo, 1961; Galerie Schmela, 1963, 65, 66; Dwan Gallery, Los Angeles, 1964, 66; Brussels/Beaux Arts, 1964; Minami Gallery, 1965; Galleria dell-Ariete, 1965; Dwan Gallery, NYC, 1966, 68, 69; Wide White Space Gallery, Antwerp, 1966; Stuttgart/ WK, 1966; Eindhoven, 1966; Wuppertal/von der Heydt, 1967; Galleria Schwarz, 1967, 71; Yvon Lambert, Paris, 1969, 75; Paris/Moderne, 1970; Hannover/Kunsterverein, 1970; Badischer Kunstverein, Karlsruhe, 1970; Fendrick Gallery, 1971; Harcus-Krakow Gallery, 1971; Angela Flowers Gallery, London, 1971; Hamburg, circ., 1972; Galerie Art in Progress, Zurich, 1972; Galerie van der Loo, Munich, 1972; Ronald Feldman Fine Arts Inc., 1972, 74; Dayton's Gallery 12, Minneapolis, 1973; Galleria A. Castelli, Milan, 1974; MOMA, 1974; U. of Wisconsin, circ., 1974; Multiples Inc., NYC, 1974; Galerie Art in Progress, Munich, 1974; Humlebaek/Louisiana, 1974; Art in Progress, Dusseldorf, 1975; 77; Galerie Arnonowitsch, Stockholm, 1975; Isy Brachot, Brussels, 1975; Pasquale Trisorio, Naples, 1975; Henie Onstad Museum, Oslo, 1975; Berger Gallery, Pittsburgh, 1975; Carl Solway Gallery, Cincinnati, 1975; Ronald Feldman Fine Arts, NYC, 1976, 79; Multiples, NYC, 1976; Galeria 42, Barcelona, 1976; Toronto, 1976; Rubicon Gallery, Los Altos, 1976; Margo Leavin Gallery, Los Angeles, 1976, 78; Delahunty Gallery, Dallas, 1976; Grupo Quince, Madrid, 1976; I.C.C. Antwerp, 1976; U. of Wisconsin, Milwaukee, 1977; Kunsthalle, Dusseldorf, 1977; Galerie Maeght, Paris, 1977, 78, 82; Museo de Arte Moderno, Bogota, 1977; Gallery Takagi, Nagoya, 1978; Berlin/National, 1978; Amsterdam/Stedelijk, 1978; Oesterreichisches Landesmuseum, Kunstsammlungen, Ludwigshafen, 1979; Seibu Museum, Tokyo, 1979; National Museum, Osaka, 1979; Gallery Takagi, Nagoya, 1980; Gloria Luria Gallery, Bay Harbor Islands, Fla., 1980; Galerie Maeght, Zurich, 1980; John Stoller & Co., Minneapolis, 1980; Arts Club of Chicago, 1981;

Hannover/K-G, 1981; Lenbachhaus, Munich, 1981; Yvon Lambert, Paris, 1982; Ronald Feldman Fine Arts, Inc., 1983, 85; Hartford/Wadsworth, 1983; Kitakyushu Museum, Kyushu, 1983; Padiglione d'Arte Contemporanea, Milan, 1984; Ridgefield/Aldrich, 1984; Arnold Herstand Gallery, NYC, 1985. **Group:** U. of Illinois, 1965, 67; MOMA, New Japanese Paintings and Sculpture, 1966; Documenta IV, Kassel, 1968; XXXV Venice Biennial, 1970; Indianapolis, 1974; Cologne, Project '74, 1974; Brooklyn Museum Print Biennial, 1974; Cincinnati/MA, Japanese Prints of the 20th Century, 1975; Hirshhorn, The Golden Door, 1876-1976, 1976; Milwaukee, From Foreign Shores, 1976; Chicago/AI, Drawings of the 70's, 1976; Berlin/National, SoHo, 1976; Documenta 6, Kassel, 1977; Chicago/ Contemporary, Words at Liberty, 1977; WMAA, Art about Art, 1978; Cleveland/ MA, 4 Contemporary Painters, 1978. **Collections:** Amsterdam/Stedelijk; Basel; Berlin; Brussels/Beaux Arts; Dayton/AI; Des Moines; Dusseldorf; Hirshhorn; MOMA; Paris/Moderne; Walker. **Bibliography:** Alloway 4; *From Foreign Shores;* Honisch and Jensen, eds.; *Art Now 74;* Calas, N. and E.; *Contemporanea; Kunst um 1970;* Danto.

ARCHIPENKO, ALEXANDER. b. May 30, 1887, Kiev, Ukraine; **d.** February 25, 1964, NYC. **Studied:** Kiev, an art school 1902-05; Academie des Beaux-Arts, Paris, 1908. To USA, 1923; citizen, 1928. Traveled Europe and USA extensively. **Taught:** U. of Washington, 1935-36; U. of Kansas; Allegheny College; opened school in Paris, 1910; opened school in NYC, 1939. **One-man Exhibitions:** Hagen, 1910, 60; X Venice Biennial, 1920; Andover/Phillips, 1928; Karl Nierendorf Gallery, NYC, 1944; Dallas/MFA, 100th One-Man, 1952; A.A.A. Gallery, NYC, 110th One-Man, 1954; Darmstadt/Kunsthalle, circ. Germany, 1955; Perls Galleries, 1957, 59; Grosvenor (Gallery), London, 1961;

Mannheim, 1962; Palazzo Barberini, Rome, 1963; Auckland, 1964; Finch College, NYC, 1967; UCLA, 1967; NCFA, 1968; Musée Rodin, Paris, 1969; Toronto, 1971; Paine Art Center and Arboretum, Oshkosh, 1971; The Pace Gallery, NYC, 1973; The Zabriskie Gallery, NYC, 1976, 79; Tel Aviv, 1981; Galerie Zabriskie, Paris, 1982; The Zabriskie Gallery, 1982; Nohra Haime Gallery, NYC, 1983; Bard College, 1985. **Retrospective:** Smithsonian, 1968. **Group:** Major international exhibitions. **Collections:** Amherst College; Andover/Phillips; Belvedere; Brandeis U.; Chicago/AI; Cleveland/MA; Cranbrook; Darmstadt/Kunsthalle; U. of Delaware; Denver/AM; Detroit/Institute; Dusseldorf; Essen; Hagen; Hanover; Honolulu Academy; U. of Kansas City; Leipzig; MOMA; Mannheim; Miami/Modern; U. of Michigan; U. of Minnesota; Municipal U. of Omaha; Northwestern U.; Omaha/Joslyn; U. of Oregon; Osaka/Municipal; Phillips; Phoenix; Rotterdam; SFMA; SRGM; San Antonio/McNay; Seattle/AM; Tel Aviv; WMAA; Yale U. **Bibliography: Alexander Archipenko, A Memorial Exhibition; Archipenko 1, 2;** Barr 1; Baur 7; Biddle 4; Bihalji-Merin; Blesh 1; Brown; Brumme; Bulliet 1; Cassou; Cheney; Draven, W.; Christensen; **Daubler and Goll;** Dorner; Dreier 2; Gertz; Giedion-Welcker 1, 2; Goodrich and Baur 1; Guggenheim, ed.; Haftman; **Hildebrandt;** Huyghe; *Index of 20th Century Artists;* Janis and Blesh 1; Janis, S.; **Karshan;** Kuh 3; Langui; Lee and Burchwood; Licht, F.; Lynton; Masten; McCurdy, ed.; Mellquist; Mendelowitz; Neumeyer; Poore; Ramsden 2; **Raynal 1;** Read 3; Rickey; Ritchie 3; Rose, B. 1; Rosenblum 1; Salvini; Selz, J.; Seuphor 3; Trier 1, 2; Valentine 2; Verkauf; Wingler, ed.; *Woodstock;* Zaidenberg, ed.; Zervos. Archives, Karshan 2; **Michaelson and Guralnik;** Rowell.

ARMAJANI, SIAH. b. Teheran, Iran, 1939. **Studied:** Macalester College,

1963, BA. To USA, 1960; Citizen. Begins making non-permanent constructions 1968-, permanent installations 1980-. **Permanent Installations:** Battery Park Commercial Center Plaza, NYC; City U. of New York; Lima Park, Sacramento, Calif.; George Mason U.; MIT; Washington Street Subway Station, Boston. **Address:** 11 Kenwood Parkway, St. Paul, Minn. 55105. **Dealer:** Max Protetch Gallery, NYC. **One-man Exhibitions:** Ohio State U., 1979; New Gallery of Contemporary Art, Cleveland, 1981; Max Protetch Gallery, 1983, 84, 85; ICA, U. of Pennsylvania, 1985. **Group:** Chicago/Contemporary, Art by Telephone, 1969; Indianapolis, 1969; MOMA, Information, 1970; Walker, Drawings: 10 Minnesota Artists, 1971; Walker, Scale and Environment, 1977; ICA, U. of Pennsylvania, Dwellings, 1978; XXXIX Venice Biennial, 1980; Hirshhorn, Metaphor, New Projects by Contemporary Sculptors, 1981; WMAA Biennial, 1981; Documenta VII, Kassel, 1982; Tate Gallery, New Art, 1983; Hirshhorn, Directions, 1983; ICA, U. of Pennsylvania, Connections, 1983; MOMA, International Survey of Recent Painting and Sculpture, 1984; RISD, Furniture, Furnishings: Subject and Object, 1984; Hirshhorn, Content: A Contemporary Focus, 1974-1984, 1984. **Collections:** Carnegie; Chicago/AI; Hirshhorn; U. of North Carolina; Omaha/Joslyn; Walker. **Bibliography: Kardon 1;** Pincus-Witten 2.

ARMAN, PIERRE. b. November 17, 1928, Nice, France. **Studied:** Ecole du Louvre; Ecole Nationale des Arts Decoratifs. US citizen, 1972. Traveled Europe, Asia, Africa, North America. **Taught:** UCLA, 1967-68. Co-founder, Groupe des Nouveaux Réalistes, 1960, and L'Ecole de Nice, 1961. **Member:** Artists Equity. **Commissions:** Le Montcel, France, 1982; Elysée Palace, Paris, 1984; Nice, France, 1985; The Centrum Project, 1985. **Theatre Commission:** *L'Heyre Espagnole* for Paris

Opera, 1985. **Awards:** IV International Biennial Exhibition of Prints, Tokyo, 1964, Second Prize; Premio Marzotto, 1966; Order of Merit, for artistic achievement, Paris, 1972. **Address:** 430 Washington Street, NYC 10013. **Dealer:** Marisa del Re, NYC; Galerie Beaubourg, Paris. **One-man Exhibitions:** (first) Galerie du Haut Pave, Paris, 1956; Iris Clert Gallery, 1958, 60; Galleria Apollinaire, Milan, 1959; Galerie Schmela, Dusseldorf, 1960, 63; Galleria Schwarz, Milan, 1961, 63, 68; Cordier and Warren, NYC, 1961; Galerie Saqqarah, Gstaad, Switzerland, 1962, 66; Dwan Gallery, Los Angeles, 1962; Galerie Lawrence, Paris, 1962, 63, 65; Sidney Janis Gallery, 1963, 64, 68; Walker, 1964; Richard Feigen Gallery, Chicago, 1965; Galerie Bonnier, Lausanne, 1965, 66, 69; Galerie de Leone, Venice, 1965; Galerie Svensk-Franska, Stockholm, 1966, 69; Ileana Sonnabend Gallery, Paris, 1967, 69; Il Punto, Turin, 1967; Galerie Françoise Meyer, Brussels, 1967; Galerie Mathias Fels, Paris, 1969; Musée des Arts Decoratifs, 1969; Humlebaek/Louisiana, 1969; Kunsthalle, Berlin, 1969; Dusseldorf/Kunsthalle, 1969; Stockholm/National, 1970; Zurich, 1970; Ileana Sonnabend Gallery, Paris, 1970; ACE Gallery, Vancouver, 1970; Galerie der Spiegel, Cologne, 1970; Galerie Lambert-Monet, Geneva, 1970; Galerie Bonnier, 1970, 71; Lawrence Rubin Gallery, NYC, 1970, 71; Galerie de la Salle, Vence, 1971; Galerie Bischofberger, Zurich, 1971; Galerie Michel Couturier & Cie., Paris, 1971; Galleria del Leone, Venice, 1972; Galeria Guillaume Campo, Antwerp, 1972; Galerie de l'Oeil, Paris, 1972; White Gallery, Lutry, 1973; John Gibson Gallery, 1973; Andrew Crispo Gallery, 1973, 74, 75; Musée d'Arles, 1974; Fort Worth, 1975; Paris/Moderne, 1975; Venice Biennial, 1976; Galerie Charles Kriwin, Brussels, 1976, 78; Wichita State U., 1977; Jollembeck Gmbh., Cologne, 1978; Andre Emmerich Gallery, NYC, 1979; Galleria Cavellini, Brescia, 1979; The Art Contact, Miami, 1979; Museo Civico da Portofino, 1980; Galerie Valeur, Nagoya, Japan, 1980; Galerie Bonnier, Geneva, 1985; Galerie Beaubourg, 1981, 82; OK Harris Works of Art, NYC, 1982; Marisa del Re, 1983, 84. **Retrospectives:** Amsterdam/Stedelijk, 1964; Krefeld/Haus Lange, 1964; Brussels/Beaux-Arts, 1966; La Jolla, circ., 1974; Galerie de la Salle, St. Paul de Vence, 1976; Hannover Kunstmuseum, 1982. **Group:** XXXIV Venice Biennial, 1968; Documenta IV, Kassel, 1968; Tokyo Biennial, 1969; Expo '70, Osaka, 1970. **Collections:** Amsterdam/Stedelijk; Antwerp; Brussels/Royaux; Buffalo/Albright; Chicago/Contemporary; Cologne; Dartmouth College; Eindhoven; France/National; Ghent/Moderne; Helsinki; Hirshhorn; Humlebaek/Louisiana; Krefeld/Haus Lange; MMA; MOMA; Munich/Modern; Musée des Arts Decoratifs, Paris; PMA; Paris/Moderne; Renault & Cie., Paris; Rome/Nazionale; U. of St. Thomas (Tex.); Societe Nationale des Arts Contemporains; Stockholm/National; Stuyvesant Foundation; Sweden/Goteborgs; Talavera; Turin/Civico; Venice/Contemporaneo; Walker; Wells, Rich, Greene, Inc., NYC. **Bibliography: Arman;** *Contemporanea;* **Hahn;** *Happening & Fluxus;* **Martin, H.** Archives. De Wilde 2; Rowell.

ARNESON, ROBERT. b. September 4, 1930, Benicia, Calif. **Studied:** College of Marin, Kentfield, Calif., 1949-51; California College of Arts and Crafts, BA, 1954; Mills College, MFA, 1958. Traveled Europe. Subject of video tape on Drawing, *California Draftsmen,* produced by The Drawing Society, NYC. m. Sanda Shannonhouse. **Taught:** Menlo-Atherton H.S., 1954-57; Santa Rosa Junior College, 1958-59; Fremont H.S., Oakland, Calif., 1960-62; Mills College, 1960-62; U. of California, Davis, 1962-. **Awards:** National Endowment for the Arts, grant, 1971, 78. **Address:** 110 East E Street, Benicia, CA 94510. **Dealer:** Allan Frumkin

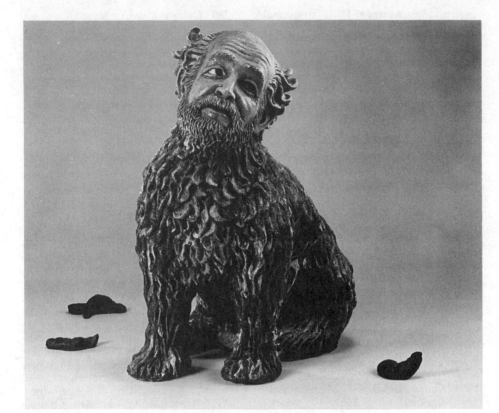

Robert Arneson   *Doggie Bob*   1982

Gallery, NYC; Fuller Goldeen, San Francisco. **One-man Exhibitions:** Oakland/AM, 1960; de Young, 1962; Barios Gallery, Sacramento, 1962; Cellini Gallery, San Francisco, 1964; Allan Stone Gallery, NYC, 1964, 69; SFMA, 1967; Candy Store Gallery, Folsom, Calif., 1969, 70, 71; Hansen-Fuller Gallery, San Francisco, 1968, 69, 70, 71, 72, 73; Fresno State College, 1970; U. of Calgary, 1971; Manolides Gallery, Seattle (two-man), 1972; Miami Dade College, 1972; U. of Nevada, Reno, 1973; Deson-Zaks Gallery, Chicago, 1974; Allan Frumkin Gallery, NYC, 1975, 78, 79, 81, 84; Fendrick Gallery, Washington, D.C., 1976, 80; Moore College of Art, Philadelphia, 1979; Frumkin & Struve, Chicago, 1980, 84; SFMA, 1981; U. of California, Davis, 1982; Sacra-mento/Crocker, 1983; Yares Gallery, Scottsdale, 1983; Fuller Goldeen Gallery, San Francisco, 1984; Karl Oskar Gallery, Westwood Hills, Kan., 1984; Metropolitan Museum & Art Center, 1984; Pittsbugh Center for the Arts, 1986. **Retrospectives:** Chicago/Contemporary, 1974; Des Moines, circ., 1986. **Group:** Oakland/AM, Sculpture, 1963; U. of California, Berkeley, Funk Art, 1967; MOMA, The Dada-Surrealist Heritage, 1968; NCFA, Objects USA, 1969; WMAA, Human Concern Personal Torment, 1969; Syracuse/Everson, Ceramics, 70, 1970; Museum of Contemporary Crafts, NYC, Clayworks: 20 Americans, 1971; SFMA, A Decade of Ceramic Art, 1962-72, 1973; U. of Illinois, 1974; WMAA Biennial, 1979; Syracuse/Everson, Nine West Coast Clay Sculptures, 1978; Amsterdam/Stedelijk, West Coast Ceramics, 1979; San Diego, Sculpture in California, 1975-1980, 1980; SFMA, Twenty American Artists, 1980; Akron/AM, The Image in American Painting and Sculpture, 1950-1980, 1981; Oakland/AM, 100 Years of California Sculpture, 1982; WMAA, Ceramic Sculpture: Six Artists, 1981; Dayton/AI, New Portraits: Behind Faces, 1982; Mount Holyoke College, The Shadow of the Bomb, 1984; Hirshhorn, Drawings 1974-1984, 1984. **Collections:** Amsterdam/Stedelijk; Canberra/National; Museum of Contemporary Crafts, NYC; Chicago/Contemporary; Des Moines; Hirshhorn; Kansas City/Nelson; Los Angeles/County MA; Mildura Art Center; Oakland Museum; PMA; Sacramento/Crocker; Santa Barbara/MA; SFMA; Seattle/AM; U. of Utah; WMAA. **Bibliography:** Adrian; *California Sculpture Show;* Gettings. Archives.

ARNOLD, ANNE. b. May 2, 1925, Melrose, Mass. **Studied:** U. of New Hampshire, 1946, BA; The Ohio State U., 1947, MA; U. of Guadalajara, 1949; ASL, 1949-53. **Taught:** Geneseo/SUNY, 1947-49; Wagner College, 1951-52; Philadelphia College of Art, 1965-68; Brooklyn College, 1971, 73-; Columbia U. Graduate School, 1975-76. **Member:** NAD; Board of Governors, Skowhegan School of Art, 1980-. **Address:** c/o Dealer. **Dealer:** Fischbach Gallery, NYC. **One-man Exhibitions:** Tanager Gallery, NYC, 1960; Fischbach Gallery, 1964, 67, 69, 71, 74, 76, 79, 86; Bard College, 1971; Galerie Dieter Brusberg, Hanover, 1972; American Kennel Club, 1981; Belfast (Me.) Free Library, 1981. **Retrospectives:** Moore College of Art, Philadelphia, 1971; U. of New Hampshire, 1983. **Group:** Riverside Museum, NYC, Twelve Sculptors, 1962; Chicago/AI Annual, 1964; Milwaukee, Pop Art and the American Tradition, 1965; Sculptors Guild, 1967, 68; PAFA An-

nual 1968; Finch College, NYC, The Dominant Woman, 1968; City Hall, Rockport, Me., Maine Coast Artists, 1969; Roko Gallery, Homage to Tanager: 1952-1962, 1971; U. of North Carolina, 1971, 72, 73; New York Cultural Center, Women Choose Women, 1973; Indianapolis, 1974; PMA/Museum of the Philadelphia Civic Center, Focus, 1974; Renwick Gallery, Washington, D.C., Object as Poet, 1977; Syracuse/Everson, The Animal Kingdom, 1978; NYU, Tracking the Marvelous, 1981; NAD, 1983; Stamford Museum, Animals! Animals! Animals!, 1984; Stamford Museum, American Art: American Women, 1985. **Collections:** Buffalo/Albright; Ciba-Geigy Corp.; Citibank, NYC; Housatonic Community College; MMA; U. of North Carolina; Norfolk/Chrysler. **Bibliography:** Schwartz 2.

ARNOLDI, CHARLES. b. April 10, 1946, Dayton, Ohio. **Studied:** Chouinard Art School, 1968. Traveled Japan, Europe. **Commission:** Hughes Corp., Calif., 1985. **Awards:** Guggenheim Foundation Fellowship, 1975; National Endowment for the Arts, 1974, 82; Chicago/AI, Witkowsky Award, 1972. **Address:** 721 Hampton Drive, Venice, Calif. 90291. **Dealer:** James Corcoran Gallery, Los Angeles. **One-man Exhibitions:** Riko Mizuno Gallery, Los Angeles, 1971; The Texas Gallery, Houston, 1972, 74, 75, 77, 79, 81, 83; Nicholas Wilder Gallery, Los Angeles, 1975, 76, 78, 79; Robert Elkon Gallery, NYC, 1975, 76, 78, 79; Charles Cowles Gallery, 1980, 85; Dobrick Gallery, Chicago, 1979; James Corcoran Gallery, 1980, 81, 82, 83, 84; Hansen Fuller Goldeen Gallery, San Francisco, 1981; Los Angeles/County MA, 1984; Fuller Goldeen Gallery, San Francisco, 1985; Thomas Babeor Gallery, La Jolla, 1985. **Retrospective:** Arts Club of Chicago, 1986. **Group:** Chicago/Contemporary, Permutations: Light & Color, 1969; Pasadena/AM, Fifteen Los Angeles Artists, 1972; Chicago/AI, Sev-

Charles Arnoldi *Untitled* 1984

entieth American Exhibition, 1972; Documenta 5, Kassel, 1972; Indianapolis, 1978; Sacramento/Crocker, Aspects of Abstract Art, 1979; WMAB Biennial, 1981; Houston/Contemporary, Americans: The Landscape, 1981; Los Angeles/County MA, Los Angeles Prints, 1883-1980, Part II, 1981; Brooklyn Museum, The American Artist as Printmaker, 1983; Corcoran Biennial, 1983; Houston/MFA, A Century of Modern Sculpture, 1882-1982, 1983; U. of California, Los Angeles, California Sculpture Show, 1984; Sacramento/Crocker, Contemporary American Wood Sculpture, 1984. **Collections:** Chicago/AI; Houston/MFA; Los Angeles/County MA; MOMA; Pasadena/AM; Santa Barbara/MA; Seattle/AM, SFMA. **Bibliography:** *California Sculpture Show*.

ARONSON, DAVID. b. October 28, 1923, Shilova, Lithuania. To USA, 1929. **Studied:** Boston Museum School, with Karl Zerbe; Hebrew Teachers College, Boston. Traveled Europe, Near East. **Taught:** Boston U., 1954-; Boston Museum School, 1942-55. **Member:** NAD. **Commissions:** Container Corp. of America, 1962. **Awards:** ICA, Boston, First Prize, 1944; ICA, Boston, First Popular Prize, 1955; VMFA, 1946; Boston Museum School, Traveling Fellowship, 1946; Boston Arts Festival, Grand Prize, 1952, 54; Boston Arts Festival, Second Prize, 1953; Tupperware Annual, First Prize, 1954; NIAL Grant, 1958; J. S. Guggenheim Fellowship, 1960; NIAL, **P.P.,** 1961; NAD, Issac N. Maynard Prize, 1975; NAD, Joseph I. Isidor Gold Medal, 1976; NAD, Henry Ward Ranger Fund **P.P.,** 1976. **Address:** 137 Brimstone Lane, Sudbury, MA 01776. **Dealer:** Pucker/Safrai Gallery, Boston. **One-man Exhibitions:** (first) Niveau Gallery, NYC, 1945, also 1956; Boris Mirski Gallery, Boston, 1951, 59, 64, 69; The Downtown Gallery, 1953; Lee Nordness Gallery, 1960, 61, 63, 69; Rex Evans Gallery, 1961; Westhampton Gallery, NYC, 1961; J. Thomas Gallery, Provincetown, Mass., 1964; Zora Gallery, Los Angeles, 1965;

Hunter Gallery, Chattanooga, 1965; Kovler Gallery, 1965; Verle Gallery, Hartford, 1967; Dannenberg Gallery, 1969, 72; Pucker-Safrai Gallery, Boston, 1978, 79; Louis Newman Gallery, Los Angeles, 1977. **Retrospective:** Brandeis U., 1979. **Group:** MOMA, Fourteen Americans, circ., 1946; Chicago/AI; U. of Illinois; MMA; ICA, Boston; WMAA; Boston/MFA; Bridgestone Museum; Palazzo di Venezia, Rome. **Collections:** Atlanta/AA; Atlanta U.; Boston/MFA; Brandeis U.; Bryn Mawr College; Carnegie; Chicago/AI; Colby College; U. of Illinois; Lincoln, Mass./De Cordoba; MOMA; Milwaukee; NCFA; U. of Nebraska; U. of New Hampshire; PAFA; Portland, Me./MA; Tupperware Museum; VMFA; WMAA; Worcester/AM. **Bibliography:** Baur 7; Genauer; Miller, ed. 2; Nordness, ed.; Pearson 2; Soby 5; Weller. Archives.

ARTSCHWAGER, RICHARD. b. December 26, 1924, Washington, D.C. **Studied:** Privately with Amedee Ozenfant; Cornell U., BA. Traveled Mexico. **Address:** 157 South Oxford, Brooklyn, N.Y. 11217. **Dealer:** Leo Castelli Inc., NYC. **One-man Exhibitions:** Leo Castelli Inc., NYC, 1965, 67, 72, 73, 75, 77, 79, 80, 81, 85; Galerie Rolf Ricke, 1969, 72; Eugenie Butler, 1970; Onasch Galerie, Berlin, 1970; LoGiudice, Chicago, 1970; Chicago/Contemporary, 1973; Dunkleman Gallery, Toronto, 1973; Weinberg Gallery, San Francisco, 1974; Jared Sable Gallery, Toronto, 1976; Neuendorf, Hamburg, 1976; Walter Kelly Gallery, Chicago, 77; Sable-Castelli Gallery, Toronto, 78; The Texas Gallery, Houston, 1978; The Clocktower, NYC, 1978; Hamburg/Kunstverein, 1978; Fisher-Faure, Los Angeles, 1980; Young-Hoffman Gallery, Chicago, 1980; RISD, 1980; Daniel Weinberg Gallery, San Francisco, 1980, 83; La Jolla, 1980; Cutting Gallery, Cambridge, Mass., 1981; Suzanne Hilberry Gallery, Detroit, 1982; Mary Boone Gallery, NYC, 1983; Basel/

Richard Artschwager *Low Overhead* 1984–85

Kunsthalle, 1984; U. of California, Berkeley, 1984; Hartford/Wads-worth, 1984; Crousel—Houssenot, Paris, 1985. **Retrospective:** Buffalo/Albright, circ., 1979. **Group:** Buffalo/Albright, 1964; Dwan Gallery, Boxes, 1964; SRGM, 1966; Jewish Museum, Primary Structures, 1966; WMAA, Contemporary American Sculpture, Selection I, 1966; Finch College, 1966; WMAA Sculpture Annuals, 1966, 68, 70, 72; MOMA, The 1960s, 1967; Ridgefield/Aldrich, 1968; Documenta IV, Kassel, 1968; Milwaukee, Directions I: Options, circ., 1968; Trenton/State, Soft Art, 1969; Berne, When Attitudes Become Form, 1969; U. of Notre Dame, 1969; Indianapolis/Herron, 1969; York U., Toronto, 1969; Hayward Gallery, London, 1969; Milwaukee, Aspects of a New Realism, 1969; Buffalo/Albright, Kid Stuff, 1971; MOMA, Information, 1971; Galerie des 4 Mouvements, Paris, Hyperrealistes americains, 1972; Documenta V, Kassel, 1972; Oakland U., American Realism—Post Pop, 1973; WMAA, American Pop Art, 1974; Leverkusen, Zeichnungen 3, USA, 1975; Musée d'Ixelles, Brussels, Je/Nous, 1975; WMAA, 200 Years of American Sculpture, 1976; XXXVII + XXXIX Venice Biennials, 1976, 80; ICA, U. of Pennsylvania, Improbable Furniture, 1977; U. of Chicago, Ideas in Sculpture 1965-1977, 1977; Buffalo/Albright, American Painting in the 1970s, 1978; MIT, Corners, 1979; Purchase/SUNY, Hidden Desires, 1980; Zurich, Reliefs, 1980; ICA, U. of Pennsylvania, Drawings: The Pluralist Decade, 1980; Brooklyn Museum, American Drawings in Black and White: 1970-1979, 1980; Basel/Kunsthalle, Amerikanische Zeichnungen der siebziger Jahre, 1981; Rice U., Variants, 1981; Documenta VII, Kassel, 1982; WMAA Biennial, 1983; Tate Gallery, New Art, 1983; RISD, Furniture, Furnishings: Subject and Object, 1984. **Collections:** Aachen/ NG; Basel; Basel/Kunstmuseum; Baxter Travenol Laboratories; Cologne; Estee Lauder Cosmetics, Inc., NYC; Kansas City/Nelson; La Jolla; Levi Strauss & Co.; MOMA; Milwaukee; NYU; Ridgefield/Aldrich; Rotterdam; R.S.M. Co., Cincinnati; Smith College; WMAA. **Bibliography:** Alloway 1, 4; Atkinson; Battcock, ed.; *Drawings: The Pluralist Decade;* Honisch and Jensen, eds.; *Kunst um 1970;* Lippard 5; Lippard, ed.; *New in the Seventies;* Sager; *When Attitudes Become Form;* **Ammann;** Kren; Murken-Altrogge.

ATHERTON, JOHN C. b. June 7, 1900, Brainerd, Minn.; **d.** 1952, New Brunswick, Canada. **Studied:** College of the Pacific; California School of Fine Arts, 1922-25. US Navy, 1918-19. Painter, illustrator, and poster artist. **Awards:** MMA, Artists for Victory, Fourth Prize, 1942; Bohemia Club, San Francisco, First Prize, 1928; Hartford/Wadsworth, First Prize, 1922. **One-man Exhibitons:** Julien Levy Galleries, NYC, 1938, 39, 42, 44, 46; A.A.A. Gallery, NYC, 1951. **Group:** U. of Illinois, 1950; MOMA; WMAA; PAFA; Chicago/AI. **Collections:** Buffalo/Albright; Chicago/AI; Hartford/ Wadsworth; MMA; MOMA; PAFA; WMAA. **Bibliography:** Baur 7; Pousette-Dart, ed.

AULT, GEORGE C. b. October 11, 1891, Cleveland, Ohio; **d.** December 30, 1948, Woodstock, N.Y. **Studied:** U. of London, Slade School; St. John's Wood Art School. Resided Great Britain 1899-1911. **One-man Exhibitions:** Sea Chest Gallery, Provincetown, 1922; Whitney Studio Club, NYC; Bourgeois Gallery, NYC, 1923; The Downtown Gallery, 1926, 28; J. B. Neumann's New Art Circle, NYC, 1927; The Little Gallery, Woodstock, N.Y. 1943; Woodstock (N.Y.) Art Gallery, 1949; The Milch Gallery, 1950; Charlotte/Mint, 1951; WMAA, 1973; The Zabriskie Gallery, 1973, 74, 78; Vanderwoude Tananbaum Gallery, NYC, 1982; WMAA, 1982; The Zabriskie Gallery, NYC, 1982. **Retrospective:** The Zabriskie Gallery, 1957, 63, 69. **Group:** Independents, NYC, 1920; WMAA; SFMA, Images of America: Precisionist Painting and Modern Photography, 1982; NMAA, Provincetown Printers: A Woodcut Tradition, 1983. **Collections:** Albany/Institute; Andover/Phillips; Brooklyn Museum; California Palace; Columbus; Cleveland/MA; Dartmouth College; Los Angeles/County MA; MMA; MOMA; Montclair/AM; U. of Nebraska; Newark Museum; U. of New Mexico; Omaha/Joslyn; PAFA; PMA; Syracuse U.; WMAA; Walker; Worcester/AM; Yale U.; Youngstown/Butler. **Bibliography:** Ault; Baur 7; Brown 2; Bulliet 1; Cahill and Barr, eds.; *Woodstock.* Archives.

AVEDISIAN, EDWARD. b. 1936, Lowell, Mass. **Studied:** Boston Museum School. **Taught:** U. of Kansas, 1969; School of Visual Arts, NYC, 1970; U. of California, Irvine, 1972; U. of Louisiana, 1973. **Awards:** Guggenheim Foundation Fellowship, 1967; National Council on the Arts Award, 1968. **Address:** 26 Warren, Hudson, NY 12534. **Dealer:** Robert Elkon Gallery; Brooke Alexander, NYC. **One-man Exhibitions:** Boylston Print Center Gallery,

Cambridge, Mass., 1957; Hansa Gallery, NYC, 1958; Tibor de Nagy Gallery, 1959, 60; Robert Elkon Gallery, 1962, 1964-68, 1970-74; Ziegler Gallery, 1964; Nicholas Wilder Gallery, 1966, 68, 69; Kasmin Ltd., 1966, 67; Bucknell U., 1970; Jack Glenn Gallery, Corona del Mar, 1971; Gallery Moos, Toronto, 1971; Janie C. Lee Gallery, Houston, 1974; The Carriage House Gallery, Buffalo, 1975; NYU (two-man) 1977; Nina Freudenheim Gallery, Buffalo, 1978. **Group:** WMAA Annuals, 1963, 65, 67; Dayton/AI, 1964; WMAA, Young America, 1965; MOMA, The Responsive Eye, 1965; Corcoran, 1966; SFMA, 1967; Expo '67, Montreal, 1967; Indianapolis, 1970; Buffalo/Albright, Six Painters, 1971. **Collections:** Hartford/Wadsworth; Los Angeles/County MA; MMA; Minneapolis/Institute; Norfolk/Chrysler, Pasadena/AM; Purchase/SUNY; Ridgefield/Aldrich; SRGM; WMAA. **Bibliography:** Wood.

AVERY, MILTON. b. March 7, 1885, Altmar, N.Y.; **d.** January 3, 1965, NYC. **Studied:** Connecticut League of Art Students, briefly 1913, with C. N. Flagg. Traveled Europe, USA. **Awards:** Chicago/AI, The Mr. & Mrs. Frank G. Logan Prize, 1929; Connecticut Academy of Fine Arts, Atheneum Prize, 1930; Baltimore Watercolor Club, First Prize, 1949; Boston Arts Festival, Second Prize, 1948; ART: USA: 59, NYC, $1,000 Award, 1959. *A Painter's World,* a 14-min., 16mm color sound film, shows him at work. **One-man Exhibitions:** (first) Opportunity Gallery, NYC, 1928; Gallery 144, NYC, 1932; Curt Valentine Gallery, NYC, 1935, 36, 38, 41; Phillips, 1943, 44; P. Rosenberg and Co., 1943, 44, 45, 46, 47, 50; Arts Club of Chicago, 1944; The Bertha Schaefer Gallery, 1944; Durand-Ruel Gallery, NYC, 1945, 46, 47, 49; Colorado Springs/FA, 1946; Portland, Me./MA, 1946; Laurel Gallery, NYC, 1950; M. Knoedler & Co., NYC, 1950; Grace Borgenicht Gallery, Inc., 1951,

Milton Avery *Artist's Wife* 1962

52, 54, 56, 57, 58, 68, 70, 74, 75, 76, 77, 78, 79, 80; Baltimore/MA, 1952; Boston/MFA, circ., 1956; U. of Nebraska, 1956, 66; Felix Landau Gallery, 1956; HCE Gallery, Provincetown, Mass., 1956, 58, 59; Otto Seligman Gallery, 1958; Philadelphia Art Alliance, 1959; Waddington Gallery, London, 1962, 66; MOMA, circ., 1965-66; Richard Gray Gallery, 1966, 70; Makler Gallery, Philadelphia, 1966; Esther Suttman Gallery, Washington, D.C., 1966; David Mirvish Gallery, 1966, 67, 69; Donald Morris Gallery, 1966, 67, 69; New Britain, 1968; Reese Palley Gallery, San Francisco, 1969; NCFA, circ., 1969; Alpha Gallery, 1969, 70; Waddington Gallery, Montreal, 1970; Brooklyn Museum, 1970; U. of California, Irvine, 1971; Cynthia Comsky Gallery, 1972; A.A.A. Gallery, 1973; Andre Emmerich Gallery, NYC, 1973; Lunn Inc., Washington, D.C., 1973, 74; U. of

Connecticut, 1976; U. of Texas, 1976; Yares Gallery, Scottsdale, 1980; Edmonton Art Gallery, 1978; Cleveland/MA (three-man), 1975; Paule Anglim Associates, San Francisco, 1981, 82; Art Gallery of Hamilton, Ont., 1981; Bard College, 1981; Grace Borgenicht Gallery, 1981, 82, 83, 85, 86; Emily Carr College of Art and Design, Vancouver, 1981; Dolly Fiterman Gallery, Minneapolis, 1981; Friedland Gallery, Toronto, 1981; Thomas Gibson Fine Art Ltd., London, 1981; Richard Gray Gallery, 1981; Greenberg Gallery, 1981; Lunn Inc., Washington, D.C., 1981; Mexico City/Moderno, circ., 1981; Santa Barbara/MA, 1981; Southern Methodist U., 1981; Waddington Galleries, London, 1981; Franz Wyans Gallery, Vancouver, 1981; Alpha Gallery, 1981, 82; Boca Raton, 1982; Harmon Gallery, Sarasota, Fla., 1982; Yares Gallery, Scottsdale, Ariz., 1982; Harmon-Meek Gallery, Naples, Fla., 1986. **Retrospectives:** A.F.A./Ford Foundation, circ., 1960; WMAA, circ., 1982. **Group:** Carnegie, 1944; PAFA, 1945; Chicago/AI; Corcoran; WMAA; U. of Illinois; Buffalo/Albright; MMA, The Painterly Print, 1980; Norfolk/Chrysler, American Figurative Painting, 1950-1980, 1980; WMAA, American Prints: Process & Proofs, 1981; Rutgers U., Realism and Realities, 1982. **Collections:** Andover/Phillips; Atlanta/AA; Baltimore/MA; Barnes Foundation; Brandeis U.; Brooklyn Museum; Bryn Mawr College; Buffalo/Albright; Chase Manhattan Bank; Dayton/AI; Evansville; Exeter; Honolulu Academy; Houston/MFA; U. of Illinois; MMA; MOMA; U. of Minnesota; U. of Nebraska; Newark Museum; PAFA; PMA; Phillips; Santa Barbara/MA; Smith College; Tel Aviv; Utica; WMAA; Walker; West Palm Beach/Norton; Witte; Yale U. **Bibliography:** Bazin; Blesh 1; Eliot; Frost; Goodrich and Baur 1; Greenberg 1; Kootz 2; **Kramer 2;** Mellquist; Nordness, ed.; Pousette-Dart, ed.; Rose, B. 1; Sandler; **Wight 2, 3;** *Woodstock: An American Art Colony 1902-1977;* **Haskell 6.** Archives.

AYCOCK, ALICE b. November 20, 1946, Harrisburg, Pa. **Studied:** Douglass College, New Brunswick, N.J., 1968, BA; Hunter College, 1971, MA, with Robert Morris. **Awards:** PBK, 1968; National Endowment for the Arts, 1975, 80; CAPS, 1976. Traveled Europe, Mexico, Egypt. **Taught:** RISD, 1977; School of Visual Arts, NYC, 1977-78, 79-82; Hunter College, 1982-85. **Address:** 62 Greene Street, NYC 10012. **Dealer:** John Weber Gallery, NYC. **One-man Exhibitions:** (first) Nova Scotia College of Art & Design, 1972; Williams College, 1974; 112 Greene Street, NYC, 1974, 77; U. of Hartford, 1976; MOMA, project room, 1977; Galerie Salvatore Ala, Milan, 1978; Cranbrook, 1978; Muhleberg College, Allentown, Pa., 1978; Philadelphia College of Art, 1978; Portland (Ore.) Center for Visual Arts, 1978; John Weber Gallery, 1978, 79, 81, 82, 84; RISD, 1978; Amherst College, 1979; Cincinnati/Contemporary, 1979; Protetch-McIntosh Gallery, Washington, D.C., 1979; SFAI, 1979; P.S. 1, Long Island City, 1980; U. of South Florida, 1980; Washington Project for the Arts, Washington, D.C., 1980; Plattsburgh/SUNY, 1981; Douglass College, 1982; Lawrence Oliver Gallery, Philadelphia, 1982; Chicago/Contemporary, 1983; Protetch-McNeill Gallery, NYC, 1983; Roanoke College, 1983; McIntosh-Drysdale Gallery, Houston, 1984; Salisbury State College, 1984; Humanic Corp., Graz, Austria, 1985; Insam Gallery, Vienna, 1985; Madison Art Center, 1985; U. of Nebraska, 1985; Serpentine Gallery, London, 1985; Vanguard Gallery, Philadelphia, 1985. **Retrospective:** Stuttgart/WK, circ., 1983. **Group:** California Institute of the Arts, C. 7500, 1974; IX Paris Biennial, 1975; Artpark, Lewiston, N.Y., 1976; Documenta VI, Kassel, 1977; Amsterdam/Stedelijk, Made by Sculptors, 1978; ICA, U. of Pennsylvania, Dwellings, 1978; XXXVIII Venice Biennial, 1978; WMAA Biennials, 1979, 81; Hirshhorn, Metaphor, New Projects by Contemporary Sculptors, 1981; Zurich,

Myth & Ritual, 1981; ICA, U. of Pennsylvania, Machineworks, 1981; Stuttgart/WK, Past-Present-Future, 1982; Antwerp, Biennale Middelheim, 1983; Citywide Contemporary Sculpture Exhibition, Toledo, 1984; Hirshhorn, Content, 1984; XVIII Sao Paolo Biennial, 1985; Fort Lauderdale, An American Renaissance: Painting and Sculpture Since 1940, 1986; Triennale di Milano, 1986. **Collections:** Antwerp/Middelheim; Basel; Brooklyn Museum; Canberra/National; Chicago/Contemporary; Cincinnati/AM; Cologne/Ludwige; Douglass College; The Hague; Humlebaek/Louisiana; La Jolla; MMA; MOMA; U. of Massachusetts; U. of Nebraska; PMA; Plattsburgh/SUNY; Roanoke College; Salisbury State U.; Stuttgart; WMAA; Walker.

AZUMA, NORIO. b. November 23, 1928, Japan. **Studied:** Kanazawa Art College, Kanazawa City, Japan; Chouinard Art Institute; ASL (with Will Barnet). **Commissions:** IBM. **Awards:** Seattle/AM; Boston Printmakers; American Color Print Society. **Address:** 276 Riverside Drive, NYC 10025. **Dealers:** A.A.A. Gallery; Weyhe Gallery; Fendrick Gallery. **One-man Exhibitions:** (first) A.A.A. Gallery, NYC, 1964, also 1969; The Print Club, Philadelphia, 1964; Tulsa/Philbrook, 1965; Benjamin Gallery, Chicago, 1965; International Monetary Fund, Washington, D.C., 1965; WGMA, 1967; Nashville, 1968; East Tennessee State U., 1969; Berman-Medalie Gallery, Massachusetts, 1969; Roanoke (Va.) Fine Arts Center, 1969. **Group:** American Color Print Society; Corcoran; Boston Printmakers; New York World's Fair, 1964-65; Brooklyn Museum Print Biennial; WMAA Sculpture Annual, 1966; SAGA. **Collections:** American Republic Insurance Co.; Boston Public Library; Brooklyn Museum; U. of California; Chase Manhattan Bank; Chicago/AI; Chouinard Art Institute; Cleveland/MA; Library of Congress; MIT; National Gallery; PAFA; PMA; Seattle/AM; Smithsonian; Trenton/State; USIA; The White House; Youngstown/Butler.

B

BABER, ALICE. b. August 22, 1928, Charleston, Ill. **d.** 1982, NYC. **Studied:** Lindenwood College; Indiana U., BA; Ecole des Beaux-Arts, Fontainebleau. Traveled Europe, Russia, Japan, Thailand, India, Middle East. **Taught:** Queens College; U. of Minnesota; Purchase/SUNY; C. W. Post College; U. of California, Santa Barbara; U. of California, Berkeley; School of Visual Arts, NYC, 1973-75; U. of New Mexico, 1979. **Member:** Women's InterArt Center. **Awards:** Yaddo Fellowship, 1958. Organized the exhibition Color Forum, U. of Texas, 1972. **One-man Exhibitions:** (first) March Gallery, NYC, 1958; Galerie de la Librairie Anglaise, Paris, 1963; New Vision Center, London, 1963; Pinacotheca Museum (two-man), 1964; A. M. Sachs Gallery, NYC, 1965, 66, 69, 71, 73, 75, 77, 78; Kölnischer Kunstverein, Cologne, 1966; Bernard Baruch College, NYC, 1968; Galerie Lambert, Paris, 1970; U. of Minnesota, 1971; Galerie fur Zeitgenossische Kunst, Hamburg, 1971; Tom Bortolazzo Gallery, Santa Barbara, 1972; Benson Gallery, 1973; Ingber Art Gallery, 1973; EuRo-Kunstgalerie, Saarbrucken, 1974; Chanakya Gallery, New Delhi, 1974; Iran-American Society, Teheran, 1974; Palm Beach Gallery, Palm Beach, 1975; American Library, Brussels, 1975; U. of Alabama, 1975; Arvil Gallery, Mexico City, 1976; Santa Barbara/MA, 1976; Kansas State U., 1976; Centro Colombo Americano, Bogota, Colombia, 1977; Centro de Arte Moderna, Guadalajara, Mexico, 1977; Henri Gallery, Washington, D.C., 1977; Allen House Galleries, Louisville, Ky., 1978; Frances Aronson Gallery, Atlanta, Ga., 1978; The Art Package, Chicago, Ill., 1979; Niagara U., 1979; Gallery West, Los Angeles, 1980; Galeria de l'Arte Nueva, Lima, Peru, 1980. **Group:** The Stable Gallery Annual, 1957; II Paris Biennial, 1961; Whitechapel Art Gallery, London, 1966; Maison de la Culture du Havre, 1966-67; Musee des Arts Decoratifs, 1966; U. of Texas, Color Forum, 1972; New York Cultural Center, Women Choose Women, 1973; Fordham U., IX Painters—IX Styles, 1973. **Collections:** Bezalel Museum; Brandeis U.; U. of California; Ciba-Geigy Corp.; Corcoran; Cornell U.; Fordham U.; MOMA; Manchester, England; Museo National, San Salvador; Newark Museum; NCFA; NYU; U. of Notre Dame; Purchase/SUNY; SRGM; Peter Stuyvesant Collection; Pinacotheca Museum; SFMA; Terre Haute/Swope; United Tanker Ltd.; Worcester/AM. **Bibliography:** *Art: A Woman's Sensibility.* Archives.

BAEDER, JOHN b. December 24, 1938, South Bend, In. **Studied:** Auburn U. **Address:** 1025 Overton Lea Road, Nashville, Tenn. 37204. **Dealer:** OK Harris Works of Art, NYC. **One-man Exhibitions:** Hundred Acres Gallery, NYC, 1972, 74, 76; Morgan Gallery, Shawnee Mission, Mo., 1973, 77; OK Harris Works of Art, 1978, 80, 82, 84; Williams College, 1979; Graphics I & Graphics II, Boston, 1980; Thomas Segal Gallery, Boston, 1982; Cumberland Gallery, Nashville, 1983. **Group:** Rice U., Gray is the Color, 1974; Darmstadt/Kunsthalle, Realism and Reality, 1975; NCFA, America As Art, 1976; Akron/AI, Contemporary

John Baeder *Moran Sq. Diner* 1986

Images in Watercolor, 1976; Indianapolis, 1976; Jacksonville/AM, New Realism, 1977; Boston/MFA, Prints of the 1970's, 1977; Tulsa/Philbrook, Realism/Photorealism, 1980; San Antonio/MA, Real, Really Real, Super Real, circ., 1981; PAFA, Contemporary American Realism Since 1960, 1981; Museum of the City of New York, Painting New York, 1983; Isetan Museum of Art, Tokyo, American Realism: The Precise Image, 1985; SFMA, American Realism (Janss), circ., 1985. **Collections:** AT&T; The Coca-Cola Co.; Denver/AM; De Pauw U.; Detroit/Institute; High Museum; Milwaukee; Newark Museum; Newark Public Library; RISD; Randolph-Macon College; Springfield, Mo./AM; Technimetrics, NYC; WMAA; West Palm Beach/Norton; Yale U. **Bibliography:** Arthur 3; Lindy.

BAER, JO. b. August 7, 1929, Seattle, Wash. **Studied:** U. of Washington, 1946-49; New School for Social Research, 1952; Resided London, 1981-84; Amsterdam, 1984-. **Taught:** School of Visual Arts, NYC, 1969-70; Brighton (Eng.) Polytechnic; G. Rietveld Academie, Amsterdam. **Awards:** National Endowment for the Arts Grant, 1969. **Address:** Rozengracht 204, Amsterdam 1016LZ, Netherlands. **One-man Exhibitions:** Fischer Gallery, 1966; Galerie Rolf Ricke, 1969, 70, 73; Locksley-Shea Gallery, 1970; Noah Goldowsky, 1970; School of Visual Arts, NYC, 1970; LoGiudice Gallery, NYC, 1972; Nicholas Wilder Gallery, 1973; Galleria Toselli, Milan, 1974; Weinberg Gallery, San Francisco, 1974; MOMA, Oxford, England, circ., 1977; Riverside Studios, London, 1981; Eindhoven, 1986. **Retrospective:** WMAA, 1975. **Group:** SRGM, Systemic Painting, 1966; Finch College, NYC, Art in Series, 1967; WMAA Annuals, 1967, 69, 73; Documenta IV, Kassel, 1968; Cologne/Kunstverein, Eine Tendenz Zeitgenossischer Malerei, 1969; Detroit/Institute, Other Ideas, 1969; Ars

69, Helsinki, 1969; Seattle/AM, Artists of the Sixties, 1969; Corcoran Biennial, 1969; Chicago/AI, Drawings, 1971; Yale U., Options and Alternatives, 1973; Chicago/Contemporary, Five Artists: A Logic of Vision, 1974; Baltimore/MA, 14 Artists, 1975; Arts Council of Great Britain, The British Art Show, circ., 1984. **Collections:** Aachen/NG; Eindhoven; MOMA; SRGM. **Bibliography:** Arthur 1; Honisch and Jensen, eds.; *Kunst um 1970;* Lippard 3; Lucie-Smith; *Options and Alternatives.*

BAILEY, WILLIAM. b. November 17, 1930, Council Bluffs, Iowa. **Studied:** U. of Kansas, 1948-51; Yale U., 1955; BFA, 1957, MFA, with Josef Albers. US Army, 1951-53, Korea, Japan. Traveled Europe, Far East; resided Paris, Rome. **Taught:** Yale U., 1957-62, 69-; Indiana U., 1962-69. **Awards:** Alice Kimball English Traveling Fellow, 1955; US State Department Grant, 1960; Guggenheim Foundation Fellowship, 1965; Ingram Merrill Foundation, grant, 1979-80. **Address:** 223 East 10th Street, NYC 10003. **Dealer:** Robert Schoelkopf Gallery, NYC; Galerie Claude Bernard, Paris; Galleria Il Gabbiano, Rome. **One-man Exhibitions:** Kanegis Gallery, 1957, 58, 61; Indiana U., 1963; U. of Vermont, 1965; Kansas City/AI, 1967; Robert Schoelkopf Gallery, 1968, 71, 74, 75, 79, 82; Galleria dei Lanzi, Milan, 1973; Galleria Il Fante di Spade, Rome, 1973; La Parisina, Turin, 1974; Dart Gallery, Inc., Chicago, 1976; Galerie Claude Bernard, Paris, 1978; Fendrick Gallery, Washington, D.C., 1979; Galleria Il Gabbiano, Rome, 1980, 85; Southern Methodist U., 1983. **Group:** U. of Illinois, 1961; Vassar College, Realism Now, 1968; Cincinnati/AM, American Paintings on the Market Today V, 1968; Swarthmore College, The Big Figure, 1969; WMAA, 22 Realists,

William Bailey   *Still Life-Noto*   1986

1970; Florida State U., Realist Painters, 1971; Cleveland/MA, 32 Realists, 1972; A.F.A., Realist Revival, 1972; Kansas City/AI, Five Figurative Artists, 1972; Yale U., Seven Realists, 1973; St. John's U., The Figure in Recent American Painting, 1975; New York Cultural Center, Three Centuries of the American Nude, 1975; Palazzo Strozzi, Florence, Biennale Internazionale della Grafica, 1977; Salon de Mai, Paris, 1978; William Patterson College, N.J., The Other Realism, 1978; WMAA, The Figurative Tradition and the WMAA, 1980; WMAA Biennial, 1981; Yale U., Twenty Artists: Yale School of Art, 1950-1970, 1981; San Antonio/MA, Real, Really Real, Super Real, 1981; PAFA, Contemporary American Realism Since 1960, 1981; Montclair/AM, Josef Albers: His Influence, 1981; Akron/AM, The Image in American Painting and Sculpture, 1950-1980, 1981; Haus der Kunst, Munich, Amerikansiche Malerie: 1930-1980, 1981; U. of California, Santa Barbara, A Heritage Renewed: Representational Drawings Today, 1983; Houston/Contemporary, American Still Life, 1945-1983, 1983; SFMA, American Realism (Janss), circ., 1985. **Collections:** Aachen/NG; Brandeis U.; U. of Connecticut; Cortland/SUNY; Des Moines; Duke U.; Hirshhorn; Indiana U.; Kalamazoo Institute; U. of Kentucky; Little Rock/MFA; Louisville/Speed; MOMA; U. of Massachusetts; Michigan State U.; Minneapolis/Institute; Montclair/AM; U. of New Mexico; NCFA; U. of North Carolina; Ogunquit; PAFA; St. Louis City; U. of Virginia; WMAA; Yale U. **Bibliography:** Arthur 1, 2; *Kunst um 1970*; Sager; Strand, ed.

BAIZERMAN, SAUL. b. December 25, 1889, Vitebsk, Russia; **d.** August 30, 1957, NYC. **Studied:** Imperial Art School, Odessa; NAD; Beaux-Arts Institute of Design, NYC. To USA, 1910. Traveled England, Russia, Italy. Fire demolished New York studio, 1931, destroying almost all his work. **Taught:**

American Artists School, NYC; U. of Southern California, summer, 1949; Baizerman Art School, 1934-40. **Awards:** PAFA, Hon. Men. 1949; AAAL Grant, 1951; Guggenheim Foundation Fellowship, 1952; PAFA, Alfred G. B. Steel Memorial Prize, 1952. **One-man Exhibitions:** (first) Dorien Leigh Galleries, London, 1924; Eighth Street Gallery, NYC, 1933; Artists' Gallery, NYC, 1938, 48, 57; Philadelphia Art Alliance, 1949; The New Gallery, NYC, 1952, 54; World House Galleries, NYC, 1963; The Zabriskie Gallery, 1967, 70, 72, 75, 80. **Retrospective:** Walker, circ., 1953; ICA, Boston, 1958; Huntington, N.Y./Heckscher, 1961. **Collections:** Andover/Phillips; Hirshhorn; U. of Minnesota; U. of Nebraska; U. of New Mexico; U. of North Carolina; PAFA; WMAA; Walker. **Bibliography:** Baur 7; Brumme; Chipp; Goodrich and Baur 1; Marter, Tarbell, and Wechsler; Pearson 2. Archives.

BALDESSARI, JOHN. b. June 17, 1931, National City, Calif. **Studied:** Otis Art Institute; Chouinard Art Institute; UCLA; U. of California, Berkeley; San Diego State College, 1953, BA, 1957, MA. Traveled Europe, Mexico, Canada, Middle East. **Taught:** San Diego Fine Arts School, 1953-54; San Diego city schools, 1956-57; San Diego State College, 1956, 59-61; Southwestern College, Chula Vista, 1962-68; U. of California, San Diego, 1962-70; La Jolla, 1966-70; California Institute of the Arts, Valencia, 1970-; Hunter College, 1971. **Awards:** National Endowment for the Arts, 1973, 74-75. **Address:** % Dealer. **Dealer:** Ileana Sonnabend Gallery, NYC. **One-man Exhibitions:** La Jolla, 1960, 66, 68; Southwestern College, Chula Vista, 1962-64, 75; Molly Barnes Gallery, Los Angeles, 1968; Eugenia Butler, 1970; Richard Feigen Gallery, 1970; Nova Scotia College of Art and Design, Halifax, 1971, 72; Art & Project, Amsterdam, 1971, 72, 75; Galerie Konrad Fischer, Dusseldorf, 1971, 73; Jack Wendler Gallery,

London, 1972, 74; Galleria Toselli, Milan, 1972, 74; Galerie MTL, Brussels, 1972, 74, 75; Ileana Sonnabend Gallery, NYC, 1973, 75, 78, 80, 81, 84; Ileana Sonnabend Gallery, Paris, 1973, 75; Galleria Schema, Florence, 1973; Galerie Volker Skulima, Berlin, 1974; Felix Handschin Gallery, Basel, 1975; Galeria Saman, Genoa, 1975; Amsterdam/Stedelijk, 1975; Modern Art Agency, Naples, 1975; The Kitchen, NYC, 1975; U. of California, Irvine, 1976; Ewing and Paton Galleries, Victoria, Australia, 1976; Auckland, 1976; U. of Akron, 1976; Ohio State U., 1976; Cirrus Editions, Los Angeles, 1976; James Corcoran Gallery, Los Angeles, 1976; Massimo Valsecchi Gallery, Milan, 1977; Hartford/Wadsworth, 1977; Robert Self Gallery, London, 1977; Julian Pretto Gallery, NYC, 1977; Portland (Ore.) Center for the Visual Arts 1978; Theatre Vanguard, Los Angeles, 1978; Artists Space, NYC, 1978; Pacific Film Archives, Berkeley, 1978; WMAA (films), 1978; ICA, Boston, 1978; InK, Zurich, 1979; New Museum, 1981; Eindhoven, 1981; CEPA Gallery, Buffalo, 1981; Buffalo/Albright, 1981; Essen, 1981; Cincinnati/Contemporary, 1982; Wright State U., 1982; Houston/Contemporary, 1982; Galerie Stampa, Basel, 1983; Marianne Deson Gallery, Chicago, 1983; Arte Viva, Basel, 1983; Douglas Drake Gallery, Kansas City, Mo., 1984; Margo Leavin Gallery, Los Angeles, 1984; Gillespie-Laage-Salomon, Paris, 1984; Centre d'Art Contemporain, Dijon, France, 1985. **Group:** La Jolla, The Uncommon Denominator—13 San Diego Painters, circ., 1960; Long Beach/MA, Arts of Southern California VIII: Drawing, circ., 1960; SFMA Annuals, 1961, 62; San Diego State College, Seven-Man Show, 1962; Long Beach/MA, Arts of Southern California: Painting, circ., 1963; La Jolla, Some Aspects of California Painting and Sculpture, 1965; U. of California, San Diego, New Work, Southern California, 1968; Hayward Gallery, London, Pop Art, 1969; Leverkusen, Konzeption, 1969; Seattle/AM, 557, 087, 1969; California College of Arts and Crafts, Space, 1969; Chicago/Contemporary, Art by Telephone, 1969; WMAA Annuals 1969, 72; Jewish Museum, Software, 1970; Oberlin College, Art in the Mind, 1970; Turin/Civico, Conceptual Art, Arte Povera, Land Art, 1970; Kyoto Municipal Museum of Art, Nirvana, 1970; MOMA, Information, 1971; Buenos Aires/Moderno, Art Systems, 1971; Dusseldorf/Kunsthalle, Prospect '71, 1971; Festival of Two Worlds, Spoleto, 1972; Documenta V, Kassel, 1972; Basel, Twelve-Man Show, 1972; Venice Biennial, 1972; VI International Theater Festival: Aspects, Belgrade, 1972; Houston/Contemporary, Five-Man Show, 1972; Minnesota College of Art and Design, I National Videotape Festival, 1972; Houston/Contemporary, Videotapes, 1972; Basel, Konzept Kunst, 1972; Pasadena/AM, Southern California Attitudes, 1972; Syracuse/Everson, Circuit, circ., 1973; Musée Galliera, Paris, Festival d'Automne, 1973; Dusseldorf/Kunsthalle, Prospect '73, 1973; Parcheggio di Villa Borghese, Rome, Contemporanea, 1974; Cologne, Project '74, 1974; Eindhoven, Kunst Informatie Centrum, 1974; Malmo, New Media, 1975; Auckland; Pan Pacific Biennial, 1976; SFMA, Painting and Sculpture in California, 1976; Fort Worth, American Artists: A New Decade, 1977; WMAA Biennials, 1977, 79; Houston/ Contemporary, American Narrative/Story Art: 1967-1977, 1978; WMAA, Art about Art, 1978; ICA, London, Wit and Wisdom, 1978; Chicago/AI, American Photography in the 70's, 1979; WMAA Biennial, 1979, 83, 85; Bochum, Words, 1979; Hayward Gallery, London, Pier and Ocean, 1980; Cologne/Stadt, Westkunst, 1981; Sydney/AG, 4th Biennial, 1982; Documenta VII, Kassel, 1982; Los Angeles/MOCA, Automobile & Culture, 1984; Paris Biennial, 1985; Carnegie, International, 1985. **Collections:** Basel, Canberra/National; Chicago/AI; Cologne; Eindhoven, Denver/AM; Houston/MFA; Institut fur Moderne

Kunst; International Museum of Photography; La Jolla; Los Angeles/County MA; Los Angeles/MOCA; MOMA; Miami-Dade; Newport Harbor; Oberlin College; The Ohio State U.; Transamerica Corp; WMAA. **Bibliography:** *Art Now 74; Contemporanea;* Meyer; *Report.*

BANNARD, DARBY. b. September 23, 1934, New Haven, Conn. **Studied:** Princeton U., BA. Contributing editor, *Artforum,* 1973-74; curator, Hans Hofmann, Hirshhorn, 1976; co-chairman, National Endowment for the Arts International Committee on the Visual Arts, 1979-. Traveled Europe, USA, Canada, Mexico. **Taught:** Columbia U., 1968; Princeton U., 1974; Brooklyn Museum, 1974; Kent State U., 1974; U. of Texas, 1975; Washington U., St. Louis, 1977; SFAI, 1979; School of Visual Arts, NYC. **Awards:** Guggenheim Foundation Fellowship, 1968; National Council on the Arts, 1968; Francis J. Greenberger Foundation Award, 1986. **Address:** Box 296, Rocky Hill, N.J. 08553. **Dealer:** Knoedler Contemporary Art; Salander-O'Reilly Galleries; NYC; Watson/de Nagy & Co., Houston. **One-man Exhibitions:** (first) Tibor de Nagy Gallery, NYC, 1965, also 1966, 67, 68, 69; Kasmin Ltd., 1965, 68, 69, 70, 72; Richard Feigen Gallery, Chicago, 1966; Nicholas Wilder Gallery, 1967; Bennington College, 1969; David Mirvish Gallery, 1969; Lawrence Rubin Gallery, NYC, 1970, 73; Joseph Helman Gallery, St. Louis, 1970; Galerie Hans R. Neuendorf, Cologne, 1971; Newport Harbor, 1972; Pasadena/AM, 1973; Tibor de Nagy Gallery, Houston, 1973, 75; M. Knoedler & Co., Inc., NYC, 1974 (twice), 75, 77, 78, 79, 80; Laguna Gloria Art Museum, Austin, Tex., 1975; Ronald Greenberg Gallery, St. Louis, 1977; Exeter, 1977; David Mirvish Gallery, Toronto, 1978; Watson/De Nagy, Houston, 1979; Wichita/Ulrich, 1980; Watson/de Nagy & Co., 1981; Martin Girard Gallery, Edmonton, Canada,

1982; M. Knoedler & Co., NYC, 1982; The Clayworks Studio Workshop, NYC, 1982. **Retrospective:** Baltimore/MA, circ., 1973. **Group:** Los Angeles/County MA, Post Painterly Abstraction, 1964; MOMA, The Responsive Eye, 1965; Chicago/Contemporary, 1965; Smithsonian, 1966; U. of Pennsylvania, 1966; WMAA Annual, 1967; Detroit/Institute, Color, Image and Form, 1967; MOMA, The Art of the Real, 1968; New Delhi, First World Triennial, 1968; Dusseldorf/Kunsthalle, Prospect '68, 1968; Corcoran Biennial, 1969; XXXV Venice Biennial, 1970; Buffalo/Albright, Color and Field: 1890-1970, 1970; Toledo/MA, The Form of Color, 1970; WMAA, The Structure of Color, 1971; Illinois State U. Biennial, 1971; Buffalo/Albright, Six Painters, 1971; Houston/MFA, Toward Color and Field, 1971; WMAA Annual, 1972; Boston/MFA, Abstract Painting in the '70s, 1972; Winnipeg (Canada) Art Gallery, Masters of the Sixties, 1972; Montreal/Contemporain, 11 Artistes Americans, 1973; Houston/MFA, The Great Decade of American Abstraction: Modernist Art 1960 to 1970, 1974; Cleveland/MA, Contemporary American Artists, 1974; WMAA (downtown), Continuing Abstraction in American Art, 1974; Indianapolis/Herron, 1978; Syracuse/Everson, New Works in Clay III, 1981. **Collections:** Brandeis U.; Baltimore/MA; Boston/MFA; Buffalo/Albright; Cleveland/MA; Dayton/AI; Harvard U.; Hofstra U.; Honolulu Academy; Houston/MFA; MOMA; Melbourne/National; Newark Museum; Oberlin College; Princeton U.; Ridgefield/Aldrich; Storm King Art Center, U. of Texas, Toledo/MA; Trenton/State; U. of Texas; SRGM; WMAA. **Bibliography:** Battcock, ed.; **Cone 2;** *The Great Decade;* Goossen 1; Rose, B., 1; Wood.

BARNES, ROBERT. b. September 24, 1934, Washington, D.C. **Studied:** Chicago Art Institute School, 1952-56; The

Robert Barnes   *Secrets Revealed by the North Sea* 1984

U. of Chicago, 1952-56, BFA; Columbia U., 1956; Hunter College, 1957-61; U. of London, Slade School, 1961-63. Traveled Great Britain, France, USA. **Taught:** Indiana U., summers, 1960, 61; Kansas City Art Institute and School of Design, 1963-64; Indiana U., 1964-. **Commissions:** New York Hilton Hotel, 1962 (edition of lithographs). **Awards:** William and Noma Copley Foundation Grant, 1961; Fulbright Fellowship, 1961, renewed 1962; Chicago/AI, 67th Annual; AAAL, **P.P.,** 1970. **Address:** % Dealer. **Dealer:** Allan Frumkin Gallery, NYC and Chicago. **One-man Exhibitions:** (first) Allan Frumkin Gallery, NYC, 1963, 68, 74, 77, 79, 83; Allan Frumkin Gallery, Chicago, 1964, 67, 75, 78; Galerie du Dragon, Paris, 1967; Coe College, 1967; Indianapolis/Herron, 1968; Quincy (Ill.) Art Club, 1971; Il Fante di Spade, Rome, 1973; Frumkin & Struve Gallery, Chicago, 1981, 83. **Group:** Chicago/AI, Exhibition Monumentum, 1952-55; Chicago/AI, Prints from the Graphic Workshop, 1955; Boston Arts Festival, 1958; Chicago/AI Annuals, 1958, 60, 61, 64; State U. of Iowa, Main Current of Contemporary American Painting, 1960; Ravinia Festival, Highland Park, Ill., 1961; WMAA Annual, 1962; Yale U., 1962; Kansas City/Nelson, 1962; SFMA, 1963; MOMA, 60 Modern Drawings, 1963; Chicago/AI, Drawings, 1963; WMAA, Young America, 1965; Salon des Jeunes Peintres, Paris, 1965; Museo Civico, Bologna, 1965;

PAFA, 1966; RISD, Recent Still Life, 1966; U. of Illinois, 1967; VMFA, Works on Paper, 1970; Indianapolis, 1972; Chicago/Contemporary, Chicago Imagist Art, 1972; Galleria Comunale d'Arte Contemporanea, Una Tendenza Americana, 1973; Joslyn/Omaha, The Chosen Object, 1977; Chicago/AI, 100 Years, 100 Artists: Alumni of the SAIC, 1979. **Collections:** Chicago/AI; Indiana U.; MOMA; U. of North Carolina. Pasadena/AM; St. Joseph/Albrecht; WMAA. **Bibliography: Robert Barnes.** Rose; B., 1.

BARNET, WILL. b. May 25, 1911, Beverly, Mass. **Studied:** Boston Museum School, with Phillip Hale; ASL, with Charles Locke. Traveled USA, Europe.

Taught: ASL, 1936-; Cooper Union, 1945-; U. of Washington, Summer, 1963; Boston Museum School, 1963; Famous Artists Schools, Inc., Guiding Faculty, 1954-64; PAFA, 1967-; Cornell U., summers, 1968, 69. **Member:** American Abstract Artists; Federation of Modern Painters and Sculptors; Century Association; NAD. Federal A.P.: Technical advisor in lithography. **Member:** Fellow, Royal Society of Arts. **Awards:** Corcoran, William A. Clark Prize; Ford Foundation/A.F.A. Artist-in-Residence; PAFA, Walter Lippincott Prize, 1968; Library of Congress, **P.P.,** 1974; NAD, Benjamin Altman Prize, 1977. **Address:** 15 Gramercy Park, NYC 10003. **Dealer:** Kennedy Galleries, Inc., NYC. **One-man Exhibitions:** (first) Hudson D. Walker Gallery,

Will Barnet *Swing* 1986

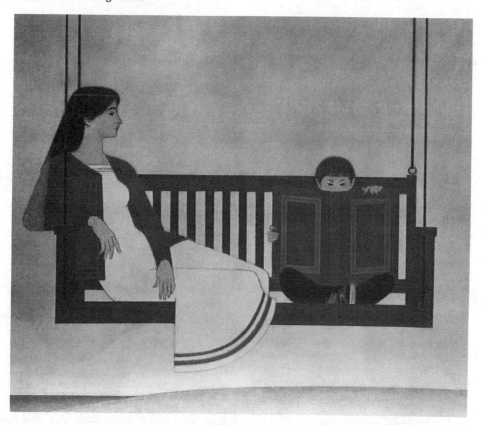

NYC, 1939; Gallery St. Etienne, NYC, 1943; The Bertha Schaefer Gallery, 1947, 49, 51, 53, 55, 60, 62; Peter H. Deitsch Gallery, 1960, 63; Mary Harriman Gallery Inc., Boston, 1963; Galleria Trastevere di Topazia Alliata, Rome, 1960; Waddell Gallery, 1965, 66, 68; Fairweather-Hardin Gallery, 1971; David/David Inc., Philadelphia, 1972; Hirschl & Adler Galleries, NYC, 1973, 76; Century Association, 1974; Harmon Gallery, 1974; Meredith Long Gallery, 1974; Prince Arthur Galleries, Toronto, 1977; Haslem Fine Arts, Inc., Washington, D.C., 1977, 79; Alice Simsar Gallery, Inc., Ann Arbor, 1978; AAA Gallery, NYC, 1978; Charlottemont, 1979; Foster Harmon Galleries of American Art, Sarasota, 1980; Le Galerie Documents, Paris, 1980; Terry Dintenfass Inc., 1982; Kennedy Galleries, Inc., 1984. **Retrospectives:** U. of Minnesota, Duluth, 1958; ICA, Boston, 1961; Albany/Institute, 1962; PAFA, 1970; A.A.A. Gallery, 1972; Print Club of Philadelphia, 1977; Purchase/SUNY, circ., 1979; Currier, circ., 1984. **Group:** American Abstract Artists since the Mid-1940's; MMA, American Paintings Today, 1950; Yale U., 1955; Corcoran, 1960; International Biennial Exhibition of Prints, Tokyo, 1960; PAFA, 1962, 68, 69; WMAA, Geometric Abstraction in America, circ., 1962; Brooklyn Museum; Carnegie; ICA, Boston; MOMA; U. of California, 1968; U. of Illinois, 1969; Expo '74, Spokane, 1974; NAD, 1975; 100th Anniversary Exhibition of ASL, 1975; IEF, Twentieth-Century American Drawings: The Figure In Context, circ., 1984. **Collections:** Boston/MFA; Brooklyn Museum; U. of California; Carnegie; Cincinnati/AM; Columbus; Corcoran; Currier; Harvard U.; Honolulu Academy; Library of Congress; MMA; MOMA; Montana State College; NAD; NMAA; NYPL; NYU; PAFA; PMA; Phillips; Rockland/Farnsworth. SRGM; Seattle/AM; U. of Texas; Utica; WMAA; Buffalo/Albright. **Bibliography:** American Artists Congress, Inc.; Doty. Farrell; Hayter 1; Janis and Blesh 1; Nordness, ed.; Reese; Smith, A. Archives.

BARRY, ROBERT. b. March 9, 1936, NYC. **Studied:** Hunter College, BFA, MA. **Awards:** National Endowment for the Arts, grant, 1976. **Address:** 1091 Emerson Avenue, Teaneck, NJ 10766. **Dealer:** Leo Castelli Inc., NYC. **One-man Exhibitions:** Westerly Gallery, NYC, 1964; Seth Siegelaub, Los Angeles, 1969; Art & Project, Amsterdam, 1969, 71, 72, 74; Gian Enzo Sperone, Turin, 1969, 70, 73, 74; Eugenia Butler, 1970, 71; Yvon Lambert, Paris, 1971, 73, 74, 77; Paul Maenz Gallery, Cologne, 1971, 72, 73, 74, 76, 77, 79; Leo Castelli Inc., NYC, 1971, 72, 74, 76, 78, 79; Galerie MTL, Brussels, 1972; Jack Wendler Gallery, London, 1972, 73, 74; Galleria Toselli, Milan, 1972, 73; Tate, 1972; Gian Enzo Sperone, Rome, 1973, 76; Galeria Foksal, Warsaw, 1973; Kabinett fur Aktuelle Kunst, Bremerhaven, 1973; Kunstmuseum, Lucerne, 1974; Rolf Preisig Gallery, Basel, 1974, 76, 79; Amsterdam/Stedelijk, 1974; Gian Enzo Sperone, NYC, 1975; Cusack Gallery, Houston, 1975; Julian Pretto Gallery, NYC, 1976; P.S. 1, Long Island City, 1976; Robert Self Ltd., London, 1977; Eindhoven, 1977; Essen, 1978; Rudiger Schottle, Munich, 1977; U. of Colorado, 1978; Francoise Lambert Gallery, Milan, 1979; Rolf Preisig Gallery, Basel, 1979; Leo Castelli, Inc., NYC, 1979, 80, 81, 83; Omaha/Joslyn, 1980; Paul Maenz Gallery, Cologne, 1980; Yvon Lambert, Paris, 1981, 84; Essen, 1982; Museum of Conceptual Art, San Francisco, 1982; Ulmer Museum, Ulm, West Germany, 1983. **Group:** Hudson River Museum, Eight Young Artists, 1964; SRGM, Systemic Painting, 1966; A.F.A., The Square in Painting, 1968; Berne, When Attitudes Become Form; Amsterdam/Stedelijk, Op Losse Schroeven, 1969; Seattle/AM, 557, 087, 1969; Dusseldorf/Kunsthalle, Prospect '69, 1969; Leverkusen, Konzeption, 1969; Oberlin College, Art in the Mind, 1970; La Jolla, Projections: Anti-Materialism, 1970; New York Cultural Center, Conceptual Art and Conceptual Aspects, 1970; MOMA, Information, 1971; Kyoto Municipal Museum of Fine Art, Nirvana, 1970;

Jewish Museum, Software, 1970; Kunsthalle, Nurnberg, Artist, Theory and Work, 1971; Munster/WK, Concept Art, 1971; Paris Biennial, 1971; Mills College, Notes and Scores for Sound, 1972; Documenta V, Kassel, 1972; Venice Biennial, 1972; Amsterdam/Stedelijk, Kunst Als Boek, 1972; Munster/WK, Das Konzept ist die Form, 1972; Parcheggio di Villa Borghese, Rome, Contemporanea, 1974; Kunsthalle, Cologne, Kunst bleibt Kunst, 1974; Sarah Lawrence College, Word, Image, Number, 1975; U. of Chicago, Ideas on Paper 1970-1976, 1976; Chicago/Contemporary, Words at Liberty, 1977; Bochum, Words, Words, 1979; Chicago/AI, Annual, 1979; U. of California, Santa Cruz, Music, Sound, Language, Theatre, circ., 1980; Centre d'Arts Plastiques Contemporains, Bordeaux, Art Povera, Antiform: Sculptures 1966-1969, 1982; Dublin/Municipal, International Quadriennial (ROSC), 1984; Paris/Beaubourg, Livres d'Artistes, 1985. **Collections:** Amsterdam/Stedelijk; Basel; Chase Manhattan Bank; Cologne; Eindhoven; Krefeld/Kaiser Wilhelm. **Bibliography:** *Art Now 74;* Celant; *Contemporanea;* Honnef; Lippard, ed.; Meyer; *When Attitudes Become Form.*

BARTH, FRANCES. b. July 31, 1946, NYC. **Studied:** Hunter College, 1968, BFA, with Doug Ohlson, Ron Gorchov, Ralph Humphrey, Vincent Longo, George Sugarman; 1970, MA, with Tony Smith, Ray Parker. Traveled Europe, Russia, USA, Japan; lived in Amsterdam, 1978. **Taught:** Bennington College, 1975-76; Princeton U., 1976-79; Sarah Lawrence College, 1979-85; Yale U., 1986-. **Commissions:** Set design for Lynne Taylor Corbett and Charles Strouse, Louisville Ballet, *Tunes,* 1984. **Awards:** CAPS, 1973; National Endowment for the Arts, 1974; Guggenheim Foundation Fellowship, 1977; National Endowment for the Arts, 1982. **Address:** 99 Van Dam Street, NYC 10013. **Dealer:** Susan Caldwell, Inc., NYC; Jan Cicero Gallery, Chicago; Nina

Freudenheim, Buffalo. **One-man Exhibitions:** (first) Susan Caldwell Inc., 1974, 75, 76, 78, 79, 80, 81, 83; Jan Cicero Gallery, 1981, 85; Jersey City Museum, 1983; Nina Freudenheim, 1985. **Group:** WMAA Annuals, 1972, 73; Corcoran Annual, 1973; SFAI, S.F./L.A./NYC, 1978; ICA, U. of Pennsylvania, Eight Abstract Painters, 1978; Buffalo/Albright, American Paintings of the 1970s, circ., 1978; NYU, American Painting: The Eighties, 1979; MOMA, New Art II, Surfaces-Textures, 1981; Indianapolis, 1984, 85. **Collections:** Akron/AI; Buffalo/Albright; American Can Corp., Greenwich, Conn.; Amerada Hess Corp., NYC; Chase Manhattan Bank, NYC; Cornell U.; Dallas/MFA; IBM Corp., NYC; MMA; Prudential Insurance Co. of America; WMAA; Lehman Brothers, NYC and Chicago; Swiss Bank Corp., NYC; MOMA.

BARTLETT, JENNIFER. b. March 14, 1941, Long Beach, Calif. **Studied:** Mills College, 1963, BA; Yale 1964, BFA, 1965, MFA, with Jack Tworkov, James Rosenquist, Al Held, Jim Dine. **Awards:** CAPS, 1974; Chicago/AI, Harris Prize, 1976; Brandeis U., Creative Art Award, 1983; AAIAL, 1983. **Taught:** School of Visual Arts, NYC; 1972-77. **Address:** % Dealer. **Dealer:** Paula Cooper Gallery, NYC. **One-man Exhibitions:** Mills College, Oakland, Calif., 1963; 119 Spring St., NYC, 1970; Reese Palley Gallery, NYC, 1972; Paula Cooper Gallery, NYC, 1974, 77, 79, 81, 82, 83, 85; Jacob's Ladder, Washington, D.C., 1973 (two-man); Galleria Saman, Genoa, 1974, 78; Garage Gallery, London, 1975 (two-man); John Doyle Gallery, Chicago, 1975; Dartmouth College, 1976; Cincinnati/Contemporary, 1976; Hartford/Wadsworth, 1977; SFMA, 1978; Hansen-Fuller Gallery, San Francisco, 1978; Baltimore/MA, 1978; Margo Leavin Gallery, Los Angeles, 1979; The Clocktower, NYC, 1979; U. of Akron, 1979; Carlton College, 1970; Heath Gallery, Atlanta, 1979, 83; Galerie Mukai, Tokyo, 1980;

Akron/AM, 1980; Buffalo/Albright, 1980; Margo Leavin Gallery, Los Angeles, 1981, 83; Omaha/Joslyn, 1982; Tate Gallery, 1981; McIntosh/Drysdale Gallery, Houston, 1982; Gloria Luria Gallery, Bay Harbor Islands, Fla., 1983; Brandeis U., 1984; Long Beach/MA, 1984; U. of California, Berkeley, 1984; U. of Miami, 1985; Walker, 1985; Knight Gallery, Charlotte, N.C., 1985; Carpenter + Hochman Gallery, Dallas, 1985; Kansas City/Nelson, 1985. **Group:** MOMA, Seven Walls, 1971; WMAA Annual, 1972, Biennials 1977, 79; Indianapolis, 1972; Walker, Painting: New Options, 1972; GEDOK, Hamburg, American Women Artists, 1972; WMAA, American Drawings: 1963-1973; Corcoran, 37th Biennial, 1975; Biennale de Paris, 1975; Chicago/AI; Annual, 1976; Akademie der Kunst, Berlin, SoHo, 1976; Dusseldorf, The Pure Form, 1976; Documenta 6, Kassel, 1977; Paris/Moderne, Historical Aspects of Constructivism and Concrete Art, 1977; WMAA, New Image Painting, 1978; U. of North Carolina, Drawings about Drawing Today, 1979; WMAA, Decade in Review, 1979; Brockton/Fuller, Aspects of the 70's: Painterly Abstraction, 1980; XXXIX Venice Biennial, 1980; Yale U., Twenty Artists: Yale School of Art, 1950-1970, 1981; WMAA Biennial, 1981; Paris/Moderne, Baroques 81, 1981; Haus der Kunst, Munich, Amerikanische Malerie: 1930-1980, 1981; Milwaukee, American Prints, 1982; WMAA, Block Prints, 1982; Bonn, Back to the USA, circ., 1983; Brooklyn Museum, The American Artist as Printmaker, 1983; Nassau County Museum, The House and Garden, 1985; AAIAL, 1985. **Collections:** Adelaide; Art Museum of South Texas; Baltimore/MA; Buffalo/Albright; Burroughs Wellcome Co.; Chicago/Contemporary; Cleveland/MA; Dallas/MFA; Goucher College; Humlebaek/Louisiana; Israel Museum; Kansas City/Nelson; Keio U., Tokyo; La Jolla; Long Beach/MA; MMA; MOMA; Oberlin College;

Omaha/Joslyn; PMA; Purchase/SUNY; RISD; St. Louis/City; Security Pacific Bank, Los Angeles; Tate Gallery; Tel Aviv; WMAA; Walker; Yale U. **Bibliography:** *Back to the USA;* Bartlett; Danto; Drawings: The Pluralist Decade; **Goldwater, Smith, and Tomkins;** Haenlein; Marshall; Murken-Altrogge.

BASKIN, LEONARD. b. August 15, 1922, New Brunswick, N.J. **Studied:** NYU, 1939-41; Yale U., 1941-43; New School for Social Research, MA, 1949; Academie de la Grande Chaumiere, 1950; Academy of Fine Arts, Florence, Italy, 1951; privately with Maurice Glickman. US Navy, 1943-46. **Taught:** Worcester Museum School, 1952-53; Smith College, 1953-74. Operates the Gehenna Press. **Awards:** Prix de Rome, Hon. Men., 1940; L. C. Tiffany Grant, 1947; Library of Congress, Pennell **P.P.,** 1952; Guggenheim Foundation Fellowship, 1953; SAGA, Mrs. A. W. Erickson Prize, 1953; Tokyo/Modern, O'Hara Museum Prize, 1954; U. of Illinois, **P.P.,** 1954; Chicago/AI, Alonzo C. Mather Prize, 1961; VI Sao Paulo Biennial, 1961; American Institute of Graphic Art, Medal of Merit, 1965; PAFA, Gold Medal, 1965; NIAL, Gold Medal, 1969. **Address:** % Dealer. **Dealer:** Kennedy Gallery. **One-man Exhibitions:** Glickman Studio, 1939; Numero Galleria d'Arte, Florence Italy, 1951; The Little Gallery, Provincetown, Mass., 1952; Mount Holyoke College, 1952; Fitchburg/AM, 1952; Boris Mirski Gallery, Boston, 1954, 55, 56, 64, 65; Grace Borgenicht Gallery, Inc., 1954, 60, 64, 66, 69; The Print Club, Philadelphia, 1956; Portland, Me./MA, 1956; Wesleyan U., 1956; U. of Minnesota, 1961; U. of Louisville, 1961; Rotterdam, 1961; Amerika Haus, Berlin, 1961; American Cultural Center, Paris, 1961; Royal Watercolor Society, London, 1962; Peale House, Philadelphia, 1966; FAR Gallery, 1970; NCFA, 1970; A. Lubin, Inc., NYC, 1970; Kennedy Gallery, NYC, 1971, 73, 74, 75, 76, 78, 86; Amon Carter Museum, 1972;

Leonard Baskin *Prodigal Son* 1922

Jewish Museum, 1974; Summit (N.J.) Art Center, 1974; SFMA, 1976; Indianapolis, 1976; Towson State College, Baltimore, 1976; Port Washington (N.Y.) Public Library, 1977; Washington U., 1978. **Retrospective:** Bowdoin College, 1962; Rotterdam, 1961; Smith College, 1963; Worcester/AM, 1957. **Group:** MOMA; WMAA; Brooklyn Museum, 1949, 52, 53, 54, 55; Library of Congress; The Print Club, Philadelphia; SAGA, 1952, 53; Sao Paulo; Bran-

deis U.; Seattle/AM. **Collections:** Allegheny College; Auburn U.; Baltimore/MA; Bezalel Museum; Boston/MFA; Bowdoin College; Brandeis U.; Brooklyn Museum; Buffalo/Albright; Amon Carter Museum; Chase Manhattan Bank; Chicago/AI; U. of Delaware; Detroit/Institute; Fitchburg/AM; Harvard U.; Hirshhorn; Holyoke Public Library; U. of Illinois; Library of Congress; MMA; MOMA; Mount Holyoke College; NYPL; National Academy of Sciences; National Gallery; U. of Nebraska; Newark Museum; New School for Social Research; Omaha/Joslyn; PAFA; PMA; Princeton U.; The Print Club, Philadelphia; Smithsonian; St. John's Abbey, Collegeville, Minn.; St. Louis/City; Seattle/AM; Skidmore College; Smith College; Trenton/State; Utica; WMAA; Wesleyan U.; Worcester/AM. **Bibliography: Baskin;** Chaet; Craven, W.; Downes, ed.; **Fern;** Geske; Goodrich and Baur 1; Honisch and Jensen, eds.; Peterdi; Read 3; Rodman 1, 3; Sachs; Soyer, R., 1; Strachan. Archives.

BAYER, HERBERT. b. April 5, 1900, Haag, Austria. d. September 30, 1985, Montecito, Calif. **Studied:** Real-Gymnasium, Linz, Austria; architecture with Prof. Schmidthammer, Linz, 1919; Bauhaus, Weimar, 1921, with Vassily Kandinsky. Traveled Europe, Central America, Japan, North Africa. To USA, 1938. **Taught:** Bauhaus, Dessau, 1925-28; New York Advertising Guild, 1939-40. Designs and plans exhibitions for museums throughout the world. Typographer and designer of typefaces, packages, posters, books, and charts. Registered architect. **Member:** American Abstract Artists; Alliance Graphique Internationale; American Institute of Architects; Aspen Institute for Humanistic Studies; International Institute of Arts and Letters. **Commissions:** (architectural) Seminar Building, Aspen Institute for Humanistic Studies; factories, Container Corp. of America; private residences; (murals) Harvard

U.; Seminar Building, Aspen Institute; Colonial Williamsburg; Elementary School, West Bridgewater, Mass.; Container Corp. of America; sculpture for Arco Plaza, Los Angeles, 1973. **Awards:** Poster competitions; art director awards and medals; Milan Triennial, 1930; Medal of the City of Salzburg; Oklahoma, First Prize; AIGA, Gold Medal for Excellence, 1970; Hon. DFA, Philadelphia College of Art, 1974; Austrian Honor Cross for Art and Science, 1978; Hon. DFA, Art Center College of Design, Pasadena, 1979; Fellow, American Academy of Arts and Sciences, 1979. **One-man Exhibitions:** (first) Galerie Povolotzki, Paris, 1929; Kunstverein, Linz, 1929; Bauhaus, Dessau, 1931; Kunstlerhaus, Salzburg, 1936; The London Gallery, London, 1937; PM Gallery, NYC, 1939; Black Mountain College, 1939; Yale U., 1940; The Willard Gallery, 1943; Art Headquarters Gallery, NYC, 1943; North Texas State Teachers College, 1943; Outline Gallery, Pittsburgh, 1944; Cleveland/MA, 1952; H. Schaeffer Galleries, Inc., NYC, 1953; Galleria II Milione, Milan, 1954; Kunst Kabinett Klihm, 1954, 57, 59, 62, 67, 78; Aspen Institute, 1955, 64; Fort Worth, 1958; Walker, 1958; Dusseldorf, 1960; Bauhaus-Archiv, 1961; Andrew-Morris Gallery, NYC, 1963; The Byron Gallery, 1965; Esther Robles Gallery, 1965; Boise (Idaho) Art Association, 1965; U. of New Hampshire, 1966; Conzen Gallery, Dusseldorf, 1967; Kunst-Amendt, Aachen, 1967; Marlborough Fine Art Ltd. 1968; Dunkelman Gallery, Toronto, 1970; Marlborough Gallery, Inc., NYC, 1971, 76, 79; Marlborough Godard Ltd., Montreal, 1972; Marlborough Galerie AG, Zurich, 1974; Arte/Contacto, Caracas, 1974; Marlborough Godard Ltd., Toronto, 1975; Die Neue Galerie der Stadt, Linz, Austria, 1976; Marion Locks Gallery, Philadelphia, 1977; A.F.A., Herbert Bayer: From Type to Landscape, circ., 1977-78; Museum Bochum, 1978; Galerie Breiting, Berlin, 1979; Aldis Browne Fine Arts, NYC, 1984; Marlborough Gallery,

Inc., NYC, 1982; Denver (Col.) Design Center, 1985. **Retrospectives:** Brown U., The Way Beyond Art, circ., USA, 1947-49; Germanisches National Museum, Nurnberg, 33 Years of Herbert Bayer's Work, circ. Germany and Austria, 1956-57; Denver/AM, 1973; Haus Deutscher Ring, Hamburg, circ., 1974. **Group:** Julien Levy Galleries, NYC, 1931, 40; MOMA, Fantastic Art, DADA, Surrealism, 1936; MOMA, Bauhaus: 1919-28, 1938; MOMA, Art and Advertising Art, circ., 1943; ART: USA: 58, NYC, 1958; American Abstract Artists Annuals, 1959-64; Marlborough Fine Art Ltd., Bauhaus, 1962; Arts Club of Chicago, 1962; Musee des Arts Decoratifs, 1966; Kunstverein, Hannover, Germany, 1967; Bauhaus Exhibition, circ. Stuttgart, London, Amsterdam, Paris, 1967-71; Berlin/National, Trends of the Twenties, 1977; Paris/Beaubourg, Paris-Berlin, 1908-1933, 1978. **Collections:** Bauhaus-Archiv; Brandeis U.; Busch-Reisinger Museum; Cologne; Denver/AM; Duisburg; Dusseldorf; Essen; Evansville; Fort Worth; Graphische Sammlung Albertina; Hagen; Hannover; Harvard U.; Hudson River Museum; Kaiserslautern; Leverkusen; Linz; MOMA; U. of Michigan; Museum des 20 Jahrhunderts, Vienna; Nurnberg; Oklahoma; Oldenburg; Omaha/Joslyn; Roswell; Rome/Nazionale; SFMA; SRGM; Saarlandmuseum; Smith College; Stuttgart; Vassar College; Wiesbaden. **Bibliography:** Barr 1; Baur 7; **Bayer 1, 2;** Blanchard; Blesh 1; Dorner; Gaunt; Haftman; Janis; McCurdy, ed.; Neff, ed.; Rickey; Rotors; Wingler, ed.

BAYNARD, EDWARD. b. September 5, 1940, Washington, D.C. Traveled Spain, England. **Address:** Bostock Road, Shokan, N.Y. 12481. **Dealer:** Bernice Steinbaum Gallery, NYC. **One-man Exhibitions:** Ivan Spence Gallery, Ibiza, 1970; The Willard Gallery, NYC, 1971 (2), 76; 98 Green Street Left, 1972; Paley & Lowe Inc., NYC, 1972; Betty

Parsons Gallery, NYC, 1973; Vick Gallery, Philadelphia, 1974; Multiples, NYC, 1977; Aronson Gallery, Atlanta, 1978; Showcase Gallery, Southfield, Mich., 1978; Alexander F. Milliken Inc., NYC, 1978, 79, 80, 82; Meridith Contemporary Art Gallery, Baltimore, 1980, 81, 84; Barbara Gladstone, NYC, 1980; John Berggruen Gallery, San Francisco, 1980; Pam Adler Gallery, NYC, 1983; Galerie 99, Bay Harbor Islands, Fla., 1984; Hagerstown/County MFA, 1984; Bernice Steinbaum Gallery, NYC, 1985. **Group:** Utica, New American Painters, 1971; MOMA, Landscape, 1972; WMAA, American Drawing 1963-1973, 1973; Cleveland/MA, Seven Contemporary Artists, 1978; Houston/Contemporary, American Still Life, 1945-1983, 1983; Walker, Prints from Tyler Graphics, 1984. **Collections:** Amerada, Hess, N.J.; Chase Manhattan Bank; Hartford/Wadsworth; High

Museum; ICA; Lehman Brothers, Inc.; MMA; MOMA; U. of Michigan; U. of Philadelphia; PMA; Prudential Insurance Co. of America; SFMA; Southeast Banking Corp; WMAA; Walker; West Palm Beach/Norton.

BAZIOTES, WILLIAM A. b. June 11, 1912, Pittsburgh, Pa.; **d.** June 4, 1963, NYC. **Studied:** NAD, 1933-36, with Leon Kroll. Federal A.P.: Teacher, 1936-38; easel painting, 1938-41. **Taught:** NYU, 1949-53; Brooklyn Museum School, 1949-52; Peoples Art Center (MOMA), 1951-53; Hunter College, 1952-63. Cofounder of a school, "Subject of the Artist," with Robert Motherwell, Barnett Newman, and Mark Rothko, NYC, 1948. **Awards:** Chicago/AI, Abstract and Surrealist Art, First Prize, 1948; U. of Illinois, **P.P.,** 1951; Chicago/AI, The Mr. & Mrs.

William Baziotes *Phantom* 1953

Frank G. Logan Medal, 1961. **One-man Exhibitions:** (first) Art of This Century, NYC, 1944; The Kootz Gallery, NYC, 1946-48, 1950-54, 1956, 58, 61; Galerie Maeght, 1947; Sidney Janis Gallery, 1961; Milwaukee, 1965; Marlborough Gallery, Inc., 1971; PAFA, 1971; Blum Helman Gallery, NYC, 1986. **Retrospective:** SRGM, 1965; Newport Harbor Art Museum, circ., 1978. **Group:** California Palace, 1948; Chicago/AI, Abstract and Surrealist Art, 1948; WMAA Annuals, 1948, 50, 1952-57; U. of Illinois, 1949-51, 1953, 55, 61; Los Angeles/County MA, 1951; U. of Minnesota, 40 American Painters, 1940-50, 1951; I & II Sao Paulo Biennials, 1951, 53; MOMA, Fifteen Americans, circ., 1952; U. of Nebraska, 1952, 54; SRGM, Younger American Painters, 1954; WMAA, The New Decade, 1954-55; Brussels World's Fair, 1958; MOMA, The New American Painting, circ., Europe, 1958-59; Documenta II, Kassel, 1959; Walker, 60 American Painters, 1960; Galerie de France, Paris, 1961; MOMA, The New American Painting and Sculpture, 1969. **Collections:** Baltimore/MA; Brandeis U.; Buffalo/Albright; Chicago/AI; Detroit/Institute; Harvard U.; U. of Illinois; MMA; MOMA; Newark Museum; New Orleans/Delgado; U. of Rochester; SRGM; San Francisco Art Association; Seattle/AM; Smith College; Tel Aviv; Vassar College; WMAA; Walker; Washington U. **Bibliography: Alloway 4;** Ashton 5; Baur 5, 7; Bazin; Biddle 4; Blesh 1; Dorner; Carleton, Hobbs, and Levin; Eliot; Finkelstein; Flanagan; Goodrich and Baur 1; Haftman; Hunter 6; Hunter, ed.; Janis and Blesh 1; Janis; McCurdy, ed.; Mendelowitz; *Metro;* Motherwell ed.; Motherwell and Reinhardt, eds.; Murken-Altrogge; Neff, ed.; Neumeyer; Nordness, ed.; Paalen; Ponente; Pousette-Dart, ed.; Read 2; Richardson, E.P.; Ritchie 1; Rodman 2; Rose, B., 1, 4; Rubin 1; Sandler 1; Soby 5; Tuchman, ed.; Tomkins 2; Weller; William Baziotes; Archives.

BEAL, GIFFORD. b. January 24, 1879, NYC; **d.** February 5, 1956, NYC. **Studied:** Princeton U., 1900; privately with William M. Chase; ASL, with Frank V. DuMond. Traveled eastern USA. **Member:** NAD, 1914; President, ASL, 1914-29. **Commissions:** (murals) Interior Department Building, Washington, D.C.; U.S. Post Office, Allentown, Pa. **Awards:** Worcester/AM, Third Prize, 1903; St. Louis Exposition, 1904, Bronze Medal; NAD, Hallgarten Prize, 1910; NAD, The Thomas B. Clarke Prize, 1913; Chicago/AI, Hon. Men., 1913; Corcoran, Third Prize, 1914; Panama-Pacific Exposition, San Francisco, 1915, Gold Medal; PMA, 1917; National Arts Club, Gold Medal, 1918; NAD, Benjamin Altman Prize, 1919, 31; Chicago/AI, Watson F. Blair Prize, 1930; Corcoran Second William A. Clark Prize, 1930; NAD Annual, Andrew Carnegie Prize, 1932; Paris World's Fair, 1937, Silver Medal; NAD, Saltus Gold Medal for Merit, 1948; NAD, Samuel F.B. Morse Gold Medal, 1954; NAD, Edwin Palmer Memorial Prize, 1955. **One-man Exhibitions:** Kraushaar Galleries, 1920-23, 1925-27, 29, 31, 33, 34, 36, 38, 41, 45, 48, 50, 56, 65, 71, 75, 79, 85; AAAL, Memorial Exhibition, 1957; Fitchburg/AM, 1960; Storm King Art Center, 1968, 71. **Retrospective:** Century Association, 1950; Cowie Galleries, Los Angeles, circ., 1953; Phillips, 1971; Montclair/AM, 1972: **Group:** Chicago/AI, 1928, 34, 37, 40, 44; Whitney Studio Club, NYC, 1929; PAFA, 1929, 30, 39, 44, 47, 51; St. Louis/City, 1930, 32; MOMA, 1930; Carnegie, 1931, 36, 51; U. of Rochester, 1932, 62; Phillips, 1932, 40, 54; WMAA, 1935, 45; New York World's Fair, 1939; NAD, 1942, 49, 51, 55; MMA, 1943; California Palace, 1945, 59; Youngstown/Butler, 1953; Hartford/Wadsworth, 1955. **Collections:** ASL; Andover/Phillips; Arizona State College; Brooklyn Museum; Chicago/AI; Detroit/Institute; Indiana U.; Kansas City/Nelson; Lehigh U.; Los Angeles/County MA; MMA; NAD; Newark Museum; New Britain; Omaha/

Joslyn; The Pennsylvania State U.; Phillips; Randolph-Macon Woman's College; Southampton/Parrish; Syracuse U.; Utica; WMAA; Washington State U. **Bibliography:** Baur 7; Bryant, L.; Cahill and Barr, eds.; Hall; Jackman; Kent, N.; Mather 1; McCurdy, ed.; Mellquist; Neuhaus; Pagano; Phillips 1; Reese. Archives.

BEAL, JACK. b. June 25, 1931, Richmond, Va. **Studied:** College of William and Mary; Virginia Polytechnic Institute; Chicago/AI School (with Kathleen Blackshear). **Taught:** U. of Indiana, 1966; Purdue U., 1967; U. of Wisconsin, 1967, 69; Cooper Union, 1968; Wagner College; Cornell U.; Skowhegan School; San Francisco Art Association; Stanford U.; Fort Worth College; Miami-Dade. **Commissions:** Washington and Lee U., 1975; US Department of the Interior, 1976; US Department of Labor, 1976. **Awards:** Chicago/AI, Emilie L. Wild Prize, 1972; National Endowment for the Arts Grant, 1972. **Address:** 67 Vestry Street, NYC 10013; 83A Delhi Stage, Oneonta, NY 13820. **Dealer:**Allan Frumkin Gallery, NYC and Chicago. **One-man Exhibitions:** (first) Allan Frumkin Gal-

Jack Beal   *Still-Life with Self Portrait*   1982

lery, NYC, 1965, also 1967, 68, 70, 72, 73, 75, 78, 80, 84, 85; Allan Frumkin Gallery, Chicago, 1966, 69, 74; Miami-Dade, 1972; Galerie Claude Bernard, Paris, 1973, 75; Colorado State U., 1976; Fullerton College, 1977; Madison Art Center, circ., 1977-78; U. of Missouri, 1979; Reynolds/Minor Gallery, Richmond, Va., 1980. **Retrospective:** VMFA, circ., 1973. **Group:** Chicago/AI, 1965; WMAA, Young America, 1965; A.F.A., 1965; RISD, Recent Still Life, 1966; Bennington College, 1967; Vassar College, 1968; SFMA, 1968; WMAA Annuals, 1968, 69; Milwaukee, Aspects of a New Realism, 1969; WMAA, 22 Realists, 1970; Boston U., The American Landscape, 1972; A.F.A. Realist Revival, 1972; Chicago/AI, 70th American Exhibition, 1972; Cleveland/MA, Aspects of the Figure, 1974; US Department of the Interior, America 1976, circ., 1976; Brooklyn Museum, Print Biennial, 1976; U. of Virginia, American Tradition and the Image of Post Modern Man in Contemporary Painting, Drawing, and Sculpture, 1979; PAFA, Seven on the Figure, 1979; Tulsa/Philbrook, Realism/Photorealism, 1980; Norfolk/Chrysler, American Figurative Painting, 1950-1980, 1980; Brooklyn Museum, American Drawings in Black and White, 1970-1979, 1980; San Antonio/MA, Real, Really Real, Super Real, circ., 1981; PAFA, Contemporary American Realism Since 1960, 1981; PAFA, Perspectives on Contemporary American Realism, 1983; IEF, Twentieth Century American Drawings: The Figure in Context, circ., 1984. **Collections:** Auckland; Bruce Museum; Brunswick Corp.; Chicago/AI; Ciba-Geigy Corp.; Delaware Art Museum; Des Moines; Exxon Corp.; Madison Art Center; MOMA; Minneapolis/Institute; Minnesota/MA; U. of North Carolina; U. of Notre Dame; Purchase/SUNY; PMA; Philip Morris Collection; Ringling; Sara Roby Foundation; SFMA; Toledo; Valparaiso U. (Ind.); U. of Vermont; U. of Virginia; WMAA; Wake Forest U.; Walker; Wilmington. **Bibliography:**

America 1976; Adrian; Arthur; Arthur 3; Arthur 4; Lucie-Smith; Rose, B., 1; Sager; Strand, ed.; Archives.

BEARDEN, ROMARE. b. September 2, 1914, Charlotte, N.C. **Studied:** NYU, BA; ASL (with George Grosz), 1938. Traveled Europe, North Africa. US Army, 1942-45. **Taught:** Williams College, 1971; Yale College, 1980. **Member:** AAIAL; Board of New York State Council on the Arts. Designed environment for the Ed Bullins play *House Rent Party,* at The American Place Theatre, NYC, 1973. **Commissions:** murals for the New Lincoln Hospital, NYC, and City Hall, Berkeley, Calif.; Baltimore Metroline, mural, 1983; Manhattan Community College, mural, 1983. **Awards:** AAAL, Painting Award, 1966; Guggenheim Foundation Fellowship, 1969; Ford Foundation Grant, 1973; New York Urban League, Frederick Douglass Medal, 1978; NAACP, James Weldon Johnson Award, 1978. **Address:** 357 Canal Street, NYC 10013. **Dealer:** Cordier & Ekstrom, Inc., NYC. **One-man Exhibitions:** (first) "G" Place Gallery, Washington, D.C., 1945; The Kootz Gallery, NYC, 1945, 46, 57; Duvuloy Gallery, Paris, 1945; Niveau Gallery, NYC, 1948; Barone Gallery, NYC, 1955; Michel Warren Gallery, NYC, 1960; Cordier & Ekstrom, Inc., 1961, 64, 67, 70, 73, 74, 75, 76, 77, 78, 81, 83; Corcoran, 1966; Waitsfield/Bundy, 1966; Spelman College, 1967; NCFA, 1971; Pasadena/AM, 1971; High Museum, 1972; Raleigh/NCMA, 1972; Studio Museum, 1972; Syracuse/Everson, 1975; Nassau College, 1976; Union College, 1977; Davidson College, 1978; Birmingham, Ala./MA, 1982; New Orleans/Contemporary, 1982; Chattanooga/Hunter, 1982; Memphis State U., 1982; Galerie Albert Loeb, Paris, 1975; Malcolm Brown Gallery, Shaker Heights, Ohio, 1982. **Retrospectives:** Albany/SUNY, 1968; MOMA, circ., 1971; Charlotte Mint, circ., 1980; Detroit/Institute, 1986. **Group:** Carnegie; WMAA; Galerie Maeght, 6 American Painters, 1948; MMA, Survey of American Art, 1951; Chicago/AI; Dallas/MFA; Boston/MFA; MOMA, The New American Painting and Sculpture, 1969; Trenton/State, Six Black Americans, 1980. **Collections:** Akron/AI; Atlanta U.; Boston/MFA; Brooklyn Museum; Buffalo/Albright; Charlotte/Mint; Davidson College; Flint/Institute; Hartford/Wadsworth; Honolulu Academy; Howard U.; MMA; MOMA; Madison Art Center; Newark Museum; PMA; Princeton U.; St. Louis/City; U. of Rochester; Studio Museum; WMAA. **Bibliography:** Dover. Archives.

BEASLEY, BRUCE. b. May 20, 1939, Los Angeles, Calif. **Studied:** Dartmouth College, 1957-59; U. of California, 1959-62. Traveled Europe, Japan, South Pacific, Central America, Mexico. Resided in France, 1973. **Commissions:** State of California; Oakland/AM; Southland Center, Hayward, Calif.; City of San Francisco; GSA, Federal Office Building, San Diego, 1975; Taubman Co., Sterling Heights, Mich., 1976; San Francisco General Hospital, 1977; City of Salinas, California, 1977; Miami International Airport, 1977. **Awards:** Oakland/AM, Adele Morrison Memorial Medal, 1960; SFAI Annual, Hon. Men., 1961; Andre Malraux, **P.P.,** Paris Biennial, 1962; Marin, Frank Lloyd Wright Memorial, **P.P.,** 1965; San Francisco Arts Festival, **P.P.,** 1967. **Address:** 322 Lewis Street, Oakland, CA 94607. **One-man Exhibitions:** RAC, 1961; Everett Ellin Gallery, Los Angeles, 1963; The Kornblee Gallery, 1964; Hansen-Fuller Gallery, 1965; David Stuart Gallery, 1966; Andre Emmerich Gallery, NYC, 1971; de Young, 1972; Santa Barbara/MA, 1973; San Diego, 1973; Fuller Goldeen Gallery, San Francisco, 1981. **Group:** RAC Annual, 1960; Oakland/AM Annual, 1960; MOMA, The Art of Assemblage, circ., 1961; III Paris Biennial, 1963; U. of California, Berkeley, Eleven American Sculptors, 1964; La Jolla, Some Aspects of California Painting and Sculpture, 1965; San Fernando Valley State College, Twenty-two Sculptors, 1966; U. of Illinois, 1969, 74; ICA, U. of Pennsylvania, Plastics and New Art, 1969; Jewish Museum, A Plastic Presence, 1969; Expo '70, Osaka, 1970; Stanford U., Sculpture Here and Now, 1970; Omaha/Joslyn, Looking West, 1970; Oakland/AM, Pierres de Fantaisie, 1970; U. of Nebraska, American Sculpture, 1970; Sacramento/Crocker Biennial, 1970; Stanford U., Sculpture 72, 1972; Salon de Mai, Paris, 1973; Salond de la Jeune Sculpture, Paris/Moderne, 1973; Oakland/AM, Public Sculpture, Urban Environment, 1974; NCFA, Across the Nation, 1980; Oakland Museum, 100 Years of California Sculpture, 1982; U. of Santa Clara, Northern California Art of the Sixties, 1982; U. of Southern California, California Sculpture Show, 1984; Oakland Museum, Art of the San Francisco Bay Area, 1945-1980, 1985; Walnut Creek (Calif.) Civic Center Arts Gallery, Going Public, 1985. **Collections:** U. of California, Berkeley; California State U., Hayward; City of Anchorage; Dartmouth College; Gallaudet College; U. of Kansas; Los Angeles/County MA; MOMA; Marin; NMAA; Oakland/AM; Paris/Moderne; Sacramento/Crocker; Santa Barbara/MA; SRGM; UCLA; Wichita/AM. **Bibliography:** *California Sculpture Show.*

BEAUCHAMP, ROBERT. b. November 19, 1923, Denver, Colo. **Studied:** U. of Denver; Cranbrook Academy of Art, BFA; Colorado Springs Fine Arts Center, with Boardman Robinson; Hofmann School. US Navy, 1943-46. Traveled Italy, 1973. **Taught:** U. of Wisconsin, 1968; Cooper Union, 1969-70; Louisiana State U., 1971; U. of Illinois, 1972; Brooklyn College, 1973; School of Visual Arts, NYC, 1974-75; U. of California, San Diego, 1977; U. of Ohio, 1978; Syracuse U., 1978; SUNY/New Paltz, 1979; U. of Arizona, 1980; U. of Georgia, 1981-85. **Member:**

Artists Equity. **Awards:** Fulbright Fellowship (Italy); Walter K. Gutman Foundation Grant; National Council on the Arts, 1966; Guggenheim Foundation Grant, 1974; National Endowment for the Arts, 1986. **Address:** 463 West Street, NYC 10014. **One-man Exhibitions:** (first) Tanager Gallery, NYC, 1953; Great Jones Gallery, NYC, 1960, 61; Sun Gallery, Provincetown, 1961, 62, 63; Green Gallery, NYC, 1961, 63; Richard Gray Gallery, 1963; Felix Landau Gallery, 1963; East End Gallery, Provincetown, 1964, 65; The American Gallery, NYC, 1965; The Graham Gallery, 1965, 67, 69; Obelisk Gallery, 1966; U. of Utah, 1967; Tirca Karlis Gallery, 1967, 68, 71, 72; Louisiana State U., 1971; Galerie Simone Stern, New Orleans, 1971; French & Co. Inc., NYC, 1972; Robert Dain Gallery, NYC, 1972, 73; U. of Southern Florida, 1974; Terry Dintenfass, Inc. NYC, 1976; Monique Knowlton Gallery, NYC, 1978, 79, 80, 81, 83, 85; Fay Gold Gallery, Atlanta, 1982; Landmark Gallery Inc., NYC, 1982. **Retrospective:** Syracuse/Everson, 1984. **Group:** Bernault Commission, circ., Asia; Carnegie, 1958, 61; WMAA Annuals, 1961, 63, 65, 67, 69; Corcoran; Chicago/AI; MOMA, Recent American Painting and Sculpture, circ., USA and Canada, 1961-62; MOMA, Recent Painting USA: The Figure, circ., 1962-63; U. of Illinois, 1963; SRGM, 10 Independents, 1972; IEF, Twentieth-Century American Drawings: The Figure in Context, circ., 1984. **Collections:** Brooklyn Museum; U. of California; Carnegie; Cornell U.; Denver/AM; Hartford/Wadsworth; Hirshhorn; IT & T; MMA; MOMA; U. of Massachusetts; National Gallery; Norfolk/Chrysler; Ridgefield/Aldrich; Seattle/AM; Syracuse/Everson; U. of Texas; WMAA. **Bibliography:** *Robert Beauchamp: An American Expressionist.* Archives.

BECHTLE, ROBERT. b. May 14, 1932, San Francisco, Calif. **Studied:** Califor-

Robert Bechtle   *Sunset Stroller*   1985

nia College of Arts and Crafts, 1954, BA, 1958, MFA; U. of California, Berkeley. Traveled Europe, Mexico. **Taught:** California College of Arts and Crafts, 1957-; U. of California, Berkeley, 1965-66, Davis, 1967-68; San Francisco State College, 1968-; SFAI, 1975. **Awards:** Oakland/AM, **P.P.,** 1957, 59; RAC, 1958, 61, 64; Bay Printmakers Society, Oakland Adell Hyde Morrison Memorial Medal, 1959, 61; SFMA, James D. Phelan Award, 1965; National Endowment for the Arts, grant, 1977. **Address:** 1250 Horton Street, Energyville, Calif. 94608. **Dealers:** OK Harris Works of Art; John Berggruen Gallery. **One-man Exhibitions:** (first) SFMA, 1959, also 1964, 67; Berkeley Gallery, Berkeley, 1965, San Francisco, 1967; RAC, 1965; Sacramento/Crolker, 1966; U. of California, Davis, 1967; Achenbach Foundation, 1969; OK Harris Works of Art, 1971, 74, 77, 81, 84; John Berggruen Gallery, San Francisco, 1973; Jack Glenn Gallery, San Diego, 1973. **Retrospective:** Sacra-mento/Crocker, 1973; San Diego, 1973. **Group:** Witte, 1965; USIA 1965-67; WMAA Annual, 1967; MOMA, The Artist as His Subject, 1967; California Palace, Painters behind Painters, 1967; U. of Illinois, 1967, 69; West Coast Now, 1968; Vassar College, 1968; Milwaukee, Aspects of a New Realism, 1969; WMAA, 22 Realists, 1970; Indianapolis, 1970; Omaha/Joslyn, Looking West, 1970; Syracuse/Everson, Cool Realism, 1970; Indiana U., American Scene: 1900-1970, 1970; Chicago/Contemporary, Radical Realism, 1971; Govett-Brewster, The State of California Painting, 1971; Documenta V, Kassel, 1972; Stuttgart/WK, Amerikanischer Fotorealismus, circ., 1972; WMAA Biennial, 1973; Hartford/Wadsworth, New/Photo Realism, 1974; Tokyo Biennial, 1974; Toledo/MA, Image, Color, and Form, 1975; Renwick Gallery, Washington, D.C., Signs of Life: Symbols in the City, 1975; Centennial Museum/Vancouver, Aspects of Realism, 1976;

Baltimore, Super Realism, 1976; Canberra/National, Illusion and Reality, 1977-78; U. of Rochester, Perceiving Time & Space through Art, 1979; Albuquerque/MA, Reflections of Realism, 1979-80; San Antonio/MA, Real, Really Real, Super Real, 1981; PAFA, Contemporary American Realism Since 1960, 1981; Long Beach, Drawings by California Painters, 1982; Laguna Beach, West Coast Realism, 1983; Isetan Museum of Art, Tokyo, American Realism: The Precise Image, 1985; SMFA, American Realism (Janss), circ., 1985. **Collections:** Aachen/NG; Achenbach Foundation; U. of California, Berkeley; Charleston/Carolina; Chase Manhattan Bank; Chattanooga/Hunter; Concordia Teachers College (Ill.); Diablo Valley College; Doane College; High Museum; U. of Miami; Govett-Brewster; Indiana National Bank; Library of Congress; U. of Miami; MOMA; Mills College; NCFA; U. of Nebraska; Oakland/MA; SFMA; SGRM; Sacramento/Crocker; San Francisco Municipal Art Commission; San Jose State College; Southland Corp., Dallas; Starr King School for the Ministry; USIA; Valparaiso U. (Ind.); WMAA. **Bibliography:** Alloway 4; *America 1976; Amerikanischer Fotorealismus;* Arthur 1, 2, 3; Honisch and Jensen, eds.; *Kunst um 1970;* Lindy; Lucie-Smith; Murken-Altrogge; Sager; *The State of California Painting.*

BECK, ROSEMARIE. b. July 8, 1923, NYC. **Studied:** Oberlin College, BA; Columbia U.; NYU. Traveled Europe. **Taught:** Vassar College, 1957-58, 61-62, 64-65; Middlebury College, 1958, 59, 63; Parsons School of Design, 1965-68; Queens College, 1968-; **Member:** NAD. **Commissions:** Ration Mfg. Co., 1956. **Awards:** Ingram Merrill Foundation Grant, 1966, 79; Yaddo Fellowship; MacDowell Colony Fellowship; National Endowment for the Arts, 1986; NAD, Benjamin Altman Prize, 1986. **Address:** 6 East 12th Street, NYC 10003. **Dealer:** Ingber Art Gallery, NYC. **One-man Exhibitions:** (first) The

Periodot Gallery, 1953, also 1955, 56, 59, 60, 63, 64, 66, 68, 70, 72; Oberlin College, 1957; Vassar College, 1957, 61; New Paltz/SUNY, 1962; Duke U., 1971; Kirkland College, 1971; Zachary Waller Gallery, Los Angeles, 1971; Poindexter Gallery, NYC, 1975, 79; Queens College, 1975; Ingber Art Gallery, NYC, 1979, 85; Middlebury College, 1979. **Retrospective:** Wesleyan U., 1960. **Group:** PAFA, 1954; U. of Nottingham (England), 1954, 57; WMAA Annuals, 1955, 57; U. of Michigan, 1956; Chicago/AI; Brooklyn Museum; Tate; Youngstown/Butler; Arts Club of Chicago; NIAL, 1969, 70, 71, 72, 73; NAD, 1973; NAD Annual, 1981. **Collections:** Corcoran; Fort Wright College; NAD; U. of Nebraska; New Paltz/SUNY; U. of North Carolina; Ration Mfg. Co., Trenton/State; Vassar College; WMAA; Yaddo; Hirshhorn. **Bibliography:** Baur 5.

BECKMAN, WILLIAM G. b. October 19, 1942, Maynard, Minn. **Studied:** U. of Minnesota, St. Cloud, BA; U. of Iowa, MA, MFA, with Byron Burford, Hans Brader, Miguel Conde. Traveled Europe. **Taught:** U. of Iowa, 1966-68. **Address:** North Towerhill Road, Wassaic, N.Y. 12592. **Dealer:** Allan Frumkin Gallery, NYC. **One-man Exhibitions:** U. of Iowa, 1969; Hudson River Museum, 1969; Allan Stone Gallery, NYC, 1970, 71, 74, 76, 78, 80; Allan Frumkin Gallery, NYC, 1982, 85, 86. **Retrospective:** Brandeis U. (two-man, with Gregory Gillespie) circ., 1984. **Group:** Indianapolis, 1970, 78; Yale U., American Drawing: 1970-1973, 1973; Boston/MFA, Trends in Contemporary Realist Painting, 1974; Chicago/AI, 71st American Exhibition, 1974; Cleveland/MA, Aspects of the Figure, 1974; William Paterson College, Wayne N.J., The Other Realism, 1978; PAFA, Seven on the Figure, 1979; Tulsa/Philbrook, Realism/Photorealism, 1980; Haus der Kunst, Munich, Amerikanische Malerie: 1930-1980, 1981; Hirshhorn, Directions,

William Beckman　*Diana, No. 6*　1983–85

1981; Newport Harbor, Inside Out: Self Beyond Likeness, 1981; PAFA, Contemporary American Realism Since 1960, 1981; San Antonio/MA, Real, Really Real, Super Real, 1981; WMMA, Focus on the Figure, 1982; SFMA, American Realism (Janss), circ., 1985; Fort Lauderdale, An American Renaissance: Painting and Sculpture Since 1940, 1986; Isetan Museum of Art, Tokyo, American Realism: The Precise Image, 1985. **Collections:** Brandeis U.; Carnegie; Chicago/AI; New Britain/American; WMAA. **Bibliography:** Adrian; Arthur 3; Arthur 4.

BEHL, WOLFGANG. b. April 13, 1918, Berlin, Germany. **Studied:** Academy of Fine Arts, Berlin, 1936–39; RISD, 1939–40. US citizen. Traveled Europe, Mexico, USA, Middle East. **Taught:** Perkiomen School, 1940-42; Lake Forest Academy, 1942-44; Layton School of Art, 1944-45; College of William and Mary, 1945-52; Silvermine Guild, 1955-57; U. of Hartford, 1955-83. **Member:** Sculptors Guild. **Commissions:** Temple Beth El Sholom, Manchester, Conn.; St. Louis Priory, Creve Coeur, Miss.; Church of St. Timothy, West Hartford, Conn.; U. of Hartford; Willow Lawn Shopping Center, Richmond, Va.; St. Joseph's Cathedral, Hartford, Conn.; Church of the Resurrection, Wallingford, Conn.; Connecticut General Insurance Co. **Awards:** Chicago/AI, Joseph N. Eisendrath Prize, 1944; Milwaukee, Wisconsin Prize for Sculpture, 1945; Connecticut Academy of Fine Arts, First Prize for Sculpture, 1961; NIAL Grant, 1963; Ford Foundation, **P.P.,** 1964. **Address:** 179 Kenyon Street, Hartford, CT 06105.

Dealer: Rosenfeld Gallery, Philadelphia. **One-man Exhibitions:** Charlotte/ Mint, 1949, 50; The Bertha Schaefer Gallery, 1950, also 1955, 63, 65, 68; Hollins College, 1951; Randolph-Macon Woman's College, 1951; Sweet Briar College, 1951; Amerika Haus, Schweinfurt, Wurzberg, and Munich; Bucknell U., 1965; U. of Connecticut, 1965; New Britain/American, 1969; Bienville Gallery, 1974; U. of New Hampshire, 1974; Hampshire College, 1976; Texann Ivy Gallery, Orlando, Fla., 1979; Rosenfeld Gallery, Philadelphia, 1979. **Retrospective:** U. of Hartford, 1983. **Group:** Chicago/AI, 1943, 44; Milwaukee, 1945; Boston Arts Festival, 1946, 47; Silvermine Guild, 1946, 47; VMFA, 1946-49, 1951; U. of Illinois, 1957; Hartford/Wadsworth, 1957; Carnegie, 1962, 64; PAFA, 1964; Harvard U., 1966; Cranbrook, 6th Biennial, National Religious Art Exhibition, 1968. **Collections:** Andover/Phillips; Cornell U.; U. of Hartford; U. of Massachusetts; U. of Miami; New Britain; New Britain/American; PAFA; Slater.

BELL, CHARLES. b. February 2, 1935, Tulsa, Ok. **Studied:** U. of Oklahoma, 1957, BA; SFAI. US Navy 1957-60. Traveled United Kingdom, Japan. **Address:** 254 West Broadway, NYC 10012. **Dealer:** Louis K. Meisel Gallery, NYC. **One-man Exhibitions:** (first) Louis K. Meisel Gallery, 1972, 74, 77, 80, 83; Morgan Gallery, Shawnee Mission, Kan., 1976; Hokin/Kaufman Gallery, Chicago, 1983. **Group:** San Jose State U., East Coast/West Coast/New Realism, 1973; Tokyo Metropolitan Art Gallery, 11th Bienniale, 1974; Hartford/Wadsworth, New/Photo Realism, 1974; Wichita State U., The New Realism: Rip-Off or Reality?, 1975; Youngstown/Butler, Midyear Show, 1975; Indianapolis, 1978; SRGM, Seven Photorealists from New York Collections, 1981; Fort Wayne/AM, Photographs by the Photorealists, 1982; Utica, An Appreciation of Realism, 1982; Saitama/ Modern, Realism Now, 1983. **Collec-**

tions: NMAA; SRGM. **Bibliography:** Arthur 3; Lindy.

BELL, LARRY. b. 1939, Chicago, Ill. **Studied:** Chouinard Art Institute, 1957-59; with Robert Irwin, Emerson Woelfer. **Awards:** Guggenheim Foundation Fellowship, 1969. **Taught:** U. of California, Berkeley; U. of California, Irvine; California State at Hayward; U. of Southern Florida; Santa Fe Museum of Fine Arts, 1986. Traveled Southeast Asia. **Commissions:** Abilene Zoological Gardens, Abilene, Tx.; GSA, Springfield, Mass. **Address:** Box 469, Ranchos de Taos, N.M. 87557. **One-man Exhibitions:** Ferus Gallery, Los Angeles, 1962, 63, 65; The Pace Gallery, 1965, 67, 70, 71, 72, 73; Ileana Sonnabend Gallery, Paris, 1967, 68; Amsterdam/Stedelijk, 1967; Walker, 1968; Buffalo/Albright, 1968; Mizuno Gallery, 1969, 71, 75; Galerie Rudolf Zwirner, 1970; Joseph Helman Gallery, St. Louis, 1971; ACE Gallery, Los Angeles, 1972; Felicity Samuel Gallery, London, 1972; Pasadena/AM, 1972; Wilmaro Gallery, Denver, 1972; Oakland/AM, 1973; Fort Worth, 1975; Galleria del Cavallino, Venice, 1975; Marlborough Galleria d'Arte, Rome, 1975; Marion Goodman/Multiples, NYC, 1978, 81; Talley Richards Gallery, Taos, 1975, 77, 78, 79, 81; Texas Gallery, Houston, 1978; Delahunty Gallery, Dallas, 1978; Hansen Fuller Goldeen Gallery, San Francisco, 1979; U. of Massachusetts (two-man), 1977; Hudson River Museum, 1981; L.A. Louver Gallery, Venice, Calif., 1981; U. of Ohio, 1981; Wildine Gallery, Albuquerque, 1981. **Retrospective:** Pasadena/AM, 1972. **Group:** Pavillion Art Gallery, Balboa, Calif., 1964; MOMA, The Responsive Eye, 1965; VIII Sao Paulo Biennial, 1965; WMAA Sculpture Annual, 1966; WMAA, Contemporary American Sculpture, Selection I, 1966; U. of California, Irvine, 5 Los Angeles Sculptors, 1966; La Jolla, 1966; Seattle/AM, 1966; MOMA, The 1960s, 1967; WGMA, A New Aesthetic, 1967; Los

Angeles/County MA, American Sculpture of the Sixties, 1967; SRGM, Sculpture International, 1967; Documenta IV, Kassel, 1968; Vancouver, 1968; Eindhoven Kompas IV, 1969; Walker, 14 Sculptors: The Industrial Edge, 1969; Princeton U., American Art since 1960, 1970; MOMA, Spaces, 1969; Tate (three-man), 1970; Hayward Gallery, London, 11 Los Angeles Artists, 1971; Detroit/Institute, Art in Space, 1973; Kennedy Center, Washington, D.C., Art Now '74, 1974; Chicago/AI, 74th American Exhibition, 1982; Leigh Yawkey Woodson Art Museum, Wausau, Wisc., Americans in Glass, 1984. **Collections:** Albuquerque Museum; Amsterdam/Stedelijk; U. of Arizona; Buffalo/Albright; Canberra/National; Caracas/Contemporaneo; Chicago/AI; Cologne/Ludwig; Dallas/MFA; Denver/AM; Des Moines; Detroit/Institute; Fort Worth; Hartford; Hirshhorn; Houston/MFA; Los Angeles/County MA; MIT; MOMA; Milwaukee; NMAA; Oakland/AM; Paris/Beaubourg; Roswell; Rotterdam; SFMA; SRGM; Santa Fe, N.M.; Norton Simon Museum; Sydney/AG; Tate Gallery; Victoria and Albert Museum; WMAA; Walker. **Bibliography:** *Art Now 74;* Calas, N. and E.; Coplans, 3; Davis, D.; Friedman, M., 2; Kozloff 3; Lucie-Smith; *Report;* Rose, B., 1; *Transparency;* Tuchman 1; *USA West Coast.*

BENGLIS, LYNDA. b. October 25, 1941, Lake Charles, La. **Studied:** Newcomb College, Tulane U., 1964, BFA, with Pat Trivigno, Ida Kohlmeyer, and Hal Carney; Brooklyn Museum Art School, 1964-65, with Rubin Tam. Traveled Greece, Great Britain, Italy, France, Indiana. **Taught:** U. of Rochester, 1970-72; Hunter College, 1972-73; Princeton U., 1975; California Institute of the Arts, 1976; Kent State U., 1977; Skowhegan School of Painting and Sculpture, 1979; U. of Arizona, 1981. **Commissions:** Atlanta Airport, 1979-80; Federal Building, Albany, N.Y., 1979-80; Fairmont Hotel, Denver;

First City Center, Dallas; O'Brien Federal Building, Albany, N.Y. **Awards:** Guggenheim Foundation Fellowship, 1975; Artpark, Grant, 1976; Australian Art Council Award, 1976; National Endowment for the Arts, Grant, 1979. **Address:** 222 Bowery, NYC 10002. **Dealer:** Paula Cooper Gallery, NYC; Margo Leavin Gallery, Los Angeles. **One-man Exhibitions:** U. of Rhode Island, 1969; Paula Cooper Gallery, NYC, 1970, 71, 74, 75, 76, 78, 80, 82, 84; Janie C. Lee Gallery, Dallas, 1970; Galerie Hans Muller, Cologne, 1970; Kansas State U., 1971; MIT, 1971; Hansen Gallery, San Francisco, 1972, 73, 74, 77, 79; Portland (Ore.) Center for the Visual Arts, 1973; Jack Glenn Gallery, Corona del Mar, 1973; The Clocktower, NYC, 1973; The Texas Gallery, Houston, 1974, 75, 79, 80, 81, 84; The Kitchen, NYC, 1975; Margo Leavin Gallery, Los Angeles, 1977, 80, 82, 85; Douglas Drake Gallery, Kansas City, 1977; Dart Gallery, Chicago, 1979, 81, 83, 85; Georgia State U., 1979; Albert Baronian, Brussels, 1979, 80, 81; Chatham College, 1980; David Heath Gallery, Atlanta, 1980, 85; Susanne Hilberry Gallery, Birmingham, Mich., 1980, 83, 85; Portland (Ore.) Center for Visual Arts, 1980; U. of Arizona, 1981; Jacksonville/MA, 1981; Okhun-Thomas Gallery, St. Louis, 1982; Fuller Goldeen Gallery, San Francisco, 1982, 86; Tilden-Foley Gallery, New Orleans, 1984. **Retrospective:** U. of South Florida, 1980; U. of Miami, 1980. **Group:** Dusseldorf/Kunsthalle, Prospect 69, 1969; Finch College, Art in Process IV, 1969; Walker, Works for New Spaces, 1971; Milwaukee, Directions 3: Eight Artists, 1971; GEDOK, Kunsthaus, Hamburg, American Women Artists, 1972; Walker, Painting: New Options, 1972; Indianapolis, 1972; Chicago/AI, 32nd Annual, 1972; Detroit/Institute, 12 Statements, 1972; WMAA Biennial, 1973; Yale U., Options and Alternatives, 1973; New Orleans Museum, Five from Louisiana, 1977; Amsterdam/Stedelijk, Made by Sculptors, 1978; Palazzo Reale, Milan, Pintura Ambiente, 1979; Houston/ Contemporary, Extensions, 1980; San Diego, Sculpture in California, 1975-1980, 1980; XXXIX Venice Biennial, 1980; Jacksonville/AM, Currents: A New Mannerism, 1981; Rice U., Variants, 1981; WMAA Biennial, 1981; Chicago/AI, 74th American Exhibition, 1982; Hannover/KG, New York Now, circ., 1982; Houston/Contemporary, The Americans: The Collage, 1982; New Museum, Early Work, 1982; Bonn, Back to the USA, circ., 1983; U. of Chicago, The Sixth Day: A Survey of Recent Developments in Figurative Sculpture, 1983; Newark Museum, American Bronze Sculpture, 1850 To The Present, 1984; Seattle/AM, American Sculpture: Three Decades, 1984. **Collections:** Betcar Corp., Northfield, Ill,; Detroit/Institute, SRGM; MOMA; Canberra/National; National Gallery of Victoria, Melbourne; PMA; Storm King Art Center; Walker; SFMA; Baltimore/MA; Buffalo/Albright; Fort Worth; Houston/MFA; Israel Museum; Kansas City/Nelson; NMAA; NYU; New Mexico State U.; New Orleans Museum; Oberlin College; U. of Rhode Island; Sapporo; Seattle/AM; WMAA. **Bibliography:** Art: A Woman's Sensibility; Drawings: The Pluralist Decade; Lucie-Smith; Back to the USA; Haenlein.

BENGSTON, BILLY AL. b. June 7, 1934, Dodge City, Kans. **Studied:** Los Angeles City College; Los Angeles State College; California College of Arts and Crafts; Los Angeles County Art Institute. **Taught:** Chouinard Art Institute, 1961; UCLA, 1962-63; U. of Oklahoma, 1967; U. of Colorado, 1969; U. of California, Irvine, 1973, 79–86. **Awards:** National Council on the Arts, 1967; Tamarind Fellowship, 1968; Guggenheim Foundation Fellowship, 1975. **Address:** 110 Mildred Avenue, Venice, CA 90291. **Dealer:** James Corcoran Galleries, Los Angeles. **One-man Exhibitions:** (first) Ferus Gallery, Los Angeles, 1957, also 1958, 1960, 61, 62, 63; Martha Jackson Gallery, 1962; SFMA,

1968; Pasadena/AM, 1969; Utah, 1969; Santa Barbara/MA, 1970; Mizuno Gallery, 1970; Galerie Hans R. Neuendorf, Cologne, 1970, 71; Galerie Hans R. Neuendorf, Hamburg, 1970, 72; Margo Leavin Gallery, 1971; La Jolla, 1971; Contract Graphics Associates, Houston, 1971; Felicity Samuel Gallery, London, 1972; Corcoran & Greenberg, Inc., Coral Gables, 1973; Nicholas Wilder Gallery, 1973 (2), 1974; Southern Methodist U., 1973; Houston/Contemporary, 1973; The Texas Gallery, 1974, 75, 76, 77, 78, 79, 81, 84; John Berggruen Gallery, 1974; Jared Sable Gallery, Toronto, 1974; Pyramid Art Galleries Ltd., Washington, D.C., 1975; Seder/Creigh Gallery, Coronado, 1975; Tortue Gallery, Santa Monica, 1975; Dootson Calderhead Gallery, Seattle, 1975; Dobrick Gallery, Chicago, 1976; Portland (Ore.) Center for the Visual Arts, 1976; U. of Montana, 1977; James Corcoran Galleries, Los Angeles, 1977, 78, 79, 81, 82, 83, 84, 85; Security Pacific National Bank, Los Angeles, 1978; John Berggruen Gallery, San Francisco, 1978; Mizuno Gallery, Los Angeles, 1978; Conejo Valley Art Museum, 1979; Acquavella Contemporary Art Gallery, NYC, 1979, 81, 83; Cantor/Lemberg Gallery, Birmingham, Mich., 1979; Honolulu Academy, 1980; Thomas Babeor Gallery, La Jolla, 1981, 82, 83, 84, 85; Corcoran, 1981; San Diego State U., 1981; Linda Farris Gallery, Seattle, 1982; John Berggruen Gallery, San Francisco, 1983; Douglas Drake Gallery, Kansas City, 1984; Smith-Andersen Gallery, Palo Alto, 1984; Angles Gallery, Santa Monica, 1985. **Retrospective:** Los Angeles/County MA, circ., Vancouver, Corcoran, 1968. **Group:** Los Angeles/County MA Annual, 1957; Pasadena/AM, Pacific Profile of Young West Coast Artists, 1961; WMAA, Fifty California Artists, 1962-63; Oakland/AM, Pop Art USA, 1963; Milwaukee, Pop Art and the American Tradition, 1965; VIII Sao Paulo Biennial, 1965; Seattle/AM, Ten from Los Angeles, 1966; WMAA Annuals, 1967,

69; U. of California, San Diego, Los Angeles to New York, 1968; Palazzo Strozzi, Florence, Italy, 1 Biennale Internazionale della Grafica, 1968; MOMA, New Media: New Methods, circ., 1969; Jewish Museum, Superlimited: Books, Boxes, and Things, 1969; MOMA, Tamarind: Homage to Lithography, 1969; Eindhoven, Kompas IV, 1969-70; Pasadena/Am, West Coast: 1945-1969, 1969; Minnesota/MA, Drawings USA, 1971; Govett-Brewster, The State of California Painting, 1971; Kunstverein, Hamburg, USA: West Coast, circ., 1972; Akron/AI, Four Artists, 1972; Corcoran Biennial, 1973; Santa Barbara/MA, Fifteen Abstract Artists, 1974; WMAA, American Pop Art, 1974; Scripps College, Painting: Color, Form and Surface, 1974; U. of California, Santa Barbara, 4 from the West, 1975; Newport Harbor, The Last Time I Saw Ferus, 1976; SFMA, Painting and Sculpture in California: The Modern Era, 1976; California Institute of Technology, Pasadena, Watercolors and Related Media by Contemporary Californians, 1977; WMAA Biennial, 1979; ICA, U. of Pennsylvania, The Decorative Impulse, 1979; U. of Miami, Fabrications, 1980; AAIAL, 1982; Houston/Contemporary, The Americans: The Collage, 1982; Nagoya City Museum, Nagoya, Japan, Exhibition of Contemporary Los Angeles Artists, 1982; ARCO Center for Visual Arts, Los Angeles Pattern Painters, 1983; Oakland Museum, On and Off the Wall; Shaped and Colored, circ., 1983; ARCO Center for Visual Arts, Los Angeles and The Palm Tree: Image of a City, 1984; Indianapolis, 1984; San Diego State U., Watercolors: A Contemporary Survey, 1984. **Collections:** A.F.A.; Amon Carter Museum; Chicago/AI; Community Arts Foundation; Fort Worth; Houston/MFA; La Jolla; Los Angeles/County MA; MOMA; Newport Harbor; Oakland/AM; Paris/Beaubourg; Pasadena/AM; Ridgefield/Aldrich; SFMA; SRGM; UCLA; WMAA. **Bibliography:** Alloway 1; Kozloff 3; Lippard 5; *The State of California Painting; USA West Coast.*

BENJAMIN, KARL. b. December 29, 1925, Chicago, Ill. **Studied:** Northwestern U.; U. of Redlands, 1949, BA; Claremont Graduate School, with Jean Ames, 1960, M.A. US Navy, 1943-46. **Taught:** General elementary school, Southern California, 1949-; Pomona College; Claremont College. **Address:** 675 West Eighth Street, Claremont, CA 91711. **Dealers:** Ruth Bachofner Gallery, Los Angeles; R. C. Erpf Gallery, NYC. **One-man Exhibitions:** U. of Redlands, 1953, 56, 62, 72, 80; Pasadena/AM, 1954; Jack Carr Gallery, Pasadena, 1955, 56; Occidental College, 1958; Long Beach/MA, 1958; Esther Robles Gallery, 1959, 60, 62, 64, 65; Scripps College, 1960; La Jolla, 1961, 70; Bolles Gallery, 1961; Santa Barbara/AM, 1962, 68; Hollis Gallery, San Francisco, 1964, 66; Jefferson Gallery, 1965; Henri Gallery, 1968; Utah, 1971; William Sawyer Gallery, 1972; Tortue Gallery, Santa Monica, 1975, 77, 78, 80; Chafey College, 1975; Francine Seders Gallery, Seattle, 1978, 79, 80, 83, 86; Cheney Cowles Memorial Museum, 1980; Whiteman College, 1980; Abraxis Gallery, Newport Beach, 1981; Chaffey College, 1981; Claremont Graduate School, 1981; Pepperdine U., 1981; Shasta College, 1981; California State U., Bakersfield, 1982; Stella Polaris Gallery, Los Angeles, 1982; Chrysalis Gallery, Claremont, 1983, 85, 86; U. of California, Santa Barbara, 1984; Ruth Bachofner Gallery, 1986; Hemmerdinger Gallery, Palm Desert, Calif., 1986. **Group:** Los Angeles/County MA Annuals; A.F.A., New Talent, circ., 1959; UCLA, California Painters under 35, 1959; Los Angeles/County MA, Four Abstract Classicists, circ., 1959-61; ICA, London, West Coast Hard Edge, 1960; Carnegie, California Artists, 1961; Pasadena/AM, Pacific Profile, 1961; WMAA, Geometric Abstraction in America, circ., 1962; Fort Worth, The Artist's Environment: The West Coast, 1962; Amon Carter Museum, circ., 1962-63; WMAA, Fifty California Artists, 1962-63; Colorado Springs/FA Annual, 1964; Denver/AM, 1965; MOMA, The Responsive Eye, 1965; SFMA, The

Colonists, 1965; M. Knoedler & Co., Art Across America, circ., 1965-67; Corcoran Biennial, 1967; U. of New Mexico, Los Angeles Abstract Painting, 1979; Pomona College, Black and White Are Colors, Paintings of the 1950s-1970s, 1979; Laguna Beach Museum of Art, Southern California Artists: 1940-1980, 1981; U. of Washington, Color in Contemporary Painting, 1982; U. of Washington, Color, Color, Color, 1984; Shasta College, Ten California Colorists, 1985. **Collections:** U. of California; Cheney Cowles Memorial Museum; City of Claremont; Haifa Museum of Modern Art, Israel; Hartford/Wadsworth; La Jolla; Long Beach/MA; Los Angeles/County MA; Harvey Mudd College; NCFA; U. of Nebraska; U. of New Mexico; Newport Harbor; Pasadena/AM; Pepsi-Cola Co.; J. Pitzer College; Pomona College; U. of Redlands; SFMA; Salk Institute; San Diego; Santa Barbara/MA; Scripps College; Seattle/AM; Utah; U. of Utah; WMAA; U. of Washington. **Bibliography:** Rickey; *Black and White Are Colors.*

BENTON, FLETCHER. b. February 23, 1931, Jackson, Ohio. **Studied:** Miami U., 1955, BFA. Traveled Northern Europe, Mediterranean, parts of Africa and Asia, 1963. US Navy, 1949-50. **Taught:** California College of Arts and Crafts, 1959; SFAI, 1964-67; California State U., San Jose, 1967. **Commissions:** Atlantic Richfield Co. **Awards:** AAAL, Distinguished Service to American Art Award, 1979. **Member:** Artists Equity. There are three films on his work, 1969, 73, 75. **Address:** 2100 Pine Street, San Francisco, CA 94115. **Dealer:** John Berggruen Gallery, San Francisco. **One-man Exhibitions:** (first) Gump's Gallery, 1957; California Palace, 1964; SFMA, 1965; Hansen Gallery, San Francisco, 1965, 66; Esther Robles Gallery, 1966, 67; SFAI, 1967; Sonoma State College, 1967; Galeria Bonino Ltd., 1967, 69; Humboldt State College, 1968; Galerie Francoise Mayer, Brussels, 1969; SFMA, 1970; Buffalo/Albright, 1970; Chico State College, 1970; London Arts, Detroit, 1970; Berkeley (Calif.) Art Center, 1970; Reed College, 1970; Galeria Bonino Ltd., Buenos Aires, 1970; Estudio Actual, Caracas, 1970; Stanford U., 1971; La Jolla, 1972; Esther Robles Gallery, 1971, 72; Danenberg Gallery, 1972; Landry-Bonino Gallery, NYC, 1972; Phoenix, 1973; U. of California, Davis, 1973; Galeria Bonino Ltd., Rio de Janeiro, 1973; Elaine Horwitch Gallery, Scottsdale, 1974; U. of Santa Clara, 1975; Smith-Andersen Gallery, San Francisco, 1975; Fresno State U., 1977; John Berggruen Gallery, San Francisco, 1977, 80, 81, 84, 86; Tortue Gallery, Los Angeles, 1978; San Jose Museum of America, 1978; Grossmont College, 1970; Arts Club of Chicago, 1979; Milwaukee, 1979; Aachen/S-L, 1980; U. of Miami, 1980; Muscatine Art Center, 1980; Newport Harbor, 1980; Oakland/AM, 1980; Portland Ore./AM, 1980; Offenbach/Klingspor, 1981; San Jose Museum of Art, 1982; Thomas Babeor Gallery, La Jolla, 1984, 86; Fresno Art Center, Calif., 1984; Yares Gallery, Scottsdale, 1984; Harcus Gallery, Boston, 1985; Brigitte Haasner, Weisbaden, 1986; Laguna Beach School of Art, 1986; Transamerica Building, San Francisco, 1986. **Retrospective:** Arts Club of Chicago, circ., 1979. **Group:** Santa Barbara/MA, 1962, 66; San Francisco Art Association, 1964; La Jolla, 1965; New York World's Fair, 1964-65; U. of California, Berkeley, Directions in Kinetic Sculpture, 1966; SFMA, 1966; U. of Illinois, 1967, 69; Los Angeles/County MA and PMA, American Sculpture of the Sixties, 1967; U. of Hawaii, 1967; Carnegie, 1967; Flint/Institute, 1967; HemisFair '68, San Antonio, Tex., 1968; Milwaukee, Directions I: Options, circ., 1968; WMAA Sculpture Annual, 1968; Lytton Art Center, Los Angeles, 1968; UCLA, Electric Art, 1969; U. of Illinois, 1969; Expo '70, Osaka, 1970; Kent State U. Annual, 1970; Indianapolis, 1970; Hayward Gallery, London, Kinetics, 1970; Omaha/Joslyn, Looking West, 1970; U. of California, Santa Barbara, Constructivist Tendencies, circ., 1970; Hudson River Museum, Kinetic Art, 1971; Stanford U., A Decade in the West, 1971; WMAA Annual, 1973; U. of California, Berkeley, Kinetic Exhibition, 1973; Philadelphia Art Alliance, Sculpture of the Sixties, 1974; Hirshhorn, Inaugural Exhibition, 1974; Huntsville Museum of Art, Ala., The California Bay Area Painting and Sculpture Update, 1977; Sonoma State U., Northern California Artists, 1978; Oakland/AM, 100 Years of California Sculpture, 1982; SFMA, 20 American Artists: Sculpture, 1982, 1982; Walnut Creek (Calif.) Civic Arts Gallery, The Planar Dimension: Geometric Abstraction by Bay Area Artists, 1983; Sonoma State U., Works in Bronze, A Modern Survey, circ., 1984; Oakland Museum, Art in the San Francisco Bay Area, 1945-1980, 1985. **Collections:** Atlantic Richfield Co.; Banque Lambert, Brussels; U. of California; Capital Research Co., Los Angeles; Denver/AM; First National City Bank of Dallas; First National Bank of Ohio, Columbus; Hirshhorn; IBM; Interchemical Corporation; La Jolla; Milwaukee; Neiman-Marcus Co.; The New York Bank for Savings; New Orleans Museum; Newport Harbor; Oakland/AM; Phoenix; Purchase/SUNY; Ridgefield/Aldrich; SFMA, Sacramento/Crocker; San Jose State U.; The Singer Company, Inc.; Stanford U.; Taubman Corp.; Thurman Arnold U. Building, Washington, D.C.; WMAA. **Bibliography:** Atkinson; *California Sculpture Show;* Davis, D.; Rickey; Selz, P., 1; Tuchman 1.

BENTON, THOMAS HART. b. April 15, 1889, Neosho, Mo.; **d.** January 19, 1975, Kansas City, Mo. **Studied:** Western Military Academy, 1906-07; Chicago Art Institute School, 1907; Academie Julian, Paris, 1908-11. Gallery director and art teacher for Chelsea Neighborhood Association, NYC, 1917. US Navy, 1918-19. Traveled Europe, USA, Canada. **Taught:** ASL, 1926-36; Kansas City Art Institute and School of Design, 1935-40; lectured at many colleges and universities. **Commissions:** (murals) New School for Social Research, with Jose Clemente Orozco, 1928; WMAA, 1932; State of Indiana, 1933 (mural now located at U. of Indiana); Missouri State Capitol, 1935-36; "Achelous and Hercules" for Harzfeld Department Store, Kansas City, 1947 (Encyclopedia Britannica filmed his progress on this mural); Lincoln U., 1952-53; Kansas City River Club, 1947; New York State Power Authority, Massena, 1957-61; Truman Library, Independence, Mo., 1958-61. **Awards:** Architectural League of New York, Gold Medal, 1933; Academia Argentina de Bellas Artes, Buenos Aires, Hon. Men., 1945; Accademia Florentina dell'Arte del Disegno, Hon. Men., 1949; Accademia Senese degli Intronati, Siena, 1949; Hon. D. Litt., Lincoln U., 1957; Hon. DFA, U. of Missouri, 1948; Hon. PBK, 1948; Hon. DFA, New School for Social Research, 1968. **One-man Exhibitions:** Lakeside Press Gallery, Chicago, 1927; Ferargil Galleries, NYC, 1934, 35; Des Moines (two-man), 1939; A.A.A. Gallery, NYC, 1939, 41, 65; A.A.A. Gallery, Chicago, 1946; U. of Arizona, circ., 1962; The Graham Gallery, 1968, 70; Madison (Wisc.) Art Center, 1971; Kansas City/Nelson, 1974; The Graham Gallery, 1968, 70, 85; U. of Kansas, 1980; Oklahoma City, 1981; Salander-O'Reilly Galleries, 1981, 82; Bard College, circ., 1984; Williams College, 1985; Little Rock/MFA, 1986. **Retrospective:** Kansas City/Nelson, 1939; Omaha/Joslyn, 1951; New Britain, 1954; U. of Kansas, 1958; Cranbrook, 1966; A.A.A. Gallery, 1969; Rutgers U., 1972. **Group:** Anderson Galleries, NYC, Forum Exhibition, 1916; The Daniel Gallery, NYC, 1919; PMA, Modern Americans, 1922; Architectural League of New York, 1924; Delphic Studios, NYC, 1928, 29; WMAA, The 1930's; A.A.A. Gallery, NYC, 1939, 40, 42. **Collections:** Andover/Phillips; Brooklyn Museum; California Palace; Canajoharie; Columbia, Mo.; Kansas City/Nelson; U. of Kansas City; MMA; MOMA; U. of Nebraska; New Britain;

Omaha/Joslyn; PAFA; St. Louis/City; Terre Haute/Swope. **Bibliography:** *Avant-Garde in America, 1910-1925;* **Baigell** 1, **2;** Baur 7; Bazin; **Benton 1, 2, 3, 4;** Biddle 4; Biederman 1; Blesh 1; Boswell 1; Brown 2; Bruce and Watson; Bryant, L.; Cahill and Barr, eds., Canaday; Cheney; Christensen; Cummings 1; **Craven, T.** 1, 2, **3;** *Cityscape 1919-39;* Danto; Downes; ed.; Eliot; **Fath, ed.;** Flanagan; Flexner; Goodrich and Baur 1; Haftman; Hall; Hunter 6; Huyghe; *Index of 20th Century Artists;* Kent, N.; Kootz 2; Lee and Burchwood; Levin 2; **Marling;** McCoubrey 1; McCurdy, ed.; Mellquist; Mendelowitz; Myers 2; Neuhaus; Newmeyer; Pagano; Pearson 1; Poore; Reese; Richardson, E.P.; Ringel, ed.; Rodman 2; Rose, B., 1, 4; Smith, S.C.K.; Soby 6; Tomkins and Time-Life Books; Wight 2; Wright 1; Zigrosser 1. Archives.

BEN-ZION. b. July 8, 1897, Old Constantin, Ukraine. **d.** January 23, 1987, NYC. Self-taught. Traveled Europe, Mexico, USA. To USA, 1920; citizen, 1936. **Taught:** Cooper Union, 1946-53; Ball State Teachers College, 1956; State U. of Iowa, 1959; Municipal U. of Omaha, 1959. Federal A.P.: Teacher. A co-founder of the Expressionist group The Ten, 1935. **Commissions:** Drawings for Wisdom of the Fathers, Limited Editions Club (1960) and Heritage Press (1962). **One-man Exhibitions:** (first) Artists' Gallery, NYC, 1936; The Willard Gallery, 1937; Buchholz Gallery, NYC; The Bertha Schaefer Gallery, Jewish Museum, 1948, 52; Curt Valentine Gallery, NYC, 1952; A.F.A., circ., 1953-54; Duveen-Graham Gallery, NYC, 1955-56; Baltimore/MA; Taft Museum; SFMA; State U. of Iowa; St. Louis/City; Bezalel Museum; Brandeis U., 1969; National Maritime Museum, Haifa, 1975, 77, 78; Terry Dintenfass Inc., NYC, 1985, 86; Berkeley, Magnes Memorial Museum, 1986. **Retrospective:** Jewish Museum, circ., 1959. **Group:** PAFA; NYU; Carnegie, 1945; WMAA, 1946. **Collections:** Ball State

U.; Bezalel Museum; Chicago/AI; Jewish Museum; Kansas City/Nelson; MMA; MOMA; NYPL; Newark Museum; Phillips; St. Louis/City; Tel Aviv; WMAA; U. of Washington. **Bibliography:** Baur 7; Pearson 2. Archives.

BERGER, JASON. b. January 22, 1924, Malden, Mass. **Studied:** Boston Museum School, 1942-43, 1946-49; U. of Alabama, 1943-44; Zadkine School of Sculpture, Paris, 1950-52. Traveled Europe, Mexico. **Taught:** Boston Museum School, 1955-69; Mount Holyoke College; Wellesley College; Buffalo/SUNY, 1969-70; Boston U., 1971-72; Art Institute of Boston, 1973-. **Awards:** Boston/MFA, James William Paige Fellowship, 1957; Boston Arts Festival, Grand Prize, 1956; Boston Arts Festival, First Prize, 1961. **Address:** 40 University Road, Brookline, MA 02146. **One-man Exhibitions:** The Swetzoff Gallery, Boston, 1952, 56; Deerfield (Mass.) Academy, 1954; Fitchburg/AM, 1955; The Peridot Gallery, 1956, 57, 58, 61; Nova Gallery, Boston, 1960; The Pace Gallery, Boston, 1961; Joan Peterson Gallery, 1962-72; MacIvor Reddie Gallery, Boston, 1979; Christian Herter Center, Boston, 1979. **Group:** Institute of Modern Art, Boston, 1943; Chicago/AI, 1952, 54; Salon de la Jeune Sculpture, Paris, 1952; ICA, Boston, 1952, 56, 60, 61; Boston Arts Festival, 1952-57, 1961; Boston/MFA, 1953-57; MOMA, Young American Printmakers, 1953; Library of Congress, 1954; Carnegie, 1954, 55; MOMA, Recent Drawings USA, 1956; PAFA, 1962; Silvermine Guild; Providence (R.I.) Art Festival, 1969; The Direct Vision Exhibitions, Boston and elsewhere, 1971, 72, 73, 74, 75, 76, 77, 78, 79. **Collections:** Brandeis U.; Chase Manhattan Bank; MOMA; Rockefeller Institute; SRGM; Smith College.

BERLANT, TONY. b. August 8, 1941, NYC. **Studied:** UCLA, 1961, BA, 1962, MA, 1963, MFA. Traveled Europe,

Tony Berlant *Untitled Romance,*
#61-1985 1985
China, Japan, Canada. **Taught:** UCLA,
1965-69. **Commissions:** San Francisco
Airport, mural; TRD, Los Angeles, mu-
ral; California Dept. of Motor Vehicles,
Davis, mural. **Address:** 1304 12th
Street, Santa Monica, Calif. 90401.
Dealer: L. A. Louver Gallery, Venice,
Calif.; Xavier Fourcade, Inc., NYC.
One-man Exhibitions: (first) David
Stuart Gallery, Los Angeles, 1963, 65,
66, 67; Hansen Gallery, San Francisco,
1964; Wichita, 1971; WMAA, circ.,
1973; Fourcade, Droll Inc., NYC, 1973;
Phyllis Kind Gallery, Chicago, 1974;
James Corcoran Gallery, 1975; The
Texas Gallery, Houston, 1976, 78; New-
port Harbor, 1978; Conejo Valley Art
Museum, Thousand Oaks, Calif., 1981;
Xavier Fourcade, Inc., 1981, 82, 84;
John Berggruen Gallery, 1982, 83;
Houston/Contemporary, circ., 1982; L.
A. Louver Gallery, 1982, 85; John
Stoller & Co., Minneapolis, 1985.
Group: Oakland/AM, Pop Art USA,
1963; Los Angeles/County MA, Five
Younger Los Angeles Artists, 1965;
WMAA Annuals, 1966, 68, 70, 73; Los
Angeles/County MA, American Sculp-
ture of the Sixties, circ., 1967; WMAA,
Human Concern/Personal Torment,

1969; Portland, Ore./AM, The West
Coast Now, circ., 1968; Omaha/Joslyn,
Looking West, 1970; Buffalo/Albright,
Working in California, 1972; Indi-
anapolis, 1974; ICA/U. of Pennsyl-
vania, Dwellings, 1978; RISD, Metals:
Cast-Cut-Coiled, 1982; Oakland/AM,
On and Off the Wall, 1983; Mexico
City/Tamayo, Boxes, 1985. **Collec-
tions:** Chicago/AI; Hirshhorn; Los An-
geles/County MA; Long Beach/MA;
PMA; WMAA; Wichita.

BERMAN, EUGENE. b. November 4,
1889, St. Petersburg, Russia; **d.** December 15, 1972; Rome. Studied privately in St. Petersburg with P.S.
Naumoff, S. Grusenberg, 1915-18; Academie Ranson, Paris, with Edouard
Vuillard, Maurice Denis, Pierre Bon-
nard, Felix Vallaton, 1920-22; with the
architect Emilio Terry, 1920. Traveled
Europe. To USA, 1935; first citizenship
papers, 1937. Became active in design-
ing for ballet, opera, 1937. **Member:**
AAAL. **Commissions:** (murals) Wright
Ludington, 1938, John Yeon, 1951; (theatre) Hartford Music Festival, 1936;
L'Opera de Quatre Sous, Paris, 1936; *Icare*
(ballet), NYC, 1939; *Concerto Barocco*
(ballet), by George Balanchine, NYC,
1951. **Awards:** Guggenheim Foundation Fellowship, 1947, 49. **One-man
Exhibitions:** (first) Galerie Granoff,
Paris, 1927; Galerie de l'Etoile, Paris,
1928; Galerie Bonjean, Paris, 1929; Bal-
zac Gallery, NYC, 1929; Galerie des
Quatre Chemins, Paris, 1929; Julien
Levy Galleries, NYC, 1932, 33, 35, 36,
37, 39, 41, 43, 46, 47; Galerie Pierre
Colle, Paris, 1933; Zwemmer Gallery,
London, 1935; Renoir and Lolle, Paris,
1937; Galerie Montaigne, Paris, 1939;
Courvoisier Gallery, San Francisco,
1941; Princeton U., 1947; Kraushaar
Galleries, 1948, 49, 54, 60; MOMA,
1945; Hanover Gallery, 1949; M.
Knoedler & Co., 1965; Richard Larcada
Gallery, 1967, 70, 72, 73; Utah, 1969;
Maxwell Galleries, Ltd., San Francisco,
1970; La Medusa Gallery; San An-
tonio/McNay, 1984. **Retrospective:**

Institute of Modern Art, Boston, circ., 1941; U. of Texas, Austin, 1975. **Group:** Galerie Drouant, Paris, 1924; MOMA; Chicago/AI; WMAA; Hartford/Wadsworth, 1931; Musée du Petit Palais, Paris, 1934; American Center, Paris, Artistes en exil 1939-1946, 1968; New York Cultural Center, Leonid and His Friends, 1974. **Collections:** Baltimore/MA; Boston/MFA; Cincinnati/AM; Cleveland/MA; Denver/AM; Graphische Sammlung Albertina; Hartford/Wadsworth; Harvard U.; U. of Illinois; State U. of Iowa; Los Angeles/County MA; MMA; MOMA; PMA; Paris/Moderne; Phillips; St. Louis/City; Santa Barbara/MA; Smith College; Tate; Vassar College; Venice/Contemporaneo; Washington U. **Bibliography:** Bazin; **Berman;** Canaday; Flanagan; Frost; Genauer; Holme 1, 2; Hunter 6; Huyghe; Kent, N.; **Levy 2;** McCurdy, ed.; Mendelowitz; Myers 2; Pearson 1, 2; Phillips 1; Richardson, E. P.; Rubin 1; Soby 1; Waldberg 4; Wight. Archives.

BERTHOT, JAKE. b. March 30, 1939, Niagara Falls, N.Y. **Studied:** New School for Social Research, 1960-61; Pratt Institute, 1960-62. **Taught:** Cooper Union; Yale U., 1982. **Awards:** Guggenheim Foundation Fellowship, 1981. **Address:** 66 Grand Street, NYC 10013. **Dealer:** David McKee Gallery. **One-man Exhibitions:** OK Harris Works of Art, 1970, 72, 75; Michael Wells Gallery, 1971, 72; Portland (Ore.) Center for the Visual Arts, 1973; Galerie de Gestlo, 1973, 77; Cunningham-Ward Gallery, 1973; Locksley-Shea Gallery, 1974; Daniel Weinberg, San Francisco, 1975; David McKee Gallery, NYC, 1976, 78, 82, 83, 86; Nigel Greenwood Gallery, London, 1979; Nina Nielsen Gallery, Boston, 1979; U. of California, Berkeley; Nielsen Gallery, Boston, 1984; Southern Methodist U., 1985. **Group:** WMAA Annuals, 1969, 73; Indianapolis, 1970; Jewish Museum, Beautiful Painting & Sculpture, 1970; Foundation Maeght, 1970;

Akron/AI, Watercolors and Drawings by Young Americans, 1970; Chicago/AI, Contemporary Drawings, 1971; U. of Rochester, Aspects of Current Painting, 1971; U. of Utah, Drawings by New York Artists, 1972; U. of California, Berkeley, Eight New York Painters, 1972; Paris Biennial, 1973; U. of Rhode Island, Drawings, 1974; Corcoran Biennial, 1975; Venice Biennial, 1976; ICA, U. of Pennsylvania, 8 Abstract Painters, 1978; Hayward Gallery, London, New Paintings—New York, 1979; Grand Palais, Paris L'Amerique aux Independents 1944-1980, 1980; MOMA, International Survey of Recent Painting and Sculpture, 1984; MOMA, Drawings: Contemporary Installation, 1984; Colby College, Landscape & Abstract Art, 1985; MOMA, Contrast of Form: Geometric Abstract Art 1910-1980, 1985. **Collections:** Baltimore/MA; Brandeis U.; U. of California, Berkeley; Canberra/National; Caracas; Carnegie; Harvard U.; High Museum; MOMA; Dallas/MFA; Prudential Insurance Co. of America, Newark; VMFA; WMAA; SRGM; U. of Kentucky; Malmo; Minneapolis/Institute; PMA. **Bibliography:** *Fundamentele Schiderkunst.*

BERTOIA, HARRY. b. March 10, 1915, San Lorenzo, Italy. **d.** October, 1978, Bally, Pa. To USA, 1930; became a citizen, 1946. **Studied:** Society of Arts and Crafts, Detroit; Cranbrook, 1936-38. Traveled Norway. Designed chairs with Charles Eames; designed the Bertoia chair for Knoll Associates, 1952. **Commissions:** General Motors Technical Center, Detroit; MIT Chapel; Manufacturers Trust Co.; Dayton Co., Minneapolis; First National Bank of Miami; First National Bank of Tulsa; Dulles International Airport, Washington, D.C.; Northwestern National Life Insurance Bldg., Minneapolis, 1964; Kodak Pavilion, New York World's Fair, 1964-65; Philadelphia Civic Center, 1967; Marshall U., 1973; Woodward Price Park, Wichita, Kan., 1974.

Awards: Architectural League of New York, Gold Medal; Graham Foundation Grant ($10,000), 1957; American Institute of Architects, Gold Medal 1973; AAAL Award, 1975. **One-man Exhibitions:** (first) Karl Nierendorf Gallery, NYC, 1940; Staempfli Gallery, 1961, 63, 68, 70, 72, 76, 78, 81, 84, 85, 86; Fairweather-Hardin Gallery; Museum of Non-Objective Art, NYC; Smithsonian, circ.; Galerie K.B., Oslo, 1977; Gross-McLeaf Gallery, Philadelphia, 1977; Allentown/AM, 1976; Fairweather-Hardin Galley, 1984. **Group:** WMAA; MOMA; Battersea Park, London, International Sculpture Exhibition, 1963. **Collections:** Buffalo/Albright; Colorado Springs/FA; Dallas Public Library; Denver/AM; Des Moines; MIT; MOMA; Omaha/Joslyn; SFMA; Utica; VMFA; WMAA. **Bibliography:** Atkinson; Baur 7; Blesh 1; Craven, W.; *From Foreign Shores;* Janis; *Metro;* **Nelson:** Ragon 2; Seuphor 3; Trier 1. Archives.

BESS, FOREST CLEMENGER. b. October 5, 1911, Bay City, Tex.; **d.** November 10, 1977, Bay City, Tex. **Studied:** Agricultural and Mechanical College of Texas, 1929-32; U. of Texas, 1932-33. Traveled Mexico, 1934-40, and USA. Corps of Army Engineers, 1940-45. **Awards:** Mark Rothko Foundation Grant, 1973. **One-man Exhibitions:** Houston/MFA, 1938; Witte, 1939; Texas Technological College, 1939; Betty Parsons Gallery, 1949, 54, 57, 59, 62, 67; Andre Emmerich Gallery, Houston, 1958; Syracuse/Everson, 1974; Agricultural and Mechanical College of Texas; New Arts Gallery, Houston. **Retrospective:** WMAA, 1981. **Group:** Corcoran, 1938; Dallas/MFA; Tulsa/Philbrook; A.F.A.; Wit and Whimsey in 20th Century Art, 1962; de Young; Stanford U. **Collections:** Boston/MFA; Brandeis U.; Houston/MFA; Witte. **Bibliography:** Archives.

BIDDLE, GEORGE. b. January 24, 1885, Philadelphia, Pa; **d.** November 6,

George Biddle   *King Street Movie, Charleston, South Carolina*   1931

1973, Croton-on-Hudson, N.Y. **Studied:** Groton School, 1904; Harvard U., 1908, BA with honors, 1911, LLB; Academie Julian, Paris, 1911. Traveled Europe, Asia, Africa, Latin America, USA. **Taught:** Columbia U.; U. of California; Colorado Springs Fine Arts Center; Artist-in-Residence, American Academy, Rome. **Member:** American Society of Painters, Sculptors and Graveurs; National Society of Mural Painters; NIAL. **Commissions** (murals): Justice Department, Washington, D.C.; Supreme Court Building, Mexico City; National Library, Rio de Janeiro. **Awards:** Yaddo, MacDowell Colony, and Huntington Hartford Foundation Fellowships. **One-man Exhibitions:** (first) The Milch Gallery, 1919; more than 100 in USA, Europe, Japan, India. **Retrospective:** PAFA, 1947; USIA, Prints, circ., 1950. **Collections:** Berlin/National; Corcoran; MMA; Mexico City/Nacional; National Gallery; Norfolk/Chrysler; Tokyo/Modern; W AA; Youngstown/Butler. **Bibliography:** American Artists Congress, Inc.; American Artists Group,

Inc.; **Biddle 1, 2, 3, 4;** Birchman; Boswell 1; Brown; Bruce and Watson; Cheney; *Index of 20th Century Artists;* Mayerson, ed.; Nordmark; Pagano; Parkes; Pearson 2; Poore; Reese; Rose, B., 1; Sachs; Zigrosser 1. Archives.

BIEDERMAN, CHARLES (Karel) JOSEPH. b. August 23, 1906. Cleveland, Ohio. **Studied:** Chicago Art Institute School, 1926-29, with Henry Poole, Laura Papalandem, John W. Norton. Resided Prague, Paris, New York. Traveled England. **Awards:** Amsterdam/Stedelijk, Sikkens Award, 1962; Ford Foundation, **P.P.,** 1964; National Council on the Arts, 1966; Walker Biennial, Donors Award, 1966; Minnesota State Arts Council, 1969; Hon. DFA, Minneapolis College of Art and Design, 1973; National Endow-

Charles Biederman *#34, Aix* 1972–74

ment for the Arts, 1973. **Address:** Route 2, Red Wing, MN 55066. **Dealer:** Grace Borgenicht Gallery, NYC. **One-man Exhibitions:** (first) Chicago Art Institute School; a movie-theater lobby in Chicago, 1930; Pierre Matisse Gallery, 1936; Arts Club of Chicago, 1941; Katherine Kuh Gallery, Chicago, 1941; St. Paul Gallery, 1954; Columbia U. School of Architecture, 1962; Georgia Institute of Technology, 1962; Rochester (Minn.) Art Center, 1967; Dayton's Gallery 12, Minneapolis, 1971; Grace Borgenicht Gallery, 1980; Matthew Hamilton Gallery, Philadelphia, 1984; Grace Borgenicht Gallery, NYC, 1985, 86. **Retrospectives:** Walker, 1965; Hayward Gallery, London, 1969; Minneapolis/Institute, 1976. **Group:** Buffalo/Albright, 1936; Reinhardt Galleries, NYC, 1936; Galerie Pierre, Paris, 1936; Amsterdam/Stedelijk, 1962; Kunstgewerbemuseum, Zurich, 1962; Marlborough-Gerson Gallery, Inc., 1964; Chicago/Contemporary, Relief/ Construction/Relief, 1968; Akron/AI, Celebrate Ohio, 1971; Dallas/MFA, Geometric Abstraction, 1926-1942, 1972; Annely Juda Fine Art, London, The Non-Objective World: 1914-1955, 1972; Rutgers U., Vanguard American Sculpture, 1919-1939, circ., 1979; Haus der Kunst, Munich, Amerikanische Malerie: 1930-1980, 1981; Carnegie, Abstract Painting and Sculpture in America, 1927-1944, 1983; Trenton/State, Beyond the Plane: American Constructions 1931-1965, circ., 1983; AAIAL, 1984. **Collections:** Buffalo/Albright; Carnegie; Chicago/AI; Chicago Public Schools; Dallas/MFA; Des Moines; U. of East Anglia; High Museum; MMA; MOMA; McCrory Corp.; Milwaukee; Minneapolis/Institute; U. of Nebraska; Newark Museum; PMA; Red Wing; Rijksmuseum Kroller-Muller; U. of Saskatchewan; Tate; Walker; WMAA. **Bibliography: Biederman 1, 2, 3, 4;** *Celebrate Ohio;* **Charles Biederman;** Hill, ed.; Lane and Larsen; Marter, Tarbell, and Wechsler; Rickey; Seuphor 3; Toher, ed.; Archives.

BIRELINE, GEORGE. b. August 12, 1923, Peoria, Ill. **Studied:** Bradley U., 1949, BFA; U. of North Carolina, 1963, MFA. **Taught:** North Carolina State College, 1957-75. **Awards:** Guggenheim Foundation Fellowship, 1967; National Council on the Arts Grant, 1968. US Army, 1942-46. **Address:** 228 East Park Drive, Raleigh, NC 27605. **One-man Exhibitions:** U. of North Carolina, 1959, 63; Winston-Salem (N.C.) Gallery of Fine Arts, 1960, 62; Andre Emmerich Gallery, NYC, 1964, 65, 67; Gallery of Contemporary Art, Winston-Salem, 1969; Meredith College, 1973; Southwestern Center for Contemporary Art, Winston-Salem, 1979. **Retrospective:** Raleigh/NCMA, 1976. **Group:** PAFA Annual, 1950; Youngstown/Butler, 1958; Raleigh/ NCMA, 1959, 61, 63; High Museum, 1960; Birmingham, Ala./MA, 1960; Columbia, S.C./MA, 1960; Los Angeles/County MA, Post Painterly Abstraction, 1964; Rockford/Burpee, 1965; U. of Illinois, 1965; Philadelphia Art Alliance, Optical Paintings, 1965; A.F.A., Fifty Artists from Fifty States, circ., 1966-68; North Carolina Annual Artists' Exhibition, 1965-67, 1969-74; Buffalo/Albright, Color and Field: 1890-1970; Mississippi Museum of Art, Jackson, Southern Realism, 1979-80;

VMFA, Painting in the South, 1983. **Collections:** Charlotte/Mint; Drake U.; East Tennessee State; Fayetteville Museum of Art; Federal Reserve Bank of Richmond, Va.; Hunter Museum; North Carolina National Bank; North Carolina State U.; Prentice Hall Inc; Raleigh/NCMA; Reynolds Metal Co. Syracuse/Everson.

BIRMELIN, A. ROBERT. b. November 7, 1933, Newark, N.J. **Studied:** Cooper Union, 1951-54; Yale U., 1954-56, BFA, 1959-60, MFA; U. of London, Slade School, 1960-61. US Army, 1957-59. Traveled Europe. **Taught:** Queens College, 1964-. **Member:** Artists Equity. **Commission:** US Dept. of Interior, 1974. **Awards:** Fulbright Fellowship, 1960-61; American Academy, Rome, Fellowship, 1961-64; PAFA, J. Henry Schiedt Memorial Prize, 1962; NIAL Grant, 1968; L. C. Tiffany Grant, 1973; National Endowment for the Arts, 1976, 82; NIAL, Childe Hassam Fund **P.P.,** 1976; New Jersey Council for the Arts, 1980. **Address:** 176 Highwood Ave., Leonia, NJ 07605. **Dealer:** Sherry French Gallery, NYC. **One-man Exhibitions:** Kanegis Gallery, 1960, 64, 66; Ross-Talalam Gallery, New Haven, 1960; The Stable Gallery, NYC, 1960,

Robert Birmelin *Noticing Separate Things* 1985

64, 67; Esther Baer Gallery, 1962; USIS Gallery, Milan, 1962; Florida State U., 1965; Jason-Teff Gallery, Montreal, 1965; Antioch College, 1965; Alpha Gallery, 1968; Terry Dintenfass, Inc., 1970, 71, 75; Queens College Art Library, N.Y., 1970; Kirkland College, 1971; Alpha Gallery, Boston, 1971, 73; Brandeis U., 1973; Cortland/SUNY, 1973; U. of California, Santa Barbara, 1976; Anapamu Gallery, Santa Barbara, 1976; Peter Rose Gallery, NYC, 1978; Capricorn Gallery, Bethesda, 1977, 79; Bowdoin College, 1980; Galerie Claude Bernard, Paris, 1980; Odyssia Gallery, NYC, 1981; Galerie Claude Bernard, Paris, 1981; Fenderick Gallery, Washington, D.C., 1982, 85; Montclair/AM, 1984; U. of Richmond, 1985. **Group:** Corcoran Biennial, 1965; XXXV Venice Biennial, 1970; Indianapolis/Herron, 1972; Omaha/Joslyn, A Sense of Place, 1973; Ball State U., XX Annual, 1974; Kalamazoo/Institute, Fifty Works, 1974; US Dept. of the Interior, America 1976, circ., 1976; MIT, The Narrative Impulse 1979. **Collections:** Andover/Phillips; U. of Washington, Seattle, Confrontations, 1984; Isetan Museum of Art, Tokyo, American Realism: The Precise Image, 1985; Seattle/AM, States of War, 1985; VMFA, Large Figurative Drawing, 1985; Boston/MFA; Bowdoin College; Brandeis U.; Brooklyn Museum; Chase Manhattan Bank; Denver/AM; First National Bank of Chicago; U. of Florida; Hirshhorn; Indiana U.; Indianapolis/Herron; Kalamazoo/Institute; Library of Congress; MMA; MOMA; U. of Massachusetts; Museum of the City of New York; NMAA; Nagaoka, Japan; U. of Nebraska; Newark Museum; U. of North Carolina; Oklahoma; Purchase/SUNY; SFMA; Terre Haute/Swope; U. of Texas; Trenton/State; Worcester/AM; WMAA; Walker; U. of Wisconsin. **Bibliography:** *America 1976;* Arthur 3.

BISCHOFF, ELMER. b. July 9, 1916, Berkeley, Calif. **Studied:** U. of Califor-

nia, Berkeley, with Margaret Peterson, Erle Loran, John Haley, 1939, MA. US Air Force, 1942-46. Traveled Europe, Morocco, Great Britain, Mediterranean Basin. **Taught:** San Francisco Art Institute, 1946-52, 1956-63; Skowhegan School, 1961; U. of California, Berkeley, 1963-; Yuba College, 1964. **Member:** NAD. **Awards:** RAC, First Prize, 1955; Oakland/AM, **P.P.,** 1957; Ford Foundation Grant, 1959; NIAL Grant, 1963; Chicago/AI, Norman Wait Harris Medal, 1964; San Francisco Art Commission, Award of Honor, 1982; Otis Art Institute, Hon. DFA, 1983. **Address:** 109 Strathmoor Drive, Berkeley, CA 94705. **Dealer:** Hirschl & Adler Modern, NYC. **One-man Exhibitions:** (first) California Palace, 1947; King Ubu Gallery, San Francisco, 1953; Paul Kantor Gallery, Beverly Hills, Calif., 1955; SFMA, 1956, 71; Staempfli Gallery, 1960, 62, 64, 69; de Young, 1961; Achenbach Foundation (three-man drawing show), 1963; Sacramento/Crocker, 1964; U. of Washington, 1968; RAC, 1969, SFAI, 1975; U. of California, Berkeley, 1975; John Berggruen Gallery, 1979, 83; San Jose Museum of Art, 1979; Arts Club of Chicago, 1980; Houston/Contemporary, 1980; Grossmont College, 1981; Sacramento/Crocker, 1981; U. of Arkansas, 1984; Hirschl & Adler Modern, 1985. **Retrospective:** SFMA, circ., 1985. **Group:** San Francisco Art Association Annuals, 1942, 46, 52, 57, 59, 63; Chicago/AI, 1947, 59, 64; California Palace, 1948, 50, 1960-63; Los Angeles/County MA, 1951; RAC, 1955, 56; Oakland/AM, 1957; Minneapolis/Institute, American Painting, 1945-57, 1957; A.F.A., New Talent, circ., 1958; ART: USA:59, NYC, 1959; U. of Illinois, 1959, 61; WMAA, 1959, 61, 63; A.F.A., West Coast Artists, circ., 1959-60; Denver/AM, 1960; Youngstown/Butler, 1960; Auckland, Painting from the Pacific, 1961; PAFA, 1962; Fort Worth, The Artist's Environment: The West Coast, 1962; SFMA, Fifty California Artists, circ., 1962; MOMA, Recent Painting USA, The Figure, circ., 1962-63; Art: USA: Now, circ., 1962-67, NIAL, 1963; Corcoran, 1963; Carnegie, 1967; Expo '70, Osaka, 1970; U. of Nebraska, 1973; U. of Illinois, 1974; Buffalo/Albright American Painting of the 1970s, circ., 1979; Corcoran, The Human Form, 1980; WMAA, The Figurative Tradition and the WMAA, 1980; Rutgers U., Realism and Realities, 1982; NYU, The Figurative Mode: Bay Area Painting, 1956-1966, circ., 1984; IEF, Twentieth Century American Drawings: The Figure in Context, circ., 1984. **Collections:** Buffalo/Albright; Chase Manhattan Bank; Chicago/AI; Hirshhorn; Honolulu Academy; U. of Kansas; MMA; MOMA; NCFA; U. of North Carolina; Oakland/AM; Purchase/SUNY; Rockefeller Institute; SFMA; Sacramento/Crocker; U. of Texas; VMFA; WMAA; U. of Wisconsin; Yale U. **Bibliography:** Downes, ed.; Goodrich and Baur 1; Nordness, ed.; Rose, B.; 1. Archives.

BISHOP, ISABEL. b. March 3, 1902, Cincinnati, Ohio. **Studied:** New York School of Applied Design; ASL, with Kenneth Hayes Miller. **Taught:** ASL, 1937; Skowhegan School. **Member:** AAAL; NAD; NIAL; SAGA; Audubon Artists. Federal A.P.: US Post Office, New Lexington, Ohio (mural). **Awards:** NAD, Isaac N. Maynard Prize; NAD, The Adolph and Clara Obrig Prize, 1942; NAD Annual, Andrew Carnegie Prize, 1945; Corcoran, Second William A. Clark Prize, 1945; AAAL Grant, 1943; PAFA, Walter Lippincott Prize, 1953; NAD, Benjamin Altman Prize, 1955; Library of Congress, Pennell **P.P.,** 1946; NAD, Joseph S. Isidora Gold Medal, 1957; Hon. DFA, Moore Institute; Brandeis U., Creative Arts Award and $1,000, 1975; Women's Caucus For Art, Outstanding Achievement Award, 1979; Hon. DFA, Bates College; Mayor's Award for Art and Culture, NYC, 1979. New York Film Co. produced a documentary film on her. **Address:** 335 West 246th Street, NYC 10471. **Dealer:** The Midtown Galleries, NYC. **One-man Exhibitions:** The Midtown Galleries, 1932, 35, 36, 39, 49, 55, 60, 67, 74, 87; Pittsfield/Berkshire, 1957; VMFA (two-man), 1960; Middendorf-Lane Gallery, Washington, D.C., 1979. **Retrospectives:** U. of Arizona, circ., 1974; Loyola U., Los Angeles, 1984. **Group:** Carnegie; VMFA; Corcoran; PAFA; New York World's Fair, 1939; Chicago/AI; WMAA; MOMA; St. Louis/City; NAD; Los Angeles/County MA, Women Artists 1940-50, 1976; Hayward Gallery, London, The Modern Spirit, 1977. **Collections:** Andover/Phillips; Atlanta U.; Baltimore/MA; Boston/MFA; British Museum; Brooklyn Museum; California Palace; Clearwater/Gulf Coast; Colorado Springs/FA; Columbus; Corcoran; Cranbrook; Dallas/MFA; Des Moines; Hartford/Wadsworth; Harvard U.; Indianapolis; Kansas City/Nelson; Library of Congress; Los Angeles/County MA; MMA; Memphis/Brooks; Morgan Library; NAD; NYPL; U. of Nebraska; Newark Museum; New Britain; PAFA; PMA; Phillips; St. Louis/City; Southampton/Parrish; Springfield, Mass./MFA; Tel Aviv; Terre Haute/Swope; Utica; VMFA; WMAA; Washburn U. of Topeka; Youngstown/Butler. **Bibliography:** Baur 7; Boswell 1; Brown 2; *Celebrate Ohio;* Cheney; Diamonstein; Downes, ed.; Goodrich and Baur 1; **Isabel Bishop;** Johnson 2; Kent, N.; Lunde; McCurdy, ed.; Mellquist; Mendelowitz; Nordness, ed.; Pagano; Richardson, E.P.; Rose, B., 1. Archives.

BISHOP, JAMES. b. October 7, 1927, Neosho, Mo. **Studied:** Syracuse U., 1950, BA; Washington U., 1951-54; Black Mountain College, 1953, with Esteban Vicente; Columbia U., 1955-56. Traveled France, 1957-66. **Taught:** Cooper Union, 1969-70; U. of California, Irvine, 1970; Carnegie-Mellon Institute, 1971; School of Visual Arts, NYC, 1972. **Awards:** Guggenheim

Foundation Fellowship, 1970. Editorial associate, *Art News*, 1969-72; National Endowment for the Arts, 1976. **Address:** 5 Lispenard Street, NYC 10013. **Dealer:** Simon/Newman Gallery, NYC. **One-man Exhibitions:** (first) Galerie Lucien Durand, Paris, 1963; Galerie Smith, Brussels, 1963; Galerie Lawrence, Paris, 1964; Fischbach Gallery, 1966, 68, 70, 72; Galerie Fournier, Paris, 1966, 71, 73; The Clocktower, NYC, 1973; Rosa Esman Gallery, 1974; Alessandro Ferranti, Rome, 1975; Galerie Annemarie Verna, Zurich, 1976, 78; Galerie Jean Fournier, Paris, 1976; Francoise Lambert, Milan, 1977; Rudiger Schottle, Munich, 1977; Droll Kolbert Gallery, NYC, 1979; Frank Kolbert Gallery, NYC, 1980; Galerie Annemarie Verna, Zurich, 1981; Daniel Weinberg Gallery, San Francisco, 1981; Simon/Newman Gallery, 1987. **Group:** Salon des Realites Nouvelles, Paris, 1962-65; Salon du Mai, Paris, 1964, 65; Musée Galliera, Paris, Promesses Tenues, 1965; Amerika Haus, Berlin, Ten Americans, 1966; WMAA, 1967, Corcoran, 1967; Expo '67, Montreal, 1967; Jewish Museum, Large Scale American Painting, 1967; Foundation Maeght, 1968, 70; U. of California, Riverside, Recent Direction, 1968; NIAL, 1971; U. of North Carolina, 1971; Yale U., Options and Alternatives, 1973; Indianapolis, 1974; Paris/Moderne, Tendences actuelles de la nouvelle peinture americaine, 1975; A.F.A., Recent Drawings, 1975; Musée de Grenoble, Art americain, 1976; Bonn, Bilder ohne Bilder, 1977; Paris, Grand Palais, L'Art moderne dans les musées francaises, 1978; Paris/Beaubourg, Dessin et couleur, 1979; Paris/Beaubourg, Nature du Dessin, 1981; P.S. 1, Long Island City, N.Y., Abstract Painting: 1960-69, 1983. **Collections:** Brooklyn Museum; U. of California, Berkeley; Canberra/National; Humlebaek/Louisiana; MOMA; Musée de Grenoble; Paris/Beaubourg; Paris/Moderne; SFMA; Tel Aviv; Zurich. **Bibliography:** *Options and Alternatives.*

BLACKWELL, TOM. b. March 9, 1938, Chicago, Ill; Autodidact. **Taught:** Keene State College, 1978; Dartmouth College, 1980; U. of Arizona, 1981. **Address:** 131 Prince Street, NYC 10012. **Dealer:** Carlo Lamagna Gallery, NYC. **One-man Exhibitions:** Roy Parsons Gallery, Los Angeles, 1961; Rex Evans Gallery, Los Angeles, 1962; Orange Coast College, Santa Ana, Calif., 1964; Sidney Janis Gallery, NYC, 1975; Morgan Gallery, Shawnee Mission, Kan., 1975; Galerie le Portail, Heidelberg, 1976; Louis K. Meisel Gallery, NYC, 1977, 80, 82; Dartmouth College, 1980; U. of Arizona, 1981. **Group:** WMAA, Human Concern/Personal Torment, 1969; Finch College, NYC, Projected Art, 1971; WMAA Annual, 1972; Indianapolis, 1972; Tokyo, Metropolitan Art Gallery, 11th Tokyo Biennale, 1974; Darmstadt/Kunsthalle, Realism & Reality, 1975; Baltimore/MA, Super Realism, 1975; Canberra/National, Illusion & Reality, 1977; SRGM, Seven Photorealists from New York Collections, 1981; San Antonio/MA, Real, Really Real, Super Real, circ., 1981; PAFA, Contemporary American Realism Since 1960, circ., 1981; Utica, An Appreciation of Realism, 1982. **Collections:** U. of Arizona; Ball State U.; Cornell U.; Currier; Detroit/Institute; Dartmouth College; Evanston/Byer; Fort Wayne/AM; MMA; MOMA; Montclair/AM; Phoenix; SRGM; U. of Texas; U. of Wisconsin. **Bibliography:** Arthur 3; Lindy.

BLADEN, RONALD. b. July 13, 1918, Vancouver, B.C., Canada. **Studied:** Vancouver School of Art; CSFA. **Awards:** SFAI, Rosenberg Fellowship; National Council on the Arts; Guggenheim Foundation Fellowship, 1970; National Council on the Arts, 1964, 77; Mark Rothko Foundation Grant, 1975. **Address:** 5 West 21st Street, NYC 10010. **Dealer:** Washburn Gallery Inc., NYC. **One-man Exhibitions:** Brata Gallery, NYC, 1953; U. of British Columbia (two-man), 1955; Six Gallery, San Fran-

Ronald Bladen *Harmon* 1985

cisco, 1956; Green Gallery, NYC, 1962; NYU (three-man), 1967; Fischbach Gallery, 1967, 70, 71, 72; Hofstra U., 1967; Vancouver (two-man), 1970; Pasadena/AM, 1972; Tyler School of Art, Philadelphia, 1972; U. of Wisconsin, Madison, 1972; Hudson River Museum, 1977; Hamilton Gallery of Contemporary Art, NYC, 1980; Washburn Gallery, Inc., 1986. **Group:** NYU, Concrete Expressionism, 1965; WMAA Annuals, 1966, 68, 73; Chicago/AI Annual, 1966; Jewish Museum, Primary Structure Sculptures, 1966; Los Angeles/County MA, Sculpture of the Sixties, 1967; A.F.A., Rejective Art, 1967; Corcoran, Scale as Content, 1967; Documenta IV, Kassel, 1968; Walker, 14 Sculptors: The Industrial Edge, 1969; U. of Nebraska, American Sculpture, 1970; Arnhem, Sonsbeek '71, 1971; SFMA, Works in Spaces, 1973; Detroit/Institute, Art in Space, 1973; U. of Miami, Less is More: The Influence of the Bauhaus on American Art, 1974; William Patterson College, N.J., Con-

temporary Drawing, 1975; Houston/Contemporary; Monumentalists in Modern Sculpture, 1975; Hirshhorn, The Golden Door: Artist Immigrants of America 1876-1976, 1976; WMAA, 200 Years of American Sculpture, 1976; Akron/AI, Project: New Urban Monuments, 1977; Trenton/State, Beyond the Plane: American Constructions 1931-1965, 1983; Montreal/MFA, Drawings by Sculptors, 1984. **Collections:** Buffalo/Albright; La Jolla; MOMA; Marine Midland Bank and Trust Co.; South Albany Mall, N.Y.; Springfield, Ohio, City Hall; Peoria, Ill., Civic Center; King Saud U., Riyadh, Saudi Arabia. **Bibliography:** Calas, N. and E.; Friedman, M., 2; *Report*; Sandler, Toher, ed.

BLAINE, NELL. b. July 10, 1922, Richmond, Va. **Studied:** Richmond (Va.) School of Art, 1939-43; Hofmann School, 1943-44; Atelier 17, NYC, with S. W. Hayter; New School for Social Research, 1952-53. Traveled Europe, Near East, West Indies, Mexico. **Taught:** Great Neck (N.Y.) Public Schools, 1943-1956, and privately. **Member:** American Abstract Artists, 1944-57; Jane Street Group, 1945-49; Artists Equity. **Commissions:** Revlon Inc. (murals); New York Hilton Hotel (lithographs). **Awards:** Norfolk, First Prize, Watercolor, 1945; MacDowell Colony Fellowship, 1957; Yaddo Fellowship, 1957, 58, 64; Ingram Merrill Grants, 1962, 64, 66; Longview Foundation Grant, 1964, 1970; CAPS, 1972; Mark Rothko Foundation Grant, 1972; Guggenheim Foundation Fellowship, 1974; Governor's award, Award for the Arts in Virginia, 1979; Honorary Degree, Moore College of Art, Philadelphia, 1980; National Endowment for the Arts, 1975; Hon. Ph.D., Virginia Commonwealth U., 1985; NAD, Benjamin Altman Prize for Landscape, 1986; Designed original logo, column headings, and styling for the *Village Voice*, 1955. **Address:** 210 Riverside

Drive, NYC 10025; Eudora Cottage, 3 Ledge Road, E. Gloucester, MA 01930. **Dealer:** Fischbach Gallery, NYC. **One-man Exhibitions:** (first) Jane Street Gallery, NYC, 1945, also 1948; VMFA, 1947, 54, 73; Southern Illinois U., 1949; Tibor de Nagy Gallery, 1953, 54; Poindexter Gallery, 1956, 58, 60, 66, 68, 70, 72, 76; New Paltz/SUNY, 1959; Stewart Richard Gallery, San Antonio, 1961; Philadelphia Art Alliance, 1961; Yaddo, 1961; Longwood College, 1962; U. of Connecticut, Storrs, 1973; Webb and Parsons, Bedford Village, N.Y., 1973; Watson/de Nagy Gallery, Houston, 1977; Fischbach Gallery, NYC, 1979, 81, 83, 85; VMFA, 1979; Hull Gallery, Washington, D.C., 1979; Jersey City Museum, 1981; Alpha Gallery, Boston, 1982; Reynolds/Minor Gallery, Richmond, Va., 1982, 85; Wyckoff Gallery, Wyckoff, N.J., 1982; Virginia Commonwealth U., 1985. **Retrospective:** Southampton/Parrish, 1974. **Group:** Art of This Century, NYC, The Women, 1944; Salon des Realites Nouvelles, Paris, 1950; Chicago/AI; Baltimore/MA; WMAA; PAFA; Corcoran; VMFA; ART:USA:59, NYC, 1959; MOMA, Abstract Watercolors and Drawings, USA, circ., Latin America and Europe, 1961-62; Festival of Two Worlds, Spoleto; MOMA, Hans Hofmann and His Students, circ., 1963-64; Hartford/Wadsworth, Figures, 1964; MOMA, Contemporary Still Life, circ., 1967-68; New School for Social Research, Humanist Tradition, 1968; NIAL, 1970, 74, 75; A.F.A., Painterly Realism, 1970; WMAA, Frank O'Hara: A Poet Among Painters, 1974; NAD, Annual, 1978; MMA, Hans Hofmann as Teacher: Drawings by His Students, 1979; Westmoreland County/MA, The New American Still Life, 1978; MMA, Hans Hofmann as Teacher: Drawings by His Students, 1979; Westmoreland County/MA, New American Still Life, 1979; Hirshhorn, The Fifties: Aspects of Painting in New York, 1980; PAFA, Contemporary American Realism Since 1960, 1981; Utica, An Appreciation of Realism, 1982; Houston/Contemporary,

American Still Life, 1945-1983, 1983; Brooklyn Museum, Homer, Sargent, and the American Watercolor Tradition, 1984; NAD, 1984; SFMA, American Realism, circ., 1985; Contemporary Arts Center, New Orleans, Landscape, Seascape, Cityscape, 1960-1985, 1986. **Collections:** Brandeis U.; Brooklyn Museum; U. of California; Chase Manhattan Bank; Ciba-Geigy Corp.; Colgate U.; U. of Connecticut; First and Merchants National Bank, Richmond, Va.; U. of Georgia; Hallmark Collection; Hirshhorn; State U. of Iowa; Longwood College; MMA; MOMA; U. of Massachusetts; Michigan State U.; NAD; New London; Newark Museum; New Paltz/SUNY; U. of North Carolina; Reader's Digest; Revlon Inc.; Southern Illinois U.; Taconic Foundation; Trade Building, Moscow; Union Carbide Corp.; Utah; VMFA; WMAA. **Bibliography:** Art: A Woman's Sensibility. Bryant, E.; Sandler 1. Archives.

BLANCH, ARNOLD. b. June 4, 1896, Mantorville, Minn.; **d.** October 23, 1968, Kingston, N.Y. **Studied:** Minneapolis Institute School, ASL, with Kenneth Hayes Miller, Boardman Robinson, John Sloan, 1916-17. Traveled USA. **Taught:** ASL, 1915-21, 1935-39, 1947-68; California School of Fine Arts, 1930-31; Colorado Springs Fine Arts Center, summers, 1939-41; U. of Minnesota, 1949, 52; Rollins College, 1950; Florida Gulf Coast Art Center, Inc., 1950-51; Woodstock, N.Y., 1950-61; Ohio U., summers, 1952, 56; Minneapolis Institute School, 1954; U. of Hawaii, 1955; Norton Gallery and School of Art, 1961-62; Michigan State U., 1964. **Commissions:** US Post Offices, Fredonia, N.Y., Norwalk, Conn., and Columbus, Wisc. (murals). **Awards:** Chicago/AI, Norman Wait Harris Prize, 1929; SFMA, **P.P.,** 1931; California Palace, 1931; Guggenheim Foundation Fellowship, 1933; PAFA, Medal, 1938; Carnegie Medal, 1938; Syracuse/Everson, National Ceramic Exhibition, 1949, 51; Silvermine Guild.

One-man Exhibitions: Rehn Galleries, 1923, 25; Philadelphia Art Alliance; Dudensing Gallery, NYC, 1928, 30; Walden-Dudensing Gallery, Chicago, 1930; Ulrich Gallery, Minneapolis, 1930; Beaux Arts Gallery, San Francisco, 1930; A.A.A. Gallery, NYC, 1943, 55, 63; Des Moines, 1952; Walker, 1952; The Krasner Gallery, 1954, 58, 59, 61, 62, 69; West Palm Beach/Norton, 1961. **Retrospective:** U. of Minnesota, 1949; Woodstock Artists Association, 1970. **Group:** Chicago/AI, 1930-43; Corcoran, 1931-45; WMAA, 1931-46, 1948-52; PAFA, 1931-45, 1948-52; New York World's Fair, 1939; MOMA; Carnegie; VMFA; MMA; Library of Congress; ART:USA, NYC. **Collections:** Abbott Laboratories; U. of Arizona; Britannica; Brooklyn Museum; California Palace; Carnegie; Cincinnati/AM; Clearwater/Gulf Coast; Cleveland/MA; Colorado Springs/FA; Cranbrook; Denver/AM; Detroit/Institute; Library of Congress; MMA; U. of Minnesota, Duluth; U. of Nebraska; U. of Oklahoma; PAFA; St. Louis/City; Utica; WMAA; Youngstown/Butler. **Bibliography:** American Artists Congress, Inc.; Baur 7; **Blanch 1, 2, 3;** Boswell 1; Cheney; *Index of 20th Century Artists;* Jewell 2; Pagano; Pearson 1; Reese; Richardson, E.P.; *Woodstock;* Zaidenberg, ed. Archives.

BLAUSTEIN, AL. b. January 23, 1924, NYC. **Studied:** Cooper Union, with Morris Kantor; Skowhegan School. US Air Force, 3 years. Traveled Mexico, Africa, the Orient; resided Rome, 1954-57. **Taught:** Pratt Institute, 1959-. Yale U. **Commissions:** Drawings for *Life* magazine and British Overseas Food Corporation, 1948-49; fresco mural for South Solon (Me.) Meeting House, 1953. **Awards:** Prix de Rome, 1954-57; Guggenheim Foundation Fellowship, 1958, 61; AAAL Grant, 1958; Childe Hassam Award, 1962-68, and **P.P.,** 1969; PAFA, Alice McFadden Eyre Medal, 1959; ART:USA:59, NYC, Graphic Prize, 1959; Youngstown/

Butler, First Prize, 1961; SAGA, First Prize, 1962; Audubon Artists, Gold Medal of Honor, 1962. **Address:** 141 East 17th Street, NYC 10003. **Dealer:** Terry Dintenfass, Inc. **One-man Exhibitions:** (first) Lee Nordness Gallery, NYC, 1959, also 1961, 62; U. of Nevada, 1961; Philadelphia Art Alliance, 1962; Walter Laubli Gallery, Zurich, 1962; Philadelphia Print Club, 1964; Franklin Siden Gallery, Detroit, 1965, 66; Randolph-Macon College, 1967; C. Troup Gallery, Dallas, 1968; Terry Dintenfass, Inc., 1969, 72. **Group:** MMA, 1950; A.F.A., 1951; Buffalo/Albright, Expressionism in American Painting, 1952; Carnegie, 1952; WMAA Annuals, 1953, 57; The Downtown Gallery, 1958; SAGA, 1962. **Collections:** Albany/Institute; Boston/MFA; Brooklyn Museum; Chicago/AI; Hartford/Wadsworth; Library of Congress; MMA; U. of Nebraska; Norfolk; PAFA; Scranton/Everhart; Syracuse U.; WMAA; Washington U.; Youngstown/Butler. **Bibliography:** Chaet; Nordness, ed. Archives.

BLEIFELD, STANLEY. b. August 28, 1924, Brooklyn, N.Y. US Navy, 1944-46. **Studied:** Stella Elkins Tyler School of Fine Arts, Temple U., with Raphael Sabatini, 1949, BFA. Traveled Israel, Mexico, and extensively in Italy; resided Rome, 1962-63. **Taught:** Weston (Conn.) Public Schools, 1950-53; New Haven State Teachers College, 1953-55; Danbury State College, 1955-63; Silvermine Guild, 1963-66; Bleifeld Studio Group, 1966-. **Member:** National Sculpture Society; Artists Equity. **Commissions:** Vatican Pavilion, New York World's Fair, 1964-65; The Margaret Sanger Award, 1966; Kokomo (Ind.) Public Library, 1969; Knights of Columbus, New Haven, CT., 1982; US Navy Memorial, Washington, D.C., 1982. **Awards:** Tyler Annual, First Prize, 1951; National Sculpture Society, John Gregory Award, 1964, Bronze Medal, 1970; elected Tyler Fellow, 1964; L. C. Tiffany

Grants, 1965, 67; NAD, Shikler Award, 1977; National Sculpture Society: Proskauer Prize, 1983, Bennett Prize, 1985. **Address:** 27 Spring Valley Road, Weston, CT 06880. **Dealers:** The Jones Gallery, La Jolla; Armstrong Gallery, NYC; Stremmel Gallery, Reno; James Fisher Gallery, Denver. **One-man Exhibitions:** The Peridot Gallery, 1963, 68; Hoffman Fuel Co., Danbury, Conn., 1962; Kenmore Galleries, Inc., Philadelphia, 1967; New Canaan (Conn.) Public Library, 1967; Fairfield U., 1967; I.F.A. Gallery, 1968, 71; FAR Gallery, 1971, 73, 77; New Britain/American, 1974. **Group:** Silvermine Guild; Stella Elkins Tyler School of Fine Arts, Temple U.; International Arts Festival, Chetwode, Newport, R.I., 1964; A.F.A., 1966-67; Temple Emanuel, Houston, Tex., 1964; Indiana U., 1966; Southampton/Parrish, Sport in Art, 1968. **Collections:** U. of Edinburgh, Scotland; Housatonic Community College; Lyndon B. Johnson Library, Austin, Texas; New Britain/American; The Pennsylvania State U.; Tampa/AI; Temple U.; Westmoreland County/MA.

BLOOM, HYMAN. b. April, 1913, near Riga, Latvia. To USA, 1920. **Studied:** West End Community Center, Boston, with Harold Zimmerman; Harvard U., with Denman W. Ross. **Taught:** Wellesley College, 1949-51; Harvard U., 1951-53. Federal A.P.: Easel Painting. **Address:** 80 Hills Ferry Road, Nashua, N.H. 03060. **Dealer:** Terry Dintenfass, Inc. **One-man Exhibitions:** Stuart Gallery, Boston, 1945; Durlacher Brothers, NYC, 1946, 48, 54; ICA, Boston; Boris Mirski Gallery, Boston, 1949; The Swetzoff Gallery, Boston, 1957; WMAA, 1968; U. of Connecticut, 1969; Terry Dintenfass, Inc., 1972, 75, 79; UCLA (two-man). **Retrospective:** Buffalo/Albright, circ., 1954. **Group:** MOMA, Americans, 1942, circ., 1942; Boston/MFA; WMAA. **Collections:** Amherst College; Andover/Phillips; First National Bank of

Hyman Bloom   *Seascape I-85*   1985

Boston; Harvard U.; Hirshhorn; Kalamazoo/Institute; Minnesota/MA; MOMA; Purchase/SUNY; Rutgers U.; St. Louis/City; Smith College; WMAA. **Bibliography:** Barker 1; Baur 7; Biddle 4; Chaet; Eliot; *From Foreign Shores*; Goodrich 1; Hess, T.B., 1; Hunter 6; Kootz 2; Kuh 3; Miller, ed., 1; Newmeyer; Pousette-Dart, ed.; Richardson, E.P.; Rodman 2, 3; Rose, B., 1; Soby 5; Wight 2; **Wight and Goodrich.** Archives.

BLUEMNER, OSCAR. b. 1867, Hanover, Germany; **d.** 1938, South Braintree, Mass. **Studied:** Academy of Fine Arts, Berlin. To USA, 1892. Practicing architect, 1894-1912. **One-man Exhibitions:** Berlin, 1885, 1912; Stieglitz Gallery, NYC, 1915; Mrs. Liebman's Art Room, NYC, 1926; Stieglitz's Intimate Gallery, NYC, 1928; Whitney Studio Club, NYC, 1929; Marie Harriman Gallery, NYC, 1935; U. of Minnesota, 1939;

Today's Gallery, Boston, 1945; The Graham Gallery, 1956, 60, 67, 72; Harvard U., 1967; New York Cultural Center, 1969; Davis Gallery, 1971; Danenberg Gallery, 1972; Hirshhorn, 1979; Monique Knowlton Gallery, NYC, 1978; Sid Deutsch Gallery, NYC, 1980; Barbara Mathes Gallery, NYC, 1985. **Group:** Anderson Galleries, NYC, Forum Exhibition, 1916; Bourgeois Gallery, NYC, 1917-23; J.B. Neumann Gallery, NYC, 1924-36; WMAA, Pioneers of Modern Art in America, 1946; WMAA, Juliana Force Memorial Exhibition, 1949; NCFA, Roots of Abstract Art in American, 1910-1930, 1967. **Collections:** Boston/MFA; MOMA; Phillips; WMAA. **Bibliography:** *Avant-Garde Painting and Sculpture;* Baur 7; Brown 2; Cheney; Frank, ed.; *From Foreign Shores;* Goodrich and Baur 1; Hunter 6; Janis; Levin 2; Mellquist; **Oscar Bluemner: American Colorist;** Rose, B., 1, 4; Wright 1. Archives.

BLUHM, NORMAN. b. March 28, 1920; Chicago, Ill. **Studied:** Illinois Institute of Technology, 1936; 1945-47, with Mies van der Rohe. US Air Force, 1941-45. Resided Paris, 1947-56. **Address:** South Brook Farm, Middletown Springs, Vt. 05757. **Dealer:** Washburn Gallery, NYC. **One-man Exhibitions:** (first) Leo Castelli Inc., 1957, also 1960; Galleria d'Arte del Naviglio, Milan, 1959; Notizie Gallery, Turin, 1961; David Anderson Gallery, NYC, 1962; Paris, 1965; Galerie Semiha Huber, Zurich, 1963; The American Gallery, NYC, 1963; Galerie Anderson-Mayer, Paris, 1963; Galerie Smith, Brussels, 1964; Galerie Stadler, Paris, 1968, 70, 72, 75; Corcoran, 1969, 77; Martha Jackson Gallery, 1970, 71, 74, 77; J. L. Hudson Art Gallery, Detroit, 1971; Syracuse/Everson, 1973; Vassar College, 1974; Galleria Venezia, Venice, 1974; Carlo Rubboli, Milan, 1974; Houston/Contemporary, 1976; Robinson Galleries, Houston, 1976; Corcoran, 1978; Galerie Stadler, Paris, 1982; Stony Brook/SUNY, 1984; Herbert

Palmer Gallery, Los Angeles, 1985; Washburn Gallery, 1986. **Group:** Carnegie, 1958; Documenta II, Kassel, 1959; ICA, Boston, 100 Works on Paper, circ., Europe, 1959; Walker, 60 American Painters, 1960; WMAA Annual, 1960; Chicago/AI Annual, 1961; SRGM, The G. David Thompson Collection; SRGM, Abstract Expressionists and Imagists, 1961; Salon du Mai, Paris, 1964; MOMA, Two Decades of American Painting, circ., 1966; Jewish Museum, Large Scale American Painting, 1967; MOMA, Dada, Surrealism, and Their Heritage, 1968; Galleria d'Arte, Cortina, Espaces Abstraits, 1969; WMAA Annual, 1972; MOMA, Color as Language, circ., 1975. **Collections:** Baltimore/MA; Buffalo/Albright; Corcoran; CNAC; Dallas/MFA; Dayton/AI; Kansas City/Nelson; MIT; MOMA; U. of Massachusetts; Melbourne/National; National Gallery; NYU; National Museum of Wales; Phillips; Reed College; Stony Brook/SUNY; Syracuse/Everson; Vassar College; WMAA. **Bibliography:** Alloway 4; *Metro;* O'Hara 1; Rubin 1; Sandler 1. Archives.

BLUME, PETER. b. October 27, 1906, Russia. To USA, 1911. **Studied:** Educational Alliance, NYC; ASL; Beaux Arts Academy, NYC. **Commissions:** Federal A.P.: US Post Offices, Cannonsburg, Pa., Rome, Ga., and Geneva, N.Y. (murals). **Awards:** Guggenheim Foundation Fellowship, 1932, 36; Carnegie, First Prize, 1934; MMA, Artists for Victory, 1942; NIAL Grant, 1947. **Address:** Rt. 1, Box 140, Church Road, Sherman, Conn. 06789. **Dealer:** Terry Dintenfass, Inc., NYC. **One-man Exhibitions:** (first) The Daniel Gallery, NYC, 1930; Julien Levy Galleries, NYC, 1937; The Downtown Gallery, 1941, 47; Durlacher Brothers, NYC, 1949, 54, 58; Kennedy Gallery, 1968; Danenberg Gallery, 1970; Coe Kerr Gallery, 1975; Terry Dintenfass, Inc., NYC, 1980. **Retrospective:** Chicago/Contemporary, 1976. **Collections:** Boston/MFA; Chicago/AI; Columbus; Hartford/

Wadsworth; Harvard U.; MMA; Newark Museum; Randolph-Macon College; WMAA; Williams College. **Bibliography:** Barker 1; Barr 3; Baur 7; Boswell 1; Brown 2; Cahill and Barr, eds.; Canaday; Cheney; Eliot; Flanagan; *From Foreign Shores;* **Getlein 3;** Goodrich and Baur 1; Haftman; Hunter 6; *Index of 20th Century Artists;* Janis; Jewell 2; Kootz 1, 2; Kuh 1; McCurdy, ed.; Mellquist; Mendelowitz; Neumeyer; Nordness, ed.; Pearson 2; Poore; Pousette-Dart, ed.; Richardson, E.P.; Ringel, ed.; Rose, B., 1; Sachs; Smith, S.C.K.; Soby 5, 6; Wight 2. Archives.

BOARDMAN, SEYMOUR. b. December 29, 1921, Brooklyn, N.Y. **Studied:** City College of New York, 1942, BS; Academie des Beaux-Arts, Academie de la Grande Chaumiere, and Atelier Fernand Leger, Paris, 1946-52. US Army, 1942-46. **Taught:** Wagner College, 1957-58. **Member:** Artists Equity. **Awards:** Longview Foundation Grant, 1963; Gottlieb Foundation Award, 1979, 83; Pollock-Krasner Foundation Grant, 1985. **Address:** 234 West 27th Street, NYC, 10001. **Dealer:** Anita Shapolsky Gallery, NYC. **One-man Exhibitions:** (first) Salon du Mai, Paris, 1951; Martha Jackson Gallery, 1955, 56; Dwan Gallery, NYC, 1960; Stephen Radich Gallery, NYC, 1960-62; Esther Robles Gallery, 1965; A. M. Sachs Gallery, 1965, 67, 68; Dorsky Gallery, 1972; Cornell U., 1971; Aaron Berman, NYC, 1978; Anita Shapolsky Gallery, 1986. **Group:** WMAA, 1955, 61, 67; Youngstown/Butler, 1955; SFMA, 1955; Carnegie, 1955; U. of Nebraska, 1956; Santa Barbara/MA, 1964; Kunsthalle, Basel, 1964; California State U., Americans in Paris: The Fifties, 1979. **Collections:** Brandeis U.; Cornell U.; Ciba-Geigy Chemical Corp.; Mexico City/Tamayo; NYU; Newark Museum; Potsdam/SUNY; SRGM; Santa Barbara/MA; Union Carbide Corp.; WMAA; Wagner College; Walker. **Bibliography:** Archives.

BOCHNER, MEL. b. 1940, Pittsburgh, Pa. **Studied:** Carnegie, 1962, BFA. **Taught:** School of Visual Arts, NYC, 1965-; Yale U., 1980-85. **Address:** 108 Franklin Street, NYC 10013. **Dealer:** Ileana Sonnabend Gallery, NYC. **One-man Exhibitions:** Visual Arts Gallery, NYC, 1966; ACE Gallery, Los Angeles, 1969; Galerie Konrad Fischer, Dusseldorf, 1969; Galerie Heiner Friedrich, Munich, 1969; Galleria Toselli, Milan, 1969, 72; MOMA, 1971; 112 Greene Street Gallery, NYC, 1971; Galerie MTL, Brussels, 1972; Galleria Marilena Bonomo, Bari, Italy, 1972; Lisson Gallery, London, 1972; Ileana Sonnabend Gallery, NYC, 1972, 73, 74, 76, 78, 80, 82, 83, 85; Ileana Sonnabend Gallery, Paris, 1972, 73, 74, 78; Galleria Schema, Florence, Italy, 1974, 78; Weinberg Gallery, San Francisco, 1974, 78; U. of California, Berkeley, 1975; Baltimore/MA, 1976; Bernier Gallery, Athens, 1977; Art in Progress, Dusseldorf, 1979; The Texas Gallery, Houston, 1981; Daniel Weinberg Gallery, San Francisco, 1981, 83; Southern Methodist U., 1981; Ab-

Mel Bochner *Palisade* 1984

baye de Senaque, Gordes, France, 1982; Pace Editions, NYC, 1983; Yarlow Salzman Gallery, Toronto, 1983; Carol Tyler Art, Dallas, 1983; Roger Ramsay Gallery, Chicago, 1984; Janet Steinberg Gallery, San Francisco, 1985. **Retrospectives:** Carnegie-Mellon U., 1985; Lucerne, 1986. **Group:** Finch College, NYC, Art in Series, 1967; Art in Process, 1969; Leverkusen, Konzeption— Conception, 1969; Seattle/AM, 557, 087, 1969; Chicago/Contemporary, Art by Telephone, 1969; Turin/Civico, Conceptual Art, Arte Povera, Land Art, 1970; New York Cultural Center, Conceptual Art and Conceptual Aspects, 1970; Oberlin College, Art in the Mind, 1970; MOMA, Information, 1971; Chicago/Contemporary, White on White, 1972; Documenta V, Kassel, 1972; Basel, Konzept Kunst, 1972; Musée Galliera, Paris, Festival d'Automne, 1973; Seattle/AM, American Art: Third Quarter Century, 1973; WMAA, American Drawings: 1963-1973, 1973; New York Cultural Center, 3D into 2D, 1973; Parcheggio di Villa Borghese, Rome, Contemporanea, 1974; Princeton U., Line as Language, 1974; Cologne, Project '74, 1974; Leverkusen, Drawings 3: American Drawings, 1975; MOMA, Drawing Now, 1976; Chicago/AI, Annual, 1976; Fort Worth, Fourteen Artists: The New Decade, 1976; WMAA, Biennial, 1977, 79; PMA, Eight Artists, 1978; Palazzo Reale, Milan, Pintura Ambiente, 1979; Paris/Beaubourg, Murs, 1981; Chicago/AI, 74th American Exhibition, 1982; Cranbrook, Viewpoint '84, 1984. **Collections:** Baltimore/AM; Brown U.; Buffalo/Albright; Carnegie; Chicago/AI; Cologne/Ludwig; Detroit/Institute; Hartford/Wadsworth; MMA; MOMA; Oberlin College; PMA; Paris/Beaubourg; St. Louis/City; Tate Gallery; WMAA; Yale U. **Bibliography:** *Contemporanea;* Johnson, Ellen H.; Gablik; Krauss 2; Lippard, ed.; Meyer; Pincus-Witten; Pincus-Witten 2; *When Attitudes Become Form.*

BOGHOSIAN, VARUJAN. b. June 26, 1926, New Britain, Conn. **Studied:** Yale U., 1956-59, BFA, MFA (with Josef Albers); Vesper George School of Art, 1946-48; US Navy, 1944-46. **Taught:** U. of Florida, 1958-59; Cooper Union, 1959-64; Pratt Institute, 1961; Yale U., 1962-64; Brown U., 1964-68; American Academy, Rome, 1967; Dartmouth College, 1968-. **Member:** AAIAL; Century Association. **Awards:** Fulbright Fellowship (Italy), 1953; Brown U., Howard Foundation Grant for Painting, 1966; New Haven Arts Festival, First Prize, 1958; Portland (Me.) Arts Festival, 1958; Boston Arts Festival, 1961; Providence Art Club, First Prize, 1967; Hon. MA, Brown U.; AAAL; NIAL; Guggenheim Foundation Fellowship, 1985. **Address:** 1 Read Road, Hanover, NH 03755. **Dealer:** Cordier & Ekstrom, Inc., NYC. **One-man Exhibitions:** (first) The Swetzoff Gallery, Boston, 1949, also 1950, 51, 53, 54, 55, 59, 63, 65; R. M. Light & Co., Boston, 1962; The Stable Gallery, 1963-66; ACE Gallery, Provincetown, Mass., 1966; U. of Massachusetts, 1968; Dartmouth College, 1968; Currier, 1968; Cordier & Ekstrom, Inc., 1969, 70, 71, 73, 75, 77, 78, 79, 80, 82, 84; Arts Club of Chicago, 1970; Alpha Gallery; 1972; U. of Connecticut, 1972; Keene (N.H.) State College, 1972. **Group:** MOMA, Young American Printmakers, 1953; MOMA, Recent Drawings USA, 1956; U. of Illinois, 1961; Chicago/AI Annual, 1961; WMAA Annuals, 1963, 64, 66, 68; Yale U., 1965; ICA, Boston, As Found, 1966; WMAA, Contemporary American Sculpture, Selection 1, 1966; Grand Rapids, Sculpture of the 60s, 1969. **Collections:** Andover/Phillips; Brandeis U.; U. of California; Dartmouth College; Indianapolis/Herron; MOMA; U. of Massachusetts; NYPL; New Britain/American; Newark Museum; Purchase/SUNY; Phoenix; RISD; Vassar College; Williams College; WMAA; Wesleyan U. (Conn.); Worcester/AM. **Bibliography:** Archives.

BOHROD, AARON. b. November 21, 1907, Chicago, Ill. **Studied:** Crane Junior College, 1925-26; Chicago Art Institute School, 1927-29; ASL, 1930-32, with Boardman Robinson, John Sloan, Richard Lahey. Traveled USA, Europe, South Pacific. **Taught:** Illinois State Normal U.; 1941-42; Ohio U., summers, 1949, 54; U. of Wisconsin, 1948-73. **Member:** NAD, Academician, 1952. Federal A.P.: Easel painting. Artist War Correspondent for *Life* magazine, 1942-45. **Commissions:** Eli Lilly & Co. (7 paintings, Medical Disciplines); *Look* magazine (14 paintings, Great Religions of America). **Awards:** Corcoran, William A. Clark Prize and Corcoran Silver Medal ($1,500); MMA, Artists for Victory, $1,000 Prize; Guggenheim Foundation Fellowship, 1936, renewed, 1937; Chicago/AI, The Mr. & Mrs. Frank G. Logan Prize, 1937, 45; PAFA, First Watercolor Prize, 1942; Illinois State Fair, First Award, 1955; Carnegie; NAD, Saltus Gold Medal for Merit, 1961; AAAL, Childe Hassam Award, 1962; Hon. DFA, Ripon College, 1960. **Address:** 4811 Tonyawatha Trail, Madison, WI 53716. **Dealers:** Harmon-Meek Gallery, Naples, Fla.; Companile Galleries, Chicago. **One-man Exhibitions:** (first) Rehn Galleries, ca. 1935; A.A.A. Gallery, NYC, 1939, 41, 43, 45, 46, 49, 52, 55; The Milch Gallery, 1957, 59, 61, 65; Agra Gallery, 1966; The Banfer Gallery, 1967; Irving Galleries, Inc., Milwaukee, 1968; Hammer Gallery, 1969; Dannenberg Gallery, 1971; Oehlschlaeger Gallery, Chicago, 1976; Milwaukee, 1979. **Retrospectives:** Madison Art Center, 1966, 80; Memphis/Brooks, 1975. **Group:** WMAA; Milwaukee; MMA; Boston/MFA; PAFA; Chicago/AI; Corcoran; Brooklyn Museum; Milwaukee, Leaders in Wisconsin Art, 1982. **Collections:** Abbott Laboratories; U. of Arizona; Beloit College; Boston/MFA; Britannica; Brooklyn Museum; Chicago/AI; Corcoran; Cranbrook; Davenport/Municipal; Detroit/Institute; Evansville; Hirshhorn; U. of Illinois; Library of Congress; Lawrence College; Los Angeles/County MA; MMA; MacNider Museum; Madison Art Center; U. of Maine; U. of Miami; Milwaukee; U. of Minnesota; Neenah/Bergstrom; New Britain/American; U. of New Mexico; Ohio U.; PAFA; Palm Springs Desert Museum; Phillipines/MA; Phoenix; Rahr-West Museum; Ripon College; St. Lawrence U.; San Antonio/McNay; Savannah/Telfair; Southern Illinois U.; Springfield, Mass./MFA; Springfield, Mo./AM; U. of Texas; Witte; Terre Haute/Swope; Syracuse U.; WMAA; Walker; West Palm Beach/Norton; U. of Wisconsin; U. of Wyoming; Youngstown/Butler. **Bibliography:** American Artists Group Inc. 2; Baur 7; Bethers; Bruce and Watson; Cheney; Christensen; Flanagan; McCurdy, ed.; Mendelowitz; Pagano; Pearson 1; Reese; Richardson, E. P.; Rose, B., 1; Wight 2. Archives.

BOICE, BRUCE. b. December, 1941, Boundbrook, N.J. **Studied:** Colgate U. US Army, 1964-66. **Taught:** School of Visual Arts, NYC, 1973-. **Awards:** National Endowment for the Arts, Grant, 1976; CAPS, 1979. **Address:** 189 Bowery, NYC 10002. **Dealer:** Sonnabend Gallery, NYC. **One-man Exhibitions:** (first) Ileana Sonnabend Gallery, NYC, 1975, 76, 77, 79; Capricorno Galleries, Venice, Italy, 1975; Galleriaforma, Genoa, Italy, 1975; Ileana Sonnabend Gallery, Paris, 1976; Galerie Rolf Ricke, Cologne, 1975; H.M., Brussels, 1976; Dart Gallery, Inc., Chicago, 1976; Thomas Segal Gallery, Boston, 1978; RAW Gallery, Hartford, Conn., 1978; Tyler School of Art, Philadelphia, 1979. **Group:** ICA, U. of Pennsylvania, Eight Abstract Painters, 1978; Cleveland/MA, Four Contemporary Painters, 1978; The University of Chicago, Ideas on Paper, 1976. **Collections:** MMA; MOMA; WMAA.

BOLLINGER, WILLIAM. b. July 15, 1939, Brooklyn, N.Y. **Studied:** Brown U., 1961. **Address:** % Dealer. **Dealer:**

OK Harris Works of Art, NYC. **One-man Exhibitions:** Paul Bianchini Gallery, NYC, 1966; Bykert Gallery, 1967, 69; Galerie Rolf Ricke, 1967, 69; Galerie Joachim Ernst, Hannover, 1969; Gian Enzo Sperone, Turin, 1969; Starrett Lehigh Building, NYC, 1970; OK Harris Works of Art, 1972, 73, 74; Bard College, 1973; U. of Rhode Island, 1976. **Retrospective:** Bennington College, 1973. **Group:** WMAA, Anti-Illusion: Procedures/Materials, 1969; WMAA Annuals, 1969, 73; MOMA, Information 1971; Storm King Art Center, Sculpture in the Fields, 1974; U. of Rhode Island, Drawings, 1974. **Collections:** Four Seasons Restaurant; Mark Twain Bankshares; Mark Twain South County Bank; U. of Rhode Island; Skidmore College; SFAI. **Bibliography:** *When Attitudes Become Form.*

BOLOMEY, ROGER. b. October 19, 1918, Torrington, Conn. **Studied:** Vevey, Switzerland, 1934-38; U. of Lausanne, 1947; Academy of Fine Arts, Florence, Italy, 1948-50; privately with Alfredo Cini, Switzerland. **Taught:** San Mateo Arts and Crafts, 1954-55;' Dutchess Community College, Poughkeepsie, N.Y. 1965-66; Barlow School, Amenia, N.Y., 1967; Hunter College, 1968; Herbert H. Lehman College, Bronx, N.Y., 1968-75; Chairman, Department of Art, 1974-; California State U., Fresno, 1975-. **Commissions:** San Jose State College Art Building; South Mall, Albany (sculptures), 1967; Southridge Shopping Center, Milwaukee, 1968; Lehman High School, Bronx, N.Y., 1969; Eastridge Mall, San Jose, Calif.; Hauppauge, 1973; Mt. Hood Community College, Gresham, Ore., 1974; North Park, Dallas, 1975. **Awards:** SFMA, **P.P.,** 1960, Sculpture Prize, 1965; Walnut Creek (Calif.) Pageant, First Prize, 1962; Waitsfield/Bundy, Bundy Sculpture Competition, First Prize, 1963. **Address:** 4014 N. Van Ness Blvd., Fresno, CA 93704. **Dealer:** Alexander Gallery, Los Angeles. **One-man Exhibitions:** (first)

SFMA, 1950; Sacramento/Crocker, 1950; Passedoit Gallery, NYC, 1951; Santa Barbara/MA, 1953; de Young, 1954; California Palace, 1958; Royal Marks Gallery, 1964; Circle Gallery, New Orleans, 1976. **Group:** SFMA Annuals, 1950, 1960-63, 65; ICA, Boston, 100 Works on Paper, circ., Europe, 1959; Chicago/AI, 1963; Salon du Mai, Paris, 1964; Carnegie, 1964; WMAA Sculpture Annual, 1964, 66; New York World's Fair, 1964-65; WMAA, Contemporary American Sculpture, Selection I, 1966; Quatrieme Exposition Suisse de Sculpture, Bienne, Switzerland, 1966; U. of Illinois, 1967; Southern Illinois U., 1967; Ridgefield/Aldrich, 1968; HemisFair '68, San Antonio, Tex., 1968; U. of Nebraska, American Sculpture, 1970; Storm King Art Center, Outdoor Sculpture Indoors, 1972; Society of Four Arts, Contemporary American Sculpture, 1974; Van Saun Park, Paramus, N.J., Sculpture in the Park, 1974. **Collections:** U. of California; Chase Manhattan Bank; Corcoran; Fontana-Hollywood Corp.; Los Angeles/County MA; MOMA; Oakland/AM; Ridgefield/Aldrich; SFAI; San Francisco Art Association; San Jose State College; WMAA; Waitsfield/Bundy. **Bibliography:** Archives.

BOLOTOWSKY, ILYA. b. July 1, 1907, Petrograd, Russia. **d.** November 22, 1981, NYC. To USA, 1923; citizen, 1929. **Studied:** College of St. Joseph, Istanbul; NAD, with Ivan Olinsky, 1924-30. US Air Force, 1942. Traveled Russia, Europe, North America. **Taught:** Black Mountain College, 1946-48; U. of Wyoming, 1948-57; Brooklyn College, 1954-56; Hunter College, 1954-56, 1963-64; New Paltz/SUNY, 1957-65; Long Island U., 1965-71; Wisconsin State College, summer, 1968; U. of New Mexico, spring, 1969; Queens College, 1973. Federal A.P.: Master easel and mural artist, teacher. **Member:** Cofounder, charter member, and former president of

Ilya Bolotowsky   *Blue Diamond*   1940–41

American Abstract Artists; cofounder and charter member of Federation of Modern Painters and Sculptors; AAAL. Produced 16 mm experimental films. Began constructivist painted columns 1961. **Commissions:** (murals) Williamsburgh Housing Project, NYC, 1936 (one of the first abstract murals); New York World's Fair, 1939; Hospital for Chronic Diseases, NYC, 1941; Theodore Roosevelt High School, NYC, 1941; Cinema I, NYC, 1962; Southampton College, Long Island U., 1968; North Central Bronx Hospital, 1973; First National City Bank, NYC 1974; P.S. 72, Brooklyn, N.Y., 1974 (tile mosaic mural); NYC, Passenger Ship terminal mural, 1978. **Awards:** Sharon (Conn.) Art Foundation, First Prize for Painting, 1959; Guggenheim Foundation Fellowship, 1941, 73; Yaddo Fellowship, 1935; L. C. Tiffany Grant, 1930, 31; NAD, Hallgarten Prize for Painting, 1929, 30; NAD, First Prize Medal for Drawing, 1924, 25; The U. of Chicago, Midwest Film Festival, First Prize (for Metanois); State U. of New York Grant, for film research, 1959, 60; NIAL, Grant, 1971. **One-man Exhibitions:** (first) G.R.D. Studios, NYC, 1930; J. B. Neumann's New Art Circle, NYC, 1946, 52; Rose Fried Gallery, 1947, 49; Pratt Institute, 1949; Grace

Borgenicht Gallery, NYC, 1954, 56, 58, 59, 61, 63, 66, 68, 70, 72, 74, 75, 76, 77, 78, 79, 80; New Paltz/SUNY, 1960; Dickinson College, 1960; Elmira College, 1962; Southampton/Parrish, 1965; Long Island U., 1965; East Hampton Gallery, East Hampton, N.Y., 1965; Buffalo/SUNY, 1965 (two-man), 1966; Gorham State College, 1967; Wisconsin State College, 1968; Stony Brook/SUNY, 1968; London Arts, London and Detroit, 1971; David Barnett Gallery, Milwaukee, 1972; Reed College, 1973; Hokin Gallery, Chicago, 1976; Washburn Gallery, NYC, 1980, 83, 84; NYU, 1983; Salt Lake Art Center, 1981; Yares Gallery, Scottsdale, Ariz., 1982; Stony Brook/SUNY, 1985; AAIAL, Memorial Exhibition, 1983; Il Punto Blu Gallery, Southampton, N.Y. 1984; River Gallery, Irvington-on-Hudson, N.Y., 1984; Pembroke Gallery, Houston, 1984. **Retrospectives:** U. of New Mexico, circ., 1970; SRGM, 1974; NCFA, circ., 1975; Houston/Contemporary, 1984. **Group:** American Abstract Artists Annuals; Federation of Modern Painters and Sculptors Annuals; WMAA Annuals; New York World's Fairs, 1939 and 1964-65; Seattle World's Fair, 1962; WMAA, Geometric Abstraction in America, circ., 1962; Corcoran, 1963; SRGM; Buffalo/Albright, Plus by Minus, 1968; Dallas/MFA, Geometric Abstraction, 1926-42, 1972; Chicago/Contemporary, Post-Mondrian Abstraction in America, 1973; Milwaukee, From Foreign Shores, 1976; Indianapolis, 1976; Philadelphia College of Art, Seventies Painting, 1978; AAIAL, Work by Newly Elected Members, 1982; Carnegie, Abstract Painting and Sculpture in America 1927-1944, 1983. **Collections:** AAAL; American Republic Insurance Co.; Andover/Phillips; Atlantic Richfield Co.; Bezalel Museum; Brandeis U.; Brooklyn Museum; Buffalo/Albright; Burlington Industries; Calcutta; Ceret; Chase Manhattan Bank; Ciba-Geigy Corp.; Cleveland/MA; Continental Grain Company; Harcourt

Brace Jovanovich, Inc.; Hirshhorn; Housatonic Community College; Indianapolis; U. of Iowa; MMA; MOMA; Manufacturers Hanover Trust Co.; U. of Michigan; The Miller Co.; Montclair/AM; NCFA; NYU; U. of Nebraska; New London; U. of New Mexico; New Paltz/SUNY; Norfolk/Chrysler; U. of North Carolina; Oklahoma; PMA; Phillips; RISD; Raleigh/NCMA; Ridgefield/Aldrich; Rock River (Wyo.) High School; SFMA; SRGM; Slater; Sweden/Goteborgs; U. of Texas; Union Carbide Corp.; Utica: U. of Vermont; WMAA; Walker; U. of Wyoming; Yale U. **Bibliography:** *Black and White Are Colors;* Blanchard; **Breeskin 2;** Brown 2; *From Foreign Shores;* Goodrich and Baur 1; Lane and Larsen; MacAgy 2; Marter, Tarbell, and Wechsler; Rickey; Rose, B., 1. Archives.

BONEVARDI, MARCELO. b. 1929, Buenos Aires, Argentina. **Studied:** U. of Cordoba, 1948-51. Traveled Italy, USA. To USA, 1958. **Taught:** National U. of Cordoba, 1956. **Awards:** Salon Annual de Santa Fe, **P.P.,** 1956; Premio de Honor J. Pellanda, Cordoba, 1957; XXXVI Salon Annual de Rosario, **P.P.,** 1957; Salon Ministerio de Obras Publicas de la Nacion, Buenos Aires, First Prize, 1957; Guggenheim Foundation Fellowship, 1958; New School for Social Research Fellowship, 1963, 64; X Sao Paulo Biennial, International Award, 1969. **Address:** 799 Greenwich Street, NYC 10014. **One-man Exhibitions:** Museo Dr. Genario Perez, Cordoba, 1956; Galeria O. Rosario, 1956; Galeria Antigona, Buenos Aires, 1957; Amigos del Arte, Rosario, 1958; Radio Nacional de Cordoba, 1958; Gallery 4, Detroit, 1959; Roland de Anelle, NYC, 1960; Latow Gallery, NYC, 1961; Galeria Bonino Ltd., NYC, 1965, 67, 69, 73, 78; J. L. Hudson Art Gallery, Detroit, 1966; Arts Club of Chicago, 1968; Galeria Bonino Ltd., Buenos Aires, 1969, 70, 76; Museo Emilio A. Caraffa, Cordoba, Argentina, 1969, 78; Quebec,

1974; Montreal/Contemporain, 1974; Galeria Pecanins, Mexico City, 1974; Galeria Ponce, Mexico, 1978; Galeria Sandiego, Bogota, Colombia, 1979; The Art Contact Gallery, 1979; Galeria del Retiro, Buenos Aires, 1979, 81, 83; Galeria Ponce, Mexico City, 1980; Promocion de Las Artes, Monterrey, 1980; Galeria Jaime Conci, Cordoba, Argentina, 1981; Museo Hara, Tokyo, 1982. **Retrospectives:** Center for Inter-American Relations, NYC, 1980; Mexico City/Moderno, 1981. **Group:** Birmingham, Ala./MA, Pan American Art, 1960; Riverside Museum, NYC, 30 Latin American Artists, 1960; ICA, Washington, D.C., Latin American Painters, 1964; U. of Illinois, 1965; Indianapolis, 1966; SRGM, The Emergent Decade, 1966; Cornell U., Latin American Art—Eight Argentines, 1966; Finch College, NYC, Art in Progress, 1967. **Collections:** Atlantic Richfield Co.; Baltimore/MA; Brooklyn Museum; Buenos Aires/Moderno; Buffalo/Albright; Caracas; Centro Artistico de Barranquilla; Chase Manhattan Bank; Ciba-Geigy Corp.; MIT; MOMA; Montreal/Contemporain; Museo de Arte Contemporaneo R. Tamayo; Museo Dr. Genaro Perez; Museo Emilio A. Caraffa; Museo Juan B. Castagnino; NYU; Owens-Corning Fiberglas Corp.; PMA; Quimica Argentina; RISD; Ridgefield/Aldrich; Southern Illinois U.; Sao Paulo/Contemporary; St. Jose Minerals Corp., NYC; Tel Aviv; U. of Texas; J. Walter Thompson Co.

BONTECOU, LEE. b. January 15, 1931, Providence, R.I. **Studied:** Bradford Junior College, with Robert Wade; ASL, 1952-55, with William Zorach, John Hovannes. Traveled Europe. **Taught:** Brooklyn College, 1971-75. **Commissions:** New York State Theater, Lincoln Center for the Performing Arts, NYC. **Awards:** Fulbright Fellowship (Rome), 1957, 58; L. C. Tiffany Grant, 1959; Corcoran, 1963. **Address:** P. O. Box 1290, East Hampton, NY 11937. **Dealer:** Leo Castelli Inc. **One-**

man Exhibitions: (first) "G" Gallery, NYC, 1959; Leo Castelli, Inc., 1960, 62, 66, 71; Ileana Sonnabend Gallery, Paris, 1965; Leverkusen, 1969; Rotterdam, 1968; Kunstverein, Berlin, 1968; Chicago/Contemporary, 1972; Wesleyan U., 1975; Halper Gallery, Palm Beach, Fla., 1976; Skidmore College, 1977. **Retrospective:** Rotterdam, 1958. **Group:** Festival of Two Worlds, Spoleto, 1958; Martha Jackson Gallery, New Media—New Forms I & II, 1960, 61; WMAA Annuals, 1961, 63, 64, 66; Carnegie, 1961, 67; MOMA, The Art of Assemblage, circ., 1961; VI Sao Paulo Biennial, 1961; Seattle World's Fair, 1962; Chicago/AI, 1962, 63, Sculpture— A Generation of Innovation, 1967; Corcoran, 1963; MOMA, Americans 1963, circ., 1963-64; Buffalo/Albright, Mixed Media and Pop Art, 1963; Documenta III, Kassel, 1964; Brandeis U., Recent American Drawings, 1964; Jewish Museum, Recent American Sculpture, 1964; U. of Texas, Drawings and. . . , 1966; Flint/Institute, I Flint Invitational, 1966; MOMA, The 1960s, 1967; WMAA Sculpture Annual, 1968; Denver/AM, Report on the Sixties, 1969; Foundation Maeght, L'Art Vivant, 1970; Carnegie, 1970; U. of North Carolina, Works on Paper, 1971; Yale U., American Drawing: 1970-1973, 1973; San Antonio/McNay, American Artists, 76, 1976; MMA, Contemporary American Prints, 1976; Corcoran, The Liberation: 14 American Artists, 1977; Dayton/AI, Skin, 1977; Albright College, Perspective 78: Works by Women, 1978; Zurich/Kunsthaus, Reliefs, 1980; Houston/Contemporary, The Americans: The Collage, 1982. **Collections:** Akron/AI; Amsterdam/Stedelijk; Basel; Buffalo/Albright; Carnegie; Chase Manhattan Bank; Chicago/AI; Cleveland/MA; Corcoran; Cornell U.; Dallas/MFA; Hirshhorn; Houston/ MFA; Little Rock/MFA; MOMA; PAFA; The Sinver Company, Inc.; Smith College; SRGM; Stockholm/ National; VMFA; WGMA; WMAA; Walker; Yale U. **Bibliography:** Battcock, ed.; Hunter, ed.; Janis and Blesh

1; Licht, F.; *Metro*; Phillips, Lisa; Rose, B., 1; Seitz 3; Trier 1; Weller; Honisch and Jensen, eds.; Johnson, Ellen H.; Toher, ed.

BOROFSKY, JONATHAN. b. 1942, Boston, Mass. **Studied:** Carnegie-Mellon U., 1964, BFA; Ecole de Fontainbleau, 1964; Yale U., 1966, MFA. **Taught:** School of Visual Arts, NYC, 1969-70; California Institute of the Arts, 1977-80. **Address:** 57 Market Street, Venice, Calif. 90291. **Dealer:** Paula Cooper Gallery, NYC. **One-man Exhibitions:** Paula Cooper Gallery, 1975, 76, 79, 80, 82, 83; Hartford/Wadsworth, 1976; U. of California, Irvine, 1976; Protetch-McIntosh Gallery, Washington, D.C., 1978; Thomas Lewallen Gallery, Los Angeles, 1978; U. of California, Berkeley, 1978; Corps de Garde, Groningen, 1978; MOMA, 1978; InK Gallery, Zurich, 1979; Portland (Ore.) Center for the Visual Arts, 1979; MIT, 1980; Houston/Contemporary, 1981; Galerie Rudolf Zwirner, Cologne, 1981; Basel/Kunsthalle, 1981; ICA, London, 1981; Rotterdam, 1982; Gemini G.E.L., Los Angeles, 1982, 85; Friedrich Gallery, Bern, 1982; Basel/Kunstmuseum, 1983; Galleria dell'Arte Graffica, Milan, 1983; Akron/AM, 1983; U. of Miami, 1984; Humlebaek/Louisiana, 1984; Carl Solway Gallery, Cincinnati, 1984; Kunsthalle Bielefeld, 1984; Seattle/AM, 1984. **Retrospective:** PMA, circ., 1984. **Group:** Seattle/AM, 557, 087, 1970; Akademie der Kunst, Berlin, Soho, 1976; U. of California, Santa Barbara, Contemporary Drawing/New York, 1978, WMAA Biennials, 1979, 81, 83; Lenbachhaus, Munich, Tendencies in American Drawings of the Late Seventies, 1979; XXXIX Venice Biennial, 1980; Indianapolis, 1980, 82; Cologne/Stadt, Westkunst, 1981; Paris/Moderne, Baroques '81, 1981; Akron/AM, The Image in American Painting and Sculpture, 1950-1980, 1981; Paris/Beaubourg, Murs, 1981; Walker, Eight Artists: The Anxious Edge, 1982; Documenta VII, Kassel, 1982; Internationale

Jonathan Borofsky   *Head in the Trees at*
2,942,771   1985

Kunstausstellung Berlin, 1982; Galeria
Politi, Milan, Transavangarde Interna-
tional, 1982; Hannover/K-G, New York
Now, circ., 1982; Hirshhorn, Direc-
tions, 1983; Bonn, Back to the USA,
circ., 1983; Tate Gallery, New Art, 1983;
SFMA, The Human Condition, 1984;
MOMA, International Survey of Recent
Painting and Sculpture, 1984;
Hirshhorn, Content: A Contemporary
Focus, 1974-1984, 1984; Cincin-
nati/Contemporary, Body and Soul,
circ., 1985; Carnegie, International,
1985; XVIII Sao Paulo Bienal, 1985; Fort
Lauderdale, An American Renaissance:
Painting and Sculpture Since 1940,
1986. **Collections:** Aachen/Ludwig;
Basel/Kunsthalle; Broida Foundation,
Los Angeles; U. of California, Berkeley;
Canberra/National; Carnegie; First
Bank of Minneapolis; Hart-
ford/Wadsworth; Los Angeles/County
MA; Los Angeles/MOCA; MOMA; Mil-
waukee; Minneapolis/Institute;
Montreal/MFA; Oberlin College; PMA;
Rotterdam; Tate Gallery; WMAA; Fred-
erick Weisman Foundation, Los An-
geles; Zurich. **Bibliography:** *Back to the
USA*; Danto; Haenlein; Hiromoto;
Joachimides and Rosenthal; *Jonathan
Borofsky: Dreams 1973-1981*; Kren;
Murken-Altrogge; Rosenthal and
Marshall.

BOSA, LOUIS. b. April 2, 1905,
Codroipo, Italy. **d.** October 20, 1981,
NYC. To USA, 1923; citizen. **Studied:**
Academy of Fine Arts, Venice, with
Mazotti; ASL, with John Sloan. Trav-
eled Europe extensively. **Taught:** ASL,
1942-53; Parsons School of Design,
1950-53; Syracuse U.; U. of Notre
Dame, summer, 1960; Cleveland Insti-
tute of Art, 1954-69. **Member:** NAD;
ASL; Audubon Artists, Federal A.P.:
Easel painting. **Awards:** Portrait of
America, NYC, $1,500 Prize, 1944;
NAD, Hon. Mem., 1944; Rockport
(Mass.) Art Association, $100 Award,
1945; Mead Painting of the Year ($500),
1947; AAAL, $1,000 Award, 1948; Los
Angeles County Fair, First Prize ($700),
1948; Pepsi-Cola $500 Award, 1948; U.

of Illinois, **P.P.** ($900), 1949; Audubon Artists, Gold Medal of Honor, 1949; Hallmark International Competition, $750 Award, 1949; NAD, Gold Medal, 1957; Hallmark International Competition, $900 Award, 1958; New Hope, Pa., First Prize, 1959, 62; Legionnaires of Pennsylvania, First Prize and Gold Medal, 1959; Younstown/Butler, First Prize ($1,000); NAD, $400 Prize, 1961. **One-man Exhibitions:** (first) Contemporary Arts Gallery, NYC, 1930; Springfield, Mass./MFA; Coy Gallery, Miami; Cleveland Institute of Art; Kleeman Gallery, NYC; Frank Oehlschlaeger Gallery, Chicago, 1954, 59, 65; The Milch Gallery, 1958, 60, 63, 65; Frank Oehlschlaeger Gallery, Saratoga, Fla., 1975; Coryell Gallery, Lambertville, N.J., 1982. **Group:** MMA; MOMA; WMAA: Carnegie; Corcoran; PMA; Boston/MFA; Toledo/MA; Buffalo/Albright; New Orleans/Delgado; Worcester/AM; Montclair/AM; Wilmington; Audubon Artists; Atlanta/AA; Cleveland/MA; Chicago/AI; Kansas City/Nelson; Argentina/Nacional; PAFA; NAD. **Collections:** AAL; Atlanta/AA; Britannica; Clearwater/Gulf Coast; Columbus, Ga.; Hartford/Wadsworth; IBM; U. of Illinois; Indianapolis/Herron; MMA; Montclair/AM; New Orleans/Delgado; U. of Notre Dame; PMA; U. of Rochester; San Diego; Springfield, Mass./MFA; Syracuse U.; Toronto; VMFA; WMAA; Wilmington; Worcester/AM; Youngstown/Butler. **Bibliography:** Kent, N.; Pagano; Watson, E.W., 2. Archives.

BOURGEOIS, LOUISE. b. December 25, 1911, Paris, France. **Studied:** Lycee Fenelon, 1932, baccalaureate; Sorbonne, 1932-35; Ecole du Louvre, 1936-37; Academie des Beaux-Arts, Paris, 1936-38; Atelier Bissiere, Paris, 1936-37; Academie de la Grande Chaumiere, 1937-38; Academie Julian, Paris,

Louise Bourgeois *Nature Study* 1986

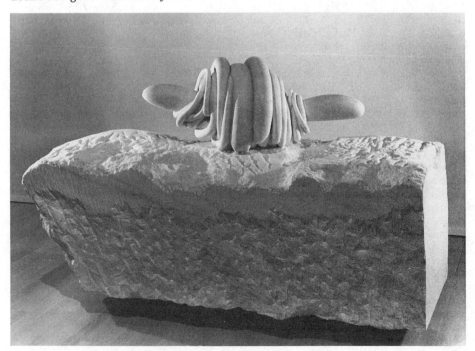

1938; Atelier Fernand Leger, Paris, 1938. Traveled Europe extensively. To USA, 1938. **Taught:** Docent at the Louvre, 1937-38; Academie de la Grande Chaumiere, 1937, 38; Great Neck (N.Y.) Public Schools, 1960; Brooklyn College, 1963, 68; Pratt Institute, 1965-67. **Awards:** Hon. DFA, Yale U., 1977; Hon. DFA, Bard College, 1981; Hon. DFA, Maryland Institute School, 1984; Officier des Arts et Lettres, France, 1984; Skowhegan School, Medal, 1985. **Member:** AAIAL; American Academy of Arts and Sciences, 1981. **Address:** 347 West 20th Street, NYC. **Dealer:** Robert Miller Gallery, NYC. **One-man Exhibitions:** The Bertha Schaefer Gallery, 1945; Norlyst Gallery, NYC, 1947; The Peridot Gallery, 1949, 50, 53; Allan Frumkin Gallery, Chicago, 1953; Cornell U., 1959; The Stable Gallery, 1964; Rose Fried Gallery, 1964; 112 Greene Street, NYC, 1974; Xavier Fourcade, Inc., NYC, 1978, 79, 80; Hamilton Gallery of Contemporary Art, NYC, 1978; U. of California, 1979; Max Hutchinson Gallery, 1980; U. of Chicago, 1981; Robert Miller Gallery, 1982, 84; Daniel Weinberg Gallery, Los Angeles, 1984; Daniel Weinberg Gallery, San Francisco, 1984; Serpentine Gallery, London, 1985; Galerie Maeght, Zurich, 1985; Galerie Maeght, Paris, 1985. **Retrospective:** MOMA, circ., 1982. **Group:** MOMA, 1943, 49, 51, 62; MMA, 1943; SFMA, 1944; Los Angeles/County MA, 1945; U. of Rochester, 1945; Brooklyn Museum, 1945; WMAA, 1945, 46, 53, 55, 57, 60, 62, 63, 68; Walker, 1954; U. of Illinois, 1957; Dallas/MFA, 1960; Claude Bernard, Paris, 1960; Salon de la Jeune Sculpture, Paris, 1965, 69; RISD, 1966; International Sculpture Biennial, Carrara, Italy, 1969; Baltimore/MA, 1969; MOMA, The New American Painting and Sculpture, 1969; WMAA, 1970, 72; Foundation Maeght, 1970; Lakeview Center, American Women: 20th Century, 1972; Storm King Art Center, The Emerging Real, 1973; PMA/Museum of the Philadelphia Civic Center, Focus, 1974;

WMAA, 200 Years of American Sculpture, 1976; New Orleans Museum Sculpture: American Directions, 1976; Brandeis U., From Women's Eyes, 1977; Albright College, Perspective '78, 1978; Purchase/SUNY, Hidden Desires, 1980; WMAA, Decade of Transition, 1940-1950, 1981; Rice U., Variants, circ., 1981; SFMA, 20 American Artists: Sculpture 1982, 1982; WMAA Biennial, 1983; AAIAL, 1983; Hirshhorn, Content: A Contemporary Focus, 1974-84, 1984; WMAA, The Third Dimension, 1984; MOMA, Primitivism in 20th Century Art, 1984; Sonoma State U., Works in Bronze, A Modern Survey, circ., 1984; Fort Lauderdale, An American Renaissance: Painting and Sculpture Since 1940, 1986. **Collections:** Calcutta; Canberra/National; Ciba-Geigy Corp.; Denver/AM; Detroit/Institute; MMA; MOMA; NYU; New Orleans Museum; Paris/Moderne; Portland, Me./AM; RISD; Storm King Art Center; WMAA. **Bibliography:** Baur 5; Giedion-Welcker 1; Goodrich and Baur 1; Lippard 3; Miller and Swenson; Motherwell and Reinhardt, eds.; Rosen 1; Seuphor 3; Trier 1. Archives.

BOWMAN, RICHARD. b. March 15, 1918, Rockford, Ill. **Studied:** Chicago Art Institute School, 1938-42, BFA; State U. of Iowa, 1947-49, MFA. Traveled Mexico, USA. **Taught:** Chicago Art Institute School, 1944-47, including summer school, 1944, 45; North Park College, 1944-46; State U. of Iowa, 1947-49; Stanford U., 1949-50, 57, 58, 63; U. of Manitoba, 1950-54; Washburn-White Art Center, Palo Alto, Calif., 1954. **Awards:** Chicago/AI, Scholarship, 1939-41; Rockford/Burpee Annual, First Prize, 1940; Edward L. Reyerson Traveling Fellowship, 1942; Chicago/AI, William R. French Memorial Gold Medal, 1945; Iowa State Fair, Second Prize, 1948; Montreal/MFA Annual, 1952; Oakland/AM, Hon. Men., 1955. **Address:** 178 Springdale Way, Redwood City, CA 94062. **One-man Exhibitions:** Beloit College, 1941; Rockford/Burpee, 1941, 47; Ras-Martin Gallery, Mexico City, 1943; The Pinacotheca, NYC, 1945; Chicago/AI, 1945; Milwaukee, 1946; U. of Illinois, 1946 (two-man, with Joan Mitchell), 1947; The Swetzoff Gallery, Boston, 1949; Pen and Palette Gallery, St. Louis, 1949; Contemporary Gallery, Sausalito, Calif. 1949, 50; Stanford U., 1950, 56; Bordelon Gallery, Chicago, 1950; Kelly Gallery, Vancouver, B.C., 1954; The Rose Rabow Gallery, San Francisco, 1959, 61, 64, 68, 70, 72, 74; SFMA, 1959 (two-man, with Gordon Onslow-Ford), 1951, 70; Harcourts Gallery, San Francisco, 1986. **Retrospectives:** Stanford U., 1956; Washington State U., circ., 1957; SFMA, 1961; Roswell, 1972. **Group:** Chicago/AI, 1940, 44, 45; SFMA, 1941, 49, 50, 55, 60; Cincinnati/AM, 1941; Art of this Century, NYC, 1945; Chicago/AI, Abstract and Surrealist Art, 1948; Chicago/AI, Exhibition Momentum, 1948; Omaha/Joslyn, 1948, 49; Iowa State Fair, 1948; Philadelphia Print Club Annual, 1949; Walker, 1949; Brooklyn Museum, 1949; Canadian Society of Graphic Art Annual, Toronto, 1952; Ottawa/National, Canadian Painters 1953, 1953; II Sao Paulo Biennial, 1953; Royal Ontario Museum, 1954; Oakland/AM, 1955; Stanford U., 50 Contemporary American Painters, 1956; SFMA, After Surrealism, circ., 1959; USIA, Contemporary American Prints, circ., Latin America, 1959-60; California Palace, 1960, 61, 62, 63, 64; Carnegie, 1961, 64; WMAA, Fifty California Artists, 1962-63; Stanford U., Some Points of View for '62, 1962; A.F.A., circ., 1966-68. **Collections:** de Young; New Britain/American; Oakland/AM; SFMA; Santa Barbara/MA; U. of Texas.

BOXER, STANLEY. b. June 26, 1926, New York City. **Studied:** Brooklyn College; Art Students League. US Navy, 1943-46. Traveled England, Germany, Canada. Designed and built set for Eric Hawkins Dance Company, *Classic Kite Tails,* 1972. **Awards:** Guggenheim Foundation Fellowship, 1975. **Address:** 37 East 18th Street, NYC 10003. **Dealer:** Andre Emmerich Gallery, NYC. **One-man Exhibitions:** (first) Perdalma Gallery, NYC, 1953, 54, 55, 56; Grand Central Galleries, NYC, 1965, 66, 67; Fischbach Gallery, NYC, 1966; Rose Fried Gallery, NYC, 1967, 68, 69; U. of Manitoba, 1967; NYU, 1968; Tibor de Nagy, NYC, 1971, 72, 73, 74, 75, 77, 82; Santa Barbara/MA, 1972; San Antonio/McNay, 1973; Watson/De Nagy Gallery, Houston, 1974, 76, 78; Galerie Andre Emmerich, Zurich, 1975; Syracuse/Everson, 1975; Andre Emmerich Gallery, NYC, 1975, 76, 77, 78, 79, 80, 81, 82, 83, 84, 85, 86; PAFA, 1976; Richard Gray, Chicago, 1977, 79; Boston/MFA, 1977; Max Protetch Gallery, Washington, D.C., 1977; Hokin Gallery, Palm Beach, Fla., 1978; Galerie Wentzel, Hamburg, 1975, 78, 80; Meredith Long Gallery, Houston, 1979, 80; Galerie Regards, Paris, 1979; Dorsky Gallery, NYC, 1980; Thomas Segal, Boston, 1980; Allrich Gallery, San Francisco, 1981; Meredith Long & Co., Houston, 1981, 83, 84, 85, 86; Hokin Gallery, Bay Harbor Island, Fla., 1980; Galerie Regards, Paris, 1980; Gallery One, Toronto, 1980, 82; Downstairs Gallery, Edmonton, 1981; Hokin Gallery, Chicago, 1982; Galerie Wentzel, Cologne, 1982, 85; Thomas Segal Gallery, Boston, 1982, 84; Galerie von Braunbehrens, Munich, 1982; Amerika Haus, Berlin, 1982; Gallery Ulysses, Vienna, 1983; Aronson Gallery, Atlanta, 1983, 84, 85; Ivory/Kimpton Gallery, San Francisco, 1983, 85; Salander-O'Reilly Gallery, NYC, 1983; Hokin/Kaufman Gallery, Chicago, 1984, 86; Woltjen/Udell Gallery, Edmonton, 1984; Thomas Smith Fine Arts, Fort Wayne, 1984; Hokin Gallery, Palm Beach, 1985; Ruth Bachofner Gallery, Los Angeles, 1985. **Retrospective:** U. of North Carolina, circ., 1978. **Group:** Syracuse/Everson, New Works in Clay, 1976; U. of Saskatchewan, Boxer, Natkin, Ferber, 1977; Indianapolis, 1978; Grand Palais, Paris, L'Amerique aux Indépendants, 1980;

Belgrade/National, Works on Paper, 1981; Baruch College, Figural Art of the New York School, 1985. **Collections:** Santa Barbara/MA; Ball State U.; Des Moines; Wichita/AM; Calcutta; Boston/MFA; Chase Manhattan Bank, NYC; IBM; Cornell U.; WMAA; Charlotte/Mint; Brandeis U.; U. of Mass.; Trenton/State; Prudential Insurance Co. of America; Buffalo/Albright; Charlotte/State; Vienna, Museum des 20. Jahrhunderts; Corcoran; Dayton/AI; Edmonton; Hirshhorn; Houston/MFA; MOMA; Milwaukee; SRGM; U. of Sydney; Syracuse/Everson; Walker.

BOYCE, RICHARD. b. June 11, 1920, NYC. US Army, 1940-44. **Studied:** Boston Museum School, 1945-49, with Karl Zerbe (highest honors in painting); assistant to O. Kokoschka, summer, 1948, Pittsfield, Mass. Traveled Europe, southern Mexico. **Taught:** Boston Museum School, 1946-49; Wellesley College, 1953-62; Boston U., 1959-61; UCLA, 1963-. **Member:** Artists Equity. **Awards:** Boston/MFA, James William Paige Fellowship, 1949-51; Boston/MFA, Bartlett Grant, 1959, 60. **Address:** 1419 W. Washington Boulevard, Venice, CA 90291. **Dealer:** Silvan Simone Gallery, Los Angeles. **One-man Exhibitions:** Boris Mirski Gallery, Boston, 1952; The Swetzoff Gallery, Boston, 1956, 59, 61, 62; Brattle Gallery, Cambridge, 1956; The Zabriskie Gallery, 1961; The Alan Gallery, NYC, 1963, 65; Felix Landau Gallery, 1966, 69; The Landau-Alan Gallery, NYC, 1968. **Group:** Johns Hopkins U., Three Young Americans, 1948; ICA, Boston, 1948, 52, 56, 62, 64; U. of Illinois, 1947, 65; Worcester/AM, 1959; Chicago/AI Annual, 1960; WMAA, 1963; PAFA Annual, 1964. **Collections:** Andover/Phillips; Harvard U.; Lincoln, Mass./De Cordova; RISD; WMAA; Wellesley College; Worcester/AM.

BOYLE, KEITH. b. February 15, 1930, Defiance, Ohio. **Studied:** State U. of Iowa, with James Lechay, BFA; Ringling School of Art, with Fred Sweet, Andrew Sanders. Traveled Europe; resided Rome. **Taught:** Lake Forest College, 1956; Barat College, 1957, 59; Sacramento State College, 1960; Stanford U., 1962-. **Commissions:** St. Thomas Episcopal Church, Sunnyvale, Calif. **Awards:** State of Iowa, Department of Education, **P.P.,** 1952; Indiana (Pa.) State Teachers College, 1953; Springfield, O./AM, 1955; The Pennsylvania State U., 1955; Chicago/AI, The Mr. & Mrs. Frank G. Logan Medal ($1,500), 1958; California Palace, Patrons of Art and Music Award, 1964; National Endowment for the Arts, 1981. **Address:** 1500 Edgewood Drive, Palo Alto, Calif. 94303. **One-man Exhibitions:** (first) Feingarten Gallery, Chicago, 1958, also 1959; Feingarten Gallery, San Francisco, 1960; Triangle Art Gallery, 1960; The Lanyon Gallery, 1963; de Young, 1964; SFMA, 1964; Stanford U., 1964, 67, 77; Hollis Gallery, San Francisco, 1967; Hansen-Fuller Gallery, 1968; Smith Andersen Gallery, Palo Alto, 1971, 72, 77; St. Mary's College, Moraga, Calif., 1972; Linda Farris Gallery, Seattle, 1973; Martha Jackson Gallery, 1974; San Jose Museum of Art, 1978; Smith Andersen Gallery, San Francisco, 1975; Pepperdine U., 1982; Stanford U., 1984. **Retrospectives:** Stanford U., 1977; San Jose Museum of Art, 1978. **Group:** Springfield, Mo./AM, 1952-55; Des Moines, 1953; Denver/AM, 1953; Walker, 1954; Washburn U. of Topeka, 1955; Younstown/Butler, 1955, 56, 58; Omaha/Joslyn, 1956; Chicago/AI, 1957-60; Ravinia Festival, Highland Park, Ill., 1957; Chicago/AI, 53 Chicago Artists, circ., France and Germany, 1957; PAFA, 1958, 60, 62; Buffalo/Albright, 1960; SFMA, 1960, 62, 64; California Palace, 1964, Painters behind Painters, 1967; U. of Michigan, 1965; SFMA, The Colorists, 1965; M. Kroedler & Co., Art Across America, circ., 1965-67; California Palace, A Century of California Painting, 1970; Omaha/Joslyn, Looking West, 1970;

Smithsonian, New American Monotypes, circ., 1978-80. **Collections:** Barat College; Dartmouth College; Indiana (Pa.) State Teachers College; U. of Iowa; Mead Corporation; NCFA; Oakland/AM; The Pennsylvania State U.; Purchase/SUNY; SFMA; Springfield, Mo./AM; Stanford U.; State of Iowa.

BOYNTON, JAMES W. b. January 12, 1928, Fort Worth, Tex. **Studied:** Texas Christian U., BFA, MFA. **Taught:** U. of Houston, 1955-57; San Francisco Art Institute, 1960-62; U. of New Mexico, 1963; Houston Museum School, 1968-69; Northwood Institute, Dallas, 1968-69; U. of St. Thomas (Tex.), 1969-70. **Awards:** Fort Worth, **P.P.,** 1951, 52, 54, 55; Texas Watercolor Society, First **P.P.,** 1951, 1953-55; Denver/AM, **P.P.,** 1952, 54, 58; Texas State Fair, **P.P.,** 1953; Houston/MFA, **P.P.,** 1955; Underwood-Neuhaus Corp., 1957; Younstown/Butler, 1957; ART: USA: 59, NYC, Hon. Men., 1959; SFMA, First Prize, 1962; Longview Foundation Grant, 1966; Tamarind Fellowship, 1967; Beaumont (Tex.) Art Museum, Second Prize, 1968. **Address:** 3723 Albans, Houston, TX 77005. **Dealer:** Moody Gallery, Houston, Texas. **One-man Exhibitions:** Fort Worth, 1955; La Escondida, Taos, N.M., 1956; Andre Emmerich Gallery, Houston, 1957; New Arts Gallery, Houston, 1957; Fairweather-Hardin Gallery, 1958; Barone Gallery, NYC, 1958; Dord Fitz Gallery, Amarillo, 1959; Bolles Gallery, San Francisco, 1959-62; Dallas Museum for Contemporary Arts, 1959; Lynchburg Art Gallery, Lynchburg, Va., 1960; Downtown Gallery, New Orleans, 1960; Haydon Calhoun Gallery, Dallas, 1960-62; Staempfli Gallery, 1961; Louisiana Gallery, Houston, 1964; David Gallery, 1966; Louise Ferrari Gallery, 1967; Chapman Kelly Gallery, 1968; Beaumont (Tex.) Art Museum, 1969; Galerie Simone Stern, New Orleans, 1970; New Orleans/Delgado, 1970; U.

of St. Thomas, Tex., 1971; Du Bose Gallery, 1975; Amarillo Art Center, 1975; Loyola U., New Orleans, 1977; Moody Gallery, Houston, 1976, 77, 79; U. of Houston, Clear Lake City, 1979. **Retrospective:** Amarillo Art Center, 1980. **Group:** Fort Worth, 1950-55; WMAA, Young America, and others; Denver/AM, 1952, 54, 56, 58; Yale U.; Corcoran; Colorado Springs/FA, 1953, 54, 57; SRGM, Younger American Painters, 1954; Carnegie, 1955; Houston/MFA, 1955, Art and the Alphabet, 1978; MOMA, Recent Drawings USA, 1956; Sante Fe, N.M., 1957; Younstown/Butler, 1957; Chicago/AI, 1957, 58; Brussels World's Fair, 1958; SFMA, After Surrealism, circ., 1959; MOMA, 1962; SFMA, 1962, 69; HemisFair '68, San Antonio, Tex., 1968; WMAA Annual, 1967; MOMA, Tamarind: Homage to Lithography, 1969; SFMA, Tamarind, 1969; International Exhibitions Foundation, Washington, D.C., Tamarind: A Renaissance of Lithography, circ., 1971-72; Houston/MFA, Wood in Art, 1979. **Collections:** Austin; Brooklyn Museum; Dallas/MFA; Denver/AM; Fort Worth; Hartford/Wadsworth; Houston/Contemporary; Houston/MFA; Inland Steel Co.; La Jolla; Los Angeles/County MA; MOMA; New Orleans/Delgado; Oak Cliff Savings and Loan; PMA; Pasadena/AM; SRGM; U. of Texas; UCLA; Underwood-Neuhaus Corp; WMAA; Witte; Youngstown/Butler. **Bibliography:** MacAgy 1. Archives.

BRACH, PAUL. b. March 13, 1924, NYC. **Studied:** Fieldston School, NYC; State U. of Iowa (with Philip Guston, Mauricio Lasansky), 1941-42, 1945-48, BFA, 1967-69, MFA. US Army, 1942-45. Traveled Spain, France, Italy; resided in California, 1967-75. **Taught:** U. of Missouri, 1949-51; New School for Social Research, 1952-55; Parsons School of Design, 1956-67; Cooper Union, 1960-62, 1978-80; U. of New Mexico, A.F.A. Visiting Artist, 1965; U. of California, San Diego, 1967-69; California Institute of the Arts, 1969-75; Fordham U., 1975-79; Lincoln Center Campus, 1975; Cooper Union, 1979-; Empire State College, 1979-. **Awards:** Tamarind Fellowship, 1964, 80, 82; **m.** Miriam Shapiro. **Address:** 393 W. Broadway, NYC 10012; Montauk Highway, East Hampton, NY 11037. **Dealer:** Bernice Steimbaum Gallery, NYC. **One-man Exhibitions:** (first) Leo Castelli Inc., 1957, also 1959; Union College (N.Y.), 1958; Dwan Gallery, 1960; Cordier and Warren, NYC, 1962; Cordier & Ekstrom Inc., 1964; U. of New Mexico, 1965; NYU, 1966; The Kornblee Gallery, 1968; Andre Emmerich Gallery, NYC, 1974; Cirrus Editions Ltd., 1975; Benson Gallery, 1975; Lerner-Heller Gallery, NYC, 1978, 80; Yares Gallery, Scottsdale, Ariz., 1979; Janus Gallery, Venice, Calif., 1980; Janus Gallery, Los Angeles, 1980; Yares Gallery, Scottsdale, Ariz., 1981; Bernice Steinbaum Gallery, 1983, 84, 85, 86. **Retrospective:** Newport Harbor and La Jolla/MA, Paul Brach and Miriam Schapiro, 1969. **Group:** WMAA; Chicago/AI; Corcoran; Baltimore/MA; St. Louis/City; Jewish Museum; Brandeis U., 1964; MOMA, The Responsive Eye, 1965; SFMA, 1965; Los Angeles/County MA, 1970; MOMA, Tamarind: Homage to Lithography, 1969; Newport Harbor, 1974; Hudson River Museum, New Vistas, 1984. **Collections:** Albion College; U. of Arizona; Avco Corp.; U. of California, San Diego; Los Angeles/County MA; MOMA; Newport Harbor; NYU; U. of Nebraska; U. of New Mexico; Nova Scotia College of Art and Design; St. Louis/City; Smith College; WMAA. **Bibliography:** Blesh 1; Sandler; Weller.

BRACKMAN, ROBERT. b. September 25, 1898, Odessa, Russia, **d.** July 16, 1980, New London, Conn. **Studied:** Ferrer School, San Francisco; NAD; and with George Bellows, Robert Henri. **Taught:** ASL, 1934-75; American Art School, NYC, 1951-80;

Brooklyn Museum School, 1936-38. **Member:** Royal Society of Arts. Consultant on the motion picture *A Portrait of Jennie,* 1950. **Awards:** Chicago/AI, 1929; NAD: The Thomas B. Clarke Prize, 1932; Saltus Gold Medal for Merit, 1941; Andrew Carnegie Prize, 1965; Gold Medal of Honor, 1966; Noel Flagg Prize, 1936; Connecticut Academy of Fine Arts, First Award, 1947; Carnegie, Hon. Men., 1949; PAFA, Carol H. Beck Gold Medal, 1958; Audubon Artists, **P.P.,** 1960; elected to Royal Society of Arts, London, 1962; Ford Foundation Grant, 1965. **One-man Exhibitions:** Macbeth Gallery, NYC, 1930, 31, 33, 34, 36, 40, 44; Grand Central, NYC, 1946. **Group:** NAD; Connecticut Academy of Fine Arts; PAFA; Audubon Artists; Montclair/AM. **Collections:** Atlanta/AA; Britannica; Brooklyn Museum; Bryn Mawr College; Canajoharie; The U. of Chicago; Colonial Williamsburg; Connecticut Life Insurance Company; U. of Connecticut; Davenport/Municipal; U. of Georgia; Harvard U.; Honolulu Academy; Houston/MFA; IBM; MMA; Memphis/Brooks; Milton Academy; Minneapolis/Institute; Montclair/AM; Newark Museum; New Britain; New Haven Public Library; Norfolk/Chrysler; Pasadena/AM; The Pentagon; Princeton U.; RISD; Radio Corporation of America; U. of Rochester; Rockford/Burpee; Toledo/MA; US Military Academy; US State Department; West Palm Beach/Norton; Wilmington; Yale U. **Bibliography:** Bates; Bazin; Boswell 1; Cheney; Hall; Jewell 2, 3; Watson, E. W., 1. Archives.

BRADY, CAROLYN. b. March 22, 1937, Chickasha, Oklahoma. **Studied:** Oklahoma State U., 1955-58; U. of Oklahoma, 1958-59, BFA, 1959-61, MFA. **Taught:** U. of Missouri, 1974. **Address:** 216 Laurens Street, Baltimore, Md., 21217. **Dealer:** Nancy Hoffman Gallery, NYC. **One-man Ex-**

hibitions: (first) Nancy Singer Gallery, St. Louis, 1974; Nancy Hoffman Gallery, 1977, 80, 83, 85; U. of Rhode Island, 1977; U. of Missouri, Kansas City, 1978; U. of Missouri, St. Louis, 1978; San Jose Museum of Art (two-man), 1978; Pittsburgh Center for the Arts, 1980; Charlotte/Mint, 1982; Columbia, S.C./MA, 1982; Jerald Melberg Gallery, Charlotte, N.C., 1985. Group: U. of North Carolina, Art on Paper, 1975; San Antonio/McNay, American Artists '76: A Celebration, 1976; Akron/AI, Contemporary Images in Watercolor, 1976; U. of Nebraska, Realists, 1978; Tulsa/Philbrook, Realism/Photorealism, 1980; Buffalo/Albright, Still-Life, 1981; PAFA, Contemporary American Realism Since 1960, 1981; San Antonio/MA, Real, Really Real, Super Real, 1981; Indianapolis, 1984; SFMA, American Realism (Janss), circ., 1985. Collections: Charlotte/Mint; Indiana U.; Louisville/Speed; MMA; New Britain/American; Oklahoma; U. of Oklahoma; U. of Rochester; St. Louis/City; San Antonio/McNay; Springfield, Mo./AM; Wilmington; Worcester/AM. Bibliography: Arthur 3.

BRAINARD, JOE. b. March 11, 1942, Salem, Ark. A poet who has published many books. Taught: Cooper Union, 1967-68. Awards: Copley Foundation Grant. Address: 8 Green Street, NYC 10013. Dealer: Fischbach Gallery, NYC. One-man Exhibitions: The Alan Gallery, NYC, 1965; The Landau-Alan Gallery, NYC, 1967, 69; Gotham Book Mart, NYC, 1968; Jerrold Morris Gallery, Toronto, 1968; Benson Gallery, 1970; Phyllis Kind Gallery, Chicago, 1970; Fischbach Gallery, NYC, 1971, 72, 74, 75; School of Visual Arts, NYC, 1972; New York Cultural Center, 1972; Utah, 1973; Vick Gallery, Philadelphia, 1976; EG Gallery, Kansas City, Mo., 1976; Suzette Schochett Gallery, Newport, R.I., 1976; Coventry Gallery, Paddington, N.S.W., 1976; Hamilton College, N.Y., 1977; Benson Gallery,

Bridgehampton, N.Y., 1977; Art 3 Associates, Savannah, Ga., 1978. Group: U. of North Carolina, 1967; MOMA, In Memory of My Feelings: Frank O'Hara, 1967; U. of Illinois, 1969; VMFA, 1968; Chicago/Contemporary, White on White, 1972; Corcoran, Seven Young Artists, 1972; Moore College of Art, Philadelphia, Artists' Books, 1973; Harvard U., New American Graphic Art, 1973; Yale U., American Drawing: 1970-73, 1973; Tyler School of Art, Philadelphia, American Drawings, 1973; William Paterson College, N.J., Contemporary Drawing, 1975. Collections: Amerada-Hess Corp., Inc., NYC; Chase Manhattan Bank, NYC; Colorado Springs/FA; Harvard U.; U. of Kansas; Liaison Films, Inc.; McCrory Corp., NYC; MOMA; RISD; Time Inc.; Utah; WMAA. Bibliography: Poets & Painters; Lucie-Smith.

BRANDT, WARREN. b. February 26, 1918, Greensboro, N.C. Studied: Pratt Institute, 1935-37; ASL, 1946, with Yasuo Kuniyoshi; Washington U., with Philip Guston, Max Beckmann, 1947-48, BFA with honors; U. of North Carolina, 1953, MFA. Traveled Mexico, Europe. Taught: Salem College, 1949-50; Pratt Institute, 1950-52; Guilford College, 1952-56; U. of Mississippi, 1957-59; Southern Illinois U., 1959-61; School of Visual Arts, NYC, 1962-63; Director, New York Studio School, 1967. Member: NAD; US Air Corps, 1940-45. Awards: John T. Milliken Traveling Fellowship. m. Grace Borgenicht. Address: 879 United Nations Plaza, NYC 10017. Dealer: Fischbach Gallery, NYC. One-man Exhibitions: (first) Sacramento State College, 1943; Nonagon Gallery, NYC, 1959; Memphis State U., 1960; New Gallery, Provincetown, 1960; Michigan State U., 1961; The American Gallery, NYC, 1961; Esther Stuttman Gallery, Provincetown, 1962; Grippi Gallery, NYC, 1963, 64; Obelisk Gallery, Washington, D.C., 1963; Grippi and Waddell Gallery, NYC, 1964; A. M. Sachs Gallery, 1966, 67, 68, 70, 72, 73, 74, 75; U. of North Carolina, 1967; Reed College, 1967; Benson Gallery, 1967; Eastern Illinois U., 1968; Salem College, 1968; Molly Barnes Gallery, Los Angeles, 1968; Cord Gallery, Southampton, N.Y., 1968; Allentown/AM, 1969; Grand Avenue Galleries, Milwaukee, 1969; Mercury Gallery, London, 1969, 72; David Barnett Gallery, Milwaukee, 1969, 71, 74, 78, 80; Allentown/MA, 1969; Agra Gallery, Washington, D.C., 1969, 70; Pratt Manhattan Center, NYC, 1970; Hooks Epstein Gallery, Houston, 1971, 73; Agra Gallery, Palm Beach, 1971; Guild Hall, East Hampton, N.Y., 1973, 74; Benson Gallery, Bridgehampton, N.Y., 1976; Vick Gallery, Philadelphia, 1976; Raleigh/NCMA, 1977; Fischbach Gallery, NYC, 1977, 80, 83, 85; Allenhouse Gallery, Louisville, Ky., 1978; Fontana Gallery, Narbeth, Pa., 1978. **Retrospectives:** Allentown/AM, 1962-1968; Beaumont Art Museum 1976; Greenhill Gallery, Greensboro, 1982. **Group:** MMA, American Watercolors, Drawings and Prints, 1952; WMAA; Brooklyn Museum, Print Biennials; VMFA, Virginia Artists Biennial; PAFA; A.F.A.; Syracuse/Everson, Provincetown Painters 1890s-1970s, 1977; U. of Missouri, American Painterly Realists, 1977; Corcoran, The Human Form: Contemporary American Figure Drawing and the Academic Tradition, 1980; AFA, the Figure in Twentieth-Century American Art, circ., 1985. **Collections:** Beaumont Art Museum; Carnegie; Chase Manhattan Bank; Ciba-Geigy Corp., Currier; Guild Hall; Hirshhorn; MMA; Michigan State U.; Milwaukee; NCFA; Norfolk/Chrysler; U. of North Carolina; New Mexico State U.; U. of Rochester; Southern Illinois U.; U. of Texas; WGMA. **Bibliography:** Archives.

BRAUNTUCH, TROY. b. 1954, Jersey City, N.J. **Studied:** California Institute of the Arts, 1975, BFA. **Address:** 182 Grand Street, NYC 10013. **Dealer:** Mary Boone Gallery, NYC. **One-man Exhibitions:** The Kitchen, NYC, 1979; Metro Pictures, NYC, 1981; Mary Boone Gallery, 1982, 83, 85; Galerie Schellman and Kluser, Munich, 1983; Akira Ikeda Gallery, Tokyo, 1984. **Group:** Cologne/Stadt, Westkunst, 1981; MIT, Figurative Aspects of Recent Art, 1981; Documenta VII, Kassel, 1982; XL Venice Biennial, 1982; Hannover/K-G, New York Now, circ., 1982; Osaka/National, Modern Nude Paintings, 1983; Bonn, Back to the USA, circ., 1983; Tate Gallery, New Art, 1983; Independent Curators Inc., NYC, Drawings after Photography, 1984; Houston/Contemporary, American Still Life, 1945-1983, 1983. **Bibliography:** Back to the USA; Haenlein.

BRECHT, GEORGE. b. 1925, NYC. **Studied:** Philadelphia College of Pharmacy and Science, BSC; Rutgers U.; New School for Social Research, with John Cage, 1958-59; Samuel S. Fleischer Art Memorial, Philadelphia. Traveled Western Europe, Mexico. **Taught:** Leeds (England) College of Art, 1968-69. Founder, *Sight Unseen*, a journal on research science and speculative art, 1968-69. **Commissions:** Music and sets for James Waring Dance Company, NYC. **Address:** Wildenburgstrasse 9, 5 Cologne-Sulz, West Germany. **One-man Exhibitions:** (first) Reuben Gallery, NYC, 1959; Fischbach Gallery, 1965; Galleria Schwarz, 1967, 69; Galerie Rudolf Zwirner, 1969; Mayer Gallery, Stuttgart, 1969; Los Angeles/County MA, 1969; Onnasch Gallery, 1973. **Group:** Martha Jackson Gallery, New Media—New Forms, I & II, 1960, 61; Stockholm/National, Art in Motion, 1961; MOMA, The Art of Assemblage, circ., 1961; Buffalo/Albright, Mixed Media and Pop Art, 1963; Oakland/AM, Pop Art USA, 1963; Hartford/Wadsworth, Black, White, and Gray, 1964; Smith College, Sight and Sound; Jewish Museum, Superlimited, 1969; Tate, Pop Art, 1969; SRGM, Eleven from the Reuben Gallery, 1965; Chicago/Contemporary, Art by Telephone, 1969; Berne, Art after Plans, 1969; Documenta V, Kassel, 1972; Rijksuniversiteit, Utrecht, Toeval, 1972. Theater Pieces: Fluxus International Festival, NYC, 1962-63; Smolin Gallery, NYC, Yam Festival: A Series of Events, 1963; Arman's Key Event, NYC, 1965. **Collections:** CNAC; MOMA; Monchengladbach. **Bibliography:** Alloway 5; Becker and Vostell; *Contemporanea;* Gerdts; Hansen; *Happening & Fluxus;* Haskell 5. Hunter, ed.; Johnson, Ellen H.; Kaprow; Lippard, ed.; *Report;* Richie; Russell and Gablik; Sandler 1.

BREER, ROBERT C. b. September 20, 1926, Detroit, Mich. **Studied:** Stanford U., BA. Resided Paris, 1949-59. Traveled Japan, 1969, Europe. **Taught:** Cooper Union, 1972-; Film Study Center, Cambridge, Mass.; Hampshire College, Amherst, Mass., 1974-79; Hampshire College, 1974-79; NYU, 1977. **Commissions:** Expo 70, Osaka, Pepsi-Cola Pavilion, 1970. **Awards:** Stanford U., Annual Painting Award, 1949; Creative Film Foundation Awards, 1957-60; Bergamo, Diplome Speciale, 1962; Oberhausen Film Festival, Max Ernst Prize, 1969; Film Culture Award, 1973; CAPS, NYC, 1975; National Endowment for the Arts, grant, 1976; American Film Institute, grant, 1977; Guggenheim Foundation Fellowship, 1978-79. **Address:** 25 Shadyside, S. Nyack, NY 10960. **One-man Exhibitions:** (first) Palais des Beaux-Arts, Brussels, 1955; Galeria Bonino Ltd., NYC, 1965, 66, 67, 70; Galerie Rolf Ricke 1968; J. L. Hudson Art Gallery, Detroit, 1972; Dag Hammarskjold Plaza, NYC, 1973; Michael Berger Gallery, Pittsburgh, 1974; IBM Plaza, Pittsburgh, 1974; MOMA (films); Buffalo/Albright, 1976; Collective for Living Cinema, NYC, 1977; Walker 1979; Millennium, NYC, 1979. **Retrospectives:** Montreux Film Festival, 1974; Film Forum, NYC, 1975; WMAA, 1977, 1980. **Group:** WGMA, The Popular Im-

age, 1963; MOMA, 1963; ICA, Boston, 1965; Stockholm/National, 1965; U. of California, Berkeley, Directions in Kinetic Sculpture, 1966; Jewish Museum, 1967; VI International Art Biennial, San Marino (Europe), 1967; Experimental Film Festival, Brussels, 1967; A.F.A., 1968; MOMA, The Machine as Seen at the End of the Mechanical Age, 1968; UCLA, Electric Art, 1969; MOMA, New Media: New Methods, circ., 1969; Hayward Gallery, London, Kinetics, 1970; Buffalo/Albright, Kid Stuff, 1971; Yale U., Options and Alternatives, 1973; Cannes Film Festival, 1974; WMAA, 1977, 1980. Paris/Beaubourg, Paris-New York, 1977; Drawing Center, NYC, Drawings for Animated Film, 1978; Hayward Gallery, London, Film as Film, 1979; New York Film Festival, 1979; WMAA Biennial, 1979. **Collections:** Anthology Film Archives; CNAC; Cinematheque de Belgique; Cinematheque Francaise; Krefeld/Kaiser Wilhelm; MOMA; NYPL; Stockholm/National. **Bibliography:** *Art Now 74;* Battcock, ed.; Davis, D.; Hulten; *Options and Alternatives;* Rickey; Selz, P., 1; Tomkins. Archives.

BRICE, WILLIAM. b. April 23, 1921, NYC. **Studied:** ASL; Chouinard Art Institute, Los Angeles. Traveled England, Spain, Greece. **Taught:** Jepson Art Institute, Los Angeles; UCLA, 1953-. **Awards:** Tamarind Fellowship, 1961; UCLA, research grants, 1964, 74, 76. **Address:** 427 Beloit Street, Los Angeles, CA 90049. **Dealer:** Robert Miller Gallery, NYC. **One-man Exhibitions:** The Downtown Gallery, 1949; Frank Perls Gallery, 1952, 55, 56, 62; The Alan Gallery, NYC, 1955, 56, 64; Santa Barbara/MA, 1958; Felix Landau Gallery, 1966; U. of California, San Diego, 1967; Colorado Springs/FA, 1967; Dallas/MFA, 1967; SFMA, 1967; The Landau-Alan Gallery, NYC, 1968; Hancock College, Santa Maria, Calif., 1975; Orange Coast College, 1975; Charles Campbell Gallery, San Francisco, 1976; U. of Redlands, 1978; ICA, Los An-

William Brice *Untitled* 1984

geles, 1978; Nicholas Wilder Gallery, Los Angeles, 1978; Robert Miller Gallery, NYC, 1980, 84; Mary Porter Sesnon Gallery, Santa Cruz, Calif. 1980; California State U., Dominquez Hills, 1981; Smith-Anderson Gallery, Palo Alto, 1983; L.A. Louver Gallery, Venice, 1984; Temple U., 1984. **Group:** Santa Barbara/MA, 1945; WMAA, 1947, 50, 51; Los Angeles/County MA, 1947-50; Sao Paulo; Carnegie, 1948, 49, 54; U. of Illinois; MMA, 1952; MOMA, 1952, 56; Chicago/AI, 1952, 56; Paris/Moderne, 1954; California Palace, 1951, 52; SFMA; de Young; VMFA, 1966; Des Moines, 1967; Laguna Beach, Museum of Art, Drawings and Illustrations by Southern California Artists before 1950, 1981; Long Beach/MA,

Drawings by Painters, 1982; IEF, Twentieth Century American Drawings: The Figure in Context, circ., 1983. **Collections:** AAAL; Andover/Phillips; Chicago/AI; Florida State U.; Hirshhorn; U. of Illinois; Israel Museum; U. of Iowa; Los Angeles/County MA; Louisiana State U.; MMA; MOMA; U. of Nebraska; San Diego; Santa Barbara/MA; Stanford U.; Utica; WMAA; Wichita/AM. **Bibliography:** Armstrong; Pousette-Dart, ed. Archives.

BRIGGS, ERNEST. b. 1923, San Diego, Calif. **Studied:** California School of Fine Arts, with Clyfford Still, David Park, Mark Rothko. US Army, 1943-45. A cofounder of Metart Gallery, San

Francisco, 1949. **Taught:** U. of Florida, 1958; Pratt Institute, 1961-; Yale U., 1967-68. **Awards:** CSFA, Albert M. Bender Fellowship, 1951; SFMA, Anne Bremer Memorial Prize, 1953; CAPS, 1975. **Address:** 50 West 29th Street, NYC 10001. **Dealer:** Gruenebaum Gallery, NYC. **One-man Exhibitions:** (first) Metart Gallery, San Francisco, 1949; The Stable Gallery, NYC, 1954, 55; CSFA, 1956; The Howard Wise Gallery, NYC, 1960, 62, 63; Yale U., 1968; Alonzo Gallery, NYC, 1969; Green Mountain Gallery, 1973; Susan Caldwell, Inc., 1975; Aaron Berman Gallery, NYC, 1977; Cape Split Place, Addison, Me. **Group:** San Francisco Art Association Annuals, 1948, 49, 53; WMAA Annuals, 1955, 56, 61; California Palace, Five Bay Area Artists, 1953; MOMA, Twelve Americans, circ., 1956; Corcoran, 1961; Carnegie, 1961; Dallas/MFA, "1961," 1962; SFMA, 1962, 63; Jewish Museum, Large Scale American Painting, 1967; AAAL, 1969, 70; Oakland/AM, San Francisco, 1945-1950, 1973; SFMA, California Painting and Sculpture: The Modern Era, 1976; Huntsville, Bay Area Update, 1977. **Collections:** Brooklyn Museum; Carnegie; CIBA-Geigy Corp.; Housatonic Community College; Michigan State U.; Oakland/AM; Rockefeller Institute; SFMA; WMAA; Walker. **Bibliography:** McChesney; Sandler 1. Archives.

BRODERSON, MORRIS (Gaylord). b. November 4, 1928, Los Angeles, Calif. **Studied:** Pasadena Museum School; U. of Southern California, with Francis De Erdely; Jepson Art Institute, Los Angeles. Traveled Europe, Japan, India, Far East. **Awards:** Pasadena Museum School, Scholarship, 1943; Los Angeles/County MA, **P.P.**, *Art in America* (magazine), New Talent, 1959; Los Angeles Art Festival, 1961; Carnegie, 1961. **Address:** % Dealer. **Dealer:** Ankrum Gallery. **One-man Exhibitions:** Dixi Hall Studio, Laguna Beach, Calif., 1954; Stanford U., 1958; Santa Bar-

bara/MA, 1958; U. of California, Riverside, 1959; Bertha Lewinson Gallery, Los Angeles, 1959, 60; Ankrum Gallery, 1961, 62, 70, 79; The Downtown Gallery, 1963, 66; Los Angeles/County MA, 1966, 68; San Diego, 1969; Staempfli Gallery, 1971. **Retrospective:** San Diego, 1969; U. of Arizona, 1975. **Group:** Santa Barbara/MA, 1958; Los Angeles/MA, 1958, 59; PAFA, 1959, 60; Ringling, 1960; WMAA, 1960; de Young, 1960; California Palace, San Diego, 1961; Carnegie, 1961, 62, 64, 67; U. of Illinois, 1963; NIAL, 1967; Hirshhorn, Inaugural Exhibition, 1974; AAAL, 1976; NAD, 1977; Springfield, Mass./MFA, Bicentennial, Watercolor, USA, 1976; Santa Barbara/MA, Images of the Mind, 1976; Minnesota/MA, Art and the Law, 1979. **Collections:** Boston/MFA; Container Corp. of America; de Young; Hirshhorn; Home Savings and Loan Association; Honolulu Academy; Kalamazoo/Institute; La Jolla; Los Angeles/County MA; NIAL; Palm Springs Desert Museum; The Pennsylvania State U.; Phoenix; SFMA; San Antonio/McNay; San Diego; Santa Barbara/MA; U. of South Florida; Stanford U.; U. of Texas; WMAA; Yale U. **Bibliography:** Weller. Archives.

BRONER, ROBERT. b. March 10, 1922, Detroit, Mich. **Studied:** Wayne State U., 1940-46, BFA, MA; UCLA, 1946-47; Society of Arts and Crafts, Detroit, 1942-45; Atelier 17, NYC, 1949-52, with S. W. Hayter; New School for Social Research, 1949-50, with Stuart Davis. **Taught:** City U. of New York, 1963-64; Society of Arts and Crafts, Detroit; Wayne State U., 1964-86; Haystack Mountain School of Crafts, 1964, 66, 68, 70, 75, 80; U. of Haifa, 1975; Cooper Union, 1983-87; Detroit Times, 1958-60 (art critic); *Art in America* magazine, 1958-63 (correspondent); *Craft Horizons* magazine, 1961-68 (correspondent); Birmingham *Eccentric*, 1962-63 (art critic); *Pictures on Exhibit* magazine, 1963-64 (reviewer); Manhattanville College, 1976-77; Parsons School of Design,

NYC, 1977; Pratt Institute, 1978. **Member:** SAGA; Philadelphia Print Club; British Printmakers Council; President, The Print Council; President, SAGA, 1981-84. **Awards:** Brooklyn Museum, Print Biennial, **P.P.**, 1964; Los Angeles Art Festival, Bronze Medal, 1948; Detroit/Institute, Michigan Artist, **P.P.**, 1961, 66; SAGA, 50th Annual Print Exhibition, $1,000 **P.P.**, 1969; Wayne State U., Faculty Research Fellowship, 1965, 69; Probus Club, Achievement Award ($500), 1969; Michigan Council for the Arts Award, 1983, 86. **Address:** 40 West 22nd Street, NYC 10010. **One-man Exhibitions:** (first) Anna Werbe Gallery, Detroit, 1953; Wellons Gallery, NYC, 1954; Philadelphia Art Alliance, 1956; Garelick's Gallery, Detroit, 1956, 61; Michigan State U., 1957; Drake Gallery, Carmel, Calif., 1960; Society of Arts and Crafts, Detroit, 1962; Feingarten Gallery, Los Angeles, 1961; Raven Gallery, Birmingham, Mich., 1963; The Ohio State U., 1969; J. L. Hudson Art Gallery, Detroit, 1971; Rina Gallery, NYC, 1973; Klein-Vogel Gallery, Royal Oak, Mich.; Delson-Richter Gallery, Tel Aviv, 1975; Troy Gallery, Mich., 1977; Manhattanville College, Purchase, N.Y., 1977; Wayne State U., 1981; Merging One Gallery, Santa Monica, 1986, 87. **Group:** MMA, American Watercolors, Drawings, and Prints, 1952; MOMA, Young American Printmakers, 1953; Brooklyn Museum, Print Biennials; USIA, circ., Europe, 1959-60 (prints); PCA, circ., Europe and France, 1959-60; PAFA, 1959, 60; Pasadena/AM, 1962; SAGA, 1962, 63; ICA, London; Salon du Mai, Paris, 1969; British International Print Biennials, 1968, 70, 72; MOMA, Pop Art Prints, Drawings, and Multiples, 1970; Paris/ Moderne, La Jeune Gravure, 1970; Bibliotheque Nationale, L'Estampe Contemporaine, 1973; Walker, Printmakers, 1973. **Collections:** Bibliotheque Nationale; Boston Public Library; Brooklyn Museum; Chicago/AI; Cincinnati/AM; Detroit/Institute; Harvard U.; Jerusalem/National; Los Angeles/County MA; MMA; MOMA; NYPL; National Gallery; PAFA; PMA; SRGM; Smithsonian; Walker. **Bibliography:** Archives.

BROOK, ALEXANDER. b. July 14, 1898, Brooklyn, N.Y.; **d.** February 26, 1980, Sag Harbor, N.Y. **Studied:** ASL, 1913-17, with R. W. Johnson, Frank V. DuMont, George Bridgeman, Dimitri Romanovsky, Kenneth Hayes Miller. Assistant Director, Whitney Studio Club, NYC. **Commissions:** US Post Office, Washington, D.C. (mural). **Awards:** Chicago/AI, The Mr. & Mrs. Frank G. Logan Medal, 1929; Carnegie, Second Prize, 1930; PAFA, Joseph E. Temple Gold Medal, 1931; Guggenheim Foundation Fellowship, 1931; Carnegie, First Prize, 1939; Los Angeles/County MA, First Prize, 1934; Paris World's Fair, 1937, Gold Medal; SFMA, Medal of Award, 1938. **One-man Exhibitions:** ACA Gallery; Curt Valentine Gallery, NYC, 1930; The Downtown Gallery, 1934, 37; Dayton/AI, 1942; Rehn Galleries, 1947, 60; M. Knoedler & Co., NYC, 1952; Richard Larcada Gallery, 1969, 74; Salander-O'Reilly Galleries, 1980; Santa Fe East Galleries, Santa Fe, 1981. **Retrospective:** Chicago/AI, 1929. **Group:** U. of Rochester, 1937; Brooklyn Museum; Carnegie; MMA; Toledo/MA; Buffalo/Albright; Chicago/AI; Newark Museum. **Collections:** Boston/MFA; Britannica; Brooklyn Museum; Buffalo/Albright; California Palace; Carnegie; Chicago/AI; Columbus; Corcoran; Dartmouth College; Detroit/Institute; de Young; Hartford/Wadsworth; IBM; Indianapolis; Kansas City/Nelson; Los Angeles/County MA; MMA; MOMA; Michigan State U.; Ogunquit; PAFA; U. of Nebraska; Newark Museum; SFMA; St. Louis/City; Toledo/MA; WMAA; Youngstown/Butler. **Bibliography:** Baur 7; Bethers; Biddle 4; Boswell 1; **Brook;** Cahill and Barr, eds.; Cheney; Eliot; Flexner; Goodrich and Baur 1; Hall; *Index of 20th Century Artists;* **Jewell 1,** 2; Kent, N.; Mellquist; Mendelowitz; Pagano; Pearson 1; Pousette-Dart, ed.; Richardson, E.P.; *Woodstock.* Archives.

BROOKS, JAMES A. b. October 18, 1906, St. Louis, Mo. **Studied:** Southern Methodist U., 1923-25; Dallas Art Institute, 1925-26, with Martha Simkins; ASL, 1927-31, with Kimon Nicolaides, Boardman Robinson; privately with Wallace Harrison. Federal A.P.: 1937-42. US Army in Middle East, 1942-45. Traveled Italy. **Taught:** Columbia U., 1947-48; Pratt Institute, 1947-59; Yale U., 1955-60; American Academy, Rome, Artist-in-Residence, 1963; New College, Sarasota, Fla., 1965-67; Miami Beach (Fla.) Art Center, 1966; Queens College, 1966-67, 1968-69; U. of Pennsylvania, 1971, 72; Cooper Union, 1975. **Member:** Century Association; NIAL. **Commissions:** (murals): Woodside, N.Y., Library; La Guardia Airport; US Post Office, Little Falls, N.Y. **Awards:** Carnegie, Fifth Prize, 1952; Chicago/AI, The Mr. & Mrs. Frank G. Logan Medal, 1957; Chicago/AI, Norman Wait Harris Silver Medal and Prize, 1961; Ford Foundation **P.P.**, 1962; Guggenheim Foundation Fellowship, 1967-68; National Endowment for the Arts, 1973; National Arts Club Gold Medal, 1985. **Address:** 128 Neck Path, The Springs, East Hampton, NY 11937. **Dealer:** Gruenebaum Gallery, Ltd., NYC. **One-man Exhibitions:** The Peridot Gallery, 1950, also 1951-53; Grace Borgenicht Gallery, Inc., 1954; The Stable Gallery, 1957, 59; The Kootz Gallery, NYC, 1961, 62; Philadelphia Art Alliance, 1966; Martha Jackson Gallery, 1968, 71, 73, 75; The Berenson Gallery, 1969; Gruenebaum Gallery, Ltd., NYC, 1979, 81, 84; Montclair/AM, 1979; Himmelfarb Gallery, Water Mill, N.Y., 1977, 78, 81; Dan Flavin Art Institute, Bridgehampton, N.Y., 1985. **Retrospectives:** WMAA, circ., 1963-64; Dallas/MFA, 1972; Finch College, NYC, circ., 1975; Portland, Me./AM, 1983.

Group: WMAA Annuals from the 1950s; Galerie de France, American Vanguard, 1952; Carnegie, 1952, 55, 58, 61; SRGM, Younger American Painters, 1954; WMAA, The New Decade, 1954-55; MOMA, Twelve Americans, circ., 1956; IV Sao Paulo Biennial, 1957; MOMA, The New American Painting, circ., Europe, 1958-59; Documenta II, Kassel, 1959; II Inter-American Paintings and Prints Biennial, Mexico City, 1960; SRGM, Abstract Expressionists and Imagists, 1961; Seattle World's Fair, 1962; Cleveland/MA, 1963; SMFA, 1963; Tate, Dunn International, 1964; MOMA, The New American Painting and Sculpture, 1969; WMAA Annuals, 1970, 72; U. of Illinois, 1971; Ball State U., Collages by American Artists, 1971; Cranbrook, Drawings by Contemporary American Artists, 1975; Corcoran Biennial, 1975; Brooklyn Museum, Thirty Years of American Printmaking, 1976; Hofstra U., Art for the People, 1978; Haus der Kunst, Munich, Amerikanische Malerie: 1930-1980, 1980; Houston/Contemporary, The Americans: The Collage, 1983; NMAA, Martha Jackson Memorial Collection, 1985. **Collections:** Boston/MFA; Brandeis U.; Brooklyn Museum; Buffalo/Albright; U. of California, Berkeley, Carnegie; Chase Manhattan Bank; Chicago/AI; Ciba-Geigy Corp.; The Coca-Cola Co.; Dallas/MFA; Detroit/Institute; Fordham U.; Hartford/Wadsworth; Harvard U.; Houston/MFA; U. of Illinois; International Minerals & Chemicals Corp.; MMA; MOMA; Mexico City/Tamayo; U. of Michigan; Miles Metal Corp.; Montclair/AM; NYU; U. of Nebraska; Owens-Corning Fiberglas Corp.; PAFA; Pepsi-Cola Co.; Philip Morris; Portland, Me./AM; Rockefeller U.; SRGM; The Singer Company Inc.; Southern Methodist U.; Tate; U. of Texas; Toledo/MA; Tulsa/Philbrook; Union Carbide Corp.; Utica; VMFA; WMAA; Walker; Yale U. **Bibliography:** Chaet; Flanagan; Goodrich and Baur 1; Haftman; Hess, T. B., 1; **Hunter** 1, 3, 6; Hunter, ed.; McCurdy, ed.; *Metro;* Motherwell and Reinhardt, eds.; Ponente; Pousette-Dart, ed.; Ritchie 1; Rodman 2; Sandler. Archives.

BROWN, JOAN. b. 1938, San Francisco, Calif. **Studied:** California School of Fine Arts, 1955; With Elmer Bischoff, Frank Lobdell, Sonia Gechtoff, Richard Diebenkorn, Manual Neri, Robert Howard, 1957-62. **Taught:** Raymond Wilkins High School, San Francisco, 1959; SFAI, 1961-; Sacramento State College, 1970-71; Academy of Art, San Francisco, 1971-73; U. of California, Berkeley, 1974-. **Awards:** SFAI, Adaline Kent Award, 1973; National Endowment for the Arts, Grant, 1976; Guggenheim Foundation Fellowship, 1977; National Endowment for the Arts, 1980. **Address:** 37 Cameo Way, San Francisco, CA **Dealer:** Allan Frumkin Gallery. **One-man Exhibitions:** Spasta Gallery, San Francisco, 1958; Staempfli Gallery, 1960 (two-man), 1961, 64; Batman Gallery, San Francisco, 1961; Ferus Gallery, Los Angeles, 1962; Hanson-Fuller Gallery, 1968, 78, 79, 80, 82; Lawson Galleries, San Francisco, 1970; SFMA, 1971; SFAI, 1973; Charles Campbell Gallery, San Francisco, 1974, 75; U. of California, Berkeley, 1974; Allan Frumkin Gallery, NYC, 1974, 76, 79, 81, 82, 83; Allan Frumkin Gallery, Chicago, 1975-77; Clarke-Benton Gallery, Santa Fe, 1977; Re: Vision Gallery, Santa Monica, 1976; Wadsworth/Hartford, 1977; U. of Akron, 1977; San Jose/MA, 1979; Newport Harbor, 1978; U. of Colorado, 1978; San Jose, 1979; U. of California, Berkeley, 1979; Whitman College, 1980; Fountain Gallery, Portland, Ore., 1981; U. of Hawaii, 1981; Koplin Gallery, Los Angeles, 1982, 83; Frumkin & Struve Gallery, Chicago, 1984; Santa Cruz County, Calif., Historical Museum, 1984; Monterey Peninsula Museum of Art, circ., 1985; U. of Redlands, 1985. **Retrospective:** U. of California, Berkeley, 1974. **Group:** Oakland/AM; RAC; SFMA; PAFA; SFAI; Drawing Invitational, 1969; WMAA, 1972; Mt. Holyoke College, Art as a Muscular

Principle, 1975; WMAA Biennial, 1977; New Museum, NYC, Bad Painting Show, 1978; U. of North Carolina, Art on Paper, 1978; American Foundation for the Arts, Miami, Story-Telling Art, 1979; PAFA, Seven on the Figure, 1979; Norfolk/Chrysler, American Figurative Painting, 1950-1980, 1980; Newport Harbor, Inside Out: Self Beyond Likeness, 1981; Columbus, American Painting of the 60's and 70's, 1981; Rutgers U., Realism and Realities, 1982; Palm Springs Desert Museum, The West as Art, 1982; WMAA, Focus on the Figure, 1982; Chicago/AI, 74th American Exhibitions, 1982; Corcoran Biennial, 1983; SFMA, The Human Condition, 1984; U. of Nebraska, San Francisco Bay Area Painting, 1984; Hirshhorn, Content: A Contemporary Focus, 1974-1984, 1984; NYU, The Figurative Mode, 1984; Oakland/AM, Art in the San Francisco Bay Area, 1945-1980, 1985. **Collections:** Buffalo/Albright; U. of California; U. of Colorado; Federal Reserve Bank, San Francisco; Long Beach/MA; Los Angeles/County MA; Miami-Dade College; MOMA; Newport Harbor; Oakland/AM; Sacramento/Crocker; SFMA; WMAA; Williams College. **Bibliography:** *Art as a Muscular Principle; Art: A Woman's Sensibility*, McChesney; Lucie-Smith; Richardson, B., 1; Schwartz, 2; Selz, P., 2. Archives.

BROWN, ROGER. b. December 10, 1941, Hamilton, Alabama. **Studied:** American Academy of Art, Chicago, 1964; Chicago Art Institute School, BFA and MFA, 1970. **Awards:** Renaissance Prize, Chicago/AI, 1969; Walter Campana prize, 1971, Chicago/AI. **Address:** 1926 N. Halsted, Chicago, IL. **Dealer:** Phyllis Kind Gallery, NYC, Chicago. **One-man Exhibitions:** Phyllis Kind Gallery, Chicago, 1971, 73, 74, 76, 77, 79, 80, 82; Phyllis Kind Gallery, NYC, 1975, 77, 79, 81, 82, 84; PAFA, 1974; Darthea Speyer Gallery, Paris, 1974; PAFA, Peale House, 1974; U. of California, Berkeley, 1980; Montgom-

Roger Brown *Corporate Farms* 1985

ery Museum, 1980; Mayor Gallery, London, 1981; Texas Gallery, Houston, 1985. **Retrospective:** U. of South Florida, circ., 1984. **Group:** Chicago/Contemporary, Don Baum Sez, "Chicago Needs Famous Artists," 1969; ICA, U. of Pennsylvania, Spirit of the Comics, 1969; Chicago/Contemporary, Chicago Imagist Art, 1972; WMAA Biennials, 1973, 79; Sao Paulo Biennial, 1974; Chicago Art Institute School, Former Famous Alumni, 1976; Sacramento/Crocker, The Chicago Connection, 1977; U. of Texas, Austin, New In the Seventies, 1977; Buffalo/Albright, American Paintings in the 1970s, 1978; Tyler School of Art, Philadelphia, Intricate Structure/Repeated Image, 1979; WMAA, The Figurative Tradition and the WMAA, 1980; Sunderland (Eng.) Arts Centre, Who Chicago?, circ., 1980; Haus der Kunst, Munich, Amerikanische Malerie: 1930-1980, 1981; Indianapolis, 1982; The New Museum, The End of the World, 1983; Los An-

geles/MOCA, Automobile and Culture, 1984; MOMA, International Survey of Recent Painting and Sculpture, 1984; Hirshhorn, Contemporary Focus, 1984; XLI Venice Biennial, 1984; Corcoran Biennial, 1985. **Collections:** Akron/AI; Atlantic Richfield Co.; AT&T; Blue Cross of Southern California; Boston/MFA; Chicago/AI; Chicago/Contemporary; Corcoran; Edinburgh/National; High Museum; Indianapolis; MMA; Montgomery Museum; Museum des 20. Jahrhunderts; MOMA; NCFA; NMAA; U. of North Carolina; Rotterdam; WMAA. **Bibliography:** Adrian; *The Chicago Connection; New in the Seventies; Who Chicago?.*

BROWN, WILLIAM THEO. b. April 7, 1919, Moline, Ill. **Studied:** Yale U., 1941, BA; U. of California, Berkeley, 1952, MA. Traveled Europe. **Taught:** U. of California, Berkeley and Davis; California School of Fine Arts. **Address:** 1151 Keeler, Berkeley, CA 94708. **One-man Exhibitions:** SFMA, 1957; Felix Landau Gallery, 1958, 60, 63, 65, 67, 71; Barone Gallery, NYC, 1961; The Kornblee Gallery, 1962; Esther Baer Gallery, 1964 (two-man, with Paul Wonner); Hollis Gallery, San Francisco, 1965; Sacramento/Crocker, 1965; The Landau/Alan Gallery, NYC, 1968. **Group:** Oakland/AM, Annuals, 1952-58; RAC Annuals, 1952-58; SFMA Annuals, 1952-58; Minneapolis/Institute, American Painting, 1945-57, 1957; Oakland/AM, Contemporary Bay Area Figurative Painting, 1957; Santa Barbara/MA, II & III Pacific Coast Biennials, 1957, 59; SFMA, West Coast Artists, circ., 1957, 59; California Palace, 1959; The Zabriskie Gallery, East-West, 1960; U. of New Mexico, circ., 1964-67; Louisville/Speed, 1965; VMFA, 1966; U. of Illinois, 1969. **Collections:** California Palace; Capitol Records, Inc.; Commerce Trust Co., Kansas City, Mo.; Davenport/Municipal; U. of Kansas; U. of Nebraska; Oakland/AM; Reader's Digest; SFMA. **Bibliography:** Archives.

BROWNE, BYRON. b. 1907, Yonkers, N.Y.; **d.** December 25, 1961. **Studied:** NAD, 1924-28, with C. W. Hawthorne, Ivan Olinsky. **Taught:** ASL, 1948-61. Charter Member, American Abstract Artists. **Awards:** U. of Illinois, **P.P.;** PAFA, **P.P;** NAD, Hallgarten Prize, 1928; La Tausca Competition, Third Prize. **One-man Exhibitions:** (first) New School for Social Research, 1936, also 1937; Artists' Gallery, NYC, 1939; The Pinacotheca, NYC, 1943, 44; The Kootz Gallery, NYC, 1946-48; Grand Central, NYC, 1949, 50, 53; Grand Central Moderns, NYC, 1950, 51, 52, 54, 55, 57, 58, 61, 62; Syracuse U., 1952; Tirca Karlis Gallery, 1960; ASL, Memorial Exhibition, 1962; Washburn Gallery, Inc., 1975, 77; Harmon Gallery, Naples, Fla., 1982; Yares Gallery, Scottsdale, Ariz., 1982; Martin Diamond Fine Arts, NYC, 1983; Gallery Schlesigner-Boisanté, NYC, 1984, 86; Harmon-Meek Gallery, Naples, Fla., 1984; Harmon Galleries, Sarasota, Fla., 1985; Meredith Long & Co., Houston, 1985; Galerie Lopes, Zurich, 1985; ASB Gallery, London, 1985. **Group:** Chicago/AI; Carnegie; WMAA; Corcoran; MOMA; MMA; ART: USA, NYC; U. of Illinois; PAFA. **Collections:** Boston/ MFA; Brown U.; Cornell U.; Dallas/ MFA; U. of Georgia; Harvard U.; High Museum; Hirshhorn; Indiana U.; MMA; MOMA; Milwaukee; U. of Minnesota; NIAL; NMAA; U. of Nebraska; Newark Museum; New Paltz/SUNY; Ohio U.; U. of Oklahoma; PAFA; Pace U.; Rio de Janeiro; U. of Rochester; Roswell; San Antonio/McNay; Syracuse/Everson; Tel Aviv; U. of Texas; Trenton/State; Utica; VMFA; WMAA; Walker; Williams College; Youngstown/Butler. **Bibliography:** Baur 7; Blesh 1; Cheney; Janis; Kootz 2; Marter; Pousette-Dart, ed.; Ritchie 1. Archives.

BROWNING, COLLEEN. b. May 18, 1929, Fermoy, County Cork, Ireland. **Studied:** Privately, and U. of London, Slade School. Traveled the world extensively. **Taught:** City College of New York, 1962-75; NAD, 1978-80. Illustrated many children's books. **Member:** NAD. **Awards:** Carnegie, Edwin Austin Abbey Fellowship; Tupperware National Competition; Yaddo Fellowship; Los Angeles County Fair, 1956; Columbia, S.C./MA, Biennial, 1957; MacDowell Colony Fellowship. **Address:** 100 La Salle Street, NYC 10027. **Dealer:** Kennedy Gallery. **One-man Exhibitions:** Robert Isaacson Gallery, NYC; Little Gallery, London, 1949; Hewitt Gallery, NYC, 1951, 52, 54; J. Seligmann and Co., 1965, 67; Lehigh U., 1966; Lane Gallery, Los Angeles, 1968; Kennedy Gallery, 1968-72, 76, 79, 86; Columbia S.C./MA, 1972; S.C. Museum, 1972; Columbus, Ga., 1972; Towson State College, Md., 1978. **Group:** A.F.A., 20th Century Realists; WMAA Annual; Chicago/AI; PAFA; NAD; NIAL; ART: USA, NYC; Walker; Carnegie; Festival of Two Worlds, Spoleto; Youngstown/Butler; Brandeis U.; U. of Rochester; U. of Illinois. **Collections:** California Palace; Columbia, S.C./MA; Corcoran; Detroit/Institute; U. of Miami; Milwaukee; NAD; New York State Museum, Albany; Randolph-Macon Woman's College; U. of Rochester; St. Louis/City; Wichita/AM; Williams College; Youngstown/Butler.

BRUCE, PATRICK HENRY. b. April 2, 1880, Long Island, Va.; **d.** November 12, 1937, NYC. **Studied:** Richmond (Va.) Art School; New York School of Art, with Robert Henri, W.M. Chase, 1901-03; with Henri Matisse in Paris, 1909. Traveled Europe; resided Paris, 1904-36. **One-man Exhibitions:** Rose Fried Gallery (three-man), 1950; Coe Kerr Gallery, 1970; Washburn Gallery, Inc., NYC, 1980; Federal Reserve Board, Washington, D.C., 1981. **Retrospective:** MOMA, 1979. **Group:** Salon d'Automne, Paris, 1907-10; The Armory Show, 1913; Herbstalon, 1913; Montross Gallery, NYC, 1916, 17; Societe Anonyme, 1920; Worcester, Mass., 1921; MacDowell Club, NYC,

1922; Vassar College, 1923; WMAA, The Decade of the Armory Show, 1963; U. of New Mexico, Cubism: Its Impact in the USA, 1967; Utica, Armory Show 50th Anniversary Exhibit, 1963; NAD; Hirshhorn, Inaugural Exhibition, 1974. **Collections:** U. of Nebraska; Yale U. **Bibliography:** *Avant-Garde Painting and Sculpture;* Baur 7; Brown 2; Dreier 2; DuBois 1; Hunter 6; Levin 2; MacAgy 2; Ritchie 1; Rose, B., 1; Seuphor 1; Wright 2. Archives.

BUCHWALD, HOWARD. b. 1943, NYC. **Studied:** Cooper Union, 1960-64, BFA; Hunter College, 1972, MA. **Taught:** Hofstra U., 1969-71; Kingsborough Community College, 1972-74; Richmond Community College, 1973-74; Queens College, 1974-75; Princeton U., 1975-82; Pratt Institute, 1972-; Columbia U., 1982-. **Awards:** Guggenheim Foundation Fellowship, 1974-75; National Endowment for the Arts, 1981; CAPS, grant, 1983. **Address:** 155 Suffolk Street, NYC, 10002. **Dealer:** Nancy Hoffman Gallery, NYC. **One-man Exhibitions:** French & Co., NYC, 1971; Nancy Hoffman Gallery, 1973, 74, 75, 76, 78, 82, 84, 85, 87; Galerie Swart, Amsterdam, 1974; Galerie Farideh Cadot, Paris, 1976, 78; Mary Boone Gallery, NYC, 1979, 80; Janet Steinberg Gallery, San Francisco, 1986. **Group:** WMAA Biennial, 1973; WMAA, American Drawings: 1963-73, 1973; Potsdam/SUNY, Abstraction Alive and Well, 1975; Indianapolis/MA, Painting and Sculpture Today 1978, 1978; NYU, The Eighties, 1979; U. of North Carolina, Art on Paper, 1983; Princeton U., A Decade of Visual Arts at Princeton, 1985. **Collections:** Bank of Oklahoma; Chase Manhattan Bank; Goldman Sachs, & Co., NYC; McCrory Corp.; Miami-Dade; WMAA.

BUCK, JOHN. b. February 14, 1946, Ames, Iowa. **Studied:** Kansas City/AI, BFA, 1964-68; U. of California, Davis, MFA, 1970-72; Skowhegan School,

1971; Gloustershire College of Art and Technology, 1972-73. **Taught:** U. of California, Davis, 1971-72; Gloustershire College of Art and Design, 1972-73; Humboldt State U., 1973-75; Miracosta College, 1975; Montana State U., 1976-. **Awards:** Skowhegan School, scholarship; National Endowment for the Arts, 1980; National Artists Award, 1984. **m.** Deborah Butterfield. **Address:** 11229 Cottonwood Road, Bozeman, Mt. 59715. **Dealer:** Zolla/Lieberman Gallery, Chicago. **One-man Exhibitions:** Miracosta College, 1974; U. of Kentucky, Lexington, 1975; Hansen Fuller Goldeen Gallery, San Francisco, 1979, 81, 83; Morgan Gallery, Shawnee Mission, Mo., 1981; U. of California, Davis, 1982; Yellowstone Art Center, circ., 1983-84; Zolla/Lieberman Gallery, 1983; Asher/Faure, Los Angeles, 1984; U. of New Mexico, Las Cruces (two-man) 1983; Carlo Lamagna Gallery, NYC, 1985. **Group:** California State U., Fullerton, Visions and Figurations, 1980; Indianapolis, 1980; Palm Springs Desert Museum, The West as Art, 1982; Fresno Art Center, Forgotten Dimension, 1982; Brooklyn Museum, The American Artist as Printmaker, 1983; Corcoran, Second Western States Exhibition, 1983; MOMA, Prints from Blocks: Gauguin to Now, 1983; Brooklyn Museum, Public and Private: American Prints Today, 1986. **Collections:** U. of California; Chicago/AI; Denver/AM; Madison Art Center; Milwaukee; Palm Springs Desert Museum; Rayovac Corp., Madison, Wisc.; SFMA; Seattle/AM; Yellowstone Art Center.

BULTMAN, FRITZ. b. April 4, 1919, New Orleans, La. **d.** July 20, 1985, Provincetown, Mass. **Studied:** Privately with Morris Graves, 1931; New Orleans Arts and Crafts School; Munich Preparatory School; New Bauhaus, Chicago, 1937-38; Hofmann School, NYC and Provincetown, 1938-41. **Taught:** Pratt Institute,

1958-63; Hunter College, 1959-64; Fine Arts Work Center, Provincetown, Mass., 1968-72. **Awards:** Italian Government Scholarship, 1950; Fulbright Fellowship, 1951, 1964-65 (Paris); Guggenheim Foundation Fellowship, 1975. **One-man Exhibitions:** (first) Hugo Gallery, NYC, 1947, also 1950; The Kootz Gallery, NYC, 1952; The Stable Gallery, NYC, 1958; Martha Jackson Gallery, 1959, 73, 74, 76; New Orleans/Delgado, 1959, 74; Galerie Stadler, Paris, 1960; Michel Warren Gallery, NYC, 1960; Gallery Mayer, NYC, 1960; Tibor de Nagy Gallery, 1963, 64; Oklahoma, 1974; Newport (R.I.) Art Association, 1974; Long Point Gallery, Provincetown, Mass., 1977, 78, 79; Landmark Gallery, Inc., NYC, 1982. **Group:** WMAA, 1950, 53; Chicago/AI; MOMA, Hans Hofmann and His Students, circ., 1963-64; IIE, 20 American Fulbright Artists, 1975. **Collections:** Brandeis U.; Ciba-Geigy Corp.; Grinnell College; Gutai Museum, Osaka; McCrory Corp.; U. of Minnesota; U. of Nebraska; New Orleans/Delgado; Norfolk/Chrysler; Union Carbide; U. of Texas; Tougaloo College; WMAA; Williams College. **Bibliography:** Pousette-Dart, ed. Archives.

BUNCE, LOUIS. b. August 13, 1907, Lander, Wyo. **d.** June 11, 1983, Portland, Ore. **Studied:** Portland (Ore.) Museum School, 1925-26; ASL, 1927-30, with Boardman Robinson, William Von Schlegell. Traveled USA, Mexico, Europe extensively. **Taught:** Salem (Ore.) Art Museum, 1937-38; Portland (Ore.) Museum School; U. of California, Berkeley; U. of British Columbia; U. of Washington; U. of Illinois; U. of Oregon, Federal A.P.: Mural Division, NYC, 1940-41. **Commissions:** Federal Building, Grants Pass, Ore., 1936-37 (mural); Portland (Ore.) International Airport 1958 (mural); Portland (Ore.) Hilton Hotel, 1963 (637 serigraphs). **Awards:** Seattle/AM, **P.P.**, 1936, 62; Northwest Printmakers Annual, 1948; U. of Washington, **P.P.**, 1950; Portland, Ore./AM, **P.P.**, 1952; SFMA, Emanuel Walter Bequest and Purchase Award, 1961; Ford Foundation, **P.P.**, 1964; Tamarind Fellowship. **One-man Exhibitions:** Seattle/AM, 1936, 53; Washburn U. of Topeka, 1937; Hollins College, 1941, 58; Portland, Ore./AM, 1945, 47, 56; U. of Washington, 1947; Harvey Welch Gallery, Portland, Ore., 1947; National Serigraph Society, NYC, 1947; Reed College, 1947, 51; Wilmette U., 1948; Santa Barbara/MA, 1948; Kharouba Gallery, Portland, Ore., 1950, 52; Cincinnati/AM, 1952; John Heller Gallery, NYC, 1953; Grants Pass (Ore.) Art League, 1953, 54; Salem (Ore.) Art Association, 1955; Morrison Street Gallery, Portland, Ore., 1955; Doris Meltzer Gallery, NYC, 1956, 57, 59, 60; Artists Gallery, Seattle, 1958; U. of California, Berkeley, 1960; Fountain Gallery, 1962, 64, 66, 72; Comara Gallery, 1964; Gordon Woodside Gallery, 1964; U. of Illinois, 1967; Fountain Gallery, Portland, Ore., 1981. **Retrospective:** Portland, Ore./AM, 1955. **Group:** Golden Gate International Exposition, San Francisco, 1939; New York World's Fair, 1939; Chicago/AI, Abstract and Surrealist Art, 1948; Worcester/AM, 1949; MMA, American Paintings Today, 1950; Colorado Springs/FA, Artists West of the Mississippi, 1951, 53, 56, 59; WMAA Annuals, 1951, 53, 54, 59, 60; Corcoran, 1953; U. of Colorado, 1953; Los Angeles/County MA; 1953; VMFA, 1954; Des Moines, 1954; U. of Nebraska, 1954, 57; Carnegie Annual, 1955; Sao Paulo, 1955, 56; Denver/AM Annuals, 1955, 56, 59, 62; Santa Barbara/MA, 1957; PAFA, 1958; Detroit/Institute, 1958; Stanford U., Fresh Point, 1958; Grand Rapids, 1961; Seattle World's Fair, 1962. **Collections:** AAAL; American Association of University Women; Auburn U.; Colorado Springs/FA; Hollins College; Library of Congress; MMA; U. of Michigan; National Gallery; PMA; Portland, Ore./AM; Reed College; SFMA; Seattle/AM; Springfield, Mo./AM; US State Department; Utica; WMAA; U. of

Washington; Youngstown/Butler. **Bibliography:** *Art of the Pacific Northwest;* **Bunce;** Clark and Cowles.

BURCHFIELD, CHARLES. b. April 9, 1893, Ashtabula Harbor, Ohio; **d.** January 10, 1967, West Seneca, N.Y. **Studied:** Cleveland Institute of Art, 1912, with Henry G. Keller, F. N. Wilcox, William J. Eastman; NAD. US Army, 1918-19. **Taught:** U. of Minnesota, Duluth, 1949; Art Institute of Buffalo, 1949-52; Ohio U., summer, 1950; U. of Buffalo, summers, 1950, 51; Buffalo Fine Arts School, 1951-52. **Member:** American Academy of Arts and Sciences: NIAL; NAD. **Commissions:** *Fortune* magazine, 1936, 37. **Awards:** Cleveland/MA, First Prize and Penton Medal, 1921; PAFA, Jennie Sesnan Gold Medal, 1929; Carnegie, Second Prize, 1935; International Arts Festival, Newport, R.I., First Prize, 1936; PAFA, Dana Watercolor Medal, 1940; Chicago/AI, Watson F. Blair Prize, 1941; NIAL, Award of Merit Medal, 1942; U. of Buffalo, Chancellor's Medal, 1944; Carnegie, Second Hon. Men., 1946; PAFA, Dawson Memorial Medal, 1947, Special Award, 1950; MMA, 1952 ($500); Buffalo/Albright, J. C. Evans Memorial Prize, 1952; Buffalo/Albright, Satter's Prize, 1955; Buffalo Historical Society, Red Jacket Medal, 1958; Hon. LHD, Kenyon College, 1944; Hon. DFA, Harvard U., 1948; Hon. DFA, Hamilton College, 1948; Hon. LLD, Valparaiso U., 1951. **One-man Exhibitions:** (first) Sunwise Turn Bookshop, NYC, 1916; Cleveland Institute of Art, 1916, 17, 21, 44; Laukhuff's Bookstore, Cleveland, 1918; Garrick Theater Library, NYC, 1919; Little Theater, Cleveland, 1919; H. Kevorkian, NYC, 1920; Chicago/AI, 1921; Grosvenor (Gallery), London, 1923; Montross Gallery, NYC, 1924, 26, 28; Eastman-Bolton Co., Cleveland, 1928; Rehn Galleries, 1930, 31, 34-36, 39, 41, 43, 46, 47, 50, 52, 54-64, 66, 71, 73; U. of Rochester, 1932; Phillips, 1934; Philadelphia Art Alliance, 1937; Town and Country Gallery, Cleveland, 1948; MOMA, 1954; Buffalo/SUNY, 1963, 71; Cleveland/MA, 1966; Danenberg Gallery, NYC, 1972; Kennedy Gallery, NYC, 1974, 75, 76, 77, 78, 79; Smithsonian, circ., 1978; Valparaiso U., 1976; WMAA, 1980; Boston Athenaeum, 1986. **Retrospectives:** Carnegie, 1938; Buffalo/Albright, 1944, 63; Cleveland/MA, 1953 (drawings); WMAA, 1956; AAAL, 1968; Oklahoma, 1984. **Group:** WMAA Annuals, Chicago/AI; U. of Illinois; MOMA; MMA; Carnegie. **Collections:** Boston/MFA; Brooklyn Museum; Buffalo/Albright; Carnegie; Chase Manhattan Bank; Chicago/AI; Cleveland/MA; Detroit/Institute; Harvard U.; IBM; U. of Illinois; Indianapolis/Herron; Kalamazoo/Institute; Kansas City/Nelson; MMA; MOMA; Muskegon/Hackley; Newark Museum; New Britain; PAFA; Phillips; RISD; St. Louis/City; San Diego; Santa Barbara/MA; Sweet Briar College; Syracuse/Everson; Terre Haute/Swope; Utica; VMFA; Valparaiso U.; WMAA; Wichita/AM; Wilmington; Youngstown/Butler. **Bibliography:** Barr 3, **Baur 1,** 7; Bazin; Beam; Blesh 1; Boswell 1; Brown; **Burchfield 1, 2, 3;** Chaill and Barr, eds.; Canaday; *Celebrate Ohio;* Cheney; Christensen; Craven 1, 2; **The Drawings of Charles E. Burchfield;** *8 American Masters of Watercolor;* Eliot; Flanagan; Flexner; Gallatin 1; Goodrich 1; Goodrich and Baur 1; Haftman; Hall; Hunter 6; *Index of 20th Century Artists;* Jewell 2; **Jones, ed.;** Lee and Burchwood; McCurdy, ed.; Mellquist; Mendelowitz; Newmeyer; Nordness, ed.; Pagano; Pearson 1; Phillips 1; Poore; Pousette-Dart, ed.; Richardson, E. P.; Ringel, ed.; Rose, B. 1, 4; Sachs; Soby 5; Sutton; Watson, E. W., 1; Weller; Wight 2. Archives.

BURDEN, CHRIS. b. 1946, Boston Mass. **Studied:** Pomona College, 1969, BA; U. of California, Irvine, 1971, MFA. **Awards:** Los Angeles/County MA, New Talent Award, 1973; National Endowment for the Arts, 1974, 76, 80,

83; Guggenheim Foundation Fellowship, 1978. Performance artist. **Address:** 1780 Will Geer Road, Topanga, Calif. 90019. **Dealer:** Ronald Feldman Fine Arts Inc., NYC. **One-man Exhibitions:** Riko Mizuno Gallery, Los Angeles, 1974, 75; Ronald Feldman Fine Arts Inc., 1974, 75, 76, 77, 80, 83; Cincinnati/Contemporary, 1974; Galleria A. Castelli, Milan, 1975; Galleria Schema, Florence, 1975; De Appel, Amsterdam, 1975; Broxton Gallery, Los Angeles, 1976; Baum-Silverman Gallery, Los Angeles, 1977; Rosamund Felsen Gallery, Los Angeles, 1979, 80, 82, 84; WMAA, 1980; Hartford/Wadsworth, 1985; U. of Miami, 1985; Lawrence Oliver Gallery, Philadelphia, 1985. **Group:** La Jolla, Body Movements, 1971; Portland (Ore.) Center for the Visual Arts, Via Los Angeles, 1975; MOMA, Projects: Video, 1975; SFMA, California Painting and Sculpture: The Modern Era, 1976; WMAA Biennial, 1977; Documenta VI, Kassel, 1977; Chicago/Contemporary, A View of a Decade, 1977; Purchase/SUNY, The Sense of Self, 1978; High Museum, Contemporary Art in Southern California, 1980; San Diego, Sculpture in California, 1975-80, 1980; Potsdam/SUNY, Usable Art, 1981; Walker, Eight Artists: The Anxious Edge, 1982; Oakland Museum, Site Strategies, 1983; MOMA, Recent Survey of International Painting and Sculpture, 1984; Hirshhorn, Content, 1984; Palm Springs Desert Museum, Return of the Narrative, 1984.

BURKHARDT, HANS GUSTAV. b. December 20, 1904, Basel, Switzerland. To USA, 1924. **Studied:** Cooper Union, 1924-25; Grand Central School, NYC, 1928-29, with Arshile Gorky, and privately with Gorky, 1930-35. Resided Mexico, 1950-52. Traveled Europe, Mexico, USA. **Taught:** Long Beach State College, summer, 1959; U. of Southern California, 1959-60; UCLA, 1962-63; California Institute of the Arts, 1962-64; Laguna Beach (Calif.) School of Art and Design, 1962-64; San Fernando Valley State College, 1963-73; Otis Art Institute, summer, 1963; California State U., Northridge, 1973. **Member:** Artists Equity. **Awards:** Los Angeles/County MA, First **P.P.**, 1946; California State Fair, **P.P.**, 1954, Second Prize, 1962; Santa Barbara/MA, Ala Story Purchase Fund, 1957; Los Angeles All-City Show, **P.P.**, 1957, 60, 61; California Watercolor Society, **P.P.**, 1962. **Address:** 1914 Jewett Drive, Los Angeles, CA 90046. **Dealer:** Jack Rutberg Fine Arts, L.A. **One-man Exhibitions:** (first) Stendahl Gallery, Los Angeles, 1939; Open Circle Gallery, 1943, 44; Chabot Gallery, Los Angeles, 1946, 47, 49; Los Angeles/County MA, 1946, 62; U. of Oregon, 1947; Hall of Art, Beverly Hills, 1948; Guadalajara, 1951; Fraymart Gallery, Los Angeles, 1951, 52; Paul Kantor Gallery, Beverly Hills, 1953; Escuela de Bellas Artes, San Miguel de Allende, Mexico, 1956, 61; Esther Robles Gallery, 1957-59; Comara Gallery, 1959; Long Beach State College, 1959; Glendale (Calif.) Public Gallery, 1960; Whittier (Calif.) Art Association, 1960; SFMA, 1961; Ankrum Gallery, 1961, 63; La Jolla, 1962; Fresno Art Center, 1962; Palm Springs Desert Museum, 1964, 79; Freie Schule, Basel, Switzerland, 1965; San Fernando Valley State College, 1965; Bay City Jewish Community Center, San Francisco, 1966; Laguna Beach (Calif.) Art Gallery, 1966; San Diego, 1968; Michael Smith Gallery, Los Angeles, 1972; Four Oaks Gallery, South Pasadena, 1972; Moorpark College, 1974; California State U., Northridge, 1975; Santa Barbara/MA, 1977; Laguna Beach Museum of Art, 1978; Cerro Coso Community College, 1978; San Fernando Mission College, 1978; Robert Schoelkopf Gallery, NYC, 1979; Santa Barbara/MA, 1977; Iannetti Gallery, San Francisco, 1977; Palm Springs Desert Museum, 1979; Robert Schoelkopf Gallery, NYC, 1979; Jack Rutberg Fine Arts, Los Angeles, 1982, 84, 85. **Retrospectives:** Falk-Raboff Gallery, Los Angeles, 1954; Pasadena/AM (10-year), 1957; Santa Barbara/MA (30-year), 1961; San Diego (40-year), 1966; Long Beach/MA, 1972; California State U., Northridge, 1973, 75; Pasquale Iannetti Assoc., San Francisco, 1977. **Group:** Los Angeles/County MA Annuals, 1940, 45, 46, 53, 54, 57, 59; Los Angeles Art Association Annuals, 1940-63; Corcoran, 1947, 51, 53; Denver/AM 1949, 53, 54; U. of Illinois, 1951; MMA, 1951; PAFA, 1951-53; WMAA Annuals, 1951, 55, 58; III Sao Paulo Biennial, 1955; Long Beach/MA, 1958, 60, 64; Kunsthalle, Basel, 1966; Trinity U., San Antonio, Tex., 1967; ICA, Los Angeles, 1974; Los Angeles Municipal Art Gallery, 1975; Hirshhorn, 1984; Milwaukee, 1984; Chapman College, 1984; IEF, Twentieth Century American Drawings: The Figure in Context, circ., 1984. **Collections:** Basel/Kunsthalle; California State U., Northridge; The Coca-Cola Co.; Columbia, S.C./MA; Corcoran; Downey Museum; Grunewald Foundation; Guadalajara; Hirshhorn; Home Savings and Loan Association; La Jolla; Long Beach/MA; Los Angeles/County MA; Lucerne; U. of Miami; Moorpark College; Norton Smith Museum (Pasadena); Oakland/AM; Omaha/Joslyn; Pasadena/AM; Portland, Ore./AM; Sacramento/Crocker; St. Louis/City; San Diego; Santa Barbara/MA; SRGM; State of California; Stockholm/National. **Bibliography:** Archives.

BURLIN, PAUL. b. September 10, 1886, NYC; **d.** March 13, 1969, NYC. Self-taught in art. Traveled Europe, North Africa, USA; resided Paris, 1921-32. **Taught:** U. of Minnesota, 1949; Washington U., 1949-54; U. of Colorado, 1951; U. of Wyoming, 1952; UCLA, 1954; Union College (N.Y.), 1954-55; Chicago Art Institute School, 1960. Federal A.P.: Easel painting. **Awards:** Portrait of America, First Prize ($2,500), 1945; ART:USA:59, NYC, First Prize, 1959; Chicago/AI, Watson F. Blair Prize ($2,000), 1960; PAFA, J. Henry Schiedt Memorial

Prize, 1963. **One-man Exhibitions:** (first) The Daniel Gallery, NYC, 1913, also 1914-20; Kraushaar Galleries, 1926, 27; Westheim Gallery, Berlin, 1927; de Hauke Gallery, NYC, 1942; Vincent Price Gallery, Los Angeles, 1944; The Downtown Gallery, 1946, 49, 52, 53; U. of Minnesota, 1949; Southern Illinois U., 1950, 60; U. of Wyoming, 1952; Washington U., circ., 1954; The Stable Gallery, 1954; Poindexter Gallery, 1958, 59; The Alan Gallery, NYC, 1959; Chicago/AI, 1960; Holland-Goldowsky Gallery, Chicago, 1960; Grace Borgenicht Gallery, Inc., 1963-66; 1970, 71, 73, 75, 81; Boston U., 1964; Hillwood Gallery, Greenville, N.Y., 1983. **Retrospective:** A.F.A. circ., 1962. **Group:** The Armory Show, 1913; WMAA Annuals; Carnegie; PAFA; WMAA, Pioneers of American Art, 1946; Walker; Corcoran; U. of Nebraska; nationally since 1913. **Collections:** Auburn U.; Britannica; Brooklyn Museum; Carleton College; Exeter; Hartford/Wadsworth; IBM; S.C. Johnson & Son, Inc.; MOMA; U. of Minnesota; NYU; Newark Museum; Southern Illinois U.; Tel Aviv; WMAA; Washington U.; Wichita/AM. **Bibliography:** Baur 7; Biddle 4; Cheney; Coke 2; Genauer; Goodrich and Baur 1; Kootz 2; Nordness, ed.; Pagano; Passloff; Pearson 1, 2; Pousette-Dart, ed.; Richardson, E. P.; Rose, B., 1; *Woodstock: An American Art Colony 1902-1977*: Zaidenberg, ed. Archives.

BURLIUK, DAVID. b. July 22, 1882, Kharkov, Ukraine; **d.** January 15, 1967, Southampton, N.Y. **Studied:** Art schools in Kazan, 1898-1902, Odessa, 1911, Munich, Moscow, 1914; Bayerische Akademie der Schonen Kunst, Munich; Academie des Beaux-Arts, Paris. To USA, 1922; citizen, 1930. Traveled Europe, the Orient, USA. **Taught:** Painting, art history. Federal A.P.: Easel painting. A founder (with W. Mayakovsky and W. Kamiensky) of Futurist art movement in Russia, 1911. A founder-member of Der Blaue Reiter and Der Sturm groups, 1910-14. Co-founder (1930) and publisher (with Marussia Burliuk) of art magazine *Color Rhyme*. Owned and operated Burliuk Gallery, Hampton Bays, N.Y. **Awards:** Pepsi-Cola, 1946. **One-man Exhibitions:** (first) Cherson, South Russia, 1904; galleries in Moscow and St. Petersburg, 1907; Societe Anonyme, NYC, 1924; J. B. Neumann Gallery, NYC, 1927; Morton Gallery, NYC, 1928; California Palace, 1931; Dorothy Paris Gallery, NYC, 1933-35; Boyer Gallery, NYC, 1935-39; Phillips, 1937; ACA Gallery, 1941-50, 1952-54, 1956, 58, 60, 63, 67, 69; Havana/Nacional, 1955; Galerie Maeght; Der Blaue Reiter, 1962; Galerie Stangl, Munich, 1962; Leonard Hutton Gallery, NYC, Der Blaue Reiter, 1963; Parrish Museum, Southampton, N.Y., 1978. **Group:** Brooklyn Museum, 1923, 26; PMA, 1962. **Collections:** Boston/MFA; Brooklyn Museum; MMA; Phillips; WMAA; Yale U. **Bibliography:** Baur 7; **Dreier 1;** Richardson, E.P.; Selz, P., 3; Soyer, R., 1. Archives.

BURTON, SCOTT. b. June 23, 1939, Greensboro, Ala. **Studied:** Columbia U., 1962, BA magna cum laude, with Trilling, Dupee, Marcus; NYU, 1963, MA; private studies 1957-60 with Leon Berkowitz, Washington, D.C., and Hans Hofmann, Provincetown, Mass. **Taught:** School of Visual Art, NYC, 1967-72; U. of North Carolina, 1976. Performance Artist & Sculptor, 1970-80. **Commissions:** Rockdale Temple, Cincinnati, 1980; National Oceanic and Atmospheric Administration, Seattle, 1983; Light Rail Rapid Transit System, Buffalo, N.Y., 1985; Pearlstone Park, Baltimore, 1985; MIT, 1985; Equitable Center, NYC, 1985. **Awards:** PBK; Woodrow Wilson Fellowship; National Endowment for the Arts, grant, 1973, 75, 79; CAPS, 1975; L. C. Tiffany Grant, 1980. **Address:** 86 Thompson Street, NYC 10012. **Dealer:** Max Protetch Gallery, NYC; Lisson Gallery, London. **One-man Exhibitions:** (first) Artists Space, NYC, 1975; Finch College, NYC, 1971; WMAA, 1972; SRGM, 1976; Droll/Kolbert Gallery, NYC, 1977, 80; Brooks Jackson Gallery Iolas, NYC, 1978; Max Protetch Gallery, Washington, D.C., 1979; U. of California, 1980; Weinberg Gallery, San Francisco, 1980; Max Protetch Gallery, NYC, 1981, 82, 85; Daniel Weinberg Gallery, Los Angeles, 1982; Cincinnati/Contemporary, 1983; McIntosh-Drysdale Gallery, Houston, 1984; Tate Gallery, 1985. **Group:** U. of Iowa, Two Evenings, 1970; Hartford/Wadsworth, Four Theater Pieces, 1970; Oberlin College, Festival of Contemporary Arts, 1973; Akademie der Kunst, Berlin, So Ho, 1976; Documenta VI & VII, Kassel, 1977, 82; Chicago/Contemporary, performance week, 1977; ICA, U. of Pennsylvania, Improbable Furniture, 1977; SRGM, Young American Artists, 1978; Purchase/SUNY, Ten Artists/Artists Space, 1979; Detroit/Institute, Image and Object in Contemporary Sculpture, 1979; WMAA Biennial, 1981; SFMA; 20 American Artists: Sculpture, 1982, 1982; Hirshhorn, Directions, 1983; RISD, Furniture, Furnishings: Subject and Object, 1984; Hirshhorn, Content: A Contemporary Focus, 1974-1984, 1984; WMAA, High Styles, 1985; Carnegie, International, 1985. **Collections:** U. of California; Chase Manhattan Bank; Dallas/MFA; Detroit/Institute; Humlebaek/Louisiana; La Jolla; Los Angeles/County MA; Los Angeles/MOCA; MOMA; Mellon Bank, Pittsburgh; Milwaukee; Omaha/Joslyn; PMA; Princeton U.; SRGM; WMAA; Walker. **Bibliography:** Pincus-Witten 1, 2.

BUTTERFIELD, DEBORAH. b. May 7, 1949, San Diego, Calif. **Studied:** San Diego State College, 1966-68; U. of California, San Diego, 1969; U. of California, Davis, 1970-72, BA; 1972-73, MFA, with Robert Arneson, William T. Wiley, Roy de Forest; Skowhegan School, 1972. **Awards:** Guggenheim Foundation Fellowship, 1980; National Endowment for the Arts, 1977, 80.

Deborah Butterfield   *Blue Roan*   1985–86

Taught: U. of Wisconsin, Madison, 1974-77; Montana State U., 1977-. **Commissions:** Corporate Center, Sacramento, Calif., 1983; Kentucky Derby Festival of Arts, Louisville, 1986. **m.** John Buck. **Address:** 11229 Cottonwood Road, Bozeman, Mt. 59715. **Dealers:** Zolla/Lieberman Gallery, Chicago. **One-man Exhibitions:** U. of California, Berkeley (two-man) 1974; Madison Art Center, 1976; Zolla/Lieberman Gallery, 1976, 77, 79, 83; Hanson Fuller Gallery, San Francisco, 1978, 81, 85; OK Harris Works of Art, 1978, 79, 84; Lee Hoffman Gallery, Birmingham, Mich., 1978; Open Gallery, Eugene, Ore., 1980; Atlantic Richfield Co., 1981; Israel Museum, 1981; RISD, 1981; Dallas/MFA, circ., 1983; Oakland/AM, 1983; San Antonio/McNay, 1983; Southeastern Center for Contemporary Art, Winston-Salem, 1983; U. of Nevada, Reno, 1984; Galerie 99, Bay Harbor Islands, Fla., 1984; Ohio State U., 1985. **Group:** Chicago/AI, Chicago and Vicinity, 1977; Buffalo/Albright, Eight Sculptors, 1979; WMAA Biennial, 1979; Dayton/AI, Woodworks One, 1980; Indianapolis, 1980; Renwick Gallery, Washington, D.C., The Animal Image, Contemporary Objects and the Beast, 1981; Fresno Art Center, Forgotten Dimensions, 1982; Oakland/AM, 100 Years of California Sculpture, 1982; Palm Springs Desert Museum, The West as Art, 1982; Philadelphia Art Alliance, S/300, 1982; Seattle/AM, American Sculpture: Three Decades, 1984; Cincinnati/Contemporary, Body and Soul, circ., 1985. **Collections:** Atlantic Richfield Co.; Chicago/Contemporary; Cincinnati/AM; Hirshhorn; Indianapolis; Israel Museum; Louisville/Speed; MMA; Oakland/AM; SFMA; WMAA; Walker.

BUTTON, JOHN. b. 1929, San Francisco. **d.** December 12, 1982, NYC. **Studied:** U. of California, Berkeley, 1947-50; California School of Fine Arts, 1949-50; U. of California Medical Center, San Francisco; and with Altina Barrett and Willard Cummings. **Taught:** Skowhegan School, 1964, 65; School of Visual Arts, NYC, 1965-82; Cornell U., 1967-68; Swarthmore College, 1969-70; U. of Pennsylvania, 1975-82. **Awards:** Artists of Los Angeles County, prize, 1952; Silvermine Guild Prize, 1964; Ingram Merrill Foundation, Grant, 1961, 69, 74, 82. **One-man Exhibitions:** Tibor de Nagy Gallery, NYC, 1956, 57; The Kornblee Gallery, 1963, 65, 67, 68, 70, 72, 73; Franklin Siden Gallery, Detroit, 1967; J. L. Hudson Gallery, Detroit, 1970; Gallery of July & August, Woodstock, N.Y., 1976; Fischbach Gallery, NYC, 1978, 79, 80; Kean College, Union, N.J., 1984; School of Visual Art, NYC, 1984. **Group:** U. of North Carolina, 1966; Vassar College, Realism Now, 1968; A.F.A., Painterly Realism, 1970; MOMA, Eight Landscape Painters, circ., 1972; Boston U., The American Landscape, 1972; School of Visual Arts, NYC, The Male Nude, 1973; Omaha-Joslyn, A Sense of Place, 1973; Hofstra U., The Male Nude, 1973; Indiana U., Contemporary Pastels and Watercolors; College of William & Mary, Contemporary Realism, 1978; Tulsa/Philbrook, Realism/Photorealism, 1980; Utica, An Appreciation of Realism, 1982; SFMA, American Realism (Janss), circ., 1985. **Collections:** Amerada Hess Corp.; AT&T; Chase Manhattan Bank; Chicago/AI; Columbia U.; Commerce Bankshares, Kansas City; Debevoise, Plimpton, Lyons and Gates; First National City Bank; Hirshhorn; MMA; MOMA; U. of North Carolina; Port Authority of New York; R.J. Reynolds Inc.; Utah. **Bibliography:** *American 1976*; Arthur 1, 2; Downes, ed.

C

CADMUS, PAUL. b. December 17, 1904, NYC. **Studied:** NAD, 1919-26; ASL, 1929-31, with Joseph Pennell, Charles Locke. Traveled Europe, the Mediterranean. Federal. A.P.: Easel painting, 1934. Designed sets and costumes for Ballet Caravan, 1938. Subject of documentary film by David Sutherland, *Paul Cadmus: Enfant Terrible at 80.* **Member:** Artists Equity; NAD; NIAL; SAGA. **Commissions** (mural): US Post Office, Richmond, Va, 1938. **Awards:** NIAL Grant, 1961; Norfolk, **P.P.,** 1967. **Address:** P.O. Box 1255, Weston, CT 06883. **Dealer:** The Midtown Galleries. **One-man Exhibitions:** The Midtown Galleries, NYC, 1937, 49, 76 (2), 78, 79, 83, 85; Baltimore/MA (three-man), 1942; The Print Cabinet, Ridgefield, Conn., 1978; Robert Samuel Gallery, NYC, 1979. **Retrospectives:** The Midtown Galleries 1968; Miami U., Oxford, Ohio, circ., 1981. **Group:** MOMA; MMA; WMAA, 1934, 36, 37, 38, 40, 41, 45; Chicago/AI, 1935; Hartford/Wadsworth; Williams College; Golden Gate International Exposition, San Francisco, 1939; PAFA, 1941; Carnegie, 1944, 45; Corcoran; NPG, American Self-Portraits: 1970-1973, 1974. **Collections:** Achenbach Foundation; Andover/Phillips; Baltimore/AM; Boston/MFA; Brooklyn Museum; Carnegie; Chicago/AI; Cleveland/AM; Columbia, S.C./MA; Cranbrook; Dallas/MFA; Dartmouth College; Fort Worth; U. of Georgia; Hartford/Wadsworth; Harvard U.; Library of Congress; Los Angeles/County MA; Louisville/Speed; MMA; MOMA; Miami U.; NMAA; NYPL; U. of Nebraska; PMA; Seattle/AM; WMAA; Williams College. **Bibliography:** American Artists Congress, Inc., 3; American Artists Group, Inc., 3; Baur 7; Bazin; Boswell 1; Brown 2; Goodrich and Baur 1; Hall; **Johnson 3;** Kent, N.; Kirstein 5; McCurdy, ed.; Nordness, ed.; Pagano; Reese; Rose, B., 1. Archives.

CAESAR, DORIS. b. November 8, 1892, NYC; d. September 8, 1971. **Studied:** ASL; Archipenko School of Art; privately with Rudolph Belling. **Member:** Federation of Modern Painters and Sculptors; Sculptors Guild; Architectural League of New York; New York Society of Women Artists; National Association of Women Artists; Audubon Artists. **One-man Exhibitions:** Wehye Gallery, 1933, 35, 37, 47, 53, 57, 59, 61, 64, 67, 69; Gallery Fifteen, NYC, 1940; Curt Valentine Gallery, NYC, 1943; Argent Gallery, NYC, 1948; Musée du Petit Palais, Paris, 1950; Katonah (N.Y.) Art Gallery, 1955; Margaret Brown Gallery, Boston, 1956; WMAA, 1959; Hartford/Wadsworth, 1960. **Group:** City of Philadelphia, Sculpture International, 1940-50; A.F.A., circ., 1953-54; MMA, 1955; New Burlington Galleries, London, 1956; I International Religious Art Biennial, Salzburg, 1958; WMAA, circ., 1959; Memphis/Brooks, 1960. **Collections:** Albion College; Andover/Phillips; Atlanta/AA; Busch-Reisinger Museum; La Casa del Libro; Cleveland/MA; Colby College; Colorado Springs/FA; Connecticut College; Dayton/AI; U. of Delaware; Father Judge Mission Seminary; Fort Worth; Grand Rapids; Hartford/Wadsworth; Harvard U.; Howard U.; Indiana U.;

State U. of Iowa; Kansas City/Nelson; Memphis/Brooks; Minneapolis/Institute; U. of Minnesota; NYU; Newark Museum; PAFA; Pasadena/AM; Phoenix; Portland, Me./MA; Rockland/Farnsworth; St. Bernard's Church, Hazardville, Conn.; St. John's Abbey, Collegeville, Minn.; Syracuse U.; Utica Public Library; WMAA; Williams College. **Bibliography:** Brumme; Bush 2; Goodrich and Baur 2. Archives.

CAJORI, CHARLES. b. March 9, 1921, Palo Alto, Calif. **Studied:** Colorado College, 1939-40, with Boardman Robinson; Cleveland Institute of Art, 1940-42; Columbia U., 1946-48, with John Herlinker, Henry Poor; Skowhegan School, summers, 1947, 48. US Air Force, 1942-46. A co-organizer of the Tanager Gallery, NYC, 1952. Traveled Europe. **Taught:** College of Notre Dame of Maryland, 1950-56; American U., 1955-56; Cooper Union, 1956-; Philadelphia Museum School, 1956-57; U. of California, Berkeley, 1959-60; Pratt Institute, 1961-62; Cornell U., summers, 1961, 63; Yale U., 1963-64; U. of Washington, 1964; New York Studio School, 1964-69, 83-; Queens College, 1965-85. **Awards:** Fulbright Fellowship (Italy), 1952; Yale U., Distinction of Arts Award, 1959; Longview Foundation Grant, 1962; Ford Foundation, **P.P.,** 1962; NIAL, 1970; Childe Hassam Fund **P.P.,** 1975, 76, 80; NIAL; L. C. Tiffany Grant, NIAL, 1979; NAD, Benjamin Altman (figure) Prize, 1983; National Endowment for the Arts, 1981. **Address:** Litchfield Road, Watertown, CT 06795. **Dealer:** Ingber Art Gallery, NYC. **One-man Exhibitions:** (first) Tanager Gallery, NYC 1956, also 1961; Watkins Gallery, Washington, D.C., 1956; The Bertha Schaefer Gallery, 1958; Oakland/AM, 1959; Cornell U., 1961; The Howard Wise Gallery, NYC, 1963; U. of Washington, 1964; Bennington College, 1969; Kirkland College, 1972; Landmark Gallery, Inc., NYC, 1974;

Ingber Art Gallery Ltd., NYC, 1976; U. of Texas, Austin, 1976; Art Academy of Cincinnati, 1976; American U., Washington, D.C. 1977; Mattatuck Historical Society Museum, 1980; Landmark Gallery Inc., NYC, 1981; Gross McCleaf Gallery, Philadelphia, 1983, 85. **Group:** Walker, Vanguard, 1955; WMAA Annuals, 1957, 62; U. of Kentucky, 1957, 61; U. of Nebraska, 1958; Festival of Two Worlds, Spoleto, 1958; Corcoran, 1959; Brooklyn Museum, 1959; ICA, Boston, 100 Works on Paper, circ., Europe, 1959; MOMA, Abstract Watercolors and Drawings: USA, circ., Latin America and Europe, 1961-62; Chicago/AI, 1964; Santa Barbara/MA, 1964; U. of Texas, 1966, 68; U. of Washington, 1967; New School for Social Research, Protest and Hope, 1967, Humanist Tradition, 1968; MMA, Recent Acquisitions, 1979; NAD Annuals, 1983, 84, 85, 86. **Collections:** Ciba-Geigy Corp.; Corcoran; Honolulu Academy Mfg. Co.; Kalamazoo/Institute; U. of Kentucky; Miami Univ.; MMA; NYU; Scovill Mfg. Co.; U. of Texas; WMAA; Wake Forest College; Walker, Wilmington.

CALCAGNO, LAWRENCE. b. March 23, 1913, San Francisco, Calif. US Air Force, 1941-45. **Studied:** California School of Fine Arts, 1947-50. Traveled Mexico, 1945-47; Europe North Africa, 1950-55; Peru, Yucatan. **Taught:** U. of Alabama, 1955-56; Buffalo/SUNY, 1956-58; U. of Illinois, 1958-59; NYU, 1960; Carnegie-Mellon U., 1965-68; Honolulu Academy School, 1968-75. **Member:** Artists Equity. **Awards:** Yaddo Fellowship, 1961-64, 1965-68; Ford Foundation Grant, 1965-68; MacDowell Colony Fellowship, 1965-68, 70, 72, 74; Wurlitzer Fellowship, 1968. **Address:** Taos, NM 87571 and 215 Bowery, NYC 10002. **Dealer:** Yares Gallery, Scottsdale, Ariz.; Stables Gallery, Taos. **One-man Exhibitions:** (first) The Little Gallery, New Orleans, 1945; College of the Pacific, 1948; Lucien Labaudt Gallery, San Francisco, 1948, 54; Numero

Galleria d'Arte, Florence, Italy, 1951-52; Galeria Clan, Madrid, 1955; Studio Paul Facchetti, Paris, 1955; Martha Jackson Gallery, 1955, 58, 60, 62; U. of Alabama, 1956; Howard College, 1956; Macon (Ga.) Art Association, 1956; Buffalo/Albright, 1956; Lima, Peru, 1957; U. of Illinois, 1959; Fairweather-Hardin Gallery, 1959; Philadelphia Art Alliance, 1960; New Arts Gallery, Houston, 1960; Mexico City U., 1961; Tirca Karlis Gallery, 1961, 62, 64; McRoberts & Tunnard Gallery, London, 1961; Galerie Kobenhavn, Denmark, 1962; Gallery 31, Birmingham, Ala., 1964; The Osborne Gallery, NYC, 1964; Carnegie, 1965; Houston/MFA, 1965; Franklin Siden Gallery, Detroit, 1965, 66; Esther Robles Gallery, 1966; Meredith Long Galleries, Houston, Tex., 1968, 70, 72; U. of New Mexico, 1973; Yares Gallery, Scottsdale, 1975; Contemporary Art Center of Hawaii, Honolulu, 1976; Yares Gallery, Scottsdale, Ariz., 1974, 75, 78; Stables Gallery, Taos, 1978; U. of Kansas, 1980; Museum of Art, Fort Collins, Colorado, 1980. **Retrospective:** Westmoreland County/MA, 1967. **Group:** Art: USA; Now, circ., 1962-67; WMAA Annuals, 1963, 65, 67; Smithsonian, 1966; Flint/Institute, Flint Invitational, 1966. **Collections:** U. of Alabama; Allentown/AM; Baltimore/MA; Boston/MFA; Buffalo/Albright; California Palace; Carnegie; Chase Manhattan Bank; Dayton/AI; Denver/AM; Honolulu Academy; Houston/MFA; ICA, Boston; U. of Illinois; Lima, Peru; Los Angeles/County MA; MOMA; McCann-Erickson, Inc.; NCFA; NYU; U. of Nebraska; New York State Art Commission, Albany; Norfolk; Norfolk/Chrysler; Phoenix; RISD; Reynolds Metals Co.; U. of Rochester; SFMA; Santa Barbara/MA; Santa Fe, N.M.; Slater; Smithsonian; Union Carbide Corp.; WGMA; WMAA; Walker; Westmoreland County/MA. **Bibliography:** Baur 5; Blesh 1; McChesney; Nordness, ed. Archives.

CALDER, ALEXANDER. b. July 22, 1898, Philadelphia, Pa.; **d.** November 11, 1976, NYC. **Studied:** Stevens Institute of Technology, 1915-19; ASL, 1923-26, with George Luks, Guy Du Bois, Boardman Robinson, John Sloan. Traveled Europe, USA, Latin America, India. To Paris, 1928. The subject of three films: *Alexander Calder: Sculpture and Constructions* (MOMA, 1944): *Alexander Calder* (Burgess Meredith and Herbert Matter, 1951); *Calder's Circus* (Pathe, 1961). Two Calder sequences are in the film *Dreams That Money Can Buy* (Hans Richter, 1948). Designed sets for *Horizons* and *Four Movements* (by Martha Graham, NYC, 1936); *Socrates* (by Eric Satie, 1936); *Happy as Larry* (by Donagh MacDonagh, NYC, 1946); *Balloons* (by Padraic Colum, Boston, 1946); *Symphonic Variations* (by Tatiana Leskova, 1949). **Member:** AAAL. **Commissions:** Spanish Pavilion, Paris World's Fair, 1937; New York World's Fair, 1939; Hotel Avila, Caracas, 1940; Terrace Plaza Hotel, Cincinnati, 1945; Aula Magna, University City, Caracas, 1952; General Motors Corp., 1954; New York International Airport, 1958; UNESCO, Paris, 1958. **Awards:** MOMA, Plexiglas Sculpture Competition, First Prize, 1939; XXVI Venice Biennial, First Prize, 1952; Sao Paulo, 1953, City of Philadelphia, Outstanding Citizen Award, 1955; Stevens Institute of Technology, Medal, 1956; Carnegie First Prize, 1958; Architectural League of New York, Gold Medal, 1960; Brandeis U., Creative Arts Award, 1962; Hon. Ph.D., Harvard U., 1966; Commander of the Legion of Honor, 1967; Gold Medal, AAAL, 1971; Grand Prix National des Arts et Lettres, France, 1974; U.N. Peace Medal, 1975. **One-man Exhibitions:** (first) Weyhe Gallery, 1928 (wire sculpture); Billiet Gallery, Paris, 1929; Neumann-Neirendorf Gallery, Berlin, 1929; 56th Street Gallery, NYC, 1930; Galerie Percier, Paris, 1931; Galerie Vignon, Paris, 1932 (first mobiles exhibited); Julien Levy Galleries, NYC, 1932; Galerie Pierre Colle, Paris, 1933; Pierre Matisse

Gallery, 1934, 36, 37, 1939-43; The U. of Chicago, 1935; Arts Club of Chicago, 1935; Honolulu Academy, 1937; Mayor Gallery, London, 1937; The Willard Gallery, 1940 (first jewelry exhibited), 1941, 42; Arts and Crafts Club, New Orleans, 1941; SFMA, 1942; Andover/Phillips, 1943; Buchholz Gallery, NYC, 1944, 45, 47, 49; The Kootz Gallery, NYC, 1945; Galerie Louis Carre, Paris, 1946; Cincinnati/AM, 1946; Berne, 1947 (two-man); Amsterdam/Stedelijk, 1947 (two-man), 1950, 59, 69; Brazilian Ministry of Education, Rio de Janeiro, 1948; Sao Paulo, 1948; Margaret Brown Gallery, Boston, 1949; Galerie Maeght, 1949, 64, 66, 71, 73, 75; Galerie Blanche, Stockholm, 1950; MIT, 1950; Lefevre Gallery, London, 1951; Gallery R. Hoffman, Hamburg, 1954; Palais des Beaux-Arts, Brussels, 1960; Kunstgewerbemuseum, Zurich, 1960; Galerie d'Art Moderne, Basel, 1962; Galleria d'Arte del Naviglio, Milan, 1964; Perls Galleries, 1966-68; Obelisk Gallery, 1967; Kiko Gallery, Houston, 1968; Wittenborn Gallery, NYC, 1968; Dayton's Gallery 12, Minneapolis, 1968; Perls Galleries, 1968, 69, 72, 73, 74, 76; Gimpel Fils, 1969, 71; Grand Rapids, 1969; Musée d'Art Moderne, Geneva, 1969; Fundacion Eugenio Mendoza, Caracas, 1969; Leonard Hutton Gallery, NYC, 1972; Corcoran, 1972; Parker Street 470 Gallery, Boston, 1972; Sala Pelaires, Palma, Majorca, 1972; Source Gallery, San Francisco, 1974; Deson-Zaks Gallery, Chicago, 1975; Haus der Kunst, Munich, 1975; AAAL, 1976; M. Knoedler & Co., NYC, 1978, 79, 80; Rolly-Michaux, Gallery, NYC, 1979; Marisa del Re Gallery, NYC, 1979; Brewster Gallery, NYC, 1976, 77; Galeria Bonino Ltd., NYC, 1977; Galerie Maeght, Barcelona, 1977; Israel Museum, 1977; M. Knoedler & Co., Inc., 1978, 80, 82, 83; Rolly-Michaux, NYC, 1978; Marisa del Re Gallery, NYC, 1979; Rolly-Michaux, Boston, 1979; Waddington Galleries, London, 1981; Mayor Gallery, London, 1981; U. of California, Berkeley, 1982; Flint/Institute, 1983; Fort Worth, 1983;

Galerie Maeght, Zurich, 1983; Rachel Adler Gallery, NYC, 1984; Caracas, 1984; M. Knoedler, Zurich, 1984; Galerie Maeght LeLong, NYC, 1985; MIT, 1986. **Retrospectives:** Springfield, Mass./MFA, 1938; MOMA, 1943; Tate, 1962; SRGM, 1964; Akademie der Kunst, Berlin, 1967; Foundation Maeght, 1969; Long Beach/MA, 1970; Chicago/Contemporary, 1974, WMAA, 1976; City of Turin, 1983. **Group:** Artists' Gallery, NYC, 1926 (first paintings exhibited); Salon des Humoristes, Paris, 1927; Salon des Artistes Independents, Paris, 1929, 30; MOMA, Painting and Sculpture, 1930; Salon des Surindependents, Paris, 1930; WMAA; Chicago/AI; SFMA; Cincinnati/AM, 1942; Berne, 1947; Yale U., 1950; Hannover/K-G, 1954; Documenta III, Kassel, 1964; Society of the Four Arts, Calder/Nevelson/David Smith, 1971; Newport, R.I., Monumenta, 1974; XXXCII Venice Biennial, 1976; Houston/MFA, A Century of Modern Sculpture, 1882-1982, 1983; WMAA, The Third Dimension: Sculpture of the N.Y. School, 1985. **Collections:** Amsterdam/Stedelijk; Andover/Phillips; U. of Arkansas; Arts Club of Chicago; Basel; Chicago/AI; Dallas/MFA; Frankfurt am Main; Hartford/Wadsworth; Honolulu Academy; Lodz; MMA; MOMA; Mannheim; Marshall Field & Co.; Montreal/MFA; Moscow/Western; Museum of Science and Industry, Chicago; PAFA: Phillips; Pittsfield/Berkshire; SRGM; St. Louis/City; U. of St. Thomas (Tex.); Sao Paulo; Smith College; Stockholm/National; Toronto; VMFA; WMAA; Washington U.; Yale U. **Bibliography:** *Abstraction creation, 1931-1936;* **Alexander Calder,** 1967; **Alexander Calder,** 1971; Baldinger; Barr 1; Battcock, ed.; Baur 5, 7; Beam; Biederman 1; Bihalji-Merin; Blesh 1; Breton 3; Brion 1; Brumme; Calas, N. and E.; **Calder 1, 2; Calder and Liedl;** Canaday; **Carandente;** Cheney; Christensen; Craven, W.; Davis, D.; Evans, ed.; Flanagan; Gaunt; Gertz; Giedion-Welcker 1, 2; Goodrich and Baur 1; Guggenheim, ed.; Haftman; Hayter 2;

Henning; Hess, T. B., 1; Honisch and Jensen, eds.; Hulten; Hunter 6; Hunter, ed.; Jakovski; Janis and Blesh 1; Janis, S.; Kozloff 3; Krauss 1, 2, 3; Lane and Larsen; Langui; Licht, F.; Lipman; Lowry; Lynton; McCurdy, ed.; Marter, Tarbell, and Wechsler; Mellquist; Mendelowitz; **Metro; Monumenta;** Moser 1; **Mulas and Arnason;** Myers 2; Neumeyer; Paalen; Pearson 2; Phillips, Lisa; Ragon 1, 2; Ramsden 1, 2; Read, 1, 3, 5, 6; Rickey; Ritchie 1, 3; Rodman 1, 3; Rose, B., 1, 4; Rowell; Rubin 1; Sachs; Selz, J.; Seuphor 2, 3; Soby 1, 5; Sutton; Strachan; **Sweeny 1,** Toher, ed.; Tomkins; Tomkins and Time-Life Books; Trier 1, 2; Tuchman 1; Valentine 2; Waldberg 4; "What Abstract Art Means to Me"; Weller; Wilenski. Archives.

CALLAHAN, KENNETH. b. October 30, 1907, Spokane, Wash. **d.** May 8, 1986, Seattle, Wash. Self-taught in art. Traveled USA, Europe, Central America, Mexico, Southeast Asia, South Pacific. **Taught:** Privately and as visiting artist in various parts of the USA; Boston U., 1954-66; Skowhegan School, 1958, 63, 66; Port Townsend Summer School, 1974. Curator, Seattle/AM, 1933-53. Subject of *Callahan the Artist*, a 30-minute color film, 1973; overall design for *MacBeth*, Seattle Repertory Theater, 1973. **Member:** Washington State Arts Commission, 1970-74; NAD, 1975. **Commissions** (murals): Maine Hospital, Seattle; US Post Offices, Centralia and Anacostes, Wash., and Rugby, N.D.; Washington State Library, Olympia, Wash.; Syracuse U., 1964; Seattle Civic Center, 1966. **Awards:** Guggenheim Foundation Fellowship, 1954; AAAL, Arts and Letters Grant, 1968; State of Washington Governor's Award, 1968; AAAL, **P.P.,** 1972. **One-man Exhibitions:** (first) American-British Art Center, NYC, 1944; Maynard Walker Gallery, NYC, 11 exhibitions, 1946-64; SFMA; Santa Barbara/MA; La Jolla; Colorado Springs/FA; Phoenix; Roswell; Williams

College; Columbia, S.C./MA; U. of Arkansas; U. of Rochester; Detroit/Institute; Renaissance Society, Chicago; Seattle/AM; Portland, Ore./AM; Spokane Art Center of Washington State U.; Tacoma; Galerie George Giraux, Brussels, 1947; Boston U., 1966; Kraushaar Gallery, NYC, 1967, 69, 71, 74, 76, 80, 82, 85; Foster-White Gallery, Seattle, 1975, 79; Fountain Gallery, Portland, Oregon, 1980. **Retrospectives:** Emily Winthrop Miles Collection, circ., 1961-64; Syracuse/Everson; Henry Art Gallery, Seattle, circ., 1973. **Group:** Japan; Formosa; Korea; Philippines; Australia; New Zealand; Brazil; USA; Great Britain; France; Italy; Sweden; Denmark; Yugoslavia; Germany; Indianapolis, 1977; Seattle/AM, 1979; AAAL, 1980; ICA, Boston, Northwest Visionaries, 1981. **Collections:** Andover/Phillips; Beloit College; Brooklyn Museum; Chase Manhattan Bank; Chicago/AI; The U. of Chicago; Colby College; Columbus; Corcoran; Des Moines; Detroit/Institute; Fort Worth; Garnett Public Library; La Jolla; MMA; MOMA; Memphis/Brooks; U. of Michigan; Minneapolis/Institute; NCFA; U. of Nebraska; Norfolk/Chrysler; PAFA; PMA; Phillips; Phoenix; Portland, Ore./AM; U. of Rochester; SFMA; SRGM; St. Louis/City; Santa Barbara/MA; Seattle/AM; Spellman College; Springfield, Mo./AM; Syracuse U.; Tacoma; Utica; WMAA; Walker; Washington; Wichita/AM. **Bibliography:** *Art of the Pacific Northwest*; Baur 7; Bruce and Watson; Cheney; Clark and Cowles; Eliot; Nordness, ed.; *Northwest Traditions*; Pousette-Dart, ed.; Richardson, E.P.; Ritchie 1. Archives.

CALLERY, MARY. b. June 19, 1903, NYC; **d.** February 12, 1977, Paris. **Studied:** ASL, with Edward McCarten; privately in Paris with Jacques Loutchansky. Resided in Paris. **Taught:** Black Mountain College. **Commissions:** Aluminum Co. of America, 1953; P.S. 34, NYC, 1954; Gen. George

W. Wingate High School, Brooklyn, N.Y., 1955; Lincoln Center; Exxon Building, NYC; Brooklyn Court House, N.Y. **One-man Exhibitions:** (first) Buchholz Gallery, NYC, 1944; Arts Club of Chicago, 1946; Curt Valentine Gallery, NYC, 1947, 49, 50-52, 55; Salon due Mai, Paris, 1949; Margaret Brown Gallery, Boston, 1951; Galerie des Cahiers d'Art, 1954; M. Knoedler & Co., NYC, 1957, 61, 65, Paris, 1962; B. C. Holland Gallery, 1968; Washburn Gallery, Inc., NYC, 1978. **Group:** Salon des Tuileries, Paris; MOMA; WMAA; Chicago/AI; Houston/MFA, 1939; St. Louis/City, 1946; PMA, 1949; Utica, 1956; Dallas/MFA, 1958; Brussels World's Fair, 1958. **Collections:** Alcoa; Andover/Phillips; CIT Corporation; Cincinnati/AM; Detroit/Institute; Eastland Shopping Center, Detroit; 525 William Penn Plaza; Hartford/Wadsworth; MOMA; NYU; Publishers Printing Co.; SFMA; Toledo/MA; WMAA. **Bibliography:** Baur 7; Gertz; Giedion-Welcker 1; Licht, F.; Ramsden 2; Read 3; Ritchie 3; Seuphor 3; Trier 1; Valentine 2; Zervos and Adams. Archives.

CAPARN, RHYS. b. July 28, 1909, Oneonta Park, N.Y. **Studied:** Bryn Mawr College; privately in Paris with Edouard Navellier; privately in New York with Alexander Archipenko. Traveled Europe; resided France. **Taught:** Dalton School, NYC, 1946-55, 1960-72. Master Institute of United Arts, Inc., NYC, 1963-. **Member:** Federation of Modern Painters and Sculptors; Sculptors Guild; American Abstract Artists; International Institute of Arts and Letters. **Commissions:** Brooklyn Botanic Garden; Wollman Library, Barnard College; National Furniture Mart, NYC; private portrait commissions. **Awards:** MMA, American Sculpture, Second Prize, 1951; New York State Fair, First Prize for Sculpture, 1958; National Association of Women Artists, Medal of Honor for Sculpture, 1960, 61. **Address:** Taunton Hill Road, Newton, CT

06470. **One-man Exhibitions:** (first) Delphic Studios, NYC, 1933, also 1935; Architectural League of New York, 1941; New York Zoological Park (Bronx), 1942; Wildenstein & Co., NYC, 1944, 47; Dartmouth College, 1949, 55; John Heller Gallery, NYC, 1953; Doris Meltzer Gallery, NYC, 1956, 59, 60; La Boetie, NYC, 1970; The New Bertha Schaefer Gallery, 1973. **Retrospective:** Riverside Museum, NYC, 1961. **Group:** MOMA, Fifteen Sculptors, circ., 1941; WMAA Annuals, 1941, 53, 54, 56, 60; Musée du Petit Palais, Paris, 1950; PAFA, 1951-53, 60, 64; ICA, London/Tate, International Unknown Political Prisoner Competition, 1953; Silvermine Guild, 1956; USIA, American Drawings, Prints, and Watercolors, circ., Europe, 1957; VMFA, American Sculpture Today, 1958; NIAL, 1968; PMA/Museum of the Philadelphia Civic Center, Focus, 1974. **Collections:** Barnard College; Brandeis U.; Bryn Mawr College; Colorado Springs/FA; Corcoran; Dartmouth College; Harvard U.; La Jolla; Museum of the City of New York; Norfolk-Chrysler; Raleigh/NCMA; St. Louis/City; WMAA; Youngstown/Butler. **Bibliography:** *Art: A Woman's Sensibility;* Seuphor 3. Archives.

CARLES, ARTHUR B. b. 1882, Philadelphia, Pa.; **d.** June 18, 1952, Chestnut Hill, Pa. **Studied:** PAFA. Traveled Spain, France, Italy. **Taught:** PAFA, 1917-25. **Awards:** PAFA: Cresson Fellowship; Walter Lippincott Prize, 1917; Stotesbury Prize, 1919; J. Henry Schiedt Memorial Prize, 1929; Joseph E. Temple Gold Medal, 1930; Chicago/AI, The Mr. & Mrs. Frank G. Logan Prize. **One-man Exhibitions:** Montross Gallery, NYC, 1922; Gimbel Gallery, Philadelphia, 1935; Marie Harriman Gallery, NYC, 1936; PAFA, 1941, 53; Philadelphia Art Alliance, 1944; Karl Nierendorf Gallery, NYC, 1944 (two-man), 1946, 70; Dubin Gallery, Philadelphia, 1953; Oberlin College (two-man), 1955;

The Graham Gallery, 1959; Peal Gallery, Philadelphia, 1967; PMA, 1970; Janet Fleisher Gallery and David David Art Galleries, Philadelphia, 1972; PAFA, Peale House, 1972; Janet Fleisher Gallery, Philadelphia, 1975; Gross McCleaf Gallery, Philadelphia, 1975; Vendo Nubes Gallery, Philadelphia, 1975; Hirshhorn, 1977; Washburn Gallery Inc., 1984. **Retrospectives:** PAFA, 1953; PAFA, Peale House, circ., 1983. **Group:** The Armory Show, 1913; WMAA, 1963; PAFA; WMAA, The 1930s, 1968; U. of Miami, French Impressionists Influence American Artists, 1971; Delaware Art Museum, Avant-Garde Painting and Sculpture in America, 1910-1925, 1975; PAFA, In this Academy, 1976; Arts Council of Great Britain, The Modern Spirit: American Painting 1908-1935, circ., 1977; Houston/MFA, Modern American Painting, 1910-1940, 1977; WMAA, Synchronism and American Color Abstraction, 1910-1925, circ., 1978; Tulsa/Philbrook, Painters of the Humble Truth, 1979. **Collections:** Chicago/AI; MOMA; U. of Nebraska; PAFA; PMA; SFMA; Syracuse U. **Bibliography:** *Avant-Garde Painting and Sculpture in America 1910-25;* Baur 7; Brown 2; Levin 2; Richardson, E. P.; Rose, B., 1, 4; **Wolani.** Archives.

CASARELLA, EDMOND. b. September 3, 1920, Newark, N.J. **Studied:** Cooper Union, 1938-42; Brooklyn Museum School, 1949-51, with Gabor Peterdi. US Army, 1944-46. Traveled Italy and Greece, 1951-52, 1960-61, France. **Taught:** Brooklyn Museum School, 1956-60; Yale-Norfolk Summer Art School, 1958; NYU, 1962; Cooper Union; ASL; Hunter College, 1963-; Columbia U., summers, 1963, 64; Pratt Graphic Art Center, 1964; Yale U., 1964-, Rutgers U., 1964-; Pratt Institute, 1964-; Finch College, NYC, 1969-74; Manhattanville College of the Sacred Heart, 1973, 74; Queens College, 1980; National Youth Administration: Designed posters. **Member:** SAGA; Sculp-

tors Guild; Artists Equity. **Commissions:** Harcourt Brace Jovanovitch, Orlando, Fla., sculpture; 325 West 52nd Street, NYC, sculpture; 1585 Broadway, NYC, sculpture. **Awards:** Fulbright Fellowship (Italy), 1951; U. of Illinois, Graphic Art exhibitions, **P.P.,** 1954, 56; L. C. Tiffany Grant, 1955; Bay Printmakers Society, Oakland, 1955, 57; Library of Congress, 1955, 56, 58; The Print Club, Philadelphia, 1956; Northwest Printmakers Annual, 1956; Boston Printmakers, 1957; New York State Fair, 1958; PCA, 1959; Brooklyn Museum, Print and Watercolor Biennials; Guggenheim Foundation Fellowship, 1960; SAGA, 100 Prints of the Year, 1962, 63. **Address:** 83 East Linden Avenue, Englewood, NJ 07631. **Dealer:** Sylvan Cole, NYC. **One-man Exhibitions:** Brooklyn Museum, 1952 (two-man); The Zabriskie Gallery, 1953, 56; Obelisk Gallery, Washington, D.C., 1956, 61; Louisiana State U., 1957; U. of Mississippi, 1957; U. of Kentucky, 1964; Rutgers U., 1964; Hudson River Museum, Yonkers, N.Y., 1965; Montclair State College, 1966; Trenton State College, 1967; Merida Gallery, Inc., 1967, 68; Louisville/Speed, 1968-69; Naroden Muzejna Bitolkiot Kraj, Bitola, Yugoslavia; Free Public Library, Fair Lawn, N.J., 1970; Cramer Gallery, 1972, 73; Landmark Gallery, NYC, 1977, 80; Sculpture Center, NYC, 1977; Bloomingdale's, Paramus, N.J., 1981; Landmark Gallery, Inc., NYC, 1981, 82; Art Center of Northern N.J., 1981; Cottage Place Gallery, Ridgewood, N.J., 1986. **Retrospectives:** Naroden Muzej na Grad Skopje, Skopje, Yugoslavia, 1967; YMHA, Hackensack, N.J., 1969; Edward Williams College, 1979; Allegheny College, 1978. **Group:** Brooklyn Museum, Print and Watercolor Biennials; International Print Exhibition, Salzburg, 1952, 58; PAFA, 1953, 59, 63; Bay Printmakers Society, Oakland, 1955-57; Library of Congress, 1955, 56, 58; Corcoran, 1955, 56, 58, 59, 63; The Print Club, Philadelphia, 1956; U. of Illinois, 50 Contemporary American Printmakers, 1956;

Boston/MFA, 1957; Grenchen, Graphics International, 1958; I Inter-American Paintings and Prints Biennial, Mexico City, 1958; The Pennsylvania State U., 10 American Printmakers, 1959; Trenton/State, Contemporary Printmakers, 1959; Victoria and Albert Museum, 1959; Gallery of Modern Art, Ljubljana, Jugoslavia, III & IV International Exhibitions of Prints, 1959, 61; WMAA, American Prints Today, 1959, 62; Yale U., 1960; Cincinnati/AM, 1960; Philadelphia Art Alliance, 1960; American Academy, Rome, 1960, 61; Memphis/Brooks, 1960-62; WMAA, American Painting, 1961; A.A.A. Gallery, NYC, 100 Prints of the Year, 1962; New York Foundation/USIA, American Prints Around the World, circ., 1963; Los Angeles/County MA, 1963; Riverside Museum, 1963; WMAA, New York Hilton Hotel Collection, 1963; USIA, Graphic Arts—USA, circ., USSR, 1963; Jewish Museum, 100 Contemporary Prints, 1964; St. Louis/City, 1964; New York World's Fair, 1964-65; I Triennale Internazionale della Zilografia Contemporanea, Capri, 1969; Mostra Internazionale della Zilografia Contemporanea, Bologna, 1971; Madrid/Nacional, Exposicion Internacional de la Zilografia Contemporanea, 1972; Landmark Gallery, NYC, 1973, 74; Bergen Community College, Outdoor Sculpture, 1974; Terrain Gallery, 25th Anniversary, NYC, 1980. **Collections:** Bibliotheque National; Brooklyn Museum; U. of Illinois; Library of Congress; Louisville/Speed; Trenton/State; Victoria and Albert Museum; Cooper Hewitt Museum, NYC. **Bibliography:** Chaet; Peterdi.

CASTELLON, FEDERICO. b. September 14, 1914, Almeria, Spain; **d.** December 27, 1971, NYC. Self-taught in art. Traveled Europe and Latin America extensively, resided Spain, 1914-21, 1961-62; France, 1934-36, 1962-63. US citizen, 1943. **Taught:** Columbia U., 1948-61; Pratt Institute, 1951-61, 1964-71; Queens College, 1964; NAD, 1964-71. **Member:** SAGA; NAD; NIAL.

Commissions: Illustrations for numerous books and magazines; two prints for International Graphic Arts Society. **Awards:** Four-year fellowship from the Spanish Repubic, 1933; Chicago/AI, The Mr. & Mrs. Frank G. Logan Prize, ca. 1940; PAFA, Alice McFadden Eyre Medal, 1940; A.A.A. Gallery, NYC, National Print Competition, First Prize, 1948; Library of Congress, First Pennell **P.P.,** 1949; Guggenheim Foundation Fellowship, 1940, 50; NIAL Grant, 1950; SAGA, 1963. **One-man Exhibitions:** (first) Raymond and Raymond, Inc., NYC; Weyhe Gallery, 1934-41; A.A.A., Gallery, NYC, 1947-52, 78; Bucknell U.; Philadelphia Art Alliance; Albany/Institute; Bennington College; Swarthmore College; Princeton U.; Columbia U.; California Palace; Madrid/Nacional; Caracas; La Paz, Bolivia; Argentina/Nacional; Asuncion, Paraguay; Montevideo/Municipal; a gallery in Paris; Bombay; Los Angeles/County MA; Slater, 1969; Martin Summers Gallery, NYC, 1978; Gallery Schlesinger-Boisanté, NYC, 1985. **Retrospective:** Syracuse U., 1978. **Group:** College d'Espagne, Paris, 1934; Corcoran; Chicago/AI; Brooklyn Museum; PAFA; WMAA; SAGA. **Collections:** Brooklyn Museum; Chicago/AI; Dartmouth College; U. of Georgia; Kalamazoo/Institute; Library of Congress; MMA; U. of Minnesota; Montclair/AM; NYPL; PAFA; PMA; Princeton U.; Syracuse U.; Utica; WMAA; Yale U. **Bibliography:** American Artists Group Inc. 3; Baur 7; Front; Goodrich and Baur 1; Mendelowitz; Pearson 1; Reese; Zigrosser 1. Archives.

CAVALLON, GIORGIO. b. March 2, 1904, Sorio, Vicenza, Italy. To USA, 1920. **Studied:** NAD, 1925-30; with C. W. Hawthorne, ca. 1929; Hofmann School, 1935-36. Resided Italy, 1930-33. **Taught:** Pratt Institute, 1952, 54 (woodworking); U. of North Carolina, 1964; Yale U., 1964; Columbia U., summer, 1969. **Member:** American Abstract Artists, 1936-57. Federal A.P.: Mural project assistant to Arshile Gorky, and easel painting. **Awards:** L. C. Tiffany Grant, 1929; Guggenheim Foundation Fellowship, 1966-67. **Address:** 178 East 95th Street, NYC 10028. **Dealer:** Gruenebaum Gallery, NYC. **One-man Exhibitions:** (first) Bottege d'Arte, Vicenza, Italy, 1932; ACA Gallery, 1934; Eighth Street Playhouse, NYC, 1940; Charles Egan Gallery, 1946, 48, 51, 54; The Stable Gallery, 1957, 59; The Kootz Gallery, NYC, 1961, 63; U. of North Carolina, 1964; A.M. Sachs Gallery, 1969, 71, 72, 74, 76; Gruenebaum Gallery, NYC, 1978, 79, 81, 82, 83, 85, 86. **Retrospective:** Purchase/SUNY, 1976. **Group:** WMAA, 1947, 48, 59, 61; Salon des Realites Nouvelles, Paris, 1950; MOMA, Abstract Painting and Sculpture in America, 1951; MMA, American Watercolors, Drawings and Prints, 1952; U. of Nebraska, 1955; Documenta II Kassel, 1959; Chicago/AI, 1959; Carnegie, 1959, 61; Walker, 1960; SRGM, Abstract Expressionists and Imagists, 1961; U. of Illinois, 1963; MOMA, 60 Modern Drawings, 1963; PAFA Annual, 1966; WMAA, The 1930s, 1968; A.F.A., 1968-69; MOMA, The New American Painting and Sculpture, 1969; A.F.A., Geometric Abstraction of the 1930s, 1972; Hirshhorn, Bicentennial Exhibition, 1976. **Collections:** American Republic Insurance Co.; Avco Corp.; Avon Products; The Bank of New York; Buffalo/Albright; U. of California; Chase Manhattan Bank; Ciba-Geigy Corp.; Continental Grain Company; MOMA; Marine Midland Bank and Trust Co.; NYU; U. of North Carolina; Prudential Insurance Co. of America; SRGM; The Singer Company, Inc.; U. of Texas; Tishman Realty & Construction Co. Inc.; Union Carbide Corp.; WMAA. **Bibliography:** Blesh 1; Hess, T. B., 1; McCurdy, ed.; O'Hara 1; Pousette-Dart, ed.; Ritchie 1; Rose, B., 1. Archives.

CELMINS, VIJA. b. 1939, Riga, Latvia. To USA, 1949. **Studied:** John Herron Art Institute, Indianapolis, 1958-62,

BFA; Yale U., 1961; UCLA, 1962-65 MFA. **Taught:** California State College, Los Angeles, 1965-66; U. of California, Irvine, 1967-72; California Institute of the Arts, Valencia, 1976. **Awards:** Cassandra Foundation, Award, 1968; National Endowment for the Arts, 1971, 76; US Department of the Interior, 1975; Guggenheim Foundation Fellowship, 1980. **Address:** 122 Mercer Street, NYC 10012. **Dealer:** David McKee Gallery, NYC. **One-man Exhibitions:** (first) David Stuart Galleries, Los Angeles, 1966; Riko Mizuno Gallery, Los Angeles, 1969, 73; WMAA, 1973; Felicity Samuel Gallery, London, 1975; Broxton Gallery, Los Angeles, 1975; Security Pacific National Bank, Los Angeles, 1978; David McKee Gallery, 1983. **Retrospective:** Newport Harbor Art Museum, circ., 1979. **Group:** California State college, Hayward, Four Painters, 1966; U. of Colorado, Boulder, NYC-L.A. Drawings of the 60s, 1967; Fort Worth, Contemporary American Drawings, 1969; WMAA Annuals, 1970, 77; La Jolla, Continuing Surrealism, 1971; Los Angeles/County MA, 24 Young Los Angeles Artists, 1971; La Jolla, Earth, Animal, Vegetable, and Mineral, 1971; MOMA, California, Prints, 1972; Brooklyn Museum, national print exhibition, 1972; WMAA, American Drawings, 1963-1973, 1973; U. of Illinois, 1974; Chicago/AI, 71st American Exhibition, 1974; US Department of the Interior, America 1976, circ., 1976; Detroit/Institute, American Artists, A New Decade, 1976; SFMA, Painting and Sculpture in California; The Modern Era, 1976; Brooklyn Museum, 30 Years of American Printmaking, 1976; SFMA, California Painting and Sculpture: The Modern Era, 1977; Brooklyn Museum, Thirty Years of American Printmaking, 1977; WMAA Biennial, 1977; MIT, Great Big Drawings, 1982; Brooklyn Museum, The American Artist as Printmaker, 1983; Houston/Contemporary, American Still Life, 1945-1983, 1983. **Collections:** WMAA; Newport Harbor; MOMA; AT&T; Los Angeles/County MA; Fort

Worth; Levi Strauss & Co., San Francisco; Paine Webber, Jackson and Curtis, Inc., NYC; SFMA. **Bibliography:** Lippard 6; *New in the Seventies; America 1976.*

CHAET, BERNARD. b. March 7, 1924, Boston, Mass. **Studied:** Tufts U., B.S. Ed.; Boston Museum School, with Karl Zerbe. Traveled Europe; resided Paris, 1949. **Taught:** Yale U., 1951-; American Academy, Rome. Contributing editor, *Arts* magazine, 1956-59. **Awards:** Silvermine Guild Award, 1955; Yale U., Senior Faculty Fellowship, 1962; St. Paul Art Center, Drawing USA, Merit Award, 1963; National Council on the Arts, Grant, 1966-67; AAIAL, Hassam and Spiecher Fund Purchase, 1981; Hon. DFA, Maryland Institute, 1985; College Art Association, Distinguished Teaching of Art Award, 1986. **Address:** 141 Cold Spring Street, New Haven, CT 06511. **Dealer:** Alpha Gallery; Marilyn Pearl Gallery, NYC. **One-man Exhibitions:** (first) Boris Mirski Gallery, Boston, 1946, also 1951, 54, 57, 59, 61, 65; The Bertha Schaefer Gallery, 1954; The Stable Gallery, 1959, 61, 67; Cornell U., 1961; Alpha Gallery, 1967, 68, 69, 71; Swarthmore College, 1971; Haslem Fine Arts, Inc., 1973; The Forum Gallery, 1975; Alpha Gallery, Boston, 1971, 75, 77, 80, 82, 84; Marilyn Pearl Gallery, NYC, 1976, 78, 79, 81, 82, 84, 86; Trinity College, 1979; Washington Art Association, Washington Depot, Conn., 1984; Delaware Art Museum, 1982. **Retrospective:** Brockton/Fuller, 1970. **Group:** U. of Illinois, 1951, 53, 61; PAFA; Los Angeles/County MA; Phillips; Chicago/AI; U. of Nebraska; ICA, Boston, 6 New England Painters, 1954; Corcoran; Contemporary American Drawings, circ., France, 1957-58; Hartford/Wadsworth, 8 From Connecticut, 1961; Detroit/Institute; MOMA; Brooklyn Museum; U. of North Carolina, 1977; U. of North Carolina, Art on Paper, 1983. **Collections:** Andover/Phillips; Boston/MFA; Boston

Public Library; Brandeis U.; Brooklyn Museum; Brown U.; U. of Connecticut; Cortland/SUNY; Dartmouth College; Harvard U.; Indiana U.; Lincoln, Mass./De Cordova; U. of Massachusetts; NYU; RISD; UCLA; Worcester/AM; Yale U.; U. of North Carolina. **Bibliography: Chaet.**

CHAMBERLAIN, JOHN. b. 1927, Rochester, Ind. **Studied:** Chicago/AI School, 1950-52; Black Mountain College, 1955-56. US Navy, 1943-46. **Awards:** Guggenheim Foundation Fellowship, 1966, 77. **Commission:** GSA, 1978. **Address:** c/o Dealer. **Dealer:** Xavier Fourcade, Inc., NYC. **One-man Exhibitions:** (first) Wells Street Gallery, Chicago, 1957; Davida Gallery, Chicago, 1958; Martha Jackson Gallery, 1960; Dilexi Gallery, Los Angeles, 1962; Dilexi Gallery, San Francisco, 1962; Leo Castelli Inc., 1962 (two-man), 1964, 65, 68, 69, 71, 73, 76, 82; Leo Castelli Warehouse, 1969; The Pace Gallery, Boston, 1963; Robert Fraser Gallery, 1963 (two-man); Dwan Gallery, Los Angeles, 1965; Cleveland/MA, 1967; Contemporary Arts Center, Cincinnati, 1968; Mizuno Gallery, 1969; LoGiudice Gallery, Chicago, 1970; Taft Museum (two-man), 1972; Dag Hammarskjold Plaza, NYC, 1973; Walter Kelly Gallery, Chicago, 1974; Houston/Contemporary, 1975; Ronald Greenberg Gallery, St. Louis, 1975; Locksley-Shea Gallery, Minneapolis (two-man), 1975; Margo Leavin Gallery, Los Angeles, 1977, 85; Dia Art Foundation, NYC, 1977, 83; Heiner Friedrich, Inc., 1977; Berne, 1979; Galerie Heiner Friedrich, Cologne, 1979; Eindhoven, 1980; Sarasota/Ringling, 1983; Youngstown/Butler, 1983; Robert L. Kidd Gallery, Birmingham, Mich., 1983; Multiples, Inc., NYC, 1983; L.A. Louver Gallery, Los Angeles, 1983; Palacio de Cristal, Madrid, 1984; Xavier Fourcade, Inc., 1984; U. of California, Santa Barbara (two-man), 1984. **Retrospective:** SRGM, 1971. **Group:** MOMA, Recent Sculpture USA, 1959; Buenos Aires

John Chamberlain *Iceberg* 1986

Museum of Modern Art, International Sculpture Exhibition, 1960; Martha Jackson Gallery, New Media—New Forms, I & II, 1960, 61; WMAA Annuals, 1960, 62, 65; Sculpture Annuals, 1966, 68; Galerie Rive Droite, Paris, Le Nouveau Realisme, 1961; VI Sao Paulo Biennial, 1961; MOMA, The Art of Assemblage, circ., 1961; Chicago/AI, 1961, 67; Carnegie, 1961, 67; Seattle World's Fair, 1962; SRGM, The Joseph H. Hirshhorn Collection, 1962; Battersea Park, London International Sculpture Exhibition, 1963; Musée Can-

tonal des Beaux-Arts, Lausanne, I Salon International de Galeries Pilotes, 1963; Pasadena/AM, New American Sculpture, 1964; New York World's Fair, 1964-65; Tate, Painting and Sculpture of a Decade, 1954-64, 1964; XXXII Venice Biennial, 1964; Jewish Museum, 1964; ICA, U. of Pennsylvania, The Atmosphere of '64, 1964, also 1965; Flint/Institute, 1965; ICA, Boston, Painting without a brush, 1965; Indianapolis/Herron, 1965, 69; WMAA, Contemporary American Sculpture, Selection I, 1966; MOMA, The 1960's, 1967; HemisFair '68, San Antonio, Tex., 1968; Swarthmore College, 1969; Trenton/State, Soft Art, 1969; York U., Toronto, 1969; ICA, U. of Pennsylvania, Highway, 1970; Indianapolis, 1970, 72; Cincinnati/Contemporary, Monumental Art, 1970; WMAA Sculpture Annual, 1970; MOMA, Younger Abstract Expressionists of the Fifties, 1971; Hofstra U., Art around the Automobile, 1971; Dusseldorf/Kunsthalle, Prospect '71, 1971; NCFA, Sculpture, American Directions, 1945-75, 1975; WMAA, 200 Years of American Sculpture, 1976; Akademie der Kunste, Berlin, SoHo, 1976; Cambridge U., Jubilation, 1977; Flint/Institute, Art and the Automobile, 1978; WMAA, Art about Art, 1978; Zurich, Soft Art, 1979; Documenta VII, Kassel, 1982; Dusseldorf/Kunsthalle, 1983; U. of North Carolina, Art on Paper, 1984; Ecole des Beaux Arts, Paris, Cinquante ans de dessins americains, 1985; Fort Lauderdale, An American Renaissance: Painting and Sculpture Since 1940, 1986. **Collections:** Buffalo/Albright; Chicago/AI; U. of Chicago; Cleveland/MA; Dallas/MFA; Detroit/Institute; Fort Worth; Frankfurt/Moderne; Hirshhorn; Kansas City/Nelson; Krefeld/Kaiser Wilhelm; Los Angeles/County MA; Los Angeles/MOCA; MOMA; Monchengladbach; Norfolk/Chrysler; U. of North Carolina; Oberlin College; Pasadena/AM; Purchase/SUNY; Rome/Nazionale; SRGM; St. Louis/City; Sarasota/Ringling; Stockholm/National; Tate Gallery; VMFA;

Vanderbilt U.; Vienna/Moderner; WMAA; Walker; Washington U. **Bibliography:** Battcock, ed.; Craven, W.; Honisch and Jensen, eds.; Hunter, ed.; Janis and Blesh 1; Kozloff 3; Kuh 3; Licht, F.; Lippard 5; *Metro; Monumenta;* Phillips, Lisa; Read 3; *Report:* Rose, B., 1; Rowell; Sandler 1; Seitz 3; Seuphor 3; **Sylvester;** Tuchman 1; Warhol and Hackett.

CHINNI, PETER. b. March 21, 1928, Mt. Kisco, N.Y. **Studied:** ASL, 1947, with Edwin Dickinson, Kenneth Hayes Miller, Julian Levi; Academy of Fine Arts, Rome, 1949-50, with Emilio Sorini. Traveled Puerto Rico, Mexico, Europe; resided in Italy 19 years. **Member:** Sculptors Guild; Artists Equity. **Commissions:** Denver/AM (bronze mural); City of Columbia, Mo., 1979; Board of Education, NYC, 1984. **Awards:** ASL, Daniel Schnackenberg Scholarship, 1948; Silvermine Guild, First Prize, 1958, 60, 61; Denver/AM, Second Prize, 1960. **Address:** 1 Andrews Place, Wappingers Falls, N.Y. 12590. **Dealer:** Adele M. Gallery and Art Service, Dallas. **One-man Exhibitions:** (first) Fairleigh Dickinson U., 1951; Galleria San Marco, Rome, 1955; Il Torcoliere, Rome, 1956; Kipnis Gallery, Westport, Conn., 1956; R. R. Gallery, Denver, 1957; Galleria Schneider, Rome, 1957; Janet Nessler Gallery, NYC, 1957, 61; Royal Marks Gallery, 1964; Albert Loeb Gallery, NYC, 1966; Loeb & Krugier Gallery, 1969; Tyler School of Art, Rome, 1979; Harcus Krakow Rosen Sonnabend Gallery, Boston, 1976; Galerie Alexandra Monett, Brussels, 1976; Galerie Bouma, Amsterdam, 1976; Musée d'Ixelles, Brussels, 1976; Beeckestijn Museum, Velsen, Holland, 1976; Hooks-Epstein Gallery, Houston, 1978; Katonah (N.Y.) Art Gallery, 1983. **Group:** Audobon Artists Annuals, 1958, 59, 61, 62; Festival of Two Worlds, Spoleto, 1960; Boston Arts Festival, 1960, 62; Connecticut Academy of Fine Arts, 1960, 62; WMAA Annuals, 1960, 62, 64, 65; Cor-

coran, 1962; Galleria Pagani del Grattacielo, Milan, 1962; Waitsfield/Bundy, 1963; Sculptors Guild, 1963, 64, 66, 68; Carnegie, 1964; Heseler Gallery, Munich, 1968; Rome/Nazionale, 1968; Utica, American Prints Today, 1970; WMAA, Art of the Sixties, 1975. **Collections:** Denver/AM; Fontana-Hollywood Corp.; St.Louis/City; WMAA; Beeckestijn Museum, Velsen, Holland; New School for Social Research; Louisville/Speed; National Gallery; MIT; Chase Manhattan Bank, Rome; Bank of New York, NYC; First National Bank, Chicago; Denver; Pace College, NYC; Middlebury College.

CHRISTENSEN, DAN. b. 1942, Lexington, Neb. **Studied:** Kansas City/AI, BFA. **Taught:** Ridgewood School of Art, 1975-77; School of Visual Arts, NYC, 1976-; NYU, 1983-. **Address:** 16 Waverly Place, NYC 10003. **Dealer:** Salander-O'Reilly Gallery, NYC. **One-man Exhibitions:** Noah Goldowsky, 1967, 68; Galerie Rudolf Zwirner, 1967; Galerie Rolf Ricke, Cologne, 1968, 71; Andre Emmerich Gallery, NYC, 1969, 71, 72, 74, 75, 76; Nicholas Wilder Gallery, 1970, 72; Edmonton Art Gallery, Alberta, 1973; Ronald Greenberg Gallery, St. Louis, 1974; Watson/De Nagy Gallery, Houston, 1977; B. R. Kornblatt Gallery, Baltimore, 1977; Douglas Drake Gallery, Kansas City, 1978, 79, 80, 81, 82, 84; Gloria Luria Gallery, Miami, 1978; Meredith Long & Co., Houston, 1978, 80, 81, 84; Meredith Long Contemporary, NYC, 1978, 79, 80; U. of Nebraska, 1980; Salander-O'Reilly Galleries, 1981, 82, 83, 84, 86; Gallery 700, Milwaukee, 1981; Gloria Luria Gallery, Bay Harbor Islands, Fla., 1981; Harcus Krakow Gallery, Boston, 1981; Ivory/Kimpton Gallery, San Francisco, 1982; Lincoln Center Gallery, NYC, 1983, 84; Carson-Sapiro Gallery, Denver, 1983; Il Punto Blu Gallery, Southampton, N.Y., 1984; Wichita State U., 1984. **Group:** WMAA, 1967, 69, 72, 73; Washington U., Here and Now, 1979; Corcoran, 1969; Buffalo/Albright,

Color and Field: 1890-1970, 1970; WMAA, The Structure of Color, 1971; WMAA, Lyrical Abstraction, 1971; Buffalo/Albright, Six Painters, 1971; Boston/MFA, Abstract Painting in the '70s, 1972; WMAA Biennial, 1973; Lehigh U., Freedom in Art, 1976; U. of Nebraska, Expressionism in the '70s, 1978; MOMA, New Work on Paper I, 1981; Houston/MFA, Miró in America, 1982; Youngstown/Butler, Midyear Show, 1982, 85. **Collections:** Boston/MFA; Buffalo/Albright; Chicago/AI; Chicago/Contemporary; Dayton/AI; Denver/AM; Edmonton; Greenville; High Museum; Hirshhorn; Houston/MFA; Indianapolis; MMA; MOMA; Mutual Benefit Life Insurance Co., Kansas City; U. of Nebraska; SRGM; St. Louis/City; Seattle/AM; Toledo/MA; WMAA. **Bibliography:** *Kunst um 1970;* Wood; *New In the Seventies.*

CHRISTO (Javacheff). b. June 13, 1935, Gabrovo, Bulgaria. **Studied:** Academy of Fine Arts, Sofia, 1951-56; theater design at Burian Theater, Prague, 1956; Academy of Fine Arts, Vienna, 1957. Moved to Geneva, 1957, to Paris, 1958, to NYC, 1964. Films of Projects: *Wrapped Coast,* 1969; *Christ's Valley Curtain,* 1972; *Running Fence,* 1973-76; Greater Miami, Surrounded Islands, Biscayne Bay, 1980-83; Paris, The Pont Neuf, Wrapped, 1985. **Address:** 48 Howard Street, NYC 10013. **Dealer:** Jeanne-Claude Christo, NYC. **One-man Exhibitions:** Galerie Haro Lauhus, Cologne, 1961; Galerie J. Paris, 1962; Galerie Schmela, 1963, 64; Galleria Apollinaire, Milan, 1963; Galleria del Leone, Venice, 1963, 68; Galleria la Salita, Rome, 1963; Galerie Ad Libitum, Antwerp, 1964; Gian Enzo Sperone, Turin, 1964; Eindhoven, 1966; Leo Castelli Inc., NYC, 1966; Walker, 1966; Wide White Space Gallery, Antwerp, 1967, 69; Galerie der Spiegel, Cologne, 1967, 69; John Gibson Gallery, 1968, 69; MOMA, 1968; ICA, U. of Pennsylvania, 1968; Chicago/Contemporary,

1969; Little Bay, Australia, Wrapped Coast, 1969; Central Street Gallery, Sydney, 1969; Melbourne/National, 1969; New Gallery, Cleveland, 1970; Francoise Lambert, Milan, 1970; Annely Juda Fine Art, London, 1971, 77, 79; Zurich, 1973; Allan Frumkin Gallery, Chicago, 1973; La Jolla, 1975; White Gallery, Lutry, 1975; Edificio Galipan, Caracas, 1975; Museo de Bellas Artes, Caracas, 1975; ICA, Boston, 1975; Galerie J. Benador, Geneva, 1975; Fabian Fine Arts, Cape Town, 1975; Galerie der Spiegel, Cologne, 1975; Museum des 20. Jahrhunderts, Vienna, 1976; SFMA, 1976; Pasadena/AM, 1976; Galerie Juan Prats, 1977; Rotterdam, 1977; Bonn, 1977; Hannover/K-G, 1977; Miami Gallery, Tokyo, 1977; Humlebaek/Louisiana, 1978; Kunstgewerbe, Zurich, 1978; Brussels/Beaux-Arts, 1978; American Foundation for the Arts, Miami, 1978; Kansas City/Nelson, 1978; Hartford/Wadsworth, 1978; Wiener Secession, Vienna, 1979; ICA, London, 1979; ICA, Boston, 1979; Corcoran, 1979; Abu Dhabi, United Arab Emirates, French Cultural Center, 1980; Cabrillo College, Aptos, Calif., 1980; Jackson/MMA, 1980; New Gallery, Cleveland, 1980; Newport Harbor, 1980; Winnepeg (Canada) Art Gallery, 1980; Albuquerque Museum, 1981; Cologne/Ludwig, 1981; Hokin Gallery, Miami, 1981; Juda-Rowan Gallery, London, 1981; Madison Art Center, 1981; Metropolitan Museum & Art Center, 1981; Montreal/Contemporain, 1981; Portland (Ore.) Center for Visual Arts, 1981; U. of Texas, El Paso, 1981; Art Gallery of Hamilton, Ont., 1982; Biuro Wystaw Artsystycznych, Sopot, Poland, 1982; U. of Calgary, 1982; Colby College, 1982; Frankfurt am Main, 1982; Kunstlerhaus Bethanien, Berlin, 1982; U. of Maine, 1982; Tokyo/Hara; U. of Wisconsin, Madison, 1982; Cincinnati/Contemporary, 1983; Delahunty Gallery, Dallas, 1983; Fukuoda, 1983; U. of Notre Dame, 1983; Osaka/National, 1983; Luther Burbank Center for the Arts, Santa Rosa, Calif., 1984; Berlin/National, 1984; Hartnell College, 1984; Henies-Onstadts Stiftelser, 1984; Indianapolis/Herron, 1984; Annely Juda Fine Art, London, 1984; Satani Gallery, Tokyo, 1984; Sun Valley (Id.) Center for the Arts and Humanities, 1984; Fondation Maeght, 1985; Hamburg, 1985; New Britain/American, 1985; Rijksmuseum Kröller-Müller, 1985; U. of West Florida, 1985; Carpenter + Hochman Gallery, Dallas, 1986; College of St. Rose, Albany, N.Y., 1986; Florida State U., 1986; Miami/Bass, 1986; Galerie Joan Prats, Barcelona, 1986; Southern Illinois U., 1986; Syracuse U., 1986. **Group:** Andover/Phillips; Harvard U.; Sorbonne; WMAA; Smithsonian; Brooklyn Museum; Boston/MFA; A.F.A., circ.; Boston Arts Festival; ICA, Boston, 1959-67, incl. View, 1960, 1960; Corcoran, 1961, 64, 65; Lincoln, Mass./De Cordova, 1966; Norfolk, 1967; AAAL, 1968; PAFA, 1969; NIAL, 1969. **Collections:** Aachen/NG; Albuquerque Museum; Amsterdam/Stedelijk; Andover/Phillips; Basel; Berlin/National; Bonn; Boston/MFA; Boston U.; Bowdoin College; Buffalo/Albright; Canberra/National; Chicago/AI; Chicago/Contemporary; Cleveland/MA; Cologne; Cologne/Ludwig; Dallas/MFA; Dartmouth College; Des Moines; Detroit/Institute; Dublin/National; Grenoble; Hamburg; Hannover/Kunstverein; Harvard U.; Houston/MFA; Humlebaek/Louisiana; Israel Museum; Kansas City/Nelson; Krefeld/Kaiser Wilhelm; La Jolla; Lincoln, Mass./De Cordova; Los Angeles/County MA; MOMA: Marseilles/Cantini U. of Massachusetts; U. of Miami; U. of Michigan; Minnesota/MA; Munich/NP; Museum des 20. Jahrhunderts; Oberlin College; PMA; Paris/Beaubourg; Paris/Moderne; Rijksmuseum Kröller-Müller; Rotterdam; SFMA; Santa Barbara/MA; Seattle/AM; Smith College; Stockholm; Stuttgart/WK Sydney/AG; U. of Sydney; Tate Gallery; U. of Tennessee; Tokyo/Hara; Toulon; VMFA; Victoria and Albert Museum; WMAA;

Walker; Wichita/AM; Worcester/AM; Yale U.; Zurich; Zurich/KS. **Bibliography:** De Wilde 2; Diamonstein; *Drawings: the Pluralist Decade;* Gettings; Honisch and Jensen, eds.; Hunter, ed.; Rowell; Strachan. Archives.

CHRYSSA. b. 1933, Athens, Greece. **Studied:** Academie de la Grande Chaumiere, 1953-54; California School of Fine Arts, 1954-55. US citizen, 1955. Traveled Europe, USA. **Awards:** Guggenheim Foundation Fellowship, 1973; MIT, grant, 1979-80. **Address:** 565 Broadway, NYC, 10012. **Dealer:** Leo Castelli Inc., NYC. **One-man Exhibitions:** (first) Betty Parsons Gallery, 1961; SRGM, 1961; Cordier & Ekstrom, Inc., 1962; Robert Fraser Gallery, 1962; The Pace Gallery, 1966, 67, 68; The Graphic Gallery, San Francisco, 1968; Galerie der Spiegel, Cologne, 1968;

Carmen Cicero *Running Scared* 1984

Harvard U., 1968; Obelisk Gallery, 1969; Galerie Rive Droite, Paris, 1969; WMAA, 1972; Galerie Denise Rene, NYC, 1973, 76; Galerie Denise Rene, Paris, 1974; Galerie Andre Emmerich, Zurich, 1974, 75; Paris/Moderne, 1979; Montreal/Contemporain, 1974; Paris/Moderne, 1979. **Group:** MOMA, Americans 1963, circ., 1963-64; Sao Paulo Biennials, 1963, 69; WMAA Annuals; Carnegie; Martha Jackson Gallery, New Media—New Forms, I, 1960; Boston Arts Festival, 1960; Seattle World's Fair, 1962; Jewish Museum; Documenta IV, Kassel, 1968; Venice Biennial, 1972; Pinacotheque National Museum, 1980. **Collections:** Berlin/National; Buffalo/Albright; Chase Manhattan Bank; U. of Chicago; Corcoran; Eindhoven; Greece/National; Hirshhorn; MIT; MMA; MOMA; Montreal/Contemporain; PMA; Princeton U.; Purchase/SUNY; Raleigh/NCMA; Rotterdam; SFMA; SRGM; Tate Gallery; WMAA; Walker. **Bibliography:** Battcock, ed.; Calas, N. and E.; Honisch; Hunter, ed.; Lippard 5; Strachan. Tuchman 1; **Waldman 2.**

CICERO, CARMEN LOUIS. b. August 14, 1926, Newark, N.J. US Army, World War II, Philippines. **Studied:** Newark State Teachers College, BA, 1947-51; Hunter College (with Robert Motherwell), 1953-55; Hofmann School, NYC. Traveled Europe. **Taught:** Sarah Lawrence College, 1959-68; School of Visual Arts, NYC, 1965-67; New School for Social Research, 1967-70; Newark State College, 1969-70; Montclair (N.J.) State College, 1969-. **Awards:** Guggenheim Foundation Fellowship, 1957, 63, 64; Ford Foundation, **P.P.,** 1961, 65. **Address:** 278 Bowery, NYC 10012. **Dealer:** The Graham Gallery, NYC. **One-man Exhibitions:** The Peridot Gallery, NYC, 1956, 57, 59, 61, 62, 64, 66, 68, 69; Arts Club of Chicago, 1958; Galerie Simone Stern, New Orleans; Kendall Gallery, Wellfleet, Mass., and Palm Beach; Rankow Gallery, 1971, 72, 74, 75;

Montclair College, 1975; Gallery Simone Stern, New Orleans, 1972; South Houston Gallery, NYC, 1975; Caldwell College, 1976; Long Point Gallery, Provincetown, Mass., 1977, 79, 81, 84; E. P. Gurewitsch Gallery, NYC, 1979; Gracie Mansion Gallery, NYC, 1982; Cincinnati, 1983; The Graham Gallery, 1985. **Group:** Corcoran, 1953; MOMA, 1953, 55; WMAA, 1955, 57, Annuals, 1960-63, 1965; U. of Nebraska, 1957; Chicago/AI, 1957; Worcester/AM, 1958; PAFA: Brooklyn Museum; Museum des 20. Jahrhunderts, 1963; St. Paul Art Center, Drawings, U.S.A., 1966; WMAA Annuals; New School for Social Research, American Drawings, 1969; Youngstown/Butler, Midyear Show, 1973; Montclair/AM, Collage: American Masters, 1979. **Collections:** Albion College; Amsterdam/Stedelijk; Brooklyn Museum; Charlotte/Mint; Cornell U.; Hirschhorn; MOMA; U. of Michigan; Montclair/AM; NYU; U. of Nebraska; Newark Museum; Purchase/SUNY; Ridgefield/Aldrich; Rotterdam; SRGM; Schiedam/Stedelijk; Southern Illinois U.; Springfield, Mass./MFA; Toronto; Trenton/State; WMAA; Worcester/AM **Bibliography:** Gerdts.

CLARKE, JOHN CLEM. b. June 6, 1937, Bend, Ore. **Studied:** Oregon State U.; Mexico City College; U. of Oregon, BFA, 1960. Traveled Mexico, Europe, USA. **Address:** 465 W. Broadway, NYC 10012. **One-man Exhibitions:** The Kornblee Gallery, 1968, 69, 71; Franklin Siden Gallery, Detroit, 1969; OK Harris Works of Art, 1970, 72, 75, 77, 79, 81, 83; Michael Walls Gallery, 1970; Galerie M. E. Thelen, Essen, 1970; Phyllis Kind Gallery, Chicago, 1971; Pyramid Art Galleries, Ltd., 1971; Galerie de Gestlo, 1971; Jack Glenn Gallery, Corona del Mar, 1972; Carl Solway Gallery, Cincinnati, 1972; D.M. Gallery, London, 1974; Morgan Gallery, Kansas City, 1977, 81; Deson-Zaks Gallery, Chicago, 1977. **Group:** WMAA, 1967, 69, 72, 75; U. of Illinois,

1969; Milwaukee, Aspects of a New Realism, 1969; WMAA, 22 Realists, 1970; Chicago/AI, 1970; Potsdam/SUNY, New Realism, 1971; Chicago/Contemporary, Radical Realism, 1971; Santa Barbara/MA, Spray, 1971; U. of Miami, Phases of New Realism, 1972; New York Cultural Center, Realism Now, 1972; Indianapolis, 1974; Hartford/Wadsworth, New/Photo Realism, 1974; Tokyo Biennial, 1974; Cleveland/MA, Aspects of the Figure, 1974; Skidmore College, New Realism, 1974; Potsdam/SUNY, The Presence and Absence of Realism, 1976; Stratford, Ontario, Aspects of Realism, circ., 1976; Indianapolis, 1976, 78; US Department of the Interior, America 1976, 1976; Fort Wayne, Hue and Far Cry of Color, 1976; Taft Museum, Look Again, 1976; Rice U., Abstract Illusionism, 1977; U. of Texas, Austin, New in the Seventies, 1977; Canberra/National, Illusion and Reality, 1977; St. Petersburg, Fla., Photo Realism, 1977; U. of Rochester, Perceiving Time and Space through Art, 1979; Aspen Center for the Visual Arts, Portraits of the Sixties/Seventies, 1979; Tulsa/Philbrook, Realism/Photorealism, 1980; Marquette U., Changes: Art in America 1881-1981, 1981; PAFA, Contemporary American Realism Since 1960, 1981; U. of Rhode Island, Diversity: New York Artists, 1985. **Collections:** Akron/AI; Baltimore/MA; Brooklyn Museum; U. of California, Berkeley; Chase Manhattan Bank; Cleveland/MA; Dallas/MFA; Flint/Institute; Fort Worth; U. of Georgia; Harvard U.; Hirshhorn; Indianapolis; Kansas City/Nelson; MMA; MOMA; Milwaukee; Security Pacific National Bank; Syracuse U.; VMFA; WMAA; Wichita State U. **Bibliography:** *Amerikanischer Fotorealismus; America 1976;* Arthur 1; *Kunst um 1970;* Lindy; Murken-Altrogge; *New in the Seventies;* Sager. Archives.

CLERK, PIERRE. b. March 26, 1928, Atlanta, Ga. **Studied:** McGill U.,

Montreal; Loyola College; Montreal/MFA; Academie Julian, Paris; Academy of Fine Arts, Florence, Italy. Traveled Canada, Europe. Resided seven years in Europe. **Commissions:** (tapestries) Skidmore, Owings & Merrill; Commerce Trust Co., Kansas City. **Awards:** Canada Council Award, 1971, 72; Tamarind Fellowship, 1972; Municipal Art Society, NYC, award, 1977; The Canada Council Award, 1980; % for the Arts Commission: Toledo, 1983. **Address:** 55 Central Park West, NYC 10023. **One-man Exhibitions:** Numero Gallery, Florence, Italy; Galleria Totti, Milan; Cittadella Gallery, Ascona, Switzerland; Beno Gallery, Zurich; Montreal/MFA; New Gallery, NYC; Galleria del Cavallino, Venice; Siegelaub Gallery, NYC, 1965, 67; Gimpel Fils, 1971; Gimpel & Hanover, 1971; Gimpel & Weitzenhoffer Ltd., 1971; Tirca Karlis Gallery, 1971; Gallery Moos, Montreal, 1972; Syracuse/Everson, 1977; Manila, 1978; USIA, sponsor, Central America and Far East tour, 1977-78; Waterside Plaza, NYC, 1977; Canadian Cultural Center, Paris, 1981. **Group:** XXVIII & XXIX, Venice Biennials, 1956, 1958; Carnegie, 1959; Expo '67, Montreal 1967; Dublin/Municipal, International Quadriennial (ROSC), 1971; Indianapolis, 1972; Bradford, England, III British Print Biennial, 1972. **Collections:** American National Fire Insurance Co.; Atlantic Richfield Co.; Avon Corp; The Bank of New York; Brandeis U.; Buffalo/Albright; Burlington Mills; Chase Manhattan Bank; First National City Bank; U. of Glasgow; Gulf Oil Corp.; Gulf and Western Industries, Inc.; Honolulu Academy; IBM; MOMA; McCrory Corporation; Mobil Oil Corp.; Montreal/Contemporain; Montreal/MFA; NYU; Newark Public Library; U. of Northern Iowa; Ottawa/National; Philip Morris; Purchase/SUNY; Quebec; Queens College; Radio Corporation of America; Rutgers U.; SRGM; The Singer Company, Inc.; Skidmore College; U. of Virginia; U.S. Steel Corp.; WMAA.

CLOAR, CARROLL. b. January 18, 1913, Earle, Ark. **Studied:** Memphis Academy of Arts; ASL, with William C. McNulty, Harry Sternberg; Southwestern College, BA. US Air Force, World War II, three years. Traveled Central and South America, Europe. **Taught:** Memphis Academy of Arts, 1956. **Member:** Artists Equity. **Awards:** MacDowell Traveling Fellowship, 1940; Guggenheim Foundation Fellowship, 1946; Youngstown/Butler, **P.P.;** Brooklyn Museum, **P.P.;** Library of Congress, **P.P.;** Mead Painting of the Year; Hon. PBK; Hon. Ph.D., Southwestern College. **Address:** 235 S. Greer, Memphis, TN 38111. **Dealer:** The Forum Gallery, NYC; **One-man Exhibitions:** (first) Memphis/Brooks, 1955, also 1957; The Alan Gallery, NYC, 1956, 58, 60, 62, 64, 65, 68; U. of Arkansas, 1956, 61; Fort Worth, 1963; Charleston Art Gallery, Charleston, W. Va.; U. of Georgia; Montgomery (Ala.) Museum of Fine Arts; Utah State Institute of Fine Arts, Salt Lake City; Columbia, S.C./MA; Dulin Gallery; Memphis/Brooks, 1957, 62, 72; Kennedy Gallery, NYC, 1973; The Forum Gallery, NYC, 1979, 81, 83, 85. **Retrospectives:** Albany/SUNY, 1968; Memphis/Brooks, 1960, 76; Tennessee State Museum, 1983. **Group:** PAFA; MMA; Carnegie; MOMA; WMAA; Brooklyn Museum; Dallas/MFA; U. of Nebraska; Brooklyn Museum, Black Folk Art in America, 1930-1980, circ., 1983. **Collections:** Abbott Laboratories; Albany/SUNY; Atlanta/AA; Brandeis U.; Bridgeport; Brooklyn Museum; Chase Manhattan Bank; Corcoran; First National Bank of Memphis; Friends of Art; Hartford/Wadsworth; Hirshhorn; Library of Congress; MMA; MOMA; Mead Corporation; Memphis/Brooks; Newark Museum; Phillips; Purchase/SUNY; St.Petersburg, Fla.; Southwestern (College) at Memphis; Tennessee State Museum; WMAA; Youngstown/Butler. **Bibliography:** Archives.

CLOSE, CHUCK (Charles). b. July 5, 1940, Monroe, Wash. **Studied:** U. of Washington, 1958-62, BA; Yale U. Summer School, Norfolk, Conn., 1961; Yale U., 1962-64; BFA, 1963, MFA, 1964; Akademie der Bildenden Kunste, Vienna, 1964-65. Traveled Europe. **Taught:** U. of Massachusetts, 1965-67; School of Visual Arts, NYC, 1967-71; NYU, 1970-73; U. of Washington, 1970; Yale U. Summer School, Norfolk, Conn., 1971, 72. **Awards:** National Endowment for the Arts, grant ($7,500), 1973. **Address:** 271 Central Park West, NYC 10024. **Dealer:** The Pace Gallery. **One-man Exhibitions:** U. of Massachusetts, 1967; Bykert Gallery, 1970, 71, 73, 75; Los Angeles/County MA, 1971; Chicago/Contemporary, 1972; MOMA, 1973; Akron/AI, 1973; Austin, 1975; Art Museum of South Texas, Corpus Christi, 1975; The Texas Gallery, Houston, 1975; Portland (Ore.) Center for the Visual Arts, 1975; Cincinnati/Contemporary, 1976; Baltimore/MA, 1976; The Pace Gallery, NYC, 1977, 79, 83, 86; Hartford/Wadsworth, 1977; Paris/Beaubourg, 1979; Munich, Kunstraum, 1979; U. of California, Riverside, 1982; Houston/Contemporary, 1985; Fuji Television Gallery, Tokyo, 1985; Pace-McGill Gallery, NYC, 1985. **Retrospectives:** Walker, circ., 1980; Cheney Cowles Memorial Museum, circ., 1984. **Group:** WMAA Annuals, 1969, 72; WMAA, 22 Realists, 1970; Oberlin College, Three Young Americans (with Ron Cooper and Neil Jenny), 1970; Dusseldorf/Kunsthalle, Prospect 72, 1971; Documenta V, Kassel, 1972; Galerie des 4 Mouvements, Paris, Hyperrealistes Americains, 1972; Stuttgart/WK, Amerikanischer Fotorealismus, circ., 1972; WMAA, American Drawings: 1963-1973, 1973; Ars 74, Helsinki, 1974; Worcester/AM, Three Realists, 1974; XI Tokyo Biennial, 1974; Corcoran, Biennial, 1975; Fort Worth, American Artists: A New Decade, 1976; Stratford, Ont., Aspects of Realism, 1976; MOMA, Drawing Now, 1976; Chicago/AI, 1976;

A.F.A., American Master Drawings and Watercolors, 1976; Daniel Weinberg, San Francisco (three-man), 1976; Akademie der Kunst, Berlin, SoHo, 1976; WMAA Biennials, 1977, 79; Documenta 6, Kassel, 1977; Canberra/National, Illusion and Reality, 1977; Minnesota/MA, American Drawings, 1927-1977, 1977; Paris/Beaubourg, Paris-New York, 1977; U. of California, Santa Barbara, Contemporary Drawing/NY, 1978; Buffalo/Albright, American Painting of the 1970's, 1978; Philadelphia College of Art, Point, 1978; Great Britain Arts Council, Hayward Gallery, The Mechanized Image, 1978; Pomona College, Black and White are Colors: Paintings of the 1950s-1970s, 1979; U. of North Carolina, Drawings About Drawing Today, 1979; NPG, American Portrait Drawings, 1980; WMAA, The Figurative Tradition and the WMAA, 1980; PAFA, Contemporary American Realism Since 1960, 1981; SRGM, Seven Photorealists from New York Collections, 1981; WMAA, American Prints: Process and Proofs, 1981; Arts Council of Great Britain, Photographer as Printmaker: 140 Years of Photographic Printmaking, 1981; MIT, Great Big Drawings, 1982; Hannover/K-G, Momentbild: Kunstlerphotographie, 1982; Maryland Institute, Drawings by Contemporary American Figurative Artists, 1984; AAIAL, 1985. **Collections:** Aachen/AG; Akron/AI; Berlin; Buffalo/Albright; Canberra/National; Chicago/Contemporary; Chicago/AI; Dayton/AI; Des Moines; U. of Georgia; Helsinki; High Museum; Indiana U.; Library of Congress; LIC; Milwaukee; MMA; MOMA; Minneapolis/Institute; U. of North Carolina; PMA; Paris/Beaubourg; Rotterdam; SRGM; Seattle/AM; Tate Gallery; Toledo/MA; Toronto; Utrecht; WMAA; Walker; Worcester/AM; Zurich. **Bibliography:** Adrian; **Amerikanischer Fotorealismus;** Arthur 2, 3, 4; Diamondstein; Gettings; Goldman 1; Honisch & Jensen, eds.; Kunst um 1970; Lindy; Murken-Altrogge; Sager; *Three Realists.*

CLUTZ, WILLIAM. b. March 19, 1933, Gettysburg, Pa. **Studied:** Mercersburg Academy, 1948-51; State U. of Iowa, with James Lechay, Stuart Edie, 1951-55, BA; ASL, 1956, with Robert Brackman. **Taught:** Artist-in-Residence, Bucknell U., 1957; Philadelphia College of Art, 1967; U. of Minnesota, 1967-68; Parsons School of Design, NYC, 1969-. **Address:** 370 Riverside Drive, NYC 10025. **Dealer:** Tatistcheff & Co., NYC. **One-man Exhibitions:** (first) Penn Hall Junior College and Preparatory School, Chambersburg, Pa., 1954; Bucknell U., 1957; Mercersburg Academy, 1958, 59; Condon Riley Gallery, NYC, 1959; David Herbert Gallery, NYC, 1962; The Bertha Schaefer Gallery, 1963, 64, 66, 69; Triangle Art Gallery, 1967; The Graham Gallery, 1972; Brooke Alexander, 1973; Exeter, 1973; Alonzo Gallery, NYC, 1977, 78, 79; Moravian College, Bethlehem, Pa., 1977; Walther-Rathenau-Saal, Rathaus, Wedding, West Berlin, 1978; Choate-Rosemary Hall School, 1979; Alonzo Gallery, NYC, 1979; Gallery 333, Dayton, Ohio, 1981; Tatistcheff & Co., 1981, 82, 84; John Stoller & Co., 1983; P. B. van Voorst van Beest Gallery, The Hague, 1984; U. of Minnesota, Duluth, 1986. **Retrospectives:** Brooklyn College, 1969; Andover/Phillips, 1973. **Group:** MOMA, Recent Drawings USA, 1956; A.F.A., The Figure, circ., 1960; Houston/MFA, The Emerging Figure, 1961; MOMA, Recent Painting, USA; The Figure, circ., 1962-63; PAFA Annuals, 1964-66; MOMA, Art in Embassies, circ.; U. of Nebraska, 1965; Norfolk/Chrysler, 1966; Purdue U., 1968; Ringling, 1969; Columbus, 1970; Smithsonian, American Drawings 1976-79; Westmoreland County/AM, The New American Still Life, 1978; Brooklyn Museum, Great East River Bridge: 1883-1983, 1983; SFMA, American Realism (Janss), circ., 1985. **Collections:** Andover/Phillips; AT&T, Ashland Oil Inc.; Ball State U.; Brooklyn College; Chase Manhattan Bank; Corcoran; Dayton/AI; Exeter; Hagertown/County MFA; Harvard U.;

Hirshhorn; MMA; MOMA; U. of Massachusetts; Miles College; Mills College; Milwaukee; Minnesota/MA; U. of Minnesota; NYU; U. of Nebraska; Newark Museum; New York School of Interior Design; J. Henry Schroder Banking Corp.; SRGM.

COATES, ROSS. b. November 1, 1932, Hamilton (Ont.), Canada. **Studied:** U. of Michigan, 1951-53; Chicago Art Institute School, 1956, BFA; NYU, 1960, MA; NYU, 1972, Ph.D., Traveled Canada, USA, Europe, resided Africa, 1968-70. **Taught:** New York Community College, 1963; Kansas City Art Institute and School of Design, 1963-64; Montclair State College, 1965-68; Canon Lawrence T.T.C., Lira, Uganda, 1968-70; Russell Sage College, 1971-76; Washington State U., 1976-. **Address:** S.W. 420 State Street, Pullman, WA 99163. **Dealer:** Space Gallery, Los Angeles. **One-man Exhibitions:** (first) Isaacs Gallery, 1957, also 1961; Camino Gallery, NYC, 1961; Louis Alexander Gallery, NYC, 1963; Galerie Niepel, Dusseldorf, 1966; Springfield College, 1966; Jerrold Morris Gallery, Toronto, 1967; Galerie Seyfried, Munich, 1967; Kansas City Jewish Community Center, 1968; Russell Sage College, 1972; Schenectady Museum, 1974; U. of Rochester, 1974; Washington State U., 1978; Spokane Falls Community College, 1979; Gordon Woodside Gallery, Seattle U., 1985; N.W. Artists Workshop, Portland, Ore., 1985. **Group:** Washington State U., Pullman, Living with the Volcano: Artists of Mt. St. Helens, 1983. **Collections:** U. of Alberta; Brandeis U.; Chase Manhattan Bank; U. of California; NYU; Springfield College; Stony Brook/SUNY; Russell Sage College.

CONGDON, WILLIAM. b. April 15, 1912, Providence, R.I. **Studied:** Yale U., BA; Cape School of Art, with Henry Hensche; PAFA; Folly Cove School of Art, with George Demetrios.

American Field Service, World War II. Active in postwar Italy with American Friends Service Committee. Traveled Mexico, North Africa, India, Cambodia, Central America, Europe. **Awards:** RISD, 1949, 50; PAFA, Joseph E. Temple Gold Medal, 1951; U. of Illinois, **P.P.,** 1951; Corcoran, William A. Clark Prize, 1952; International Novara, Trieste, Gold Medal, 1961; Hon. DFA, U. of Portland, 1969. **Address:** Via Marconi 33, 20090 Buccinasco (Mi.), Italy. **One-man Exhibitions:** (first) Betty Parsons Gallery, 1949, also 1950, 52, 53, 54, 56, 59, 62, 67; ICA, Boston, 1951; Margaret Brown Gallery, Boston, 1951, 56; Phillips, 1952; L'Obelisco, Rome, 1953, 58; Providence (R.I.) Art Club, 1953; Santa Barbara/MA, 1954; UCLA, 1954; Arts Club of Chicago, 1954; Art of This Century (Peggy Guggenheim), 1957; Denver/AM, 1957; MIT, 1958; Arthur Jeffress Gallery, London, 1958; Michigan State U., 1959; Pro-Civitate-Christiana, 1961; Palazzo Reale, Milan, 1962; U. of Notre Dame, circ., 1964-65; New York World's Fair, Vatican Pavilion, 1964-65; Cambridge U., 1968; Galleria Cadario, Milan, 1969-70; Palazzo Diamante, Ferrara, Italy, 1981; Basilica San Francesco, Como, Italy, 1983; Casa G. Cini, Ferrara, Italy, 1986. **Retrospectives:** RISD, 1965; Galleria Cadario, 1969. **Group:** PAFA, 1936-38, 1951-53, 1956, 58, 60; NAD, 1939; Carnegie, 1940-52, 58; Andover/Phillips, 1941; MMA, American Painters under 35, 1950; WMAA, 1950, 51, 53, 56, 58; Buffalo/Albright, 1952; California Palace, 1952; U. of Illinois, 1952, 53, 55, 57, 59; Chicago/AI, 1952, 54, 57; XXVI & XXIX Venice Biennials, 1952, 58; WMAA, The New Decade, 1954-55; Walker, Expressionism, 1900-1955, 1956; International Novara, Trieste, 1961, 66; Musée Cantonal des Beaux-Arts, Lausanne, Il Salon de Galeries Pilotes, 1966; Hartford/Wadsworth; Cincinnati/AM; Lincoln, Mass./De Cordova. **Collections:** Andover/Phillips; Boston/MFA; Carnegie; Cleveland/MA; Detroit/Institute; Hartford/Wadsworth; Houston/MFA; U. of Illinois; MMA;

MOMA; Phillips; Pro-Civitate-Christiana; RISD; U. of Rochester; St. Louis/City; Santa Barbara/MA; Smithsonian; Toledo/MA; Venice/Contemporaneo; WMAA. **Bibliography:** McCurdy, ed.; Nordness, ed.; Pousette-Dart, ed.; Rodman 2.

CONLON, WILLIAM. b. July 30, 1941, Albany, N.Y. **Studied:** U. of Notre Dame, 1959-60; School of Visual Arts, with Michael Lowe, George Ortman; Yale U., 1965-67, BFA, MFA, with Jack Tworkov, Al Held. **Taught:** Yale U. 1967-70; Hunter College, 1971-72; U. of California, Irvine, 1972-75; Sarah Lawrence College, 1975-79; Fordham U., 1979-. Designed sets for Bat-Dorf Dance Co., 1968. **Awards:** Graham Foundation, grant, 1965; CAPS, 1974; National Endowment for the Arts, 1977. **Address:** 461 Broome Street, NYC 10013. **Dealer:** Andre Emmerich Gallery, NYC. **One-man Exhibitions:** (first) Reese Palley Gallery, NYC, 1970, 72; Andre Emmerich Gallery, 1977, 80, 81, 85, 86. **Retrospective:** Carnegie, 1981. **Group:** Dallas/MFA, Four Painters: Conlon, Cote, Hacklin, Rafoss, 1971; WMAA Annual, 1972; Corcoran Biennial, 1975; NYU, American Painting: The Eighties, 1979; Brooklyn Museum, American Drawings in Black and White: 1970-1979, 1980; Indianapolis, 1980; Maryland Institute, Six Abstract Painters, 1982. **Collections:** Brooklyn Museum; Buffalo/Albright; Carnegie; Dallas/MFA; Grand Rapids; Syracuse/Everson.

CONNER, BRUCE. b. November 18, 1933, McPherson, Kans. **Studied:** U. of Nebraska, BFA; U. of Wichita; Brooklyn Museum School, with Reuben Tam; Kansas City Art Institute and School of Design; U. of Colorado. **Taught:** California College of Arts and Crafts, 1965-66; SFAI, 1966, 67, 72; UCLA, summer, 1973; San Jose State U., 1974; San Francisco State U., 1976. Produced the light show for the Avalon Ballroom; filmmaker. Traveled Japan. **Awards:** IV International Art Biennial, San Marino (Europe), Gold Medal, 1963; The U. of Chicago, Midwest Film Festival, First Prize; SFMA, Nealie Sullivan Award, 1963; Ford Foundation Grant, 1964; Tamarind Fellowship, 1965; Copley Foundation Award, 1965; National Endowment for the Arts, grant, 1973; American Film Institute, grant, 1974; Francis Scott Key Award, 1975; Guggenheim Foundation Fellowship, 1975; Brandeis U. Creative Art Award for Film, 1979; National Endowment for the Arts, 1984; San Francisco Arts Commission, Award of Honor, 1985; Hon. DFA, SFAI, 1986. **Address:** 45 Sussex Street, San Francisco, CA 94131. **Dealer:** Frankel Gallery, San Francisco. **One-man Exhibitions:** Rienzi Gallery, NYC, 1956; East West Gallery, San Francisco, 1958; Designers Gallery, San Francisco, 1958; Spatsa Gallery, San Francisco, 1959; The Alan Gallery, NYC, 1960, 61, 63, 64, 65, 66; Batman Gallery, San Francisco, 1960, 62; Glantz Gallery, Mexico City, 1962; Antonio Suza Gallery, Mexico City; Ferus Gallery, Los Angeles, 1963; Wichita/AM, 1963; The Swetzoff Gallery, Boston, 1963; George Lester Gallery, Rome, 1964; Robert Fraser Gallery, London, 1964, 66; Brandeis U., 1965; Western Association of Art Museums, circ., 1965-66; of British Columbia, 1965; Galerie J, Paris, 1965; Quay Gallery, 1966, 72, 74; ICA, U. of Pennsylvania, 1967; SFAI, 1967, 71; Molly Barnes Gallery, Los Angeles, 1971; Reese Palley Gallery, San Francisco, 1971, 72; Martha Jackson Gallery, 1972; The Texas Gallery, 1972, 73; Nicholas Wilder Gallery, 1972; Jacqueline Anhalt Gallery, 1973; Tyler (Tex.) Museum of Art, 1974; Smith Andersen Gallery, Palo Alto, 1974; de Young, 1974; Braunstein/Quay Gallery, San Francisco, 1975, 76; Frankel Gallery, 1983, 86; Smith-Anderson Gallery, Palo Alto, 1986. **Retrospective:** ICA, U. of Pennsylvania, 1967; de Young, circ., 1974-75. **Group:** SFAI Annuals, 1958, 63; San Francisco Episcopal Diocese, Church

Art Today, 1960; U. of Illinois, 1961; MOMA, The Art of Assemblage, circ., 1961; WMAA, Fifty California Artists, 1962-63; IV International Art Biennial, San Marino, 1963; Chicago/AI, 66th Annual, 1963; Brandeis U., Recent American Drawings, 1964; ICA, Boston, Selection 1964, 1964; U. of California, Berkeley, Funk, 1967; Omaha/Joslyn, Nebraska Art Today, 1967; Los Angeles/County MA, American Sculpture of the Sixties, circ., 1967; WMAA, Human Concern/Personal Torment, 1969; Dallas/MFA, Poets of the Cities, 1974; Newport Harbor, A Drawing Show, 1975; Dallas/MFA, Poets of the Cities, circ., 1974. **Collections:** U. of California, Berkeley; Brandeis U.; Chicago/AI; Indiana U.; Kansas City/Nelson; Los Angeles/County MA; MOMA; U. of Missouri; U. of Nebraska; Netherlands Film Museum; Oakland/AM; Pasadena/AM; SFMA; WMAA; Wichita/AM; Worcester/AM. **Bibliography:** *Art as a Muscular Principle*; **Bruce Conner Drawings;** Janis and Blesh 1; Lippard 5; Rose, B., 1; Selz, P., 2; Siegfried; Tuchman 1. Archives.

CONOVER, ROBERT. b. July 3, 1920, Trenton, N.J. **Studied:** Philadelphia Museum School, 1938-42; ASL, with Morris Kantor, Cameron Booth, Will Barnet; Brooklyn Museum School, with Max Beckermann, John Ferren, Reuben Tam, William Kienbusch, William Baziotes. Corps of Army Engineers, World War II. Traveled Europe, Canada. **Taught:** New School for Social Research, 1957-; Brooklyn Museum School, 1961-; Newark (N.J.) School of Fine and Industrial Art 1967-. **Member:** American Abstract Artists; SAGA; Federal A.P.: National Youth Act, Philadelphia, 1939-41. **Commissions:** International Graphic Arts Society, 1957, 62 (woodcuts); New York Hilton Hotel, 1963; *Business Week* magazine, 1963. **Awards:** MacDowell Colony Fellowship; Brooklyn Museum, **P.P.,** 1951, 56; The Print Club, Philadelphia, **P.P.;** PAFA, Samuel S. Fleisher Memorial

P.P.; SAGA, **P.P.,** 1976 ($1,000), 1969; Trenton/State, **P.P.,** 1969; SAGA, Vera List Award, 1979; CAPS, 1976. **Address:** 162 East 33 Street, NYC 10016. **Dealer:** A.A.A. Gallery. **One-man Exhibitions:** (first) Laurel Gallery, NYC, 1949; The New Gallery, NYC, 1951, 53, 55; The Zabriskie Gallery, 1957, 59, 61; New School for Social Research, 1968, 74; New School for Social Research, NYC, 1977, 86. **Group:** WMAA Annuals, 1950, 51, 53, 54, 55, 61; PAFA, 1951-53; Chicago/AI; Cincinnati/AM; MOMA, Abstract Painting and Sculpture in America, 1951; Brooklyn Museum, 1952, 54, 56, 58, 60, 62, 64, 66, 68; Newark Museum; Los Angeles/County MA; Memphis/Brooks; Walker, The Classic Tradition, 1953; MOMA, Young American Printmakers, 1953; WMAA, American Prints Today, 1958; ART: USA: 59, NYC, 1959; New York World's Fair, 1964-65; SAGA, 1965-69; American Abstract Artists, 1966-69; International Graphic Arts Exhibition, Zagreb; WMAA, Landscape in American Art; Pratt Institute, circ., Japan, 1967; Newark Museum, 1968; Trenton/State, 1968, 69; Library of Congress, 1969; MOMA, Prints from Blocks: Gauguin to Now, 1983; NAD Annual, 1984; Cooper-Hewitt Museum, SAGA Annual, 1985. **Collections:** Baltimore/MA; Brooklyn Museum; Canberra/National; Ciba-Geigy Corp.; Cincinnati/AM; Cooper Hewitt Museum, NYC; Detroit/Institute; U. of Illinois; Library of Congress; MMA; MOMA; Museum of the City of New York; NCFA; NYPL; National Gallery; PAFA; PMA; Syracuse/Everson; Tokyo/Modern; Trenton/State; VMFA; WMAA. **Bibliography:** Baur 5; Ritchie 1. Archives.

COOK, HOWARD. b. July 16, 1901, Springfield, Mass., **d.** June 24, 1980, Santa Fe, New Mexico. **Studied:** ASL, 1919-21, with George Bridgeman, Wallace Morgan, Joseph Pennell, Andrew Dasburg, Maurice Sterne. Artist War Correspondent, South Pacific, World

War II. Traveled extensively, USA, North Africa, the Orient, Europe. **Taught:** U. of Texas, 1942-43; Minneapolis Institute School, 1945-50; U. of New Mexico, 1947; U. of California, Berkeley, 1948; Colorado Springs Fine Arts Center, 1949; Scripps College, 1951; Washington U., 1954; New Mexico Highlands U., 1957. **Member:** NAD; SAGA. Federal A.P.: Mural painting. **Commissions** (murals): Hotel Tasqueno, Taco, Mexico; Law Library, Springfield, Mass.; Federal Court House, Pittsburgh, Pa.; US Post Offices, Alamo Plaza (San Antonio) and Corpus Christi; Mayo Clinic, Rochester, Minn. **Awards:** Two Guggenheim Foundation Fellowships; Architectural League of New York, Gold Medal; NAD, Samuel F.B. Morse Gold Medal; MMA, **P.P.**, 1942; PMA, **P.P.**; Denver/AM, **P.P.**; Tupperware National Competition, **P.P.**, 1956; Orlando, **P.P.**; Oklahoma, First Painting Award; Tucson Fine Arts Association, Art Prize. **One-man Exhibitions:** (first) Denver/AM, 1928; Weyhe Gallery, 1929, 31, 34, 37, 41; Springfield, Mass./MFA, 1936; The Print Club, Philadelphia, 1937; Kennedy Gallery, 1942, 44; National Gallery, 1944; Rehn Galleries, 1945, 50; Dallas/MFA, 1945, 53; Minneapolis/Institute, 1950; Grand Central Moderns, NYC, 1951, 53, 56, 60, 64; San Diego, 1952, Santa Barbara, MA, 1952; de Young, 1952; Kansas City/Nelson, 1953; Omaha/Joslyn, 1953; G.W.V. Smith Art Museum, Springfield, Mass., 1954; Houston/MFA, 1954; Dartmouth College, 1954; Montclair/AM, 1954; Carnegie, 1958; Raymond Burr Gallery, Los Angeles, 1962, 63; Prakapas Gallery, NYC, 1976. **Retrospective:** Roswell, 1975. **Group:** WMAA, 20th-Century Drawings from the Permanent Collection, 1975. **Collections:** Baltimore/MA; Chicago/AI; Denver/MFA; Dartmouth College; Denver/AM; de Young; Harvard U.; MMA; MOMA; Minneapolis/Institute; Oklahoma; Omaha/Joslyn; Orlando; PMA; U. of Rochester; Santa Barbara/MA; Santa Fe, N.M.; WMAA. **Bibliography:** American Artists Congress, Inc.; American Artists Group Inc. 1, 3; Bethers; Bruce and Watson; Cheney; Coke 2; Hall; Kent, N.; Mellquist; Pearson 1; Pousette-Dart, ed.; Reese; Wheeler; Zigrosser 1. Archives.

COPLEY, WILLIAM N. (CPLY) b. January 24, 1919, NYC. **Studied:** Andover; Yale U. Self-taught artist. Proprietor of the Copley Gallerie in Beverly Hills, 1947-48. Designed sets and costumes for *Crosswalk*, by George Skibine, for the Harkness Ballet Co., 1965. Publisher of the S.M.S. Press. **Address:** 1 Frisbie Road, Roxbury, CT 06783. **Dealer:** Phyllis Kind Gallery, NYC. **One-man Exhibition:** (first) Royer's Bookstore, Los Angeles, 1947; Galerie Nina Dauset, Paris, 1953; Galerie Monte Napoleone, Milan, 1954; Galerie du Dragon, 1956; Iolas Gallery, NYC, 1956, 58, 60, 63, 65, 66, 67, 70, 71, 72, 76, 78; Brooks Jackson Gallery Iolas, NYC, 1979, 80; Galerie Furstenburg, Paris, 1959; Galleria Naviglio, Milan,

William Copley *It's Raining in Chicago* 1985–86

1960; Galleria Cavalino, Venice, 1960; ICA, London, 1960; Galerie Schwarz, Milan, 1961; Galerie Iris Clert, Paris, 1961, 62; Hanover Gallery, London, 1962; David Stuart Gallery, Los Angeles, 1964, 70, 72; Hanover Gallery, London, 1962; Louisiana Gallery, Houston, 1965; Southwestern College, Chula Vista, 1965; Allan Frumkin Gallery, Chicago, 1965; Galerie Iolas, Paris, 1966, 72; Bodley Gallery, NYC, 1968; Galerie Neundorf, Hamburg, 1968; Galerie Springer, Berlin, 1968, 70, 72, 78; Merida Gallery, Louisville, 1969; Galerie Aspects, Brussels, 1972; Galerie Iolas, Milan, 1972; Gallery Saxe, San Francisco, 1972; Galeria II Fauno, Torino, 1973; Moore College of Art, Philadelphia, 1974; Onnasch Gallery, NYC, 1974; Gallerie Onnasch, Cologne, 1974; Erik Nord Gallery, Nantucket, 1975; Galerie Renate Fassbender, Munich, 1978; Galerie Zwirner, Cologne, 1978; Rice U., 1979; Lens Fine Art, Anvers, 1980; Galerie Klewan, Munich, 1981; Kunstler Werkstatt, Munich, 1981; Brooks Jackson Gallery Iolas, NYC, 80, 81; Phyllis Kind Gallery, Chicago, 1977, 82; Reinhard Onnasch Gallery, Berlin, 1983; Phyllis Kind Gallery, NYC, 1982, 83, 85; The Quay Gallery, San Francisco, 1985; The New Museum, NYC, 1986. **Retrospective:** Amsterdam/Stedelijk, 1966; Berne, circ., 1980. **Group:** Nagaoka, Exposition International de l'art actuel, 1956; Salon de Mai, Paris, 1957, 58, 59, 61; Stockholm/National, Objects in Motion, 1961; Pasadena/AM, Collage out of California, 1962; Paris/Decoratifs, L'Antagonisme de l'objet, 1962; Oakland, Pop Art, 1963; Brandeis U., New Directions in American Painting, 1964; Huntington, N.Y./Heckscher, Whence Pop, 1965; U. of California, Santa Barbara, Surrealism, 1966; New School for Social Research, NYC, Erotic Art, 1971; New York Cultural Center, Three Generations of the American Nude, 1975; The New Museum, NYC, Bad Painting Show, 1977; Los Angeles/County MA; Cooper-Hewitt Museum, NYC, Box Museum, 1978;

WMAA, The Figurative Tradition, 1980; Westkunst, Cologne, 1981; Documenta VII, Kassel, 1982; Los Angeles/MOCA, Arto and Culture, 1984; Ecole National Superiere des Beaux Arts, Paris, Cinquante ans de Dessins Americains, circ., 1985. **Collections:** Amsterdam/Stedelijk; Chicago/AI; MOMA; Oberlin College; Paris/Beaubourg; Paris/Moderne; Pasadena/AM; PMA; Princeton U.; U. of Sydney; Tate; WMAA. **Bibliography:** Hunter, ed. Archives.

CORBETT, EDWARD. b. August 22, 1919, Chicago, Ill.; **d.** June 6, 1971, Provincetown, Mass. **Studied:** California School of Fine Arts, two years. Traveled Mexico, USA, Philippines. US Army, US Navy, Merchant Marine, 1941-44. **Taught:** San Francisco State Teachers College, 1947; California School of Fine Arts, 1947-50; U. of California, Berkeley, 1950; Mount Holyoke College, 1953-62; U. of New Mexico, 1955; U. of Minnesota, 1960-61; Santa Barbara, 1967-68. **Awards:** Abraham Rosenberg Foundation Fellowship, 1951. **One-man Exhibitions:** Grace Borgenicht Gallery, Inc., 1956, 59, 61, 64, 70, 73, 81; Quay Gallery, 1967. **Retrospective:** MIT, 1959; Walker, 1961; SFMA, 1969. **Group:** California Palace, 1957, 60; Riverside Museum, 1948; Chicago/AI, American Abstract Artists, 1948; de Young, 1951; MOMA, Fifteen Americans, circ., 1952; WMAA Annuals, 1953, 55, 58, 61, 63, 65-68; U. of Illinois, 1954; U. of Nebraska, 1955; Carnegie, 1955; Corcoran, 1956, 1966-68; Walker, 1961; Sao Paulo, 1962; NCFA, 1966; WMAA, Art of the U.S. 1670-1966, 1966. **Collections:** Andover/Phillips; Baltimore/AM; Bankers Trust Company; Buffalo/Albright; Burlington Mills Collection; U. of California, Berkeley; Carnegie; Chase Manhattan Bank; Chicago/AI; Corcoran; Harcourt, Brace & World, Inc.; MOMA; Michigan State U.; Mount Holyoke College; National Gallery; Newark Museum; Oakland/AM; Phillips; SFMA;

SRGM; Sweet Briar College; Tate Gallery; Trenton/State; WMAA; Walker. **Bibliography:** McChesney. Archives.

CORNELL, JOSEPH. b. December 24, 1903, Nyack, N.Y.; **d.** December 29, 1972, NYC. **Awards:** Copley Foundation Grant, 1954; Chicago/AI, Ada S. Garrett Prize, 1959; AAAL, Award of Merit, 1968. **One-man Exhibitions:** (first) Julien Levy Galleries, NYC, 1932, also 1933, 39; 40; Hugo Gallery, NYC, 1946; Copley Gallery, Hollywood, 1948; Charles Egan Gallery, 1949, 50; Allan Gallery, Chicago, 1953; Walker, 1953; The Stable Gallery, 1957; Bennington College, 1959; Richard Feigen Gallery, Chicago, 1960 (three-man); Ferus Gallery, Los Angeles, 1962; Robert Schoelkopf Gallery, NYC, 1966; J. L. Hudson Art Gallery, Detroit, 1966; Brandeis U., 1968; Allan Stone Gallery, 1972; Buffalo/Albright, 1972; Chicago/Contemporary, 1973; Castelli, Feigen, Corcoran Gallery, NYC, 1978, 79, 80; ACA Gallery, NYC, 1975, 77; Wichita State U., 1980; Greenberg Gallery, Clayton, Mo., 1976; Rice U., 1977; Baudoin Lebon, Paris, 1977; Castelli Feigen Corcoran, NYC, 1982; Chicago/AI, 1982; Betsy Rosenfeld Gallery, Chicago, 1982; NMAA, 1983; Acme Art, San Francisco, 1985. **Retrospectives:** Pasadena/AM, 1966; SRGM, 1967; MOMA, 1980. **Group:** MOMA, Fantastic Art, Dada, Surrealism, 1936; Galerie des Beaux Arts, Paris, Exposition Internationale du Surréalisme, 1938; Art of This Century, NYC, 1942; Carnegie, 1958; MOMA, The Art of Assemblage, 1961; Seattle World's Fair, 1962; WMAA Annuals, 1962, 66; NYU, Boxes and Collages, 1963; Chicago/AI, 1964; Musée Rodin, Paris, Sculpture of the 20th Century, 1965; U. of Illinois, 1967. **Collections:** Boston/MFA; MOMA; Pasadena/AM; WMAA. **Bibliography: Ashton, ed.;** Baur 7; Blesh 1; Breton 2; Calas, N. and E.; Downes, ed.; Finch; Flanagan; Guggenheim, ed.; Hunter 6; Hunter, ed.; Janis and Blesh 1; Janis, S.; Johnson, Ellen H.; Kozloff 3; Licht, F.; Marter, Tarbell, and Wechsler; McShine, ed.; *Metro;* Neff, ed.; O'Doherty; Read 3; Rickey; Rose, B., 1; Rowell; Rubin 1; Steitz 3; Seuphor 3; *7 Decades;* Tuchman 1; **Waldman 3.** Archives.

CORNELL, THOMAS. b. March 1, 1937, Cleveland, Ohio. **Studied:** Amherst College, 1959, BA, with Leonard Baskin; Yale U., 1960-61, with N. Welliver, Wm. Bailey, B. Chaet. US Marine Corps, 1956-63. Traveled Europe and U.S. **Taught:** U. of California, Santa Barbara, 1960-62; Princeton U., 1969-71; Bowdoin College, Maine, 1963-. **Member:** CAA; Alliance of Figurative Artists; NAD. **Commissions:** IGAS, print edition, 1966; many portrait commissions; John Hancock Mutual Life Ins. Co., Boston, 1984. **Awards:** I. C. Tiffany Grant, 1961; National Endowment for the Arts, grant, 1966; Ford Foundation, grant, 1969. **Address:** 305 Maine Street, Brunswick, Me. 04011. **Dealer:** G. W. Einstein Co., NYC. **One-man Exhibitions:** (first) Esther Baer Gallery, Santa Barbara, 1961, 63; Rex Evans Gallery, Los Angeles, 1962; Sabarsky Gallery, Los Angeles, 1965; Yale U., 1965; Princeton U., 1971; Dartmouth College, 1966; Tragos Gallery, Boston, 1966; Block Gallery, St. Louis, 1968; Bowdoin College, 1971; A.A.A. Gallery, NYC, 1972; Optik Gallery, Amherst, 1972; Frishman Gallery, Boston, 1974; Muhlenberg College, 1976; Barridoff Galleries, Portland, Me., 1977; A. M. Sachs Gallery, NYC, 1979, 81; U. of Redlands, Calif., 1979; Santa Barbara/MA, 1980; U. of North Carolina, 1982. **Group:** MOMA, Contemporary Painters and Sculptors as Printmakers, 1964; Brooklyn Museum, Print Biennial, 1960; Grolier Club, 1966; Ringling, Young New England Painters, 1969; The Pennsylvania State U., Contemporary Artists and the Figure, 1974; Southern Connecticut State College, In Their Own Image, 1976; Brooklyn Museum, Thirty Years of American Printmaking, 1976; NPG,

American Portrait Drawings, 1980; Youngstown U., Annual, 1982; IEF, Twentieth Century Drawings: The Figure in Context, circ., 1984. **Collections:** Amherst College; Bibliotheque Nationale, Paris; Bowdoin College; U. of California, Berkeley, Los Angeles, and Santa Barbara; Cleveland/MA; Harvard U.; MIT, MOMA; NCFA; U. of Nebraska; U. of North Carolina; NYPG; Princeton U. Library; Smith College; Yale U.

COTTINGHAM, ROBERT. b. September 26, 1935, Brooklyn, N.Y. **Studied:** Pratt Institute, 1959-64, Associate Degree in Advertising Art. US Army, 1955-58. At one time art director for Young and Rubicam, New York and Los Angeles. **Taught:** Art Center College of Design, Los Angeles, 1969-70. **Awards:** National Endowment for the Arts, 1974. **Address:** 16 Blackman Road, Newtown, CT 06470. **Dealer:** Fendrick Gallery, Washington, D.C. **One-man Exhibitions:** Molly Barnes Gallery, Los Angeles, 1968, 69, 70; OK Harris Works of Art, 1971, 74, 76, 78; D.M. Gallery, London, 1975; Galerie de Gestlo, Hamburg, 1975, Cologne, 79; John Berggruen Gallery, San Francisco, 1976; Morgan Gallery, Kansas City, 1978; Bethel Art Gallery, Bethel, Conn., 1978; Ridgefield/Aldrich, 1979; Beaver College, 1979; Landfall Press Gallery, Chicago, 1977, 79; Delta Gallery, Rotterdam, 1979; Galerie de Gestlo, Cologne, 1979; Ridgefield/Aldrich, 1979; Thomas Segal Gallery, Boston, 1980; Coe Kerr Gallery, NYC, 1982; Wichita/AM, 1983; Fendrick Gallery, 1981, 84; Springfield, Mo./AM, 1984; The Art Guild, Framington, Conn., 1985; Little Rock/MFA, circ., 1985. **Group:** Fresno State College, The Persistent Image, 1970; ICA, U. of Pennsylvania, Highway, 1970; Chicago/Contemporary, Radical Realism, 1971; Potsdam/SUNY, New Realism, 1971; Documenta V. Kassel, 1972; Stuttgart/WK, Amerikanischer Fotorealismus, circ., 1972; New York Cultural Center, Realism Now, 1972; Lincoln, Mass./De Cordova, The Super-Realist Vision, 1973; Los Angeles Municipal Art Gallery, Separate Realities, 1973; Cincinnati/Contemporary, Options, 73/30, 1973; CNAC, Hyperrealistes Americains/Realistes Europeens, 1974; Hartford/Wadsworth, New Photo Realism, 1974; Tokyo Biennial, 1974; Toledo/MA, Image, Color and Form—Recent Paintings by Eleven Americans 1975; Wichita State U., The New Realism: Rip-Off or Reality? 1975; Nordjyllands Kunstmuseum, Aalborg, Tendenser i Modern Kunst, 1975; Renwick Gallery, Washington, D.C., Signs of Life: Symbols in the City, 1975; NCFA, Recent American Etchings, circ., 1975; Baltimore/MA, Super Realism, 1975; Brooklyn Museum, Thirty Years of American Printmaking, 1976; NCFA, America as Art, 1976; Canberra/National, Illusion and Reality, circ., 1977; U. of Texas, Austin, New in the '70's, 1977; Tulsa/Philbrook, Realism-Photorealism, 1980; PAFA, Contemporary American Realism Since 1960, 1981; San Antonio/MA, Real, Really Real, Super Real, circ., 1981. **Collections:** Ackland; Arts Council of Great Britain; Baltimore/MA; Carnegie; Cincinnati/AM, Cleveland/MA; Cornell U.; Currier; Dartmouth College; Detroit/Institute; Harvard U.; High Museum; Hirshhorn; Honolulu Academy; Indianapolis; U. of Iowa; U. of Kansas; Little Rock/MFA; Long Beach/MA; New Orleans Museum; NCFA; NMAA; Notre Dame U.; PMA; RISD; Rotterdam; Rutgers U.; Springfield, Mass./MFA; Syracuse U.; U. of Utah; U. of Virginia; Wesleyan U. (Conn.); Williams College; WMAA; Yale U. **Bibliography:** *Amerikanischer Fotorealismus;* Arthur 3, 4; Lindy; Murken-Altrogge; Sager; *The State of California Painting.*

COVERT, JOHN. b. 1882, Pittsburgh, Pa.; **d.** December 24, 1960, NYC. **Studied:** Pittsburgh School of Design, 1902-08; in Munich, 1908-12, on a German government scholarship. Traveled France, Germany, England. A founder and director of the Society of Independent Artists, 1916. The collection of the Societé Anonyme was started with a gift of six of his paintings in 1923. Stopped painting between 1923 and 1949. **One-man Exhibitions:** Salander-O'Reilly Galleries, 1984. **Group:** Paris Salon, 1914; Independent Artists, NYC, 1917; PAFA, 1921; Societé Anonyme, 1921; Vassar College, 1923; Detroit/Institute, 1923; Brooklyn Museum, 1926; Delphic Studios, NYC, 1936; Dallas Museum for Contemporary Arts, 1961; WMAA, 1963; Hirshhorn, 1976. **Collections:** MOMA; PMA; Seattle/AM; Yale U. **Bibliography:** *Avante-Garde Painting and Sculpture; Avante-Garde Painting and Sculpture in America, 1910-1925;* Baur 7; Brown 2; Hunter 6; Rose, B., 1; Tashjian.

CRAMER, KONRAD. b. November 9, 1888, Wurzburg, Germany; **d.** January, 1965, Woodstock, N.Y. **Studied:** Academy of Fine Arts, Karlsruhe, Germany. **Taught:** Bard College, 1940. Founder, Woodstock (N.Y.) School of Photography, 1936. **One-man Exhibitions:** Woodstock (N.Y.) Art Gallery, 1952; New Paltz/SUNY, 1952; Long Island U., 1958; Rochester Institute of Technology, 1966; The Zabriskie Gallery, 1963, 73, 80, 82; Ellen Sragow Gallery, NYC, 1981; Martin Diamond Fine Arts, NYC, 1984; WMAA, 1984. **Retrospectives:** Bard College, circ., 1981; U. of Texas, 1983. **Group:** MacDowell Club, NYC, 1912; Whitney Studio Club, NYC, 1924; WMAA, Abstract Painting in America, 1935; PAFA, 1936; Carnegie, 1937, 38; Corcoran, 1938, 39; WMAA, Pioneers of Modern Art in America, 1946; Woodstock (N.Y.) Art Gallery; WMAA, The Decade of the Armory Show, 1963; U. of New Mexico, Cubism, Its Impact in the U.S.A., 1910-1930, 1967; Delaware Art Museum, Avant-Garde Painting and Sculpture in America, 1910-1925, 1978. **Collections:** International Museum of

Photography; MMA; MOMA; NCFA; U. of North Carolina; PMA; San Diego; U. of Texas; WMAA. **Bibliography:** *Avant-Garde Painting and Sculpture;* Bauer 7; Brown 2; Janis, S.; Levin 2; Rose, B., 1; Tuchman 3; Woodstock. Archives.

CRAWFORD,   RALSTON.   b. September 25, 1906, St. Catharines (Ont.), Canada; **d.** April 27, 1978, Houston, Texas. **Studied:** Otis Art Institute, Los Angeles, 1926-27; PAFA, 1927-30, with Henry Breckenridge, Henry McCarter; Barnes Foundation, 1927-30; Academie Colarossi and Academie Scandinave, Paris, 1932-33; Columbia U., 1933. Traveled Europe, Canada, South Pacific, North Africa, USA, Mediterranean. **Taught:** Art Academy of Cincinnati, 1940-41, 1949; Buffalo Fine Arts Academy, 1942; Honolulu Academy School, summer,

Ralston Crawford *H.M.S. Queen Mary* 1952

1947; Brooklyn Museum School, 1948-49; U. of Minnesota; Louisiana State U., 1949-50; New School for Social Research, 1952-57; U. of Colorado, summer, 1953; U. of Michigan, summer, 1953; lecture tour of U.S.A. for American Association of Colleges, 1956; Hofstra College, 1960-62; U. of Southern California, summer, 1961; U. of Nebraska, 1965; U. of Illinois, 1966. **Awards:** L. C. Tiffany Grant, 1931; Wilmington, 1933; Mary Curtis Bok Foundation Fellowship, 1937; MMA, **P.P.**, 1942; Tamarind Fellowship, 1966; NAD, Palmer Memorial Prize, 1972. **One-man Exhibitions:** (first) Maryland Institute, 1934; Boyer Gallery, Philadelphia, 1937, NYC, 1939; Philadelphia Art Alliance, 1938; Cincinnati/AM, 1941; Flint/Institute, 1942; Artists' Gallery, Philadelphia, 1943; The Downtown Gallery, 1943, 44, 46, 50; Arts Club of Chicago, 1945 (three-man); Portland, Ore./AM, 1946; Santa Barbara/MA, 1946; Howard U., 1947; Mac-Murray College, 1949; Hofstra College, 1952; U. of Alabama, 1953; Grace Borgenicht Gallery, Inc., 1954, 56, 58; Louisiana State U., 1956; Milwaukee, 1958; Lee Nordness Gallery, NYC, 1961, 63; U. of Nebraska, 1965; U. of Illinois, 1966; The Zabriskie Gallery, 1973, 76; Ronald Greenberg Gallery, St. Louis, 1974; Corcoran & Greenberg Gallery, Inc., Coral Gables; Middendorf-Lane Gallery, Washington, D.C., 1977; Century Association, NYC, 1978; U. of Maryland, 1983; UCLA, 1983; Long Island U., 1983; Robert Miller Gallery, 1983. **Retrospectives:** U. of Alabama, 1953; Milwaukee, 1958; U. of Kentucky, 1961; U. of Minnesota, 1961; Creighton U., 1968; U. of Nebraska (photographs); Utica; Montgomery Museum; WMAA, circ., 1986. **Group:** PAFA; WMAA; MOMA; MMA; Corcoran; Phillips; Chicago/AI. **Collections:** American Export Isbrandtsen Lines, Inc.; Auburn U.; Baltimore/MA; Baton Rouge; Brooklyn Museum; Buffalo/Albright; Carnegie; Chicago/AI; Cincinnati/AM; U. of Delaware; Denver/AM; Des Moines; Detroit/Institute;

Flint/Institute; U. of Georgia; Hamline U.; Harvard U.; Hirshhorn; Hofstra U.; Honolulu Academy; Houston/MFA; Howard College; U. of Illinois; Illinois Wesleyan U.; Library of Congress; Los Angeles/County MA; MMA; MOMA; MacMurray College; Michigan State U.; The Miller Co., Milwaukee; U. of Minnesota; NMAA; Newark Museum; U. of Oklahoma; PMA; Phillips; SFMA; Toledo/MA; Utica; Vassar College; WMAA; Walker, Wesleyan U.; Youngstown/Butler. **Bibliography:** Agee 2; *America 1976;* Baur 7; Boswell 1; Danto; *From Foreign Shores;* Frost; Halpert, Janis, S.; Kootz 2; McCurdy, ed.; Nordness, ed.; Pagano; Reese; Ritchie 1; Rodman 2; Rose, B., 1. Archives.

CREMEAN, ROBERT. b. September 28, 1932, Toledo, Ohio. **Studied:** Alfred U., 1950-52; Cranbrook Academy of Art, 1954, BA, 1956, MFA. **Taught:** The Detroit Institute of Arts; UCLA, 1956-57; Art Center in La Jolla, 1957-58. **Awards:** Fulbright Fellowship (Italy), 1954; Tamarind Fellowship, 1966. **Address:** % Dealer. **Dealer:** Braunstein Gallery, San Francisco. **One-man Exhibitions:** Esther Robles Gallery, 1960-66, 73; The Landau-Alan Gallery, NYC, 1968; Wisconsin State U., 1969; Melbourne/National, 1970; Archer Gallery, London, 1972; Santa Barbara/MA, 1975; de Young, 1976; Braunstein-Quay Gallery, San Francisco, 1977. **Group:** Detroit/Institute, 1956; Houston/MFA, 1957; Santa Barbara/MA, 1957; U. of Nebraska, 1958; Chicago/AI, 1960, 61; Los Angeles/County MA, The Image Retained, 1961; SFMA, Bay Area Artists, 1961; California Palace, 1961; WMAA Annuals, 1961, 62; U. of Illinois, 1961, 63; Western Association of Art Museum Directors, Light, Space, Mass, circ., 1962; WMAA, Fifty California Artists, 1962-63; XXXIV Venice Biennial, 1968. **Collections:** Cleveland/MA; Detroit/Institute; Los Angeles/County MA; U. of Miami; U. of Michigan; U. of Nebraska; St. Louis/City; Santa Barbara/MA;

Toledo/MA; UCLA. **Bibliography:** Geske.

CRILE, SUSAN. b. 1942, Cleveland, Ohio. **Studied:** Bennington College, 1960-62, 64-65, BA; NYU, 1962-64; Hunter College, 1971-72. **Taught:** Fordham U., 1972-76; Princeton U., 1974-76; Sarah Lawrence College, 1976-79; School of Visual Arts, NYC, 1976-82; U. of Pennsylvania, 1980; Barnard College, 1983-; Hunter College, 1983-. **Awards:** MacDowell Colony Grant, 1972; Ingram Merrill Foundation Grant, 1972; Yaddo Grant, 1970, 71, 75, 78; National Endowment for the Arts, 1982. **Address:** 168 West 86th Street, NYC 10024. **Dealer:** The Graham Gallery, NYC. **One-man Exhibitions:** Kornblee Gallery, NYC, 1971, 72, 73; Fischbach Gallery, NYC, 1974, 75, 77; Brooke Alexander Gallery, NYC, 1976; Phillips, 1976; The New Gallery, Cleveland, 1977; Bucknell U., 1978; Droll/Kolbert Gallery, NYC, 1978, 80; Ivory/Kimpton Gallery, San Francisco, 1981, 84; Janie C. Lee Gallery, Houston, 1982; Mattingly/Baker, Dallas, 1982; Carson-Sapiro Gallery, Denver, 1982; Van Straaten Gallery, Chicago, 1983; Lincoln Center Gallery, NYC, 1983; Cleveland Center for Contemporary Art, 1984; Nina Freudenheim, Buffalo, 1984; The Graham Gallery, 1985; Adams-Middleton Gallery, Dallas, 1986. **Group:** WMAA Annual, 1972; Indianapolis, 1972, 74; Chicago/AI, 1972; Corcoran Biennial, 1973; NYU, American Painting: The Eighties, 1979; Brooklyn Museum, American Drawings in Black and White: 1970-1979, 1980; Brooklyn Museum, 22nd National Print Exhibition, 1981; WMAA, Block Prints, 1982; Brooklyn Museum, The American Artist as Printmaker, 1983; Columbus, American Art Now!, 1985. **Collections:** Brooklyn Museum; Buffalo/Albright; Carnegie; Chase Manhattan Bank; Chemical Bank; Cleveland/MA; Hirshhorn; MMA; NYU; Phillips.

CRISS, FRANCIS H. b. April 26, 1901, London, England; **d.** November 27, 1973; NYC. **Studied:** PAFA; ASL, with Jan Matulka. **Taught:** Brooklyn Museum School; Albright Art School; ASL; Graphic Sketch Club, Philadelphia. **Awards:** PAFA, Cresson Fellowship; Guggenheim Foundation Fellowship, 1934. **One-man Exhibitions:** (first) Contemporary Arts Gallery, NYC; Mellon Galleries, Philadelphia, 1933, 34; Philadelphia Art Alliance, 1953; School of Visual Arts, NYC. **Retrospective:** School of Visual Arts, NYC, 1967. **Group:** WMAA, 1936, 37, 38, 40, 42, 51; Corcoran, 1939; PAFA, 1939, 41, 43, 45; MMA, 1941; Chicago/AI, 1942, 43; Carnegie, 1944; 45. **Collections:** Kansas City/Nelson; La France Art Institute; National Gallery; PMA; WMAA. **Bibliography:** Baur 7; Pagano. Archives.

CRONBACH, ROBERT M. b. February 10, 1908, St. Louis, Mo. **Studied:** Washington School of Fine Arts, 1926, with Victor Holm; PAFA, 1927-30, with Charles Grafly, Albert Laesslie; assistant in Paul Manship Studio, NYC and Paris, 1930. Traveled Europe extensively. **Taught:** Adelphi College, 1947-62; North Shore Community Art Center, 1949-54; Skowhegan School, summers, 1959, 60, 64. **Member:** Sculptors Guild; Architectural League of New York; Artists Equity. Federal A.P.: Willerts Park Housing Project, Buffalo, N.Y., 1939 (sculpture). **Commissions** (architectural): St. Louis (Mo.) Municipal Auditorium, 1933, Social Security Building, Washington, D.C., 1940; Cafe Society Uptown, NYC, 1940; Hotel Hollenden, Cleveland, 1946; Hopping Phillips Motor Agency, Newark, N.J., 1948; 240 Central Park South, NYC, 1954; Dorr-Oliver Building, Stamford, Conn., 1957; Adelphi College, 1958; Ward School, New Rochelle, N.Y., 1959; National Council for U.S. Art, 1960 (a gift to the United Nations); Temple Chizuk Amuno, Baltimore, 1962, 68; Federal Building, St. Louis

1964; Temple Israel, St. Louis, 1964; Charleston (W. Va.) Public Library, 1965. **Awards:** PAFA, Stewardson Prize, 1938; PAFA, Cresson Fellowship, 1929, 30; National Sculpture Competition for Social Security Building, Washington, D.C., First Award, 1939; National Sculpture Society, Henry Hering M.M., 1985. **Address:** 420 East 86th Street, NYC 10028. **One-man Exhibitions:** (first) Hudson D. Walker Gallery, NYC, 1939; The Bertha Schaefer Gallery, 1951 (two-man), 1952, 1960 (two-man), 1967, 71; The New Bertha Schaefer Gallery, 1974; Nassau County Center for Fine Arts, Roslyn Harbor, N.Y., 1976; Adelphi U., 1981; Century Association, 1984. **Group:** New York World's Fairs, 1939, 1964-65; Sculptors Guild, 1939-42, 1945-62, 1967; City of Philadelphia Sculpture International, 1940, 49; MMA, 1943; Denver/AM, The Modern Artist and His World, 1947; WMAA Annuals, 1948, 1956-59; Riverside Museum, 1947; Silvermine Guild, 1947, 58, 60; Brussels World's Fair, 1958; ART: USA: 59, NYC, 1959; HemisFair '68, San Antonio, Tex., 1968; PAFA Architectural League of New York; Brooklyn Museum; St. Louis/City; Houston/MFA; MOMA. **Collections:** U. of Minnesota; Rosenthal China Co.; St. Louis/City; Springfield, Mo./AM; Walker. **Bibliography:** Baur 7; Archives.

CRONIN, ROBERT. **b.** 1936, Lexington, Mass. **Studied:** RISD, 1959, BFA; Cornell U., 1962, MFA. **Taught:** Bennington College; Brown U.; Michigan State U.; Worcester Museum School; St. John's U. **Awards:** R. S. Reynolds Memorial Sculpture Award, 1982. **Address:** 325 West 16th Street, NYC 10011. **Dealer:** Gimpel & Weitzenhoffer Ltd., NYC. **One-man Exhibitions:** Brown U., 1958; Wheaton College, 1959; Nexus Gallery, Boston, 1961; Cornell U., 1961; Bennington College, 1967, 74; Botolph Gallery, Boston, 1968; ICA, Boston, 1971; Worcester/AM, 1974; The Zabriskie Gallery,

NYC, 1974; Helen Shlien Gallery, Boston, 1979; Sculpture Center, NYC, 1981; Carnegie, 1981; Gimpel Fils, London, 1982; Gimpel & Weitzenhoffer Ltd., 1982, 84; Watson de Nagy Gallery, Houston, 1983; G.M.B. Gallery, Birmingham, Mich., 1983; Clark Gallery, Lincoln, Mass., 1983; Gimpel-Hanover & Galerie Andre Emmerich, Zurich, 1983; Klonaridis Gallery, Toronto, 1984. **Group:** Minneapolis/Institute, Biennial, 1963; ICA, Los Angeles, Art Words/Book Works, 1978; Brooklyn Museum, American Drawings in Black and White: 1970-1979, 1980; RISD, Metals: Cast-Cut-Coiled, 1982. **Collections:** Boston/MFA; Boston Public Library; Brooklyn Museum; Carnegie; Cornell U.; U. of Oklahoma; Worcester/AM; Worceste Polytechnic Institute.

CURRY, JOHN STEUART. **b.** November 14, 1897, Dunavant, Kans.; **d.** 1946, Madison, Wisc. **Studied:** Kansas City Art Institute and School of Design, 1916; Chicago Art Institute School, 1916-18, with E. J. Timmons, John W. Norton; Geneva College, 1918-19; Studio of B. Schoukhaieff, Paris, 1926-27. Traveled France. **Taught:** Cooper Union, 1932-34; ASL, 1932-36; U. of Wisconsin, 1936. **Commissions** (murals): Justice Department, Washington, D.C., 1936-37; Kansas State Capitol, 1938-40; U. of Wisconsin, 1940-42. **Awards:** Carnegie, 1933; PAFA, Gold Medal, 1941; MMA, Artists for Victory, Second Prize, 1942. **One-man Exhibitions:** (first) Whitney Studio Club, NYC, 1930; Feragil Galleries, NYC, 1933, 35; U. of Wisconsin, 1937; Hudson D. Walker Gallery, NYC, 1938, Milwaukee, 1946; A.A.A. Gallery, NYC, 1947; Syracuse U., 1956; U. of Kansas, 1957; NCFA, 1971. **Group:** WMAA; Chicago/AI; Wichita/AM; Milwaukee. **Collections:** Andover/Phillips, Britannica; Chicago/AI; First National Bank, Madison; Kansas State College; MMA; Muskegon/Hackley; U. of Nebraska; St. Louis/City; WMAA; Wichita/AM.

Bibliography: American Artists Group, Inc., 1; Baigell 1; Baur 7; Bazin; Benton 1; Biddle 4; Blesh 1; Boswell 1; Brown 2; Bruce and Watson; Cahill and Barr, eds.; Canaday; Cheney; Christensen; Crayen, T., 1; **Curry 1, 2, 3;** Flanagan; Flexner; Goodrich and Baur 1; Hall; Hunter 6; *Index of 20th Century Artists;* Jewell 2; McCurdy, ed.; Mellquist; Mendelowitz; Newmeyer; Pagano; Pearson 1; Reese; Richardson, E.P.; Rose, B., 1; **Schmeckebler 2;** Wight 2. Archives.

D

DALLMAN, DANIEL. **b.** March 12, 1942, St. Paul, Minn. **Studied:** U. of Minnesota, 1965, BS; U. of Iowa, 1968, MA; 1969, MFA. Traveled Europe; resided Rome, 1974-76. **Taught:** Tyler School of Art, Temple U., 1969-. **Address:** 847 Horsham Road, North Wales, Pa. 19454. **Dealer:** Robert Schoelkopf Gallery, NYC. **One-man Exhibitions:** (first) The Print Club, 1972; Hemingway Gallery, Nantucket, 1973; Paul Kramer Gallery, St. Paul, 1973; West Chester State College, 1973; Ronnie Brenner Gallery, New Orleans, 1974; Gallery Four, Alexandria, Va., 1976; Tyler School of Art, Rome, 1976; Charlotte/Mint, 1977; Robert Schoelkopf Gallery, 1980, 84; Philadelphia College of Art, 1982; Louisville/Speed (two-man), 1984. **Group:** Krakow/National, Print Biennial, 1974; Brooklyn Museum, Thirty Years of American Printmaking, 1976; San Antonio/MA, Real, Really Real, Super Real, circ., 1981; U. of North Carolina, Art on Paper, 1982; Hudson River Museum, New Vistas, 1984; SMFA, American Realism (Janss), 1985; Hudson River Museum, Form or Formula: Drawing and Drawings, 1986. **Collections:** AT&T; Ball State U.; Carleton College; Chemical Bank; Chicago/AI; Cleveland/MA; U. of Delaware; U. of Iowa; Kemper Insurance Co., Chicago; Louisville/Speed; Mellon Bank; Metropolitan Life, NYC; NMAA; PMA; Readers Digest.

DAPHNIS, NASSOS. **b.** July 23, 1914, Krockeai, Greece. To USA, 1930; citizen. Self-taught; US Army Corps of Engineers, 1942-45. Traveled USA, Greece, Italy, France. Leading tree-peony hybridizer. **Taught:** Horace Mann School, Riverdale, N.Y., 1953-58. **Member:** American Abstract Artists. **Awards:** Ford Foundation, 1962; National Council on the Arts, 1966; National Endowment for the Arts, 1971; New England 350th Celebration Exhibition, 1972; A. P. Saunders Medal, Tree Peony Award, 1973; National Endowment for the Arts, 1971; Guggenheim Foundation Fellowship, 1977. **Dealer:** Leo Castelli Inc., NYC; Kouros Gallery, NYC; Andre Zarre Gallery, NYC. **Address:** 362 West Broadway, NYC 10012. **One-man Exhibitions:** (first) Contemporary Arts Gallery, NYC, 1938, also 1947, 49; Charlotte/Mint, 1949; Galerie Colette Allendy, Paris, 1950; Leo Castelli Inc., 1959-61, 1963, 65, 68, 71, 73, 75, 80, 83, 85, 86; Galleria Toninelli, Milan, 1961; Iris Clert Gallery, 1962; Franklin Siden Gallery, Detroit, 1967; Syracuse/Everson, 1969; Brockton/Fuller, 1970; Andre Zarre Gallery, NYC, 1974, 76; Kingpitcher Gallery, Pittsburgh, 1976; Muhlenberg College, 1980; Eaton/Shoen Gallery, San Francisco, 1980; Omega Gallery, Athens, Greece, 1983; Andre Zarre Gallery, 1983, 85; Kouros Gallery, 1985. **Retrospectives:** Buffalo//Albright, 1969; Syracuse/Everson, 1969. **Group:** Carnegie, 1955, 58, 61, 70; Corcoran Biennial, 1959, 63, 69; WMAA Annuals, 1960-65, 1967; Walker, Purist Painting, 1961; American Abstract Artists Annual, 1961; SRGM, Abstract Expressionists and Imagists, 1961; Seattle World's Fair, 1961; WMAA, Geometric Abstraction in America, circ., 1962; Musée Cantonal des Beaux-Arts, Lausanne, I Salon International de Galeries Pilotes, 1963; Lincoln, Mass./De Cordova, 1965; U. of Illinois, 1969;

Carnegie, International, 1970; Syracuse/Everson, Provincetown Painters, 1890s-1970s, 1977; Brooklyn Museum, Noemata, 1977. **Collections:** Akron/AI; Baltimore/MA; Buffalo/Albright; Carnegie; Corcoran; Basil Goulandris Museum, Andros, Greece; Hirshhorn; MOMA; U. of Michigan; Norfolk; Norfolk-Chrysler; RISD; Reading/Public; Ridgefield/Aldrich; SRGM; Ian Vores Museum, Peonia, Athens, Greece; South Mall, Albany; Syracuse/Everson; Tel Aviv; Union Carbide Corp.; Utica; WMAA. **Bibliography: Murdock 2.** Archives.

D'ARCHANGELO, ALLAN. b. June 16, 1930, Buffalo, N.Y. **Studied:** U. of Buffalo, 1948-52, BA (history and government); City College of New York; New School for Social Research, 1953-54; Mexico City College, 1957-59, with Dr. John Golding, Fernando Belain; studio work with Boris Lurie, NYC, 1956-66. Traveled Mexico, USA, Japan, Far East, North Africa. **Taught:** NYC public schools, 1956-62; School of Visual Arts, NYC, 1963-68; Cornell U., 1968; Syracuse U., 1971; U. of Wisconsin, 1972; St. Cloud State College, 1972; Memphis Academy of Arts, 1975; Brooklyn College, 1973-. **Member:** SAGA. **Commissions:** Transportation and Travel Pavilion, New York World's Fair, 1964-65 (mural). **Awards:** Municipal U. of Omaha, First **P.P.**, 1966; NIAL, 1970. **Address:** Kenoza Lake, NY 12750. **Dealer:** Grace Borgenicht Gallery, NYC. **One-man Exhibitions:** Galerie Genova, Mexico City, 1958 (two-man); Long Island U., 1961; Fishbach Gallery, 1964, 65, 67, 69; Ileana Sonnabend Gallery, Paris, 1965; Galerie Rudolf Zwirner, 1965; Galerie Hans R. Neuendorf, Hamburg, 1965; Galerie Muller, 1965; Dwan Gallery, Los Angeles, 1966; Wurttembergischer Kunstverein, Stuttgart, 1967; Galerie Rolf Ricke, Kassel, 1967; Minami Gallery, 1967; Obelisk Gallery, 1967 (two-man), 1970; Franklin Siden Gallery, Detroit, 1968, 72; Lambert Gallery, Paris, 1968; Wisconsin State U., Eau Claire, 1970; Marlborough Gallery, Inc., NYC, 1971, 75; U. of Wisconsin, Madison, 1972; Hokin Gallery, Chicago, 1974; Patricia Moore Inc., Aspen, 1974; Russell Sage College, 1974; Kingpitcher Gallery, Pittsburgh, 1975; Buffalo/SUNY, 1979; Grace Borgenicht Gallery, 1982. **Retrospective:** ICA, U. of Pennsylvania, 1971. **Group:** Sarah Lawrence College, Popular Imagery, 1963; ICA, London, 1963; Oakland/AM, Pop Art USA 1963; Buffalo/Albright, Mixed Media and Pop Art, 1963; Salon du Mai, Paris, 1964; The Hague, New Realism, 1964; Salon des Comparaisons, Paris, 1964; Dwan Gallery, Los Angeles, Boxes, 1964, also 1965; Milwaukee, 1965; Galerie Hans R. Neuendorf, Hamburg, 1965, 66; Galerie Friedrich & Dahlem, Munich, 1966; V. International Biennial Exhibition of Prints, Tokyo, 1966; Amsterdam/Stedelijk, New Shapes of Color, 1966; Expo '67, Montreal, 1967; Detroit/Institute, Color, Image and Form, 1967; Torcuato di Tella, Buenos Aires, 1967; WMAA Annual, 1967; Brandeis U., 1968; Foundation Maeght, 1968; MOMA, Social Comment in America, circ., 1968; ICA, U. of Pennsylvania, Highway, 1970; Utica, American Prints Today, 1973; WMAA, American Pop Art, 1974. **Collections:** Atlantic Richfield Co.; Brandeis U.; Brooklyn Museum; Buffalo/Albright; Chase Manhattan Bank; Cleveland/MA; Detroit/Institute; Gelsenkirchen; The Hague; Hannover/Kunstverein; The Hertz Corp.; Hirshhorn; MIT; MOMA; Munster/WK; NYU; Nagaoka, Japan; New Orleans/Delgado; Ridgefield/Aldrich; Skopje/Modern; WMAA; Walker; U. of Wisconsin. **Bibliography:** Alloway 4; Battcock, ed.; Calas, N. and E.; Honisch and Jensen, eds.; Hunter, ed.; *Kunst um 1970;* Lippard 5.

DARROW, PAUL GARDNER. b. October 31, 1921, Pasadena, Calif. **Studied:** Art Center School, Los Angeles;

Colorado Springs Fine Arts Center, with Boardman Robinson; Claremont Graduate School, with Millard Sheets, Sueo Serisawa, Henry McFee, Howard Cook. **Taught:** Coronado School of Fine Arts, summers, 1953, 55; Brigham Young U., 1954; Otis Art Institute, 1955-69; Claremont Graduate School, 1955-69, 1970-; Laguna Beach (Calif.) School of Art and Design, 1960-69. **Commissions** (murals): Richmond (Calif.) Youth Center, 1952, Convair Aircraft Corp., San Diego, 1953; National American Insurance Co., Los Angeles, 1954; Kaiser Aluminum Corp.; Disneyland, Calif., 1955; Broadway Dept. Stores, Anaheim and Van Nuys, Calif., 1955; Gourmet Shop, Hollywood, 1955; Air France, International Airport, Los Angeles, 1960-61; Home Insurance Co., Los Angeles. Traveled Japan, Taiwan, Philippines, Okinawa. US Navy artist correspondent, Vietnam. **Awards:** California State Fair, 1950; Los Angeles/County MA, First Prize Watercolor, 1954; Pasadena/AM, **P.P.**, 1954, 58; NEH, grant, 1973. **Address:** 690 Cuprien Way, Laguna Beach, CA 92651. **One-man Exhibitions:** Philadelphia Art Alliance, 1948; Mezzanine Gallery, Oakland, Calif., 1953; Gump's Gallery, 1954; RAC, 1954; Pasadena/AM, 1955; Scripps College, 1958; Drake Gallery, Carmel, Calif., 1960; Comara Gallery, 1961, 64, 68; San Joaquin Pioneer Museum and Haggin Art Galleries, Stockton, Calif., 1963; Sacramento State College, 1966; Hartnell College, 1968; California Institute of Technology, Pasadena, 1970; Muckenthaler Cultural Center, Fullerton, Calif., 1971; Newport Harbor, 1972; Galleria Forma, El Salvador, 1975. **Retrospective:** Scripps College, 1973. **Group:** U. of Vienna, 1951; Los Angeles/County MA, 1951-54; Santa Barbara/MA, 1952-55; SFMA, 1952, 53; Seattle/AM, 1953; Youngstown/Butler, 1953, 54; PAFA, 1954; Denver/AM, 1954; Corcoran, 1954; Sao Paulo, 1955; Smithsonian, circ., 1955-56, Long Beach/MA, 1958-61; Oakland/AM; Newport Harbor Art Museum, Balboa,

Calif., 1964; Laguna Beach/MA, Southern California 100, 1977; Claremont Galleries, California Photographers, 1978. **Collections:** Long Beach/MA; Los Angeles Times; U. of Michigan; Newport Harbor; Palos Verdes; Pasadena/AM; Scripps College.

DASBURG, ANDREW. b. May 4, 1887, Paris, France. To USA, 1892, **d.** August 13, 1979, Ranchos de Taos, N.M. **Studied:** ASL, with Kenyon Cox, Frank V. DuMond; privately with Birge Harrison; also with Robert Henri. **Awards:** Pan-American Exhibition, Los Angeles, 1925; Carnegie, 1927, 31; Guggenheim Foundation Fellowship, 1932; Ford Foundation Grant; Arizona Governor's Art Award, 1976. **One-man Exhibitions:** Dallas/MFA, 1957; Rehn Galleries, 1958; U. of New Mexico, 1966; Governor's Gallery, Santa Fe, 1975, 76; Mission Gallery, Taos, 1978; Salander-O'Reilly Galleries, 1985. **Retrospective:** A.F.A./Ford Foundation, circ., 1959; U. of New Mexico, Albuquerque, circ., 1979. **Group:** WMAA; SFMA; MMA; Denver/AM; Santa Fe, N.M. **Collections:** Barnes Foundation; California Palace; Cincinnati/AM; Colorado Springs/FA; Dallas/MFA; Denver/AM; Fort Worth; Hirshhorn; U. of Kansas; Kansas City/Nelson; Los Angeles/County MA; MMA; U. of Nebraska/Sheldon; U. of Nebraska; U. of New Mexico; San Antonio/McNay; SFMA; Santa Barbara/MA; Santa Fe, N.M.; WMAA. **Bibliography:** *Avant-Garde Painting and Sculpture;* Baur 7; Brown, 1, 2; **Bywaters 1, 2;** Cahill and Barr, eds.; Cheney; Coke 2; Goodrich and Baur 1, Hunter 6; *Index of 20th Century Artists;* Janis, S.; Levin 2; McCurdy, ed.; Neuhaus; Richardson, E.P.; Rose, B., 1, 4; *Woodstock;* Wright 1. Archives.

DASH, ROBERT. b. June 8, 1934, NYC. **Studied:** U. of New Mexico, BA (anthropology and English). Traveled Italy, Mexico, USA, Ireland, West Germany. **Taught:** Southampton College, 1976, 82, 84, 86; Dodfitz School, Amarillo, 1977, 82, 84; Long Island U., 1972. **Member:** Fellow, Royal Horticultural Society. **Awards:** New York State Board of Regents Scholarship. **Address:** Sagaponack, NY 11962. **Dealer:** Schutz & Co., NYC. **One-man Exhibitions:** (first) The Kornblee Gallery, 1961, also 1962, 63; The Osborne Gallery, NYC, 1964, 65, 66; The Graham Gallery, 1964, 68, 69, 70; Crane-Kalman Gallery, London, 1966; Munich/Modern, 1969; FAR Gallery, 1972, 73; Vick Gallery, Philadelphia, 1974; Fischbach Gallery, NYC, 1975, 77; Hirschl & Adler Gallerie, NYC, 1978. **Retrospective:** Southampton/Parrish, 1969; Allentown/AM, 1971. **Group:** Yale U., The New York Season, 1961; MOMA, Eight American Painters of the Landscape, circ., 1964; Corcoran; U. of Colorado; Norfolk, Contemporary Art USA, 1966; AAAL; Childe Hassam Fund Exhibition, 1973; Omaha/Joslyn, A Sense of Place, 1973; Lincoln, Mass./De Cordova, Candid Painting, 1975; U. of North Carolina, Art on Paper, 1976; U. of Missouri, American Painterly Realists, 1977. **Collections:** Allentown/AM; AT&T; The Bank of New York; Bristol-Meyers Co.; Brooklyn Museum; U. of California; Chase Manhattan Bank; Brooklyn Museum; Commerce Bank, Kansas City; Continental Grain Corp.; Corcoran; Federal Deposit Insurance Corporation; First National Bank of Memphis; The Grace Line; Hirshhorn; Munich/Modern; NYU; NATO Headquarters, Brussels; U. of North Carolina; PMA; Southampton/Parrish; Suffolk County National Bank; Xerox Corp.; Youngstown/Butler. **Bibliography:** Downes, ed. Archives.

DAVIS, GENE. b. August 22, 1920, Washington, D.C. **d.** April 6, 1985, Washington, D.C. **Studied:** U. of Maryland; Wilson Teachers College. **Taught:** The Corcoran School of Art, 1967-68, 1970-85; American University, 1968-70; Skidmore College, 1969; U. of Virginia, 1972. **Member:** Washington Project for the Arts, vice-president, 1980. **Commissions:** South Mall, Albany, 1969 (mural); Neiman-Marcus Co., Bal Harbour, Fla., 1970 (mural). **Awards:** Corcoran, Bronze Medal for Painting and $1,000 Award, 1965; National Council on the Arts, $5,000 Grant, 1967; Guggenheim Foundation Fellowship, 1974. **One-man Exhibitions:** (first) The Catholic U. of America, 1953; American U., 1955; Bader Gallery, Washington, D.C., 1956; Jefferson Place Gallery, 1959, 61, 63, 67; Poindexter Gallery, 1963, 65-67; Corcoran, 1964, 68, 70, 77, 78; Hofstra U., 1966; MIT, 1967; Des Moines, 1967; Galerie Rolf Ricke, 1967; Fischbach Gallery, 1967-69, 1970, 71, 72, 73, 75, 77, 78; SFMA, 1968; WGMA, 1968; Jewish Museum, 1968; Henri Gallery, 1968-70; Chapman Kelly Gallery, 1969; Axiom Gallery, London, 1969; Nova Scotia College of Art and Design, 1970; Galerie Annemarie Verna, Zurich, 1971; Dunkelman Gallery, Toronto, 1971-73; J. L. Hudson Art Gallery, Detroit, 1972; U. of Utah, 1972; Omaha/Joslyn, 1972; Max Protetch Gallery, Washington, D.C., 1972, 77; Michael Berger Gallery, Pittsburgh, 1973; Quay Gallery, 1973; New Gallery, Cleveland, 1974; Tibor de Nagy, Houston, 1974; Reed College, 1975; Harcus Krakow Rosen Sonnabend, Boston, 1976; Walker, 1978; Dayton/AI, 1978; Protetch-McIntosh Gallery, Washington, D.C., 1978, 80; Droll/Kolbert Gallery, Inc., NYC, 1979, 80; Charles Cowles Gallery, 1982, 84; College of William & Mary, 1983; Omaha/Joslyn, 1984; Middendorf-Lane Gallery, Washington, D.C., 1983; Washington Project for the Arts, Washington, D.C., 1983; U. of Missouri, 1984; Tampa/AM, 1985; Wilmington, 1983; Middendorf Gallery, Washington, D.C., 1984. **Retrospective:** Brooklyn Museum, 1982. **Group:** WGMA, The Formalists 1963; Brandeis U., New Directions in American Painting, 1963; Los Angeles/County MA,

Post Painterly Abstraction, 1964; MOMA, The Responsive Eye, 1965; WGMA, circ., 1965; MOMA, Two Decades of American Painting, circ., Japan, India, Australia, 1967; Corcoran Biennial, 1967, 75; Detroit/Institute, Color, Image and Form, 1967; WMAA Annuals, 1968, 71, 73; Milwaukee, Directions I, circ., 1968; Art Fair, Cologne, 1968; Edmonton Art Gallery, Alberta, Ten Washington Artists: 1950-1970, 1970; Baltimore/MA, Washington Art: 1950-1970, 1970; ICA, U. of Pennsylvania, Two Generations of Color Painting, 1970; WMAA, The Structure of Color, 1971; U. of Texas, Color Forum, 1972; West Palm Beach/Norton, The Vincent Melzac Collection—Part One: The Washington Color Painters, 1974; SRGM, Within the Decade, 1974; Indianapolis, 1978; U. of Southern Florida, Miami, Two Decades of Abstraction, 1979. **Collections:** Akron/AI; AT&T; Bank of America; Brandeis U.; Buffalo/Albright; Carnegie; Chicago/AI; Chase Manhattan Bank, NYC; Cleveland/MA; Corcoran; Dallas/MFA; Dayton/AI; Denver/AM; Des Moines; Federal Reserve Bank of Boston; Federal Reserve Bank of Richmond, Virginia; Florsheim Foundation; Hirshhorn; High Museum; Indianapolis/Herron; Jacksonville/AM; Louisville/Speed; MIT; MMA; MOMA; Milwaukee; NCFA; NMAA; National Gallery; U. of Nebraska; Oklahoma; Omaha/Joslyn; Phillips; PMA; Princeton U.; RISD; Ringling; SFMA; SRGM; Tate Gallery; Toronto; Utah; WMAA; Walker; Wasington U; Wellesley College; Woodward Foundation; Xerox; Yale U. **Bibliography:** *Art Now 74*; Atkinson; Davis, D.; **Gene Davis; Gene Davis: Drawings; Naifeh and White.** Archives.

DAVIS, JERROLD. b. November 2, 1926, Chico, Calif. **Studied:** U. of California, Berkeley, BA, 1953, MA. Traveled Latin America, Europe. **Taught:** U. of California, summer, 1967. **Awards:** Sigmund Martin Heller Trav-

eling Fellowship, 1953; Guggenheim Foundation Fellowship, 1958; Ford Foundation Artist-in-Residence, 1964. **Address:** 66 Twain Avenue, Berkeley, CA 94708. **Dealer:** Jacqueline Anhalt Gallery. **One-man Exhibitions:** Instituto Brasil-Estados-Unidos, Rio de Janeiro, 1951; California Palace, 1957; Everett Ellin Gallery, Los Angeles, 1958; The Rose Rabow Gallery, San Francisco, 1963, 74; Esther Robles Gallery, 1964; Flint/Institute, 1964; Gallery of Modern Art, 1965; Quay Gallery, 1967, 68; Fleischer Anhalt Gallery; 1968; Jacqueline Anhalt Gallery, 1970; Newport Harbor, 1973. **Retrospective:** Richmond Art Center, Calif., 1980. **Group:** Sao Paulo Biennial, 1951; Oberlin College, 3 Young Painters, 1958; Carnegie, 1958; U. of Illinois, 1959, 61, 63; California Palace, 1960-64; Flint/Institute, 1964; Phoenix, 1964; Los Angeles/County MA, 1965; U. of Arizona, 1967; Omaha/Joslyn, A Sense of Place, 1973. **Collections:** Bank of America; Carnegie; Flint/Institute; Los Angeles/County MA; Oakland/AM; SFMA; Santa Barbara/MA.

DAVIS, RONALD. b. June 29, 1937, Santa Monica, Calif. **Studied:** U. of Wyoming, 1955-56; San Francisco Art Institute (with Jack Jefferson, Frank Lobdell), 1960-64; Yale-Norfolk Summer Art School (with Philip Guston), 1962. **Taught:** U. of California, 1967. **Awards:** National Council on the Arts Grant, 1968. **Address:** 6950 Grasswood Avenue, Malibu, CA 90265. **Dealers:** Blum-Helman Gallery, NYC. **One-man Exhibitions:** (first) Nicholas Wilder Gallery, 1965, also 1967, 69, 73, 77; Tibor de Nagy Gallery, 1966; Leo Castelli Inc., 1968, 74, 75; Kasmin Ltd., 1968, 71; David Mirvish Gallery, 1970, 75; Pasadena/AM, 1971; Galleria dell-Ariete, Milan, 1972; Joseph Hellman Gallery, St. Louis, 1972; John Berggruen Gallery, San Francisco, 1973, 78; Corcoran & Greenberg, Coral Gables, 1974; Gemini G.E.L., Los Angeles, 1974; Western Galleries, Cheyenne,

Ronald Davis   *Star Drips Near Malibu*   1981

1974; Boise State U., 1975; Greenberg Gallery, St. Louis, 1975; Aspen Gallery of Art, 1976; Seder/Creigh Gallery, Coronado, Calif., 1976; U. of Nevada, 1977; Pepperdine U., 1979; Blum-Helman Gallery, New York, 1979, 81, 84; **Group:** San Francisco Art Festival, 1961-63; SFMA, Arts of San Francisco, 1964; RAC, 1964; U. of Illinois, 1965; WGMA, A New Aesthetic, 1967; WMAA Annual, 1967; Documenta IV, Kassel, 1968; Corcoran Biennial, 1967; Venice Biennial, 1972; Montreal/Contemporain, II Artistes Americains, 1973; The Greenberg Gallery, St. Louis, 1979; Nicholas Wilder Gallery, Los Angeles, 1979; San Diego State U., 1980; Middendorf/Lane Gallery, Washington, D.C., 1980; John Berggruen Gallery, San Francisco, 1980, 82; Gemini G.E.L., Los Angeles, 1981; Asher Faure, Los Angeles, 1982, 83; Thomas Babeor Gallery, La Jolla, 1984; Margo Leavin Gallery, Los Angeles, 1984. **Retrospective:** Oakland, 1976. **Group:** Indianapolis, 1974; Corcoran Biennial, 1975; Leverkusen, Zeichnungen 3, USA, 1975; Cleveland/MA, Four Contemporary Painters, 1978; Indianapolis, 1974; Santa Barbara/MA, Fifteen Abstract Artists, 1974; Corcoran Biennial, 1975; Leverkusen, Drawings 3: American

Drawings, 1975; ICA, Los Angeles, Current Concerns, 1975; MOMA, Color as Language, circ., 1975; SFMA, California Painting and Sculpture. The Modern Era, 1977; U. of California, Santa Barbara, Photographs by Southern California Painters and Sculptors, 1977; Cleveland/MA, Four Contemporary Painters, 1978; Honolulu Academy, California: 3 by 8 Twice, 1978; Buffalo/Albright, American Painting of the 1970s, 1978; Los Angeles/County MA, Art in Los Angeles, 1981; Houston/MFA, Miró in America, 1982. **Collections:** Baltimore/MA; Bowdoin College; Buffalo/Albright; Los Angeles/County MA; MOMA; Oakland/AM; SFMA; Seattle/AM; Tate Gallery; WMAA. **Bibliography:** Davis, D.; *New in the Seventies; Report: The State of California Painting; USA West Coast;* Wood.

DAVIS, STUART. b. December 7, 1894, Philadelphia, Pa.; **d.** June 24, 1964, NYC. Studied with Robert Henri, 1910-13, US Army Intelligence, World War I. Traveled Europe, Cuba, USA. **Taught:** ASL, 1931-32; New School for Social Research, 1940-50; lectured at museums and universities. Federal A.P.: 1933-39. Editor: *Art Front* magazine. **Commissions** (murals): Radio City Music Hall, NYC, 1932; Indiana U., 1938; New York World's Fair, 1939; Municipal Broadcasting Co., NYC, 1939; Drake U., 1955; Heinz Research Center, Pittsburgh, 1957. **Awards:** Pepsi-Cola, 1944; Carnegie, Hon. Men. 1944; PAFA, J. Henry Schiedt Memorial Prize, 1945; Chicago/AI; Norman Wait Harris Silver Medal, 1948; La Tausca Competition, **P.P.,** 1948; VMFA, John Barton Payne Medal, 1950; Chicago/AI, Ada S. Garrett Prize, 1951; Guggenheim Foundation Fellowship, 1952; Hallmark International Competition, 1956; PAFA, Hon. Men., 1956; Brandeis U., Creative Arts Award, 1957; Guggenheim International, 1958, 60; Chicago/AI, Floral Mayer Witkowsky Prize, 1961; PAFA, Joseph E. Temple Gold Medal, 1964; Chicago/AI, The Mr. & Mrs. Frank G. Logan Medal and Prize. **One-man Exhibitions:** Sheridan

Square Gallery, NYC, 1917; Ardsley Gallery, 1918; Newark Museum, 1925; Whitney Studio Club, NYC, 1926-29; The Downtown Gallery, 1927, 30, 31, 32, 34, 43, 46, 52, 54, 56, 60, 62; Curt Valentine Gallery, NYC, 1928; Crillon Galleries, Philadelphia, 1931; Katherine Kuh Gallery, Chicago, 1939; Modern Art Society, Cincinnati, 1941 (two-man); Arts Club of Chicago, 1945; MOMA, 1945; Baltimore/MA, 1946; Santa Barbara/MA, 1949 (three-man); XXVI Venice Biennial, 1952; Contemporary Arts Gallery, NYC, 1955, 59; Brandeis U., 1957; Peale House, Philadelphia, 1964; Lawrence Rubin Gallery, NYC, 1971; The Zabriskie Gallery, NYC, 1976; Grace Borgenicht Gallery, NYC, 1979, 80, 83, 86; Hirschl & Adler Gallery, NYC, 1978; Esther Robles Gallery, Los Angeles, 1979; WMAA, 1980; Washburn Gallery Inc., 1983; Columbus, 1986. **Retrospectives:** Walker,

Stuart Davis *Town Square* 1924

1947; NCFA, 1965; Brooklyn Museum, 1978. **Group:** The Armory Show, 1913; Independents, NYC, 1916; Golden Gate International Exposition, San Francisco, 1939; Tate, American Painting, 1946; I Sao Paulo Biennial, 1951; MOMA, 12 Modern American Painters and Sculptors, circ., Europe, 1953-55; MOMA, Modern Art in the United States, circ., Europe, 1955-56; I Inter-American Paintings and Prints Biennial, Mexico City, 1958; American Painting and Sculpture, Moscow, 1959; WMAA, The 1930's, 1968; Brown U., Graham, Gorky, Smith & Davis, 1977. **Collections:** AAAL; Andover/Phillips; Arizona State College; U. of Arizona State College; U. of Arizona; Baltimore/MA; Bezalel Museum; Brandeis U.; Britannica; Brooklyn Museum; Buffalo/Albright; Carnegie; Chicago/AI; Cincinnati/AM; Cranbrook; Dartmouth College; U. of Georgia; Hartford/Wadsworth; Harvard U.; Honolulu Academy; IBM; U. of Illinois; State U. of Iowa; U. of Kentucky; Library of Congress; Los Angeles/County MA; MMA; MOMA; Milwaukee; Minneapolis/Institute; U. of Nebraska; Newark Museum; New Trier High School; Ogunquit; U. of Oklahoma; PAFA; PMA; The Pennsylvania State U.; Phillips; Randolph-Macon Woman's College; Sara Roby Foundation; U. of Rochester; Roswell; SFMA; SRGM; St. Louis/City; San Diego; Seattle/AM; Utica; VMFA; Vassar College; WMAA; Walker; Washington U.; Wellesley College; Wichita/AM; Yale U. **Bibliography: Arnason 3, 4;** *Avant-Garde Painting and Sculpture in America, 1910-25;* Baigell 1; Barker 1; Barr 3; Battcock, ed.; Baur 5, 7; Bazin; Beekman; Biddle 4; Biederman 1; **Blesh 1, 2;** Brown 2; Cahill and Barr, eds.; Cheney; Chipp; Christensen; *Cityscape 1919-39;* Coke 2; **Davis S.;** Eliot; **Elliott;** Flanagan; Flexner; Frost; Genauer; Gerdts; Goodrich and Baur 1; **Goossen 4;** Greengood; Haftman, Graham, Gorky, *Smith & Davis in the Thirties;* Halpert; Hess, T.B., 1; Honisch and Jensen, eds.; Hunter 1, 6; Hunter, ed.; Huyghe;

Janis, S.; Johnson, Ellen H.; **Kelder;** Kepes 2; Kootz 2; Kozloff 3; Kuh 2, 3; Lane and Larsen; Lee and Burchwood; Lippard, 5; Levin 2; McCurdy, ed.; Mendelowitz; Munsterberg; Murken-Altrogge; **Myers, ed.** Newmeyer; Nordness, ed.; O'Doherty; Pagano; Pearson 1; Phillips 1; Pousette-Dart, ed.; Read 2; Richardson E.P.; Rickey; Ringel, ed.; Ritchie 1; Rodman 2; Rose, B., 1, 4; Rosenblum, 1; Sachs; Sandler; Seuphor 1; Sutton; **Sweeney 4;** Tashjian; Weller; "What Abstract Art Means to Me"; Wheeler; Wight 2. Archives.

DE ANDREA, JOHN. b. December 24, 1941, Denver, Colo. **Studied:** U. of Colorado, 1964, BFA. Traveled Europe, Mexico, USA. **Taught:** U. of New Mexico, 1965. **Awards:** National Endowment for the Arts, 1974. **Address:** 1235 Pierce Street, Lakewood, CO 80214. **Dealer:** Carlo Lamagna Gallery, NYC. **One-man Exhibitions:** OK Harris Works of Art, 1970, 71, 73, 76, 78, 85; Carlo Lamagna Gallery, 1987. **Group:** Chicago/Contemporary, Radical Realism, 1971; VII Paris Biennial, 1971; Documenta V, Kassel, 1972; Galerie des 4 Mouvements, Paris, Hyperrealistes Americains, 1972; Harvard U., Recent Figure Sculpture, 1972; New York Cultural Center, Realism Now, 1972; Lunds Konsthall, Sweden, Amerikansk Realism, 1973; Lincoln, Mass./ De Cordova, The Super-Realist Vision, 1973; Hofstra U., The Male Nude, 1973; CNAC, Hyperrealistes Americains/ Realistes Europeens, 1974; Hartford/Wadsworth, New/Photo Realism, 1974; Wichita State U., Photo-Realism, 1975; Baltimore/MA, Super Realism, 1975; Vancouver, Aspects of Realism, 1976; Stamford Museum, American Salon des Refuses, 1976; Canberra/National, Illusion and Reality, 1977; Venice Biennial, 1978; PAFA, Seven on the Figure, 1979; Paris/Beaubourg, Copie Conforme, 1979. **Collections:** Aachen/NG; Belger Cartage Service, Kansas City, Mo.; Syracuse/Everson; U. of Virginia. **Bibliography:** *Kunst um*

1970; Lindy; Lucie-Smith; *Recent Figure Sculpture;* Sager.

DE CREEFT, JOSE. b. November 27, 1884, Guadalajara, Spain. **d.** September 11, 1982, NYC. **Studied:** Atelier of Don Augustin Querol, Barcelona, 1906; apprenticed to Idalgo de Caviedas; Academie Julian, Paris, 1906; Maison Greber, Paris, 1910-14. To USA, 1929; citizen, 1940. **Taught:** New School for Social Research, 1932-48, 1957-62; ASL, 1934-62. **Member:** Artists Equity (founding member); Audubon Artists; National Sculpture Society; Federation of Modern Painters and Sculptors (president, 1943); NIAL, 1955; NAD, 1964; AAAL; Sculptors Guild. **Commissions:** Saugues (Puy de Dome), France, 1918 (World War I Memorial); Fortress of Ramonje, Mallorca, 1932 (200 pieces of sculpture); Fairmount Park, Philadelphia, 1950; Central Park, NYC, 1959 (Alice in Wonderland group); Bronx (N.Y.) Municipal Hospital, 1962 (mosaic for nurses' residence); New Public Health Laboratory, NYC, 1966. **Awards:** Officier de l'Instruction Publique, France; MMA, Artists for Victory, First Prize, 1942; PAFA, George D. Widener Memorial Gold Medal, 1945; Audubon Artists, Gold Medal of Honor, 1954, 57; Ford Foundation Traveling Retrospective, 1960; National Sculpture Society, Therese and Edwin Richard Prize for Portrait Sculpture, 1969; Comendador de la Orden de Isabel la Catolica, 1973; National Arts Club, Gold Medal, 1975. **m.** Lorrie Goulet. **One-man Exhibitions:** (first) El Circulo de Bellas Artes, Madrid, 1903; Seattle/AM, 1929; Ferargil Galleries, NYC, 1929; Arts Club of Chicago, 1930; Philadelphia Art Alliance, 1933; Passedoit Gallery, NYC, 1936, 1938-49; Santa Barbara/MA, 1937; St. Paul Gallery, 1943; College of William and Mary, 1944; West Palm Beach/Norton, 1949, 50; The Contemporaries, NYC, 1956, 58, 60, 64, 65; Kennedy Gallery, 1970, 71, 72, 75, 79; Sid Deutsch Gallery, NYC,

1985; NMAA, 1983. **Retrospectives:** A.F.A./Ford Foundation, circ., 1960; New School for Social Research, 1974. **Group:** Salon d'Automne, Paris, 1910-29; Chicago/AI Annuals, 1939-51; MMA, National Sculpture Exhibition, 1942, 51; WMAA Annuals, 1942-57; PAFA Annuals, 1944-62; Carnegie; MOMA, Sculpture of the XXth Century, 1953; Worcester/AM; Brooklyn Museum; Sculptors Guild Annuals; Audubon Artists Annuals; Federation of Modern Painters and Sculptors; Artistes Francais; Societe Nationale des Beaux Arts, Paris; Salon des Artistes Independents, Paris. **Collections:** Bezalel Museum; Brooklyn Museum; Columbia U.; Hirshhorn; IBM; MMA; MOMA; Museum of the City of New York; U. of Nebraska; New Paltz/SUNY; PAFA; U. of Puerto Rico; SFMA; Seattle/AM; Trenton/State; U. of Tucson; Utica; WMAA; West Palm Beach/Norton; Wichita/AM. **Bibliography:** Baur 7; Brumme; **Campos;** Cheney; Craven, W.; **de Creeft; Devree;** Goodrich and Baur 1; McCurdy, ed.; Marter, Tarbell, and Wechsler; Pearson 2; Ritchie 3; Selz, J.; Seuphor 3. Archives.

DEEM, GEORGE. b. August 18, 1932, Vincennes, Ind. **Studied:** Vincennes U.; The U. of Chicago; Chicago Art Institute School, with Paul Wieghardt, Boris Margo, 1958, BFA. Traveled Europe; resided in England, 1966-67, Italy, 1970-77. US Army, 1951-53. **Taught:** School of Visual Arts, NYC, 1965-66; Leicester Polytechnic, England, 1966-67; U. of Pennsylvania, 1968-69; Museum of Arts and Sciences, Evansville, Ind., 1979; Illinois State U., 1982. **Awards:** MacDowell Colony Fellowship, 1977, 79. **Address:** 10 West 18th Street, NYC 10011. **Dealer:** Nancy Hoffman Gallery, NYC. **One-man Exhibitions:** (first) Allan Stone Gallery, 1962, also 1963-66, 68, 69, 75, 77; Merida Gallery, Inc., Louisville, 1964, 68, 69, 78, 83; James Goodman Gallery, Buffalo, 1965; Ferrier Gallery, Houston,

George Deem   *School of Caravaggio*   1984

1969; Sneed-Hillman Gallery, Rockford, Ill., 1968, 69, 72, 76, 80, 81; M. E. Thelen Gallery, Essen, 1970; Indianapolis, 1975; Evansville, 1979; Ronald Greenberg Gallery, St. Louis, 1979; Witte, 1984. **Group:** Corcoran; Baltimore/MA, 1962; Buffalo/Albright, 1962; Chicago/AI, 1963, 65; MOMA; Barnard College; Silvermine Guild; The Hague, New Realism, 1964; Brandeis U., 1964; Cornell U., 1965; ICA, U. of Pennsylvania, 1965; U. of Illinois, 1965, 74; Indianapolis, Biennial, 1972, 76, 78; WMAA, Art about Art, 1978; Duisburg, Mona Lisa in the 20th Century, circ., 1978; PAFA, Contemporary American Realism Since 1960, 1981; Allentown/AM, The Artist's Studio in American Painting, 1840-1983, 1983; Fort Wayne/AM, Indiana Influence, 1984. **Collections:** Houston/MFA; Aachen/NG; Evansville; Houston/MFA; Indianapolis; Louisville/Speed; Miami U.; U. of Nebraska; Oberlin College; U. of North Carolina; U. of Rochester; Rockford/Burpee; SFMA; The Singer Company, Inc.; Vassar. **Bibliography:** *Kunst um 1970*; Murken-Altrogge; Sager; Weller.

DE FOREST, ROY DEAN. b. February 11, 1930, North Platte, Neb. **Studied:** Yakima Valley Junior College, 1950, AA; California School of Fine Arts, 1950-52, with Edward Corbett, Hassel Smith, David Park; San Francisco State College, 1953, BA, 1958, MA, with Seymour Locks, Alexander Nepote. Traveled Paris, London, 1971. **Taught:** SFMA, 1955-58; Yakima Jr. College,

1958-60; Contra Costa Jr. College, 1960-61; Jr. Center of Arts and Sciences, Oakland, Calif. 1964-65; San Quentin Prison, 1964; California College of Arts and Crafts, 1964-65; U. of Calif., Davis, 1965-82. **Awards:** Bay Printmakers Society, Oakland, **P.P.,** 1956; San Francisco Art Association, 1956; SFMA, Nealie Sullivan Award, 1962; National Endowment for the Arts, 1972. **Address:** P.O. Box 47, Port Costa, CA 94569. **Dealers:** Fuller Goldeen, San Francisco; Allan Frumkin Gallery, NYC; Darthea Speyer Gallery, Paris. **One-man Exhibitions:** (first) The East-West Gallery, San Francisco, 1955, also 1958; Stonecourt Gallery, Yakima, Wash., 1960; Dilexi Gallery, San Francisco, 1960, 63; Dilexi Gallery, Los Angeles, 1962; San Francisco Art Association, 1962, 65; Allan Frumkin Gallery, NYC, 1966, 73, 75, 77, 79; Peninsula Gallery, Menlo Park, Calif., 1966; Sacramento City College Art Gallery, 1967; Allan Frumkin Gallery, Chicago, 1966, 77; Candy Store Art Gallery, Folsom, Calif., 1969; Mabikudes Gallery, Seattle, 1971; California Palace, 1971; Hansen-Fuller Gallery, 1971, 73, 74, 75, 78; Glenbow Alberta Institute, Calgary, 1974; Darthea Speyer Gallery, 1974, 77; Gallery Allen, 1974; Clark/Benton Gallery, Santa Fe, 1977, 81; 603 East 3rd Street Gallery, Los Angeles, 1979; Fresno State U., 1979; Michael Berger Gallery, Pittsburgh, 1979; U. of California, Davis, 1980, 83; Triton Museum of Art, Santa Clara, 1980; Fountain Gallery, Portland, Ore., 1980; Blackfish Gallery, Portland, Ore., 1980; Susan Whitney Gallery, Regina, 1980; Sacramento/Crocker, 1980; Marian Locks Gallery, Philadelphia, 1980; Hansen Fuller Goldeen Gallery, San Francisco, 1981, 84; California State U., Chico, 1982. **Retrospective:** SFMA, circ., 1974. **Group:** Cincinnati/AM, 1952; SFMA, 1952, 63, 64; Sao Paulo, 1955; Reed College, 1957; California Palace, 1960, 63; WMAA, 1962; Pasadena/AM, 1962; Buffalo/Albright, 1963; Walker, 1963; U. of Illinois, 1964, 69; U. of California, Berkeley, Funk 1967; Portland,

Ore./AM, The West Coast Now, 1968; WMAA, Extraordinary Realities, 1973; Sacramento Sampler 2, 1973; SFMA, Painting and Sculpture in California: The Modern Era, 1976; Washington State U., 6 from California, 1976; Halifax, 3 from California, 1976; U. of Texas, Austin, New in the Seventies, 1977; SFMA, Downtown Center, Dog Images through the Century, 1978; ICA, Boston, Roy de Forest, Robert Hudson, 1977; XXXIX Venice Biennial, 1980; Brooklyn Museum, American Drawings in Black and White, 1970-1979, 1980; Sacramento/Crocker, Welcome to the Candy Store, 1981; Columbus, American Paintings of the 60's and 70's, 1981; Palm Springs Desert Museum, The West as Art, 1982; U. of Southern California, Idioms of Surrealism, 1984; Sioux City Art Center, Beasties, 1984. **Collections:** Arizona State U.; Brooklyn Museum; U. of California, Berkeley; California College of Arts and Crafts; Chicago/AI; Cornell U.; Des Moines; Indianapolis; U. of Kansas; La Jolla; Madison Art Center; Memphis/Brooks; U. of New Mexico; U. of North Carolina; Oakland/AM; Omaha/Joslyn; PMA; Paris/Beaubourg; RISD; U. of Rochester; SFMA; Sacramento/Crocker; San Francisco Civic Center; Stanford U.; U. of Utah; U. of Virginia; WMAA; Yakima (Calif.) Public Library. **Bibliography:** *Drawings: The Pluralist Decade;* Humphrey; Janis and Blesh 1; *New in the Seventies;* Selz, P., 2; The State of California Painting. Archives.

DEHN, ADOLF ARTHUR. b. November 22, 1895, Waterville, Minn.; **d.** May 19, 1968, NYC. **Studied:** Minneapolis Institute School; ASL. **Taught:** Famous Artists Schools, Inc. **Member:** NAD. **Awards:** Philadelphia Art Alliance, 1936; The Print Club, Philadelphia, 1939; Guggenheim Foundation Fellowship, 1939, 51; Chicago/AI, 1943; Library of Congress, Pennell **P.P.,** 1946. **One-man Exhibitions:** Macbeth Gallery, NYC, 1933; A.A.A. Gallery, NYC,

1941, 51; Brooklyn Public Library, 1944; Dayton/AI, 1946; The Milch Gallery, 1957, 60, 68; FAR Gallery, 1964, 65; Studio North, Towson, Md., 1969; Kennedy Gallery, 1971; Hirschl & Adler Galleries, Inc., NYC, 1976; Harmon Gallery, Naples, Fla., 1981, 82; Mary Ryan Gallery, 1982; Fine Arts America, Inc., Richmond, Va., 1983; Harmon-Meek Gallery, Naples, Fla., 1985. **Retrospective:** Amon Carter Museum. **Group:** MMA; MOMA; NYPL; Brooklyn Museum; Chicago/AI; Boston/MFA; WMAA. **Collections:** Boston/MFA; Brooklyn Museum; Chicago/AI; Cincinnati/AM; Cleveland/MA; Indianapolis/Herron; Lehigh U.; MMA; MOMA; Minneapolis/Institute; NYPL; Newark Museum; Standard Oil Co.; US Navy; Utica; WMAA. **Bibliography:** American Artists Group Inc. 1, 2, 3; Brown; Dehn; Goodrich 1; Goodrich and Baur 1; *Index of 20th Century Artists;* Mellquist; Mendelowitz; Pagano; Pearson 1, 2; Pousette-Dart, ed.; Reese; Zigrosser 1. Archives.

DEHNER, DOROTHY. b. December 23, 1901, Cleveland, Ohio. **Studied:** UCLA; Skidmore College, BS (Art). Pasadena Playhouse, with Gilmor Brown; ASL, with Kimon Nicolaides, Boardman Robinson, Jan Matulka, Kenneth Kayes Miller. Traveled Europe, USSR, Mexico, USA. Began as a painter, became a sculptor in 1955. **Taught:** New York State Extension Program, 1952-54; Barnard School, NYC, 1954-56; Parsons School of Design, NYC, 1950-; Boas Dance Studio, Bolton Landing, N.Y.; and privately. **Member:** Sculptors Guild; Federation of Modern Painters and Sculptors. **Commissions:** Great Southwest Industrial Park (outdoor relief), 1969; Union Camp Corp., Wayne, N.J., 1971; Rockefeller Center, 1972. **Awards:** Audubon Artists, First Prize, 1949; ART: USA: 59, NYC, Second Prize for Sculpture, 1959; Tamarind Fellowship, 1965; Kane Memorial Exhibition, Providence, R.I., First Prize

for Sculpture, 1962; Yaddo Fellowship, 1971. **Address:** 33 Fifth Avenue, NYC 10003. **Dealer:** Twining Gallery, NYC. **One-man Exhibitions:** Albany/Institute, ca. 1944 (two-man, with David Smith), also 1954; Skidmore College, 1948, 53, 59; Rose Fried Gallery, 1952; Howard U., 1954; U. of Virginia, 1954; Chicago/AI, 1955; The Willard Gallery, 1955, 57, 59, 61, 63, 66, 70, 73; Wittenborn Gallery, NYC, 1956; Gres Gallery, Washington, D.C., 1959; Columbia U., 1961; Philadelphia Art Alliance, 1962; U. of Michigan, 1963; Cornell U., 1964; Fort Wayne/AM, 1975; Benson Gallery, Bridgehampton, 1975; Jane Weis Gallery, Cleveland, 1974; Parsons-Dreyfus Gallery, NYC, 1978; Barbara Fiedler Gallery, Washington, D.C., 1980; Twining Gallery, 1986. **Retrospective:** Jewish Museum, 1965; Hyde Collection, 1967; Jacksonville/Cummer; Fort Wayne/AM; Design Corner, Cleveland; Storm King Art Center, 1978. **Group:** Brooklyn Museum; Sculptors Guild Annuals; Baltimore/MA; Los Angeles/County MA; Utica; PAFA; Walker; Hartford/Wadsworth; New Sculpture Group, NYC; Rome/Nazionale; SFMA, 1944; WMAA Annuals, 1950, 51, 54, 60, 63; MMA, 1953; Carnegie, 1961; MOMA, 1962, 64. **Collections:** AT&T; Bankers Trust Company; Calcutta; Chase Manhattan Bank; Cleveland/MA; Columbia U.; Columbus; First National Bank of Chicago; Free Library of Philadelphia; Great Southwest Industrial Park; Hemisphere Club; Hyde Collection; Jacksonville/Cummer; MMA; MOMA; Minnesota/MA; NYPL; U. of New Mexico; The New York Bank for Savings; U. of North Carolina; St. Lawrence U.; Seattle/AM; Skidmore College; US State Department; Utica; Wellesley College; Wichita State U.; U. of Wisconsin. **Bibliography:** Bihalji-Merin; Moser 1. Archives.

DE KNIGHT, AVEL. b. 1933, NYC. **Studied:** Ecole des Beaux-Arts, Paris,

1955-56; Academie de la Grande Chaumiere, Paris, 1956-57; Academie Julien,
Paris, 1957-58. Art critic for *France-
Amérique*, 1958-68. **Taught:** New School
for Social Research, 1967; Brooklyn Mu-
seum School, 1969-70; NAD. **Member:**
NAD; American Watercolor Society.
Awards: NAD, Palmer Memorial Prize,
1958, Ranger Fund, **P.P.**, 1958, 64, 66;
AAAL, Childe Hassam Fund **D.P.**,
1960, 70; US State Department Ex-
change Grant to travel USSR, 1961;
NAD, Grumbacher Award, 1962, 64,
Samuel F. B. Morse Medal, 1966, Wil-
liam A. Paton Prize, 1967, 71; American
Watercolor Society, Grand Prize and
Gold Medal, 1967; Audubon Artists
Medal of Honor, 1969. **Address:** 81
Perry Street, NYC 10014. **Dealer:** The
Babcock Gallery. **One-man Exhibi-
tions:** Richard Larcada Gallery, 1968,
71; The Babcock Gallery, 1973. **Group:**
Youngstown/Butler, 1958-73; PAFA,
1965; Boston/MFA, Black Artists; New
York and Boston, 1970; WMAA, Con-
temporary Black Artists in America,
1971; Finch College, NYC, Projected
Art, 1971; Jacksonville/Cummer, Rem-
nants of Things Past, 1971. **Collec-
tions:** Chase Manhattan Bank; Denison
U.; Lehigh U.; MMA; Massilon Museum; Miles College; NAD; Norfolk;
Southern Vermont Art Center; Springfield, Mo./AM; Walker. **Bibliography:**
Archives.

DE KOONING, ELAINE. b. March 20,
1920, NYC. **Studied:** Leonardo da
Vinci Art School, NYC, 1937; American
Artists School, NYC, 1938, with Con-
rad Marca-Relli; privately with Willem
de Kooning, 1938-43. Traveled France,
Belgium, Spain. **Taught:** U. of New
Mexico, 1959; The Pennsylvania State
U., 1960; U. of California, Davis,
1963-64; Yale U., 1967; Pratt Institute,
1968; Carnegie-Mellon U., 1968-70; U.
of Pennsylvania, 1971-72; Wagner Col-
lege, 1971; New York Studio School,
Paris, 1974; Parsons School of Design,
NYC, 1974-75; U. of Georgia, 1976-79;
Skowhegan School, 1979; Bard College.

Member: Artists Equity. Commis-
sioned by President Harry S Truman to
paint portrait of John F. Kennedy,
1963. **Awards:** Hon. DFA, Webster
College, 1964; Moore College of Art,
Philadelphia, 1972; Hon. DFA, Adelphi
U., 1985; Hon. DFA, U. of Maryland,
1986. **Address:** P.O. Box 1437, East
Hampton, L.I., NY 11937. **Dealer:**
Gruenebaum Gallery, NYC. **One-man
Exhibitions:** The Stable Gallery, NYC,
1954, 56; Tibor de Nagy Gallery, NYC,
1957; U. of New Mexico, 1958; Santa
Fe, N.M., 1959; Gump's Gallery, 1959;
Dord Fitz Gallery, Amarillo, 1959; Hol-
land-Goldowsky Gallery, Chicago,
1960; The Howard Wise Gallery,
Cleveland, 1960; Ellison Gallery, Fort
Worth, 1960; Tanager Gallery, NYC,
1960; The Graham Gallery, 1960, 61, 64,
75, 81; De Aenlle Gallery, NYC, 1961;
Drew U., 1966; Montclair/AM, 1973;
Benson Gallery, 1973; Illinois Wesleyan
U., 1975; St. Catherine's College, St.
Paul, 1975; Greenberg Gallery, 1982;
Gruenebaum Gallery, 1982, 86; Phoenix
II Gallery, Washington, D.C., 1982;
Port Washington (N.Y.) Library, 1982;
Arts Club of Chicago, 1983; Guild Hall,
1983; Adelphi U., 1984; C. Grimaldis
Gallery, Baltimore, 1984, 85; Vered Gal-
lery, East Hampton, N.Y., 1984. **Retrospective:** New London, 1959. **Group:**
The Kootz Gallery, NYC, New Talent,
1950; International Biennial Exhibition
of Paintings, Tokyo; Walker, Expressionism, 1900-1955, 1956; Carnegie,
1956; A.F.A., Sports in Art, 1957; Jewish Museum, The New York School,
Second Generation, 1957; MOMA,
Younger American Painters, circ., 1957,
59; Houston/MFA, Action Painting,
1958; Walker, 60 American Painters,
1960; Hallmark Art Award, 1960;
WMAA Annuals 1963, 74; Carnegie,
1964; PMA/Museum of the Philadelphia Civic Center, Focus, 1974; NPG,
American Self-Portraits: 1670-1973;
1974. **Collections:** U. of Arkansas;
Ciba-Geigy Corp.; Elmira College; Kennedy Library; MOMA; Montclair/AM;
NYU; Purchase/SUNY; Harry S
Truman Library. **Bibliography:** Blesh

1; Chipp; Downes, ed.; Hunter 6; Janis and Blesh 1; O'Hara 1. Archives.

DE KOONING, WILLEM. b. April 24, 1904, Rotterdam, Holland. **Studied:** Academie voor Beeldende Kunsten ed Technische Wetenschappen, Amsterdam, 1916-24. To USA, 1926. Federal A.P.; Mural painting, 1935-39. **Taught:** Black Mountain College, 1948; Yale U., 1950-51. **Member:** NIAL; Akademie der Kunst, Berlin, 1982; Hon. Member, Royal Academy for the Visual Arts, Netherlands, 1982; Royal Academy of Fine Arts, Sweden, 1986. **Commissions** (murals): New York World's Fair, 1939; French Line Pier, NYC (with Fernand Leger); Williamsburg Housing Project, NYC. **Awards:** State Academy Medal, Rotterdam; Academy of Plastic Arts, Rotterdam, Silver Medal; Chicago/AI, The Mr. & Mrs. Frank G. Logan Medal, 1951; The President's Medal, 1963; Presidential Medal of Honor, 1964; Talen Prize, Amsterdam, 1968; Brandeis U., Creative Arts Award, 1974; MacDowell Colony Medal, 1975; AAIAL, Gold Medal for Painting, 1975; Officer of the Order of Orange-Nassau, Netherlands, 1979; Carnegie, Andrew W. Mellon Prize shared with Eduardo Chillida, 1979; Goslarer Kaisseringes, 1984; Max Beckmann Prize, 1984; Mayor's Liberty Medal, NYC, 1986; National Medal of the Arts, 1986. **Address:** Woodbine Drive, East Hampton, NY 11973. **Dealer:** Xavier Fourcade, Inc., NYC. **One-man Exhibitions:** (first) Charles Egan Gallery, 1948, also 1951; Arts Club of Chicago, 1951; Sidney Janis Gallery, 1953, 56, 59, 62, 72; Boston Museum School, 1953; Workshop Art Center, Washington, D.C., 1953; Martha Jackson Gallery, 1955; Paul Kantor Gallery, Beverly Hills, Calif., 1961, 65; Allan Stone Gallery, 1962 (two-man), 1964, 65, 71, 72; The Goodman Gallery, Buffalo, 1964; Smith College, 1965; M. Knoedler & Co., NYC, 1967, 69, 71, Paris, 1968, 71; Betty Gold, Los Angeles, 1971; Fourcade, Droll, Inc.,

Willem de Kooning *Untitled III* 1984

NYC, 1972, 75; Richard Gray Gallery, 1974; Walker, 1974; Galerie Biedermann, Munich, 1974; West Palm Beach/Norton, 1975; Seattle/AM, 1976; Amsterdam/Stedelijk, 1976, 83; Musée de Grenoble, 1977; Corcoran Gallery, Los Angeles, 1976, 77; Gimpel Fils, London, 1976; Gimpel Fils, Zurich, 1976; Xavier Fourcade, Inc., NYC, 1976, 77, 78, 79, 84, 85; Galerie Daniel Templon, Paris, 1977; U. of Houston, 1976; Belgrade, 1977-78; Duisburg, 1977; SRGM, 1978; U. of Northern Iowa, 1978; Carnegie, 1979; Richard Gray Gallery, Chicago, 1980; Richard Hines Gallery, Seattle, 1980; Guild Hall, 1981; Janie C. Lee Gallery, Houston, 1981; Galerie Maeght Lelong, NYC, 1983; Colorado State U., 1984; Lincoln Center, Fort Collins, 1984; Mönchehause Museum, Goslar, 1984; Galerie Daniel Templon, Paris, 1984; Hans Strelow Gallery, Dusseldorf, 1984; Anthony d'Offay Gallery, London, 1985; Studio Marconi, Milan, 1985; Margo Leavin Gallery, Los Angeles, 1986. **Retrospectives:** Amsterdam/Stedelijk, 1968; MOMA, 1968; WMAA, circ., 1983; Stadelsches Kunst

Institute, Frankfurt, 1984. **Group:** MOMA, New Horizons in American Art, 1936; WMAA Annuals, 1948, 50, 51; VMFA, American Painting, 1950; California Palace, 1950; XXV, XXVI, & XXVIII Venice Biennials, 1950, 52, 56; MOMA, Abstract Painting and Sculpture in America, 1951; Sao Paulo, 1951, 53; Chicago/AI, 1951, 54; Buffalo/Albright, Expressionism in American Painting, 1952; Carnegie, 1952, 55; Baltimore/MA, 1953; WMAA, The New Decade, 1954-55; WMAA, Nature in Abstraction, 1958; Brussels World's Fair, 1958; MOMA, The New American Painting, circ., Europe 1958-59; Hartford/Wadsworth, Continuity and Change, 1962; Seattle World's Fair, 1962; Art: USA: Now, circ., 1962-67; SRGM, Guggenheim International, 1964; Tate, Painting and Sculpture of a Decade, 1954-64, 1964; SRGM, American Drawings 1964; Los Angeles/County MA, New York School, 1965; U. of Illinois, 1967; Melbourne/National, Two Decades of American Painting, 1967; Frankfurter Kunstverein, Kompass New York, 1968; ICA, London, The Obsessive Image, 1968; MOMA, The New American Painting and Sculpture, 1969; Corcoran Biennial, 1979; U. of California, Berkeley, Matrix, 1978; National Gallery, American Art Mid-Century, 1978; PAFA, Seven on the Figure, 1979; Sunderland (Eng.) Arts Center, Drawings in Air, 1983; Chicago/Terra, Woman, 1984; Hirshhorn, Drawings 1974-1984, 1984; Southampton/Parrish, Painting Naturally: Fairfield Porter and His Influences, 1984; National Gallery, Gemini G.E.L.: Art and Collaboration, 1984; Amsterdam/Stedelijk, La Grande Parade, 1984; Ecole des Beaux Arts, Paris, American Drawing: 1930-1980, 1985; U. of Nebraska, Contemporary Bronze: Six in the Figurative Tradition, 1985. **Collections:** Amsterdam/Stedelijk; Baltimore/MA; Brooklyn Museum; Buffalo/Albright; Canberra/National; Carnegie; Chicago/AI; Container Corp. of America; Hartford/Wadsworth; Hirshhorn; Inland Steel Co.; Kansas City/Nelson; Los An-geles/County MA; MMA; MOMA: National Gallery; U. of Nebraska; U. of North Carolina; Ottawa; PMA; Phillips; SRGM; RISD; Stockholm/National; Toronto; Vassar College; WMAA; Walker; Washington U. **Bibliography:** Alloway 4; Ashton 5; Barr 3; Battcock, ed.; Baur 5, 7; Becker and Vostell; Biddle 4; Bihalji-Merin; Blesh 1; Brion 1; Brown 2; Calas, N. and E.; Canaday; Carmean and Rathbone; **Cummings, Merkett, and Stullig;** Chipp; Danto; **de Kooning;** De Wilde 1, 2; Downes, ed.; Eliot; Elsen 1; Finch; Flanagan; *from Foreign Shores;* **Gaugh;** Gettings; Goodrich and Baur 1; Greenberg 1; Haftman; Henning; **Hess, T.B., 1, 4, 5;** Hobbs and Levin; Hunter 1, 6; Hunter, ed.; **Janis and Blesh 1, 2;** Janis, S.; Johnson, Ellen H.; Kozloff 3; Kuh 3; Lane and Larsen; Langui; **Larson and Schjeldahl;** Lippard 5; Lynton; McCoubrey 1; McCurdy, ed.; Mendelowitz; **Metro; Monumenta;** Motherwell and Reinhardt, eds.; Murken-Altrogge; Neumeyer; Nordness, ed.; O'Doherty; Plous; *Poets & Painters;* Ponente; Pousette-Dart, ed.; Ragon 1; Read 2; Richardson, E.P.; Rickey; Ritchie 1; Rodman 1, 2, 3; Rose, B., 1, 4; **Rosenberg;** Rothschild; Sandler; Seitz 1, 3; Seuphor 1; Soby 6; Tomkins 1, 2; Tomkins and Time-Life Books; Tuchman, ed.; Weller; "What Abstract Art Means to Me". Archives.

DE LAP, TONY. b. November 4, 1927, Oakland, Calif. **Studied:** California College of Arts and Crafts; Menlo Junior College; Academy of Art, San Francisco; Claremont Graduate School, AA. Traveled in Europe for 3 months, 1954. **Taught:** Academy of Art, San Francisco, 1957-59; California College of Arts and Crafts, 1961-63; U. of Wisconsin, summer 1963; Scripps College, U. of California, Davis, 1964-65; Claremont Colleges, 1964; San Francisco Art Institute, 1964-67; U. of California, Irvine, 1965-. Art Commissioner, San Francisco Municipal Art Commission. **Commissions:** Brooks

Hall, San Francisco; Carborundum Co., 1969; C.C.H. Building, San Rafael, Calif., 1972; City of Inglewood, Calif., 1973. **Awards:** San Francisco Art Festival, First Prize, Mural Competition, 1957; SFMA, Nealie Sullivan Award, 1964; Ford Foundation/A.F.A. Artist-in-Residence, 1966; Long Beach/MA., **P.P.,** 1969; 1st Prize, Los Angeles Department of Airports, sculpture competition, 1976. **Address:** 225 Jasmine Street, Corona del Mar, CA 92625. **Dealers:** Robert Elkon Gallery; Janus Gallery, Venice, Calif. **One-man Exhibitions:** (first) Gump's Gallery; SFMA; RAC, 1954; Oakland/AM, 1960; Dilexi Gallery, San Francisco, 1963, 67; Robert Elkon Gallery, 1965, 66, 68, 70, 73, 75, 77, 79; Felix Landau Gallery, 1966, 69; Mt. San Antonio College, 1969 (two-man); Nicholas Wilder Gallery, 1972, 74, 76; California State U., Long Beach, 1974; John Berggruen Gallery, 1974, 76; California Institute of Technology, Pasadena, 1975; Newport Harbor, 1977; Jack Glenn Gallery, Newport Beach, 1976; Casat Gallery, La Jolla, 1977; California State College, Chico, 1979; Janus Gallery, Venice City, 1979; Janus Gallery, Los Angeles, 1981, 83; Jan Turner Gallery, Los Angeles, 1987; Klein Gallery, Chicago, 1985. **Retrospective:** U. of California, Irvine, Tony De Lap: The Last Five Years: 1963-68, 1969. **Group:** Stanford U., 1961; Kaiser Center, Oakland, Sculpture Today, 1964; Carnegie, 1964; WMAA, 1964; Chicago/AI; MOMA, 1964, The Responsive Eye, 1965, The 1960's, 1967; La Jolla, 1965, 66; Jewish Museum, Primary Structures, 1966; WMAA, Contemporary American Sculpture, Selection 1, 1966; Musée Cantonal des Beaux-Arts, Lausanne, II Salon de Galeries Pilotes, 1966; Seattle/AM, 1966; Los Angeles/County MA, American Sculpture of the Sixties, 1967; Scripps College, 1967; San Marino (Europe), Nuove Tecniche dell'immagine, 1967; Portland, Ore./AM, 1968; U. of California, Irvine, A Los Angeles Esthetic, 1969; Pasadena/AM, West Coast; 1945-1969, 1969; La Jolla, The

Wall Object, 1973; Newport Harbor, Modern and Contemporary Sculpture, 1974; Corcoran, Biennial, 1978; SFMA, California Painting and Sculpture: The Modern Era, 1976. **Collections:** Arizona State U.; Atlantic Richfield Co.; Claremont College; Hartford/Wadsworth; Hirshhorn; Los Angeles/County MA; MOMA; Oakland/AM; Ridgefield/Aldrich; SFMA; San Francisco Municipal Art Commission; Santa Barbara/MA; State of California; Tate; WMAA; Walker. **Bibliography:** Tuchman 1.

DELLA-VOLPE, RALPH. b. May 10, 1923, New Jersey. **Studied:** NAD; ASL (with Edwin Dickinson, Will Barnet, Harry Sternberg). Traveled USA, Mexico. US Army, 1942-45. **Taught:** Bennett College, Millbrook, N.Y., 1949-77; Marist College, Poughkeepsie, 1977-79. **Member:** College Art Association; Association of American University Professors. **Awards:** MacDowell Colony Fellowship, 1963; Library of Congress, Pennell **P.P.;** NIAL, Drawing Prize, 1963, 64. **Address:** Altamont Road, RD #2, Box 295, Millbrook, NY 12545. **Dealer:** Munson Gallery, New Haven, CT. **One-man Exhibitions:** Bennett College, 1949-63; Three Arts Gallery, Poughkeepsie, N.Y., 1951; Artists' Gallery, NYC, 1959; The Babcock Gallery, 1960, 62, 63; Lehigh U., 1963; Mansfield State College, 1964; Pittsfield/Berkshire, 1964; Cobleskill/SUNY, 1968; Dutchess Community College, Poughkeepsie, N.Y.; Centenary College, Hackettstown, N.J.; The Hotchkiss School, Lakeville, Conn.; Wolfe Street Gallery, Washington, D.C., 1974, 77; Talking of Michelangelo Gallery, Washington, D.C., 1974; Barrett House Art Gallery, Poughkeepsie, N.Y., 1978. **Retrospectives:** The Gallery, West Cornwall, Conn., 1974; Columbia, S.C./MA, 1975. **Group:** PAFA; Library of Congress; NIAL; American Color Print Society; Youngstown/Butler; Bradley U.; Brooklyn Museum; Hartford/Wadsworth; San Antonio/McNay; Vassar College; Newport (R.I.) Art Association; Audubon Artists, NYC. **Collections:** ASL; Chase Manhattan Bank; Library of Congress; Mansfield State College; Slater; Wichita/AM.

DE MARIA, WALTER. b. October 1, 1935, Albany, Calif. **Studied:** U. of California, BA, MA (with David Park). Traveled Europe. **Commissions:** Dia Art Foundation, NYC, 1977, 79, 81. **Films:** *Three Circles & Two Lines in the Desert*, 1969; *Hard Core*, 1969. **Address:** 421 East 6th Street, NYC 10009. **Dealer:** Xavier Fourcade, Inc., NYC. **One-man Exhibitions:** (first) Nine Great Jones Street, NYC (two-man, with Robert Whitman), 1963; Paula Cooper Gallery, 1965; Cordier & Ekstrom, Inc., 1966; Nicholas Wilder Gallery, 1968; Galerie Heiner Friedrich, Munich, 1968, 79; Dwan Gallery, 1969, 70; Cinema Odeon, Turin, 1969; Iris Clert Gallery, 1969; Gian Enzo Sperone, Turin, 1969, 70; Basel, 1972; Darmstadt/ Hessisches, 1974; Heiner Friedrich, NYC, 1977; Dia Art Foundation, NYC, 1979, 80; Darmstadt/Kunsthalle, 1974;

Paris/Beaubourg, 1981; Rotterdam, 1984. **Group:** Jack London Outdoor Art Annual, Oakland, Calif., 1959; Douglass College, 1964; Jewish Museum, Primary Structures, 1966; WMAA Sculpture Annual, 1967, 68; Museum of Contemporary Crafts, 1967; Los Angeles/County MA, American Sculpture of the Sixties, 1967; A.F.A., circ., 1967; Milwaukee, Directions I: Options, circ., 1968; Documenta IV, Kassel, 1968; Prospect '68, Dusseldorf, 1968; Berne, When Attitudes Become Form, 1969; Amsterdam/Stedelijk, 1969; MOMA, circ., 1969; MOMA, Information, 1970; Dusseldorf/Kunsthalle, Prospect 71, 1971; SRGM, Guggenheim International, 1971; Philadelphia College of Art, Line, 1976; WMAA, 200 Years of American Sculpture, 1976; Chicago/AI, 1976; Hayward Gallery, London, Pier and Ocean, 1980; Venice Biennial, 1980; ROSC, Dublin, 1980; Documenta VI, Kassel, 1977; Cologne/Stadt, Westkunst, 1981; WMAA, Blam!, 1984. **Collections:** Dia Art Foundation; MOMA; Rotterdam; SRMG; Stockholm/ National; WMAA. **Bibliography:** Adrian; Atkinson; Battcock, ed.; Calas, N. and E.; Celanti; *Contemporanea;*

Walter De Maria   *Large Rod Series: Circle/Rectangle 9*   1986

Davis, D.; *Happening & Fluxus; Kunst um 1970;* Haskell 5; Lippard, ed.; Muller; *Report;* Ruhe; Tuchman 1; *When Attitudes Become Form.* Archives.

DEMUTH, CHARLES. b. November 8, 1883, Lancaster, Pa.; **d.** October 23, 1935. **Studied:** Franklin and Marshall College; Drexel Institute of Technology, 1901; Pennsylvania School of Industrial Art, Philadelphia; PAFA, 1905-08, with Thomas Anshutz, Henry McCarter; Academie Colarossi, Academie Moderne, and Academie Julian, Paris, 1912-14. Traveled Europe, eastern USA. **One-man Exhibitions:** (first) The Daniel Gallery, NYC, 1915, also 1916, 17, 18, 20, 22, 23, 24, 25; Stieglitz's Intimate Gallery, NYC, 1926, 29; An American Place (Gallery), NYC, 1931; The Downtown Gallery, 1931, 50, 54, 58; Smith College, 1934; WMAA, 1935; WMAA Memorial Exhibition, 1937; U. of Minnesota, 1937; Franklin and Marshall College, 1941, 48; Cincinnati/AM, 1941; Phillips, 1942; PMA, 1944; The U. of Chicago, 1946; Graphische Sammlung Albertina, 1949; Ogunquit, 1959; U. of California, Santa Barbara, 1971; Kennedy Gallery, 1971; Salander-O'Reilly Galleries, 1981; Tacoma, 1981; Carnegie, 1983. **Retrospective:** MOMA, 1949; Harrisburg, Pa./State Museum, 1966. **Group:** MOMA; WMAA; MMA; PAFA; Phillips; Pomona College, Stieglitz Circle, 1958. **Collections:** Amherst College; Andover/Phillips; Arizona State College; Baltimore/MA; Barnes Foundation; Boston/MFA; Brooklyn Museum; Buffalo/Albright; Chicago/AI; Cleveland/MA; Columbus; Detroit/Institute; Fisk U.; Hartford/Wadsworth; Harvard U.; Honolulu Academy; MMA; MOMA; Milwaukee; National Gallery; U. of Nebraska; Newark Museum; New Britain; Ogunquit; PMA; Phillips; Princeton U.; RISD; San Antonio/McNay; Santa Barbara/MA; Toledo/MA; Utica; WMAA; Walker; Wellesley College; West Palm Beach/Norton; Wichita/AM; Worcester/AM; Yale U. **Bibliography:** *Avant-Garde Painting and Sculpture in America, 1910-25;* Barnes; Baur 7; Bazin; Biddle 4; Blesh 1; Born; Brown; Brown 2; Cahill and Barr. eds.; **Charles Demuth;** Cheney; Christensen; Dijkstra, ed.; *8 American Masters of Watercolor;* Eliot; **Farnham;** Forerunners; Frost; Gallatin 1; Goodrich and Baur 1; Haftman; Hall; Hunter 6; Huyghe; **Index of 20th Century Artists;** Janis, S.; Jewell 2; Kootz 1, 2; Lane; Mather 1; McCoubrey 1; McCurdy, ed.; Murken-Altrogge; Murrell 1; Neuhaus; Phillips 2; Poore; Richardson, E.P.; Rigel, ed.; **Ritchie 2;** Rose, B., 1; Rosenblum 1; Sachs; Sager; Schwartz 2; Soby 5; Sutton; Tashjian; Tomkins and Time-Life Books; Wight 2. Archives.

DENBY, JILLIAN. b. NYC. **Studied:** Pratt Institute, 1971, BFA; Brooklyn College, 1973, MFA. **Awards:** National Endowment for the Arts, 1985. **Address:** 87 Franklin Street, RD #3, Box 198, Greenwich, NY 12834. **Dealer:** Tatistcheff & Co., NYC. **One-man Exhibitions:** A. M. Sachs Gallery, NYC, 1974, 75, 77; Tyler School of Art, Philadelphia, 1978; Alexander F. Milliken, NYC, 1981; Tatistcheff & Co., 1985. **Group:** U. of Miami, Phase of New Realism, 1972; Hofstra U., The Male Nude, 1973; The Pennsylvania State U., Contemporary Artists and the Figure, 1974; U. of North Carolina, Art on Paper, 1974, 77; Lehigh U., American Figure Drawings, circ., 1976; U. of Missouri, Kansas City, The Opposite Sex: A Realistic Viewpoint, 1979; Utica, An Appreciation of Realism, 1982. **Collections:** Roswell; Union College, Schenectady.

DE NIRO, ROBERT. b. May 3, 1922, Syracuse, N.Y. **Studied:** Syracuse Museum School, 1935-39; Hofmann School, Provincetown, summers, 1939, 40; Black Mountain College, with Josef Albers. Traveled France; resided Paris. **Taught:** New School for Social Research, 1966-; School of Visual Arts,

NYC, 1966-70; Buffalo/SUNY, summers, 1969, 70, 71; Wagner College, 1970, 71; Cooper Union, 1971-; The Pennsylvania State U., 1973; Fine Arts Work Center, Provincetown, Mass., 1973; Michigan State U., 1974; New York Studio School, Paris, 1974; U. of California, Santa Cruz, 1979. **Awards:** V Hallmark International Competition; Longview Foundation Grant; Guggenheim Foundation Fellowship, 1968; Tamarind Institute Grant, 1974. **Address:** 465 West Broadway, NYC 10012. **Dealer:** The Graham Gallery, NYC. **One-man Exhibitions:** (first) Art of This Century, NYC, 1946; Charles Egan Gallery, 1950, 52, 54; Poindexter Gallery, 1955, 56, 76; The Zabriskie Gallery, 1958, 60 (2), 62, 65, 70; (2), 67, 68, 70; Ellison Gallery, Fort Worth (two-man), 1959; Buffalo/SUNY, 1967; Galleries Reese Palley, Atlantic City and San Francisco, 1968, 69; Bard College, 1969; Brenner Gallery, Provincetown, 1971; The Pennsylvania State U., 1973; Kansas City/AI, 1974; The Graham Gallery, NYC, 1979, 80, 82, 84, 86; Swain School of Design, New Bedford, Mass., 1979; Charles Campbell Gallery, San Francisco, 1978, 79; David Stuart Gallery, Los Angeles, 1978; Hobart College, 1980; Charlotte/Mint, 1981; Asheville Art Museum, 1981; Foster White Gallery, Seattle, 1981; David Hamilton Gallery, Charleston, S.C., 1983; St. Paul's School, Concord, 1984; Crane Kalman Gallery, London, 1986. **Group:** WMAA Annuals; Jewish Museum, The New York School, Second Generation, 1957; ICA, Boston, 100 Works on Paper, circ., Europe, 1959; U. of Nebraska, 1960; A.F.A., The Figure, circ., 1960; Felix Landau Gallery, Los Angeles-New York, 1960; Colorado Springs/FA Annual, 1961; MOMA, Recent Painting USA; The Figure, circ., 1962-63; Illinois Wesleyan U. Annual, 1962; New School for Social Research, Portraits from the American Art World, 1965; IEF, Twentieth Century American Drawings: The Figure in Context, 1984; Hudson River Museum, Form or Formula, 1986. **Collections:** Baltimore/MA; Brandeis U.; Brooklyn Museum; Charlotte/Mint; Corcoran; Hirshhorn; Houston/MFA; Longview Foundation; MMA; U. of North Carolina; Oakland/AM; Syracuse/Everson; Yellowstone Art Center. **Bibliography:** Sandler 1. Archives.

DE RIVERA, JOSE. b. September 18, 1904, West Baton Rouge, La. **d.** March 19, 1985, NYC. **Studied:** Studio School, Chicago, with John W. Norton, 1928-30. Traveled USA, Europe, Mediterranean, North Africa. Federal A.P.: Mural painting, 1937-38. US Army Air Corps, 1942-43. **Taught:** Brooklyn College, 1953; Yale U., 1954-55; North Carolina School of Design, Raleigh, 1957-60. **Member:** NIAL. **Commissions:** Cavalry Monument, El Paso, 1938-40; Newark Airport, 1938; Soviet Pavilion, New York World's Fair, 1939; Wm. Kaufman Inc., NYC, 1955; Hotel Statler-Hilton, Dallas, 1956; Moore-McCormack Lines Inc., SS *Argentina*, 1958; Reynolds Metals Co., 1958; City of Lansing, Mich. **Awards:** Chicago/AI, Watson F. Blair Prize, 1957; NIAL Grant, 1959; Hon. Ph.D., Washington U. **One-man Exhibitions:** Harvard U. (two-man, with Burgoyne Diller), 1945; Mortimer Levit Gallery, NYC, 1946; Grace Borgenicht Gallery Inc., 1952, 56, 57, 58, 59, 60, 72, 78, 80, 85; Walker, 1957. **Retrospective:** A.F.A./Ford Foundation, circ., 1961; La Jolla, 1972. **Group:** Chicago/AI, 1934; Brooklyn Museum, 1938; WMAA Annuals, 1938-; MOMA, Twelve Americans, circ., 1956; Brussels World's Fair, 1958; American Painting and Sculpture, Moscow, 1959; MOMA, Recent Sculpture USA, 1959; Public Education Association, NYC, 1966; U. of New Mexico, 1966; Los Angeles/County MA, Sculpture of the Sixties, circ., 1967. **Collections:** The M. L. Annenberg Foundation; Brooklyn Museum; Chicago/AI; Des Moines; Fort Dodge/Blandend; Hirshhorn; La Jolla; Lembke Construction Co.; MMA; MOMA; Newark Museum; U. of New Mexico; U. of Pennsylvania; Pur-

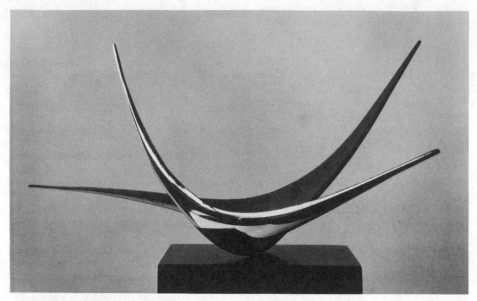

José de Rivera   *Maquette for Hilton Hotel Commission, Dallas, Texas*   1955

chase/SUNY; Ridgefield/Aldrich; U. of Rochester; SFMA; St. Louis/City; Smithsonian; Tate Gallery; Toronto; Utica; VMFA; WMAA. **Bibliography:** Baur 7; Brumme; Craven, W.; Flanagan; Gerdts; Goodrich and Baur 1; **Jose de Rivera;** Licht, F.; Marter, Tarbell, and Wechsler; McCurdy, ed.; Mendelowitz; Read 3; Rickey; Ritchie 1, 3; Rodman 3; Seuphor 3; Trier 1. Archives.

DESHAIES, ARTHUR. b. July 6, 1920, Providence, R.I. **Studied:** Cooper Union, 1939-42; RISD, 1947-48, BFA; Indiana U., 1948-50, MFA; self-taught as a printmaker. Traveled Mexico, USA, Europe. **Taught:** RISD, 1947-48; Indiana U., 1949-56; Pratt Institute, 1956-57; Pratt Graphic Art Center, 1962; Florida State U., 1963-75; lectures and writes extensively on art and printmaking. **Awards:** Indiana U., Faculty Research Grant for Painting, 1950; Fulbright Fellowship, 1952; MacDowell Colony Fellowship, winters, 1959, 60, 61, 62; Yaddo Fellowship, 1960; L. C. Tiffany Grant, 1960; Guggenheim Foundation Fellowship, 1961; Brooklyn Museum; Bradley U.; Oklahoma Print Society; Indianapolis/Herron; U. of Kentucky, **P.P.;** Otis Art Institute, Los Angeles; Memphis/Brooks, **P.P. Address:** 1314 Dillard Street, Tallahassee, FL 32303. **One-man Exhibitions:** (first) Weyhe Gallery, 1940; Philadelphia Art Alliance; Galerie Paul Fachetti, 1954; Coker College, Hartsville, S.C., 1957; The Little Gallery, Tallahassee, 1964. **Group:** PCA, American Prints Today, circ., 1959-62; Brooklyn Museum; III International Biennial Exhibition of Prints, Tokyo, 1962; Otis Art Institute; WMAA. **Collections:** Bibliotheque Nationale; Bradley U.; British Museum; Brooklyn Museum; MMA; MOMA; RISD. **Bibliography:** Hayter 1; Peterdi.

DEUTSCH, DAVID. b. 1943, Los Angeles. **Studied:** UCLA, 1966, BA; California Institute of the Arts, 1968. **Address:** 225 West 13th Street, NYC 10011. **Dealer:** Blum Helman Gallery, NYC. **One-man Exhibitions:** Michael

Walls Gallery, Los Angeles, 1972; Gagosian/Nosei-Weber Gallery, NYC, 1980; 112 Greene Street, NYC, 1980; Annina Nosei Gallery, NYC, 1981, 82; MIT, 1983; Gallery 5, Stockholm, 1984; Blum Helman Gallery, 1985, 87. **Group:** Pomona College, Six Attitudes, 1969; La Jolla, Projections: Anti-materialism, 1970; Kassel, Documenta V, 1972; MIT, Great Big Drawings, 1982; XL Venice Biennial, 1982; Newport Beach, Shift-L.A./N.Y., 1982; MOMA, International Survey of Recent Painting and Sculpture, 1984. **Collections:** Cincinnati/AM; Los Angeles/County MA; MOMA; Mexico City/Tamayo; Phoenix.

DICKINSON, EDWIN. b. October 11, 1891, Seneca Falls, N.Y.; **d.** December 2, 1978, Orleans, Mass. **Studied:** Pratt Institute, 1910-11; ASL, 1911-12, with William M. Chase; Provincetown, summers, 1912, 13, 14, with C. W. Hawthorne. US Navy, 1917-19. Traveled Europe, Near East, North Africa, Greece. **Taught:** Buffalo Fine Arts Academy, 1916, 39; ASL, 1922-23, 1944-66; Provincetown Art Association, 1929-30; Stuart School, Boston, 1940-41; Association of Art and Music, Cape Cod, 1941; Cooper Union, 1945-49; Midtown School, NYC, 1946-47;

David Deutsch *Curved Garden* 1983

Brooklyn Museum School, 1946-47; Pratt Institute, 1950-58; Dennis Foundation, Dennis, Mass., 1951; Skowhegan School, 1956, 58; Cornell U., 1957; Boston U., 1961. **Member:** NAD, 1948; NIAL; AAAL; Audubon Artists; The Patteran Society. Federal A.P.: Easel painting, 1934. **Awards:** NAD, Benjamin Altman Prize, 1929, 58; Benjamin West Medal; NAD, First Prize, 1949; Century Association, Medal; NIAL Grant, 1954; Brandeis U., Creative Arts Medal, 1959; Ford Foundation Grant, 1959. **One-man Exhibitions:** (first) Buffalo-Albright, 1927, 77; Worcester/AM, Boston/MFA; Houston/MFA; U. of Rochester; Cornell U.; Provincetown/Chrysler; Passedoit Gallery, NYC, 1939; Wood Memorial Gallery, Provincetown, 1939; Wellesley College, 1940; Nantucket Museum, 1943; Cushman Gallery, Houston, 1958; MOMA (circ. only), 1961; The Graham Gallery, 1961, 65, 68, 72; Kansas City/Nelson, 1964 (two-man, with Lennart Anderson); Peale House, Philadelphia, 1966; Katonah (N.Y.) Art Gallery, 1966; Gilman Galleries, Chicago, 1966; Provincetown Art Association, 1967; Bristol (R.I.) Art Museum, 1970; Pratt Manhattan Center, 1970; Wellfleet (Mass.) Art Gallery, 1970; Cape Cod Conservatory, Barnstable, 1970, 74; ICA, Boston, 1970; Wellfleet (Mass.) Historical Society, 1972; Hammelbacker Gallery, Nashville, 1975; Wellfleet Art Gallery, 1975; Provincetown Art Association, 1976; Buffalo/SUNY, Burchfield Center, circ., 1977; Hirschl and Adler Modern, NYC, 1983, 86. **Retrospective:** Boston U., 1958; WMAA, 1965. **Group:** MOMA, Fifteen Americans, circ., 1952; WMAA; Brooklyn Museum; Boston/MFA; PMA; PAFA; Carnegie; U. of Rochester; XXXIV Venice Biennial, 1968. **Collections:** Atlanta/AA; Bowdoin College; Brooklyn Museum; Buffalo/Albright; Chicago/AI; Cornell U.; Hirshhorn; MMA; MOMA; Montpelier/Wood; NAD; U. of Nebraska; Sara Roby Foundation; Springfield, Mass./MFA; Syracuse U.; Yale U. **Bibliography:** *America 1976;* Goodrich 2, 5; Goodrich and Baur

1; Haftman; Kuh 2; McCurdy, ed.; Mellquist; Nordness, ed.; Pousette-Dart,
ed.; Rose B., 1; Soyer, R. 1. Archives.

DIEBENKORN, RICHARD. b. April
22, 1922, Portland, Ore. **Studied:** Stanford U., 1940-43; U. of California,
Berkeley, 1943-44; CSFA, 1946; Stanford U., 1949, BA; U. of New Mexico,
1952, MA. US Marines, 1943-45. Traveled USSR. **Taught:** U. of Illinois,
1952-53; California College of Arts and
Crafts, 1955-57; SFAI, 1959-63; Stanford
U., 1963-64; UCLA, 1966-73; U. of Colorado; U. of California at Los Angeles,
1966-73. **Member:** National Council on
the Arts, 1966-69; AAIAL, 1985.
Awards: CSFA, Albert M. Bender Fellowship, 1946; Rosenberg Traveling
Fellowship, 1959; Olivet College, **P.P.;**
NIAL, 1962; PAFA, Gold Medal, 1968;
Skowhegan School, Medal for Painting,
1979; MacDowell Colony Medal, 1978.
Address: 334 Amalfi Drive, Santa
Monica, CA 90402. **Dealer:** M.
Knoedler & Co., Inc. **One-man Exhibitions:** (first) California Palace, 1948,
also 60; U. of New Mexico, 1951; Paul
Kantor Gallery, 1952, 54; SFMA, 1954,
73; Allan Frumkin Gallery, Chicago,
1954; Poindexter Gallery, 1955, 58, 61,
63, 66, 68; Phillips, 1958, 61; de Young,
1963; Stanford U., 1964; Pavilion Art
Gallery, Newport Beach, Calif., 1965;
Waddington Galleries, London, 1965,
67; U. of Washington, 1967; Kansas
City/Nelson, 1968; RAC, 1968; Los An-
geles/County MA, 1969; Irving Blum
Gallery, Los Angeles, 1971; Marlborough Gallery, Inc., NYC, 1971, 74;
James Corcoran Galleries, Los Angeles,
1975; John Berggruen Gallery, San
Francisco, 1975, 83; UCLA, 1976; M.
Knoedler & Co. Inc., NYC, 1977, 79,
82, 84, 85; U. of California, Berkeley,
1981; Marlborough Gallery, 1981;
Crown Point Gallery, Oakland, 1982;
Brooklyn Museum, 1982; L. A. Louver
Gallery, Venice, Calif., 1984; U. of
Nebraska, 1985; Patricia Heesy Gallery,

NYC, 1985. **Retrospectives:** Pas-
adena/AM, 1960; WGMA, 1964; Jewish
Museum, 1964; UCLA, circ., 1976; Min-
neapolis/Institute, circ., 1981; SFMA,
1983. **Group:** SRGM, Younger American Painters, 1954; WMAA Annuals,
1955, 58, 61; Carnegie, 1955, 58, 61, 70;
IV Sao Paulo Biennial, 1957; Brussels
World's Fair, 1958; MOMA, New Images of Man, 1959; Tate, Paintings and
Sculpture of a Decade, 1964; Edin-
burgh/National, Two American Painters: Sam Francis Richard Diebenkorn,
1965; WMAA, Art of the United States:
1670-1966, 1966; XXIV Venice Biennial,
1968, 78; SFMA, Untitled 1968, 1968;
Eindhoven, Kompas IV, 1969-70;
Omaha/Joslyn, Looking West, 1970;
Boston U., Drawings: Elmer Bischoff
and Richard Diebenkorn, 1974;
Oakland/AM, California Landscape,
1975; Corcoran Biennial, 1975; PAFA,
Young American, 1975; Newport Harbor, The Last Time I Saw Ferus, 1976;
Buffalo/Albright, American Paintings
of the 1970's, 1978; Brooklyn Museum,
American Drawings in Black and
White: 1970-1979, 1981; Corcoran Biennial, 1981; Long Beach/MA, Drawings
by Painters, 1982; Hirshhorn, Drawing
1974-1984, 1984; NYU, The Figurative
Mode: Bay Area Painting, 1956-1966,
1984; IEF, Twentieth Century American
Drawings: The Figure in Context, circ.,
1984; Houston/Contemporary, Amer-
ican Still Life, 1945-1983, 1983;
Oakland/AM, Art in the San Francisco
Bay Area, 1945-1980, 1985; MOMA,
Contrasts of Form: Geometric Abstract
Art 1910-1980, 1985. **Collections:** Al-
bany/SUNY; U. of Arkansas; Bal-
timore/MA; Brooklyn Museum; Buf-
falo/Albright; California Palace; U. of
California, Berkeley; Carnegie; Chi-
cago/AI; Cincinnati/AM; Cleveland/
MA; Colorado Springs; Corcoran; Des
Moines; Fort Worth; Grand Rapids;
Hirshhorn; Houston/MFA; U. of Iowa;
Kansas City/Nelson; Little Rock/MFA;
Los Angeles/County MA; U. of Michi-
gan; MMA; MOMA; U. of Nebraska; U.
of New Mexico; Norfolk/Chrysler; Oklahoma; Oakland/AM; Oberlin College;

Olivet College; PAFA; Pasadena/AM; Phillips; Phoenix; Purchase/SUNY; Raleigh/NCMA; Readers Digest; SFMA; SRGM; Santa Barbara/MA; Skidmore College; Stanford U.; Toronto; WMAA; Washington U.; Witte. **Bibliography:** Arthur 2; Blesh 1; Geske; Gettings; Johnson; Mendelowitz; Murken-Altrogge; Neumeyer; Nordness, ed.; Read 2; Rose, B., 1; *Richard Diebenkorn;* Sandler 1.

DILL, LADDIE JOHN. b. September 14, 1943, Long Beach, Calif. **Studied:** Chouinard Art Institute, Los Angeles, 1968, BA; with M. Kanamitsu, E. Woelffer, R. Irwin. Traveled Europe, South Seas, Mexico, and Central America. **Taught:** U. of California, Irvine, 1974; UCLA, 1975-86. **Awards:** National Endowment for the Arts, 1975, 82; Guggenheim Foundation Fellowship, 1979. **Address:** 1625 Electric Avenue, Venice, Calif. 90291. **Dealer:** James Corcoran, Los Angeles; Charles Cowles Gallery, NYC; Fuller Goldeen, San Francisco. **One-man Exhibitions:** (first) Ileana Sonnabend Gallery, NYC, 1971, 72; Pasadena/AM, 1971; Portland State U., 1971; The Morgan Gallery, Shawnee Mission, Kans., 1972; Mizuno Gallery, Los Angeles, 1973; James Corcoran Gallery, Los Angeles, 1974, 75, 77, 78, 79, 82, 83, 86; Douglas Drake Gallery, Kansas City, 1975, 78; Kansas State U., 1976; Dootson Calderhead Gallery, Seattle, 1976; Seder/Creigh Gallery, Coronado, 1976; Dobrick Gallery, Chicago, 1976, 78; Grapestake Gallery, San Francisco, 1977; Landfall Press, Chicago, 1978; California Institute of Technology, Pasadena, 1978; Linda Farris Gallery, Seattle, 1980, 82, 84; Osuna Gallery, Washington, D.C., 1980; Charles Cowles Gallery, 1981, 83, 86; Thomas Babeor Gallery, La Jolla, 1981, 83, 85; Grapestake Gallery, San Francisco, 1981; Landfall Press Gallery, Chicago, 1981; U. of Redlands, 1981; Zolla Lieberman, Chicago, 1981, 84; ICA, Los Angeles, 1982; California

State U., Long Beach, 1983; West Beach Cafe, Los Angeles, 1983; Fuller Goldeen, 1984; Ochi Gallery, Boise, 1984; San Jose State U., 1985. **Retrospectives:** California Institute of Technology, 1978; Long Beach/MA, 1986. **Group:** California State U., Los Angeles, Venice, California, 70, 1970; Los Angeles/County MA, 24 Young Los Angeles Artists 1971; Walker, Works for New Spaces, 1971; Govett-Brewster Art Gallery, New Plymouth, N.Z., The State of California Painting, 1972; California State U., Fullerton, Guy Dill/Laddie John Dill, 1972; Webster College, St. Louis, Some California Artists, 1973; Santa Barbara/MA, 15 Abstract Artists, 1974; Scripps College, Claremont, Light, 1974; Newport Harbor/Art Museum, Modern and Contemporary Sculptures, 1975; Brandeis U., Three California Painters, 1975; SFMA, Painting and Sculpture in California; The Modern Era, 1976; Kansas City/AI, Spectrum 77, 1977; Indianapolis, 1978; Buffalo/Albright, Painting of the Seventies, 1979; Sacramento/Crocker, Aspects of Abstraction, 1979; AAAL, 1979; Municipal Art Gallery, Los Angeles, It's All Called Painting, 1980; La Jolla, Artists Quilts: Quilts by Ten Artists, 1981; Houston/Contemporary, The Americans: The Collage, 1982; Paris/Moderne, Echange entre artistes, 1931-1982, Pologne-USA, 1982; Corcoran, Second Western States Exhibition, 1983; Palo Alto (Calif.) Cultural Center, Unity of Opposites: Art About Architecture, 1985. **Collections:** Corcoran; Greenville; Kansas City/Nelson; Los Angeles/County MA; Miami-Dade; Newport Harbor; Oakland/AM; SFMA; Seattle/AM; Norton Simon Museum. **Bibliography:** *California Sculpture Show.*

DILLER, BURGOYNE. b. 1906, NYC; **d.** January 30, 1964, NYC. **Studied:** Michigan State College; ASL. US Navy, World War II. **Taught:** Brooklyn College, 1945-64; Pratt Institute, 1945-64. **Member:** American Abstract Artists.

Federal A.P.: Head, Mural Division, 1935-40; Assistant Technical Director, New York Art Project, 1940-41; Director, New York Art Project, 1940-41; Director, New York City Art Section, 1939-42. **Awards:** Ford Foundation, **P.P.**, 1963. **One-man Exhibitions:** Harvard U., 1945 (two-man, with Jose de Rivera); The Pinacotheca, NYC, 1946; Galerie Chalette, 1961, 64; Goldowsky Gallery, 1968, 72; Los Angeles/County MA, 1968; Washburn Gallery, Inc., NYC, 1978; Meredith Long Gallery, Houston, 1979; Meredith Long Contemporary, NYC, 1979; Andre Emmerich Gallery, 1981, 84, 86; Meredith Long & Co., 1984. **Retrospectives:** Trenton/State, 1966; Walker, circ., 1971. **Group:** American Abstract Artists Annuals to 1940; WMAA; Geometric Abstraction in America, circ., 1962; VII Sao Paulo Biennial, 1963; Corcoran, 1963; WMAA, 1964; Colorists 1950-1965, 1965; SRGM, Guggenheim International, 1967; WMAA, The 1930s, 1968; MMA, New York Painting and Sculpture: 1940-1970, 1969-70; U. of New Mexico, America Abstract Artists, 1977; Yale U. Mondrian and Neoplasticism in America, 1979; Walker, De Stijl, 1917-1931: Visions of Utopia, circ., 1982. **Collections:** Baltimore/MA; Buffalo/Albright; Chicago/AI; Chicago/Contemporary; Corcoran; The Hague; Hirshhorn; MMA; MOMA; Milwaukee; NYU; Newark Museum; SRGM; Springfield, Mass./MFA; Trenton/State; WMAA; Yale U. **Bibliography:** Blesh 1; Brown 2; Gerdts; Hess, T.B., 1; Janis and Blesh, 1; Janis, S.; Lane and Larsen; **Larson;** MacAgy 2; McCurdy, ed.; Marter, Tarbell, and Wechsler; Rickey; Ritchie 1; Rose, B., 1, 4; Seuphor 1, 3; Toher, ed. Archives.

DINE, JIM. b. June 16, 1935, Cincinnati, Ohio. **Studied:** U. of Cincinnati; Boston Museum School; Ohio U., 1957; BFA, and 1958. An early creator of Happenings and Environments. Subject of a 16mm. sound film, *Jim Dine*, directed by Lane Slate, produced by National Educational Television; Subject of film, *Jim Dine*, 16mm., 28 min., produced by Blackwood Productions, Inc. **Member:** AAIAL, 1980. **Address:** 522 West End Avenue, NYC 10024. **Dealer:** The Pace Gallery, NYC. **One-man Exhibitions:** Judson Gallery, NYC, 1959 (two-man, with Claes Oldenburg); Reuben Gallery, NYC, 1959 (two-man, with Oldenburg); Reuben Gallery, NYC, 1960; Martha Jackson Gallery, 1952; Galleria dell'Ariete, 1962; Ileana Sonnabend Gallery, Paris, 1963, 69, 72, 75, NYC, 71, 73, 74; Brussels/Beaux-Arts, 1963, 70; Sidney Janis Gallery, 1963, 64; Galleria Sperone, Turin, 1965; Oberlin College, 1965; Robert Fraser Gallery, London, 1965, 66, 69; Galerie Rolf Ricke, Kassel, 1967; Galerie Rudolf Zwirner, 1967; The Gallery Upstairs, Buffalo, 1967; Harcus-Krakow Gallery, 1967; Toronto, circ., 1967 (three-man, with Oldenburg, George Segal); MOMA, Jim Dine Designs for "A Midsummer Night's Dream," 1967; Sidney Janis Gallery, 1967; Amsterdam/Stedelijk, 1967; Cornell U., 1967; MOMA, 1969; Dunkelman Gallery, Toronto, 1970; Turin/Civico, 1970; Dusseldorf/Kunsthalle, 1970; Hannover/K-G, 1970; Rotterdam, 1970; Berlin Festival, 1970; Gimpel & Hanover, Gallery, 1972; Aronson Gallery, Atlanta, Ga., 1972; Modern Art Agency, Naples, 1972; Gimpel Fils, 1973; D. M. Gallery, London, 1973; Felicity Samuel Gallery, London, 1973; Galerie Sonnabend, Geneva, 1974; La Jolla, 1974; Dartmouth College, 1974; Petersburg Press, NYC, 1974; Centre d'Arts Plastiques Contemporains, Bordeaux, 1975; Gian Enzo Sperone, Rome, 1975; Williams College, 1976; The Pace Gallery, NYC, 1977, 78, 80, 81, 84; Waddington, Tooth Galleries II, London, 1977; Makler Gallery, Philadelphia, 1978; The Pace Gallery, Columbus, 1978; MOMA, 1978; Katonah Gallery, Katonah, 1979; Galerie Claude Bernard, Paris, 1979; California State U., Long Beach, circ., 1979; Galerie Alice Pauli, Lausanne, 1980; Janie C. Lee Gallery, Houston,

1980; Harcus-Krakow Gallery, Boston, 1980; Pace Gallery, Columbus, 1981; Galerie Isy Brachot, Brussels, 1981; Waddington Galleries, London, 1981; Richard Gray Gallery, Chicago, 1983, 85; Los Angeles/County MA, 1983; John Berggruen Gallery, San Francisco, 1984; Barbara Krakow Gallery, Boston, 1984; Fay Gold Gallery, Atlanta, 1984; Cantor Lemberg Gallery, Detroit, 1984; Thorden Wetterling Galleries, Goteborg, 1984; Toni Birckhead Gallery, Cincinnati, 1985. **Retrospectives:** WMAA; Walker, circ., 1984. **Happenings:** Judson Gallery, NYC, The Smiling Workman, 1959; Reuben Gallery, NYC, Car Crash, 1960; Jim Dine's Vaudeville, 1960, The Shining Bed, 1960; First New York Theatre Rally, NYC, Natural History (The Dreams), 1965. **Group:** Cornell U., Young Americans, 1960; Martha Jackson Gallery, New Media—New Forms, I, 1960; USIA Gallery, London, Modern American Painting, 1961; Dallas/MFA, "1961," 1961; Sidney Janis Gallery, The New Realists, 1962; Philadelphia YM-YWHA Arts Council, Art, A New Vocabulary, 1962; Pasadena/AM, New Paintings of Common Objects, 1962; International Biennial Exhibition of Paintings, Tokyo; SRGM, Six Painters and the Object, circ., 1963; Houston/MFA, Pop Goes the Easel, 1963; WGMA, The Popular Image, 1963; ICA, London, The Popular Image, 1963; Buffalo/Albright, 1963; Cincinnati/AM, An American Viewpoint, 1963; Jewish Museum, Black and White, 1963; Hartford/Wadsworth, Black, White and Gray, 1964; Tate, Gulbenkian International, 1964; Chicago/AI, 1964, 69; Milwaukee, Popular Art and the American Tradition, 1965; Worcester/AM, New American Realism, 1965; WMAA, A Decade of American Drawings, 1965; WMAA, Art of the U.S. 1670-1966, 1966; Dublin/Municipal, I International Quadrennial (ROSC), 1967; Expo '67, Montreal, U.S. Pavilion, 1967; Honolulu Academy, Signals of the 60's, 1967; Corcoran Annual, 1967; Documenta IV, Kassel, 1968;

Hayward Gallery, London, 1969; Cincinnati/AM, 1973; WMAA, American Drawings: 1963-1973, 1973; Musée Galliera, Paris, Festival d'Automne, 1973; Parcheggio di Villa Borghese, Contemporanea, 1974; Dallas/MFA, Poets of the Cities, 1974; Moore College of Art, Philadelphia, 1975; Hayward Gallery, London, The Human Clay, 1976; Documenta 6, Kassel, 1977; Chicago/AI, Drawings of the 70's, 1977; U. of North Carolina, Drawings about Drawing, 1979; SFMA, Twenty American Artists, 1980; WMAA, Blam!, 1984; Cincinnati/Contemporary, Body and Soul, circ., 1985. **Collections:** Amsterdam/Stedelijk; Ball State U.; Baltimore/MA; Boston/MFA; Brandeis U.; Brooklyn Museum; Buffalo/Albright; Carnegie; Chicago/AI; Chicago/Contemporary; Cincinnati/AM; Cleveland/MA; Dallas/MFA; Dayton/AI; Detroit/Institute; Eindhoven; Harvard U.; High/Atlanta; Hirshhorn; Indiana U.; Indianapolis; Jewish Museum; Los Angeles/County MA; La Jolla; MMA; MOMA; NCFA; New Orleans Museum; NYU; Oberlin College; Ohio U.; Paris-Beaubourg; Princeton U.; RISD; SRGM; Stockholm/National; St. Louis/City; Tate; Toronto; VMFA; WGMA; WMAA; Walker, Western Australia Art Gallery, Perth; Williams College; Worcester; Woodward Foundation; Yale U. **Bibliography:** Allen, V.; Alloway 1, 4; Battcock, ed.; Becker and Vostell; Bihalji-Merin; Calas, N. and E.; *Celebrate Ohio; Contemporanea;* De Wilde 2; Diamonstein; Dienst 1; Finch; Gettings; **Glenn;** Goldman 1; Hansen; *Happening & Fluxus;* Haskell 5; Honisch and Jensen, eds.; Hunter, ed.; Janis and Blesh 1; Johnson, Ellen H.; Kaprow; Kirby; Kozloff 3; Lippard 5; *Metro;* Rose, B. 1; Rubin 1; *Poets & Painters;* Russell and Gablik; Sager; Sandler 1; Sontag; Tomkins 2; Tomkins and Time-Life Books.

DI SUVERO, MARK. b. September 18, 1933, Shanghai, China. To USA, 1941.

Studied: California School of Fine Arts, 1953-54; U. of California, Santa Barbara, 1954-55, with Robert Thomas; U. of California, Berkeley, BA in Philosophy, 1956, with Stephen Novak. Traveled USA, Mexico. **Awards:** Longview Foundation Grant; Walter K. Gutman Foundation Grant; Chicago/AI, 1963; National Endowment for the Arts, grant; Brandeis U., Creative Arts Award; Skowhegan School Award for Sculpture. **Address:** P.O. Box 2128, Long Island City, N.Y. 11102. **Dealer:** Oil & Steel Gallery, Long Island City, N.Y. **One-man Exhibitions:** (first) Green Gallery, NYC, 1960; Dwan Gallery, Los Angeles, 1965; Park Place Gallery, NYC, 1966; Goldowsky Gallery, 1968; LoGiudice Gallery, Chicago, 1968; Eindhoven, 1972; Duisburg, 1972; City of Chalon-sur-Saone, 1973; Le Jardin des Tuileries, Paris, 1975; Janie C. Lee Gallery, Houston, 1978; ConStruct Gallery, Chicago, 1979; Oil & Steel Gallery, 1983, 85; Esprit Park, San Francisco, 1983; Storm King Art Center, 1985; Hill Gallery, Birmingham, Mich., 1986. **Retrospective:** WMAA, 1975. **Group:** Green Gallery, NYC, 1961, 62, 63; Hartford/Wadsworth, Continuity and Change, 1962; March Gallery, NYC (three-man); Chicago/AI, 1963; 79 Park Place Gallery, NYC, 1963, 64; Peace Tower, Los Angeles, 1966; Los Angeles/County MA, American Sculpture of the Sixties, 1967; WMAA, 1966, 67, 68, 70; SFMA, 1969; MMA, New York Painting and Sculpture: 1940-1970, 1969-1970; Cincinnati/Contemporary, Monumental Art, 1970; Walker, Works for New Spaces, 1971; WMAA, American Drawings: 1963-1973, 1973; Seattle/AM, American Art—Third Quarter Century, 1973; Vassar College, Contemporary College, 1974; Venice Biennial, 1975; SFMA, California Painting and Sculpture: The Modern Era, 1976; Fine Arts Gallery, San Diego, Drawing Invitational, 1977; U. of Chicago, Ideas in Sculpture, 1977; Hayward Gallery, London, The Condition of Sculpture, 1975; Akron/AM, Project/New Urban Movements, 1977; WMAA, American

Sculpture, 1980; Nassau County Museum, Sculpture: The Tradition in Steel, 1983; Los Angeles/MOCA, The First Show, 1984. **Collections:** Baylor U. Medical Center; Chicago/AI; Cincinnati/AM; City of Chalon-sur-Saone; City of Toronto; Dallas/MFA; Federal Reserve Bank, Dade County, Fla.; Hartford/Wadsworth; Hirshhorn; Honeywell Corp., Minneapolis; U. of Iowa; Los Angeles/County MA; Los Angeles/MOCA; MIT; Muhlenberg College; NYU; U. of Nebraska; Otterlo; RISD; St. Louis/City; Storm King Art Center; Toledo/MA; WMAA; Walker, Western Washington State College. **Bibliography:** Battcock, ed.; Hunter, ed.; Krauss 2; Phillips, Lisa; MacAgy 2; *Report;* Rose, B., 1; Rowell; Sandler 1; Tuchman 1.

DOBKIN, ALEXANDER. b. May 1, 1908, Genoa, Italy; **d.** March 21, 1975, Saint-Martin, West Indies. **Studied:** City College of New York, BS; Columbia U., MA; ASL, with George Bridgeman, Dimitri Romanovsky, Jose Clemente Orozco. Traveled Europe, Scandinavia, Israel; resided Paris. **Taught:** Lecturer, A Century of Progress, Chicago, 1933-34; New Art School, NYC, 1937-41; City College of New York; Educational Alliance, NYC, Art Director, 1934-55, Director, 1955-75. **Member:** Artists Equity. Federal A.P.: Easel painting for public buildings. **Awards:** Augustus Saint-Gaudens Medal from Cooper Union, 1930; Roosevelt Memorial Award, 1936; AAAL, Childe Hassam Award, 1947; Library of Congress, Pennell **P.P.,** 1949, 55; AAAL, **P.P.,** 1956. **One-man Exhibitions:** (first) ACA Gallery, 1935, also 1938, 47, 51, 58; Philadelphia Art Alliance, 1957; Garelick's Gallery, Detroit, 1957; Michel Galerie, Paris, 1959; A.A.A. Gallery, NYC, 1960, 69; The Forum Gallery, 1962, 68. **Retrospective:** A.A.A. Gallery, NYC, 1969. **Group:** A Century of Progress, Chicago, 1933-34; ART:USA: 58, NYC, 1958; Brooklyn Museum; Chicago/AI;

MOMA; PMA; PAFA; Carnegie; Corcoran; Festival of Two Worlds, Spoleto; Library of Congress; New York World's Fair, 1964-65. **Collections:** Harvard U.; Library of Congress; MOMA; Newark Museum; PMA; Phoenix; Tel Aviv; WMAA; Youngstown/Butler. **Bibliography:** Archives.

DODD, LAMAR. b. September 22, 1909, Fairburn, Ga. **Studied:** Georgia Institute of Technology, 1926-27; ASL, 1929-33, with George Luks, Boardman Robinson, John Steuart Curry, Jean Charlot, George Bridgeman. Traveled USA. Europe. **Taught:** Five Points, Ala., 1927-28; U. of Georgia, 1937-76; emeritus, 1976-. **Member:** NAD; Audubon Artists. Federal A.P.; Easel painting. **Awards:** Chicago/AI, 1936; Pepsi-Cola, 1947, 48; LHD, LaGrange College, 1947; VMFA, Virginia Artists Biennial, **P.P.,** 1948; NIAL Grant, 1950; NAD, Edwin Palmer Memorial Prize, 1953; PAFA, **P.P.,** 1958; WMAA, **P.P.,** 1958; DFA, U. of Chattanooga, 1959; DFA, Florida State U., 1968. **Address:** 590 Springdale, Athens, GA 30606. **One-man Exhibitions:** (first) Ferargil Galleries, NYC, 1933; Columbia, S.C./MA, 1961; LaGrange College, Ga., 1964, 78; College of St. Catherine, 1964; Grand Central Moderns, NYC, 1948, 52, 55, 57, 61, 64, 65, 67, 68; U. of Georgia, 1969; Clemson U. 1972; Georgia Southern College, 1977. **Retrospective:** High Museum, 1970; U. of Georgia, circ., 1971; Columbia, S.C., 1954. **Group:** U. of Nebraska; PAFA; NIAL; Audubon Artists; Chicago/AI; Corcoran; Boston/MFA; NAD; U. of Illinois; Santa Barbara/MA; Carnegie, 1936; WMAA Annuals, 1937-57; Golden Gate International Exposition, San Francisco, 1939; New York World's Fair, 1939. **Collections:** Andover/Phillips; Atlanta/AA; Chicago/AI; CIT Corporation; Cranbrook; High Museum; U. of Georgia; IBM; MMA; Montclair/AM; Montgomery Museum; PAFA; Pepsi-Cola Co.; U. of Rochester; Savannah/Telfair; VMFA;

WMAA; Wilmington. **Bibliography:** Baur 7; Bethers; Cheney; Wheeler. Archives.

DODD, LOIS. b. April 22, 1927, Montclair, N.J. **Studied:** Cooper Union, with Byron Thomas, Peter Busa. Traveled Italy, France, Switzerland. **Taught:** Philadelphia College of Art, 1963, 65; Wagner College, 1963-64; Brooklyn College, 1965-69, 1971-. A co-founder of the Tanager Gallery, NYC. **Member:** Board of Governors, Skowhegan School. **Commissions:** New York Hilton Hotel (lithographs). **Awards:** Italian Government Scholarship, 1959-60; Longview Foundation Grant, 1962; Ingram Merrill Foundation Grant, 1971; AAIAL, award, 1986. **Address:** 30 East Second Street, NYC 10003. **Dealer:** Fischbach Gallery, NYC. **One-man Exhibitions:** (first) Tanager Gallery, NYC, 1954, also 1957, 58, 61, 62; Purdue U., 1965; Ithaca College, 1966; Wilmington, 1967; Green Mountain Gallery, 1969, 70, 71, 74, 76; Colby College, Waterville, Me., 1977; Washington (Conn.) Art Association, 1977; Cape Split Place, Addison, Me., 1977, 83; Fischbach Gallery, NYC, 1978, 82, 86; New London, 1980; Trenton/State, 1981; Louisiana State U., Baton Rouge, 1984. **Retrospective:** Cape Split Place, circ., 1979. **Group:** The Stable Gallery Annuals, 1956, 58; USIA, Americans in Rome, Rome, 1960; U. of Kentucky, Drawings, 1961; Yale U., Drawings and Watercolors, 1964; A.F.A., Painterly Realism, 1970; U. of Vermont, New England Landscapes, 1971; New York Cultural Center, Women Choose Women, 1973; Omaha/Joslyn, A Sense of Place, 1973; Queens Museum, New Images, 1974; Brooklyn College, Brooklyn College Art Department: Past and Present 1942-1977, 1977; Queens Museum, Flushing, N.Y., New Images, 1974; AAIAL, 1986. **Collections:** AT&T; Brooklyn Museum; Chase Manhattan Bank; Ciba-Geigy Corp; Colby College; Commerce Bank of Kansas City;

Cooper Union; First National City Bank; Hartford/Wadsworth; Kalamazoo/Institute; Reynolds Metals Co.; New York Hilton Hotel; WMAA. **Bibliography:** Archives.

DOLE, WILLIAM. b. September 2, 1917, Angola, Ind. **d.** January 13, 1983, Santa Barbara, Calif. **Studied:** Olivet College (with George Rickey, Harris King Prior), 1937, BA; Mills College, 1940, 49; U. of California, Berkeley, 1947, MA. Traveled Mexico, Europe; resided Florence, Rome. **Taught:** U. of California, Berkeley, 1947-49, Santa Barbara, 1949-83. **Member:** Trustee, Santa Barbara/MA. **Awards:** DFA, Olivet College, 1978; AAIAL, 1978. **One-man Exhibitions:** (first) Santa Barbara/MA, 1951, also 1954, 58, 62, 68; de Young, 1951; Mills College, 1951; Geddis-Martin Studios, Santa Barbara, 1952; Rotunda Gallery, San Francisco, 1954; La Jolla, 1954, 64; Bertha Lewinson Gallery, Los Angeles, 1955; Eric Locke Gallery, San Francisco, 1956; Galerie Springer, Berlin, 1956, 64; Galleria Sagittarius, Rome, 1957; U. of California, Santa Barbara, 1958; Duveen-Graham Gallery, NYC, 1958, 60; Esther Baer Gallery, 1960, 61, 63, 65, 67, 70, 71, 73; Galeria Antonio Souza, Mexico City, 1961; The Thatcher School, Ojai, Calif., 1961; Rex Evans Gallery, 1961, 63, 64, 65, 67, 68, 69; California Palace, 1962; McRoberts & Tunnard Gallery, London, 1966; San Antonio/McNay, 1969; U. of California, Santa Cruz, 1969; Mary Moore Gallery, 1971; Jodi Scully Gallery, 1971, 74, 77; Graphics Gallery, 1972; Mount Holyoke College, 1974; Staempfli Gallery, 1974, 76, 78, 80, 82, 83, 84; William Sawyer Gallery, San Francisco, 1977; Loyola Marymount U., Los Angeles, 1980; William Sawyer Gallery, San Francisco, 1980, 82; Cheekwood, 1981; Mekler Gallery, 1981; Santa Cruz City Museum, 1981; U. of Redlands, 1982; Santa Barbara/MA, 1983. **Retrospectives:** U. of California, Santa Barbara, 1965; Los Angeles Municipal Art Gallery, circ.,

1976; Oakland/AM, 1980. **Group:** California Palace, 1947, 52; Denver/AM, 1948; SFMA, 1948-51; California State Fair, 1950, 51; PAFA, 1950, 60, 65, 68; Los Angeles County Fair, 1951; Hallmark Art Award, 1958; Long Beach/MA, 1953, 60, 63, 69; Santa Barbara/MA, 1955, 57; Los Angeles/County MA, 1958; AAIAL, NYC, 1978. **Collections:** Allentown/AM; Amherst College; Atlantic Richfield Co.; Brooklyn Museum; U. of California; Chase Manhattan Bank; Fort Worth; Harvard U.; Hirshhorn; Honolulu Academy; Long Beach/MA; Mills College; Minnesota/MA; Mount Holyoke College; Newark Museum; Olivet College; Phillips; Phoenix; Rockefeller Institute; Santa Barbara/MA; Storm King Art Center; Walker. **Bibliography:** Archives.

DONATI, ENRICO. b. February 19, 1909, Milan, Italy. To USA, 1934; citizen, 1945. **Studied:** U. of Pavia, Italy; New School for Social Research; ASL. Traveled Europe, India, USA. **Taught:** Yale U., 1960-62. **Member:** Advisory Board of Brandeis U., 1956-; Jury of Fulbright Program, 1954-56; 1963-64; Yale U. Council for Arts and Architecture, 1962-72; belonged to the Surrealist group of Andre Breton, to 1950. **Address:** 222 Central Park South, NYC 10019. **Dealer:** Gimpel & Weitzenhoffer Gallery, NYC. **One-man Exhibitions:** New School for Social Research, 1942; Passedoit Gallery, NYC, 1942, 44; Arts Club of Chicago, 1944, 59; Durand-Ruel Gallery, NYC, 1945, 46, 47, 49; Galerie Drouant, Paris, 1947; P. Rosenberg and Co., 1950; L'Obelisco, Rome, 1950; Galleria II Milione, Milan, 1950; Alexander Iolas Gallery, 1952; Galleria del Cavallino, Venice, 1952; Galleria d'Arte del Naviglio, Milan, 1953; Betty Parsons Gallery, 1954, 55, 57, 59, 60; Syracuse U., 1958; Neue Galerie, Munich, 1962; Staempfli Gallery, 1962, 64, 66, 68, 70, 72, 74, 76, 80; MIT, 1964; J.L. Hudson Art Gallery, Detroit, 1964, 66, 69; Obelisk Gallery, 1965; Minnesota/MA,

1977; Ankrum Gallery, Los Angeles, 1977, 79; Norfolk/Chrysler, 1977; Phillips, Washington, D.C., 1979; Grand Palais, Paris, 1980; Fairweather Hardin Gallery, Chicago, 1977; Chattanooga/Hunter, 1978; West Palm Beach/Norton, 1979; Osuna Gallery, Washington, D.C., 1979; Palm Springs Desert Museum, 1980; Gimpel & Weitzenhoffer Gallery, 1984, 86; Staempfli Gallery, 1982. **Retrospective:** Palais des Beaux-Arts, Brussels, 1961. **Group:** Carnegie, 1950, 52, 54, 56, 58, 61; Venice Biennial; Sao Paulo, 1953; International Biennial Exhibition of Paintings, Tokyo; A.F.A., The Embellished Surface, circ., 1953-54; Chicago/AI, 1954, 57; WMAA Annuals, 1954, 56, 58, 59, 61, 62, 64, 70; Santa Barbara/MA, 1954; SRGM, Younger American Painters, 1954; Utica, 1955; SFMA, 1955; Indiana U., 1957, 59; PAFA, 1957; VMFA, American Painting, 1958; Inter-American Paintings and Prints Biennial, Mexico City, 1958; U. of Illinois, 1959; Lincoln, Mass./De Cordova, Decade in Review, 1959; A.F.A., V International Exhibition, 1959; Corcoran, 1960; St. Paul Gallery, 1960; Walker, 60 American Painters, 1960; SRGM, Abstract Expressionists and Imagists, 1961; New York World's Fair, 1964-65. **Collections:** American Republic Insurance Co.; Arthur Anderson & Co.; Anderson Clayton Company; Atlantic Richfield Co.; Avon Products; Baltimore/MA; Bezalel Museum; Brussels/Moderne; Buffalo/Albright; U. of California; Chase Manhattan Bank; Detroit/Institute; Doane College; Ford Motor Company; High Museum; Houston-MFA; J.L. Hudson Co.; IBM; Indian Head Mills, Inc.; International Institute for Aesthetic Research; Johns Hopkins U.; MIT; MOMA; Michigan Consolidated Gas Co.; U. of Michigan; Milan; Minnesota/MA; Needham, Harper & Steers, Inc.; Newark Museum; Northwestern National Life Insurance Co.; Oslo/National; Owen-Corning Fiberglas Corp.; Palm Beach Company; Prudential Life Insurance Co.; St.

Louis/City; The Singer Company, Inc.; Temple Beth El; U. of Texas; Tougaloo College; Turin/Civico; U.S. Steel Corp.; WGMA; WMAA; Washington U.; Yale U. **Bibliography:** Breton 2, 3; Goodrich and Baur 1; Read 2; Rubin 1; Wolff.

DOVE, ARTHUR G. b. August 2, 1880, Canandaigua, N.Y.; **d.** November 1946, Centerport, N.Y. **Studied:** Cornell U., 1903. Commercial illustrator, 1903-07. Traveled Europe, 1907-9, with Alfred Maurer and Arthur B. Carles, Jr. Met Alfred Stieglitz, 1910. **One-man Exhibitions:** (first) Photo-Secession, NYC, 1912; Scott Thurber Gallery, Chicago, 1912; Stieglitz's Intimate Gallery, NYC, 1926, 27, 29; An American Place (Gallery), NYC, annually, 1930-46; Springfield, Mass./MFA, 1933; Phillips, 1937; Vanbark Studios, Studio City, Calif., 1947; Utica, 1947; The Downtown Gallery, 1949, 52, 54, 55, 56, 67; Houston/MFA, 1951; Walker, 1954; Deerfield (Mass.) Academy, 1956; Paul Kantor Gallery, Beverly Hills, Calif., 1956; U. of Maryland, 1967; Terry Dintenfass, Inc., 1970, 71, 77, 78, 79, 80, 84; Asher/Faure, Los Angeles, 1981; Hobart and William Smith College, Geneva, N.Y., 1981; Barbara Mathes Gallery, 1984; Salander-O'Reilly Galleries, 1984. **Retrospectives:** The Downtown Gallery, 1947; Cornell U., 1954; UCLA, circ., 1958-59; SFMA, circ., 1974; Phillips, circ., 1981. **Group:** Salon d-Automne, Paris, 1908, 09; National Arts Club Annual, NYC, 1914; Anderson Galleries, NYC, Forum Exhibition, 1916; Society of Independent Artists, NYC, 1917; PAFA, 1921; Wildenstein & Co., NYC, Tri-National Art, 1926; Brooklyn Museum, International Exhibition of Modern Art (assembled by Societe Anonyme), 1926; Salons of America, NYC, 1929; MOMA, Paintings by 19 Living Americans, 1929; Cleveland/MA Annuals, 1931, 32, 35; WMAA Annuals, 1932, 34; A.F.A., Abstraction, 1932; A Century of Progress, Chicago, 1933-34; WMAA, Abstract Painting in America, 1935; Buffalo/Albright, 1935; U. of Minnesota, 1937; Cleveland/MA, American Painting from 1860 until Today, 1937; Worcester/AM, 1938; Musée du Jeu de Paume, Trois Siecles d'Art aux Etats-Unis, 1938; MOMA, Art in Our Time; 10th Anniversary Exhibition, 1939; Boston/MFA, 10 American Watercolor Painters, 1939; Golden Gate International Exposition, San Francisco, 1939; Cornell U., 1940; MOMA, Cubist and Abstract Art, 1942; PMA, History of an American, Alfred Stieglitz: "291" and After, 1944. **Collections:** American U.; Andover/Phillips; Arizona State College; Baltimore/MA; Boston U.; Brittania; Brooklyn Museum; Buffalo/Albright; Carnegie; Chicago/AI; Colorado Springs/FA; Columbus; Cornell U.; Des Moines; Detroit/Institute; Fisk U.; Fort Worth; Hartford/Wadsworth; Honolulu Academy; IBM; Inland Steel Co.; MMA; MOMA; Milwaukee; U. of Minnesota; National Gallery; U. of Nebraska; Omaha/Joslyn; PMA; Phillips; Phoenix; Randolph-Macon Woman's College; U. of Rochester; SFMA; Smith College; Springfield, Mass./MFA; Utica; WMAA; Washington U.; Wellesley College; West Palm Beach/Norton; Wichita/AM; Wilmington; Yale U. **Bibliography: Arthur Dove: The Years of Collage;** Ashton 5; *Avant-Garde Painting and Sculpture in America, 1920-25;* Barr 3; Baur 5, 7; Blanchard; Blesh 1; Brown 2; Cahill and Barr, eds.; Cheney; Downes, ed.; *8 American Masters of Watercolor;* Eliot; *Forerunners;* Frank, ed.; Frost; Gerdts; Goodrich and Baur 1; Haftman; **Haskell 1;** Hess, T. B., 1;

Hunter 6; Janis and Blesh; Janis, S.; Kootz 1; Kozloff 3; Mather 1; McCurdy, ed.; Mellquist; Mendelowitz; Morgan; Neuhaus; Newmeyer; Phillips 1, 2; Poore; Read 2; Richardson, E.P.; Ringel, ed.; Ritchie 1; Rodman 2; Rose, B., 1, 4; Rosenblum 2; Rubin 1; Schwartz 2; Seitz 3; Sutton; Tashijan; Tuchman 3; Wight 2; Wright 1. Archives.

DOWNES, RACKSTRAW, b. November 8, 1939, England. **Studied:** Cambridge U., BA, 1961, with Donald Davie; Yale U., MFA, 1964, with Neil Welliver, Alex Katz, Al Held; U. of Pennsylvania, post-graduate fellowship, 1964-65. **Taught:** Parsons School of Design, 1964-67; U. of Pennsylvania, 1967-79; Skowhegan School, 1975; Yale U., 1979-80; New York Studio School, 1981-82. Art critic and writer. **Member:** Board of Governors, Skowhegan School. **Awards:** Yaddo Fellowship, 1970; Ingram Merrill Foundation Grant, 1974; CAPS, 1978. **Address:** 16 Hudson Street, NYC 10013. **Dealer:** Hirschl & Adler Modern, NYC. **One-man Exhibitions:** (first) Swarthmore College, 1969; The Kornblee Gallery, NYC, 1972, 74, 75, 78, 80; McLeaf Gallery, Philadelphia, 1969; Swain School of Design, New Bedford, Mass., 1978; Tatistcheff & Co., NYC, 1980; Hirschl & Adler Modern, NYC, 1984. **Group:** A.F.A., Painterly Realism, 1970-72; Colgate U., Painters of the Land and Sky, 1972; Omaha/Joslyn, A Sense of Place, 1973; Queens County Art and Cultural Center, New Images in American Painting,

Rackstraw Downes   *Portland Water District Wastewater Treatment Plant*   1984

1974; US Department of the Interior, America 1976, 1976; Los Angeles/County MA, Eighteen Artists, 1976; AAAL, 1977; Brooklyn Museum, American Drawings in Black and White: 1970-1979, 1980; San Antonio/MA, Real, Really Real, Super Real, circ., 1981; Haus der Kunst, Munich, Amerikanische Malerei, 1930-1980, 1981; WMAA Biennial, 1981; PAFA, Contemporary American Realism Since 1960, 1981; Utica, An Appreciation of Realism, 1982; Carnegie, International, 1983; U. of California, Santa Barbara, A Heritage Renewed: Representational Drawings Today, 1983; PAFA, Perspective on Contemporary American Realism, 1983; Hudson River Museum, Form or Formula: Drawing and Drawings, 1986. **Collections:** U. of California, Santa Barbara; Carnegie; Chase Manhattan Bank, NYC; Corcoran; Hirshhorn; MMA; U. of North Carolina; PAFA; WMAA. **Bibliography:** *America 1976*; Arthur 3.

DOYLE, TOM. b. May 23, 1928, Jerry City, Ohio. **Studied:** Miami U.; The Ohio State U. (with Roy Lichtenstein, Stanley Twardowicz), BFA, MA. Traveled Europe. **Taught:** Brooklyn Museum School, 1961-68; New School for Social Research, 1961-68; School of Visual Arts, NYC, 1969; Queens College, CUNY, 1970-. **Member:** American Abstract Artists. **Commissions:** GSA, for Fairbanks, Alaska, 1980. **Awards:** Ohio State Fair, two First and two Second Prizes; Guggenheim Foundation Fellowship, 1982. **Address:** 130 West 18th Street, NYC 10011. **One-man Exhibitions:** (first) The Ohio State U., 1956; Allan Stone Gallery, 1961, 62; Dwan Gallery, 1966, 67, 72; Brata Gallery, NYC, 1972; 55 Mercer Steet, NYC, 1974, 76; Colgate U., 1976; Sculpture Now, Inc., 1978; Max Hutchinson Gallery, 1982; Miami-Dade, 1982. **Group:** Cornell U., 1960; Martha Jackson Gallery, New Media—New Forms, I & II, 1960, 61; Oberlin College, 1961; Carnegie, 1961; Seattle World's Fair, 1962;

Berne, 1964; WMAA Annual, 1966, 67; Los Angeles/County MA, American Sculpture of the Sixties, 1967; Jewish Museum, Primary Structures, 1967; Los Angeles/County MA, American Sculpture of the Sixties, 1967; Documenta, Kassel, 1972; Taft Museum, Painting and Sculpture Today, 1974; Indianapolis, 1974; Pratt Institute, Sitesights, 1980; NMAA, Across the Nation, 1980; Stockholm/National, Flyktpunkter–Vanishing Points, 1984; Queens College, The Ways of Wood, 1984; Bronx Museum, American Abstract Artists 50th Anniversary Celebration, circ., 1986. **Collections:** Bard College; Brooklyn Museum; Carnegie; Fairbanks, Alaska, Federal Building and Court House; Manhattanville College; Nassau County Museum; Ohio State U.; Purchase, N.Y.; South Dakota State U.; Wright State U. **Bibliography:** Atkinson; Tuchman 1. Archives.

DREWES, WERNER. b. July 27, 1899, Canig, Germany. **d.** June 21, 1985, Reston, Va. **Studied:** Gymnasium, Brandenburg/Havel, 1909-17; Charlottenburg Technische Hochschule, Berlin, 1919; Stuttgart School of Architecture, 1920; Stuttgart School of Arts and Crafts, 1921; Bauhaus, Weimar, 1921-22, with Josef Itten, Paul Klee; Bauhaus, Dessau, 1927-28, with Vassily Kandinsky, Lyonel Feininger. To USA, 1930; citizen, 1936. Traveled Europe, South and Central America, Asia, USA. **Taught:** Columbia U., 1937-40; Master Institute of United Arts, Inc., NYC, 1940; Brooklyn College, 1944; Institute of Design, Chicago, 1945; Washington U., 1946-65. Federal A.P.: Instructor, Brooklyn Museum, 1934-36; Technical Supervisor, Graphic Art Project, 1940-41. **Member:** American Artists Congress; co-founder, American Abstract Artists, 1936. **Commissions:** International Graphic Arts Society, 1954, 57. **Awards:** 50 Best Prints of the Year, 1932, 44; PAFA, **P.P.,** 1933; MOMA; Plexiglas Sculpture Competition, Third Prize, 1939; MOMA, Textile

Design Competition, First and Second Prizes, 1941; The Print Club, Philadelphia, Hon. Men., 1946; A.A.A. Gallery, NYC, **P.P.**, 1959; St. Louis Artists' Guild, Bader Art Prize, 1960. **One-man Exhibitions:** Madrid/Nacional, 1923; Montevideo/Municipal, 1924; St. Louis Public Library, 1924; Gump's Gallery, 1926; Flechtheim and Kahnweiler, Frankfurt, 1928; Galerie del Vecchio, Leipzig, 1929; Morton Gallery, NYC, 1932, 33; New School for Social Research, 1935; Artists' Gallery, NYC, 1939, 41; Lilienfeld Gallery, NYC, 1945; Indiana U., 1945; Kleemann Gallery, NYC, 1945, 46, 47, 49; Princeton U., 1946 (four-man); Smithsonian, 1948; Pen and Palette Gallery, St. Louis, 1949; Lutz and Meyer Gallery, Stuttgart, 1951; Argent Gallery, NYC, 1951; Neue Gallerie Gurlitt, 1952; St. Louis Artists' Guild, 1953; Beloit College, 1954, 77; Schermahorn Gallery, Beloit, 1955, 56; Los Angeles/County MA, 1956; Memphis/Brooks, 1957; Springfield, Mo./AM, 1958; Oregon State College, circ., 1959; Cleveland/MA, 1961; Washington U., 1962; Hom Gallery, Washington, D.C., 1971; Princeton Gallery of Fine Art, 1972, 76; Haslem Fine Arts, Washington, D.C., 1978; Tobey C. Moss Gallery, Los Angeles, 1983; AAA Gallery, 1986. **Retrospectives:** California Palace, 1962; Washington U., 1965; Smithsonian, 1969; US Embassy Program, Turkey, 1974; St. Olaf College, circ., 1978. **Group:** Carnegie; Brooklyn Museum; Chicago/AI; MMA; USIA; WMAA; U. of Illinois; PAFA; SRGM; Bennington College. **Collections:** U. of Alabama; Andover/Phillips; Bibliotheque Nationale; Boston/MFA; Boston Public Library; Brooklyn Museum; Chicago/AI; Cleveland/MA; Cologne; Frankfurt am Main; Hartford/Wadsworth; Harvard U.; Honolulu Academy; U. of Illinois; Kansas City/Nelson; Karsruhe; Library of Congress; Los Angeles/County MA; MOMA; Memphis/Brooks; Mills College; NCFA; NYPL; National Gallery; Newark Public Library; PAFA; RISD; SFMA; SRGM St. Louis/City; Seat-

tle/AM; Springfield, Ill./State; Springfield, Mo./AM; Trenton/State; Victoria and Albert Museum; Washington U.; Wells College; Wichita/AM; Worcester/AM; Yale U. **Bibliography:** American Artists Congress, Inc.; Baur 7; Bazin; Cheney; Lane and Larsen. Archives.

DRUMMOND, SALLY HAZELET. b. June 4, 1924, Evanston, Ill. **Studied:** Rollins College, 1942-44; Columbia U., with John Heliker, Peppino Mangravite, 1946-48, BA; Institute of Design, Chicago, 1949-50, with Hugo Weber, Emerson Woelffer; U. of Louisville, with Ulfert Wilke, 1950-52, MA. Traveled Italy, France, England. A co-organizer of the Tanager Gallery, NYC. **Taught:** Skowhegan School, 1973. **Awards:** Fulbright Fellowship (Italy), 1952; Guggenheim Foundation Fellowship, 1967-68. **Address:** 371 Wilton Road East, Ridgefield, CT 06877. **One-man Exhibitions:** (first) Hadley Gallery, Louisville, 1952, also 1961; Art Center Association, Louisville, 1955; Tanager Gallery, NYC, 1955, 57, 60; Green Gallery, NYC, 1962; Louisville/Speed, 1967 (two-man); Fischbach Gallery, 1968, 72, 78; Ridgefield/Aldrich, 1981; Merida Gallery, Louisville, 1982; Artists Space, NYC, 1984. **Retrospective:** Corcoran, 1972. **Group:** American Embassy, Rome, 1953; Bordighera, 1953; A.F.A., Fulbright Artists, circ., 1958; Houston/MFA, 1959; WMAA Annual, 1960; A.F.A., Lyricism in Abstract Art, circ., 1962-63; MOMA; Americans, 1963, circ., 1963-64; Trenton/State, Focus on Light, 1967; Silvemine Guild, 1970; PMA, FOCUS, 1974; Stamford Museum, American Art-American Women, 1986. **Collections:** Avco Corp.; Chase Manhattan Bank; Ciba-Geigy Corp.; Corcoran; Currier; Hirshhorn; Interchemical Corporation; U. of Iowa; Louisville/Speed; MOMA; MMA; U. of North Carolina; Union Carbide Corp.; WMAA.

DU BOIS, GUY PENE. b. January 4, 1884, Brooklyn, N.Y.; **d.** July 18, 1958, Boston, Mass. **Studied:** W. M. Chase School, NYC, 1899-1905, with J. C. Beckwith, Frank V. DuMond, Robert Henri, Kenneth Hayes Miller; Academie de la Grande Chaumiere, with Theophile A. Steinlen. Traveled USA, Europe. Reporter and critic for *New York American, New York Tribune, New York Evening Post;* editor of *Arts and Decoration* magazine for seven years. **Awards:** Pan-American Exhibition, Los Angeles, 1925, Third Prize; Chicago/AI Norman Wait Harris Silver Medal, 1930; NAD, Benjamin Altman Prize, 1936; Corcoran Second William A. Clark Prize, 1937. **One-man Exhibitions:** Kraushaar Galleries, 1922, 24, 30, 32, 35, 36, 38, 42, 43, 46; Staten Island, 1954; The Graham Gallery, 1961, 63, 79, 83; Northwestern U., 1981. **Retrospective:** Hagerstown/County MFA, 1940. **Group:** Salon des Beaux-Arts, Paris, 1906; Corcoran; Chicago/AI; PAFA; WMAA. **Collections:** Amherst College; Andover/Phillips; Baltimore/MA; Barnes Foundation; Brooklyn Museum; Chicago/AI; Cleveland/MA; Detroit/Institute; Los Angeles/County MA; MOMA; Milwaukee; Newark Museum; New Britain; PAFA; PMA; Phillips; San Diego; Toledo/MA; WMAA. **Bibliography:** Baur 7; Bazin; Brown 2; Bruce and Watson; Cahill and Barr, eds.; Cheney; **Cortissoz 2; Du Bois 1, 2, 3, 4, 5, 6;** Ely; Gerdts; Glackens; *Cityscape 1919-39;* Goodrich and Baur 1; Hall; Hunter 6; *Index of 20th Century Artists;* Jewell 2; Kent, N.; Mather 1; Mc-Coubrey 1; **Medford;** Mellquist; Neuhaus; Pagano; Pearson 1; Phillips 2; Poore; Richardson, E.P.; Ringel, ed.; Rose, B., 1, 4; Smith, S.C.K. Archives.

DUCHAMP, MARCEL. b. July 28, 1887, Blainville, near Rouen, France; **d.** October 1, 1968, Neuilly, France. **Studied:** Academie Julian, Paris, 1904. To USA, 1915; citizen, 1955. Traveled Europe, Argentina, USA. Founding member, Society of Independent Artists, 1916. Cofounder (with Man Ray and Francis Picabia) of DADA group, NYC, 1917. Co-organizer (with Katherine S. Dreier and Man Ray) of Societe Anonyme (Museum of Modern Art), 1920. Published one issue of *New York DADA* with Man Ray, 1921. Produced a film, *Anemic Cinema,* 1925. **One-man Exhibitions:** Montross Gallery, NYC, 1916 (four-man); Arts Club of Chicago, 1937; Rose Fried Gallery, 1952 (three-man); SRGM, 1957 (three-man); Galerie de l'Institut, Paris, 1957; Signey Janis Gallery, 1958, 59; La Hune, Paris, 1959; Pasadena/AM, 1963; Eva de Buren Gallery, Stockholm, 1963; Walker, 1965; Milwaukee, 1965; Cordier & Ekstrom, Inc., 1965, 67, 68; Tate, 1966; Fourcade, Droll, Inc.; Galerie Rene Block, Berlin, 1971; Galleria Civica d'Arte Moderna, Ferrara, 1971; Galleria Schwarz, 1972; Jerusalem/National, 1972; L'Uomo e l'Arte, Milan, 1973; Dayton's Gallery 12, Minneapolis, 1973, 74; Holly Solomon Gallery, 1977; L.A. Louver Gallery, Venice, Calif., 1982; Gallery Yves Arman, NYC, 1984; Florida International U., 1985; Arnold Herstand & Co., NYC, 1986; Luhring, Augustine & Hodes, NYC, 1987. **Retrospectives:** Gimpel Fils Ltd., 1964; Galleria Solaria, Milan, 1967; Paris/Moderne, 1967; Cologne, 1968; PMA, 1969, 73. **Group:** Salon des Artistes Independents, Paris, 1909-12; Salon d'Automne, Paris, 1909-12; Salon de la Section d'Or, 1912, The Armory Show, 1913; Societe Anonyme, NYC, 1920; Salon DADA, Paris, 1920; A Century of Progress, Chicago, 1933-34; MOMA, Cubism and Abstract Art, 1936; MOMA, Fantastic Art, DADA, Surrealism, 1936; WMAA, European Artists in America, 1945; MOMA, Eleven Europeans, 1946; XXIV Venice Biennial, 1948; California Palace, 1948; Chicago/AI, 1949; MOMA, The Machine, 1968; Haus der Kunst, Munich, Der Surrealismus, 1922-1942, 1972. **Collections:** MOMA; Ottawa/National; PMA; SRGM; Yale U. **Bibliography:** Alloway 4; Barr 1, 3; Battcock, ed.; Baur 7; Becker and Vostell;

Biddle 4; Biederman 1; Bihalji-Merin; Blesh 1; Breton 2; Brion 2; Brown; Bulliet 1, 2; **Cabanne;** Calas, N. and E.; Canaday; Cassou; Chipp; Christensen; Coplans 3; Davidson 1; Davis, D.; De Vries; **D'Harnoncourt and McShine, eds.;** Dorival; Dorner; Dreier 2; **Duchamp 1, 2;** Elsen 1; Finch; Flanagan; Frost; Gablik; Gascoyne; Gaunt; Gerdts; Giedion-Welcker 1, 2; Guggenheim, ed.; Haftman; **Hamilton, R.;** Honnef; Hulten; Hunter 6; Hunter, ed; Huyghe; Janis and Blesh 1; Johnson, Ellen H.; Kepes 2; Kozloff 3; Krauss 2, 3; Kuh 1, 2, 3; Kyrou; Langui; Lippard 3; **Lebel;** Lee and Burchwood; Licht, F.; Lippard 5; Lippard, ed.; Lowry; Lynton; McCurdy, ed.; Marter, Tarbell, and Wechsler; Mellquist; Metro; Motherwell 1; Murken-Altrogge; Neff, ed.; Neumeyer; Newmeyer; Pach 2, 3; Ramsden 1; **Raymond Duchamp-Villon/Marcel Duchamp;** Raynal 3, 4; Read 2, 3; Richardson, E. P.; Richter; Rickey; Rose, B., 1, 4; Rosenblum 1; Rowell; Rubin 1; Sager; **Schwarz 1, 2;** Sandler 1; Seitz 3; Selz, J.; Seuphor 1, 3; Soby 1, 5, 6; **Sweeney 2;** Tashijian; Tomkins; Tomkins and Time-Life Books; Tomkins 2; Trier 1, 2; Tuchman 3; Valentine 2; Verkauf; Waldberg 2, 3, 4; Weller. Archives.

DUFF, JOHN. b. 1943, Lafayette, Indiana. **Studied:** SFAI, 1967, BFA. **Address:** 5 Doyer Street, NYC 10013. **Dealer:** Blum Helman Gallery, NYC. **One-man Exhibitions:** Brady Gallery, San Francisco, 1967; David Whitney Gallery, NYC, 1970, 71; Galerie Rolf Ricke, Cologne, 1971; Irving Blum Gallery, Los Angeles, 1972; Janie C. Lee Gallery, Dallas, 1972; John Bernard Myers Gallery, NYC, 1972, 73; Daniel Weinberg Gallery, San Francisco, 1974, 75, 77, 80; Willard Gallery, NYC, 1975, 76, 77, 78; Galerie Swart, Amsterdam, 1978; Sonoma State U., 1979; Margo Leavin Gallery, Los Angeles, 1981, 84; Blum Helman Gallery, 1985; The Clocktower, NYC, 1985. **Group:** WMAA, Anti-Illusion Procedures/

Materials, 1969; WMAA Annual, 1970; SRGM, Nine Young Artists, 1977; WMAA Biennial, 1973, 85; West Palm Beach/Norton, Material Matters, circ., 1980; WMAA, Developments in Recent Sculpture, 1981. **Collections:** ICA, Boston; Los Angeles/County MA; MOMA; SRGM; WMAA; Walker.

DUGMORE, EDWARD. b. February 20, 1915, Hartford, Conn. **Studied:** Hartford Art School, 1934-38; California School of Fine Arts (with Clyfford Still), 1948-50; U. of Guadalajara, 1951-52, MA. US Marine Corps, 1943-44. Traveled Mexico, USA extensively, Europe, 1966-67. **Taught:** St. Joseph College, 1946-49; Southern Illinois U.; Pratt Institute, 1964-72; U. of Minnesota, 1970; Des Moines, 1972; Maryland Institute, 1973, 74. A cofounder of Metart Gallery, San Francisco. **Awards:** Chicago/AI, The M.V. Kohnstamm Prize, 1962; Guggenheim Foundation Fellowship, 1966-67; National Endowment for the Arts, 1976, 85; AAAL Award, 1980. **Address:** 118 West 27th Street, NYC 10001. **One-man Exhibitions:** (first) Metart Gallery, San Francisco, 1949; The Stable Gallery, 1953, 54, 56; Holland-Goldowsky Gallery, Chicago, 1959; The Howard Wise Gallery, Cleveland, 1960; The Howard Wise Gallery, NYC, 1960, 61, 63; Green Mountain Gallery, 1971, 73; Des Moines, 1972. **Group:** Carnegie, 1955; Walker, Vanguard, 1955; WMAA Annual, 1959; SRGM, Abstract Expressionists and Imagists, 1961; Chicago/AI Annual, 1962; SFMA, Directions— Painting U.S.A., 1963; U. of Texas, Recent American Painting, 1964, also 1968; Green Mountain Gallery, 1971; Buffalo/Albright, Abstract Expressionism: First and Second Generations, 1972; Oakland/AM, A Period of Exploration, 1973; SFMA, California Painting and Sculpture: The Modern Era, 1976; NCFA, 1977; AAAL, 1980. **Collections:** Buffalo/Albright; Ciba-Geigy Corp.; Des Moines; Housatonic Community College; Michigan State U.; Minneapolis/Institute; U. of North Carolina; Southern Illinois U.; Walker. **Bibliography:** McChesney; Sandler. Archives.

DURAN, ROBERT. b. 1938, Salinas, Calif. **Studied:** Richard Stockton State College, 1958-60; San Francisco School of Fine Arts, 1960-61. Traveled Mexico, USA, Morocco, Europe, India. **Address:** 431 Broome Street, NYC 10013. **One-man Exhibitions:** Bykert Gallery, 1968 (two-man), 1970 (two-man), 1971, 72, 73; The Texas Gallery, 1973; Susan Caldwell Gallery, NYC, 1975, 77. **Group:** Park Place Gallery, NYC, 1966; Ithaca College, Drawings, 1967, 1967; A.F.A., Rejective Art, 1967; ICA, U. of Pennsylvania, Between Object and Environment, 1969; WMAA, 1969, 73; Columbus, Beaux-Arts, Twenty-Fifth Anniversary Exhibition, 1971; Corcoran Biennial, 1971; Indianapolis, 1972; Storm King Art Center, 1972; WMAA Biennial, 1973; Vassar College, New American Abstract Painting, 1973; Akron/AI, Contemporary Images in Watercolor, 1976; Georgia State U., Ten Painters, 1976. **Collections:** Amerada Hess Corp., N.J.; Amstar Corp.; Betcar Corp.; Business Card, Inc.; Columbus; General Reinsurance Corp.; Lehman Brothers, NYC; MOMA; National Gallery; Port Authority of New York & New Jersey; Prudential Insurance Co. of America, N.J.; J. Henry Schroeder Banking Corp.; Two Trees; United Mutual Savings; WMAA.

DZUBAS, FRIEDEL. b. April 20, 1915, Berlin, Germany. To USA, 1939. Traveled Europe extensively. **Taught:** U. of South Florida, 1962; Artist-in-Residence, Dartmouth College, 1962, Aspen Institute, 1965, 66; Cornell U., 1967, 1969-74; U. of Pennsylvania, 1968; Sarah Lawrence College, 1968-69. **Commissions:** National Shawmut Bank of Boston (mural). **Awards:** Guggenheim Foundation Fellowship, 1966; J. S. Guggenheim Fellowship, 1968; National Council on the Arts, 1968. **Ad-**

dress: Lakeville, CT 06039. **Dealers:** Knoedler Contemporary Art; David Mirvish Gallery; Watson/De Nagy. **One-man Exhibitions:** Tibor de Nagy Gallery, 1952, 76; Leo Castelli Inc., 1958; French & Co., Inc., NYC, 1959; Dwan Gallery, 1960; Robert Elkon Gallery, 1961-65; Kasmin Ltd., 1964, 65; Nicholas Wilder Gallery, 1966; Andre Emmerich Gallery, 1966, 67, 68; Jack Glenn Gallery, Corona del Mar, 1971; Lawrence Rubin Gallery, NYC, 1971, 72, 73; Gallerie Hans Strelow, Cologne, 1971, 72; David Mirvish Gallery, 1973, 74, 75, 76; Knoedler Contemporary Art, 1974, 75, 76; Watson/De Nagy Gallery, Houston, 1976; Margo Leavin Gallery, Los Angeles, 1976; John Berggruen Gallery, San Francisco, 1977, 79; M. Knoedler & Co., NYC, 1977, 78, 79, 80, 82; Kunsthalle, Bielefeld, 1977; Dart Gallery, Chicago, 1978; Thomas Segal Gallery, Boston, 1982; Galerie Ninety-Nine, Bay Harbor Islands, Fla., 1982; Martha White Gallery, Louisville, 1982; M. Knoedler & Co., Zurich, 1982. **Retrospectives:** Houston/MFA, 1974; Boston/MFA, 1975. **Group:** Chicago/AI Annuals, 1942, 43, 44; MMA, American Painters under 35, 1950; Ninth Street Exhibition, NYC, 1951; WMAA Annuals, 1958, 59, 64; Corcoran, 1959, 63, Biennial, 1967; The Kootz Gallery, NYC, New Talent, 1960; Carnegie, 1961; SRGM, Abstract Expressionists and Imagists, 1961; Dayton/AI, 1963; Jewish Museum, Black and White, 1963; Los Angeles/County MA, Post Painterly Abstraction, 1964; Detroit/Institute, Color and Image and Form, 1967; U. of Illinois, 1967; Expo '67, Montreal, 1967; Buffalo/Albright, Color and Field, 1890-1970, 1970; Boston/MFA, Abstract Painting in the '70s, 1972; Houston/MFA, The Great Decade of American Abstraction: Modernist Art 1960 to 1970, 1974; Corcoran Biennial, 1975; Syracuse/Everson, New Works in Clay, 1976; US Embassy, Ottawa, Eighteen Contemporary Masters, 1977. **Collections:** Baltimore/MA; Boston/MFA; Brandeis U.; Buffalo/Albright; Chase Manhattan Bank;

Cornell U.; Dayton/AI; Dartmouth College; Hirshhorn; Houston/MFA; MMA; Manufacturers Hanover Trust; Memphis/Brooks; NYU; Oberlin College; Phillips; Ridgefield/Aldrich; Rutgers U.; SFMA; SRGM; St. Louis/City; Syracuse/Everson; Tufts Dental College; Utica; WMAA; Wellesley College; Yale U. **Bibliography:** *The Great Decade*; Rose, B., 1; Sandler 1.

E

EDDY, DON. b. November 4, 1944, Long Beach, Calif. **Studied:** Fullerton Junior College; U. of Hawaii, 1967, BFA, 1969, MFA; U. of California, Santa Barbara, 1969-70. US Navy, 1967-68. **Taught:** U. of Hawaii, 1967-69; NYU, 1973-78; School of Visual Arts, NYC, 1977-. **Address:** 30 Christopher Street, NYC 10014. **Dealer:** Nancy Hoffman Gallery. **One-man Exhibitions:** Ewing Krainin Gallery, Honolulu, 1968; Molly Barnes Gallery, Los Angeles, 1970, 71; Esther Baer Gallery, 1970; Galerie M. E. Thelen, Essen and Cologne, 1970; Galerie de Gestlo, 1971; French & Co. Inc., NYC, 1971; Aktionsgalerie, Bern (two-man), 1971; Nancy Hoffman Gallery, 1973, 74, 76, 79, 83, 86; Galerie Petit, Paris, 1973; Williams College, Williamstown, Mass., 1975; Miami-Dade Community College, 1976; U. of Hawaii, Manoa, 1982. **Group:** Stockton, Beyond the Actual, 1970; Sacramento/Crocker, West Coast '70, 1970; Munster/WK, Verkehrskultur, 1971; Santa Barbara/MA, Spray, 1971; VII Paris Biennial, 1971; Potsdam/SUNY, New Realism, 1971; Documenta V, Kassel, 1972; Cleveland/MA, 32 Realists, 1972; Stuttgart/WK, Amerikanischer Fotorealismus, circ., 1972; Kunsthalle und Spritzpistole, 1973; Los Angeles Municipal Art Gallery, Separate Realities, 1973; U. of Illinois, 1974; Hartford/Wadsworth, New/Photo Realism, 1974; Toledo, Image, Color and Form, 1975; Baltimore/MA, Super Realism, 1976; Canberra/National, Illusion and Reality, circ., 1977; Dayton/AI, Photo Images, 1977; U. of Texas, New in the 70's, 1977; Kansas City/Sheldon, Things Seen, 1978; Tulsa/Philbrook,

Realism/Photorealism, 1980; Brooklyn Museum, American Drawings in Black and White: 1970-1979, 1980; San Antonio/MA, Real, Really Real, Super Real, circ., 1981; PAFA, Contemporary American Realism Since 1960, 1981. **Collections:** Aachen/NG; American Republic Insurance Co.; Akron/AI; Claremont College; Cleveland/MA; Des Moines; Fort Wayne/AM; Harvard U.; Honolulu Academy; Israel Museum; Louisville/Speed; U. of Massachusetts; Museo de Arte Moderno, Bogota; U. of Nebraska; Oklahoma; RISD; SRGM; St.-Etienne; San Antonio/McNay; Santa Barbara/MA; Springfield, Mo./AM; Storm King Art Center; Toledo/MA; Utrecht; Warner Bros., Los Angeles; Williams College; WMAA. **Bibliography:** Alloway 4; *Amerikanischer Fotorealismus;* Arthur 4; Honisch and Jensen, eds.; *Kunst um 1970;* Lindy; *New in the Seventies;* Sager.

EDMONDSON, LEONARD. b. June 21, 1916, Sacramento, Calif. **Studied:** Los Angeles City College, 1934-37; U. of California, Berkeley, 1937-42, BA (1940), MA (1942). US Army Intelligence, 1942-46. Traveled Europe, 1978. **Taught:** Los Angeles County Art Institute, 1954-56; Pasadena City College, 1947-54, 1956-64; U. of California, Berkeley, summers, 1960, 64; Pratt Institute, summer, 1961; Los Angeles State College, 1964-74; Otis Art Institute, 1974-76; California State U., Los Angeles, 1976-. **Member:** Board of Directors, Pasadena/AM, 1957-63; Los Angeles, Printmaking Society, president, 1966; Pasadena Society of Artists, president, 1967; AAAL, Hassam and

Speicher Fund **P.P.**, 1977. **Commissions** (prints): International Graphic Arts Society, 1960; New York Hilton Hotel, 1962. **Awards:** SFMA, First **P.P.**, 1946, Second Prize, 1951, 52, James D. Phelan Award, 1951, 53, **P.P.**, 1957; California State Fair, First Prize for Etching, 1951, Second **P.P.**, 1952, 56; Brooklyn Museum, 1951, 56; Oakland/AM, First Prize, Etching, 1952; Seattle/AM, **P.P.**, 1952, 53, 54, 59; Pasadena/AM, **P.P.**, 1952, 54, 57, 58, 59, 62; L. C. Tiffany Grant, 1952, 55; U. of Illinois, **P.P.**, 1954, 55; MMA, $500; American Color Print Society, Prize for Etching, 1954, 55; Los Angeles/County MA, Patronnaires Prize, 1957; Library of Congress, Pennell **P.P.**, 1957, 63; J. S. Guggenheim Fellowship, 1960; Los Angeles State College, Foundation Grants, 1965, 67; U. of North Carolina, **P.P.**, 1966; Los Angeles Printmaking Society, **P.P.**, 1968; and many others; AAAL/Hassam and Speicher Fund **P.P.**, 1977. **Address:** P.O. Box 26765, Los Angeles, Calif. 90026. **One-man Exhibitions:** (first) Felix Landau Gallery, 1950, also 1953, 55, 58, 60; de Young, 1952; Pasadena/AM, 1953; Santa Barbara/MA, 1953, 66; SFMA, 1956, 67; The Gallery, Denver, 1963; Comara Gallery, 1963; Laguna Beach (Calif.) Art Gallery, 1964; Oklahoma City U., 1964; Adele Bednarz Gallery, 1965, 68; Lincoln, Mass./De Cordova, 1967; Ventura College, 1969; Heath Gallery, Atlanta, 1969; Louisiana State U., 1969; California State College, Dominguez Hills, 1969; California Institute of the Arts, Valencia, 1970; U. of Colorado, 1972; Mount St. Mary's College, Los Angeles, 1979. **Group:** MMA, 1952; WMAA, 1952, 53, 55, 56, 58; U. of Illinois, 1953, 55, 58, 59, Fifty Contemporary American Printmakers, 1956; SRGM, Younger American Painters, 1954; Carnegie, 1955; Sao Paulo, 1955; SFMA, Art in the Twentieth Century, 1955; Corcoran, 1957, 59; Chicago/AI, 1957; VMFA, 1958; PCA, American Prints Today, circ., 1959-62; USIA, 30 Contemporary American Prints, circ., 1964; Taiheiyo Art Association, Tokyo,

I International, LX Annual, 1964; California Society of Printmakers, 50th Anniversary Exhibition, 1964; New York World's Fair, 1964-65; Temple U., Rome, 1967; Brooklyn Museum, Print Biennial, 1968; Santa Barbara/MA, Artist-Teachers in Southern California, 1975; SFMA, Painting and Sculpture in California: The Modern Era, 1976; Laguna Beach Art Museum, Southern California 100, 1977; The College of St. Rose, Albany, N.Y., Draw 80, 1980. **Collections:** Bibliotheque Nationale; Brooklyn Museum; California State U., Los Angeles; Cornell U.; Cranbrook; Detroit/Institute; U. of California; U. of Colorado; Dallas/MFA; U. of Delaware; Grunwald Foundation; U. of Illinois; Ithaca College; Karachi; Library of Congress; Lincoln, Mass./De Cordova; Lindenwood College; Los Angeles/County MA; MMA; Montana State U.; NYPL; National Gallery; U. of North Carolina; U. of North Dakota; Oakland/AM; Olivet College; Orange Coast College; Otis Art Institute; PMA; Pasadena/AM; Potsdam/SUNY; SFMA; St. Lawrence U.; Seattle/AM; Southern Illinois U.; State of California; USIA; Utica; VMFA; Victoria and Albert Museum; Western Michigan U.; Western New Mexico U.; U. of Wisconsin; College of Wooster.

ENGMAN, ROBERT. b. 1927, Belmont, Mass. **Studied:** RISD, 1948-52, BFA; Yale U. (with Josef Albers, Jose de Rivera), 1952-54, MFA. US Navy, 1944-46. **Taught:** Yale U., 1954-64; U. of Pennsylvania, 1963-; RISD, 1951-52. **Awards:** NAD, Samuel F. B. Morse Fellowship, 1963-64. **Commissions:** MIT, Independence Park, Jerusalem; City of New York; Girard Bank, Philadelphia; U. of Pennsylvania. **Address:** 37 Maple Dr., Haverford, PA 19041. **Dealer:** Fischbach Gallery, NYC. **One-man Exhibitions:** (first) The Stable Gallery, 1960, also 1962; Kanegis Gallery, 1967; John Bernard Myers Gallery, NYC, 1972; Fischbach Gallery, NYC, 1978. **Retrospective:** MIT, 1966. **Group:** ICA, Boston, 1959; MOMA, Recent Sculpture USA, 1959; Sao Paulo, 1961; SRGM, 1962; WMAA, 1965; Los Angeles/County MA, American Sculpture of the Sixties, 1967. **Collections:** Franchard Corp.; Container Corp. of America, NYC; MOMA; Revere; WMAA; MIT; Wellesley College; Yale U. **Bibliography:** Downes, ed.

ERLEBACHER, MARTHA MEYER. b. 1937, Jersey City, N.J. **Studied:** Gettysburg College, 1955-56; Pratt Institute, 1956-60, BA, Industrial Design, 1963, MFA, Ed. **Taught:** School Art League, NYC, 1962, 64; Pratt Institute, 1964-65; Parsons School of Design, NYC, 1965-66; Philadelphia College of Art, 1966-. **Awards:** Yaddo Fellowship, 1966, 77; Ingram Merrill Foundation, grant, 1978; National Endowment for the Arts, 1982. **Address:** c/o Dealer. **Dealer:** Schoelkopf Gallery, NYC. **One-man Exhibitions:** The Other Gallery, Philadelphia, 1967; Robert Schoelkopf Gallery, 1973, 75, 78, 79, 85; Dart Gallery, Chicago, 1976, 83; U. of Connecti-

Martha Mayer Erlebacher *Girl on Cushions* 1983

cut (two-man), 1977; PFA, 1978; U. of North Carolina, 1983. **Group:** St. Cloud State College, New Realism, '69, 1969; Yale U., American Drawing, 1970-1973, 1973; PMA/Museum of the Philadelphia Civic Center, Woman's Work, 1974; Library of Congress, National Exhibition of Prints, 1975; St. Joseph/Albrecht, Drawing-America: 1976, 1976; PMA, 300 Years of American Art, 1976; Chicago/AI, Drawings of the '70s, 1977; PMA, Contemporary Drawings, II, 1979; U. of Missouri, Kansas City, The Opposite Sex: A Realistic Perspective, 1979; Brooklyn Museum, Drawings in Black and White: 1970-1979, 1980; PAFA, Contemporary American Realism, 1981; U. of California, Santa Barbara, A Heritage Renewed: Representational Drawings Today, 1983; SFMA, American Realism (Janss), circ., 1985. **Collections:** Ball State U.; Cleveland/MA; Flint/Institute; Fort Wayne/AM; Harvard U.; Library of Congress; U. of Michigan; U. of North Carolina; U. of Notre Dame; PAFA; PMA; The Pennsylvania State U.; St. Joseph/Albrecht; Yale U.

ERNST, JIMMY. b. June 24, 1920, Cologne, Germany. **d.** February 6, 1984, NYC. **Studied:** Cologne-Lindenthal Real-Gymnasium; Altona Arts and Crafts School. To USA, 1938. **Taught:** U. of Colorado, summers, 1954, 56; Museum of Fine Arts of Houston, 1956; Brooklyn College, 1951-; Pratt Institute; lectures extensively. Sent by US State Department to USSR, 1961. **Commissions:** General Motors Technical Center, Detroit (10-ft. mural); NBC-TV, "Producers' Showcase," 1954 (plastic sculpture signature); Abbott Laboratories, 1955; *Fortune* magazine, 1955, 61 (paintings); NBC-TV, "Playwrights '56" (welded steel sculpture signature, with Albert Terris); American resident Lines, USS *President Adams*, 1956 (mural); Continental National Bank, Lincoln, Neb., 1956 (96-ft. mural); Envoy Towers, 300 East 46th Street, NYC, 1960 (relief mural). **Awards:** Pasadena/AM, Hattie Brooks Stevens Memorial **P.P.**, 1946; WMAA, Juliana Force Memorial **P.P.**, 1951; Chicago/AI, Norman Wait Harris Bronze Medal, 1954; Brandeis U., Creative Arts Award, 1957; Guggenheim Foundation Fellowship, 1961. **One-man Exhibitions:** (first) Norlyst Gallery, NYC, 1941; Philadelphia Art Alliance, 1948; Grace Borgenicht Gallery, Inc., 1951-55, 1957, 61, 62, 68, 71, 72, 76; Walker, 1954; Silvermine Guild, 1955; Houston/MFA, 1956; Brandeis U., 1957; Detroit/Institute, 1963; PAFA, 1965; West Palm Beach/Norton, 1965; Des Moines, 1966; Arts Club of Chicago, 1968; Harmon Gallery, Naples, Fla., 1981; Guild Hall, 1985; Century Association, 1985. **Group:** Pasadena/AM, 1946; Brooklyn Museum, Watercolor Biennial; California Palace, 1952; U. of Colorado, 1953, 54, 56; Detroit/Institute, 1953, 59; *Life* magazine, Painters under 35, NYC, 1954; MMA, 100 Years of American Painting, 1954; SRGM, Younger American Painters, 1954; American Embassy, Paris, American Drawing, 1954; Toronto, 1954; Toledo/MA, 1954, 55; Carnegie, 1955; WMAA, Young America, 1955; XXVIII Venice Biennial, 1956; U. of Nebraska, 1956; U. of Illinois, 1957; Brooklyn Museum, Golden Years of American Drawing, 1957; Brussels World's Fair, 1958; NIAL, 1958, 60, 65; PAFA, 1959, 65; Chicago/AI, Directions in American Painting, 1960; WMAA Annual, 1966; Washburn U. of Topeka, 1966; WMAA, Art of the U.S. 1670-1966, 1966; Honolulu Academy, 1967. **Collections:** Allentown/AM; Bielefeld; Brandeis U.; Brooklyn Museum; Buffalo/Albright; Chicago/AI; Clearwater/Gulf Coast; Cologne; U. of Colorado; U. of Connecticut; Corcoran; Cranbrook; Detroit/Institute; Hartford/Wadsworth; Houston-MFA; Lehigh U.; MMA; MOMA; Michigan State U.; U. of Michigan; NCFA; NYU; U. of Nebraska; PAFA; Pasadena/AM; SFMA; SRGM; Southern Illinois U.; Toledo/MA; Toronto; Tulsa-Philbrook; Utica; VMFA; WMAA; Walker; West Palm

Beach/Norton. **Bibliography:** Baur 7; Beekman; Blesh 1; Goodrich and Baur 1; Guggenheim, ed.; McCurdy, ed.; Janis and Blesh 1; Janis, S.; Mendelowitz; Motherwell and Reinhardt, eds.; Nordness, ed.; Pousette-Dart, ed.; Read 2; Ritchie 1; Archives.

ESTES, RICHARD. b. May 14, 1936, Evanston, Ill. **Studied:** Chicago/AI School, 1952-56. **Address:** 300 Central Park West, NYC 10024. **Dealer:** Allan Stone Gallery. **One-man Exhibitions:** Allan Stone Gallery, 1968, 69, 70, 72, 74, 83; Hudson River Museum, 1968; Chicago/Contemporary, 1974; New Gallery of Contemporary Art, Cleveland (three-man), 1979; Boston/MFA, 1978. **Group:** Milwaukee, Aspects of a New Realism, 1969; U. of Illinois, 1969; Newport Harbor, Directly Seen: New Realism in California, 1970; WMAA, 22 Realists, 1970; Syracuse/Everson, Cool Realism, 1970; Chicago/Contemporary, Radical Realism, 1971; Documenta V, Kassel, 1972; Stuttgart/WK, Amerikanischer Fotorealismus, circ., 1972; California State U., San Jose, East Coast/West Coast/New Realism, 1973; Serpentine Gallery, London, Photo Realism, 1973; Seattle, American Art: Third Quarter Century, 1973; Worcester/AM, Three Realists, 1974; VMFA, Twelve American Painters, 1974; US Department of the Interior, America 1976, 1976; NCFA, America as Art, 1976; Australian Council, Illusion and Reality, 1976; A.F.A., American Master Drawings and Watercolors, 1977; WMAA Annual, 1977; SRGM, Seven Photorealists from New York Collections, 1981; San Antonio/MA, Real, Really Real, Super Real, 1981; Fort Wayne, Photographs by the Photorealists, 1982; PAFA, Contemporary American Realism, circ., 1981; Huntington/Heckscher, Through the Looking Glass: Reflected Images in Contemporary Art, 1984. **Collections:** Aachen/Ludwig; American Broadcasting Co.; Chicago/AI; Chicago/Contemporary; Hirshhorn; Ivest-Wellington Corp.; Kansas City/Nelson; NMAA; SRGM; Toledo/MA; WMAA. **Bibliography:** *America 1976; Amerikanischer Fotorealismus;* Arthur 1, 2, 3; Honish and Jensen, eds.; Hunter, ed.; Lindy; Sager; *Three Realists.*

ETTING, EMLEN. **b.** August 24, 1905, Philadelphia, Pa. **Studied:** Harvard U., 1928; Academie de la Grande Chaumiere; with Andre Lhote in Paris. **Taught:** Philadelphia Museum School; Stella Elkins Tyler School of Fine Arts, Temple U.; Philadelphia College of Art. **Member:** President and co-founder, Philadelphia chapter of Artists Equity; National President of Artists Equity, 1955-57; Hon. President of The Alliance Française of Philadelphia; Society of Cincinnati; National Society of Mural Painters; Philadelphia Art Alliance and Athenaeum. **Commissions** (murals): Market Street National Bank, Philadelphia; Italian Consulate, Philadelphia. **Awards:** Italian Star of Solidarity; Chevalier de la Legion d'Honneur. **Address:** 1927 Panama Street, Philadelphia, PA 19103. **Dealer:** The Midtown Galleries. **One-man Exhibitions:** The Midtown Galleries, NYC, 1940, 43, 44, 46, 48, 50, 51, 57, 66, 71, 75, 80, 84; ICA, Boston; Cleveland/MA; Warwick Gallery, Philadelphia; Philadelphia Art Alliance, 1946; Phoenix, 1965; Century Association, 1979. **Retrospectives:** Florida Southern College, 1973; Allentown/MA, 1974. **Group:** WMAA; Corcoran; PAFA; Florida Southern College; VMFA; NAD; Audubon Artists; St. Louis/City; Philadelphia Art Alliance; Youngstown/Butler; Dayton/AI; Indiana U.; Illinois Wesleyan U.; West Palm Beach/Norton. **Collections:** Andover/Phillips; Atwater Kent Museum, La France Institute; PAFA; WMAA. **Bibliography: Etting;** Frost; Hall. Archives.

EVERGOOD, PHILIP HOWARD FRANCIS DIXON. **b.** October 26, 1901, NYC; **d.** March 11, 1973, Bridgewater, Conn. **Studied:** Eton College, England, 1914-18; Trinity Hall, Cambridge, 1918-20; U. of London, Slade School, 1920-23, with Henry Tonks; ASL, 1923-25, with George Luks, William Von Schlegell; Academie Julian, Paris, 1925, with Jean Paul Laurens, Andre Lhote. Traveled North Africa, USA and Europe, extensively. **Taught:** The Kalamazoo Institute of Arts; American Artists School, NYC; Contemporary School of Art, NYC; Iowa State College, 1952-58; U. of Minnesota, Duluth, 1955; Muhlenberg College; Settlement Music School, Philadelphia; extensive lecturing. Wrote for *Art Front* and *Direction* magazines. **Member:** NIAL; Artists Equity. Federal A.P.: Mural painting; Managing Supervisor, Easel Painting Division; mural for Richmond Hill (N.Y.) Public Library. **Commissions** (murals): Kalamazoo College; US Post Office, Jackson, Ga. **Awards:** Chicago/AI, The M.V. Kohnstamm Prize, 1935; MMA, **P.P.,** 1942; Carnegie, Hon. Men., 1945; Chicago/AI, W.H. Tuthill **P.P.,** 1946; Carnegie, Second Prize, 1949; PAFA, Carol H. Beck Gold Medal, 1949, Joseph E. Temple Gold Medal, 1958; Corcoran, Second Prize, 1951; AAAL Grant, 1956; Ford Foundation, **P.P.,** 1962. **One-man Exhibitions:** (first) Dudensing Gallery, NYC, 1927; Montross Gallery, NYC, 1929, 33, 35; Balzac Gallery, NYC, 1931; Denver/AM, 1936; Atheneum Gallery, Melbourne, 1937; ACA Gallery, 1938, 40, 42, 44, 46, 48, 51, 53, 1955-62; Kalamazoo/Institute, 1941; Norlyst Gallery, NYC, 1948; State U. of Iowa; Utica; Hartford/Wadsworth; Halkins College, 1953; Garelick's Gallery, Detroit, 1953, 55; Tulane U., 1957; Gallery 63, Inc., Rome, 1963, NYC, 1964; Hammer Gallery, 1967; Kennedy Gallery, 1972; Terry Dintenfass, Inc., 1974, 85; Hirshhorn, 1978; Bucknell U., 1986; ACA Gallery, NYC, 1986. **Retrospective:** U. of Minnesota, Duluth, 1955; WMAA, 1960. **Group:** An American

Group (Gallery), NYC; American Society of Painters, Sculptors and Graveurs; Salon d'Automne, Paris, 1924; NAD; Independent Artists, NYC; WMAA Annuals since 1934; PAFA; Chicago/AI; Brooklyn Museum; Corcoran; Carnegie; Venice Biennial. **Collections:** Arizona State College; Atlanta/AA; Baltimore/MA; Boston/MFA; Britannica; Brooklyn Museum; Carnegie; Chicago/AI; Corcoran; Cornell U.; Dallas/MFA; Denver/AM; Free Library of Philadelphia; Grolier Club; Hartford/Wadsworth; Harvard U.; IBM; U. of Illinois; Kalamazoo/ Institute; Lehigh U.; Library of Congress; Los Angeles/County MA; U. of Louisville; MMA; MOMA; Melbourne/National; Muhlenberg College; PAFA; Pepsi-Cola Co.; Santa Fe, N.M.; Smith College; Syracuse U.; WMAA; Youngstown/Butler. **Bibliography:** American Artists Congress, Inc.; **Baur 6, 7;** Biddle 4; Cheney; Eliot; Finkelstein; Genauer; Goodrich and Baur 1; Haftman; Kootz 2; **Lippard 3,** 5; McCurdy, ed.; Mendelowitz; Nordness, ed.; Pagano; Pousette-Dart, ed.; Reese; Richardson, E.P.; Rose, B., 1; Shapiro, ed. Archives.

F

FAHLSTROM, OYVIND. b. 1928, Sao Paulo, Brazil. **d.** November 9, 1976, Paris. To Sweden, 1939; to USA, 1961. Wrote plays, poetry, journalism, criticism, 1950-55; manifesto for concrete poetry (Stockholm), 1953; produced happenings, 1966-68. **Awards:** Sao Paulo Biennial, Hon. Men., 1959; Guggenheim Foundation Fellowship, 1964. **One-man Exhibitions:** (first) Numero Gallery, Florence, Italy, 1952; Daniel Cordier, Paris, 1959, 62; Galerie Blanche, Stockholm, 1959; Cordier & Ekstrom, Inc., 1964; Sideny Janis Gallery, 1967, 69, 71, 73; MOMA, circ., 1969; Galerie Rudolf Zwirner, 1969; U. of Minnesota, 1969; Baudoin Lebon Gallery, Paris, 1977; Redbird Galleries, Brooklyn, 1978; Arnold Herstand Gallery, NYC, 1984. **Group:** Exposition Phases, Paris, 1956; V Sao Paulo Biennial, 1959; Carnegie, 1960, 67; Venice Biennials, 1964, 66; EAT, NYC, 1966; Chicago/Contemporary, Pictures to Be Read/Poetry to Be Seen, 1967; Musée des Arts Decoratifs, 1967; Documenta IV, Kassel, 1968; ICA, U. of Pennsylvania, The Spirit of the Comics, 1969; Hayward Gallery, London, Pop Art, 1969; Los Angeles/County MA, Art & Technology, 1971; Tokyo/Modern, Swedish Art 1972, 1972. **Collections:** Cologne; Los Angeles/County MA; Stockholm/National; Stuttgart.

FAULKNER, FRANK. b. July 24, 1946, Sumter, South Carolina. **Studied:** U. of North Carolina, BFA, 1968, MFA, 1972. **Awards:** National Endowment for the Arts, 1974; SECCA 1976; American Institute of Architects, Collaborating Artist Award, 1976. **Address:** 150 West 26th Street, NYC 10010. **One-man Exhibitions:** North Carolina Central U., 1968; The Other Ear Gallery, Chapel Hill, N.C., 1968; Art Gallery of Chapel Hill (two-man), 1971; Southeastern Center for Contemporary Art, 1974, 77; Monique Knowlton Gallery, NYC, 1976, 77, 79, 80, 81, 82, 83; East Tennessee State U., 1977; Alexandra Monett Gallery, Brussels, 1978; Roy Boyd Gallery, Chicago, 1979; Davidson College, 1979; Galerie Haberman, Cologne, 1980; Arts Club of Chicago, 1981. **Group:** WMAA Biennial, 1975; The Pennsylvania State U., The Material Dominant, 1977; High Museum, Southwestern Painters and Sculptors, 1977; Phoenix, New York Now, 1979; Buffalo/Albright, Patterns, 1979; Wesleyan U., Bloomington, Pattern Painters, 1980. **Collections:** Becton Dickinson, & Co., Paramus, N.J.; Buffalo/Albright; Chase Manhattan Bank; Delaware Art Museum; The Hanes Corp.; Harris Bank, Chicago; Henkel Co., GMBH; Hirshhorn; Hollywood (Fla.) Federal Savings and Loan Assn.; NCFA; North Carolina State U.; U. of North Carolina; Owens-Corning Fiberglas Corp; The Pennsylvania State U.; Raleigh/NCMA; R.J. Reynolds Corp.; Smith College; Southeastern Baking Corp., Miami; Springfield, Mo./AM; Toledo/MA.

FEELEY, PAUL. b. July 27, 1913, Des Moines, Iowa; **d.** June 10, 1966, NYC. **Studied:** Menlo Junior College; privately with Hobart Jacobs, in California, and Cecilia Beaux, in NYC; ASL, with Thomas Hart Benton, George Bridgeman; Beaux-Arts Institute of Design, NYC. Traveled Spain, Morocco, Greece, USA. **Taught:** Cooper Union, 1936-39; Bennington College, 1940-66. US Marine Corps, 1943-46. **Member:** National Society of Mural Painters. **One-man Exhibitions:** (first) Palo Alto (Calif.) Public Library, 1929; New School for Social Research, 1948; Santa Barbara/MA, 1950; The Rose Rabow Gallery, San Francisco, 1951; Stanford U., 1951; Mills College, 1951; SFMA, 1951; Tibor de Nagy Gallery, 1955, 57, 58; Betty Parsons Gallery, 1960, 1962-66, 1970, 71; Kasmin Ltd., 1964, 65, 67; Nicholas Wilder Gallery, 1966; Smithsonian, 1970; Andre Emmerich Gallery, NYC, 1976. **Retrospective:** SRGM, 1968. **Group:** Walker, 1950; ICA, Boston, 1952; PAFA; The Kootz Gallery, NYC, New Talent, 1954; Chicago/AI; Lincoln, Mass./De Cordova, New Experiments in Art, 1963; Los Angeles/County MA, Post Painterly Abstraction, 1964; SRGM, American Drawings, 1964, also 1965; Systemic Painting, 1966; SFMA, The Colorists, 1965; MOMA, The Responsive Eye, 1965; Amsterdam/Stedelijk, New Shapes of Color, 1966; Mexico City/Nacional, 19th Olympiad, 1968. **Bibliography:** Alloway 3, 4; **Baro;** Battcock, ed.; Goossen 1. Archives.

FEININGER, LYONEL. b. July 17, 1871, NYC; **d.** January 13, 1956, NYC. Studied the violin with his father and played in concerts from the age of 12; went to Germany in 1880 to study music, but changed to painting. **Studied:** Kunstgewerbeschule, Hamburg; Academy of Fine Arts, Berlin, with Ernst Hancke, Woldemar Friedrich; Jesuit College, Liege, Belgium, 1887-91; Academie Colarossi, Paris, 1892-93. Traveled Europe, USA. **Taught:** Bauhaus, Weimar, 1919-24; Bauhaus, Dessau, 1925-33; Mills College, summers, 1936, 37. Cartoonist and illustrator for *Ulk* and *Lustige Blätter*, Berlin, 1893-1906; *Le Temoin*, Paris, 1906-07; and Chicago *Sunday Tribune*. A member of the Blue Four, 1924 (with Vassily Kandinsky,

Paul Klee, and Alexej von Jawlensky). **Commissions:** New York World's Fair, 1939 (murals for Marine Transport Building and Masterpieces of Art Building). **One-man Exhibitions:** Emil Richter Gallery, Dresden, 1919; Anger-Museum, Erfurt, Germany, 1920, 27, 29, 30; Kunst und Bucherstube, Erfurt, 1921; Goldschmidt-Wallerstein, Berlin, 1922, 25; Anderson Galleries, NYC, 1923; Wiesbaden, 1925; Neue Kunstfides, Dresden, 1925, 26, 31; Brunswick, 1926; Kassel, 1927; Staatliche Galerie Moritzburg, Halle, Germany, 1928; Anhalt Gallery, Dessau, 1929; Kunstverein, Prague, 1930; Mills College, 1936, 37; SFMA, 1937; Los Angeles/County MA, 1937; Seattle/AM, circ., 1937; Andover/Phillips, 1938; Curt Valentine Gallery, NYC, 1941, 44, 46, 48, 50, 52, 54; Buchholz Gallery, NYC, 1941, 43, 44; Karl Nierendorf Gallery, NYC, 1943; The Willard Gallery, 1943, 44; Dalzell Hatfield Gallery, 1944; Fort Worth, 1956; Harvard U., 1958; Detroit/Institute, 1964; R. N. Ketterer, Campione, Switzerland, 1965; Pasadena/AM, 1966; LaBoetie Gallery, NYC, 1966; MOMA, 1967; Marlborough-Gerson Gallery, Inc., 1969; A.A.A. Gallery, 1972; Serge Sabarsky Gallery, NYC, 1972, 74, 79; Haus der Kunst, Munich, 1973; Marlborough Gallery, Inc., NYC, 1974; Society of the Four Arts, 1976; AAA, NYC, 1974; Achim Moeller Fine Art Ltd., NYC, 1985; Acquavella Galleries, NYC, 1985; Phillips, 1985. **Retrospective:** Berlin, 1931, MOMA, 1944 (two-man); ICA, Boston, 1949; Jeanne Bucher, Paris, circ., Europe, 1950-51; Print Club of Cleveland, 1951; Hannover, circ., Europe, 1954-55; SFMA, circ., 1959-61. **Group:** Salon des Artistes Independants, Paris, 1911; Der Sturm, Berlin, 1917; Documenta I, Kassel, 1955; WMAA; Tate; Mannheim; Allentown/AM, The Blue Four and German Expressionism, 1974. **Collections:** Baltimore/MA; Buffalo/Albright; Chicago/AI; Cranbrook; U. of Houston; Kansas City/Nelson; Lehigh U.; MMA; MOMA; U. of Michigan; Milwaukee;

Minneapolis/Institute; PMA; Phillips; RISD; Raleigh/NCMA; SRGM; San Antonio/McNay; Seattle/AM; Toledo/MA; Utica; WMAA; Walker; Washington U. **Bibliography:** Barr 1; Baur 5, 7; Bazin; Beekman; Biddle 4; Blanchard; Blesh 1; Born; Brion 2; Brown; Bulliet 1; Cassou; Cheney; *Cityspace 1919-39*; Eliot; Feininger, T.L.; Flanagan; Frost; Goodrich and Baur 1; Haftman; Hess, H.; Hess, T.B., 1; Hulten; Hunter 6; Huyghe; Janis S.; Kouvenhoven; Kuh 1; Langui; Lee and Burchwood; MacAgy 2; McCurdy, ed.; Mendelowitz; Munsterberg; Murken-Altrogge; **Ness, ed.;** Neumeyer; Newmeyer; Pousette-Dart, ed.; Raynal 3, 4; Read 2; Richardson, E.P.; Rickey; Ritchie 1; Rose, B., 1; Rosenblum 1, 2; Roters; Sachs; Scheyer; Selz, P., 3; Sutton; Valentine 2; Verkauf; Wight 2; Wingler, ed. Archives.

FEITELSON, LORSER, b. 1898, Savannah, Ga.; **d.** May 24, 1978, Los Angeles, Calif. **Taught:** Art Center School, Los Angeles. **One-man Exhibitions:** The Daniel Gallery, NYC, 1924; San Diego, 1928; California Palace, 1928, 32; Los Angeles/County MA, 1929, 44; SFMA, 1944; Lucien Labaudt Gallery, San Francisco, 1949; San Antonio/McNay, 1955; Paul Rivas Gallery, Los Angeles, 1959 (two-man); Scripps College, 1958, 61; Long Beach/MA, 1962; Chapman College, Los Angeles, 1963; Occidental College, Los Angeles, 1965; Los Angeles, Art Association Galleries, 1968, 79; David Stuart Gallery, Los Angeles, 1977; WMAA, 1978; Jan Baum Gallery, Los Angeles, 1982; Tobey C. Moss Gallery, Los Angeles, 1983, 85. **Retrospectives:** Pasadena/AM, 1952; Los Angeles Municipal Art Gallery, 1972; SFMA, 1980. **Group:** Brooklyn Museum, 1936; SFMA, 1936; MOMA, Fantastic Art, DADA, Surrealism, 1936; Chicago/AI, Abstract and Surrealist Art, 1948; U. of Illinois, 1950, 51, 53, 65; Sao Paulo, 1955; WMAA, 1955, Annuals, 1965, 67; MOMA, The Responsive Eye, 1965;

Sacramento/Crocker, 1967, 68; Pasadena/AM, West Coast: 1945-1969, 1969; Museum of Fine Arts, St. Petersburg, Color in Control, 1969; Sacramento/Crocker, Century of California Painting, 1970; VMFA, American Painting, 1970; Painting and Sculpture in California: The Modern Era, 1976; Rutgers U.; Surrealism and American Art: 1931-47, 1977. **Collections:** Atlantic-Richfield Co.; Bank of Omaha; Brooklyn Museum; Craig Elwood Associates; Great Western Savings and Loan Association; Hirshhorn; Industrial Electronics Engineers, Inc.; Lansing Sound Corp.; Long Beach/MA; Los Angeles/County MA; MOMA; SFMA; Xerox Corp. **Bibliography:** *Avant-Garde Painting and Sculpture;* Baur 7; *Black and White Are Colors;* **Feitelson and Lundeberg;** Flanagan; Rickey. Archives.

FELTUS, ALAN. b. May 1, 1943, Washington, D.C. **Studied:** Tyler School of Art, Philadelphia, 1961-62;

Alan Feltus *Another Summer* 1984

Cooper Union, 1966, BFA; Yale U., 1968, MFA, with Jack Tworkov, Lester Johnson; Jerry Farnsworth School, No. Truro, Mass, 1959. Traveled Europe, Guatemala. **Taught:** Dayton Art Institute School, 1968-70; American U., 1972-85. **Awards:** National Endowment for the Arts, 1981; L. C. Tiffany Grant, 1980; Prix de Rome Fellowship, 1970-72. **Address:** Route 1, Box 344, Hughesville, Md. 20736. **Dealer:** The Forum Gallery, NYC. **One-man Exhibitions:** (first) American Academy, Rome, 1972; Jacobs Ladder Gallery, Washington, D.C., 1973; The Forum Gallery, 1976, 80, 83, 85; Northern Virginia Community College, Annandale, 1976. **Group:** AAIAL, 1977, 79, 81; Corcoran, Ten Plus Ten Plus Ten, 1982; NAD, 1982, 84, 86. **Collections:** California Palace; Dayton/AI; Hirshhorn; Little Rock/MFA; NMAA; Oklahoma; Springfield, Mass./MFA; Trenton/State; U. of Virginia, Charlottesville.

FERBER, HERBERT. b. April 30, 1906, NYC. **Studied:** City College of New York, 1923-26; Columbia U. School of Dental and Oral Surgery, 1927, BS, 1930, DDS; Beaux-Arts Institute of Design, NYC, 1927-30; NAD, 1930. Associate Fellow, Morse College, Yale U., 1967-. **Taught:** U. of Pennsylvania, 1963-64; Columbia U. School of Dental and Oral Surgery; Rutgers U., 1965-67; Yale U., 1967-; Rice U., 1979. **Commissions:** B'nai Israel Synagogue, Millburn, N.J., 1950; Brandeis U., Jewish Chapel, 1955; Temple Anshe Chesed, Cleveland, 1955; Temple of Aaron, St. Paul, 1955; WMAA, Sculpture as Environment, 1961; Rutgers U., 1968; John F. Kennedy Federal Office Building, Boston, 1969; American Dental Association Building, Chicago, 1974. **Awards:** Beaux-Arts Institute of Design, NYC, Paris Prize, 1929; L. C. Tiffany Grant, 1930; MMA, Artists for Victory, $1,000 Prize, 1942; ICA, London/Tate, International Unknown Political Prisoner Competition, 1953; Guggenheim Foundation Fellowship, 1969; AFA, Reynolds Metal Award, 1979. **Address:** 44 MacDougal Street, NYC 10012. **Dealer:** M. Knoedler & Co. Inc., NYC. **One-man Exhibitions:** (first) The Midtown Galleries, 1937, also 1943; Betty Parsons Gallery, 1947, 50, 53; The Kootz Gallery, NYC, 1955, 57; Columbia U., 1960; Andre Emmerich Gallery, 1960, 62, 67, 69, 70, 71, 72, 73, 75, 76, 77; U. of Vermont, 1964; Rutgers U., 1968; M. Knoedler & Co., Inc., NYC, 1978, 79, 80, 81, 83, 84, 85, 86; Roy Boyd Gallery, Chicago, 1978; Des Moines, 1981; Martha White Gallery, Louisville, 1981; Weintraub Gallery, NYC, 1983; Hokin Gallery, Palm Beach, Fla., 1984; M. Knoedler & Co., Inc., Zurich, 1984; Pittsfield/Berkshire, 1984; Adams-Middleton Gallery, Dallas, 1985. **Retrospectives:** Bennington College, 1958; WMAA, 1961; SFMA, 1962; Walker, circ., 1962-63; Houston/MFA, circ., 1981. **Group:** NAD, 1930; Brooklyn Museum; PAFA, 1931, 42, 43, 45, 46, 54, 58; Corcoran, 1932; Philadelphia Art Alliance, 1933; American Artists Congress, 1936, 40; Musée du Jeu de Paume, 1938; Sculptors Guild, 1938-42, 1944, 48, 64; Golden Gate International Exposition, San Francisco/AI, 1940, 41, 45; WMAA Annuals, 1940, 42, 1945-; Federation of Modern Painters and Sculptors, 1941-49; A.F.A., Sculpture in Wood, 1941; MMA, 1942; Sao Paulo, 1951; MOMA, Abstract Painting and Sculpture in America, 1951; MOMA, Fifteen Americans, circ., 1952; Tate, 1953; WMAA, The New Decade, 1954-55; Brussels World's Fair, 1958; Carnegie, 1958; A.F.A., God and Man in Art, circ., 1958-59; Documenta II, Kassel, 1959; St. Paul Gallery, Drawings, USA, 1961; Baltimore/MA; Cranbrook; Battersea Park, London, International Sculpture Exhibition, 1963; Musée Rodin, Paris, 1965; MOMA, The New American Painting and Sculpture, 1969; Newport, R.I., Monumenta, 1974; NCFA; Sculpture, American Directions, 1945-1975, 1975; Indianapolis, 1978; Rutgers U., Vanguard American Sculpture, 1919-1939, 1979; WMAA, Decade of Transition, 1940-1950, 1981; Newark Museum, American Bronze Sculpture, 1850 to the Present, 1984; WMAA, The Third Dimension, 1984; Sarah Lawrence College, Sculpture Expressions, 1985. **Collections:** Bennington College; Brandeis U.; Buffalo/Albright; Carnegie; Cranbrook; Detroit/Institute; Grand Rapids; Houston/MFA; U. of Indiana; Indiana U.; MMA; MOMA; NYU; National Gallery; Newark Museum; Paris/Beaubourg; Pasadena/AM; Pittsfield/Berkshire; Princeton U.; Purchase/SUNY; Rutgers U.; Storm King Art Center; U. of Vermont; WMAA; Walker; Williams College; Yale U. **Bibliography:** Baur 5, 7; Blesh 1; Brumme; Chipp; Craven, W.; Flanagan; Giedion-Welcker 1; Goodrich and Baur 1; **Goosen 5;** Henning; Hunter 6; Hunter, ed.; Krauss 2; McCurdy, ed.; Marter, Tarbell, and Wechsler; *Monumenta;* Motherwell and Reinhardt, eds.; Phillips, Lisa; Read 3; Ritchie, 3; Rose, B., 1; Rubin 1; Seuphor 3; Strachan; Trier 1. Archives.

FERRARA, JACKIE. b. 1929, Detroit, Mich. Autodidact. **Commissions:** Minneapolis College of Art, 1978; Federal Building, Carbondale, Ill., 1980; Laumeier Sculpture Park, St. Louis, Mo., 1981; Memorial Lake Park, Norwalk, Ohio, 1984; Columbus, 1984; Loch Haven Art Center, 1985. **Awards:** CAPS, 1971, 75; National Endowment for the Arts, 1973, 77; Guggenheim Foundation Fellowship, 1976. **Address:** 121 Prince Street, NYC 10012. **Dealer:** Max Protetch Gallery, NYC. **One-man Exhibitions:** (first) A.M. Sachs Gallery, NYC, 1973, 74; Daniel Weinberg Gallery, San Francisco, 1975; Max Protetch Gallery, Washington, D.C., 1975; Max Protetch Gallery, NYC, 1975, 76, 77, 78, 79, 81, 82, 83, 84; Ohio State U., 1977; Minneapolis College of Art, 1978; U. of Rhode Island, 1979; Glen Hanson Gallery, Minneapolis, 1979; U. of Southern California, 1980; U. of Massachusetts, 1980; Okhun-Thomas Gallery, St. Louis,

1980; Laumeier Sculpture Park, St. Louis, 1981; Marianne Deson Gallery, Chicago, 1981; U. of Miami, 1982; Galleriet, Lund, Sweden, 1983; Janus Gallery, Venice, Calif., 1983; U. of North Carolina, 1983; Susan Montezinos Gallery, Philadelphia, 1984. **Group:** WMAA Annual, 1970; GEDOK, Hamburg, American Woman Artist Show, 1972; WMAA Biennials, 1973, 79; Indianapolis, 1974, 80; U. of North Carolina, 1979; XXXIX Venice Biennial, 1980; ICA, U. of Pennsylvania, Connections, 1983; Cleveland Center for Contemporary Art, Artists + Architects, Challenges in Collaboration, 1985. **Collections:** Baltimore/MA; Carnegie; Cincinnati/AM; Columbus; Cornell U.; Des Moines; Humlebaek/Louisiana; Indianapolis; Laumeier Sculpture Park; Loch Haven Art Center; MMA; MOMA; U. of Massachusetts, Amherst; U. of Miami; Minneapolis College of Art; NCFA; U. of North Carolina; St. Lawrence U.; St. Louis/City; WMAA.

FERREN, JOHN. b. October 17, 1905, Pendleton, Ore.; **d.** July 24, 1970, Southampton, N.Y. **Studied:** Academie de la Grande Chaumiere; Sorbonne; U. of Florence; U. of Salamanca; Academie Ranson, Paris; Academie Colarossi, Paris. Traveled Europe, USA, Middle East; resided, worked in Paris, 1931-38. Civilian employee of War Department and OWI, 1941-45; Psychological Warfare Division, SHAEF (Propaganda Chief, Italian Radio Section); Algiers headquarters (Chief of Publications for France); received Bronze Star. **Taught:** Brooklyn Museum School, 1946-50; Cooper Union, 1947-54; Art Center School, Los Angeles, summer, 1948; Queens College, 1952-70; UCLA, summer, 1953; privately in New York; U. of Saskatchewan, summer, 1960; Yale U., summer, 1962; lectured extensively and published essays. Advisory work on *The Trouble with Harry* (1955) and *Vertigo* (1958), films directed by Alfred Hitchcock. **Member:** Advisory Council to the School of Art and Architecture, Yale U., 1959-62. **One-man Exhibitions:** Art Center, San Francisco, 1930; Galerie Zak, Paris, 1932; Gallerie Pierre, Paris, 1936; Pierre Matisse Gallery, 1936, 37, 38; Minneapolis/Institute, 1936; Howard Putzell Gallery, Hollywood, 1936; SFMA, 1936, 52; Arts Club of Chicago, 1937; Galerie Beaune, Paris, 1938; The Willard Gallery, 1942; Art Project Gallery, Hollywood, 1942; Kleemann Gallery, NYC, 1947, 49; Santa Barbara/MA, 1952; Tacoma, 1952; Portland (Ore.) Arts Club, 1952; Alexander Iolas Gallery, 1953; UCLA, 1953; U. of Washington, 1953; The Stable Gallery, 1954, 55, 56, 57, 58; Phillips, 1958; U. of Wisconsin, 1959; Glassboro State College, 1959; Trenton State College, 1959; Rose Fried Gallery, 1962, 1965-68; Queens College, 1963; Centre d'Art Gallery, Beirut, Lebanon, 1964; American Embassy, London, 1965; Pageant Gallery, Florida, 1968; Southampton College, 1968 (two-man); A.M. Sachs Gallery, 1969, 72, 74, 75, 77, 82, 83, 85; Southampton/Parrish, 1969; The Century Assn., NYC, 1971; Katharine Rich Perlow Gallery, NYC, 1985, 86. **Group:** Los Angeles/County MA Annuals, 1925-29; SFMA Annuals, 1925-29; California Palace, 1931; American Abstract Artists 1934, 35, 37; Musée de l'Orangerie, Paris, 1937; Salon des Surindependants, Paris, 1937; Royal Institute of the Arts, Copenhagen, 1937; Corcoran, 1940; Chicago/AI, 1947; Brooklyn Museum, 1949; U. of Minnesota, Pioneers in American Abstract Art, 1951; Ninth Street Exhibition, NYC, 1951; MOMA, Abstract Painting and Sculpture in America, 1951; WMAA Annuals, 1952, 55, 56, 58, The 1930's, 1968; Carnegie 1955; MOMA, 7 American Watercolorists, circ., Europe, 1956; Chicago/AI, 1956; U. of Illinois, 1957; WMAA, Nature in Abstraction, 1958; U. of Kentucky, Graphics, 1958, 59; Pasadena/AM, A Decade in the Contemporary Gallery, 1959; ART:USA:59, NYC, 1959; Walker, 60 American Painters, 1960; SRGM, Abstract Expressionists and Imagists, 1961; A.F.A., Affinities, circ., 1962; PAFA, 1964, 66; Gallery of Modern Art, NYC, 1965. **Collections:** Allentown/AM; Art of This Century (Peggy Guggenheim); Arts Club of Chicago; Birmingham, Ala./MA; Brandeis U.; Buffalo/Albright; California Palace; U. of California; Cedar Rapids/AA; Cleveland/MA; Detroit/Institute; Hartford/Wadsworth; High Museum; Hirshhorn; Los Angeles/County MA; MOMA; NYU; U. of Nebraska; Norfolk/Chrysler; Oklahoma; PMA; Phillips; SFMA; SRGM; Sacramento/Crocker; Santa Barbara/MA; Scripps College; Tel Aviv; U. of Texas; Tougaloo College; WGMA; WMAA; Washington U.; Yale U. **Bibliography:** Baur 5, 7; Chipp; Downes, ed.; Eliot; Frost; Goodrich and Baur 1; Guggenheim, ed.; Hayter 2; Janis, S.; Lane and Larsen; Passloff; Ritchie 1; Rose, B., 1, 4; Sandler 1. Archives.

FIENE, ERNEST. b. November 2, 1894, Eberfeld, Germany; **d.** August 10, 1965, Paris, France. To USA, 1912; citizen 1928. **Studied:** NAD, 1914-18; Beaux-Arts Institute of Design, NYC, 1916-18; ASL, 1923; Academie de la Grande Chaumiere, 1929; Florence, Italy (fresco painting), 1932. Traveled Europe, Mexico, USA. **Taught:** Westchester County Center, 1930-31; Colorado Springs Fine Arts Center, 1935; Cooper Union, 1938-39; ASL, 1938-65; Ogunquit School of Painting, 1950-51; Famous Artists Schools, Inc., 1956-65; NAD, 1960-65. **Member:** Artists Equity (Hon. President); NAD; Century Association; ASL. **Commissions** (portraits): Columbia U.; New York Hospital; Ohio U.; Abbott Laboratories; (series of paintings); Scruggs, Vandervoort, and Barney; Gimbel's, Philadelphia; Central Needle Trades High School of New York; (murals): International Ladies' Garment Workers Union, NYC; Abraham Lincoln High School, Brooklyn (2); US Post Office, Canton, Mass.; New Interior Building, Washington, D.C. **Awards:** Guggenheim Foundation Fellowship, 1932; Chicago/AI, Norman Wait Harris Prize, 1937; Corcoran, William A. Clark Prize, 1938; Carnegie, Hon. Men., 1938; Chicago/AI, Ada S. Garrett Prize, 1940; Library of Congress, Pennell **P.P.**, 1940; Library of Congress, First Pennell **P.P.**, 1944; NAD, Edwin Palmer Memorial Prize, 1961. **One-man Exhibitions:** (first) Whitney Studio Club, NYC, 1923; The New Gallery, NYC, 1924; Kraushaar Galleries, 1927; The Downtown Gallery, 1928, 33, 36; Rehn Galleries, 1930-32; Western Association of Art Museum Directors, circ., 1938; A.A.A. Gallery, NYC, 1938-41, 1945; M. Knoedler & Co., 1949-51; The Midtown Galleries, 1959; Stonington Gallery, Conn., 1963; Bay Head Art Center, 1964; Washington Irving Gallery, NYC, 1969; ACA Gallery, 1981. **Group:** WMAA, 1930-45; Carnegie, 1930-45; PAFA, 1930-45; NAD; MOMA; Youngstown/Butler; Chicago/AI, 1930-33, 1936-45; Corcoran, 1931-45; MMA; Boston/MFA. **Collections:** ASL; Abbott Laboratories; Boston/MFA; Bowdoin College; Britannica; Brooklyn Museum; California Palace; Chicago/AI; Cleveland/MA; Columbia U.; Dartmouth College; Denver/AM; Detroit/Institute; Drake U.; Library of Congress; Los Angeles/County MA; MIT; MMA; MOMA; NAD; NYPL; U. of Nebraska; Newark Museum; Ogunquit; Ohio U.; PAFA; Phillips; SFMA; Syracuse U.; Tel Aviv; Terre Haute/Swope; Tulsa/Philbrook; WMAA; Yale U. **Bibliography:** American Artists Congress, Inc.; American Artists Group Inc. 1, 2, 3; Cahill and Barr, eds.; Goodrich and Baur 1; Hall; Pearson 1; Phillips 1; Reese; Richardson, E.P.; *Woodstock: An American Art Colony, 1902-1977.* Archives.

FISCHL, ERIC. b. 1948, NYC. **Studied:** California Institute of the Arts, 1972, BFA. **Taught:** Nova Scotia College of Art, 1974-78. **Address:** 77 Reade Street, NYC 10007. **Dealer:** Mary Boone Gallery, NYC. **One-man Exhibitions:** Dalhousie Art Gallery, Halifax, 1975; Studio, Halifax, 1976; Galerie B., Montreal, 1976, 78; Edward Throp Gallery, NYC, 1980, 81, 82; U. of Akron, 1980; Sable-Castelli Gallery, Ltd., Toronto, 1981, 82, 85; U. of Colorado, 1982; U. of Montreal, 1983; Larry Gagosian Gallery, Los Angeles, 1983; Mario Diacono Gallery, Rome, 1983; Mary Boone Gallery, 1984, 86, 87; Multiples, 1983; Mendel Art Gallery, Saskatoon,

Eric Fischl *Salad Days (from "The Rooms of the House")* 1985

Canada, 1985; Eindhoven, circ., 1985. **Retrospective:** WMAA, 1986. **Group:** P. S. 1, Long Island City, The Big Drawing Show, 1978; WMAA, Focus on the Figure, 1982; WMAA Biennial, 1983, 85; Bonn, Back to the USA, circ., 1983; Indianapolis, 1984; MOMA, International Survey of Contemporary Painting and Sculpture, 1984; XLI Venice Biennial, 1984; Biennale de Paris, 1985; Carnegie, International, 1985. **Collections:** Houston/MFA; MMA; MOMA; National Gallery; SFMA; WMAA. **Bibliography:** Danto; Murken-Altrogge; Pincus-Witten 2.

FISH, JANET. b. May 18, 1938, Boston, Mass. **Studied:** Smith College, BA, 1960; Yale U., MFA, 1963. **Awards:** Chicago/AI; MacDowell Colony Fellowship, 1968, 69, 72; Norman Wait Harris Award, 1974; Australia Council for the Arts, Grant, 1975. **Taught:** Skowhegan School, 1973, 74; School of Visual Arts, NYC, 1968-69; U. of Bridgeport, 1971; Parsons School of Design, NYC, 1974; Syracuse U., 1974; U. of Chicago, 1976. **Member:** Board of Governors, Skowhegan School. **Address:** 101 Prince Street, NYC 10012. **Dealer:** Robert Miller Gallery, Inc., NYC. **One-man Exhibitions:** (first) Fairleigh Dickinson U., 1967; Stony Brook/SUNY, 1967, 78; Ours Gallery, NYC, 1968; Mercer Street, NYC, 1969; The Kornblee Gallery, NYC, 1971, 72, 73, 74, 75, 76; Pace College, NYC, 1972; Russell Sage College, 1972; Galerie Alexandra Monett, Brussels, 1974; Galerie Kostiner-Silvers, Montreal, 1974; Hogarth Gallery, Paddington, Sydney, Australia, 1975; Tolarno Gallery, Stokitha, Victoria, 1975, 77; Phyllis Kind Gallery, Chicago, 1976; Robert Miller Gallery, Inc., NYC, 1978, 79, 80, 83, 85; Union College, 1981; Wilmington, 1982; Texas Gallery, Houston, 1983, 85; Columbus (Ga.) College, 1983; Columbia, S.C./MA, 1984; Smith College, 1985. **Group:** A.F.A., Still Life Today, 1970-71; NIAL, 1972; Chicago/AI, 1972, 74; Indi-

Janet Fish   *Flying Kites*   1986

anapolis, 1972; Lakeview Center, American Women; 20th Century, 1972; Randolph-Macon College, Paintings by Some Contemporary American Women, 1972; Cleveland/MA, 32 Realists, 1972; A.F.A., The Realist Revival, 1972; WMAA, American Drawings: 1963-1973, 1973; Yale U., 7 Realists, 1973; PMA/Museum of the Philadelphia Civic Center, Focus, 1974; Tokyo Biennial, 1974; Queens Museum, New Images, 1974; U. of North Carolina, 1975, 78; Ohio State U., Concept of Reality: Recent Art, 1975; Minnesota/MA, Drawings USA/75, 1975; Baltimore/MA, Super Realism, 1975; US Department of the Interior, America 1976, circ., 1976; PAFA, 8 Contemporary American Realists, 1977, Centro Colombo Americano, Bogota, 16 Realists, 1979; Lincoln, Mass./De Cordova, Born in Boston, 1979; Tulsa/Philbrook, Realism-Photorealism, 1980; NAD, 1980; Yale U., Twenty Artists: Yale School of Art, 1950-1970, 1981; San Antonio/MA, Real, Really Real, Super Real, circ., 1981; AAIAL, 1982, 84; Houston/Contemporary, American Still Life, 1945-1983, 1983. **Collections:**

A.F.A.; Art Museum of South Texas; AT&T; American Airlines, Amstar Corp.; Buffalo/Albright; Chase Manhattan Bank; Chicago/AI; Cleveland/MA; Colby College; Commerce Bank of Kansas City; Dallas/MFA; Heublein Inc.; U. of Indiana; MMA; Minneapolis/Institute; IBM; Minnesota/MA; National Gallery; Newark Museum; New York State Health and Hospitals Corp.; Oberlin College; Oklahoma; PAFA; Port Authority of New York & New Jersey; RISD; Union Camp Corp.; U. of Sydney; WMAA; Wellington Management Corp; Westmoreland County/MA; Yale U. **Bibliography:** *America 1976;* Arthur 1, 2, 3, 4; Goodyear; *New in the Seventies.*

FISHER, JOEL. b. June 6, 1947, Salem, Ohio. **Studied:** Kenyon College, 1969, BA, magna cum laude. Traveled Europe; resided England, 1977-82. **Member:** Artists Equity. **Awards:** PBK, 1969; Kress Foundation Fellowship, 1967, 68; Thomas J. Watson Traveling Fellowship, 1969; DAAD Grant, 1973-74; National Endowment for the Arts, 1984; Howard Foundation Fellowship, 1986. **Taught:** Shiller College, Berlin, 1973-74; Goldsmith College, London, 1979; Bath Academy of Art, 1980-82; RISD, 1985. **Address:** 350 Bowery, NYC 10012. **Dealer:** Diane Brown Gallery, NYC. **One-man Exhibitions:** Robert Brown Gallery, Gambier, Ohio, 1968; The Mansfield (Ohio) Arts Center, 1970; Whitney Museum Independent Study Program, NYC, 1970; Corso's Wine Shop, Salem, Ohio, 1971; Nigel Greenwood Inc., Ltd., London, 1971, 76, 78, 79, 82, 86; Victoria & Albert Museum, 1971; Galeria Marilena Bonomo, Bari, Italy, 1972, 76; Galerie Sonnabend, Paris, 1972, 74; New Gallery, Cleveland, 1973; Galerie Stampa, Basel, 1973; Aachen/NG, 1974; Galerie Folker Skulima, Berlin, 1974, 75; Galerie Joachim Ernst, Hannover, 1975; Galleria Forma, Genoa, 1975; 112 Greene Street, NYC, 1975; Monchengladbach, 1975; Max Protetch

Joel Fisher   *Family*   1987

Gallery, Washington, D.C., 1975; Galerie Salvatore Ala, Milan, 1976, 78; Galeria 2, Stuttgart, 1976; Max Protetch Gallery, NYC, 1976, 77; Galleric Akumulatory, Poznan, Poland, 1977; Brussels/Beaux-Arts, 1977; Oliver Dowling Gallery, Dublin, 1977; Galerie Kiki Maier-Hahn, Dusseldorf, 1977; Lia Rumma Studia d'Arte, Naples, 1977; Amsterdam/Stedelijk, 1978; Galeria Foksal, Warszawa, 1978; Galerie Michele Lachowsky, Brussels, 1979, 81; Matt's Gallery, London, 1979, 84; Graeme Murray Gallery, Edinburgh, 1979; Galerie Farideh Cadot, 1980, 83, 86; Galerie Toni Gerber, Bern, 1980, 84; New 57 Gallery, Edinburgh, 1980; LYC Museum, Banks, Cumbria, 1981; Galleriet, Lund, Sweden, 1981; Spectro Arts Workshop, Newcastle, 1981; Riverside Studios, London, 1982; Diane Brown Gallery, 1984, 85; Lucerne, 1984; Munster/WK, 1984; Galerij S. 65, Aalst,

Belgium, 1985; Dart Gallery, Inc., Chicago, 1986; Anders Tornberg Gallery, Lund, Sweden, 1986. **Group:** Youngstown/Butler, 1962, 65, 67, 69; Sir George Williams U., Montreal, 45° 39'N - 73° 36'W, Conceptual Art, 1970; Documenta V, Kassel, 1972; VIII Paris Biennial, 1973; Leverkusen, Drawings 3: American Drawings, 1975; MOMA, Handmade Paper Prints & Unique Works, 1976; Wrokaw Ministry of Culture and Art, The International Drawing Triennial, 1978; U. of North Carolina, Drawings, 1979; MOMA, International Survey of Contemporary Painting and Sculpture, 1984; Harvard U., Smart Art, 1985; Muhlenberg College, Allentown, Pa., Archaic Echos, 1986. **Collections:** Amsterdam/Stedelijk; Berlin; Berne; Canberra/National; Chase Manhattan Bank; Cincinnati/AM; Gent/Contemporary; Groningen; Kenyon College; Leeds/Municipal; Monchengladbach; Paris/Beaubourg; Stockholm/National; Tate Gallery; VMFA; Victoria & Albert Museum; Youngstown/Butler.

FLACK, AUDREY. b. May 30, 1931, NYC. **Studied:** Cooper Union, 1951; Yale U., 1952 with J. Albers; NYU; Institute of Fine Arts, 1953. Traveled USA, Europe, India. **Taught:** Pratt Institute, 1960-68; NYU, 1960-68; Riverside Museum Master Institute, 1966-67; School of Visual Arts, NYC, 1970-74; Bridgeport U., 1975. **Awards:** Hon. Ph.D., Cooper Union, 1977; Cooper Union, Saint-Gauden's Medal, 1982; NYC Art Teachers Association, Teacher of the Year, 1985. **Commissions:** Time Magazine, Man of the Year cover, Anwar Sadat, 1979. **Address:** 110 Riverside Drive, NYC 10024. **Dealer:** Louis K. Meisel Gallery, NYC. **One-man Exhibitions:** Roko Gallery, NYC, 1959, 63; French & Co., Inc., NYC, 1972; Louis K. Meisel Gallery, NYC, 1974, 76, 78; U. of Hartford, 1974; U. of Bridgeport, 1975; Louis K. Meisel Gallery, 83; Carnegie-Mellon U., 1984; Cooper Union, 1986. **Retrospective:**

U. of South Florida, Tampa, 1981. **Group:** NAD, 1948; The Stable Gallery, Annual, NYC, 1960; School of Visual Arts, NYC, 65 Self-Portraits, 1965; WMAA, 22 Realists, 1970; WMAA, Annual, 1972; Indianapolis, 1972; Cleveland/MA, 32 Realists, 1972; WMAA, American Drawings, 1963-73, 74; Serpentine Gallery, London, Photo Realism, 1973; U. of Illinois, 1974; Tokyo Metropolitan Art Gallery, 11th Tokyo Biennale, 1974; PMA/Museum of the Philadelphia Civic Center, Women's Work: American Art 1974, 1974; California Institute of the Arts, Art: A Woman's Sensibility, 1975; Toledo/MA: Image, Color and Form, 1975; Wichita State U., The New Realism, 1975; Baltimore/MA, Super Realism, 1975; Stratford, Ont., Aspects of Realism, circ., 1976-78; WMAA, Art about Art, circ., 1978; Akron/AM, The Image in American Painting and Sculpture, 1950-1980, 1981; PAFA, Contemporary American Realism Since 1960, 1981; San Antonio/MA, Real, Really Real, Super Real, circ., 1981; WMAA, Sacred Images in Secular Art, 1986. **Collections:** Akron/AI; U. of Arizona; Brandeis U.; Canberra/National; MMA; MOMA; NMWA; NYU; Oberlin College; SRGM; St. Louis/City; WMAA. **Bibliography:** *Art: A Woman's Sensibility;* Arthur 3; Lindy; *New in the Seventies.*

FLANNAGAN, JOHN. b. April 7, 1895, Fargo, N.D.; **d.** January 6, 1942, NYC. **Studied:** Minneapolis Institute School, 1914-17, with R. Koehler. US Merchant Marine, 1914-17. Traveled Ireland, USA, France. **Awards:** Guggenheim Foundation Fellowship, 1932; MMA, Alexander Shilling Prize, 1940. **One-man Exhibitions:** Whitney Studio Club, NYC, 1925; Weyhe Gallery, 1927, 28, 30, 31, 34, 36, 38, 73, 78; Arts Club of Chicago, 1934; Vassar College, 1936; Bard College, 1937; Buchholz Gallery, NYC, 1942 (2); VMFA, 1946; A.F.A., circ., 1959; International Exhibitions Foundation, Washington, D.C.,

1965-76. **Group:** WMAA; MOMA; MMA; Brooklyn Museum; Carnegie, Forerunners of American Abstraction, 1971. **Collections:** Andover/Phillips; Cincinnati/AM; Cleveland/MA; Detroit/Institute; Dublin/Municipal; Harvard U.; Honolulu Academy; MMA; U. of Nebraska; Oberlin College; Vassar College; WMAA; Wichita/AM. **Bibliography:** *Avant-Garde Painting and Sculpture;* Baur 7; Brumme; Cheney; Craven, W.; Fierens; *Forerunners;* Goodrich and Baur 1; Hunter 6; Jackman; Licht, F.; Marter, Tarbell, and Wechsler; McCurdy, ed.; Mellquist; Mendelowitz; **Miller, ed., 3;** Ritchie, 3; Rose, B., 1, 4; Selz J.; Seuphor 3; Seymour; **Valentine 1, 2;** Wheeler. Archives.

FLAVIN, DAN. b. April 1, 1933, NYC. **Studied:** Cathedral College of the Immaculate Conception, 1947-52; US Air Force Meteorological Technician Training School, 1953; U. of Maryland (Extension, Korea), 1954-55; New School for Social Research, 1956; Columbia U., 1957-59. **Address:** Garrison, NY 10524. **Dealers:** Leo Castelli Inc., NYC; John Weber Gallery. **One-man Exhibitons:** Judson Gallery, NYC, 1961; Kaymar Gallery, NYC, 1964; Green Gallery, NYC, 1964; Ohio State U., 1965; Galerie Rudolf Zwirner, 1966; Nicholas Wilder Gallery, 1966; The Kornblee Gallery, 1967; Chicago/Contemporary, 1968; Galleria Sperone, Turin, 1968; Galerie Heiner Friedrich, Munich, 1968; Konrad Fischer Gallery, Dusseldorf, 1969; Irving Blum Gallery, Los Angeles, 1969; Galerie Bischofberger, Zurich, 1969; Ottawa/National, 1969; Vancouver, 1970; Jewish Museum, 1970; Dwan Gallery, NYC, 1970; Leo Castelli Inc., NYC, 1970, 71, 72, 73, 74, 75, 76, 78, 79, 81, 84, 85; Los Angeles/County MA, 1970; Galerie Heiner Friedrich, Munich, 1970; ACE Gallery, Los Angeles, 1971, 77; John Weber Gallery, 1971, 73; Galerie Heiner Friedrich, Cologne, 1971, 73; Janie C. Lee Gallery, Dallas, 1971; Rice U., 1972; St. Louis/City, 1973; U. of Bridgeport,

1973; Locksley-Shea Gallery, 1973; Lisson Gallery, London, 1973; Ronald Greenberg Gallery, St. Louis, 1974; Jared Sable Gallery, Toronto, 1974; Pasquale Trisorio Naples, 1974; Weinberg Gallery, San Francisco, 1974; Rotterdam, 1975; Basel, 1975; Charlotte Square Gallery, Edinburgh, 1976; Portland (Ore.) Center for the Visual Arts, 1976; Heiner Friedrich, Inc., NYC, 1976, 77, 78 (two-man); Otis Art Institute, 1977; Chicago/AI, 1977; ACE Canada, Vancouver, 1977; Cincinnati/Contemporary, 1977; Austin, 1979; Ottawa/National, 1979; Laguna Gloria, 1980; SRGM, 1982; Ottawa, 1980; Melinda Wyatt Gallery, Venice, Calif., 1983; Margo Leavin Gallery, 1984; Corcoran, 1984; Galerie Daniel Templon, Paris, 1984; Bordeaux/Contemporain, 1985; Galerie Onnasch, Berlin, 1985. **Retrospective:** Fort Worth, 1976; Southampton/Parrish, circ., 1978; Los Angeles/MOCA, 1984. **Group:** Hartford/Wadsworth, Black, White and Gray, 1964; ICA, Boston, 1966; U. of California, Irvine, 5 Los Angeles Sculptors, 1966; Jewish Museum, Primary Structures, 1966; Finch College, 1966; Eindhoven, Kunst-Licht-Kunst, 1966; Los Angeles/County MA, PMA, American Sculpture of the Sixties, 1967; Trenton/State, Focus on Light, 1967; Goethe U., Frankfurt, Germany, 1967; WGMA, A New Aesthetic, 1967; VI International Art Biennial, San Marino (Europe), 1967; Buffalo/Albright, Plus by Minus, 1968; The Hague, Minimal Art, 1968; Documenta IV, Kassel, 1968; WMAA, Light: Object and Image, 1968; UCLA, Electric Art, 1969; MMA, New York Painting and Sculpture, 1940-1970, 1969-70; Fort Worth, Drawings, 1969; U. of California, Irvine, Five Sculptors, 1969; MOMA, Spaces, 1969; WMAA Annual, 1970; SRGM, Guggenheim International, 1971; Buffalo/Albright, Kid Stuff, 1971; Walker, Works for New Spaces, 1971; Los Angeles/County MA, Art & Technology, 1971; High Museum, The Modern Image, 1972; Detroit/Institute, Art in Space, 1973; MOMA, Some Recent

American Art, circ., 1973; Musée Galliera, Paris, Festival d'Automne, 1973; Parcheggio di Villa Borghese, Rome, Contemporanea, 1974; Indianapolis, 1974; U. of North Carolina, Light/Sculpture, 1975; NCFA, Sculpture; American Directions 1945-1975, 1975; MOMA, Drawing Now, 1976; WMAA, 200 Years of American Sculpture, 1976; Chicago/AI, 1976; U. of Chicago, Ideas in Sculpture 1965-1977, 1977; ICA, Boston, The Reductive Object, 1979; Zurich, Reliefs, 1980; Cologne, International, 1981; Grand Palais, Paris, La rime et la raison, 1984; Dublin/Municipal, International Quadriennial (ROSC), 1984; WMAA, Blam!, 1984; Bordeaux/Contemporain, Art Minimal I, 1985. **Collections:** Amsterdam/Stedelijk; Basel; Cologne; Eindhoven; Harvard U.; Krefeld/Kaiser Wilhelm; Los Angeles/County MA; MOMA; Ottawa/National; Pasadena/AM; RISD; SRGM; Tate; WMAA; Walker. **Bibliography:** *Art Now 74*; Battcock, ed.; Calas, N. and E.; *Contemporanea*; **Dan Flavin;** Davis, D.; De Vries; Gablik; Haskell 5; Honisch and Jensen, eds.; Johnson, Ellen, H.; Krauss 2; Lippard 4, 5; MacAgy 2; Muller; *Report*; Rowell; Tuchman 1.

FLEISCHNER, RICHARD. b. 1944, NYC. **Studied:** RISD, 1962-66, BFA, 66-68, MFA. **Taught:** Rhode Island Council on the Arts, 1971-74; Brown U., 1971-74; RISD, 1977. **Awards:** Tiffany Fellowship, 1972; AAAL/NIAL Award, 1974; National Endowment for the Arts, 1975, 80; Rhode Island Governor's Award, 1986. **Address:** 95 Greenwood Avenue, Rumford, R.I. 02916. **Dealer:** McIntosh/Drysdale Gallery, Washington, D.C. **One-man Exhibitions:** Dartmouth, 1971; Terry Dintenfass Inc., NYC, 1971, 73, 75; Dag Hammerskjold Plaza, NYC, 1976; U. of Massachusetts, 1977; RISD, 1980; Max Protetch Gallery, NYC, 1980, 81; Philadelphia College of Art, 1983; U. of Rhode Island, 1983; Harcus Gallery, Boston, 1986; McIntosh/Drysdale Gal-

lery, 1987. **Group:** AAAL/NIAL, 1974; Newport, R.I., Monumenta, 1974; Documenta VI, Kassel, 1977; Hirshhorn, Probing the Earth, 1977; Seattle/AM, Earthworks, 1979; ICA, Boston, Drawing/Structures, 1980; XXXIX Venice Biennial, 1980; NCFA, Across the Nation, 1980; WMAA Biennial, 1981; PAFA, Form and Function, 1982; WMAA, New American Art Museum, 1982; La Jolla, Sitings, 1986; Los Angeles/MOCA, Individuals, 1986. **Collections:** U. of California, San Diego; Dallas/MFA; High Museum; U. of Massachusetts; RISD; SRGM; WMAA.

FORAKIS, PETER. b. October 2, 1927, Hanna, Wyo. **Studied:** San Francisco Art Institute, with Bud Dixon, Thomas Hardy, Nathan Oliveira, 1954-57, BA. US Army, 1951-53. Traveled Japan, Philippines, and Pacific Islands. **Taught:** San Francisco Art Institute, 1958; Brooklyn Museum School, 1961-63; The Pennsylvania State U., 1965; Carnegie, 1965; U. of Rhode Island, 1966; Windham College, 1968-74; U. of California, Berkeley, 1980; U. of Kentucky, 1980-82. **Commissions:** Mural for a motion-picture theater, San Francisco, 1956; North Jersey Culture Council, Paramus; Great Southwest Industrial Park; U. of Houston, 1971; Kingsborough College, 1980; Claremont Resort Hotel, Oakland, Calif., 1982. **Awards:** National Endowment for the Arts, 1972, 83. Editor, publisher, *Grope* magazine, 1964-66. **Address:** RFD 1, Box 5, Putney, VT 09346. **Dealer:** Paula Cooper Gallery. **One-man Exhibitions:** (first) Gallery Six, San Francisco, 1955, also 1956, 58; Spasta Gallery, San Francisco, 1959; David Anderson Gallery, NYC, 1961 (two-man); Tibor de Nagy Gallery, 1962, 64; Park Place Gallery, NYC, 1966; Windham College, 1967; Paula Cooper Gallery, 1968, 70; Sunne Savage Gallery, Boston, 1977; Sculpture Now, Inc., NYC, 1978; U. of Kentucky, 1981; U. of Cincinnati, 1981; Sunne Savage Gallery, 1982; Max Hutchinson

Gallery, 1983; Gallery 30, San Mateo, Calif., 1983, 84. **Group:** Uiano Museum, Tokyo, 1952, 53; SFMA, 1955-58; Oakland/AM, 1957; Martha Jackson Gallery, New Media—New Forms, 1, 1960; SRGM, Drawings and Prints, 1964; Jewish Museum, Primary Structure Sculptures, 1966; Los Angeles/County MA, American Sculpture of the Sixties, circ., 1967; Milwaukee, Directions I: Options, circ., 1968; Indianapolis, 1970; Storm King Art Center, Sculpture 1973, 1973; U. of Vermont, Vermont '73, 1973; Hirshhorn, Inaugural Exhibition, 1974; Georgetown (Ky.) College, Sculpture Invitational, 1981. **Collections:** Bergen Community College; Buffalo/SUNY; Dartmouth College; Hirshhorn; U. of Houston; U. of Kentucky; Northwood Institute; Oakland/AM; Ridgefield/Aldrich.

FORST, MLES. b. August 18, 1923, Brooklyn, N.Y. **Studied:** New School for Social Research; Veterans Art Center, MOMA, with Mervin Jules; ASL, with Morris Kantor; Hofmann School, NYC. Traveled Europe, Mexico, Nova Scotia. **Taught:** Assistant to Hans Hofmann at his school, 1952-53; Great Neck (N.Y.) Adult Education Program, 1958-60; School of Visual Arts, NYC, 1964-71; U. of California, Davis, 1965-66; Brooklyn Museum School, 1966-69; U. of California, San Francisco, 1971-72; Otis Art Institute, 1971-. **Awards:** Laurian Fund Award, 1954; Walter K. Gutman Foundation Grant 1960, 62, 65; Longview Foundation Grant, 1961, 62; Ford Foundation Fellowship, 1965; MacDowell Colony Fellowship, 1965, 67. **Address:** 14 Westminster Avenue, Venice, CA 90291. **One-man Exhibitions:** (first) Hansa Gallery, NYC, 1953, also 1954, 55, 58; Wittenborn Gallery, NYC, 1955; The Drawing Shop, NYC, 1964; Goldowsky Gallery, 1964. **Group:** Chicago/AI, 1953; SRGM, 1954; A.F.A., Collage in America, circ., 1957-58; Cornell U., 1958; Carnegie, 1959; A.F.A., The Figure, circ., 1960; Green Gallery, NYC,

1961, 62; MOMA, Hans Hofmann and His Students, circ., 1963-64; Hartford/Wadsworth, 1964; U. of Illinois; Gallery of Modern Art, NYC, 1965; 112 Greene Street, NYC, 1974; Otis Art Institute, 1975. **Collections:** Allentown/AM; Bowdoin College; Charlotte/Mint; Dillard U.; Hartford/Wadsworth; MIT; Newark Museum; Newport/Chrysler; Tulane U. **Bibliography:** Sandler 1.

FOULKES, LLYN. b. November 17, 1934, Yakima, Wash. **Studied:** Central Washington College, 1953; U. of Washington, 1952-54; Chouinard Art Institute, 1957-59, with Richards Ruben, Emerson Woelffer, Don Graham. US Army, Germany, 1955-56. Traveled Europe, North Africa, USA. **Taught:** UCLA, 1965-71; Art Center College of Design, Pasadena, 1971-77; U. of California, Irvine, 1981; California State U., Long Beach, 1982-. **Awards:** Chouinard Art Institute, First Prize, 1959; SFMA, First Prize, 1963; V Paris Biennial, First Prize, 1967; Guggenheim Foundation Fellowship, 1977. **Address:** 2002 Tuna Canyon, Topanga, Calif. 90290. **Dealer:** Asher/Faure, Los

Llyn Foulkes   *That Old Black Magic*   1985

Angeles. **One-man Exhibitions:** (first) Ferus Gallery, Los Angeles, 1961; Pasadena/AM, 1962, 67 (four-man); Rolf Nelson Gallery, Los Angeles, 1963-65; Oakland/AM, 1964; Robert Fraser Gallery, 1966 (four-man); David Stuart Gallery, 1969, 74; Darthea Speyer Gallery, 1970, 75; The Willard Gallery, 1975; Gruenebaum Gallery, NYC, 1977; Chicago/Contemporary, 1978; Asher/Faure, 1983; ICA, Los Angeles, 1984; Zolla/Liberman Gallery, Chicago, 1984. **Retrospective:** Newport Harbor, 1974. **Group:** Los Angeles/County MA Annuals, 1960, 61, 63; Pomona College, Object Makers, 1961; SFMA, West Coast Artists, circ., 1961; SMFA, Directions—Painting U.S.A., 1963; Pasadena/AM, Directors Choice, 1964; Sao Paulo, 1964; New York World's Fair, 1964-65; SRGM, 1966; V Paris Biennial, 1967; WMAA Annuals, 1967, 69, 71, 74; IX Sao Paulo Biennial, 1967; Brandeis U., 1968; Foundation Maeght, 1968; Los Angeles/County MA, 5 Los Angeles Artists, 1968; VMFA, American Painting, 1970; ICA, U. of Pennsylvania, The Topography of Nature: The Microcosm and Macrocosm, 1972; Los Angeles Municipal Art Gallery, Separate Realities, 1973; Chicago/AI, 71st American Exhibition, 1974; Corcoran Biennial, 1975; ARCO Center, Los Angeles, Los Angeles and the Palm Tree, 1984. **Collections:** Chicago/AI; La Jolla; Los Angeles/County MA; MOMA; Museum des 20. Jahrhunderts; Newport Beach; Oakland/AM; Paris/Beaubourg; Pasadena/MA; Rotterdam; SFMA; SRGM; Stanford U.; UCLA; WMAA. **Bibliography:** *New in the Seventies;* Weller.

FRANCIS, SAM. b. June 25, 1923, San Mateo, Calif. **Studied:** U. of California, Berkeley, 1941-43; 1949, BA; 1950, MA; Atelier Fernand Leger, Paris. US Air Force, 1943-45. Began painting under the encouragement of David Park while hospitalized in 1945. Traveled Europe, Japan, USA; resided and worked in Paris, 1950-57. Subject of films: *Sam Francis: These are My Footsteps,* WNED-TV, 1972; *Sam Francis,* 1975, Blackwood Productions, Inc. **Commissions:** (murals): Kunsthalle, Berne, 1957; Sofu School of Flower Arrangement, Tokyo, 1957; Chase Manhattan Bank, NYC, 1959. **Awards:** III International Biennial Exhibition of Prints, Tokyo, First Prize, 1963; Hon. DFA, U. of California, 1969; Legion of Honor, 1981; Skowhegan School, Medal for Painting, 1983. **Address:** 345 West Channel Road, Santa Monica, Calif. **Dealers:** Pierre Matisse Gallery, NYC; Minami Gallery, Tokyo; Andre Emmerich Gallery, NYC; Brooke Alexander, NYC. **One-man Exhibitions:** (first) Galerie Nina Dausset, Paris, 1952; Galerie du Dragon, 1952; Galerie Rive Droite, Paris, 1955, 56; Martha Jackson Gallery, 1956, 58, 63, 64, 68, 70; Gimpel Fils Ltd., 1957; Klipstein & Kornfeld, Berne, 1957, 61, 66, 68, 73, 76; Zoe Dusanne Gallery, Seattle, 1957; Tokyo Department Store Gallery, 1957; Kintetsu Department Store Gallery, Osaka, 1957; Phillips, 1958; Seattle/AM, 1959; SFMA, 1959, 67; Esther Baer Gallery, 1962, 63; Galerie Engelberts, Geneva, 1962; Galerie Pauli, Lausanne, 1962; A. Tooth & Sons, London, 1965; Pierre Matisse Gallery, 1967; Houston/MFA, 1967; U. of California, 1967; Kunstverein, Basel, 1968; Galerie Gunther Franke, Munich, 1968; CNAC, 1968; Shasta College, 1969; Minami Gallery, 1969, 74; Andre Emmerich Gallery, NYC, 1969, 70, 71, 72, 73, 74, 75, 76, 78, 79, 81, 82, 83, 84, 86; Felix Landau Gallery, 1970; Los Angeles/County MA, 1970; Nicholas Wilder Gallery, 1970, 71, 73, 75, 78; Pace Editions, NYC, 1973; Galerie Fournier, Paris, 1973-75, 76, 78, 79, 81, 83, 85; Margo Leavin Gallery, 1974; Jack Glenn Gallery, San Diego, 1975; Minami Gallery, Tokyo, 1961, 64, 66, 68, 70, 74, 77, 78, 79; Smith-Anderson Gallery, Palo Alto, 1972, 73, 76, 78; Smith-Anderson Gallery, San Francisco, 1975; Richard Gray Gallery, Chicago, 1975; Kornfeld and Klipstein, Zurich, 1975; Humlebaek/Louisiana,

1977; Otis Art Institute, 1978; Paris/Beaubourg, 1978; Honolulu, 1977; Ace Gallery, Vancouver, 1970; Maxwell Davidson Gallery, NYC, 1979; Thomas Segal Gallery, Boston, 1979, 83; The Elkon Gallery, NYC, 1979, 84; Brooke Alexander, Inc., NYC, 1979, 84; Richard Hines Gallery, Seattle, 1979; Los Angeles/County MA, 1980; Mizuno Gallery, Los Angeles, 1980; James Corcoran Gallery, Los Angeles, 1980; Abbaye de Senaque, Gordes, France, 1980; Foster Goldstrom Gallery, San Francisco, 1980; Pal Sui Loong Galleries, Hong Kong, 1981; Ace Gallery, Venice, Calif., 1981; Ruth S. Schaffner Gallery, Santa Barbara, 1981; Flow Ace Gallery, Venice, Calif., 1982; Nantenshi Gallery, Tokyo, 1982, 83; Richard Gray Gallery, Chicago, 1982; Makler Gallery, Philadelphia, 1982; Studio Marconi, Milan, 1983; John Berggruen Gallery, San Francisco, 1983; Art Attack Gallery, Boise, Id., 1983; Jane Kahan Gallery, NYC, 1983; Foundation Maeght, 1983; Thomas Babeor Gallery, La Jolla, 1984; Knoedler Gallery, London, 1984; Gemini G.E.L., Los Angeles, 1984; Hokin Gallery, Bay Harbor Islands, Fla., 1985. **Retrospectives:** Berne, 1960; Hannover/K-G, 1963; Amsterdam/Stedelijk, 1968; CNAC, 1969; Buffalo/Albright, circ., 1972; ICA, Boston, 1979; Phillips, 1980. **Group:** Salon du Mai, Paris, 1950; Studio Paul Facchetti, Signifiants de l'Informal, 1952; Studio Paul Facchetti, Un Art Autre, 1953; ICA, London, Opposing Forces, 1953; Berne, Tendances Actuelles, 1955; Carnegie, 1955; MOMA, Twelve Americans, circ., 1956; International Biennial Exhibition of Paintings, Tokyo; Arts Council Gallery, London, New Trends in Painting, 1957; Brussels World's Fair, 1958; MOMA, The New American Painting, circ., Europe, 1958-59; American Cultural Center, Paris, 3 Americans, 1958; Brooklyn Museum, 1959; Sao Paulo, 1959; III International Biennial Exhibition of Prints, Tokyo, 1962; Chicago/AI, 1962; Musée Cantonal des Beaux-Arts, Lausanne, I Salon International de Galeries Pilotes, 1963; Tate, Dunn International, 1964; Gulbenkian International, 1964; Flint/Institute, The Coming of Color, 1964; WMAA, Annuals, 1964, 65; Toronto, 1964; SRGM, American Drawings, 1964; Los Angeles/County MA, Post Painterly Abstraction, 1964; U. of Arkansas, 1965; Dayton/AI, 1966; Tokyo/Modern, 1966; II Internationale der Zeichnung, Darmstadt, 1967; Kunsthalle, Cologne, 1968; Carnegie, 1970; Buffalo/Albright, Color and Field, 1890-1970, 1970; Foundation Maeght, L'Art Vivant, 1970; VMFA, American Painting, 1970; Indianapolis, 1970; Chicago/AI Annual, 1970; Wilmington, 1970; Corcoran Biennial, 1971; Chicago/Contemporary, White on White, 1971-72; Toledo/MA, The Fresh Air School, 1973; Buffalo/Albright, Abstract Expressionism: The First and Second Generations, 1972; U. of Illinois, Contemporary American Painting and Sculpture, 1974; Santa Barbara/MA; 15 Abstract Artists, 1974; U. of California, Riverside, A View of Lithography in Los Angeles, 1975; SFMA, Painting and Sculpture in California: The Modern Era, 1977; California State U., Northridge, Americans in Paris, The 50's, 1979; Grand Palais, Paris, Societé des Artistes, 1980; MMA, The Painterly Print, 1980; SFMA, Twenty American Artists, 1980; Los Angeles/County MA; Art in Los Angeles, 1981; Haus der Kunst, Munich, Amerikansiche Malerie: 1930-1980, 1981; Cologne/Stadt, Westkunst, 1981; WMAA, American Prints: Process and Proofs, 1981; Milwaukee, American Prints, 1982; SFMA, Fresh Paint, 1982; Brooklyn Museum, The American Artist as Printmaker, 1983. **Collections:** Amsterdam/Stedelijk; Basel/Offentliche; Berlin/National; Berne; Buffalo/Albright; U. of California; Carnegie; Dallas/MFA; Dayton/AI; Dusseldorf/KN-W; Eindhoven; Essen; Fort Worth; Hamburg; Hannover/K-G; Hirshhorn; Humlebaek/Louisiana; Idemitsu Museum; Kansas City/Nelson; Los Angeles/County MA; MOMA; Montreal/MFA; NCFA; National Gallery; National Museum of Western Art, Tokyo; OBD/Basel; Ohara Art Museum; Paris/Beaubourg; Paris/Moderne; Pasadena/AM; Phillips; SFMA; SRGM; St. Louis; Santa Barbara/MA; Seattle/AM; Sofu School of Flower Arrangement; Stockholm/National; Stuttgart; Tate; Toronto; WMAA; Washington U.; Yale U.; Zurich. **Bibliography:** Blesh 1; Goldman 1; Haftman; Honisch and Jensen, eds.; Hunter 1; Hunter, ed.; Langui; Lippard 5; Lynton; McCurdy, ed.; *Metro*; Nordness, ed.; Ponente; Read 2; *Report*; Restany 2; Rickey; Rose, B., 1; **Sam Francis;** Sandler 1; Schneider; Seuphor 1; *The State of California Painting*; **Sweeney 3;** Tapie 1; Weller. Archives.

FRANK, MARY. b. February 4, 1933, London, England. **Studied:** NYC, with Max Beckmann, 1950; Hans Hofmann, 1951. Traveled Spain, France, England. **Taught:** New School for Social Research, 1970-75; Queens College, 1970-75; Skowhegan School, 1976. **Member:** AAIAL, 1984. **Awards:** Ingram Merrill Foundation Grant, 1962; Longview Foundation Grant, 1964-66; National Council on the Arts, 1969; Guggenheim Foundation Fellowship, 1973; CAPS, 1973; Brandeis U., Creative Arts Award, 1977; Guggenheim Foundation Fellowship, 1983. **Address:** 139 West 19th Street, NYC 10003. **Dealer:** The Zabriskie Gallery, NYC. **One-man Exhibitons:** (first) Stephen Ràdich Gallery, 1961, also 1963, 66; Boris Mirski Gallery, Boston, 1964, 66; The Drawing Shop, NYC; Bennett College, 1966; The Zabriskie Gallery, 1968, 70, 71, 73, 75, 77, 78, 79, 81, 83, 84, 85; Donald Morris Gallery, 1968; Richard Gray Gallery, 1969; U. of Connecticut, 1975; Harcus Krakow Gallery, Boston, 1976; Connecticut College, 1976; Arts Club, Chicago, 1976; Hobart College, 1976; Alice Simsar Gallery, Ann Arbor, 1976; U. of Bridgeport, 1976; Makler Gallery, Philadelphia, 1982; Quay Gallery, San Francisco,

Mary Frank   *Flowers: Auras and Reflections*   1984

1984; Marsha Mateyka Gallery, Washington, D.C., 1985. **Retrospective:** Purchase/SUNY, 1978. **Group:** MIT; Yale U.; Brandeis U.; MOMA, Hans Hofmann and His Students, circ., 1963-64; SRGM, 10 Independents, 1972; GEDOK, Hamburg, American Woman Artist Show, 1972; WMAA Annuals, 1972, 73; PMA/Museum of the Philadelphia Civic Center, Focus, 1974; New York Cultural Center, Three Centuries of the American Nude, 1975; Philadelphia College of Art, Private Notation; Artists' Sketchbooks, 1976; Brooklyn Museum Contemporary Women, 1977; Chicago/AI, 1977; PMA, Eight Artists, 1978; Albright College, Perspective 78, 1978; WMAA Biennial, 1979; MMA, The Painterly Print, 1980; WMAA, The Figurative Tradition and the WMAA, 1980; Brooklyn Museum, The American Artist as Printmaker, 1983; Cincinnati/Contemporary, Body and Soul, circ., 1985. **Collections:** Akron/AI; Brandeis U.; Brown U.; Chicago/AI; Bank of Chicago; Des Moines; Hirshhorn; Kalamazoo/Institute; Library of Congress; MMA; MOMA; U.

of Massachusetts; U. of New Mexico; U. of North Carolina; Purchase/SUNY; Southern Illinois U.; Syracuse/Everson; VMFA; WMAA; Wichita/AM; Worcester/AM; Yale U. **Bibliography:** *Woodstock: An American Art Colony, 1902-1977.*

FRANKENTHALER, HELEN. b. December 12, 1928, NYC. **Studied:** Dalton School, NYC, with Rufino Tamayo; Bennington College; with Paul Feeley, 1945-49, BA; ASL, with Vaclav Vytlacil, 1946; with Wallace Harrison, NYC, 1948; with Hans Hofmann, 1950. Traveled Europe extensively. **Taught:** NYU, 1958; U. of Pennsylvania, 1958; Yale U., 1967, 70; School of Visual Arts, NYC, 1967; Hunter College, 1970; U. of Rochester, 1971; Bennington College, 1972; Brooklyn Museum School, 1973; Swarthmore College, 1974; Drew U., 1975. **Member:** NIAL, 1974. Trustee, Bennington College, 1967-82; Fellow, Calhoun College, Yale U., 1968. Member of the Corporation of Yaddo, 1974. Designed and executed set for *Of Love* for Erick Hawkins Dance Company, 1971. **Commissions:** Temple of Aaron, St. Paul (ark curtain tapestry); First Wisconsin National Bank, Milwaukee, 1973; North Central Bronx Hospital (mural), 1973-74; The Fourth National Bank, Wichita (tapestry), 1974. **Awards:** I Paris Biennial, First Prize, 1959; PAFA; Joseph E. Temple Gold Medal, 1968; Honorary Doctor of Humane Letters, Skidmore College, 1969; Albert Einstein College, Spirit of Achievement Award, 1970; Chicago/AI, Ada S. Garrett Prize, 1972; III Biennale della Grafica d'Arte, Florence, Italy, Gold Medal, 1972; Hon. DFA, Smith College, 1973; Hon. DFA, Moore College of Art, Philadelphia, 1974; Creative Arts Award, American Jewish Congress, National Women's Division, 1974; Hon. DFA, Bard College, 1976; Hon. Ph.D., Radcliffe College 1978; Hon. Ph.D., Amherst College, 1979; Hon. DFA, NYU, 1979; Hon. DFA, Philadelphia College of Art, 1980; Hon. DFA, Williams College, 1980; Hon.

DFA, Harvard U., 1980; Hon. DFA, Yale U., 1981; Hon. DFA, Brandeis U., 1982; Hon. DFA, U. of Hartford, 1983; Hon. DFA, Syracuse U., 1985. Subject of the film *Frankenthaler: Toward a New Climate*, 1978, produced and directed by Perry Miller Adato. **Address:** 173 East 94th Street, NYC 10028. **Dealer:** Andre Emmerich Gallery, NYC. **One-man Exhibitions:** (first) Tibor de Nagy Gallery, 1951, also 1952-58; Andre Emmerich Gallery, NYC, 1959-63, 1965, 66, 68, 69, 71, 72, 73, 77, 78, 79, 82, 83, 84; Jewish Museum, 1960; Everett Ellin Gallery, Los Angeles, 1961; Bennington College, 1962, 78; Galerie Lawrence, Paris, 1961, 63; Galleria dell'Ariete, 1962; Kasmin, Ltd., 1964; David Mirvish Gallery, 1965, 71, 73, 75; St. John, N.B., 1966 (three-man, with Kenneth Noland, Jules Olitski); Gertrude Kasle Gallery, 1967; Nicholas Wilder Gallery, 1967; Heath Gallery, Atlanta, 1971; Fendrick Gallery, 1972, 74; Portland, Ore./AM, 1972; Waddington Galleries, London, 1973, 74; Janie C. Lee Gallery, Dallas, 1973; MMA, 1973; Swarthmore College, 1974; Corcoran, 1975; SRGM, 1975; John Berggruen Gallery, San Francisco, 1976, 79, 82, 86; Fendrick Gallery, Washington, D.C., 1974, 79, 80; Janie C. Lee Gallery, Houston, 1975, 76, 78, 79, 80, 82; SRGM, 1975; ACE Gallery, Vancouver, 1975; Rosa Esman Gallery, NYC, 1975; Diane Gilson Gallery, Seattle, 1976; Greenberg Gallery, St. Louis, 1977; Galerie Wentzel, Hamburg, 1977; Knoedler Gallery, London, 1978, 81, 83, 85; Jacksonville, Fla., 1978; Kansas City/Nelson, 1978; Saginaw, circ., 1980; Gallery Ulysses, Vienna, 1980; Brandeis U., 1981; Thomas Segal Gallery, Boston, 1981; Getler/Pall Gallery, NYC, 1982; Gallery One, Toronto, 1983, 85; Katonah Gallery, 1985. **Retrospectives:** WMAA, 1969; John Berggruen Gallery (prints) 1972; Corcoran, circ., 1975; International Communications Agency (World Tour), 1978; Williamstown/Clark, circ., 1980; IEF, circ., 1984. **Group:** The Kootz Gallery, NYC, New Talent, 1951; Ninth Street Exhibition, NYC, 1951; WMAA Annuals, 1955, 58, 61, 63, 67, 69, 70, 71, 72, 73, Young America, 1957, Nature in Abstraction, 1958, The Structure of Color, 1971; Carnegie, 1955, 58, 61; Sao Paulo, 1958; International Biennial Exhibition of Paintings, Tokyo; Documenta II, Kassel, 1959; U. of Illinois, 1959, 63, 65, 67; SRGM, Abstract Expressionists and Imagists, 1961; Chicago/AI, 1961, 63; Seattle World's Fair, 1962; PAFA Annuals, 1963, 66, 68; Los Angeles/County MA, Post Painterly Abstraction, 1964; New York World's Fair, 1964-65; U. of Michigan, 1965; Detroit/Institute, 1965, Color, Image and Form, 1967; ICA, Boston, Painting without a Brush, 1965; XXXIII Venice Biennial, 1966; Public Education Association, NYC, 1966; Expo '67, Montreal, 1967; Corcoran Biennial, 1967; MOMA, Two Decades of American Painting, circ., Japan, India, Australia, 1967; U. of Oklahoma, East Coast—West Coast Paintings, 1968; SFMA, Untitled 1968, 1968; Washington U., The Development of Modernist Painting, 1969; MMA, New York Painting and Sculpture, 1940-1970, 1969-70, Prints by Four New York Painters, 1969; Baltimore/MA, Washington Art: 1950-1970, 1970; Boston U., American Artists of the Nineteen Sixties, 1970; Foundation Maeght, L'Art Vivant, 1970; Buffalo/Albright, Color and Field: 1890-1970, 1970; ICA, U. of Pennsylvania, Two Generations of Color Painting, 1970; Boston/MFA, Abstract Painting in the '70s, 1972; Lakeview Center, American Women: 20th Century, 1972; Museum of Fine Arts, St. Petersburg, Flowing Form, 1973; Houston/MFA, The Great Decade of American Abstraction: Modernist Art 1960-1970, 1974; A.A.A. Gallery, One Hundred Prints, 1975; Wesleyan U., Middletown, Recent American Etching, 1975; Syracuse/Everson, New Work in Clay, 1976; PAFA, In This Academy, 1805-1976, 1976; Baltimore/MA, 200 Years of American Painting, 1976; Brooklyn Museum, 30 Years of American Printmaking, 1977; Syr-

acuse/Everson, New Works in Clay, 1976; Chicago/AI, Drawings of the 70's, 1977; Syracuse/Everson, Provincetown Painters, 1977; Grand Rapids, Two Centuries of American Art, 1977; Buffalo/Albright, American Painting of the 70s, 1978; U. of Tampa, Two Decades of American Abstraction, 1979; MMA, Hans Hofmann as Teacher, 1979; Montgomery/Museum, Art, Inc., 1979; Syracuse/Everson, A Century of Ceramics in the U.S., 1979; Brockton/Fuller, Aspects of the 70's: Painterly Abstraction, 1980; MOMA, Printed Art: A View of Two Decades, 1980; Sierra Nevada Museum of Art, Artists in the American Desert, circ., 1980; Centre d'Arts Plastiques Contemporains de Bordeaux, France, Depuis la couleur, 1958/1964, 1981; Haus der Kunst, Munich, Amerikanische Malerie: 1930-1980, 1981; Houston/MFA, Miró in America, 1982; WMAA, American Prints: Process and Proofs, 1982; MOMA, The Modern Drawing, 1983; MOMA, Prints from Blocks: Gauguin to Now, 1983; Walker, Prints from Tyler Graphics, 1984; Stamford Museum, American Art: American Women, 1985; Fort Lauderdale, An American Renaissance: Painting and Sculpture Since 1940, 1986; Independent Curators Inc., NYC, After Matisse, 1986. **Collections:** Auckland; Baltimore/MA; Belfast/Ulster; Bennington College; Boston/MFA; Brooklyn Museum; Buffalo/Albright; U. of California, Canegie; Carnberra/National; Chicago/AI; Cincinnati/AM; Cleveland/MA; Cologne; Columbia U.; Columbus; Corcoran; Detroit/Institute; Fort Worth; Hartford/Wadsworth; Harvard U.; High Museum; Hirshhorn; Honolulu Academy; Houston/Contemporary; Houston/MFA; Jerusalem/National; Johannesburg/Municipal; Kansas City/ Nelson; Louisville/Speed; MMA; MOMA; Mexico City/Nacional; Melbourne/National; Milwaukee; NCFA; NYU; Nagaoka, Tokyo; U. of Nebraska; Newark Museum; Omaha/Joslyn; Paris/Beaubourg; Pasadena/MA; Phoenix; PMA; Purchase/SUNY; RISD; San Antonio/McNay; Seattle/AM; SFMA; SRGM; St. Louis/City; Smithsonian; U. of Sydney; Syracuse/Everson; U. of Texas; Ulster Museum; Victoria and Albert Museum; Vienna/Stadt; WGMA; WMAA; Walker; Wichita/AM; U. of Wisconsin; Yale U. **Bibliography:** Alloway 4; Battcock, ed.; Baur 5; Friedman, ed.; Goldman 1; Goodrich and Baur 1; Goossen 3; *The Great Decade;* Hunter 1, 6; Honisch and Jensen, eds.; Hunter, ed.; Janis and Blesh 1; Kozloff 3; *Metro;* Murken-Altrogge; O'Hara 1; **Rose, B.,** 1, 3; Sandler 1; Schwartz 2; Wilken, K. Archives.

FRASCONI, ANTONIO. b. April 28, 1919, Montevideo, Uruguay. **Studied:** Circulo de Bellas Artes, Montevideo; ASL, 1946 with Yasuo Kuniyoshi; New School for Social Research, 1947, with Camilio Egas. To USA, 1945. **Taught:** New School for Social Research, 1951-52; Brooklyn Museum School; Pratt Institute; Vassar College; Atlanta Art Institute; Purchase/SUNY, 1973-. **Member:** SAGA; Educational Film Library. **Awards:** Guggenheim Foundation Fellowship, 1952; NIAL Grant, 1954; Venice International Film Festival, 1960, Grand Prix for *The Neighboring Shore* (15 minutes, more than 300 woodcuts); US Post Office Department, Design Competition, 1963; Connecticut State Commission on the Arts, 1974; IX International Biennial Exhibition of Prints, Tokyo; NAD, Cannon Prize, 1979. **Address:** 26 Dock Road, South Norwalk, CT 06854. **Dealers:** Terry Dintenfass, Inc., NYC; Weyhe Gallery. **One-man Exhibitions:** Ateneo Gallery, Montevideo, 1939; Montevideo YMCA, 1940; Agrupacion Intelectual, Montevideo, 1944; Brooklyn Museum, 1946; San Jose State College, 1946; Pasadena/AM, 1946; Santa Barbara/MA, 1946, 50, 51, 55, 77; New School for Social Research, 1947; Philadelphia Art Alliance, 1948; Weyhe Gallery, 1948-54, 1956, 60; Pan-American Union, Washington, D.C., 1949; Utica, 1949; San Diego, 1950; SFMA, 1950, 75; Princeton Print Club, 1950, 52; Art Association, Madison, Wisc.; 1951; Prang Institute, NYC, 1951; U. of Delaware, 1951; Bennington College, 1952; Louisville/Speed, 1953; Detroit/Institute, 1953; Los Angeles/County MA, 1953; Currier, 1955; Chattanooga/AA, 1955; Fort Worth, 1955; Wesleyan U., 1956; U. of Maine, 1956; Scripps College, 1958; Berea College, 1958; Collectors Art Center, Tallahassee, 1958; Atlanta/AA, 1959; Carnegie, 1959; San Antonio/McNay, 1959; Terry Dintenfass, Inc., 1962, 63, 64, 66, 69, 71, 76, 79, 83; The Print Club, Philadelphia, 1963; The Pennsylvania State U., 1963; Ankrum Gallery, 1963; Esther Baer Gallery, 1967, 75; Bridgeport, 1967; Lincoln, Mass./De Cordova, 1967; Haslem Fine Arts, Washington, D.C., 1976; Dunne/Steen Fine Arts, Old Greenwich, Ct., 1981. **Retrospectives:** Cleveland/MA, 1952; Smithsonian, circ., 1953-55; Montevideo/Municipal, 1961; Baltimore/MA, 1963; Brooklyn Museum, 1964; Missouri State Council of the Arts, circ., 1976; Musedel Grabado, San Juan, Obra Grafica 1943-1975, 1976. **Group:** Brooklyn Museum; Corcoran; Boston/MFA; Detroit/Institute; Hartford/Wadsworth; PAFA; Newark Museum; MOMA; Carnegie; St. Louis/City; San Diego; Baltimore/MA; New School for Social Research, Protest and Hope, 1967; XXXIV Venice Biennial, 1968; Intergraphic 76, Berlin, 1976; Smithsonian, American Prints from Wood, circ., 1976; York U., Toronto, Spain 1936-1976, 1976; Purchase/SUNY, Americans, 1977. **Collections:** Akron/AI; Albion College; Allegheny College; Alverthorpe Gallery, U. of Arizona; Arts Council of Great Britain; Atlanta/AA; Baltimore/MA; Boston/MFA; Boston Public Library; Brandeis U.; Brooklyn Museum; U. of California, Berkeley; Carnegie; La Casa del Libro; Chicago/AI; Cincinnati/AM, Cleveland/MA; Dartmouth College; U. of Delaware; Des Moines; Detroit/Institute; Fort Worth; Genesco/SUNY; Georgia State U.;

Grand Rapids; Hamilton College; Hartford/Wadsworth; Harvard U.; Honolulu Academy; Hunter College; State College of Iowa; Kalamazoo/Institute; U. of Kentucky; Lawrence College; Library of Congress; Louisville/Speed; MMA; MOMA; U. of Maine; Memphis/Brooks; U. of Michigan; U. of Minnesota; Minnesota/MA; Montclair/AM; Montevideo/Municipal; NYPL; Newark Museum; New Britain; New Paltz/SUNY; U. of Notre Dame; Omaha/Joslyn; PAFA; PMA; The Pennsylvania State U.; Princeton U.; RISD; U. of Rochester; Rutgers U.; St. Louis/City; San Diego; Santa Barbara/MA; Seattle/AM; Smith College; Smithsonian; Springfield, Mo./AM; Uruguay/Nacional; Utica; Wake Forest U.; Washington U.; Wesleyan U.; College of William and Mary; Williams College; U. of Wisconsin. **Bibliography: Frasconi;** Sachs. Archives.

FRECKELTON, SONDRA. b. June 23, 1936, Dearborn, Mich. **Studied:** U. of Chicago; School of the Art Institute of Chicago; Exhibited sculpture 1959-65 under the name Sondra Beal. **Taught:** Downtown Community School, NYC, 1960-63; Cooper Union, 1966. **Awards:** Ingram Merrill Foundation Grant, 1960; Michigan Artists Show, Prize, 1965; 6th British Interaction Print Biennial, prize, 1979. **m.** Jack Beal. **Address:** 83A Delhi Stage, Oneonta, NY 13820; and 67 Vestry Street, NYC 10013. **Dealer:** Robert Schoelkopf Gallery, NYC. **One-man Exhibitions:** (first) Tibor de Nagy, NYC, 1960, 61, 63; B.C. Holland Gallery, Chicago, 1965; LoGuidice Gallery, Chicago, 1970; Brooke Alexander, Inc., NYC, 1976, 79, 80, 81; Allan Frumkin Gallery, Chicago, 1978; Fendrick Gallery, Washington, D.C., 1980; John Berggruen Gallery, San Francisco, 1982; Robert Schoelkopf Gallery, 1985, 86. **Group:** MOMA, Recent Sculpture USA, 1959; Chicago/AI, American Exhibition, 1962, 65; WMAA, Annual, 1964; A.F.A., Colored Sculpture, circ.,

Sondra Freckelton *Cut Flowers* 1979

1965; Chicago/AI, 100 Artists—100 Years, 1976; Brooklyn Museum, Print Exhibition, 1978; Bradford Art Gallery, England, print biennial, 1979; PAFA, Contemporary American Realism Since 1960, 1981; PAFA, Perspective on Contemporary American Realism, 1983; SFMA, American Realism, circ., 1985. **Collections:** Amerada Hess Corp., Inc.; Best Products Co.; Madison Art Center; Prudential Insurance Co. of America; Reader's Digest; Sara Roby Foundation; Southeast Banking Corp.; Springfield Mo./AM; VMFA. **Bibliography:** Arthur 2.

FREILICHER, JANE. b. November 19, 1924, NYC. **Studied:** Brooklyn College, BA; Columbia U., MA; Hofmann School. Traveled Europe, Morocco. Designed set for *Red Robbins,* by Kenneth Koch. Designed sets for *The Heroes* by John Ashberry for Eye & Ear Theatre, NYC, 1981. **Taught:** Great Neck (N.Y.) Adult Education Program; New Jersey public schools; U. of Pennsylvania, 1968; Skowhegan School, 1968; Boston U., 1968; Swarthmore College, 1969; Carnegie-Mellon Institute, 1971; Cooper Union, 1972; Louisiana State U., 1973; Galveston Arts Center, 1973; Maryland Institute, 1973. Brandeis U.,

1979; American U., 1979. **Member:** NAD. **Awards:** Hallmark International Competition, 1960; *Art News* magazine, 10 Best Shows of 1962; National Endowment for the Arts, 1976. **Address:** 51 Fifth Avenue, NYC 10003. **Dealer:** Fischbach Gallery, NYC. **One-man Exhibitions:** (first) Tibor de Nagy Gallery, 1952, also 1953-64, 70; John Bernard Myers Gallery, NYC, 1971; Benson Gallery, 1972, 74; Fischbach Gallery, 1975, 77, 79, 80, 83, 85; Hartford/Wadsworth, 1976; Utah, 1979; Louise Himmelfarb Gallery, Water Mill, N.Y., 1980; Kornbluth Gallery, Fair Lawn, N.J., 1980; College of the Mainland, Texas City, Tx., 1982; Kansas City/AI, 1983; Currier, circ., 1986. **Retrospective:** Southampton/Parrish, 1986. **Group:** RISD, Four Young Americans, 1955; MOMA, Recent Drawings, USA, 1956; WMAA Annual, 1958; PAFA, 1961; U. of Nebraska, 1963; MOMA, Hans Hofmann and His Students, circ., 1963-64; Chicago/AI; Brooklyn Museum; Yale U.; Corcoran; A.F.A.; 1965; MOMA, 1966; A.F.A., Painterly Realism, 1970; Omaha/Joslyn, A Sense of Place, 1973; PMA/Museum of the Philadelphia Civic Center, Focus, 1974; AAAL, 1975; US Department of the Interior, America 1976, 1976; U. of Missouri, American Painterly Realists, 1977; Westmoreland County/MA, The New American Still Life, 1979; Denver/AM, Poets and Painters, 1979; Houston/Contemporary, American Still Life, 1945-1983, 1983; Brooklyn Museum, Public & Private: American Prints Today, 1984; NAD, 1985; SFMA, American Realism (Janss), circ., 1985. **Collections:** AT&T; Brandeis U.; Brooklyn Museum; Chase Manhattan Bank; Colby College; Commerce Bank of Kansas City; Corcoran; Greenville; Hampton Institute; Hirshhorn; Lehman Brothers; MMA; MOMA; NAD; NYU; U. of North Carolina; Prudential Insurance Co. of America; RISD; Rahr-West Museum; San Antonio/McNay; Southampton/Parrish; Stratford College; Union Carbide Corp.; Utah; U. of Utah; WMAA. **Bibliography:** *America 1976;*

Art: A Woman's Sensibility; Arthur 1, 2; Doty, ed.; Downes, ed.; *Poets & Painters;* Sandler 1; Strand, ed. Archives.

FRENCH, JARED. b. February 4, 1905, Ossining, N.Y. **Studied:** ASL, with Thomas Hart Benton, Boardman Robinson, Kimon Nicolaides; Amherst College, 1925, BA, with Robert Frost. Traveled Europe, 1927-28, 31-33; northern USA. Federal A.P.: US Post Offices, Richmond, Va., and Plymouth, Pa., 1935-39 (murals). Designed costumes and sets for the ballet *Billy the Kid.* **Awards:** NIAL Grant, 1967. **Address:** Hartland, VT 05048; Piazza Cucchi, 3, Rome 00152 Italy. **One-man Exhibitions:** (first) Julien Levy Galleries, NYC, 1939; Hewitt Gallery, NYC, 1950; Robert Isaacson Gallery, NYC; The Banfer Gallery, 1967. **Retrospective:** The Banfer Gallery, 1969. **Group:** Arts Club of Chicago; PAFA; WMAA; Chicago/AI; Carnegie; NAD; Walker; U. of Rochester, 1964-65; Youngstown/Butler, 1967. **Collections:** Baltimore/MA; Baseball Museum; Dartmouth College; WMAA. **Bibliography:** Baur 7; Goodrich and Baur 1.

FRIEDENSOHN, ELIAS. b. December 12, 1924, NYC. **Studied:** Stella Elkins Tyler School of Fine Arts, Temple U., 1942-43, with Rafael Sabatini; Queens College, with Cameron Booth, 1946-48, AB; NYU, Institute of Fine Arts, 1949-50; privately with Gabriel Zendel in Paris. Traveled Europe and Tunisia. **Taught:** Queens College, 1959-; Kirkland College, 1970-71. **Member:** College Art Association. **Awards:** Joe and Emily Lowe Foundation Award, 1951; Fulbright Fellowship (Italy), 1957; U. of Illinois, **P.P.,** 1957; National Arts Club Annual, NYC, Stephens Award, 1958; Guggenheim Foundation Fellowship, 1960; MacDowell Colony Fellowship, 1969, 70; AAAL, **P.P.** 1972; New Jersey Council on the Arts Grant, 1981, 85; CUNY, University Research Foundation Grant, 1981, 85. **Address:**

209 Hillcrest Avenue, Leonia, NJ 07605. **One-man Exhibitions:** (first) Roko Gallery, NYC, 1951; Hewitt Gallery, NYC, 1955, 57, 59; Vassar College, 1958; Robert Isaacson Gallery, NYC, 1960; Feingarten Gallery, NYC, San Francisco, Los Angeles and Chicago, 1961, 62; Feingarten Gallery, Los Angeles, 1964; The Contemporaries, NYC, 1964; Terry Dintenfass, Inc., NYC, 1967, 70, 74, 76, 80, 85; Kirkland College, 1972; Moravian College, 1977; Jersey City State College, 1978; Magnes Memorial Museum, 1981; Pine Library, Fairlawn, N.J., 1985. **Retrospective:** Jersey City State College, 1982. **Group:** Audubon Artists Annual 1957; WMAA, Young America, 1957, Fulbright Artists, 1958, Annuals, 1958, 59, 60, 62; Chicago/AI Annuals, 1957, 59; U. of Illinois, 1957, 59, 61, 63; National Arts Club Annual, NYC, 1958; Galleria Schneider, Rome, Fulbright Artists, 1958; Festival of Two Worlds, Spoleto, 1958; Corcoran Annuals, 1960, 62; Denver/AM, 1962; Smithsonian; Buffalo/Albright; Philadelphia Art Alliance; Syracuse U.; U. of Wisconsin; PAFA Annual, 1967; New School for Social Research, 1969; Minnesota/MA, Drawings USA, 1971, 73; NAD, 1971; VMFA, Works on Paper, 1974. **Collections:** Chicago/AI; Hampton Institute; U. of Illinois; Huntington, N.Y./Heckscher; Indianapolis; Kalamazoo/Institute; Kirkland College; Little Rock/MFA; The Joe and Emily Lowe Foundation; U. of Massachusetts; NMAA; U. of Oklahoma; Queens College; St. Mary's College, Md.; Sara Roby Foundation; WMAA; Walker. **Bibliography:** Weller.

FULLER, SUE. b. August 11, 1914, Pittsburgh, Pa. **Studied:** with Hans Hofmann, 1934; with S. W. Hayter, 1943-44; privately with Josef Albers, T. Tokuno; Carnegie Institute of Technology, 1936, BA; Teachers College, Columbia U., 1939, MA. Traveled Europe, Africa, Japan. **Taught:** U. of Minnesota, 1950; Stourbridge (England) School of Arts and Crafts, 1951; U. of Georgia, 1951, 52; Teachers College, Columbia U., 1958; Pratt Institute, 1964-65. **Commissions:** All Souls Unitarian Church, NYC, 1980; Tobin Library, San Antonio/McNay, 1984. **Awards:** Charles M. Rosenbloom Prize, 1942; The Print Club, Philadelphia, 1944, 1945, Charles M. Lea Prize, 1949; Northwest Printmakers Annual, **P.P.,** 1945; Society of American Etchers and Engravers, NYC, 1947; L. C. Tiffany Grant, 1948; Guggenheim Foundation Fellowship, 1949; NIAL Grant, 1950; Eliot D. Pratt Foundation Fellowship, 1966, 67, 68; Carnegie-Mellon U., Alumni Merit Award, 1974. **Address:** P.O. Box 1580, Southampton, NY 11968. **One-man Exhibitions:** Village Art Center, NYC, 1947; Corcoran, 1951; U. of Georgia, 1951; The Bertha Schaefer Gallery, 1952, 55, 56, 61, 65, 67, 69; Nishi Machi School, Tokyo, 1954; Fort Worth, 1956; Currier, 1956; San Antonio/McNay, 1956, 66; Grand Rapids, 1957; Charlotte/Mint, 1957; Grinnell College, 1960; Chatham College, 1960; Eleanor Rigelhaupt Gallery, Boston, 1965; Storm King Art Center, 1966; Norfolk, 1967; McNay Art Institute, 1967; Southern Vermont Art Center, 1968; Chatanooga/AA, 1969; Port Washington Public Library, 1978; Benson Gallery, Bridgehampton, 1978; Plum Gallery, Kensington, Md., 1978. **Group:** MOMA, Master Prints from the Museum Collection, 1949, Abstract Painting and Sculpture in America, 1951, The Responsive Eye, 1965; SAGA, 1951; Sao Paulo Biennial, 1951; WMAA Annuals, 1951, 53, 54, 56, The New Decade, 1954-55, Geometric Abstraction in America, circ., 1962; Salon du Mai, Paris, 1952; PMA, A Decade of American Printmaking, 1952, also 1964; III Biennial of Spanish-American Art, Barcelona, 1955; Brooklyn Museum, 14 Painter-Printmakers, 1955; Chicago/AI Annual, 1957; A.F.A., 14 Painter-Printmakers, circ., 1957, Collage in America, circ., 1957-58, The New Landscape in Art and Science, circ., 1958-59, Explorers of Space, circ., 1961-62, Hayter and Atelier 17, circ., 1961-62; USIA,

American Prints, circ., Middle East, 1957-59, Plastics—USA, circ. USSR, 1961; Corcoran Biennials, 1963, 65; Buffalo/Albright, Box Show, 1966; Cornell U., Small Sculpture, 1967; Flint/Institute, Made of Plastic, 1968; Denver/AM, Report on the Sixties, 1969; Colgate U., Viewpoints 3, 1969; Skidmore College, Contemporary Women Artists, 1970; U. of Nebraska, American Sculpture, 1970; Finch College, NYC, Projected Art, 1971; Potsdam/SUNY, Women in Art, 1971; PMA/Museum of the Philadelphia Civic Center, Focus, 1974; Sculptors Guild, NYC, 1983, 85; Carnegie-Mellon U., 75 Years of Pittsburgh Art, 1985; Stamford Museum, American Art: American Women, 1985. **Collections:** Albion College; American Republic Insurance Co.; Amherst College; Andover/Phillips; Baltimore/MA; Boston/MFA; British Museum; Brooklyn Museum; CIT Corporation; Carnegie; Chase Manhattan Bank; Chicago/AI; Des Moines; Ford Foundation; Hartford/Wadsworth; Harvard U.; Honolulu Academy; NYPL; National Gallery; Norfolk; PMA; Peabody Institute; Ridgefield/Aldrich; St. Louis/City; San Antonio/McNay; Seaton Hall, Inc.; Storm King Art Center; Tate; Union Carbide Corp.; WMAA. **Bibliography:** Hayter 2; Janis and Blesh 1; Moser; Newmeyer; Reese; Ritchie 1. Archives.

G

GABLIK, SUZI. b. September 26, 1934, NYC. **Studied:** Black Mountain College, 1951; Hunter College, NYC, BA, 1955, with Robert Motherwell. Author, critic, and lecturer. **Taught:** U. of the South, 1982; U. of California, Santa Barbara, 1985, 86. **Member:** International Association of Art Critics. **Address:** 5 Westmoreland Street, London W1, England. **One-man Exhibitions:** Alan Gallery, NYC, 1963, 66; Landau-Alan Gallery, NYC, 1967; Henri Gallery, Washington, D.C., 1971; Terry Dintenfass, Inc., 1972, 78; Hester van Royen Gallery, London, 1978. **Group:** SRGM, The Photographic Image, 1966; ICA, London, Young and Fantastic, 1969; New York Cultural Center, Women Choose Women, 1973. **Collections:** Sara Roby Foundation; Hirshhorn.

GABO, NAUM NEEMIA PEVSNER. b. August 5, 1890, Briansk, Russia; **d.** August 23, 1977, Waterbury, Conn. **Studied:** U. of Munich, medical faculty, 1910, natural science, 1911; Polytechnic Engineering School, Munich, 1912. Traveled Italy, Scandinavia, Great Britain, USA, Russia. To USA, 1946; citizen, 1952. **Taught:** Harvard U., 1953-54. Designed set for *La Chatte* (Ballet Russe, 1926). Edited *Circle* (with Leslie Martin and Ben Nicholason), 1937. **Member:** AAAL, 1965. **Commissions:** Bijenkorf Building, Rotterdam, 1955; U.S. Rubber Co. Building, NYC, 1956. **Awards:** ICA, London/Tate, International Unknown Political Prisoner Competition, Second Prize, 1953; Guggenheim Foundation Fellowship, 1954; Chicago/AI, The Mr. & Mrs. Frank G.

Logan Medal, 1954; Hon. DFA, Royal College of Art, London, 1967; NIAL. **One-man Exhibitions:** Gallery Percier, Paris, 1924; Little Review Gallery, NYC, 1926; Hannover/K-G, 1930; Arts Club of Chicago, 1934, 1952 (two-man); Lefevre Gallery, London, 1936; Musée du Jeu de Paume, 1937; The London Gallery, London, 1937; Julien Levy Galleries, NYC, 1938; Hartford/Wadsworth, 1938, 53; Museum of the City of London, 1942; MOMA, 1948; Baltimore/MA, 1950; MIT, 1952; Pierre Matisse Gallery, 1953; France/National, Paris, 1971; Berlin/National, 1971. **Retrospectives:** Amsterdam/Stedelijk, circ., 1965-66; Buffalo/Albright, 1968; Dallas/MFA and Dusseldorf/KN-W, circ., 1986. **Group:** Golden Gate International Exposition, San Francisco, 1939; MOMA; WMAA; Chicago/AI; Paris/Moderne. **Collections:** Buffalo/Albright; Hartford/Wadsworth; MOMA; Princeton U.; Tate; U.S. Rubber Co.; WMAA; Yale U. **Bibliography:** *Abstraction creation 1931-36*; Baldinger; Barr 1; Battcock, ed.; Baur 7; Biederman 1; Bihalji-Merin; Blanchard; Blesh 1; Calas, N. and E.; Canaday; Cassou; Chipp; Craven, W.; Davis, D.; Flanagan; **Gabo;** Gaunt; Gertz; Giedion-Welcker 1, 2; Goodrich and Baur 1; Guggenheim, ed.; Henning; Hess, T.B., 1; Hulten; Hunter, ed.; Janis and Blesh 1; Janis, S.; Kepes 2; Kepes, ed.; Krauss 2; Kuh 1, 2, 3; Langui; Licht, F.; Lowry; Lynton; MacAgy 2; McCurdy, ed.; **Martin, Nicholson, and Gabo, eds.;** Mendelowitz; *Metro*; Murken-Altrogge; Myers 2; Nash and Merkert, eds.; Neumeyer; Newmeyer; Newton 2; **Olson and Chanin;** Ramsden 1, 2; Read 1, 3,

6; **Read and Martin;** Rickey; Ritchie 3; Rose, B., 1; Rowell; Selz, J.; Pela, P. 3; Seuphor 3; Seymour; Trier 1, 2; Valentine 2; Zervos. Archives.

GALLATIN, ALBERT E. b. 1882, Villanova, Pa.; **d.** June 17, 1952. **Studied:** Cutler School, Vermont; New York Law School. Traveled Europe, USA. Founder of Museum of Living Art, now housed at the Philadelphia Museum of Art. **One-man Exhibitions:** (first) Galerie Pierre, Paris, 1938; Passedoit Gallery, NYC, 1938, 42; Pittsfield/Berkshire, 1939; J. Seligmann and Co., 1939 (three-man); The Willard Gallery, 1941; Mortimer Brandt, NYC, 1945; Durand-Ruel Gallery, NYC, 1947, 48; The Pinacotheca, NYC, 1950; The Zabriskie Gallery, 1972. **Retrospective:** Rose Fried Gallery. **Group:** Salon des Surindependants, Paris, 1938; American Abstract Artists Annuals, 1938-48; New York World's Fair, 1939; Arts Club of Chicago, 1940; MOMA, 1942; Federation of Modern Painters and Sculptors, 1943; PMA, 1945; Corcoran, 1947. **Collections:** Black Mountain College; MMA; MOMA; PMA; Phillips; Pittsfield/Berkshire; SFMA; SRGM. **Bibliography:** American Abstract Artists, ed.; Baur 7; Bazin; Blesh 1; Frost; **Gallatin 1, 2, 3, 4, 5, 6, 7, 8;** Lane and Larsen; McCurdy, ed.; Morris; Ritchie 1; Rose, B., 1. Toher, ed. Archives.

GALLO, FRANK. b. 1933, Toledo, Ohio. **Studied:** Toledo/MA, 1954, BFA; Cranbrook, 1955; U. of Iowa, 1959, MFA. **Taught:** U. of Illinois, 1959-64, 68; U. of Iowa, 1967-68. **Awards:** Des Moines, First Prize, 1958, 59; Guggenheim Foundation Fellowship, 1966. **Address:** 1101 North High Cross, Urbana, Ill. 61801. **Dealer:** Circle Galleries Ltd., NYC and other cities. **One-man Exhibitions:** Toledo/MA, 1955; Gilman Galleries, Chicago, 1963-66; Sherry-Netherland Hotel, NYC, 1964; The Graham Gallery, 1965, 67; Felix Landau Gallery, 1966; Time, Inc., 1966; Danen-

berg Gallery, 1972; Puck Gallery, NYC, 1974; Jack Gallery, NYC; Circle Gallery Ltd., 1974, 82; Spencer-Howard Gallery, Laguna Beach, 1978; Cherry Creek Gallery of Fine Art, Denver, 1980; Old Town Gallery, San Diego, 1980; Collectors Fine Arts Gallery, Cleveland, 1981; U. of Nebraska, 1981; G. Oatis Gallery, Houston, 1981; Pioneer Square Gallery, Seattle, 1981; Akron/AM, 1982; Carolyn Summers Gallery, New Orleans, 1982; ArtExpo, NYC, 1983, 84. **Retrospectives:** Paine Art Center and Arboretum, Oshkosh, 1981; Colorado State U., 1984. **Group:** Des Moines, 1958, 59; U. of Illinois, 1963-65; Chicago/AI, 1964; WMAA Annual, 1964-67; Youngstown/Butler, 1965; WMAA, Young America, 1965; Toronto International Sculpture Symposium, 1967; XXXIV Venice Biennial, 1968; Owens-Corning Fiberglas Corp., Corning, N.Y., 1970; Harvard U., Recent Figure Sculpture, circ., 1972. **Collections:** Baltimore/MA; Caracas; Chicago/AI; Cleveland/MA; Colorado State U.; Hirshhorn; U. of Illinois; Los Angeles/County MA; MOMA; Melbourne/National; U. of Nebraska; Princeton U.; RISD; St. Louis/City; Toronto; WMAA; U. of Wisconsin. **Bibliography:** Geske; *Recent Figure Sculpture.*

GANSO, EMIL. b. April 4, 1895, Halberstadt, Germany; **d.** April 18, 1941, Iowa City, Iowa. To USA, 1912. **Studied:** NAD. **Taught:** Lawrence College, 1940; State U. of Iowa, 1941. **Awards:** Guggenheim Foundation Fellowship, 1933. **One-man Exhibitions:** Weyhe Gallery, 1926-28, 1930-36, 1944, 46; Washington Irving Gallery, NYC, 1960; Kenan Center, Lockport, N.Y., 1969; U. of Connecticut, 1976; Martin Sumers Graphics, 1978, 80. **Retrospectives:** WMAA, 1941; Brooklyn Museum, 1944; U. of Iowa, 1979. **Group:** WMAA; Salons of America, NYC; Brooklyn Museum; Chicago/AI; Cleveland/MA; PAFA; Corcoran; NAD. **Collections:** Boston/MFA; Dartmouth

College; Denver/AM; MMA; U. of Rochester; WMAA. **Bibliography:** American Artists Group, Inc. 1, 3; Cahill and Barr, eds.; Cheney; Hall; *Index of 20th Century Artists;* Jewell 3; Mellquist; Moser 2; Pearson 1; Reese; Ringel, ed.; *Woodstock: An American Art Colony, 1902-1977;* Zigrosser 1. Archives.

GARET, JEDD. b. 1955, Los Angeles. **Studied:** RISD, 1975-76; School of Visual Arts, NYC, 1977, BFA. **Address:** 99 East 7th Street, NYC 10009. **Dealer:** Robert Miller Gallery, NYC. **One-man Exhibitions:** Robert Miller Gallery, 1979, 81, 83, 84; Felicity Samuel Gallery, London, 1979; Galerie Bischofberger, Zurich, 1980; Larry Gagosian Gallery, Los Angeles, 1981; Texas Gallery, Houston, 1982, 85; John Berggruen Gallery, San Francisco, 1982; Michael Lord Gallery, Milwaukee, 1983; Stephen Wirtz Gallery, San Francisco, 1984; Betsy Rosenfield Gallery, Chicago, 1984; ICA, U. of Pennsylvania, 1984; Texas Gallery, Houston; Totah-Stelling Art, NYC, 1985; Galerie Daniel Templon, Paris, 1986. **Group:** Norfolk/Chrysler, American Figure Painting, 1950-1980, 1980; XXXIX & XLI Venice Biennials, 1980, 84; WMAA Biennials, 1981, 85; Cincinnati/ Contemporary, Dynamix, circ., 1982; Hannover/K-G, New York Now, circ., 1982; Indianapolis, 1982, 84; XVII Sao Paulo Biennale, 1983; Houston/ Contemporary, American Still Life, 1945-1983, 1983; Bonn, Back to the USA, circ., 1983; New Museum, The 1970s: New American Painting, 1984; MOMA, International Survey of Recent Painting and Sculpture, 1984; SFMA, The Human Condition, 1984; Houston/ Contemporary, The Heroic Figure, circ., 1984; Indianapolis, 1984; ICA, U. of Pennsylvania, Investigations, 1984; U. of North Carolina, Art on Paper, 1985. **Collections:** Bowdoin College; Harvard U.; Honolulu Academy; MOMA; Tate Gallery, WMAA. **Bibliography:** *Back to the USA;* Haenlein.

GATCH, LEE. b. September 10, 1902, Baltimore, Md. **d.** November 10, 1968, Trenton, N.J. **Studied:** Maryland Institute, 1924; Academie Moderne, Paris, 1924, with Andre Lhote, Moise Kisling. Traveled France, Italy. **Member:** NIAL, 1966. **Commissions:** (murals) US Post Offices, Mullins, S.C., and Elizabethtown, Pa. **Awards:** Chicago/AI, Watson F. Blair Prize, 1957; Corcoran, 1960. **One-man Exhibitions:** (first) J. B. Neumann's New Art Circle, NYC, 1927, also 1932, 37, 46, 49; The Willard Gallery, 1943; Grace Borgenicht Gallery, Inc., 1954; Phillips, 1954, 56, 60; World House Galleries, NYC, 1958; Staempfli Gallery, 1963, 67, 72, 74; NCFA, 1971; Newark Museum, 1981. **Retrospective:** WMAA, 1960. **Group:** XXV & XXVIII Venice Biennials, 1950, 56; Santa Barbara/MA, 1952; Detroit/Institute, 1959; U. of Illinois, 1961. **Collections:** Andover/Phillips; Atlanta U.; Baltimore/MA; Boston/MFA; Detroit/Institute; Hartford/Wadsworth; U. of Illinois; Los Angeles/County MA; MMA; MOMA; U. of Nebraska; PAFA; PMA; Phillips; St. Louis/City; Utica; WMAA; Washington U. **Bibliography:** Baur 5; Blesh 1; *Cityscape 1919-37;* Eliot; Frost; Gerdts; Goodrich and Baur 1; Hess, T. B., 1; Janis and Blesh 1; Janis, S.; McCurdy, ed.; Nordness, ed.; Pousette-Dart, ed.; Richardson, E.P. Archives.

GECHTOFF, SONIA. b. September 25, 1926, Philadelphia, Pa. **Studied:** Philadelphia Museum School, BFA. Traveled Europe. **Taught:** California School of Fine Arts, 1957-58; NYU, 1961-70; Queens College, 1970-74; U. of New Mexico, 1974-75. **Member:** National Advisory Board, Tamarind Institute; Artists Equity. **Awards:** SFMA, **P.P.,** Santa Barbara/MA, **P.P.;** Tamarind Fellowship, 1963; Phoenix Art Museum, drawing award, 1975. **m.** James Kelly. **Address:** 463 West Street, NYC 10014. **Dealer:** Gruenebaum Gallery, Ltd., NYC. **One-man Exhibitions:** (first) Dubin Gallery, Philadelphia, 1949; Lucien

Labaudt Gallery, San Francisco, 1952, 53; Gallery Six, San Francisco, 1955; de Young, 1957; Ferus Gallery, San Francisco, 1957, 59; Poindexter Gallery, 1959, 60; East Hampton Gallery, 1963, 67, 68; Montclair State College, 1974; Cortella Gallery, NYC, 1976, 78; Gruenebaum Gallery, Ltd., NYC, 1979, 80, 82, 83, 85. **Group:** SFMA Annuals, 1952-58; SRGM, Younger American Painters, 1954; Brussels World's Fair, 1958; Carnegie, 1958; I Paris Biennial, 1959; WMAA Annual, 1959; WMAA, Young America, 1960; Walker, 60 American Painters, 1960; VI Sao Paulo Biennial, 1961; MOMA, Abstract American Drawings and Watercolors, circ., Latin America, 1961-63; U. of Texas, 1966; Florida State U., 1967; Los Angeles/County MA, 1968; New York Cultural Center, Women Choose Women, 1973; SFMA, California Painting and Sculpture: The Modern Era, 1976; MOMA, Extraordinary Women, 1977; MOMA, American Drawn and Matched, 1977; U. of California, Davis, Directions in Bay Area Painting, 1983; Stamford Museum, American Art: American Women, 1985. **Collections:** Achenbach Foundation; AT&T; U. of California; Amon Carter Museum; Baltimore/MA; Chase Manhattan Bank; U. of Iowa; La Jolla; Little Rock/MFA; Los Angeles/County MA; MMA; MOMA; U. of Massachusetts; Oakland/AM; Pasadena/AM; SFAI; SFMA; SRGM; The Singer Company, Inc.; Woodward Foundation. **Bibliography:** *Art: A Woman's Sensibility.* Archives.

GEORGE, THOMAS. b. July 1, 1918, NYC. **Studied:** Dartmouth College, 1940, BA; ASL; Academie de la Grande Chaumiere; Academy of Fine Arts, Florence, Italy. US Navy, 1942-46. Traveled Europe, Far East, North Africa, China. **Taught:** Dartmouth College, 1979; Art League of San Juan, Puerto Rico, 1982. **Member:** MacDowell Colony. **Awards:** Brooklyn Museum, **P.P.,** 1955; Rockefeller Foundation Grant, 1957; Ford Foundation,

P.P., 1962, 63. **Address:** 20 Greenhouse Drive, Princeton, NJ 08540. **Dealer:** Betty Parsons Gallery, NYC. **One-man Exhibitions:** Ferargil Galleries, NYC, 1951, 53; Korman Gallery, NYC, 1954; Dartmouth College, 1956, 79; The Contemporaries, NYC, 1956; Bridgestone Museum, 1957; Diamaru, Osaka, 1957; Betty Parsons Gallery, NYC, 1959, 70, 72, 74, 76, 78, 81; The Reid Gallery, London; Bennington College, 1967; U. of California, Santa Cruz, 1967; Axiom Gallery, London, 1968; Esther Baer Gallery, 1969; Delaware Art Museum, 1971; Henies-Onstadts Stiftelser, 1971; Tranegarden Gallery, Hellerup, Copenhagen, 1971; Princeton Gallery of Fine Art, 1972, 74; Oslo Kunstforening, 1973; Jefferson Place Gallery, Washington, D.C., 1974; Princeton U., 1975; NCFA, 1977; Artes Galleri, Oslo, 1979; Oslo/National, 1980; Galerie Ravel, Austin, 1981; Riis Gallery, Oslo, 1982, 84; Maxwell Davidson Gallery, NYC, 1983, 85; Princeton Gallery of Fine Art, 1983, 85. **Retrospective:** Dartmouth College, 1965. **Group:** MOMA, Recent Drawings, USA, 1956; Carnegie, 1958, 61; WMAA, Annuals, 1960-62, 1965; PAFA, 1962; Corcoran, 1963; International Biennial Exhibition of Paintings, Tokyo; Lincoln, Mass./De Cordova, 1963; San Antonio/McNay, 1964; SFMA, 1965; Musée Cantonal des Beaux-Arts, Lausanne, II Salon International de Galeries Pilotes, 1966; NCFA, 1968; US Mission to the United Nations; New School for Social Research, NYC, American Drawings of the Sixties, 1970; Trenton/State, New Jersey 6, 1971. **Collections:** Brandeis U.; Bridgestone Museum; Brooklyn Museum; Buffalo/Albright; U. of California, Santa Cruz; Chase Manhattan Bank; Colby College; Dartmouth College; Delaware Art Museum; Flint/Institute; Ford Motor Company; Henie-Onstadts Stiftelser; Houston/MFA; Library of Congress; MOMA; Musée Cantonal des Beaux-Arts; NCFA; Oklahoma; Oslo/National; Princeton U.; U. of Rochester; SFMA;

SRGM; Tate Gallery; U. of Texas; Trenton/State; WGMA; WMAA; Yale U.

GEORGES, PAUL. b. 1923, Portland, Ore. **Studied:** U. of Oregon; Hofmann School; Atelier Fernand Leger in Paris, 1949-52. Traveled France, USA. **Taught:** U. of Colorado, 1960; Dartmouth College, 1961; Yale U., 1964; Brandeis U., 1977-85. **Awards:** Longview Foundation Grant; Hallmark International Competition, **P.P.,** 1961; PAFA, Carol H. Beck Gold Medal, 1964; NAD, Benjamin Altman Prize, 1981; NAD, Andrew Carnegie Prize, 1982; AAIAL, 1986. **Address:** Sagaponack, NY 11962 and 85 Walker Street, NYC 10013. **Dealer:** Anne Plumb Gallery, NYC. **One-man Exhibitions:** Reed College, 1948, 56, 61; Tibor de Nagy Gallery, 1955, 57; The Zabriskie Gallery, 1959; Great Jones Gallery, NYC, 1960, 61; Allan Frumkin Gallery, NYC and Chicago, 1962, 64, 66, 67, 68; Dorsky Gallery, 1968; Fischbach Gallery, 1974, 76; Green Mountain Gallery, 1975; Union College, Cranford, N.J., 1979; Meghan Williams Gallery, Los Angeles, 1979; Northern Illinois U., 1980; Brandeis U., 1981; Zolla/Lieberman Gallery, Chicago, 1982; College of the Mainland, 1983; Charles Moore Gallery, Philadelphia, 1983; Manhattan Art, NYC, 1984; Amherst College, 1985; Anne Plumb Gallery, 1986. **Group:** Salon du Mai, Paris, 1949; The Kootz Gallery, NYC, New Talent, 1952; PAFA, 1952, 64; Corcoran, 1962; Chicago/AI, 1962; WMAA, 1962, 63; MOMA; U. of Colorado; U. of Kentucky, Drawings, 1963; MOMA, Hans Hofmann and His Students, circ., 1963-64; Boston U., 1964; Silvermine Guild, 1964; Youngstown/Butler, 1964. **Collections:** Corcoran; 57th Madison Corp.; Guild Hall; Hallmark Collection; Hirshhorn; Indianapolis; MIT; MOMA; U. of Massachusetts; NYU; Newark Museum; U. of North Carolina; Purchase/SUNY; Reed College; WMAA. **Bibliography:** Adrian; Downes, ed. Archives.

GIBRAN, KAHLIL. b. November 29, 1922, Boston, Mass. **Studied:** Boston Museum School, 1940-43, with Karl

Paul Georges   *Goodbye Sagaponack*   1983–84

Zerbe. Changed from painting to sculpture, 1953-54. **Taught:** Wellesley College, 1958; Boston U. **Member:** National Sculpture Society; New England Sculptors Association. **Awards:** PAFA, George D. Widener Memorial Gold Medal, 1958; Guggenheim Foundation Fellowship, 1959, 60; NIAL Award, 1961; Boston Arts Festival Grand Prize, 1964. **Address:** 160 West Canton Street, Boston, MA 02118. **Dealer:** Bologna-Landi Gallery, East Hampton, N.Y. **One-man Exhibitions:** (first) Stuart Gallery, Boston, 1944; Mortimer Levitt Gallery, NYC; Margaret Brown Gallery, Boston; U. of Kansas; Lee Nordness Gallery, NYC, 1962 (sculpture); Cambridge (Mass.) Art Association, 1969, 1977. **Group:** WMAA Annual, 1960; Boston Arts Festival; Carnegie; Dallas/MFA; NAD; Chicago/AI; ICA, Boston. **Collections:** Brockton/Fuller; Kansas City/Nelson; Nashville; Norfolk; Norfolk/Chrysler; PAFA; Terre Haute/Swope. **Bibliography:** Pousette-Dart, ed. Archives.

GIKOW, RUTH. b. January 6, 1915, Russia. **d.** April 22, 1982, NYC. **Studied:** Cooper Union, 1932-35, with John Steuart Curry, Austin Purvis; American Art School, NYC, with Raphael Soyer. Traveled Europe, Mexico, Asia, USSR. **Taught:** New School for Social Research, ca. 1961-71. Illustrated *Crime and Punishment* (World Publishing Co.) and *History of the Jews in America* (Jewish Theological Seminary). Subject of a film demonstrating the cutting and printing of linoleum blocks, produced by Walter O. Gutjohn, 1943. **Member:** Artists Equity. Federal A.P.; Mural painter and graphic artist; mural for Bronx County Hospital, 1940. **Commissions** (murals): New York World's Fair, 1939; Rockefeller Center, NYC, 1943. **Awards:** NIAL Grant, 1961. **m.** Jack Levine. **One-man Exhibitions:** (first) National Serigraph Society, 1943, also 1947; Weyhe Gallery, 1946; Grand Central Moderns, NYC, 1948, 50; Philadelphia Art Alliance, 1949; Ganso Gallery,

NYC, 1952, 53, 54; Rehn Galleries, 1956, 57, 59; Lee Nordness Gallery, NYC, 1961, 63; The Forum Gallery, 1970; Kennedy Gallery, 1972, 76; The Margo Feiden Galleries, NYC, 1974. **Group:** Carnegie; Corcoran; Utica; Youngstown/Butler; MMA; MOMA; U. of Nebraska; PAFA; Springfield, Mass./MFA; WMAA; State U. of Iowa; SFMA; Toledo/MA; San Diego. **Collections:** Brandeis U.; Colby College; MMA; MOMA; NCFA; NIAL; NYU; PMA; Portland; Me./MA; Smithsonian; Springfield, Mass./MFA; Syracuse/Everson; Terre Haute/Swope; WMAA. **Bibliography:** Bethers; Nordness, ed. Archives.

GILLESPIE, GREGORY. b. November 29, 1936, Roselle Park, New Jersey. **Studied:** Cooper Union, 1945-60; SFAI, BA, MFA, 1960-62. **Awards:** Fulbright Fellowship, 1962, 65; Chester Dale Fellowship, 1964, 65; L. C. Tiffany Grant, 1960; NAD, Childe Hassam Fund **P.P.,**

Gregory Gillespie *Self Portrait* 1985

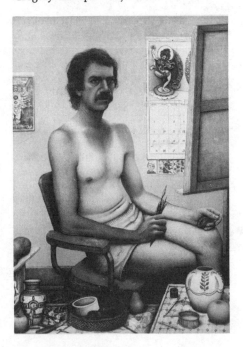

1965. Resided Italy, 1962-70. **Address:** % Dealer. **Dealer:** Forum Gallery, NYC. **One-man Exhibitions:** Forum Gallery, NYC, 1966, 68, 70, 73, 76, 79, 82, 84, 86; American Academy, Rome, 1969; U. of Georgia, 1970; Alpha Gallery, Boston, 1971, 74; Smith College, 1971; Galleria il Fante de Spade, Rome, 1974; Alpha Gallery, Boston, 1982; John Berggruen Gallery, San Francisco, 1983; College of William and Mary, 1983; Brandeis U., (two-man) 1984; Duke U., 1986. **Retrospective:** Hirshhorn, 1977. **Group:** AAAL, 1961, 64, 69; WMAA Annuals, 1965, 68; NAD, 1971, 72, 79; MOMA, 1975; U. of Bridgeport, 1980; New York Cultural Center, Realism Now, 1972; Ringling, After Surrealism, 1977; Haus der Kunst, Munich, Amerikanische Malerie: 1930-1980, 1981; NAD, 1983. **Collections:** Boston/MFA; U. of Georgia; Hirshhorn; Lincoln/Woods; Little Rock/MFA; MMA; NMAA; U. of Nebraska; The Pennsylvania State U.; Trenton/State; VMFA; U. of Virginia; West Virginia U.; WMAA. **Bibliography:** Lucie-Smith.

GILLIAM, SAM. b. 1933, Tupelo, Mississippi. **Studied:** U. of Louisville, 1952-56, BA; 1958-61, MA, with Mary Spencer Nay, Charles Crodel, Eugene Leake, Ulfert Wilke. **Awards:** National Endowment for the Arts, grant, 1967, 73, 74; Chicago/AI, Norman B. Harris Prize, 1969; Longview Grant, 1970; Guggenheim Foundation Fellowship, 1971. **Address:** 1752 Lamont Street, N.W., Washington, DC 20010. **Dealer:** Middendorf/Lane, Washington, D.C. **One-man Exhibitions:** U. of Louisville, 1956; Frame House Gallery, Louisville, 1963; Alan Morgan Gallery, Washington, D.C., 1963, 64; Jefferson Place Gallery, Washington, 1965, 66, 67, 68, 70, 71; Phillips Gallery, 1967; Byron Gallery, NYC, 1968; Galerie Darthea Speyer, Paris, 1970, 73; MOMA, 1971; New Gallery, Cleveland, 1973; Greenberg Gallery, St. Louis, 1973; U. of California, Irvine, 1973; Maison de la Culture, Rennes, 1973; Linda Farris

Gallery, Seattle, 1974, 75; Phoenix Gallery, Seattle, 1974; Solway Gallery, Cincinnati, 1974; Fendrick Gallery, Washington, D.C., 1975, 76, 78; PMA, 1975; Collectors Gallery, Baltimore, 1975; Louisville/Speed, 1976; U. of Kentucky, 1978; Virginia Commonwealth U., 1978; Solway Gallery, NYC, 1978; Nina/Freudenheim Gallery, Buffalo, 1979; Middendorf/Lane Gallery, Washington, D.C., 1979, 80, 84; Hamilton Gallery of Contemporary Art, NYC, 1979, 80; Monique Knowlton Gallery, NYC, 1985; Davis/McClair Gallery, Houston, 1987. **Group:** ICA, Washington, D.C., Artists in Washington, 1966; UCLA, The Negro in American Art, 1966; First World Festival of Negro Arts, Dacca, 1966; Minneapolis/MA, Thirty Contemporary Black Artists, 1968; Corcoran, three-man, 1969; MOMA, Works on Paper, 1970; U. of Texas, Color Forum, 1972; Venice Biennial, 1972; Corcoran Biennial, 1975; Brooklyn Museum, 30 Years of American Printmaking, 1976; NAD, 1979; Trenton/State, 6 Black Americans, 1980. **Collections:** Chicago/AI; Baltimore/MA; Carnegie; Corcoran; Howard U.; Madison/Art Center; Phillips; U. of Iowa; MOMA; Smithsonian; Oberlin College; Oklahoma; Walker; MMA; Rotterdam; Tate; Princeton U.; Museum of African Art, Washington, D.C.; NCFA.

GINNEVER, CHARLES. b. August 28, 1931, San Mateo, Calif. Studied with Ossip Zadkine, William Stanley Hayter, Paris, 1953-55; SFAI, 1955-57, BFA; Cornell U., 1957-59, MFA. Traveled Europe, USA. USAF, 1951-52. **Taught:** Cornell U., 1957-59; Pratt Institute, 1963; New School for Social Research, NYC, 1964; Brooklyn Museum School, 1964-65; Newark School of Fine and Industrial Art, 1965; Dayton/AI, 1966; Aspen (Colo.) School of Contemporary Art, 1966; Orange County Community College, Middletown, N.J., 1966; Windham College, 1967-75. **Commissions:** GSA, St. Paul Courthouse, 1974;

Walker, 1976; City of Houston, 1977; U. of Michigan, National Endowment for the Arts, 1977; Albany/SUNY, 1978; U. of Houston, 1979; K & B Plaza, New Orleans, 1979; Charleston, West Virginia, 1980; Dayton/AI, 1980; Buffalo/SUNY, 1981; Hurd Development Corp., Dallas, 1983; Hewlett-Packard Corp., Palo Alto, Calif., 1985. **Awards:** Vermont State Council on the Arts, 1971; Guggenheim Foundation Fellowship, 1974; National Endowment for the Arts, 1975. **Address:** P.O. Box 411, Putney, VT 05346. **Dealer:** Fuller Goldeen, San Francisco; Marlborough Gallery, NYC. **One-man Exhibitions:** (first) Allan Stone Gallery, 1961; Bennington College, 1965; Washington Square Park, 1968; Battery Park, NYC, 1969-74; Paula Cooper Gallery, 1970-72; Dag Hammarskjold Plaza, NYC, 1973; Sculpture Now, NYC, 1978, 79; Max Hutchinson Gallery, Houston, 1978; Max Hutchinson Gallery, NYC, 1978; Smith-Anderson Gallery, Palo Alto, 1978, Long Beach/AM, 1978; Galerie Simone Stern, New Orleans, 1978; Construct, Chicago, 1979, 81; Max Hutchinson Gallery, NYC, 1980; Storm King Art Center, 1980; Marlborough Gallery, 1983; Fuller Goldeen, 1984, 86; Lee Park, Dallas, 1984; Hurd Development Corp., Dallas, 1984; Max Hutchinson's Sculpture Fields, Kenoza Lake, N.Y., 1986. **Retrospective:** Sculpture Now, Inc., NYC, 1975. **Group:** SFMA Annuals, 1955, 56; SFMA, Bay Area Sculpture, 1956; Cornell U., New York Artists, 1961; Martha Jackson Gallery, NYC, New Forms—New Media, 1960; Riverside Museum, NYC, 10 New York Sculptors, 1963; Walker, Sculpture Made in Place, 1976; A.F.A., Color Sculpture, 1965; Greenwich, Conn., Sculpture '76, 1976; Washington State U., Two Decades 1957-77, 1977; Lake George Arts Project, Lake George, N.Y., Prospect Mountain Sculpture Show, An Homage to David Smith, 1979; NCFA, Across the Nation, 1980; Palo Alto (Calif.) Cultural Center, Outdoor Sculpture Invitational, 1982; Nassau

County Museum, Sculpture: The Traditional in Steel, 1983; AAIAL, 1985. **Collections:** Chicago; Cornell U.; Hartford/Wadsworth; Hirshhorn; U. of Houston; U. of Michigan; Norfolk/Chrysler; Park 470 Corp.; Storm King Art Center; Walker.

GIOBBI, EDWARD. b. July 18, 1926, Waterbury, Conn. US Army, 1944-46. **Studied:** Whitney School of Art, 1946, 47; Vesper George School of Art, 1947-50; ASL, 1950-51; Academy of Fine Arts, Florence, Italy, 1951-54, 1955-56. Traveled Europe. **Taught:** Memphis Academy of Arts, 1960, 61 (Artist-in-Residence); Dartmouth College, 1972. **Member:** Century Association. **Awards:** Joe and Emily Lowe Foundation Award, 1951, and Special Grant, 1952; Yaddo Fellowship, 1957; Ford Foundation, 1966; Guggenheim Foundation Fellowship, 1971. **Address:** 161 Croton Lake Road, Katonah, NY 10536. **Dealer:** Irving Galleries Inc., Palm Beach, Fla. **One-man Exhibitions:** (first) Ward Eggleston Gallery, NYC, 1950, also 1952; Galerie An der Reuss, Lucerne, 1953 (two-man); Nexus Gallery, Boston, 1956 (two-man); Artists' Gallery, NYC, 1956; John Heller Gallery, NYC, 1957, 58; The Contemporaries, NYC, 1960, 61, 63; Memphis/Brooks, 1961, 70; Memphis Academy, 1962; Katonah (N.Y.) Art Gallery, 1963, 69, 75; The New Art Centre, 1964, 67, 70; The Bear Lane Gallery, Oxford, 1964; The Queen Square Gallery, Leeds, 1964; Tirca Karlis Gallery, 1965-66; Mickelson's Gallery, Washington, D.C., 1966; The Alan Gallery, NYC, 1966; Waddell Gallery, 1967, 69; Obelisk Gallery, 1968; Gertrude Kasle Gallery, 1968, 70; Galleria Obelisco, Rome, 1974; Crane Kalman Gallery, London, 1975; Galleria del Naviglio, Milan, 1976; Purchase/SUNY, 1977; Gruenebaum Gallery, NYC, 1978, 79, 82; Lee Hoffman Gallery, Detroit, 1978; Mattatuck Museum, Waterbury, Conn., 1978; Irving Gallery, Palm Beach, 1978. **Group:** WMAA

Annuals, 1957, 61, 66, Young America, 1961, Forty Artists under Forty, circ., 1962; MOMA, Recent Drawings USA, 1956, Recent Painting USA: The Figure, circ., 1962-63; PAFA, 1961; U. of Arkansas, 1966; Finch College, 1967. **Collections:** Allentown/AM; Baltimore/MA; Boston/MFA; Brandeis U.; Brooklyn Museum; Buffalo/Albright; Cambridge; Chicago/AI; Dartmouth College; Detroit/Institute; Florence, Italy; Mattatuck Museum, Waterbury, Conn.; Memphis/Brooks; U. of Michigan; Oxford; Poole Technical College; San Antonio/McNay; Spelman College; Syracuse U.; Tate Gallery; WMAA; Wesleyan College; Williams College; U. of Wisconsin.

GLACKENS, WILLIAM. b. March 13, 1870, Philadelphia, Pa.; **d.** May 22, 1938, Westport, Conn. **Studied:** Central High School, Philadelphia, BA; PAFA. Traveled France, Spain, Canada. Newspaper illustrator for many years. **Member:** Society of Independent Artists, NYC (first president, 1916-17); The Eight; NAD, 1937 (Associate, 1896); NIAL. **Awards:** Buffalo/Albright, Gold Medal, 1901; St. Louis Exposition, 1904, Silver and Bronze Medals; Carnegie, Hon. Men., 1905; Panama-Pacific Exposition, San Francisco, 1915, Bronze Medal; PAFA, Joseph E. Temple Gold Medal, 1924; Carnegie, Second Prize, 1929; PAFA, Carol H. Beck Gold Medal, 1933; PAFA, Jennie Sesnan Gold Medal, 1936; Paris World's Fair, 1937, Grand Prix; PAFA, J. Henry Schiedt Memorial Prize, 1938. **One-man Exhibitions:** (first) New Arts Club, NYC; Academy of Fine Arts, Berlin, 1910; Kraushaar Galleries, 1925, 28, 35, 42, 57, 85; Andover/Phillips, 1936; Louisville/Speed, 1939; 10 West Ninth Street, NYC, Memorial Exhibition, annually, 1939-49; NCFA, 1972. **Retrospectives:** WMAA, 1938, 67; Carnegie, 1939; Kraushaar Galleries, 1949; Dartmouth College, 1960; St. Louis/City, 1966; NCFA, 1967. **Group:** Paris Salon, 1895, 1900; Macbeth Gallery, NYC, The Eight, 1908; Independents, NYC, 1910; The Armory Show, 1913; WMAA, New York Realists, 1937; Brooklyn Museum, The Eight, 1943; PMA, Artists of the Philadelphia Press, 1945; Renaissance Society, Chicago, 1955; Syracuse/Everson, The Eight, 1958. **Collections:** Andover/Phillips; Barnes Foundation; Boston/MFA; Buffalo/Albright; Chicago/AI; Columbus; Detroit/Institute; MMA; U. of Nebraska; Newark Museum; PMA; Sweet Briar College; WMAA. **Bibliography:** Barnes; Bazin; Biddle 4; Born; Bulliet 1; Canaday; Cheney; **Du Bois 5, 6;** Gallatin 2; **Glackens;** Hall; Hartmann; Huyghe; *Index of 20th Century Artists;* Jackman; **Katz;** Kent, N.; McCoubrey 1; McCurdy, ed.; Neuhaus; Pach 1; Perlman; Phillips 2; Poore; Ringel, ed.; Rose, B., 1, 4; Sachs; **Watson, F.** Archives.

GLARNER, FRITZ. b. July 20, 1899, Zurich, Switzerland; **d.** September 18, 1972, Locarno, Switzerland. **Studied:** Academy of Fine Arts, Naples. To USA, 1936. **Commissions:** Time & Life Building, lobby, NYC, 1960 (mural); Dag Hammarskjold Library, United Nations, NYC. **Awards:** Corcoran, 1957. **One-man Exhibitions:** Galerie Povolotzki, Paris, 1930; Civic Club, NYC, 1931; The Kootz Gallery, NYC, 1945; Rose Fried Gallery, 1949, 51; Galerie Louis Carre, Paris, 1952, 55; ICA, U. of Pennsylvania, 1971; SFMA, 1971; Gimpel & Hanover Gallery, 1972; Gimpel Fils, 1972; Graham Gallery, NYC (three-man), 1980. **Retrospective:** Berne, 1972. **Group:** Buffalo/Albright, 1931; American Abstract Artists, 1938-44; Chicago/AI, 1947, 58, 64; Toronto, 1949; California Palace, 1950; WMAA, 1950, 51, 53, 54, 55; VMFA, 1950, 58; Sao Paulo, 1951; Brooklyn Museum, 1951; U. of Minnesota, 1951; MOMA, 1951, 52, 54, 55; U. of Illinois, 1952, 65; Carnegie, 1952, 58, 61; Tokyo/Modern, 1953; SRGM, 1954; U. of Nebraska, 1955; Documenta I, Kassel, 1955; Corcoran, 1955, 57, 60;

Zurich, 1956; Musée Neuchatel, 1957; Kunstverein, Winterthur, 1958; Kongresshalle, Berlin, 1958; XXIX & XXXII Venice Biennials, 1958, 64; Heimathaus, Zurich, 1960; Seattle World's Fair, 1962; WMAA, Geometric Abstraction in America, circ., 1962; WGMA, The Formalists, 1963; St. Paul Gallery, Drawing USA 1963; Tate, Dunn International, 1964; Musée Cantonal des Beaux-Arts, Lausanne, 1964; MOMA, Contemporary Painters and Sculptors as Printmakers, 1964; Indiana U., 1965; PAFA, 1965. **Collections:** Baltimore/MA; Boston/MFA; Brandeis U.; Brooklyn Museum; Buffalo/Albright; Chase Manhattan Bank; Florida State U.; Karachi; MOMA; Minnesota/MA; NYU; National Gallery; U. of Nebraska; PMA; Phillips; Rockefeller Institute; Smithsonian; WMAA; Walker; Yale U.; Zurich. **Bibliography:** *Abstraction Creation 1931-1936;* Baur 7; Biddle 4; Blesh 1; **Fritz Glarner;** Haftman; Hess, T.B., 1; Janis, S.; Lane and Larsen; MacAgy 2; McCurdy, ed.; Neumeyer; Pousette-Dart, ed.; Read 2; Rickey; Ritchie 1; Rose, B., 1; Seuphor 1; Staber; "What Abstract Art Means to Me."

GLASCO, JOSEPH. b. January 19, 1925, Paul's Valley, Okla. **Studied:** U. of Texas, 1941-43; Jepson Art Institute, Los Angeles; Art Center School, Los Angeles, 1946-48; privately with Rico Lebrun, 1946-48; Escuela de Bellas Artes, San Miguel de Allende, Mexico, 1948; ASL, 1949. US Army Air Force, 1943-45, Infantry, 1945-56. Traveled Mexico, Europe, Africa. **Member:** National Society of Literature and the Arts. **Commissions:** Amarillo (Tex.) Air Field (mural). **Address:** 100 Greene Street, NYC 10012. **Dealer:** Gimpel & Weitzenhoffer, Ltd. **One-man Exhibitions:** (first) Perls Galleries, 1950; Caterine Viviano Gallery, 1951, 52, 53, 54, 56, 58, 61, 63, 70; Arts Club of Chicago, 1954, 57; U. of Oklahoma, 1965 (three-man); Rizzoli Gallery, NYC, 1967; Kiko Gallery, Houston, 1968, 69, 70; Louisiana Gallery, Houston, 1973,

75; Gimpel & Weitzenhoffer, NYC, 1979, 82. **Retrospective:** Houston/Contemporary, 1986. **Group:** MOMA, New Talent; MMA; WMAA; Corcoran; SRGM; Brooklyn Museum; Chicago/AI; Dallas/MFA; Detroit/Institute; Los Angeles/County MA; U. of Illinois; U. of Nebraska; Carnegie, 1958; PAFA; WMAA Forty Artists under Forty, 1963; Houston/MFA, Fresh Paint, circ., 1985. **Collections:** Brooklyn Museum; Buffalo/Albright; Corcoran; Detroit/Institute; High Museum; Hirshhorn; Houston/MFA; MMA; MOMA; Newark Museum; Princeton U.; SRGM; WMAA; Yale U. **Bibliography:** Goodrich and Baur 1; Mendelowitz; Rodman 1; Tapie 1.

GOINGS, RALPH. b. May 9, 1928, Corning, Calif. **Studied:** California College of Arts and Crafts, 1953, BFA; Sacramento State U., 1966, MA. US Army, 1946-48. Traveled England, Europe. **Taught:** La Sierra High School, 1969; U. of California, Davis, 1971. **Address:** Charlotteville, NY 12036. **Dealer:** OK Harris Works of Art, NYC. **One-man Exhibitions:** Artists Cooperative Gallery, Sacramento, 1960, 62, 68; OK Harris Works of Art, 1970, 73, 77, 80, 83, 85; MOMA, 1977. **Group:** SFMA Annual, 1961; Milwaukee, Aspects of a New Realism, 1969; Newport Harbor, Directly Seen: New Realism in California, 1970; Potsdam/SUNY, New Realism, 1971; Hamburg/Kunstverein, USA; West Coast, circ., 1972; Documenta V, Kassel, 1972; Stuttgart/WK, Amerikanischer Fotorealismus, circ., 1972; Cincinnati/Contemporary, Options, 73/30, 1973; Randers Kunstmuseum, Denmark, Amerikanske Realister, 1973; Tokyo Biennial, 1974; CNAC, Hyperrealistes Americains/Realistes Europeens, 1974; Akron/AI, Selections in Contemporary Realism, 1974; Hamilton College, California Climate, 1974. **Group:** Queens Museum, Urban Aesthetics, 1976; Akron/AI, Contemporary Images in Watercolor, 1976; Albright College,

Buffalo, Perspective 1976, 1976; Canberra/National, Illusion and Reality, circ., 1977; U. of Nebraska, Things Seen, circ., 1978; Tulsa/Philbrook, Realism/Photorealism, 1980; PAFA, Contemporary American Realism Since 1960, 1981; San Antonio/MA, Real, Really Real, Super Real, circ., 1981; Houston/Contemporary, American Still Life: 1945-1983, 1983; Los Angeles/MOCA, Automobile and Culture, 1984; Isetan Museum of Art, Tokyo, American Realism, The Precise Image, 1985; SFMA, American Realism, circ., 1985. **Collections:** Borgon Associates; Chicago/Contemporary; Essen/NG; F.T.D. Association; Hamburg/Kunstverein; ICA, U. of Pennsylvania; U. of Miami; MOMA; U. of Nebraska; Portland, Ore./AM; SRGM; Tampa/AI; WMAA. **Bibliography:** Alloway 4; *Amerikanischer Fotorealismus;* Arthur 1, 3, 4; Goings; Honisch and Jensen, eds.; *Kunst um 1970;* Sager; *The State of California Painting; USA West Coast.*

GOLDBERG, MICHAEL. b. 1924, NYC. **Studied:** ASL, 1938-42, 1946, with Jose de Creeft; City College of New York, 1940-42, 1946-47; Hofmann School, 1941-42, 1948-50. US Army 1942-46. **Taught:** U. of California, 1961-62. **Address:** 222 Bowery, NYC 10012. **Dealer:** Ileana Sonnabend Gallery, NYC. **One-man Exhibitions:** (first) Tibor de Nagy Gallery, 1953; Poindexter Gallery, 1956, 58; Martha Jackson Gallery, 1960, 64, 66; Paul Kantor Gallery, Beverly Hills, Calif., 1960; Holland-Goldowsky Gallery, Chicago, 1960 (two-man); B.C. Holland Gallery, 1961; Galerie Anderson-Mayer, Paris, 1963; Bob Keene, Southampton, N.Y., 1963; Paley & Lowe Inc., NYC, 1971 (two-man), 1972, 73; Vancouver, 1971 (two-man); Cunningham-Ward Gallery, NYC, 1975, 76; Ghent Gallery, Norfolk, Va., 1973; Galerie Hecate, Paris, 1975; Galerie Denise Rene, NYC, 1977; Galerie Sonnabend, Paris, 1978; Galerie December, Dusseldorf, 1978;

Young-Hoffman Gallery, Chicago, 1978; Loyse van Oppenheim Gallery, Geneva, 1978; Daniel Weinberg Gallery, San Francisco, 1978; Sonnabend Gallery, NYC, 1979, 80, 81, 83; Thomas Segal Gallery, Boston, 1979; Artline, The Hague, 1980; Galerie Art in Progress, Dusseldorf, 1980; L.A. Louver Gallery, Venice, Calif., 1981, 82; Cleveland/MA, 1981; Plurima, Udine, Italy, 1982, 84; Roberto Peccolo, Livorno, Italy, 1982, 84; Virginia Commonwealth U., 1983; Young Hoffman Gallery, Chicago, 1983; Vanderwoude Tananbaum Gallery, NYC, 1984, 85; Nadia Bassanese, Trieste, 1984; U. of Nebraska, 1984; Jack Tilton Gallery, NYC, 1985; Galerie Biedermann, Munich, 1985. **Group:** Ninth Street Exhibition, NYC, 1951; The Stable Gallery Annuals, 1952-57; Sidney Jarvis Gallery, Four Younger Americans, 1956; Carnegie, 1958; WMAA Annuals, 1958, 67; Gutai 9, Osaka, 1958; Turin Art Festival, 1959; Documenta II, Kassel, 1959; Walker, 60 American Painters, 1960; Columbus, Contemporary American Painting, 1960; MOMA, Hans Hofmann and His Students, circ., 1963-64; Musée Cantonal des Beaux-Arts, Lausanne, I Salon International de Galeries Pilotes, 1963; Lehigh U., 1966; Smithsonian, 66; Star Turtle Gallery, NYC, The Tenants of Sam Wapnowitz, 1969; Corcoran, 1969; Salon de Mai, Paris, 1969; WMAA Annual, 1973; Indianapolis, 1978; Hirshhorn, The Fifties, 1980; Newport Harbor, Action/Precision, circ., 1984. **Collections:** Baltimore/MA; Buffalo/Albright; U. of California, Berkeley; Chicago/AI; Corcoran; Cornell U.; Hartford/Wadsworth; Hirshhorn; Israel Museum; Lincoln, Mass./De Cordova; MOMA; Norfolk/Chrysler; PMA; SRGM; Tokyo/Modern; WMAA; Walker. **Bibliography:** Downes, ed.; Janis and Blesh 1; O-Hara; Sandler 1. Archives.

GOLDIN, LEON. b. January 16, 1923, Chicago, Ill. **Studied:** State U. of Iowa, with Mauricio Lasansky, 1948, BFA, 1950, MFA; Chicago Art Institute School, with Robert Von Neuman. Traveled Europe extensively; resided Paris, 1952-53, Rome, 1955-58. **Taught:** California College of Arts and Crafts, 1950-52, 1954-55; Philadelphia Museum School, 1960-62; Queens College, 1960-62; Cooper Union, 1961-64; Columbia, U., 1962-. **Awards:** L. C. Tiffany Grant, 1951; Fulbright Fellowship (France), 1952; SFMA, H.S. Crocker Co. Award, 1952; Prix de Rome, 1955, renewed 1956-57; Guggenheim Foundation Fellowship, 1959; Ford Foundation, **P.P.**, 1960; PAFA, Jennie Sesnan Gold Medal, 1965; National Endowment for the Arts Grant, 1966; NIAL Grant, 1968; National Endowment for the Arts, 1980; CAPS grant, 1981; and many print awards. **Address:** 438 West 116th Street, NYC, 10027. **Dealer:** Kraushaar Galleries. **One-man Exhibitions:** (first) Oakland/AM, 1955; Felix Landau Gallery, 1956, 57, 59; Galleria L'Attico, Rome, 1958; Kraushaar Galleries, 1960, 64, 68, 72; U. of Houston, 1981. **Group:** Chicago/AI Annuals, 1946, 48; SFMA Annuals, 1948, 51-54; Los Angeles/County MA, 1949, 50; MMA, American Paintings Today, 1950; PAFA, 1951, 1960-64; MOMA, Contemporary American Painting, 1953; Santa Barbara/MA, 1955; MOMA, Recent Drawings, USA, 1956; Corcoran, 1963; Carnegie, 1964. **Collections:** Andover/Phillips; Arts Council of Great Britain; Ball State U.; Baltimore/MA; Brooklyn Museum; Cincinnati/AM; Los Angeles/County MA; Louisville/Speed; Morgan State College; NCFA; U. of Nebraska; Oakland/AM; PAFA; Portland, Me./AM; RAC; St. Louis/City; Santa Barbara/MA; U. of Southern California; Syracuse/Everson; Utica; VMFA; Worcester/AM. **Bibliography:** Nordness, ed.

GOLUB, LEON. b. January 23, 1922, Chicago, Ill. **Studied:** The U. of Chicago, 1942, BA; Chicago Art Institute

School, with Paul Wieghardt, Kathleen Blackshear, Robert Lifuendahl, 1949, BFA, 1950, MFA. US Army, 1942-46. Traveled Europe; resided Italy, 1956-57, Paris, 1959-64. **Taught:** Illinois Institute of Technology, 1955-56; Indiana U., 1957-59; Wright Junior College; Northwestern U.; Stella Elkins Tyler School of Fine Arts; Temple U., 1965-66; School of Visual Arts, NYC, 1966-69; Fairleigh Dickinson U., 1969; Rutgers U., 1970-. **Awards:** Chicago/AI, Florsheim Memorial Prize, 1954; Ford Foundation Grant, 1960; Chicago/AI, Watson F. Blair Prize; II Inter-American Paintings and Prints Biennial, Mexico City, Hon. Men., 1960; Cassandra Foundation Grant, 1967; Guggenheim Foundation Fellowship, 1968; AAAL; NIAL, 1973; Hon. DFA, Chicago Art Institute School, 1982; Hon. DFA, Swarthmore College, 1985. **Address:** 530 LaGuardia Place, NYC 10012. **Dealer:** Barbara Gladstone, NYC. **One-man Exhibitions:** (first) Contemporary Gallery, Chicago, 1950; Purdue U., 1951; Wittenborn Gallery, NYC, 1952, 57; Kerrigan-Hendricks Gallery, Chicago, 1954; Artists' Gallery, NYC, 1954; Allan Frumkin Gallery, Chicago, 1955, 60, 64, NYC, 1959, 61, 63; Feigl Gallery, NYC, 1955, 56; Chicago Public Library, 1956; Pomona College, 1956; Pasadena/AM, 1956; ICA, London, 1957, 82; Indiana U., 1958; American Cultural Center, Paris, 1960; Iris Clert Gallery, 1962; Hanover Gallery, 1962; Gallery A. Melbourne, 1963; The U. of Chicago, 1966; Pro Graphica Arte, 1968; MIT, 1970; Melbourne/Nacional, 1970; Darthea Speyer Gallery, 1971; Herbert H. Lehman College, Bronx, N.Y., 1972; Bienville Gallery, 1972; Stony Brook/SUNY, 1975; Trenton/State, 1975; Haverford College, 1976; SFAI, 1976; Olympia Galleries, Glen Cove, Pa. 1977; Walter Kelly Gallery, Chicago, 1977; Colgate U., 1978; School of Visual Arts, NYC, 1979; Protetch-McIntosh Gallery, Washington, D.C., 1980; Swarthmore College (two-man) 1981; Susan Caldwell, Inc., 1982, 84; Kipnis Works of Art, Atlanta, 1982; Young

Hoffman Gallery, Chicago, 1982; U. of California, Berkeley, 1983; College of Art and Design, Detroit, 1983; Honolulu Academy, 1983; U. of Houston, circ., 1983; U. of New Mexico (two-man) 1983; Paule Anglim Associates, San Francisco, 1984; Installation Gallery, San Diego, 1984; Rhona Hoffman Gallery, Chicago, 1985; Printworks, Chicago, 1985; Darthea Speyer Gallery, 1985; Stanford U., 1985; Donald Young Gallery, Chicago, 1985; Barbara Gladstone, 1986. **Retrospectives:** Temple U., 1964; Chicago/Contemporary, 1974; New York Cultural Center, 1975; New Museum, circ., 1984. **Group:** Chicago/AI, Exhibition Momentum, 1948-58; SRGM, Younger American Painters, 1954; Chicago/AI, 1954, 62; Carnegie, 1955, 64, 67; Premio Marzotto; U. of Illinois, 1957, 61, 63; MOMA, New Images of Man, 1959; Documenta II & III, Kassel, 1959, 64; Sao Paulo, 1962; Corcoran, 1962; Salon des Realites Nouvelles, Paris, 1962; MOMA, Recent Painting, USA: The Figure, circ., 1962-63; Art: USA: Now, circ., 1962-67; SFMA, Directions—Painting U.S.A., 1963; Smithsonian, Graphics, circ., USA, 1963; Ghent, Figuration d'Aujourd'hui, 1964; Paris/Moderne, Mythologiques Quotidiennes, 1964; PAFA Annuals, 1964, 65; New York World's Fair, 1964-65; VMFA, American Painting, 1966, 70; II Internationale der Zeichnung, Darmstadt, 1967; Paris/Moderne, Le Monde en Question, 1967; ICA, London, The Obsessive Image, 1968; Madrid/Nacional, II Biennial, 1969; Chicago/Contemporary, Chicago Imagist Art, 1972; Chicago Art Institute School, Visions, 1976; Paris/Beaubourg, Paris—New York, 1977; U. of Michigan, Chicago: The City and its Artists, 1945-78, 1977; Chicago/AI, Centennial Exhibition, 1979; Brandeis U., Aspects of the 70's—Mavericks, 1980; Indianapolis, 1982; Rutgers U., Realism & Realities, 1982; Contemporary Arts Center, New Orleans, Sex and Violence, 1983; WMAA Biennial, 1983; Hirshhorn, Content: A Contemporary Focus 1974-1984, 1984; Studio Museum, Transition and Conflict: Images of a Turbulent Decade, 1984; Grande Halle de la Villette, Paris, Nouvelle Biennale de Paris, 1985; Seattle/AM, States of War, 1985; Fort Lauderdale, An American Renaissance: Painting and Sculpture Since 1940, 1986. **Collections:** Allentown/AM; Amon Carter Museum; U. of California; Chicago/AI; Chicago/Contemporary; U. of Chicago; Corcoran; Des Moines; Grunwald Foundation; Hampton Institute; Hirshhorn; Indiana U.; Kansas City/Nelson; Jewish Museum; Kent State U.; La Jolla; Los Angeles; MOMA; Melbourne/National; Montreal/MFA; NCFA; Nashville; Nashville/State; U. of North Carolina; Pasadena/AM; Seattle/AM; Southern Illinois U.; Tel Aviv; U. of Texas. **Bibliography:** Adrian; Danto; **Kuspit;** Nordness, ed.; Sandler 1; Schulze. Archives.

GONZALEZ, JUAN J. b. January 12, 1945, Cuba. **Studied:** U. of Miami, BFA, MFA. US Citizen. **Taught:** School of Visual Arts, NYC, 1977-. **Awards:** Cintas Fellowship, 1973, 75; CAPS, 1976; National Endowment for the Arts, 1980, 85. **Address:** 42 West 17th Street, NYC 10011. **Dealer:** Nancy Hoffman Gallery, NYC. **One-man Exhibitions:** (first) Allan Stone Gallery, NYC, 1972; Corcoran and Corcoran, Miami, 1973; Nancy Hoffman Gallery, 1975, 78, 82, 85; Union College, Cranford, N.J., 1978; Miami-Dade, 1980; Center for Inter-American Relations, 1981. **Group:** Miami-Art Center, Thirty-Three Miami Artists, 1971; WMAA Annual, 1972; Indianapolis, 1974; Center for Inter-American Relations, 6 Cuban Painters Working in New York, 1975; Rice U., Drawing Today in New York, circ., 1977; Bronx Museum, Images of Horror and Fantasy, 1977; IEF, Recent Latin American Drawings 1969-1976, 1977; IEF, Twentieth Century American Drawings: The Figure in Context, circ., 1984; SFMA, American Realism (Janss), circ., 1985.

Juan Gonzalez *New York, Year 1986* 1986

Collections: Carnegie; Danforth Museum; Hirshhorn; Indianapolis; MMA; U. of Oklahoma; Vassar College. **Bibliography:** Arthur 3.

GONZALEZ, XAVIER. b. February 15, 1898, Almeria, Spain. US citizen, 1930. **Studied:** Chicago/AI. Traveled Greece, Crete, USA; resided Paris, 1930-40; Orient. **Taught:** H. Sophie Newcomb Memorial College; Brooklyn Museum School; Western Reserve U., 1953-54; Summer School of Art, Wellfleet, Mass. President, National Society of Mural Painters. **Member:** NAD; Century Association; Trustee, Lewis Comfort Tiffany Foundation. **Awards:** AAAL Grant; PAFA, Dawson Memorial Medal, 1946; Guggenheim Foundation Fellowship, 1947; Audubon Artists, Gold Medal of Honor; National Arts Club, Gold Medal, 1978. **Address:** 222

Central Park South, NYC 10019. **Dealers:** Oehlschlaeger Gallery, Sarasota, Fla; The Milch Gallery, NYC; Wellfleet Art Gallery, Wellfleet, Mass. **One-man Exhibitions:** Joseph Luyber Galleries, NYC, 1946, 47; Arts and Crafts Club, New Orleans, 1948; Philadelphia Art Alliance, 1949; Norlyst Gallery, NYC; Shore Studio, Boston; Grand Central Moderns, NYC, 1951, 52, 53; The Howard Wise Gallery, Cleveland, 1958; Widdifield Gallery, NYC, 1958; The Milch Gallery, 1960, 63; Richard Larcada Gallery, 1974. **Group:** PAFA; Corcoran; U. of Nebraska; Carnegie; Brooklyn Museum; WMAA; Indianapolis/Herron. **Collections:** Wellesley College. **Bibliography:** Biddle 4; Cheney; Pearson 2; Pousette-Dart, ed. Archives.

GOODE, JOE. b. March 23, 1937, Oklahoma City, Okla. **Studied:** Chouinard Art Institute. Traveled Mexico, England, Europe, South America, India, Iceland. **Awards:** Cassandra Foundation Grant. **Address:** 1159 S. Hayworth, Los Angeles, CA 90035. **Dealer:** Charles Cowles Gallery, NYC. **One-man Exhibitions:** Nicholas Wilder Gallery, 1966, 69, 70, 72, 74, 75, 78, 79; Rowan Gallery, London, 1967; Gallery Hans R. Neuendorf, Hamburg, 1970, 72, 73, 75; Galleria Milano, Milan, 1971; La Jolla, 1971; Mueller Gallery, 1971; Felicity Samuel Gallery, London, 1972, 73; Fort Worth, 1973; Houston/Contemporary, 1973; Contract Graphics, Houston, 1972, 75; Cirrus Gallery, Los Angeles, 1974; California State College, Northridge, 1974; Seder/Creigh Gallery, Coronado, 1975; James Corcoran Gallery, Los Angeles, 1976; Washington U., 1976; St. Mary's College, L.A., 1977; Texas Gallery, Houston, 1979; Charles Cowles Gallery, NYC, 1980; Texas Gallery, Houston, 1979; Charles Cowles Gallery, NYC, 1980; Texas Gallery, Houston, 1979; Arco Center for the Visual Arts, Los Angeles, 1982; Braunstein Gallery, San Francisco, 1985.

Group: WMAA Annuals, 1966, 67, 69; Carnegie, 1967; Portland, Ore./AM, The West Coast Now, 1968; WMAA, American Pop Art, 1974; Chicago/AI, 1974; School of Visual Arts, NYC, 4 Los Angeles Artists, 1975; LAICA, Current Concerns, Part I, 1975; SFMA, California Painting and Sculpture: The Modern Era, 1976; Austin (two-man), 1976; Scripps College, Claremont, Black and White Are Colors, 1978; Buffalo/Albright, American Painting in the Seventies, 1978; Sacramento/Crocker, Aspects of Abstract, 1978. **Collections:** Fort Worth; Los Angeles/County MA; MOMA; Oklahoma; Pasadena/AM. **Bibliography:** Alloway 1; *Black and White Are Colors; New in the Seventies; The State of California Painting; USA West Coast.*

GOODMAN, SIDNEY. b. January 19, 1936, Philadelphia, Pa. **Studied:** Philadelphia Museum School, 1958, with Jacob Landau, Larry Day, Morris Berd. US Army, 1958-59. Traveled Europe. **Taught:** Philadelphia College of Art, 1960-78; Tyler School, Philadelphia, 1977; PAFA, 1978-; Skowhegan School, 1985; Maryland Institute, 1986; Illinois State U., 1986. **Awards:** PAFA, First Watercolor Prize, 1961; Guggenheim Foundation Fellowship, 1963; Ford Foundation Fellowship, 1963; Ford Foundation, **P.P.,** Yale-Norfolk Summer School Fellowship; National Endowment for the Arts, 1974; PAFA, Fellowship Prize, 1974; Governor's Award for Excellence in the Arts in Pennsylvania, 1986. **Address:** 413 South 24th Street, Philadelphia, Pa. 19146. **Dealer:** Terry Dintenfass, Inc., NYC. **One-man Exhibitions:** (first) The Print Club, Philadelphia, 1958, also 1963; Terry Dintenfass, Inc., 1961, 1963-1966, 68, 75, 77, 78, 80, 82, 84, 85; Bard College, 1968; George Washington U., 1969; PAFA, Peale House, 1969 (two-man), 1975 (two-man); U. of Rhode Island, 1974; Moravian College, 1974; The Schenectady Museum, 1977; Rhode Island College, 1979; College of

William and Mary, 1979; VMFA, 1981; Boston U., 1982; Wichita/AM, 1984; PMA, 1985. **Retrospective:** Queens Museum, circ., 1980. **Group:** PAFA, 1960-64, 67, 68; MOMA, 1962; NAD, 1962, 77, 78; WMAA, Forty Artists under Forty, circ., 1962; MOMA, Recent Painting USA: The Figure, circ., 1962-63; WMAA Annuals, 1962-64, 1967-68; 73; Corcoran, 1963; Brooklyn Museum, 1963, 1968-69; Newark Museum, 1967; New School for Social Research, Protest and Hope, 1967; Vassar College, 1968; U. of Miami, 1968; U. of Kentucky, 1968; Indianapolis/Herron, 1969; U. of Illinois, 1969; Southern Methodist U., 1969; Tulsa/Philbrook, 1969; Iowa State U., American Drawing, 1971; Boston U., The American Landscape, 1972; Cleveland/MA, 32 Realists, 1972; Sweden/Gotenborgs, Warmwind: American Realists, 1972; Omaha/Joslyn, A Sense of Place, 1973; VMFA, Works on Paper, 1974; AAAL, 1974; Harrisburg, Pa./State Museum, The Figure in American Art, 1975; PMA, Three Centuries of American Art, 1976; Queens Museum, Urban Aesthetics, 1976; US Department of the Interior, America, 1976, 1976; U. of North Carolina, Art on Paper, 1977; PMA, Contemporary Drawing; Philadelphia II, 1979; WMAA, 20th Century Drawings from the Whitney Museum of American Art, circ., 1979-81; PAFA, Contemporary American Realism Since 1960, 1981; NAD, 1982; IEF, Twentieth Century American Drawings: The Figure in Context, circ., 1984; SFMA, American Realism (Janss), circ., 1985. **Collections:** U. of Arkansas; Brandeis U.; Brooklyn Museum; Chicago/AI; Delaware Art Museum; Grinnell College; Hirshhorn; Kalamazoo/Institute; Library of Congress; MMA; MOMA; U. of Maine; Miami-Dade; Minnesota/MA; Moravian College; NAAL; NAD; U. of Nebraska; U. of North Carolina; PAFA; PMA; The Pennsylvania State U.; Syracuse U.; WMAA; Wake Forest U. **Bibliography:** *America 1976;* Goodyear; Arthur 2.

GOODNOUGH, ROBERT. b. October 23, 1917, Cortland, N.Y. **Studied:** Syracuse U., BFA; NYU, MA; New School for Social Research; Hofmann School; Ozenfant School of Art, NYC. **Taught:** Cornell U.; NYU; Fieldston School, NYC. Critic for *Art News* magazine, 1950-57. Secretary, Documents of Modern Art (edited by Robert Motherwell), 1951. **Commissions:** Manufacturers Hanover Trust Co. **Awards:** Syracuse U., Hiram Gee Fellowship; Chicago/AI, Ada S. Garrett Prize, 1962; Ford Foundation, **P.P.,** 1962. **Address:** 15 Barrow Street, NYC 10014. **Dealer:** Andre Emmerich Gallery, NYC. **One-man Exhibitions:** (first) Tibor de Nagy Gallery, 1952, also 1953-70; RISD, 1956; Dwan Gallery, 1959-62; Jefferson Place Gallery, 1960; Ellison Gallery, Fort Worth, 1960; Nova Gallery, Boston, 1961; U. of Minnesota; U. of Notre Dame, 1964; Arts Club of Chicago, 1964; New Vision Center, London, 1964; USIS Gallery, London, 1964; Gertrude Kasle Gallery, 1966, 69, 72, 74; Reed College, 1967; Buffalo/Albright, 1969; Axiom Gallery, London, 1969; Cayuga Museum of History and Art, Auburn, N.Y., 1969; Galerie Simone Stern, New Orleans, 1969, 70; Kasmin Ltd., 1970; Harcus-Krakow Gallery, 1972; Nicholas Wilder Gallery, 1972; Syracuse U., 1972; Andre Emmerich Gallery, NYC, 1972, 73, 74, 80, 82; David Mirvish Gallery, 1973, 75; Waddington, Tooth Galleries II, London, 1975; M. Knoedler & Co., NYC, 1977; Hokin Gallery, Chicago, 1978; Nina Freudenheim Gallery, Buffalo, 1978; Watson/De Nagy, Houston, 1979, 81, 83; Wichita State U., 1978; Tibor de Nagy, NYC, 1984, 85; Klonaridis, Inc., Toronto, 1979, 81; Klonaridis, Inc., NYC, 1982, 86; Modern Master Tapestries, Inc., NYC, 1982; Martha White Gallery, Louisville, 1982; Nina Freudenheim, 1983; Lincoln Center, NYC, 1983; Elca London Gallery, Montreal, 1985. **Group:** The Kootz Gallery, NYC, New Talent, 1950; Sidney Janis Gallery, Four Younger Americans, 1956; WMAA; Yale U.; Carnegie; Chicago/AI; NIAL, 1964; MOMA, The New American Painting and Sculpture, 1969; U. of Illinois, 1969; Indianapolis, 1969; XXV Venice Biennial, 1970; AAAL, 1971; Grand Palais, Paris, L'Amerique aux Indépéndants, 1980; Houston/Contemporary, The Americans: The College, 1982; St. Lawrence U., Pre Postmodern: Good in the Art of Our Time, 1985. **Collections:** Baltimore/MA; Birmingham, Ala./MA; Boston/MFA; Buffalo/Albright; Chase Manhattan Bank; Chicago/AI; Hartford/Wadsworth; MMA; MOMA; Manufacturers Hanover Trust Co.; Michigan State U.; NYU; Newark Museum; U. of Notre Dame; The Pennsylvania State U.; RISD; Raleigh/NCMA; SRGM; Syracuse U.; WMAA. **Bibliography:** Baur 5; Blesh 1; **Bush and Moffett;** Downes, ed.; Friedman, ed.; Goodrich and Baur 1; Guest and Friedman; Janis and Blesh 1; Nordness, ed.; Rose, B., 1; Sandler 1; Seitz 3.

GOODYEAR, JOHN. b. October 22, 1930, Los Angeles, Calif. **Studied:** U. of Michigan (with Richard Wilt, Chet LaMore, Gerome Kamrowski), B. Design, 1952, M. Design, 1954. US Army, 1954-56. Traveled Mexico, Western Europe; resided USA, Japan. **Taught:** U. of Michigan; U. of Massachusetts, Douglass College 1964-. **Member:** American Abstract Artists. **Awards:** Graham Foundation Fellowship, 1962, 70; Trenton/State, Gov. Hughes P.P., 1967; MIT, Center for Advanced Visual Studies Grant, 1970-71. **Address:** RD #2, Box 94A, Lambertville, N.J. 08530. **One-man Exhibitions:** The Amel Gallery, NYC, 1964-66; ICA, Boston, 1971; Musée de Quebec, 1971; Electric Gallery, Toronto, 1971; Cornell U., 1972; Syracuse U., 1972; Allegheny College, 1972; Inhibodress Gallery, Sydney, 1972; New Jersey State Cultural Center, 1975; Currier, 1976; MIT, 1976; Trenton/State, 1981; U. of Michigan, Ann Arbor, 1981. **Group:** MOMA, The Responsive Eye, 1965; Buffalo/Albright, 1965; ICA, Boston, 1965; Harvard U., 1965; WMAA, Art of the U.S.

1670-1966, 1966; Walker and Milwaukee, Light Motion Space, 1967; Buffalo/Albright, Plus by Minus, 1968; Milwaukee, Directions I: Options, circ., 1968; WMAA Sculpture Annual, 1968; Newark Museum, 1969; Jewish Museum, Software, 1970; Boston/MFA, Elements of Art, 1971; Centro de Arte y Communicacion, Buenos Aires, Arte de Sistemas, II, 1972; MIT, Interaction, 1973; New Jersey Cultural Central, Constructivist Art, 1975; Purchase/SUNY, Spirit of Constructivism, 1980; Trenton/State, Beyond the Plane, 1983. **Collections:** Corcoran; Cornell U.; MOMA; U. of Massachusetts; Mills College; Milwaukee; Muskegon/Hackley; NMAA; NYU; Newark Museum; New Jersey Cultural Center; Norfolk/Chrysler; U. of North Carolina; Princeton U.; Purchase/SUNY; Quebec; Smith College; Spelman College; SRGM; U. of Texas; Trenton/State; WMAA. **Bibliography:** Atkinson; MacAgy 2; Rickey; Toher, ed.

GORCHOV, RON. b. April 5, 1930, Chicago, Ill. **Studied:** U. of Mississippi, 1947-48; Roosevelt College; Chicago/AI School, 1948-50; U. of Illinois, 1950-51. Traveled USA, Europe. **Taught:** Hunter College, 1962-. Designed Stage sets for Theater Club of New York production of Lorca's *Shoemaker's Prodigious Wife*, 1957. **Awards:** Ingram Merrill Foundation Grant, 1959; National Arts Club Annual, NYC, Hon. Men., 1959. **Address:** 461 Broome Street, NYC 10013. **Dealer:** Marlborough Gallery, NYC. **One-man Exhibitions:** Tibor de Nagy Gallery, NYC, 1960, 63, 66; Syracuse/Everson, 1972; The Texas Gallery, 1974; Fischbach Gallery, 1975; Henri 2, Washington, D.C. (two-man), 1975; Texas Gallery, Houston, 1976; Suzanne Hilberry Gallery, Birmingham, Mich., 1977, 79; Galerie M, Bochum, Germany (two-man), 1978; U. of California, Berkeley, 1978; Palazzo Reale, Milan, 1979; P.S.7, Long Island

City, 1979; Young-Hoffman Gallery, Chicago, 1979; Hamilton Gallery of Contemporary Art, NYC, 1979; Marlborough Gallery, 1983. **Group:** The Stable Gallery, NYC, Invitational, 1958; National Arts Club Annual, NYC, 1959; WMAA, Young America, 1960; VMFA, 1964; Syracuse/Everson, 1971; Akademie der Kunst, Berlin, SoHo, 1976; Brockport/SUNY, Recent Abstract Painting, 1976; California State U., Los Angeles, New Work/New York, 1976; New Museum, NYC, Early Work by Five Contemporary Artists, 1977; WMAA Biennial, 1977; NYU, American Painting of the 1980s, 1979. **Collections:** Chicago/AI; Detroit/Institute; Glen Alden Corp.; Hartford/Wadsworth; MOMA; MMA: SRGM; Syracuse/Everson; WMAA.

GORDIN, SIDNEY. b. October 24, 1918, Cheliabinsk, Russia. **Studied:** Cooper Union, 1937-41, with Morris Kantor, Carol Harrison, Leo Katz. **Taught:** Pratt Institute, 1953-58; Brooklyn College, 1955-58; New School for Social Research, 1956-58; Sarah Lawrence College, 1957-58; U. of California, Berkeley, 1958-86. **Commissions:** (sculpture): Temple Israel, Tulsa, Okla., 1959; Envoy Towers, 300 East 46th Street, NYC, 1960. **Address:** 903 Camilia Street, Berkeley, Calif. **Dealers:** Newspace, Los Angeles; Gallery Paule Anglim, San Francisco. **One-man Exhibitions:** Bennington College, 1951; Peter Cooper Gallery, NYC, 1951; Grace Borgenicht Gallery, Inc., 1953, 55, 58, 60, 61; New School for Social Research, 1957; Dilexi Gallery, San Francisco, 1959, 63, 65; de Young, 1962; Los Angeles/County MA, 1963; Zabriskie Gallery, NYC, 1979; Sid Deutsch Gallery, NYC, 1980; Newspace, 1979, 84; Gallery Paule Anglim, 1981, 84. **Retrospectives:** De Young, 1961; Berkeley Art Center, 1967. **Group:** MMA, 1951; WMAA Annuals, 1952-57; MOMA; Chicago/AI; PAFA, 1954, 55; Brooklyn Museum; Newark Museum; SFMA; Oakland/AM; Tulsa/Philbrook,

1960. **Collections:** Chicago/AI; Corcoran; Newark Museum; Norfolk/Chrysler; Oakland/AM; Southern Illinois U.; WMAA. **Bibliography:** Goodrich and Baur 1; Mendelowitz; Seuphor 3; Toher, ed. Archives.

GORDY, ROBERT. b. October 14, 1933, Jefferson Island, Louisiana. **Studied:** Louisiana State U., Baton Rouge, BA, MA; Yale U., 1953, and with Hans Hofmann. **Awards:** National Council of the Arts, grant, 1967; National Endowment for the Arts, 1978. **Address:** 2630 Bell Street, New Orleans, LA 70119. **Dealer:** Phyllis Kind Gallery, Chicago and NYC. **One-man Exhibitions:** Emily Lowes Gallery, New Orleans, 1965; Glade Gallery, New Orleans, 1967, 68; Tampa Bay Art Center, 1969; Hank Baum Gallery, San Francisco, 1969, 71, 73; Cranfill Gallery, Dallas, 1971; Glasgow College of Arts, Scotland, 1972; Galerie Simone Stern, New Orleans, 1968, 70, 71, 72, 73, 80, 81, 83; Mills College, 1973; Long Beach/MA, 1975; Phyllis Kind Gallery, Chicago, 1976; Delahunty, Inc., Dallas, 1977; Phyllis Kind Gallery, NYC, 1979, 85; Carol Shapiro Gallery, St. Louis, 1983; Mobile/FAMS, 1984; New Orleans Museum, circ., 1984; Arthur Roger Gallery, New Orleans, 1984; U. of South Florida, circ., 1985. **Retrospective:** New Orleans Museum, 1981. **Group:** ICA, U. of Pennsylvania, The Spirit of the Comics, 1969; Fort Worth, Contemporary Drawings, 1969; WMAA Biennials, 1967, 73; Memphis/Brooks, American Painting and Sculpture, 1973; NCFA, Divergent Representation, 1973; WMAA, Extraordinary Realists, 1973; Moore College of Art, Philadelphia, North, East, South, West, and Middle, 1975; Brooklyn Museum, 21st National Print Exhibition, 1978; Brooklyn Museum, American Drawings in Black and White, 1970-1979; Norfolk/Chrysler, American Figurative Painting, 1950-1980, 1980; WMAA, The Figurative Tradition and the WMAA, 1980; Brooklyn Museum, The American

Artist as Printmaker, 1983; Houston/Contemporary, Southern Fictions, 1983; IEF, Twentieth Century Drawings: The Figure in Context, circ., 1984; New Orleans, Louisiana World Exposition, 1984; Southeastern Center for Contemporary Art, Winston-Salem, N.C., The Art of New Orleans, 1984. **Collections:** Chicago/Contemporary; Corcoran; Dallas/MFA; Fort Worth; Greenville; MMA; Mobile/FAMS; Montgomery; NMAA; New Orleans Museum; U. of North Carolina; Oklahoma; Tampa Bay Art Center; WMAA; Wichita/AM; Witte.

GORKY, ARSHILE (Vosdanig Manoog Adoian). b. April 15, 1904, Khorkom Vari Haiyotz Dzor, Armenia; **d.** July 21, 1948, Sherman, Conn. To USA, 1920. **Studied:** Polytechnic Institute, Tiflis, 1916-18; RISD; Providence (R.I.) Technical High School; New School of Design, Boston, 1923; NAD, 1925. Subject of *Arshile Gorky*, Cort Productions, 1982; *Windows to Infinity: The Life and Work of Arshile Gorky*, Armenian General Benevolent Union of America, 1979. **Taught:** New School of Design, Boston, 1924; Grand Central School, NYC, 1925-31. **Commissions:** Federal A.P.: Newark (N.J.) Airport 1935-38 (mural). Aviation Building, New York World's Fair, 1939 (mural). Fire destroyed 27 paintings in his studio, January 1946. **One-man Exhibitions:** (first) Guild Art Gallery, NYC, 1932, also 1935, 36; Mellon Galleries, Philadelphia, 1934; Boyer Gallery, Philadelphia, 1935; Boyer Gallery, NYC, 1938; The Kootz Gallery, NYC, 1942, 50, 51; Julien Levy Galleries, NYC, 1945, 46, 47, 1948 (two-man, with Howard Warshaw); WMAA, Memorial Exhibition, 1951; Princeton U., 1952; Paul Kantor Gallery, Beverly Hills, Calif., 1952; Sidney Price Gallery, NYC, 1952, 55, 57; U. of Maryland, 1969; M. Knoedler & Co., 1969, 70, 73, 75; Dunkelman Gallery, Toronto, 1972; Galatea Galleria d'Arte, Turin, 1972; Allan Stone Gallery, NYC, 1973; Richard Feigen Gal-

Arshile Gorky   *Fireplace in Virginia*   1946

lery, NYC, 1973; U. of Texas, Austin, 1975; Oxford/MOMA, 1975; Washburn Gallery, NYC, 1978; Newark Museum, 1978; Xavier Fourcade, Inc., NYC, 1979; Hirshhorn, 1979; Jeremy Stone Gallery, San Francisco, 1983. **Retrospectives:** SFMA, 1941; MOMA, 1963; SRGM, 1981. **Group:** WMAA Annuals; MOMA, 46 Painters and Sculptors under 35 Years of Age, 1930; WMAA, Abstract Painting in America, 1935; MOMA, Fourteen Americans, circ., 1946; Galerie Maeght, 6 Surrealists in 1947, 1947; XXIV & XXV Venice Biennials, 1948, 50; Galerie de France, Paris, 1952; MOMA, The New American Painting, circ. Europe, 1958-59; MOMA, The New American Painting and Sculpture, 1969; 20th Century American Drawing; Three Avant-Garde Generations, 1976; Hirshhorn, The Golden Door, 1976; MOMA, The Natural Paradise; Painting in America 1800-1950, 1976; Milwaukee, From Foreign Shores, 1976; Oswego/SUNY, The New Deal for Art, 1977; Brown U., Graham, Gorky, Smith and Davis in the Thirties, 1977; Paris/Beaubourg, Paris—New York, 1977; Houston/MFA, American Paintings, 1910-1949, 1977; Royal Scottish Academy, Edinburgh, Modern Spirit in American Painting, 1908-1935, 1977; Cornell U., Abstract Expressionism: The Formative Years, 1978; National Gallery, Washington, D.C., American Art at Mid-Century, 1978; Cleveland/MA, The Spirit of Surrealism, 1979. **Collections:** U. of Arizona; Baltimore/MA; Brooklyn Museum; Buffalo/Albright; Canberra/National; Chicago/AI; Cleveland/MA; High Museum; Hirshhorn; Indiana U.; Kansas City/Nelson; Los Angeles/County MA; MMA; MOMA; NYU; National Gallery; Oberlin College; Art Gallery of Ontario, Toronto; SFMA;

SRGM; Seattle; Tate; U. of Texas, Austin; Utica; WMAA; Washington U.; Yale U. **Bibliography:** Ashton 5; Barr 3; Baur 5, 7; Blesh 1; Breton 2, 3; Calas; Cheney; Chipp; De Wilde 1; Eliot; Flanagan; Gerdts; Goodrich and Baur 1; Greenberg 1; Haftman; Hess, T.B., 1; Hunter 1, 6; Hunter, ed.; Janis, S.; Jordan and Goldwater; **Joyner;** Kozloff 3; Lader; Lane and Larsen; Langui; **Levy 1;** Lynton; McCoubrey 1; McCurdy, ed.; Miller, ed. 2; Murken-Altrogge; Myers 2; Neff, ed.; Neumeyer; Newmeyer; Passloff; Ponente; Pousette-Dart, ed.; Ragon 1; Rand; Read 2; Richardson, E.P.; Ritchie 1; Rodman 2; Rose, B., 1, 4; **Rosenberg 1;** Rubin 1; Sandler; **Schwabacher; Seitz 1, 2;** Seuphor 1; Soby 6; Tomkins and Time-Life Books; Tuchman, ed.; Waldbert 3, 4; **Waldman 7;** Weller. Archives.

GOTO, JOSEPH. b. January 7, 1920, Hilo, Hawaii. **Studied:** Chicago/AI School; Roosevelt U. **Taught:** College of William and Mary, 1958-59; U. of Michigan, 1959-63; RISD, 1963-65; U. of Illinois, 1965; Carnegie, 1958; Brandeis U., 1970. **Awards:** Chicago/AI, **P.P.,** 1957; Graham Foundation Fellowship, 1957; John Hay Whitney Fellowship; Chicago/AI, Watson F. Blair Prize; Chicago/AI, The Mr. & Mrs. Frank G. Logan Prize; Chicago/AI, Pauline Palmer Prize; J.S. Guggenheim Fellowship, 1969; Rhode Island, Governor's Arts Award, 1972. **Address:** 17 Sixth Street, Providence, R.I. **One-man Exhibitions:** Allan Frumkin Gallery, NYC and Chicago, 1962; Stephen Radich Gallery, NYC, 1964, 65, 67; Honolulu Academy, 1973; Contemporary Arts Center of Hawaii, Honolulu, 1973; The Zabriskie Gallery, 1973. **Retrospective:** RISD, 1972. **Group:** Chicago/AI; Carnegie; U. of Illinois; Louisville/Speed, WMAA; Chicago/AI; Exhibition Momentum; Denver/AM; Houston/MFA, 1957; VMFA, 1958; Carnegie, 1970. **Collections:** Chicago/AI; Indiana U.; MOMA; U. of Michigan;

Union Carbide Corp. **Bibliography:** Joseph Goto; Rubin 1.

GOTTLIEB, ADOLPH. b. March 14, 1903, NYC; **d.** March 4, 1974, NYC. **Studied:** ASL, 1919, with John Sloan, Robert Henri; Academie de la Grande Chaumiere, 1921; Parsons School of Design, 1923. Exhibited with The Ten, NYC, 1935-40. President, Federation of Modern Painters, 1944-45. **Taught:** Pratt Institute, 1958; UCLA, 1958. **Awards:** Winner of Dudensing National Competition, 1929; US Treasury Department, Mural Competition, 1939; Brooklyn Museum, First Prize, 1944; U. of Illinois, **P.P.,** 1951; Carnegie, Third Prize, 1961; VII Sao Paulo Biennial, First Prize, 1963; American Academy of Achievement, 1965; Flint/Institute **P.P.,** 1966. **One-man Exhibitions:** (first) Dudensing Gallery, NYC, 1930; Uptown Gallery, NYC, 1934; Theodore A. Kohn Gallery, NYC, 1934; Artists' Gallery, NYC, 1942, 43; Wakefield Gallery, NYC, 1944; "67" Gallery, NYC, 1945; Karl Nierendorf Gallery, NYC, 1945; The Kootz Gallery, NYC, 1947, 1950-54; J. Seligmann and Co., 1949; Area Arts Gallery, San Francisco, 1953; Williams College, 1954; The Kootz Gallery, Provincetown, Mass., 1954; Martha Jackson Gallery, 1957; HCA Gallery, Provincetown, Mass., 1957; Andre Emmerich Gallery, 1958, 59, 77, 78, 79; Galerie Rive Droite, Paris, 1959; Paul Kantor Gallery, Beverly Hills, Calif., 1959; ICA, London, 1959; French & Co. Inc., NYC, 1960; Sidney Janis Gallery, 1960, 62; Galleria dell' Ariete, 1961; Galerie Handschin, Basel, 1961; Walker, 1963; Marlborough-Gerson Gallery, Inc., 1964-66, 71, 72, 73, 74; MIT, 1966; Arts Club of Chicago, 1967; U. of Maryland, 1970; Galleria Lorenzelli, Bergamo, 1970; Gertrude Kasle Gallery, 1970, 74; Marlborough Fine Art Ltd., London, 1972; MOMA, 1974; Edmonton Art Gallery, Alberta, circ., 1977-78; Thomas Segal Gallery, Boston, 1978; Klonaridis Inc., Toronto, 1979; Currier, 1979; Omaha/Joslyn, 1979; Phoenix, 1979;

Andre Emmerich Gallery, 80; Corcoran, circ., 1981; Klondaridis, Inc., 1982; M. Knoedler & Co., Inc., NYC, 1982; M. Knoedler & Co., Inc., Zurich, 1983; Muhlenberg College, 1984; Galerie Wentzel, Cologne, 1984. **Retrospectives:** Bennington College, 1954; Jewish Museum, 1957; WMAA and SRGM, 1968; Tel Aviv, 1983. **Group:** WMAA Annuals, 1944, 45, 46, 48, 51, 53, 55, 61; PAFA; Walker; Chicago/AI, Abstract and Surrealist Art, 1948; Carnegie, 1952, 55, 58, 61; SRGM, Younger American Painters, 1954; WMAA, The New Decade, 1954-55; MOMA, The New American Painting, circ., Europe, 1958-59; Documenta II, Kassel, 1959; Seattle World's Fair, 1962; VII Sao Paulo Biennial, 1963; Tate, Gulbenkian International 1964, Dunn International, 1964; Chicago/AI Annual, 1966; Flint/Institute, Flint Invitational, 1966; Corcoran, 1966, Biennial, 1967; Winnipeg Art Gallery, 1967; MOMA, The New American Painting and Sculpture, 1969; Boston/MFA, Abstract Painting in the 70's, 1972; WMAA Biennial, 73; Cornell U., Abstract Expressionists: The Formative Years, 1978; Sao Paulo, Biennial, circ., 1979; MMA, The Painterly Print, 1980; Nassau County Museum, Sculpture: The Tradition in Steel, 1983; Vassar College, The Artist's Perception 1948/1984, 1984. **Collections:** Andover/Phillips; Atlanta/AA; Ball State U.; Bezalel Museum; Brandeis U.; Brooklyn Museum; Buffalo/Albright; Carnegie; Chicago/AI; Columbia U.; Corcoran; Cornell U.; Dallas/MFA; Des Moines; Detroit/Institute; Flint/Institute; Hartford/Wadsworth; U. of Illinois; Jewish Museum; Los Angeles/County MA; MMA; MOMA; U. of Miami; NYU; U. of Nebraska; U. of Nevada; Newark Museum; New Orleans/Delgado; Pasadena/AM; Phillips; SRGM; San Jose Library; Santa Barbara/MA; Seagram Collection; Smith College; Society of the Four Arts; Tel Aviv; Utica; VMFA; WMAA; Walker; Yale U.; Youngstown/Butler. **Bibliography:** Alloway 4; Ashton 5; Barr 3; Baur 5, 7; Blesh 1;

Chipp; Eliot; **Friedman, M., 1;** Goodrich and Baur 1; *The Great Decade;* Greenberg 1; Haftman; Hess, T.B., 1; Hobbs and Levin; Hunter 1, 6; Hunter, ed.; Janis, S.; Kootz 2; Mendelowitz; *Metro:* Motherwell and Reinhardt, eds.; Myers 2; Neumeyer; Nordness, ed.; Pousette-Dart, ed.; Read 2; Richardson, E.P.; Rodman 1, 2, 3; Rose, B., 1, 4; Rosenblum 2; Rubin 1; Sandler; Seuphor 1, Soby 5; Tomkins 2; Tuchman, ed.; Tuchman 3; Weller; Wight 2. Archives.

GOULET, LORRIE. b. August 17, 1925, Riverdale, N.Y. **Studied:** Black Mountain College, 1943-45, with Josef Albers, Jose de Creeft. Traveled USA, Europe. **Taught:** Scarsdale Art Workshop, and privately, 1957-61; MOMA School, 1957-64; New School for Social Research, 1961-75; ASL, 1981-. **Member:** Sculptors Guild; Artists Equity; Audubon Artists. **Commissions:** Grand Concourse (Bronx) Public Library, 1958 (ceramic relief); Nurses Residence and School, Bronx Municipal Hospital Center, 1961 (relief); 48th Precinct Police and Fire Station, Bronx, 1971. CBS-TV, lecture-demonstrations on sculpture for children's series "Around the Corner," 1964, 66, 67, 68. **Awards:** West Palm Beach/Norton, First Prize, 1949, 50; Westchester (N.Y.) Art Society, First Prize, 1964; Audubon Artists, Solten Engel Memorial Award, 1966. **m.** Jose de Creeft. **Address:** 241 West 20th Street, NYC 10011. **Dealer:** Kennedy Galleries, NYC. **One-man Exhibitions:** (first) Clay Club, NYC, 1948; Sculpture Center, 1955; The Contemporaries, NYC, 1959, 62, 66, 68; New School for Social Research, 1968; Temple Emeth, N.J., 1969; Kennedy Galleries, 1971, 72, 75, 78, 80, 83, 86. **Group:** PAFA, annually since 1948; Audubon Artists, annually since 1948; WMAA Annuals, 1948, 49, 50, 53, 55; Philadelphia Art Alliance, 1950; MMA, 1951; Sculptors Guild, annually since 1960; AAAL, 1961; A.F.A., Mother and Child in Modern Art, circ., 1963; Carroll Reece Memorial Museum, Johnson City, Tenn.; Black Mountain College, 1964; New York World's Fair, 1964-65; NAD, 1966; New School for Social Research, Erotic Art, 1973; National Arts Club, NYC, 1978. **Collections:** Hirshhorn; NMWA; Trenton/State; WMAA; Wichita/AM. **Bibliography:** Archives.

GRAHAM, JOHN D. b. January 9, 1881, Kiev, Russia; **d.** June 27, 1961, London, England. **Studied:** U. of Kiev, degree in law, 1911; ASL, 1921, with John Sloan. To USA, 1920; became a citizen. Traveled Europe, Asia, Africa, USA. **Taught:** Wells College, 1932. **One-man Exhibitions:** (first) Baltimore/MA, 1926; Galerie Zborowski, Paris, 1929; Societe Anonyme, NYC, 1931; Eighth Street Gallery, NYC, 1933; Artists' Gallery, NYC, 1941; The Pinacotheca, NYC, 1946; Dudensing Gallery, NYC; The Stable Gallery, 1954; Gallery Mayer, NYC, 1960; Arts Club of Chicago, 1963; U. of Minnesota, 1964; Andre Emmerich Gallery, 1966; MOMA, 1968; Phyllis Kind Gallery, Chicago, 1970; Donald Morris Gallery, 1972; Allan Stone Gallery, NYC, 1973, 81; The Zabriskie Gallery, 1973; Andre Emmerich Gallery, NYC; School of Visual Arts, NYC, 1984. **Group:** MOMA; WMAA; U. of Minnesota; Societe Anonyme, NYC; Brown U., Graham, Smith, Gorky, & Davis in the Thirties, 1977; Minnesota/MA, American Drawing, 1927-1977, circ., 1977; Carnegie, Abstract Painting and Sculpture in America 1927-1944, 1983. **Collections:** Carnegie; MOMA; Nashville; Phillips; WMAA. **Bibliography:** Baur 7; Brown 2; Downes, ed.; *From Foreign Shores;* **George 2; Graham;** *Graham, Gorky, Smith & Davis in the Thirties;* Hunter 6; Janis, S.; Kootz 2; Lane and Larsen; Passloff; Phillips 1; Rose, B., 1, 4; Sandler. Archives.

GRAHAM, ROBERT. b. August 19, 1938, Mexico, D.F. **Studied:** San Jose State College, 1961-63; SFAI, MFA, 1963-64. Traveled Germany, Switzerland, England. US Citizen. **Address:** 69 Windward Avenue, Venice, CA 90291. **Dealer:** Robert Miller Gallery, NYC. **One-man Exhibitions:** The Lanyon Gallery, 1964; Nicholas Wilder Gallery, 1966, 67, 69, 74, 75, 77; M.E. Thelen Gallery, Essen, 1967; The Kornblee Gallery, 1968, 69; Galerie Hans R. Neuendorf, Hamburg, 1968, 70, 74, 76, Cologne, 1968, 70; Galerie Rudolf Zwirner, 1970; Galerie Rene Block, Berlin, 1970; Whitechapel Art Gallery, London, 1970; Ileana Sonnabend Gallery, NYC, 1971; Hamburg/Kunstverein, 1971; Galerie Herbert Meyer-Ellingen, Frankfurt, 1972; Dallas/MFA, 1972; Felicity Samuel Gallery, London, 1974; Gimpel & Hanover, 1975; Greenberg Gallery, St. Louis, 1975; Texas Gallery, Houston, 1975; Rosenthal Gallery, Chicago, 1975; Galerie Neuendorf, Hamburg, 1976; Gimpel Fils, London, 1976; John Stoller Gallery, Minneapolis, 1977; Robert Miller Gallery, NYC, 1977, 79, 82; Galerie Hans R. Neuendorf, Hamburg, 1979; Dag Hammarskjold Plaza, NYC, 1979; Dorothy Rosenthal Gallery, Chicago, 1980, 81, 84; School of Visual Arts, NYC, 1981; Badischer Kunstverein, Karlsruhe, 1983; Gemini G.E.L., Los Angeles, 1984; ARCO Center, Los Angeles, 1984. **Retrospective:** Walker, circ., 1981. **Group:** WMAA Sculpture Annuals, 1966, 69, 71; Washington U. (St. Louis), Here and Now, 1969; Victoria and Albert Museum, Three Americans, 1971; Hamburg/Kunstverein, USA: West Coast, circ., 1972; NCFA, Sculpture: American Directions 1945-1975, 1975; Los Angeles/County MA, Los Angeles—Eight Artists, 1975; SFMA, Painting and Sculpture in California: The Modern Era, 1976; Rutgers U., Contemporary Artists Series Number 1, 1978; WMAA Biennial, 1979; Los Angeles/County MA, The Museum as Site, 1981; PAFA, Contemporary American Realism Since 1960, 1981; SFMA, 20 American Artists, Sculpture 1982, 1982; Oakland/AM, 100

Years of California Sculpture, 1982; Hirshhorn, Content: A Contemporary Focus, 1974-1984, 1984. **Collections:** Aachen; Bank of America; Cologne; Dallas/MFA; Des Moines; Hamburg/Kunstmuseum; Hirshhorn; Los Angeles/County MA; MOMA; National Museum of Wales; Oakland Museum; Paris/Moderne; Pasadena/AM; Rotterdam; SFMA; Smith College; UCLA; Victoria and Albert, London; WMAA; Walker. **Bibliography:** *Kunst um 1970; Sager; USA West Coast.*

GRANLUND, PAUL. b. October 6, 1925, Minneapolis, Minn. **Studied:** Gustavus Adolphus College, 1952, BA; U. of Minnesota; Cranbrook Academy of Art, 1954, MFA. **Taught:** Cranbrook Academy of Art, 1954; Minneapolis Institute School, 1955-68; U. of California, summer, 1959; Gustavus Adolphus College, 1968-. **Awards:** Cranbrook, George A. Booth Scholarship, 1953; Fulbright Fellowship, 1954; Guggenheim Foundation Fellowship, 1957, 58. **Address:** % Art Department, Gustavus Adolphus College, St. Peter, MI 56082. **One-man Exhibitions:** Minnesota State Fair, 1957; Minneapolis/Institute, 1959; Walker, 1965; Gustavus Adolphus College, 1956, 60; Allan Frumkin Gallery, Chicago, 1959, 66, 68, NYC, 1960, 63; Esther Robles Gallery, 1962; California Palace, 1962; Gethsemane Lutheran Church, Seattle, 1962; U. of Nebraska, 1964; Washington U., 1965. **Group:** American Academy, Rome, 1959; U. of Illinois, 1961; Cincinnati/AM, 1961; Corcoran, 1961; U. of Colorado, 1962; Buffalo/Albright, 1962; VMFA, 1962; Louisiana State U., 1964; Minneapolis School of Art, Art of Two Cities, 1965. **Collections:** A.F.A.; American Swedish Institute; Cranbrook; Minneapolis/Institute; VMFA; Walker.

GRAVES, MORRIS COLE. b. August 28, 1910, Fox Valley, Ore. Studied with Mark Tobey. Traveled Europe, the Ori-

ent, USA. Federal A.P.: Easel painting, 1936-39. US Army, 1943. **Awards:** Seattle/AM, Northwest Annual, $100 Award, 1933; Guggenheim Foundation Fellowship, 1946; Chicago/AI, Norman Wait Harris Medal, 1947; Chicago/AI, Watson F. Blair Prize, 1949; U. of Illinois, **P.P.,** 1955; NIAL Grant, 1956; Windsor Award, 1957. **Address:** Box 90, Loleta, CA 95551. **Dealer:** The Willard Gallery. **One-man Exhibitions:** (first) Seattle/AM, 1936, also 1956; The Willard Gallery, 1942, 44, 45, 48, 53, 54, 55, 59, 71, 73, 81; Arts Club of Chicago, 1943; U. of Minnesota, 1943; Detroit/Institute, 1943; Phillips, 1943, 54; Philadelphia Art Alliance, 1946; Santa Barbara/MA, 1948; Los Angeles/County MA, 1948; Chicago/AI, 1948; Margaret Brown Gallery, Boston, 1950; Beaumont (Tex.) Art Museum, 1952; Kunstnernes hus Oslo, 1955; La Jolla, 1957; Bridgestone Museum, 1957; Phoenix, 1960; Roswell, 1961; Kalamazoo/Institute, 1961; Richard White Gallery, Seattle, 1969; Foster/White Gallery, Seattle, 1980; Charles Campbell Gallery, San Francisco, 1979. **Retrospectives:** California Palace, 1948; WMAA, circ., 1956; Pavilion Gallery, Balboa, Calif., 1963; U. of Oregon, 1966; Tacoma, 1971. **Group:** Seattle/AM; WMAA; U. of Illinois; Chicago/AI; Phillips; MOMA, Americans 1942, circ., 1942; Houston/MFA, 1956; ICA, London, 1957; Brussels World's Fair, 1958; Seattle World's Fair, 1962; ICA, Boston, American Art since 1950, 1962; Amon Carter Museum, The Artist's Environment, West Coast, 1962; PAFA, 1963; Columbia, S.C./MA, Ascendancy of American Painting, 1963; Tate, American Painting, 1963; St. Louis/City, 200 Years of American Painting, 1964; U. of Michigan, One Hundred Contemporary American Drawings, 1965; MOMA, The Object Transformed, 1966; U. of Illinois, 1969; Minnesota/MA, Drawings USA, 1971; St. Joseph/Albrecht, Drawing—America: 1973, 1973; NAD, 1974. **Collections:** Baltimore/MA; Boston/MFA; Buffalo/Albright; U. of California; Chi cago/AI; Cincinnati/AM; Cleveland/MA; Denver/AM; Detroit/Institute; Fort Wayne/AM; Hartford/Wadsworth; Harvard U.; Hirshhorn; U. of Illinois; MMA; MOMA; Milwaukee; NIAL; U. of Nebraska; Ogunquit; Pasadena/AM; Phillips; Portland, Ore./AM; Purchase/SUNY; SFMA; SRGM; Santa Barbara/MA; Seattle/AM; Tacoma; U. of Texas; Toronto; Upjohn Co.; Utica; WMAA; U. of Washington; Wilmington; Worcester/AM. **Bibliography:** *Art of the Pacific Northwest;* Baldinger; Barker 1; Barr 3; Baur 7; Bazin; Beekman; Blesh 1; **Cage;** Canaday; Clark and Cowles; Flanagan; Flexner; Frost; Goodrich and Baur 1; Graves; Haftman; Honisch and Jensen, eds.; Hunter 6; Janis, S.; **Kass;** Kootz 2; Kuh 1, 2; Langui; McCurdy, ed.; Mendelowitz; Miller, ed., 1; Munsterberg; Neumeyer; Nordness, ed.; *Northwest Traditions;* Pousette-Dart, ed.; Ragon 1; Read 2, 3; Richardson, E.P.; Rodman 1, 2; Rose, B., 1; Sachs; Soby 5; Sutton; Tuchman 3; Valentine 2; Weller; Wight 2; **Wight, Baur, and Phillips.** Archives.

GRAVES, NANCY STEVENSON. b. December 23, 1940, Pittsfield, Mass. **Studied:** Vassar College, 1961, BA; Yale U., 1962, BFA, 1964, MFA. **Awards:** Fulbright Fellowship, 1965; Vassar College Grant, 1971; Paris Biennial Grant, 1971; National Endowment for the Arts, 1972; CAPS, 1973; American Academy, Rome, Fellowship, 1979; Skowhegan School, Medal for Drawing/Graphics, 1980; Yale Arts Medal for Distinguished Artistic Achievement, 1985. Also produces films. Designed sets and costumes for Trisha Brown's *Lateral Pass,* 1985. **Address:** 69 Wooster Street, NYC 10012. **Dealer:** M. Knoedler & Co., Inc., NYC. **One-man Exhibitions:** The Graham Gallery, 1968; WMAA, 1969; Ottawa/National, 1970, 71, 73; Reese Palley Gallery, NYC, 1971, Aachen/NG, 1971; Vassar College, 1971; MOMA, 1971; New Gallery, Cleveland, 1972; Janie C. Lee Gallery, Dallas, 1972, 73, 75; ICA, U. of Pennsylvania, 1972; Janie C. Lee Gallery, Houston, 1974, 75, 76, 77, 78, 83, 84; Pittsfield/Berkshire, 1973; Art Museum of South Texas, Corpus Christi, 1973; Andre Emmerich Gallery, NYC, 1974, 77; Buffalo/Albright, 1974, 80; Galerie Andre Emmerich, Zurich, 1977; Galerie im Schloss, Munich, 1977; M. Knoedler & Co., Inc., NYC, 1978, 79, 80, 81, 82, 84; Diane Gilson Gallery, Seattle, 1978; Richard Gray Gallery, 1981; M. Knoedler & Co., Inc., Zurich, 1982; Gloria Luria Gallery, Bay Harbor Islands, Fla., 1983; Santa Barbara (Calif.) Contemporary Arts Forum, 1983. **Retrospective:** Buffalo/Albright, circ., 1980. **Group:** WMAA Annuals, 1970, 71, 73; MOMA, Information, 1971; Corcoran, Depth and Presence, 1971; Dusseldorf/Kunsthalle, Prospect '71, 1971; Chicago/Contemporary, Six Sculptors, 1971; VII Paris Biennial, 1971; Kunsthaus, Hamburg, American Women Artists, 1972; Documenta V, Kassel, 1972; New York Cultural Center, 3D into 2D, 1973; WMAA, American Drawings, 1963-1973, 1973; Cologne, Project 74, 1974; Sarah Lawrence College, Drawings by Women, 1975; Corcoran, The Liberation, 1976; US Department of the Interior, America 1976, circ., 1976; WMAA, 200 Years of American Sculpture, 1976; Kassel, Documenta VI, 1977; U. of Texas, Austin, New in the Seventies, 1977; U. of California, Santa Barbara, Contemporary Drawing/New York, 1977; Albright College, Perspective 78, 1978; Buffalo/Albright, American Painting of the 1970s, circ., 1978; Zurich/Kunsthaus, Weich und Plastisch—Soft Art, 1979; ICA, U. of Pennsylvania, Masks; Tents, Vessels, Talismans, 1979; NYU, American Painting: The Eighties, 1979; XXXIX Venice Biennale, 1980; U. of Kansas, 4 Artists and the Map: Image/Process/Data/Place, 1981; Houston/Contemporary, In Our Time, 1982; Stuttgart/WK, Past-Present-Future, 1982; Yale U.; Prints by Contemporary Sculptors, 1982; WMAA Biennial, 1983; MOMA, Primitivism in 20th

Century Art, 1984; Newark Museum, American Bronze Sculpture, 1850 To The Present, 1984; Purchase/SUNY, Hidden Desires, 1984; Seattle/AM, American Sculpture: Three Decades, 1984; Sonoma State U., Works in Bronze, A Modern Survey, circ., 1984; Williams College, Six in Bronze, circ., 1984. **Collections:** Aachen/NG; Akron/AI; Art Museum of South Texas; Buffalo/Albright; CNAC; U. of California, Berkeley; Chicago/AI; Cologne; Corcoran; Dallas/MFA; Des Moines; Fort Worth; Houston/MFA; La Jolla; Los Angeles/County MA; Memphis/ Brooks; MMA; MOMA; U. of North Carolina; Oberlin College; Ottawa/ National; Vienna/Stadt; Purchase/ SUNY; SRGM; Vassar College; WMAA; Walker. **Bibliography:** *America 1976; Art: A Woman's Sensibility; Art Now 74; Drawings: The Pluralist Decade; Kunst um 1970;* Lippard 3; Lucie-Smith; *New in the Seventies;* **Nancy Graves,** 1973; **Nancy Graves,** 1971; Sager. Archives.

GRAY, CLEVE. b. September 22, 1918, NYC. **Studied:** Princeton U., 1940, BA summa cum laude, PBK; Academie Andre Lhote; privately with Jacques Villon in Paris. US Army, 1943-46. Traveled in Europe, USA. **Taught:** Honolulu Academy, 1970-71; American Academy, Rome, 1980. **Member:** Century Association; Trustee, New York Studio School, 1970-. **Awards:** U. of Illinois, **P.P.,;** Ford Foundation, **P.P. Address:** Cornwall Bridge, Cornwall, CT 06754. **Dealers:** Fairweather-Hardin Gallery, Chicago; Armstrong Gallery, NYC. **One-man Exhibitions:** (first) J. Seligmann and Co., 1947, also 1948, 49, 50, 52, 54, 57, 59; Staempfli Gallery, 1960, 62, 64; Galleria Pagani del Grattacielo, Milan, 1963; Jerrold Morris Gallery, Toronto, 1963; Oklahoma, 1963; Saidenberg Gallery, 1965, 67; Hargate Art Center, Concord, Mass., 1969; Betty Parsons Gallery, 1970, 72, 74, 76, 80, 82; Sneed-Hillman Gallery, 1970, 73, 74; Honolulu Academy, 1970, 71;

Princeton U., 1970; Purchase/SUNY, 1972, 74, 79, 83, 84; Buffalo/Albright, 1977; Columbus, 1977; U. of Illinois, 1977; Museum of Art, Providence, R.I., 1978; Mattatuck Museum, 1980; Caracas, 1980; Yale U., 1981; American Embassy, Prague, 1984; Robert L. Kidd Gallery, Birmingham, Mich., 1984; Griffin-Haller Gallery, Washington Depot, Ct., 1984; Gallery Two Nine One, Atlanta, 1984; Armstrong Gallery, 1984; Fairweather-Hardin Gallery, 1984. **Group:** WMAA Annuals; Chicago/AI; SRGM, Abstract Expressionists and Imagists, 1961; Hartford/Wadsworth; PAFA; El Retiro Parquet, Arte de America y Espana, 1963; Andover/Phillips, Decades, 1969; Minnesota/MA, Drawings USA, 1973. **Collections:** Andover/Phillips, Brandeis U.; Buffalo/Albright; U. of California; Corcoran; Columbia U.; Columbus; Hartford/Wadsworth; Honolulu Academy; U. of Illinois; Jewish Museum; MMA; Minnesota/MA; NCFA; NYU; Nashville; U. of Nebraska; New School for Social Research; U. of Notre Dame; Oklahoma; Phillips; Princeton U.; Purchase/SUNY; RISD; SRGM; St. Paul Gallery; Vanderbilt U.; WMAA; West Palm Beach/Norton; Williams College; Yale U. **Bibliography:** Goodrich and Baur 1; *7 Decades.* Archives.

GREEN, ART. b. May 13, 1941, Frankfort, Ind. Canadian Citizen, 1976. **Studied:** Chicago Art Institute School, 1965, BFA, with Ray Yoshida, Vera Berdich, Paul Weighart, T. Kapsalis. Traveled Canada, USA, England. **Taught:** Wright Jr. College, Chicago, 1967-68; Kendall College, Evanston, Ill, 1968-69; Nova Scotia College of Art & Design, Halifax, 1969-71; U. of British Columbia, 1975; U. of Waterloo, 1977-. **Awards:** Cassandra Foundation Grant, 1970; The Canada Council Award, 1971, 72, 76. **Address:** 5 Elizabeth Street, Stratford, Ont., Canada N5A 4ZI. **Dealer:** Phyllis Kind Gallery, NYC & Chicago. **One-man Exhibitions:** (first) Kendall College, 1968; Mt. Al-

Art Green   *Common Knowledge*   1985

lison U., 1973; Phyllis Kind Gallery, NYC, 1976, 79; Phyllis Kind Gallery, Chicago, 1974, 75, 78, 80, 81, 83, 86; Bau-Xi Gallery, Toronto, 1973, 79, 83; PAFA, Peale House, 1976; The Gallery, Stratford, Ont., 1979; U. of Waterloo, 1979; Burnaby (B.C.) Art Gallery, 1979. **Group:** Hyde Park Art Center, Chicago, The Hairy Who, 1966, 67; School of Visual Arts, NYC, The Hairy Who–Drawings, 1969; Chicago/Contemporary, Don Baum Sez, "Chicago Needs Famous Artists," 1969; WMAA, Human Concern/Personal Torment, 1969; Ottawa/National, What They're Up To in Chicago, 1972; 12th Sao Paulo Biennial, 1973; WMAA, Extraordinary Realities, 1973; Sunderland (Eng.) Arts Center, Who Chicago?, circ., 1980; Kansas City/AI, Chicago Imagists, 1982; Fort Wayne/MA, Indiana Influence, 1984. **Collections:** Chicago/AI; Chicago/Contemporary; Dalhousie U., Halifax; Madison Art Center; NMAA; New Orleans Museum; Northern Illinois U.; Ottawa/National; Vienna/Moderner; U. of Waterloo.

GREEN, GEORGE D. b. June 24, 1943, Portland, Ore. **Studied:** Oregon State U., 1961-62; U. of Oregon, 1965, BS, with Jack Wilkenson, Gordon Gilkey; Washington State U., 1968, MFA. **Taught:** U. of Texas, 1969-72; SUNY, 1972-80. **Address:** 451 West Broadway, NYC 10012. **Dealer:** Louis K. Meisel Gallery, NYC. **One-man Exhibitions:** Boise College, 1968; Eastern Washington State College, 1968; Clarke College, 1969; Lawson Galleries, San Francisco, 1969; Winn Galleries, Austin, 1969, 70, 71; Comora Gallery, Los Angeles, 1970; Witte, 1970; Artists' Space, NYC, 1974; Hansen Gallery, NYC, 1974; Potsdam/SUNY (two-man), 1974; Missoula/MA, 1976; Montana State U., 1976; Salem (Ore.) Art Museum, 1976; Corvallis Art Center, 1977; Triangle Art Gallery, San Francisco, 1977, 80; Syracuse/Everson, 1978; Louis K. Meisel Gallery, 1978, 79, 81, 82, 83, 84, 85; Hokin Gallery, Chicago, 1981; St. Lawrence U., 1981; Union College, Cranford, N.J., 1982; Hokin Gallery, Palm Beach, 1983; Hokin-Kaufman Gallery, Chicago, 1984. **Collections:** Akron/AM; Brandeis U.; Cheney Cowles Memorial Museum; Chicago/AI; Cornell U.; Currier; Dartmouth College; Denver/AM; Detroit/Institute; Fort Worth; Indianapolis; Jacksonville/AM; Los Angeles/County AM; Marquette U.; U. of Oklahoma; U. of Oregon; Portland (Ore.)/AM; Potsdam/SUNY; SRGM; St. Lawrence U.; Syracuse/Everson; U. of Texas; Utica. **Bibliography:** Toher, ed.

GREENE, BLACOMB. b. May 22, 1904, Shelby, N.Y. **Studied:** Syracuse U., 1922-26, AB; Columbia U., 1927; U. of Vienna, 1926-27; NYU, 1943, MA; self-taught in art. Traveled Europe extensively. **Taught:** Dartmouth College

(English), 1928-31; Carnegie, 1942-59. Editor, *Art Front* magazine, 1935-36. Fire in New York studio, 1941, destroyed many early paintings. **Member:** American Abstract Artists (first chairman, 1936-37, 1938-39, 1940-41); International Institute of Arts and Letters; Cosmopolitan Club, NYC. Federal A.P. Mural Division: New York World's Fair, 1939, Federal Hall of Medicine (mural); Bronx (N.Y.) High School of Science (stained-glass window); Williamsburg Housing Project, Brooklyn, 1939 (mural); NIAL. **Awards:** *Art News* (magazine) Critics Choice, 1950, 53, 55, 56; PAFA, Carol H. Beck Gold Medal, 1961; NAD, Benjamin Altman Prize for Figure Painting, 1976. **Address:** 315 East 68th Street, NYC 10021; Montauk Point, N.Y. **Dealer:** ACA Gallery, NYC; Katharine Rich Perlow Gallery, NYC; Harmon Gallery, Naples, Fla. **One-man Exhibitions:** (first) a gallery in Paris, 1932; J. B. Neumann's New Art Circle, NYC, 1947; The Bertha Schaefer Gallery, 1952, 54, 55, 56, 58, 59, 61; Arts and Crafts Center, Pittsburgh, 1953, 66; American U., 1957; Brookhaven National Laboratory, 1959; American Cultural Center, Paris, 1960; Saidenberg Gallery, 1962, 63, 65, 67, 68; Feingarten Gallery; Los Angeles, 1963, 64; La Jolla, 1965; U. of Florida, 1965; Tampa/AI, 1965; James David Gallery, Miami, 1965, 66; Main Street Gallery, Chicago, 1966; Santa Barbara/MA, 1966; Phoenix, 1966; Adele Bednarz Gallery, 1966-69; Occidental College, 1967; The Berenson Gallery, 1967, 68, 69; Makler Gallery, Philadelphia, 1968; The Forum Gallery, 1970, 73, 74, 75; Fairweather-Hardin Gallery, Chicago, 1972, 73; Harmon Gallery, Naples, Florida, 1974, 75, 76, 77; International Oceanographic Institute, Key Biscayne, Fla., 1976; ACA Gallery, NYC, 1977, 79, 82; Harmon Gallery, 1979; Yares Gallery, Scottsdale, Az., 1979; Katharine Rich Perlow Gallery, 1986. **Retrospectives:** WMAA/A.F.A., circ., 1961; Guild Hall, East Hampton, 1978. **Group:** American Abstract Artists Annuals; WMAA Annuals; U. of Illinois;

Chicago/AI; Walker; SRGM; Brooklyn Museum; Carnegie. **Collections:** Ball State U.; Baltimore/MA; Brooklyn Museum; Carnegie; Chiago/AI; Corcoran; Guild Hall; Hartford/Wadsworth; Houston/MFA; Indianapolis/Herron; U. of North Carolina; MIT; MMA; MOMA; U. of Miami; NCFA; U. of Nebraska; U. of North Carolina; Omaha/Joslyn; PAFA; Pasadena/AM; Portland, Ore./AM; Purchase/SUNY; SRGM; U. of Texas; Vassar College; U. of Virginia; WMAA; Walker; Youngstown/Butler. **Bibliography:** Baur 5, 7; Flanagan; Frost; Goodrich and Baur 1; Hess, T.B., 1; Janis, S.; Kootz 2; Lane and Larsen; Newmeyer; Nordness, ed.; Pousette-Dart, ed.; Read 2; Richardson, E.P.; Ritchie 1; Rodman 3; Rose, B., 4; Archives.

GREENE, STEPHEN. b. September 19, 1918, NYC. **Studied:** ASL, with Morris Kantor, 1937; State U. of Iowa, with Philip Guston, 1939-42, 1944-45, BFA, MA. Traveled Europe, North Africa. **Taught:** Indiana U., 1945-56; Washington U., 1946-47; Pratt Institute, 1959-64; Parsons School of Design; NYU; Princeton U., Artist-in-Residence, 1956-59; ASL, 1959-65; Columbia U., 1961-68; Stella Elkins Tyler School of Fine Arts, Temple U., 1968-85; Princeton U., 1985-86. **Member:** Trustee, Louis Comfort Tiffany Foundation. **Awards:** Prix de Rome, 1949; Corcoran, William A. Clark Prize and Corcoran Medal, 1966; National Council on the Arts, $5,000, 1966; NIAL, $2,500, 1967; NAD, Andrew Carnegie Prize, 1970; NAD, Obrig Award, 1985. **Address:** 408A Storms Road, Valley College, NY 10989. **Dealers:** Marilyn Pearl Gallery, NYC; Galeria Ponce, Mexico City. **One-man Exhibitions:** (first) Durlacher Brothers, 1947, also 1949, 52; Grace Borgenicht Gallery, Inc., 1955, 57, 58; Staempfli Gallery, 1961 (circ., 1964), 64, 66, 69; William Zierler, Inc., 1971, 72, 73; U. of Wisconsin, 1972; U. of Alberta, circ., 1972; Galleria d'Arte l'Obelisco, 1975; College of William and

Mary, 1977; U. of Connecticut, 1977; Marilyn Pearl Gallery, NYC, 1978, 80, 83, 85; Galeria Ponce, Mexico City, 1977, 79, 82; Ruth Bachofner Gallery, Los Angeles, 1985; Matthew Hamilton Gallery, Philadelphia, 1984. **Retrospectives:** Corcoran, 1963; Lincoln, Mass./De Cordova, 1953; Akron/AI, circ., 1978. **Group:** MMA, American Paintings Today, 1950; Chicago/AI, Contemporary Drawings from 12 Countries, 1952; Walker, Reality and Fantasy, 1954; Paris/Moderne, American Drawings, 1954; WMAA, The New Decade, 1954-55; MOMA, Recent Drawings USA, 1956; I International Religious Art Biennial, Salzburg, 1958; VI Sao Paulo Biennial, 1961; WMAA Annuals; SRGM, Abstract Expressionists and Imagists, 1961; Corcoran; Carnegie; Chicago/AI; El Retiro Parquet, Madrid, Arte de America y Espana, 1963; Internationale der Zeichnung, Darmstadt, 1964; MMA, American Paintings, Drawings and Watercolors from the Museum's Collections, 1969; WMAA, Human Concern/Personal Torment, 1969; Foundation Maeght, L'Art Vivant, 1970; Museo Comunale, Prato, Italy, American Painters in Europe, 1973; SRGM, American Painters through Two Decades, 1973; Rome Quadriennial, 1977; WMAA, The Figurative Tradition and the WMAA, 1980; NAD, 1981, 85; WMAA, Decade of Transition 1940-1950, 1981; AAIAL, 1982; Rutgers U., Realism and Realities, 1982. **Collections:** American Republic Insurance Co.; Andover/Phillips; Atlantic Richfield Co.; Brandeis U.; Brooklyn Museum; Carnegie; Chase Manhattan Bank; Chicago/AI; Columbia U.; Corcoran; Dayton/AI; Detroit/Institute; Hamline U.; Hartford; High Museum; Hirshhorn; U. of Illinois; Indiana U.; Indianapolis/Herron; Kalamazoo/Institute; Kansas City/ Nelson; U. of Kentucky; MMA; MOMA; Minnesota/MA; NYU; Nashville; New Orleans/Delgado; New Orleans Museum; Owens-Corning Fiberglas Corp.; Pasadena/AM; Princeton U.; SFMA; SRGM; St. Louis/City; Santa

Barbara/MA; Tate; Trenton/State; Utica; VMFA; WMAA; Yale U. **Bibliography:** Baur 7; Bazin; Genauer; Mendelowitz; Sachs; Soby 5. Archives.

GREENLY, COLIN. b. January 21, 1928, London, England. **Studied:** Harvard U., 1948, AB; American U. (with Robert Gates); Columbia U. (with Oronzio Maldarelli, Peppino Mangravite). Traveled western USA, France, Italy, England. **Taught:** Established art programs for employee groups at Standard Oil, Metropolitan Life Insurance Co., Union Carbide Corp., New York Life Insurance, all NYC, 1951-53; US Dept. of Agriculture, Graduate School, 1954-56; Madeira School, Greenway, Va., 1955-68; Colgate U., 1972-73; Central Michigan U., 1972; Finch College, NYC, 1974; Windham College, 1976. **Commissions:** New York State Office Building, Utica (twelve color panels), 1973. **Awards:** Corcoran, **P.P.,** 1956; The Corcoran School of Art, National Playground Sculpture Competition, First Prize, 1967; National Council on the Arts, Grant, 1967; CAPS, 1972, 77; Committee for the Visual Arts Grant, NYC, 1974. **Address:** RD1, Box 545, Campbell Hall, NY 10916. **One-man Exhibitions:** (first) Jefferson Place Gallery, 1958, also 1960, 63, 65; The Bertha Schaefer Gallery, 1964, 66, 68; Corcoran, 1968; Royal Marks Gallery, 1968, 70; Syracuse/Everson, 1971; Cornell U., 1972; Fredonia/SUNY, 1973; Colgate U., 1973; The Schenectady (N.Y.) Museum, 1973; Alfred/SUNY, 1974, 75; Nassau Community College, Garden City, N.Y., 1974; Finch College, NYC, 1974; Creative Arts Workshop, New Haven, 1975; 112 Greene Street, NYC, 1976. **Retrospective:** Corcoran, 1968. **Group:** MOMA, Young American Printmakers, 1953; Corcoran, 1955-57; Lincoln, Mass./De Cordova, 1965; Flint/Institute, Made of Plastic, 1968; Grand Rapids, Sculpture of the 60s, 1969; Baltimore/MA, Washington; Twenty Years, 1970; New York State

Fair, Enviro-Vision, circ., 1972; U. of Illinois, 1974. **Collections:** Buffalo/Albright; Corcoran; Cornell U.; Des Moines; High Museum; MOMA; Manufacturers and Traders Trust Co., Buffalo, N.Y.; NCFA; National Gallery; PMA; Virginia National Bank.

GREGOR, HAROLD LAURENCE. b. September 10, 1929, Detroit, Mich. **Studied:** Wayne State U., 1951, BS, Ed., with Jane Betsy Welling, Earl Weilley; Michigan State U., 1953, MS, with Louis Raynor, Murray Jones; Ohio State U., 1960, PhD., with Hoyt Sherman. Traveled Europe, USA. US Army, 1953-55. **Taught:** Ohio State U., 1957-60; San Diego State College, 1960-62; Purdue U., 1963-66; Chapman College, 1966-70; Illinois State U., 1970-. **Awards:** National Endowment for the Arts, 1973. **Address:** 107 West Market Street, Bloomington, Ill. 61701. **Dealer:** Richard Gray Gallery, Chicago; Tibor de Nagy Gallery, NYC. **One-man Exhibitions:** (first) Jefferson Gallery, La Jolla, 1963; Countryside Gallery, Arlington Heights, Ill, 1973; Virginia Commonwealth U., 1973; Metropolitan State College, 1973; Fresno State U., 1973; 118: An Art Gallery, Minneapolis, 1974; Central Michigan U. (two-man), 1975; Cynthia Comsky Gallery, Beverly Hills, 1976; Northern Indiana Art Association, Hammond, 1976; Western Illinois U., 1977; Parkland College, Champaign, Ill., 1984; Nancy Lurie Gallery, Chicago, 1974, 76, 77, 78, 79, 80, 81, 83; Richard Gray Gallery, 1983; Tibor de Nagy Gallery, 1977, 78, 79, 81, 82; Peoria (Ill.) Art Guild, 1985. **Group:** Omaha/Joslyn, Midwest Biennial, 1972; West Palm Beach/Norton, Imagist Realism, 1974; Sacramento/Crocker, The Chicago Connection, circ., 1976; Youngstown/Butler, National Mid-year Show, 1976; Chicago/AI, 1978; U. of Nebraska, Things Seen, circ., 1979; U. of North Carolina, 1979; PAFA, Contemporary American Realism Since 1960, circ., 1981. **Collections:** Brandeis U.; Chicago/Contemporary; Dartmouth

College; U. of Georgia; U. of Guam; Illinois State Museum; The Pennsylvania State U.; Rockford/Burpee; San Diego; Southwestern College; Syracuse U.; Western Illinois U.; Yavapai College.

GRIEFEN, JOHN ADAMS. b. November 24, 1942, Worcester, Mass. **Studied:** Williams College, 1966 BA; Bennington College, 1965-66, with Jules Olitski; Hunter College, 1966-68; Chicago/AI, 1964-65. Traveled Europe. **Taught:** Bennington College, 1968. **Address:** 57 Laight Street, NYC 10013. **Dealer:** Salander-O'Reilly Galleries, NYC. **One-man Exhibitions:** (first) The Kornblee Gallery, NYC 1969, 70, 73; Harcus/Krakow Gallery, Boston, 1972; Phyllis Kind Gallery, Chicago, 1973; Frank Watters Gallery, Sydney, Australia, 1975; Deitcher/O'Reilly Gallery, NYC, 1976; William Edward O'Reilly Inc., NYC, 1978; B.R. Kornblatt Gallery, Baltimore, Md., 1978; Diane Brown Gallery, Washington, D.C., 1978; Martha Jackson Gallery, NYC, 1979; Sunne Savage Gallery, Boston, 1979; Galerie Wentzel, Hamburg, 1980; Williams College, 1980; Martin Gerard Gallery, Edmonton, 1981; Gallery Moos, Toronto, 1981; Salander-O'Reilly Galleries, 1981, 82, 85; W. R. Mitchell & Associates, Calgary, 1983; Edmonton Art Gallery, 1984. **Group:** Ridgefield/Aldrich, Lyrical Abstraction, 1970; Akron/AI, Watercolors and Drawings by Young Americans, 1970; Indianapolis, 1970, 72; WMAA, Lyrical Abstraction, 1971; Edmonton Art Gallery, The Threshold of Color, 1982; Youngstown/Butler, 1985. **Collections:** Barnard College; Boston/MFA; Brandeis U.; Brooklyn Museum; Carnegie; Chase Manhattan Bank; Detroit/Institute; Edmonton Art Gallery; Hirshhorn; MMA; MOMA; U. of Massachusetts; Mechanics National Bank, Worcester; Newark Museum; Oberlin College; Ridgefield/Aldrich; Sydney/AG; St. Lawrence U.; U. of Texas; Utica; WMAA; Williams College; Worcester/AM.

GRILLO, JOHN. b. July 4, 1917, Lawrence, Mass **Studied:** Hartford Art School, 1935-38; California School of Fine Arts, 1946; Hofmann School, NYC, 1949-50. US armed forces, 1944-46. **Taught:** Southern Illinois U., 1960; School of Visual Arts, NYC, 1961; U. of California, Berkeley, 1962-63; New School for Social Research, 1964-66; Pratt Institute, 1965-66; State U. of Iowa, 1967-; U. of Massachusetts, Artist-in-Residence, 1968-69. **Awards:** CSFA, Albert M. Bender Fellowship, 1947; Ford Foundation Fellowship (Tamarind Lithography Workshop and Youngstown/Butler), 1964. **Address:** 19 Page Street, Amherst, MA 01002. **One-man Exhibitions:** Daliel Gallery, Berkeley, 1947; Artists' Gallery, NYC, 1948; Tanager Gallery, NYC, 1952, 60; Tibor de Nagy Gallery, NYC, 1953, 70; The Bertha Schaefer Gallery, 1955, 57, 59; HCE Gallery, Provincetown, Mass., 1959, 62; The Howard Wise Gallery, NYC, 1961, 62, 63; Ankrum Gallery, 1962; U. of California, Berkeley, 1962; East End Gallery, Provincetown, 1963; Youngstown/Butler, 1964; Waitsfield/Bundy, 1966; New School for Social Research, 1967; State U. of Iowa, 1967; Simmons College, 1968; Eleanor Rigelhaupt Gallery, Boston, 1968; Benedict Art Center, St. Joseph, Minn. 1969; Horizon Gallery, NYC, 1969; Robert Dain Gallery, NYC, 1970; Landmark Gallery Inc., NYC, 1973; Borgenicht Gallery, Inc., NYC, 1975, 77, 78; Pisces Gallery, Wellfleet, Mass., 1977; Union College, Cranford, N.J., 1977; Art Association of Newport, R.I., 1979; Jean Lumbard Fine Arts, NYC, 1983. **Retrospective:** The Olsen Foundation, Inc., circ., USA, 1956-60. **Group:** The Kootz Gallery, NYC, Fifteen Unknowns, 1950; Walker, Vanguard, 1955; WMAA Annual, 1959; Walker, 60 American Painters, 1960; SRGM, Abstract Expressionists and Imagists, 1961; Yale U., Contemporary Painting, 1961; Dallas/MFA, 1961, 62; Seattle World's Fair, 1962; MOMA, Hans Hofmann and His Students, circ., 1963-64; SFMA, Directions—Painting U.S.A.,

1963, Buffalo/Albright, 1964; Brooklyn Museum Print Biennial, 1970; Oakland/AM, California Artists, 1944-1952, 1973; SRGM, 40 Modern Masters, 1977; Syracuse/Emerson, Provincetown Painters, 1890's—1970's, 1977; MMA, Hans Hofmann as Teacher: Drawings by His Students, 1979. **Collections:** Baton Rouge; Bennington College, Brooklyn Museum; Ciba-Geigy Corp.; Dartmouth College; Hartford/Wadsworth; Hayden, Shearson, Inc., NYC; Los Angeles/County MA; MMA; Newark Museum; Norfolk/Chrysler; The Olsen Foundation, Inc.; Pittsburgh; Portland, Me./MA; SRGM; Smith College; Southern Illinois U.; U. of Texas; Union Carbide Corp.; WMAA; Waitsfield/Bundy; Walker; Westinghouse; Youngstown/Butler. **Bibliography:** Blesh 1; McChesney; Sandler 1.

GRIPPE, PETER. b. August 8, 1912, Buffalo, N.Y. **Studied:** Albright Art School; Buffalo Fine Arts Academy, with E. Wilcox, Edwin Dickinson, William Ehrich; Atelier 17, NYC. Traveled Europe. **Taught:** Black Mountain College, 1948; Pratt Institute, 1949-50; Smith College, 1951-52; Atelier 17, NYC, 1951-52; Brandeis U., 1953-. Federal A.P.: Taught sculpture and drawing, 1939-42. **Commissions:** Creative Arts Award Medallion design for Brandeis U., 1954; Puerto Rican Information Center, NYC, 1958 (two sculpture murals); Theo Shapiro Forum, Brandeis U., 1963 (sculpture). **Awards:** Brooklyn Museum, **P.P.,** 1947; MMA, $500 First Prize, 1952; The Print Club, Philadelphia, Charles M. Lea Prize, 1953; National Council for United States Art, $1,000 Sculpture Award, 1955; Boston Arts Festival, First Prize for Sculpture, 1955; Rhode Island Arts Festival, Sculpture Award, 1961; Guggenheim Foundation Fellowship, 1964, 70. **Address:** 1190 Boylston St., Newton, MA 02164. **One-man Exhibitions:** (first) Orrefors Galleries, NYC, 1942; The Willard Gallery, 1944, 45, 46, 48; Brandeis U., 1957;

The Peridot Gallery, 1957, 59; Lee Nordness Gallery, NYC, 1960, 63; College of the Holy Cross, Worcester, 1986. **Group:** MMA, Contemporary American Art, 1942; WMAA Annuals, 1944, 45, 47, 48, 50, 51, 52, 54, 56, 57, 60, 62; Federation of Modern Painters and Sculptors, 1944, 45, 52; American Abstract Artists Annuals, 1946, 47, 49; Carnegie, 1946, 48; Brooklyn Museum, 1947, 48, 49, 53, 56, 58; Detroit/Institute, Origins of Modern Sculpture, 1948; Chicago/AI, Abstract and Surrealist Art, 1948; A.F.A., Tradition and Experiment in Modern Sculpture, circ., 1950-51; MMA, National Sculpture Exhibition, 1951; MOMA, Abstract Painting and Sculpture in America, 1951; Ninth Street Exhibition, NYC, 1951; MOMA, From Sketch to Sculpture, 1952; PAFA, 1952, 59; U. of Illinois, 50 Contemporary American Printmakers, 1956; ART:USA:59, NYC, 1959; PCA, American Prints Today, circ., 1959-62; ICA, Boston, View, 1960; U. of Illinois, 1961; Chicago/AI, 1961; Smithsonian, Drawings by Sculptors, circ., USA, 1961-63; A.F.A., Hayter and Atelier 17, circ., 1961-62; Hartford/Wadsworth, Eleven New England Sculptors, 1963; MOMA, The New American Painting and Sculpture, 1969; Brandeis U., 1973. **Collections:** Andover/Phillips; Brandeis U.; Brooklyn Museum; Buffalo/Albright; Fort Dodge/Blanden; U. of Georgia; Library of Congress; MMA; MOMA; U. of Michigan; Milwaukee-Downer College; NYPL; National Gallery; Newark Museum; Norfolk/Chrysler; PCA; PMA; The Print Club, Philadelphia; Raleigh/NCMA; Simmons College; Tel Aviv; Toledo/MA; USIA; WMAA; Walker; Washington U. **Bibliography:** Baur 7; Blesh 1; Brumme; Flanagan; Hayter 1; Mendelowitz; Moser 1; Motherwell and Reinhardt, eds.; Ritchie 1; Seuphor 3; Trier.

GROOMS, RED. b. June 2, 1937, Nashville, Tenn. **Studied:** Peabody College; privately with J. Van Sickle; New School for Social Research; Chicago Art Institute School; Hofmann School, Provincetown. Traveled Europe, Near East. Sets and costumes for *Guinevere,* a play by Kenneth Koch, 1964; Designed sets for *Red Robins,* play by Kenneth Koch, 1978; Sets and costumes for *City Junketh,* play by Kenward Elmslie for Eye and Ear Theatre, NYC, 1980; Set for *Creation of the World,* dance by Jacques d'Artoise, 1984. **Commissions:** Center for Modern Culture, Florence, Italy (mural, with Mimi Gross); Hudson River Museum, Bookstore, 1978; Northern Kentucky U., 1978; ICA, U. of Pennsylvania, 1982. **Awards:** Ingram Merrill Foundation Grant, 1968; AAAL Grant, 1969; CAPS, 1970. **Address:** 85 Walker Street, NYC 10013. **Dealer:** Marlborough Gallery, Inc., NYC. **One-man Exhibitions:** (first) Sun Gallery, Provincetown, 1958; City Gallery, NYC, 1958-59; Reuben Gallery, NYC, 1960; Tibor de Nagy Gallery, NYC, 1963, 65, 66, 67, 69, 70; Artists Guild, Nashville, 1962; Walker, 1970; John Bernard Myers Gallery, 1971, 74; Allan Frumkin Gallery, Chicago, 1972; Fendrick Gallery, 1972; Graphics 1 & Graphics 2, Boston, 1972; Nashville, 1972; Rutgers U., 1973; Brooks Alexander Gallery, NYC, 1975; Marlborough Gallery, NYC, 1976, 77, 81, 84; Galerie Roger d'Amecourt, Paris, 1977; Van Straaten, Gallery, Chicago, 1976; Benjamin Mangel Gallery, Bala Cynwyd, 1977; Santa Barbara 1977; New Gallery, Cleveland, 1977; Showcase Galleries, Southfield, Mich., 1977; Martin Wiley Gallery, Nashville, 1978; Purchase/SUNY, 1978; Hudson River Museum, 1979; Virginia Commonwealth U., 1979; Colorado State U., 1980; Camp Gallery, St. Louis, Mo., 1980; U. of Miami, 1980; Aspen Center for the Visual Arts, 1981; Montgomery Bell Academy, Nashville, 1981. **Happenings:** Fire, Sun Gallery, Provincetown, 1958; Walking Man, Sun Gallery, Provincetown, 1959; Burning Building, Delancey Street Museum, NYC, 1959; Magic Train Ride, Reuben Gallery, NYC, 1960; U. of California, Berkeley,

1968; Ruckus Studio, NYC, 1972; *In 32 Chromosomes*, by Elizabeth Ross, 99 Prince Street, NYC, 1980. **Movies:** *Unwelcome Guests*, 1961; *Shoot the Moon*, 1962; *Miracle on the BMT*, 1963; *Lurk*, 1964; *Spaghetti Trouble*, 1964; *Man or Mouse*, 1964; *Umbrellas, Bah!*, 1965; *Big Sneeze*, 1965; *Secret of Wendel Sampson*, 1965-66; *Before 'n' After*, 1966; *Washington's Wig Whammed!* 1966; *Fat Feet*, 1966; *Meow, Meow!*, 1967; *Tappy Toes*, 1969-70; *Hippodome Hardware*, 1972-73; *The Conquest of Libya by Italia*, 1913-1912. 1972-73; *Ruckus Manhattan*, 1975-76; *Little Red Riding Hood*, 1978; *Hippodrome Hardware*, 1980. **Group:** Delancey Street Museum, NYC, 1959, 60; Chicago/AI, 1964; Province-town/Chrysler; SRGM, 1965; South-ampton/Parrish, 1965; Worcester/AM, 1965; A.F.A., 1965-66; Chicago/AI, Twenty Americans, 1966; MOMA, 1966; XXXIV Venice Biennial, 1968; Cologne/Kunstverein, Happening & Fluxus, circ., 1970; ICA, U. of Pennsylvania, The Spirit of the Comics, 1969; SRGM, 10 Independents, 1972; Harvard U., Recent Figure Sculpture, 1972; WMAA, Extraordinary Realities, 1973; Hirshhorn Inaugural Exhibition, 1974; Dallas/MFA, Poets of the Cities, 1974; Fort Worth, The Great American Rodeo, 1975; Stamford, Conn., American Salon des Refuses, 1976; Potsdam/SUNY, Off the Beaten Path, 1977; WMAA, Art about Art, 1978; Chicago/AI, Centennial Exhibition, 1979; Denver/AM, Poets and Painters, 1979; XXXIX Venice Biennial, 1980; Dublin/Municipal, International Quadriennial (ROSC), 1980; Brooklyn Museum, Drawings in Black and White: 1970-1979, 1980; PAFA, Contemporary American Realism Since 1960, 1981; Carnegie, International, 1983; Brooklyn Museum, The Great East River Bridge, 1883-1983, 1983; California State U., Long Beach, Figurative Sculpture, 1984; WMAA, Blam!, 1984. **Collections:** Brooklyn Museum; Caracas/Contemporaneo; Carnegie; Charlotte/Mint; Chicago/AI; Chicago/Contemporary; Delaware Art Museum; Den-

ver/AM; Fort Worth; Hirshhorn; Little Rock/MFA; MMA; MOMA; Nashville/Cheekwood; New School for Social Research; Norfolk/Chrysler; Northern Kentucky U.; Oberlin College; Raleigh/NCMA; Stockholm/National; Syracuse/Everson; Trenton/State. **Bibliography:** Arthur 2; Becker and Vostell; Drawings, The Pluralist Decade; *Figures/Environments*; Geske; *Happening & Fluxus*; Haskell 5; Honisch and Jensen, eds.; Janis and Blesh 1; Kaprow; Kirby; Lippard 5; *Poets & Painters; Recent Figure Sculpture*; Sandler 1; Sontag. Archives.

GROPPER, WILLIAM. b. December 3, 1897, NYC; **d.** January 4, 1977, Manhasset, N.Y. **Studied:** Ferrar School, San Francisco, with Robert Henri, George Bellows, 1912-13; NAD, 1913-14; New York School of Fine and Applied Art, with Howard Giles, Jay Hambridge, 1915-18. Traveled Europe, USA, USSR. Staff Artist, *New York Tribune*, 1919-21; *New York World*, 1925-27. **Taught:** American Art School, NYC, 1946-48. **Member:** Artists Equity; NIAL, 1968; NAD. **Commissions:** New Interior Building, Washington, D.C.; Northwestern Postal Station, Detroit; US Post Office, Freeport, N.Y.; Schenley Industries, Inc., NYC. **Awards:** Young Israel Prize; Los Angeles/County MA. **P.P.;** Indianapolis/Herron, Prize for Lithography; *Collier's* (magazine) Prize for Illustration, 1920; Harmon Foundation Award, 1930; J. S. Guggenheim Fellowship, 1937; Carnegie, Third Prize; MMA, Artists for Victory, Lithography Prize, 1942; Tamarind Fellowship, 1967; NAD, Thomas B. Clarke Prize, 1973; Andrew Carnegie Prize, 1975. **One-man Exhibitions:** ACA Gallery, 1983. **Retrospectives:** Phoenix; Evansville; Palm Springs Desert Museum; Syracuse U.; U. of Miami, 50 Years of Drawing and Cartoons, circ., 1968. **Group:** MMA; WMAA; Chicago/AI; MOMA; Los Angeles/County MA. **Collections:** Abbott Laboratories; U. of

Arizona; Brandeis U.; Britannica; Canton Art Institute; Chicago/AI; Cornell U.; Evansville; Hartford/Wadsworth; Harvard U.; Hirshhorn; Library of Congress; Los Angeles/County MA; MMA; MOMA; Montclair/AM; Moscow/Western; NYPL; Newark Museum; PAFA; Phillips; St. Louis/City; Sofia; Storm King Art Center; Syracuse U.; Tate; U. of Tucson; WMAA; Walker; Youngstown/Butler. **Bibliography:** American Artists Congress, Inc.; Barr 3; Baur 7; Bazin; Boswell 1; Brown; Brown 2; Canaday; Cheney; Christensen; **Freundlich;** Goodrich and Baur 1; Hall; Kootz 2; McCurdy, ed.; Mellquist; Mendelowitz; Pagano; Pearson 1; Reese; Richardson, E.P.; Rose, B., 1; Shapiro, ed.; Wight, 2. Archives.

GROSS, CHAIM. b. March 17, 1904, Kolomea, East Austria. To USA, 1921. **Studied:** Kunstgewerbe Schule; Educational Alliance, NYC; Beaux-Arts Institute of Design, with Elie Nadelman; ASL, with Robert Laurent. Traveled Europe, Israel, Turkey. **Taught:** Educational Alliance, NYC; New School for Social Research. **Member:** Sculptors Guild (President); Artists Equity; Federation of Modern Painters and Sculptors; NIAL. Federal A.P.: Teacher, supervisor, sculptor. **Commissions:** Main Post Office, Washington, D.C. 1936; Federal Trade Commission Building, Washington, D.C., 1938; France Overseas Building, New York World's Fair, 1939; US Post Office, Irwin, Pa., 1940; Reiss-Davis Child Guidance Clinic, Beverly Hills, 1961; Hadassah Hospital, Jerusalem, 1964; Temple Shaaray Tefila, NYC, 1964; U. of Rhode Island, 1972; International Synagogue, Kennedy International Airport, 1972. **Awards:** L. C. Tiffany Grant, 1933; Paris World's Fair, 1937, Silver Medal; MMA, Artists for Victory, $3,000 Second Prize, 1942; Boston Arts Festival, Third Prize for Sculpture, 1954; PAFA, Hon. Men., 1954; Audubon Artists, Prize for Sculpture, 1955; NIAL Grant, 1956; Boston Arts Festival, First Prize,

1963; NIAL, Award of Merit Medal, 1963; Hon. DFA, Adelphi U., 1980; Hon. DHL, Yeshiva U., 1978. **Address:** 526 West Broadway, NYC. **Dealer:** The Forum Gallery, NYC. **One-man Exhibitions:** (first) Gallery 144, NYC, 1932; Boyer Gallery, Philadelphia, 1935; Boyer Gallery, NYC, 1937; A.A.A. Gallery, NYC, 1942, 69; Massilon Museum, Akron/AI, 1946; Youngstown/Butler, 1946; New Paltz/SUNY, 1952; Jewish Museum, 1953; Shore Studio, Boston, 1954; Muriel Latow Gallery, Springfield, Mass., 1956; Duveen-Graham Gallery, NYC, 1957; WMAA, circ., 1959; The Marble Arch Gallery, Miami Beach, 1961; Anna Werbe Gallery, Detroit, 1962; The Forum Gallery, 1962, 64, 67, 72, 73, 74, 77, 80, 87; Irving Galleries, Inc., Milwaukee, 1963; New School for Social Research, 1971; NCFA, 1974; Leonard Hutton Gallery, NYC, 1974; U. of Miami, Fla., 1977; Montclair/AM, 1977; Jewish Museum, NYC, 1977; Prince Arthur Galleries, Toronto, 1977. **Group:** WMAA Sculpture Annuals; Sculptors Guild Annuals; PAFA; A.F.A., Sculpture in Wood, circ., 1941-42; American Painting and Sculpture, Moscow, 1959; MOMA, The Making of Sculpture, circ., 1961-62; Smithsonian, Drawings by Sculptors, circ., USA, 1961-63; New York World's Fair, 1964-65. **Collections:** Ain Harod; Andover/Phillips; Atlanta/AA; Baltimore/MA; Bezalel Museum; Boston/MFA; Brandeis U.; Brooklyn Museum; Bryn Mawr College; Chicago/AI; Colby College; Dayton/AI; Des Moines; Fairleigh Dickinson U.; U. of Georgia; Haifa; Jewish Museum; Kalamazoo/Institute; Kansas City/Nelson; U. of Kansas; La Jolla; MMA; MOMA; Massillon Museum; Milwaukee; U. of Minnesota; Newark Museum; Ogunquit; PAFA; PMA; Phoenix; Queens College; Reading/Public; Reed College; Rutgers U.; Scranton/Everhart; Scripps College; Smith College; Tel Aviv; WMAA; Walker; West Palm Beach/Norton; Worcester/AM; Youngstown/Butler. **Bibliography:** Baur 7; Brumme; Cheney; Craven, W.;

Flanagan; **Getlein 1; Goodrich and Baur, 1, 2; Gross;** Lombardo; Martin; McCurdy, ed.; Marter, Tarbell, and Wechsler; Mendelowitz; Sutton; Wheeler. Archives.

GROSSER, MAURICE. b. October 23, 1903, Huntsville, Ala.; **d.** December 22, 1986, NYC. **Studied:** Harvard U., 1920-24, with M. Mower. Traveled Europe, USA, Latin America, Africa. Art Critic for *The Nation*, 1961-67. **Taught:** U. of Ife, Nigeria, 1970. **Member:** The Travelers, London, NAD. Librettist of the Gertrude Stein-Virgil Thomson Operas *Four Saints in Three Acts* and *The Mother of Us All*. **One-man Exhibitions:** Grace Horne Galleries, Boston, 1925; Grand Central Palace, NYC, 1928; Galerie Vignon, Paris, 1931; Galerie des Quatre Chemins, Paris, 1933, 39; Hendrix, Inc. (Gallery), NYC, 1935; Arts Club of Chicago, 1939; Julien Levy Galleries, NYC, 1940, 41, 42, 44, 46; High Museum, 1941; Houston/MFA, 1942; M. Knoedler & Co., 1948, 50; Hugo Gallery, NYC, 1954; Alexander Iolas Gallery, 1955; Carstairs Gallery, NYC, 1957, 60, 62; Garlen Gallery, Philadelphia, 1958; The Banfer Gallery, 1963, 65; U. of Ife, 1970; Hirschl & Adler Galleries, 1971; Capricorn Gallery, Washington, D.C., 74; Boston Atheneum, 1975; Richard Larcada Gallery, NYC, 1975, 77; Fischbach Gallery, NYC, 1979, 80, 82. **Group:** U. of Minnesota; MOMA; WMAA; Cleveland/MA; VMFA. **Collections:** The Bank of New York; Brooklyn Museum; Cleveland/MA; Columbus; MOMA; U. of Minnesota; Rockland/Farnsworth; Springfield Art Center; VMFA; U. of Vermont. **Bibliography: Grosser, 1, 2.** Archives.

GROSSMAN, NANCY. b. April 28, 1940, NYC. **Studied:** Pratt Institute, BFA. **Taught:** Boston Museum School, 1985. **Member:** Sculptors Guild; Foundation for the Community of Artists. **Awards:** Ida C. Haskell Scholarship for

Foreign Travel, 1962; Guggenheim Foundation Fellowship, 1965; Pratt Institute, Inaugural Contemporary Achievement Award, 1966; AAAL, 1974; National Endowment for the Arts, 1984. **Address:** 105 Eldridge Street, NYC 10002. **Dealer:** Heath Gallery, Atlanta. **One-man Exhibitions:** The Krasner Gallery, 1964, 65, (2), 67; Cordier & Ekstrom, Inc., 1969, 76 (two-man), 1971, 73, 75; U. of Nevada, Reno, 1978; Barbara Gladstone, 1980; Heath Gallery, 1981; Terry Dintenfass, Inc., 1984. **Retrospective:** U. of Nevada, Reno. **Group:** PAFA, 1963; Corcoran, 1963; WMAA Annuals, 1968, 73, Contemporary American Sculpture, 1968-69, Human Concern/Personal Torment, 1969; Museum of Contemporary Crafts, Face Coverings, 1970-71; Harvard U., Recent Figure Sculpture, 1972; PMA/Museum of the Philadelphia Civic Center, Focus, 1974; Soho Center for Visual Artists, Drawing Now: Ten Artists, 1976; Brooklyn Museum, Works on Paper—Women Artists, 1977; Kohler Art Center, Sheboygan, Wis., Unpainted Portrait, 1979; Dade Community College, Miami, Fla., The Figure of 5, circ., 1979, 80; NYU, Perceiving Modern Sculpture, 1980; MIT, Body Language, circ., 1981; Houston/Contemporary, The Americans: The Collage, 1982; WMAA, The Sculptor as Draftsman, circ., 1983; Hofstra U., Maelstrom, 1986. **Collections:** Alcoa; Baltimore/MA; U. of California, Berkeley; Columbia Broadcasting System; Cornell U.; Dallas/MFA; Hamline U.; Kutztown State College; Minneapolis/MA; Pratt Institute; Princeton U.; Ridgefield//Aldrich; Rotterdam; U. of Utah; WMAA. **Bibliography:** Lucie-Smith; Nemser; *Recent Figure Sculpture*.

GROSVENOR, ROBERT. b. 1937, NYC. **Studied:** Ecole des Beaux-Arts, Dijon, 1956; Ecole Nationale des Arts Decoratifs, 1957-59; Universita di Perugia, 1958. Traveled France, England, Italy, Germany, USA, Mexico. **Taught:**

Robert Grosvenor   *Untitled*   1981–83

School of Visual Arts, NYC. **Awards:** National Council on the Arts, 1969. **Address:** 543 Broadway, NYC 10013. **Dealer:** Paula Cooper Gallery. **One-man Exhibitions:** Park Place Gallery, NYC, 1962-66; Dwan Gallery, Los Angeles, 1966; NYU, 1967; Galerie Rolf Ricke, 1970; Fischbach Gallery, 1970; Paula Cooper Gallery, NYC, 1970, 71, 74, 75, 78, 79, 81, 85; La Jolla, 1971; City U. of New York Graduate Center, NYC, 1973; Francoise Lambert, Milan, 1974; Galerie Stampa, Basel, 1975; Galerie Eric Fabre, Paris 1975, 77; Pasquale Trisorio, Naples, 1975; The Clocktower, NYC, 1976; P.S. 1, Long Island City, N.Y., 1984. **Group:** New York World's Fair, 1964-65; Jewish Museum, Primary Structures, 1966; ICA, U. of Pennsylvania, 1967; Buffalo/Albright, Plus by Minus, 1968; The Hague, Minimal Art, 1968; WMAA Sculpture Annual, 1968-69; U. of Minnesota, 1969; Walker, 1969; Chicago/Contemporary, 1969; ICA, Boston, Art on Paper, 1970; Cincinnati/Contemporary, Monumental Art, 1970; Arnhem, Sonsbeek '71, 1971; Middelheim Park, Antwerp, XI Sculpture Biennial, 1971; Houston/Contemporary, Eight, 1972; WMAA, 1973; Newport, R.I., Monumenta, 1974; Leverkusen, Zeichnungen III, 1975; Paris/Moderne, Tendances actuelles de la peinture americaine, 1975; WMAA, 200 Years of American Sculpture, 1976; Sydney/AG, Biennale, 1976; Documenta 6, Kassel, 1977; Minnesota/MA, American Drawings, 1927-1977, 1977; U. of Rochester, Drawings and Prints—New York, 1977; Lenbachhaus, Munich, Tendencies in American Drawings of the Late Seventies, 1979; U. of South Florida, Objects, Structures, Artifice, 1983. **Collections:** Lannan Foundation; Lipschultz Foundation; MIT; MOMA; NYU; Ridgefield/Aldrich; WMAA; Walker. **Bibliography:** Battcock, ed.; Friedman, M. 2; Kren; Lippard; MacAgy, 2; *Monumenta*; Tuchman 1. Archives.

GROSZ, GEORGE. b. July 26, 1893, Berlin, Germany; **d.** July 6, 1959, Berlin, Germany. **Studied:** Royal Saxon Academy of Fine Art, Dresden, 1909-11, R. Muller. O. Schindler, R.

Sterl. R. Wehle; School of Fine and Applied Arts, Berlin, 1911, with E. Orlik; Academie Colarossi, Paris, 1913. German Army, 1914-16, 1917-18. Traveled Russia, Europe, USA. To USA, 1932; citizen, 1938. **Taught:** Maurice Sterne School, NYC, 1933; ASL, 1933-36, 1940-42, 1943-44, 1950-53; Columbia U., 1941-42. Designed sets for Max Reinhardt Theatre, 1920-30. **Commissions:** A. Harris & Co., Dallas (portfolio of drawings entitled *Impressions of the City*). **Awards:** Chicago/AI, Watson F. Blair Prize, 1931, 40; Guggenheim Foundation Fellowship, 1937; PAFA, Carol H. Beck Gold Medal, 1940; Carnegie, Second Prize, 1945. **One-man Exhibitions:** (first) Goltz Gallery, Berlin, 1918; Gallery A. Flechtheim, Berlin, 1926; M. Wasservogel, Berlin, 1926; A.A.A. Gallery, NYC, 1926, 41, 43, 46, 48, 54; Club of Chicago, 1933; Crillon Galleries, Philadelphia, 1933; Milwaukee, 1933; Mayor Gallery, London, 1934; An American Place (Gallery), NYC, 1935; Contemporary Arts Gallery, NYC, 1935; Harvard U., 1935, 49, 73; Municipal U. of Omaha, 1936; Smith College, 1936 (three-man); Chicago/AI, 1938; Currier, 1939; Hudson D. Walker Gallery, NYC, 1938 (2), 1941; MOMA, 1941, 69; Denver/AM, 1943; Baltimore/MA, 1944; Leicester Gallery, London, 1946; Print Club of Cleveland, 1949; The Swetzoff Gallery, Boston, 1950; Dallas/MFA, 1952; Vera Lazuk, Cold Spring Harbor, N.Y., 1959; The Forum Gallery, 1963; E. V. Thaw, NYC, 1963; Arts Council of Great Britain, circ., 1963; Paul Kantor Gallery, Beverly Hills, Calif., 1964; Graphische Sammlung Albertina, 1965; Claude Bernard, Paris, 1966; Ira Spanierman Gallery, NYC, 1967, 69; Donald Morris Gallery, 1968; Peter H. Deitsch Gallery 1968, 69; LoGiudice Gallery, Chicago, 1969; Stuttgart/WK, 1969; La Medusa Gallery, 1970; Richard Feigen Gallery, NYC, 1971; Harvard U., 1973; Lunn Inc., Washington, D.C., 1974; Serge Sabarsky Gallery, NYC, 1975; Weintraub Gallery, NYC, 1978; Huntington/Hecksher, 1977; Hirshhorn,

1978. **Retrospective:** WMAA, 1954. **Group:** WMAA Annuals; MOMA; Chicago/AI; Los Angeles/County MA; SFMA; Newark Museum; St. Louis/City; Dallas/MFA. **Collections:** Berlin/National; Boston/MFA; Chicago/AI; Cleveland/MA; Detroit/Institute; Essen; Galerie des 20. Jahrhunderts; Harvard U.; Huntington, N.Y./Heckscher; MOMA; Newark Museum; Stuttgart; WMAA. **Bibliography: Ballo, ed.; Baur 2, 7; Bazalgette;** Bazin; Biddle 4; Bihalji-Merin; **Bittner;** Blesh 1; Bulliet 1, 2; Canaday; Cassou; Cheney; Christensen; *Cityscape 1919-39*; Craven, T., 1, 2; Davidson 2; *Dessins et Aquarelles*; Flanagan; Frost; Genauer; *George Grosz*; Goodrich and Baur 1; **Grosz 1, 2, 3, 4, 5;** Haftman; Hess, T. B., 1; Hulten; Hunter, ed.; Huyghe; Janis, S.; Kent, N.; Kouvenhoven; Kuh 1, 3; Langui; Lynton; McCurdy, ed.; **Mehring;** Mendelowitz; Murken-Altrogge; Newmeyer; Pagano; Pearson 1, 2; Pousette-Dart, ed.; Read 2; Richardson, E.P.; Richter; Rodman 3; Rose, B., 7; Rubin 1; Sachs; Salvini; Sietz 3; Selz, P. 3; **Tavolato;** Verkauf; Wingler, ed. Archives.

GUERRERO, JOSE. b. October 29, 1914, Granada, Spain. **Studied:** Escuela de Artes y Oficios Artisticos, Granada, 1930-34; Real Academia de Bellas Artes de San Fernando, Madrid, 1940-44; Academie des Beaux-Arts, Paris, 1945-46. Traveled Europe, 1947-49; resided Spain, 1965-68. To USA, 1949; citizen, 1952. **Taught:** New School for Social Research, 1962-; Cleveland Institute of Art, 1974; Atlanta College of Art, 1975; Iowa State U., 1978. **Awards:** *Art in America* magazine, New Talent, 1958; Graham Foundation Grant, 1958-59; Chevalier of the Order of Arts and Letters (France), 1959; Society for Contemporary American Art annual prize donation to The Art Institute of Chicago, 1959; Officer Order of Arts and Letters, 1979. **Address:** 406 West 20th Street, NYC 10011; and Cuenca, Spain. **Dealers:** Gruenebaum Gallery, Ltd.,

NYC; Galleria Juana Mordo, Madrid. **One-man Exhibitions:** Galerie Altarriba, Paris, 1946 (two-man); Galleria Secolo, Rome, 1948; Lou Cosyn Gallery, Brussels, 1948; St. George's Gallery, London, 1949 (two-man); Buchholz Gallery, Madrid, 1950; Arts Club of Chicago, 1954 (two-man); Betty Parsons Gallery, 1954, 57, 58, 60, 63; Rose Fried Gallery, 1964; Galeria Juana Mordo, 1964, 67, 71, 75, 76; Buchholz Gallery, Lisbon, 1967; French & Co. Inc., 1967, 70; Galleri Ostermalm, Stockholm, 1970; The Graham Gallery, 1970; Vali 30 Gallery, Valencia, 1972; Mikelki Gallery, Bilbao, 1972; A. M. Sachs Gallery, 1974; Galerie Wolfgang Ketterer, Munich, 1975; Juana de Azipuru Gallery, Seville, 1976; Hoover Gallery, San Francisco, 1976, 78; Museo Provincial de Bellas Artes, Victoria, Spain, 1977; Museo Provincial de Bellas Artes, Bilbao, Spain, 1976; Galeria Luzaro, Bilbao, 1978; Gruenebaum Gallery, Ltd., NYC, 1978, 80; Galeria Fucares, Almagro, Spain, 1979; Galerie Ditesheim, Neuchatel, Switzerland, 1979. **Group:** SRGM, Younger American Painters, 1954; Galerie de France, 10 Jeune Peintres de l'Ecole de Paris, 1956; Salon des Realites Nouvelles, Paris, 1957; Worcester/AM, 1958; Dallas/MFA, 1958; Rome-New York Foundation, Rome, 1958; Buffalo/Albright, 1958; I Inter-American Paintings and Prints Biennial, Mexico City, 1958; WMAA Annuals, 1958, 59, 62; American Abstract Artists, 1958, 61, 62; Carnegie, 1958, 61, 63; Corcoran, 1959; Spanish Art Today, circ., Germany, Holland, Denmark, 1967-68; Spanish Culture Institute, Munich, 1968; Sweden/Goteborgs, Spanish Painters, 1970; Dublin/Municipal, International Quadriennial (ROSC), 1971; Madrid, March Foundation Collection, circ., 1973-74; Mexico City/Nacional, Masters of Spanish Contemporary Art, 1974. **Collections:** Belgian Ministry of National Education; Beloit College; Brooklyn Museum; Buffalo/Albright; California Palace; Carnegie; Chase Manhattan Bank; Chicago/AI; Cornell

U.; Cuenca; Dartmouth College; French Ministry of National Education; Fundacion Juan March, Madrid; Harvard U.; Houston/MFA; Humlebaek/Louisiana; Indianapolis; Madrid/Nacional; Mobil Oil Co.; NYU; New School for Social Research; PAFA; Prudential Insurance Co. of America, Newark; Purchase/SUNY; RISD; SRGM; Sweden/Goteborgs; Toronto; WMAA; Westinghouse Electric Corp.; Yale U. **Bibliography:** Moser 1. Archives.

GUGLIELMI, O. LOUIS. b. April 9, 1906, Cairo, Egypt; **d.** September 3, 1956, Amagansett, N.Y. To USA, 1914. **Studied:** NAD, 1920-25. Corps of Army Engineers, 1943-45. **Taught:** Louisiana State U., 1952-53; New School for Social Research, 1953. Federal A.P.: Easel painting. **Awards:** L.C. Tiffany Grant, Yaddo Fellowship, and MacDowell Colony Fellowship, 1925-32; Chicago/AI, Ada S. Garrett Prize, 1943; Pepsi-Cola, Hon. Men., 1944; Carnegie, Hon. Men., 1944; AAAL Grant, 1946; PAFA, Joseph E. Temple Gold Medal, 1952. **One-man Exhibitions:** (first) The Downtown Gallery, 1938, also 1942, 46, 47, 51, 67; New Art Center, NYC; J. Seligmann and Co.; Julien Levy Galleries, NYC; Lee Nordness Gallery, NYC, 1958, 61, 62; WMAA, 1981. **Retrospective:** Rutgers U., 1980. **Group:** Musée du Jeu de Paume; New York World's Fair, 1939; MOMA, Americans 1943; Realists and Magic-Realists, circ., 1943; Chicago/AI, 1943; WMAA, The Precisionists, 1961; PAFA; Pepsi-Cola Co.; Newark Museum; U. of Minnesota; Denver/AM; PMA. **Collections:** Auburn U.; Britannica; Chicago/AI; Cornell U.; Cranbrook; U. of Georgia; MMA; MOMA; Newark Museum; SFMA; Tel Aviv; WMAA; Walker. **Bibliography:** Baur 7; Bethers; Blesh 1; *From Foreign Shores*; Genauer; Goodrich and Baur 1; Haftman; Hall; Halpert; Janis, S.; McCurdy, ed.; Pagano. Archives.

GUSSOW, ALAN. b. May 8, 1931, NYC. **Studied:** Middlebury College, 1952, AB; Cooper Union, 1952-53, with Morris Kantor; Atelier 17, NYC. Traveled Europe, USA, Central America, Australia; resided Rome, two years. **Taught:** Parsons School of Design, 1956-68, Chairman, Department of Fashion Illustration, 1959-68; Sarah Lawrence College, 1958-59; U. of Massachusetts, 1968-69; Rockland Community College, Suffern, N.Y., 1974; Pace U. 1977; Bard College, 1978; New York Studio School, 1980, 82; Queens College, 1983. **Film:** *A Sense of Place, The Artist and the American Land,* 1973; Creative consultant, *The Shadow Project,* 1982, on anti-nuclear art work; narrator, *Gustave Stickley and the American Craftsman Movement,* 1983, produced by Nabisco. Designed costumes, lighting, posters, choreography for Avodah Dance Ensemble, 1985. **Commissions:** Skidmore, Owings and Merrill, Architects (mural). **Awards:** Prix de Rome, 1953-54, renewed 1954-55; Artist-in-Residence, Cape Cod National Seashore, 1968; CAPS, 1971; AFE Grant, Artist-in-Residence, Delaware Water Gap, 1974-75. US Department of the Interior, National Parks Service, Environmental Consultant, 1968-; AAIAL, 1977. **Address:** 121 New York Avenue, Congers, NY 10920. **One-man Exhibitions:** (first) Hagerstown/County MFA, 1961; Middlebury College, 1961, 77; The Peridot Gallery, 1962, 63, 66, 67, 69, 70; Kendall Gallery, Wellfleet, Mass., 1971; The Joe and Emily Lowe Art Gallery, Syracuse, 1972; Washburn Gallery Inc., 1972, 73, 77, 80; Jacobs Ladder Gallery, Washington, D.C., 1974; Joe deMers Gallery, Hilton Head Island, S.C., 1978; VMFA, 1979; St. Paul's School, Concord, N.H., 1979; Hull Gallery, Washington, D.C., 1980, 83; William Sawyer Gallery, San Francisco, 1980; U. of California, Santa Cruz, 1981; Hopper House Gallery, Nyack, 1983; Sid Deutsch Gallery, NYC, 1984; Iowa State U., 1984. **Retrospectives:** Portland, Me./MA, 1971; Arnot, 1975; Rockland Center for the Arts, West Nyack, N.Y., 1978; Marywood College, 1984. **Group:** III Mostra di Pittura Americana, Bordighera, 1955; Maine State Art Festival, 1961; Youngstown/Butler, 1963; U. of Nebraska; PAFA Annual, 1966; A.F.A., Maine—50 Artists of the 20th Century, circ., 1966; AAAL, 1966; Colgate U., Viewpoints 7, 1972; Omaha/Joslyn, A Sense of Place, 1973; Queens Museum, New Images, 1974; AAIAL, 1977. **Collections:** Arnot; Bowdoin College; U. of California, Santa Cruz; Corcoran; Guild Hall; Middlebury College; Montgomery Museum; U. of Nebraska; Portland, Me./MA; VMFA; Wichita/AM.

GUSSOW, ROY. b. November 12, 1918, Brooklyn, N.Y. **Studied:** New York State Institute of Applied Agriculture (Farmingdale), 1938; Institute of Design, Chicago, 1945, with Lazlo Moholy-Nagy, and 1946, with Alexander Archipenko, 1948, BS. Traveled Europe and USA extensively. **Taught:**

Roy Gussow   *Stelae 10-24-84*   1984

Bradley U., 1948; Colorado Springs Fine Arts Center, 1949-51; North Carolina State College, 1951-62; Pratt Institute, 1962-68; Columbia U., 1981-85. **Member:** Sculptors Guild, President, 1976-; Artists Equity Association of New York; Artists Equity Association of N.Y., Vice-President, 1980-84, President, 1985-. **Commissions:** US Commerce Department Trade Fair, circ., Bangkok and Tokyo, 1956 (American Pavilion); Lenoir-Rhyne College, 1957; Cooperative Savings & Loan Association, Wilmington, N.C., 1959; North Carolina State College, 1961; North Carolina State College Faculty Club, 1962; San Francisco Museum of Science and Industry, 1962; Phoenix-Mutual Building, Hartford, Conn., 1963 (8-ft stainless-steel structure commissioned by Max Abramovitz); Reynolds Metal Co., 1967; Tulsa Civic Center, 1968; Xerox Corp., 1968; Creedmore State Hospital, Queens, N.Y., 1970; Heublein Inc., Farmington Conn., 1974; Family Court Building, NYC, 1975; Combustion Engineering Corp., Stamford, Conn., 1976; City of Reading, Pa., 1979; City Hall, Harrisburg, Pa., 1983; J. C. Penney Co., Plano, Tx., 1985. **Awards:** Raleigh/NCMA, **P.P.,** 1957, 61; PAFA, Hon. Men., 1958; Ford Foundation, **P.P.,** 1960, 62; National Gold Medal Exhibition for the Building Arts, NYC, NYC, 1962. **Address:** 4040 24th Street, Long Island City, NY 11101. **Dealer:** Grace Borgenicht Gallery, Inc., **One-man Exhibitions:** (first) Design Associates Gallery, Greensboro, N.C., 1952; The Pennsylvania State U., 1959; Grace Borgenicht Gallery, Inc., 1964, 71, 73, 77, 80; Chicago/AI, 1947, 48, 49; U. of Arkansas, 1948; Omaha/Joslyn, 1949, 50; Denver/AM, 1949-51; SFMA, 1951; MMA, 1951; PAFA, annually 1951-59; Raleigh/NCMA, annually 1952-61; WMAA, 1956; Oakland/AM, 1959; WMAA, Sculpture Annual, 1964, 66, 68; WMAA, Contemporary American Sculpture, Selection II, 1969; Albright College, 1979; Nassau Community College, Garden City, N.Y., 1985. **Collections:** American Tobacco Co.; Atlanta/AA; Brooklyn Museum; California Academy of Science; Equitable Life Assurance Society; MOMA; Newark Museum; U. of North Carolina; Radcliffe College; Raleigh/NCMA; Tulsa/Philbrook; WMAA. **Bibliography:** Craven, W. Archives.

GUSTON, PHILIP. b. June 27, 1913, Montreal, Canada; **d.** June 9, 1980, Woodstock, N.Y. To USA, 1916. **Studied:** Otis Art Institute, Los Angeles, for 3 months, 1930. Traveled Spain, Italy, France, USA. **Taught:** State U. of Iowa, 1941-45; Washington U., 1945-47; U. of Minnesota, 1950; NYU, 1951-59; Pratt Institute, 1953-57; Yale U., 1963; Brandeis U., 1966; Columbia U., 1969, 70, 74; New York Studio School; Skidmore College, 1968; Boston U., 1973-80. **Commissions:** Federal A.P., 1935-40, murals: WPA Building, New York World's Fair, 1939 (facade); Queensbridge Housing Project, 1940; Forestry Building, Laconia, N.H., 1941. Section of Fine Arts (murals), Social Security Building, Washington, D.C., 1942; US Post Office, Commerce, Ga., 1938. Trustee, American Academy, Rome. **Member:** NIAL. **Awards:** Carnegie, First Prize, 1945; Guggenheim Foundation Fellowship, 1947, renewed 1968; Prix de Rome, 1948; AAAL Grant, 1948; Ford Foundation Grant, 1948, $10,000, 1959; Hon. DFA, Boston U., 1970; College Art Association, Distinguished Teaching of Art Award, 1975; Brandeis U., Creative Arts Award, 1980. **One-man Exhibitions:** (first) The Midtown Galleries, 1945; Boston Museum School, 1947; Utica, 1947; U. of Minnesota, 1950; The Peridot Gallery, 1952; Charles Egan Gallery, 1953; Sidney Janis Gallery, 1956, 58, 60, 61; Dwan Gallery, Los Angeles (two-man, with Franz Kline), 1962; Jewish Museum, 1966; Santa Barbara/MA, 1966, 67; Gertrude Kasle Gallery, 1969, 73, 74; Marlborough Gallery Inc., NYC, 1970; Boston U., 1970, 74; La Jolla,

1971; MOMA, 1973; David McKee Gallery, 1974, 76, 77, 78, 79, 80, 82, 83, 85; Allan Frumkin Gallery, Chicago, 1978; MIT, 1984; Reconnaisance Gallery, Fitroy, Australia, 1985; Greenville, 1986; Phillips, circ., 1980; Whitechapel Art Gallery, London, circ., 1982; Melbourne/National, circ., 1984. **Retrospectives:** V Sao Paulo Biennial, 1950; XXX Venice Biennial, 1960; SRGM, 1962; Amsterdam/Stedelijk, 1962; Los Angeles/County MA, 1963; Brandeis U., 1966; SFMA, circ., 1980-81. **Group:** U. of Illinois, 1944, 67; Walker, Contemporary American Painting, 1950; U. of Minnesota, 40 American Painters, 1940-50, 1951; MOMA, Abstract Painting and Sculpture in America, 1951; Baltimore/MA, Abstract Expressionists, 1953; MOMA, Twelve Americans, circ., 1956; Sao Paulo, 1957; WMAA, Nature in Abstraction, 1958; I Inter-American Paintings and Prints Biennial, Mexico City, 1958; MOMA, The New American Painting, circ., Europe, 1958-59; St. Louis/City, Modern American Painting, 1959; WMAA, 18 Living American Artists, 1959, also Annuals; Documenta II, Kassel, 1959; Ringling, 1961; SRGM/USIA, American Vanguard, circ., Europe, 1961-62; PAFA; SFMA; Chicago/AI; Corcoran; SRGM, circ., 1963; Tate, Painting and Sculpture of a Decade, 1954-64, 1964; Carnegie, 1964; Los Angeles/County MA, New York School: The First Generation, 1965; U. of St. Thomas (Tex.), 1967; ASL, 1967-68; MOMA, The New American Painting and Sculpture: The First Generation, 1969; MMA, New York Painting and Sculpture: 1940-1970, 1969-70; Ente Manifestazioni Genovesi, Immagine per la Citta, Genoa, 1972; National Gallery, American Art at Mid-Century, 1973; MIT, Drawings by Five Abstract Expressionist Painters, 1975; Buffalo/Albright, American Painting in the 1970s, 1978; Hayward Gallery, London, New Painting—New York, 1979; WMAA Biennial, 1979; Denver/AM, Poets-Painters, 1979; Akron/AI, Dialogue, 1980; Brandeis U., Mavericks, 1980; Houston/Contemporary, American Still Life, 1945-1983, 1983; MOMA, The Modern Drawing, 1983; AFA, Social Concern and Urban Realism, circ., 1984; IEF, Twentieth Century American Drawings: The Figure in Context, circ., 1984; Los Angeles/MOCA, Automobile and Culture, 1984; National Gallery, Gemini G.E.L.: Art and Collaboration, 1984; Amsterdam/Stedelijk, La Grande Parade, 1984; Ecole des Beaux Arts, Paris, American Drawing: 1930-1980, 1985; Fort Lauderdale, An American Renaissance: Painting and Sculpture Since 1940, 1986; ICA, London, Komik Ikonoklasm, 1986. **Collections:** Allentown/AM, Baltimore/MA; Bezalel National Museum, Jerusalem; Brandeis U.; Buffalo/Albright; Canberra/National; Carnegie; Chicago/AI; Cleveland/MA; Denver/AM; Detroit/Institute; Harvard U.; High Museum; Hirshhorn; IBM; U. of Illinois; Illinois Wesleyan U.; State U. of Iowa; Los Angeles/County MA; MMA; MOMA; Minneapolis/Institute; NCFA; U. of Nebraska; Phillips; Purchase/SUNY; SFMA; SRGM; St. Louis/City; San Jose State College; Seagram Collection; Tate; U. of Texas; Utica; VMFA; WMAA; Washington U.; Worcester/AM; Yale U. **Bibliography:** Arnason 2; Ashton 2, 3, 5, 6; Baur 5; Bazin; Biddle 4; Blesh 1; Canaday; De Wilde 1; *From Foreign Shores;* Genauer; Goodrich and Baur 1; Haftman; Henning; **Hunter** 1, 6, **7;** Hunter, ed.; Kozloff 3; Lucie-Smith; McCoubrey 1; McCurdy, ed.; Nordness, ed.; *Poets and Painters;* O'Hara 1; Ponente; Read 2; Ritchie 1; Rose, B., 1; Sandler 1; Seuphor 1; Tuchman, ed.; Tuchman, ed.; Weller; *Woodstock: An American Art Colony, 1902-1977.* Archives.

GUY, JAMES. b. 1910, Middletown, Conn.; **d.** March 14, 1983, Moodus, Conn. **Studied:** Hartford Art School, with Albertus Jones, Kimon Nicolaides. Traveled Mexico, Europe, USA. **Taught:** Bennington College, 1945-46; MacMurray College, Jacksonville, Ill.,

1946-54; Wesleyan U., 1963-75. Film-maker during the 1930s with the Film and Photo League. Articles on fishing for leading outdoor publications. Federal A.P.: Easel painting; mural for Hartford (Conn.) High School. **One-man Exhibitions:** (first) Boyer Gallery, NYC, 1939, also 1940; Ferargil Galleries, NYC, 1941, 42, 44; a gallery in Hollywood, Calif., 1945; Lehigh U., 1945; Bennington College, 1947; Carlebach Gallery, NYC, 1949, 50; MacMurray College, 1949; St. Louis/City, 1952; Hartford College for Women, 1960; Wesleyan U., 1961; Rose Fried Gallery; Charles Egan Gallery, 1969. **One-man Exhibitions:** Mattatuck Historical Society Museum; Martin Diamond Fine Arts, NYC, 1983. **Retrospective:** Hartford College for Women, 1970; Wesleyan U., 1976. **Group:** Paris World's Fair, 1937; New York World's Fair, 1939; Golden Gate International Exposition, San Francisco, 1939; WMAA Annuals, MOMA; MMA; Chicago/AI; Rutgers U., Surrealist & American Art: 1931-1947, 1977. **Collections:** Hartford/Wadsworth, The Miller Co.; Mattatuck Historical Society Museum; MIT; The Olsen Foundation Inc.; SRGM; Society of the Four Arts. **Bibliography:** Hall.

GWATHMEY, ROBERT. b. January 24, 1903, Richmond, Va. **Studied:** North Carolina State College, 1924-25; Maryland Institute, 1925-26; PAFA, 1926-30, with George Harding, Daniel Garber. Traveled Europe, Caribbean, Mexico, Egypt. **Taught:** Beaver College, 1930-37; Carnegie Institute of Technology, 1938-42; Cooper Union, 1942-68; Boston U., 1968-69; Syracuse U., 1970. **Member:** Artists Equity; NIAL; NAD. **Commissions:** US Post Office, Eutaw, Ala. **Awards:** PAFA, Cresson Fellowship, 1929, 30; US Government 48-State Mural Competition winner, 1939; San Diego, First Prize, Watercolors, 1940; Carnegie, Second Prize, 1943; Lessing J. Rosenwald Fund Fellowship, 1944; AAAL Grant, 1946; Corcoran, Fourth Prize, 1957; NAD, Joseph Isidor Gold Medal, 1971; NAD, Saltus Gold Medal, 1977; Adolph and Clara Obrig Prize, 1978; Benjamin Altman Prize (figure) 1979. **Address:** Bluff Road, Amagansett, NY 11930. **Dealer:** Terry Dintenfass, Inc. **One-man Exhibitions:** (first) ACA Gallery, 1940, also 1946, 49; VMFA; Terry Dintenfass, Inc., NYC, 1961, 64, 68, 71, 74, 76, 80. **Retrospectives:** Randolph/Macon Woman's College, 1967; Boston U., 1969; St. Mary's College of Maryland, 1976. **Group:** WMAA Annuals; Corcoran; PAFA; MMA; Boston/MFA; Carnegie, 1964, 65; U. of Illinois, 1965; NAD, 1973; St. Joseph/Albrecht, Drawing—America: 1973, 1973; Ball State U. Annual, 1974; Skidmore College, An Exhibition of Twentieth-Century Drawings, 1975; Youngstown/Butler, Midyear show, 1973, 78, 81. **Collections:** Alabama Institute; Auburn U.; Birmingham, Ala./MA; Boston/MFA; Brandeis U.; Brooklyn Museum; California Palace; Carnegie; U. of Georgia; Guild Hall; Hirshhorn; IBM; U. of Illinois; Los Angeles/County MA; U. of Nebraska; U. of Oklahoma; PAFA; PMA; Randolph-Macon Woman's College; U. of Rochester; St. Joseph/Albrecht; San Diego; Sao Paulo; Savannah/Telfair; Springfield, Mass./MFA; U. of Texas; VMFA; WMAA; Youngstown/Butler. **Bibliography:** Baldinger; Baur 7; Bazin; Goodrich and Baur 1; McCurdy, ed.; Mendelowitz; Nordness, ed.; Pousette-Dart, ed.; Reese. Archives.

H

HAAS, RICHARD. b. August 29, 1936, Spring Green, Wisc. **Studied:** U. of Wisconsin, Milwaukee 1954-58, BS; U. of Wisconsin, with Joseph Friebert, Robert von Neuman, Harold Altman; U. of Minnesota, 1961-64, MFA, with Jack Tworkov, Peter Busa, Malcolm Myers. Traveled Mexico, Europe, Morocco. US Army, 1959. **Taught:** Lincoln High School, Milwaukee, 1959-61; School of Visual Arts, NYC, 1966-80; U. of Minnesota, 1963-64; Michigan State U., 1964-68; Bennington College, 1968-80; School of Visual Arts, NYC, 1976-80. **Member:** Art Commission of the City of New York, 1978-80; Architectural League of New York, vice-president, 1978-80. Board of Directors, Public Art Fund, 1981-; Board of Governors, Skowhegan School, 1982-; Century Association. **Commissions:** Numerous wall murals indoors-outdoors nationwide. **Awards:** Taliesen Fellowship, 1955, 56; Ford Foundation **P.P.,** 1964; CAPS, 1972; National Endowment for the Arts grant, 1978; AIA, Medal of Honor, 1978; Municipal Art Society, NYC, award, 1979; Guggenheim Foundation Feloowship, 1983. **Address:** 20 Overcliff Street, Yonkers, N.Y. 10705. **Dealers:** Brooke Alexander, NYC; Young-Hoffman Gallery, Chicago. **One-man Exhibitions:** Bennington College, 1968, 71, 74; Hundred Acres Gallery, Ltd., 1971, 73, 74; Brooke Alexander, 1972, 75, 80, 82, 85; Contract Graphics Associates, Houston, 1973; Boston U., 1973; WMAA, 1974; Harcus-Krakow Gallery, Boston, 1975; Delahunty Gallery, Dallas, 1976; Marion Locks Gallery, Philadelphia, 1976; Tyler School of Art, Philadelphia, 1977; The Art Center, Waco, 1977; Quincy College, 1978; Young-Hoffman Gallery, Chicago, 1978; Galerie Biedermann, Munich, 1978; Swain's Art Store, Plainfield, N.J., 1979; Brooke Alexander, Inc., NYC; SFMA, 1980; Municipal Art Society, NYC, 1981; Young Hoffman Gallery, Chicago, 82; American Institute of Architects Foundation, Washington, D.C., 1982; Norfolk/Chrysler, 1983; Rhona Hoffman Gallery, Chicago, 1983; U. of Tennessee, 1984; Chattanooga/Hunter, 1984. **Retrospective:** West Palm Beach/Norton, 1977. **Group:** Walker, Five Young Minnesota Artists, 1963; Indianapolis, 1972; Yale U., American Drawing: 1969-1973, 1973; Brooklyn Museum Print Biennial, 1974; Akron/AI, Contemporary Images in Watercolor, 1976; Davidson, N.C., Art on Paper 1976; U. of North Carolina, Art on Paper, 1976; A.F.A., American Master Drawings and Watercolors, 1976; Brooklyn Museum, Thirty Years of American Printmaking, 1976; US Department of the Interior, America, 1976, 1976; Library of Congress and NCFA, 25th National Exhibition of Prints, 1977; Cooper-Hewitt Museum, Ornament in the 20th Century, 1978; Tulsa/Philbrook, Realism/Photorealism, 1980; Architectural League of NY, Collaboration: Artists & Architects, circ., 1981; PAFA, Contemporary American Realism Since 1960, 1981; Cooper-Hewitt Museum, Urban Documents, 1983; Paris/Beaubourg, Images et Imaginaires d'Architecture, 1984. **Collection:** Allentown/AM; Boston/MFA, Boston Public Library; Chicago/AI; Detroit/Institute; Fort Worth; Free Library of Philadelphia; Hartford/Wadsworth; Harvard U.;

High Museum; Houston/MFA; Library of Congress; MOMA; MMA; Minneapolis/Institute; NCFA; Newark Museum; NYPL; San Antonio/McNay; Walker; West Palm Beach/Norton: WMAA; Yale U. **Bibliography:** *America 1976;* Arthur 1, 2, 3; *Richard Haas: An Architecture of Illusion.*

HADZI, DIMITRI. b. March 21, 1921, NYC. **Studied:** Brooklyn Polytechnic Institute, 1940-43; Cooper Union, NYC, 1946-50; Brooklyn Museum School, 1948-50; Polytechnion, Athens, 1950-51, Museo Artistico Industriale, Rome, 1952-53. US Air Force, 1943. Traveled Europe, USA. **Taught:** Dartmouth College, 1969; Fullerton Junior College, 1973; U. of Oregon, summer, 1974; Harvard U., 1975, 77-. **Member:** AAIAL, 1983. **Commissions:** MIT; Philharmonic Hall, Lincoln Center for the Performing Arts, NYC; sculpture for the Reynolds Metal Co. Memorial Award; Sun Life Insurance Co., Baltimore; John F. Kennedy Federal Office Building, Boston; Federal Reserve Bank, Minneapolis, 1971; St. Paul's Church, Rome; Lane County's Public Service Building; Federal Office Building, Portland, Ore., 1976; Johnson Wax Co., Racine, Wis., 1978-79; Dallas Center, Dallas, 1978-79; Harvard Square, Cambridge, 1979; City of Columbus, Ohio, 1980; Owens-Illinois Co., Toledo, 1980; City of Appleton, Wisc., 1981; Stanford U., 1981; Copley Place sculpture fountain, Boston, 1982; Carleton College, 1985. **Awards:** Fulbright Fellowship (Greece), 1950; L. C. Tiffany Grant, 1955; Guggenheim Foundation Fellowship, 1957; NIAL, 1962; American Academy, Rome, 1973-74; Hon. MA, Harvard U., 1977; American Academy of Arts and Sciences, fellow, 1978; Art Directors Club, Gold Medal Awards, 1978. **Address:** 7 Ellery Square, Cambridge, MA 02138. **Dealers:** Gruenebaum Gallery, Ltd., NYC; Richard Gray Gallery, Chicago. **One-man Exhibitions:** Galleria Schneider, Rome, 1958, 60; Seiferheld Gallery,

NYC, 1959; Galerie Van der Loo, Munich, 1961; Stephen Radich Gallery, 1961; Gallery Hella Nebelung, Dusseldorf, 1962; MIT, 1963; Temple U., Rome, Temple Abroad, 1968; Felix Landau Gallery, 1969; Dartmouth College, 1969; Alpha Gallery, 1971, 77; Richard Gray Gallery, 1972; Jodi Scully Gallery, 1973; Galleria d'Arte l'Obelisco, 1974; Harvard U., 1975, 76; Mekler Gallery, Los Angeles, 1978, 80, 82; Gruenebaum Gallery, Ltd., NYC, 1978, 81, 84; Harvard U., 1984. **Retrospective:** MIT, 1963; Tyler School, Temple U., Rome, 1968. **Group:** MOMA, New Talent, 1956; Middelhelm Park, Antwerp, Outdoor Sculpture, 1957, 59, 71; Carnegie, 1958, 61; MOMA, Recent Sculpture, USA, 1959; Smith College, New Sculpture Now, 1960; WMAA, Business Buys American Art, 1960; RISD, Bronze Figure Sculpture Today, 1960; U. of Nebraska, 1960; Claude Bernard, Paris, Aspects of American Sculpture, 1960; WMAA Annuals, 1960, 63; Boston Arts Festival, 1961; XXXI Venice Biennial, 1962; Seattle World's Fair, 1962; Battersea Park, London, International Sculpture Exhibition, 1963; New York World's Fair, 1964-65; Hannover/Kunstverein, 1965; The White House, Washington, D.C., 1965; Musée Rodin, Paris, 1966; Rome/Nazionale, 1970; Athens Panhellenic Exhibitions, 1973; Quadriennale, Rome, 1977; AAAL, 1978; Boston Athenaeum, Four Sculptors, 1982; Sonoma State U., Works in Bronze, A Modern Survey, 1983; Antwerp/ICC, Europalia, 1982. **Collections:** Andover/Phillips; Buffalo/Albright; Chase Manhattan Bank; U. of Chicago; Ciba-Geigy Corp.; City of Tilburg; Cleveland/MA; Currier; Dallas/MFA; Fullerton Junior College; Harvard U.; Hirshhorn; U. of Massachusetts; MIT; MOMA; Montreal/MFA; Mount Holyoke College; Newark Museum; New School for Social Research; NYU; PMA; Phoenix; Princeton U.; UCLA; RISD; U. of Chicago; SRGM; Seattle/AM; Smith College; U. of Southern

California, Los Angeles; Sweet Briar College; UCLA; Union Carbide Corp.; U. of Vermont; WMAA; Yale U. **Bibliography:** Craven, W.

HALE, NATHAN CABOT. b. July 5, 1925, Los Angeles, Calif. **Studied:** Chouinard Art Institute, Los Angeles, 1945; ASL, 1945-50; Santa Monica City College, 1952; Saratoga Springs/SUNY, Empire State College, 1975, BS in Morphology; Union College (N.Y.), 1976, Ph.D. in Organomic Morphology. Traveled Mexico, Europe, South Pacific, USA, Greece, Israel. **Taught:** Los Angeles City Art Education and Recreation Program, 1956-57; Pratt Institute, 1963-64; ASL, 1966-72; Sculptor's Society of Ireland, 1982; Walden U., 1978-; ASL, 1985-. Designed sets for off-Broadway production of *The Affairs of Anatole*, 1958. Senior Editor *Art/World*, 1985-. **Member:** Architectural League of New York; Municipal Art Society of New York. **Commissions:** Architectural and portrait; sculpture for St. Anthony of Padua, East Northport, N.Y. **Awards:** Los Angeles/County MA, **P.P.** for Sculpture, 1953; Audubon Artists, 1974. **Address:** Sheffield Road, Amenia, NY 12501. **Dealer:** The Midtown Galleries. **One-man Exhibitions:** (first) Felix Landau Gallery, 1957; Washington Irving Gallery, NYC, 1960; Feingarten Gallery, NYC and Chicago, 1961; The Midtown Galleries, NYC, 1964, 68, 74; Hazleton Art League, 1966; Fort Wayne/AM, 1966; Queens College, 1966; Franklin and Marshall College, 1967; NYU, 1967; Quinata Gallery, Nantucket, 1968. **Group:** J. Seligmann and Co., 1947-49; Roko Gallery, NYC, 1948-50; Los Angeles/County MA, 1953-55; Colorado Springs/FA, 1961; Hirschl & Adler Galleries, Inc., NYC, Continuing Traditions of Realism in American Art, 1962; Lehigh U., 1963; Corcoran, 1963, 64; Buffalo/Albright, 1963, 68; Wayne State U., 1964; United States Government, Art in the Embassies, 1964-66; National Art Museum of Sport, NYC, 1969. **Collections:** Indi-

anapolis/Herron; Los Angeles/County MA; Sara Roby Foundation; Wake Forest U.

HALEY, JOHN CHARLES. b. September 21, 1905, Minneapolis, Minn. **Studied:** Minneapolis Institute School, with Cameron Booth; Hofmann School, Munich and Capri; Scuola Mosaico, Ravenna, Italy. US Navy, World War II. Traveled Europe, USA. **Taught:** U. of California, Berkeley, 1930-72. Federal A.P.; Fresco painter, briefly. **Commissions:** Stained glass in churches in St. Paul, Duluth, Rochester, and Benson, Minn.; a fresco at Government Island. **Awards:** San Francisco Art Association, 1936, 39, 44, 51, 53, 56; California State Fair, 1950, 51; RAC, 1956, 58. **Address:** 771 Ocean Avenue, Richmond, Calif. 94807. **One-man Exhibitions:** (first) SFMA, mid 1930; Mortimer Levitt Gallery, NYC, 1949, 52; U. of California, Worth Ryder Gallery, 1962; de Young, 1962; Chico State College, 1963; Four Winds Gallery, Kalamazoo, 1974; De Young, 1980. **Group:** SFMA Annuals, 1932-; California Palace Annuals; U. of Illinois Annuals, 1948-51; III & VI Sao Paulo Biennials, 1955, 61; Chicago/AI; MMA; PAFA; Dallas/MFA; Denver/AM; RAC; Pasadena/AM; Colorado Springs/FA; Santa Barbara/MA; St. Louis/City; MOMA, circ. **Collections:** U. of California, Berkeley; Chico State College; First National Bank of Nevada; IBM; Mills College; MMA; Oakland/MA; Phillips; SFMA.

HAMMERSLEY, FREDERICK. b. January 5, 1919, Salt Lake City, Utah. **Studied:** U. of Idaho, 1936-38; San Francisco Junior College, 1938-39; Academy of Advertising Art, San Francisco, 1939-40; Chouinard Art Institute, Los Angeles, 1940-42; 1946-47, with Henry McFee; Jepson Art Institute, Los Angeles, 1947-49, with Rico Lebrun; Academie des Beaux-Arts, Paris, 1945. US Army, 1942-46. **Taught:** Jepson Art Institute, Los Angeles, 1949-51;

Pomona College, 1953-62; Pasadena Museum School, 1956-61 (children's painting class); 1963- (adult classes); occasional private lessons; Chouinard Art Institute, 1964-68; U. of New Mexico, 1968-71. **Awards:** Laguna Beach Art Gallery, First Prize, 1949; City of Claremont, First Prize, 1960; Youngstown/Butler, **P.P.**, 1961; Guggenheim Foundation Fellowship, 1973; National Endowment for the Arts, Grant, 1975, 77. **Address:** 608 Carlisle S.E., Albuquerque, NM 87106. **Dealer:** Hoshour Gallery, Albuquerque. **One-man Exhibitions:** (first) Fullerton (Calif.) Art Museum, 1959; Pasadena/AM, 1961; Heritage Gallery, Los Angeles, 1961, 63; Occidental College, 1962; California Palace, 1962; La Jolla, 1963; Santa Barbara/MA; Hollis Gallery, San Francisco; Whittier College; U. of New Mexico; U. of New Mexico, 1969-75; L. A. Louver Gallery, Venice, Calif., 1978, 81; Middendorf Lane Gallery, Washington, D.C. (two-man), 1977; Hoshour Gallery, 1984. **Retrospective:** U. of New Mexico, 1975. **Group:** SFMA, Abstract Classicists, circ., Los Angeles/County MA; ICA, London; USIA, Drawings from California, circ., Europe, 1958-59; Queens U., Belfast, 1959-60; Western Association of Art Museum Directors, circ., 1960-61; A.F.A., Purist Painting, circ., 1960-61; WMAA, Geometric Abstraction in America, circ., 1962; WMAA, Fifty California Artists, 1962-63; MOMA, The Responsive Eye, 1965; M. Knoedler & Co., Art Across America, circ., 1965-67; U. of Nebraska, Geometric Abstraction, 1974; Los Angeles/County MA, California, 5 Footnotes to Modern Art History, 1977; Corcoran Biennial, 1977; Denver/AM Biennial, 1979; Albuquerque Museum, Here and Now, 1980. **Collections:** U. of California, Berkeley; City of Claremont; Corcoran; Foote, Cone & Belding Communications, Inc., Los Angeles; U. of New Mexico; Oakland/AM; SFMA; Santa Barbara/MA; US Navy; Youngstown/Butler. **Bibliography:** Archives.

HANSEN, JAMES LEE. b. June 13, 1925, Tacoma, Wash. **Studied:** Portland (Ore.) Museum School. **Taught:** Oregon State U., 1957-58; U. of California, Berkeley, 1958; Portland (Ore.) State College, 1964-69. Founder of The Fine Arts Collaborative, 1959. **Commissions:** Vancouver (Wash.) Federal Savings and Loan Building; Land Title Building, Vancouver, Wash.; Sacred Heart Nurses Dormitory, Eugene, Ore.; Corvallis (Ore.) First Federal Savings and Loan; Alder Way Building, Portland, Ore.; St. Louis Church, Bellevue, Wash.; Providence Heights College, Pine Lake, Wash.; St. Mary's Mission, Pioneer, Wash.; Fresno (Calif.) Civic Mall; St. Ann's Church, Butte, Mont., 1966; Holy Trinity Parish, Bremerton, Wash., 1967; Graphic Arts Center, Portland, Ore., 1968; Harrison Square, Portland (Ore.) Civic Center; State Capitol Campus, Olympia, Wash.; U. of Oregon; Clark College; Stadium Plaza, Pullman, Wash.; Civic Center Fountain, Salem, Ore.; BLM Regional Headquarters, Medford, Ore. **Awards:** SFMA, First **P.P.**, 1952, 60; Seattle/AM, First **P.P.**, 1952; SFMA, American Trust Co. Award, 1956; Seattle/AM, Norman Davis **P.P.**, 1958, Fellow of the International Institute of Arts and Letters. **Address:** 6423 N.E. 248th Street, Battle Ground, Wash. 98604. **Dealers:** Hodges/Banks Gallery, Seattle; Abante Gallery, Portland, Ore. **One-man Exhibitions:** Kraushaar Galleries, 1952; Dilexi Gallery, San Francisco; The Morris Gallery, NYC, 1951; Fountain Gallery, 1966, 69; U. of Oregon, 1969; Cheney Cowles Memorial Museum, Spokane, 1972; Polly Friedlander Gallery, 1973, 78; Fountain Gallery, Portland, Ore., 1977, 81, 84; Hodges/Banks Gallery, 1983, 85. **Retrospective:** Portland, Ore./AM, 1971. **Group:** Portland, Ore./AM, 1951-60; Santa Barbara/MA; U. of Oregon; Fort Worth; U. of Washington; SFMA, 1952, 56, 60; Seattle/AM, 1952-57, 1959, 60, Northwest Annual, 1967; Denver/AM, 1952, 61; WMAA, 1953; San Diego; The Morris Gallery, NYC, 1961; State of

Washington Governor's Invitational, circ., 1964-75; U. of Washington, Seattle, An American Tradition: Abstraction, 1981. **Collections:** The Bank of California, N.A., Portland, Ore.; First Federal Savings and Loan Association of Corvallis; First National Bank of Oregon; First National Bank of Seattle; U. of Oregon; Portland, Ore./AM; SFMA; Seattle/AM. **Bibliography:** *Art of the Pacific Northwest; Recent Figure Sculpture.*

HANSEN, ROBERT. b. January 1, 1924, Osceola, Neb. **Studied:** U. of Nebraska, with Kady Faulkner, Dwight Kirsch, 1948, AB, BFA; Escuela de Bellas Artes, San Miguel de Allende, Mexico, with Alfredo Zalce. US Army, 1943-46. Resided Mexico, Hawaii, India, Spain. **Taught:** Bradley U., 1949-55; Occidental College, 1956-. **Commissions** (murals): Public School and State Library, Morelia, Mexico. **Awards:** Fulbright Fellowship (India), 1961; Guggenheim Foundation Fellowship, 1961; Tamarind Fellowship, 1965. **Address:** 1974 Addison Way, Los Angeles, CA 90041. **One-man Exhibitions:** (first) Peoria (Ill.) Art Center, 1951; Occidental College, 1957; Ferus Gallery, Los Angeles, 1958; Bertha Lewinson Gallery, Los Angeles, 1959; Huysman Gallery, Los Angeles, 1961; Comara Gallery, 1963, 64, 66, 68, 70, 72, 75. **Retrospective:** Long Beach/MA, 1967; Los Angeles Municipal Art Gallery, 1973. **Group:** SFMA Annuals, 1957-59; Ball State Teachers College Annuals, 1957, 58, 60; U. of Nebraska, 1958; Oakland/AM Annuals, 1958, 60; UCLA, California Painters under 35, 1959; Pasadena/AM, Pacific Profile, 1960; Carnegie, 1961, 1964; WMAA, Fifty California Artists, 1962-63; MOMA, Recent Painting USA, 1963; Pasadena/AM, Ten Californians, 1964; WMAA Annual, 1965; US State Department, circ., 1968-70; MOMA, 1969. **Collections:** Long Beach/MA; Los Angeles/County MA; MOMA; U.

of Nebraska; Princeton U.; San Diego; WMAA.

HANSON, DUANE. b. January 17, 1925, Alexandria, Minn. **Studied:** Luther College, 1943-44; U. of Washington, 1944-45; Macalester College, 1945-56, BA; Cranbrook, 1950-51, MFA. Traveled Western Europe, Egypt, USSR, Mexico, Canada, West Indies; resided seven years in Germany. **Taught:** public High Schools, 1946-47, 49-50, 52-53, 60-62; US Army schools,

Duane Hanson *Working Cowboy* 1987

Germany, 1953-60; private school, Greenwich, Conn., 1951-52; Oglethorpe U., 1963-65; Miami-Dade Junior College, 1965-69; U. of Miami, 1979. **Commissions:** Chase Manhattan Bank, 1975; Kansas City/Nelson, 1975. **Awards:** Harvard U., Ella Ayman Cabot Trust, 1963; Chicago/AI, Blair Award, 1974; DAAD Grant (Berlin), 1974; Hon. DHL, Nova U., Ft. Lauderdale. **Address:** 6109 Southwest 55 Court, Davie, FL 33314. **Dealer:** OK Harris Works of Art, NYC. **One-man Exhibitions:** Cranbrook, 1951; Wilton (Conn.) Gallery, 1952; Galerie Netzel, Bremen, 1958; U. of South Florida, 1968; West Palm Beach/Norton, 1968; Ringling, 1968; OK Harris Works of Art, 1970, 72, 74, 76, 80, 84; Onnasch Galerie, Berlin, 1972; Berlin/Adademie der Kunst, 1975; Humlebaek/Louisiana, 1975; U. of Nebraska, 1976; Des Moines, 1977; U. of California, Berkeley, 1977; Portland, Ore./AM, 1977; Kansas City/Nelson, 1977; Colorado Springs/FA, 1977; VMFA, 1977; Corcoran, 1977; WMAA, 1978; Jacksonville/AM, circ., 1980; Wichita State U., circ., 1984; Cranbrook, 1985. **Retrospectives:** Stuttgart/WK, circ., 1974; Wichita State U., 1976. **Group:** WMAA, Human Concern/Personal Torment, 1969; WMAA Annuals, 1970, 73; Walker, Figures/Environments, circ., 1970-71; Aachen/NG, Klischee und Antiklischee, 1970; Corcoran, Depth and Presence, 1971; Chicago/Contemporary, Radical Realism, 1971; Documenta V, Kassel, 1972; Galerie des 4 Mouvements, Paris, Hyperrealistes Americains, 1972; Harvard U., Recent Figure Sculpture, 1972; Lunds Konsthall, Sweden, Amerikansk Realism, 1973; Lincoln, Mass./De Cordova, The Super-Realist Vision, 1973; Randers Kunstmuseum, Denmark, Amerikanske Realister, 1973; Hartford/Wadsworth, New/Photo Realism, 1974; Chicago/AI, 1974; CNAC, Hyperrealistes Americains/Realistes Europeens, 1974; Baltimore/MA, Super Realism, 1975; PAFA, 8 Contemporary American Realists, 1977; Yale U., Seven Realists, 1976; Berlin/National, Aspekts

der 60er Jahre, 1978; Denver/AM, Reality of Illusion, 1979; WMAA, The Figurative Tradition and the WMAA, 1980; San Antonio/MA, Real, Really Real, Super Real, circ., 1981; WMAA Biennial, 1981; PAFA, Contemporary American Realism Since 1960, 1981; California State U., Long Beach, Figurative Sculpture, 1984; Sydney/AG, Pop Art, circ., 1985. **Collections:** Aachen/NG; Adelaide; Caracas; Cologne; Duisburg; Edinburgh/National; Hannover/K-G; Lewis and Clark College; U. of Miami; Milwaukee; RAC; Rotterdam; Hartford/Wadsworth; Kansas City/AI; Kansas City/Nelson; Utrecht; West Palm Beach/Norton; VMFA; WMAA. **Bibliography:** Adrian; *Figures/Environments*; Goodyear; *Kunst um 1970*; Lindy; Sager.

HANSON, PHILIP. b. January 8, 1942, Chicago, Ill. **Studied:** U. of Chicago, BA, 1965; Chicago Art Institute School, 1969, MFA. **Taught:** Chicago Art Institute School, 1969-72; Illinois Institute of

Philip Hanson   *Tantric Jacket*   1983

Technology, 1970-72. **Awards:** Cassandra Foundation Grant, 1973; National Endowment for the Arts, 1978, 83. **Address:** 5008 North Hermitage, Chicago, Ill. 60640. **Dealer:** Phyllis Kind Gallery, Chicago and NYC. **One-man Exhibitions:** (first) Phyllis Kind Gallery, Chicago, 1975, 76, 82; Phyllis Kind Gallery, NYC, 1984. **Group:** Chicago/AI, Chicago and Vicinity, 1969; Chicago/Contemporary, Don Baum Sez, "Chicago Needs Famous Artists," 1969; Chicago/Contemporary, Chicago Imagist Art, 1972; Ottowa/National, What They're Up To In Chicago, 1972; 12th Sao Paolo Biennial, 1973; Sacramento/Crocker, The Chicago Connection, circ., 1976; Sunderland (Eng.) Arts Center, Who Chicago?, circ., 1980; Kansas City/AI, Chicago Imagists, 1982. **Collections:** AT&T; Ball State U.; Chicago/Contemporary; Elmhurst College; NMAA; Vienna/Moderner.

HARDY, DeWITT. b. June 25, 1940, St. Louis, Mo. **Studied:** Syracuse U., 1956-62, BA. Curator and Assoc. Dir., Ogunquit, 1964-; Scenic designer, Hackmatack Theater, Benwick, Me., 1978-81. **Address:** Oak Woods Road, North Berwick, Me. 03906. **Dealer:** Robert Schoelkopf Gallery, NYC. **One-man Exhibitions:** Pietrantonio Gallery, NYC, 1959; Syracuse U., 1962; The Gallery, Wellesley, Mass., 1963; Pinetree Designs, Ogunquit, Me., 1961, 63; Argus Gallery, Madison, N.J., 1965, 66; Rehn Gallery, NYC, 1966-77; 10 Oak Gallery, Springvale, Me., 1967; The Point Gallery, Kittery, Me., 1967; Shore Gallery, Boston, 1968; Ogunquit, 1968-77; Nasson College, 1968, 71; Frost Gully Gallery, Freeport, Me., 1972, 74; Lehigh U., 1972; Thayer Academy, 1972; Cove Bookstore, Ogunquit, Me., 1973, 74, 75, 76, 77; U. of Maine, 1973, 74, 75, 76, 77; Tomlinson Gallery, Baltimore, Md., 1974; Polk Public Museum, 1974; Bates College, 1975; Ogunquit Gallery, 1975; Wilkes College, 1976; Robert Schoelkopf Gallery, 1981, 83. **Group:** Youngs-

town/Butler, National Mid-year Shows, 1969; The Pennsylvania State U., Living American Artists and the Figure, 1974; U. of North Carolina, Art on Paper, 1981. **Collections:** Beloit College; Bowdoin College; British Museum; Chattanooga/Hunter; Cleveland/MA; Davidson College; Dayton/AI; Drake U.; Emory U.; Indiana State U.; Kalamazoo/Institute; Library of Congress; Madison Art Center; U. of Maine; Minneapolis/Institute; U. of Nebraska; U. of Nevada; U. of North Carolina; Ringling; Rockford College; St. Lawrence U.; U. of Washington; Youngstown/Butler.

HARE, DAVID. b. March 10, 1917, NYC. Studied in New York, Arizona, Colorado (majored in experimental color photography). Researched and published a portfolio of color photographs on the American Indian, in collaboration with Dr. Clark Whissler of the American Museum of Natural History, 1940. Editor, *VVV* (surrealist magazine), 1942-44. Lectured extensively. **Taught:** Philadelphia College of Art, 1964-65; U. of Oregon. **Commissions** (sculpture): NYC; Massachusetts; Rhode Island; Illinois. **Awards:** Hon. DFA, Maryland Institute of Arts. **Address:** 34 Leroy Street, NYC 10014. **Dealer:** Gruenebaum Gallery, NYC. **One-man Exhibitions:** (first) Hudson D. Walker Gallery, NYC, 1939; Julien Levy Galleries, NYC, 1946; Art of This Century, 1946, 47; The Kootz Gallery, NYC, 1946, 48, 51, 52, 55, 56, 58, 59; SFMA, 1947; Galerie Maeght, 1948; Saidenberg Gallery, 1960-63; Staempfli Gallery, 1969; Tibor de Nagy, Houston, 1974; Alessandra Collection, NYC, 1976; SRGM, 1977; Hamilton Gallery of Contemporary Art, NYC, 1978; Zolla-Lieberman, Chicago, 1978; NYU (two-man) 1982; Hamilton Gallery, NYC, 1978, 80; Gruenebaum Gallery, 1987. **Retrospective:** PMA, 1969. **Group:** MOMA, Fourteen Americans, circ., 1946; I & IV Sao Paulo Biennials, 1951, 57; WMAA, The New Decade, 1954-55;

MOMA, Modern Art in the United States, circ., Europe, 1955-56; Musée Rodin, Paris, International Sculpture, 1956; Seattle/AM, circ., Far East and Europe, 1958; Brussels World's Fair, 1958; Chicago/AI, 1961; Seattle World's Fair, 1962; Pittsburgh Bicentennial, 1962; WMAA, 1962; MOMA, Dada, Surrealism and Their Heritage, 1968; MOMA, The New American Painting and Sculpture, 1969; Foundation Maeght, L'Art Vivant, 1970; Baltimore/MA, The Partial Figure in Modern Sculpture, 1970; WMAA, 200 Years of American Sculpture, 1976; Washington, D.C./Renwick Gallery, Object as Poet, 1977; Arts Council of Great Britain, Dada and Surrealism Revisited, 1978; Buffalo/Albright, American Painting in the 1970s, circ., 1978. **Collections:** Akron/AI; Brandeis U.; Brooklyn Museum; Buffalo/Albright; Carnegie; Hartford/Wadsworth; MMA; MOMA; New Orleans/Delgado; SFMA; SRGM; WMAA; Washington U.; Yale U. **Bibliography:** Baur 5; Biddle 4; Blesh 1; Breton 3; Brumme; Calas; Craven, W.; Giedion Welcker 1; Goodrich and Baur 1; **Goossen 5;** Hess, T.B., 1; Hunter 6; Janis and Blesh 1; Janis, S.; Muane 2; McCurdy, ed.; Mendelowitz; Miller, ed. 2; Motherwell and Reinhardt, eds.; Paalan; Read 3; Ritchie 3; Rodman 1; Rose, B., 1; Rubin 1; Seuphor 3; Trier 1; Waldbert 4. Archives.

HARING, KEITH. b. May 4, 1958, Kutztown, Pa. **Studied:** School of Visual Arts, NYC, 1978-79, with Joseph Kosuth, Keith Sonnier, Barbara Schwartz. Traveled world-wide. **Taught:** Fort Green Day Care Center, Brooklyn, N.Y., 1982. **Address:** 676 Broadway, NYC 10012. **Dealer:** Tony Shafrazi Gallery, NYC. **One-man Exhibitions:** (first) Pittsburgh Center for the Arts, 1978; Westbeth Gallery, NYC, 1981; Club 57, NYC, 1982; Rotterdam Arts Council, 1982; Tony Shafrazi Gallery, 1982, 83, 85; Lucio Amelio Gallery, Naples, Italy, 1983; Fun Gallery, NYC, 1983; Hartford/Wadsworth, 1983;

Galerie Watari, Tokyo, 1983; Galeria Salvatore Ala, Milan, 1984; Galerie Corinne Hummel, Basel, 1984; U. of Iowa, 1984; Paul Maenz Gallery, Cologne, 1984; Paradise Garage, NYC, 1984; Semaphore East, NYC, 1984; Bordeaux/Contemporain, 1985; Leo Castelli Inc., 1985; Galerie Schellmann & Klüser, Munich, 1985; Amsterdam/Stedelijk, 1986; WMAA (Stamford), 1986. **Group:** NYC, Times Square Show, 1980; New Museum, Events: Fashion Moda, 1980, P.S. 1, Long Island City, New York/New Wave, 1981; Documenta VII, Kassel, 1982; Kunsthalle, Nurmberg, 2. Internationale Jugendtriennale, circ., 1982; P.S. 1, Long Island City, Beast: Animal Imagery in Recent Painting, 1982; Bonn, Back to the USA, circ., 1983; Palacio de Velasquez, Madrid, Tendencias en Nueva York, circ., 1983; 12th Sao Paolo Biennial, 1983; WMAA Biennial, 1983; Hirshhorn, Content: A Contemporary Focus 1974-1984, 1984; Montreal/Contemporain, Via New York, 1984; SFMA, The Human Condition, 1984; XLI Venice Biennial, 1984; La Biennale de Paris, 1985; Fort Lauderdale, An American Renaissance: Painting and Sculpture Since 1940, 1986; WMAA, Sacred Images in Secular Art, 1986. **Collections:** Amsterdam/Stedelijk; WMAA. **Bibliography:** *Back to the USA*; Danto; *Keith Haring*; Murken-Altrogge.

HARRIS, PAUL. b. November 5, 1925, Orlando, Fla. **Studied:** with Jay Karen Winslow, Orlando, Fla.; Chouinard Art Institute; New School for Social Research (with Johannes Molzahn); U. of New Mexico; Hans Hofmann School. US Navy, W.W. II. **Taught:** U. of New Mexico; Knox College, Jamaica, W. I.; New Paltz State College; Montclair State College; California Institute of the Arts, Valencia; Universidad Catolica, Santiago; California College of Arts and Crafts, 1968-; Editorial Associate, *Art News* magazine, 1955-56; U. of California, Berkeley. **Commissions:** U. of

New Mexico. **Awards:** Fulbright Fellowship (Chile), 1962-63; Tamarind Fellowship, 1969-70; Guggenheim Foundation Fellowship, 1979; MacDowell Colony Fellowship, 1977; Longview Foundation Grant, 1978. **Address:** P.O. Box 930, Bolinas, CA 94924. **One-man Exhibitions:** Poindexter Gallery, 1961, 63, 67, 70, 72; The Lanyon Gallery, 1965; Berkeley Gallery, San Francisco, 1965, Candy Store Art Gallery, Folsom, Calif., 1967; William Sawyer Gallery, 1969, 71; M. E. Thelen Gallery, Essen, 1970; SFMA, 1972; U. of California, Santa Barbara, 1972; U. of New Mexico, 1973; Arkansas Art Center, Little Rock, 1974; Loch Haven Art Center, 1981; Greenville, 1982; Stanford U., 1982; Fuller Goldeen, 1983. **Group:** New School for Social Research; U. of New Mexico; MOMA, Recent Sculpture USA, 1959; Hans Hofmann and His Students, circ., 1963; Chicago/AI, 1965; New York World's Fair, 1964-65; IX Sao Paulo Biennial, 1967; Los Angeles/County MA, American Sculpture of the Sixties, circ., 1967; Dusseldorf/Kunsthalle, Prospect '68, 1968; NCFA, New American Figurative, 1968; Trenton/State, Soft Art, 1969; International Exhibitions Foundation, Washington, D.C., Tamarind: A Renaissance of Lithography, circ., 1971-72. **Collections:** Aachen/NG; Los Angeles/County MA; MOMA; U. of New Mexico; Yale U. **Bibliography:** Tuchman 1.

HARTELL, JOHN. b. January 30, 1902, Brooklyn, N.Y. **Studied:** Cornell U. (Architecture), 1925; Royal Academy of Fine Arts, Stockholm. Traveled Europe, Puerto Rico, England. **Taught:** Clemson College (Architecture), 1927-28; U. of Illinois, 1928-30; Cornell U., 1930-68. **Awards:** Utica, 1948, 52; Illinois Wesleyan U., 1950; New York State Fair, 1951; U. of Rochester, 1953; Fellow of the American Scandinavian Foundation. **Address:** 319 The Parkway, Ithaca, NY 14850. **Dealer:** Kraushaar Galleries. **One-man Exhibi-**

tions: Kleemann Gallery, NYC, 1937; Kraushaar Galleries, 1943, 45, 49, 53, 57, 63, 66, 69, 72, 75, 77, 80, 83; Cornell U., 1943, 46, 53, 57, 62, 66, 84; Wells College, 1945, 49, 55; Utica, 1952; U. of Rochester, 1954; Upstairs Gallery, Ithaca, N.Y., 1968, 73, 80; Lehigh U., 1971. **Retrospective:** Cornell U., 1982. **Group:** Architectural League of New York, 1932; U. of Rochester, 1943, 53, 54; ICA, Boston; Cincinnati/AM, 1945; St. Louis/City, 1945; Carnegie, 1945-47; WMAA, 1946, 50, 53; Utica, 1948, 51, 52, 54; Illinois Wesleyan U., 1950, 57; U. of Illinois, 1951; PAFA, 1953; US State Department, Traveling Show to Australia, 1967-68; Indianapolis/Herron, 1970. **Collections:** Atlanta U.; Cornell U.; Illinois Wesleyan U.; U. of Nebraska; Northern Trust Co., Chicago, Ill.; E. R. Squibb Co., Princeton; Utica; Wake Forest U.

HARTIGAN, GRACE. b. March 28, 1922, Newark, N.J. Studied with Isaac Lane Muse, NYC, mid 1940s. Traveled Europe; resided Mexico, 1949. Designed set for *Red Riding Hood*, by Kenneth Koch, for the Artists Theater, NYC, 1953. **Taught:** Maryland Institute, Artist-in-Residence, 1967-; Bard College, 1983. **Awards:** Moore Institute of Art, Science and Industry, Hon. DFA, 1969; AAAL, Childe Hassam Fund **P.P.**, 1975. **Address:** 1710½ Eastern Avenue, Baltimore, MD 21231. **Dealer:** Gruenebaum Gallery, NYC. **One-man Exhibitions:** (first) Tibor de Nagy Gallery, 1951, also 1952-55, 1957, 59; Vassar College, 1954; Gres Gallery, Washington, D.C., 1960; Chatham College, 1960; Carnegie, 1961; Martha Jackson Gallery, 1962, 64, 67, 70; U. of Minnesota, 1963; Franklin Siden Gallery, Detroit, 1964; Kent State U., 1966; The U. of Chicago, 1967; Maryland Institute, 1967; Gertrude Kasle Gallery, 1968, 70, 72, 74, 76; Grand Rapids, 1968 (two-man); William Zierler Inc., 1975; American University, Washington, D.C., 1975; Genesis Galleries, NYC, 1977, 78; U. of Maryland, 1979; Gri-

maldis Gallery, Baltimore, 1979; Platts-
burg/SUNY, 1980; Hamilton Gallery of
Contemporary Art, NYC, 1981; Gri-
maldis Gallery, Baltimore, 1979, 81,
82, 84; Lafayette College, 1983;
Gruenebaum Gallery, 1984, 86;
Charlotte/Mint, 1981; Baltimore/MA,
1980; U. of Maryland, 1980. **Retrospec-
tive:** Fort Wayne, 1981. **Group:** Ninth
Street Exhibition, NYC, 1951; U. of
Minnesota, Rising Talent, 1955;
MOMA, Modern Art in the United
States, circ., Europe, 1955-56; MOMA,
Twelve Americans, circ., 1956; Jewish
Museum, The New York School, Sec-
ond Generation, 1957; International
Biennial, Exhibition of Paintings,
Tokyo; IV Sao Paulo Biennial, 1957;
MOMA, The New American Painting,
circ., Europe, 1958-59; Brussels World's
Fair, 1958; ART:USA:59, NYC, 1959;
Documenta II, Kassel, 1959; Walker, 60
American Painters, 1960; SRGM, Ab-
stract Expressionists and Imagists,
1961; SRGM/USIA, American Van-
guard, circ., Europe, 1961-62; WMAA
Annual, 1963; PAFA, 1963, 68; Ghent,
The Human Figure since Picasso, 1964;
White House Festival of the Arts,
Washington, D.C., 1965; Drexel Insti-
tute of Technology, 1966; Flint/
Institute, 1966; U. of Illinois, 1967, 69;
Ball State U., Collages by American
Artists, 1971; Delaware Art Museum,
American Painting since World War II,
1971; WMAA, Frank O'Hara; A Poet
Among Painters, 1974; Corcoran Bien-
nial, 1975; NCFA, Poets & Painters,
1976; Syracuse/Everson, Critics Choice,
1977; Hirshhorn, Art of the Fifties,
1980; National Gallery, Contemporary
American Prints and Drawings,
1940-1980, 1981; Houston/Contempo-
rary, The Americans: The Collage, 1982;
Newport Harbor, Action/Precision,
1984. **Collections:** American Republic
Insurance Co.; American U.; Bal-
timore/MA; Bezelel Museum; Brandeis
U.; Brooklyn Museum; Buffalo/
Albright; Carnegie; Chicago/AI; The U.
of Chicago; Flint/Institute; Grand
Rapids; Hartford/Wadsworth; Kansas
City/Nelson; MMA; MOMA; Minneap-
olis/Institute; NCFA; New Paltz/SUNY;
New School for Social Research; Okla-
homa; PAFA; PMA; Princeton U.; RISD;
Raleigh/NCMA; Ringling; SRGM; St.
Louis/City; Vassar College; WGMA;
WMAA; Walker; Washington U.;
Woodward Foundation. **Bibliography:**
Art: A Woman's Sensibility; Downes, ed.;
Friedman, ed.; Goodrich and Baur 1;
Haftman; Hunter 1, 6; Hunter, ed.; Mc-
Curdy, ed.; Metro; Nemser; Nordness,
ed.; Read 2; Sandler 1.

HARTL, LEON. b. January 31, 1889,
Paris, France; **d.** December 1973, Schenectady, N.Y. To USA, 1912; citizen,
1922. Self-taught. Expert on aniline
dyes. **Taught:** Brooklyn Museum
School. **Member:** Artists Equity. Federal A.P.: Easel painting. **Awards:**
NIAL, Marjorie Peabody Waite Award,
1959; Youngstown/Butler, Hon. Men.,
1960; MacDowell Colony Fellowship,
1959-61; Yaddo Fellowship, 1960, 61,
63; Ingram Merrill Foundation Grant,
1968. **One-man Exhibitions:** (first)
Whitney Studio Club, NYC, 1925, also
1926; Curt Valentine Gallery, NYC,
1927, 30, 36; Joseph Brummer Gallery,
NYC, 1934, 38; The Peridot Gallery,
1954, 55, 58, 60, 62, 64, 66; The
Zabriskie Gallery, 1967; Ingber Art Gallery, 1971, 76. **Group:** Youngs-
town/Butler; Carnegie; Chicago/AI;
Corcoran; Independent Artists, NYC,
1917, 18, 19; NIAL; Palazzo del Parco,
Bordighera; PAFA; U. of Nebraska.
Collections: Corcoran; Hallmark Collection; Hartford/Wadsworth; U. of
Nebraska; Phillips; Society of New York
Hospitals; Syracuse U.; WMAA. **Bibliography:** Downes, ed. Archives.

HARTLEY, MARSDEN. b. January 4,
1877, Lewiston, Me.; **d.** September 2,
1943, Ellsworth, Me. **Studied:**
Cleveland Institute of Art, 1892, with

C. Yates, N. Waldeck, C. Sowers; privately with John Semon; W. M. Chase School, NYC, 1898-99, with Frank V. DuMond, William M. Chase, F. L. Mora; NAD, 1900, with F. C. Jones, E. M. Ward, G. W. Maynard, E. H. Glashfield, F. J. Dillman, F. S. Hartley. Traveled USA extensively; Germany, France, Mexico. Federal A.P.: Easel painting. **Awards:** Guggenheim Foundation Fellowship, 1931. **One-man Exhibitions:** (first) Photo-Secession, NYC, 1909, also 1912, 14; The Daniel Gallery, NYC, 1915; Montross Gallery, NYC, 1920; Anderson Galleries, NYC, 1921; Stieglitz's Intimate Gallery, NYC, 1926-29; Arts Club of Chicago, 1928, 45; An American Place (Gallery), NYC, 1930, 36, 37; The Downtown Gallery, 1932; Galeria de la Escuela Nacional de Artes Plasticas, Mexico City, 1933; Hudson D. Walker Gallery, NYC, 1938, 39, 40; Carlen Gallery, Philadelphia, 1938; Symphony Hall, Boston, 1939; Portland, Ore./AM, 1940; California Palace, 1940; Walker, 1940; M. Knoedler & Co., 1942, 44, 68; Phillips, 1943; P. Rosenberg and Co., 1944, 47, 48, 50, 55; Macbeth Gallery, NYC, 1945; Indianapolis/Herron, 1946; The Bertha Schaefer Gallery, 1948, 56; U. of Minnesota, 1952, Minneapolis, 1952, 79; Santa Fe, N.M., 1958; The Babcock Gallery, 1959-61, 75; Shore Studio, Boston, 1962; Alfredo Valente Gallery, NYC, 1966; La Jolla, 1966; Colby College, 1967; U. of Southern California, 1968; Tucson Art Center, 1969; U. of Texas, 1969; Danenberg Gallery, 1969; U. of Kansas, 1972; C. W. Post College, 1977; Bates College, 1978; Washburn Gallery, NYC, 1978; Florida International U., Miami, 1984; Robert Miller Gallery, 1984; Salander-O'Reilly Galleries, 1985; Portland Me./AM, 1985. **Retrospectives:** Cincinnati/AM, 1941; MOMA, 1944; A.F.A., circ., 1960; Danenberg Gallery, 1969; WMAA, 1980. **Group:** The Armory Show, 1913; The Forum Gallery, 1916; Brooklyn Museum, 1926; WMAA, 1935, 38; U. of Minnesota, 1937; Baltimore/MA, 1942; Delaware Art Museum, Avant-Garde Painting and Sculpture in America, 1910-1925, 1975; U. of California, Santa Barbara, O'Keefe, Hartley and Marin in the Southwest, 1975; SRGM, 20th Century American Drawings, 1976; MOMA, The Natural Paradise, 1976; Royal Scottish Academy, Edinburgh, The Modern Spirit: American Painting 1908-1935, 1977; WMAA, William Carlos Williams and the American Scene, 1978; WMAA, Synchronism and American Color Abstraction, 1978; Dusseldorf, Two Decades of American Painting, 1929-1940, 1979. **Collections:** Andover/Phillips; Barnes Foundation; Boston/MFA; Bowdoin College; Brooklyn Museum; Buffalo/Albright; Carnegie; Amon Carter Museum; Cleveland/MA; Colorado Springs/FA; Columbus; Cornell U.; Denver/AM; Des Moines; Detroit/Institute; U. of Georgia; Hartford/Wadsworth; Indiana U.; Kalamazoo/Institute; Lewiston (Me.) Public Library; Los Angeles/County MA; Louisville/Speed; MMA; MOMA; U. of Michigan; Milwaukee; U. of Minnesota; U. of Nebraska; Newark Museum; Omaha/Joslyn; PMA; Pasadena/AM; Phillips, Phoenix; Portland, Ore./AM; SFMA; St. Louis/City; San Antonio/McNay; Santa Barbara/MA; Santa Fe, N.M.; Smith College; U. of Texas; Utica; VMFA; Vassar College; WMAA; Walker; Wichita/AM; Williams College; Worcester/AM; Yale U.; Youngstown/Butler. **Bibliography:** *Avant-Garde Painting and Sculpture in America, 1910-25;* Barker 1; Baur 7; Bazin; Biddle 4; Blesh 1; Born; Brown; Brown 2; Cahill and Barr, eds.; Canaday; Chipp; Coke 2; Dijkstra, ed.; Eliot; Flexner; Frank, ed.; Frost; Goldwater and Treves, eds.; Goodrich and Baur 1; Haftman; **Hartley;** Haskell 4; Hunter 6; *Index of 20th Century Artists;* Janis, S.; Kootz 1, 2; Levin 2; **McCausland;** McCoubrey 1; McCurdy, ed.; Mellquist; Mendelowtiz; Phillips 2; Read 2; Richardson, E.P.; Ritchie 1; Rodman 2; Rose, B., 1, 4; Schwartz 2; Soby 6; Sutton; Tashjian; Tuchman 3; **Well, ed.;** Wight 2; Wright 1. Archives.

HARTMAN, ROBERT. b. December 17, 1926, Sharon, Pa. **Studied:** U. of Arizona, BFA, MA; Colorado Springs/FA, with Peppino Mangravite, 1947, with Vaclav Vytlacil, Ludwig Sander, Emerson Woelffer, 1951; Brooklyn Museum School, with William King, Hui Ka Swong, 1953-54. **Taught:** U. of Arizona, 1952-53; Texas Technological College, 1955-58; U. of Nevada, 1958-61; U. of California, 1961-. **Awards:** Youngstown/Butler, **P.P.,** 1955; La Jolla, 1962; SFMA, Emanuel Walter Bequest and Purchase Award, 1966; IV International Young Artists Exhibit, America-Japan, Tokyo, Hon. Men., 1967. **Address:** 1265 Mountain Boulevard, Oakland, CA 94611. **Dealer:** Bluxome Gallery, San Francisco. **One-man Exhibitions:** (first) Kipnis Gallery, Westport, Conn., 1954; Roswell, 1957; U. of Nevada, 1958; U. of California, 1961; RAC, 1963; Comara Gallery, 1963, 65; Berkeley Gallery, 1965, 67, 68; The Bertha Schaefer Gallery, 1966, 69, 74; Santa Barbara/MA, 1973; Hank Baum Gallery, San Francisco, 1973, 78; Shirley Cerf Gallery, San Francisco, 1980; San Jose Museum of Art, 1983; Wesleyan U., 1983; Bluxome Gallery, 1985; U. of California, Berkeley, 1985. **Group:** New York World's Fair, 1964-65; U. of Illinois, 1965; M. Knoedler & Co., Art Across America, 1965-67; San Francisco Art Association, 1966; VMFA, American Painting, 1966; U. of Washington, 1967; Colorado Springs/FA, 1967; IV International Young Artists Exhibit, America-Japan, Tokyo, 1967; Redding Museum, Art and Aviation, 1984; Pacific, Artists Invitational, 1985. **Collections:** Achenbach Foundation; Colorado Springs/FA; Dublin/Municipal; Kaiser Industries, Oakland, Calif.; Long Beach/MA; Mead Corporation; NCFA; Oakland/AM; Redding Museum; Roswell; SFAI; San Jose Museum of Art; U. of Washington; Youngstown/Butler; Zischke Organization, San Francisco, Calif.

HARVEY, ROBERT. b. September 16, 1924, Lexington, N.C. **Studied:** Ringling School of Art, with Elmer Harmes, Georgia Warren; San Francisco Art Institute with Nathan Oliveira, Sonia Gechtoff. Traveled Great Britain, France, North Africa, Italy; Resides Spain, 1966-. **Awards:** Corcoran, Hon. Men. and Ford Foundation Purchase 1963; San Francisco Art Festival, Award of Merit, 1963; Western Washington State College, **P.P.,** 1965; Mead Painting of the Year, 1967; Hon. Men., 1st Concurso de Pintura, L'Oréal, Madrid, 1985. **Address:** La Huerta del Angel, Macharaviaya, Malaga, Spain. **Dealer:** Gump's Gallery, San Francisco; Mussavi Arts Center, NYC. **One-man Exhibitions:** (first) Saidenberg Gallery, 1954; Gump's Gallery, 1959, 61, 63, 64, 83, 86; La Escondida, Taos, N.M., 1962; Bedell Gallery, Santa Fe, N.M., 1962; Terry Dintenfass, Inc., 1963; Phoenix, 1964; Jefferson Gallery, 1964; David Stuart Gallery, 1964, 65, 67, 69; 75; Wichita/AM, 1965; Sacramento/Crocker, 1965; The Krasner Gallery, 1967-74, 78; San Diego, 1968; Richard White Gallery, Seattle, 1969; Owen Gallery, Denver, 1970-74; Charles Campbell Gallery, 1972, 74, 77; Parlade, Marbella, 1972; Galeria Diaz Lario, Malaga, 1975; Gallery Malacke, 1975; Centro Cultural de los Estados Unidos, Madrid, 1977; David Marshall Gallery, Puerto Banus, Spain, 1979; Galeria Estudio, Cordoba, 1981; Galeria Harras, Malaga, 1982; Castillo Bil-Bil, Benaladena, 1983; La Alhambra, Granada (two-man), 1984; Woodwrith Gallery, Toronto, 1985. **Retrospective:** Ringling, 1970; Sacred Heart College, Atherton, Calif., 1974. **Group:** Corcoran, 1963, Biennial, 1967; deYoung, New Images of San Francisco; Oakland/AM; California Palace; Kansas City/Nelson; Denver/AM; Santa Barbara/MA; Phoenix; Santa Fe, N.M.; Raleigh/NCMA, 1965; VMFA, American Painting, 1966; Youngstown/Butler, 1966; U. of Illinois, 1967, 69; San Diego, Invitational American Drawing Exhibition, 1977; Oakland/AM,

Bay Area Artist, 1977; City of Zamora, 6th Biennial of Painting, 1981; Alicante, 7th Convocatoria de Artes Plasticas, 1986. **Collections:** City of Benalnadena; City of San Francisco; Corcoran; Crown Zellerbach Foundation; Hirshhorn; L'Oréal; Mead Corp.; Mobile/FAMS; Museo Municipal, La Coruña, Spain; Stanford U.; Storm King Art Center; Western Washington State College; Wichita/AM.

HATCHETT, DUANE. b. May 12, 1925, Shawnee, Okla. **Studied:** U. of Oklahoma (with John O'Neill), 1950, BFA, 1952, MFA; US Army Air Corps, 1943-46. **Taught:** U. of Oklahoma, 1949-50; Oklahoma City U., 1951-54; U. of Tulsa, 1954-64; The Ohio State U., 1964-65; Buffalo/SUNY, 1968-80. **Commissions:** First National Bank of Tulsa; Boston Avenue Methodist Church, Tulsa; Trader's National Bank, Kansas City, Mo.; Northeastern State College; Tulsa Fire Department. **Address:** 347 Starin Avenue, Buffalo, NY 14216. **Dealer:** Nina Freudenheim Gallery, Buffalo, N.Y. **One-man Exhibitions:** Haydon Calhoun Gallery, Dallas; U. of Oklahoma; Oklahoma State U.; Oklahoma; Bryson Gallery, Columbus, Ohio; Royal Marks Gallery, 1966, 68, 69, 70; Tulsa/Philbrook (three-man), 1973; Rochester Institute of Technology, 1973; Buffalo/Albright, 1974; Nina Freudenheim Gallery, Buffalo, N.Y., 1976, 77. **Group:** New York World's Fair, 1964-65; WMAA Sculpture Annual, 1966, 68; U. of Illinois, 1967; Los Angeles/County MA, American Sculpture of the Sixties, 1967; Carnegie, 1967; HemisFair '68, San Antonio, 1968; U. of Minnesota, 1969; U. of Nebraska, American Sculpture, 1970; Carnegie, 1970. **Retrospective:** Buffalo/Albright, 1974. **Collections:** Alcoa; Andover/Phillips; Atlanta Corp.; Carnegie; Columbus; Dallas/MFA; First National Bank of Tulsa; Fort Worth; State U. of Iowa; Milwaukee; U. of Minnesota; The Ohio State U.; Oklahoma; U. of Oklahoma; Ridgefield/

Aldrich; San Antonio/McNay; Traders National Bank, Kansas City, Mo.; WMAA. **Bibliography:** Tuchman 1.

HAVARD, JAMES P. b. June 29, 1937, Galveston, Texas. **Awards:** Cresson scholar, 1964; PAFA, J. Henry Schiedt Memorial Prize, 1965; PAFA, Mabel Wilson Woodrow Award, 1962. **Studied:** Sam Houston State College, 1959, BS; Atelier Chapman Kelley, Dallas, 1960; PAFA, 1965. **Address:** 20 North Moore Street, NYC 10013. **Dealer:** Louis K. Meisel Gallery, NYC. **One-man Exhibitions:** Chapman Kelley Gallery, Dallas, 1965, 70; Temple U. 1967; Vanderlip Gallery, Philadelphia, 1969; Marian Locks Gallery, Philadelphia, 1970, 73, 74, 77; Henri Gallery, Washington, D.C., 1970; OK Harris Works of Art, NYC, 1971; Galerie Reckermann, Cologne, 1973; Gimpel & Weitzenhoffer, Ltd., NYC, 1973; Gallerie Arnesen, Copenhagen, 1974; Galleriet Lunda, Sweden, 1974; Gallerie Fabian Carlsson, Goteborg, 1974; Gallerie Ahlner, Stockholm, 1974; Deson-Zaks Gallery, Chicago, 1975; Louis K. Meisel Gallery, NYC, 1975, 77, 79, Gallerie Krakeslatt, Bromolla, Sweden, 1975; Delahunty Gallery, Dallas, 1976; Morgan Gallery, Shawnee Mission, Kansas, 1976; Galerie le Portail, Heidelberg, 1977; Hanson-Cowles Gallery, Minneapolis, 1977; Irving Galleries, Palm Beach, 1978; Janus Gallery, Venice, Calif., 1978; Janus Gallery, Los Angeles, 1984; Jeremy Stone Gallery, San Francisco, 1985. **Group:** PAFA, Annuals 1962-67; A.F.A., Recent Drawing, 1967; Silvermine, Annual, 1969; PAFA, Sculpture: New Forms, New Materials, 1970; U. of North Carolina, Art on Paper, 1975; PAFA, Three Centuries of American Art, 1976; SRGM, 1977; Springfield, Mass./MFA, Abstract Illusionism, circ., 1979. **Collections:** Atlantic Richfield Co.; AT&T; First Pennsylvania Banking & Trust Co., Philadelphia; Kemper Insurance Co., Chicago, Ill.; NCFA; NYU; PAFA; PMA; Prudential Insurance Co. of

America, N.J.; SRGM; Stockholm/ National; Temple U.; Westinghouse Corp., NYC; Witte. **Bibliography:** Lucie-Smith.

HAYES, DAVID V. b. March 15, 1931, Hartford, Conn. **Studied:** U. of Notre Dame, with Antony Lauck, 1949-53, AB; Indiana U., with Robert Laurent, David Smith, 1955, MFA; Ogunquit School of Painting; Atelier 17, Paris, with Stanley Hayter. Traveled, resided Paris, 1961-68. US Navy, 1955-57; Traveled USA, Europe. **Taught:** Harvard U., 1972-73. **Awards:** Hamilton Easter Field Foundation Scholarship, 1953; Silvermine Guild, Sculpture Award, 1958; Fulbright Fellowship, 1961; Guggenheim Foundation Fellowship, 1961; Chicago/AI, The Mr. & Mrs. Frank G. Logan Medal, 1951; NIAL, 1965. **Address:** P.O. Box 109, Coventry, CT 06238. **Dealer:** Christopher Colt, NYC. **One-man Exhibitions:** (first) Indiana U., 1955; Wesleyan U., 1958; New London, 1959; The Willard Gallery, 1961, 63, 64, 66, 69, 71; David Anderson Gallery, Paris, 1966; Galerie de Haas, Rotterdam, 1968; Bard College, 1969; U. of Arizona, 1969; U. of Connecticut, 1970; Manchester Community College, 1970; St. Joseph College, West Hartford, Conn., 1970; Connecticut College, 1971; Agra Gallery, Washington, D.C., 1971, 72; Gallery 5 East, East Hartford, Conn., 1971, 73; Harvard U., 1972; New Britain, 1972; Munson Gallery, 1973; Sunne Savage Gallery, 1973, 74; Albany/Institute, 1973; Copley Square, Boston, 1974; Martha Jackson Gallery, 1974; Columbus, 1974; Syracuse/Everson, 1975; Brockton Art Center, 1975; Bader Gallery, Washington, D.C., 1977; George Washington U., Washington, D.C., 1977; Lincoln, Mass./De Cordova, 1977; Springfield, Mass/MFA, 1978; Albany/SUNY, 1978; Dartmouth College, 1978; Amherst College, 1979; Nassau County Museum, 1979; Shippee Gallery, NYC, 1986. **Retrospectives:** U. of Notre Dame, 1962; Utica, 1963; New London, 1966. **Group:** MOMA, New Talent; SRGM,

1958; MOMA, Recent Sculpture USA, 1959; Boston Arts Festival, 1960; Claude Bernard, Paris, 1960; Chicago/AI, 1961; Forma Viva sculpture symposium, Portoroz, Yugoslavia, 1963; Salon du Mai, Paris, 1966, Musée Rodin, International Sculpture, 1966; Houston Festival of Arts, 1966; Carnegie, 1967; Paris/Moderne, 1968; Galerie D'Eendt NV, Amsterdam, Three Americans, 1970; Lincoln, Mass./De Cordova, Sculpture in the Park, 1972; Corcoran, 1973. **Collections:** Andover/Phillips; Albany/ SUNY; Arizona State U.; Boston Public Library; Brooklyn Museum; Carnegie; U. of Connecticut; Columbus; Currier; Dallas/MFA; Dartmouth College; Detroit/Institute; Elmira College; First National Bank of Chicago; Great Southwest Industrial Park; Hartford/ Wadsworth; Harvard U.; Hirshhorn; Houston/MFA; Indiana U.; Lincoln, Mass./De Cordova; Lydall Inc.; MOMA; U. of Michigan; Moriarty Brothers; Musée des Arts Decoratifs; The Norton Co., Worcester, Mass; NCFA; U. of Notre Dame; Price, Waterhouse, Inc., Hartford, Conn; Ringling; SRGM; Michael Schiavone & Sons Inc.; Syracuse/Emerson; U. of Vermont; Williams College. **Bibliography:** Archives.

HEBALD, MILTON. b. May 24, 1917, NYC. **Studied:** ASL, with Ann Goldwaithe, 1927-28; NAD, with Gordon Samstag, 1931-32; Roerich Master Institute of Arts, Inc., NYC, 1931-34; Beaux-Arts Institute of Design, NYC, 1932-35. US Army, 1944-46. Traveled Europe, Near East, North Africa, USSR; resided Italy, 1955-. **Taught:** Brooklyn Museum School, 1946-51; Cooper Union, 1946-53; U. of Minnesota, 1949; Skowhegan School, summers, 1950-52; Long Beach State College, summer, 1968, 74. Federal A.P.: Taught sculpture and worked on sculpture project, three years. **Member:** Sculptors Guild, 1937-86. **Commissions:** Ecuador Pavilion, New York World's Fair, 1939 (façade); US Post Office, Toms River,

N.J., 1940 (relief); Republic Aviation Trophy, 1942; Isla Verde Aeropott, San Juan, P.R., 1954; East Bronx (N.Y.) TB Hospital, 1954; AAAL, 1957 (portrait bust of Archibald MacLeish); Pan American Airways Terminal, NYC, 1957-58 (110-ft. bronze relief, *Zodiac*); 333 East 79th Street Building, NYC, 1962 (bronze fountain); U. of North Carolina, 1962; James Joyce Monument, Zurich, 1966; Central Park, NYC, 1973; C.V. Starr Memorial, Tokyo, 1974; Augenhaug Press, Oslo, 1975; Central Park, NYC, 1979; YMCA, Los Angeles, 1986. **Awards:** ACA Gallery Competition, Exhibition Prize, 1937; Brooklyn Museum, First Prize, 1950; Prix de Rome, 1955-59. **Address:** Travi Quatro Del Lago 13, Brassiano, Italy 00062. **Dealer:** Harmon-Meeks Gallery, Naples, Fla. **One-man Exhibitions:** ACA Gallery (prize show), 1937, also 1940; Grand Central Moderns, NYC, 1949, 52; Galleria Schneider, Rome, 1957, 63; Lee Nordness Gallery, NYC, 1959-61, 1963, 66; Michelson's Gallery, Washington, D.C., 1963, 67, 79; Cheekwood, 1966; Penthouse Gallery, San Francisco, 1966; Gallery of Modern Art, 1966, 68; VMFA, 1967; Kovler Gallery, 1967-70; London Arts; Cincinnati/AM; West Palm Beach/Norton, 1969; Mickelson Gallery, Washington, D.C., 67, 79; Kovler Gallery, Chicago, 1968-70; Heritage Galleries, Los Angeles, 1978; Yares Gallery, Scottsdale, 1976-78; Harmon Gallery, Naples, Fla., 1978; Randall Galleries, NYC, 1978; Byck Gallery, Louisville, Ky., 1978; Cheekwood, Nashville, 1978; Sestiero Galleria, Rome, 1975; Ostaehag Gallery, Oslo, 1975; Foster Harmon Gallery, Sarasota, Fla., 1981; Harmon-Meek Gallery, 1981, 83; Randall Galleries, NYC, 81; Academy of Art College, San Francisco, 1983. **Group:** Sculptors Guild, 1937-46; WMAA Annuals, 1937-63; PAFA, 1938-64; Arte Figurativo, Rome, 1964, 67; Carnegie, 1965. **Collections:** AAAL; U. of Arizona; Bezalel Museum; Billedgalleri, Bergen, Norway; Brandeis U.; Calcutta; Cheekwood; James Joyce Museum; Lit-

tle Rock/MFA; MOMA; Museum of the City of New York; U. of North Carolina; U. of Notre Dame; Oslo U.; PAFA; PMA; Pan American Airways, NYC; Tel Aviv; VMFA; WMAA; Yale U. **Bibliography:** Brumme; Cheney.

HEIZER, MICHAEL. b. 1944, Berkeley, Calif. **Studied:** SFAI, 1963-64. **Address:** % Dealer. **Commissions:** Seattle, Wash., 1976; MMA, 1979; Capitol Plaza, Lansing, Mich., 1977; Oakland Museum, 1980; Wells Fargo Building, Los Angeles, 1982; IBM Building, NYC, 1982. **Dealer:** Xavier Fourcade, Inc., NYC. **One-man Exhibitions:** Gallerie Heiner Friedrich, Munich, 1969; Dwan Gallery, NYC, 1970; Detroit/Institute, 1971; ACE Gallery, Los Angeles, 1974, 77; Fourcade, Droll Inc., 1974; Xavier Fourcade, Inc., 1976, 77, 79, 80, 82, 83, 85; ACE Gallery, Venice, Calif., 1977; Galerie am Promenadenplatz, Heizer und Kinnius, Munich, 1977; Richard Hines Gallery, Seattle, 1979; St. Louis/City, 1980; Janie C. Lee Gallery, 1981, 84; Flow Ace Gallery, Venice, Calif., 1982; Oil and Steel, Long Island City, N.Y., 1983; Barbara Krakow Gallery, Boston, 1983; Patricia Heesy Gallery, NYC, 1983; Los Angeles/MOCA, 1984; Rice U., 1984; WMAA, 1985. **Retrospective:** Essen, 1979. **Group:** WMAA, 1968, 70; Amsterdam/Stedelijk, Op Losse Schroeven, 1969; Detroit/Institute, Other Ideas, 1969; Berne, When Attitudes Become Form, 1969; Dusseldorf/Kunsthalle, Prospect '70, 1970; XXXV Venice Biennial, 1970; Cornell U., Earth Art, 1970; SRGM, Guggenheim International, 1971; Durer Centennial, Nurnberg, 1971; Rijksmuseum Kroller-Muller, Diagrams and Drawings, 1972; WMAA, American Drawings: 1963-1973, 1973; New York Cultural Center, 3D into 2D, 1973; MIT, Interventions in Landscape, 1974; Chicago/AI, 71st American Exhibition, 1974; MOMA, Drawing Now, 1975; Chicago/AI, 1976, 79; WMAA, 200 Years of American Sculpture, 1976;

Documenta 6, Kassel, 1977; U. of Texas, New in the Seventies, 1977; Hirshhorn, Probing the Earth, 1977; Indianapolis, 1978; Purchase/SUNY, Hidden Desires, 1980; Sierra Nevada Museum of Art, Artists in the American Desert, 1980; Houston/Contemporary, The Americans: The Landscape, 1981; Rice U., Variants, 1981; SFMA, 20 American Artists: Sculpture, 1982, 1982; National Gallery, Gemini G.E.L.: Art and Collaboration, 1984; Ecole des Beaux Arts, Paris, American Drawing: 1930-1950, 1985; Fort Lauderdale, An American Renaissance: Painting and Sculpture Since 1940, 1986. **Collections:** MMA; MOMA; WMAA. **Bibliography:** Alloway 4; *Art Now 74;* **Brown, Julia, ed.;** Calas, N. and E.; Celant; *Contemporanea;* Honisch and Jensen, eds.; *Kunst um 1970;* Lippard, ed.; Lucie-Smith; Muller; *New in the Seventies; When Attitudes Become Form.*

HELD, AL. b. October 12, 1928, Brooklyn, N.Y. **Studied:** ASL, with Kimon Nicolaides, Robert B. Hale, Harry Sternberg; Academie de la Grande Chaumiere; Siquieros in Mexico, 1949. US Navy, 1945-47. Traveled France, USA. **Taught:** Yale U., 1962-80. **Member:** Board of Trustees, American Academy, Rome, 1982-; AAIAL, 1984. **Commissions:** Tower East, Cleveland, Oh., 1967; Empire State Plaza, Albany, N.Y., 1976; Social Security Building, Philadelphia, 1977; Southland Center, Dallas, 1983; Akron (Oh.) Government Building, 1985. **Awards:** Chicago/AI, The Mr. and Mrs. Frank G. Logan Medal, 1964; Guggenheim Foundation Fellowship, 1966; Brandeis U., Creative Arts Award, 1983. **Address:** 435 West Broadway, NYC 10012. **Dealer:** Andre Emmerich Gallery, NYC; Robert Miller Gallery, NYC. **One-man Exhibitions:** (first) Galerie Huit, Paris, 1952; Poindexter Gallery, 1958 (two-man), 1959, 61, 62; Galeria Bonino, Buenos Aires, 1961; Ziegler Gallery, 1964, 70; Galerie Gunar, Dusseldorf, 1964; Andre Emmerich Gallery, NYC, 1965, 67, 68, 70, 72, 73, 75, 76, 78, 79, 80, 82, 84, 85, 86; Amsterdam/Stedelijk, 1966; Galerie

Muller, 1966; SFMA, 1968; Corcoran, 1968; ICA, U. of Pennsylvania, 1968; Houston/Contemporary, 1969; Current Editions, Seattle; Donald Morris Gallery, 1971, 74; Andre Emmerich Gallery, Zurich, 1974, 77; Jared Sable Gallery, Toronto, 1975; Adler Castillo Gallery, Caracas, 1975; Galerie Rene Ziegler, Zurich, 1977; Galerie Roger d'Amecourt, Paris, 1977; Annely Juda Fine Art, London, 1977, 80; Donald Morris Gallery, Birmingham, Mich., 1977; ICA, Boston, 1978; Friedland Gallery, Toronto, 1978; Janus Gallery, Venice, Calif., 1979; Robert Miller Gallery, 1980, 82; Gimpel-Hanover and Andre Emmerich Galleries, Zurich, 1980, 84; Annely Juda Fine Art, London, 1980; Quadrat Gallery, Bottrop, 1980; Galerie Andre Emmerich, Zurich, 1980; American Academy, Rome, 1982; Juda-Rowan Gallery, London, 1982; Donald Morris Gallery, Birmingham, Mich., 1983; Richard Gray Gallery, Chicago, 1984; Friedland Gallery, Toronto, 1984. **Retrospective:** WMAA, 1974. **Group:** SRGM, Abstract Expressionists and Imagists, 1961; Marlborough Fine Art, Ltd., 1961; ICA, Boston, 1961; Carnegie, 1961; Dallas/MFA, 1961, 62; MOMA, Abstract American Drawings and Watercolors, circ., Latin America, 1961-63; WMAA; Geometric Abstraction in America, circ., 1962; Yale U., 1962; Corcoran, 1962; Jewish Museum, Toward a New Abstraction, 1963; Chicago/AI, 1963, 64; Los Angeles/County MA, Post Painterly Abstraction, 1964; WMAA Annuals, 1964, 65, 67, 69, 72, 73; Kunsthalle, Basel, Signale, 1965; U. of Michigan, 1965; NYU, 1965; Amsterdam/Stedelijk, New Shapes of Color, 1966; WMAA, Art of the U.S. 1670-1966, 1966; SRGM, Systematic Painting, 1966; Flint/Institute, I Flint Invitational, 1966; Jewish Museum, 1967; Documenta IV, Kassel, 1968; Chicago/AI, 1969; Fort Worth Art Museum, Drawings, 1969; VMFA, 1970; Dublin/Municipal, International Quadriennial (ROSC), 1971; Indianapolis/Herron, 1974; Corcoran Biennial, 1975; Tulane U., Drawing Today in New York, 1977, 1976-77; Chicago/AI, Drawings of the 70's, 1976; Documenta, Kassel, 1977; U. of Texas, New in the Seventies, 1977; Minnesota/MA, American Drawing 1927-1977, 1977; Philadelphia College of Art, Point, 1978; Pomona College, Black and White Are Colors, 1979; Purchase/SUNY, Hidden Desires, 1980; Brooklyn Museum, American Drawings in Black and White, 1970-1979, 1980; WMAA Biennial, 1981; Haus der Kunst, Minich, Amerikanische Malerie: 1930-1950, 1981; Brooklyn Museum, The American Artist as Printmaker, 1983; Newport Harbor, Action/Precision, circ., 1984; Independent Curators, Inc., NYC, Concepts in Construction, circ., 1983. **Collections:** Akron/AI; Berlin/National; Brandeis U.; Buffalo/Albright; Canberra/National; Ciba-Geigy Corp.; Cleveland/MA; Cleveland Trust Co.; Dallas/MFA; Dartmouth College; Delaware Art Museum; Dayton/AI; First National Bank of Seattle; Greenville; Harvard U.; High Museum; Hirshhorn; Kunsthalle, Basel; MMA; MOMA; Milwaukee; U. of North Carolina; SFMA; Stuttgart; Syracuse/Everson; Treadwell Corp.; WMAA; Yale U.; Zurich. **Bibliography:** Al Held; Alloway 3; Battcock, ed.; *Black and White Are Colors;* Calas, N. and E.; Honisch and Jensen, eds.; Hunter, ed.; Lucie-Smith; *New in the Seventies;* Rose, B., 1; Sandler 1; Tucker. Archives.

HELIKER, JOHN EDWARD b. January 16, 1909, Yonkers, N.Y. **Studied:** ASL, 1927-29, with Kimon Nicolaides, Thomas Hart Benton, Kenneth Hayes Miller, Boardman Robinson. Traveled Europe; resided Italy, two years. **Taught:** Colorado Springs Fine Arts Center; Columbia U. Federal A.P.: Easel painting. **Membership:** NIAL, 1969, vice-president, 1971-74. **Awards:** Corcoran, First Prize, 1941; Pepsi-Cola, 1946; Prix de Rome, 1948; NAD, The Adolph and Clara Obrig Prize, 1948; Guggenheim Foundation Fellowship 1952; NIAL Award, 1957; Ford Foundation, **P.P.,** 1960, 61; AAAL, Award of Merit Medal and $1,000, 1967; NAD;

Benjamin Altman Prize for Landscape, Benjamin Altman Prize for Figure, 1977. **Address:** 865 West End Avenue, NYC. **Dealer:** Kraushaar Galleries. **One-man Exhibitions:** (first) Maynard Walker Gallery, NYC, 1936, also 1938, 41; Kraushaar Galleries, 1945, 51, 54, 68, 71, 74, 77; Lehigh U., 1970; Drew U., Madison, N.J., 1971; Saint-Gaudens National Historical Site, Cornish, N.H., 1972; Edmonton Art Gallery, Alberta, 1974; New York Studio School, NYC, 1982. **Retrospective:** WMAA, 1968. **Group:** MOMA; MMA; Corcoran; VMFA; WMAA, 1941-46, 1955-57; Chicago/AI, 1942, 43, 45; Toldeo/MA, 1942, 43, 45; Carnegie, 1943-45; PAFA, 1944, 46; WMAA, The New Decade, 1954-55; Brussels World's Fair, 1958; U. of Illinois, 1961; New York World's Fair, 1964-65; Expo '70, Osaka, 1970; Huntington, N.Y./Heckscher, Windows and Doors, 1972; ASL Centennial, 1975; US Department of the Interior, America 1976, circ., 1976. **Collections:** Arizona State College; Atlanta U.; Atlantic Richfield Co.; Ball State U.; Britannica; Brooklyn Museum; Chicago/AI; Clearwater/Gulf Coast; Cleveland/MA; Colby College; Colorado Springs/FA; Columbia U.; Commerce Trust Co., Kansas City, Mo.; Corcoran; Currier; Denver/AM; Des Moines; Hartford/Wadsworth; Harvard U.; Hirshhorn; Illinois Wesleyan U.; U. of Illinois; Kansas City/Nelson; Lehigh U.; Louisville/Speed; MMA; U. of Miami; NCFA; U. of Nebraska; New Britain/American; U. of Notre Dame; Ogunquit; PAFA; PMA; The Pennsylvania State U.; RISD; U. of Rochester; SFMA; Savannah/Telfair; Storm King Art Center; U. of Texas; Utica; WMAA; Walker; Washington U.; Whitney Communications Corp.; Wichita/AM. **Bibliography:** *America 1976;* Baur 5, 7; Goodrich and Baur 1; **Goodrich and Mandel;** Kent, N.; Nordness, ed.; Pagano; Pousette-Dart, ed.; Ritchie 1. Archives.

HENDLER, RAYMOND. b. February 22, 1923, Philadelphia, Pa. **Studied:**

Academie de la Grande Chaumiere; Contemporary School of Art, NYC; Temple U.; PAFA; Philadelphia Museum School; Graphic Sketch Club, Philadelphia, intermittently 1938-51. US Army in Europe, 1942-45. Traveled Europe extensively; resided Paris. **Taught:** Assistant to Moses Soyer in NYC, adult classes; Philadelphia public school system; Contemporary School of Art, Brooklyn, N.Y., 1948-49; Fleicher Art Memorial, Philadelphia, 1953-55; Moore College of Art, Philadelphia, 1955-56; Minneapolis College of Art, 1958-62; Parsons School of Design, NYC, 1962-65; Pratt Institute, 1964-66; School of Visual Arts, NYC, 1966-68; Long Island U., 1968; U. of Minnesota, 1968-. A co-organizer of Galerie Huit, Paris, 1949. Director of the Hendler Gallery, Philadelphia, 1952-54. **Awards:** Longview Foundation Grant, 1963. **Address:** 2212 Seabury Avenue South, Minneapolis, MI 55406. **One-man Exhibitions:** (first) Galerie Huit, Paris, 1951; Dubin Gallery, Philadelphia, 1952; Hendler Gallery, Philadelphia, 1953; Minneapolis/Institute, 1959; Rose Fried Gallery, 1962, 64, 67. **Group:** Newark Museum; Paris/Moderne; Salon d'Art Libre, Paris; U. of Pennsylvania; U. of South Carolina; Montreal/MFA; Stanford U.; U. of Manitoba; Massillon Museum; Houston/MFA; Minneapolis/Institute; Walker; NYU. **Collections:** Calcutta; Ciba-Geigy Corp.; Minneapolis College of Art; NYU; U. of Notre Dame; PAFA; PMA; J. Walter Thompson Co.; Walker.

HESSE, EVA. b. January 11, 1936, Hamburg, Germany; **d.** May 29, 1970, NYC. **Studied:** Cooper Union, 1954-57; Yale U. Summer School, Norfolk, Conn., 1957; Yale U., 1969, BFA. **Taught:** School of Visual Arts, NYC, 1968; Oberlin College, 1968. **One-man Exhibitions:** Allan Stone Gallery, 1963; Dusseldorf/Kunsthalle, 1965; Fischbach Gallery, 1968, 70; School of Visual Arts, NYC, 1971; Droll/Kolbert Gallery,

Eva Hesse   *Accession II*   1967

NYC, 1977; Whitechapel Art Gallery, circ., 1979; Mayor Gallery, London, 1979; Metro Pictures, NYC, 1983; Brandeis U., 1985. **Retrospectives:** SRGM, circ., 1972; Oberlin College, circ., 1982. **Group:** Brooklyn Museum, Watercolor Biennial, 1961; Riverside Museum, NYC, American Abstract Artists, 1966; Ithaca College, Drawings, 1967, 1967; U. of North Carolina, 1967; New York State Fair, Art Today: 1967, 1967; Finch College, NYC, Art in Process, 1967, 69; Moore College of Art, Philadelphia, American Drawings, 1968; Milwaukee, Directions I: Options, circ., 1968; A.F.A., Soft Sculpture, 1968; WMAA, 1968; Fort Worth Art Museum, Drawings, 1969; Trenton/State, Soft Art, 1969; ICA, U. of Pennsylvania, Plastics and New Art, 1969; Seattle/AM, 557, 087, 1969; Milwaukee, A Plastic Presence, circ., 1969; Berne, When Attitudes Become Form; 1969; WMAA, Anti-Illusion: Procedures/Materials, 1969; Princeton U., American Art since 1960, 1970; Foundation Maeght, 1970; ICA, U. of Pennsylvania, Projected Art, 1970; New York Cultural Center, 3D into 2D, 1973; WMAA (downtown), Sculpture of the Sixties, 1975; WMAA, 200 Years of American Sculpture, 1976; New Orleans Museum, Sculpture:

American Directions, 1976; Documenta VI, Kassel, 1977; U. of Chicago, Ideas in Sculpture, 1977; Amsterdam/Stedelijk, Made by Sculptors, 1978; Purchase/SUNY, Hidden Desires, 1980; Cologne/Stadt, Westkunst, 1981; Fort Lauderdale, An American Renaissance: Painting and Sculpture Since 1940, 1986. **Collections:** Cologne; Dusseldorf/Kunsthalle; Krefeld Museum; MOMA; Milwaukee; U. of North Carolina; Oberlin College; Ridgefield/ Aldrich; WMAA. **Bibliography:** Celant; **Eva Hesse: A Memorial Exhibition;** Nemser; Rowell; *When Attitudes Become Form.* Archives.

HEUBLER, DOUGLAS. b. October 27, 1924, Ann Arbor, Mich. **Studied:** U. of Michigan, Ann Arbor, MFA; Cleveland School of Art; Academie Julien, Paris. US Marine Corps. **Taught:** Harvard U. **Address:** Box 102, Turo, Mass. 02666. **Dealer:** Leo Castelli Inc., NYC. **One-man Exhibitions:** Phillips Gallery, Detroit, 1953; Obelisk Gallery, Boston, 1967; Windham College, 1968; Seigelaub Gallery, NYC, 1968; Eugenia Butler Gallery, Los Angeles, 1969; Konrad Fischer Gallery, Dusseldorf, 1970, 71, 72, 74; Andover/Phillips, 1970; Gian Enzo Sperone, Turin, 1970, 74; Yvon Lambert, Paris, 1970, 74, 80; Art & Project, Amsterdam, 1970, 71; Leo Castelli Inc., 1971, 72, 73, 76, 78, 81, 83; California Institute of the Arts, Valencia, 1972; Galleria Toselli, Milan, 1972; Jack Wendler Gallery, London, 1972, 73, 74; Boston/MFA, 1972; Munster/WK, 1973; Kunsthalle, Kiel, 1973; Kunsthalle, Bielfeld, 1973; Fischer Sperone Galleria, Rome, 1973; Israel Museum, 1973; Galerie MTL, Brussels, 1973, 74, 79; Oxford/MOMA, 1973; Nova Scotia College of Art and Design, 1973; Lia Rumma Studio, Naples, 1974; Rolf Preisig Gallery, Basel, 1974; Francoise Lambert, Milan, 1975; Barbara Cusack Gallery, Houston, 1975; Sperone Westwater Fischer Inc., NYC, 1976; Galleric Akumulatory, Poznan, Poland, 1977; Thomas Lewallen Gallery, Los Angeles, 1977; Rudiger Schöttle, Munich, 1978, 79; U. of California, San Diego, 1979; Eindhoven, 1979; Los Angeles/County MA, 1979; Northwestern U., 1980; Los Angeles/Contemporary, 1984; Los Angeles Center for Photographic Studies, 1984. **Group:** Corcoran Biennial, 1957; WMAA Annual, 1966; The Pennsylvania State U., Six Sculptors, 1967; Berne, When Attitude Becomes Form, 1969; Amsterdam/Stedlijk, Op Losse Schroeven, 1969; Seattle/AM, 557, 087, 1969; Dusseldorf/Kunsthalle, Prospect 69, 1969; MOMA, Information, 1970; Arnhem, Sonsbeek '71, 1971; Basel, Konzept Kunst, 1972; Documenta V, Kassel, 1972; Chicago/AI, 72nd American Exhibition, 1976; Houston/Contemporary, American Narrative/Story Art, 1977; ICA, Boston, Narration, 1978; Wichita State U., Artists and Books, 1979. **Collections:** Amsterdam/ Stedelijk; Andover/Phillips; Brandeis U.; Columbia, S.C./MA; Israel Museum; MOMA; Ottawa; Tate Gallery.

HILLSMITH, FANNIE. b. March 13, 1911, Boston, Mass. **Studied:** Boston Museum School, with Burns, Guthrie; U. of London, Slade School, 1930-34; ASL, 1934-35, with Alexander Brook, Yasuo Kuniyoshi, William Zorach, John Sloan; Atelier 17, NYC, 1946-50, with S. W. Hayter. **Taught:** Black Mountain College, 1945; Cornell U., 1963. **Awards:** Boston Arts Festival, First Prize, 1957, 63; Boston Museum School, Traveling Scholarship, 1958; Portland Me./MA, First Prize, 1958. **Address:** % Wedgewood, Jaffrey, NH 03452. **One-man Exhibitions:** Norlyst Gallery, NYC, 1943; Charles Egan Gallery, 1949, 54; The Swetzoff Gallery, Boston, 1949, 50, 54, 57, 63; Colby College, 1950; Santa Barbara/MA, 1950; Milton Academy, 1952; Currier, 1954; Dayton/AI, 1954; ICA, Boston, 1954; Lincoln, Mass./De Cordova, 1954, 58; The Peridot Gallery, 1957, 58, 62, 65; Cornell U., 1963; Green Mountain College, 1965; Weeden Gallery, Boston, 1967; Fitchburg/AM, 1969; Jaffrey Civic Center, 1970; Brockton/Fuller, 1971; Thorne Gallery, Keene, N.H., 1972; Brattleboro (Vt.) Museum and Art Center, 1974. **Group:** Art of This Century, NYC; Corcoran; Phillips; A.F.A.; MOMA; Boston/MFA; Brooklyn Museum; The Print Club, Philadelphia; American Abstract Artists, 1946-58; Chicago/AI, 1947, 48, 54; WMAA, 1949, 51, 55; Walker, 1953, 54; SRGM, 1954; Carnegie, 1955; U. of Illinois, 1955, 57, 59; Federation of Modern Painters and Sculptors, 1956-58; AAAL, 1964; Hartford/Wadsworth, 1966. **Collections:** Andover/Phillips; Boston/MFA; Currier; Harvard U.; MOMA; NYPL; PMA. **Bibliography:** Janis. S.

HINMAN, CHARLES. b. December 29, 1932, Syracuse, N.Y. **Studied:** Syracuse U., BFA, 1955; ASL (with Morris Kantor), 1955-56. Played professional baseball, Milwaukee Braves, 1954-55. US Army, 1956-58. Traveled Japan, India, Europe, and around the world. **Taught:** Staten Island Academy, 1960-62; Woodmere Academy, 1962-64; Aspen Institute, Artist-in-Residence; Cornell U., 1968-69; Syracuse U., 1971; Pratt Institute, 1975; School of Visual Arts, NYC, 1976; Cooper Union, NYC, 1977. **Member:** Artists Equity. **Commissions:** Neiman-Marcus Co., Atlanta (sculpture); Grand Hyatt Hotel, NYC; Madison Green Building, NYC; Mack Plaza, Tampa, Fla. **Awards:** Syracuse U., Augusta Hazard Fellowship, 1955-56; Nagaoka, Japan, First Prize, 1965; Flint/Institute, First Prize, 1966; Torcuato di Tella, Buenos Aires, Special Mention, 1967; National Endowment for the Arts, 1980. **Address:** 231 Bowery, NYC 10002. **One-man Exhibitions:** (first) Richard Feigen Gallery, NYC, 1964, also 1966, 67; Feigen-Palmer Gallery, Los Angeles, 1964; Oberlin College (three-man), 1965; Richard Feigen Gallery, Chicago, 1965, 66; Tokyo Gallery, 1966; Galerie Denise

Rene/Hans Mayer, Krefeld, W. Germany, 1970; Galerie Denise Rene, Paris, 1971, NYC, 1972, 73, 75; Hokin Gallery, Chicago, 1976, 79; Hokin Gallery, Palm Beach Fla., 1977; Irving Galleries, Milwaukee, 1976; Donald Morris Gallery, Birmingham, Mich., 1979; Bellman Gallery, NYC, 1983. **Retrospective:** Lincoln Center, 1969. **Group:** Riverside Museum, 1965; WMAA, Young America, 1965; Chicago/AI, 1965, 66, 69; SFMA, The Colorists, 1965; Nagaoka, Japan, 1975; U. of Notre Dame, 1965; Finch College, 1966; WMAA, Art of the U.S. 1670-1966; U. of Illinois, 1967; VI International Art Biennial, San Marino (Europe), 1967; Carnegie, 1967; WMAA Annual, 1967; Honolulu Academy, 1968; Jewish Museum, Superlimited, 1969; A.F.A., 1969; Indianapolis/Herron, 1969; Princeton U., American Art since 1960, 1970; NCFA, Disappearance and Reappearance of the Image, circ., 1969; U. of Illinois, 1971; Indianapolis, 1976. **Collections:** American Republic Insurance Co.; Aspen Institute; Boise-Cascade Corp.; Buffalo/Albright; Chase Manhattan Bank; Continental Grain Corp.; Delaware Art Museum; Detroit/Institute; Fort Lauderdale; Hirshhorn; U. of Illinois; Lehigh U.; Los Angeles/County MA; MIT; MOMA; McCrory Corp.; Milwaukee; Nagaoka, Japan; U. of North Carolina; Oberlin College; The 180 Beacon Collection: The Pennsylvania State U.; Princeton U.; Ridgefield/Aldrich; U. of Texas; WMAA; Williams College. **Bibliography:** Battcock, ed.; Hunter, ed.; Johnson, Ellen H.

HIRSCH, JOSEPH. b. April 25, 1920, Philadelphia, Pa. **d.** Sept. 25, 1981, NYC. **Studied:** Philadelphia Museum School, 1927-31; privately with Henry Hensche in Provincetown; with George Luks in NYC. Traveled Europe, the Orient, USA; resided France, five years. **Taught:** Chicago Art Institute

School; American Art School, NYC; U. of Utah; ASL, 1959-; Dartmouth College, 1966; Utah State U. 1967; Brigham Young U., 1971; NAD. Artist war correspondent, 1943-44. **Member:** Artists Equity (founder and first treasurer); NAD; Philadelphia Watercolor Club; NIAL, 1967. Federal A.P.: Easel painting; first WPA murals in Philadelphia, for Amalgamated Clothing Workers Building and Municipal Court. **Awards:** Scholarship from the City of Philadelphia; PAFA, Walter Lippincott Prize; American Academy, Rome; International Institute of Education Fellowship, 1935-36; New York World's Fair, 1939, First Prize; Guggenheim Foundation Fellowship, 1942-43; Library of Congress, Pennell **P.P.**, 1944, 45; NIAL Grant, 1947; Carnegie, Second Prize, 1947; Chicago/AI, Watson F. Blair Prize; Fulbright Fellowship, 1949; MMA, 1950; NAD, Benjamin Altman Prize, 1959, 66; NAD Annual Andrew Carnegie Prize, 1968; Davidson College, **P.P.**, 1972, 73; Oklahoma, **P.P.**, 1974; NAD, Altman Prize for Figure Painting, 1978. **One-man Exhibitions:** ACA Gallery, Philadelphia; A.A.A. Gallery, NYC, 1946, 48, 54; The Forum Gallery, 1965, 69, 74; Oklahoma, 1974; Century Association, NYC, 1980; Kennedy Gallery, NYC, 1975, 76, 78, 80. **Group:** WMAA; Newark Museum; Walker; MMA; Kansas City/Nelson; PAFA. **Collections:** AAAL; Andover/Phillips; U. of Arizona; Boston/MFA; Dartmouth College; U. of Georgia; IBM; Kansas City/Nelson; Library of Congress; MMA; MOMA; Museum of Military History; NAD; U. of Oklahoma; PMA; Southampton/Parrish; Springfield, Mass./MFA; Harry S. Truman Library; WMAA; Walker; College of Wooster. **Bibliography:** Baur 7; Cheney; Genauer; **Joseph Hirsch;** Miller, ed. 1; Nordness, ed.; Pagano; Phillips 2; Reese; Richardson, E.P.; Wight 2. Archives.

HOFMANN, HANS. b. March 21, 1880, Weissenberg, Bavaria, Germany; **d.** February 17, 1966, NYC. **Studied:** Gymnasium, Munich; Academie de la Grande Chaumiere, 1904. Resided Paris, 1904-14, with the patronage of Phillip Freudenberg, department-store owner and art collector. US citizen, 1941. **Taught:** Opened first art school, 1915, in Munich; held summer sessions at Ragusa, 1924, Capri, 1925-27, Saint-Tropez, 1928, 29; Chouinard Art Institute, Los Angeles, 1930; U. of California, Berkeley, summer, 1930; ASL, 1932-33; Thurn School, Provincetown, summers, 1923, 33; opened own school in NYC, 1933, own summer school in Provincetown, 1934. Stopped teaching 1958, to devote full time to painting. **Awards:** U. of Illinois, **P.P.**, 1950; Society for Contemporary American Art, Chicago, **P.P.**, 1952; PAFA, J. Henry Schiedt Memorial Prize, 1952; Chicago/AI, The Mr. & Mrs. Frank G. Logan Medal, 1953; Chicago/AI, Flora Mayer Witkowsky Prize, 1959; II Inter-American Paintings and Prints Biennial, Mexico City, 1960, Hon. Men.; Chicago/AI, Ada S. Garrett Prize, 1961; hon. degree, Dartmouth College, 1962; hon. degree, U. of California, 1964; elected to the NIAL, 1964. **One-man Exhibitions:** (first) Paul Cassirer Gallery, Berlin, 1910; California Palace, 1931; New Orleans/Delgado, 1940; Art of This Century, NYC, 1944; "67" Gallery, NYC, 1944, 45; Betty Parsons Gallery, 1946, 47; The Kootz Gallery, NYC, 1947, 49, 1950-55, 1957, 58, 1960-64, 1966; Galerie Maeght, 1949; Boris Mirski Gallery, Boston, 1954; Baltimore/MA, 1954; Rutgers U., 1956; Dartmouth College, 1962; Stamford U., 1966; Andre Emmerich Gallery, NYC, 1967-69, 1972, 73, 74, 75, 76, 77, 78, 79, 80, 82, 83, 84, 85, 86; Richard Gray Gallery, 1968, 72, 80; Obelisk Gallery, 1969; David Mirvish Gallery, 1969, 73, 74; MMA, 72; John Berggruen Gallery, 1973; Buffalo/Albright, 1973; Art Museum of South Texas, Corpus Christi, 1974; Santa Ana/Bowers, 1975; MMA, 1974; Waddington Galleries, Montreal,

1975; Garage Gallery, Birmingham, Ala., 1975; Fendrick Gallery, Washington, D.C., 1975; Deutsch Gallery, NYC, 1976; Schaffner Gallery, Los Angeles, 1976; Janie C. Lee Gallery, Houston, 1977; B. R. Kornblatt Gallery, 1977; David Mirvish Gallery, Toronto, 1977; Hokin Gallery, Chicago, 1977; Freudenheim Gallery, Buffalo, 1978; Thomas Segal Gallery, Boston, 1978; Richard Gray Gallery, Chicago, 1978; Hokin Gallery, Palm Beach, 1978; MMA, Hans Hofmann as Teacher, 1979; Friedland Gallery, Toronto, 1979, 81, 82, 84, 86; Gallery 609, Denver/AM, 1979; MMA, 1980; Provincetown Art Association, 1980; Waddington Gallery, Montreal, 1980; Asher/Faure, 1981; Harcus-Krakow Gallery, Boston, 1981; Makler Gallery, Philadelphia, 1981; Martha White Gallery, Louisville, 1981; Edmonton Art Gallery, 1982; Douglas Drake Gallery, Kansas City, 1984; B.R. Kornblatt Gallery, Washington, D.C., 1983; Yares Gallery, Scottsdale, 1984; Thomas Babeor Gallery, La Jolla, 1985; Fort Worth, 1985; C. Grimaldis Gallery, Baltimore, 1986. **Retrospectives:** Arts Club of Chicago, 1944; Andover/Phillips, 1948; Bennington College, 1955; Philadelphia Art Alliance, 1956; WMAA, circ., 1957; The Kootz Gallery, NYC, 1959; Germanisches National Museum, Nurnberg, circ., Germany, 1962; MOMA, circ., USA, Latin America, and Europe, 1963. **Group:** Chicago/AI; U. of Illinois; Carnegie; Documenta II, Kassel, 1959; XXX & XXXIV Venice Biennials, 1960, 68; WMAA Annual, 1965; Corcoran Biennial, 1965; Marlborough-Gerson Gallery, Inc., 1967; MOMA, The New American Painting and Sculpture, 1969; Albright/Buffalo, Color and Field 1890-1970, 1970; WMAA, The Structure of Color, 1971; Birmingham, Alabama, American Watercolors 1850-1972, 1972; National Gallery, American Art at Mid Century, 1973; Houston/MFA, The Great Decade of American Abstraction, 1974; Kennedy Gallery, NYC, The Art Students League, 1875-1975, 1975; Harvard U., The New York School: From the First Generation, 1975; SRGM, Twentieth Century Drawings, 1976; A.F.A., American Master Drawings and Watercolors, 1976; Bonn, 200 Years of American Painting, 1976; Baltimore/MA, 200 Years of American Painting, 1977; Syracuse/Everson, Provincetown Painters, 1977; Cornell U., Abstract Expressionism, The Formative Years, 1978; Flint/Institute, Art and the Automobile, 1978; Sierra Nevada Museum of Art, The New York School, 1940-1960, 1979; Grande Palais, Paris, L'Amerique aux Independants, 1980; Hirshhorn, The Fifties: Aspects of Painting in New York, 1980; Cologne/Stadt, Westkunst, 1981; Houston/Contemporary, The Americans: The Collage, 1982; Houston/MFA, Miró in America, 1982; NYU, Tracking the Marvelous, 1981; Carnegie, Abstract Painting and Sculpture in America, 1927-1944, circ., 1983; Ecole des Beaux-Arts, Paris, American Drawing: 1930-1980, 1985; Hofstra U., Avant-Garde Comes to New York, 1985; Fort Lauderdale, An American Renaissance: Painting and Sculpture Since 1940, 1986. **Collections:** Abbott Laboratories; Andover/Phillips; Art of This Century (Peggy Guggenheim); Baltimore/MA; Buffalo/Albright; U. of California (Museum Hofmann); Canberra/National; Carnegie; Chicago/AI; Cleveland/MA; Columbia Broadcasting System; Dallas/MFA; Dayton/AI; Fort Dodge/Blanden; Grenoble; High Museum; Hirshhorn; U. of Illinois; Indianapolis/Herron; International Minerals & Chemicals Corp.; Louisville/Speed; MMA; MOMA; U. of Michigan; Montreal/MFA; U. of Nebraska; Newark Museum; PMA; U. of Rochester; SRGM; Santa Barbara/MA; Tate Gallery; Toledo/MA; Toronto; WMAA; Walker; Washington U.; Wilmington; Yale U. **Bibliography:** Alloway 4; Ashton 5; Barker 1; Baur 5, 7; Biddle 4; Blesh 1; Brion 1; Cheney; Chipp; Danto; Eliot; Goodrich and Baur 1; *From Foreign Shores; The Great Decade;* **Greenberg** 1, **2;** Haftman; Henning; Hess, T. B., 1; Hobbs and Levin;

Hofmann; Hunter 1, 2, 6; Hunter, ed., Janis and Blesh 1; Janis, S.; Kozloff 3; Kuh 2; Lane and Larsen; **Loran 2;** Mc-Curdy, ed.; Mendelowitz; *Metro;* Motherwell and Reinhardt, eds.; Murken-Altrogge; Newmeyer; Nordness, ed.; Ponente; Pousette-Dart, ed.; Read 2; Richardson, E.P.; Ritchie 1; Rose, B., 1, 4; Rothschild; Sandler 1; **Seitz** 1, **4;** Tapie 1; Tomkins 2; Tuchman, ed.; Weller; **Wight 1.** Archives.

HOLLAND, TOM. b. June 15, 1936, Seattle, Wash. **Studied:** Wilamette U., 1954-56; U. of California, Santa Barbara and Berkeley, 1957-59. Traveled Chile. **Awards:** Fulbright Fellowship, 1960; National Endowment for the Arts, 1975; Guggenheim Foundation Fellowship, 1979. **Taught:** SFAI, 1962-67, U. of California, Berkeley; San Francisco Art Institute, 1961-68, 72-80; U. of California, Los Angeles, 1968-70; U. of California, Berkeley, 1978-79; Cornish Institute, Seattle, 1978. **Awards:** National Endowment for the Arts, grant, 1976; Guggenheim Foundation Fellowship, 1980-81. **Address:** 28 Roble Road, Berkeley, CA 94705. **Dealers:** Charles Cowles Gallery, NYC; James Corcoran Gallery, Los Angeles. **One-man Exhibitions:** Universidad Catolica, Santiago, 1961; RAC, 1962; New Mission Gallery, San Francisco, 1962; Hansen-Fuller Gallery, 1962-66, 68, 70, 72, 73, 74, 76, 77, 80; The Lanyon Gallery, 1963-65; Nicholas Wilder Gallery, 1965, 68, 72, 73, 75, 76, 77, 79; Robert Elkon Gallery, 1970; Galerie Hans R. Neuendorf, Cologne, 1971; Lawrence Rubin Gallery, NYC, 1972; Ronald Greenberg Gallery, St. Louis, 1972, 75, 83; Corcoran and Greenberg, Inc., Miami, 1972; Multiples, Los Angeles, 1972; Felicity Samuel Gallery, London, 1973; Knoedler Contemporary Art, NYC, 1973, 75; Current Editions, Seattle, 1973; Dootson Calderhead Gallery, Seattle, 1975; Sedar/Creigh Gallery, Coronado, Calif., 1975; Watson/DeNagy Gallery, Houston, 1977; Smith Andersen Gallery, Palo Alto,

Tom Holland *Pine* 1981

1978; Charles Casat Gallery, La Jolla, 1978; Droll-Kolbert Gallery, NYC, 1978; SFAI, 1979; Linda Farris Gallery, Seattle, 1979, 81, 83; Blum Helman, NYC, 1979, 81; Watson-Willour & Co., Houston, 1979; Smith Anderson Gallery, Palo Alto, 1982; James Corcoran Gallery, Los Angeles, 1980, 82, 83, 86; South Alberta Art Gallery, 1981; John Berggruen Gallery, 1984, 86; Arts Club of Chicago, 1985; Charles Cowles Gallery, 1981, 83, 84, 85, 86. **Retrospective:** RAC, 1975. **Group:** SFMA, Bay Area Artists, 1964; Stanford U., Current Painting and Sculpture of the Bay Area, 1964; La Jolla, 1965; PAFA, 1968; Ringling, California Painters, 1968; U. of Illinois, 1969; Corcoran, 1969; WMAA Annual, 1969; Pasadena/AM, West Coast: 1945-69, 1969; SFAI Centennial Exhibition, 1971; Hamburg/Kunstverein, USA: West Coast, circ., 1972; U. of Illinois Biennial, 1974;

SFMA, California Painting and Sculpture: The Modern Era, 1976; Invitational American Drawing Exhibition, San Diego, 1977; U. of Texas, New in the Seventies, 1977; Sacramento/Crocker, Aspects of Abstract Art, 1979; MOMA, New Works on Paper I, circ., 1981; Oakland/AM, On and Off the Wall, 1983; Cranbrook, Viewpoint '84, 1984. **Collections:** U. of California, Berkeley; Chicago/AI; Hirshhorn; Honolulu Academy; MOMA; U. of Nebraska; Oakland/AM; Phoenix; Ridgefield/Aldrich; RISD; St. Louis/City; Seattle AM; SFMA; SRGM; Stanford U., Walker; WMAA. **Bibliography:** *California Sculpture Show; New in the Seventies; The State of California Painting; USA West Coast.*

HOLTY, CARL ROBERT. b. June 21, 1900, Freiburg, Germany; **d.** March 23, 1973, NYC. To USA, 1900; citizen, 1906. US Army, 1917-18. **Studied:** Marquette U., 1918-19; NAD, 1920-22; Academy of Fine Arts, Munich, 1925-26; Hofmann School, Munich. Traveled Europe. **Taught:** ASL, 1939-40, 1950-51; U. of Georgia, 1948-50; U. of California, Berkeley, summer, 1951; U. of Florida, 1952-53; Brooklyn College, 1955-60, 1964-73; U. of Wisconsin, 1961; U. of Louisville, 1962-63; lectured extensively. **Member:** Abstraction-Creation, Paris, 1931-32; American Abstract Artists, 1936-43. **Awards:** U. of Illinois, **P.P.,** 1948; Ford Foundation, 1963. **One-man Exhibitions:** J. B. Neumann Gallery, NYC, 1936-44; Karl Nierendorf Gallery, NYC, 1938; The Kootz Gallery, NYC, 1946, 48; J.B. Neumann's New Art Circle, 1951, 52; Duveen-Graham Gallery, NYC, 1956; The Graham Gallery, 1959-62, 64, 67; Poindexter Gallery, 1972; City U. of New York Graduate Center, 1972; Andrew Crispo Gallery, 1974; Milwaukee, 1981; The Graham Gallery, 1983. **Group:** WMAA; PAFA; Corcoran; Chicago/AI; MMA; St. Louis/City; Los Angeles/County MA; Cincinnati/AM; Columbus. **Collec-**

tions: U. of Arkansas; U. of California; Chattanooga/AA; Exeter; U. of Georgia; U. of Illinois; Louisville/Speed; Milwaukee; NYU; U. of Nebraska; SRGM; St. Louis/City; Seattle/AM; U. of Tennessee; U. of Texas; WMAA; U. of Wisconsin; Youngstown/Butler. **Bibliography:** Baur 7; Blesh 1; **Carl Holty Memorial Exhibition;** Hess, T. B., 1; Janis, S.; Kootz 2; Lane and Larsen; McCurdy, ed.; Passloff; Ritchie 1; Seuphor 1. Archives.

HOOD, DOROTHY. b. August 22, 1919, Bryan, Texas. **Studied:** RISD; ASL, NYC. Traveled Mexico, South and Central America, Europe, extensively. Subject of documentary film by Carl Colby, *Dorothy Hood: The Color of Life*, 1985. **Taught:** Museum School of Fine Arts, Houston, 1963-77; Colorado State U., 1976. **Commissions:** Mural, St. Worth National Bank, 1972; mural, Lumm's Tower Building, Houston, 1980; sets for several ballet companies. **Awards:** National Scholastic Scholar, 1937-41; NAAL Childe Hassam **P.P.,** 1973; Brown Foundation, travel grant, 1973; Italian Academy of Arts & Labor, 1978. **Address:** 819 Highland Avenue, Houston, Tx. 77009. **Dealer:** Meredith Long Gallery, Houston. **One-man Exhibitions:** (first) The Willard Gallery, NYC, 1950; Proteo Gallery, Mexico City, 1955; Duveen-Graham Gallery, NYC, 1958; Galerie Genova, Mexico City, 1955; Philadelphia Art Alliance, 1958; Atelier Chapman Kelley, Dallas, 1961; Witte, 1965; Houston/Contemporary, 1970; Syracuse/Everson, 1972; Rice U., 1971; Houston Art Museum of South Texas, Corpus Christie, 1975; Houston/MFA, 1974; Tibor de-Nagy, NYC, 1974; Potsdam/SUNY, 1974; Davis & Long Company, NYC, 1975; U. of Texas, 1975; Meredith Long Gallery, Houston, 1962, 64, 66, 68, 70, 72, 74, 76, 82; Marianne Friedland Gallery, Toronto, 1976; Meredith Long Contemporary, NYC, 1978, 80; San Antonio/McNay, 1978; Meredith Long

Contemporary, NYC, 1982; Wallace Wentworth Gallery, Washington, D.C., 1986. **Retrospectives:** San Antonio/McNay, 1978; Syracuse/Everson, circ., 1980. **Group:** Brooklyn Museum, Golden Years of American Drawing, 1905-56, 1956; RISD, Four Young Americans, 1959; MOMA, Young American Printmakers, 1953; Potsdam/SUNY, Women in Art, 1972; Syracuse/Everson, New Works in Clay by Contemporary Painters and Sculptors, 1976; Houston/Contemporary, The Americans: The Collage, 1982; Houston/MFA, Fresh Paint, 1985. **Collections:** Boston/MFA; Brooklyn Museum; California State College, Long Beach; Dallas/MFA; Fort Worth; U. of Houston; Houston/Contemporary; Jolla; Mexico City Nacional; MOMA; Montreal Contemporary; National Gallery; The New Harmony Gallery of Contemporary Art; PMA; Potsdam/SUNY; Rice U.; RISD; San Antonio/McNay; Santa Barbara/MA; SFMA; Syracuse/Everson; U. of Texas; Texas A & M; WMAA; Worcester/AM. **Bibliography:** Archives.

HOPKINS, BUDD. b. June 15, 1931, Wheeling, W. Va. **Studied:** Oberlin College, 1949-53, BA. Traveled Europe. Published author on UFOs. **Taught:** Wagner College, 1955; MOMA, summers, 1955, 56; WMAA, 1957-60; Pratt Institute, 1959, Provincetown, summer, 1974; RISD, 1967, 68, 69, 76, 77; U. of Minnesota, 1975. **Commissions:** Provincetown/Chrysler, 1958 (large painting). **Awards:** West Virginia Arts and Humanities Council; Guggenheim Foundation Fellowship, 1976; National Endowment for the Arts, grant, 1979; NY State Council on the Arts, special project grant, 1982. **Member:** American Abstract Artists; Provincetown Art Assn. **Address:** 246 West 16th Street, NYC 10011. **Dealer:** Marilyn Pearl Gallery, NYC. **One-man Exhibitions:** (first) Poindexter Gallery, 1956, also 1962, 63, 66, 67, 69, 71; Tirca Karlis Gallery, 1958, 60, 1962-69, 73, 75; The Zabriskie Gallery, 1959; Kasha Heman, Chicago, 1962, 63; Art Galleries Ltd., Washington, D.C., 1963; Athena Gallery, New Haven, 1964; Bradford Junior College, 1965; Obelisk Gallery, 1966; Reed College, 1967; Exeter, 1968; William Zierler Inc., 1972, 73, 74, 76; Galerie Liatowitsch, Basel, 1974; Landmark Gallery, NYC, 1975; Pelham-von Stoffler Gallery, Houston, 1977; Andre Zarre Gallery, NYC, 1978; Middlebury College, Vt., 1978; Lerner-Heller Gallery, NYC, 1977, 78, 80, 81, 82; Cultural Activities Center, Temple, Texas, 1979; Fedele Fine Arts, NYC, 1981; Long Point Gallery, Provincetown, 1978, 80, 82; U. of Vermont, 1981; Marilyn Pearl Gallery, 1985. **Retrospectives:** Huntington, W. Va., 1973; U. of North Carolina, 1974; Michigan State U., 1974. **Group:** Wagner College, 1957; Oberlin College, 3 Young Painters, 1957; Festival of Two Worlds, Spoleto, 1958; WMAA, 1958, 63, Annuals, 1965, 67, 72; WMAA, Young America, 1960; Charlotte/Mint, 1960; PAFA, 1964; Cincinnati/AM, 1968; WMAA, Free Form Abstraction, 1972; SRGM, American Painters through Two Decades, 1973; New School for Social Research, Erotic Art, 1973; Montclair/AM, Collage, 1979; U. of North Carolina, American Abstract Artists, 1983. **Collections:** Ashland Oil Co.; Auckland; Block Drug Co.; Bradford Junior College; Brooklyn Museum; Ciba-Geigy Corp.; Conesta International Hotels; Corcoran; Delaware Art Museum; Hirshhorn; Historical Society of Montana; Hotel Corp. of America; Huntington, W. Va.; International Minerals and Chemicals Corp.; Litton Industries; U. of Massachusetts; MIT; Michigan State U.; Montana Historical Society; Norfolk/Chrysler; U. of North Carolina; Oberlin College; Oklahoma State Art Collection; Pepsi-Cola Co.; Pet Milk Co.; Pioneer Aerodynamic Systems; Reading/Public; Reed College; SRGM; SFMA; Simmons College; United Aircraft Corp.; United Grain Co.; WMAA; Westinghouse; Williams College. **Bibliography:** Archives.

HOPPER, EDWARD. b. July 22, 1882, Nyack, N.Y.; **d.** May 15, 1967, NYC. **Studied:** New York School of Art, 1900-06, with Kenneth Hayes Miller, Robert Henri, George Luks, A.B. Davies; a commercial art school, NYC, 1899-1900; Paris, 1906-07, 1909-10. Traveled USA, France. **Awards:** US Shipping Board, Poster Prize, 1918; Los Angeles/County MA, W. A. Bryan Prize, 1923; Chicago Society of Etchers, The Mr. & Mrs. Frank G. Logan Medal, 1923; NIAL, Gold Medal; Baltimore/MA, Hon. Men., 1931; Brooklyn Museum, 1931; PAFA, Joseph E. Temple Gold Medal, 1935; Worcester/AM, First **P.P.,** 1935; Corcoran, William A. Clark Prize, 1937; Chicago/AI, The Mr. & Mrs. Frank G. Logan Medal, 1945; Chicago/AI, Hon. Men. 1946; Chicago/AI, Hon. DFA, 1950; Hon. Litt. D., Rutgers U., 1953; Hallmark International Competition, 1957; Edward MacDowell Medal, 1966. **One-man Exhibitions:** (first) Whitney Studio Club, NYC, 1919, also 1922; Rehn Galleries, 1924, 27, 29, 46, 48, 65; PAFA, 1925, 71; Arts Club of Chicago, 1934; Carnegie, 1937; Currier, 1959; U. of Arizona, 1963; WMAA, 1971; Rutgers U., 1985. **Retrospective:** MOMA, 1933; WMAA, 1960, 64, 80. **Group:** WMAA; Chicago/AI; Boston/MFA; PAFA; Corcoran; The Armory Show, 1913; Smith College, Five Americans, 1934; Cincinnati/AM, 1948; IX Sao Paulo Biennial, 1967. **Collections:** Andover/Phillips; U. of Arizona; Boston/MFA; Brooklyn Museum; California State Library; Carnegie; Chicago/AI; Cleveland/MA; Corcoran; Hartford/Wadsworth; Harvard U.; IBM; Indianapolis/Herron; Kansas City/Nelson; Library of Congress; MMA; MOMA; Montclair/AM; Muskegon/Hackley; NYPL; U. of Nebraska; Newark Museum; New Orleans/Delgado; PAFA; Phillips; Randolph-Macon College; Terre Haute/Swope; Toledo/MA; Victoria and Albert Museum; WMAA; Walker; West Palm Beach/Norton; Wichita/AM; Worcester/AM; Yale U.; Youngstown/Butler. **Bibliography:** Alloway 4;

Barker 1; **Barr 2,** 3; Baur 7; Bazin; Blesh 1; Boswell 1; Brown 2; Canaday; Cheney; Christensen; *Cityscape 1919-39;* **Du Bois 2;** Eliot; Flexner; Goldwater and Treves, eds.; **Goodrich** 1, **3, 4;** Goodrich and Baur 1; Haftman; Hall; **Hopper;** Hunter 6; *Index of 20th Century Artists;* Jewell 2; Kozloff 3; Kuh 1, 2; Langui; Levin 1; McCoubrey 1; McCurdy, ed.; Mellquist; Mendelowitz; Murken-Altrogge; Neuhaus; Newmeyer; Nordness, ed.; O'Doherty; Pagano; Pearson 1; Phillips 1, 2; Poore; Pousette-Dart, ed.; Print Council of America; Reese; Richardson, E.P.; Ringel, ed.; Rodman 1; Rose, B., 1, 4; Sachs; Sager; Soby 5, 6; Soyer, R. 1; Sutton; Tomkins and Time-Life Books; Weller; Wight 2. Archives.

HORIUCHI, PAUL. b. April 12, 1906, Yamanashiken, Japan. Self-taught. **Commissions:** Seattle World's Fair, 1962 (free-standing mural). **Awards:** Ford Foundation, **P.P.;** Tupperware National Competition; Rockford/Burpee, 1966; U. of Puget Sound, Hon. H.H.D.; Hon. DFA, St. Martin College, 1979; and some 30 other awards. **Address:** 9773 Arrowsmith Avenue So., Seattle, WA 98118. **Dealer:** Woodside-Braseth Gallery, Seattle. **One-man Exhibitions:** (first) Seattle/AM, 1954, also 1958; Little Rock/MFA, 1958; Zoe Dusanne Gallery, Seattle, 1959, 63; Everett Junior College, 1960; U. of Arizona, 1962; Lee Nordness Gallery, NYC, 1963, 65; Felix Landau Gallery, 1963; 66; Reed College, 1964; Spelman College, 1965; Utica, 1965; Gordon Woodside Gallery, Seattle, 1965, 67, 72, 74, 76, 78; San Francisco, 1966, 68; Tacoma, 1967; Fountain Gallery, Portland, Ore. **Retrospective:** U. of Oregon, 1969; Seattle/AM, 1969. **Group:** Rome-New York Foundation, Rome, 1959; ART: USA:59, NYC, 1959; SFMA Annuals; Denver/AM; Seattle/AM; Carnegie, 1961; Seattle World's Fair, 1962; Rikkikai (Group), Tokyo, 1963; M. Knoedler & Co., Art across America, circ., 1965-67; VMFA, American Painting, 1966; Expo '74, Spokane, 1974; NCFA, Art of the Pacific Northwest, 1974. **Collections:** U. of Arizona; Chase Manhattan Bank; Colorado Springs/FA; Denver/AM; Everett Junior College; First National Bank of Seattle; Fort Worth; Hartford/Wadsworth; Harvard U.; Imperial Household, Tokyo; Little Rock/MFA; Lytton Savings and Loan Association; Marylhurst College; Mead Corporation; National Economics Research Association; U. of Oregon; Reed College; SFMA; Safeco Building; Santa Barbara/MA; Seattle/AM; Seattle Civic Center; Seattle Public Library; Seattle U.; Spelman College; Spokane Coliseum; Tacoma; Tokyo/Modern; Tupperware Museum; U.S. Steel Corp.; Utica; Vancouver; Victoria (B.C.); U. of Washington. **Bibliography:** *Art of the Pacific Northwest;* Clark and Cowles; *Northwest Traditions.*

HORNAK, IAN. b. January, 1944, Philadelphia, Pa. **Studied:** U. of Michigan, Wayne State U., BFA, MFA. Traveled Europe. **Taught:** Wayne State U., 1965-67; Henry Ford College, Dearborn, 1966-67. **Address:** Hands Creek Road, East Hampton, N.Y. 11937. **Dealer:** Armstrong Gallery, NYC. **One-man Exhibitions:** (first) Tibor de Nagy Gallery, NYC, 1971, 72, 73, 74, 75, 76; Fischbach Gallery, NYC, 1977, 79; Wood Gallery, Philadelphia, 1979; Gertrude Kasle Gallery, Detroit, 1974; Jacob's Ladder Gallery, Washington, D.C., 1971, 72; Sneed Gallery, Rockford, Ill., 1976; Selby Museum, Sarasota, 1980; The John Pence Gallery, San Francisco, 1980; Fischbach Gallery, 1981, 83; Selby Museum of Botany and Art, Sarasota, Fla., 1981; Armstrong Gallery, 1985. **Group:** Moore College of Art, Philadelphia, The New Landscape, 1971; Indianapolis, 1972, A.F.A., The Realist Revival, 1972; Oklahoma Art Center, Contemporary Landscape, 1975; Potsdam/SUNY, Landscape/Cityscape, 1978; Guild Hall, East Hampton, N.Y., Artists and East

Hampton, 1976; Huntington, N.Y./ Heckscher, Aspects of Change: Drawing Today, 1978; Potsdam/SUNY, Contemporary Realism, 1982. **Collections:** AT&T; Canton Art Institute; Chase Manhattan Bank; Citibank Corp.; Dartmouth College; Commerce Bank, Kansas City; Corcoran; Detroit/Institute; Indianapolis; IT&T; U of Maryland; NMAA; Oberlin College; Owens-Corning Fiberglas Corp.; Rutgers U.; St. Joseph/Albrecht; Toldeo/MA; Wayne State U.; Xerox Corp., NYC.

HOWARD, CHARLES. b. January 2, 1899, Montclair, N.J.; **d.** 1978, Ponte, Italy. **Studied:** U. of California, Berkeley, 1921; Harvard U.; Columbia U. Traveled USA. Europe. **Taught:** Camberwell School, London, 1959. Federal A.P.: Design Supervisor, mural at US Naval Air Station, Alameda, Calif. **Awards:** SFMA, **P.P.,** 1940; SFMA, 1942; MMA, Artists for Victory, 1942; Pasadena/AM, Third Prize, 1946; California Palace, First Prize; La Tausca Competition, **P.P.,** 1947. **One-man Exhibitions:** (first) Whitney Studio Club, NYC, 1926; Julien Levy Galleries, NYC, 1933; Bloomsbury Gallery, London, 1935; Guggenheim Jeune (Gallery), London, 1939; Courvoisier Gallery, San Francisco, 1941; U. of California, Berkeley, 1941; SFMA, 1942; Karl Nierendorf Gallery, NYC, 1946; Hanover Gallery, 1949; Heller Gallery, Cambridge, England, 1951; Santa Barbara/MA, 1953; St. George's Gallery, London, 1958; The Howard Wise Gallery, 1965. **Retrospective:** California Palace, 1946; Whitechapel Art Gallery, London, 1956. **Group:** Salons of America, NYC, 1933; New Burlington Galleries, London, International Surrealist Exhibition, 1936; Sao Paulo, 1938; SFMA, 1940-46; Carnegie, 1941, 46; MOMA, Americans 1942, circ., 1942; Chicago/AI, 1942, 46, 48; MMA, 1942, 52; WMAA, 1943-46; Corcoran, 1943-47; California Palace, 1945-59; Tate, American Painting, 1946; Salon des Realites Nouvelles, Paris, 1949. **Collections:** Chicago/AI; Container Corp. of America; Dallas/MFA; Jesus College; MMA; Pasadena/AM; SFMA; SRGM. **Bibliography:** Baur 7; Blesh 1; Frost; Genauer; Guggenheim, ed.; **Howard;** Janiz, S.; McCurdy, ed.; Miller, ed. 1; Ragon 2; Read 2; Richardson, E.P.; Ritchie 1; **Robertson 1.**

HUDSON, ROBERT H. b. September 8, 1938, Salt Lake City, Utah. **Studied:** San Francisco Art Institute, BFA, MFA. **Taught:** U. of California, Berkeley, 1966-73; Davis; SFAI, 1976-. **Awards:** RAC, 1959; San Francisco Art Festival, **P.P.,** 1961; SFMA, 1963; San Jose State College, **P.P.,** 1964; SFMA, Nealie Sullivan Award, 1965; Guggenheim Foundation Fellowship, 1976. **Address:** 392 Eucalyptus Avenue, Cotati, CA 94928. **Dealer:** Fuller Goldeen, San Francisco. **One-man Exhibitions:** RAC, 1961; Batman Gallery, San Francisco, 1961; Bolles Gallery, San Francisco, 1962; The Lanyon Gallery, 1964; San Francisco Art Institute, 1965; Allan Frumkin Gallery, Chicago, 1964, 68, 72; NYC, 1965, 71, 76, 78, 80, 81, 84; Nicholas Wilder Gallery, 1967; Michael Walls Gallery, 1970; U. of California, Berkeley, 1971, 72; Hansen-Fuller Gallery, San Francisco, 1973, 75, 77; Moore College of Art, Philadelphia, 1977; Miami-Dade Community College, 1979; Hansen Fuller Goldeen Gallery, San Francisco, 1979, 82; U. of California, Davis, 1983; Morgan Gallery, Shawnee Mission, Kan., 1983. **Retrospectives:** Moore College of Art, Philadelphia, 1977; SFMA, circ., 1985. **Group:** RAC, 1959-61; La Jolla, 1961; Oakland/AM, 1961, 63; Stanford U., Some Points of View for '62, 1962; SFM, 1962, 64; WMAA Sculpture Annual, 1964, 67, 68; WMAA, Young America, 1965; Westmoreland County/MA, 1966; U. of California, Berkeley, Funk, 1967; Los Angeles/County MA, American Sculpture of the Sixties, 1967; Chicago/AI, 1967; Walker, 1969; ICA, U. of Pennsylvania, The Spirit of the Comics, 1969;

Robert Hudson *Gaze* 1985–86

Walker, 14 Sculptors: The Industrial Age, 1969; U. of California, Berkeley, Impossible Dreams (two-man), 1970; U. of California, Santa Barbara, Six Californians, 1971; Corcoran Biennial, 1975; Hayward Gallery, London, The Condition of Sculpture, 1975; ICA, Boston, Hudson and De Forest, 1977; U. of Texas, New in the Seventies, 1977; SFMA, Aesthetics of Graffiti, 1978; Hirshhorn, Directions, 1979; Oakland/AM, 100 Years of California Sculpture, 1982. **Collections:** American Republic Insurance Co.; Amsterdam/Stedelijk; Los Angeles/County MA; Oakland/AM; SFMA. **Bibliography:** *California Sculpture Show;* Friedman, M. 2; *New in the Seventies;* Selz, P., 2; Tuchman 1.

HULTBERG, JOHN. b. February 8, 1922, Berkeley, Calif. **Studied:** Fresno

State College, 1939-43, BA; ASL, 1941-51, with Morris Kantor, California School of Fine Arts, with Clay Spohn, Richard Diebenkorn, David Park, Clyfford Still, Mark Rothko. US Navy, 1943-46. **Taught:** Boston Museum School, 1958; ASL, summer 1960; Portland, Ore./AM, Artist-in-Residence, 1964. **Member:** AAIAL; NAD. **Commissions:** *Fortune* magazine (portfolio of drawings of Newport News Shipbuilding Co.). **Awards:** CSFA, Albert M. Bender Fellowship, 1949; Corcoran, First Prize, 1955; Congress for Cultural Freedom, First Prize, 1955; Carnegie, Hon. Men., 1955; Guggenheim Foundation Fellowship, 1956; Hallmark International Competition, 1957; Chicago/AI, Norman Wait Harris Medal, 1962; Ford Foundation/A.F.A. Artist-in-Residence, 1964; NAD, Benjamin Altman Prize, 1972, 85; National Endowment for the Arts, 1981. **Address:** Box 14, Monhegan, Me. 04852. **Dealer:** Anita Shapolsky Gallery, NYC. **One-man Exhibitions:** (first) Contemporary Gallery, Sausalito, Calif., 1949; Korman Gallery, NYC, 1953; Martha Jackson Gallery, 1955, 58, 59, 61, 63, 66, 67, 69, 79; ICA, London, 1956; Galerie Rive Droite, Paris, 1957; The Swetzoff Gallery, Boston, 1957; Phoenix, 1957; Galerie du Dragon, Paris, 1957, 59, 70; Numero Galleria d'Arte, Florence, Italy, 1958; Main Street Gallery, NYC, 1961; Piccadilly Gallery, 1961, 65; Museum of Malmo, Sweden, 1962; Esther Baer Gallery, 1962, 64; Roswell, 1963; Galerie Pauli, Lausanne, 1965; Galerie Anderson-Mayer, Paris, 1966; Museum of Contemporary Crafts Council, 1966; Honolulu Academy, 1967; Gallery of Modern Art, 1967; Apiaw (Gallery), Paris, 1968; Long Island U., 1968; American Cultural Center, Paris, 1968; David Anderson Gallery, NYC, 1978. **Group:** California Palace, 1947; MOMA, New Talent; Corcoran, 1955; WMAA Annuals, 1955, 64, 68; XXVIII Venice Biennial, 1956; Gutai 9, Osaka, 1958; Carnegie, 1958; ART:USA:59, NYC, 1959; Chicago/AI, 1962; Brooklyn

John Hultberg *Habitable Void* 1979

Museum, 1964; Salon du Mai, Paris, 1964; Ghent, 1964; VIII Sao Paulo Biennial, 1965; Museo Civico, Bologna, 1965; U. of Kentucky, 1968; PAFA, 1968; AAAL, 1969; VMFA, American Painting, 1970; U. of Illinois, American Painting & Sculpture, 1948-1969, 1971. **Collections:** U. of Arizona; Atlanta/AA; Baltimore/MA; Boston U.; U. of California; Carnegie; Chase Manhattan Bank; Dallas/MFA; Davenport/Municipal; Dayton/AI; Eindhoven; Honolulu Academy; U. of Illinois; Indianapolis/Herron; MIT; MMA; MOMA; U. of Michigan; Musée Cantonal des Beaux-Arts; NYU; U. of Nebraska; New School for Social Research; Philadelphia Art Alliance; Phoenix; Quaker Ridge School; RISD; Roswell; St. Louis/City; Santa Barbara/MA; The Singer Company Inc.; Stamford Museum; Stockholm/National; WMAA; Walker. **Bibliography:** Blesh 1; Janis and Blesh 1; Hunter, ed.; McChesney; Nordness, ed. Archives.

.

HUMPHREY, RALPH. b. 1932, Youngstown, Ohio. **Studied:** Youngstown U., 1951-52, 1954-56. **Taught:** ASL; Harley House, NYC, 1959-60; Bennington College, 1961-63; New School for Social Research; Hunter College. **Address:** 323 West 21 Street, NYC 10011. **One-man Exhibitions:** Tibor de Nagy Gallery, 1959, 60; Gallery Mayer, NYC, 1961; Green Gallery, NYC, 1965; Bykert Gallery, 1967, 68, 69, 70, 72, 73, 74, 75; Dunkleman Gallery, Toronto, 1970; Andre Emmerich Gallery, NYC, 1971; The Texas Gallery, 1973; Daniel Weinberg Gallery, San Francisco, 1975; John Weber Gallery, NYC, 1976, 77; Daniel Weinberg Gallery, Los Angeles, 1983; Willard Gallery, NYC, 1982. **Group:** SRGM, Abstract Expressionists and Imagists, 1961; SRGM, Systemic Painting, 1966; Ithaca College, 1967; Trenton/State, Focus on Light, 1967; ICA, U. of Pennsylvania, A Romantic Minimalism, 1967; MOMA, The Art of the Real,

1968; WMAA, 1969; Buffalo/Albright, Color and Field; 1890-1970, 1970; WMAA, The Structure of Color, 1971; Indianapolis, 1972; Chicago/AI, 1974; UCLA, Fourteen Abstract Painter, 1975; Baltimore/MA, Fourteen Artists, 1975; U. of Chicago, Ideas on Paper, 1970-1976, 1976; WMAA Biennial, 1979; ICA, Boston, The Reductive Object, 1979. **Collections:** Bennington College; Brandeis U.; Canberra/National; Dayton/AI; Hartford/Wadsworth; MOMA; U. of North Carolina; SFMA; VMFA; WMAA. **Bibliography:** Alloway 3; Battcock, ed.; Goossen 1; *New in the Seventies.*

HUNT, BRYAN. b. June 7, 1947, Terre Haute, Indiana. **Studied:** U. of South Florida, Tampa, 1966-68; Otis Art Institute, Los Angeles, 1969-70; BFA; WMAA, Independent Study Program, 1972. Traveled Europe 1969, around the world 1979-80. **Taught:** School of Visual Arts, NYC, 1978. **Commissions:** Edgar Kaufman, *Falling Water,* scupture for Frank Lloyd Wright, 1979. **Address:** 9 White Street, NYC, 10013. **Dealer:** Blum Helman Gallery, NYC. **One-man Exhibitions:** The Clocktower, NYC, 1974; Jack Glenn Gallery, Corona del Mar, 1974; Brussels Beaux-Arts, 1976; Weinberg Gallery, San Francisco, 1976, 78; Blum Helman Gallery, NYC, 1977, 78, 79, 81, 83, 85; Greenberg Gallery, St. Louis, 1978; Bernard Jacobson Gallery, London, 1979; Galerie Bischofberger, Zurich, 1979; Margo Leavin Gallery, Los Angeles, 1980; Akron/AM, 1981; Galerie Hans Strelow, Dusseldorf, 1981; Jean Bernier Gallery, Athens, 1982; Weinberg Gallery, San Francisco, 1982; Amerika Haus, Berlin, 1983; Los Angeles/County MA, 1983; Margo Leavin Gallery, Los Angeles, 1983; John C. Stoller & Co., Minneapolis, 1984; M. Knoedler & Co., Zurich, 1985. **Retrospective:** California State U., Long Beach, 1983. **Group:** Portland Oregon, Center for the Visual Arts, Via Los Angeles, 1976; SRGM, Young American Artists, 1978; Amsterdam/Stedelijk,

Bryan Hunt *Dancers* 1985

Made by Sculptors, 1978; WMAA Biennial, 1979; Venice Biennial, 1980; Akron/AM, The Image in American Painting & Sculpture, 1950-1980, 1981; Rice U., Variants, 1981; WMAA Biennials, 1981, 85; Chicago/AI, 74th American Exhibition, 1982; Cincinnati/Contemporary, Dynamix, circ., 1982; Indianapolis, 1982; Houston/MFA, A Century of Modern Sculpture, 1882-1982, 1983; Palacio de Velazquez, Madrid, Tendencias en Nueva York, circ., 1983; MOMA, International Survey of Contemporary Painting and Sculpture, 1984; Newark Museum, American Bronze Sculpture, 1850 To The Present, 1984; Purchase/SUNY, Hidden Desires, 1984; Seattle/AM, American Sculptures, Three Decades, 1984. **Collections:** Akron/AM; Amsterdam/Stedelijk; Boston/MFA; Buf-

falo/Albright; Chicago/AI; Dallas/MFA; Duisburg; Harvard U.; High Museum; Houston/MFA; Humlebaek/Louisiana; MMA; MOMA; Newport Harbor; SRGM; Vassar College; Vienna/Moderner; WMAA; Yale U.

HUNT, RICHARD. b. September 12, 1935, Chicago, Ill. **Studied:** U. of Illinois; The U. of Chicago; Chicago Art Institute School, 1959, BA. Ed. US Army, 1958-60. Traveled Europe. **Taught:** U. of Illinois, 1960-62; Chicago Art Institute School, 1960-61; Yale U., 1964; Chouinard Art Institute, Los Angeles, 1964-65; Purdue U., 1965; Northern Illinois U., 1968; Northwestern U., 1968-69; Wisconsin State U., Oshkosh, 1969; Southern Illinois U., 1969; Western Illinois U., 1970; U. of Indiana, 1975; U. of Georgia, 1977; Washington U., 1977-78; U. of Arizona, 1980; Utah State U., 1982. **Member:** National Council on the Arts, 1968-74; Illinois Arts Council, 1970-75; Board of Trustees, Chicago/Contemporary, 1975-79; Board of Trustees, American Academy in Rome, 1980-82; Commissioner, NMAA, 1980-; Board of Trustees, The Institute for Psychoanalysis, 1981-; President/Founder, Chicago Sculpture Society, 1982-. **Commissions:** Louisiana State U., 1960; Johnson Publishing Co., Chicago, 1974; U. of Chicago, 1975; U. of California, Los Angeles, 1975; U. of Illinois, Chicago Campus, 1975; Martin Luther King Community Service Center, Chicago, 1975; U. of Michigan, 1975; Social Security Center, Richmond, Calif., 1976; Roosevelt Square, NYC, 1976; Justice Center, Cleveland, 1977; Cartwright Park, Evanston, Ill., 1977; Martin Luther King Memorial, Memphis, Tenn., 1977; Carter Woodson Library, Chicago, 1977; Prairie View A. & M. U., 1978; Howard U., 1978; Greenville, 1978; Cultural Activities Center, Temple, Tex., 1979; Northwestern U., 1979. **Awards:** Chicago/AI, James Nelson Raymond Traveling Fellowship, 1957; Guggenheim

Foundation Fellowship, 1962; Chicago/AI, The Mr. & Mrs. Frank G. Logan Prize; Cassandra Foundation Fellowship, 1970. **Address:** 1035 West Lill Avenue, Chicago, IL 60614. **Dealer:** Terry Dintenfass, Inc., NYC. **One-man Exhibitions:** (first) The Alan Gallery, NYC, 1958, also 1960, 63; Stewart Rickard Gallery, San Antonio, 1960, 64; B. C. Holland Gallery, 1961, 63, 70, 76; U. of Tulsa, 1964; Wesleyan College, 1964; Felix Landau Gallery; Cleveland/MA; Milwaukee; U. of Illinois; U. of Notre Dame; The Ohio State U.; Dorsky Gallery, 1968, 69, 71, 73, 75, 76, 77, 79; Wisconsin State U., Oshkosh, 1969; Southern Illinois U., 1970; MOMA, 1971; Indianapolis, 1973; U. of Iowa, 1975; Sears Bank and Trust Co., Chicago, 1976; Greenville, 1978; Terry Dintenfass, Inc., 1983, 84, 86; Springfield, Mo./AM, 1981. **Retrospectives:** MOMA, 1971; Chicago/AI, 1971; Milwaukee, 1967. **Group:** New Sculpture Group, NYC, 1960, 61; U. of Illinois; MOMA; WMAA; Michigan State U.; Smith College; Yale U.; Newark Museum; Carnegie; Seattle World's Fair, 1962; HemisFair '68, San Antonio, Tex., 1968. **Collections:** Bezalel Museum; Buffalo/Albright; Chicago/AI; Cleveland/MA; Cincinnati/AM; Hirshhorn; Kansas City/Nelson; Los Angeles/County MA; MMA; MOMA; Milwaukee; Museum des 20. Jahrhunderts; Trenton/State; WMAA; Wichita/AM. **Bibliography:** *The Chicago Connection;* Dover.

HUOT, ROBERT. b. September 16, 1935, Staten Island, N.Y. **Studied:** Wagner College, BS; Hunter College. Traveled Europe, Africa, Greenland, Iceland, California. **Taught:** Hunter College, 1963-. **Awards:** National Council on the Arts. **Address:** RD 1, New Berlin, NY 13411. **Dealer:** Filmmakers Coop, 175 Lexington Avenue, NYC. **One-man Exhibitions:** (first) Stephen Radich Gallery, 1964, also 1965-67; Galerie Muller, 1967; Ziegler Gallery, 1968, 70; Galerie Schmela, 1968; Paula Cooper Gallery, 1969, 73; Colgate U., 1975; Paula Cooper Gallery, 1974. **Group:** Hudson River Museum, Yonkers, N.Y., 1964; Vassar College, 1964; SRGM; Systemic Painting, 1966; IV International Young Artists Exhibit, American-Japan, Tokyo, 1967; A.F.A., 1967; MOMA, The Art of the Real, 1968. **Collections:** Torrington Mfg. Corp. **Bibliography:** Alloway 3; Battcock, ed.; Goosen 1; Lippard, ed.; Murdock 1.

I

INDIANA, ROBERT. b. September 13, 1928, New Castle, Ind. **Studied:** John Herron Art Institute, 1945-46; Munson-Williams-Proctor Institute, Utica, N.Y., 1947-48; Chicago Art Institute School, 1949-53, BFA; Skowhegan School, summer, 1953; U. of Edinburgh, Edinburgh College of Art, 1953-54; Aspen Institute, Artist-in-Residence, summer, 1968. Traveled USA, Mexico, Europe. **Commissions:** New York State Pavilion, New York World's Fair, 1964-65 (mural); New York State Theater, Lincoln Center for the Performing Arts, NYC (poster); costumes, sets, and poster for the Walker Art Center Opera Company's production of the Virgil Thomson-Gertrude Stein opera *The Mother of Us All*, Tyrone Guthrie Theater, Minneapolis, 1967; 8¢ US postage stamp (400,000,000 printed), 1973; Numerous Posters, banners, and several volumes of poetry with Robert Creely. **Awards:** Chicago/AI, Traveling Fellowship, 1953; Hon. DFA, Franklin and Marshall College, 1970; Indiana State Commission on the Arts Award, 1973; Hon. DFA, U. of Indiana, 1977. **Address:** Vinalhaven, ME 04863. **One-man Exhibitions:** (first) The Stable Gallery, 1962, also 1964, 66; ICA, Boston, 1963; Walker, 1963 (two-man, with Richard Stankiewicz); Rolf Nelson Gallery, Los Angeles, 1965; Dayton's Gallery 12, Minneapolis, 1966; Galerie Schmela, 1966; Eindhoven, 1966; Krefeld/Haus Lange, 1966; Wurttembergischer Kunstverein, Stuttgart, 1966; ICA, U. of Pennsylvania, 1968; San Antonio/McNay, 1968; Indianapolis/Herron, 1968; Toledo/MA, 1968; Hunter Gallery, Aspen, Colo., 1968; Creighton U., 1969; St. Mary's College (Ind.), 1969; Colby College, 1969; Dartmouth College, 1970; Bowdoin College, 1970; Brandeis U., 1970; Badischer Kunstverein, Karlsruhe, 1971; Humlebaek/Louisiana, 1972; Galerie Denise Rene, NYC, 1972, 75, 76; Didrichsenin Konsmuseum, Helsinki, 1972; Santa Fe, N.M., 1976; U. of Texas, Austin, 1977; Norfolk/Chrysler, 1977; Indianapolis, 1978; Purchase/SUNY, 1978; Art Center, South Bend, 1978; Flint/Institute, 1984; NMAA, 1984. **Group:** MOMA, The Art of Assemblage, circ., 1961; Chicago/AI Annual, 1963; WMAA, New Directions in American Painting, 1963; ICA, London, The Popular Image, 1963; Bertrand Russell Peace Foundation, Woburn Abbey, England, 1963; MOMA, Americans 1963, circ., 1963-64; Tate, Dunn International, 1964; Tate, Painting and Sculpture of a Decade, 1954-64, 1964; Museum des 20. Jahrhunderts, 1964; New York World's Fair, 1964-65; WMAA Annuals, 1964, 65, 67, Sculpture Annual, 1966; Corcoran Biennial, 1965; Palais des Beaux-Arts, Brussels, 1965; WMAA, A Decade of American Drawings, 1965; SRGM, 1965; Milwaukee, 1965; U. of Illinois, 1965, 67; PAFA, 1966; ICA, Boston, 1966; Eindhoven, Kunst-Licht-Kunst, 1966; Expo '67, Montreal 1967; VI International Art Biennial, San Marino (Europe), 1967; IX Sao Paulo Biennial, 1967; Carnegie, 1967; Dublin/Municipal, I International Quadrennial (ROSC), 1967; Documenta IV, Kassel, 1968; Chicago/Contemporary, 1968; WMAA, Contemporary American Sculpture, Selection II, 1969; Cologne, 1969; Fine Arts Academy of Finland, Helsinki, 1969; Jewish Museum, Superlimited, 1969; WMAA, Seventy Years of American Art, 1969; Hayward Gallery, London, Pop Art, 1969; ICA, U. of Pennsylvania, Highway, 1970; Cincinnati/Contemporary, Monumental Art, 1970; Foundation Maeght, L'Art Vivant, 1970; Museo de Arte Contemporaneo, Cali, Colombia, S.A., I Bienal Graficas, 1971; Dusseldorf, Zero Raum, 1973; WMAA (downtown), Nine Artists/Coenties Slip, 1974; WMAA, American Pop Art, 1974; Newport, R.I., Monumenta, 1974; Hirshhorn, Inaugural Exhibition, 1974; Corcoran, 1975; MOMA, American Art since 1945, 1975; Philadelphia College of Art, Artists' Sets and Costumes, 1977; Indianapolis, Perceptions of the Spirit in 20th Century American Art, 1977. **Collections:** Aachen/NG; Allentown/AM; Amsterdam/Stedelijk; Baltimore/MA; Brandeis U.; Brigham Young U.; Buffalo/Albright; Carnegie; Cologne; Detroit/Institute; Delaware Art Museum; U. of Dublin; Eindhoven; Honolulu Academy; Humlebaek/Louisiana; ICA, U. of Pennsylvania; U. of Illinois; Indianapolis; Indianapolis/Herron; Krefeld/Kaiser Wilhelm; Los Angeles/County MA; MMA; MOMA; U. of Michigan; U. of Nebraska; Oklahoma; Purchase/SUNY; Ridgefield/Aldrich; SFMA; Spelman College; Stanford U.; U. of Texas; Toronto; VMFA; WGMA; WMAA; Walker; Wuppertal/von der Heydt. **Bibliography:** Alloway 1; Calas, N. and E.; Dienst 1; Diamonstein; Honisch and Jensen, eds.; Hunter, ed.; *Kunst um 1970;* Lippard 5; **McCoubrey 2;** *Monumenta;* Russell and Gablik; Seitz 3; Weller. Archives.

INGLE, JOHN S. b. September 18, 1933, Evansville, Ind. **Studied:** U. of Arizona, BFA, 1964, MFA, 1966; Musées Royaux des Beaux-Arts de Belgique, Brussels. **Taught:** U. of Minnesota, Morris, 1966-. **Awards:** Minnesota State Fair, 1st Prize, watercolor, 1976, 77, 78. Traveled Europe. **Address:** 210 Colorado Avenue, Morris,

John Stuart Ingle   *Still Life with Daguerrotypes* 1985

Minn. 56267. **Dealer:** Tatistcheff & Co., NYC. **One-man Exhibitions:** (first) U. of Arizona, Tucson, 1966; Springfield College, 1975; Southwest State U., Marshall, Minn., 1976; Capricorn Gallery, Bethesda, Md., 1979; Tatistcheff & Co., 1981, 83, 85; Transco Energy Gallery, Houston, 1985. **Group:** Springfield, Mo./AM, Watercolor USA, 1976, 77, 78; PAFA, Contemporary American Realism Since 1960, circ., 1981; Chicago/AI, Perspectives on Contemporary American Realism, 1983; SFMA, American Realism (Janss), circ., 1985. **Collections:** Allied Bank of Texas, Houston; Chemical Bank; Evansville; Little Rock/MFA; MMA; McCrory Corporation, NYC; Metropolitan Life Ins. Oc., NYC; St. Louis/City; Philip Morris Collection; Springfield, Mo./AM.

INSLEY, WILL. b. October 15, 1929, Indianapolis, Ind. **Studied:** Amherst College, BA, 1951; Harvard U., B. Arch., 1955. Traveled USA, Europe. US Army, 1955-57. **Taught:** Oberlin College, Artist-in-Residence, 1966; U. of North Carolina, 1967-68; Cornell U., 1969; School of Visual Arts, NYC, 1969; Cooper Union, 1972. **Commissions:** Great Southwest Industrial Park, 1968; Cambridge Arts Council, 1978. **Awards:** National Council on the Arts, 1966; Guggenheim Foundation Fellowship, 1969-70. **Address:** 231 Bowery, NYC 10002. **Dealers:** Max Protetch, NYC; Galerie Annemarie Verna, Zurich; Paul Maenz, Cologne. **One-man Exhibitions:** (first) Amherst College, 1951; The Stable Gallery, NYC, 1965-68; Oberlin College, 1967; U. of North Carolina, 1967; Walker, 1968; Buffalo/Albright, 1968; Cornell U. (three-man), 1969; ICA, U. of Pennsylvania, 1969; John Gibson Gallery, 1969; MOMA, 1971; School of Visual Arts, NYC, 1972; Paul Maenz Gallery, Cologne, 1972; Krefeld/Haus Lange, 1973; Fischbach Gallery, NYC, 1973, 74, 76; Galerie Annemarie Verna, Zurich, 1974; Stuttgart/WK, 1974; Wisconsin State U., Max Protetch, NYC, 1977, 80, 82, 84; Protetch/McIntosh, Washington, D.C., 1977; Galerie Orny, Munich, 1978; SRGM, 1984. **Group:** WMAA Annuals, 1965, 67; Riverside Museum, 1966; SRGM, Systemic Painting, 1966; U. of Illinois, 1967; VI International Art Biennial, San Marino (Europe), 1967; U. of North Carolina, 1967; Ridgefield/Aldrich, 1968; J. L. Hudson Art Gallery, Detroit, 1968; New Delhi, First World Triennial, 1968; ICA, U. of Pennsylvania, 1969; Fort Worth, Drawings, 1969; Foundation Maeght, L'Art Vivant, 1970; Finch College, NYC, Projected Art, 1971; Arnhem, Sonsbeek '71, 1971; U. of Washington, Drawing from New York, 1972; ICA, U. of Pennsylvania, Grids, 1972; Documenta V, Kassel, 1972; WMAA, American Drawings: 1963-1973, 1973; Tyler School of Art, Philadelphia, American Drawings, 1973; Kennedy Center, Art Now '74, 1974; Minnesota/MA, Drawings USA '75, 1975; Stamford (Conn.)/Museum, American Salon des Refuses, 1976; Rice U., Drawing Today in New York, 1976; Documenta VI, Kassel, 1977; ICA, U.

of Pennsylvania, Dwellings, 1978; U. of North Carolina, Drawings about Drawings, 1979; Hayward Gallery, London, Pier and Ocean, 1980; Humlebaek/Louisiana, American Drawings of the Seventies, circ., 1981; ICA, U. of Pennsylvania, Connections, 1983; Hirshhorn, Dreams and Nightmares, 1984; Fort Wayne/AM, Indiana Influence, 1984. **Collections:** Brandeis U.; Colby College; U. of North Carolina. **Bibliography:** Alloway 3; *Art Now 74*; Battcock, ed.; Kren; Lucie-Smith.

IPPOLITO, ANGELO. b. November 9, 1922, St. Arsenio, Italy. **Studied:** Ozenfant School of Art, NYC, 1946-47; Brooklyn Museum School, 1948; Instituto Meschini, Rome, 1949-50. Traveled Europe. **Taught:** Cooper Union, 1956-59, 1962-64; Sarah Lawrence College, 1957; Yale U., Visiting Critic, 1961; U. of California, Berkeley, 1961-62; Queens College, 1963-64; Michigan State U., Artist-in-Residence, 1966-67; Binghamton/SUNY, 1971-. A cofounder of the Tanager Gallery, NYC. **Commissions:** New York Hilton Hotel, 1963. **Awards:** Fulbright Fellowship (Italy), 1959. **Address:** Friendsville Stage, Binghamton, NY 13903. **Dealer:** Grace Borgenicht Gallery, NYC. **One-man Exhibitions:** (first) Galleria della Rotondo, Bergamo, 1950; Tanager Gallery, NYC, 1954, 62; The Bertha Schaefer Gallery, 1956, 58; HCE Gallery, Provincetown, Mass., 1957, 61; Massillon Museum; Canton (Ohio) Museum; Cleveland Institute of Art, 1960; U. of California, 1961; Michigan State U., 1962; Bolles Gallery, 1962 (two-man, with Harold P. Paris); Grace Borgenicht Gallery, NYC, 1962, 64, 67, 72, 75, 77, 84; Jesse Besser Museum, Alpena, Mich., 1968; Albion College, 1969; Western Michigan U., 1969; Grand Valley State College, Allandale, Mich., 1970; City Hall, Binghamton, N.Y., 1982. **Retrospective:** Binghamton/SUNY, 1975. **Group:** Arts Club of Chicago, 1953; Walker, Vanguard,

Angelo Ippolito *August Landscape* 1973

1955; Utica, 1955, 57; SMAA Annuals, 1955, 57, 59, 62; USIA, 20th Century Graphics, circ., 1956-58; WMAA, Young America, 1957; A.F.A., College in America, circ., 1957-58; WMAA, Nature in Abstraction, 1958; VI Sao Paulo Biennial, 1961; Silvermine Guild, 1963; IIE, 1975. **Collections:** U. of California; Chase Manhattan Bank; CIT Corporation; General Electric Corp.; Hirshhorn; Lehman Bros.; IIE; MMA; MOMA; Massillon Museum; Michigan State U.; U. of Michigan; Milwaukee; Montreal Trust Co.; NYU; Norfolk/Chrysler; Phillips; Purchase/SUNY; Sarah Lawrence College; Utica; WMAA. **Bibliography:** Baur 5; Goodrich and Baur 1; Janis and Blesh 1; Sandler 1.

IRWIN, ROBERT. b. 1928, Long Beach, Calif. **Studied:** Otis Art Institute, 1938-50; Jepson Art Institute, Los Angeles, 1951. **Taught:** Chouinard Art Institute, 1957-58; UCLA, 1962; U. of California, Irvine, 1968-69. **Awards:** MacArthur Fellowship, 1984-89. **Address:** 2926 Kellogg Street, San Diego, Calif. 92106. **Dealer:** The Pace Gallery, NYC. **One-man Exhibitions:** Felix Landau Gallery, 1975; Ferus Gallery, Los Angeles, 1959, 60, 62, 64; Pasadena/AM, 1960, 68; The Pace Gallery, 1966, 68, 69, 71, 73, 74, 85; Los Angeles/County MA (two-man), 1966; Jewish Museum, 1968; Fort Worth (two-man), 1969; MOMA, 1970; Walker, 1971, 76; ACE Gallery, Los Angeles, 1972; Harvard U., 1972; Ileana Sonnabend Gallery, Paris, 1972; Wright

State U., 1974; U. of California, Santa Barbara, 1974; Mizuno Gallery, Los Angeles, 1972, 74, 76; Fort Worth, 1975; Chicago/Contemporary, 1975; Palomar College, San Marcos, Calif., 1975; Walker, 1976; Mizuno Gallery, Los Angeles, 1976; U. of California, San Diego, 1983; Public Safety Building, Seattle, 1984; Humlebaek/Louisiana, 1982. **Retrospective:** WMAA, 1977. **Group:** Los Angeles/County MA, Annual, 1952-53, 1956-60; WMAA Annual, 1957; UCLA, 1960; SFMA, Fifty California Artists, circ., 1962; MOMA, The Responsive Eye, 1965; VIII Sao Paulo Biennial, 1965; Vancouver, 1968; Documenta IV, Kassel, 1968; Walker, 1968; Eindhoven, Kompas, 1970; U. of Washington, 1971; Corcoran, 1971; Hayward Gallery, London, 11 Los Angeles Artists, 1971; SMFA, Works in Spaces, 1973; Kennedy Center, Art Now '74, 1974; Long Beach State U., Transparencies, 1975; WMAA, 200 Years of American Sculpture, 1976; Philadelphia College of Art, Projects for PCA, 1976; ICA, U. of Pennsylvania, Urban Encounters, 1980. **Collections:** Art Gallery of New South Wales; Buffalo/Albright; U. of California, Berkeley; U. of California, San Diego; Boston/MFA; Chicago/AI; Cleveland/MA; Des Moines; Fort Worth; Harvard U.; La Jolla; Los Angeles/County MA; MOMA; Melbourne/National; Omaha/Joslyn; Pasadena/AM; Public Safety Building, Seattle, Wash.; RISD; SFMA; Sydney/AG; Tate Gallery; Vancouver; WMAA; Walker; Wellesley College.

Bibliography: Art Now 74; Davis, D.; Drawings of the Pluralist Decade; Robert Irwin; Report; The State of California Painting; Transparency; Tuchman 3; USA West Coast.

ITO, MIYOKO. b. 1918, Berkeley, Calif.; **d.** August 18, 1983, Chicago, Ill. **Studied:** U. of Calif., Berkeley, BA, 1942; Smith College; School of the Art Institute of Chicago. **Awards:** MacDowell Colony Fellowship, 1970-77; Guggenheim Foundation Fellowship, 1977. **One-man Exhibitions:** Hyde Park Art Center, Chicago, 1971; Phyllis Kind Gallery, Chicago, 1973, 80, 81; Kornblee Gallery, NYC, 1976; Phyllis Kind Gallery, NYC, 1978, 82, 85. **Retrospective:** U. of Chicago, 1980. **Group:** WMAA Biennial, 1975; School of the Art Institute of Chicago, Former Famous Alumni, 1976; U. of Illinois, 1976; Sacramento/Crocker, The Chicago Connection, 1977; Chicago Public Library Cultural Center, Masterpieces of Chicago Art, 1977; U. of Northern Iowa, Contemporary Chicago Painters, 1978; Chicago/AI, Chicago and Vicinity, 1981. **Collections:** AT&T, NYC; Atlantic Richfield, Co., San Francisco; Chicago/AI; Illinois State U.; U. of Illinois; Kemper Insurance Co.; Madison Art Center; McDermott, Will and Emery, Chicago; NMAA; PAFA; SFMA; Vulcan Materials Co., New Orleans. **Bibliography:** Adrian; Chicago Connection.

J

JACQUETTE, YVONNE. **b.** December 15, 1934, Pittsburgh, Pa. **Studied:** RISD, 1952-56, with John Frazier; privately with Herman Cherry. Traveled Europe, Japan. **Taught:** Moore College of Art, Philadelphia, 1972; U. of Pennsylvania, 1972-75, 79-84; Tyler School of Art, Philadelphia, 1974; Parsons School of Design, NYC, 1974-78. **Member:** Artists Equity. **Commissions:** North Central Bronx Hospital, N.Y.; GSA, federal building and post office, Bangor, Maine. **Awards:** Ingram Merrill Foundation grant, 1975; CAPS, grant, 1979; N.Y. Foundation for the Arts, grant, 1985. **m.** Rudolph Burckhardt. **Address:** 50 West 29th Street, NYC 10001. **Dealer:** Brooke Alexander, Inc. **One-man Exhibitions:** (first) Swarthmore College, 1965; Fischbach Gallery, NYC, 1971, 74; Tyler School of Art, Philadelphia, 1972; Brooke Alexander, Inc., NYC, 1974, 76, 79, 81, 82, 83, 86; St. Louis/City, 1983; Seibu Museum of Art, Tokyo, 1985. **Group:** Vassar College, Realism Now, 1968; U. of North Carolina, Art on Paper, 1969; Buffalo/Albright, Cool Realism, 1970; WMAA Annual, 1972; New York Cultural Center, Women Choose Women, 1972; WMAA, Drawings 1963-1973; 1973; Chicago/AI, Small Scale in Contemporary Art, 1975; Minnesota/MA, Drawings USA, 1975; San Antonio/McNay, American Artists '76, 1976; P.S. 1, Long Island City, Couples, 1979; Brooklyn Museum, American Drawings in Black & White, 1970-1979, 1980; MOMA, New Work on Paper I, circ., 1981; Brooklyn Museum, The American Artist as Printmaker, 1983; Hirshhorn, Drawing 1974-1984, 1984; MOMA, International Survey of Con-

temporary Painting and Sculpture, 1984; Taft Museum, Night Lights, 1985. **Collections:** Akron/AI; Colby College; Corcoran; Minnesota/MA; MMA; U. of North Carolina; Pomona College; RISD; Yale U. **Bibliography:** Arthur 2; Gettings; Lippard 3; *Poets and Painters.*

JAUDON, VALERIE. **b.** August 6, 1945, Mississippi. **Studied:** Mississippi U. for Women, 1963-65; U. of the Americas, Mexico City, 1966-67; St. Martin's School of Art, London, 1968-69; Memphis Academy of Arts, 1965. Traveled Mexico, Europe. **Taught:** School of Visual Arts, NYC, 1983-84; Hunter College, 1986. **Commission:** ceiling mural, Insurance Co. of North America, Philadelphia, 1977. **Awards:** CAPS, 1980; Mississippi Institute of Arts & Letters, art award, 1981. **Address:** 139 Bowery, NYC 10002. **Dealer:** Sidney Janis Gallery, NYC. **One-man Exhibitions:** (first) Holly Solomon Gallery, NYC, 1977, 78, 79, 81; PAFA, 1977; Galerie Bischofberger, Zurich, 1979; Galerie Hans Strelow, Dusseldorf, 1980; James Corcoran Gallery, Los Angeles, 1981; Amerika Haus, Berlin, 1983; Dart Gallery, Chicago, 1983; Sidney Janis Gallery, 1983, 85; Quadrat Gallery, Bottrop, 1983; Fay Gold Gallery, Atlanta, 1985; McIntosh/Drysdale Gallery, Washington, D.C., 1985. **Group:** Sarah Lawrence College, Painting 1975-77, 1977; P.S. 1, Queens, Pattern Painting at P.S. 1, 1977; Utica, Critic's Choice, 1976-77, 1977; Rice U., Pattern and Decoration, 1978; Rutgers U., Decorative Art: Recent Work, 1978; Claremont College, Black and White Are Colors, 1979; Day-

Valerie Jaudon *File* 1986

ton/AI, Patterns Plus, 1979; Brussels/Beaux-Arts, Patterning Painting, 1979; Mannheimer Kunstverein, Mannheim, Dekor, 1980, Aachen, Les Nouveau Fauves/Die Neuen Wilden, 1980. **Collections:** Aachen/Ludwig; Harvard U.; Hirshhorn; Humlebaek/Louisiana; Indiana U.; Ridgefield/Aldrich. **Bibliography:** *Black and White Are Colors.*

JENKINS, PAUL. b. July 12, 1923, Kansas City, Mo. **Studied:** Kansas City Art Institute and School of Design, 1938-41; US Naval Air Corps, 1943-45; ASL, 1948-51. Also resides Paris, 1953-. Published *Anatomy of A Cloud,* autobiography, 1983. **Member:** The Century Association. **Awards:** Corcoran Biennial, Silver Medal, 1966; Golden Eagle Award for a film, *The Ivory Knife,* of which he is the subject, 1966; Honorary Doctor of Humanities, Linwood College, 1973. Officer des Arts et Lettres, 1980; Commandeur des Arts et Lettres, France, 1983. **Address:** 169 East 94th Street, NYC 10028; studio: 831 Broadway, NYC 10003. **Dealers:** Gimpel & Weitzenhoffer Ltd., NYC; Elaine Horwitch Gallery, Scottsdale, Ariz.; Galerie Michel Delorme, Paris; Gallery Art

Point, Tokyo. **One-man Exhibitions:** (first) Studio Paul Facchetti, Paris, 1954; Zimmergaleries Franck, Frankfurt am Main, 1954; Zoe Dusanne Gallery, Seattle, 1955; Martha Jackson Gallery, 1956, 58, 60, 61, 64, 66, 68, 69, 70, 71; Galerie Stadler, Paris, 1957, 59; A. Tooth & Sons, London, 1960, 63; Galerie Karl Flinker, 1960, 61, 63, 65, 73, 76; Galleria Toninelli, Milan, 1962; Galerie Charles Leinhard, Zurich, 1962; Galleria Odyssia, Rome, 1962; Cologne/Kunstverein, 1962; Esther Robles Gallery, 1963; Eva de Buren Gallery, Stockholm, 1963; Hannover/K-G, 1964; Tokyo Gallery, 1964; Court Gallery, Copenhagen, 1964; Gutai Museum, Osaka, 1964; Gertrude Kasle Gallery, 1965, 71; Gallery of Modern Art, 1965, 66; Makler Gallery, Philadelphia, 1966; SRGM, 1966; Moss Gallery Ltd., Toronto, 1968; Daniel Gervis Gallery, Paris, 1968; Bernard Raeder Gallery, Lausanne, 1968; Richard Gray Gallery, 1971; Suzanne Saxe Gallery, San Francisco, 1971; SFMA, 1972; Images Gallery, Toledo, 1972; Gimpel Fils, London, 1972, 80, 82, 86; Corcoran, 1972; Baukunst Galerie, Cologne, 1974; Gimpel & Weitzenhoffer Ltd., 1974, 76, 78, 79, 81, 83, 85; Galerie Ulysses, Vienna, 1974; Galerie Tanit, Munich, 1975; Galerie Farber, Brussels, 1975; Ohio U., 1975; Miami U., Oxford, 1975; Ft. Lauderdale, 1975; Carone Gallery, Ft. Lauderdale, 1975; A.B. Classon Co., Cincinnati, 1975, 77; Tampa Bay Art Center, 1975; Montgomery Museum, 1975; Columbus, 1975; Haslem Fine Arts, Inc., Washington, D.C., 1976; Gimpel & Hanover, Zurich, 1977; La Galerie Cour St.-Pierre, Geneva, 1977; Contemporary Gallery, Dallas, 1977; Tulsa/Philbrook, 1977; Diane Gilson Gallery, Seattle, 1977; Galleria d'Arte Narciso, Turin, 1978; Balcon des Arts, Paris, 1978; Elaine Horwitsch Gallery, Scottsdale, 1978, 79, 80; Carone Gallery, Fort Lauderdale, Fla., 1981, 84; Galerie Georges Fall, Paris, 1982, 83, 85; Maison Internationale du Theatre, Theatre du Rond-Point, Paris, 1981; Samuel Stein Gallery, Chicago, 1981;

Paul Jenkins *Phenomena White Shadow* 1984

Nicoline Pon Gallery, Zurich, 1982; Contemporary Gallery, Dallas, 1982, 83; Amherst College, 1983; Dunkerque/MAC, 1984; Gallery Moos, Toronto, 1985; Galerie Sapone, Nice, 1985; Gallery Art Point, Tokyo, 1986. **Retrospectives:** Hannover/KG, 1964; Houston/MFA, 1971; Palais des Beaux Arts, Charleroi, Belgium, 1974; Palm Springs Desert Museum, 1980. **Group:** Musée du Petit Palais, Paris, 1955; MOMA, Recent Drawings USA, 1956; Arts Council Gallery, London, New Trends in Painting, 1957; WMAA, Young America, 1957; WMAA, Nature in Abstraction, 1958; Carnegie, 1958, 61; Corcoran, 1958, 66; SRGM, Abstract Expressionists and Imagists, 1961; Salon du Mai, Paris, 1962; Seattle World's Fair, 1962; WMAA Annuals, 1962, 65; Art:USA:Now, circ., 1962-67; Salon des Realites Nouvelles, Paris, 1963; Tate, Painting and Sculpture of a Decade, 1954-64, 1964; PAFA, 1965; ICA, Boston, Painting without a Brush, 1965; M. Knoedler & Co., Art Across America, circ., 1965-67; Smithsonian, 1966; U. of Illinois, 1967, 68; U. of Oklahoma, 1968; Indianapolis, 1969; U. of California, Santa Barbara, 1970; VMFA, American Painting 1970, 1970; Brooklyn Museum, Annual, 1970; Musée des Beaux Arts de Caen, Peinture Contemporaine, 1970; U. of Illinois, 1971; Indianapolis, 1974, 76; Springfield, Mass./MFA, Watercolor USA, 1977; Butler/Youngstown, Midyear Show, 1978, 85; Brooklyn Museum, Homer, Sargent and the American Watercolor Tradition, 1984. **Collections:** Amsterdam/Stedelijk; Baltimore/MA; Bezalel Museum; Brooklyn Museum; Buffalo/Albright; Busch-Reisinger Museum; U. of California, Berkeley; Cologne/Kunstverein; Columbus; Corcoran; Dallas/MFA; Des Moines; Detroit; France/National; Hannover/K-G; Hirshhorn; U. of Illinois; Indianapolis; Jewish Museum; Liverpool/Walker; Los Angeles/County MA; Louisville State; MIT; Milwaukee; MOMA; Musée Guimet; NCFA; National Museum of Western Art, Tokyo; Niigata Museum; Norfolk/Chrysler; Paris/Beaubourg; PMA; Seattle/AM; SRGM; Stanford U.; Stuttgart; Tate; U. of Texas; Toronto; Victoria and Albert Museum; U. of Virginia; Walker; WMAA; Worcester/AM. **Bibliography: Elsen 1; Jenkins with Jenkins; Nordland 4;** Sandler 1. Archives.

JENNEY, NEIL. b. 1945, Torrington, Conn. Autodidact. **Address:** 69 Wooster Street, NYC 10012. **Dealer:** Blum Helman Gallery, NYC. **One-man Exhibitions:** (first) Galerie Rudolf Zwirner, Cologne, 1968; Noah Goldowsky Gallery, NYC, 1970; David Whitney Gallery, NYC, 1970; Blum Helman Gallery, 1975; Hartford/Wadsworth, 1975. **Group:** Cornell U., Earthart, 1969; Berne, When Attitude Becomes Form, circ., 1969; WMAA, Anti-Illusion: Procedures/Materials, 1969; WMAA, New Image Painting, 1978; Amsterdam/Stedelijk, '60–'80 Attitudes/Concepts/Images, 1982. **Collections:** WMAA. **Bibliography:** *Back to the USA;* De Wilde 2; Murken-Altrogge; Rosenthal.

JENNIS, STEVAN. b. 1945, Newark, N.J. **Studied:** San Fernando Valley College, 1967, BFA; UCLA, 1970, MA; U. of Massachusetts, 1973, MFA. **Taught:** Mount Holyoke College, 1973; U. of Massachusetts, 1973-74. **Awards:** CAPS grant, 1979. **Address:** 434 Greenwich Street, NYC 10013. **Dealer:** Barbara Toll Gallery, NYC. **One-man Exhibitions:** ICA, Boston, 1972; Hundred Acres Gallery, NYC, 1972, 75; Westfield State College, 1976; Robert Feidus Gallery, NYC, 1978; Barbara Toll Gallery, 1979, 80, 82, 85; Connecticut

College, 1979. **Group:** U. of North Carolina, Art on Paper, 1975, 82; WMAA, Recent Drawings by Younger Artists, 1978; Buffalo/Albright, With Paper, About Paper, 1980; ICA, Los Angeles, Wallpaper/Roompaper, 1981; Chicago/Contemporary, Dogs!, 1983; Denver/AM, Another Great Love Affair, 1983; Hudson River Museum, New Vistas, 1984. **Collections:** U. of Massachusetts; Newark Museum; U. of North Carolina; Purchase/SUNY; Washington and Jefferson College.

JENSEN, ALFRED. b. December 11, 1903, Guatemala City, Guatemala; **d.** April 4, 1981, Livingston, N.J. **Studied:** San Diego Fine Arts School, 1925; Hofmann School, Munich, 1927-28; Academie Scandinave, Paris, with Charles Despiau, Charles Dufresne, Othon Friesz, Marcel Gromaire, Andre Masson. Traveled USA, Europe. **Taught:** Maryland Institute, 1958. **Commissions:** Time Inc. (mural). **Awards:** Tamarind Fellowship, 1965. **One-man Exhibitions:** (first) John Heller Gallery, NYC, 1952; Tanager Gallery, NYC, 1955; The Bertha Schaefer Gallery, 1957; Martha Jackson Gallery, 1957, 59, 61, 67; SRGM, 1961; Fairleigh Dickinson U., 1963; The Graham Gallery, 1963-65; Klipstein & Kornfeld, Berne, 1964; Rolf Nelson Gallery, Los Angeles, 1964; Kunsthalle, Basel, 1964 (two-man, with Franz Kline); Amsterdam/Stedelijk, 1964; Ziegler Gallery, 1966; Cordier & Ekstrom, Inc., 1967, 68, 70; The Pace Gallery, NYC, 1972, 73, 76, 83, 84; Hannover/K-G, 1973; Humlebaek/Louisiana, 1973; Kunsthalle, Baden-Baden, 1973; Dusseldorf/Kunsthalle, 1973; Berne, 1973; SRGM, 1984. **Retrospective:** Buffalo/Albright, circ., 1977. **Group:** San Diego; Baltimore/MA; MOMA; The Stable Gallery, 1954-57; II Inter-American Paintings and Prints Biennial, Mexico City, 1960; ICA, Boston, 1960; Chicago/AI, 1961; Corcoran Biennial, 1962; WMAA, Geometric Abstraction in America, circ.,

1962; WMAA Annual, 1963; Los Angeles/County MA, Post Painterly Abstraction, 1964; XXXII Venice Biennial, 1964; International Biennial Exhibition of Paintings, Tokyo; Buffalo/Albright, Plus by Minus, 1968; Documenta IV, Kassel, 1968; Lafayette College, Black-White, 1969; Indianapolis, 1970; VMFA, 1970; WMAA, The Structure of Color, 1971; ICA, U. of Pennsylvania, Grids, 1972; Documenta V, Kassel, 1972; WMAA Biennials, 1973, 77; Sao Paulo Biennial, 1977; Brandeis U., Aspects of the 70's: Mavericks, 1980. **Collections:** American Republic Insurance Co.; Baltimore/MA; Brandeis U.; Chase Manhattan Bank; Dayton/AI; Health and Hospital Corp.; MOMA; SRGM; San Diego; Time Inc.; WMAA. **Bibliography: Alfred Jensen;** Calas, N. and E.; *From Foreign Shores;* Honisch and Jensen, eds.; *Kunst um 1970;* MacAgy 2; Sandler 1; Tuchman 3.

Bill Jensen   *Denial*   1983–86

JENSEN, BILL. b. November 26, 1945, Minneapolis, Minn. **Studied:** U. of Minnesota, BFA, 1964, MFA, 1970, with Peter Busa. **Taught:** U. of Minnesota, 1968-70; Brooklyn Museum School, 1971-75. **Awards:** CAPS, 1978; National Endowment for the Arts, 1985. **Address:** 429 West 14th Street, NYC, 10014. **Dealer:** Washburn Gallery Inc., NYC. **One-man Exhibitions:** (first) U. of Minnesota, 1970; Fischback Gallery, 1973, 75; Washburn Gallery, 1980, 81, 82, 84, 86; MOMA, 1986. **Group:** P.S. 1, Long Island City, Rooms, 1976; P.S. 1, Long Island City, A Painting Show, 1977; WMAA Biennial, 1981; MIT, Affinities, 1983; U. of Chicago, The Meditative Surface, 1984; MOMA, International Survey of Recent Painting and Sculpture, 1984; WMAA, Five Painters in New York, 1984; Carnegie, International, 1985; Los Angeles/County AM, The Spiritual in Art, 1986. **Collections:** Carnegie; Chase Manhattan Bank; Harvard U.; Los Angeles/County MA; MMA; MOMA; Paine Webber Inc., NYC; WMAA;

Worcester/AM. **Bibliography:** Armstrong and Marshall; Tuchman 3.

JESS (COLLINS). b. 1923, Long Beach, Calif. **Studied:** California Institute of Technology, BS, 1948; California School of Fine Arts, 1949-51, with Clyfford Still, Edward Corbett, Elmer Bischoff, David Park, and Hassel Smith. Opened the King Ubu Gallery, San Francisco, in 1953, with Harry Jacobus and Robert Duncan. Traveled Europe. **Address:** 3267 20th Street, San Francisco, CA 94110. **Dealer:** Odyssia Gallery, NYC. **One-man Exhibitions:** The Place (a bar), San Francisco, 1954; Gump's Art Gallery, San Francisco, 1959; City Lights Book Shop, San Francisco, 1959; Dilexi Gally, San Francisco, 1960; Borregaard's Museum, San Francisco, 1961; Rolf Nelson Gallery, Los Angeles, 1965; Cheney Cowles Museum, Spokane, 1967; SFMA, 1968; Odyssia Gallery, NYC, 1971, 78; Chicago/Contemporary, 1972; MOMA, 1974; Hartford/Wadsworth, 1975; Galleria Odyssia, Rome, 1975; Dallas/MFA, circ., 1977; Newport Harbor, 1984; Gallery Paule Anglim, San Francisco, 1983. **Group:** King Ubu Gallery, San Francisco, 1953; MOMA, The Art of Assemblage, 1961; Oakland/AM, Pop Art USA, 1963; U. of New Mexico, The Painter and the Photograph, 1964; SFMA, Looking Back, 1968; ICA, U. of Pennsylvania, The Spirit of the Comics, 1969; Hayward Gallery, London, Pop Art Redefined, 1969; Chicago/AI, 70th American Exhibition, 1972; WMAA, Extraordinary Realities, 1973; U. of Illinois, 1974; Dallas/MFA, Poets of the Cities, 1974; SFMA, California Painting and Sculpture: The Modern Era, 1976; Indianapolis, Perceptions of the Spirit in 20th Century American Art, 1977; ICA, Boston, Narration, 1978. **Collections:** Chicago/AI; Dallas/MFA; MMA; MOMA; PMA. **Bibliography:** Tuchman 3.

JOHNS, JASPER. b. May, 1930, Augusta, Ga. **Studied:** U. of South Carolina. Artistic adviser to Merce Cunningham Dance Company. A director of the Foundation for Contemporary Performance Arts since 1963. **Member:** NIAL, 1973. **Awards:** Gallery of Modern Art, Ljubljana, Yugoslavia, VII International Exhibition of Prints, First Prize, 1967; IX Sao Paulo Biennial, 1967; Skowhegan School, Award for Graphics, 1977; New York City Mayor's Award of Honor for Arts and Culture, 1978; AAIAL, Gold Medal, 1986. **Address:** 225 East Houston Street, NYC 10002; St. Martin, French West Indies. **Dealer:** Leo Castelli Inc., NYC. **One-man Exhibitions:** Leo Castelli Inc., 1958, 60, 61, 63, 66, 68, 70, 71, 76, 77, 79, 81, 82, 84; Galleria d'Arte del Naviglio, Milan, 1959; Galerie Rive Droite, Paris, 1959, 61; Columbia, S.C./MA, 1960; U. of Minnesota, 1960; Ferus Gallery, Los Angeles, 1960 (two-man); Ileana Sonnabend Gallery, Paris, 1962; Everett Ellin Gallery, Los Angeles, 1962; Whitechapel Art Gallery, London, 1964; Pasadena/AM, 1965;

Jasper Johns *Untitled* 1984

Ashmolean Museum, Oxford, England, 1965; American Embassy, London, 1965; Minami Gallery, 1965; NCFA, 1966; MOMA, circ., 1968; Eva de Buren Gallery, Stockholm; Castelli-Whitney, NYC, 1969; PMA, 1970; U. of Iowa, 1970; MOMA, 1970; Minneapolis/Institute, 1971; Dayton's Gallery 12, Minneapolis, 1971; Chicago/Contemporary, 1971; MOMA, Thirty Lithographs: 1960-68, circ., 1972; Fendrick Gallery, Washington, D.C., 1972; Houston/MFA, 1972; Hofstra U., 1972; Lo Spazio, Rome, 1974; Modern Art Agency, Naples, 1974; Galerie Folker Skulima, Berlin, 1974; Galerie Mikro, Berlin, 1974; Museum of Modern Art, Oxford, England, 1974; Arts Council of Great Britain, Drawings, 1975; Janie C. Lee Gallery, Houston, 1976, 79; Brooke Alexander, NYC, 1977; Margo Leavin Gallery, Los Angeles, 1978, 81; Galerie Nancy Gillespie, Paris, 1978; Galerie Valeur,

Nagoya, 1978, 79; Baltimore/MA, 1978; John Berggruen Gallery, San Francisco, 1978; Basel, circ., 1979; Tucson Museum of Art, 1979; Getler/Pall and Patricia Heesey Fine Art, NYC, 1980; Greenberg Gallery, 1980; Toledo/MA, 1980; Tyler, Texas, 1980; Thomas Segal Gallery, Boston, 1981; Tate Gallery, 1981; L. A. Louver Gallery, Venice, Calif., 1982; WMAA, 1982; Akira Ikeda Gallery, Tokyo, 1983; Delahunty Gallery, Dallas, 1983; Lorence/Monk Gallery, NYC, 1985; Brooke Alexander, Inc., NYC, 1985; St. Louis/City, 1985. **Retrospectives:** Jewish Museum, 1964; Whitechapel Art Gallery, London, 1964; Pasadena/AM, 1965; WMAA, circ., 1977; MOMA, 1986. **Group:** Jewish Museum, The New York School, Second Generation, 1957; A.F.A., Collage in America, circ., 1957-58; Houston/MFA, Collage International, 1958; XXIX & XXXII Venice Biennials, 1958, 64; Carnegie, 1958, 61, 64, 67; Houston/MFA, Out of the Ordinary, 1959; Daniel Cordier, Paris, Exposition Internationale de Surrealisme, 1959; Columbus, Contemporary American Painting, 1960; A.F.A., School of New York—Some Younger American Painters, 1960; Martha Jackson Gallery, New Media—New Forms, I & II, 1960, 61; WMAA, Annuals, 1960, 61, 62, 64, 65; SRGM, Abstract Expressionists and Imagists, 1961; Dallas/MFA, 1961-62; SRGM/USIA, American Vanguard, circ., Europe, 1961-62; MOMA, Abstract Watercolors and Drawings: USA, circ., Europe, 1961-62; MOMA, Lettering by Hand, 1962; Seattle World's Fair, 1962; Berne, 4 Americans, 1962; Chicago/AI, 1962; Stockholm/National; Amsterdam/Stedelijk; Salon du Mai, Paris, 1962, 64; SRGM, Six Painters and the Object, circ., 1963; WGMA, The Popular Image, 1963; Musée Cantonal des Beaux-Arts, Lausanne, I Salon International de Galeries Pilotes, 1963; ICA, London, The Popular Image, 1963; Buffalo/Albright, Mixed Media and Pop Art, 1963; El Retiro Parquet, Madrid, Arte de America y Espana, 1963; Jewish Museum, Black and White, 1963; Hartford/Wadsworth, Black, White, and Gray, 1964; Tate, Dunn International, 1964; Tate, Painting and Sculpture of a Decade, 1954-64; SRGM, 1964; Documenta III & IV, Kassel, 1964, 68; Palais des Beaux-Arts, Brussels, 1965; MOMA, Art in the Mirror, 1966; Jewish Museum, 1966; Expo '67, Montreal, 1967; IX Sao Paulo Biennial, 1967; Gallery of Modern Art, Ljubljana, Yugoslavia, VII International Exhibition of Prints, 1967; MOMA, Dada, Surrealism and Their Heritage, 1968; Vancouver, 1969; Cincinnati/Contemporary, Monumental Art, 1970; Dublin/Municipal, International Quadriennial (ROSC), 1971; Chicago/Contemporary, White on White, 1971-72; ICA, U. of Pennsylvania, Grids, 1972; WMAA Biennial, 1973; New York Cultural Center, 3D into 2D, 1973; Seattle/AM, American Art— Third Quarter Century, 1973; Parcheggio di Villa Borghese, Rome, Contemporanea, 1973; Art Museum of South Texas, Corpus Christi, Eight Artists, 1974; Chicago/AI, Idea and Image in Recent Art, 1974; WMAA, American Pop Art, 1974; Walker, Eight Artists, 1974; NCFA, Sculpture, American Directions 1945-1975, 1975; MOMA, Drawing Now, 1976; Chicago/AI, 1976; A.F.A., American Master Drawings and Watercolors, 1976; Cambridge, Jubilation, 1977; Minnesota/MA, American Drawing, 1927-1977, circ., 1977; Amsterdam/Stedelijk, At Second Sight, 1978; WMAA, Art About Art, circ., 1978; Buffalo/Albright, American Painting of the 1970's, circ., 1978; Corcoran Biennial, 1979; WMAA, American Prints: Process and Proofs, 1981; Amsterdam/Stedelijk, '60–'80: Attitudes, Concepts, Images, 1982; MOMA, A Century of Modern Drawing, circ., 1982; Brooklyn Museum, The American Artist as Printmaker, 1983; Houston/Contemporary, American Still Life, 1945-1983, circ., 1983; MOMA, The Modern Drawing, 1983; Amsterdam/Stedelijk, La Grande Parade, 1984; WMAA, Blam!, 1984; MOMA, Pop Art: 1955-1970, circ., 1985; WMAA Biennial,

1985. **Collections:** Amsterdam/ Stedelijk; Basel; Buffalo/Albright; Cologne; Dallas/MFA; Des Moines; Hartford/Wadsworth;   Hirshhorn; Houston/MFA; MOMA; Ohara Art Museum; SFMA; Seibu Museum of Art, Tokyo; Stockholm/National; Tate; Victoria and Albert Museum; WMAA. **Bibliography:** Alloway 1; Battcock, ed.; Becker and Vostell; Bihalji-Merin; Calas, N. and E.; *Contemporanea;* **Crichton;** Danto; Davis, D.; De Vries, ed.; De Wilde 1, 2; Dienst 1; Downes, ed.; Finch; Friedman, ed.; Gablik; Gettings; Goldman 1; Haskell 5; Krauss 2, 3; Honnef; Hunter, ed.; Janis and Blesh 1; Honisch and Jensen, eds.; **Kozloff 2,** 3; Johnson, Ellen H.; Licht, F.; Lippard 5; Lynton; *Metro;* Murken-Altrogge; *Poets & Painters;* Rickey; Rodman 3; Rose, B., 1, 4; Rubin 1; Russell and Gablik; Sandler; Shapiro; Seitz 3; **Steinberg, L.;** Tomkins; Tomkins 2; Tomkins and Time-Life Books; Tuchman 3; Warhol and Hackett; Weller.

JOHNSON, BUFFIE. b. February 20, 1912, NYC. **Studied:** ASL; Atelier 17, Paris, with S. W. Hayter (engraving); UCLA, MA. Traveled extensively, Europe, Mexico, USA. **Taught:** Parsons School of Design, 1946-50; US State Department lecturer; UCLA; Aegina Art Center, Greece, 1973. **Member:** Artists Equity. **Commissions:** Astor Theater, NYC, 1959 (murals). **Awards:** Le Salon International de la Femme, Nice, Second Prize, 1970; Yaddo Fellowship, 1974. **Address:** 102 Greene Street, NYC 10012. **Dealer:** Ingber Art Gallery, NYC. **One-man Exhibitions:** (first) Jake Zeitlin Gallery, Los Angeles, 1937; Galerie Rotge, Paris, 1939; Wakefield Gallery, NYC, 1939; Vose Gallery, Boston, 1942; Caresse Crosby, Washington, D.C., 1944; "67" Gallery, NYC, 1945; Ringling, 1948; Galleria del Cavallino, Venice, 1948; Hanover Gallery, 1949; Galerie Colette Allendy, Paris, 1949; Betty Parsons Gallery, 1950; Choate School, Wallingford, Conn., 1951; Galleries Bing, Paris, 1956, 60;

Bodley Gallery, NYC, 1960; Thibaut Gallery, NYC, 1961; Granville Gallery, NYC, 1964; Galeria Antonio Souza, Mexico City, 1964; Max Hutchinson Gallery, 1973; Palm Beach Gallery, Palm Beach, Fla., 1975; New School for Social Research; Andre Zarre Gallery, NYC; Stamford Museum; Ringling; Landmark Gallery, NYC. **Group:** Carnegie, 1941; Art of This Century, NYC, 1943; Salon des Realites Nouvelles, Paris, 1949, 50; Baltimore/MA; Walker; Brooklyn Museum, 1950, 54; WMAA; U. of Illinois, 1955; Kunsthaus, Hamburg, American Women Artists, 1972; New York Cultural Center, Women Choose Women, 1973; WMAA Biennial; Cranbrook, Waves, 1974. **Collections:** Baltimore/MA; Bezalel Museum; Boston/MFA; Brooklyn Museum; Calcutta; Ciba-Geigy Corp.; Cincinnati/AM; City Investing Corp; Corcoran; Cornell U.; U. of Illinois; International Nickel Co.; Israel Museum; Layton School of Art; U. of Michigan; NCFA; NYU; Newark Museum; U. of New Mexico; New Orleans Museum; The Ohio State U.; Purchase/SUNY; RISD; Santa Barbara/MA; SRGM; Tanger Museum, Morocco; U. of Texas; Utica; Valley Bank of Springfield; WMAA; Walker; Yale U. **Bibliography:** Archives.

JOHNSON, LESTER. b. January 27, 1919, Minneapolis, Minn. **Studied:** Minneapolis Institute School (with Alexander Masley, Glen Mitchell), St. Paul School of Art (with Cameron Booth), Chicago Art Institute School, 1942-47. Traveled Europe. **Taught:** St. Bernard School, NYC, 1955-61; The Ohio State U., 1963; U. of Wisconsin, 1964; School of Visual Arts, NYC, 1964; Yale U., 1964-; American Center, Paris, summer, 1966; Director of Studies, Graduate Painting, Yale U., 1969-74. **Awards:** Alfred Pillsbury Scholarship; St. Paul Gallery Scholarship; Midwestern Artists Competition, First Prize, 1942; Guggenheim Foundation Fellowship, 1973; Brandeis U., Creative

Lester Johnson   *Untitled*   1983

Arts Award, Painting, 1978. **Address:** 191 Milbank Avenue, Greenwich, Conn., 06830. **Dealer:** Zabriskie Gallery, NYC & Paris. **One-man Exhibitions:** (first) Artists' Gallery, NYC, 1951; Korman Gallery, NYC, 1954; The Zabriskie Gallery, 1955, 57, 58, 59, 61; Sun Gallery, Provincetown, 1956-59; City Gallery, NYC, 1959; HCE Gallery, Provincetown, 1960-62; Minneapolis/Institute, 1961; B.C. Holland Gallery, 1962; Dayton/AI, 1962; Fort Worth; The Ohio State U.; Martha Jackson Gallery, NYC, 1962, 63, 66, 69, 71, 73, 74, 75; Donald Morris Gallery, Detroit, 1965, 74; 78; Smithsonian, 1968; Alpha Gallery, 1972; Gallery Moos, Toronto, 1973; Richard Gray Gallery, 1973; Ruth S. Schaffner Gallery, Santa Barbara, 1973, 74; Smith-Anderson Gallery, Palo Alto, 1974; Peter M. David Gallery, Minneapolis, 1974, 78; Livingstone-Learmonth Gallery, NYC, 1975; U. of Connecticut, Storrs, 1975; Alpha Gallery, Boston, 1976; Gimpel & Weitzenhoffer Ltd., NYC, 1977, 80; Gallery Moos Ltd., Toronto, 1977; Ruth S. Schaffner Gallery, Los Angeles, 1978; Louisiana State U., 1979; Gimpel Fils, London, 1979; Gimpel-Hanover, Zurich, 1980; Galerie Andre Emmerich, Zurich, 1980; Swain School of Art, New Bedford, Conn., 1980; Donald Morris Gallery, Birmingham, Mich., 1981; U. of Virginia, 1981; Alpha Gallery, Boston, 1982; Gimpel & Weitzenhoffer Gallery, NYC, 82; Paperwork Gallery, Larchmont, 1983; Zabriskie Gallery, NYC, 1983, 85; Kansas City/AI, 1984; U. of Hartford (two-man), 1984; David

Barnett Gallery, Milwaukee, 1985; Walter Moos Gallery, Toronto, 1986; Munson Gallery, New Haven, 1986. **Group:** PAFA; Minneapolis/Institute; Jewish Museum, The New York School, Second Generation, 1957; Minneapolis/Institute, American Painting, 1945-57; 1957; Baltimore/MA, Critics Choice, 1958; WMAA, 1958; 68, Annual 1967; ICA, Boston, 100 Works on Paper, circ., Europe, 1959; A.F.A., The Figure, circ., 1960; ICA, Boston, Future Classics, 1960; A.F.A., Graphics '60, 1960; Carnegie, 1961, 68; MOMA, Recent American Painting and Sculpture, circ., USA and Canada, 1961-62; Chicago/AI, Recent Trends in Painting, USA, 1962; MOMA, Recent Painting USA, The Figure, circ., 1962-62; Lehigh U., 1967; MOMA, The 1960's, 1967; Dublin/Municipal, I International Quadrennial (ROSC), 1967; U. of Kentucky, 1968; Madrid/Nacional, II Biennial, 1969; Star Turtle Gallery, NYC, The Tenants of Sam Wapnowitz, 1969; Philadelphia Art Alliance, 1969; Smithsonian, Neue Figuration USA, circ., 1969; Brooklyn Museum Print Biennial, 1970; Carnegie, 1970; U. of North Carolina, Works on Paper, 1971; SRGM, 10 Independents, 1972; Chicago/AI, 70th American Exhibition, 1972; Minnesota/MA, 1973; WMAA, 1973; NAD, 1974; Indianapolis, 1976; Provincetown Art Association, Provincetown Artists, 1977; Chicago/AI, 100 Years—100 Artists, 1979; Oklahoma, Masters of the Portrait, 1979; Ridgefield/Aldrich, Homo Sapiens: The Many Images, 1982; MMA, Aspects of the City, 1984; MOMA, Naked/Nude; Contemporary, 1986. **Collections:** U. of Arizona; Baltimore/MA; Buffalo/Albright; California College of Arts and Crafts; Chase Manhattan Bank; Chicago/AI; Ciba-Geigy Corp.; Dayton/AI; Detroit/Institute; Fort Worth; Goldring International; Hirshhorn; Hartford/Wadsworth; MOMA; U. of Michigan; Minneapolis/Institute; NCFA; U. of Nebraska; New School for Social Research; Norfolk/Chrysler; Northwestern U.; Ohio State U.; PMA; Philip Morris Collection; Phoenix; Purchase/SUNY; SRGM; Smithsonian; Stony Brook/SUNY; Tulsa/Philbrook; U.S. Steel Corp.; Walker; U. of Wisconsin; Yale U. **Bibliography:** Sandler 1.

JOHNSON, RAY. b. October 16, 1927, Detroit, Mich. **Studied:** ASL; Black Mountain College (with Josef Albers, Robert Motherwell, Mary Callery, Ossip Zadkine), 1945-48. **Member:** American Abstract Artists, 1949-52. Operates the New York Correspondence School. **Awards:** NIAL Grant, $2,000, 1966; National Endowment for the Arts, 1976, 77; CAPS, 1977. **Address:** 44 West Seventh Street, Locust Valley, NY 11560. **Dealer:** Brooks Jackson Gallery Iolas, NYC. **One-man Exhibitions:** (first) The Willard Gallery, 1965, also 1966, 67; Richard Feigen Gallery, Chicago, 1966, NYC, 1968, 70, 71; Wooster Community Art Center, Danbury, Conn., 1968; Kunstmarkt, Cologne, 1968; U. of Virginia, 1968; U. of British Columbia (two-man), 1969; Boylston Print Center Gallery, Cambridge, Mass.; U. of Sacramento, 1969; WMAA, New York Correspondence School, 1970; Betty Parsons Gallery, 1972; Angela Flowers Gallery, London, 1972; Jacob's Ladder Gallery, Washington, D.C., 1972; Chicago/AI, Correspondence Show, 1972; Marion Locks Gallery, Philadelphia, 1973; Gertrude Kasle Gallery, 1975; Massimo Valsecchi Gallery, Milan, 1975; Brooks Jackson Gallery Iolas, NYC, 1978; Sid Deutsch Gallery, NYC, 1976; Nassau County Museum of Fine Art, Roslyn Harbor, 1984. **Retrospective:** Raleigh/NCMA, 1976. **Group:** American Abstract Artists, 1949-52; MOMA, Art in the Mirror, 1966; Chicago/Contemporary, Pictures to be Read/Poetry to be Seen, 1967; Finch College, NYC; A.F.A., circ., 1967; Hayward Gallery, London, Pop Art, 1969; U. of British Columbia, Concrete Poetry, 1969; Fort Worth, Drawings, 1969; Dallas/MFA, Poets of the Cities, 1974. **Collections:** Chicago/AI; Dulin Gallery; Houston/MFA; Lincoln, Mass./

De Cordova; MOMA. **Bibliography:** Alloway 4; Becker and Vostell; *Correspondence;* Hansen; *Happening & Fluxus;* Ruhe; Russell and Gablik. Archives.

JOHNSTON, YNEZ. b. May 12, 1920, Berkeley, Calif. **Studied:** U. of California, Berkeley, BA, 1946, MA. Traveled Europe, USA, India, England, Italy, Japan. **Taught:** Colorado Springs Fine Arts Center, summers, 1945, 55; U. of California, Berkeley, 1950-51; Otis Art Institute; Fullerton College, 1982; Laguna Beach School of Art, 1984. **Commissions:** International Graphic Arts Society, 1958, 60. **Awards:** Guggenheim Foundation, Fellowship, 1952; MMA; 1952; L.C. Tiffany Grant, 1955; SFMA, James D. Phelan Award, 1958; Tamarind Fellowship, 1966; National Endowment for the Arts, 1976, 86. **Address:** 569 Crane Boulevard, Los Angeles, CA 90065. **Dealers:** Mekler Gallery, Los Angeles; Worthington Gallery, Inc., Chicago. **One-man Exhibitions:** SFMA, 1943; U. of Redlands, 1947; American Contemporary Gallery, Hollywood, 1948; Fraymont Gallery, Los Angeles, 1952; Chicago/AI, 1952 (two-man); Santa Barbara/MA, 1952, 57; Paul Kantor Gallery, Beverly Hills, Calif., 1952, 53, 57, 58, 59, 64; Pasadena/AM, 1954; Colorado Springs/FA, 1955; California Palace, 1956; Ohana Gallery, London, 1958; California State U., Long Beach, 1967; Moore Galeries, Inc., San Francisco, 1968; Benjamin Galleries, Chicago, 1969; Jodi Scully Gallery, 1971, 72, 74; Tokyo-Shoten Gallery, NYC, 1976; Elizabeth Weiner Gallery, NYC, 1977; Mitsukoshi Gallery, Tokyo, 1977; Cornell U., 1978; Mekler Gallery, Los Angeles, 1978, 82, 84; Ericson Gallery, NYC, 1979; Worthington Galleries, Inc., Chicago, 1979, 83, 86; Fullerton College, 1982; San Diego Print Club, 1982; Laguna Beach School of Art, 1984; Hank Baum Gallery, San Francisco, 1985. **Retrospective:** Mount San Antonio College, 1974. **Group:** WMAA, 1951-55; U. of Illinois, 1951-54; Carnegie, 1955; SFMA; Los Angeles/County MA; MOMA, New Talent; Ohio U., Ultimate Concerns, 1968; Palazzo Strozzi, Florence, Italy, I Biennale Internazionale della Grafica, 1968; California State U., Los Angeles, Small Images, 1969; California Institute of Technology, Pasadena, Four Printmakers, 1969; U. of Kentucky, Graphics '71, 1971; International Exhibitions Foundation, Washington, D.C., Tamarind; A Renaissance of Lithography, circ., 1971-72; Scripps College, California Women Artists, 1972; SFMA, Painting and Sculpture in California: The Modern Era, 1976; SFMA, World Print, 1977; College of St. Rose, Albany, N.Y., Drawing Invitational, 1980; Taipei, Taiwan, Second International Print Exhibition, 1985. **Collections:** Albion College; California State U., Los Angeles; Cedars-Sinai Medical Center, Los Angeles; Cornell U.; Fresno Art Center; Hartford/Wadsworth; Hirshhorn; U. of Illinois; Israel Museum; La Jolla; Los Angeles/County MA; MMA; MOMA; Michigan State U.; U. of Michigan; Milwaukee; Montclair/AM; Oakland; PMA; Pasadena/AM; RISD; St. Louis/City; San Diego; Santa Barbara/MA; Santa Fe, N.M.; Schaeffer School of Design; Tulsa/Philbrook; Tusculum College; WMAA. **Bibliography:** Pousette-Dart, ed.

JONES, JOHN PAUL. b. November 18, 1924, Indianola, Iowa. **Studied:** State U. of Iowa, 1949, BFA, 1951, MFA. Traveled Europe; resided Great Britain, 1960-61. **Taught:** U. of Oklahoma, 1951-52; State of Iowa, 1952-53; UCLA, 1953-63; U. of California, Irvine 1969-. **Awards:** L. C. Tiffany Grant, 1951; Guggenheim Foundation Fellowship, 1960; and more than 40 others. **Address:** 22370 Third Avenue, South Laguna, CA 92677. **Dealer:** Mekler Gallery, Los Angeles. **One-man Exhibitions:** Iowa Wesleyan College, 1951; Des Moines, 1951; Fort Dodge/Blanden, 1951; San Antonio/

McNay, 1951; U. of Oklahoma, 1952; Los Angeles/County MA, 1954 (two-man); Kalamazoo/Institute, 1955; Oakland/AM, 1956; Felix Landau Gallery, 1956, 58, 62, 64, 67, 70; Laguna Blanca School, Santa Barbara, 1958; Santa Barbara/MA, 1958; Pasadena/AM, 1959; Taft College, 1959; Galleria Cadario, 1961; Arizona State U., 1962; U. of Minnesota, 1963; U. of Nebraska, 1963; Terry Dintenfass, Inc., 1963, 65; Louisville/Speed, 1964; San Jose State College, 1965; Container Corp. of America, 1965; Brook Street Gallery, London, 1965; The Landau-Alan Gallery, NYC, 1967, 69; La Jolla, 1970; Graphics Gallery, 1973; Jodi Scully Gallery, 1973, 75; Charles Campbell Gallery, 1974; U. of California, Riverside, 1975; The Works Gallery, Long Beach, Calif., 1987. **Retrospectives:** Brooklyn Museum, 1963; Los Angeles/County MA, 1965. **Group:** Youngstown/Butler; U. of Illinois; State U. of Iowa; MOMA; WMAA; Oakland/AM; Santa Barbara/MA; SFMA; Pasadena/AM; Library of Congress; Brooklyn Museum; U. of Minnesota. **Collections:** Achenbach Foundation; Ball State U.; Bibliotheque Nationale; Bradley U.; Brooklyn Museum; U. of Calgary; California State Fair; UCLA; Coos Bay; Dallas/MFA; Des Moines; Fort Dodge/Blanden; U. of Illinois; Iowa State Fair; Iowa Wesleyan College; State U. of Iowa; Kalamazoo/Institute; Kansas City/Nelson; Kansas State College; Karachi; Kentucky Southern College; La Jolla; Library of Congress; Los Angeles/County MA; Lytton Savings and Loan Association; MOMA; Michigan State U.; Minnesota/MA; NYPL; National Gallery; U. of Nebraska; Oakland/AM; Omaha/Joslyn; Otis Art Institute; Palomar College; Pasadena/AM; SFMA; San Diego; Santa Barbara/MA; Seattle/AM; Texas Western College; Tulane U.; Utica; Victoria and Albert Museum; Walker; Youngstown/Butler. **Bibliography:** Murken-Altrogge.

Donald Judd *Untitled* 1986

JUDD, DON. b. June 3, 1928, Excelsior Springs, Mo. **Studied:** College of William and Mary, 1948-49; Columbia U., BS, 1949-53, MFA; ASL, with Johnson, Stewart Klonis, Robert Beverly Hale, Louis Bouche, Will Barnet. Traveled western Europe, southwestern USA. Critic for *Arts Magazine* 1959-65. **Taught:** Allen Stevenson School, 1957-61; Hunter College, 1966; Yale U., 1967. **Awards:** Swedish Institute Grant, 1965; U.S. Government Grant, 1967; Guggenheim Foundation Fellowship, 1968. **Address:** 101 Spring Street, NYC 10012; Box 218, Marsa, Tx. 79843. **Dealer:** Paula Cooper Gallery, NYC. **One-man Exhibitions:** (first) Green Gallery, NYC, 1964; Leo Castelli Inc., 1966, 67; WMAA, 1968; Ileana Sonnabend Gallery, Paris, 1969; Galerie Rudolf Zwirner, 1969; Eindhoven, 1970; Joseph Helman Gallery, St. Louis, 1970; Essen, 1970; Hannover/Kunstverein, 1970; Whitechapel Art Gallery, London, 1970; Locksley-

Shea Gallery, 1970, 73; Janie C. Lee Gallery, Dallas, 1970, Houston, 1976; Galerie Heiner Friedrich, Munich, 1971, 78; Ronald Greenberg Gallery, St. Louis, 1972; Galerie Rolf Ricke, 1972; Leo Castelli Inc., NYC, 1973, 76, 78, 79, 81, 83, 84; Galerie Daniel Templon, Paris, 1973, 75; Gian Enzo Sperone and Galerie Konrad Fischer, Rome, 1973; Gian Enzo Sperone, Turin, 1973; Galerie Annemarie Verna, Zurich, 1973, 79, 80, 83, 85; Lisson Gallery, London, 1974, 75; Portland (Ore.) Center for the Visual Arts, 1974; Basel, circ., 1976; Sable-Castelli Gallery Ltd., Toronto, 1976; Heiner Friedrich Gallery, NYC, 1977, 78; Corpus Christi, 1977; Cincinnati/Contemporary, 1977; Heiner Friedrich, Cologne, 1977, 79; Moderne Galerie, Bottrop (Switzerland), 1977; ACE Gallery, Venice, Calif., 1977; Berlin/National, 1978; Foyer MGB, Zurich, 1978; Vancouver, 1978; Kroller Muller, Otterlo, 1978; Young-Hoffman Gallery, Chicago, 1978; Eindhoven, 1979; Akron/AI, 1979; Thomas Segal Gallery, Boston, 1979; Newport Harbor, 1981; Larry Gagosian Gallery, Los Angeles, 1982; Carol Taylor Gallery, Dallas, 1983; Knight Gallery, Charlotte, N.C., 1983; Blum Helman Gallery, NYC, 1983; Max Protetch Gallery, NYC, 1984; 101 Spring Street, NYC, 1984; Margo Leavin Gallery, Los Angeles, 1984; Purchase/SUNY, 1984; Texas Gallery, Houston, 1985; Lia Rumma Studio d'Arte, Naples, Italy, 1985; Rhona Hoffman Gallery, Chicago, 1985; Galerie Barbel Grasslin, Frankfurt-am-Main, 1985. **Retrospectives:** WMAA; Ottawa/National, 1975. **Group:** VIII Sao Paulo Biennial, 1965; ICA, U. of Pennsylvania, 1965; Stockholm/National, 1965; Jewish Museum, Primary Structures, 1966; WMAA, Contemporary American Sculpture, Selection I, 1966; Walker, 1966; WMAA Sculpture Annuals, 1966, 68, 70, 73; Los Angeles/County MA, American Sculpture of the Sixties, 1967; Detroit/Institute, Color, Image and Form, 1967; WGMA, A New Aesthetic, 1967;

SRGM, Sculpture International, 1967; Walker, 1969; Vancouver, 1969; Expo '70, Osaka, 1970; Indianapolis, 1970; Princeton U., American Art since 1960, 1970; Brooklyn Museum, Attitudes, 1970; Cincinnati/Contemporary, Monumental Art, 1970; SRGM, Guggenheim International, 1971; Dublin/Municipal, International Quadriennial (ROSC), 1971; High Museum, The Modern Image, 1972; Rijksmuseum Kroller-Muller, Diagrams and Drawings, 1972; New York Cultural Center, 3D into 2D, 1973; Musée Galliera, Paris, Festival d'Automne, 1973; Parcheggio di Villa Borghese, Rome, Contemporanea, 1974; Art Museum of South Texas, Corpus Christi, Eight Artists, 1974; Cologne/Kunstverein, Kunst uber Kunst, 1974; Otterlo, Functions of Drawing, 1975; NCFA; Sculpture: American Direction, 1945-1975, 1975; MOMA, Drawing Now, 1976; MOMA, Oxford, Eng. (four-man), 1976; WMAA, 200 Years of American Sculpture, 1976; Dallas/MFA, American Art since 1945, 1976; Venice Biennial, 1976; Cambridge U., Jubilation, 1977; U. of Chicago, Ideas in Sculpture, 1965-1977, 1977; Kansas City/AI, Project Drawings, 1978; WMAA, 20th Century American Masters of the 60s and 70s, 1978; ICA, Boston, The Reductive Object, 1979; Milwaukee, Emergence & Progression, circ., 1979; Documenta VII, Kassel, 1982; WMAA, Block Prints, 1982; WMAA, The Sculptor as Draftsman, 1983; WMAA, Minimalism to Expressionism, 1983; Sunderland (Eng.) Arts Center, Drawing in Air, 1983; WMAA, Blam!, 1984; WMAA Biennial, 1985; MOMA, Contrasts in Form: Geometric Abstract Art 1910-1980, 1985; WMAA, High Styles, 1985; SRGM, Transformation in Sculpture, 1985; Fort Lauderdale, An American Renaissance: Painting and Sculpture Since 1940, 1986. **Collections:** Art Gallery of Ontario; Basel; Chicago/AI; Detroit/Institute; Fort Worth; Krefeld/Kaiser Wilhelm; Los Angeles/County MA; MOMA; Ottawa/National; Pasadena/AM; SRGM; St. Louis/City; Stockholm/National;

WMAA; Walker. **Bibliography:** Alloway 4; *Art Now 74*; Battcock ed.; *Black and White Are Colors*; Calas, N. and E.; *Contemporanea*; Danto; Davis, D.; De Vries, ed.; Friedman, M. 2; Friedman and van der Marck; Gablik; Goossen 1; Haskell 5; Honnef; Honisch and Jensen, eds.; Hunter, ed.; Johnson, Ellen H.; Kozloff 3; Krauss 2; Lippard 3, 4, 5; Lucie-Smith; MacAgy 2; *Report*; Rickey; Rose, B., 4; Rowell; Sandler 1; **Smith., B.,** 1975; Toher, ed.; Trier 1; Tuchman 1. Archives.

K

KACERE, JOHN. b. June 23, 1920, Walker, Iowa. **Studied:** Mizen Academy of Art, Chicago, 1938-42; State U. of Iowa, BFA, 1946-49, MFA, 1950-51. **Taught:** State U. of Iowa, 1949-50 (graduate assistant to Mauricio Lasansky); U. of Manitoba, 1950-53; U. of Florida, 1953-65; Cooper Union; Parsons School of Design, NYC; U. of New Mexico. **Address:** 152 Wooster Street, NYC 10013. **Dealer:** OK Harris Works of Art. **One-man Exhibitions:** The Little Art Gallery, Cedar Rapids, Iowa, 1942; U. of Florida, 1953, 57; Korman Gallery, NYC, 1954; Mirell Gallery, Miami, Fla., 1955; Cedar Rapids/AA, 1955; The Zabriskie Gallery, 1956; Louisiana State U., 1957; Allan Stone Gallery, 1963; OK Harris Works of Art, 1971, 73, 75, 78, 80, 82, 84; Galerie de Gestlo, Hamburg, 1972, 73; Lavignes-Bastille, Paris, 1981, 83. **Group:** Walker, circ., USA, Canada, South America, 1949-51; MOMA; Chicago/AI; PMA; Omaha/Joslyn; Dallas/MFA; Ringling; Jacksonville/AM; U. of Georgia; Corcoran, 1963; U. of Illinois, 1965; John Michael Kohler Arts Center, Sheboygan, The Human Image, 1970; Chicago/Contemporary, Radical Realism, 1971; Cleveland/MA, 32 Realists, 1972; MOMA, The Realist Revival, 1972; Stuttgart/WK, Amerikanischer Fotorealismus, circ., 1972; Lincoln, Mass./De Cordova, The Super-Realist Vision, 1973; Tokyo Biennial, 1974; Chicago/AI, 1974; Wichita State U., Photo-Realism, 1975; Xerox Art Exhibition, Rochester, N.Y., Unordinary Realities, 1975; WMAA, downtown branch, Nothing but Nudes, 1977; Williamstown/Clark, The Dada/Surrealist Heritage, 1977; PAFA, Contemporary American Realism Since 1960, circ., 1981; Potsdam/SUNY, Contemporary Realism, 1982; Isetan Museum of Art,

John Kacere *Lauren* 1984

Tokyo, American Realism: The Precise Image, 1985. **Collections:** Amsterdam/Stedelijk; Brandeis U.; Hartford/Wadsworth; Louisville/Speed; Mt. Holyoke College; Portland, Ore./AM; Yale U. **Bibliography:** *Amerikanischer Fotorealismus;* Arthur 3; Honisch and Jensen, eds.; Hunter, ed.; Sager.

KAHN, WOLF. b. October 4, 1927, Stuttgart, Germany. To Great Britain, 1939; to USA, 1940. **Studied:** Hofmann School, 1947-49; The U. of Chicago, 1950-51, BA. Traveled Europe, Mexico, USA. **Taught:** U. of California, Berkeley, 1960; Cooper Union, 1961-77; Haystack School, Deer Isle, Me., 1961, 62; Columbia U. 1978; RISD, 1978-79. **Member:** Associate, NAD; AAIAL. **Commissions:** Jewish Theological Seminary, NYC (portraits). **Awards:** Ford Foundation, **P.P.,** 1962; Fulbright Fellowship, 1962, 64; J.S. Guggenheim Fellowship, 1966-67; NAD, Ranger Fund, **P.P.,** 1977; AAAL, Childe Hassam Fund, **P.P.,** 1978, AAAL, Award, 1979. **m.** Emily Mason. **Address:** % Dealer. **Dealers:** Grace Borgenicht Gallery, NYC. **One-man Exhibitions:** (first) Hansa Gallery, NYC, 1953, also 1954; Grace Borgenicht Gallery, NYC, 1956, 58, 60, 61, 62, 65, 67, 69, 71, 73, 74, 75, 77, 79, 81, 83, 85, 86; U. of California, 1960; U. of Michigan, 1961; Ellison Gallery, Fort Worth, 1961; RISD, 1961; 79; Kansas City/Nelson 1962; Michigan State U., 1963; Stewart Richard Gallery, San Antonio, 1964; Obelisk Gallery, 1964; Nashville, 1964; Sabarsky Gallery, Los Angeles, 1966; Marlboro College, 1967; Princeton Gallery of Fine Art, 1970, 72, 74, 75; Meredith Long Gallery, Houston, 1971, 73, 74, 76, 77, 78, 80, 82, 85; Harcus Krakow Rosen Sonnabend, 1972; U. of Nebraska, 1973; Norfolk/Chrysler, 1973; Rudolph Galleries, Coral Gables, 1974; David Barnett Gal-

Wolf Kahn
Barn in a Warm Tonality 1982

lery, Milwaukee, 1972, 75, 77; L. Kornbluth Gallery, Fairlawn, N.J., 1978, 79, 82; Harcus Krakow Gallery, Boston, 1976; L. Kornbluth Gallery, Fairlawn, N.J., 79, 82; RISD, 1979; Waddington Gallery, London, 1980; Arts Club of Chicago, circ., 1981; Cheekwood, 1981; Thomas Segal Gallery, Boston, 1981, 83, 84, 85; The Schenectady Museum, 1982; Utica, 1982; Dartmouth U., circ., 1984; San Diego, circ., 1984. **Group:** The Stable Gallery Annuals, 1954, 55; WMAA Annuals, 1958, 60, 61; Utica, 1959; ART: USA 59, NYC, 1959; WMAA, Young America, 1960; International Biennial Exhibition of Paintings, Tokyo; SFMA, 1961; PAFA, 1961, 65; American Art Gallery, Copenhagen, 1963; MOMA, Hans Hofmann and His Students, circ., 1963-64; Omaha/Joslyn, A Sense of Place, 1973; IIE, 20 American Fulbright Artists, 1975; US Department of the Interior, America 1976; MMA, Hans Hofmann as Teacher: Drawings by His Students, 1979; SFMA, American Realism (Janss), circ., 1985. **Collections:** Boston/MFA; Brandeis U; Brooklyn Museum; U. of California; Carnegie Mellon U.; Charlotte/Mint; Chase Manhattan Bank; Corcoran; Los Angeles County/MA; MMA; Dallas/MFA; Fort Worth; Houston/MFA; ICA, Boston; U. of Illinois; Jewish Museum; Lincoln Life Insurance Co.; Springfield, Mass./MFA; MOMA; U. of Massachusetts; Michigan State U.; NAD; U. of Nebraska; U. of Nevada; U. of Rochester; San Diego; St. Louis/City; Union Carbide Corp.; VMFA; WMAA. **Bibliography:** Blesh 1; Downes, ed. Archives.

KAISH, LUISE. b. September 8, 1925, Atlanta, Ga. **Studied:** Syracuse U., with Ivan Mestrovic, BFA, MFA, Escuela de Pintura y Escultura, Mexico City, with Alfredo Zalce, J.G. Galvan. Traveled Europe, Scandinavia, Italy, Israel, Middle East. **Taught:** Columbia U., 1974-75, 80-; Dartmouth College, 1974; U. of Washington, Seattle, 1979.

Member: Sculptors Guild; Trustee, American Academy in Rome, 1973-; Trustee, The Augustus Saint Gaudens Memorial, National Park Service, 1978-; executive board, The Sculptors Guild, 1974-. **Commissions:** Temple B'rith Kodesh, Rochester, N.Y.; Container Corp. of America; Syracuse U.; Amoco Building, NYC; Jewish Museum; Temple Beth Shalom, Washington, Del.; Temple Israel, Westport, Conn.; Holy Trinity Mission Seminary, Silver Spring, Md.; Beth El Synagogue Center, New Rochelle, N.Y.; Temple B'nai Abraham, Essex County, N.J.; U.A.H.C., Jerusalem, Israel. **Awards:** Guggenheim Foundation Fellowship; L.C. Tiffany Grant; Audubon Artists, Medal; Ball State Teachers College, **P.P.;** Joe and Emily Lowe Foundation Award; National Association of Women Artists; U. of Rochester; Syracuse/Everson; American Academy, Rome, Fellowship, 1970-71. **Address:** 610 West End Avenue, NYC 10024. **Dealer:** Staempfli Gallery, NYC. **One-man Exhibitions:** U. of Rochester, 1954; Sculpture Center, NYC, 1955, 58; Staempfli Gallery, NYC, 1968, 81, 84; St. Paul Gallery, 1969; Dartmouth College (two-man), 1974; U. of Haifa (two-man), 1985. **Retrospective:** Jewish Museum, 1973. **Group:** MMA, National Sculpture Exhibition, 1951; WMAA, 1955, 62, 64, 66; MOMA, Recent Sculpture USA, 1959; U. of Nebraska; Ball State Teachers College; U. of Notre Dame; Ohio U.; NAD; Sculptors Guild; Buffalo/Albright; AAAL; Newark Museum, Women Artists of America, 1966; U. of Illinois, 1968; New School for Social Research, Drawings by Painters and Sculptors, 1967; U. of Nebraska, American Sculpture, 1970; Minnesota/MA, Drawings, USA, 1970; Finch College, NYC, Artists at Work, 1970; USIS, Rome, 1973; Minnesota/MA, Drawings USA, 1976. **Collections:** Export Khleb, Moscow; General Mills Corp., Minneapolis; High Museum; Jewish Museum; MMA; Minnesota/MA; NMAA; U. of Rochester; Syracuse U.; WMAA.

KAMIHIRA, BEN. b. March 16, 1925, Yakima, Wash. **Studied:** Art Institute of Pittsburgh; PAFA, 1948-52. US Army, 1944-47. **Taught:** The Pennsylvania State U.; Philadelphia Museum School; PAFA, 1953-. **Awards:** PAFA, Cresson Fellowship, 1951; PAFA, J. Henry Schiedt Scholarship, 1952; NAD, Hallgarten Prize, 1952; L.C. Tiffany Grant, 1952, 58; Guggenheim Foundation Fellowship, 1955, 56; PAFA, Walter Lippincott Prize, 1958; NAD, Benjamin Altman Prize, 1958, 62; Corcoran, First William A. Clark Prize, 1961; NAD, Gold Nedal, 1975. **Address:** 957 North 5th Street, Philadelphia, PA. 19123. **One-man Exhibitions:** Dubin Gallery, Philadelphia, 1952; Philadelphia Art Alliance, 1954; PAFA, 1956; Janet Nessler Gallery, NYC, 1951; Durlacher Brothers, NYC, 1964; The Forum Gallery, NYC, 1966, 73, 76; Maxwell Gallery, San Francisco, 1969. **Group:** NAD, 1952, 54, 56, 58, 61; Youngstown/Butler, 1953, 1958-61; PAFA, 1954, 58, 60; WMAA, 1958; Corcoran, 1961; PAFA, Seven on the Figure, 1979. **Collections;** Colorado Springs/FA; Dallas/MFA; NAD; PAFA; Ringling; WMAA. **Bibliography:** Goodrich and Baur 1.

KAMROWSKI, GEROME. b. January 29, 1914, Warren, Minn. **Studied:** St. Paul School of Art, with L. Turner, Cameron Booth; ASL; Hofmann School. **Taught:** U. of Michigan, 1946-84. Federal A.P.: mural painting in Minnesota and New York. **Awards:** Guggenheim Foundation Fellowship; Detroit/Institute, 1949, 54, 55, 61, Merit Prize, 1967; Cranbrook, Horace H. Rackham Research Grant, 1957. **Address:** 1501 Beechwood Drive, Ann Arbor, MI 48103. **One-man Exhibitions:** Mortimer Brandt, NYC, 1946; Betty Parsons Gallery, 1948; Alexander Iolas Gallery, Galerie Creuze, Paris, 1950, 58; Hugo Gallery, NYC, 1951; U. of Michigan, 1952, 59, 61; The Saginaw Museum, 1954; Jackson Art Association; Cranbrook, 1947; Gallery Mayer, NYC,

1961; S.W. Wind Gallery, Ann Arbor; Eastern Michigan U. (two-man); Monique Knowlton Gallery, NYC, 1978. **Group:** Chicago/AI, 1945, 46; Buffalo/Albright, 1946; Galerie Maeght, 6 American Painters, 1947; WMAA Annuals, 1947, 48, 51, 53; Detroit/Institute, 1948, 50, 52, 54, 58; U. of Illinois, 1950; Sidney Janis Gallery, Surrealist and Abstract Art; MOMA; SRGM; U. of Michigan (four-man); 12 Canadian and American Painters, NYC; Hayward Gallery, London, Dada and Surrealism Revisited, 1978; Rutgers U., Surrealism and American Art, 1931-1947, 1947; U. of New Mexico, American Abstract Artists, 1977; MMA, Hans Hofmann as a Teacher, 1979. **Collections:** Detroit/Institute; Flint/Institute; Simon Frazer U.; Knoll Associates, Inc.; MMA; MOMA; Minnesota/MA; U. of New Mexico; U. of North Carolina; Phillips; WMAA. **Bibliography:** Baur 7; Breton 3; Calas; Janis, S.; Ritchie 1.

KAMYS, WALTER. b. June 8, 1917, Chicago, Ill. **Studied:** Chicago Art Institute School, 1943, with Hubert Ropp, Boris Anisfeld, privately in Mexico with Gordon Onslow-Ford, 1944. Traveled Mexico, Europe. **Taught:** The Putney School, Vermont, 1945; G. W. V. Smith Art Museum, Springfield, Mass., 1947-60; U. of Massachusetts, 1960-. Director, Art Acquisition Program, U. of Massachusetts Collection, 1962-74. **Awards:** Prix de Rome, 1942; Chicago/AI, Anna Louise Raymond Fellowship, 1942-43; Chicago/AI, Paul Trebilcock **P.P.,** 1943; Chicago/AI, James Nelson Raymond Traveling Fellowship, 1943-44; Boston Arts Festival, Second Prize, 1955; State College at Westfield, **P.P.,** 1968; Polish Ministry of Culture, grant, 1978. **Address:** North Main Street, Sunderland, MA 01375. **One-man Exhibitions:** (first) Cliff Dwellers Club, Chicago, 1944; Dartmouth College, 1946; Margaret Brown Gallery, Boston, 1949; The Little Gallery, Springfield, Mass., 1951; Mortimer Levitt Gallery, NYC, 1954; Muriel Latow Gallery, Springfield, Mass., 1954; The Bertha Schaefer Gallery, 1955, 57, 61; Deerfield (Mass.) Academy, 1956, A Painter with a Camera (abstract photos), 1960; Concordia College, 1957; Springfield, Mass./MFA, 1948, 59; New Vision Center, London, 1960; Univision Gallery, London, 1960; U. of Massachusetts, 1961; Stanhope Gallery, Boston, 1963; Ward-Nasse Gallery, Boston, 1968; East Hampton Gallery, N.Y., 1970; Pisces Gallery, Wellfleet, Mass., 1976; Danco Gallery, Northampton, Mass., 1978; Castleton (Vt.) State College, 1981; Greenfield (Mass.) College, 1985. **Group:** Chicago/AI; Salon des Realities Nouvelles, Paris; PAFA; Carnegie; USIA, 20th Century American Graphics, circ.; Corcoran; ICA, Boston, Younger New England Graphic Artists, 1954; MOMA, Recent Drawings, 1956; ICA, Boston, View, 1960; Northeastern U., 1965; Silvermine Guild, 1967; Smithsonian, The Art of Organic Forms, 1968; U. of Connecticut, New England Artists, 1971; G.W.V. Smith Museum, Springfield, Mass., 1973. **Collections:** Albion College; Hampshire College; Harvard U.; U. of Massachusetts; Mount Holyoke College; NYU; Smith College; U. of Vermont; WDAY; Westfield; Wright State U.; Yale U. **Bibliography:** Janis and Blesh 1.

KANEMITSU, MATSUMI. b. May 28, 1922, Ogden, Utah. **Studied:** Atelier Fernand Leger, Paris (painting); ASL, with Yasuo Kuniyoshi, Harry Sternberg, C.P. Austin, Byron Browne, privately with Karl Metzler in Baltimore (sculpture). US Army, 1941-46. Traveled Europe, USA, the Orient. **Taught:** Chouinard Art Institute, 1965-67; 1969-72; U. of California, Berkeley, 1966, 1970-71; Honolulu Academy School, 1967-68; Otis Art Institute, 1971; U. of California, Santa Barbara, 1972-73; California Institute of the Arts, Valencia, 1971-72. **Awards:** Ford Foundation Grant for Tamarind, 1961; Longview Foundation Grant, 1962, 64; Ford Foundation/A.F.A. Artist-in-Residence, 1964. **Address:** 854 South Berendo Street, Los Angeles, CA 90005. **Dealer:** Janus Gallery. **One-man Exhibitions:** (first) Fort Riley, Kans., 1942; Gallery 77, New Haven, 1953; Western Maryland College, 1954; Baltimore/MA, 1954; Zoe Dusanne Gallery, 1955; The New Gallery, NYC, 1957; Widdifield Gallery, NYC, 1959; Dwan Gallery, 1960, 61, 63; Stephen Radich Gallery, 1961, 62; Southern Illinois U., 1961; i Gallery, La Jolla, 1963; Akron/AI, 1964; Occidental College, 1966; U. of California, 1966; Honolulu Academy, 1967; Paul Gallery, 1967; Chouinard Art Institute, 1968; Serisawa Gallery, 1970; Michael Smith Gallery, Los Angeles, 1972; Pacific Culture Asia Museum, Pasadena, 1973; Jodi Scully Gallery, 1974. **Group:** Baltimore/MA, 1948-52; Corcoran, 1950; Chicago/AI, 1952; Academy of Fine Arts, Berlin, 1954; MOMA, 1956; WMAA, 1956; Dallas/MFA, 1960; WMAA Annual, 1962; MOMA, Art in Embassies, circ. internationally, 1963 64; MOMA, Americans 1963, circ., 1963-64. **Collections:** Akron/AI; U. of Arizona; Baltimore/MA; Baltimore/Walters; Chicago/AI; Cincinnati/AM; Corcoran; Dillard U., Fort Worth; Hall of Justice; Hiroshima State Museum; Honolulu Academy; Housatonic Community College; Kansas City/Nelson; La Jolla; Los Angeles/County MA; MOMA; NCFA; Nagoya City Hall; National Museum of Wales; U. of New Mexico; Norfolk/Chrysler; Osaka/Municipal; SFMA; Santa Barbara/MA; Tokyo/Modern; Tougaloo College; Turin/Civico; UCLA; Worcester/AM.

KANOVITZ, HOWARD. b. February 9, 1929, Fall River, Mass. **Studied:** Providence College, 1949, BS; RISD, 1949-51; ASL, Woodstock, 1951; with Yasuo Kuniyoshi; New School for Social Research, 1949-52; U. of Southern California, 1958; NYU, 1960-61. Traveled Europe, North Africa, 1956-58. **Taught:** Brooklyn College, 1961-64; Pratt Institute, 1964-66; Long Island U., 1977-78; School of Visual Arts, 1981-85. **Awards:** DAAD Fellowship, 1979. **Address:** 463 Broome Street, NYC 10013. **Dealer:** Alex Rosenberg Gallery, NYC. **One-man Exhibitions:** The Stable Gallery, NYC, 1962; Fall River (Mass.) Association, 1964; Jewish Museum, 1966; Waddell Gallery, 1969, 71; Everyman Gallery, NYC, 1970; M.E. Thelen Gallery, Cologne, 1970, 73; Benson Gallery, Bridgehampton, N.Y., 1970, 71, 77; Galleri Ostergren, Malmo, 1971; Hedendaagse Kunst, Utrecht, 1973; Duisburg, 1974; Stefanotty Gallery, NYC, 1975; Galerie Jollembeck, Cologne, 1977, 80; Alex Rosenberg Gallery, NYC, 1978, 82; Guild Hall, East Hampton, N.Y., 1978; Hamburg/Kunstverein, 1979; Akademie der Kunst, Berlin, 1979; Hannover/K-G, 1979; Forum Kunste, Rottweil, 1980; Kunstverein, Freiburg, 1980; Indianapolis (two-man), 1985; Benson Gallery, Southampton, N.Y., 1986. **Retrospective:** Akademie der Kunste, 1979. **Group:** Chicago/AI, 1961; U. of Illinois, 1963; WMAA, 1965, 67, 72; Riverside Museum, NYC, Paintings from the Photo, 1969; Sweden/Goteborgs, Warmwind, 1970; WMAA, 22 Realists, 1970; VMFA, American Painting, 1970; Chicago/Contemporary, Radical Realism, 1971; NIAL, 1972; Stuttgart/WK, Amerikanischer Fotorealismus, circ., 1972; Kunsthalle, Recklinghausen, Mit Kamera, Pinsel und Spritzpistole, 1973; Documenta 6, Kassel, 1977; Guild Hall, East Hampton, Aspects of Realism, 1977; Berlin/National, 1979; Youngstown/Butler, 1983; Los Angeles/MOCA, Automobile and Culture, 1984; Kunstverein Frankfurt, Von Zeichnen, circ., 1986. **Collections:** Aachen/NG; Cologne; Cologne/Ludwig; Duisburg; F.T.D. Association; Guild Hall; Helsinki; Hirshhorn; Indianapolis; Kunsthaus zu Kiel; Los Angeles/County AM; Moderne Galerie, Landessammlung, Salzburg; Rotterdam; Staatliche Museen Berlin-Dahlem;

Sweden/Goteborgs; Utrecht; Vienna/Moderner; WMAA. **Bibliography:** *Amerikanischer Fotorealismus;* Honisch and Jensen, eds.; **Howard Kanovitz;** *Kunst um 1970;* Sager.

KAPROW, ALLAN. b. August 23, 1927, Atlantic City, N.J. **Studied:** NYU, 1945-49, BA; Hofmann School, NYC, 1947-48; Columbia U., with Meyer Schapiro, 1950-52, MA (art history); privately with John Cage in NYC, 1956-58. Traveled Europe, USA. **Taught:** Rutgers U., 1953-61; Pratt Institute, 1960-61; Stony Brook/SUNY, 1961-69; California Institute of the Arts, Los Angeles, 1969-. A co-founder of Hansa Gallery, NYC, 1952, and Reuben Gallery, NYC, 1959. Designed sets and costumes for Eileen Passloff Dance Co., 1958. Initiated the first Environments and Happenings, 1958. **Awards:** Katherine White Foundation Grant, 1951; Rutgers U., Research Fund Grant, 1957; Copley Foundation Grant, 1962; Guggenheim Foundation Fellowship, 1967. **Address:** 1225 Linda Rose Avenue, Los Angeles, CA 90041. **One-man Exhibitions:** (first) Hansa Gallery, NYC, 1953, also 1955, 57; Rutgers U., 1953, 55; Urban Gallery, NYC, 1955, 56; Sun Gallery, Provincetown, 1957; John Gibson Gallery, NYC, 1969; Galerie Rene Block, Berlin, 1970; Galleria Bertesca, Milan, 1973; Stefanotty Gallery, NYC, 1974; U. of Northern Iowa, 1979. **Environments:** Hansa Gallery, NYC, 1958; Judson Gallery, NYC, 1960; Martha Jackson Gallery, 1961; U. of Michigan, 1961; Rijksmuseum, Amsterdam, and Stockholm/National, 1961; Smolin Gallery, NYC, and Stony Brook/SUNY, 1962; Smolin Gallery, NYC, 1964. **Happenings:** Douglass College, 1958; Reuben Gallery, NYC, 1959, 61; Judson Memorial Church, NYC, 1960; U. of Michigan, 1961; Maidman Playhouse, NYC, 1962; Walker, 1962; Theatre des Nations, Paris, 1963; Edinburgh, Scotland, 1963; Southern Illinois U., 1964; Miami, Fla., 1964; U. of California, Berkeley, 1964; Cornell U., 1964; Florida State U., 1965; Judson Hall, NYC, 1965; ICA, Boston, 1966; Central Park, NYC, 1966; Westchester Art Society, White Plains, N.Y., 1966; Stony Brook/SUNY, 1967; Aspen Design Conference, 1970; Merriewold West Gallery, Far Hills, N.J., 1975; and many others. **Retrospective:** Pasadena/AM, 1967. **Group:** Boston Arts Festival, 1957; A.F.A., College in America, circ., 1957-58; Cornell U., 1958; Carnegie, 1958; A.F.A., New Talent, circ., 1958; Rijksmuseum, Amsterdam, and Stockholm/National, 1960; MOMA, Hans Hofmann and His Students, circ., 1963-64; Jewish Museum, Work, 1969, Software, 1970; Cologne/Kunstverein, Happening & Fluxus, circ., 1970; WMAA, Blam!, 1984. **Bibliography:** Alloway 4; Battcock, ed.; Becker and Vostell; *Contemporanea;* Danto; Davis, D.; Downes, ed.; Hansen; *Happening & Fluxus;* Haskell 5; Honisch and Jensen, eds.; Hunter, ed.; Janis & Blesh 1; Johnson, Ellen H.; **Kaprow;** Kirby; Kozloff 3; Lippard 5; Lippard, ed.; *Metro;* Rubin 1; Sandler; Sontag.

KARFIOL, BERNARD. b. May 6, 1886, Budapest, Hungary; **d.** 1952. **Studied:** Academie Julian, Paris, 1901, with Jean Paul Laurens; Academie des Beaux-Arts, Paris; Pratt Institute, 1899; NAD, 1900. Traveled Mexico, Europe, West Indies. **Awards:** Pan-American Exhibition, Los Angeles, 1925; Carnegie, 1927, 29; Corcoran, First William A. Clark Prize and Corcoran Gold Medal, 1928; Fort Dodge/Blanden, **P.P.,** 1940; VMFA, **P.P.,** 1942. **One-man Exhibitions:** (first) Joseph Brummer Gallery, NYC, 1924, also 1925, 27; The Downtown Gallery, 1931, 33, 35, 41, 43, 46, 50, 56; Baltimore/MA, 1939; Vanbark Studios, Studio City, Calif., 1946; Grover Cronin Gallery, Waltham, Mass., 1957; The Forum Gallery, NYC, 1967, 78. **Group:** Grand Salon, Paris, 1903; Salon d'Automne, Paris, 1904; The Armory Show, 1913; MOMA, Paintings by 19 Living Americans,

1929; Carnegie; Corcoran; Baltimore/MA, Six Americans 1939. **Collections:** AAAL; Andover/Phillips; Baltimore/MA; Brandeis U.; Britannica; Brooklyn Museum; California Palace; Carnegie; Corcoran; Dartmouth College; Detroit/Institute; Fisk U.; Fort Dodge/Blanden; Los Angeles/County MA; MMA; MOMA; Newark Museum; New Britain; New London; Ogunquit; Phillips; Southhampton/Parrish; Upjohn Co.; VMFA; WMAA; Wellesley College; Wichita/AM. **Bibliography:** Bethers; Blesh 1; Brown; Cahill and Barr, eds.; Cheney; Goodrich and Baur 1; Hall; Halpert; Huyghe; *Index of 20th Century Artists;* Jewell 2; **Karfiol;** Kootz 1, 2; McCurdy, ed.; Mellquist; Neuhaus; Pagano; Phillips 2; Pousette-Dart, ed.; Richardson, E.P.; Ringel, ed.; **Slusser;** Wight 2. Archives.

KASTEN, KARL. b. March 5, 1916, San Francisco, Calif. **Studied:** U. of California, with Worth Ryder, John Haley, Erie Loran; State U. of Iowa, with Mauricio Lasansky; Hofmann School; San Francisco Art Institute (AB, MA). Traveled Europe, Turkey, Morocco, Russia, Far East. **Taught:** San Francisco Art Institute, 1941; U. of Michigan, 1946-47; San Francisco State College, 1947-50; U. of California, 1950-. **Member:** California Society of Printmakers. **Commissions:** North American Title Co., Berkeley, Calif. (Mural). **Awards:** U. of California Institute for Creative Work in the Arts, 1964-65; Tamarind Fellowship, 1968. **Address:** 1884 San Lorenzo Avenue, Berkeley, CA 94707. **Dealer:** Rorick Gallery, San Francisco. **One-man Exhibitions:** (first) U. of Michigan, 1946; SFMA; Galerie Breteau, Paris; Rennes; California Palace; The Lanyon Gallery; Hollis Gallery, San Francisco; St. Mary's College (Ind.); Oakland/AM; Lanai Gallery; Chico State College; Bolles Gallery; 1965, 68, 71, 73; RAC, 1968; The Catholic U. of America, 1968; Dohan Gallery, Sherman Oaks, Calif., 1969; Sacramento/Crocker 1969; Achenbach Foundation, 1975; Turkish-American Gallery, Ankara, 1975; Arlene Lind Gallery, 1975; Achenbach Gallery, 1975; U. of Alaska, 1976; Fairbanks Civic Art Gallery, 1976; Wellesley College, 1976; Arlene Lind Gallery, San Francisco, 1980; Gallerita, Milan, 1981; Rorick Gallery, 1982, 85; Worth Ryder Gallery, 1983. **Retrospectives:** Walnut Creek Civic Arts Gallery, 1973; Valley Art Center, 1978; Valley Art Center, Clarkson, Wash., 1978. **Group:** de Young; SFMA; WMAA; MMA; Chicago/AI; Detroit/Institute; Seattle/AM; Pasadena/AM; Oakland/AM; I & III Sao Paulo Biennials, 1951, 55; U. of Illinois, 50 Contemporary American Printmakers, 1956, Contemporary American Painting and Sculpture, 1969; Pomona College, California Drawing, 1957. Art Center, Berkeley, 1967; Los Angeles Printmakers Society, 1968; Moore College of Art, Philadelphia, American Drawings, 1968; U. of the Pacific, 1969; U. of Illinois, 1969. **Collections:** Achenbach Foundation; Auckland; U. of California; de Young; College of Idaho; Ithaca College; Los Angeles/County MA; MOMA; Mills College; NYPL; Oakland/AM; U. of Oklahoma; U. of the Pacific; Pasadena/AM; Rennes; SFMA; San Francisco State College; US State Department; Victoria and Albert Museum. **Bibliography:** Archives.

KATZ, ALEX. b. July 24, 1927, NYC. **Studied:** Cooper Union; Skowhegan School, 1959; Yale U., 1960-61; Pratt Institute, 1963-66; School of Visual Arts, NYC, 1965, 66; New York Studio School, 1968-69. Stage sets and costumes for Paul Taylor Dance Company, Festival of Two Worlds, Spoleto, 1960, 64; Kenneth Koch's *George Washington Crossing the Delaware*, 1962; Artists Festival Theater, Southampton, *Little Eyolf*, by Henrik Ibsen, 1968. **Commissions:** Mural, Federal Courthouse Annex, NYC. Designed sets for Paul Taylor Dance Co., *Polaris*, sets and costumes, and set for *Diggity*, 1979; Kenneth

Alex Katz *Rudy* 1980

Koch's *Red Robin*, 1977-78; Sets and Cutouts for National Dance Institute's collaboration between USA and the People's Republic of China, 1986. **Awards:** Guggenheim Foundation Fellowship, 1972; National Endowment for the Arts, 1976; US Government Cultural Exchange Grant to USSR, 1978; Cooper Union, Saint-Gaudens

Medal, 1980; Skowhegan School, Medal for Painting, 1980; Art Direction Magazine Award for *Time* magazine cover, 1982; Graphic Design USA Award for *Time* magazine cover, 1983; Hon. DFA, Colby College, 1984. **Address:** 435 West Broadway, NYC 10013. **Dealer:** Marlborough Gallery, NYC; Robert Miller Gallery, NYC. **One-man Exhibitions:** Roko Gallery, 1954, 57; The Pennsylvania State U., 1957; Sun Gallery, Provincetown, 1958; Tanager Gallery, NYC, 1959, 62; The Stable Gallery, NYC, 1960; Martha Jackson Gallery, 1962; Fischbach Gallery, 1962-68, 70, 71; Thibaudt Gallery, NYC, 1963; Tanager Gallery, NYC (two- and three-man shows), 1953, 57, 60; David Stuart Gallery, 1966; Bertha Eccles Art Center, Ogden, Utah, 1968; Phyllis Kind Gallery, Chicago, 1969, 71; Galerie Dieter Brusberg, Hanover, 1971; M.D. Thelen Gallery, 1971; Reed College, 1972; Sloan O'Sickey Gallery, Cleveland, 1972; Carlton Gallery, NYC, 1973; Assa Galleria, Helsinki, 1973; Marlborough Gallery, NYC, 1973, 76, 78, 80, 82, 83; Colgate U., 1974; Wesleyan U. (Conn.), 1974; Marlborough Godard Ltd., Toronto and Montreal, 1974, 76, 78; Marlborough Fine Art Ltd., London, 1975, 82; Galerie Arensen, Copenhagen, 1975; American Foundation for the Arts, Miami, 1976; Marlborough Gallerie AG, Zurich, 1977; Galerie Roger d'Amecourt, Paris, 1977; Fresco Arts Center, Calif., circ., 1977-78; Brandeis U., 1978; Beaver College, 1978; Benjamin Mangel Gallery, Bela Cynwyd, Pa., 1978-79; Susanne Hilberry Gallery, Birmingham, Mich., 1978, 82, 83, 84; Hokin Gallery, Chicago, 1978, 82; Brooke Alexander, NYC, 1979, 82; Robert Miller Gallery, NYC, 1980, 81, 84, 85; Queens Museum, 1980; Mira Godard Gallery, Toronto, 1980, 81, 82, 84; Benjamin Mangel Gallery, Bala Cynwyd, Penn., 1980, 84; Stony Brook/SUNY, 1980; Gallery Odin, Port Washington, N.Y., 1980; Fay Gold Gallery, Atlanta, 1980; Hokin Gallery, Palm Beach, 1980, 83; Midden-

dorf/Lane Gallery, Washington, D.C., 1980; Hartnell College, 1980; Portland, Ore./AM, 1981; Cincinnati/Contemporary, 1981; U. of California, Santa Barbara, 1981; John Stoller & Co., Inc., Minneapolis, 1982; Texas Gallery, Houston, 1983; McIntosh/Drysdale Gallery, Houston, 1983; Michael Lord Gallery, Milwaukee, 1984; Colgate U., 1984; Asher/Faure Gallery, Los Angeles, 1984; Cooper Union, NYC, 1985; Marlborough Gallery, Tokyo, 1985; Cleveland Center for Contemporary Arts, 1985; Bowdoin College, 1985; Wichita State U., 1985; O'Farrel Gallery, Brunswick, Me., 1985; Mario Diacono Gallery, Boston, 1985. **Retrospectives:** U. of Utah, circ., 1971; WMAA, circ., 1974; Centro Colombo-Americano, Bogota, 1980; WMAA, circ., 1986. **Group:** New York Art Alliance, Younger Artists, 1959; PAFA, 1960; WMAA, Young America, 1960; Annual, 1967-68; Houston-MFA, 1961; Chicago/AI, 1961, 62, 64; Colby College, Maine and Its Artists, 1963; Swarthmore College, Two Generations of American Art, 1964; MOMA, 1964-65, American Collages, 1965, The Inflated Image, circ., 1968; RISD, Recent Still Life, 1966; Milwaukee, 1966; Bennington College, 1967; U. of California, San Diego, The Impure Image, 1969; Tulsa/Philbrook, The American Sense of Reality, 1969; Milwaukee, Aspects of a New Realism, 1969; Walker, Figures/Environments, circ., 1970-71; Sweden/Goteborgs, Warmwind, 1970; Corcoran Biennial, 1971; PAFA, Contemporary Realism, 1971; SFMA, Color/Constructivism/Realism in Contemporary Graphics, 1971-72; WMAA Annuals 1972, 73; Boston U., The American Landscape, 1972; WMAA, American Drawings: 1963-1973, 1973; Cleveland/MA, 1974; Lincoln, Mass./De Cordova, Candid Painting: American Genre 1950-1975, 1975; US Department of the Interior, America 1976, 1976; Tulane U., Drawing Today in New York, 1977; Philadelphia College of Art, Artists' Sets and Costumes, 1977; Aspen Center for the Visual Arts,

American Portraits of the Sixties and Seventies, 1979; Brooklyn Museum, American Drawings in Black and White: 1970-1979, 1980; San Antonio/MA, Real, Really Real, Super Real, 1981; PAFA, Contemporary American Realism Since 1960, 1981; WMAA, Focus on the Figure, 1982; Houston/Contemporary, American Still Life, 1945-1983, circ., 1983; MOMA, Pop Art: 1955-1970, circ., 1985. **Collections:** Aachen/NG; Allentown/AM; Atlantic-Richfield Corp., Los Angeles; Berlin; Boston/MFA; Bowdoin College; Brandeis U.; Chase Manhattan Bank; Chicago/AI; Ciba-Geigy Corp.; Cincinnati/AM; Cleveland; Colby College; Commerce Bank of St. Louis; Dartmouth College; Delaware; Des Moines; Detroit/Institute; Hartford/Wadsworth; Harvard U.; Hirshhorn; Helsinki; MMA; MOMA; Madison Art Center; Mexico City/Tamayo; Miami-Dade; Milwaukee; Museum of Contemporary Art, Utrecht; NCFA; NYU; U. of North Carolina; Oberlin College; Omaha/Joslyn; Rice U.; RISD; Scranton/Everhart; J. Henry Schroeder Banking Corp.; U. of Southern California; Syracuse U.; Trenton/State; US State Department; Utah; WMAA; Wake Forest U.; Wichita/AM. **Bibliography:** Alloway 4; *America 1976*; Arthur 1; Arthur 2; Downes, ed.; *Figures/Environments*; Honisch and Jensen, eds.; Hunter, ed.; *Kunst um 1970*; Lippard 5; O'Hara 1; *Poets & Painters*; Sandler 1; Sager; Schwartz 2; Strand, ed. Archives.

KATZMAN, HERBERT. b. January 8, 1923, Chicago, Ill. **Studied:** Chicago Art Institute School, 1940-46. Traveled Great Britain; resided Paris, Florence. **Taught:** Rockland Foundation, 1952-53; Pratt Institute; School of Visual Arts, NYC, 1959-. **Awards:** Chicago/AI, Traveling Fellowship, 1946; Chicago/AI, Campana Prize, 1951; PAFA, J. Henry Schiedt Memorial Prize, 1954; Fulbright Fellowship, 1956; AAAL Grant, 1958; National Council on the Arts, 1967; Guggenheim Foundation Fellowship, 1968. **Address:** 463 West Street, NYC 10014. **Dealer:** Terry Dintenfass, Inc., NYC. **One-man Exhibitions:** (first) The Alan Gallery, NYC, 1954, also 1957, 59; Terry Dintenfass, Inc., NYC, 1962, 64, 66, 68, 71, 72, 75, 78; U. of Illinois; Brooklyn Museum. **Group:** Chicago/AI, 1951; MOMA, Fifteen Americans, circ., 1952; U. of Illinois; PAFA, 1952, Annuals, 1967, 69; Carnegie, 1953, 55; WMAA, The New Decade, 1954-55. XXVIII Venice Biennial, 1956; WMAA, Forty Artists under Forty, circ., 1962; Gallery of Modern Art, NYC, 1967-68; New School for Social Research, 1968; Skidmore College, Contemporary Drawings, 1975; U. of North Carolina, Art on Paper, 1977; Indianapolis, 1978; NAD, 1979. **Collections:** Chicago/AI; Hirshhorn; MOMA; U. of Massachusetts; Minnesota/MA; NCFA; Sacramento/Crocker; St. Lawrence U.; WMAA; Wright State U. **Bibliography:** Nordness, ed.; Pousette-Dart, ed.

KAUFFMAN, CRAIG. b. March 31, 1932, Eagle Rock, Calif. **Studied:** U. of Southern California, 1950-52; UCLA, BA, MA, 1952-56. Traveled Europe, 1956-57; resided Paris, 1960-62. **Taught:** U. of California, 1967-. **Awards:** National Endowment for the Arts, grant, 1968; Chicago/AI, Prize, 1970. **Address:** 4988 Mount Royal Drive, Los Angeles, CA 90041. **Dealer:** Asher/Faure, Los Angeles. **One-man Exhibitions:** (first) Felix Landau Gallery, 1953; Dilexi Gallery, San Francisco, 1958, 60; Ferus Gallery, Los Angeles, 1958, 63, 65, 67; The Pace Gallery, 1967, 69, 70, 73; Ferus/Pace Gallery, Los Angeles, 1967; Irving Blum Gallery, Los Angeles, 1969, 72; Pasadena/AM, 1970; U. of California, Irvine, 1970; Darthea Speyer Gallery, 1973; Mizuno Gallery, 1975; Robert Elkon Gallery, NYC, 1976; Cynthia Comsky Gallery, Los Angeles, 1976; Arco Center for Visual Arts, Los Angeles, 1978; Blum Helman Gallery, NYC, 1979, 82; Janus Gallery, Venice,

Calif., 1979; Grapestake Gallery, San Francisco, 1979; Asher/Faure, 1981, 83; Cirrus Gallery, Los Angeles, 1982; Thomas Segal Gallery, Boston, 1982. **Retrospective:** La Jolla, circ., 1981. **Group:** SFMA Annual, 1952, 54, 59-61; UCLA, California Painters under 35, 1959; U. of Illinois, 1961, 67; Seattle/AM, 1966; Detroit/Institute, Color, Image and Form, 1967; MOMA, The 1960's, 1967; WGMA, A New Aesthetic, 1967; V. Paris Biennial, 1967; CSCS, Los Angeles, 1968; Des Moines, Painting Out from the Wall, 1968; Vancouver, 1968; Pasadena/AM, West Coast: 1945-1969, 1969; Jewish Museum, Using Walls, 1970; Govett-Brewster, The State of California Art, 1971; Corcoran Biennial, 1973; Chicago/AI, 71st American Exhibition, 1974; WMAA (downtown), Illuminations and Reflections, 1974; U. of Illinois, 1974; ICA, Los Angeles, Current Concerns, 1975; Newport Harbor, The Last Time I Saw Ferus, 1976; Indianapolis, 1976; SFMA, 75 Years of California Art, 1976; SFMA, Painting and Sculpture in California: The Modern Era, 1977; Laguna Beach Museum of Art, Southern California 100, 1977; WMAA Biennial, 1979; Laguna Beach Museum of Art, Southern California Artists, 1981; Los Angeles/County MA, Art in Los Angeles, 1981; Long Beach/MA, Drawings by Painters, 1982. **Collections:** Arco Corp.; U. of Arizona; Australia; Buffalo/Albright; Chicago/AI; Fort Worth; Laguna Beach/AM; Long Beach/MA; Los Angeles/County MA; Milwaukee; MOMA; Pasadena/AM; Philip Morris Collection; Newport Harbor; Ridgefield/Aldrich; Santa Barbara/MA; Seagram Collection; SFMA; Tate; U. of Sydney, Australia; WMAA; Walker. **Bibliography:** Davis, D.; Friedman, M. 2; *The State of California Painting.*

KEARL, STANLEY. b. December 23, 1913, Waterbury, Conn. **Studied:** Yale U., 1941, BFA, 1942, MFA; State U. of Iowa, 1948, Ph.D. Traveled the world

extensively; resided Rome, nine years. **Taught:** U. of Minnesota, Duluth, 1947-48; Pratt Institute, 1967; YMHA, Scarsdale, 1974-75. Federal A.P.: Easel painting. **Awards:** Fulbright Exchange Professor to Rome U., Italy, 1949-50; Institute of Contemporary Arts, Florence, Italy, 1952; Connecticut Academy Sculpture Prize, 1958. **Address:** 344 Sprain Road, Scarsdale, NY 10583. **Dealer:** Ingber Art Gallery, NYC. **One-man Exhibitions:** (first) L'Obelisco, Rome, 1950; Galerie d'Art Moderne, Basel, 1951; Samlaren Gallery, Stockholm, 1951; Marbach Galerie, Berne, 1952; Galerie 16, Zurich, 1952; Beaux Arts Gallery, London, 1956; Galleria Selecta, Rome, 1957; Obelisk Gallery, Washington, D.C., 1958; Wakefield Gallery, NYC, 1961; D'Arcy Gallery, NYC, 1962; Hudson River Museum, Yonkers, N.Y., 1964; Grand Central Moderns, NYC, 1965, 68; IIE, NYC, 1967; Benson Gallery, Bridgehampton, N.Y., 1976. **Group:** XXVI Venice Biennial, 1952; PAFA, 1959; MOMA, 1961; WMAA Annual, 1962; Hudson River Museum Yonkers, N.Y., 1963; Institute of International Education; The Graham Gallery, 1969; Stamford Museum, 1974. **Collections:** State U. of Iowa; Marbach Galerie; U. of Minnesota; Northland College; Rome/Nazionale; Stockholm/National; Sweden/Goteborgs. **Bibliography:** Seuphor 3.

KEARNS, JAMES. b. August 7, 1924, Scranton, Pa. **Studied:** Chicago Art Institute School; De Paul U.; The U. of Chicago, 1946-50 (BFA). **Taught:** School of Visual Arts, NYC, 1959-; Skowhegan School, summer, 1961-64; Fairleigh Dickinson U., 1962-63. Illustrated *Can These Bones Live?* by Edward Dahlberg (New Directions, 1960), and *The Heart of Beethoven*, by Selman Rodman (Shorewood Press, 1962). **Awards:** NIAL Grant in Art, 1959; Montclair/AM, First Prize for Painting, 1961. **Address:** 452 Rockaway Road, Dover, NJ 07801. **One-man Exhibitions:** (first)

Grippi Gallery, 1956, also 1957, 60, 62, 68; Fairleigh Dickinson U., 1962; Scranton/Everhart, 1963; Lee Nordness Gallery, NYC, 1964; Bloomfield College, 1967; David Gallery, 1969, 71; Bloomfield College, 1972; Free Public Library, Fair Lawn, N.J., 1972; Sculpture Center, NYC, 1973; River Run Gallery, Edgartown, Mass., 1975, 77; Somerset Art Association, Bernardsville, N.J., 1975; Cramer Gallery, Glen Rock, N.J., 1976; Caldwell College, N.Y., 1976; Spook Farm Gallery, Far Hills, N.J., 1977. **Group:** A.F.A., Drawings, 1959; WMAA Annuals, 1959-61; A.F.A., New Talent, circ., 1960; A.F.A., Private Worlds, 1960; Newark Museum, Survey of American Sculpture, 1962; PAFA Annual; New York World's Fair, 1964-65; Monmouth Museum, Three Centuries of Art in New Jersey, 1969; San Diego, National Invitational Print Show, 1969; SAGA Annual, 1971; Schenectady Museum, Sculpture, 1976; NYC Audubon Artists, 1977. **Collections:** Caldwell College; Colby College; Hirshhorn; MMA; MOMA; Montclair/AM; NCFA; Newark Museum; Scranton/Everhart; Topeka Public Library; Trenton/State; WMAA. **Bibliography:** Gerdts; Nordness, ed.; Rodman 1, 3.

KELLY, ELLSWORTH. b. May 31, 1923, Newburgh, N.Y. **Studied:** Boston Museum School; Academie des Beaux-Arts, Paris; Pratt Institute, 1941-42. US Army, 1943-46. Traveled France, 1948-54. **Taught:** Norfolk House Center, Boston, 1946; American School, Paris, 1950-51. **Commissions:** Transportation Building, Philadelphia, 1957 (sculpture); Eastmore House, NYC (mural); New York State Pavilion, New York World's Fair, 1964-65 (sculpture); UNESCO, Paris, 1969 (mural); Central Trust Co., Cincinnati, 1979; Lincoln Park, Chicago, 1979; Lincoln Park, Chicago, 1981; Dallas/MFA, 1983. Designed sets and costumes for Paul Taylor Dance Co. **Member:** NIAL. **Awards:** Brandeis U., 1962; Carnegie,

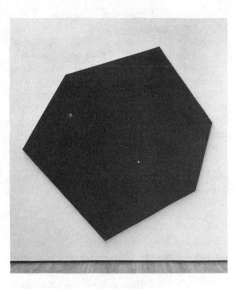

Ellsworth Kelly   *Dark Blue*   1986

1962, 64; International Biennial Exhibition of Paintings, Tokyo; Chicago/AI; Flora Mayer Witkowsky Prize, 1964; Chicago/AI, Painting Prize, 1974; Skowhegan School, award for sculpture, 1981. **Address:** Box 151, Spencertown, N.Y. 12165. **Dealers:** Leo Castelli Inc., NYC; Blum Helman Gallery, NYC; Margo Leavin Gallery, Los Angeles; Janie C. Lee, Houston. **One-man Exhibitions:** (first) Galerie Arnaud, 1951; Betty Parsons Gallery, 1956, 57, 59, 61, 63; Galerie Maeght, 1958, 64; A. Tooth & Sons, London, 1962; WGMA, 1964; ICA, Boston, 1964; Ferus Gallery, Los Angeles, 1965; Sidney Janis Gallery, 1965, 67, 71; Irving Blum Gallery, Los Angeles, 1967, 68, 73; Galerie Denise Rene/Hans Mayer, Dusseldorf, 1972; Buffalo/Albright, 1972; Leo Castelli Inc., NYC, 1973, 75 (2), 77 (2), 80, 81, 84 85; Ronald Greenberg Gallery, St. Louis, 1973; ACE Gallery, Venice, Calif., 1975; Blum Helman Gallery, NYC, 1975, 77, 79, 81, 82, 84, 85, 86; Janie C. Lee Gallery, Houston, 1976; Margo Leavin Gallery, Los Angeles, 1977, 82, 84; MOMA, 1978; MMA, 1979; Amsterdam/Stedelijk, circ., 1979-80; Buffalo/Albright, 1980; Larry

Gagosian Gallery, Los Angeles, 1981; John Berggruen Gallery, 1982; The Greenberg Gallery, 1982; Katonah (N.Y.) Gallery, 1985; Thomas Segal Gallery, Boston, 1982; Ann Weber Gallery, Georgetown, Me., 1985. **Retrospectives:** MOMA, 1973; Walker, 1974; Detroit/Institute, 1974; WMAA, 1982. **Group:** Salon des Realites Nouvelles, Paris, 1950, 51; Galerie Maeght, Tendence, 1951, 62; Brussels World's Fair, 1958; Carnegie, 1958, 62, 64, 66, 67; MOMA, Sixteen Americans, circ., 1959; SRGM, Abstract Expressionists and Imagists, 1961; VI Sao Paulo Biennial, 1961; Chicago/AI, 1961, 62, 64, 66; Seattle World's Fair, 1962; Jewish Museum, Toward a New Abstraction, 1963; Los Angeles/County MA, Post Painterly Abstraction, 1964; Tate, Gulbenkian International, 1964; SRGM, American Drawings, 1964; Tate, Dunn International, 1964; MOMA, The Responsive Eye, 1965; Amsterdam/Stedelijk, New Shapes of Color, 1966; SRGM, Systemic Painting, 1966; Jewish Museum, Primary Structures, 1966; XXXIII Venice Biennial, 1966; Brandeis U., 1966; WMAA, Sculpture Annuals, 1966, 68, Annual, 1967; Tokyo/Modern, 1966-67; Detroit/Institute, Color, Image and Form, 1967; Expo '67, Montreal, 1967; Los Angeles/County MA, American Sculpture of the Sixties, 1967; SRGM, 1967; MOMA, The Art of the Real, 1968; Buffalo/Albright, Plus by Minus, 1968; Documenta IV, Kassel, 1968; Pasadena/AM, Serial Imagery, 1968; WMAA, Contemporary American Sculpture, 1968-69; WMAA Annuals, 1969, 73; MMA, New York Painting and Sculpture, 1940-1970, 1969-70; Chicago/Contemporary (four-man), 1970; WMAA, The Structure of Color, 1971; MOMA, Technics and Creativity; Gemini G.E.L., 1971; ICA, U. of Pennsylvania, Grids, 1972; Kunstmuseum, Lucerne, 1973; Musée Galliera, Paris, Festival d'Automne, 1973; Parcheggio di Villa Borghese, Rome, Contemporanea, 1974; Rijksmuseum/Kroller-Muller, Functions of Drawing, 1975; NCFA, Sculpture: American Directions

1945-1975, 1975; MOMA, Drawing Now, 1976; SRGM, 20th Century American Drawings, 1976; Chicago/AI Annual, 1976; WMAA, 200 Years of American Sculpture, 1976; A.F.A., American Master Drawing and Watercolors, 1976; Paris/Beaubourg, Paris-New York, 1977; Cambridge, Jubilation, 1977; Minnesota/MA, American Drawings 1927-1977, 1977; Venice, Biennial, 1978; Buffalo/Albright, American Painting of the 1970's, 1978; WMAA Biennial, 1979; Corcoran Biennial, 1979; California State U., Northridge, Americans in Paris, the 50s, 1979; Brooklyn Museum, American Drawings in Black and White: 1970-1979, 1980; MOMA, Printed Art: A View of Two Decades, 1980; SFMA, Twenty American Artists, 1980; Walker, Artist and Printer, 1980; Cologne, International, 1981; Cologne/Stadt, Westkunst, 1981; Paris/Beaubourg, Paris-Paris/Créations en France 1937-57, 1981; Toulon, Espace Peint, Espace Traverse: La Danse, 1981; WMAA Biennials, 81; ARS 83, Helsinki, 1983; Sunderland (Eng.) Arts Centre, Drawing in Air, 1983; Amsterdam/Stedelijk, La Grande Parade, 1984; Boston/MFA, 10 Painters and Sculptors Draw, 1984; National Gallery and Yale U., The Folding Image, 1984; Carnegie, International, 1985; Ecole des Beaux Arts, Paris, Cinquante Ans de Dessins Americains, 1930-1980, 1985; MOMA, Contrasts of Form, 1985; Fort Lauderdale, An American Renaissance: Painting and Sculpture Since 1940, 1986; Los Angeles/County MA, The Spiritual in Art, 1986; Purchase/SUNY, The Window in Twentieth Century Art, 1986; Tate Gallery, Forty Years of Modern Art, 1945-1985, 1986; Whitechapel Art Gallery, London, In Tandem: The Painter-Sculptor in the Twentieth Century, 1986. **Collections:** Amsterdam/Stedelijk; Baltimore/MA; Berlin/National; Brandeis U.; Buffalo/Albright; Canberra/National; Carnegie; Chicago/AI; Cincinnati/AM; Cleveland/MA; Cologne; Corcoran; Dallas/MFA; Dartmouth College; Detroit/Institute; Dusseldorf/KN-W; Eindhoven; Fort

Worth; Foundation Maeght; Grenoble; Harvard U.; High Museum; Hirshhorn; Humlebaek/Louisiana; La Jolla; Los Angeles/County MA; MMA; MOMA; Milwaukee; Munster/WK; Omaha/Joslyn; PMA; Paris/Moderne; Pasadena/AM; Portland, Ore./AM; RISD; Rijksmuseum Kroller-Muller; St. Louis/City; SFMA; SRGM; Seattle/AM; Stockholm/National; Tate Gallery; U. of Texas; Toronto; VMFA; WGMA; WMAA; Walker; Worcester/AM; Yale U. **Bibliography:** Alloway 3; Battcock, ed.; *Black and White Are Colors*; Calas, N. and E.; *Contemporanea*; **Coplans 1,** 3; Davies; Davis, D.; De Wilde 1, 2; Friedman, M. 2; Gaunt; **Goossen** 1, **2**; Honisch and Jensen, eds.; Hunter, ed.; Kozloff 3; *Kunst um 1970*; Lippard 5; MacAgy 2; Murken-Altrogge; Nordness, ed.; *Report*; Rickey; Rose, B., 1; Sandler 1; Seuphor; Sims and Pulitzer; Toher, ed.; Tuchman 1, 3; Weller.

KELLY, JAMES. b. December 19, 1913, Philadelphia, Pa. **Studied:** Philadelphia Museum School, 1937; PAFA, 1938; Barnes Foundation, 1941; California School of Fine Arts, 1951-54. US Air Force, 1941-45. **Taught:** U. of California, Berkeley, 1957. **Member:** Artists Equity. **Awards:** Ford Foundation Grant for Tamarind, 1963. **Address:** 463 West Street, NYC 10014. **One-man Exhibitions:** (first) California Palace, 1954; SFMA, 1956; The Stryke Gallery NYC, 1963; East Hampton Gallery, N.Y., 1965, 69; Albright College, Reading, Pa., 1966; Long Island U., 1968; Westbeth Gallery, NYC, 1971, 72. **Group:** PAFA, 1951; SFMA Annuals, 1955-58; U. of Minnesota, California Painters, 1956; Minneapolis/Institute, American Painting, 1945-57, 1957; Santa Barbara/MA, II Pacific Coast Biennial, 1957; A.F.A., West Coast Artists, circ., 1959-60; Los Angeles/County MA, Late Fifties at the Ferus, 1968; Oakland/AM, A Period of Exploration, 1973; Newport Harbor, The Last Time I Saw Ferus, 1976; SFMA, California

Painting: The Modern Era, 1976; Oakland/AM, Art in the San Francisco Bay Area, 1945-1980, 1985. **Collections:** Amon Carter Museum; Chase Manhattan Bank, NYC; Chicago/AI; Fort Worth; La Jolla; Los Angeles/County MA; MOMA; U. of Massachusetts; Oakland/AM; Pasadena/AM; Richmond (Calif.) Art Center; Sacramento/Crocker; SFMA; UCLA; Westinghouse. **Bibliography:** McChesney. Archives.

KELLY, LÉON (Léon Kelly y Corrons). **b.** October 21, 1901, Philadelphia. **d.** June 28, 1982, Loveladies Harbor, N.J. **Studied:** Philadelphia Museum School; PAFA; privately with Arthur B. Carles, Jr., and Earl Horter. Traveled Europe, North Africa, USA; resided Paris, 1924-30. Federal A.P.; Supervisor of Artists in Philadelphia; mural and easel painting. Designed sets and costumes for several ballet companies including the Ballet Russe de Monte Carlo. **Taught:** Brooklyn Museum School. **Commissions:** Portraits. Awards: PAFA, Cresson Fellowship, 1924; William and Noma Copley Foundation Grant, 1959. **One-man Exhibitions:** (first) Little Gallery of Contemporary Art, Philadelphia, 1925, also 1932; Galerie du Printemps, Paris, 1926; Contemporary Arts Gallery, NYC, 1933; Julien Levy Galleries, NYC, 1942, 44, 45; Philadelphia Art Alliance, 1943; Hugo Gallery, NYC, 1950; Galleria Amici di Francia, Milan, 1954; Hewitt Gallery, NYC, 1956; Alexandre Iolas Gallery, NYC, 1959, 61; The Zabriskie Gallery, 1963; Washburn Gallery Inc., 1981. **Retrospectives:** Philadelphia Art Alliance, 1928; International Gallery, Baltimore, 1965. **Group:** European International 1927: A Century of Progress, Chicago, 1933-34; WMAA Annuals; Carnegie; U. of Nebraska; PMA; Chicago/AI; Corcoran; Newark Museum, 1968. **Collections:** Allentown/AM; Andover/Phillips; Chicago/AI; Clearwater/Gulf Coast; Hartford/Wadsworth; La France Art Institute; MMA; MOMA; Museo Nacional de Historia; National Arts Foundation; U. of Nebraska; Newark Museum; PAFA; PMA; The Pennsylvania State U.; Steuben Glass; Tel Aviv; Utica; WMAA. **Bibliography:** *Avant-Garde Painting and Sculpture in America;* Gerdts; Janis, S. Archives.

KENT, ROCKWELL. b. June 21, 1882, Tarrytown Heights, N.Y.; **d.** March 13, 1971, Plattsburg, N.Y. **Studied:** Columbia U., 1906-10, with William M. Chase, Robert Henri, Kenneth Hayes Miller, Abbott Thayer, Traveled Canada, USA, Europe, Latin America, Greenland. **Member:** NIAL; Hon. Member, Academy of Fine Arts of the USSR. **Commissions** (murals): US Post Office, Washington, D.C.; Federal Building, Washington, D.C. **One-man Exhibitions:** Clausen Galleries, NYC, 1908, 19; Wildenstein & Co., NYC, 1925, 42; Macbeth Gallery, NYC, 1934; Richard Larcada Gallery, 1966, 69, 72; Bowdoin College, 1969; Plattsburgh/SUNY, 1982; Santa Barbara/MA, 1985. **Retrospectives:** Wildenstein & Co., NYC, 1924; Syracuse/Everson, 1937; Bowdoin College, 1969. **Group:** NAD, 1905; Academy of Fine Arts, Berlin, 1910; Century Association, 1940; Cleveland/MA; WMAA. **Collections:** American Car and Foundry Co.; Andover/Phillips; Baltimore/MA; Boston/MFA; British Museum; Brooklyn Museum; Chicago/AI; Cleveland/MA; Columbus; Corcoran; Detroit/Institute; Harvard U.; Honolulu Academy; Houston/MFA; Indianapolis/Herron; Library of Congress; MMA; NYPL; Newark Museum; Phillips; Victoria and Albert Museum; WMAA; Yale U. **Bibliography:** American Artists Congress, Inc.; American Artists Group Inc. 1, 3; **Armitage;** Baur 7; Biddle 4; Birchman; Blesh 1; Brown; Cahill and Barr, eds.; Cheney; Cummings 1; Finklestein; Goodrich and Baur 1; Hall; Hartmann; *Index of 20th Century Artists;* Jackman; **Jones, D.B.;** Kent, N.; **Kent, R. 1, 2, 3; Kent R., ed.;**

Lee and Burchwood; Mather 1; Mellquist; Narodny; Neuhaus; Pagano; Pearson 1; Phillips 1, 2; Reese; Richardson, E.P.; Ringel, ed.; Ritchie 1; Rose, B., 1; Smith, S.C.K.; Zigrosser 1. Archives.

KEPES, GYORGY. b. October 4, 1906, Selyp, Hungary. **Studied:** Academy of Fine Arts, Budapest, 1924-28. **Taught:** New Bauhaus, Chicago, 1937-43; a foundling collaborator, with Lazlo Moholy-Nagy and Robert Wolff, of the Institute of Design, Chicago, 1938-42; MIT, 1946-. Codirector, Rockefeller Foundation Research Project: Perceptual Form of Cities. **Commissions** (murals): Harvard U. Graduate Center; KLM Royal Dutch Airlines, NYC; Travelers Insurance Companies, Los Angeles; Sheraton Hotels, Dallas and Chicago; Children's Library, Fitchburg, Mass.; American Housing Exhibit, Paris, 1946. **Awards:** American Institute of Graphic Art, 1944, 49; U. of Illinois. **P.P.,** 1954; Guggenheim Foundation Fellowship, 1960-61; Art Directors Club, Chicago, 1963. **Address:** 90 Larchwood Drive, Cambridge, MA 02138. **Dealer:** Saidenberg Gallery. **One-man Exhibitions:** Katherine Kuh Gallery, Chicago, 1939; Chicago/AI, 1944, 54; Outline Gallery, Pittsburgh, 1945; Royal Academy, Copenhagen, 1950; Margaret Brown Gallery, Boston, 1951, 55; San Diego, 1952; Amsterdam/Stedelijk, 1952; Long Beach/MA, 1952; U. of California, Berkeley, 1952; SFMA, 1952, 54; Currier, 1953; Cranbrook, 1954; ICA, Boston, 1954; Syracuse/Everson, 1957; Houston/MFA, 1958; Dallas/MFA, 1958; L'Obelisco, Rome, 1958; Ivrea Gallery, Florence, Italy, 1958; The Howard Wise Gallery, Cleveland, 1959; Baltimore/MA, 1959; Saidenberg Gallery, 1960, 66, 68; Lincoln, Mass./De Cordova, 1969; NCFA, 1970, Saidenberg Gallery, NYC, 1970, 72, 80; Alpha Gallery, 1970, 72, 74; Museum of Science and Hayden Planetarium, Boston, 1973; Dartmouth College, 1977; Prakapas Gallery,

NYC, 1977; Alpha Gallery, Boston, 1986; ICP, NYC, 1984; Galereabon, Budapest, 1986; MIT, 1984. **Retrospective:** MIT, 1978. **Group:** MOMA, 1947, 52; Chicago/AI, 1951, 53, 57; U. of Illinois, 1952, 53; SFMA; Cranbrook; Dallas/MFA; Andover/Phillips; San Diego, WMAA; Denver/AM, 1953; Carnegie, 1955. **Collections:** Andover/Phillips, Boston/MFA; Buffalo/Albright; Chase Manhattan Bank; Cranbrook; Dallas/MFA; Des Moines; Houston/MFA; U. of Illinois; Indianapolis/Herron; Lincoln, Mass./De Cordova; MIT; MOMA; SFMA; San Diego; VMFA; WMAA. **Bibliography: Alfieri;** Davis, D.; Janis and Blesh 1; Janis, S.; **Kepes 1, 2; Kepes, ed.;** Kuh 1; Nordness, ed.; Pearson 1; Rickey. Archives.

KEYSER, ROBERT b. July 27, 1924, Philadelphia, Pa. **Studied:** U. of Pennsylvania; Atelier Fernand Leger, Paris, 1949-51. US Navy, World War II (three years). Traveled Europe, North Africa (two years). **Taught:** Philadelphia Museum School, 1963; Temple U., Rome, 1975-77. **Address:** Box 328 R.D. #4, Quakertown, PA, 18951. **Dealer:** Marion Locks Gallery, Philadelphia. **One-man Exhibitions:** (first) Galerie Huit, Paris, 1951; Hendler Gallery, Philadelphia, 1952; Parma Gallery, NYC, 1954, 56, 58; P. Rosenberg and Co., 1959, 60, 62, 66, 71, 75, 79; Gimpel Fils, 1962; Gallery Marc, Washington, D.C., 1972; Marion Locks Gallery, Philadelphia, 1974, 1979; Temple U., Rome, 1977. **Group:** PAFA Annual; WMAA Annual; A.F.A., Collage in America, circ., 1957-58; Joachim Gallery, Chicago, 1960; U. of Illinois, 1961; Salon du Mai, Paris, Salon d'Automne, Paris; Salon des Realites Nouvelles, Paris; Corcoran, 1975; PMA, 300 Years of American Art, 1976; PAFA, Contemporary Drawing: Philadelphia I, 1978. **Collections:** AT&T; Brandeis U.; New London; PMA; Phillips; Utica; Vassar College.

KIENBUSCH, WILLIAM b. April 13, 1914, NYC; **d.** March 23, 1980, NYC. **Studied:** Princeton U., 1936, BA, PBK (fine-arts major); ASL, 1936-37; Colorado Springs Fine Arts Center, with Henry Poor; Academie Colarossi, Paris; privately with Anton Refregier and Stuart Davis in New York. US Army, World War II. **Taught:** Brooklyn Museum School, 1948-1979. **Awards:** Brooklyn Society of Artists Annual, First Prize, 1952; MMA, Drawing Prize, 1952; Columbia, S.C./MA, First **P.P.,** Watercolors, 1957; Guggenheim Foundation Fellowship, 1958; Ford Foundation, **P.P.,** 1961; Boston Arts Festival, First Prize for Watercolor, 1961; NIAL, Childe Hassam Fund, 1970. **One-man Exhibitions:** Kraushaar Galeries, 1949, 52, 56, 59, 63, 65, 69, 72, 78, 83; U. of Maine, 1956; Cornell U., 1958; Princeton U., 1962; Fort Worth, 1964 (two-man); Portland, Me./AM, 1973; Drew U., 1973. **Retrospectives:** Carnegie, 1954 (two-man, with Dioda); Colby College, circ., 1981. **Group:** Buffalo/Albright; Chicago/AI; MMA, 1952; Brooklyn Museum, 1953, 59; WMAA, The New Decade, 1954-55; Carnegie, 1955; WMAA, 1955; Walker, MOMA, Twelve Americans, circ., 1956; Brussels World's Fair, 1958; PAFA Annuals, 1962, 65, 67; New York World's Fair, 1964-65; WMAA, Art of the U.S. 1670-1966, 1966; Indianapolis, 1969; Omaha/Joslyn, A Sense of Place, circ., 1973; VMFA, American Marine Painting, 1976. **Collections:** Atlanta U.; Boston/MFA; Bowdoin College; Brooklyn Museum; Buffalo/Albright; Carnegie; Colorado Springs/FA; Columbia, S.C./MA; Commerce Trust Co.; Currier; Dartmouth College; U. of Delaware; Des Moines; Detroit/Institute; Fort Worth; Hartford/Wadsworth; Houston/MFA; Kansas City/Nelson; Lehigh U.; MMA; MOMA; U. of Maine; U. of Michigan; U. of Minnesota; Montclair/AM; NCFA; U. of Nebraska; Newark Museum; New Britain; Norfolk/Chrysler; PAFA; PMA; Portland, Me./MA; U. of Rochester; Toledo/MA; Toronto; Utica;

VMFA; WMAA; Wichita/AM; Williams College. **Bibliography:** Baur 5; Eliot; Goodrich and Baur 1; McCurdy, ed.; Nordness, ed.; Pousette-Dart, ed.; Ritchie 1; Seitz 3. Archives.

KIENHOLZ, EDWARD. b. 1927, Fairfield, Wash. **Studied:** Eastern Washington College of Education. Founded the Now Gallery, Los Angeles, 1956, and later the Ferus Gallery, Los Angeles. **Address:** Hope, Idaho 83836. **One-man Exhibitions:** (first) Cafe Galleria, Los Angeles, 1955; Syndell Studios, Los Angeles, 1956; Exodus Gallery, San Pedro, Calif.; Ferus Gallery, Los Angeles (three-man), 1958, (two-man), 1959, 60, 62; Pasadena/AM, 1961; Alexander Iolas Gallery, 1963; Dwan Gallery, Los Angeles, 1963-65; Dwan Gallery, NYC, 1967 (2); WGMA, 1967; Gallery 699, Los Angeles, 1968; Eugenia Butler, 1969; Stockholm/National, 1970; Dusseldorf/Kunsthalle, 1970; CNAC, 1970; Zurich, 1971; ICA, London, 1971; Wide White Space Gallery, Antwerp, 1972; Galerie Onnasch, Cologne, 1973; Galleria Bocchi, Milan, 1974; Humlebaek/Louisiana, 1976; Chicago/Contemporary, 1985; Portland (Ore.) Center for the Visual Arts, 1986; Trinity College, Dublin, 1981; Galerie Maeght, Paris, 1983; Art Museum of South Texas, 1982; Braunstein Gallery, San Francisco, 1984. **Group:** MOMA, The Art of Assemblage, circ., 1961; WMAA, Fifty California Artists, 1962; Los Angeles/County MA, Sculpture of the Sixties, 1967; MOMA, The Machine, 1968; MOMA, Dada, Surrealism and Their Heritage, 1968; WMAA, Human Concern/Personal Torment, 1969; Documenta IV & V, Kassel, 1968, 72; XXXVIII, Venice Bienniale, 1976; WMAA, 200 Years of American Sculpture, 1976; WMAA Biennial 1981. **Collections:** Aachen/NG; Amsterdam/Stedelijk; Los Angeles/County MA; MOMA; Tokyo/Modern; WMAA. **Bibliography:** Battcock, ed.; Calas, N. and E.; Davis, D.; De Wilde 2; Hulten;

Edward Kienholz; Edward Kienholz: **11 + 11 Tableaux;** Kozloff 3; Lippard 5; Lippard, ed.: Rose, B., 1; Rubin 1; Russell and Gablik; Tuchman 1, 2; *When Attitudes Become Form.*

KIESLER, FREDERICK, J. b. 1890, Vienna, Austria; **d.** December 27, 1965, NYC. To USA, 1926; citizen. Scenic Director, Julliard School of Music, NYC, 1933-57. Registered Architect; designed and built the Art of This Century Gallery, NYC (1940); the Galerie Maeght, Paris (1947); the World House Galleries, NYC (1957); and the Kamer Gallery, NYC (1959). **One-man Exhibitions:** MOMA, 1951 (sculpture); MOMA, Endless House, 1960, also 1966; U. of Houston, Architectural Plans, 1960; Leo Castelli Inc., 1961, 62; SRGM, Environmental Sculpture, 1964; The Howard Wise Gallery, NYC, 1969; Andre Emmerich Gallery, NYC, 1979, 80; Alfred Kren Gallery, NYC and Jason McCoy, Inc., NYC, 1986. **Retrospective:** Galerie Nachst Skt. Stephan, Vienna, 1975. **Group:** WMAA; A.F.A., Universal Theater, circ., 1961-64; WMAA, The Third Dimension, 1984. **Collections:** MOMA. **Bibliography:** Arp; Barr 1; Blesh 1; Breton 3; Calas; *Frederick Kiesler;* Janis and Blesh 1; Janis, S.; *Metro;* Phillips, Lisa; Rose, B., 1; Rubin 1; Seuphor 3; Tuchman 1. Archives.

KING, WILLIAM DICKEY. b. February 25, 1925, Jacksonville, Fla. **Studied:** U. of Florida, 1942-44; Cooper Union 1945-48, with Milton Hebald, John Hovannes; Brooklyn Museum School, 1948-49, with Hebald; Central School of Arts and Crafts, London, 1952. Traveled Italy, Greece. **Taught:** Brooklyn Museum School, 1953-60; U. of California, Berkeley, 1965-66; ASL, 1968-69; U. of Pennsylvania, 1972-73; SUNY 1974-75. **Commissions:** (murals) SS *United States,* 1952; Bankers Trust Company, NYC, 1960; Miami-Dade, 1972; Potsdam/SUNY, 1973-74; Detroit Medi-

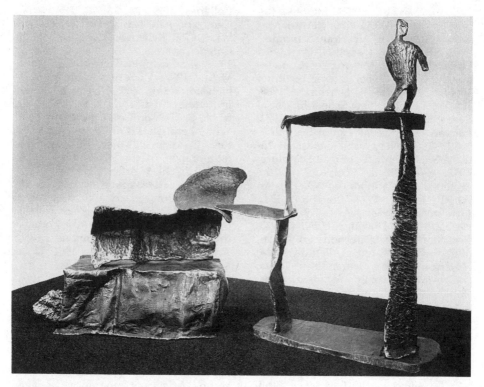

Frederick Kiesler   *Arch as Triumph of Man*   1964

cal Center, 1979; Madison Art and Civic Center, Wisconsin, 1979; Lincoln Library, Fort Wayne, 1980; Orlando (Fla.) International Airport, 1983; Florida Atlantic U., 1984; Sterling Plaza, NYC, 1985. **Awards:** Cooper Union, Sculpture Prize, 1948, Augustus Saint-Gaudens Medal, 1964; Fulbright Fellowship (Italy), 1949; Margaret Tiffany Blake Competition, First Prize, 1951; Moorehead Patterson Award (sculpture/to AMF Company), 1960; CAPS, 1974. **Address:** % Dealer. **Dealer:** Terry Dintenfass, Inc., NYC. **One-man Exhibitions:** The Alan Gallery, NYC, 1954, 55, 61; Terry Dintenfass, Inc., 1962, 64-71, 1973, 74, 76, 80, 81, 82, 83, 86; The Gallery, Norwalk, Ohio, 1963; Donald F. Morris Gallery, Detroit, 1964; Washington Federal Savings & Loan Association of Miami Beach, Fla., 1965; Felix Landau Gallery, 1966; Berkeley Gallery, San Francisco, 1966; Feigen-Palmer Gallery, Los Angeles, 1966; U. of Miami, 1967; Guild Hall, 1969; Galerie Ann, Houston, 1970; The Berenson Gallery, 1970; SFMA, 1970, circ., 74; Alpha Gallery, 1971; U. of Nebraska, 1972; U. of Connecticut, 1973; Aronson Gallery, Atlanta, 1973; Moravian College, 1974; San Antonio/McNay, circ., 1973; Davis Stuart Galleries, Los Angeles, 1974; U. of Connecticut, 1979; Wingspread Gallery, Northeast Harbor, Me., 1981; Albany/SUNY, 1981; Alpha Gallery, Boston, 1982. **Retrospective:** SFMA, circ., 1970, 74. **Group:** City of Philadelphia, Sculpture International, 1949; MOMA, New Talent; Brooklyn Museum, 1949, 50, 54, 55, 57, 58; WMAA Annuals, 1950-56, 1958-60, 1962-64, 1966, 68; U. of Illinois, 1954, 56, 62, 63, 65; New Sculpture Group, NYC,

1957-60; Carnegie, 1958; MOMA, Recent Sculpture USA, 1959; Newark Museum, Survey of American Sculpture, 1962; SRGM, The Joseph H. Hirshhorn Collection, 1962; Museum of Contemporary Crafts, 1966; Drexel Institute, 1966; Indianapolis/Herron, 1968; AAAL, 1970, 74; New School for Social Research, Humor, Satire, Irony, 1972; Harvard U., Recent Figure Sculpture, 1972; Art Gallery of Budapest, II International Biennial of Small Sculpture, 1973; San Diego, Sculpture in the Street, 1973; Cranbrook, WAVES, An Artist Selects, 1974; Newport, R.I., Monuments, 1974; AAAL, 1974; Minnesota/MA, Drawings/USA, 1975; Potsdam/SUNY, Directions in Metal, 1982. **Collections:** Allentown/AM; American Export Isbrandtsen Lines, Inc., Andover/Phillips; U. of Arkansas; Bankers Trust Company; Brandeis U.; U. of California; Columbus; Cornell U.; Creekwood; Dartmouth College; First National Bank of Chicago; Guild Hall; Little Rock/MFA; MMA; U. of Massachusetts; Miami-Dade; NYU; U. of North Carolina; Potsdam/SUNY; SRGM; Syracuse U.; Temple U. **Bibliography:** Downes, ed.; Lippard 5; *Monumenta: Recent Figure Sculpture;* Seuphor 3. Archives.

KIPNISS, ROBERT. b. February 1, 1931, NYC. **Studied:** Wittenberg College, 1948-50; State U. of Iowa, 1950-54, BA (English literature), MFA (painting and art history); ASL, with Alice Murphy. US Army, 1956-58. **Member:** Board of Directors of Audubon Artists; NAD. **Awards:** SAGA, 1979; Audubon Artists, 1976, 78; NAD, 1976; Hon. Ph.D., Wittenberg U., 1979. **Address:** Hudson House, Box 7099, Ardsley-on-Hudson, N.Y. 10503. **One-man Exhibitions:** (first) Creative Gallery, NYC, 1951; The Salpeter Gallery, NYC, 1953; The Contemporaries, NYC, 1959, 60, 66, 67; Alan Auslander Gallery, NYC, 1963; Gallery Vendome, Pittsburgh, 1964; U. of Louisville, 1965; FAR Gallery, 1968, 70, 72, 75; Merrill Chase Galleries, 1972, 74, 76, 77, 78, 79, 80; Centro de Arte Actual, Pereira, Colombia, 1975; Kalamazoo/Institute, 1975; Galerie Sandiego, Bogota, Colombia, 1975, 77; Xochipili Gallery, Rochester, Mich., 1977; Quadrum Gallery, Marblehead, Mass., 1977, 78; River Gallery, Irvington-on-Hudson, N.Y., 1977, 78, 80; A. B. Closson Co., Cincinnati, 1979; Wittenberg U., 1979; Canton Art Institute, Ohio, 1979; Museo de Arte Contemporanco, Cali, Colombia, 1975, 1980; Hirschl & Adler Galleries, NYC, 1977, 80. **Retrospective:** Museo de Arte Contemporaneo, Cali, Colombia, S.A., 1975; AAA, Ten Years of Lithography, 1977. **Group:** Youngstown/Butler, 1951; Columbus, 1958; A.F.A., New Talent, circ., 1961; U. of Minnesota, Duluth; A.F.A., circ., 1963-65; Indianapolis/Herron, 1964; Utah State Institute of Fine Arts, Salt Lake City, 1964; Cornell U., 1964; Cranbrook, 1964; Corcoran, 1966, 67; Buffalo/Albright, 1966, 67; MOMA, 1966, 67; Massillon Museum, 1967; NAD, 1974; NYPL, 1974; NAD, 1974, 76, 77; SAGA, 1979; AAIAL, 1978; Museo de Arte Contemporanea, III Biennal Graficas, 1976. **Collections:** AT&T; Atlantic Richfield Co.; Ball State U.; Buffalo/Albright; Canton Art Institute; Chase Manhattan Bank, NYC; Chicago/AI; Cleveland/MA; Continental Grain Company, NYC; Detroit/Institute; Esmark, Chicago; Flint/Institute; Glen Alden Corp., NYC; IBM, Chicago; U. of Iowa; Irving Trust Co.; Los Angeles/County MA; Library of Congress; Miami U.; Minnesota/MA; NCFA; Notre Dame U.; NYPL; Ohio U.; RISD; Singer Company, Inc., NYC; WMAA; Wittenberg U.; Yale U.

KIPP, LYMAN. b. December 24, 1929, Dobbs Ferry, N.Y. **Studied:** Pratt Institute, 1950-54; Cranbrook, 1952-53. Traveled Europe, India, Morocco, Australia. **Taught:** Bennington College, 1960-63; Hunter College, 1963-86; Herbert H. Lehman College, Bronx, N.Y.,

1968-75; Dartmouth College, 1969. **Member:** American Association of University Professors; Artists Equity. **Commissions:** Lambert Corp., Dallas; General Services Administration, Federal Office Building and Post Office, Van Nuys, Calif.; Lake Placid, N.Y. **Awards:** Guggenheim Foundation Fellowship, 1965; Fulbright Fellowship, 1965. **Address:** Route 100, Somers, N.Y. 10589. **One-man Exhibitions:** Cranbrook, 1954; Betty Parsons Gallery, 1954, 56, 58, 60, 62, 64, 65, 68; Arizona State College, 1957; Myrtle Todes Gallery, Glencoe, Ill, 1956, 60; Bennington College, 1961; Dartmouth College, 1965; Buffalo/Albright, 1967; Katonah (N.Y.) Art Gallery, 1968; Obelisk Gallery, 1969; A.M. Sachs Gallery, 1970; Chapman Kelley Gallery, Dallas, 1971; Adam Gallery, NYC, 1972; City U. of New York Graduate Center, 1972; Richard Gray Gallery, 1973; Galerie Denis Rene, NYC (two man), 1974; Bridge Gallery, White Plains, N.Y., 1975; Greenway Plaza, Houston, 1975; Laguna Gloria Museum, Austin, Texas, 1976; The Art Center, Waco, Texas, 1976; Nielson Memorial Museum, Amarillo, Texas, 1977; U. of Alabama, 1977; Max Hutchinson Gallery, NYC, 1977; Sculpture Now, Inc., NYC, 1978; Construct, Chicago, 1978, 80; William Patterson College (three-man), 1979; Calvin College, Grand Rapids, Mich., 1979; Carolyn Schneebeck Gallery, Cincinnati, 1980; Irving Sculpture Gallery, Glebe, N.S.W., Australia, 1985; Robert L. Kidd Gallery, Birmingham, Mich., 1985. **Group:** RISD, Four Young Americans, 1955; WMAA Annuals, 1956, 60, 62, 66, 68; Pensacola, Freedom of Inspiration, 1958; Claude Bernard, Paris, 1960; U. of Illinois, 1961; Carnegie, 1961, 62; Chicago/AI, 1961, 62; Sao Paulo, 1963; Drawing Society, National Exhibition, 1965; Jewish Museum, Primary Structures, 1966; Musée Cantonal des Beaux-Arts, Lausanne, II Salon International de Galeries Pilotes, 1966; Los Angeles/County MA, American Sculpture of the Sixties, 1967; Ridgefield/Aldrich, 1968; MOMA, The Art of the Real, 1968; U. of Nebraska, American Sculpture, 1970; San Diego, Art Is for People, 1973; Grand Rapids, Sculpture off the Pedestal, 1973; Newport, R.I., Monumenta, 1974; Akron/AI, Project: New Urban Monuments, circ., 1977-79. **Collections:** U. of Alaska; Andover/Phillips; Buffalo/Albright; U. of California; Cranbrook; Dartmouth College; Fort Worth; High Museum; Jackson/MMA; U. of Kentucky; MIT; U. of Michigan; U. of Nebraska; New York Bank for Savings; PMA; The Pennsylvania State U.; South Mall, Albany; State College at Salem; Storm King Art Center; WMAA. **Bibliography:** Battcock, ed.; Goossen 1; MacAgy 2; *Monumenta*; Seuphor 3; Tuchman 1.

KIRSCHENBAUM, JULES. b. March 25, 1930, NYC. **Studied:** Brooklyn Museum School, 1948-50. **Awards:** Joe and Emily Lowe Foundation Award, 1950; PAFA, Dana Watercolor Medal, 1952; NAD, Hallgarten Prize, 1953; NAD, Isaac N. Maynard Prize, 1954; NAD, S. J. Wallace Truman Prize, 1955; Fulbright Fellowship (Italy), 1956; PAFA, Hon. Men., 1957; AAAL, Childe Hassam Award, 1957; Youngstown/Butler, First Prize, 1957; NAD, First Prize, Figure Painting, 1960; NAD, Thomas R. Proctor Prize, 1983; NAD, Grumbacher Award and Gold Medal, 1984; NAD, Emil and Dines Carlsen Award, 1985. **Address:** 2829 Forest Drive, Des Moines, IA 50312. **Dealer:** The Forum Gallery. **One-man Exhibitions:** The Salpeter Gallery, NYC, 1955, 56; Des Moines, 1964; The Forum Gallery, NYC, 1969, 1977, 85. **Group:** MMA, 1952; MOMA; PAFA, 1952, 53, 54, 57; WMAA, 1953-57; Brooklyn Museum; NYU; Chicago/AI, 1957; U. of Illinois, 1957; Youngstown/Butler, 1957; Corcoran; Festival of Two Worlds, Spoleto, 1958; Santa Barbara/MA; Pasadena/AM; Houston/MFA; Dallas/MFA. **Collections:** Des Moines; U. of Nebraska; WMAA; Youngstown/Butler.

KITAJ, R. B. b. October 19, 1932, Cleveland, Ohio. Traveled Europe, North Africa. U.S. Army 1955-57. **Studied:** Cleveland/MA, Children's Classes, 1937-42; Cooper Union, 1950, with Sidney Delevante; Akademie der Bildenden Kunste, Vienna, 1951-54, with A. P. von Gutersloh, Fritz Wotruba; U. of Oxford, Ruskin School of Drawing and Fine Art, 1957, 1959, certificate of Fine Art; Royal College of Art, 1960-62. **Taught:** Camberwell School of Art and Crafts, Ealing Technical College, 1961-63; Slade School of Fine Art, 1963, 64, 66, 67; Dartmouth College, 1978. **Organized:** *The Human Clay*, exhibition for the Hayward Gallery, London, 1976. **Address:** 62 Elm Park Road, London S.W. 3, England. **Dealer:** Marlborough Gallery Inc., NYC and Marlborough Fine Art Ltd., London. **One-man Exhibitions:** (first) Marlborough Fine Art Ltd., London, 1963, 70, 77, 80, 85; Marlborough Gallery, Inc., NYC, 1965, 74, 79, 86; Los Angeles/County MA, 1965; Cleveland/MA, 1967; Amsterdam/Stedelijk, 1967; U. of California, Berkeley, 1967; Galerie Mikro, Berlin, 1969; Hannover/K-G, 1970; Graphic Gallery, San Francisco, 1971; Amerika Haus, Berlin, 1973; New 57 Gallery, Edinburgh, 1975; Petersburg Press, NYC, 1975, 76; Mala Galerija, Ljubljana, 1976; Ikon Gallery, Birmingham, England, 1977; Dartmouth College, 1978. **Retrospective:** Hirshhorn, circ., 1981. **Group:** Royal College of Art, London, Young Contemporaries, 1961; Eindhoven, Lompass 2, 1962; Beaverbrook Art Gallery, Fredericton, New Brunswick, Canada, Dunn International, 1963; SRGM, Guggenheim International, 1964; Tate Gallery, Painting and Sculpture of a Decade, 1964; XXXII & XXXV Venice Biennials, 1964, 70; Documenta III, Kassel, 1964; Museum des 20. Jahrhunderts, Pop, etc., 1964; Carnegie, International, 1964, 67; Brussels/Beaux-Arts, Pop Art, 1965; WMAA Annuals, 1965, 67; U. of Illinois, 1967; Chicago/Contemporary, Pictures to be Read/Poetry to be Seen, 1967; ICA, London, The Obsessive Image, 1968; Musée des Arts Decoratifs, Paris, Peintres européens d'aujourd'hui, 1968; Hayward Gallery, London, Pop Art, 1969; Los Angeles/County MA, Art & Technology, 1971; Hayward Gallery, London, British Painting '74, 1974; Los Angeles/County MA, European Painting in the Seventies, 1975; Hayward Gallery, London, The Human Clay, circ., 1976; Hayward Gallery, London, Hayward Annual, 1977; Royal Academy, London, A New Spirit in Painting, 1981. **Collections:** Berlin/National; Edinburgh/National; MOMA; Rotterdam; Tate Gallery. **Bibliography:** Gettings; Murken-Altrogge.

KLINE, FRANZ. b. May 23, 1910, Wilkes-Barre, Pa.; **d.** May 13, 1962, NYC. **Studied:** Girard College; Boston U., 1931-35; Heatherley School of Fine Art, London, 1937-38. **Taught:** Black Mountain College, 1952; Pratt Institute, 1953; Philadelphia Museum School, 1954. **Awards:** NAD, S. J. Wallace Truman Prize, 1944; Chicago/AI, 1957; XXX Venice Biennial, 1960. **One-man Exhibitions:** (first) Charles Egan Gallery, 1950, also 1951, 54; Margaret Brown Gallery, Boston, 1952; Institute of Design, Chicago, 1954; Allan Frumkin Gallery, Chicago, 1954; Sidney Janis Gallery, 1956, 58, 60, 61, 63; La Tartaruga, Rome, 1958; Galleria d'Arte del Naviglio, Milan, 1958; Arts Club of Chicago, 1961; Collectors Gallery, NYC, 1961; New Arts Gallery, Atlanta, 1961; Galerie Lawrence, Paris, 1962; Dwan Gallery, 1962 (two-man, with Philip Guston); Kunsthalle, Basel, 1964 (two-man, with Alfred Jensen); Marlborough-Gerson Gallery, Inc., 1967; Marlborough Fine Art Ltd., London, 1972; David McKee Gallery, NYC, 1975; Binghamton/SUNY, 1977; Phillips, 1979. **Retrospectives:** WGMA, 1962; Whitechapel Art Gallery, London, 1964; WMAA, 1968; Cincinnati/AM, circ., 1985. **Group:** NAD, 1942-45; Galerie de France, Paris, 1952;

10th Inter-American Conference, Caracas, 1954; WMAA, The New Decade, 1954-55; MOMA, Twelve Americans, circ., 1956; Tate Gallery, 1956; XXVIII & XXX Venice Biennials, 1956, 60; Sao Paulo, 1957; MOMA, The New American Painting, circ., Europe, 1958-59; Baltimore/MA, 1960/SRGM, 1961; Hartford/Wadsworth, 1962; WMAA, 1966, 69; U. of St. Thomas (Tex.), 1967; MOMA, The New American Painting and Sculpture, 1969. **Collections:** Baltimore/MA; Buffalo/Albright; Carnegie; Cleveland; Houston/MFA; International Minerals & Chemicals Corp.; Kansas City/Nelson; Kunsthalle, Basel; MMA; MOMA; Norfolk/Chrysler; PMA; Raleigh/NCMA; Rockefeller Institute; SRGM; Tate; Toronto; Utica; WMAA. **Bibliography:** Ashton 5; Baur 5; Bihalji-Merin; *Black and White Are Colors*; Blesh 1; **Breeskin 1;** Calas, N. and E.; Danto; **Dawson;** Eliot; Elsen 2; Flanagan; Gaunt; Goodrich and Baur 1; **Gordon 1;** Greenberg 1; Haftman; Henning; Hess, T.B., 1; Honisch and Jensen, eds.; Hunter 1, 6; Hunter, ed.; Janis and Blesh 1; Johnson, Ellen H.; Kuh 2, 3; Langui; Lynton; McCoubrey 1; McCurdy, ed.; Mendelowitz; Murken-Altrogge; Neumeyer; Nordness, ed.; O'Hara 1, 3; Ponente; Pousette-Dart, ed.; Read 2; Rodman 1, 3; Rose, B., 1, 4; Sandler; Sandler 1; Seuphor 1; Tomkins and Time-Life Books; Tomkins 2; Tuchman, ed.; Weller. Archives.

KNATHS, KARL. b. October 21, 1891, Eau Claire, Wis.; **d.** March 9, 1971, Provincetown, Mass. **Studied:** Chicago Art Institute School. **Taught:** The Phillips Gallery School; Bennington College. **Member:** Audubon Artists. Federal A.P. (murals); Falmouth (Mass.) High School; US Post Office, Rehoboth Beach, Del.; Provincetown (Mass.) Town Hall. **Awards:** Chicago/AI, Norman Wait Harris Prize, 1928; Boston Tercentenary Art Exhibit, Gold Medal; Carnegie, First Prize, 1946; Carnegie International, Third Hon. Men., 1950;

Chicago Art Institute School, Hon. DFA, 1951; elected to NIAL, 1955; Brandeis U., Creative Arts Award, 1961; NAD Annual, Andrew Carnegie Prize, 1962. **One-man Exhibitions:** (first) The Phillips Gallery and The Daniel Gallery, NYC. (concurrently); P. Rosenberg and Co., NYC, 1946-69, 1974-75; Bard College, 1982; Phillips, 1982; Syracuse/Everson, 1982. **Retrospective:** Provincetown Art Association, 1974. **Group:** WMAA; Corcoran; Chicago/AI; Carnegie; U. of Illinois; PAFA; MMA. **Collections:** Boston/MFA; Brooklyn Museum; Buffalo/Albright; California Palace; Chicago/AI; Corcoran; Currier; Dayton/AI; Des Moines; Ford Foundation; Hartford/Wadsworth; U. of Illinois; Indianapolis/Herron; Los Angeles/County MA; MMA; MOMA; Mary Washington College; U. of Nebraska; PAFA; PMA; Phillips; U. of Rochester; Rockefeller Institute; St. Louis/City; Santa Barbara/MA; Stanford U.; Toledo/MA; Utica; WMAA; Walker; West Palm Beach/Norton; Wilmington; Woodward Foundation; Worcester/AM. **Bibliography:** American Abstract Artists, ed.; Baur 5, 7; Bazin; Bethers; Blanchard; Blesh 1; Cheney; Eliot; Frost; **Goodrich and Baur** 1, **2;** Hess, T.B., 1; Janis, S.; Jewell 2; Kootz 2; Leepa; McCurdy, ed.; Mellquist; **Mocsanyi;** Morris; Nordness, ed.; Pearson 1; Phillips 1, 2; Pousette-Dart, ed.; Read 2; Richardson, E.P.; Ringel, ed.; Ritchie 1; Wight 2. Archives.

KNIPSCHILD, ROBERT. b. August 17, 1927, Freeport, Ill. **Studied:** U. of Wisconsin, with Alfred Sessler, 1947-50, BA, 1950, MFA, 1951; Cranbrook, with Zoltan Sepeshy. Traveled USA, Canada, Mexico, China, Japan. US Army, 1945-47. **Taught:** Baltimore/MA, 1951-52; American U., 1952; U. of Connecticut, 1954-56; U. of Wisconsin, 1956-60; U. of Iowa, 1960-66; U. of Cincinnati, 1966-. **Address:** 3245 Bishop Street, Cincinnati, OH 45220. **One-man Exhibitions:**

Cranbrook, 1951; Baltimore/MA, 1952-53, 55; American U., 1952; The Alan Gallery, NYC, 1953-55, 57, 58, 61; U. of Iowa, 1960; U. of Wisconsin, 1960-65; Lubetkin Gallery, Des Moines, 1962; Sneed-Hillman Gallery, 1962, 64, 67, 68, 75; Skidmore College, 1969; Louisiana State U., 1970; U. of Massachusetts, Madison College, 1972; U. of Cincinnati, 1974; Western Michigan U., 1975; Birmingham Gallery, Inc., Birmingham, Mich., 1975; Miami U., 1976; Findlay College, Ohio, 1976; Virginia Beach Art Center, 1976; Piedmont Gallery, Augusta, 1977, 78, 79; Yares Gallery, Scottsdale, Ariz., 1978; Ohio Wesleyan U., 1978; Western Kentucky U., 1978; Toni Birckhead Gallery, Cincinnati, 1982; Case Western Reserve U., 1982; Gallery K, Washington, D.C., 1984; Idaho State U., 1986. **Retrospectives:** U. of Cincinnati, 1974; Western Michigan U., 1975. **Group:** MMA, American Painting Today, 1950; PAFA Biennial, 1951, 53; WMAA Annual, 1952; Youngstown/Butler Biennial, 1954; Corcoran; Carnegie. **Collections:** AT&T; Baltimore/MA; Brandeis U.; Bell Telephone Co.; Cedar Rapids/AA; Chase Manhattan Bank; U. of Cincinnati; Corcoran; Cranbrook; Davenport/Municipal; Grinnell College; Hirshhorn; Hope College; Illinois Wesleyan U.; Library of Congress; Madison College; U. of Michigan; Milwaukee Journal; U. of Minnesota; Murray State U.; PAFA; Phillips; Skidmore College; Springfield, Ill./State; Stephens College; Tucson Museum of Art; Upjohn Co.; U. of Wisconsin; Wisconsin State U. **Bibliography:** Archives.

KOCH, JOHN. b. August 18, 1909, Toledo, Ohio; **d.** April 19, 1978, NYC. Self-taught in art. Traveled France, Great Britain; resided Paris, 1929-33. **Taught:** ASL, 1944-45; Chairman of the School Committee, NAD. **Member:** NAD; Century Association; Lotus Club; Audubon Artists; NIAL. **Awards:** Salon de Printemps, Paris, Hon. Men., 1929; Carnegie, First Hon.

Men., 1943; NAD, 1952; NAD, Benjamin Altman Prize, 1959; NAD, 137th Annual, Saltus Gold Medal for Merit; Youngstown/Butler, Dr. John J. McDonough Award, 1962; Lotus Club, 1964. **One-man Exhibitions:** (first) Bonestell Gallery, Detroit, 1927; Curt Valentine Gallery, NYC, 1935; Kraushaar Galleries, NYC, 1939, 41, 43, 46, 49, 51, 54, 58, 61, 65, 69, 72, 80; Kansas City/Nelson, 1940; J. L. Hudson Art Gallery, 1941; Whyte Gallery, Washington, D.C., 1944; Philadelphia Art Alliance, 1945; Portraits, Inc., NYC; Syracuse/Everson, 1951; Cowie Galleries, Los Angeles, 1951; 460 Park Avenue Gallery, NYC, 1951; Colgate U., 1977; The Pennsylvania State U., 1977. **Retrospective:** Suffolk Museum, Stony Brook, N.Y., 1951; Museum of the City of New York, 1963; Pittsfield/Berkshire, 1963; VMFA, 1962; Louisville/Speed, 1971; Akron/AI, 1971; Columbia (S.C.), 1978. **Group:** Salon de Printemps, Paris, 1929; Salon des Tuileries, Paris, 1929; NAD, 1939-. **Collections:** ASL; Bennington College; Boston/MFA; Brooklyn Museum; California Palace, Canajoharie; Chicago/AI; Des Moines; Detroit/Institute; U. of Georgia; Kansas City/Nelson; Lehigh U.; MMA; MOMA; NAD; Newark Museum; New Britain; Norfolk; Omaha/Joslyn; U. of Rochester; Southampton/Parrish; Springfield, Mass./MFA; Storm King Art Center; Toledo/MA; VMFA; Youngstown/Butler. **Bibliography:** Celebrate Ohio; **Eliot; Koch, J.;** Soyer, R. 1. Archives.

KOENIG, JOHN FRANKLIN b. October 24, 1924, Seattle, Wash. **Studied:** U. of California, Berkeley; Washington State College; U. of Washington, 1948, BA (Romance Languages); U. of Biarritz; Sorbonne, MA. US Army, 1943-45. Traveled Europe and the Orient extensively. General Secretary, *Cimaise* (art magazine), Paris, 1953-58. Resided Paris, 1948-79. Was codirector of Galerie Arnaud, Paris. **Taught:** School of Applied Arts, Istanbul, 1976. **Commissions:** Hopital St. Antoine, Paris, 1964; Theatre de Poche, Paris, 1949; Pacific Northwest Ballet, 1982. **Awards:** Paris/Moderne, (Third) Prix des Peintres Etrangers, 1959; I Paris Biennial, 1959; Prix des Critiques d'Art de la Presse Parisienne; Officier l'Ordre des Arts et des Lettres, France, 1985; Medaille Vermeil de la Ville de Paris, 1986. **Address:** 400 18th Avenue East, Seattle, Wash. 98112. **Dealer:** Foster-White Gallery, Seattle. **One-man Exhibitions:** Librairie Selection, Paris, 1948; Galerie Arnaud, 1952 (collages), 1953, 55, 57, 59-61, 1963, 66, 68, 72, 74, 75; La Citadella d'Arte Internazionale e d'Avanguardia, Ascona, Switzerland, 1955, 57; Galleria del Cavallino, Venice, 1957; Brussels/Beaux-Arts, 1957; Grange (Gallery), Lyon, 1958; Zoe Dusanne Gallery, Seattle, 1958, 60; Tokyo Gallery, 1960, 62; Seattle/AM, 1960, 61, 70, 71; Gordon Woodside Gallery, Seattle and San Francisco, 1962, 65, 67; The Willard Gallery, 1963, 65; Musée de Verviers, 1963; San Antonio/McNay, 1963; Le Lutrin, Lyon, 1965, 66; Montreal/Contemporain, 1966, 73; Holst Halvorsen Konsthandel, Oslo, 1966, 69; Quebec, 1966; Portland, Ore./AM, 1966; Tacoma, 1967; Musée Vivenel, Compiegne, 1969; Galleria Lorenzelli, Bergamo, 1970; Galerie Gilles Corbeil, Montreal, 1970, 71; Jongeward Gallery, Seattle, 1971; Galleria San Fedele, Milan, 1972; Foster-White Gallery, 1973, 74, 77; American Cultural Center, Istanbul, 1975; i.e. Graphics, Copenhagen, 1975; American Cultural Center, Katmandu, 1975; Galerie Kutter, Annenberg, 1976; Triveni Gallery, New Delhi, 1976; American Cultural Center, Madras, circ., 1976; American U., Calcutta, 1977; Galerie Influx, Marseilles, 1977; Fuji Television Gallery, Tokyo, 1977; Ochano-mizu Gallery, Tokyo, 1977; The John Pence Gallery, San Francisco, 1978, 81; Galerie Erval, Paris, 1979, 82; Ecole de Poto-Poto, Brazzaville, Congo, 1979; La Petite Galerie, Lyon, 1980; Galerie Jourdain, Montreal, 1981; Paris Art Center, Paris, 1982; Galerie d'Art International, Chicago, 1982; College St. Pierre, Port-au-Prince, Haiti, 1982; Greg Kucera Gallery, Seattle, 1983, 86; Free Atelier Gallery, Kuwait, 1985; Shoshana Wayne Gallery, Los Angeles, 1985; Paris/Moderne, 1986; Grace Gallery, Vancouver, 1986. **Retrospectives:** Musée Vivenel, Compiegne, 1969; Seattle/AM, 1970; Galerie Arnaud, Paris, 1974; Tacoma, 1980; Reykjavik, 1985. **Group:** International Congress of Museums, Marseilles, 1953; ICA, London, Collages and Objects, 1954; Palais des Beaux-Arts, Brussels, 1954; Amsterdam/Stedelijk, 1956; Palais des Beaux-Arts, Charleroi, Belgium, L'Arte de XX-Ieme Siecle, 1958; ICA, Boston, 100 Works on Paper, circ., Europe, 1959; Salon des Realites Nouvelles, Paris, Artistes Americains en France, circ., France, 1960; Tate, Ecole de Paris, 1962; Havana/Nacional; Carnegie, 1964; USA: Nouvelle Peinture, circ., French museums, 1965; Musée de Lyon, USA: Groupe 68, 1968; Musée Municipal, Brest, 21 Peintres Americains, 1968; Salon des Realities Nouvelles, 1973; Menton Biennale de Tapisserie, 1975. **Collections:** Basel; Bellevue (Wash.) Art Museum; Bibliotheque Nationale; CNAC; Grenoble; Houston/MFA; MMA; Montreal/Contemporain; Montreal/MFA; Musée de Verviers; NYPL; Nantes; National Museum of Western Art, Tokyo; Osaka/National; Ottawa/National; Paris/Moderne; Reykjavik; St.-Etienne; Salzburg; San Antonio/McNay; Seattle/AM; Seattle Public Library; Tacoma; Tokyo/Modern; Seafirst Mortgage Corporation; Venice/Contemporaneo. **Bibliography:** Ragon 1; Read 4; **Restany 1,** 2. Archives.

KOHN, GABRIEL. b. 1910, Philadelphia, Pa., **d.** May 21, 1975, Los Angeles, Calif. **Studied:** Cooper Union, 1929; Beaux-Arts Institute of Design, NYC, 1930-34; Zadkine School of Sculpture, Paris, 1946. **Awards:** Augustus Saint-Gaudens Medal from

Cooper Union, 1925; Beaux-Arts Institute of Design, NYC, 14 awards in sculpture, 1929-32, and a Silver Medal, 1932; Nicholas Roerich Society, First Prize, 1932; Cranbrook, George A. Booth Scholarship, 1952; ICA, London/Tate, International Unknown Political Prisoner Competition, 1953; Ford Foundation Grant, 1960; Guggenheim Foundation Fellowship, 1967; Mark Rothko Foundation Grant, 1971. **One-man Exhibitions:** Atelier Mannucci, Rome, 1948; Galleria Zodiaco, Rome, 1950; Cranbrook, 1953; Tanager Gallery, NYC, 1958; Leo Castelli Inc., 1959; Otto Gerson Gallery, NYC, 1963; Ringling, 1964; La Jolla, 1963; David Stuart Gallery, 1963-66, 1972; The Zabriskie Gallery, NYC, 1972-77; Midtown Galleries, NYC, 1986. **Retrospective:** Newport Harbor, circ., 1971; Corcoran, 1977. **Group:** Pershing Hall, Paris, American Veterans in Paris, 1948; Salon de la Jeune Sculpture, Paris, 1950; Los Angeles/County MA, 1950; Salon d'Art Libre, Paris, 1951; MMA, National Sculpture Exhibition, 1951; PAFA, 1953; WMAA Annuals, 1953, 60, 62; II Sculpture Biennial, Antwerp, 1953; MOMA, New Talent; MOMA, Recent Sculpture USA, 1959; Sao Paulo, 1959; Claude Bernard, Paris, Aspects of American Sculpture, 1960; New School for Social Research, Mechanism and Organism, 1961; Seattle World's Fair, 1962; MOMA, Americans 1963, circ. 1963-64; Ringling, 1964; WMAA, The Third Dimension, 1984. **Collections:** Buffalo/Albright; Cranbrook; Hirshhorn; MOMA; Pasadena/AM; Ringling; WMAA. **Bibliography:** Downes ed.; Goodrich and Baur 1; Hunter, ed.; Phillips, Lisa; Read 3; Rose, B., 1; Sandler 1; Seuphor 3; Tuchman 1.

KOHN, MISCH. b. March 26, 1916, Kokomo, Ind. **Studied:** John Herron Art Institute, 1939; in Mexico, 1943-44, with Jose Clemente Orozco, Mendez, Diego Rivera. **Taught:** Institute of Design, Chicago; Illinois Institute of Technology, 1949-75; Indiana U.; California State U., Hayward, 1972-80. **Awards:** PAFA, Alice McFadden Eyre Medal, 1949; Seattle/AM, **P.P.,** 1950; Brooklyn Museum, **P.P.,** 1950, 51; The Print Club, Philadelphia, 1950, 51, 55, 56, 58; Chicago/AI, 1951, 52, 58; PAFA, Pennell Memorial Medal, 1952; Guggenheim Foundation Fellowship, 1952, 54; Indianapolis/Herron, 1952, 56; NAD, 1955; Salon du Mai, Paris, 1960; Gallery of Modern Art, Ljubljana, Yugoslavia, IV International Exhibition of Prints, 1961; Tamarind Fellowship, 1961; Ford Foundation Grant. **Address:** 1860 Grove Way, Castro Valley, CA 94546. **One-man Exhibitions:** Philadelphia Art Alliance; Chicago/AI; St. Amands Gallery, Sarasota, Fla., 1969; Weyhe Gallery, 1970; Los Angeles/County MA; Kansas City/Nelson. **Retrospectives:** A.F.A./Ford Foundation, 1961; Brooklyn Museum, 1981. **Group:** PAFA, 1949, 52, 56; Brooklyn Museum, 1949-57; Boston/MFA; Seattle/AM; Chicago/AI, 1949-58; The Print Club, Philadelphia, 1949-58; Salon du Mai, Paris, 1952, 53. **Collections:** Brooklyn Museum; Chicago/AI; Library of Congress; MOMA; NYPL; National Gallery; PMA; Rio de Janeiro; Stockholm/National. **Bibliography:** Hayter 1; Peterdi.

KONZAL, JOSEPH. b. November 5, 1905, Milwaukee, Wis. **Studied:** ASL, with Max Weber, Walt Kuhn, Robert Laurent, 1926-30; Layton School of Art, 1927; Beaux-Arts Institute of Design, NYC, 1928-30. **Taught:** Brooklyn Museum School, 1949-71; Adelphi U., 1954-71; Newark (N.J.) Public School for Fine and Industrial Art, 1960-67; Queens College, 1966-69; Kent State U., 1971-76; Federal A.P.: Supervised Federal Art Project Gallery; architectural sculpture project. **Awards:** Brooklyn Museum Biennial, 2 First Prizes; Guggenheim Foundation Fellowship, 1966. **Address:** 360 West 21st Street, NYC 10011. **Dealer:** Andre Zarre Gallery, NYC. **One-man Exhibi-**

tions: (first) Eighth Street Playhouse, NYC, 1938; Contemporary Arts Gallery, NYC, 1950, 52, 55; The Bertha Schaefer Gallery, 1960, 63, 65, 67, 71; Canton Art Institute, 1974, 75; Andre Zarre Gallery, NYC, 1978, 80. **Retrospectives:** Adelphi U., 1965; Kent State U., 1971. **Group:** Chicago/AI, 1938; MOMA, Subway Art, 1938; New York World's Fair, 1939; Sculptors Guild Annuals, 1941-71; WMAA Annuals, 1948, 61, 62, 64, 66, 68; Riverside Museum, NYC, 14 Sculptors, 1958; MOMA, Recent Sculpture USA, 1959; Newark Museum, 1961, 64; Carnegie International, 1962; WMAA, Geometric Abstraction in America, circ., 1962; New York World's Fair, 1964-65; Federation of Modern Painters and Sculptors Annuals, 1964-71; Cleveland/MA, 1972; Canton Art Institute, 1973; Dayton/AI, 1974. **Collections:** American Sugar Co.; American Can Corp.; Canton Art Institute; Garcia Corp.; Kent State U.; R. H. Macy & Co.; New School for Social Research; San Antonio/McNay; Storm King Art Center; Tate; Trenton/State; Union Carbide Corp.; WMAA. **Bibliography:** Archives.

KOPPELMAN, CHAIM. b. 1920, Brooklyn, N.Y. **Studied:** Brooklyn College, 1938; Educational Alliance, NYC, 1938; American Artists School, NYC, 1939, with Eugene Morley, Carl Holty; New School for Social Research, with Amedee Ozenfant; Art College of Western England; Bristol, 1944; Ecole Regionale de Beaux-Arts, Reims, 1945; ASL, 1946, with Will Barnet, Jose de Creeft; privately with Amedee Ozenfant, 1946-49 (and served concurrently as his assistant). US Air Force, 1942-45. **Taught:** NYU; Brooklyn College; New Paltz/SUNY; School of Visual Arts, 1959-; Aesthetic Realism Foundation, NYC, 1971-. **Member:** Society for Aesthetic Realism; NAD, Associate, 1979. **Commissions:** International Graphic Arts Society, 1958; A.A.A. Gallery, NYC, 1959, 61, 64. **Awards:** L.C.

Tiffany Grant, 1956, 59; PAFA, Hon. Men., 1959; Audubon Artists, Medal for Graphics, 1960; Library of Congress, Pennell **P.P.**, SAGA, List Prize ($1,000), 1967; IBM Gallery of Arts and Sciences, NYC, III International Miniature Print Exhibition, 1968; Brooklyn Museum, Print Biennial, 1968; CAPS, 1976; NAD, Cannon Prize, 1986. **Address:** 498 Broome Street, NYC 10012. **Dealers:** Yvonne Rapp Matchmaker Arts Space, Louisville. **One-man Exhibitions:** (first) Outline Gallery, Pittsburgh, 1943; "67" Gallery, NYC, 1945; The Terrain Gallery, 1956, 69 (two-man, with wife, Dorothy), 74, 83; Philadelphia Art Alliance, 1959; Kornbluth Gallery, Paterson, N.J., 1964; Hinckley and Brohel Galleries, Washington, D.C. 1967; A.A.A. Gallery, NYC, 1973; AFS Gallery, Binghamton, N.Y., 1973; U. of Maine, 1974; Warwick (Eng.) Gallery (two-man), 1975; Yvonne Rapp Matchmaker Arts Space, 1985. **Retrospectives:** AAA, NYC, Prints, 1973; The Terrain Gallery, NYC, Drawings, 1974. **Group:** Boston/MFA; Los Angeles/County MA; Chicago/AI; Walker; Baltimore/MA; Detroit/Institute; Brooklyn Museum Print Biennial; WMAA Annuals, 1948, 50, 61, 63; Yale U., 1949, 60; Documenta II, Kassel, 1959; USIA, Contemporary American Prints, circ., Latin America, 1959-60; II Inter-American Paintings and Prints Biennial, Mexico City, 1960; MOMA, Recent Painting USA: The Figure, circ., 1962-63; Graphics: USA, Moscow, 1964; St. Paul Gallery, 1966; Mexico City/Nacional, 1967; IBM Gallery of Arts and Sciences, NYC, 1968; Cranbrook, 6th Biennial, National Religious Art Exhibition, 1968; Western New Mexico U., 1969; Library of Congress Print Annual, 1969; A.F.A., The Indignant Eye, 1971; Purdue U., Print Invitational, 1972; Utah State U. Print Invitational, 1972; Anchorage, Print Invitational, 1972, 74; NAD, Annuals 1978, 79, 80; The Terrain Gallery NYC, 25th Anniversary Exhibition, 1980; NAD, 1986. **Collections:** Anchorage; Boston/MFA; Brooklyn Museum; CSCS, Long Beach;

Caracas; Long Beach State College; MMA; MOMA; National Gallery; Otis Art Institute; Peabody Museum; Syracuse U.; US State Department; Victoria and Albert Museum; Walker; Western New Mexico U.; Yale U. **Bibliography:** Archives.

KORTLANDER, WILLIAM CLARK. b. February 9, 1925, Grand Rapids, Mich. **Studied:** Michigan State U., BA; State U. of Iowa, MA, Ph.D. US Army, 1943-46. Traveled USA, Western Europe; resided Western Europe, 1967-68. **Taught:** State U. of Iowa, 1950-54; Lawrence U., 1954-56; U. of Texas, 1956-61; Michigan State U., 1960; Ohio U., 1961-. **Awards:** Mead Painting of the Year, 1965; Ohio U., Baker Award, 1967-68. **Address:** Angel Ridge, Route 4, Box 182, Athens, OH 45701. **One-man Exhibitions:** (first—NYC) A.M. Sachs Gallery, 1967, also 1968; The Jewish Center, Columbus, Ohio, 1964; Bryson Gallery, Columbus, 1965; Denison U., 1965; Otterbein College, 1965; Battelle Memorial Institute, Columbus, 1966; George Bennett Gallery, Toledo, Ohio, 1966; Western Electric Co., Columbus, 1966; West Virginia State College, 1966; Zanesville/AI, 1966; Merida Gallery, Inc., 1967; Montana State College, 1969; Gallery 200, Columbus, Ohio, 1974; Springfield Art Center, Ohio, 1974; Northern Ohio U., 1974; Haber/Theodore Gallery, NYC, 1980, 82, 84; Mercersburg Academy, Mercersburg, Pa., 1986. **Retrospectives:** Springfield Art Center, 1974; Ohio U., 1976; Southeastern Ohio Cultural Arts Center, Athens, Ohio, 1984. **Group:** Dallas Museum for Contemporary Arts, 1959; Witte, 1961; Ball State U., Drawings and Sculpture Annual, 1964-65; PAFA Annual, 1965; Dayton/AI, 1965; Villanova U., 1968; U. of Wisconsin, 1968; U. of North Carolina, 1970; New School for Social Research, American Drawings of the Sixties, 1970; Roanoke Fine Arts Center, Va., 1978; Marietta College, 1980; Northern Ohio U., 1985. **Collections:** Abraham

and Straus, Brooklyn; AT&T; Chemical Bank Chubu Institute, Nagoya; Columbus; Huntington, W. Va.; Mead Corporation; The Ohio Co.; Ohio U.; Oppenheimer Co., NYC; Otterbein College; Wylain Corp., Fort Worth; West Virginia State College; Zanesville/AI.

KOSUTH, JOSEPH. b. January 13, 1945, Toledo, Ohio. **Studied:** Toledo Museum School of Design, with Line Bloom Draper, 1955-62; Cleveland Institute of Art, 1963-64; private study; with Roger Barr, Paris, 1964-65; School of Visual Arts, NYC, 1965-67; New School for Social Research, 1971-72. Traveled Europe, South America, Asia, the Orient, Pacific Islands. **Taught:** School of Visual Arts, NYC, 1968. Founded and directed the Museum of Normal Art, NYC, 1967. **Member:** The Editorial Board of the Art and Language Press. **Award:** Cassandra Foundation Grant, 1968. **Address:** 591 Broadway, NYC 10012. **Dealer:** Leo Castelli Inc., NYC. **One-man Exhibitions:** Museum of Normal Art, NYC, 1967; Gallery 669, Los Angeles, 1968; Bradford Junior College (two-man), 1968; Douglas Gallery, Vancouver, 1969; Instituto Torcuato di Tella, Buenos Aires, 1969; Nova Scotia College of Art and Design, Halifax, 1969; St. Martin's School of Art, London, 1969; Art & Project, Amsterdam, 1969; Coventry (Eng.) College of Art and Design, 1969; Gian Enzo Sperone, Turin, 1969, 70; A 37 90 89, Antwerp, 1969; Pinacotheca, St. Kilda, Virginia, Australia, 1969; Leo Castilli, Inc., NYC, 1969, 71, 72 (2), 1975, 79, 82, 85; Toronto, 1969, 81; Pasadena/AM, 1970; Iysk Kunstgalerie, Copenhagen, 1970; Galerie Daniel Templon, Paris, 1970; Paul Maenz Gallery, Cologne, 1971; Protetch-Rivkin, Washington, D.C., 1971; Centro de Arte y Comunicacion, Buenos Aires, 1971; Lia Rumma Studio d'Arte, Naples, 1971, 75; Carmen Lamanna Gallery, Toronto, 1971, 72, 74, 78, 81; Galeria Toselli, Milan, 1971; Gian Enzo Sperone and Konrad Fischer

Gallery, Rome, 1972, 74; Galerie Gunter Sachs, Hamburg, 1973; Paul Maenz Gallery, Brussels, 1973; Cologne, 1979; Kunstmuseum, Lucerne, 1973; Claire S. Copley Gallery, Los Angeles, 1974; Galeria La Bertesca, Dusseldorf, 1974; Galleria Peccolo, Livorno, 1975; Galerie MTL, Brussels, 1975; Durand-Desert Gallery, Paris, 1975; U. of Chicago, 1976; International Cultural Center, Antwerp, 1976; Ghent, 1977; Eindhoven, 1978; Museum of Modern Art, Oxford, 1978; New 57 Gallery, Edinburgh, 1979; Galerie Eric Fabre, Paris, 1979, 82; Rudiger Schottle, Munich, 1979; Galeria Samon, Genoa, 1979, 81; Musée de Charters, 1979; P.S. 1, Queens, 1980; Françoise Lambert, Milan, 1981; Stuttgart, 1981; Galerie Mario Diacono, Rome, 1982; Michelle Larchowsky, Antwerp, 1982; France Morin Gallery, Montreal, 1982; Galerie Ghislain Mollet-Vieville, Paris, 1982; Centre d'Art Contemporain, Geneva, 1985. **Group:** Lannis Gallery, NYC, Non-Anthropomorphic Art, 1967; U. of Rochester, New York Art, 1968; A.F.A., The Square in Painting, 1968; UCLA, Electric Art, 1969; Berne, When Attitudes Become Form, 1969; Amsterdam/Stedelijk, Op Losse Schroeven, 1969; Seattle/AM, 557,087, 1969; Dusseldorf/Kunsthalle, Prospect '69, 1969; Chicago/Contemporary, Art by Telephone, 1969; WMAA Annual, 1969; Turin/Civico, Conceptual Art, Arte Povera, Land Art, 1970; Jewish Museum, Software, 1970; Galerie im Taxispalais, Innsbruck, Concept Art, 1970; MOMA, Information, 1971; SRGM, Guggenheim International, 1971; VII Paris Biennial, 1971; Buenos Aires/Moderno, Art Systems, 1971; Kunsthalle, Nurnberg, Biennial, 1971; Munster/WK, Das Konzept ist die Form, 1972; Kunstmuseum, Lucerne, Joseph Kosuth; Investigationen uber Kunst and 'Problemkreise' seit 1965, 1973; Chicago/AI, Idea and Image in Recent Art, 1974; Kennedy Center, Art Now, '74, 1974; Cologne/Kunstverein, Kunst uber Kunst, 1974; Indianapolis, 1974; Chicago/AI Annual, 1976; Can-

berra/National Illusion & Reality, circ., 1977; Berlin/Akademie der Kunst; SoHo, 1976; Museum Bochum, Words, 1979; MOMA, Printed Art: A View of Two Decades, 1980; Amsterdam/Stedelijk, '60-'80: Attitudes/Concepts/Images, 1982; Documenta VII, Kassel, 1982; Hirshhorn, Content, 1984. **Collections:** Amsterdam/Stedelijk; Canberra/National; Eindhoven; Ghent; MOMA; Melbourne/National; Oberlin College; Ottawa/National; Paris/Beaubourg; SRGM; Tate Gallery; WMAA. **Bibliography:** Art Now 74; Celant; *Contemporanea*; Davis, D.; De Wilde 2; Honisch and Jensen, eds.; Honnef; Lippard, ed.; Meyer; Sager; *When Attitudes Become Form.*

KRASNER, LEE. b. October 27, 1908, Brooklyn, N.Y. **d.** June 19, 1984, NYC. **Studied:** Cooper Union; NAD; Hofmann School, 1938. Federal A.P.: Mural Painting. **Commissions:** 2 Broadway Building, NYC (86-ft. mural). Subject of the film *Lee Krasner: The Long View,* made by Barbara Rose. **Awards:** Cooper Union, Saint-Gaudens Medal, 1974; Chevalier de l'Ordre des Arts et des Lettres, France, 1982; Hon. DFA, Stony Brook/SUNY. **m.** Jackson Pollock (1944). **One-man Exhibitions:** (first) Betty Parsons Gallery, 1950; The Stable Gallery, 1955; Martha Jackson Gallery, 1958; The Howard Wise Gallery, NYC, 1961, 62; Arts Council Gallery, London, circ., 1966; U. of Alabama, 1967; Marlborough Gallery, Inc., NYC, 1968, 69, 73; Reese Palley Gallery, San Francisco, 1969; WMAA, 1973; Miami-Dade, 1974; Gibbes Art Gallery, Charleston, S.C., 1974; The Pace Gallery, NYC, 1977, 79, 81; Susanne Hilberry Gallery, Birmingham, Mich., 1977; Janie C. Lee Gallery, Houston, 1978, 81; Tower Gallery, Southampton, 1980; Guild Hall (two-man), 1981; Robert Miller Gallery, 1982, 85; Brooklyn Museum, 1985; Cooper Union, NYC, 1985; Meredith Long Gallery, Houston, 1985. **Retrospectives:**

Whitechapel Art Gallery, London, circ., 1965; Corcoran, circ., 1975; Houston/MFA, 1983. **Group:** MacMillin Gallery, NYC, French and American Painting, 1942; Howard Putzell Gallery, Hollywood, 1945; Marlborough Fine Arts Ltd., London, The New, New York Scene, 1961; PAFA, 1962; PMA; MOMA, Hans Hofmann and His Students, circ., 1963-64; SRGM, American Drawings, 1964; Gallery of Modern Art, NYC, 1965; U. of Illinois, 1969; MOMA, The New American Painting and Sculpture; The First Generation, 1969; Finch College, NYC, Projected Art, 1971; WMAA, 1973; PMA/Museum of the Philadelphia Civic Center, Focus, 1974; Cornell U., Abstract Expressionism: The Formative Years, 1978; Buffalo/Albright, American Painting of the 1970's, 1978; MMA, Hans Hofmann as Teacher: Drawings by His Students, 1979; NYU, Tracking the Marvelous, 1981; Carnegie, International, 1982; Houston/Contemporary, The Americans: The Collage, 1982; WMAA, Reflections of Nature, 1984. **Collections:** U. of Alabama; Buffalo/Albright; Brooklyn Museum; Canberra/National; Dallas/MFA; Flint/Institute; Hartford/Wadsworth; High Museum; Houston/MFA; IBM; Indianapolis; MMA; MOMA; NYU; PMA; Purchase/SUNY; SRGM; Sony Corp.; Tate Gallery; WMAA; Yale U. **Bibliography:** *Art: A Woman's Sensibility*; Danto; Diamonstein; Hunter 6; Janis and Blesh 1; Janis, S.; Hobbs and Levin; Nemser. Archives.

KRIESBERG, IRVING. b. March 13, 1919, Chicago, Ill. **Studied:** Chicago Art Institute School, 1941, BFA; Escuela Nacional de Artes Plasticas, Mexico City, 1941-44; NYU, 1972, MA (cinema). Traveled Mexico, India, Japan. **Taught:** Parsons School of Design, NYC, 1955-61; Pratt Institute, 1961-72; Yale U., 1962-69; City U. of New York, 1969-72; SUNY, 1972-76; Columbia U., 1977, 78. **Awards:** Ford Foundation, **P.P.,** 1946; Fulbright Fellowship (In-

dia), 1965-66; CAPS (films), 1974; CAPS (Painting), 1974; Guggenheim Foundation Fellowship, 1977; National Endowment for the Arts, 1981. **Address:** 160 Sixth Avenue, NYC 10013. **Dealer:** The Graham Gallery, NYC. **One-man Exhibitions:** Curt Valentine Gallery, NYC; Chicago/AI, 1946; MOMA, 1953; St. Louis/City, 1954; Detroit/Institute, 1954; The Graham Gallery, Delhi, 1966; Yale U., 1967; Terry Dintenfass, Inc., NYC, 1978, 80, 82; Fairweather-Hardin Gallery, Chicago, 1979; Syracuse/Everson, 1980; Brandeis U., 1980; Galerie Elizabeth, Chicago, 1980; Brandeis U., 1981; Fiedler Gallery, Washington, D.C., 1981; Jack Gallery, NYC, 1981, 83; Washington U., 1982; Zenith Gallery, Pittsburgh, 1982; The Graham Gallery, 1985. **Retrospective:** Jewish Museum, NYC, 1962. **Group:** Chicago/AI, 1946; MOMA, New Talent; MOMA, Fifteen Americans, circ., 1952; Detroit/Institute, 1953; St. Louis/City 1954; Milwaukee, Directions 1; Options, circ., 1968; SRGM, 1972; SRGM, Ten Independents, 1972; AALA, 1978. **Collections:** Baltimore/MA; Brandeis U.; Chase Manhattan Bank, NYC; Cincinnati/AM; Corcoran; Detroit/Institute; Mead Corporation; MOMA; The Naropa Institute, Boulder; Santa Barbara/MA; St. Louis/City, WMAA. **Bibliography:** Atkinson.

KROLL, LEON. b. December 6, 1894, NYC; **d.** October 25, 1974, NYC. **Studied:** ASL, with John Henry Twachtman; NAD; Academie Julian, Paris, with Jean Paul Laurens. Traveled France, USA. **Taught:** NAD and ASL, 1911-73; Marland Institute, 1919-21; Chicago Art Institute School, 1924-25; PAFA, 1929-30. **Member:** NAD; AAAL; NIAL. Federal A.P.: Mural Division. **Commissions** (mural): US Justice Department, Washington, D.C., 1936-37; Worcester (Mass.) War Memorial Building, 1938-41; Johns Hopkins U.; US Military Cemetery, Omaha Beach, France. **Awards:** Chicago/AI, The Mr. & Mrs. Frank G. Logan Prize, 1919, 32,

35; NAD, Benjamin Altman Prize, 1923, 32, 35; Chicago/AI, Potter Palmer Gold Medal, 1924; PAFA, Joseph E. Temple Gold Medal, 1927; Carnegie, First Prize, 1936; Chevalier of the Legion of Honor; and more than 20 others. **One-man Exhibitions:** (first) NAD, 1910; Buffalo/Albright, 1929; Toronto, 1930 (three-man); Worcester/AM, 1937; Cleveland/MA, 1945; French & Co. Inc., NYC, 1947; The Milch Gallery, 1947, 59; Danenberg Gallery, 1970. **Retrospectives:** Museum of Art, Ft. Lauderdale, Fla., 1980; ACA Gallery, 1984. **Group:** The Armory Show, 1913; Chicago/AI; Cleveland/MA; St. Louis/City; U. of Nebraska; WMAA; Detroit/Institute; Baltimore/MA; MMA. **Collections:** Baltimore/MA; Britannica; Carnegie; Chicago/AI; Cleveland/MA; Corcoran; Dayton/AI; Denver/AM; Detroit/Institute; U. of Illinois; Indianapolis/Herron; Los Angeles/County MA; MMA; MOMA; Minneapolis/Institute; Municipal U. of Omaha; U. of Nebraska; PAFA; SFMA; St. Louis/City; San Diego; WMAA; West Palm Beach/Norton; Wilmington. **Bibliography:** Baur 7; Biddle 4; Boswell 1; Brown; Bruce and Watson; Bryant, L.; Cheney; Coke 2; Eliot; Gerdts; Hall; *Index of 20th Century Artists;* Jackman; Jewell 2; Kent, N.; **Kroll 1, 2;** Mather 1; McCurdy, ed.; Mellquist; Narodny; Neuhaus; Pagano, Poore; Watson 1; *Woodstock: An American Art Colony 1902-1977.* Archives.

KRUSHENICK, NICHOLAS. b. May 31, 1929, NYC. **Studied:** ASL, 1948-50; Hofmann School, NYC, 1950-51. US Army, 1947-48. **Taught:** U. of Wisconsin, 1969; Dartmouth College, 1969; Yale U., 1969, 70; Cornell U., 1970; Ball State U., 1971; Herbert H. Lehman College, Bronx, N.Y., 1972; California State U., Long Beach, 1973; U. of Alabama, 1973; St. Cloud State College, 1973; U. of California, Berkeley, 1973-74; The Ohio State U., 1974; U. of Washington, 1974. **Commissions:** Designed production of Haydn's *Man in the Moon,* Guthrie Theater, Minneapolis, 1968. **Awards:** Longview Foundation Grant, 1962; Tamarind Fellowship, 1965; Guggenheim Foundation Fellowship, 1967. **Address:** 140 Grand Street, NYC 10013. **One-man Exhibitions:** (first) Camino Gallery, NYC, 1956; Brata Gallery, NYC, 1958, 60; The Graham Gallery, 1962, 64; Cinema I and Cinema II, NYC, 1964; Fischbach Gallery, 1965; WGMA, 1965; Galerie Muller, 1966, 67; Ileana Sonnabend Gallery, Paris, 1967; The Pace Gallery, 1967, 69, 72; Galerie Nachst Skt. Stephan, Vienna, 1967; Walker, 1968; Galerie der Spiegel, Cologne, 1968; Galerie Rene Ziegler, Zurich, 1969, 70; Dartmouth College, 1969; Harcus-Krakow Gallery, 1969; U. of Southern Florida, 1970; Galerie Beyeler, 1971; Herbert H. Lehman College, Bronx, N.Y., 1972; Hannover/K-G, 1972; Galerie Denise Rene/Hans Mayer, Dusseldorf, 1973; U. of Alabama, 1973; Jack Glenn Gallery, Corona del Mar, 1973; California State U., Long Beach, 1974; ADI Gallery, San Francisco, 1974; Portland (Ore.) Center for the Visual Arts, 1974; Reed College, 1974; Foster-White Gallery, 1975; Bucknell U., 1977; Newport Art Association, 1978; Pyramid Gallery, Washington, D.C., 1978; Hokin Gallery, Chicago, 1978; Elizabeth Weiner Gallery, NYC, 1978; Suzette Schochett Gallery, Newport, L.I., 1977; Carnegie Mellon U., 1981; Gallery K, Washington, D.C., 1981; Ridgefield/Aldrich, 1981; Kaber Gallery, NYC, 1982; Medici/Berenson Gallery, Miami, 1982; River Gallery, Westport, Ct., 1982; 18th Street Gallery, Santa Monica, Calif., 1984. **Retrospective:** Walker, 1968. **Group:** Wagner College, 1958; Galerie Creuze, Paris, 1958; Tokyo/Modern, 1959, 66; The Howard Wise Gallery, Cleveland, 1960; Barnard College, 1962; Lincoln, Mass./De Cordova, 1962; WMAA Annuals, 1963, 65, 67; Los Angeles/County MA, Post Painterly Abstraction, 1964; MOMA, Contemporary Painters and Sculptors as Printmakers, 1964; Corcoran Biennial, 1965; MOMA,

American Collages, 1965; SRGM, Systemic Painting, 1966; Amsterdam/Stedelijk, New Shapes of Color, 1966; Expo '67, Montreal, 1967; Documenta IV, Kassel, 1968; Ars 69, Helsinki, 1969; ICA, U. of Pennsylvania, The Spirit of the Comics, 1969; Humlebaek/Louisiana, Amerikanst Kunst, 1950-1960, 1969; Berlin/National, 1973; WMAA Biennial, 1973; Long Beach/MA, Mixing Masters, 1974. **Collections:** Albany/SUNY; Albright/Buffalo; Amsterdam/Stedelijk; Ball State U.; Baruch College; Bibliotheque National, Paris; Chase Manhattan Bank; Cornell U.; Dallas/MFA; Essen; Fort Lauderdale; Guild Hall; Kalamazoo/Institute; Los Angeles/County MA; MMA; MOMA; NMAA; Norfolk; Norfolk/Chrysler; Ridgefield/Aldrich; VMFA; WGMA; WMAA; Walker. **Bibliography:** Alloway 3; Honisch and Jensen, eds.; Lippard 5; Rose, B., 1. Archives.

KUHN, WALT. b. October 27, 1877, Brooklyn, N.Y.; **d.** July 13, 1949, NYC. **Studied:** Academie Colarossi, Paris, 1901; Academy of Fine Arts, Munich, 1901, with H. von Zugel; Artists Sketch Class, NYC, 1905. **Taught:** New York School of Art, 1908-09. Executive Secretary, Association of American Painters and Sculptors, sponsor of The Armory Show, NYC, 1913. Founder of the Penguin Club, 1917-19. Designed sets and directed many revue skits for Broadway in the 1920s. **One-man Exhibitions:** (first) Madison Gallery, NYC, 1910, also 1911; Montross Gallery, NYC, 1914, 15, 22, 24, 25; DeZayas Gallery, NYC, 1920; Grand Central, NYC, 1927; M. Knoedler & Co., 1928; The Downtown Gallery, 1928; Marie Harriman Gallery, NYC, 1930-42; Durand-Ruel Gallery, NYC, 1944, 45, 46, 48; Colorado Springs/FA, 1947, 64; Maynard Walker Gallery, NYC, 1954, 57, 62, 66; Amon Carter Museum, 1964; Kennedy Galleries, NYC, 1967, 68, 72, 77, 80; Salander-O'Reilly Galleries, 1985. **Retrospectives:** Phillips, 1944

(two-man); A.F.A., circ., 1951; Albany/Institute, 1958; Cincinnati/AM, 1960; Fort Worth, 1964; U. of Arizona, 1966. **Group:** WMAA; Chicago/AI; Detroit/Institute; Cincinnati/AM; MOMA. **Collections:** Buffalo/Albright; Cincinnati/AM; Colorado Springs/FA; Columbus; Currier; Denver/AM; Des Moines; Detroit/Institute; New York Cultural Center; Indianapolis/Herron; Kansas City/Nelson; MMA; MOMA; U. of Nebraska; Ogunquit; Phillips; WMAA; Wellesley College; Wichita/AM. **Bibliography: Adams 1, 2;** Baur 7; Bazin; Biddle 4; **Bird;** Blesh 1; Brown 1, 2; Bulliet 1; Cahill and Barr, eds.; Cheney; Eliot; Flanagan; Genauer; Gerdts; Goodrich and Baur 1; Hunter 6; *Index of 20th Century Artists;* Janis, S.; Jewell 2; Kootz 1; **Kuhn 1, 2;** Marter, Tarbell, and Wechsler; McCurdy, ed.; Mellquist; Mendelowitz; Newmeyer; Pagano; Phillips 2; Poore; Richardson, E. P.; Ringel, ed.; Rose, B., 1; Smith, S.C.K.; Wight 2. Archives.

KULICKE, ROBERT. b. March 9, 1924, Philadelphia, Pa. **Studied:** Temple U., Philadelphia Museum School, Atelier Fernand Leger, 1946-50. **Taught:** U. of California, 1964, 1970; Kulicke Cloisonne Workshop, NYC, 1964-. **Awards:** American Institute of Interior Designers, International Design Award, 1968. **Address:** 2231 Broadway, NYC 10024. **Dealer:** Davis & Langdale Co., Inc., NYC. **One-man Exhibitions:** Parma Gallery, NYC, 1960; Allan Stone Gallery, 1962, 63; Multiples, 1966; The Kornblee Gallery, 1968, 69, 72; Benson Gallery, 1968, 69; Davis & Long Co., Inc., NYC, 1977, 78, 79, 80, 81, 82, 83, 84, 85, 86; Columbia, S.C./MA, 1983; John Stoller & Co., Minneapolis, 1985. **Retrospective:** The Pennsylvania State U., 1978. **Group:** WGMA, 1964; Silvermine Guild, 1964; Chicago/AI, Dayton/AI; A.F.A., 100 Years of American Realism, 1965; WMAA, 1969. **Collections:** PMA. **Bibliography:** Archives.

KUNIYOSHI, YASUO. b. September 1, 1893, Okayama, Japan; **d.** May 14, 1953, NYC. To USA, 1906. **Studied:** Los Angeles School of Art, three years; NAD; Robert Henri School, 1910; Independent School of Art, 1914-16, with Homer Boss; ASL, 1916-20, with Kenneth Hayes Miller. Traveled Europe, Japan, USA. **Taught:** ASL, 1933-53; New School for Social Research, 1936-53; Brooklyn Museum School. **Member:** Salons of America, 1922-38 (director); Hamilton Easter Field Foundation; American Artists Congress; An American Place (president, 1939-44); Artists Equity (president, 1947-50, Hon. president until his death). Federal A.P.: Graphics Division, two years, ca. 1936. **Commissions:** Radio City Music Hall, NYC (mural). **Awards:** Carnegie, Hon. Men., 1931, Second Prize, 1939, and First Prize, 1944; Los Angeles/County MA, Second Prize, 1934; PAFA, Joseph E. Temple Gold Medal, 1934; Guggenheim Foundation Fellowship, 1935; Golden Gate International Exposition, San Francisco, 1939, First Prize, PAFA, J. Henry Schiedt Memorial Prize, 1944; VMFA, **P.P.**, 1944; Chicago/AI, Norman Wait Harris Bronze Medal and Prize, 1945; La Tausca Competition, Fifth Award, 1947, 48; *Look* magazine poll of "Ten Best Painters," February, 1948; MMA, Second Prize, 1950. **One-man Exhibitions:** The Daniel Gallery, NYC, 1922, also 1928, 30; Tokyo/Modern and Osaka/Municipal, 1931-32; The Downtown Gallery, 1933, 36, 39, 40, 41, 45, 48, 50, 52, 55, 61, 65; ASL, 1936; Baltimore/MA, 1939; Boston Museum School, 1950; Woodstock (N.Y.) Art Gallery, 1956; FAR Gallery, 1970; Paul Gallery, 1971; U. of Texas, 1975; Salander O'Reilly Galleries, 1981, 82; WMAA (Philip Morris) circ., 1986; The Zabriskie Gallery, 1986. **Retrospectives:** The Downtown Gallery, benefit for United China Relief, 1942; WMAA, 1948; Tokyo/Modern, 1954; Boston U., 1961; U. of Florida, 1969. **Group:** Society of Independent Artists, NYC; Penguin Club, NYC, 1917; MOMA, Paintings by 19 Living Americans, 1929; MOMA, Twentieth Century Portraits, 1942; The U. of Chicago, 1948; Portland, Me./MA, 1949; XXVI Venice Biennial, 1952; U. of Illinois; U. of Nebraska. **Collections:** AAAL; Agricultural and Mechanical College of Texas; Andover/Phillips; Arizona State College; U. of Airzona; Atlanta/AA; Auburn A.; Baltimore/MA; Britannica; Brooklyn Museum; Buffalo/Albright; Carnegie; Chicago/AI; Cincinnati/AM; Clearwater/Gulf Coast; Cleveland/MA; Columbus; Cranbrook; Dallas/MFA; Des Moines; Detroit/Institute; Hamilton Easter Field Foundation; Fort Worth; U. of Georgia; Hartford/Wadsworth; Honolulu Academy; Houston/MFA; U. of Illinois; Indiana U.; Indianapolis/Herron; Kalamazoo/Institute; Kansas City/Nelson; Library of Congress; MMA; MOMA; U. of Michigan; Milwaukee; U. of Nebraska; Newark Museum; New London; Ogunquit; PMA; Phillips; Portland, Ore./AM; Santa Barbara/MA; Sao Paulo; Tel Aviv; Tokyo/Modern; Utica; VMFA; WMAA; Walker; Washington U.; West Palm Beach/Norton; Wichita/AM; Wilmington; Youngstown/Butler. **Bibliography:** American Artists Congress, Inc.; American Artists Group, Inc. 3; Barker 1; Baur 7; Bazin; Bethers; Biddle 4; Blesh 1; Boswell 1; Brown 2; Cahill and Barr, eds.; Cheney; Coke 2; Eliot; *From Foreign Shores;* Genauer; Goodrich 8; Goodrich and Baur 1; Goodrich and Imgizumi; Haftman; Hall; Halpert; Hunter, ed.; *Index of 20th Century Artists;* Jewel 2; Kootz 1, 2; **Kuniyoshi;** McCurdy, ed.; Mellquist; Newmeyer; Pagano; Pearson 1, 2; Poore; Pousette-Dart, ed.; Reese; Richardson, E.P.; Ringel, ed.; Rose, B., 1; Wheeler; Wight 2; *Woodstock: An American Art Colony 1902-1977;* Zaidenberg, ed.; Zigrosser 1. Archives.

KUNTZ, ROGER. b. January 4, 1926, San Antonio, Tex., **d.** August, 1975, Laguna Beach, Calif. **Studied:** Pomona College, 1943-44, 1946-48, BA; Claremont Graduate School, 1948-50, MFA; in France and Italy, 1950. **Awards:** Arizona State Fair, Second Prize, 1949, and First Prize, 1950; NAD Annual, Andrew Carnegie Prize, 1952; Denver/AM, **P.P.**, 1952, 53; Los Angeles/County MA, **P.P.**, 1953, 55, and First Prize, 1954; U. of Illinois, **P.P.**, 1955; Jose Drudis Foundation **P.P.**, ($400), 1956; Guggenheim Foundation Fellowship, 1956; Los Angeles Art Festival, 1959; Chaffey College, First Award, 1960. **One-man Exhibitions:** Scripps College, 1950, 54; San Diego, 1951; Felix Landau Gallery, 1952, 54, 56, 58, 62, 64; Pasadena/AM, 1953, 63; Urban Gallery, NYC, 1955; Barone Gallery, NYC, 1957; Gump's Gallery, 1957; Sierra Madre (Calif.) Public Library, 1958; San Bernardino Valley College, 1959; Whittier (Calif.) Art Association, 1960; Mount San Antonio College, 1961. **Group:** Los Angeles/County MA, California Centennial Art Exhibition, 1949, Annuals, 1951, 53, 57; NAD, 1952, 53; Denver/AM, 1952, 53, 54, 55; PAFA, 1952, 55; Corcoran, 1953; Carnegie, 1955, 64; Sao Paulo, 1955; U. of Illinois, 1955, 57; Santa Barbara/MA, I West Coast Biennial, 1958; Long Beach/MA, Arts of Southern California II, 1958; Oakland/AM, Pop Art USA, 1963. **Collections:** Denver/AM; U. of Illinois; Los Angeles/County MA; NAD; Pasadena/AM; Scripps College.

KUSHNER, ROBERT. b. August 19, 1949, Pasadena, Calif. **Studied:** U. of California, San Diego, BA. Traveled Iran, Afghanistan, Europe, India. **Commission:** Exxon Building, Houston. Designed sets and costumes for theatrical and dance groups. **Awards:** National Endowment for the Arts, 1977, 79. **Address:** 17 East 16th Street, NYC 10003. **Dealer:** Holly Solomon Gallery, NYC. **One-man Exhibitions:** (first) Holly Solomon Gallery, NYC, 1975, 77, 79 (2), 81, 82, 83, 85; U. of Kentucky, 1975; Thorpe Intermedia Gallery, Sparkill, N.Y., 1977; Philadelphia College of Art, 1977; Lunn Gallery, Washington, D.C., 1978; F. H. Mayor Gallery, London, 1979, 80, 81, 85; Daniel Templon, Paris, 1979; Dart Gallery, Chicago, 1980, 83; Akira Ikeda Gallery, Nagoya, Japan, 1981; Asher/Faure, Los Angeles, 1981; Galerie Bischofberger, Zurich, 1981; American Graffiti Gallery, Amsterdam, 1982; Castelli-Goodman-Solomon, East Hampton, 1982; U. of Colorado, 1982; U. of Southern California, Los Angeles, 1982; Studio Marconi, Milan, 1982; Galerie Rudolf Zwirner, Cologne, 1982, 86; Brentwood Gallery, St. Louis, 1984; Brooklyn Museum, 1984; Galleria Guilia, Rome, 1984; McIntosh/Drysdale Gallery, Houston, 1984; WMAA, 1984; Capricorno Gallerie, Venice, 1985; Crown Point Press, NYC, 1985; Rugg Road Gallery, Boston, 1986. **Retrospective:** ICA, U. of Pennsylvania, 1987. **Group:** U. of California, San Diego, Costumes for Moving Bodies, 1971; Museum of Contemporary Crafts, NYC, Vegetables and Flowers Weeks, 1973; WMAA Biennials, 1975, 81, 85; American Foundation for the Arts, Miami, Patterning and Decoration, 1977; U. of North Carolina, Art on Paper, 1977; P. S. 1, Long Island City, N.Y., Projects of the 70's, 1977; Cincinnati/Contemporary, Arabesque, 1978; Rice U., Pattern and Decoration, 1978; Brussels/Beaux-Arts, Patterning Painting, 1978; Dayton/AI, Patterns +, 1979; Buffalo/Albright, Patterns, 1979; Aspen Center for the Visual Arts, American Portraits of the 60's and 70's, 1979; ICA, U. of Pennsylvania, The Decorative Impulse, 1979; Mannheim, Dekor, 1980; Aachen/NG, Les nouveaux fauves—Die neuen Wilden, 1980; XXXIX & XLI Venice Biennials, 1980, 84; Hannover/KG, New York Now, circ., 1982; Houston/Contemporary, The Americans: The Collage, 1982; Sydney/AG, 4th Biennial, 1982; WMAA, Focus on the Figure, 1982; Bonn, Back to the USA, circ., 1983. **Bibliography:** *Back to the USA; Drawings: The Pluralist Decade;* Haenlein; Hiromoto; Lucie-Smith; Murken-Altrogge.

L

LABAUDT, LUCIEN. b. May 14, 1880, Paris, France; **d.** December 13, 1943, Assam, India. Primarily self-taught. To London 1903; to USA, 1906; became a citizen. French Army, World War I; US War Department, World War II. Artists War Correspondent for *Life* magazine, 1943. **Commissions** (murals): Coit Memorial Tower, San Francisco; George Washington High School, San Francisco; Beach Chalet, San Francisco; US Post Office, Los Angeles; US Court House, Los Angeles; California State Building and Auditorium, Golden Gate International Exposition, San Francisco, 1939. **Awards:** SFMA, Anne Bremer Memorial Prize, 1927; Gump's Gallery, First Prize, 1932; Radical Group, Los Angeles, First Prize, 1937; SFMA, First Municipal **P.P.**, 1937. **One-man Exhibitions:** Beaux Arts Gallery, San Francisco; California Palace; Stanley Rose Gallery, Hollywood; Stendhal Gallery, Los Angeles; Oakland/AM; San Joaquin Pioneer Museum and Haggin Art Galleries, Stockton, Calif.; SFMA, 1940; SFMA, Memorial Exhibition, 1944; Lucien Labaudt Gallery, San Francisco, Memorial Exhibition, annually. **Group:** SFMA Annuals, 1920-43; Salon des Artistes Independants, Paris, 1921-26; Society of Independent Artists, NYC, 1922-31; Salon d'Automne, Paris, 1924-26; Paris Salon, 1928; Carnegie, 1931, 1933-37; MOMA, 1933, 34, 36; Brooklyn Museum, 1936. **Collections:** SFMA; San Francisco Municipal Art Commission. **Bibliography:** Cheney. Archives.

LACHAISE, GASTON. b. March 19, 1882, Paris, France; **d.** October, 1935, NYC. **Studied:** Ecole Bernard Palissy, Paris, 1895; Academie des Beaux-Arts, Paris, 1898-1904, with G. J. Thomas. Worked for Rene Lalique. To USA, 1906. Worked for H. H. Kitson in Boston, 1906-12. **Commissions:** Electricity Building, A Century of Progress, Chicago, 1933-34; Rockefeller Center, NYC; Fairmount Park, Philadelphia. **One-man Exhibitions:** (first) Bourgeois Gallery, NYC, 1918, also 1920; Stieglitz's Intimate Gallery, NYC, 1927; Joseph Brummer Gallery, NYC, 1928; Philadelphia Art Alliance, 1932; WMAA, 1937; Brooklyn Museum, 1938; M. Knoedler & Co. 1947; Weyhe Gallery, 1956; Margaret Brown Gallery, Boston, 1957; MOMA, circ. only, 1962; Robert Schoelkopf Gallery, 1964, 66, 69, 73; Felix Landau Gallery, 1965; Cornell U., 1974; UCLA, 1975; The Zabriskie Gallery, 1975; U. of Rochester, 1979; WMAA, 1980; Palm Springs Desert Museum, 1982; Robert Schoelkopf Gallery, NYC, 1982. **Retrospective:** MOMA, 1935; Los Angeles/County MA, 1963; SFMA, 1967. **Group:** MOMA; WMAA; Phillips; Hartford/Wadsworth; Harvard U., Three American Sculptors and the Female Nude, 1980. **Collections:** Andover/Phillips; Arizona State College; Cincinnati/AM; Cleveland/MA; Hartford/Wadsworth; Harvard U.; Los Angeles/County MA; MMA; MOMA; Museum of the City of New York; New London; PMA; Phillips; U. of Rochester; Santa Barbara/MA; Smith College; U. of Texas; WMAA. **Bibliography:** *Avant-Garde Painting and Sculpture in America 1910-25*; Baur 7; Biddle 4; Blesh 1; Brumme; Cahill and Barr, eds.; Cheney; Elsen 2; Fierens; *From*

Foreign Shores; **Gallatin 4;** Goodrich and Baur 1; Hunter 6; **Kramer 3;** Lee and Burchwood; Marter, Tarbell, and Wechsler; McCurdy, ed.; **Nordland 1, 2;** Parkes; Ringel, ed.; Ritchie 3; Rose, B., 1, 4; Schwartz 2; Selz, Jr.; Seuphor 3; Seymour; Sutton; Archives.

LADERMAN, GABRIEL. b. October 26, 1929, Brooklyn, N.Y. **Studied:** Hans Hofmann School, 1949; privately with Willem de Kooning, 1949-50; Brooklyn College, 1948-52, BA; Atelier 17, Paris, 1949-50, 1952-53; Cornell U., 1955-57, MFA; Academy of Fine Arts, Florence, Italy, 1962-63. **Taught:** Cornell U., 1955-57; New Paltz/SUNY, 1957-59; Art Center of Northern New Jersey, 1960-64; Brooklyn College, 1961-62, 1967-68; Queens College, 1965-66, 1968-75; Pratt Institute, 1959-68, 1968-75; Yale U., 1968-69; Louisiana State U., 1966-67. **Awards:** L. C. Tiffany Award, 1969; Yaddo Fellowship, 1960, 61, 65; Fulbright Fellowship, 1962-63; Ingram Merrill Foundation Grant, 1975. **Address:** 760 West End Avenue, NYC. **Dealer:** Robert Schoelkopf Gallery, NYC. **One-man Exhibitions:** Cornell U., 1957; New Paltz/SUNY, 1958; Woodstock (N.Y.) Artists' Association, 1958, 59; Three Arts Gallery, 1959; Montclair State College (three-man), 1961; Pratt Institute, 1961; Robert Schoelkopf Gallery, 1964, 67, 69, 72, 74, 75, 76, 77; Felix Landau Gallery (four-man), 1965; Louisiana State U., 1966; Gallery 331, New Orleans, 1967; Hobart and William Smith College, 1970; U. of Rhode Island, 1970; Tyler School of Art, Philadelphia, 1971; Harwood Gallery, Springfield, Mo., 1972; Tanglewood, Mass., 1973; IIE, 1978. **Group:** Laurel Gallery, NYC, 1949; Brooklyn College, 1951, 57, 58, 60; Library of Congress, 1955, 56, 57; Philadelphia Print Club, 1955, 56, 58; Tanager Gallery, NYC, 1957, 62; Utica, 1957; SAGA, 1960; Cornell U.; Arts Festival, 1961; Boston U., Nine Realists, 1964; Columbia U., The Natural Vision, 1965; U. of North Carolina, 1966, 67;

Tulsa/Philbrook, The American Sense of Reality, 1969; Milwaukee, Aspects of a New Realism, 1969; Indiana U., Six Figurative Artists, 1969; New Paltz/SUNY, 20 Representational Artists, 1969; WMAA, 22 Realists, 1970; Trenton/State, Four Views, 1970; Lincoln, Mass./De Cordova, Landscape, 1971; A.F.A., Realist Revival, 1972; Boston U., The American Landscape, 1972; AAAL, 1972; Arts Club of Chicago, American Landscape, 1973; The Pennsylvania State U., Contemporary Artists and the Figure, 1974; Boston/MFA, Trends in Contemporary Realist Painting, 1974; Museum of Fine Arts, St. Petersburg, Fla., The Figure as Form: American Painting 1930-1975, 1975; NAD, 1977; PAFA, Contemporary American Realism Since 1960, circ., 1981; Houston/Contemporary, American Still Life, 1945-1983, 1983; Florida International U., American Art Today: Still Life, Annual President's Choice Exhibition, 1985. **Collections:** Chase Manhattan Bank; Cornell U.; Fidelity Bank, Philadelphia; Montclair State College; New Paltz/SUNY; Uris-Hilton Hotels. **Bibliography:** *America 1976;* Sager.

LA MANTIA, PAUL. b. January 20, 1938, Chicago. **Studied:** Chicago Art Institute School, 1968, BFA, MFA. Worked as advertising designer in Chicago, 1960-64. **Taught:** Chicago Public Schools, 1966-. **Address:** % Dealer. **Dealer:** Zaks Gallery, Chicago. **One-man Exhibitions:** Milwaukee, 1968; Illinois Arts Council Gallery, Chicago, 1970; Deson-Zaks Gallery, Chicago, 1974; Douglas Kenyon Gallery, Chicago, 1975; U. of Illinois, 1977; Zaks Gallery, 1977, 81. **Retrospective:** Hyde Park Art Center, Chicago, 1982. **Group:** Momentum, Chicago, 1962; Chicago/AI, Chicago and Vicinity, 1962, 64, 71, 78, 84; Chicago/Contemporary, Violence in Recent American Art, 1968; AAAL, 1975; Moore College, North, East, West, South, and Middle, circ., 1975; Chicago

Art Institute School, Visions, 1976; Sacramento/Crocker, The Chicago Connection, 1976; NCFA, Chicago Currents, circ., 1979; Madison Art Center, Chicago/Some Other Traditions, circ., 1983; Hyde Park Art Center, Chicago, Then and Now, 1985. **Collections:** AT&T; Chicago/AI; U. of Chicago; Madison Art Center; NCFA. **Bibliography:** Adrian.

LAMIS, LEROY. b. September 27, 1925, Eddyville, Iowa. **Studied:** New Mexico Highlands U., BA, 1953; Columbia U., MA, 1956. Traveled Europe, Canada, Mexico, England. **Taught:** Cornell College, 1956-60; Indiana State U. (Terre Haute), 1961–; Dartmouth College, Artist-in-Residence, 1970. **Member:** American Abstract Artists. **Commissions:** New York State Council on the Arts, 1970. **Award:** New York State Council on the Arts, 1970. Ceased producing plastic sculpture in 1978. Founded *PC ART*, 1983, dedicated to learning and teaching computer graphics. **Address:** 3101 Oak Street, Terre Haute, IN 47803. **One-man Exhibitions:** (first) Staempfli Gallery, 1966, also 1969; Gilman Galleries, Chicago, 1967; Fort Wayne/AM, 1968; Louisville/Speed, 1969; Indianapolis/Herron, 1969; Des Moines, 1969; La Jolla, 1969; Dartmouth College; Indiana State U., 1976; Sheldon Swope Art Gallery, Terre Haute, Ind., 1979. **Group:** Buffalo/Albright, Mixed Media and Pop Art, 1963, Art Today, 1965; WMAA Sculpture Annual, 1964, 66, 68; MOMA, The Responsive Eye, 1965; Ridgefield/Aldrich, 1965-66; Riverside Museum, 1965-67; U. of Illinois, 1965-69; Flint/Institute, I Flint Invitational, 1966. **Collections:** Brooklyn Museum; Buffalo/Albright; Des Moines; Evansville; Hirshhorn; Indianapolis; Louisville/Speed; Lytton Savings and Loan Associations; Ridgefield/Aldrich; Terre Haute/Swope; WMAA; Walker.

LANDAU, JACOB. b. December 17, 1917, Philadelphia, Pa. **Studied:** Philadelphia Museum School, with Franklin Watkins, H. C. Pitz; New School for Social Research, 1947-48, 1952-53; Academie de la Grande Chaumiere, Paris, 1949-52. US Army, 1943-46. **Taught:** School of Visual Arts, NYC, 1954; Philadelphia College of Art, 1954-56; Pratt Institute, 1957-82. **Member:** Philadelphia Watercolor Club; NAD; SAGA. **Commissions:** International Graphic Arts Society; A.A.A. Gallery; National Broadcasting Co.; The Limbach Co.; McGraw Hill, Inc. **Awards:** The Print Club, Philadelphia, Lessing J. Rosenwald **P.P.,** 1955, 59; L. C. Tiffany Grant, 1962; PAFA, Watercolor Prize, 1963; Tamarind Fellowship, 1965; National Council on the Arts, Sabbatical Leave Grant ($7,500), 1966; Guggenheim Foundation Fellowship, 1968; AAAL, Childe Hassam **P.P.,** 1973; Ford Foundation Grant, 1974; SAGA, **P.P.,** 1977, 79. **Address:** 2 Pine Drive, Roosevelt, NJ 08555. **Dealers:** A.A.A. Gallery, NYC. **One-man Exhibitions:** (first) Galerie Le Bar, Paris, 1952; Philadelphia Art Alliance, 1954; Samuel S. Fleisher Art Memorial, Philadelphia, 1959; A.A.A. Gallery, NYC, 1960, 70; U. of Maine, 1961, 71; Cober Gallery, 1961, 63; Zora Gallery, Los Angeles, 1964; Glassboro State College, 1966; Manhattanville College of the Sacred Heart, 1966; Earlham College, 1967; Instituto General Electric, Montevideo, 1967; U. of Notre Dame, 1969; U. of New Hampshire, 1970; U. of Connecticut, 1971; Galeria Pecanins, Mexico City, 1972; The Ohio State U., 1973; Imprint, San Francisco, 1973; ACA Gallery, 1976; Schneider-Sato Gallery, Karlsruhe, 1977; Evangelische Akademie, Arnoldshain, 1978; U. of Arizona, 1979; Daberkow Gallery, Frankfurt, 1979; U. of Northern Iowa, 1979; U. of Northern Michigan, 1979; U. of Georgia, 1982; Mary Ryan Gallery, NYC, 1982. **Retrospectives:** Trenton/State, 1981; Western Carolina U., 1982. **Group:** NAD Annual, 1953; Boston/MFA, 1955; Seattle/AM, 1957; Cober Gallery, The Insiders, 1960; Brooklyn Museum Biennials, 1960, 62; SAGA; PAFA Annuals, 1961, 63; St. Paul Gallery, Drawings, USA, 1961, 68; A.A.A. Gallery, NYC, 100 Prints of the Year, 1962; MOMA, Recent Painting USA: The Figure, circ., 1962-63; USIA, Graphic Arts—USA, circ., USSR, 1963; Library of Congress, 1963; PCA-USIA, 30 Contemporary Prints, circ., Europe, 1964; Corcoran, 1964; Otis Art Institute, 1964; New York World's Fair, 1964-65; PMA, 1965; New Jersey Tercentenary Exhibition, New Brunswick, 1965; WMAA Annual, 1966; U. of Southern California, 1967; Mexico City/Nacional, 1967; U. of Kentucky, 1968; MOMA, Tamarind: Homage to Lithography, 1969; SAGA, Fifty Years of American Printmaking, 1969; WMAA, Human Concern/Personal Torment, 1969; A.F.A., The Indignant Eye, 1971; Museo de Arte Contemporaneo, Cali, Colombia, S.A., 1971, 73; Sao Paulo, American and Brazilian Printmakers, 1972; NAD, 1974; NCFA, Print Annual, 1977; Hirshhorn, Dreams and Nightmares, 1984. **Collections:** Baltimore/MA; Bibliotheque Nationale; Brooklyn Museum; U. of California; High Museum; U. of Kentucky; Library of Congress; Los Angeles/County MA; MMA; MOMA; U. of Maine; Malmo; U. of Minnesota; Montclair/AM; NMAA; NYPL; Newark Museum; New Orleans/Delgado; Norfolk; Nurnberg; PAFA; PMA; Princeton U.; Rutgers U.; San Antonio/McNay; Slater; Syracuse U.; Trenton/State; Utica; VMFA; WMAA; Yale U.; Youngstown/Butler. **Bibliography:** Archives.

LANDFIELD, RONNIE. b. 1947, NYC. **Studied:** Kansas City AI; SFAI, 1963-65. **Taught:** School of Visual Arts, NYC, 1975–. **Awards:** Cassandra Foundation Grant, 1969; National Endowment for the Arts, 1983. **Address:** 31 Desbrosses Street, NYC 10013. **Dealer:** Stephen Haller Fine Art, NYC. **One-man Exhibitions:** David Whitney Gallery, NYC, 1969, 71; Helman Gallery, St. Louis, 1970; Jack Glenn Gallery,

Corona Del Mar, 1970; Corcoran and Corcoran Gallery, Coral Gables, 1971, 74, 76; Andre Emmerich Gallery, NYC, 1973, 74, 75; B. R. Kornblatt Gallery, Baltimore, 1976, 78, 80, 84; Sara Rentschler Gallery, NYC, 1978, 79; Linda Farris Gallery, Seattle, 1978, 81, 84; Medici-Berensen Gallery, Miami, 1979, 81, 83; Charles Cowles Gallery, NYC, 1980, 82, 83, 84; Bank of America, San Francisco, 1981; Nexus Gallery, Atlanta, 1982. **Group:** WMAA Annuals, 1967, 69; ICA, U. of Pennsylvania, Two Generations of Color Painting, 1970; Houston/MFA, Toward Color and Field, 1971; WMAA, Lyrical Abstraction, 1971; WMAA Biennial, 1973; NYU, The Big Picture Show, 1978. **Collections:** Art Museum of South Texas; Chicago/AI; Cornell U.; Greenville; Hirshhorn; Kansas City/Nelson; MMA; MOMA; Munich/SG; NYU; U. of Nebraska; Oberlin College; RISD; Raleigh/NCMA; Ridgefield/Aldrich; Seattle/AM; Norton Simon Museum; Smith College; Stanford U.; Udine; Utica; WMAA; Walker.

LANDON, EDWARD. b. March 13, 1911, Hartford, Conn. **Studied:** Hartford Art School; ASL, with Jean Charlot; privately in Mexico with Carlos Merida. Traveled Europe, Scandinavia, Mexico. **Taught:** privately (serigraphy). Subject of a film, *How to Make a Serigraph*, produced by the Harmon Foundation. **Member:** Charter member and past president National Serigraph Society; Boston Printmakers; American Color Print Society; The Print Club, Philadelphia. Federal A.P.: Easel painting and murals. **Awards:** Northwest Printmakers Annual, 1944, 46, 52; Brooklyn Museum, 1947; American Color Print Society, 1947, 54, 57, 58; Boston Printmakers, 1979; San Francisco Art Association, 1949; Fulbright Fellowship (Norway), 1950, 51. **Address:** Lawrence Hill Road, Weston, VT 05161. **Dealer:** Gallery 2, Woodstock, Vt.; Gallery North Star, Grafton, Vt. **One-man Exhibitions:** (first)

Boston/MFA, 1934; Smith College, 1941; Norlyst Gallery, NYC, 1945; Unge Kunstneres Samfund, Oslo, 1950; The Print Club, Philadelphia, 1953; Fine Arts Gallery, Hartford, 1954; Doris Meltzer Gallery, NYC, 1957, 58; Bennington, Vt., 1967; Sunapee, N.H., 1968; Woodstock, Vt., 1969; Southern Vt. Artists Assn., Manchester; Garden Gallery, Londonderry, Vt., 1984. **Retrospective:** Wenniger Graphics, Boston, 1986. **Group:** Brooklyn Museum; Northwest Printmakers Annuals; American Color Print Society; National Serigraph Society; MOMA; Library of Congress; MMA; Cooper Union, 1968; Lincoln, Mass./De Cordova, By the People, for the People: New England, 1947. **Collections:** Bezalel Museum; Bibliotheque Nationale; Brooklyn Museum; Buffalo/Albright; Library of Congress; Kansas City/Nelson; MMA; MOMA; NCFA; PMA; SFMA; Tel Aviv; Turku Museum, Finland; Victoria and Albert Museum; Worcester/AM. **Bibliography:** American Artists Congress, Inc.; Landon; Reese. Archives.

LANE, LOIS. b. January 6, 1948, Philadelphia. **Studied:** Philadelphia College of Art, 1969, BFA; Yale U., Summer School, 1968; Yale U., 1971, MFA. **Awards:** CAPS grant, 1977; National Endowment for the Arts, 1978. **Address:** 155 Wooster Street, NYC 10012. **One-man Exhibitions:** Artists Space, NYC, 1974; The Willard Gallery, NYC, 1977, 79, 83, 85; Greenberg Gallery, St. Louis, 1980; Akron/AM, 1980; PAFA, 1982; Nigel Greenwood Gallery, London, 1982. **Group:** WMAA, New Image Painting, 1978; WMAA Biennial, 1979; Purchase/SUNY, Ten Artists, 1979; NYU, American Painting: The Eighties, 1979; Indianapolis, 1980; Bonn, Back to the USA, 1983; Youngstown/Butler, Mid-year Show, 1983. **Collections:** Akron/AM; Art Museum of South Texas; Buffalo/Albright; Des Moines; Houston/MFA; MOMA; Na-

tional Gallery; WMAA. **Bibliography:** *Back to the USA.*

LANG, DANIEL S. b. March 17, 1935, Tulsa, Ok. **Studied:** Tulsa U., BFA, with Alexandre Hogue and Louis Weinberg; U. of Iowa, MFA, with Mauricio Lasansky and James Lechay; ASL, Woodstock, N.Y., with Yasuo Kuniyoshi. US Army, 1954-56. Resided London 9 years; Italy 15 years. **Taught:** Chicago Art Institute School, 1962-64; Washington U., 1964-65; U. of South Florida; U. of Ohio; U. of Utah. **Member:** Artists Equity. Designed sets for the Kent Opera (England) and Jonathan Miller's production of Monteverdi's *Orfeo*, filmed by BBC, 1979. **Awards:** Yaddo Fellowship; MacDowell Fellowship. **Address:** 46 MacDougal Street, NYC 10012 and via Osppedate, 1, Montone 06014, Italy. **Dealer:** Sherry French Gallery, NYC. **One-man Exhibitions:** (first) Boston/MFA, 1961; U. of Chicago, 1965; Ivan Spence Gallery, Ibiza, Italy, 1966; Boston Public Library, 1970; Arthur Tooth & Sons, London, 1971, 74; Fairweather Hardin Gallery, Chicago, 1971, 80; French & Co. Inc., NYC, 1972; Galerie Alexandra Monett, Brussels, 1973; Tampa/AI, 1974; Gimpel & Weitzenhoffer Ltd., 1974, 75; Il Gabbiano Gallery, Rome, 1975; Fischback Gallery, 1977, 79; Graphic International, Stuttgart, 1979; Galleria Il Bisonte, Florence, 1981; Watson/deNagy Gallery, Houston, 1981; Richard Demarco Gallery, Edinburgh, 1981, 83; David Findlay Jr. Gallery, NYC, 1981, 83; Galleria Gina Ferrari, Milan, 1984; Sherry French Gallery, 1984; William Hardie, Ltd., Glasgow, 1986. **Group:** ICA, U. of Pennsylvania, Highway, 1970; Omaha/Joslyn, A Sense of Place, circ., 1973; U.S. Department of the Interior, America 1976, circ., 1976. **Collections:** AT&T; Boston Public Library; California Palace; Carlton Steel; Chicago/AI; Citicorp; Dallas/MFA; IBM; U. of Illinois; Kansas City/Nelson; Lanvin-Charles of the Ritz; Library of Congress; MOMA; U.

of Massachusetts; Oklahoma State Art Collection; J. C. Penney; St. Joseph/Albrecht; Springfield, Ill./State; Tulsa/Philbrook; Victoria & Albert Museum.

LANGLAIS, BERNARD. b. July 23, 1921, Old Town, Me.; **d.** December 27, 1977, Portland, Me. **Studied:** The Corcoran School of Art; Skowhegan School; Brooklyn Museum School; Academie de la Grande Chaumiere; Academy of Art, Oslo. US Navy, 1942-48. **Taught:** The Pennsylvania State U., 1972; U. of Pennsylvania, 1974. **Member:** Maine State Commission on the Arts and Humanities. **Commissions:** Samoset Hotel, Rockland, Me., 1974; GSA, Federal Building, Sandpoint, Idaho. **Awards:** Fulbright Fellowship (Norway), 1954; Ford Foundation, **P.P.,** 1963, Guggenheim Foundation Fellowship, 1972; Maine State Commission on the Arts and the Humanities Award, 1972; Hon. DFA, U. of Maine; National Endowment for the Arts, grant, 1977. **One-man Exhibitions:** Roko Gallery, NYC, 1956; Area Gallery, NYC, 1959; U. of Maine, 1960, 67, 74; Leo Castelli Inc., 1961; Allan Stone Gallery, 1962; Grippi and Waddell Gallery, NYC, 1964; Seton Hall U., 1965; Makler Gallery, 1966, 72; Portland, Me./MA, 1968; Maine Art Gallery, 1969; Marlboro (Vt.) College, 1969; Bowdoin College, 1969; Lee Ault & Co. NYC, 1971, 76; Alpha Gallery, 1972, Exeter, 1972; Governor Dummer Academy, Byfield, Mass., 1973; Frost Gully Gallery, 1974; Bates College, 1974; Colby College, 1974; Farnesworth, Rockland, Me., 1978; Ahima Gallery, Wellfleet, Mass., 1976; Hobe Sound Gallery, Fla., 1978; Manchester Institute of Arts and Sciences, Manchester, N.H., 1977; Unity College, Unity, Me., 1976; Waldoboro Gallery, Waldoboro, Me., 1977; Hobe Sound Gallery, Hobe Sound, Fla., 1978; Hurlbutt Gallery, Greenwich, Ct., 1978; Rockland/Farnsworth, 1978; Wingspread Gallery, Northeast Harbor, Me.,

1978, 81; Maine Coast Artists Gallery, Rockport, Me., 1978, 84; U. of Maine, 1981; Payson-Weisberg Gallery, NYC, 1981, 82, 84; Ann Weber Gallery, Georgetown, Me., 1984; Midtown Galleries, 1986. **Group:** ART:USA:58 and ART:USA:59, NYC, 1958, 59; Yale U., Best of Contemporary Painting from New York Galleries, 1960; Boston Arts Festival, 1960, 61; Martha Jackson Gallery, New Media—New Forms, I & II, 1960, 61; Chicago/AI Annuals, 1960, 61, 64; WMAA Annuals, 1960, 63; Houston/MFA, New Media, 1961; MOMA, The Art of Assemblage, circ., 1961; Carnegie, 1961; A.F.A., circ., 1961-62; Colby College, Maine and Its Artists, 1963, Drawing Exhibition, 1970; Queens Museum, American Sculpture: Folk & Modern, 1977. **Collections:** Chase Manhattan Bank; Chicago/AI; Chrysler Corp.; Colby College; U. of Indiana; U. of Maine; Norfolk/Chrysler; Ogunquit; Olsen Foundation Inc.; PMA; Philadelphia Zoological Gardens; Rockland/Farnsworth; The Singer Company, Inc.; J. Walter Thompson Co.; WMAA. **Bibliography:** Archives.

LANING, EDWARD. b. April 26, 1906, Petersburg, Ill. **d.** May 6, 1981, NYC. **Studied:** The U. of Chicago; ASL, with Boardman Robinson, Max Weber, John Sloan, Kenneth Hayes Miller; Academy of Fine Arts, Rome. Traveled USA, Europe, North Africa. **Taught:** Cooper Union, 1938-41; Kansas City Art Institute and School of Design, 1945-50; Pratt Institute, 1952-56; ASL, 1952-75. **Member:** NAD; ASL; National Society of Mural Painters. Federal A.P. (murals): Ellis Island; New York Public Library; US Post Offices, Rockingham, N.C., and Bowling Green, Ky. **Commissions:** *Life* magazine (paintings); murals for Sheraton Corporation hotels in Los Angeles, Dallas, Louisville, Niagara Falls, NYC; US Department of Interior, Bureau of Reclamation, 1969; Union Station, Ogden, Utah, 1979.

Awards: Guggenheim Foundation Fellowship, 1945; AAAL Grant; VMFA, 1945; Chicago/AI, 1945; Fulbright Fellowship, 1950. **One-man Exhibitions:** (first) Dudensing Gallery, NYC, 1932; The Midtown Galleries; Kansas/Nelson, 1945; Hewitt Gallery, NYC, 1950; The Griffin Gallery, NYC, 1963; Dannenberg Gallery, 1969; NAD, 1973. **Group:** WMAA; MMA; Chicago/AI; Cleveland/MA; VMFA; NAD; Audubon Artists. **Collections:** Kansas City/Nelson; MMA; WMAA. **Bibliography:** Boswell 1; Cheney; Hall. Archives.

LANSNER, FAY. b. June 21, 1921, Philadelphia, Pa. **Studied:** Wanamaker Institute, 1939-41; Stella Elkins Tyler School of Fine Arts, Temple U., 1945-47; Columbia U., 1947-48; ASL, 1947-48, with Vaclav Vytlacil; Hofmann School, 1948; Atelier Fernand Leger, Paris, 1950; Academie Andre Lhote, Paris, 1950. Traveled Europe extensively; resided Paris, 1950-52. **Taught:** New School for Social Research, 1974-75; coproducer, writer, editor, *The Circle of Charmion von Wiegand, 1977,* videotape, for WNET. **Address:** 317 West 80th Street, NYC 10024. **Dealer:** Ingber Art Gallery, NYC. **One-man Exhibitions:** (first) Galerie Huit, Paris, 1951; Le Gerrec, Paris, 1952; Peretz Johannes Gallery, NYC, 1952; Hansa Gallery, NYC, 1955, 56, 58; Hood College, 1961; David Herbert Gallery, NYC, 1961; The Zabriskie Gallery, 1963; The Kornblee Gallery, 1963, 65; James David Gallery, Miami, 1965; Douglass College, 1975; Lehigh U., 1976; Ingber Art Gallery, NYC, 1980, 83; Benson Gallery, Bridgehampton, N.Y., 1970, 72, 76. **Group:** Finch College, NYC, Paul Magriel Collection; Southampton/Parrish; Houston/MFA, The Emerging Figure, 1961; Louis Alexander Gallery, NYC, Recent American Drawings, 1962; Stanhope Gallery, Boston, Works on Paper; New School for Social Research, International Year of the Woman, 1975; Huntington,

N.Y./Heckscher, Aspects of Change: Drawing Today, Guild Hall, East Hampton, N.Y., 1978; Tenth Street Days—The Coops of the 50s, 1978; Denver, Poets and Painters, 1979; MMA, Hans Hofmann as Teacher, 1979. **Collections:** Ciba-Geigy Corp.; Corcoran; Douglass College; Lehigh U.; MMA; NYU; Newsweek; U. of North Carolina; Purchase/SUNY. **Bibliography:** *Art: A Woman's Sensibility;* **Fay Lansner;** *Poets & Painters.* Archives.

LANYON, ELLEN. b. December 21, 1926, Chicago, Ill. **Studied:** Chicago Art Institute School; The U. of Chicago; Roosevelt College (with Max Kahn, Kathleen Blackshear, Joseph Hirsch, 1944-48, BFA); State U. of Iowa, with Mauricio Lasansky, Eugene Ludnis, 1948-50, MFA; Courtauld Institute, 1950-51. **Taught:** Chicago/AI, 1952-54 (Junior School), 1964-65, 73; Rockford College, 1954; Saugatuck Summer School of Painting, 1961, 62, 67, 68, 69; U. of Illinois, 1966; Oxbow Summer School, 1970, 71, 72, 73; U. of Wisconsin, 1972; Stanford U., 1973; U. of California, Davis, 1973; Sacramento State U., 1973; The Pennsylvania State U., 1974; Boston U., 1975; U. of Iowa, 1975; Cooper Union, 1979-80; Parsons School of Design, NYC, 1979-80; Director Oxbow Summer School of Painting, Workshop, 1978; School of Visual Arts, 1980. **Member:** Chicago/AI Exhibition Momentum, 1948-52; CAA, Women's Caucus for Art. **Awards:** Chicago/AI, Mr. & Mrs. Frank H. Armstrong Prize, 1946, 55, 77; Denver/AM, **P.P.,** 1950; Library of Congress, Pennell **P.P.,** 1950; Fulbright Fellowship (England), 1950; Chicago/AI, Martin B. Cahn Award, 1961; Chicago/AI, Pauline Palmer Prize, 1962, 64; Dallas/MFA, 1965; Chicago/AI, Vielehr Award, 1967; Cassandra Foundation Grant, 1971; Yaddo Fellowship, 1974, 75, 76; National Endowment for the Arts, grant, 1974; Herewood Lester Cook Foundation, grant, 1981. **m.** Roland Ginzel. **Ad-**

dress: 138 Prince Street, NYC 10012. **Dealers:** Richard Gray Gallery, Chicago. **One-man Exhibitions:** (first) Carlebach Gallery, NYC, 1949; Bordelon's, Chicago, 1952; Superior Street Gallery, Chicago, 1958; Stewart Rickard Gallery, San Antonio, 1962, 65 (two-man); Fairweather-Hardin Gallery, 1962; The Zabriskie Gallery, 1962, 64, 69, 72; Haydon Calhoun Gallery, Dallas, 1963; B.C. Holland Gallery, 1965, 68; Fort Wayne/AM, 1967; Kendall College, 1967; Richard Gray Gallery, 1970, 73, 76, 79; Wabash Transit Gallery, Chicago, 1972; Madison Art Center, 1972; NCFA, 1972; Stephens College, 1973; U. of California, Davis, 1974, 80; The Pennsylvania State U., 1974; Odyssia Gallery, Rome, 1975, 76; Documenta Gallery, Rome, 1975; Harcus Krakow Rosen Sonnabend, Boston, 1976; U. of Illinois, 1976; Oshkosh Public Museum, 1976; U. of Missouri, 1976; The Woman's Building, L.A., 1977; Lake Forest College, 1977; Fendrick Gallery, Washington, D.C., 1978; U. of Houston, 1977; Culver-Stockton College, 1978; Kentucky State U., 1978; Bradley U., 1979; Illinois Wesleyan U., 1979; Landfall Press Gallery, Chicago, 1980; U. of California, Davis, 1980; Landfall Press, Chicago, 1980; Odyssia Gallery, 80; Alverno College, Milwaukee, 1981; Richard Gray Gallery, 1982, 85; Susan Caldwell Gallery, NYC, 1983; St. Louis Community College, 1984. **Retrospectives:** Rockford College 1970; One Illinois Center, Chicago, 1973; John Michael Kohler Arts Center, Sheboygan, 1974; Kansas State U., 1976; U. of Missouri, 1976; Northern Illinois U., 1978; N.A.M.E. Gallery, Chicago, 1983; U. of Illinois, 1987. **Group:** PMA, 1946, 47, 50, 54; Chicago/AI Annuals, 1946, 47, 51, 53, 55, 57, 58, 60, 61, 62, 66, 69; Chicago/AI, Exhibition Momentum, 1948, 50, 52, 54, 56; Omaha/Joslyn, 1949, 58; Library of Congress, 1950, 52; Denver/AM, 1951, 52; MMA, 1952; U. of Illinois, 1953; MOMA, Young American Printmakers, 1953, The Downtown Gallery, Chicago Artists—1954; Chicago/AI, Prints from The Graphic Workshop, 1955; Corcoran, 1961; MOMA, Recent Painting USA: The Figure, circ., 1962-63; Northern Illinois U., 1966; Illinois Arts Council, circ., 1967-69; Chicago/ Contemporary, 1968, Chicago Imagist Art, 1972; Moore College of Art, Philadelphia, Artists' Books, 1973; Galleria Comunale d'Arte Contemporanea, Una Tendenza Americana, 1973; Sacramento State U., National Print Annual, 1974; US Department of the Interior, America 1976, circ., 1976; Illinois Arts Council, Naive Art in Illinois, 1839-1976, 1976; Purdue U., Chicago Art, 1976; San Antonio/McNay, American Artists, 76, 1976; Sacramento/Crocker, The Chicago Connection, circ., 1976; Chicago Culture Center, Masterpieces of Chicago Art, 1977; U. of Michigan, Chicago: The City & Its Artists, 1945-78, 1978; Los Angeles/County MA, Private Images: Photographs by Painters, 1977; Chicago/AI, 100 Artists, 100 Years, 1979; Chicago/AI, Chicago and Vicinity, Prizewinners Revisited, 1980; Milwaukee, American Prints 1960-1980, 1982; Rutgers U., Realism and Realities, 1982; San Antonio/McNay, The Artist and the Quilt, 1983; Indianapolis, 1984; SFMA, American Realism (Janss), circ., 1985. **Collections:** Albion College; AT&T; Borg-Warner International Corporation; Boston Public Library; Brandeis U.; Brooklyn Museum; Chicago/AI; Container Corp. of America; Crocker Bank, San Francisco; U. of Dallas; Denver/AM; Des Moines; F.T.D. Association; First National Bank of Chicago; Galleria Comunale d'Arte Contemporanea; IIE; Illinois Bell Telephone Company; U. of Illinois; Illinois Wesleyan U.; Kansas State U.; Library of Congress; Madison Art Center; U. of Massachusetts; NCFA; The Singer Company, Inc.; Springfield, Ill./State; Trenton/State; Walker. **Bibliography:** Adrian; *Art: A Woman's Sensibility*, Arthur 2. Archives.

LASANSKY, MAURICIO. b. October 12, 1914, Buenos Aires, Argentina. **Studied:** Superior School of Fine Arts, Buenos Aires. Traveled Europe, Latin America. To USA, 1943; citizen, 1952. **Taught:** Director, Free Fine Arts School, Villa Maria, Argentina, 1936; Taller Manualidad, 1939; Atelier 17, NYC; State U. of Iowa, 1954-. **Awards:** Guggenheim Foundation Fellowship (USA), 1943, renewed 1944; Seattle/AM, Seattle International, First Prize, 1944; The Print Club, Philadelphia, **P.P.,** 1945, 48; Library of Congress, Pennell **P.P.,** 1945, 48, 50, 56, 59, 62, 63; Denver/AM, **P.P.,** 1946, 47; Des Moines, **P.P.,** 1946, 49, 51, 57, 58; Iowa State Fair, First Prize, 1947; Society of American Etchers and Engravers, NYC, 1947; PAFA, Alice McFadden Eyre Medal, 1948, 57; Brooklyn Museum, **P.P.,** 1948, 58; Northwest Printmakers Annual, **P.P.,** 1948, 51, 55, 59, 61; Walker, First and Second Prizes, 1949; The Print Club, Philadelphia, Charles M. Lea Prize, 1951, 57, 62; Printmakers of Southern California, **P.P.,** 1952; Bradley U., **P.P.,** 1952; Des Moines, IV Annual, Edmundson Award, 1952; Des Moines, V Annual, Special Commendation, 1953; Des Moines, Prize in Painting, 1955; Des Moines Younkers Professional Award, 1956; I Inter-American Paintings and Prints Biennial, Mexico City, Posada Award, 1958; Silvermine Guild, **P.P.,** 1958; Walker Biennial, **P.P.,** 1958; De Pauw U., **P.P.,** 1959; Hon. DFA, Illinois Wesleyan College, 1959; Kansas City/Nelson, **P.P.,** 1960; II Inter-American Paintings and Prints Biennial, Mexico City, Special Hon. Men. with Gold Medal, 1960; PAFA, Hon. Men. and one-man exhibition, 1961; Pasadena/AM, **P.P.,** 1962; Ford Foundation, **P.P.,** 1962; Guggenheim Foundation Fellowship (Spain and France), 1963, 64; Hon. DFA, Pacific Lutheran U., 1969; Philadelphia Print Club Annual, Bertha von Moschzisker Prize, 1971; Dickinson College Arts Award, 1974. **Address:** Quail Creek Condominium, Rural Route 1, North Lib-

erty, Iowa 52317. **One-man Exhibitions:** (first) Fort General Roca, Rio Negro, Argentina, 1935; Whyte Gallery, Washington, D.C., 1945; SFMA, 1945, 50; Chicago/AI, 1947; U. of Louisville, 1948; Walker, 1949; Houston/MFA, 1949; Milwaukee, 1949; Purdue U., 1949; Santa Barbara/MA, 1950; Northwestern U., 1950; Cornell U., 1951; Tulane U., 1952; Memphis/Brooks, 1953; Madrid/Nacional, 1954; Oakland/AM, 1958; USIA, Intaglios (one-man and his students), circ., Latin America and USA, 1959-61; PAFA Annual, 1961; Des Moines, 1967; Carleton College, 1965; PMA, circ., 1966; Dickinson College, 1972; Fort Dodge/Blanden, 1973; Jane Haslem Gallery, Washington, D.C., 1982. **Retrospectives:** State U. of Iowa, 1957; A.F.A./Ford Foundation, circ., 1960-62; Iowa State U., 1967; U. of Iowa, 1976. **Group:** Carnegie, American Prints, 1949; Sao Paulo, 1951; U. of Illinois, Graphic Art, USA, 1954; France/National, 50 Ans d'Art aux Etats-Unis, circ., Europe, 1955; Gallery of Modern Art, Ljubljana, Yugoslavia, I, II, and V International Exhibitions of Prints, 55, 57, 63, 67, 71; Michigan State U., 20 American Printmakers, 1956; Achenbach Foundation, Prints since the 14th Century, 1957; SAGA, 1957; U. of California, Berkeley, Modern Master Prints, 1958; I and II Inter-American Paintings and Prints Biennials, Mexico City, 1958, 60; ICA, Boston, 100 Works on Paper, circ., Europe, 1959; PAFA, 1959, 60; PCA, American Prints Today, circ., 1959-62; Yale U., American Prints, 1950-60, 1960; USIA, Graphic Arts—USA, circ., USSR, 1963; I & II International Print Biennials, Kracow, 1966, 68; MOMA, The Artist as His Subject, 1967; National Academy of Fine Arts, Amsterdam, American Prints, 1968; Bradford, England, British Print Biennial, 1969; XXXV Venice Biennial, 1970; San Juan, Puerto Rico, Biennial del Grabado, 1970, 72, 74; Graphische Sammlung Albertina, Graphik der Welt, 1971; WMAA, Oversized Prints, 1971. **Collections:** Albion College; American

Life and Casualty Insurance Co.; Argentina/Nacional; Barcelona; Bradley U.; Brooklyn Museum; Buenos Aires/Municipal; Cedar Rapids/AA; Chicago/AI; Colorado Springs/FA; Cordoba/Municipal; Cordoba/Provincial; U. of Delaware; De Pauw U.; Des Moines; Detroit/Institute; First National Bank, Iowa City; Flint/Institute; U. of Georgia; Gettysburg College; IBM; Illinois State Normal U.; U. of Illinois; Indiana U.; Iowa Wesleyan College; State College of Iowa; State U. of Iowa; Kansas City/Nelson; La Plata; Library of Congress; Louisiana State U.; Luther College; MOMA; Madrid/Nacional; U. of Maine; Melbourne/National; Mendoza; U. of Michigan; Millikin U.; U. of Minnesota; Museo Rosario; NYPL; National Gallery; U. of Nebraska; New Britain; Oakland/AM; Omaha:/Joslyn; PAFA; PMA; Pasadena/AM; Portland, Ore./AM; Rio Cuarto; SFMA; St. Louis/City; Salt Lake City Public Library; Seattle/AM; Silvermine Guild; Southwest Missouri State College; Springfield, Mo./AM; Syracuse U.; Time Inc.; USIA; U. of Utah; Walker; Washburn U. of Topeka; Washington U.; U. of Washington; Wesleyan U.; Yale U. **Bibliography:** *From Foreign Shores;* Hayter 1, 2; Marter, Tarbell, and Wechsler; **Honig;** Moser 1; Reese; Soyer, R. 1; **Zigrosser 2.**

LASSAW, IBRAM. b. May 4, 1913, Alexandria, Egypt. To USA, 1921; citizen, 1928. **Studied:** City College of New York; Clay Club, 1926-30; Beaux-Arts Institute of Design, NYC, 1930-31; Ozenfant School of Art, NYC. Traveled Europe. US Army, 1942-44. **Taught:** American U., 1950; Duke U., 1962-63; Long Island U., 1966-; U. of California, Berkeley, 1965-66; Brandeis U., 1972; Mt. Holyoke College, 1978; and privately. **Member:** A founder and member of American Abstract Artists (president, 1946-49); charter member, Artist's "Club," 1949. Federal A.P.: 1933-42; Artists Equity; AAIAL. **Commissions:**

Beth El Temple, Springfield, Mass.; Beth El Temple, Providence, R.I.; Temple of Aaron, St. Paul; Temple Ansche Chesed, Cleveland; Kneses Tifereth Israel Synagogue, Port Chester, N.Y.; House of Theology of the Franciscan Fathers, Centreville, Ohio; Washington U., 1959; New York Hilton Hotel; Yale & Towne Inc.; Rockefeller Center, NYC, Celanese Building; Long Island Hall of Fame; Springfield, Mass./MFA. **Awards:** AAIAL, 1975. **Address:** P. O. Box 487, East Hampton, N.Y. 11937. **Dealer:** Sid Deutsch Gallery, NYC. **One-man Exhibitions:** (first) The Kootz Gallery, NYC, 1951, also 1952, 54, 58, 60, 63, 64; Duke U., 1963; Benson Gallery, 1966; Gertrude Kasle Gallery, 1968; Carnegie-Mellon U., 1969; Vanderbilt U., 1970; Guild Hall, East Hampton, 1971; The Zabriskie Gallery, NYC, 1977; Yares Gallery, Scottsdale, 1970; Phoenix II Gallery, Washington, D.C., 1982; Sid Deutsch Gallery, 1986. **Retrospective:** MIT, 1957; Huntington, N.Y./Heckscher, 1973. **Group:** WMAA Annuals, 1936-46; American Abstract Artists Annuals, 1937-; Salon des Realites Nouvelles, Paris, 1950; MOMA, Abstract Painting and Sculpture in America, 1951; MOMA, Sculpture of the XXth Century, 1953; XXVII Venice Biennial, 1954; Chicago/AI, 1954; WMAA, The New Decade, 1954-55; U. of Illinois, 1955, 57, 59, 61; MOMA, Twelve Americans, circ., 1956; IV Sao Paulo Biennial, 1957; Brussels World's Fair, 1958; Documenta II, Kassel, 1959; Cleveland/MA, Paths of Abstract Art, 1960; Carnegie, 1961; Seattle World's Fair, 1962; WGMA, Sculptors of Our Time, 1963; WMAA, Between the Fairs, 1964; Musée Rodin, Paris, 1965; Indianapolis/Herron, 1965; Public Education Association, NYC, 1966; WMAA, Art of the U.S. 1670-1966, 1966; WMAA, The 1930's, 1968; MOMA, The New American Painting and Sculpture, 1969; Washburn Gallery Inc., Art of the 1940s, 1972; Duke U., 1972; Katonah (N.Y.) Art Gallery, Drawing in Space, 1972; Society of the Four Arts, Contemporary American Sculpture, 1974;

NIAL, 1974; Sculpture-American Directions, 1945-75, 1976; Hirshhorn, The Golden Door, 1976; WMAA, 200 Years of American Sculpture, 1976; Rutgers U., Vanguard American ·Sculpture 1919-1939, 1979; Rutgers U., Vanguard American Sculpture, 1919-1939, 1979; MMA, An American Choice, 1981; Hirshhorn, Five Distinguished Alumni, 1982; WMAA, The Third Dimension, 1984. **Collections:** Buffalo/Albright; Calcutta; U. of California; Carnegie; U. of North Carolina; Chase Manhattan Bank; Cornell U.; Hartford/Wadsworth; Harvard U.; MOMA; Metalcraft Corp.; NCFA; Newark Museum; Rio de Janeiro; SRGM; Springfield, Mass./MFA; WMAA; Washington U.; Wichita/AM; Williams College; Worcester/AM. **Bibliography:** Baur 5, 7; Blesh 1, Brumme; Craven, W.; Giedion-Welcker 1; Goodrich and Baur 1; *From Foreign Shores;* **Goossen 5;** Henning; Hunter 6; Hunter, ed.; Lane and Larsen; Marter Tarbell, and Wechsler; Mendelowitz, Myers 2; Phillips, Lisa; Read 3; Ritchie 1, 2; Rose B., 1; Seuphor 3; Toher, ed.; Trier 1; Weller. Archives.

LAURENT, JOHN. b. November 27, 1921, Brooklyn, N.Y. **Studied:** Syracuse U.; Indiana U. (MFA); Academie de la Grande Chaumiere (with Walt Kuhn, Othon Friesz, Stephen Greene). Traveled France, Italy. **Taught:** Virginia Polytechnic Institute, 1949-53; Ogunquit School of Painting, 1946-60; U. of New Hampshire, 1954-. **Commissions:** U. of New Hampshire (mural for Student Union building). **Awards:** L.C. Tiffany Grant; Syracuse U., Traveling Fellowship; Silvermine Guild, Larry Aldrich Prize; National Council on the Arts, Sabbatical Leave Grant ($7,500), 1966. **Address:** Mill Lane Road, York, ME 03909. **Dealer:** Sunne Savage Gallery, Boston. **One-man Exhibitions:** (first) Kraushaar Galleries, 1955; Smithsonian; U. of New Hampshire,

1956, 67; Lincoln, Mass./De Cordova, 1959; Bowdoin College, 1959; Indiana U.; Currier, Ogunquit, 1967; Frost Gully Gallery, Portland, Me., 1977: St. Paul's School, Concord, Vt., 1978. **Retrospective:** Andover/Phillips, 1973. **Group:** WMAA Annual; PAFA, 1951, 54; ART:USA:58, NYC, 1958; Boston Arts Festival; U. of Nebraska; MMA; Carnegie; Corcoran; Chicago/AI; Audubon Artists; Newark Museum. **Collections:** Andover/Phillips; Colby College; Hollins College, Illinois Wesleyan U.; U. of Illinois; Indiana U.; Lehigh U.; U. of Nebraska; Syracuse U. **Bibliography:** Archives.

LAURENT, ROBERT. b. June 29, 1890, Concarneau, France; **d.** April 20, 1970, Cape Neddick, Me. **Studied:** British School, Rome, 1908-09, with Frank Burty; also with Hamilton Easter Field, Maurice Sterne, Giuseppe Doratore. US Naval Aviation, World War I. Traveled Europe, Cuba, Canada, Mexico, USA; resided France, Italy. **Taught:** ASL, fifteen years intermittently (sculpture); Vassar College, 1939-40; Goucher College, 1940-41; The Corcoran School of Art, 1940-42; Indiana U., 1942-60 (prof. emeritus, 1960-69). **Member:** Sculptors Guild; National Sculpture Society; Audubon Artists; Indiana Artists; New England Sculptors Association, Cambridge, Mass. Federal A.P.: Federal Trade Building, Washington, D.C. (relief); New York World's Fair, 1939; US Post Office, Garfield, N.J. **Commissions:** Fairmount Park, Philadelphia (sculpture); Radio City Music Hall, NYC; Indiana U. (a relief, a fountain, and several sculptures); many portrait busts. **Awards:** Chicago/AI, First Prize, and The Mr. & Mrs. Frank G. Logan Medal, 1924, 38; Fairmount Park (Philadelphia), International Sculpture Competition, 1935 (monument); Brooklyn Museum, First Prize, 1942; Audubon Artists, 1945; Indianapolis/Herron, five First Prizes; Louisville/Speed, First Prize, 1954; Artist-in-Residence, American Academy, Rome, 1954-55. **One-man Exhibitions:** (first) The Daniel Gallery, NYC, 1915; Bourgeois Gallery, NYC; Curt Valentine Gallery, NYC; Worcester/AM; Arts and Crafts Club, New Orleans; Vassar College; Corcoran; Indiana U.; Indianapolis/Herron; Kraushaar Galleries; Galleria Schneider, Rome; Art Association of Richmond, Ind.; New England Sculptors Association, Cambridge, Mass. **Retrospectives:** Indiana U., Laurent; Fifty Years of Sculpture, 1961; U. of New Hampshire, 1972. **Group:** Salons of America, NYC; Society of Independent Artists, NYC; Audubon Artists; Sculptors Guild; American Society of Painters, Sculptors and Graveurs; National Sculpture Society; WMAA; MMA; Brooklyn Museum; Newark Museum; Portland, Me./MA; Boston/MFA; Colby College; Riverside Museum; Louisville/Speed; Indianapolis/Herron; Chicago/AI; PMA; American Painting and Sculpture, Moscow, 1959. **Collections:** Barnes Foundation; Brookgreen Gardens; Brooklyn Museum; Chicago/AI; Colby College; Hartford/Wadsworth; IBM; Indiana U.; MMA; MOMA; U. of Nebraska; Newark Museum; Ogunquit; PAFA; Society of the Four Arts; Vassar College; WMAA. **Bibliography:** *Avant-Garde Painting and Sculpture;* Baur 7; Blesh 1; Brumme; Cahill and Barr, eds.; Cheney; Craven, W.; Goodrich and Baur 1; *Index of 20th Century Artists;* **Moak;** Parkes; Richardson, E.P.; Ringel, ed.; Rose, B., 1; *Sculpture of the Western Hemisphere.* Archives.

LAWRENCE, JACOB. b. September 7, 1917, Atlantic City, N.J. **Studied:** College Art Association, Harlem Workshop, 1932, with Charles Alston, Federal Art Project class, NYC, 1934-37, with Henry Bannarn; American Artists School, NYC, 1937-39, with Anton Refregier, Sol Wilson, Eugene Morley. Traveled USA, British West Indies, Africa. **Taught:** Black Mountain College, summer, 1947; Five Towns Music and Art Foundation, Cedarhurst, N.Y., 1956-60; Pratt Institude, 1956-71; Brandeis U., 1965; New School for Social Research, 1966-70; ASL, 1967-71; U. of Washington, 1971-83; California State College, Hayward, 1970-71. **Member:** NIAL. Federal A.P.: Easel painting, 1938-39; Artists Equity; NAD; American Academy and Institute of Arts and Letters. **Commissions:** *Fortune* magazine, 1947 (10 paintings); Mural for Kingdome Stadium, Seattle; Howard U. **Awards:** Scholarship to American Artists School, NYC, 1937; Lessing J. Rosenwald Fund Fellowship, 1940, 41, 42; MMA, Sixth **P.P.,** 1942; Guggenheim Foundation Fellowship, 1946; PAFA, Hon. Men., 1948; Brooklyn Museum, Hon. Men., 1948; Chicago/AI, Norman Wait Harris Silver Medal, 1948; NIAL Grant, 1953; Chapelbrook Foundation Grant, 1954; NAACP, Springarn Medal, 1970; NAD, 1971; Hon. DFA, Pratt Institute, 1972; Hon. Ph.D., Colby College and Dennison U. **Address:** 4316 37 Avenue, N.E., Seatle WA 98105. **Dealer:** Francine Seders Gallery, Seattle. **One-man Exhibitions:** (first) Harlem YMCA, NYC, 1938; Baltimore/MA, 1938; Columbia U., 1940; The Downtown Gallery, 1941, 43, 45, 47, 50, 53; Portland, Me./MA, 1943; MOMA, 1944; Institute of Modern Art, Boston, 1945; Trenton/State, 1947; The Alan Gallery, NYC, 1957, 60; Terry Dintenfass, Inc., 1963, 65, 68, 73, 78; Seattle/AM, 1974; St. Louis/City, 1974; Birmingham, Ala./MA, 1974; Kansas City, 1975; Norfolk/Chrysler, 1979; **Retrospectives:** A.F.A., circ., 1960; WMAA, 1974. **Group:** WMAA; Brooklyn Museum; Phillips; PAFA Annuals, 1966, 67; City College, 1967; Johnson C. Smith U., 1968; Dartmouth College 1968; Carnegie, 1968; MOMA, The Artist as Adversary, 1971; Princeton U., Fragments of American Life, 1976; Lewis and Clark College, Blacks in the Arts, 1979. **Collections:** Alabama Polytechnic; Andover/Phillips; U. of Arizona; Atlanta U.; Auburn U.; Baltimore/MA; Boston/MFA; Brandeis U.; Brooklyn Museum; Buffalo/Albright;

U. of California; Container Corp. of America; Cornell U.; Detroit/Institute; George Washington Carver Junior College; Harmon Foundation, Inc.; Hirshhorn; Howard U.; IBM; Johnson Publishing Co.; Karamu House; MMA; MOMA; Milwaukee; NCFA; Newark Public Library; Olympia State Capitol Museum; Omaha/Joslyn; Phillips; Portland, Me./MA; RISD; Sao Paulo; Southern Illinois U.; Spelman College; Tougaloo College; Trenton/State; The Vatican, Rome; VMFA; WMAA; Wichita/AM; Worcester/AM. **Bibliography:** Dover; Eliot; Finkelstein; Goodrich and Baur 1; Halpert; McCurdy, ed.; Newmeyer; Nordness, ed.; Pearson 2; Richardson, E.P.; Shapiro, ed. Archives.

LEBRUN, RICO. b. December 10, 1900, Naples, Italy; **d.** May 10, 1964, Malibu, Calif. **Studied:** Academy of Fine Arts, Naples, 1919-21. Italian army, 1917-18. To USA, 1924. Traveled USA, Europe. **Taught:** ASL, 1936-37; Chouinard Art Institute, Los Angeles, 1938-39; H. Sophie Newcomb Memorial College, 1942-43; Colorado Springs Fine Arts Center, 1945; Jepson Art Institute, Los Angeles, 1947-50; Escuela de Bellas Artes, San Miguel de Allende, Mexico, 1953; Yale-Norfolk Summer Art School, 1956; UCLA, summers, 1956, 57; Yale U., 1958-59; American Academy, Rome, 1959-60; Santa Barbara Museum School, 1962. **Commissions** (murals): Pomona College; Pennsylvania Station, NYC, 1936-38. **One-man Exhibitions:** San Diego, 1940; Faulkner Gallery, Santa Barbara, 1940, 47; de Young, 1942; Santa Barbara/MA, 1942, 47, 51, 56 (three-man, with Channing Peake and Howard Warshaw); Julien Levy Galleries, NYC, 1944; Colorado Springs/FA, 1945; Philadelphia Art Alliance, 1945, 50; Jepson Art Institute, Los Angeles, 1947, 49; A.F.A., Drawings, 1949; J. Seligmann and Co., 1950, 51; Los Angeles/County MA, 1950, 61; Frank Perls Gallery, 1958; Chicago/AI, 1955; Whyte Gallery,

Washington, D.C., 1956; Pomona Gallery, 1956; Toronto, 1958; Yale U., 1958; Boston U.; Boris Mirski Gallery, Boston, 1959, 62; U. of California, Santa Barbara, 1960; Esther Baer Gallery, 1960; Princeton U., 1961; Obelisk Gallery, Washington, D.C., 1962; Cornell U., 1962; Syracuse U., 1962; Nordness Gallery, NYC, 1962, 64, 69; AAAL, 1965; Antioch College, 1966. **Retrospective:** Los Angeles/County MA, 1967. **Group:** U. of Illinois; MOMA; Chicago/AI; SFMA; Oakland/AM; Carnegie, 1945, 52, 55, 59; WMAA, 1948, 50, 52, 57, 58, 60; XXV Venice Biennial, 1950; PAFA, 1951, 52, 53, 56. **Collections:** Andover/Phillips; Boston/MFA; Britannica; Colby College; de Young; Denver/AM; Harvard U.; U. of Hawaii; U. of Illinois; Kansas City/Nelson; Los Angeles/County MA; MMA; MOMA; Mills College; U. of Nebraska; Pomona College; RISD; Santa Barbara/MA; Syracuse U.; Toronto; Utica; WMAA. **Bibliography:** Barker 1; Baur 7; Biddle 4; Frost; Getlein, F. and D.; Goodrich and Baur 1; Mendelowitz; Miller, ed. 1; Nordness, ed.; Pearson 2; Pousette-Dart, ed.; Rodman 1, 2, 3; Sachs; **Seldis;** Weller; Wight 2. Archives.

LECHAY, JAMES. b. July 5, 1907, NYC. **Studied:** U. of Illinois, 1928, BA; privately with Myron Lechay. Traveled Canada, Europe, USA. **Taught:** State U. of Iowa, 1945–; Stanford U., 1949; NYU, 1952; Skowhegan School, summer, 1961. Federal A.P.: Easel painting; Chinese U. of Hong Kong, 1976. **Awards:** Chicago/AI, Norman Wait Harris Medal, 1941; PAFA, Lambert **P.P.,** 1942; Society for Contemporary American Art, Presentation Prize, 1942; Chicago/AI, Hon. Men., 1942, 43; Portrait of America Prize, 1945; Iowa State Fair, First Prize, 1946, Second Prize, 1951; Denver/AM, Hon. Men., 1946; Walker, First Prize, 1947; Des Moines, Edmundson Trustee Prize, 1950, Davenport/Municipal, 1950; Des Moines, First Prize, 1952, 53;

Hon. DFA, Coe College, 1961; two University Fellowships, 1962, 67; Tamarind Fellowship, 1973; AAAL, Childe Hassam Fund **P.P.**, 1974; NAD, Benjamin Altman Prize for Landscape, 1977; NAD, Ranger Fund, **P.P.**, 1979. **Address:** 1191 Hotz Avenue, Iowa City, IA 52240; summer, Box 195, Wellfleet, MA 02667. **Dealers:** Kraushaar Galleries; Cherry Stone Gallery. **One-man Exhibitions:** (first) Another Place, NYC, 1936; Artists' Gallery, NYC, 1938, 40; Ferargil Galleries, NYC, 1942, 43; Toledo/MA, 1943; Wally Findlay Galleries, Chicago, 1944; American-British Gallery, NYC, 1945; Macbeth Gallery, NYC, 1946, 47, 50; Cedar Rapids/AA, 1946; Springfield (Ill.) Art Association, 1946; Louisville (Ky.) Art Center, 1949; Des Moines, 1951, 60; U. of Iowa, 1951, 55, 59, 64, 67, 72; Fort Dodge/Blanden, 1952; Wesleyan U. (Conn.), 1953; Kraushaar Galleries, 1955, 64, 68, 70, 73, 77, 81, 85; Cedar Falls Art Association, 1955; Davenport/Municipal, 1956; Sioux City (Iowa) Art Center, 1958; Omaha/Joslyn, 1958; Coe College, 1959; Dubuque/AA, 1961; Rochester (Minn.) Art Center, 1962; U. of Northern Iowa, 1962; Lubetkin Gallery, Des Moines, 1963; Hollins College, 1964; Waterloo, 1970; MacNider Museum, 1971; Luther College, 1971; Cherry Stone Gallery, Wellfleet, Mass., 1975, 79; Iowa Arts Council, 1976; La Lanterna, 1974; Provincetown Art Association, 1984. **Retrospective:** U. of Iowa, 1972. **Group:** Toledo/MA; MMA; Corcoran; RAC; WMAA; Carnegie; Arts Club of Chicago; St. Louis/City; Worcester/AM; California Palace; U. of Illinois; Indiana U.; Phillips; NAD, 1982, 83, 85, 86. **Collections:** American Life and Casualty Insurance Co.; Andover/Phillips; U. of Arizona; Brooklyn Museum; Chicago/AI; Coe College; Davenport/Municipal; Des Moines; First National Bank of Chicago; First National Bank, Iowa City; Grinnell College; Hirshhorn; Illinois Wesleyan U.; State College of Iowa; State U. of Iowa; Luther College; Memphis/Brooks; NCFA; U. of Nebraska; New Britain; U. of Northern Iowa; Omaha/Joslyn; PAFA; Potsdam/SUNY; Rensselaer Polytechnic Institute; U. of Rochester; Syracuse U.; Tulsa/Philbrook; Washburn U. of Topeka; Waterloo; Wichita/AM.

LEIBER, GERSON. b. November, 1921, Brooklyn, N.Y. **Studied:** Academy of Fine Arts, Budapest; ASL, with Will Barnet, Louis Bosa, Vaclav Vytlacil, Morris Kantor; Brooklyn Museum School, with Gabor Peterdi. US Armed Forces, 1943-47. Traveled Europe. **Taught:** Creative Graphic workshop, NYC (five years); Newark (N.J.) School of Fine and Industrial Art, 1959-66. **Member:** Boston Printmakers; SAGA; California Society of Printmakers; American Color Print Society; ASL; NAD; SAGA, president, 1978-80. **Awards:** L. C. Tiffany Grant (2); Audubon Artists, Joseph Mayer Award, Gold Medal of Honor, Presidents Award; Brooklyn Museum, **P.P.**; Arden Prize; Francesca Wood Award; A.A.A. Gallery, NYC, National Print Competition, Second Prize; Henry B. Shope Prize; Hunterdon County (N.J.) Art Center, **P.P.**; SAGA, $1,000 **P.P.**, 1968; American Color Print Society, Sonia Wather Award, 1968; NAD, John Taylor Arms Memorial Prize, 1971; Los Angeles Printmaking Society, **P.P.**; NAD, Benjamin Altman Prize, 1985. **Address:** 7 Park Avenue, NYC 10016. **Dealer:** Alex Rosenberg Gallery, NYC. **One-man Exhibitions:** Oakland/AM, 1960; Matrix Gallery, NYC, 1960; A.A.A. Gallery, NYC, 1961-64; Roko Gallery, NYC, 1961-64, 72; East Side Gallery, NYC, 1963; Riverdale-on-the-Hudson Museum, Riverdale, N.Y., 1963; Queens College; Raleigh/NCMA, 1964. **Group:** Library of Congress; Cincinnati/AM; Cincinnati International Biennial of Contemporary Color Lithography; PCA, American Prints Today, circ., 1959-62; Brooklyn Museum; PAFA; WMAA; Oakland/AM; Lincoln, Mass./De Cordova; MMA; Cincinnati/AM; SAGA; Ohio State U., 1968;

Workshop Gallery of Letterio Calapai, Ill., 1969, 70; Ro-Ko Gallery, NYC, 1972; Artist's Proof Gallery, East Hampton, N.Y., 1982; Benson Gallery, Bridgehampton, 1985; Alex Rosenberg Gallery, 1985. **Collections:** Abbot Academy; Anchorage; Boston/MFA; Brooklyn Museum; Cincinnati/AM; Clairol Inc.; Cooper Union; U. of Delaware; Free Library of Philadelphia; Guild Hall; Hamilton College; Karachi; Library of Congress; Lincoln, Mass./De Cordova; Lindenwood College; MMA; U. of Maine; Malmo; Memphis/Brooks; Minneapolis/Institute; Montclair/AM; NCFA; NYPL; NYU; National Gallery; U. of Nebraska; New York Hilton Hotel; Norfolk; The Ohio State U.; PMA; Potsdam/SUNY; Rutgers U.; Seattle/AM; Topeka Public Library; USIA; US State Department; Victoria and Albert Museum; WMAA; Wilmington; Walker; Wesleyan U.; Yale U.

LEKAKIS, MICHAEL. b. March 1, 1907, NYC. Self-taught, US Army Air Corps, 1942-45. Traveled Mexico, Europe, Egypt, Greece. **Awards:** Guggenheim Foundation Fellowship; Pollock-Krasner Foundation, grant, 1985. **Address:** 345 West 29th Street, NYC 10001. **Dealer:** Kouros Gallery, NYC. **One-man Exhibitions:** Artists' Gallery, NYC, 1941; San Antonio/McNay, 1946; The Bertha Schaefer Gallery, 1946, 48; American U., 1949; Signa Gallery, East Hampton, N.Y., 1959; The Howard Wise Gallery, NYC, 1961; Dayton/AI, 1968, 69; Flair Gallery, Cincinnati, 1968, 69; WMAA, 1973; Kouros Gallery, 1983, 84. **Group:** WMAA Annuals, 1948-52, 1958, 60, 62; SRGM, Sculpture and Drawings, 1958; Cleveland/MA, 1961; Boston Arts Festival, 1961; Hartford/Wadsworth, Continuity and Change, 1962; Seattle World's Fair, 1962; MOMA, Americans 1963, circ., 1963-64; WMAA, The Third Dimension, circ., 1984. **Collections:** Dayton/AI; Greece/National; Guild Hall; Hartford/Wadsworth; U. of Kentucky;

MOMA; U. of Nebraska; U. of North Carolina; PMA; Pinakothiki, Athens; Portland, Ore./AM; SRGM; Seattle/AM; Tel Aviv; WMAA. **Bibliography:** Phillips, Lisa; *Sculpture and Drawings.* Archives.

LEONG, JAMES C. b. November 27, 1929, San Francisco, Calif. **Studied:** California College of Arts and Crafts, 1951-53, BFA, MFA; San Francisco State College, 1954, MA. US Army, 1952-53. Traveled Europe, USA; U. of Oslo, 1956-58. **Taught:** U. of Georgia, 1971. Prologue sequence for *Freud,* directed by John Huston, 1962. **Commissions** (murals): Chung Mei Home for Boys, El Cerrito, Calif., 1950; Ping Yuen Federal Housing Project, San Francisco, 1951; San Francisco State College, 1951. **Awards:** Fulbright Fellowship; Guggenheim Foundation Fellowship; San Francisco Art Festival, Third Prize, 1951; SFMA, 1962. **Address:** Piazza del Biscione 95, Interno 4, Rome 00186, Italy. **One-man Exhibitions:** (first) Hungry i, San Francisco, 1951; Baronc Gallery, NYC, 1955, 56, 57, 60; American Gallery, Los Angeles, 1955; Holst Halvorsen Gallery, Oslo, 1956; Galerie Paletten, Oslo, 1957; Erling Haghfelt, Copenhagen, 1957; L'Obelisco, Rome, 1960, 61; Feingarten Gallery, NYC, 1962; Galleria dell'-Ariete, 1962; Royal Athena II, NYC, 1963, 67; Temple U., Rome, 1967; Cerberus Gallery, 1969; Gloria Luria Gallery, 1970; U. of Georgia, 1971; Middle Tennessee State U., 1971; The Pennsylvania State U., 1971; Kama Studio, 1975; Richard Larcada Gallery, 1975; Galleria Galtung, Oslo, 1976; Gallery 47, Copenhagen, 1976; Gallerie Oljemark, Helsinki, 1976; Studiodue, Rome, 1976; Galleria Il Ponte, Rome, 1985, 86. **Group:** SFMA; de·Young, WMAA, 1955; American Academy, Rome; MOMA, 1960; Internazionale di Arte Astratta, Prato, Italy, 1960; Brooklyn Museum, 1961; Carnegie, 1961; U. of Rochester, 1962; Rome National Art Quadrennial, 1967;

NIAL, 1967; AFA, Inverse Illusionism, 1971-72; USIA, Rome, Four American Artists, 1972; Rome, V Quadriennial, 1977. **Collections:** Brooklyn Museum; Dallas/MFA; U. of Georgia; Harvard U.; Indianapolis; MIT; Middle Tennessee State U.; NYU; U. of North Carolina; Princeton U.; Purchase/SUNY; U. of Rochester; U. of Texas. **Bibliography:** Archives.

LESLIE, ALFRED. b. October 29, 1927, NYC. Studied with Tony Smith, William Baziotes, Hale Woodruff, John McPherson; NYU, 1956-57; Pratt Institute; ASL. US Coast Guard, 1945-46. **Taught:** Great Neck (N.Y.) Adult Education Program, 1956-57; San Francisco Art Institute, summer, 1964. Codirector-producer (with Robert Frank and Jack Kerouac) of the film *Pull My Daisy.* **Awards:** Guggenheim Foundation Fellowship, 1969; Butler Institute of American Art, First Prize, 1977. **Address:** 1641 South East Street, South Amherst, MA 01002; 8 West 13th Street, NYC 10011. **Dealer:** Oil & Steel Gallery, Long Island City, N.Y. **One-man Exhibitions:** (first) Tibor de Nagy Gallery, 1951, also 1952, 53, 54, 57; Martha Jackson Gallery, 1959, 60; Holland-Goldowsky Gallery, Chicago, 1960; Noah Goldowsky, 1968, 69, 71; Allan Frumkin Gallery, NYC, 1975, 78; Allan Frumkin Gallery, Chicago, 1977; Youngstown State U., 1977; U. of Connecticut, 1978; Texas Gallery, Houston, 1986. **Group:** Festival of Two Worlds, Spoleto, 1958; Paris/Moderne, Young Americans, 1958; V Sao Paulo Biennial, 1959; Walker, Sixty American Painters, 1960; Carnegie, 1961; Stockholm/National, Four Americans, 1961; WMAA Annuals, 1961, 65, 67, 68, 71, 72, 73; Kunsthalle, Basel, 4 Americans, 1963; Bennington College, Recent Figurative Art, 1967; MOMA, In Memory of My Feelings; Frank O'Hara, 1967; WMAA, 22 Realists, 1970; MIT, Contemporary Views of Man, 1971; WMAA, American Drawings: 1963-1973,

1973; St. John U., The Figure in Recent American Painting, 1974; New York Cultural Center, Three Centuries of the American Nude, 1975; St. Petersburg, Fla./MFA, The Figure as Form: American Painting 1930-1975, 1975; Venice Biennial, 1976; US Department of the Interior, America '76, circ., 1976; Youngstown/Butler, 41st Annual Midyear Show, 1977; Indianapolis, Perceptions of the Spirit in 20th Century American Art, 1977; PAFA, 8 Contemporary American Realists, 1977. **Collections:** Aachen; U. of Alabama; Amsterdam/Stedelijk; Buffalo/Albright; Chicago/AI; Cornell U.; Hirshhorn; Kunsthalle, Basel; MOMA; Milwaukee; Minneapolis/Institute; Norfolk/Chrysler; PAFA; Stockholm/National; U. of Virginia; WMAA; Walker. **Bibliography:** *America 1976*; Arthur 2, 3; Downes, ed.; Friedman, ed.; Goodyear; Hunter 1; Hunter, ed.; Janis and Blesh 1; *Kunst um 1970*; Sager; Sandler 1. Archives.

LE VA, BARRY. b. 1941, Long Beach, Calif. **Studied:** Los Angeles Art Center School; Otis Art Institute, Los Angeles, BA, MFA, 1964-67. **Taught:** Minneapolis College of Art and Design, 1969-70; Princeton U., 1973-74; Yale U., 1976. **Awards:** Los Angeles County/MA, Young Talent Grant, 1968; Guggenheim Foundation Fellowship, 1974; National Endowment for the Arts, 1976. **Address:** % Dealer. **Dealer:** Sonnabend Gallery, NYC. **One-man Exhibitions:** Minneapolis School of Art, 1969; Galerie Ricke, Cologne, 1970, 71, 72, 73, 76; Nigel Greenwood Gallery, London, 1971; U. of Utrecht, 1971; Bykert Gallery, NYC, 1972, 73, 74, 75; Gallery Projection, Cologne, 1972; Felix Handshin Gallery, Basel, 1973; Zwirner Gallery, Cologne, 1973; The Texas Gallery, Houston, 1974, 76, 78; Hartford (Conn.) Art School, 1974; Galleria Toselli, Milan, 1974; Daniel Weinberg Gallery, San Francisco, 1975, 76; Claire Copley Gallery, Los Angeles, 1975,

Barry LeVa *Sculptured Activities: Silver Green* 1986–87

76; Espace 5, Montreal, 1975; Montreal/ Contemporain, 1975; Sonnabend Gallery, NYC, 1976, 78, 79, 81, 83; Galerie Sonnabend, Paris, 1976; Wright State U., 1977; Texas Gallery, Houston, 1978, 85; Hartnell College, 1979; Nigel Greenwood Gallery, London, 1980; Michelle Lachowsky Gallery, Bruxelles, 1980; ICA, Los Angeles, 1980; The New Gallery, Cleveland, 1981; P. S. 1, Long Island City, 1982; Beaver College, 1982; Yarlow-Salzman Gallery, Toronto, 1982; Daniel Weinberg Gallery, San Francisco, 1982. **Retrospective:** The New Museum, NYC, 1979. **Group:** California State College, Los Angeles, 2 Painters, 1 Sculptor, 1968; SFA, Conception-Perception, 1968; WMAA, Anti-Illusion, 1969; Seattle/AM, 557,087, 1969; La Jolla, Projections, 1970; MOMA, Information, 1970; WMAA Annuals, 1971, 76; Dusseldorf/Kunsthalle, Prospect, 1971; Documenta 5, Kassel, 1971; 1971; Yale U., Options and Alternatives, 1973; Cincinnati/Contemporary, Bochner, La Va, Rockburne, Tuttle, 1975; Baltimore/MA, Fourteen Artists, 1975; Leverkusen, U.S.A. Drawings III, 1975; WMAA, 200 Years of American Sculpture, 1976; Philadelphia College of Art, Line, 1976; U. of

Chicago, Installations, 1977; U. of Santa Barbara, Contemporary Drawing New York, 1978; U. of North Carolina, Drawings about Drawing Today, 1979; XXXIX Venice Biennial, 1980; Humlebaek/Louisiana, Drawing Distinctions, 1981; Documenta VII, Kassel, 1982; MIT, Great Big Drawings, 1982; New Museum, Language, Drama, Source & Vision, 1983; Wesleyan U., Large Drawings, 1984. **Collections:** Los Angeles County/MA; WMAA. **Bibliography:** *Drawings: The Pluralist Decade;* Gablik; Kren; Pincus-Witten.

LEVEE, JOHN. b. April 10, 1924, Los Angeles, Calif. **Studied:** UCLA, BA (philosophy); New School for Social Research, with Stuart Davis, Yasuo Kuniyoshi, Adja Yunkers, Abraham Rattner; Academie Julian, Paris. Traveled Europe, North Africa, Middle East; resides Paris, 1949–. **Taught:** U. of Illinois, 1965; Washington U. (St. Louis) 1967, 68; NYU, 1967-68; U. of Southern California, Los Angeles, 1971. **Commissions:** Hôtel de Vaudreuil, Paris; Parc de Noiseil, France; Prudential Insurance Co. of America, Los Angeles; Lycee d'Enseignement Professionel, Château Chinon, France. **Awards:** Deauville Salon, 1951; California Watercolor Society, 1955, 56; I Paris Biennial, First Prize, 1959; VMFA, Virginia Artists Biennial, **P.P.,** 1966; Tamarind Fellowship, 1969; Woolmark Foundation Prize, 1974. **Address:** 119 rue Notre Dame des Champs, Paris 6, France. **Dealers:** Margo Leavin Gallery; Andre Emmerich, NYC. **One-man Exhibitions:** (first) Galerie Huit, Paris, 1951; Twenster, Rotterdam, 1953; Felix Landau Gallery, 1954; Andre Emmerich Gallery, NYC, 1956, 58, 59, 62, 65, 66; Gimpel Fils Ltd., 1958, 60, 66; Galerie de France, Paris, 1958, 61, 62, 64, 69; Esther Robles Gallery, 1962, 63, 65; Haifa, 1964; Phoenix, 1964; U. of Illinois, 1965; Walker, 1965; Margo Leavin Gallery, 1970; Galerie Henri Mayer, Lausanne, 1971; Galerie Liatowitsch,

Basel, 1972; American Embassy, London, 1974; Palm Springs Desert Museum, 1976, 77. **Retrospectives:** Tel Aviv, 1969; Galerie la Tortue, Paris, 1975; Galerie Callu Merite, Paris, 1986; Galerie Le Gall, Paris, 1986. **Group:** Carnegie, 1955, 58; Corcoran, 1956, 58, 66; WMAA, Young America, 1957; Brooklyn Museum, Watercolor Biennials; MOMA, Younger American Painters, circ., 1957-59; Arts Club of Chicago, 1958; Smithsonian, American Painters in France, circ., USA; WMAA Annuals, 1958, 59, 65, 66; Foundation Maeght, l'Art Vivant, circ., French museums, 1966, 67; UNESCO, 1975; Comparison Salon, Paris, 1978; American Cultural Center, Paris, 1981. **Collections:** Allentown/AM; Amsterdam/Stedelijk; U. of Arizona; Baltimore/MA; Basel; CNAC; U. of California, Berkeley; Carnegie; Cincinnati/AM; Columbus; Corcoran; Dallas/MFA; Des Moines; Djakarta Museum; Grenoble; Haifa; Harvard U.; Hirshhorn; Honolulu Academy; Los Angeles/County MA; MOMA; Musée du Havre; NYPL; Oberlin College; Oklahoma; Palm Springs Desert Museum; Phoenix; SRGM; Santa Barbara/MA; Smith College; U. of Sydney; Tel Aviv; Towner Art Gallery; VMFA; WGMA; WMAA; Walker; Washington U.; Yale U. **Bibliography:** Juin; Read 2.

LEVI, JOSEF. b. February 17, 1938, NYC. **Studied:** U. of Connecticut (with Walter Meigs), BA; Columbia U. Traveled Spain, France, Belgium, Holland, England, Mexico, Middle East. US Army, 1960-67. **Taught:** Appalachian State U., Artist-in-Residence, 1969, Fairleigh Dickinson U., 1971. Director, Encounter, Inc. (drug rehabilitation program), NYC, 1974. **Taught:** Pennsylvania State U., 1977. **Awards:** U. of Illinois, **P.P.,** 1967. **Member:** Artists Equity. **Address:** 171 West 71st Street, NYC 10023. **Dealer:** OK Harris Works of Art, NYC. **One-man Exhibitions:** (first) The Stable Gallery, NYC, 1966, also 1967, 69, 70; Arts Club of

Chicago, 1968; Louisville/Speed, 1968; Appalachian State U., 1969; Lambert Studios, Inc., Los Angeles, 1971; Jacobs Ladder Gallery, Washington, D.C., 1972; Images Gallery, Toledo, 1972; A.M. Sachs Gallery, NYC, 1975, 76, 78; OK Harris Works of Art, 1983, 85; Adams-Middleton Gallery, Dallas, 1986. **Group:** Houston/Contemporary, 1966; Kansas City/Nelson, Sound, Light, Silence, 1966; U. of Illinois, 1967; Walker, Light Motion Space, 1967; MOMA, The 1960's, 1967; Flint/Institute, 1967; Indianapolis/Herron, 1968; WMAA Annual, 1968; Brooklyn Museum, 1969; RISD, 1972; WMAA, Art about Art, 1978; U. of Rochester, Uncommon Visitations, 1979; Worcester/AM, Illusions of Light, 1981. **Collections:** Albion College; AT&T; The Bank of New York; Buffalo/Albright; Chrysler Corp.; Corcoran; Des Moines; Exxon Corp., NYC; U. of Illinois; Louisville/Speed; Minolta Corp., NYC; MOMA; U. of Maryland; Newark Museum; U. of Notre Dame; Ridgefield/Aldrich; Spelman College; Storm King Art Center; VMFA; Worcester/AM. **Bibliography:** Archives.

LEVI, JULIAN. b. June 20, 1900, NYC. **Studied:** PAFA, with Henry Breckenridge, Arthur B. Carles, Jr.; and five years in France and Italy. **Taught:** ASL; PAFA, 1964-77; New School for Social Research. **Awards:** PAFA, Cresson Fellowship, 1920; Chicago/AI, The M.V. Kohnstamm Prize, 1942; Chicago/AI, Norman Wait Harris Medal, 1943; Carnegie, Hon. Men., 1945; NAD, The Adolph and Clara Obrig Prize, 1945; U. of Illinois, 1948; PAFA, Fellowship, 1954; NIAL Grant, 1955; elected to the NIAL, 1960. **Address:** 79 West 12th Street, NYC 10011; summer: 791 Fireplace Road, East Hampton, NY 11937. **Dealer:** Babcock Gallery, NYC. **One-man Exhibitions:** Crillon Galleries, Philadelphia, 1933; The Downtown Gallery, 1940, 42, 45, 50, Philadelphia Art Alliance, 1953, 63; The

Alan Gallery, NYC, 1955; Lee Nordness Gallery, NYC, 1961; Anna Werbe Gallery, Detroit, 1961. **Retrospective:** Boston U., 1962; New Britain; Rehn Galleries, 1974. **Group:** Detroit Institute, 1961; PAFA; NAD; U. of Illinois; WMAA; Newark Museum; Youngstown/Butler. **Collections:** U. of Arizona; Britannica; Buffalo/Albright; Chicago/AI; Cranbrook; Des Moines; Detroit/Institute; U. of Georgia; U. of Illinois; MMA; MOMA; Michigan State U.; NAD; NCFA; U. of Nebraska; Newark Museum; New Britain; PAFA; Reed College; Santa Barbara/MA; Scripps College; Springfield, Mass./MFA; Toledo/MA; WMAA; Walker/Wilmington; Youngstown/Butler. **Bibliography:** Baur 7; Blesh 1; Halpert; Hess, T.B., 1; Kootz 2; Nordness, ed.; Pagano; Passloff; Rose, B. 1; Watson, E.W., 2; Wheeler. Archives.

LEVINE, JACK. b. January 3, 1915, Boston, Mass. Studied with Denman W. Ross, Harold Zimmerman. Traveled Europe, Mexico; resided Rome, one year. **Member:** NIAL; American Academy of Arts and Sciences; Artists Equity. Federal A.P.: Easel painting. **Taught:** American Art School, NYC; PAFA; Skowhegan School; Cleveland/MA; Chicago/AI; U. of Illinois. **Awards:** Carnegie, 1946; Corcoran, 1959; PAFA, 1948; NIAL, 1946; Guggenheim Foundation Fellowship, 1946; Hon. DFA, Colby College; NAD, Benjamin Altman Prize, 1975. **m.** Ruth Gikow. **Address:** 68 Morton Street, NYC 10014. **Dealer:** Kennedy Gallery. **One-man Exhibitions:** The Downtown Gallery, NYC, 1939, 48, 52; Boris Mirski Gallery, Boston, 1950; The Alan Gallery, NYC, 1953, 57, 59, 63, 66; Chicago/AI, 1955; Philadelphia Art Alliance, 1955; Colby College, 1956; Randolph-Macon Woman's College, 1960; New Art Center, Detroit, 1962; B'nai B'rith Building, Washington, D.C., 1965; Kovler Gallery, Chicago, 1966; Athena Gallery, New Haven,

1967; Graphics, Inc., NYC, 1967; George Washington U., 1967; Galeria Colibri, San Juan, 1968; Lincoln, Mass./De Cordova, 1968; Galleria d'Arte il Gabbiano, Rome, 1968; Muggleton Art Gallery, Auburn, N.Y., 1968; Art Harris Art Gallery, L.A., 1970; Kennedy Gallery, NYC, 1972, 73, 75, 77; Rodman Hall Arts Center, St. Catherines, Ont., 1978. **Retrospectives:** Long Beach/MA, 1971. **Group:** MOMA, New Horizons in American Art, 1936; WMAA Annuals, 1937 to 1967; Musée du Jeu de Paume, Paris, Three Centuries of American Art, 1938; Carnegie, International Exhibition, 1938-1955; MOMA; Art in Our Time, 1939; PAFA Annuals, 1940-1968; MOMA, Thirty-Five under Thirty-Five, circ., 1940; Institute of Modern Art, Boston, Painting by 50 Oncoming Americans, 1941; MMA, Artists for Victory, 1942; WAC, 92 Artists, 1943; NAD, 1946; Tate Gallery, London, American Painting from the Eighteenth Century to the Present Day, 1946; Corcoran Biennials, 1947-1959; ICA, Boston, American Painting in Our Century, circ., 1949; U. of Illinois, 1949-1967; MMA, American Painting Today, 1950; U. of Minnesota, 40 American Painters, 1940-1950; Sao Paulo, Biennial, 1951; Youngstown/Butler, The American Jew in Art, 1955; MOMA, Modern Art in the U.S.A., circ. internationally, 1955; XXVIII Venice, Biennial, 1956; Smithsonian, Fulbright Painters, circ., 1958, U.S. Dept. of State, American Painting and Sculpture, circ. internationally, 1959; Milwaukee Art Center, ART: USA: NOW, 1962; Washington (D.C.) Gallery of American Art, US Government Art Projects: Some Distinguished Alumni, 1963; Minneapolis/Institute, Four Centuries of American Art, 1963; MMA, Three Centuries of American Paintings, 1965; Corcoran, Two Hundred Fifty Years of American Art, 1966; Cleveland/MA, Four Centuries of American Art, 1966; WMAA, Art in the United States, 1670-1966, 1966; WMAA, The 1930s; Painting and Sculpture in America, 1968; Omaha/

Joslyn, The Thirties Decade: American Artists and Their European Contemporaries, 1971; Pushkin Museum, Moscow, Representations of America, circ., 1977. **Collections:** Andover/Phillips; Boston/MFA; Brooklyn Museum; California Palace; Chicago/AI; Harvard U.; State U. of Iowa; U. of Kansas; MMA; MOMA; U. of Nebraska; U. of Oklahoma; PAFA; Phillips; Portland, Ore./AM; Utica; WMAA; Wichita/AM; Walker. **Bibliography:** Barker 1; Baur 7; Blesh 1; Cheney; Christensen; Eliot; Finkelstein; Frost; Genauer; **Getlein 2;** Getlein, F. and D; Goodrich and Baur 1; Halpert; Hunter 6; Kootz 2; McCurdy, ed.; Mendelowitz; Miller, ed., 1; Munsterberg; Newmeyer; Nordness, ed.; Pousette-Dart, ed.; Read 2; Richardson, E.P.; Rodman 1, 2, 3; Rose, B., 1: Sachs; Shapiro, ed.; Soby 5, 6; Soyer, R. 1; Wight 2. Archives.

LEVINE, LES. b. October 6, 1935, Dublin, Ireland. **Studied:** Central School of Arts and Crafts, London. To Canada, 1958; to USA, 1966. Traveled Australia, Europe, South America. Founder/President, The Museum for Mott Art, Inc., 1970. **Taught:** NYU, 1972-73; William Paterson College; Nova Scotia College of Art and Design, 1973. Artist-in-Residence, Aspen Institute, 1967, 69; U. of Illinois, 1975-76; Columbia U., 1978. Produced *Levine's Restaurant*, NYC, 1969. **Member:** National Arts Club. **Awards:** National Endowment for the Arts, 1974; CAPS, 1980; The Architectural League of New York, Grant, 1972; National Endowment for the Arts, 1980; National Endowment for the Arts, Sculpture Award, 1974; CAPS, Video Award, 1979; International Video Festival, San Francisco, Award, 1983. **Address:** 20 East 20th Street, NYC 10003. **Dealer:** Ted Greenwald Gallery, NYC. **One-man Exhibitions:** U. of Toronto, 1964; Blue Barn Gallery, Ottawa, 1964, 66; David Mirvish Gallery,

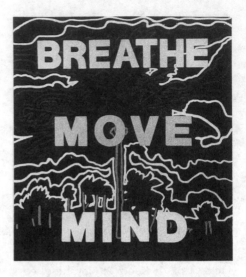

Les Levine   *Breathe, Move, Mind*   1985

1965; Isaacs Gallery, 1965, 67, 70, 73; Fischbach Gallery, 1966, 67, 68, 69, 70, 72, 73; Toronto, 1966; Lofthouse Gallery, Ottawa, 1966; Walker, 1967; MOMA, 1967; York U., 1968; John Gibson Gallery, 1968; Molly Barnes Gallery, Los Angeles, 1969; ICA, Chicago, 1969; U. of Michigan, 1969; Rowan Gallery, London, 1969; Phyllis Kind Gallery, Chicago, 1969; NYU, 1969; Galerie de Gestlo, 1971, 73, 74; Finch College, NYC, 1972; Rivkin Gallery, Washington, D.C., 1972; Nova Scotia College of Art and Design, 1973; Vancouver, 1974; U. of California, San Diego, 1974; Stefanotty Gallery, NYC, 1974; The Video Distribution Inc., 1974; Gallerie Gilles Gheerbrant, Montreal, 1976; M. L. D'Arc Gallery, NYC, 1976, 77; Hartford/Wadsworth, 1976; California State U., Los Angeles, 1976; Art Gallery of New South Wales, Adelaide, Australia, 1976; National Gallery of Victoria, Melbourne, Australia, 1976; U. of Melbourne, Australia, 1976; Syracuse/Everson, 1977; Buffalo/Albright, 1977; Galerie de Gestlo, Hamburg, 1977; Isaacs Gallery, Toronto, 1977; Vehicule Art, Inc., Montreal, 1977; Galerie Arnesen, Copenhagen, 1977; International Cultural Centrum, Antwerp,

1978; Rotterdamse Kunststichting, Rotterdam, 1978; Station Gallery, Whitby, Canada, 1978; Laurentian U., 1978; Parry Sound Public Library, Canada, 1979; Canadian Cultural Center, Paris, 1979; Northwestern Illinois U., 1979; Ronald Feldman Fine Arts, NYC, 1979, 83; Galerie Jollembeck, Cologne, 1979; PMA, 1979; Plattsburgh/SUNY, 1979; Alberta College of Art, Calgary, 1979; Marion Goodman Gallery, NYC, 1980; Carpenter & Hochman Gallery, NYC, 1986; ICA, London, 1985; Ted Greenwald Gallery, 1984. **Group:** Ottawa/National, Canadian Sculpture Exhibitions, 1964, 65, 67; MOMA, The Object Transformed, 1966; ICA, Boston, Nine Canadians, 1967; Expo '67, Montreal, 1967; MOMA, Dada, Surrealism, and Today, 1967; MOMA, Canadian Prints Today, 1967; Union Carbide Corp., NYC, Canada '67, 1967; ICA, Boston, The Projected Image, 1967; Finch College, NYC, Schemata 7, 1967; U. of North Carolina, Works on Paper, 1968; Newark College of Engineering, Light as Art, 1968; Edinburgh Festival; 1968; Finch College, NYC, Destructionists, 1968; HemisFair '68, San Antonio, Tex., 1968; Brandeis U., Vision and Television, 1969; Milwaukee, A Plastic Presence, circ., 1969; Edmonton Art Gallery, Alberta, Place and Process, 1969; X Sao Paulo Biennial, 1969; ICA, U. of Pennsylvania, Between Object and Environment, 1969; Buffalo/Albright, Manufactured Art, 1969; UCLA, Electric Art, 1969; Cincinnati/Contemporary, Monumental Art, 1970; Moore College of Art, Philadelphia, Recorded Image, 1970; ICA, London, Multiple Art, 1970; Jewish Museum, Software, 1970; MOMA, Information, 1971; Montreal/Contemporain, Conceptual Decorative, 1971; Dalhousie U., Halifax, Morbus Exhibition, 1973; Walker, New Learning Spaces, 1974; Cologne, Project '74, 1974; ICA, U. of Pennsylvania, Video and Television, 1975; ICA, Philadelphia, Video and Television, 1975; XII Sao Paulo Biennial, 1975; U. of California, Berkeley, Milwaukee, From Foreign Shores, 1976, Commissioned Video Tapes, 1976; Philadelphia College of Art, Artists' Maps, 1977; Kunsthaus, Zurich, Painting and Photography in Dialogue from 1840 to Today, 1977; Documenta 6, Kassel, 1977; Smith College, Artists' Stamps, 1977; Museum of Contemporary Crafts, NYC, The Great American Foot, 1978-80; Purchase/SUNY, The Sense of Self, 1978; ICA, Boston, Wit and Wisdom, 1978; Hirshhorn, Content, 1984. **Collections:** Art Gallery of Ontario; Art Gallery of South Australia; Brown U.; Corcoran; U. of Georgia, Athens; Hartford/Wadsworth; Honolulu Academy; Lenbachhaus, Munich; MMA; MOMA; NYPL; National Gallery of Australia; National Gallery, Victoria; New Orleans Museum; Ottawa/National; PMA; Paris/Beaubourg; Sydney/AG; Toronto; WMAA. **Bibliography:** Calas, N. and E.; Davis, D.; *From Foreign Shores;* Lippard, ed.; *Report.* Archives.

LEVINSON, MON. b. January 6, 1926, NYC. **Studied:** U. of Pennsylvania, 1948, BS Econ.; self-taught in art. US Army, 1945-46. Traveled Mexico, Europe. **Taught:** Boston Museum School, 1969; C. W. Post College, 1970-72. **Commissions:** Betsy Ross Flag & Banner Co. 1963 (banner); MOMA, 1964 (greeting card); Astor Foundation Grant, 1967 (sculpture for P.S. 166, NYC); Housing and Redevelopment Board, NYC, 1967-69 (murals for demountable vest-pocket parks); Great Southwest Industrial Park, 1968 (mural); Machpelah Cemetery, Flint, Mich., 1969 (sculpture). **Awards:** Cassandra Foundation Grant, 1972; CAPS, New York State Council on the Arts, 1974; National Endowment for the Arts, 1976. **Address:** 309 West Broadway, NYC 10013. **One-man Exhibitions:** (first) The Kornblee Gallery, 1961, also 1963-66, 1968, 69, 71, 72; Cinema I and Cinema II, NYC, 1965; Franklin Siden Gallery, Detroit, 1965-67, 69; Obelisk Gallery, 1968; C.

W. Post College, 1970; A Clean Well-Lighted Place, Austin, Tex., 1970; Southern Methodist U., 1971; John Weber Gallery, 1973; Gertrude Kasle Gallery, 1975; Rosa Esman Gallery, NYC, 1976 (two-man), 77; Deson-Zaks Gallery, Chicago, 1976; Suzette Schochett Gallery, Newport, R.I., 1976. **Group:** Martha Jackson Gallery, New Media—New Forms, I, 1960; MOMA, 1962, 63; Sidney Janis Gallery, 1964; Chicago/AI, 1964; A.F.A., circ.; Buffalo/Albright, 1964; RISD, 1965; Staatliche Kunsthalle, Baden-Baden, 1965; MOMA, 1967; Buffalo/Albright, Plus by Minus, 1968; Finch College, 1968; Museum of Contemporary Crafts, 1968; Flint/Institute, Made of Plastic, 1968; Grand Rapids, 1969; Jewish Museum, Superlimited, 1969; Foundation Maeght, L'Art Vivant, 1970; WMAA, 1970, 73; Lincoln, Mass./De Cordova, Refracted Images, 1973; Indianapolis, 1973; U. of Miami, Less Is More: The Influence of the Bauhaus on American Art, 1974; Renwick Gallery, Washington, D.C., The Object as Poet, 1978; NCFA, New Ways with Paper, 1978; NYU, Drawing and Collage, 1977; Albright/Buffalo, Paper about Paper, 1980. **Collections:** Brandeis U.; Caracas; Cornell U.; NYU; Princeton U.; Spelman College; Springfield, Mo./AM; Storm King Art Center: WMAA. **Bibliography:** MacAgy 2, Rickey.

LEVITAN, ISRAEL. b. June 13, 1912, Lawrence, Mass. **Studied:** Chicago Art Institute School; Ozenfant School of Art, 1948; Hofmann School, NYC, 1948-50; Zadkine School of Sculpture, Paris, 1950-51. US Navy, 1942-47. Traveled Europe, USA extensively; India. **Taught:** Cooper Union, 1955; Brooklyn Museum School, 1956-60; NYU, 1956-65, 1967; U. of California, Berkeley, 1962; Philadelphia Museum School, 1962-66; Florida Humanistic Institute, St. Petersburg, Fla.; and privately. **Commissions:** Interchurch Center, NYC. **Awards:** MacDowell Colony Fellowship, 1956; Guild Hall, First Prize, Sculpture, 1960. **Address:** 1348 High Bluff Drive, Largo, FL 33540; summer: 45 Alewive Brook Road, East Hampton, NY 11937. **One-man Exhibitions:** (first) Artists' Gallery, NYC, 1952; Weyhe Gallery, 1953; Barone Gallery, NYC, 1957, 59, 60; U. of California, Berkeley, 1962; PMA, 1963; Grand Central Moderns, NYC, 1964; The Gallery, Memphis, 1964; Benson Gallery, 1970; Artist Market Gallery, Clearwater, Fla., 1963-73; Eckerd College, St. Petersburg, Fla., 1978. **Retrospective:** U. of California, Berkeley, 1962. **Group:** WMAA Annuals, 1952-53; American Abstract Artists, 1953-57; PAFA; Paris/Moderne; SFMA; Brooklyn Museum; PMA; Claude Bernard, Paris, Aspects of American Sculpture, 1960; Clearwater/Gulf Coast, 1972. **Collections:** Guild Hall; Interchurch Center, NYC. **Bibliography:** Seuphor 3.

LEWANDOWSKI, EDMUND D. b. July 3, 1914, Milwaukee, Wis. **Studied:** Layton School of Art, 1932-35. **Taught:** Florida State U., 1949-54; Layton School of Art, 1945-49, 1954-72; Winthrop College, 1973-84. **Commissions:** Commemorative Stamp, Polish Millennium. **Awards:** Hallmark International Competition, 1950, 53, 57; Milwaukee, Medal, 1940. **Address:** 537 Meadowbrook Lane, Rockhill, SC 29730. **Dealer:** Sid Deutsch Gallery, NYC. **One-man Exhibitions:** Layton School of Art; Minnesota State Fair; Florida State U., 1950; Fairweather-Hardin Gallery, Chicago, 1973, 1978; Sid Deutsch Gallery, NYC, 1983, 85. **Group:** Chicago/AI; Carnegie; Corcoran; PAFA; Brooklyn Museum; New York World's Fair, 1939, Phillips. **Collections:** AAAL; Allen-Bradley Co. Inc.; Andover/Phillips; Beloit College; Boston/MFA; Brooklyn Museum; Chicago/AI; Corcoran; Dartmouth College; Flint/Institute; Florida State U.; Gimbel Bros.; Grand Rapids; Hallmark Collection; High Museum; Krakow/National;

Layton School of Art; MOMA; Marquette U.; Milwaukee; U. of Oklahoma; Queens College; St. Patrick's, Mensasha, Wis.; Shell Oil Co.; US Maritime Commission; Warsaw; Warsaw/National; Winthrop College; U. of Wisconsin. **Bibliography:** Baur 7; Cheney; Halpert; Pousette-Dart, ed.; Ritchie, 1.

LEWIS, NORMAN. b. July 23, 1909, NYC; **d.** August 27, 1979, NYC. **Studied:** Columbia U., with Augusta Savage. **Taught:** Junior high school, NYC, 1935; Harlem Art Center, NYC, 1937; Thomas Jefferson School, NYC, 1944-49; Indian Hill Music School, Stockbridge, Mass., 1954; HARYOUACT, 1965-70; ASL, 1972-78. Traveled Europe, North Africa, Greece. Organized an art center at Bennett College under government sponsorship, 1938. Supervised a mural for Thomas Jefferson High School, St. Albans, N.Y., 1939; cofounder of Cinque Gallery, NYC. **Awards:** Carnegie, Popularity Prize, 1955; AAAL, 1970; NIAL, 1971; Mark Rothko Foundation, 1972; National Endowment for the Arts, 1972. **One-man Exhibitions:** Harlem Artists Guild, 1936; Fisk U., 1939; Baltimore/MA, 1939; The Willard Gallery, 1949, 51, 52, 54, 56. **Retrospective:** City U. of New York, 1976. **Group:** Carnegie, 1955; XXVIII Venice Biennial, 1956; U. of Illinois; NIAL; PAFA; PMA; Library of Congress; Boston, MFA, Black Artists: New York and Boston, 1970. **Collections:** Andover/Phillips, Chicago/AI; IBM; MOMA; Manufacturers Hanover Trust Co.; Utica. **Bibliography:** Baur 5; Dover; Motherwell and Reinhardt, eds.; *Norman Lewis: A Retrospective*; Ritchie 1. Archives.

LE WITT, SOL. b. 1928, Hartford, Conn. **Studied:** Syracuse U., 1945-49, BFA. **Taught:** MOMA School, 1964-67; Cooper Union, 1967. **Commissions:** GSA, Syracuse, N.Y., 1979; Hartford (Conn.) Coliseum, 1980. DANCE, in collaboration with Lucinda Childs and Philip Glass, Brooklyn Academy of Music, 1979; New Mexico State U., Las Cruces, 1981; Light Rail Transit System, 1984; Pittsburgh, Pa.; 10 West Jackson Street, Chicago, 1985; The Equitable Center, NYC, 1985; BOC Group, Windlesham, Surrey, England, 1985. **Address:** 117 Hester Street, NYC 10002. **Dealer:** John Weber Gallery; Paula Cooper Gallery, NYC. **One-man Exhibitions:** The Daniel Gallery, NYC, 1965; Dwan Gallery, NYC, 1966, 68, 70, 71; Dwan Gallery, Los Angeles, 1967; Galerie Bischofberger, Zurich, 1968; Galerie Heiner Friedrich, Munich, 1968; Konrad Fischer Gallery, Düsseldorf, 1968, 69, 71, 75, 77, 79, 84; ACE Gallery, Los Angeles, 1968; Galleria l'Attico Rome, 1969, 73; Galerie Ernst Joachim, Hanover, 1969; Krefeld/Haus Lange, 1969; Wisconsin State U., 1970; Art & Project, Amsterdam, 1970, 71; Yvon Lambert, Paris, 1970, 73, 74, 79, 81, 84; The Hague, 1970; Pasadena/AM, 1970; Protetch-Rivkin, Washington, D.C., 1971; Galleria Toselli, Milan, 1971; Lisson Gallery, London, 1971, 73, 74, 77, 79; John Weber Gallery, 1971, 73, 74, 77, 78, 80, 82; Dunkelman Gallery, Toronto, 1971; MIT, 1972; Harkus-Krakow Gallery, 1972; Dayton/AI, 1972; Berne, 1972, 74; Rosa Esman Gallery, 1973, 79; Vehicule Art Inc., Montreal, 1973; Museum of Modern Art, Oxford, England, 1973; Galerie MTL, Brussels, 1973; Portland (Ore.) Center for the Visual Arts, 1973; Cusack Gallery, Houston, 1973; Max Protetch Gallery, Washington, D.C., 1974; Galerie December, Munster, 1974; Brussels/Beaux-Arts, 1974; Rijksmuseum Kroller-Muller, 1974; Amsterdam/Stedelijk, 1974, 75; Douglas Christmas, Los Angeles, 1974; Daniel Weinberg Gallery, San Francisco, 1974, 81, 85; Gian Enzo Sperone, Turin, 1970, 74, 75; Vancouver, 1974; Galerie Vega, Liege, 1974; Sperone Westwater Fisher Inc., NYC, 1974; Galleria Scipione, Macerata, Italy, 1975; Young-Hoffman Gallery, Chicago, 1979, 80, 82; Israel Museum 1975;

Basel/Kunsthalle 1975; National Gallery of Victoria, 1977; Sydney/AG, 1977; Brooklyn Museum, 1978; Art & Project, Amsterdam, 1970, 71, 72, 73, 75; Galeria Genoa, Italy, 1974, 75, 77; Galerie Annemarie Verna, Zurich, 1975, 81, 84; Hartford, 1976; Utah, 1977; Galerie Watari, Tokyo, 1980; Protetch/McIntosh Gallery, Washington, D.C., 1980; Ugo Alessandro Ferranti Gallery, Rome, 1980, 82, 83; Texas Gallery, Houston, 1980; Paula Cooper Gallery, NYC, 1981; Miami-Dade Community College, 1981; Larry Gagosian Gallery, Los Angeles, 1981; Bellman Gallery, Toronto, 1981, 82; Max Protetch Gallery, NYC, 1981; New Mexico State U., Las Cruces, 1981; Hartford/Wadsworth, 1981; Graeme Murray Gallery, Edinburgh, 1981; Marilena Conomo Gallery, Bari, Italy, 1982, 84; Aronowitsch Gallery, Stockholm, 1982; Rudiger Schottle Gallery, Munich, 1982; Barbara Toll Gallery, NYC, 1982; Eindhoven, 1983, 84; Centre d'Art Contemporaine, Geneve, 1983; Lisson Gallery, London, 1983, 84; Brooke Alexander Gallery, NYC, 1983; U. of California, Berkeley, 1983; Amsterdam/Stedelijk, 1984; Gallery A, Amsterdam, 1984; Raum für Kunst, Hamburg, 1984; Galerie Daniel Templon, Paris, 1984. **Retrospectives:** SFMA (drawings), circ., 1974-76; MOMA, circ., 1978. **Group:** World House Galleries, NYC, 1965; Finch College, 1966, 67; WMAA Sculpture Annual, 1967; Los Angeles/County MA; PMA, American Sculpture of the Sixties, 1967; Ridgefield/Aldrich, 1968; The Hague, Minimal Art, 1968; Documenta IV, Kassel, 1968; Prospect '68, Dusseldorf, 1968; Munich/Modern, New Art: USA, 1968; Stadtische Kunsthalle, Dusseldorf, 1969; U. of British Columbia, 1969; U. of Illinois, 1969; Berne, When Attitudes Become Form, 1969; ICA, U. of Pennsylvania, Between Object and Environment, 1969; Seattle/AM, 557,087, 1969; Chicago/Contemporary, Art by Telephone, 1969; Chicago/AI, 1970; Tokyo Biennial, 1970; Turin/Civico, Conceptual Art, Arte Povera, Land Art, 1970; MOMA, Information, 1971; SRGM, Guggenheim International, 1971; Arnhem, Sonsbeek '71, 1971; Chicago/Contemporary, White on White, 1971-72; ICA, U. of Pennsylvania, Grids, 1972; Walker, Painting; New Options, 1972; New York Cultural Center, 3D into 4D, 1973; Basel, Diagrams and Drawings, 1973; WMAA, American Drawings; 1963-1973, 1973; Hartford Art School, Drawings: Seventies, 1973; Princeton U., Line as Language, 1974; Cologne/Kunstverein, Kunst uber Kunst, 1974; Neuer Berliner Kunstverein, Berlin, Multiples, 1974; Indianapolis, 1974; Documenta 6, Kassel, 1977; Cleveland/MA, Book Art, 1978; La Jolla, Numerals, 1978; ICA, Boston, The Reductive Object, 1979; Dublin/Municipal, 1980; Hayward Gallery, London, Pier and Ocean, 1980; Hayward Gallery, London, Pier & Ocean, 1980; Brooklyn Museum, American Drawings in Black and White, 1970-1979, 1980; Cologne/Stadt, Westkunst, 1981; MOMA, A Century of Modern Drawing, 1982; Amsterdam/Stedelijk, '60-'80: Attitudes, Concepts, Images, 1982; Documenta VII, Kassel, 1982; WMAA, The Sculptor as Draftsman, circ., 1983; Ars 83, Helsinki, 1983; Trenton/State, Beyond the Plane: American Constructions 1931-1965, 1983; Stockholm/National, Flyktpunkter-Vanishing Points, 1984; Amsterdam/Stedelijk, La Grande Parade, 1984; Bordeaux/Contemporain, Art Minimal 1, 1985; Ridgefield/Aldrich, A Second Talent, 1985. **Collections:** Akron/AM; Amsterdam/Stedelijk; Baltimore/MA; Basel; Bordeaux/Contemporain; Bowdoin College; Brooklyn Museum; Buffalo/Albright; Canberra/National; Chicago/AI; Columbus; Dallas/MFA; Dayton/AI; Detroit/Institute; Edinburgh/Modern; Edinburgh/National; Eindhoven; Gilman Paper Corp.; Grenoble; Hartford/Wadsworth; Humlebaek/Louisiana; U. of Illinois; Indianapolis; Israel Museum; Krefeld/Kaiser Wilhelm; La Jolla; Los Angeles/County MA; MMA; MOMA;

U. of Massachusetts; Milwaukee; Minneapolis/Institute; New Britain/American; Oberlin College; PMA; Paris/Beaubourg; RISD; Rijksmuseum Kroller-Muller; Rotterdam; SFMA; SRGM; St. Louis/City; Stockholm/National; Storm King Art Center; Tate Gallery; Toronto; WMAA; Walker. **Bibliography:** Alloway 4; *Art Now 74*; Battcock, ed.; Calas, N. and E.; *Contemporanea*; De Vries, ed.; De Wilde 1, 2; *Drawings: The Pluralist Decade*; Gilsok; Goossen 1; Honnef; Honisch and Jensen, eds.; Johnson, Ellen H.; Krauss 2, 3; Lippard 2, 3, 4; Lippard, ed.; Meyer; Muller; Pincus-Witten, 1, 2; Rowell; *Sol Le Witt*, Toher, ed.; Tuchman 1, *When Attitudes Become Form*. Archives.

LIBERMAN, ALEXANDER. b. 1912, Kiev, Russia. **Studied:** Academie Andre Lhote, Paris, 1929-31 (painting); Academie des Beaux-Arts, Paris, with August Perret (architecture). With the Louvre Museum, made *La Femme francaise*, 1936, one of the first color films on painting. US citizen, 1946. Art editor of *VU*, 1933-37. Joined *Vogue* magazine, 1941; became its art director, 1943; became art director of Condé Nast Publications, Inc., USA and Europe, 1944, and the organization's editorial director, 1962. **Commissions:** Grand Bay Hotel, Coconut Grove, Miami, 1983; San Diego Tech Center, 1983; Designed 1984 Governor's Art Award, New York State Council on the Arts; TRW, Inc., Lyndhurst, Ohio, 1985; Seattle Center, Wash., 1985. **Awards:** Henry Moore Grand Prize, The Hakone Open-Air Museum, Japan, 1983. **Address:** 173 East 70th Street, NYC 10021. **Dealer:** Andre Emmerich Gallery, NYC. **One-man Exhibitions:** MOMA, The Artist in His Studio, 1959; Betty Parsons Gallery, 1960, 62, 63, 64, 67, 69; Robert Fraser Gallery, 1964; Bennington College, 1964; Galleria dell'Ariete, 1965; Galeria d'Arte, Naples, 1965; Jewish Museum, 1966; Andre Emmerich Gallery, 1967-69, 73, 74 (two-man), 79 (two-man), 80, 81, 83; Janie C. Lee Gallery, Houston, 1974; Van Straaten Gallery, Chicago, 1977; Vernissage, Rome, 1978; Greenberg Gallery, St. Louis, 1979; Landau/Alexander Gallery, Los Angeles, 1979; Arts Gallery Limited, Baltimore, 1979; Hokin Gallery, Bay Harbor Islands, Fla., 1981, 83, 85; Galerie Ulysses, Vienna, 1982; Michael H. Lord Gallery, Milwaukee, 1982; Heath Gallery, Atlanta, 1982; Galleria Il Ponte, Rome, 1983; Palazzo Dei Leone, Messina Italy, 1983; Fort Worth, 1985. **Retrospectives:** Houston/MFA, 1970; Corcoran, 1970; Honolulu Academy, 1972; Storm King Art Center, 1977. **Group:** SRGM, Younger American Painters, 1954; A. Tooth & Sons, London, Six American Painters, 1961; MOMA, Modern American Drawings, circ., Europe, 1961-62; Chicago/AI, 1961, 62; WMAA, Geometric Abstraction in America, circ., 1962; III International Biennial Exhibition of Prints, Tokyo, 1962; WMAA Annuals, 1962, 63, 65; Corcoran, 1963; Roswell, 1963; Hartford/Wadsworth, 1964; Los Angeles/County MA, Post Painterly Abstraction, 1964; MOMA, Contemporary Painters and Sculptors as Printmakers, 1964; SRGM, American Drawings, 1964; Galerie Denise Rene, Paris, Hard Edge, 1964; New York World's Fair, 1964-65; PAFA, 1965; MOMA, The Responsive Eye, 1965; Amsterdam/Stedelijk, New Shapes of Color, 1966; WMAA Sculpture Annuals, 1966, 69; Los Angeles/County MA, American Sculpture of the Sixties, 1967; U. of Illinois, 1967; HemisFair '68, San Antonio, Tex., 1968; MOMA, The Art of the Real, 1968; PMA, 1969; MOMA, The New American Painting and Sculpture, 1969; Newport, R.I., Monumenta, 1974; MOMA, Color as Language, circ., 1975; Pomona College (Calif.), Black and White Are Colors, 1979; Houston/MFA, Miro in America, 1982; Ridgefield/Aldrich, A Second Talent, 1985. **Collections:** Akron/AI; Andover/Phillips; Atlantic Richfield Co., Los Angeles; Brandeis U.; Buffalo/Albright; U. of

California, Berkeley; Chase Manhattan Bank; Chicago/AI; Civic Center Synagogue, NYC; Corcoran; Dayton/AI; Hartford/Wadsworth; Houston/MFA; MMA; MOMA; Memphis/Brooks; Mexico City/Tamayo; U. of Minnesota; NCFA; NMAA; U. of Nebraska; Oklahoma; U. of Pennsylvania; Purchase/SUNY; RISD; SRGM; Seattle/AM; Smith College; Storm King Art Center; Tate Gallery; VMFA; WGMA; WMAA; Woodward Foundation; Yale U. **Bibliography: Alexander Liberman;** Alloway 4; Battcock, ed.; *Black and White Are Colors;* Calas, N. and E.; Goossen 1; *Monumenta;* Rickey; Tuchman 1.

LICHTENSTEIN, ROY. b. October 27, 1923, NYC. **Studied:** The Ohio State U., 1940-43, BFA, 1946-49, MA; ASL, 1940, with Reginald Marsh. US Army, 1943-46. **Taught:** The Ohio State U., 1946-51; New York State College of Education, Oswego, 1957-60; Douglass College, 1960-63. **Member:** American Academy of Arts and Science. **Commissions:** New York State Pavilion, New York World's Fair, 1964-65 (mural). **Award:** Skowhegan Award for Graphics, 1977; Hon. DFA, California Institute of the Arts, 1977. **Address:** P.O. Box 1369, Southampton, NY 11968. **Dealer:** Leo Castelli Inc. **One-man Exhibitions:** (first) Carlebach Gallery, NYC, 1951; John Heller Gallery, NYC, 1952, 53, 54, 57; Leo Castelli Inc., NYC, 1962-65, 67, 69, 71, 72, 73, 74, 75, 77, 78, 79, 80, 81, 83, 84, 85; Ferus Gallery, Los Angeles, 1963; Ileana Sonnabend Gallery, Paris, 1963, 65, 70; Il Punto, Turin, 1964; Galleria Apollinaire, Milan, 1965; Cleveland/MA, 1966; Contemporary Arts Center, Cincinnati, 1967; Amsterdam/Stedelijk, 1967; Berne, 1968; Irving Blum Gallery, Los Angeles, 1968, 69,

Roy Lichtenstein *Mountain Village* 1985

70; Hannover/KG, 1969; U. of Puerto Rico, 1970; Kansas City/Nelson, 1970; Chicago/Contemporary, 1970; Seattle/AM, 1970; Columbus, 1970; U. of California, Irvine, 1970; Houston/Contemporary, 1972; Ronald Greenberg Gallery, St. Louis, 1973; Galerie Beyeler, 1973; Galerie Mikro, Berlin, 1974; Margo Leavin Gallery, 1974, 76; Current Editions, Seattle, 1974; F.H. Mayor Gallery, London, 1974, 76, 77; CNAC, 1975; ACE Gallery, Los Angeles, Calif., 1975, 78; Albert White Gallery, Toronto, 1975; Galerie de Gestlo, Hamburg, 1976; Seattle, 1976; School of Visual Arts, NYC, 1976; California State U., Long Beach, 1977; Mannheim, 1977; Blum Helman Gallery, NYC, 1977; Washington Gallery, Indianapolis, 1978; ICA, Boston, 1978; U. of Miami, 1979; Stony Brook/SUNY, 1979; Mayor Gallery, London, 1980; Portland (Ore.) Center for the Visual Arts, 1980; U. of Wisconsin, 1980; Getler/Paul Gallery, NYC, 1981; Magnuson-Lee Gallery, Boston, 1981; Gallerie Andre Emmerich, Zurich, 1982; Gimpel & Hanover, Zurich, 1982; Mattingly Baker Gallery, Dallas, 1982; Colorado State U., 1982; Nantenshi Gallery, Tokyo, 1983; Ohio State U., 1983; Galerie Daniel Templon, Paris, 1983; Columbus, 1984; Galerie Beyeler, Basel, 1984; James Goodman Gallery, NYC, 1984; Richard Gray Gallery, 1984; Galerie Humanite Nagoya, 1984. **Retrospectives:** Pasadena/AM, 1967; Tate Gallery, 1968; SRGM, 1969; St. Louis/City, circ., 1981. **Group:** Dayton/AI, 1962; Pasadena/AM, New Paintings of Common Objects, 1962; Sidney Janis Gallery, The New Realists, 1962; Galerie Saqqarah, Gstaad, Switzerland, The Figure and the Object from 1917 to the New Vulgarians, 1962; Chicago/AI, 1963; SRGM, Six Painters and The Object, circ., 1963; WGMA, The Popular Image, 1963; ICA, London, The Popular Image, 1963; Houston/Contemporary Pop Goes the Easel, 1963; Brandeis U., New Directions in American Painting, 1963; Festival of Two Worlds, Spoleto, 1965;

SRGM, Word and Image, 1965; WMAA Annuals, 1965, 68; ICA, U. of Pennsylvania, The Other Tradition, 1966; RISD, Recent Still Life, 1966; XXXIII Venice Biennial, 1966; Expo '67, Montreal, 1967; U. of St. Thomas (Tex.), 1967; Carnegie, 1967; IX Sao Paulo Biennial, 1967; Documenta IV, Kassel, 1968; Brooklyn Museum, Print Biennial, 1968; Turin/Civico, 1969; Ars 69, Helsinki, 1969; WMAA Annuals, 1970, 72, 73; Expo '70, Osaka, 1970; Foundation Maeght, L'Art Vivant, 1970; Cincinnati/Contemporary, Monumental Art, 1970; Corcoran Biennial, 1971; Buffalo/Albright, Kid Stuff, 1971; Chicago/AI, 70th American Exhibition, 1972; Indianapolis, 1972; Detroit/Institute, Art in Space, 1973; Art Museum of South Texas, Corpus Christi, Eight Artists, 1974; Chicago/AI, Idea and Image in Recent Art, 1974; WMAA, American Pop Art, 1974; MOMA, Works from Change, 1974; MOMA, Drawing Now, 1976; SRGM, 20th Century American Drawings, 1976; Cambridge U., Jubilation, 1977; Minnesota/MA, American Drawing 1927-1977, circ., 1977; Syracuse/Everson, The Cartoon Show, 1978; WMAA, Art about Art, circ., 1978; Philadelphia College of Art, Point, 1978; Dusseldorf/Kunsthalle, About the Strange Nature of Money, circ., 1978; Buffalo/Albright, American Painting of the 1970s, 1978; U. of Illinois, 1979; Aspen Center for the Visual Arts, American Portraits of the Sixties and Seventies, 1979; Milwaukee, Emergence and Progression, circ., 1979; Brooklyn Museum, American Drawings in Black & White: 1970-79, 1980; Hirshhorn, The Fifties: Aspects of Painting in New York, 1980; Instituto di Cultura di Palazzo Grassi, Venice, Pop Art: Evolution of A Generation, 1980; MOMA, Printed Art: A View of Two Decades, 1980; Purchase/SUNY, Hidden Desires, 1980; Société des Artistes Indépendants, Paris, 91st Annual Exhibition, 1980; Walker, Artist and Printer, 1980; Amsterdam/Stedelijk, '60-'80; Attitudes/Concepts/Images,

1982; WMAA, Block Prints, 1982; Houston/Contemporary, American Still Life, 1945-1983, circ., 1983; Krefeld/Haus Lange, Sweet Dreams Baby!: American Pop Graphics, 1983; Boston/MFA, 10 Painters and Sculptors Draw, 1984; XL Venice Biennale, 1984; WMAA, Blam!, 1984; Sydney/AG, Pop Art 1955-70, 1985. **Collections:** Aachen/Ludwig; Amsterdam/Stedelijk; Baltimore/MA; Brandeis U.; Buffalo/Albright; Chicago/AI; Cologne; Corcoran; Darmastadt/Hessisches; Dayton/AI; Denver/AM; Des Moines; Detroit/Institute; Dusseldorf/KN-W; Hirshhorn; Houston/MFA; Humlebaek/Louisiana; Indiana U.; Kansas City/AI; Kansas City/Nelson; Library of Congress; Los Angeles/County MA; MMA; MOMA; Milwaukee; U. of Minnesota; NMAA; NPG; National Gallery; PMA; Pasadena/AM; RISD; SFMA; SRGM; St. Louis/City; Stockholm/National; Syracuse/Everson; Tate; Tokyo/Seibu; Victoria and Albert Museum; Vienna/Moderner; WMAA; Walker; Wellesley College; Wolverhampton; Yale U. **Bibliography:** Alloway 1, 4; Battcock, ed.; Becker and Vostell; **Beeren;** Bihalji-Merin; Calas, N. and E.; *Contemporanea;* **Coplans 2; Coplans, ed.;** Danto; Davis, D.; De Wilde 2; Dienst 1; Diamonstein; Downes, ed.; Finch; Haskell 5; Honisch and Jensen, eds.; Hunter, ed.; Johnson, Ellen H.; Kozloff 3; *Kunst um 1970;* Lippard 5; Lucie-Smith; *Metro;* Murken-Altrogge; *Report;* Rose, B., 1, 4; Rubin 1; Rublowsky; Russell and Gablik; Sandler 1; Tomkins 2; Tomkins and Time-Life Books; Warhol and Hackett; Weller. Archives.

LIGARE, DAVID. b. 1945, Oak Park, Ill. **Studied:** Art Center College of Design, Los Angeles. **Address:** 19518 Creek Side Court, Salinas, Calif. 93908. **Dealer:** Robert Schoelkopf Gallery, NYC. **One-man Exhibitions:** Wickersham Gallery, NYC, 1969; Monterey, 1970; Andrew Crispo Gallery, NYC, 1974, 78; Hall Galleries, Fort Worth, 1983; Koplin Gallery, Los Angeles, 1983; Robert Schoelkopf Gallery, 1985. **Group:** Santa Barbara/MA, Photo-realist Painting in California: A Survey, 1980; Houston/MFA, Modern American Painting, circ., 1982; U. of California, Santa Barbara, A Heritage Renewed: Representational Drawings Today, 1983; Laguna Beach Museum of Art, West Coast Realism, circ., 1983; SFMA, American Realism (Janss), circ., 1985. **Collections:** Canton Art Institute; Fairleigh Dickinson U.; U. of Georgia; Hartford/Wadsworth; U. of Kansas; MOMA; NMAA; Newark Museum; Syracuse U.

LINDNER, RICHARD. b. November 11, 1901, Hamburg, Germany; **d.** April 16, 1978, Paris. **Studied:** School of Fine and Applied Arts, Nurnberg; Academy of Fine Arts, Munich, 1924; in Berlin, 1927-28. Concert pianist, 1919-23. To Paris, 1933-39; English army, 1939-41; to USA, 1941; citizen, 1948. Traveled Europe, Mexico. **Taught:** Pratt Institute, 1951-63; Yale U., 1963. **Awards:** Copley Foundation Grant, 1957. **One-man Exhibitions:** Betty Parsons Gallery, 1954, 56, 59; Cordier and Warren, NYC, 1961; Robert Fraser Gallery, 1962; Cordier & Ekstrom, Inc., 1963-67; Claude Bernard, Paris, 1965; Galleria d'Arte Contemporanea, Turin, 1966; Il Fante di Spade, Rome, 1966; Leverkusen, 1968; Hannover/K-G, 1968; Kunstverein Museum, Berlin, 1969; Staatliche Kunsthalle, Baden-Baden, 1969; U. of California, Berkeley, 1969; Galerie Rudolph Zwirner, 1969; Spencer A. Samuels & Co., NYC, 1971; Kunstsalon Wolfsberg, Zurich, 1971; Fischer Gallery, London, 1972; Rotterdam, 1974; Dusseldorf/Kunsthalle, 1974; Harold Reed Gallery, NYC, 1977; Galerie Maeght, Paris, 1977; Hooks-Epstein Galleries, Houston, 1985. **Retrospective:** Paris/Moderne, 1974; Chicago/Contemporary, 1977. **Group:** Walker, 1954; Chicago/AI, 1954, 57, 66; Brooklyn Museum, 1955; Yale U., 1955;

WMAA, 1959, 60, 61, 67; MOMA, Americans 1963, circ., 1963-64; Tate, Dunn International, 1964, Gulbenkian International, 1964; Documenta III, Kassel, 1964; Brandeis U., Recent American Drawings, 1964; Corcoran, 1965; Milwaukee, 1965; Worcester/AM, 1965; International Biennial Exhibition, Tokyo; SFMA, 1966; Flint/Institute, I Flint Invitational, 1966; Detroit/ Institute, Color, Image, and Form, 1967; U. of Colorado, 1967; IX Sao Paulo Biennial, 1967; ICA, London, The Obsessive Image, 1968. **Collections:** Chicago/AI; Cleveland/MA; MOMA; Tate; WMAA. **Bibliography: Ashton 4; Battcock, ed.; Dienst 2;** Honisch and Jensen, eds.; Hunter, ed.; Lippard 5; **Tillim.** Archives.

LIPCHITZ, JACQUES, b. August 22, 1891, Druskieniki, Lithuania; **d.** March 26, 1973, NYC. **Studied:** Academie des Beaux-Arts, Paris, 1909-11, with Jean Antonine Ingalbert, Dr. Richet; Academie Julian, Paris, with Raoul Verlet; Academie Colarossi, Paris. Became French citizen, 1924; to USA, 1941. Traveled Europe, Middle East, USA. Fire destroyed Manhattan studio, 1952. **Commissions:** Dr. Albert Barnes, 1922 (5 bas-reliefs); Vicomte Charles de Noailles, Hyeres, France, 1927 (Joy of Life); Paris World's Fair, 1937 *(Prometheus);* Brazilian Ministry of Health and Education, 1943 *(Prometheus Strangling the Vulture);* Notre Dame de Toute-Grace, Assy, Haute-Savoie, France, 1956 (baptismal font); Mrs. John D. Rockefeller III, 1950 (bas-relief); Fairmount Park Association, Philadelphia, 1958 (sculpture); Presidential Scholars Medallion (USA), 1965; U. of Minnesota, Duluth, 1964 (9-ft. statue of Sieur Duluth). **Awards:** Academie Julian, Paris. First Prize for Sculpture, 1909; Paris World's Fair, 1937, Gold Medal; Legion of Honor (France), 1946; PAFA, George D. Widener Memorial Gold Medal, 1952; Hon. DFA, Brandeis U., 1958; AAAL, Gold Medal, 1966.

One-man Exhibitions: (first) Leonce Rosenberg Gallery, Paris, 1920; Galerie de la Renaissance, Paris, 1930; Joseph Brummer Gallery, NYC, 1935; Musée du Petit Palais, Paris World's Fair, 1937; Buchholz Gallery, NYC, 1942, 43, 46, 48, 51; Galerie Maeght, 1946; Petite Galerie Seminaire, Brussels, 1950; Portland, Ore./AM, 1950; SFMA, 1951, 63; Cincinnati/AM, 1951; Frank Perls Gallery, 1952, 57; Santa Barbara/MA, 1952; XXVI Venice Biennial, 1952; MOMA, 1954; Walker, 1954, 63; Cleveland/MA, 1954; Otto Gerson Gallery, NYC, 1957, 59, 61; Amsterdam/Stedelijk, 1958; Rijksmuseum Kroller-Muller, 1958; Brussels/Royaux, 1958; Basel, 1958; Paris/Moderne, 1959; Tate, 1959; Cornell U., 1961; Denver/AM, 1962; UCLA, 1963; Fort Worth 1963; Buffalo/Albright, 1963; Des Moines, 1964; PMA, 1964; Omaha/Joslyn, 1964; Marlborough-Gerson Gallery Inc., 1964, 66; Newark Museum, 1965; Boston U., 1965; AAAL, 1966; Dunkelman Gallery, Toronto, 1967; Marlborough Gallery Inc., NYC, 1968, 77, 79, 81, 85; Tel Aviv, 1971; Marlborough Godard Ltd., Toronto, 1972; Marlborough Fine Art Ltd., London, 1973; Makler Gallery, 1973; MIT, 1985. **Retrospectives:** Berlin/National, 1971; MMA, 1972. **Group:** Salon d'Automne, Paris, 1913; WMAA; MOMA; Tate; Paris/Moderne; Chicago/AI. **Collections:** Baltimore/MA; Barnes Foundation; Buffalo/Albright; Carleton College; Chicago/AI; Cleveland/MA; Cornell U.; Currier; Dartmouth College; Des Moines; Detroit/Institute; Harvard U.; Hunt Foods & Industries; Jewish Museum; Los Angeles/County MA; MOMA; Mansion House Project; U. of Minnesota; Montreal/MFA; U. of Nebraska; New Orleans/Delgado; PMA; Paris/Moderne; Phillips; Princeton U.; Regina/MacKenzie; Rijksmuseum Kroller-Muller; Rouen; SRGM; St. Louis/City; Syracuse U.; Tate; Tel Aviv; Toronto; Utica; Zurich. **Bibliography:** Barr 1; Baur 7; Biddle 4; Biederman 1; Bihalji-Merin; Blesh 1; Canaday; Cassou; Craven, W.; Elsen 2;

Fierens; George 1; Gertz; Giedion-Welcker 1, 2; Goodrich and Baur 1; Greenberg; Hayter 1, 2; Henning; Hess, T.B., 1; **Hope;** Huyghe; **Jacques Lipchitz;** Kuh 2, 3; Langui; Licht, E.; Lowry; McCurdy ed.; Mendelowitz; *Metro;* Moser 1; Myers 2; Neumeyer; **Raynal 2;** Read 1, 3; Rickey; Rodman 1; Rose, B., 1; Roseblum 1; Rothschild; Rowell; Rubin 1; Sachs; Salvini; Selz, J.; Seuphor 3; Seymour; Strachan; Tomkins and Time-Life Books; Trier 1, 2; Valentine 2; **Van Bork;** Waldberg 4; Wingler, ed.; Zervos.

LIPPOLD, RICHARD. b. May 3, 1915, Milwaukee, Wisc. **Studied:** The U. of Chicago and Chicago Art Institute School, 1933-37, BFA (industrial design). Traveled Mexico, Europe, Greece, Turkey, North Africa. **Taught:** Layton School of Art, 1940-41; U. of Michigan 1941-44; Goddard College, 1945-47; Trenton Junior College (Head of Art Department), 1947-52; Queens College, 1947-48; Black Mountain College, 1948; Hunter College, 1952-68. Designer, Chicago Corporation, 1937-41. Began wire constructions, 1942. **Member:** American Academy of Arts & Letters. **Commissions:** Harvard U. Law School, 1950; MMA, 1952-56; Inland Steel Building, Chicago, 1957; Longview Bank, Longview, Tex., 1958; Four Seasons Restaurant, NYC, 1959; Festival of Two Worlds, Spoleto, 1959 (stage set); Benedictine Chapel, Portsmouth, R.I., 1960; Musée du Vin, Chateau Mouton Rothschild, Pouillac, France, 1960; J. Walter Thompson, NYC, 1960; Pan-Am Building, NYC, 1961; Philharmonic Hall, Lincoln Center for the Performing Arts, NYC, 1961; Jesse Jones Hall, Houston, Tex.; Cathedral of St. Mary, San Francisco, 1969; North Carolina National Bank, Charlotte, 1969; Fairlane, Dearborne, 1974; Christian Science Center, Boston, 1974; Hyatt Regency Hotel, Atlanta, 1975; National Air and Space Museum, Washington, D.C., 1975; Hyatt Regency, Milwaukee, 1980; Atrium Tower Building, NYC, 1981; Shiga Sacred Garden, Kyoto, Japan, 1981; One Financial Center, Boston, 1984; Deutsche Bank, Frankfurt, 1985; First Interstate Bank, Seattle, 1985; Crystal City, Virg., 1986; Seoul, S. Korea, 1986; Singapore, 1986; SoHio Oil Co., Cleveland, 1986. **Awards:** ICA, London/Tate, International Unknown Political Prisoner Competition, Third Prize, 1953; Brandeis U., Creative Arts Award, 1953, 58; American Institute of Architects, Chicago Chapter, Honors Award, 1958; American Institute of Architects, New York Chapter, Silver Medal, 1960; Hon. PBK, NYC, 1961; Municipal Art Society of New York, Citation, 1963; elected to NIAL, 1963; Hon. DFA, Ripon College, 1968; American Institute of Architects, Fine Arts Medal, 1970; Guild for Religious Architecture, Honorary member, 1970. **Address:** P.O. Box 248, Locust Valley, NY 11560. **One-man Exhibitions:** (first) The Willard Gallery, NYC, 1947, also 1948, 50, 52, 68, 73; Arts Club of Chicago, 1953; Brandeis U., 1958; Corcoran, 1954; Utica, 1959; U. of Chicago, 1965; Boston/MFA (two-man), 1966. **Group:** MOMA, Fifteen Americans, circ., 1952; PMA, Sculpture of the Twentieth Century, 1953; ICA, London/Tate, International Unknown Political Prisoner Competition, 1953; WMAA, The New Decade, 1954-55; France/National, 50 Ans d'Art aux Etats-Unis, circ., Europe, 1955; Brooklyn Museum, Sculpture in Silver, 1955; Newark Museum, Abstract Art, 1910 to Today, 1956; WMAA, Geometric Abstraction, 1962; NCFA, Sculpture; American Directions, 1945-1975, 1975; WMAA, 200 Years of American Sculpture, 1976; Indianapolis, Perception of the Spirit in 20th Century American Art, circ., 1978; Chicago/AI, 100 Artists—100 Years, 1979; WMAA, The Third Dimension, 1984. **Collections:** Andover/Phillips; Des Moines; Detroit/Institute; Harvard U.; Hartford/Wadsworth; MMA; MOMA; Memphis/Brooks; Milwaukee; Mobile Art Center and Gallery, Ala.; Musée du

Vin; Newark Museum; Utica; VMFA; WMAA; Yale U. **Bibliography:** Baur 7; Blesh 1; Brumme; Craven, W.; Flanagan; Giedion-Welcker 1; Hunter 6; Licht, F.; McCurdy, ed.; Mendelowitz; *Metro*; Motherwell and Reinhardt, eds.; Neumeyer; Phillips, Lisa; Read 1, 3; Rickey; Ritchie 1, 3; Rose, B. 1; Seuphor 3; Trier 1; Weller. Archives.

LIPTON, SEYMOUR. b. November 6, 1903, NYC. **d.** December 5, 1986, Glen Cove, N.Y. **Studied:** City College of New York, 1922-23; Columbia U., 1923-27. **Taught:** Cooper Union, 1943-44; Newark State Teachers College, 1944-45; Yale U., 1957-59; New School for Social Research, 1940-64. **Member:** NIAL, 1975. **Commissions:** Temple Israel, Tulsa, Okla.; Temple Beth-El, Gary, Ind.; Manufacturers Hanover Trust Co., NYC; Inland Steel Building, Chicago; Reynolds Metals Co. (NYC); International Business Machines Corp. (Yorktown Heights, N.Y.); Dulles International Airport, Washington, D.C.; Golden Gateway Redevelopment Project, San Francisco; Philharmonic Hall, Lincoln Center for the Performing Arts, NYC; Milwaukee Center for the Performing Arts, 1967. **Awards:** Chicago/AI, 1957; IV Sao Paulo Biennial, Acquisition Prize, 1957; NIAL, 1958; Guggenheim Foundation Fellowship, 1960; New School for Social Research, 1960; Ford Foundation Grant, 1961; PAFA, George D. Widener Memorial Gold Medal, 1968. **One-man Exhibitions:** ACA Gallery, 1938; Gallery St. Etienne, NYC, 1943; Betty Parsons Gallery, 1948, 50, 52, 54, 58, 62; Watkins Gallery, Washington, D.C., 1951; New Paltz/SUNY, 1955; Troy, N.Y., 1961; Phillips, 1964; Marlborough-Gerson Gallery, Inc., 1965; Milwaukee, 1969; U. of Wisconsin, 1969; Marlborough Gallery, Inc., NYC, 1971, 76; MIT, 1971; VMFA, 1972; Cornell U., 1973; Syracuse/Everson, 1973; Marlborough Galerie AG, Zurich, 1974; C. W. Post College, Long Island U., 1984. **Retrospectives:** NCFA, 1979;

Charlotte/Mint, 1983. **Group:** WMAA Annuals since 1941; IV Sao Paulo Biennial, 1957; XXIX Venice Biennial, 1958; Carnegie, 1958, 61; Brussels World's Fair, 1958; Seattle World's Fair, 1962; New York World's Fair, 1964-65; Chicago/AI Annual, 1966; Flint/Institute, 1 Flint Invitational, 1966; MOMA, Dada, Surrealism and Their Heritage, 1968; PAFA Annual 1968; Smithsonian, 1968; MOMA, The New American Painting and Sculpture; WMAA, The Third Dimension, 1984. **Collections:** Baltimore/MA; Brooklyn Museum; Buffalo/Albright; Cornell U.; Davenport/Municipal; Des Moines; Detroit/Institute; Didrichsen Foundation; Franklin Institute; Hartford/Wadsworth; H. J. Heinz Co.; Hirshhorn; IBM; Inland Steel Co.; U. of Kansas; MMA; MOMA; Manufacturers Hanover Trust Co.; U. of Massachusetts; U. of Michigan; NCFA; New School for Social Research; NYU; Pepsico Museum; RISD; Reynolds Metals Co.; Santa Barbara/MA; South Mall, Albany; Purchase/SUNY; Sperry Rand Corp.; Tel Aviv; Toronto; Utica; VMFA; WGMA; WMAA; Yale U. **Bibliography:** Baur 5, 7; Biddle 4; Blesh 1; Brumme; Chaet; Craven, W.; Christensen; Elsen 1, 3; Flanagan; Goodrich and Baur 1; Henning; Hunter 6; Hunter, ed.; Krauss 2; Langui; McCurdy, ed.; Marter, Tarbell, and Wechsler, Rand; Mendelowitz; *Metro*: Myers 2; Neumeyer, Phillips, Lisa; Read 3; Ritchie 1, 3; Rose, B., 1; Seuphor 3; Strachan; Trier 1; Weller. Archives.

LOBDELL, FRANK. b. 1921, Kansas City. Mo. **Studied:** St. Paul School of Art, 1938-39, with Cameron Booth; California School of Fine Arts, 1947-50; US Army, 1942-46. Resided Paris, 1950-51. **Taught:** California School of Fine Arts, 1957-65; Stanford U., 1965-. **Awards:** SFMA, Artists Council Prize, 1948; SFMA, **P.P.,** 1950; SFMA, Nealie Sullivan Award, 1960; Tamarind Fellowship, 1966; A Knight of Mark

Frank Lobdell   *Winter 1979*   1979

Twain, 1971. **Address:** 340 Palo Alto Avenue, Palo Alto, CA 94301. **Dealer:** Oscarsson Siegeltuch & Co., NYC. **One-man Exhibitions:** (first) Lucien Labaudt Gallery, San Francisco, 1949; Martha Jackson Gallery, N.Y., 1958, 60, 63, 72, 74, 77; de Young, 1959; Pasadena/AM, 1961; Ferus Gallery, Los Angeles, 1962; Galerie D. Benador, Geneva, 1964; Galerie Anderson-Mayer, Paris, 1965; Pasadena/AM and Stanford U., 1966; Maryhurst College, 1967; SFMA, 1969; St. Mary's College, Moraga, Calif., 1970, 71. Smith-Anderson Gallery, Palo Alto, 1978, 81; Oscarsson Hood Gallery, NYC, 1983, 84, 85; Portland, Me./AM, 1985. **Retrospectives:** Pasadena/AM, 1963; SFMA, 1983. **Group:** San Francisco Art Association Annual, 1950; III Sao Paulo Biennial, 1955; WMAA, Fifty California Artists, 1962-63; SRGM, American Drawings, 1964; U. of Washington, Drawings by Americans, 1967; Albany/SUNY, Giant Prints, 1967; Eindhoven, Kompas IV, 1969-70; Pasadena/AM, West Coast, 1945-69, 1969; Corcoran, 1971; WMAA Annual, 1972; U. of Illinois; Oakland/AM, A Period of Exploration,

1973; U. of Illinois, 1974; Newport Harbor, The Last Time I Saw Ferus, 1976; SFMA, California Painting and Sculpture: The Modern Era, 1976; U. of North Carolina, Art on Paper, 1983. **Collections:** Los Angeles/County MA; Oakland/AM; Pasadena/AM; SFMA; Stanford U. **Bibliography: Hopps.**

LOBERG, ROBERT W. b. December 1, 1927, Chicago, Ill. US Marine Corps, 1946-47. **Studied:** Glendale College, 1948, City College of San Francisco, 1948-50, AA; U. of California, Berkeley, 1950-52, BA, 1953-54, MA (painting, with Karl Kasten, Ward Lockwood, John Haley, Erie Loran, James McCray, Glenn Wessels, Worth Ryder, Felix Ruvulo, William H. Calfee, Carl Holty, Kyle Morris); Hofmann School, Provincetown, 1956, with Hans Hofmann. Traveled northern China, Japan, Europe. **Taught:** U. of California, Berkeley, 1955, 56, 58, 59, 65; California College of Arts and Crafts, 1961-62; San Francisco Art Institute, 1962-66; U. of Washington, 1967-68. **Awards:** California State Fair, Hon. Men., 1955; RAC, Prize in Graphics, 1955; Yaddow Fellowship, 1957; RAC, Prize in Watercolors, 1959; MacDowell Colony Fellowship, 1959, 60; SFMA, Anne Bremer Memorial Prize, 1961; San Francisco Art Festival, **P.P.,** in Painting, 1962; La Jolla, Prize in Painting, 1962. **Address:** 2020 Vine Street, Berkeley, CA 94709. **One-man Exhibitions:** (first) Artist's Gallery, NYC, 1959; SFMA (three-man), 1961, Staempfli Gallery, 1962; David Stuart Gallery, 1962, 64; Richard White Gallery, Seattle, 1968; California College of Arts and Crafts, 1969; Berkeley Gallery, 1969; California College of Arts and Crafts, 1969; Berkeley Craft Center, 1977; San Jose Museum 1978; Paule Anglim Gallery, San Francisco, 1979. **Retrospective:** U. of Washington, 1968. **Group:** Chicago/AI, 1948, 62; RAC; Oakland/AM; SFMA Annuals since 1955; de Young; California Palace; Carnegie, 1959; SFMA, Abstract Expressionism, in the West, circ.,

1961; SFMA, Collage in San Francisco, 1962; WMAA, Fifty California Artists, 1962-63; SFMA, New Paintings, 1964. **Collections:** California College of Arts and Crafts; Chicago/AI; Oakland/AM; Portland, Ore./AM; San Francisco Municipal Art Commission; WGMA; U. of Washington. Archives.

LOEW, MICHAEL. b. May 8, 1907, NYC. **d.** November 14, 1985, NYC. **Studied:** City College of New York; ASL, 1926-29, with Richard Lahey, Boardman Robinson; Academie Scandinave, Paris, 1930, with Othon Friesz; Hofmann School, NYC, 1947-49; Atelier Fernand Leger, Paris, 1950, with F. Leger. US Navy "Seabees," Battalion Artist, Pacific theater, 1943-46. Traveled France, Germany, Italy, Africa, Mexico, Central America, Spain, England. **Taught:** Portland (Ore.) Museum School, 1956-57; U. of California, Berkeley, 1960-61; 1967; School of Visual Arts, NYC, 1958-85. **Member:** American Abstract Artists; Federation of Modern Painters and Sculptors. Federal A.P.: Gustave Straubenmuller Junior High School, NYC (series of 5 murals); U. of California, Berkeley, 1960-61, 1966. **Commissions:** (murals) Hall of Man and Pharmacy Building, New York World's Fair, 1939; US Post Offices, Amherst, Ohio, and Belle Vernon, Pa. **Awards:** Sadie May Fellowship, 1929; Section of Fine Arts, National Mural Competition for Social Security Building and War Department Building, Washington, D.C., Hon. Men., 1941, 42; Ford Foundation, **P.P.,** 1964; Chicago/AI Annual, 1964; National Endowment for the Arts, grant, 1976; Guggenheim Foundation Fellowship, 1979. **One-man Exhibitions:** (first) Artists' Gallery, NYC, 1949; Rose Fried Gallery, 1953, 55, 57, 59; Portland, Ore./AM, 1956; Rutgers U. (two-man), 1959; T.K. Gallery, Provincetown, Mass., 1959; Holland-Goldowsky Gallery, Chicago, 1960; U. of California, Berkeley, 1960, 67; The Stable Gallery, NYC, 1961, 62, 64, 65;

Landmark Gallery, Inc., NYC, 1973, 76; Marilyn Pearl Gallery, NYC, 1977, 79, 81, 82, 84, 86. **Retrospectives:** Holland-Goldowsky Gallery, Chicago, 1960; The Stable Gallery, 1962. **Group:** American Abstract Artists Annuals, 1949-; Salon des Realites Nouvelles, Paris, 1950; WMAA, 1950, 61; MMA, 1952; Walker, The Classic Tradition, 1953; International Association of Plastic Arts, Contemporary American Painting, circ., Europe, 1956-57; A.F.A., Collage in America, circ., 1957-58; Douglass College, 1959; ART:USA:59, NYC, 1959; Federation of Modern Painters and Sculptors Annuals, 1959-; WMAA, Geometric Abstraction in America, circ., 1962; MOMA, Hans Hofmann and His Students, circ., 1963-64; Chicago/AI, 1964; Colby College, 100 Artists of the 20th Century, 1964; PAFA, 1966; Allentown/AM, Monhegan Island Painters, 1974; Newark Museum, Geometric Abstraction and Related Works, 1978; Portland, Me./MA, Maine Drawing Biennial, 1984. **Collections:** Buffalo/Albright; Calcutta; U. of California, Berkeley; Carnegie; Ciba-Geigy Corp.; Hampton Institute; Hirshhorn; Humlebaek/Louisiana; Lehman Bros.; McCrory Corp.; U. of Nebraska; PMA; Portland, Me./AM; St. Lawrence U.; Union Carbide Corp.; WMAA; Wichita State U. **Bibliography:** Archives.

LONGO, ROBERT. b. 1953, Brooklyn, N.Y. **Studied:** Buffalo/SUNY, BFA, 1975. Active as a performer and designer of installations. **Address:** % Dealer. **Dealer:** Metro Pictures, NYC. **One-man Exhibitions:** Hallwalls, Buffalo, 1976; The Kitchen, NYC, 1979; Studio Cannaviello, Milan, 1980; U. of Rhode Island, 1981; Metro Pictures, 1981, 83, 84; Larry Gagosian Gallery, Los Angeles, 1981, 84; Texas Gallery, Houston, 1982; Brooke Alexander Gallery, NYC, 1983; Galerie Schellmann & Klusher, Munich, 1983; Akron/AM, 1984; Amsterdam/Stedelijk, 1985; Brooklyn Museum, 1985; U. of Iowa,

1985; Lia Rumma Gallery, Naples, 1985. **Group:** MIT, Body Language, circ., 1980; Cologne/Stadt, Westkunst, 1981; Cincinnati/Contemporary, Dynamix, 1982; Documenta VII, Kassel, 1982; Milwaukee, New Figuration in America, 1982; WMAA, Focus on the Figure, 1982; Walker, Eight Artists: The Anxious Edge, 1982; Bonn, Back to the USA, circ., 1983; Hirshhorn, Directions, 1983; WMAA, Biennial, 1983; Cincinnati/Contemporary, Disarming Images, 1984; Hirshhorn, Content, 1984; Houston/Contemporary, The Heroic Figure, 1984; MOMA, International Survey of Recent Painting and Sculpture, 1984; SFMA, The Human Condition, 1984; Sydney/AG, 5th Biennale, 1984; Carnegie, International, 1985; Fort Lauderdale, An American Renaissance: Painting and Sculpture Since 1940, 1986. **Collections:** Buffalo/Albright; High Museum; MOMA; U. of North Carolina; SRGM; U. of Sydney; Tate Gallery; WMAA; Walker. **Bibliography:** *Back to the USA;* Pincus-Witten 2.

LONGO, VINCENT. b. February 15, 1923, NYC. **Studied:** Cooper Union, with Leo Katz, Sidney Delevant, 1942-46; Brooklyn Museum School, 1950, with Max Beckmann, 1953, with Louis Schanker. Traveled Europe. **Taught:** Brooklyn Museum School, 1955-56; Yale U. Summer School, Norfolk, Conn., 1967-68; Bennington College, 1957-67; Hunter College, 1967-. **Member:** SAGA; American Abstract Artists. **Awards:** Fulbright Fellowship (Italy), 1951; Philadelphia Print Club, First Prize, 1954; Yaddo Fellowship, 1954; Guggenheim Foundation Fellowship, 1971; Cooper Union, Achievement Citation, 1973; National Endowment for the Arts, 1974. **Address:** 50 Greene Street, NYC 10013. **Dealer:** Condeso/Lawler Gallery, NYC. **One-man Exhibitions:** Regional Arts Gallery, NYC, 1949; Korman Gallery,

NYC, 1954; The Zabriskie Gallery, 1956; Yamada Art Gallery, Kyoto, 1959; Area Gallery, NYC, 1960; Wheaton College, 1969; Thibault Gallery, NYC, 1963; U. of Vermont, 1965; Reese Palley Gallery, NYC, 1970; Susan Caldwell Inc., 1974; Bard College, 1975; U. of Notre Dame, 1976; Andrew Crispo Gallery, NYC, 1976, 80; Alfred U., 1978; Adam Gimbel Gallery, NYC, 1981; Condeso/Lawler Gallery, 1984, 85. **Retrospectives:** Bennington College, 1970; Corcoran, 1970; Detroit/Institute, 1970. **Group:** WMAA Annuals, 1951, 71; PAFA Annual, 1953; MOMA, Young Printmakers, 1954; Brooklyn Museum, 1954, 55; Philadelphia Print Club (three-man), 1955; MOMA, Drawings USA, 1956; American Abstract Artists, 1957, 58, 59; New York Coliseum, ART:USA:59, 1959; U. of Kentucky, Graphics '60, 1960; USIA, Contemporary American Woodcut and Its Variations, 1962; PCA, American Prints Today, 1962; Brooklyn Museum, Two Decades of American Prints, 1969; WMAA, American Drawings, 1963-1973, 1973; WMAA, American Prints: Process and Proofs, 1982; WMAA, Block Prints, 1982; Hunter College, Repetitions, 1985. **Collections:** Bibliotheque Nationale; Brooklyn Museum; Chemical Bank; Ciba-Geigy Corp.; Corcoran; Detroit/Institute; Guild Hall; Library of Congress; Milwaukee-Downer Institute; MMA; MOMA; NCFA; NYPL; National Gallery; New London; Oakland/AM; PMA; Stockholm/National; Syracuse/Everson; U. of Vermont; Washington U.; WMAA. **Bibliography:** Goldman 1. Archives.

LORAN, ERLE. b. October 3, 1905, Minneapolis, Minn. **Studied:** U. of Minnesota; Minneapolis Institute School, with Cameron Booth; Hofmann School, 1954. Traveled Europe extensively. **Taught:** U. of California, Berkeley. Federal A.P.: Easel painting, teaching. **Awards:** Chaloner Prize Foundation Award ($6,000), 1926; SFMA, Artists' Fund Prize, 1944; Pepsi-Cola Bronze Medal, 1949; San Francisco Art Association, **P.P.**, 1956; California Palace, H.S. Crocker Co. Award, 1963; U. of Illinois, **P.P.**, 1965; Minneapolis Institute School, Hon. MFA, 1968; and some 20 others. **Address:** 10 Kenilworth Court, Berkeley, CA 94707. **Dealer:** John Berggruen Gallery, San Francisco. **One-man Exhibitions:** (first) Kraushaar Galleries, 1931; SFMA, 1936, 39, 44; Artists' Gallery, NYC, 1938; Pasadena/AM, 1947; Santa Barbara/MA, 1947, 50; Dalzell Hatfield Gallery, 1949; de Young, 1949, 54, 63; Catherine Viviano Gallery, 1952, 54; Comara Gallery, 1964; The Bertha Schaefer Gallery, 1965; Arleigh Gallery, 1969; Oakland/AM, 1981. **Group:** MOMA, 1935; Oakland/AM, 1936, 46; SFMA, 1936-64; WMAA, 1937, 41, 44, 48, 51, 52; Chicago/AI, 1938, 39, 43, 44, 46, 48; Carnegie, 1941; Toledo/MA, 1943; PAFA, 1945; U. of Illinois, 1949, 52, 53, 63, 65, 69; MMA, 1951, 53; Cranbrook, 1953; Sao Paulo, 1955, 56, 61; California Palace, 1961, 62, 63; MOMA, Hans Hofmann and His Students, circ., 1963-64. **Collections:** Brigham Young U.; U. of California; Denver/AM; IBM; U. of Illinois; U. of Minnesota; SFMA; San Diego; Santa Barbara/MA; Smithsonian; US State Department; Utah State U. **Bibliography:** Bethers; Blanchard; Cheney; Flanagan; **Loran 1, 2;** Pousette-Dart, ed. Archives.

LORBER, STEPHEN. b. August 30, 1943, Brooklyn, N.Y. **Studied:** Pratt Institute, BFA, 1961-66; Brooklyn College, MFA, 1966-68; Yale, 1964. Resided Rome, 1969-70; New Mexico, 1973-74. **Taught:** Roswell, 1973-74. **Awards:** Stoeckel Fellow, Yale U., 1964; Yaddo Fellowship, 1971, 75; National Endowment for the Arts; Fellowship, 1976. **Address:** R.D. 3, Box 198, Greenwich, NY 12834. **Dealer:** Alexander F. Milliken, NYC. **One-man Exhibitions:** (first) A. M. Sachs Gallery, NYC, 1974,

75, 76, 77, 78; Russell Sage College, Troy, N.Y., 1976; Delahunty Gallery, Dallas, 1975, 77, 80; Roswell, 1974; Alexander F. Milliken, 1981, 83, 84, 85; Dubins Gallery, Los Angeles, 1983. **Group:** PAFA, 1969; U. of North Carolina, Art on Paper, 1974, 76; Minnesota/MA, American Drawing, 1927-77, circ., 1977; U. of Nebraska, Things Seen, 1978; Utica, A Painter's Appreciation of Realism, 1982. **Collections:** AT&T; Amerada Hess Corp.; American Airlines; Atlantic Richfield Corp.; A.G. Beck Co., Inc.; Chase Manhattan Bank; Chemical Bank; Chicago/AI; E.F. Hutton, Inc.; U. of Illinois; Lehman Bros.; Mobil Oil Corp.; U. of North Carolina; Oklahoma; Owens-Corning Fiberglas Corp.; Prudential Insurance Co. of America; Reynolds Tobacco, Inc.; Roswell; 3M Corp.; Western New Mexico U.

LOSTUTTER, ROBERT. b. 1939, Emporia, Kan. **Studied:** Chicago Art Institute School, 1958-63. **Awards:** Chicago/AI, Tuthill Prize, 1977; Illinois Arts Council Grant, 1984. **Address:** 207 West St. Paul Avenue, Chicago, Ill. 60614. **Dealer:** Dart Gallery, Chicago. **One-man Exhibitions:** Deson-Zaks Gallery, Chicago, 1971, 73, 75; Richard Demarco Gallery, Edinburgh, 1972; Dart Gallery, Chicago, 1976, 78, 80, 84, 87; Nancy Lurie Gallery, Chicago, 1978; Monique Knowlton Gallery, NYC, 1981, 84; U. of Chicago, 1984. **Group:** Chicago/AI, Chicago and Vicinity, 1971, 73; Ringling, After Surrealism, 1972; Indianapolis, 1972; Brooklyn Museum, Biennial, 1974; Sacramento/Crocker, The Chicago Connection, circ., 1976; Chicago Art Institute School, Visions, 1976; Chicago/AI, Drawings of the '70s, 1977; Madison Art Center, Chicago/Some Other Traditions, circ., 1983; ICA, Boston, Currents, 1984; Corcoran, Biennial, 1985. **Collections:** Brooklyn Museum; Chicago/AI; Chicago/Contemporary; Illinois State U.; Madison Art Center;

Springfield, Mo./AM. **Bibliography:** Adrian.

LOUIS, MORRIS. b. November 28, 1912, Baltimore, Md.; **d.** September 7, 1962, Washington, D.C. **Studied:** Maryland Institute, 1920-33. **One-man Exhibitions:** (first) Martha Jackson Gallery, 1957; French & Co. Inc., NYC, 1959, 60; ICA London, 1960; Bennington College, 1960; Galleria dell'-Ariete, 1960; Galerie Neufville, Paris, 1961; Galerie Schmela, 1962; Galerie Lawrence, Paris, 1962; Galerie Muller, 1962; Andre Emmerich Gallery, NYC, 1961, 62, 65, 68, 69, 72, 78, 79, 82; Zurich, 1973, 81; Ziegler Gallery, 1964; Staatliche Kunsthalle, Baden-Baden, 1965; WGMA, 1966; Seattle/AM, 1967; MOMA (three-man), 1968; Lawrence Rubin Gallery, NYC, 1970, 73, 74; David Mirvish Gallery, 1971; National Gallery, 1976; Walker, 1977; NCFA, 1979; Asher/Faure, Los Angeles, 1979; Medici-Berenson Gallery, Bay Harbor Islands, Fla., 1979; Waddington Gallery, London, 1979; Israel Museum, 1980; Wichita State U., 1980; M. Knoedler & Co., 1983. **Retrospectives:** SRGM, 1963; XXXII Venice Biennial, 1964; WGMA, 1967; Boston/MFA, circ., 1967; NMAA, circ., 1979; MOMA, 1986. **Group:** The Kootz Gallery, NYC, New Talent, 1954; Rome-New York Foundation, Rome, 1960; SRGM, Abstract Expressionists and Imagists, 1961; Seattle World's Fair, 1962; WMAA, 1962; Jewish Museum, Toward a New Abstraction, 1963; Tate, Painting and Sculpture of a Decade, 1954-64, 1964; Corcoran; Los Angeles/County MA, Post Painterly Abstraction, 1964; Documenta III & IV, Kassel, 1964, 68; MOMA, The Responsive Eye, 1965; SFMA, The Colorists, 1965; WGMA, 1965-66; WMAA, Art of the U.S. 1670-1966, 1966; Chicago/AI Annual, 1966; Wurttembergischer Kunstverein, Stuttgart, 1967; Detroit/Institute, Color, Image and Form, 1967; Trenton/State, Focus on Light, 1967; MOMA, The Art of the Real,

1968; Pasadena/AM, Serial Imagery, 1968; MOMA, The New American Painting and Sculpture, 1969; WMAA, 1970; Edmonton Art Gallery, Alberta, Ten Washington Artists: 1950-1970, 1970; Auckland, 1971; Hayward Gallery, London, 1974; Houston/MFA, The Great Decade of American Abstraction, Modernist Art 1960 to 1970, 1974; Norfolk/Chrysler, 300 Years of American Art, 1976; Baltimore/MA, Two Hundred Years of American Painting, 1977; Milwaukee, Washington Color Painters, 1980; Grand Palais, Paris, L'Amerique aux Indépendants, 1980; Purchase/SUNY, Hidden Desires, 1980; Cologne/Stadt, Westkunst, 1981; Haus der Kunst, Munich, Amerikanische Malerie: 1930-1980, 1981; Oklahoma, American Masters of the Twentieth Century, 1982; SRGM, The New York School: Four Decades, 1982; U. of Maryland, 350 Years of Art & Architecture in Maryland, 1984. **Collections:** Allentown/AM; Amsterdam/Stedelijk; Belfast; Berlin/National; Boston/MFA; Brandeis U.; Buffalo/Albright; Canberra/National; Chicago/AI; Cologne; Corcoran; Dayton/AI; Detroit/AI; Eindhoven; Fort Worth; Harvard U.; Hirshhorn; Honolulu; Houston/MFA; Humlebaek/Louisiana; Israel Museum; Jerusalem/National; MMA; MOMA; Michigan State U.; Milwaukee; National Gallery; PMA; Phillips; Raleigh/NCMA; SFMA; SRGM; St. Louis/City; Sydney/AG; Syracuse/Everson; Tate Gallery; Tel Aviv; Toronto; WGMA; WMAA; Walker. **Bibliography:** Battcock, ed.; Calas, N. and E.; Coplans 3; Davis, D.; Elderfield; Fried 1, 2; Goossen 1; Headley; Honisch and Jensen, eds.; *The Great Decade;* Hunter, ed.; Kozloff 3; Murken-Altrogge; Rickey; Sandler; Tomkins 2; Weller. Archives.

LOZOWICK, LOUIS. b. December 10, 1892, Ludvinovka, Russia; **d.** September 9, 1973, South Orange, N.J. To USA, 1906. **Studied:** The Ohio State

U., 1915-1918, BA; NAD, with Carlson, Ivan Olinsky, 1912-15. US Army, 1918-19. Traveled Europe, Russia, the Orient. **Taught:** Educational Alliance, NYC; and privately. **Member:** SAGA; Boston Printmakers. Federal A.P.: Main Post Office, NYC. (mural); printmaker. **Awards:** Brewster Prize for Lithography; PMA, International Print Competition, First Prize; Society of American Etchers and Engravers, NYC, Knobloch Prize; Brooklyn Museum, **P.P.;** U. of Rochester, 150 Years of Lithography, Second Prize; SAGA; Audubon Artists. **One-man Exhibitions:** (first) Heller Gallery, Berlin, 1923; Weyhe Gallery; Courvoisier Gallery, San Francisco; Stendahl Gallery, Los Angeles; Casson Gallery, Boston; J. B. Neumann's New Art Circle, NYC; The Zabriskie Gallery, 1961, 71, 72; Galerie Zak, Paris; Smithsonian; Argus Gallery, Madison, N.J., 1965; Heritage Art Gallery, South Orange, N.J., 1967; WMAA, 1972; Robert Dain Gallery, NYC, 1973; Lynn Gallery, Washington, D.C., 1975; Hirschl & Adler Gallery, NYC, 1980; Summit Art Gallery, NYC, 1983; Vanderwoude Tananbaum Gallery, NYC, 1985. **Retrospectives:** Newark Public Library, 1969; Seton Hall U., South Orange, N.J., 1975; Long Beach/MA, 1975; NCFA, 1975. **Group:** Brooklyn Museum, 1926; Chicago/AI, 1929; Carnegie, 1930, 39; Corcoran, 1932; A Century of Progress, Chicago, 1933-34; WMAA Annuals, 1933, 41; New York World's Fair, 1939; MMA, 1942; MOMA, 1943; Youngstown/Butler, 1960; Gallery of Modern Art, NYC, 1965; Boston/MFA. **Collections:** Boston/MFA; Cincinnati/AM; Cleveland/MA; Honolulu Academy; Houston/MFA; Library of Congress; Los Angeles/County MA; MMA; MOMA; Montclair/AM; Moscow/Western; NYPL; Newark Museum; PMA; U. of Rochester; Syracuse/Everson; Trenton/State; Victoria and Albert Museum; WMAA. **Bibliography:** American Artists Congress, Inc.; American Artists Group Inc. 3; Baur 7; Brown 2; Gerdts; *Index of 20th Century*

Artists; Cityscape 1917-39; Mellquist; Reese. Archives.

LUCCHESI, BRUNO. b. July 31, 1926, Fibbiano, Italy. To USA, 1957. **Studied:** Institute of Art, Lucca, 1953, MFA. **Taught:** Academy of Fine Arts, Florence, 1952-57; New School for Social Research, 1962-. **Commissions:** Trade Bank and Trust Co., NYC; Cornell U. **Awards:** NAD, Elizabeth N. Watrous Gold Medal, 1961; Guggenheim Foundation Fellowship, 1962; National Arts Club, NYC, Gold Medal, 1963; NAD, Samuel F. B. Morse Medal, 1965; NAD, Gold Medal, 1970, 74; City of Lucca, Medal for Honoring Italy Abroad, 1976; National Sculpture Society, Gold Medal, 1977; The Italian Cultural Society, The Lion of San Marco, 1981; NAD, Artists Fund Prize for Sculpture, 1983. **Address:** 14 Stuyvesant Street, NYC 10003. **Dealer:** The Forum Gallery, NYC. **One-man Exhibitions:** The Forum Gallery, 1961, 63, 66, 72, 75, 76, 80, 84, 85; Washington & Lee U., 1979; Shirlee Raushbach Gallery, Bay Harbor Islands, Fla., 1983; Blue Hill Cultural Center, Pearl River, N.Y., 1984; Foster Harmon Galleries, Sarasota, 1980, 86; Casey Gallery, Scottsdale, 1986. **Group:** Corcoran; NAD; PAFA; WMAA. **Collections:** Brooklyn Museum; Columbia, S.C./MA; Dallas/MFA; Hirshhorn; PAFA; Ringling; WMAA.

LUND, DAVID. b. October 16, 1925, NYC. **Studied:** Queens College, with Vaclav Vytlacil, Cameron Booth, 1944-48, BA (major in painting); NYU, 1948-50, with Hale Woodruff; New School for Social Research, with Yasuo Kuniyoshi. Traveled Europe, southwestern USA, Mexico. **Taught:** Cooper Union, 1955-57, 1959-69; Parsons School of Design, 1963-66, 1967-; Queens College, 1964-66; Washington U. (St. Louis), 1966-67; Columbia U. 1969-82. **Awards:** Fulbright Fellowship (Rome), 1957-58, renewed 1958-59;

David Lund   *Coral Bluff*   1980

WMAA Annual, Ford Foundation Purchase, 1961; AAAL, Childe Hassam Fund **P.P.**, 1978. **Address:** 470 West End Avenue, NYC 10024. **Dealer:** Grace Borgenicht Gallery, NYC. **One-man Exhibitions:** (first) Grand Central Moderns, NYC, 1954; Galleria Trastevere di Topazia Alliata, Rome, 1955; Grace Borgenicht Gallery, NYC, 1960, 63, 67, 69, 76, 78, 80, 83, 86; Martin Schweig Gallery, 1966; U. of Alaska, 1983; Allport Associates, San Francisco, 1984; Washington U., 1985. **Group:** Tanager Gallery, NYC, Invitational; The Stabe Gallery Annual, 1956; Galleria Schneider, Rome, Fulbright Artists, 1958, 59; WMAA, Fulbright Artists, 1958; Hirschl & Adler Galleries, Inc., NYC, Experiences in Art, I, 1959; WMAA, Young America, 1960; WMAA Annual, 1961; WMAA, Forty Artists under Forty, circ., 1962; PAFA, 1965, 69; School of Visual Arts, NYC, 1966; Omaha/Joslyn, A Sense of Place, 1973; City Hall, Rockport, Me., Maine Coast Artists, 1974; Oklahoma, Contemporary American Landscape Painting, 1975; IIE, 20 American Fulbright Artists, 1975; NAD, 1977; Youngstown/Butler, Mid-year Shows, 1978, 84. **Collections:** AAIAL; Baltimore/MA; Brandeis U.; Bristol-Meyers Co., NYC; Buffalo/Albright; Burlington Industries, NYC; Chase Manhattan Bank; Colby College; Commerce Trust Co., Corcoran; J.C. Penney Co., NYC; Kansas City, Mo.; Fort Worth; Harcourt Brace Jovanovich Inc.; Manufacturers Hanover Trust Co.; U. of Massachusetts; Mellon Bank; Montclair/AM; McDonnell & Co. Inc.; U. of Nebraska; Prudential Insurance Co. of America, Newark; The New York Times; The Pure Oil Co., NYC.; South County Bank; Toronto; Union Carbide Corp. NYC; WMAA; Wilmington.

LUNDEBERG, HELEN. b. June 1908, Chicago, Ill. **Studied:** Privately with Lorser Feitelson, Federal A.P.: Painting, lithography, mural designer. **m.** Lorser Feitelson. **Address:** 8307 West 3 Street, Los Angeles, CA 90048. **Dealer:** Tobey C. Moss Gallery, Los Angeles. **One-man Exhibitions:** (first) Stanley Rose Gallery, Hollywood, 1933; Mid-20th Century Art Gallery, Los Angeles, 1947; Art Center School, Los Angeles (two-man); Lucien Labaudt Gallery, San Francisco (two-man), 1949; Pasadena/AM; Santa Barbara, 1958; Paul Rivas Gallery, Los Angeles, 1959; Long Beach/MA, 1963; Occidental College, 1965; David Stuart Gallery, 1970, 71, 77; The Graham Gallery, 1982; Tobey C. Moss Gallery, 1982, 83, 84, 85; Palm Springs Desert Museum, 1983. **Retrospectives:** Pasadena/AM, 1953; La Jolla, 1971; Los Angeles Municipal Art Gallery, 1979; SFMA, 1980; UCLA, 1981. **Group:** Brooklyn Museum, 1936; SFMA, 1936; MOMA, Fantastic Art, DADA, Surrealism, 1936; MOMA, Americans 1942, circ., 1942; Chicago/AI, Abstract and Surrealist Art, 1948; U. of Illinois, 1950-52, 55, 57, 65; Carnegie, 1952; III Sao Paulo Biennial, 1955; WMAA, Geometric Abstraction in America, circ., 1962; WMAA, Fifty California Artists, 1962-63; WMAA Annuals, 1965, 67; Sacramento/Crocker, 1968; Los Angeles Institute of Contemporary Art, 1974; MOMA, Painting and Sculpture in California: The Modern Era, 1976; San Antonio/McNay, American Artists '76, 1976; Rutgers U., Surrealism and American Art: 1931-1947, 1977; Denver/AM Biennial, 1979; Laguna Beach Museum of Art, Southern California Artists: 1940-1980, 1981; Rutgers U., Realism and Realities, 1982. **Collections:** Atlantic Richfield Co.; Bank of Tulsa, Tulsa; Boston/MFA; Chaffey College; Craig Ellwood Associates; Great Western Savings and Loan Association; Hirshhorn; Honolulu Academy; La Jolla; Lansing Sound Corp.; Los Angeles/County MA; NCFA; NYPL; Oakland/AM; Palm Springs Desert Museum; Pasadena/AM; SFMA; Santa Barbara/MA; Xerox Corp.; WMAA. **Bibliography: Feitelson and Lundeberg;** Rickey. Archives.

LYE, LEN. b. July 5, 1901, Christchurch, New Zealand; **d.** May 15, 1980, Warwick, N.Y. **Studied:** Wellington Technical College; Canterbury College of Fine Arts. To London, 1926; to USA, 1946; became a citizen. Traveled Samoa, Europe, USA, around the world, 1968. **Taught:** City College of New York (film technique); NYU. International awards for experimental films. Began kinetic constructions in the 1920s. Created "direct animation" technique, working directly on film strip without camera, 1935. National Endowment for the Arts, grant, 1979. **One-man Exhibitions:** London Film Society (*Tusalava*), 1928; MOMA, Tangible Motion Sculpture, 1961; St. Luke's School, NYC, Wind Wands, 1962; The Howard Wise Gallery, 1965; Buffalo/Albright, 1965; Govett-Brewster Gallery, New Plymouth, N.Z., 1977; Auckland Gallery, N.Z., 1980. **Group:** Seven & Five Society, London, 1928-33; a Surrealists group, London, 1937; Amsterdam/Stedelijk, Art in Motion, circ., Europe, 1961-62; WMAA Annual, 1962; The Howard Wise Gallery, NYC, On The Move, 1963. **Collections:**

Buffalo/Albright; U. of California, Berkeley; Chicago/AI; Tel Aviv; WMAA. **Film Collections:** U. of California, Berkeley; London Film Society; MOMA. **Bibliography:** Battcock, ed.; Bihalji-Merin; Calas, N. and E.; Davis, D.; Kuh 3; Read 5; *Report:* Rickey; Selz, P., 1; Tuchman 1.

LYTLE, RICHARD. b. February 14, 1935, Albany, N.Y. **Studied:** Cooper Union, with Nicholas Marsicano, Victor Candell; Yale U., with Josef Albers (whom he assisted as teaching fellow in color and drawing), James Brooks, Bernard Chaet, 1957, BFA, 1960, MFA. Traveled Europe, northeastern USA. **Taught:** Yale U., 1960-63, 1966-?; Dean, Silvermine Guild, 1963-66. **Commissions:** Fairfield U. (concrete relief mural). **Awards:** Scholarship to the Cummington School of Fine Arts, 1956; Fulbright Fellowship (Italy), 1958; New Haven Arts Festival, First Prize, 1958. **Address:** Sperry Road, Woodbridge, CT 06525. **Dealer:** Marilyn Pearl Gallery, NYC. **One-man Exhibitions:** (first) Grace Borgenicht Gallery, Inc., 1961, also 1963, 64, 66, 68, 72; Silvermine Guild, 1964; Cortland/SUNY, 1969; U. of Hartford, 1970; U. of Connecticut, 1973; Lincoln, Mass./De Cordova, 1974; Marilyn Pearl Gallery, NYC, 1977, 79, 82, 84; Munson Gallery, New Haven, 1979, 83; Munson Gallery, Santa Fe, 1980. **Group:** Brooklyn Museum, 1956; A.F.A., American Art, circ., Europe, 1956-59; Boston Arts Festival, 1958; MOMA, Sixteen Americans, circ., 1959; Chicago/AI Annuals, 1960, 61; Houston/MFA, The Emerging Figure, 1961; Seattle World's Fair, 1962; PAFA, 1962, 63, 64; Art: USA: Now, circ., 1962-67; WMAA, 1964; Silvermine Guild, 1964; U. of Illinois, 1967; Yale U., 1967; Ringling, Young New England Painters, 1969; Yale U., American Drawing, 1970-1973, 1973; Harvard U., Works by Students of Josef Albers, 1974; IIE, 20 American Fulbright Artists, 1975; U. of North Carolina, 1978, 80; Buffalo/Albright, Works on Paper,

1979; Montclair/AM, Josef Albers: His Influence, 1981. **Collections:** AT&T; Chase Manhattan Bank; Cincinnati/AM; Citicorp, NYC; Columbia U.; Lincoln, Mass./De Cordova; MOMA; U. of Massachusetts; Minneapolis/Institute; NCFA; St. Joseph/Albrecht; Williams College; Yale U. **Bibliography:** Nordness, ed.

M

MAC CONNEL, KIM. b. 1946, Oklahoma City, Oklahoma. **Studied:** U. of California, San Diego, BA, honors, 1969; MFA, honors, 1972. **Awards:** California State Scholar, 1970. **Address:** % Dealer. **Dealer:** Holly Solomon Gallery, NYC. **One-man Exhibitions:** Holly Solomon Gallery, NYC, 1975, 77, 78, 79, 80, 86; Metropolitan Museum and Art Center, Miami, 1975; La Jolla, 1975; Galerie Ehrensperger, Zurich, 1976; U. of California, Berkeley, 1978; Galerie Bischoisberger, 1978; F. H. Mayor Gallery, London, 1978; Dart Gallery, Chicago, 1979, 80. **Group:** U. of California, San Diego, Decorations, 1971; The Clocktower, NYC, Toys Artists Make, 1974; WMAA Biennials, 1975, 77, 79; American Foundation for the Arts, Miami, Patterning and Decoration, 1977; Philadelphia College of Art, Artists, Sets and Costumes, 1977; ICA, U. of Pennsylvania, Improbable Furniture, 1977; La Jolla, Southern California, Styles of the 60's and 70's, 1978; Rice U., Pattern and Decoration, 1978; Cincinnati/Contemporary, Arabesque, 1978; ICA, U. of Pennsylvania, The Decorative Impulse, 1979; Hirshhorn, Directions, 1979; Buffalo/Albright, Patterns, 1979; Mannheim, Dekor, 1980; Aachen/NG, Les Nouveaux Fauves—/Di neuen Wilden, 1980; Bonn, Back to the USA, circ., 1983. **Bibliography:** *Back to the USA; Drawings: The Pluralist Decade;* Haenlein; Lucie-Smith; Murken-Altrogge.

MacDONALD-WRIGHT, STANTON. b. July 8, 1890, Charlottesville, Va.; **d.** August 24, 1973, Pacific Palisades, Calif. **Studied:** Sorbonne; Academie des Beaux-Arts, Paris; Academie Colarossi, Paris; Academie Julian, Paris; ASL, with W. T. Hedges, J. Greenbaum. Met Morgan Russell in Paris, 1912, and with him founded the Synchromist movement in 1913. Studied the color theories of Michel Eugene Chevruel, Herman von Helmholz, and O. N. Rood. Returned to USA, 1916. Traveled Japan, 1937, 1952-53. **Taught:** U. of California, 1942-50; U. of Southern California; Scripps College, 1946; U. of Hawaii, 1949; Fulbright Exchange Professor to Japan, 1952-53; lectured on art history and Oriental aesthetics. Federal A.P.: California State Director, 1935-42, and technical advisor to seven western states. **Commissions** (murals): Santa Monica (Calif.) Public Library; Santa Monica City Hall; Santa Monica High School (mosaic). **One-man Exhibitions:** (first) Photo-Secession, NYC, 1917; Stendahl Gallery, Los Angeles, 1942 (two man); Rose Fried Gallery, 1955; Duveen-Graham Gallery, NYC, 1956; Esther Robles Gallery, 1965; UCLA, 1970; Suzuki Graphics, NYC, 1972; St. Petersburg Museum, Fall, 1977; Harmon Gallery, Naples, 1975, 78; The Forum Gallery, NYC, 1982; Joseph Chowning Gallery, San Francisco, 1984. **Retrospectives:** Los Angeles/County MA, 1956; NCFA, 1967. **Group:** Salon d'Automne, Paris, 1910; The Synchromists, Munich and Paris, 1913; Salon des Artistes Independants, Paris, 1913-14; MMA; Brooklyn Museum; Honolulu Academy. **Collections:** Boston/MFA; Brooklyn Museum; Carnegie; Chicago/AI; Columbus; Corcoran; Denver/AM; Detroit/Institute; Grand Rapids; Los Angeles/County MA; MMA; MOMA; U. of Minnesota;

Newark Museum; Omaha/Joslyn; PMA; Pasadena/AM; San Diego; Santa Barbara/MA; Toledo/MA; WMAA; Walker. **Bibliography:** *Avant-Garde Painting and Sculpture in America, 1910-25;* Baur 7; Blanchard; Blesh 1; Brown 2; Cheney; Chipp; Christensen; Craven, T., 1; Goodrich and Baur 1; Haftman; Hess, T. B., 1; Hunter 6; Huyghe; Jackman; Janis, S.; Levin 2; McCurdy, ed.; Mellquist; Neuhaus; Read 2; Richardson, E.P.; Rickey; Ringel, ed.; Ritchie 1; Rose, B., 1, 4; **Scott;** Seuphor 1, 2; Wright 1, 2. Archives.

MacIVER, LOREN. b. February 2, 1909, NYC. **Studied:** ASL, 1919-20. Traveled Europe. Lighting and decor for four Coffee Concerts, MOMA, 1941. **Member:** NIAL, 1959. Federal A.P.: 1936-39, New York; Artists Equity. **Commissions** (murals): Moore-McCormack Lines, Inc., SS *Argentina,* 1947; American Export Lines, SS *Excalibur,* SS *Exeter,* SS *Exochorda,* SS *Excambion,* 1948. **Awards:** Corcoran, First Prize, 1957; Ford Foundation Grant, 1960; Mark Rothko Foundation Grant, 1972; Guggenheim Foundation Fellowship, 1976. **Address:** 61 Perry Street, NYC 10014. **Dealer:** Pierre Matisse Gallery, NYC. **One-man Exhibitions:** (first) East River Gallery, NYC, 1938; Pierre Matisse Gallery, NYC, 1940, 44, 49, 56, 61, 70, 81; Arts Club of Chicago, 1941; MOMA, circ., 1941; Baltimore/MA, 1945; Vassar College, circ., 1950; Santa Barbara/MA, 1951; Margaret Brown Gallery, Boston, circ., 1951; Phillips, 1951; Corcoran, 1956; Fairweather-Hardin Gallery, 1959; Southern Vermont Art Center, Manchester, Vt., 1968; Paris/Moderne, 1968; Musées Classes de Nice, 1968; Rutgers U., 1982. **Retrospectives:** WMAA, circ., 1953; Paris/Moderne, 1968; Newport Harbor, 1985. **Group:** WMAA annuals; MOMA, Fourteen Americans, circ., 1946; Corcoran. **Collections:** Andover/Phillips; Baltimore/MA; Bibliotheque Nationale;

Brooklyn Museum; Chicago/AI; Corcoran; Detroit/Institute; Hartford/Wadsworth; Harvard U.; Hirshhorn; Los Angeles/County MA; MMA; MOMA; NMAA; National Gallery; Newark Museum; U. of Oklahoma; PMA; Phillips; SFMA; Smith College; Utica; Vassar College; WMAA; Walker; Williams College; Yale U. **Bibliography:** Barr 3; **Baur 4,** 5, 7; Bazin; Blesh 1; Eliot; Flanagan; Genauer; Goodrich and Baur 1; Hunter 6; Janis, S.; McCurdy, ed.; Mendelowitz; Miller, ed. 2; Newmeyer; Nordness, ed.; Pousette-Dart, ed.; Read 2; Richardson, E.P.; Soby 5, 6; Wight 2. Archives.

MADSEN, LOREN. b. March 29, 1943, Oakland, Calif. **Studied:** Reed College; UCLA, BA, 1966; MA, 1970. Traveled Switzerland, 1959-60, Europe, 1963-64. **Taught:** UCLA. **Commissions:** Prudential Insurance Co., Florham Park, N.J., 1974; Los Angeles Museum of Art, Calif., 1977; Prudential Insurance Co., Woodland Hills, Calif.; Cedars-Sinai Medical Center, Beverly Hills, Calif., 1977; Michael's Restaurant, Santa Monica, Calif., 1979; Newport Harbor Art Museum, Newport Beach, Calif., 1980; First Bank Atrium, Pillsbury Center, Minneapolis, Minn.; SSA Metro West (G.S.A.), Baltimore, Md.; Stamford Town Center, Stamford, Conn.; Iowa State University, Ames, Iowa, 1980-81; 1st Bank Atrium, Pillsbury Center, Minneapolis, 1981; Brookhollow Atrium, San Antonio, 1984; RepublicBank, San Antonio, 1984; Horton Plaza, San Diego, 1985; Quorum, Dallas, 1985. **Awards:** Los Angeles/County MA, New Talent, **P.P.,** 1975; National Endowment for the Arts, Fellowship, 1975 and 1980. **Address:** 428 Broome Street, NYC 10013. **Dealer:** David McKee Gallery, NYC. **One-man Exhibitions:** (first) Mizuno Gallery, Los Angeles, 1973, 74; MOMA, 1975; David McKee Gallery, NYC, 1976, 77, 82, 84; Site, San Francisco, 1976; L. A. Louver Gallery, Los Angeles, 1976; Zolla-Lieberman, Chicago, 1978; Wright State U., 1980; Hansen Fuller Goldeen Gallery, San Francisco, 1980; U. of Massachusetts, 1981; Miami-Dade, 1984. **Group:** Scripps College, Young Sculptors, 1972; Long Beach/MA, Constructions, 1974; Los Angeles/County MA, Six Artists, 1974; Los Angeles Municipal Art Gallery, 24 from Los Angeles, 1974; SFAI, 8 Los Angeles Artists, 1974; Hayward Gallery, The Condition of Sculpture, 1975; Walker, Dill, Ginnever, Madsen, 1975; Omaha/Joslyn, L.A. in the Seventies, 1979; Hirshhorn, Directions, 1979; Sacramento/Crocker, Aspects of Abstract Art, 1979; San Diego Museum of Art, Sculpture in California, 1975-80, 1980; Newport Harbor, Shift— L.A./N.Y., 1983. **Collections:** Akron/AM; Hirshhorn; Israel Museum; Los Angeles/County MA; MOMA; Newport Harbor; Paris/Beaubourg; Vancouver; Walker.

MALLARY, ROBERT. b. December 2, 1917, Toledo, Ohio. **Studied:** La Escuela de las Artes del Libro, Mexico City, 1938; privately with Koloman Sokol (graphics), Mexico City and New York, 1941-42. **Taught:** Pratt Institute, 1959-67; The Pennsylvania State U., 1962; U. of California, Davis, 1963, 67; U. of Minnesota, 1965; U. of Massachusetts, 1967-. Director, ARSTECNICA, U. of Massachusetts/Amherst College. **Commissions:** Beverly Hilton Hotel, Beverly Hills, Calif., 1954-55 (mural, with Dale Owen); New York State Pavilion, New York World's Fair, 1964-65. **Awards:** Tamarind Fellowship, 1962; Guggenheim Foundation Fellowship, 1964. **Address:** P.O. Box 48, Conway, MA. 01341. **Dealer:** Allan Stone Gallery. **One-man Exhibitions:** SFMA, 1944; Sacramento/Crocker, 1944, 52; Santa Barbara/MA, 1952; Gump's Gallery, 1953; San Diego, 1953; Urban Gallery, NYC, 1954; U. of New Mexico, 1956-59; Jonson Gallery, Albuquerque, N.M., 1957-59; Santa Fe, N.M., 1958; Allan Stone Gallery, 1961, 62, 66; Yale U. (two-man), 1965; Purdue U., 1974.

Retrospective: Potsdam/SUNY, 1969. **Group:** Salon de Grabado, Mexico City, 1942; SFMA, 1945; Los Angeles/County MA Annuals, 1951, 53, 56; Denver/AM Annual, 1955; III & VII Sao Paulo Biennials, 1955, 63; Smithsonian, California Painters, circ., USA, 1956-58; MOMA, Recent Sculpture USA, 1959; MOMA, Sixteen Americans, circ., 1959; SRGM, Guggenheim International, 1960; WMAA Annuals, 1960, 62; MOMA, The Art of Assemblage, circ., 1961; Martha Jackson Gallery, New Media—New Forms, II, 1961; Seattle World's Fair, 1962; A.F.A., Relief Sculpture, circ., 1964; Brandeis U., Recent American Drawings, 1964; ICA, London, Cybernetic Serendipity, 1968; WMAA, Human Concern/Personal Torment, 1969; Akron/AI, Celebrate Ohio, 1971. **Collections:** Brandeis U.; Buffalo/Albright; U. of California; Houston/MFA; Kalamazoo/Institute; Los Angeles/County MA; MOMA; U. of New Mexico; U. of North Carolina; Roswell; Smith College; U. of Texas; WMAA. **Bibliography:** *Celebrate Ohio;* Davis, D.; Hunter, ed.; Janis and Blesh 1; *Report;* Seitz 3; Weller.

MANGOLD, ROBERT. b. 1937, North Tonawanda, N.Y. **Studied:** Cleveland Institute of Art, 1956-59; Yale U., 1959, 1960-62, BFA, 1963, MFA. **Taught:** School of Visual Arts, NYC, 1963-; Hunter College, 1964-65; Skowhegan School, 1968; Yale U. Summer School, Norfolk, Conn., 1969; Cornell U., 1970. **Address:** Bull Road, Washingtonville, N.Y. **Dealer:** John Weber Gallery, NYC; Paula Cooper Gallery, NYC. **One-man Exhibitions:** Thibaut Gallery, NYC, 1964; Fischbach Gallery, 1965, 67, 69, 70, 71, 73; Galerie Muller, 1968; SRGM, 1971; Yvon Lambert, 1973; Galleria Toselli, Milan, 1973; Lisson Gallery, 1973; Galerie Annemarie Verna, Zurich, 1973, 80; Galleria Marilena Bonomo, Bari, Italy, 1973; Max Protetch, Washington, D.C., 1973; Weinberg Gallery, San Francisco,

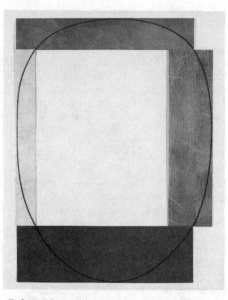

Robert Mangold *Four Color Frame Painting #15 (Variant)* 1985

1973; John Weber Gallery, 1974, 76, 77, 79, 80; Konrad Fischer Gallery, Dusseldorf, 1974, 82; Protetch-McIntosh Gallery, Washington, D.C., 1978; Bielefeld, Kunsthalle, 1980; Young Hoffman Gallery, Chicago, 1980; Texas Gallery, Houston, 1980; Richard Hines Gallery, Seattle, 1980; Lisson Gallery, London, 1981; Hoshour Gallery, Albuquerque, 1981; Carol Taylor Gallery, Dallas, 1981; Sidney Janis Gallery, NYC, 1982; Amsterdam/Stedelijk, 1982; Daniel Weinberg Gallery, Los Angeles, 1983; U. of California, Berkeley, 1983; Paula Cooper Gallery, NYC, 1984; Akron/AM, circ., 1985. **Group:** SRGM, Systemic Painting, 1966; Yale U., Twelve Yale Artists, 1966; ICA, U. of Pennsylvania, A Romantic Minimalism, 1967; Ithaca College, Selected New York Artists, 1967; Trenton/State, Focus on Light, 1967; WMAA, Artists under Forty, 1968; Buffalo/Albright, Modular Paintings, 1970; Documenta V, Kassel, 1972; WMAA, American Drawings, 1963-1973, 1973; Parcheggio di Villa Borghese, Rome, Contemporanea, 1973; Chicago/Contemporary,

Five Artists: A Logic of Vision, 1974; MOMA, Color as Language, circ., 1975; MOMA, Drawing Now, 1976; Documenta VI, Kassel, 1977; Buffalo/Albright, American Paintings of the 1970s, 1978; U. of North Carolina, Drawings about Drawing Today, 1979; ICA, Boston, The Reductive Object, 1979; Lenbachhaus, Munich, Tendencies in American Drawings of the Late Seventies, 1979; Paris/Beaubourg, Nature du Dessin, 1981; Documenta VII, Kassel, 1982; SRGM, The New York School: Four Decades, 1982; WMAA, Biennial, 1983, 85; Amsterdam/Stedelijk, La Grande Parade, 1984. **Collections:** Amsterdam/Stedelijk; Los Angeles/County MA; MOMA; McCrory Corporation; Oberlin College; RISD; Ridgefield/Aldrich; SRGM; WMAA. **Bibliography:** *Art Now 74; Contemporanea;* De Wilde 1; *Fundamentele Schilderkunst;* Gablik; Honisch and Jensen, eds.; Lippard 2; Murdoch 1; Murken-Altrogge; *Options and Alternatives;* **Waldman 4.**

MANGOLD, SYLVIA PLIMACK. b. September 18, 1938. **Studied:** Cooper Union, NYC, 1956-59; Yale U., BFA, 1961. **Taught:** School of Visual Arts, NYC, 1970-71. **Address:** Bull Road, Washingtonville, N.Y. **Dealer:** Brooke Alexander, NYC. **One-man Exhibitions:** Fischbach Gallery, NYC, 1974, 75; Daniel Weinberg Gallery, San Francisco, 1974; Droll/Kolbert Gallery, NYC, 1978, 80; Galerie Annemarie Verna, Zurich, 1978; Ohio State U., 1980; Young Hoffman Gallery, Chicago, 1980; Hartford/Wadsworth, 1981; Houston/Contemporary, 1981; Duke U., 1982; Madison Art Center, circ., 1982; Brooke Alexander, 1982, 84; Rhona Hoffman Gallery, Chicago, 1985. **Group:** Vassar College, Realism Now, 1968; U. of North Carolina, Art on Paper, 1968; Potsdam/SUNY, New Realism, 1972; WMAA Annual, 1972; Yale U., American Drawing 1970-1973, 1973; Yale U., Seven Realists, 1974; California Institute of the Arts, Valencia, Anonymous Was a Woman, 1974; Skidmore College, 20th Century Drawings, 1975; San Antonio/McNay, American Artists, '76, 1976; Akron/AI, Contemporary Images in Watercolor, 1976; Indianapolis, 1976; Documenta 6, Kassel, 1977; Buffalo/Albright, American Painting of the 1970's, 1978; Ljubljana, 13th Print Biennial, 1979; Denver, The Reality of Illusion, 1979; Walker, Eight Artists; The Elusive Image, 1979; XXXIX Venice Biennial, 1980; PAFA, Contemporary American Realism Since 1960, 1981; San Antonio/MA, Real, Really Real, Super Real, circ., 1981; Hudson River Museum, New Vistas, 1985; Stamford Museum, American Art: American Women, 1985. **Collections:** Buffalo/Albright; Dallas/MFA; Detroit/Institute; Hartford/Wadsworth; Houston/MFA; Indianapolis; MOMA; Madison Art Center; Milwaukee; U. of North Carolina; Oberlin College; Utah; U. of Utah; WMAA; Walker; Yale U. **Bibliography:** *Art: A Woman's Sensibility; Drawings: The Pluralist Decade;* Lindy; Lippard 3.

MAN RAY (Emmanuel Radinski). b. August 27, 1890, Philadelphia, Pa; **d.** November 18, 1976, Paris. **Studied:** NAD, 1908; ASL; Ferrer Center, NYC, with Robert Henri and George Bellows. Cofounder (with Marcel Duchamp and Francis Picabia) of DADA group, NYC, 1917. Co-organizer (with Katherine S. Dreier and Marcel Duchamp) of Societe Anonyme (Museum of Modern Art), 1920. Published one issue of *New York DADA* with Marcel Duchamp, 1921. To Paris, 1921, and became a member of the DADA and Surrealist groups, 1924-39. Developed the rayography technique in photography, 1921. Created abstract and surrealist films: *Le Retour de la Raison,* 1923; *Emak Bakia,* 1926; *L'Etoile de Mer,* 1928; *Les Mysteres du Chateau de Des,* 1929. Resided Hollywood, 1940-50; returned to Paris. **One-man Exhibitions:** (first) Daniel Gallery, NYC, 1915, also 1916, 19; Librairie Six,

Paris, 1922; Galerie Surrealiste, Paris, 1926; Myrbor Galerie, Paris, 1929; Galerie Vanleer, Paris, 1929; Galerie Vignon, Paris, 1932; Curt Valentine Gallery, NYC, 1936; Galerie Beaune, Paris, 1939; The London Gallery, London, 1939; Frank Perls Gallery, 1941; Julien Levy Galleries, NYC, 1945; Copley Gallery, Hollywood, Calif., 1948; Paul Kantor Gallery, Beverly Hills, 1953; Galerie Furstenberg, Paris, 1954; Galerie Rive Droite, Paris, 1959; Bibliotheque Nationale, 1962; Cordier & Ekstrom, Inc., 1963, 70; Princeton U., 1963; Galleria Schwarz, 1964, 71; Los Angeles/County MA, 1966; Martha Jackson Gallery, 1968; Galerie der Spiegel, Cologne, 1968, 75; Hanover Gallery, 1969; Trenton/State, 1969; Noah Goldowsky, 1971; La Boetie, NYC, 1972; MMA, 1973; Alexandre Iolas Gallery, NYC, 1974; Galleria Il Fauno, Turin, 1974; Studio Marconi, Milan, 1975; Chicago/Contemporary, 1975; Stephen Wirtz Gallery, San Francisco, 1982; The Zabriskie Gallery, 1982, 85; Robert Miller Gallery, 1983; Center for Photography, Film and Television, Zagreb, Yugoslavia, 1985; Light Gallery, NYC, 1985; G. Ray Hawkins Gallery, Los Angeles, 1986. **Retrospectives:** Paris/Moderne, 1971; New York Cultural Center, 1974; Paris/Beaubourg, 1981. **Group:** Societe Anonyme, NYC, 1920; Brooklyn Museum, 1926; Springfield, Mass./MFA, 1929; MOMA, 1936; WMAA, 1946; Yale U., 1948. **Collections:** MOMA. **Bibliography:** Ammann and Bussmann; *Avant-Garde Painting and Sculpture in America, 1910-25;* Barr 1; Baur 7; Biddle 4; Blesh 1; **Bourgeade;** Breton 1, 2, 3; Brown 2; Cassou; Christensen; Crespelle; Davis, D.; Flanagan; Gascoyne; Gerdts; Guggenheim, ed.; Haftman; Hulten; Honisch and Jensen, eds; Hunter 6; Hunter, ed.; Kozloff 3; Krauss 2, 3; Kyrou; **Langsner; Man Ray 1, 2, 3, 4; Man Ray;** McCurdy, ed.; Marter, Tarbell, and Wechsler; Mellquist; Motherwell 1; Murken-Altrogge; Neff, ed.; **Penrose;** Raynal 3; Read 2, 3, 5; **Ribemont-Dessaignes;** Richter;

Ritchie 1; Rose, B., 1; Rowell; Rubin 1; Seitz 3; Soby 1; Tashijian; Tomkins; Tomkins and Time-Life Books; Verkauf; Waldberg 2, 3, 4; Wright 1; Zervos.

MANSHIP, PAUL. b. December 25, 1885, St. Paul, Minn.; **d.** February 1, 1966, NYC. **Studied:** St. Paul School of Art, 1892-1903; ASL, 1905; PAFA, 1906-08; American Academy, Rome, 1909-12. Traveled Europe, USA; resided Paris, 1922-26. **Taught:** PAFA, 1943-46. **Member:** (Federal) Commission of Fine Arts (president, 1937-41); National Sculpture Society (president, 1939-42); AAAL (president, 1948-53); Century Association (president, 1950-54); Academy of St. Luca, Rome, 1952. **Commissions:** Designed coinage for Irish Free State, 1927. **Awards:** NAD, Helen Foster Barnett Prize, 1913, 17; PAFA, George D. Widener Memorial Gold Medal, 1914; Panama-Pacific Exposition, San Francisco, 1915, Gold Medal; NAD, 1920; elected to the NIAL, 1920; American Independent Artists Medal, 1921; American Institute of Architects, Gold Medal, 1921; NAD, Saltus Gold Medal for Merit, 1924; Philadelphia Art Week, Gold Medal, 1925; Philadelphia Sesquicentennial, Gold Medal, 1926; Legion of Honor, 1929; elected to the AAAL, 1932; Paris World's Fair, 1937, Diplome d'Honneur; National Sculpture Society, Medal of Honor, 1939; NIAL, Gold Medal, 1945. **One-man Exhibitions:** Architectural League of New York, 1912; A.F.A., 1914; Corcoran, 1920, 37; Leicester Gallery, London, 1921; PMA, 1926; U. of Rochester, 1927; Toronto, 1928; Averell House, NYC, 1933; Tate Gallery, 1935; Century Association, 1935; VMFA, 1936; Arden Gallery, NYC, 1941; AAAL, 1945; Walker, 1948; St. Paul Gallery, 1967; Robert Schoelkopf Gallery, 1971, 72; Hamline U., 1972; Hudson River Museum, 1985. **Retrospectives:** Smithsonian, 1958; NCFA, 1966. **Group:** Corcoran, 1920; PAFA; NAD; WMAA; MMA; and many others in America and abroad. **Collec-** **tions:** American Academy, Rome; Andover/Phillips; Chicago/AI; Cochran Memorial Park; Detroit/Institute; Harvard U.; League of Nations; MMA; Minneapolis/Institute; New York Coliseum; Pratt Institute; Rockefeller Center; St. Louis/City; Smith College; West Palm Beach/Norton. **Bibliography:** Baur 7; **Beggs;** Birnbaum; Brumme; Cahill and Barr, eds.; Cortissoz 1; **Gallatin 7;** *Index of 20th Century Artists;* Jackman; Lee and Burchwood; **Leach;** Licht, F.; Mather 1; Mellquist; Mendelowitz; **Murtha;** Pach 1; *Paul Manship: Changing Taste in America;* Poore; Rose, B., 1; **Vitry.** Archives.

MANSO, LEO. b. April 15, 1914, NYC. **Studied:** Educational Alliance, NYC, 1929; NAD, 1930-34; New School for Social Research. Traveled Mexico, Africa, India, Nepal, Italy, Sicily, Tunisia. **Taught:** Cooper Union, 1947-70; NYU, 1950-72; Columbia U., 1950-55; NYC, 1950-1980; Provincetown Workshop, 1959 (cofounder); ASL, 1974, 1977-; New School for Social Research, 1975. **Member:** American Abstract Artists; NAD; Artists Equity. **Commissions:** Public Library, Lincoln, Neb. (mural), 1965. **Awards:** U. of Illinois, **P.P.,** 1951, Audubon Artists, 1952, 57; Ford Foundation, **P.P.,** 1963; AAAL, Childe Hassam Award, 1968; AAIAL, grant, 1981; Guggenheim Foundation Fellowship, 1983. **Address:** 460 Riverside Drive, NYC 10027. **Dealer:** Long Point Gallery, Provincetown, Mass.; Arras Gallery, NYC. **One-man Exhibitions:** (first) Norlyst Gallery, NYC, 1947; Guadalajara Institute, Mexico, 1948; Mortimer Levitt Gallery, NYC, 1950; The Babcock Gallery, 1953, 56; Columbia U., 1954; NYU, 1957; Grand Central Moderns, NYC, 1957, 60, 61, 63, 64; Philadelphia Art Alliance, 1961, 69; Tirca Karlis Gallery, 1963, 65, 67, 69, 70, 72, 73; Arts Council of Winston-Salem (N.C.), 1966; Rose Fried Gallery, 1966, 68, 70; George Washington U., 1968; Rehn Galleries, 1974; E. P. Gurewitsch Gallery, NYC, 1975, 78;

Syracuse/Everson, 1976; Long Point Gallery, Provincetown, Mass., 1977, 79, 80, 83, 85; American Academy, Rome, 1979; AAIAL, 1981; Arras Gallery, 1983; Pace U., 1983; Dartmouth College, 1985. **Group:** PAFA, 1947-50, 1952, 54, 61, 62, 64, 68; WMAA Annuals, 1948-66; U. of Illinois, 1950, 51, 52, 54, 57; A.F.A., circ., U. of Nebraska Annual; American Abstract Artists Annual; Brooklyn Museum, Watercolor Biennials; ART: USA:58, NYC, 1958; MOMA, The Art of Assemblage, circ., 1961; NIAL, 1961, 68; MOMA, 1965. **Collections:** Alcoa; Boston/MFA; Brandeis U.; Brooklyn Museum; Cape Town; Charleston, W. Va.; Corcoran; Dartmouth College; Hirshhorn; U. of Illinois; MOMA; Michigan State U.; Mount Holyoke College; NAD; NYU; U. of Nebraska; Norfolk; PAFA; Portland, Ore./AM; RISD; Safad; Syracuse U.; WMAA; Wesleyan U.; West Palm Beach/Norton; Worcester/AM. **Bibliography:** Seitz 3. Archives.

MARCA-RELLI, CONRAD. b. June 5, 1913, Boston, Mass. **Studied:** Cooper Union, one year; mostly self-taught. US Army, 1941-45. Traveled Europe, USA, Mexico. **Taught:** Yale U., 1954-55, 1959-60; U. of California, Berkeley, 1958; New College, Sarasota, Fla., 1966. Federal A.P.: Easel and mural painting; also art teacher. **Member:** NIAL, 1976. **Awards:** Chicago/AI, The Mr. & Mrs. Frank G. Logan Medal, 1954; Ford Foundation, 1959; Detroit/Institute, **P.P.,** 1960; II Inter-American Paintings and Prints Biennial, Mexico City, 1960, Hon. Men.; Chicago/AI, The M.V. Kohnstamm Prize, 1963. **Address:** Box 1367, Apaquogue Road, East Hampton, NY 11937; Urbanization Can Pepsimo Ibiza (Baleares), Spain. **Dealer:** Marisa del Re, NYC. **One-man Exhibitions:** (first) Niveau Gallery, NYC, 1948, also 1950; The New Gallery, NYC, 1951; The Stable Gallery, 1953-58 (4); Frank Perls Gallery, 1956; La Tartaruga, Rome, 1957, 62; The Kootz Gallery, NYC,

1959-64; Bolles Gallery, 1961; Galerie Schmela, 1961 (two-man, with Robert Motherwell), 71; Lima, Peru, 1961; Joan Peterson Gallery, 1961; Galerie de France, Paris, 1962; Galerie Charles Leinhard, Zurich, 1963; Tokyo Gallery, 1963; James David Gallery, Miami, 1966, 67; Makler Gallery, 1967, 74; WMAA, 1967; Brandeis U., 1967-68; U. of Alabama, 1968; Buffalo/Albright, 1968; Alpha Gallery, 1968; Reed College, 1969; Seattle/AM, 1969; Marlborough Gallery, Inc., NYC, 1970, 75; U. of Maryland, 1970; West Palm Beach/Norton, 1970; Fort Lauderdale, 1971; U. of Miami, 1971; Galeria Carl van der Voort, Ibiza, 1972; Darthea Speyer Gallery, 1972; Galerie Numaga, Auvernier, Switzerland, 1973; Galeria Inguanzo, Madrid, 1973; Marlborough Galerie AG, Zurich, 1974; Marlborough Godard Ltd., Toronto, 1975; Alex Rosenberg Gallery, NYC, 1984; Marisa del Re, 1985; R.H. Love Modern, Chicago, 1986. **Retrospective:** WMAA, 1967. **Group:** Ninth Street Exhibition, NYC, 1951; WMAA Annuals; Chicago/AI; U. of Illinois; U. of Nebraska; Carnegie; Venice Biennial; Yale U.; Corcoran; Arts Club of Chicago; Rome-New York Foundation, Rome; Boston Arts Festival; Minneapolis/Institute; PAFA; Montreal/MFA; Brussels World's Fair, 1958; Documenta II, Kassel, 1959; American Painting and Sculpture, Moscow, 1959; Sao Paulo Biennial; Seattle World's Fair, 1962; A.F.A., 1967-68; MOMA, The New American Painting and Sculpture, 1969; WMAA Annual, 1969; New School for Social Research, NYC, American Drawings of the Sixties, 1969; U. of California, Santa Barbara, Trends in Twentieth Century Art, 1970; VMFA, American Painting, 1970; NAD, Annual, 1972; AAAL, Newly Elected Members, 1976. **Collections:** U. of Alabama; Brandeis U.; Buffalo/Albright; Carnegie; Chase Manhattan Bank; Chicago/AI; Cleveland/MA; Colby College; Columbia Broadcasting System; Detroit/Institute; Hartford/Wadsworth; Harvard U.; High Museum; Hirshhorn; Houston/MFA;

Indianapolis/Herron; International Minerals & Chemicals Corp.; Los Angeles/County MA; MMA; MOMA; U. of Michigan; Minneapolis/Institute; Minnesota/MA; NCFA; U. of Nebraska; PAFA; U. of Rochester; SFMA; SRGM; Seattle/AM; The Singer Company Inc.; U. of Texas; Union Carbide Corp.; Utica; WMAA; Waitsfield/Bundy; Walker; Washington U.; Yale U. **Bibliography: Agee; Arnason 1;** Chaet; Goodrich and Baur 1; Henning; Hunter, ed.; Janis and Blesh 1; *Metro;* Nordness, ed.; Rodman 3; Rose, B., 1; Seitz 3; **Tyler, P., 2.**

MARCUS, MARCIA. b. January 11, 1928, NYC. **Studied:** NYU 1943-47, BFA; Cooper Union, 1950-52; ASL, 1954, with Edwin Dickinson. Traveled Europe. **Taught:** Purdue U.; Moore Institute of Art, Science and Industry; RISD; Cooper Union, 1970-71; Louisiana State U., 1972; NYU, 1972; Vassar College, 1973-74; Cornell U., 1975; Iowa State U., 1979-80; Colorado State U., 1984; Northern Arizona U., 1984. **Member:** Artists Equity. **Awards:** Ingram Merrill Grant, 1964; NIAL, Richard and Hinda Rosenthal Foundation Award, 1964; Ford Foundation Grant, 1966; Gottlieb Foundation Grant, 1983. **Address:** 80 North Moore Street, NYC 10013. **One-man Exhibitions:** (first) March Gallery, NYC, 1957; Delancey Street Museum, NYC, 1960; Cober Gallery, 1961; The Alan Gallery, NYC, 1962; RISD, 1966; The Graham Gallery, 1966; Tirca Karlis Gallery, 1966, 67; The Zabriskie Gallery, 1970; Makler Gallery, 1972; Louisiana State U., 1972; Vassar College, 1974; ACA Gallery, 1974; Syracuse/Everson, 1975; Bloomsburg College, 1976; Benson Gallery, Bridgehampton, N.Y., 1978; Terry Dintenfass Inc., NYC, 1979; Wheaton College, 1980; Cedar Rapids Art Center, 1980. **Retrospective:** Canton Art Institute, 1984. **Group:** WMAA, Young America, 1960; WMAA Annual, 1963; NIAL, 1964; MOMA, Contemporary Portraits, circ.; New York Cultural Center, Women Choose Women, 1973; PMA/Museum of the Philadelphia Civic Center, Focus, 1974; Syracuse/Everson, Provincetown Painters, 1977; Indianapolis, 1978; U. of Missouri, Kansas City, The Opposite Sex: A Realistic Viewpoint, 1979; Lehigh U., The Revival of Realism, 1979. **Collections:** Canton Art Institute; Hampton Institute; Hirshhorn; Housatonic Museum, Bridgeport, Conn.; NIAL; Newark Museum; Phoenix/SUNY; Phoenix; Purdue U.; RISD; Randolph Macon Jr. College; Syracuse/Everson; WMAA; Williamstown/Clark; U. of Wyoming. **Bibliography:** *Art: A Woman's Sensibility.* Archives.

MARDEN, BRICE. b. October 15, 1938, Bronxville, N.Y. **Studied:** Boston U., 1958-61, BFA; Yale U. Summer School, Norfolk, Conn., 1961; Yale U., 1961-63, MFA. Traveled USA, France, Greece, Middle East, Asia. **Taught:** School of Visual Arts, NYC, 1969-74. **Address:** 276 Bowery, NYC 10012. **Dealer:** Mary Boone Gallery, NYC. **One-man Exhibitions:** (first) Swarthmore College, 1964; Bykert Gallery, 1966, 68, 69, 70, 72, 73, 74; Yvon Lambert, 1969, 73; Francoise Lambert, Milan, 1970; Gian Enzo Sperone, Turin, 1971, 77; U. of Utah, 1971; Locksley-Shea Gallery, Minneapolis, 1972, 74; Jack Glenn Gallery, Corona del Mar, 1973; Konrad Fischer Gallery, Dusseldorf, 1972, 73, 75, 80; John Berggruen Gallery (two-man), 1972; Cirrus Editions, Ltd., 1974; Jared Sable Gallery, Toronto, 1974; SRGM, 1975; Alessandro/Ferranti, Rome, 1975; Sperone, Westwater, Fischer, NYC, 1976; Brown, U., 1977; Jean and Karen Bernier, Athens, 1977; Max Protetch Gallery, Washington, D.C., 1977; The Pace Gallery, NYC, 1978, 80, 82, 84; Kunstraum, Munich, 1979; Institut fur Moderne Kunst, Nuremberg, 1980; Rice U. (three-man), 1975; InK, Zurich, 1980; Amsterdam/Stedelijk, 1981; Whitechapel Art Gallery, London, 1981; Mizuno Gallery, Los Angeles,

Brice Marden   *Untitled 3*   1986–87

1982; Daniel Weinberg Gallery, Los Angeles, 1984. **Group:** New London, Drawings by New England Artists, 1960; U. of Illinois, 1967; Ithaca College, Drawings, 1967, 1967; ICA, U. of Pennsylvania, A Romantic Minimalism, 1967; WMAA Annuals 1968, 73; Buffalo/Albright, Modular Painting, 1970; Foundation Maeght, L'Art Vivant, 1970; WMAA, The Structure of Color, 1971; U. of Utah, 1971; U. of Rochester, Aspects of Current Painting, 1971; Chicago/Contemporary, White on White, 1971-72; Indianapolis, 1972; U. of California, Berkeley, Eight New York Painters, 1972; Chicago/AI, 1972; Walker, Painting: New Options, 1972; Documenta V, Kassel, 1972; Yale U., Options and Alternatives, 1973; WMAA, American Art: Third Quarter Century, 1973; MOMA, Some Recent American Art, circ., 1973; Chicago/Contemporary, Five Artists: A Logic of Vision, 1974; MOMA, Eight Contemporary Artists, 1974; UCLA, 14 Abstract Painters, 1975; Paris/Moderne, Tendances Actuelles de la Nouvelle Peinture Americaine, 1975; Amsterdam/Stedelijk, Fundamental Painting,

1975; Rijksmuseum Kroller-Muller, Functions of Drawings, 1975; MOMA, Drawing Now, 1976; WMAA Biennial, 1977; Brooklyn Museum, American Drawings in Black and White: 1970-1979, 1980; Royal Academy, London, A New Spirit in Painting, 1981; MIT, Affinities, 1983. **Collections:** Amsterdam/Stedelijk; Buffalo/Albright; Fort Worth; Musée de Grenoble; Harvard U.; National Gallery of Canada; MOMA; SRGM; WMAA; Walker. **Bibliography:** *Contemporanea;* De Wilde 1, 2; *Fundamentele Schilderkunst;* Honisch and Jensen, eds.; Licht, J.; Murdoch 1; Murken-Altrogge; *New in the Seventies; Options and Alternatives;* **Shearer;** Tuchman 3. Archives.

MARGO, BORIS. b. November 7, 1902, Wolotschisk, Russia. **Studied:** Polytechnic School, Odessa, 1919; Futemas, Moscow, 1924; Filonoy School, Leningrad, 1927. To USA, 1930; citizen, 1937. Traveled Western Europe, Israel, 1968; Hawaii. **Taught:** Master Institute of United Arts, Inc., 1932; American U., 1946; U. of Michigan, 1957; Chicago Art Institute School, 1957; Michigan State U., 1959; U. of Illinois, 1960; U. of Minnesota, Duluth, 1962; U. of North Carolina, 1963; Ford Foundation/A.F.A., Artist-in-Residence, 1965; Syracuse U., 1966-67; The Ohio State U., 1968; Honolulu Academy, 1973; Potsdam/SUNY, 1974; Fine Arts Work Center, Provincetown, Mass., 1974. **Member:** SAGA. Federal A.P.: Newark (N.J.) Airport (assisted Arshile Gorky on a mural). **Commissions:** Honolulu Academy (sculpture), 1973. **Awards:** Chicago/AI, Watson F. Blair Prize, 1947; Brooklyn Museum, Print Exhibitions, 1947, 53, 55, 60, 64, 68; Portland, Me./MA, **P.P.,** 1960; National Endowment for the Arts, grant, 1974. **m.** Jan Gelb. **Address:** 749 West End Avenue, NYC 10025. **One-man Exhibitions:** (first) Artists' Gallery, NYC, 1939, also 1941, 42; Norlyst Gallery, NYC, 1943; Mortimer Brandt, NYC, 1946, 47; American U., 1946, 47;

J. Seligmann and Co., 1947; Brooklyn Museum, 1947; Smithsonian, 1948; Betty Parsons Gallery, 1950, 53, 55, 57, 60; World House Galleries, NYC, 1964; Honolulu Academy, 1973; Monique Knowlton Gallery, NYC, 1974. **Retrospectives:** Syracuse U., 1966; A.A.A. Gallery, NYC, 1967. **Group:** MMA, Artists for Victory, 1942; Mortimer Brandt, NYC, Abstract and Surrealist Art in the U.S., circ., western museums, 1944; NAD, 1946; Library of Congress, 1946; Carnegie, 1946, 52; WMAA Annuals, 1947-50, 1953-55; Chicago/AI, Abstract and Surrealist Art, 1948; U. of Illinois, 1950, 52; Chicago/AI, 1950, 54; I Sao Paulo Biennial, 1951; MOMA, XXVth Anniversary Exhibition, 1954; Federation of Modern Painters and Sculptors Annual, 1955; XXXV Venice Biennial, 1970; U. of Illinois, 1971. **Collections:** Albion College; Andover/Phillips; Baltimore/MA; Brooklyn Museum; Brown U.; Buffalo/Albright; Chase Manhattan Bank; Chicago/AI; Cincinnati/AM; Corcoran; Cornell U.; Currier; Dartmouth College; Evansville; U. of Georgia; U. of Illinois; Kalamazoo/Institute; Los Angeles/County MA; Louisville/Speed; MIT; MMA; MOMA; U. of Maine; U. of Michigan; U. of Minnesota; NYPL; National Gallery; New Orleans/Delgado; U. of North Carolina; The Ohio State U.; Omaha/Joslyn; PMA; Phoenix; RISD; SFMA; San Jose State College; Sao Paulo; Slater; Syracuse U.; Utica; WMAA; Yale U. **Bibliography:** Baur 5, 7; Blesh 1; Hayter 1; Janis, S.; Peterdi; Pousette-Dart, ed.; Reese; **Schmeckebier 1.** Archives.

MARIN, JOHN. b. December 3, 1870, Rutherford, N.J.; **d.** October 1, 1953, Cape Split, Me. **Studied:** Hoboken Academy; Stevens Preparatory School; Stevens Institute of Technology; PAFA, 1899-1901, with Thomas Anshutz, Henry Breckenridge; ASL, 1901-03, with Frank V. DuMond. Worked as a free-lance architect. Traveled Europe, 1905-11. **Member:** AAAL, 1945. **Awards:** Philadelphia Watercolor Club, 1940; American Institute of Architects, 1948; Hon. DFA, U. of Maine, 1940; MMA, 1952; PAFA, Joseph E. Temple Gold Medal, 1954; Hon. DFA, Yale U. **One-man Exhibitions:** (first) Photo-Secession, NYC, 1909, also 1910, 13, 15; Brooklyn Museum, 1922; Montross Gallery, NYC, 1922, 24; Stieglitz's Intimate Gallery, NYC, 1925, 28; An American Place (Gallery), NYC, 1929-35, 1937-42, 1944-50; Cleveland/MA, 1939; The Downtown Gallery, 1939, 48, 1950-54, 1963; ICA, Boston, 1947; de Young, 1949; XXV Venice Biennial, 1950; A.F.A., 1952-54; Detroit/Institute, 1954; Philadelphia Art Alliance, 1954; The Willard Gallery, 1965; La Jolla, 1966; M. Knoedler & Co., 1967; U. of Utah, 1969; PMA, 1969; Los Angeles/County MA, 1970; Marlborough Gallery Inc., NYC, 1972, 77, 78; Kennedy Galleries, Inc., 1981, 86; Portland Me./AM, 1985; Phillips, 1985. **Retrospectives:** The Daniel Gallery, NYC, 1920; MOMA, 1936; Trenton/State, 1950; U. of Michigan, 1951; Houston/MFA, 1953; AAAL, 1954; UCLA, 1955. **Group:** Salon d'Automne, Paris, 1908; Salon des Artistes Independants, Paris, 1904; The Armory Show, 1913; WMAA; MOMA; Chicago/AI; Detroit/Institute; Cleveland/MA; Walker; Cincinnati/AM; SFMA; Toronto; Dallas/MFA; Utica; Corcoran; MMA. **Collections:** Andover/Phillips; Arizona State U.; Auburn U.; Baltimore/MA; Brooklyn Museum; Buffalo/Albright; Chicago/AI; Cleveland/MA; Colorado Springs/FA; Columbus; Cranbrook; Denver/AM; Des Moines; Detroit/Institute; Fisk U.; U. of Georgia; Hagerstown/County MFA; Hartford/Wadsworth; Harvard U.; Houston/MFA; IBM; Indiana U.; Indianapolis/Herron; Lane Foundation; MMA; MOMA; U. of Maine; The Miller Co.; National Gallery; U. of Nebraska; Newark Museum; New Britain; Ogunquit; Omaha/Joslyn; PAFA; Phillips; U. of Rochester; Roswell; SFMA; St. Louis/City; San Antonio/McNay; San

Diego; Santa Barbara/MA; Springfield, Mo./AM; Utica; WMAA; Walker; Wellesley College; West Palm Beach/Norton; Wichita/AM; Wilmington; Yale U.; Youngstown/Butler. **Bibliography:** American Artists Group Inc. 3; *Avant-Garde Painting and Sculpture in America, 1910-25*; Baldinger; Becker 1; Barr 3; Baur 5, 7; Bazin; Beekman; Benson; Bethers; Biddle 4; Blesh 1; Born; Brown 1, 2; Bryant, L.; Cahill and Barr, eds.; Canaday; Cassou; Cheney; Chipp; Christensen; *Cityscape 1919-39*; Coke 2; Craven, T., 1; Downes, ed.; Dijkstra, ed.; *8 American Masters of Watercolor*; Eliot; Elsen 2; Flanagan; Flexner; Flockhart; *Forerunners*; Frank, ed.; Frost; Gallatin 1; Gaunt; Gerdts; Goldwater and Treves, eds.; Goodrich 1; Goodrich and Baur 1; Haas; Haftman; Hartmann; **Helm; Helm and Wight;** Hess, T. B., 1; Hunter 6; Huyghe; *Index of 20th Century Artists*; Janis, S.; Jewell 2; Johnson, Ellen H; Kootz 1, 2; Kuh 1, 3; Lane; Langui, Lee and Burchwood; Leepa; Mather 1; **McBride;** McCoubrey 1; McCurdy, ed.; Mellquist; Mendelowitz; Munsterberg; Neuhaus; Newmeyer; **Norman; Norman, ed.;** Pach 1; Pearson 2; Phillips 1, 2; Pousette-Dart, ed.; Raynal 3, 4; Read 2; Richardson, E.P.; Ritchie 1; Rodman 2; Rose, B., 1, 4; Rosenblum 1; Rubin 1; Sachs; **Seligmann, ed.;** Soby 5, 6; Sutton; Tashijan; Tomkins and Time-Life Books; Valentine 2; Wight 2; Wright 1; Zigrosser 1. Archives.

MARISOL (Escobar). b. May 22, 1930, Paris, France. **Studied:** ASL, 1950, with Yasuo Kuniyoshi; Hofmann School, 1951-54; Academie des Beaux-Arts, Paris, 1949; New School for Social Research, 1951-54. Traveled Venezuela, USA, Europe. Designed sets for Martha Graham and Louis Falco dance companies. **Awards:** Academy of Achievement, San Diego; Hon. DFA, Moore College of Art. **Taught:** State U. of Montana. **Member:** AAAL. **Address:** 427 Washington Street, NYC

Marisol *Portrait of William Burroughs* 1981

10013. **Dealer:** Sidney Janis Gallery, NYC. **One-man Exhibitions:** (first) Leo Castelli Inc., NYC, 1957; The Stable Gallery, NYC, 1962, 64; Arts Club of Chicago, 1965; Sidney Janis Gallery, NYC, 1966, 67, 73, 75, 81, 84; Hanover Gallery, 1967; XXIV Venice Biennial, 1968; Moore College of Art, Philadelphia, 1970; Worcester/AM, 1971; New York Cultural Center, 1973; Ohio U., 1974; Estudio Actual, Caracas, 1974; Makler Gallery, Philadelphia, 1975; Houston/Contemporary, 1977. **Group:** Festival of Two Worlds, Spoleto, 1958; Dallas/MFA, Humor in Art, 1958; Chicago/AI, Pan American Art, 1959; Carnegie, 1959, 64, 67; U. of Illinois, 1961; MOMA, The Art of Assemblage, circ., 1961; A.F.A., Wit and Whimsy in 20th

Century Art, circ., 1962-63; WMAA Annuals, 1962, 64, 66; MOMA, Americans 1963, circ., 1963-64; Chicago/AI, 1963, 66, 68; Tate, Painting and Sculpture of a Decade, 1954-64, 1964; The Hague, New Realism, 1964; WMAA, Art of the U.S. 1620-1966, 1966; II Internationale der Zeichnung, Darmstadt, 1967; Los Angeles/County MA, American Sculpture of the Sixties, 1967; Houston Festival of Arts, 1967; ICA, London, 1968; MOMA, circ., 1968-70; Finch College, NYC, The Dominant Woman, 1968; Chicago/AI, 1969; Hayward Gallery, London, Pop Art, 1969; Carnegie, 1970; Foundation Maeght, 1970; Skidmore College, Contemporary Women Artists, 1970; Potsdam/SUNY, Contemporary Women Artists, 1972; Baltimore/MA, Drawing Exhibition, 1973; Art Students League, 100th Anniversary, NYC, 1975; New York Cultural Center, The Nude in America, 1975; Hirshhorn, The Golden Door, 1976; Williamstown/Clark, The Dada/Surrealist Heritage, 1976; Bronx Museum, The Year of the Woman, 1976; San Antonio/McNay, Women Artists, 1976, 1977; Brooklyn Museum, Contemporary Women, 1977; U. of Missouri, The Opposite Sex, 1979; Ridgefield/Aldrich, New Dimensions in Drawing, 1981; Hirshhorn, Drawings 1974-1984, 1984. **Collections:** Arts Club of Chicago; Brandeis U., Buffalo/Albright; Caracas/Contemporaneo; Chicago/AI; Chicago/Contemporary; Cologne; Hakone Open Air Museum, Japan; MMA; MOMA; Memphis/Brooks; Ringling; WMAA. **Bibliography:** Bihalji-Merin; Calas, N. and E.; Craven, W.; *From Foreign Shores;* Gettings; Hunter, ed.; Lippard 5; **Medina;** Nemser; Seitz 3; Seuphor 3; Trier 1; Tuchman 1; Weller. Archives.

MARKMAN, RONALD. b. May 29, 1931, Bronx, N.Y. **Studied:** Yale U., BFA, 1957, MFA, 1959. US Army, 1952-54. Resided in Rome and London. **Taught:** U. of Florida, 1959; Chicago/AI, 1960-64; Indiana U., 1964.

Commissions: Murals for Riley Children's Hospital, Indianapolis, 1986. **Awards:** Fulbright Fellowship, 1962. **Address:** 719 South Jordan, Bloomington, IN 47401. **Dealers:** Terry Dintenfass, Inc., NYC; Dart Gallery, Inc., Chicago; Patrick King Gallery, Indianapolis. **One-man Exhibitions:** Terry Dintenfass, Inc., 1965, 66, 68, 71, 72, 76, 79, 82, 84, 85; Reed College, 1966; U. of Manitoba, 1972; Curwen Gallery, London (two-man), 1971; The Gallery, Bloomington, Inc., 1972, 79; Queens College, N.Y., 1972; Indianapolis, 1974; Indianapolis/Herron, 1976; Tyler School of Art, Philadelphia, 1976; Franklin College, 1980; J. Walter Thompson, NYC, 1977; Dart Gallery, Inc., 1981; Patrick King Gallery, 1983, 86; Indianapolis/Herron, 1985. **Group:** Boston Arts Festival, 1959, 60; WMAA, Young America, 1960; Chicago/AI, 1964; Ball State U., 1966; PAFA Annual, 1967; Anderson (Ind.) Fine Arts Center, 1967; Brooklyn Museum, Print Biennial; Indianapolis/Herron, 1968, 69; New School for Social Research, Humor, Satire, and Irony, 1972; Indianapolis, 1972, 74; Harvard U., Work by Students of Josef Albers, 1974; AAIAL, 1977; U. of New Mexico, Works on Paper, 1980. **Collections:** U. of Alberta; U. of Arkansas; Brooklyn Museum; Chicago/AI; Cincinnati/AM; Library of Congress; Cornell U.; Hirshhorn; Indiana U.; U. of Manitoba; MMA; MOMA; Worcester/AM.

MARSH, REGINALD. b. March 14, 1898, Paris, France; **d.** July 3, 1954, Dorset, Vt. **Studied:** The Lawrenceville School, 1915-16; Yale U., 1916-20, AB; ASL, 1919, 1920-24, 1927-28, with John Sloan, Kenneth Hayes Miller, George Bridgeman, George Luks. Traveled Europe extensively. Artist War Correspondent for *Life* magazine, 1943. **Taught:** ASL; Moore Institute of Art, Science and Industry, Philadelphia, 1953-54. **Commissions:** US Post Office, Washington, D.C., 1937; US Customs House, NYC, 1937. **Awards:**

MARSICANO, NICHOLAS 437

Chicago/AI, The M. V. Kohnstamm Prize, 1931; Wanamaker Prize, 1934; NAD, The Thomas B. Clarke Prize, Limited Editions Club, 1938; Chicago/AI, Watson F. Blair Prize, 1940; PAFA, Dana Watercolor Medal, 1941; NAD, 1943; Corcoran, First William A. Clark Prize, 1945; Salmagundi Club, NYC, T. J. Watson Prize, 1945; NIAL, 1946; NIAL, Gold Medal for Graphics, 1954. **One-man Exhibitions:** (first) Whitney Studio Club, NYC, 1924, also 1928; Curt Valentine Gallery, NYC, 1927; Weyhe Gallery, 1928; Marie Sterner Gallery, NYC, 1929; Rehn Galleries, 1930-34, 36, 38, 40, 41, 43, 44, 46, 48, 50, 53, 62, 64, 65, 70, 73; Yale U., 1937; Andover/Phillips, 1937; McDonald Gallery, NYC, 1939; Carnegie, 1946; Print Club of Cleveland, 1948 (two-man); Philadelphia Art Alliance, 1950; Martha Jackson Gallery, 1953; Steeplechase Park, Coney Island, NYC, 1953; Moravian College, 1954; Kennedy Gallery, 1964; Danenberg Gallery, 1969, 71; U. of Arizona, 1969; City Center Gallery, NYC, 1969; Sid Deutsch Gallery, NYC, 1981; WMAA (Phillip Morris), 1983; Richard Gray Gallery, 1984; Hirschl & Adler Galleries, 1986. **Retrospectives:** Gallery of Modern Art, NYC, 1964; Newport Harbor, 1972. **Group:** WMAA; MMA; MOMA; Corcoran; Carnegie. **Collections:** Andover/Phillips; Boston/MFA; Chicago/AI; Hartford/Wadsworth; MMA; U. of Nebraska; PAFA; Springfield, Mass./MFA; WMAA. **Bibliography:** American Artists Group Inc. 1, 3; Baigell 1; Barker 1; Baur 7; Bazin; Boswell 1; Brown 2; Bruce and Watson; Cahill and Barr, eds.; Canaday; Cheney; Christensen; *Cityscape 1919-39;* Craven, T., 2; Eliot; Flanagan; Flexner; Gerdts; **Goodrich** 1, **11;** Goodrich and Baur 1; Hall; Hunter 6; Kent, N.; Kuh 1; McCoubrey 1; McCurdy, ed.; **Marsh;** Mellquist; Mendelowitz; Moser 1; Newmeyer; Nordmark; Pagano; Pearson 1; Reese; Richardson, E.P.; Ringel, ed.; Rose, B., 1, 4; **Sasowsky;** Soyer, R. 1; Sutton; Wight 2. Archives.

MARSICANO, NICHOLAS. b. October 1, 1914, Shenandoah, Pa. **Studied:** PAFA and Barnes Foundation, 1931-34; abroad, 1933-36. Traveled Europe, North Africa, Mexico, USA. **Taught:** Cooper Union, 1948-; U. of Michigan, summer, 1950; Yale U., summers, 1951-54; Brooklyn Museum School, 1951-58; Pratt Institute, 1957-60; Cornell U., summer, 1959; Silvermine College of Fine Arts, 1965-69; Davenport/Municipal, summer, 1972; Purchase/SUNY, 1974. **Awards:** PAFA, Cresson Fellowship, and Barnes Foundation Scholarship, 1933-36; V. Hallmark International Competition, Second Prize, 1960; Guggenheim Foundation Fellowship, 1974. **Address:** 42 West 15th Street, NYC 10011. **Dealer:** Gruenebaum Gallery, NYC. **One-man Exhibitions:** The Salpeter Gallery, NYC, 1948; The Bertha Schaefer Gallery, 1957, 59, 60, 61; San Joaquin Pioneer Museum and Haggin Art Galleries, Stockton, Calif., 1959; Stewart Richard Gallery, San Antonio, 1959; The Howard Wise Gallery, NYC, 1963; Des Moines, 1963, 64; Huntington, W. Va., 1967; A. M. Sachs Gallery, 1971, 72, 73; Davenport/Municipal, 1972; Landmark Gallery, NYC, 1976; Utica, 1979; Gruenebaum Gallery, NYC, 1980. **Group:** U. of Nebraska, 1954, 58, 60; Walker, Vanguard, 1955; II Inter-American Paintings and Prints Biennial, Mexico City, 1960; A.F.A., The Figure, circ., 1960; WMAA Annuals, 1960-62; Chicago/AI, 1961, 64; Dallas/MFA, 1961, 62; MOMA, Abstract American Drawings and Watercolors, circ., Latin America, 1961-63; PAFA, 1962-64; MOMA, Recent Painting USA; The Figure, circ., 1962-63; U. of Kentucky, 1963; U. of Texas, 1968; MOMA, The New American Painting and Sculpture, 1969. **Collections:** Amarillo; Baltimore/MA; Chicago/AI; Ciba-Geigy Corp.; Dallas/MFA; Davenport/Municipal; Des Moines; Hallmark Collection; Housatonic Community College; Huntington, W. Va.; ICA, Boston; MIT; MOMA; U. of Massachusetts; NYU; U. of North Carolina;

Ridgefield/Aldrich; SFMA; U. of Texas. **Bibliography:** Archives.

MARTIN, AGNES. b. March, 1912, Maklin, Canada. **Studied:** Columbia U. Teachers College, 1941-42, 1951-52, with Arthur Young; Columbia U., MFA; Western Washington College; U. of New Mexico. To USA, 1932; citizen, 1950. Traveled the world; resided many U.S. locations. Stopped painting, 1967-74. **Awards:** National Endowment for the Arts Grant, $5,000, 1966. Did not paint 1967-74. Hon. DFA, New Mexico State U.; Skowhegan Medal for Painting, 1978. **Address:** Cuba, NM 87013. **Dealer:** The Pace Gallery, NYC. **One-man Exhibitions:** Betty Parsons Gallery, 1958, 59, 61; Robert Elkon Gallery, NYC, 1961, 63, 66, 70, 72, 76; Nicholas Wilder Gallery, 1966, 67, 73; Visual Arts Gallery, NYC, 1971; Kunstraum, Munich, 1973; Pasadena/AM, 1973; ICA, U. of Pennsylvania, 1973; MOMA, 1973; The Pace Gallery, 1975, 76, 77, 78, 79, 80, 81, 83, 84, 85; F.H. Mayor Gallery, London, 1978, 84; Galerie Rudolf Zwirner, Cologne, 1978; Harcus-Krakow Gallery, Boston, 1978; Margo Leavin Gallery, Los Angeles, 1979, 85; Santa Fe, N.M., 1979; Wichita State U., circ., 1980; Richard Gray Gallery, Chicago, 1981. **Retrospective:** Hayward Gallery, London, circ., 1977. **Group:** Carnegie, 1960; WMAA, Geometric Abstraction, 1962; Hartford/Wadsworth, Black, White, and Grey, 1964; SRGM, American Drawings, 1964, Systemic Painting, 1966; MOMA, The Responsive Eye, 1965; ICA, U. of Pennsylvania, A Romantic Minimalism, 1967; WMAA Annual, 1967; Detroit/Institute, Color, Image and Form, 1967; Corcoran, 1967; PMA, The Pure and Clear, 1968; Chicago/Contemporary, White on White, 1971-72; ICA, U. of Pennsylvania, Grids, 1972; Documenta V, Kassel, 1972; WMAA (downtown), Nine Artists/Coenties Slip, 1974; Amsterdam/Stedelijk, Fundamental Painting, 1975; U. of Massachusetts, Critical Per-

spectives in American Art, 1976; Venice Biennial, 1976; MOMA, Drawing Now, 1976; WMAA Biennial, 1977; Cleveland/MA, Four Contemporary Painters, 1978; Buffalo/Albright, American Painting of the 1970's; 1978; ICA, Boston, The Reductive Object, 1979; XXXIX Venice Biennial, 1980; Dublin/Municipal, International Quadriennial (ROSC), 1980; Corcoran Biennial, 1981; MOMA, Contrasts of Form: Geometric Abstract Art 1910-1980, 1985; AAIAL, 1983, 85. **Collections:** Aachen/NG; Amsterdam/Stedelijk; Albright/Buffalo; Canberra/National; Hartford/Wadsworth; High Museum; Hirshhorn; Israel Museum; La Jolla; Los Angeles/County MA; MOMA; NYU; Ontario; Pasadena/AM; Ridgefield/Aldrich; RISD; SRGM; Tate; Walker; WMAA; Worcester/AM; Yale U. **Bibliography:** DeWilde 2; *Fundamentele Schilderkunst;* Lippard 3; *Options and Alternatives.*

MARTIN, FRED. b. June 13, 1927, San Francisco, Calif. **Studied:** U. of California (with James McCray, Glenn Wessels), BA, 1949, MA, 1954; California School of Fine Arts (with David Park, Clyfford Still, Mark Rothko), 1949-50. **Taught:** Oakland/AM, 1954-56; San Francisco Art Institute, 1958-; Director, 1965-. **Awards:** National Council on the Arts Fellowship, 1971. **Address:** 232 Monte Vista, Oakland, CA 94611. **Dealer:** Quay Gallery, San Francisco. **One-man Exhibitions:** (first) Contemporary Gallery, Sausalito, Calif., 1949; Lucien Labaudt Gallery, San Francisco, 1950; Zoe Dusanne Gallery, Seattle, 1952; de Young, 1954, 64; 6 Gallery, San Francisco, 1955; Oakland/AM, 1958; SFMA, 1958; Spasta Gallery, San Francisco, 1959; Dilexi Gallery, San Francisco, 1961, 66, 68; Cain Gallery, Aspen, Colo., 1962; Minami Gallery, 1963; The Lanyon Gallery, 1964; Royal Marks Gallery, 1965, 66, 68, 70; RAC, 1969; Berkeley Gallery, San Francisco, 1970, 71; SFAI, 1972; SFMA, 1973; Quay Gallery, San Francisco, 1979. **Group:** de Young; California Palace; SFMA, Bay Area 1945-1962, 1968; WMAA Annual, 1969, Extraordinary Realities, 1973. **Collections:** Achenbach Foundation; Oakland/AM; Pasadena/AM; RAC; SFMA; WMAA. **Bibliography:** *Art as a Muscular Principle.* Archives.

MARTIN, KNOX. b. February 12, 1923, Barranquilla, Colombia. **Studied:** ASL. US Coast Guard, 1941-45. **Taught:** Yale U., 1965-71; ASL, 1972, 1974-; U. of Minnesota, 1972. **Member:** Society of American Magicians. **Commissions:** City Walls Inc., NYC, 1971; Mercor, Inc., Fort Lauderdale, 1972; Nieman Marcus Co., White Plains, N.Y., 1980; Mural for John Wayne School, Brooklyn, N.Y., 1982. **Address:** 128 Fort Washington Avenue, NYC. **One-man Exhibitions:** Charles Egan Gallery, 1954, 61; Avant Garde Gallery, NYC, 1956; Holland-Goldowsky Gallery, Chicago, 1958; Rose Fried Gallery, 1963; Fischbach Gallery, 1964, 66; Galeria Bonino Ltd., 1972, 74; Ingber Art Gallery, 1974, 76, 80, 82; IKI Dusseldorf, 1974; National Arts Club, NYC, 1975; Gallery G., Wichita, 1975; Jack Gallery, NYC, 1978; Jankovsky Gallery, NYC, 1975; River Gallery, Irvington-on-Hudson, 1980, 82; John Wayne School, Brooklyn, 1982. **Group:** WGMA, 1963; Chicago/AI, 1963; Baltimore/MA, 1963; Buffalo/Albright, 1963; WMAA, 1972; Bradford, England, British Print Biennial, 1974; Ljubljana (Yugoslavia) Biennial, 1981. **Collections:** Austin; Baltimore/MA; Bibliotheque Nationale, Paris; U. of California, Berkeley; Chicago/AI; Corcoran; Denver/AM; U. of Illinois; MOMA; U. of Miami; NYU; U. of North Carolina; WMAA.

MARTINELLI, EZIO. b. November 27, 1913, West Hoboken, N.J. **d.** 1981, Saugerites, N.Y. **Studied:** Academy of Fine Arts, Bologna, Italy, 1931; NAD, 1932-36, with Leon Kroll, Gifford Beal,

Robert Aitken (sculpture), Ivan Olinsky. Traveled France, Italy. **Taught:** Pennsylvania School of Industrial Art, Philadelphia, 1946-49; Philadelphia Museum School, 1946-49; Sarah Lawrence College, 1947-75; Parsons School of Design, 1953-78; American Academy, Rome, Artist-in-Residence, 1964-65 (appointed trustee, 1966). Painted only until 1952; began sculpture in 1938. Federal A.P.: Teacher, NYC; easel painter and unit supervisor, 1937-41. **Commissions:** United Nations General Assembly Building, NYC (30-ft. sculpture); Joint Industries Board, 1964 (bronze); Revere Aluminum Co., 1966 (aluminum). **Awards:** L. C. Tiffany Grant, 1936, 64; Guggenheim Foundation Fellowship, 1958, 62; NAD, President's Award; Ford Foundation, **P.P.,** 1963; appointed to the Jury of Selection, John Simon Guggenheim Memorial Foundation, 1963; Ford Foundation/A.F.A., Artist-in-Residence, Sarasota, 1964; NIAL, 1966. **One-man Exhibitions:** Philip Ragan Gallery, Philadelphia, 1943; The Willard Gallery, 1946, 47, 52, 55, 64, 66; Seattle/AM; U. of Minnesota; Chicago/AI; Benson Gallery, 1968. **Group:** Art of This Century, 1942-44; PAFA, 1944, 58, 64, 67; Brooklyn Museum, 1947; Chicago/AI, Abstract and Surrealist Art, 1948; WMAA Annuals, 1948, 61, 62, 66; Chicago/AI, Drawings, 1952; Contemporary American Drawings, circ., France, 1954; Walker, Expressionism, 1900-1955, 1956; A.F.A., Major Work in Minor Scale, circ., 1957; USIA, Eight American Artists, circ., Europe and Asia, 1957-58; VMFA, American Sculpture Today, 1958; Carnegie, 1959; NIAL, 1959, 66; WMAA, Business Buys American Art, 1960; Claude Bernard, Paris, Aspects of American Sculpture, 1960; Newark Museum, Survey of American Sculpture, 1962; Gallery of Modern Art, NYC, 1965; Lincoln, Mass./De Cordova, 1965; U. of St. Thomas (Tex.) 1966. **Collections:** Brooklyn Museum; Chicago/AI; U. of Illinois; Memphis/Brooks; Newark Museum; PMA; SRGM; Seattle/AM; United Nations; WMAA; U. of Wisconsin. **Bibliography:** Moser 1; Seuphor 3. Archives.

MARYAN. b. January 1, 1927, Poland; **d.** June 1977, NYC. **Studied:** Bezalel Art School; l'Ecole National Superieure des Beaux-Arts, Paris, 1951-53. Traveled Israel, Europe, USA; resided Paris, 1950-62; resided NYC, 1962-77; citizen, 1969. Produced film, *Ecce Homo*, 1975. **Awards:** Prix des Critiques d'Art a Paris, 1959; Order of Arts and Letters, France. **One-man Exhibitions:** (first) Jerusalem, Israel, 1949; Galerie Breteau, Paris, 1952; Galerie Le Miroir, Brussels, 1954; Tourcoing, 1956; Galerie Rive Gauche, Paris (two-man), 1957; Galerie de France, Paris, 1958, 60, 65, 78; Galerie Kunstnernes Kunsthandel, Copenhagen, 1959; Andre Emmerich Gallery, 1960; Allan Frumkin Gallery, NYC, 1963-66, 68, 69, 85; Chicago, 1963-66, 70; Galleria Juana Mordo, 1964; David Stuart Gallery, 1964; Galerie D. Benador, Geneva, 1966; Galerie Van der Loo, Munich, 1966; Galerie Nova Spectra; The Hague, 1966, 71; Claude Bernard, Paris, 1966, 70; Galeria Sen., Madrid, 1970; Galerie Nord, Lille, 1970; Eindhoven, 1970; Galerie Nicholas, Amsterdam, 1971, 73; Galeria d-Arte la Bussola, Turin, 1971; Galerie Espace, Amsterdam, 1973, 74; Galerie Ariel, Paris, 1977; U. of Haifa, 1979. **Retrospective:** Galerie de France, Paris, 1974. **Group:** Salon des Surindependants, Paris, 1952, 53; Salon du Mai, Paris, 1953-65; Festival de l'Art d'Avant-Garde, Marseilles, 1956; Paris Biennial, Musée de Nantes, 1958; Festival de Bayreuth, 1958; Walker, 1958, 59; XXX Venice Biennial, 1960; Carnegie, 1961, 64, 67; SFMA, Directions—Painting U.S.A., 1963; Torcuato di Tella, Buenos Aires, 1963; Ghent, The Human Figure since Picasso, 1964; The Hague, New Realism, 1964; Chicago/AI, 1964; Paris/Moderne, 1965; PAFA Annual, 1965; Foundation Maeght, 1967; U. of Colorado, 1967; MOMA, 1969; SRGM, 10

Independents, 1972. **Collections:** Carnegie; Chicago/AI; LeHavre/Municipal; MOMA; Museum des 20. Jahrhunderts; Paris/Moderne; Tel Aviv; Tourcoing.

MASON, ALICE TRUMBULL. b. November 16, 1904, Litchfield, Conn.; **d.** June 28, 1971, NYC. **Studied:** British School, Rome, 1972; NAD, 1923; privately with C. W. Hawthorne, 1924, and Arshile Gorky, 1926. Traveled Italy and around the world, 1920. **Member:** American Abstract Artists; Federation of Modern Painters and Sculptors; SAGA; American Color Print Society. **Awards:** The Print Club, Philadelphia, Charles M. Lea Prize, 1945; Longview Foundation Grant, 1963. **One-man Exhibitions:** (first) Museum of Living Art, NYC, 1948; Hansa Gallery, NYC, 1958; The XXth Century Gallery, NYC, 1967; Washburn Gallery, Inc., NYC, 1974, 77, 80, 82, 84, 85; Tulane U., 1982. **Retrospectives:** Nassau Community College, Garden City, N.Y., 1967; WMAA, circ., 1974. **Group:** Federation of Modern Painters and Sculptors Annuals; A.A.A. Gallery, NYC, Annuals: PMA, "8 × 8," 1945; Brooklyn Museum, 1949; Chicago/Contemporary, Post-Mondrian Abstraction in America, 1973; Springfield, Mass./MFA, Three American Purists, 1975; Los Angeles/County MA, Women Artists 1550-1950, 1976; Houston/MFA, Miró in America, 1982. **Collections:** Brooklyn Museum; Free Library of Philadelphia; Hirshhorn; ICA, Washington, D.C.; Library of Congress; MMA; MOMA; NYPL; U. of Nebraska; PMA; The Pennsylvania State U.; SRGM; Springfield, Mass./MA; WMAA. **Bibliography:** Lane and Larsen; Moser 1; Reese. Archives.

MATULKA, JAN. b. November 7, 1890, Vlachovo Brezi, Bohemia; **d.** June 22, 1972, Queens, N.Y. To USA, 1907. **Studied:** NAD, with G.W. Maynard, 1908-17. ASL, 1924-25. Traveled Europe, USA. **Taught:** ASL, 1929-31. Federal A.P.: Mural for a hospital in Brooklyn, N.Y. **Awards:** Pulitzer Scholarship for Painting. **One-man Exhibitions:** (first) The Artists' Gallery, NYC, 1925; Whitney Studio Club, NYC, 1926, 29; Art Center, NYC, 1926; Modern Gallery, NYC, 1927, also 1930; Rehn Galleries, 1928, 29, 31, 32, 33, 35, 56; The Zabriskie Gallery, 1965; SRGM; Columbia U., 72; ACA Gallery, NYC, 1944; Robert Schoelkopf Gallery, NYC, 1970, 72, 79; Bartholet Gallery, NYC, 1969, 79, 83. **Retrospective:** NCFA, 1979. **Group:** WMAA, 1944; MMA; Chicago/AI; Carnegie, 1944; U. of New Mexico, 1967; Galleries of the Societe Anonyme, NYC, Second Exhibition of Modern Art, 1920; Brooklyn Museum, 1923; Salon des Independants, Paris, 1924; AIGA, Annual, 1925, 26; PAFA, Annual, 1930, 31, 32, 33; Carnegie Annual, 1930, 33; WMAA, First Annual, 1931, 33, 36, 41, 44; WMAA, Abstract Painting in America, 1935; Delaware Art Museum, Avant-Garde Painting and Sculpture in America 1910-25, 1975; NCFA, America as Art, 1976; Houston/MFA, Modern American Painting 1910-40, 1977; WMAA, Synchromism and American Color Abstraction 1910-1925, 1978. **Collections:** ASL; Boston/MFA; Brooklyn Museum; Chicago/AI; Cincinnati/AM; Des Moines; Detroit/Institute; Hartford/Wadsworth; Hirshhorn; MMA; MOMA; Nashville; NCFA; U. of Nebraska; Newark Public Library; U. of New Mexico; U. of North Carolina; NYPL; PAFA; Portland (Ore.)/AM; Prague/National; Seattle/AM; SFMA; St. Louis/City; SRGM; Syracuse/Everson; WMAA; Yale U. **Bibliography:** *Avant-Garde Painting & Sculpture in America, 1910-25;* Blesh 1; Hunter; Hunter 6; Jan Matulka, Janis, S.; Lane and Larsen; Rose, B., 1.

MAYHEW, RICHARD. b. April 3, 1924, Amityville, N.Y. **Studied:** Brooklyn Museum School, with Edwin Dickinson, Reuben Tam. Traveled Eu-

rope, England. **Taught:** ASL, to 1969; Smith College, 1969-70; Pratt Institute; Hunter College, 1971-75; The Pennsylvania State U., 1977-. **Member:** NAD. **Awards:** John Hay Whitney Fellowship, 1958; Ingram Merrill Foundation Grant, 1960; L.C. Tiffany Grant, 1963; NAD, **P.P.,** 1964; NIAL Grant, 1966; NAD, Benjamin Altman Prize, 1970; NAD, Grumbacher Art Award and Gold Medal, 1983. **Address:** 539 Orlando Avenue, State College, Pa. 16803. **Dealer:** Osuna Gallery, Washington, D.C. **One-man Exhibitions:** The Morris Gallery, NYC, 1957; Washington Irving Gallery, NYC, 1958; Robert Isaacson Gallery, NYC, 1959, 61, 62; Durlacher Brothers, NYC, 1963, 66; The Contemporaries, NYC, 1967; The Midtown Galleries, 1969, 71, 73, 74; Grand Central Galleries, NYC; Hampton U. **Retrospective:** Studio Museum, 1978. **Group:** NAD, 1955, 59; Brooklyn Society of Artists Annual, 1956; ART: USA: 58, NYC, 1958; Chicago/AI, 1961; Youngstown/Butler, 1961; Carnegie, 1961; Brooklyn Museum, 1961; WMAA Annuals; U. of Illinois, 1963. **Collections:** Brooklyn Museum; MMA; Minnesota/MA; Museum of African Art, Washington, D.C.; NAD; NMAA; Newark Museum; Studio Museum; WMAA; Youngstown/Butler.

MAZUR, MICHAEL B. b. November 2, 1935, NYC. **Studied:** Amherst College, 1954-58, BA; Academy of Fine Arts, Florence, Italy, 1956-57; Yale U., with Gabor Peterdi, Rico Lebrun, Josef Albers, Jon Schueler, Bernard Chaet, Nicholas Carone, 1959-61, BFA, MFA; privately with Leonard Baskin (printmaking), 1956-58. **Taught:** Yale U., 1960-61, 1972; RISD, 1961-64; Yale U. Summer School, Norfolk, Conn., 1963; Brandeis U., 1965, 1972-; Queens College, 1973; Brown U., 1974; U. of California, Santa Barbara, 1974, 75. **Commissions:** US Department of the Interior; MIT, monotype mural, 1983. **Awards:** Memphis/Brooks, **P.P.,** 1961, 62; Boston Printmakers, **P.P.,** 1962;

L.C. Tiffany Grant, 1962; Guggenheim Foundation Fellowship, 1964; NIAL, 1964; Library of Congress, Pennell **P.P.**, SAGA, Second Prize; Tamarind Fellowship, 1968; NAD, 1974; Philadelphia Print Club, **P.P. Address:** 5 Walnut Avenue, Cambridge, MA 02140. **Dealers:** Barbara Krakow Gallery, Boston; Barbara Mathes Gallery, NYC; John Stoller & Co., Minneapolis; Jan Turner Gallery, Los Angeles. **One-man Exhibitions:** (first) The Kornblee Gallery, 1961, also 1962, 63, 65; The Gallery, Northampton, Mass., 1963; Boris Mirski Gallery, Boston, 1964; Silvermine Guild, 1964; Alpha Gallery, 1966, 68, 74; Juniata College, 1966; A.A.A. Gallery, NYC, 1968; Finch College, NYC, 1971; U. of Connecticut, 1972; Exeter, 1972; Kutztown State College, 1973; Cortland/SUNY (two-man), 1973; The Ohio State U., 1975; Colgate U., 1973; Terry Dintenfass, Inc., NYC, 1974, 76; Robert Miller Gallery, Inc., NYC, 1978, 80; Harcus Krakow Gallery, Boston, 1978, 80; College of William and Mary, 1981; The Greenberg Gallery, St. Louis, 1981; Rutgers U., 1981; John Stoller & Co., 1981, 85; Gustavus Adolphus College, St. Peter, Minn., 1982; Harcus Krakow Gallery, Boston, 1982; Smith-Anderson Gallery, Palo Alto, Calif., 1982; Janus Gallery, Venice, Calif., 1982, 84; MIT, 1983; Barbara Mathes Gallery, 1983, 84; Barbara Krakow Gallery, 1984; Arts Club of Chicago, 1985; Beaver College, 1986. **Retrospectives:** Brandeis U., 1969; Colgate U., 1973. **Group:** USIA, 10 American Printmakers, circ., Europe; MOMA, 60 Modern Drawings, 1963, also 1965; Library of Congress; Seattle/AM; Kansas City/Nelson; Smith College; The Print Club, Philadelphia; Boston Arts Festival; WMAA Annual, 1967; PAFA, 1967, 69; ICA, Boston, Boston Now; Boston/MFA, Prints of the Sixties; Salon du Mai, Paris, 1969; Museo de Arte Contemporaneo, Cali., Colombia, S.A., I & II Biennials Graficas; XXXV Venice Biennial, 1970; Pratt Graphics Center, NYC, Monotypes, 1972; Library of Congress, 1972,

73, 74; Cleveland/MA, 32 Realists, 1972; Omaha/Joslyn, A Sense of Place, 1973; MOMA, American Prints: 1913-1963, 1974-75; Smithsonian, New American Monotypes, circ., 1978-80; Brussels/Beaux Arts, La Nouvelle Subjectivite, 1979; MMA, The Painterly Print, 1980; Brooklyn Museum, American Drawings in Black and White: 1970-1979; 1980; WMAA, American Prints: Process and Proofs, 1981; Boston/MFA, Contemporary Realist Paintings, 1983; PAFA, Perspectives on Contemporary American Realism, 1983; IEF, Twentieth Century American Drawings: The Figure in Context, circ., 1984; SFMA, American Realism (Janss), circ., 1985. **Collections:** Amherst College; Andover/Phillips; Boston/MFA; Boston Public Library; Brandeis U.; Brooklyn Museum; Chicago/AI; Cincinnati/AM; Colgate U.; Cortland/SUNY; Delaware Art Museum; Fredonia/SUNY; Harvard U.; Kalamazoo/Institute; Library of Congress; Los Angeles/County MA; MIT; MMA; MOMA; U. of Maine; U. of Massachusetts; Memphis/Brooks; Minneapolis/Institute; Montreal/MFA; The Ohio State U.; PMA; The Pennsylvania State U.; Portland, Ore./AM; RISD; Rutgers U.; Smith College; Toledo/MA; USIA; WMAA; Wellesley College; Westminster Foundation; Worcester/AM; Yale U. **Bibliography:** *America 1976; Arthur 2; Goldman 1.*

McCHESNEY, ROBERT P. b. January 16, 1913, Marshall, Mo. **Studied:** Washington U., with Fred Conway; Otis Art Institute, Los Angeles. Resided Mexico, one year. Traveled around the world, Mexico, Cuba. **Taught:** California School of Fine Arts, 1949-51; Santa Rosa Junior College, 1957-58. Federal A.P.: Federal Building, Golden Gate International Exposition, San Francisco, 1939 (mural). **Member:** San Francisco Art Institute, board of trustees. **Commissions:** SS *Monterey* (wall decoration); San Francisco Social Service Building (mural), 1978.

Awards: San Francisco Municipal Art Commission, **P.P.,** 1950, 69; WMAA Annual, **P.P.,** 1955; SFMA, First Prize, 1960; San Francisco Art Festival, Prize, 1979. **Address:** 2955 Sonoma Mountain Road, Petaluma, CA 94952. **One-man Exhibitions:** (first) Raymond and Raymond, Inc., San Francisco, 1944; Pat Wall Gallery, Monterey, 1946; Lucien Labaudt Gallery, San Francisco, 1947, 51; Marquis Gallery, Los Angeles, 1949; SFMA, 1949, 53, 57, 64; Daliel Gallery, Berkeley, 1950; Gump's Gallery, 1952, 53, 55; Myrtle Todes Gallery, Glencoe, Ill., 1958; Bolles Gallery, NYC, 1960; San Francisco, 1960, 61; Parsons Gallery, Los Angeles, 1960, 61; Marshall Art Gallery, Marshall, Calif., 1964; Twentieth Century West Gallery, NYC, 1965; Triangle Art Gallery, 1966; San Francisco Theological Seminary, San Anselmo, Calif., 1966, 69; California State College, Sonoma, 1970; Both-Up Gallery, Berkeley, Calif., 1973, 74; Santa Rosa City Hall, Calif., 1974; California State U., Hayward, 1977; Capricorn Asunder Gallery, San Francisco, 1974; Lincoln Arts Center, Santa Rosa, 1978; Marin County Civic Center, 1980. **Retrospective:** Capricorn Asunder Gallery, San Francisco, 1974. **Group:** SFMA, 1945, 50, 53, 60; Phillips, 1947; de Young, 1947, 51, 53, 59, 60, 61; Chicago/AI Annuals, 1947, 54, 60, 61; Los Angeles/County MA, 1949; Sao Paulo, 1955; WMAA Annual, 1955; Corcoran, 1957; California Palace, 1962, 64; Oakland/AM, 1972; Reed College, 1973; UCLA Extension Gallery, 1975. **Collections:** Chicago/AI; Oakland/AM; SFMA; San Francisco Municipal Art Commission; WMAA. **Bibliography:** McChesney. Archives.

McCRACKEN, JOHN. b. December 9, 1934, Berkeley, Calif. **Studied:** California College of Arts and Crafts, 1962, BFA, and 1962-65. **Taught:** U. of California, Irvine and Los Angeles, 1965-68; School of Visual Arts, NYC, 1968-69; Hunter College, NYC, 1971; U. of Nevada. **Address:** % Dealer.

Dealer: Elkon Gallery, NYC. **One-man Exhibitions:** Nicholas Wilder Gallery, 1965, 67, 68; Robert Elkon Gallery, 1966, 67, 68, 72, 73; Ileana Sonnabend Gallery, Paris, 1969, Toronto, 1969, NYC, 1970; ACE Gallery, Vancouver, 1970; Pomona College, 1971; U. of Nevada, 1974. **Retrospective:** P.S. 1, Long Island City, 1986. **Group:** Barnsdall Park Municipal Art Gallery, Los Angeles, Los Angeles Sculpture, 1965; Jewish Museum, Primary Structure Sculptures, 1966; WMAA, 1966, 68, 70; Seattle/AM, Ten from Los Angeles, 1966; Los Angeles/County MA, Sculpture of the Sixties, circ., 1967; WGMA, A New Aesthetic, 1967; Paris/Moderne, 1967; Milwaukee, Directions 1: Options, circ., 1968; MOMA, The Art of the Real, 1968; ICA, U. of Pennsylvania, Between Object and Environment, 1969; Eindhoven, Kompas IV, 1969-70; Chicago/AI, 1970; Chicago/Contemporary, Permutations: Light & Color, 1970; MOMA, Ways of Looking, 1971; Documenta V, Kassel, 1972. **Collections:** Chicago/AI; Los Angeles/County MA; MOMA; Milwaukee; Pasadena/AM; SRGM; Toronto; WMAA. **Bibliography:** *Report; USA West Coast.*

McFEE, HENRY LEE. b. April 14, 1886, St. Louis, Mo.; **d.** 1953, Claremont, Calif. **Studied:** Washington U. School of Fine Arts; ASL, Woodstock, N.Y., 1908, with Birge Harrison; Stevenson Art Center, Philadelphia. **Awards:** Carnegie, Hon. Men., 1923; Corcoran, Fourth William A. Clark Prize, 1928; Carnegie, First Hon. Men., 1930; VMFA, **P.P.,** 1935; PAFA, Joseph E. Temple Gold Medal, 1937; Los Angeles County Fair, **P.P.,** 1940, 49; Guggenheim Foundation Fellowship, 1941; NIAL, 1945; elected an associate of the NAD, 1949. **One-man Exhibitions:** Rehn Galleries, 1927, 29, 33, 36, 50; Pasadena/AM, 1950; Bucknell U., 1986. **Retrospective:** Scripps College, 1950. **Group:** Panama-Pacific Exposition, San Francisco, 1915; Detroit/Institute; Cleveland/MA; Anderson Galleries,

NYC, Forum Exhibition, 1916; Carnegie, 1923-49; Corcoran, 1924, 26, 1928-44; PAFA; Chicago/AI; St. Louis/City; U. of New Mexico, Cubism: Its Impact in the USA, 1967. **Collections:** Brooklyn Museum; Buffalo/Albright; Carnegie; Cleveland/MA; Columbus; Corcoran; Detroit/Institute; Los Angeles County Fair Association; MMA; PMA; Phillips; St. Louis/City; Scripps College; Taft Museum; VMFA; WMAA. **Bibliography:** Barker 2; Baur 7; Brown; Brown 2; Cahill and Barr, eds.; Cheney; Hall; Hunter 6; Huyghe; *Index of 20th Century Artists*; Janis, S.; Kent, N.; Mellquist; Mendelowitz; **Miller 1;** Pearson 2; Poore; Pousette-Dart, ed.; Richardson, E.P.; Smith, S.C.K.; Watson, E.W., 2; *Woodstock: An American Art Colony 1902-1977*; Wright 1.

McGARRELL, JAMES. b. February 22, 1930, Indianapolis, Ind. Resides Italy, 1971-. **Studied:** Indiana U., with Alton Pickens, Leo Steppat, AB; UCLA, with John Paul Jones, Gordon Nunes, MA; Skowhegan School; Academy of Fine Arts, Stuttgart. Traveled USA, Europe; resided Paris, 1964-65. **Taught:** Reed College, 1956-59; Indiana U., 1959-; Skowhegan School, summers, 1964, 68. Foreign correspondent member of the Academie des Beaux-Arts de l'Institut de France, 1970. **Member:** CAA, board of directors, 1969-73; National Advisory Board, Tamarind Institute, 1977-. **Awards:** Fulbright Fellowship, 1955; Tamarind Fellow, 1962; NIAL, Grant, 1963; Ford Foundation, **P.P.**, 1963, 64; J.S. Guggenheim Fellowship, 1964; National Council on the Arts, Sabbatical Grant to Artists Who Teach. **Address:** 5699 East Lampkins Ridge Road, Bloomington, IN 47401; Polgeto, 06019 Umbertide, Italy. **Dealer:** Allan Frumkin Gallery, NYC and Chicago; Galleria II Fante Di Spade, Milan; Galerie Claude Bernard, Paris. **One-man Exhibitions:** (first) Frank Perls Gallery, 1955, also 1957, 58, 62, 64; Portland, Ore./AM, 1959, 62; Indiana U., 1960, 63; Allan Frumkin Gallery,

Chicago, 1960, 62, 65, 67, 71, 74; Salt Lake Art Center, Salt Lake City, 1962; Gallery 288, St. Louis, 1963; U. of Florida, 1964; Galleria Galatea, Turin, 1965, 66, 68; Pittsfield/Berkshire, 1966; Tragos Gallery, Boston, 1967; Galleria II Fante de Spada, Rome, 1967, 71, 72, 74, 76; Claude Bernard, Paris, 1967, 68, 74; Galleria dei Lanzi, Milan, 1970, 72; Utah, 1972; Allan Frumkin Gallery, NYC, 1961, 64, 66, 71, 73, 78, 81, 84; Bedford House Gallery, London, 1973; Clark-Benton Gallery, Santa Fe, 1977; Frumkin & Struve Gallery, Chicago, 1979; Yares Gallery, Scottsdale, 1980; U. of Nebraska, 1980; Fountain Gallery, Portland, Ore., 1980, 82; Galleria Gian Ferrari, Milan, 1981; U. of New Mexico, 1982; Wentz Gallery, Portland, Ore., 1983; U. of Bridgeport, 1984; St. Louis/City, 1985; Southern Methodist U., 1985. **Group:** WMAA Annuals, 1957, 59, 60, 67; MOMA, New Images of Man, 1959; U. of Illinois, 1959, 61, 63; Carnegie, 1959, 64; III International Biennial Exhibition of Prints, Tokyo, 1962; WMAA, Fifty California Artists, 1962-63; Chicago/AI Annual, 1963; Tate, Dunn International, 1964; Documenta III, Kassel, 1964; PAFA, 1964; U. of Kentucky, 1966, Graphics 1968, 1968; XXXIV Venice Biennial, 1968; SFMA, 1968; Smithsonian, 1969; Indiana U., American Scene: 1900-1970, 1970; Le Centre Cultural Americain, Paris (fourman), 1971; Kansas City/AI, Narrative Painting, 1972; Dayton/AI, Eight American Painters, 1972; Galleria Communale d'Arte Contemporanea, Una Tendenza Americana, 1973; MOMA, American Prints 1913-1963, 1974-75; Boston U., Drawings by American Realists, 1977; WMAA, Art about Art, 1978; Venice Biennale, 1980; Houston/Contemporary, Modern American Paintings, circ., 1982. **Collections:** Baltimore/MA; Boston/MFA; Brooklyn Museum; Chicago/AI; Hamburg; Hirshhorn; Indiana U.; Kansas City/AI; Kansas City/Nelson; MOMA; U. of Massachusetts; National Gallery; U. of Nebraska; U. of Oregon; PAFA; Paris/Beaubourg; Paris/Moderne; Portland, Ore./AM; Reed College; SFMA; Santa Barbara/MA; U. of Texas; Utah; WMAA; U. of Wichita. **Bibliography:** Arthur 2; Geske; Honisch and Jensen, eds.

McLAUGHLIN, JOHN. b. May 21, 1898, Sharon, Mass.; **d.** March 1976, Dana Point, Calif. **Studied:** Roxbury Latin School; Andover/Phillips; self-taught in art. US Army Intelligence, 1941-45. Traveled the Orient, resided Japan for many years beginning 1935. Began to paint 1938. **Awards:** Tamarind Fellowship, 1963; Corcoran Biennial, Bronze Medal, 1967; National Council on the Arts, Visual Arts Award, 1967. **One-man Exhibitions:** Felix Landau Gallery, 1953, 58, 62, 63, 66; U. of California, Riverside, 1958; Long Beach/MA, 1960; K. Kazimir Gallery, Chicago, 1964; Occidental College, 1968; The Landau-Alan Gallery, NYC, 1968; U. of California, Irvine, 1971; Nicholas Wilder Gallery, 1972, 79; Andre Emmerich Gallery, NYC, 1972, 74, 79, 82; Corcoran and Corcoran, Coral Gables, 1973; Felicity Samuel Gallery, London, 1975; Galerie Andre Emmerich, Zurich, 1976, 81, 82; U. of California, Santa Barbara, 1978; Annely Juda Fine Art, London, 1981; Modern Galerie, Quadrat Bottrop, West Germany, 1981; Galerie Mueller-Roth, Stuttgart, 1981; James Corcoran Gallery, Los Angeles, 1982; Ulmer Museum, Ulm, West Germany, 1982; Gatodo Gallery, Tokyo, 1983, 85. **Retrospectives:** Pasadena/AM, 1956, 63; Corcoran, 1968; WMAA, 1974; La Jolla, 1973. **Group:** Los Angeles/County MA Annuals, 1949, 50, 54-60; California State Fair, 1950; Los Angeles/County MA; Contemporary Painting in the United States, 1951; Sao Paulo, 1955; SFMA, Art in the Twentieth Century, 1955; Corcoran, 1955; Long Beach/MA, Fifteen Americans, circ., 1956; Walker, 1956; Houston/MFA, The Sphere of Mondrian, 1957; VMFA, American Painting, 1958; U. of Nebraska, 1958;

Denver/AM, 1958; Los Angeles/County MA, Four Abstract Classicists, circ., 1959-61; ICA, London, 1960; A.F.A., Purist Painting, circ., 1960-61; SFMA, Fifty California Artists, circ., 1962; WMAA, Geometric Abstraction in America, circ., 1962; Chicago/AI, 1964; MOMA, The Responsive Eye, 1965; Corcoran, 1967; Pasadena/AM, West Coast: 1945-1969, 1969; Hayward Gallery, London, 11 Los Angeles Artists, 1971; MOMA, Color as Language, circ., 1975; Los Angeles/County MA, Los Angeles Hard Edge, 1977; Los Angeles/County MA, California: Five Footnotes to Modern Art History, 1977; Lincoln, Mass./De Cordova, Born in Boston, 1979; Claremont Colleges, Black and White Are Colors, 1979; Los Angeles/County MA, Art in Los Angeles, 1981; P.S. 1, Long Island City, Underknown, 1984; MOMA, Contrasts of Form: Geometric Abstract Art 1910-1980, 1985. **Collections:** Amherst College; Andover/Phillips; Bowdoin College; U. of California; Corcoran; Hartford/Wadsworth; Long Beach/MA; Los Angeles/County MA; MIT; MMA; MOMA; NCFA; U. of New Mexico; Oakland/AM; Pasadena/AM; Santa Barbara/MA; Stanford U. **Bibliography:** *Black and White Are Colors;* **John McLaughlin;** *7 Decades; The State of California Painting;* Tuchman 3; Weller. Archives.

McLEAN, RICHARD. b. April 12, 1934, Hoquiam, Wash. **Studied:** California College of Arts and Crafts, 1958, BFA; Mills College, 1962, MFA; Oakland/AM, 1962. US Army, 1958-60. Traveled Asia, Australia, Europe. **Taught:** San Francisco State U., 1963-; California College of Arts and Crafts, 1963-65. **Awards:** National Endowment for the Arts, 1986. **Address:** 5840 Heron Bridge, Oakland, CA 94718. **Dealer:** OK Harris Works of Art. **One-man Exhibitions:** Lucien Labaudt Gallery, San Francisco, 1957; RAC, 1963; Berkeley Gallery, San Francisco, 1964, 66, 68; Valparaiso U. (Ind.), 1965; U. of

Omaha, 1967; OK Harris Works of Art, NYC, (two-man) 1971, 73, 75, 78, 81, 83, 85; Galerie de Gestlo, Hamburg, 1976; John Berggruen Gallery, San Francisco, 1976; Lavignes-Bastille, Paris, 1984. **Group:** SFAI Annuals, 1961, 62, East Bay Realists, circ., 1966; Hayward Gallery, London, Four Painters, 1967; U. of Arizona, 80 Contemporaries in the West, 1967; U. of California, Davis, People Painters, 1970; WMAA, 22 Realists, 1970; Expo '70, Osaka, 1970; Chicago/Contemporary, Radical Realism, 1971; Documenta V. Kassel, 1972; Buffalo/Albright, Working in California, 1972; Stuttgart/WK, Amerikanischer Fotorealismus, cir., 1972; Cleveland/MA, 32 Realists, 1972; New York Cultural Center, Realism Now, 1972; Lunds Konsthall, Sweden, Amerikansk Realism, 1973; Los Angeles Municipal Art Gallery, Separate Realities, 1973; CNAC, Hyperrealistes Americains/Realistes Europeens, 1974; Hartford/Wadsworth, New/Photo Realism, 1974; Tokyo Biennial, 1974; Wichita State U., The New Realism, Rip-Off or Reality? 1975; Reed College, American Realism, 1975; Purchase/SUNY, Photo-Realist Watercolors, 1976; SFMA, Painting and Sculpture in California; The Modern Era, 1976; Stratford, Ontario, Aspects of Realism, 1976; California State U., Chicago, A comparative Study of 19th Century California Painting and Contemporary California Realism, 1977; Canberra/National, Illusion and Reality, 1977; Santa Barbara/MA; Photo-Realist Painting in California, 1980; Akron/AM, The Image in American Painting and Sculpture, 1981; PAFA, Contemporary American Realism Since 1960, 1981; San Antonio/MA, Real, Really Real, Super Real, circ., 1981; Palm Springs Desert Museum, The West as Art, 1982; U. of Santa Clara, Northern California Art of the Sixties, 1982; U. of California, Davis, Directions in Bay Area Painting, 1983; Laguna Beach Museum of Art, West Coast Realism, circ., 1983; Saitama/Modern, Realism Now, 1983;

U. of Nebraska, San Francisco Bay Area Painting, 1984; Isetan Museum of Art, Tokyo, American Realism: The Precise Image, 1985; Oakland/AM, Art in the San Francisco Bay Area, 1945-1980, 1985. **Collections:** Aachen/NG; A.V. Gunuchian, Inc.; Hannover/K-G; Milwaukee; NMAA; Oakland/AM; Omaha/Joslyn; Portland, Ore./AM; Reed College; Rotterdam; SFMA; SRGM; VMFA; WMAA. **Bibliography:** *Amerikanischer Fotorealismus;* Arthur 3; *Kunst un 1970;* Lindy; Sager; *The State of California Painting.*

McNEIL, GEORGE. b. February 22, 1908, NYC. **Studied:** Pratt Institute, 1927-29; ASL, 1930-33; Hofmann School, 1933-36; Columbia U., BS, MA, Ed.D. US Navy, 1943-46. Traveled Cuba, Europe, North Africa, the Orient. **Taught:** Pratt Institute, 1946-; U. of Wyoming, 1946-48; U. of California, Berkeley, 1955-56; Syracuse U., 1974; Columbia U., 1975. Federal A.P.: Designed abstract murals, 1935-40. **Awards:** Ford Foundation, **P.P.,** 1963; National Council on the Arts, 1966; Guggenheim Foundation Fellowship, 1969. **Address:** 195 Waverly Avenue, Brooklyn, NY 11205. **Dealer:** M. Knoedler & Co., Inc., NYC. **One-man Exhibitions:** (first) Lyceum Gallery, Havana, 1941; Black Mountain College, 1947; U. of Wyoming, 1948; U. of New Mexico, 1948; U. of Colorado, 1948; Charles Egan Gallery, Boston, 1953; Hendler Gallery, Philadelphia, 1954; Poindexter Gallery, 1957, 59; The Howard Wise Gallery, NYC, 1960, 62, 64, 67; Nova Gallery, Boston, 1961; Colby Junior College, 1965; U. of Texas, 1966; Great Jones Gallery, NYC, 1966; Des Moines, 1969; Pratt Institute, Manhattan Center, NYC, 1973; U. of California, Santa Cruz, 1974; Northern Arizona U., 1975; Landmark Gallery, NYC, 1975; Aaron Berman Gallery, NYC, 1977; Terry Dintenfass, Inc., NYC, 1979; Fort Lauderdale, 1982; U. of Connecticut, 1982; Gruenebaum Gallery, 1981, 83, 85. **Group:** American

Abstract Artists, 1936; MOMA, New Horizons in American Art, 1936; New York World's Fair, 1939; Chicago/AI, Abstact Painting and Sculpture in America, 1951; WMAA Annuals, 1953, 57, 61; Carnegie, 1953, 55, 58; Walker, 60 American Painters, 1960; Cleveland/MA, Some Contemporary American Artists, 1961; SRGM, Abstract Expressionists and Imagists, 1961; USIA, American Painting, circ., Latin America, 1961; PAFA, 1962; Hartford/Wadsworth, 1962; Chicago/AI, 1963; MOMA, Hans Hofmann and His Students, circ., 1963-64; WMAA, The 1930's, 1968; MOMA, The New American Painting and Sculpture, 1969; U. of New Mexico, American Abstract Artists, 1977. **Collections:** Alcoa; Brooklyn Museum; Ciba-Geigy Corp.; Cornell U., Fort Lauderdale; Havana/Nacional; U. of Michigan; MOMA; NYU; Newark Museum; U. of New Mexico; U. of North Carolina; Oklahoma; U. of Texas; WGMA; WMAA; Waitsfield/ Bundy; Walker. **Bibliography:** Passloff; Pousette-Dart, ed.; Ritchie 1; Sandler. Archives.

MEEKER, DEAN JACKSON. b. May 18, 1920, Orchard, Colo. **Studied:** Chicago Art Institute School, BFA, MFA; Northwestern U.; U. of Wisconsin. **Taught:** U. of Wisconsin, 1946-. **Awards:** Milwaukee, Medal of Honor, 1952, 56; Guggenheim Foundation Fellowship, 1959. **Address:** % Art Department, U. of Wisconsin, Madison, WI 33706. **Dealer:** Jane Haslem Fine Arts, Washington, D.C. **One-man Exhibitions:** Milwaukee, 1950; Lawrence College, 1953; U. of North Dakota, 1954; U. of Wisconsin, 1955; Chicago/AI, 1956; U. of New Mexico, 1956; Los Angeles/County MA, 1957; La Gravure, Paris, 1959; Maxwell Galleries, Ltd., San Francisco, 1968; Haslem Fine Arts, Inc., 1969; Jacques Baruch Gallery, 1974. **Group:** PAFA, 1946-53; Brooklyn Museum, 1951-55; Chicago/AI, 1952; SFMA, 1952-54; Walker, 1952-54; Chicago/AI, Exhibition Momentum,

1952-54; Milwaukee; Connecticut College; U. of Missouri; Lawrence College; Library of Congress, 1952, 54, 55; MMA, 1953; Seattle/AM, 1953-1955; The Hague, 1954; Boston/MFA, 1954-56; MOMA, 1955; Los Angeles/County MA, 1959. **Collections:** Beloit College; Bibliotheque Nationale; Boston/MFA; Brooklyn College; Carleton College; Cornell U.; Dallas/MFA; Denison U.; Denver/AM; Kansas City/Nelson; Library of Congress; Lincoln, Mass./De Cordova; MOMA; Milwaukee; U. of Oklahoma; PAFA; The Print Club, Philadelphia; SFMA; Seattle/AM; USIA; Victoria and Albert Museum; U. of Wisconsin. **Bibliography:** Hayter 1.

MEIGS, WALTER. b. September 21, 1918, NYC. **Studied:** Ecole des Beaux-Arts, Fontainebleau, Diplome, 1939; Syracuse U., BFA, 1941; State U. of Iowa, MFA, 1949; and with R. Lotterman. US Army, more than three years, World War II. Traveled France, Greece; resided Greece, 1961-64, Spain, 1965-. **Taught:** U. of Nebraska, 1949-53; U. of Connecticut, 1953-61. **Awards:** Walker, 1951; Silvermine Guild, 1954; Slater, First Prize, 1955, 56; Boston Arts Festival, Grand Prize, 1956; and some 20 others. **Address:** Candelaria, Tenerif, Canarias, Spain. **Dealer:** Harmon-Meek Gallery, Naples, Fla. **One-man Exhibitions:** (first) The Downtown Gallery; U. of Nebraska, 1952; The Alan Gallery, NYC, 1954; Wesleyan U., 1956; New London, 1956; Boris Mirski Gallery, Boston, 1957; Lee Nordness Gallery, NYC, 1958, 64, 67; Lincoln, Mass./De Cordova, 1959; Frank Oehlschlaeger Gallery, Sarasota, Fla., 1965; Harmon Gallery, Naples, Fla., 1966, 70-80; Florida Southern College, 1979; Harmon-Meek Gallery, 1981. **Group:** Walker Biennial, 1951; Omaha/Joslyn, 1952; Boston Arts Festival; Berkshire Art Festival; Youngstown/Butler, 1957; Carnegie; WMAA Annuals; U. of Illinois. **Collections:** Amherst College; Birmingham,

Ala./MA; Denver/AM; Fort Worth; Hartford/Wadsworth; Lincoln, Mass./ De Cordova; The Pennsylvania State U.; Springfield, Mo./AM; USIA; Utica; Youngstown/Butler. **Bibliography:** Nordness, ed. Archives.

MENKES, SIGMUND. b. May 7, 1896, Lwow, Poland. **Studied:** In Europe. Traveled France. To USA, 1936. **Member:** NAD; Federation of Modern Painters and Sculptors. **Awards:** Corcoran, 1941, First Prize, Gold Medal, 1947; PAFA, Medal, 1945; NIAL, 1955; ART:USA:58, NYC, 1958; Audubon Artists, Gold Medal of Honor, 1965, Silver Anniversary Medal, 1967; Polish Institute of Arts and Sciences, Award for Collective Work, 1968. **Address:** 5075 Fieldstone Road, Riverdale, N.Y. **One-man Exhibitions:** Mrs. Cornelius J. Sullivan Gallery, NYC; Le Portique, Paris, 1928; A.A.A. Gallery, NYC, 1936-54; Durand-Ruel Gallery, NYC, 1941. **Group:** Carnegie; Chicago/AI; Corcoran; PAFA; U. of Nebraska; Cleveland/MA; American U.; State U. of Iowa; Cranbrook; MMA; WMAA; Toronto. **Collections:** Abbott Laboratories; Belgrade/National; Britannica; Brooklyn Museum; Cranbrook; Davenport/Municipal; Denver/AM; Greece/ National; Hirshhorn; Jerusalem/ National; MMA; U. of Miami; Montclair/AM; Musée du Jeu de Paume; NIAL; PAFA; Tel Aviv; WMAA; Walker; Warsaw/National; Wichita/ AM. **Bibliography:** Genauer; Pousette-Dart, ed.; Zaidenberg, ed.

MESIBOV, HUGH. b. December 29, 1916, Philadelphia, PA. **Studied:** Graphic Sketch Club, Philadelphia; PAFA; Barnes Foundation. Traveled Europe, Mediterranean, Israel, USA. **Taught:** Lenox Hill Neighborhood Association, NYC, 1949-57; Wiltwyck School for Boys, Esopus, N.Y., 1957-66; Rockland Community College, Suffern, N.Y., 1966-86. **Member:** PAFA Fellowship Association; Philadelphia Watercolor Club. Federal A.P.: Graphics, drawings, watercolors, oils, mural design. **Commissions:** US Post Office, Hubbard, Ohio (mural). **Awards:** The Print Club, Philadelphia, 1941, 46; Hallmark International Competition, 1952; PAFA, 1952, 58; Philadelphia Watercolor Club, Thornton Oakley Memorial Prize, 1968, 76. **Address:** 377 Saddle River Road, Chestnut Ridge, NY 10952. **One-man Exhibitions:** (first) Carlen Gallery, Philadelphia, 1940; Philadelphia Art Alliance, 1945; Chinese Gallery, NYC, 1947; Bookshop Gallery, Aspen, Colo., 1951, 53; The Morris Gallery, NYC, 1954; Pied Piper Gallery, Aspen, Colo., 1954; Artists' Gallery, NYC, 1956, 58; Sunken Meadow Gallery, Kings Park, N.Y., 1958; Gallery Mayer, NYC, 1959; Elizabeth Nelson Gallery, Chicago, 1962; Rockland Community College, 1964-68, 69, 72; Mansfield State College, 1968; High Point Galleries, Lenox, Mass., 1968; Tappan Zee Theater, Nyack, N.Y., 1967, 68, 69; St. Thomas Aquinas College, Sparkhill, N.Y., 1971; Finkelstein Memorial Library, Spring Valley, N.Y., 1978; Hopper House Gallery, Nyack, N.Y., 1979, 82; Ringwood Manor Art Association, Ringwood, N.J., 1983. **Group:** New York World's Fair, 1939; Carnegie, 1939; Philadelphia Art Alliance, 1940, 41, 45; Harrisburg, Pa.; PAFA, 1943, 1952-55, 57; Library of Congress, 1951; Brooklyn Museum, 1951, 1953-55; WMAA, 1956-59; Corcoran, 1959; MOMA, 1961; Philadelphia Art Alliance, 1967; AAAL, 1967. **Collections:** Albion College; Barnes Foundation; Canadian Society of Graphic Art; Carnegie; Free Library of Philadelphia; MMA; NYU; New York Hilton Hotel; U. of Oregon; PAFA; PMA; WMAA; U. of Wyoming.

MIDDAUGH, ROBERT. b. 1935, Chicago, Ill. **Studied:** U. of Illinois, 1954-55; Chicago Art Institute School, 1960-64, BFA. **Address:** 1318 West Cornelia, Chicago, Ill. 60657. **Dealer:** Fairweather-Hardin Gallery, Chicago. **One-**

man Exhibitions: Kovler Gallery, Chicago, 1965, 67, 69; Covenant Club, Chicago, 1966; Barat College, 1970; Martin Schweig Gallery, St. Louis, 1970, 72, 79, 83; Deson-Zaks Gallery, Chicago, 1974; St. Mary's College, 1975; U. of Wisconsin, Milwaukee, 1976; Fairweather-Hardin Gallery, 1977, 80, 83; Racine, 1980; Countryside Art Center, Arlington Heights, Ill., 1981; Evanston, 1982; Fine Arts Forum, Chicago, 1982; Lake Forest College, 1982; U. of Wisconsin, Marinette, 1982. **Group:** Chicago/AI, 2nd Biennial, 1964; U. of Illinois, Biennial, 1965; Chicago/AI, Chicago and Vicinity, 1966, 73, 78; PAFA, Annual, 1967; U. of Chicago, The Chicago Style: Graphics, 1974; AAIAL, 1975; Chicago/AI, 100 Artists-100 Years, 1979; U. of Wisconsin, Other Realities, 1981. **Collections:** Boston/MFA; Chicago/AI; Davenport; Des Moines; Los Angeles/County MA; Mobile/FAMS; Northern Illinois U.; Phoenix; Portland, Ore./AM; Springfield, Ill./State; Worcester.

MILLER, KENNETH HAYES. b. March 11, 1878, Oneida, N.Y. **d.** January 1, 1952, NYC. **Studied:** ASL, with H.S. Mowbray, Kenyon Cox, F.L. Mora, Frank V. DuMond. Traveled Europe. **Taught:** New York School of Art, 1899-1911; ASL, 1911-35, 1937-43, 1945-52. **Member:** NAD; Artists Equity; NIAL. **Awards:** Chicago/AI, Ada S. Garrett Prize, 1945; NAD, Gold Medal, 1943; NIAL, 1947. **One-man Exhibitions:** Montross Gallery, NYC, 1922, 23, 25, 28; Rehn Galleries, 1929, 35; Utica, 1953; ASL, 1953; The Zabriskie Gallery, NYC, 1970, 71, 79; AAA, NYC, 1979; Bethesda Art Gallery, Bethesda, Md., 1981. **Group:** Chicago/AI; The Armory Show, 1913; Buffalo/Albright; RISD, PAFA; Musée de Luxembourg; Paris; Brooklyn Museum; Carnegie; Corcoran; NAD; WMAA. **Collections:** Andover/Phillips; Bibliotheque Nationale; Chicago/AI; Cleveland/MA; Columbus; Hartford/Wadsworth; Hirshhorn; Library of

Congress; Los Angeles/County MA; MMA; MOMA; NMAA; NYPL; PAFA; Phillips; San Diego; Utica; VMFA; WMAA; Youngstown/Butler. **Bibliography:** Brown 2. Archives.

MILLER, RICHARD. b. March 15, 1930, Fairmount, W. Va. **Studied:** PAFA, with Franklin Watkins, 1948; American U., with William H. Calfee, BA, 1949-53; Columbia U., with John Heliker, MA, 1956. Traveled Europe and USA extensively. **Taught:** Kansas City/AI, 1968-69; Scarsdale Studio School, 1970-75; Rye Art Center, 1976-80; Westchester Community College, 1979-86; privately. Professional actor-singer. **Commissions:** General Motors Building, NYC. **Awards:** Gertrude V. Whitney Scholarship, 1948, 56; Fulbright Fellowship (Paris), 1953. **Address:** 222 West 83rd Street, NYC 10024. **One-man Exhibitions:** (first) Washington D.C., Public Library, 1945; Trans-Lux Gallery, Washington, D.C., 1948; Watkins Gallery, Washington, D.C., 1951; Bader Gallery, Washington, D.C., 1954, 61; Baltimore/MA, 1955; The Graham Gallery, 1960, 62, 63, 65; Jefferson Place Gallery, 1966; Drew U., 1967; Jewish Community Center, Kansas City, Mo., 1969; Albrecht Gallery, St. Joseph, Mo., 1969; Long Island U., 1973; Rye (N.Y.) Library Gallery, 1980; Westbeth Gallery, NYC, 1982; Aaron Berman, NYC, 1983. **Group:** WMAA Annual; PAFA Annual; WMAA, Fulbright Artists, 1958; Salon National, Paris; Pan-American Union, Washington, D.C.; U. of Nebraska; San Antonio/McNay, 1960; Carnegie, 1961; Corcoran, 1961; Finch College; V International Biennial Exhibition of Prints, Tokyo, 1966. **Collections:** U. of Arizona; Columbia U.; Hirshhorn; Phillips; U. of Rochester; St. Joseph/Albrecht.

MILLER, RICHARD McDERMOTT. b. April 30, 1922, New Philadelphia, Ohio. **Studied:** Cleveland Institute of

Art, 1940-42, 1949-52. US Army, 1942-46. Traveled Mexico, Europe, China. **Taught:** Queens College, City University of New York, 1967-. **Members:** Sculptors Guild; NAD Alliance of Figurative Artists. **Awards:** May Page Scholarship, Cleveland Institute of Art, 1951; Youngstown/Butler, **P.P.,** 1970; NAD, Elizabeth N. Watrous Gold Medal, 1974; AAIAL, 1978. **Address:** 61 Grove Street, NYC 10014. **One-man Exhibitions:** Peridot Gallery, 1964, 66, 67, 69; Holland Gallery, 1965; Feingarten, 1966; Duke U., 1967; Raleigh/NCMA, 1967; Cleveland/MA 1968; Alwin Gallery, London, 1968; Columbia, S.C./MA, 1969; Duke U. (two-man), 1971; Washburn Gallery, Inc., 1971, 74, 75, 77; Joe deMers Gallery, Hilton Head, S.C., 1971; Queens College, N.Y., 1978; Canton Art Institute, 1980; Imprimature Gallery, Minneapolis, 1985; Springfield, Mo./AM, 1985. **Retrospective:** Artist's Choice Museum, NYC, 1985. **Group:** WMAA, Sculpture Annual, 1964; NIAL, 1965; New Paltz/SUNY, 20 Representational Artists, 1969; Baltimore/MA, The Part Is the Whole, 1969; Youngstown/Butler, Sculpture Annual, 1970, 71; U. of Nebraska, American Sculpture, 1970, 73; St. Cloud State College, New Realism, '70, 1970; WMAA Biennial, 1971; The Pennsylvania State U., Living American Artists and the Figure, 1974; New York Cultural Center, Three Centuries of the American Nude, 1975; Sculptors Guild Annual, NYC, 1977; Nassau County Museum, Monuments and Monoliths: A Metamorphosis, 1978; PAFA, Contemporary American Realism Since 1960, 1981; Pratt Institute, Sculpture of the 70s: The Figure, 1981. **Collections:** Ashland Oil Inc., NYC; Canton Art Institute; Columbia, S.C./MA; Duke U.; Hirshhorn; U. of Houston; Massillon Museum; U. of Nebraska; U. of North Carolina; Union National Bank & Trust Co., Kansas City, Mo.; WMAA; Youngstown/Butler.

MITCHELL, FRED. b. November 24, 1923, Meridian, Miss. **Studied:** Carnegie Institute of Technology, 1942-43; Cranbrook Academy of Art, 1946-48, BFA, MFA; Academy of Fine Arts, Rome. **Taught:** Cranbrook Academy of Art, 1955-59; Positano (Italy) Art Workshop, 1956; NYU, 1961-; Cornell U., 1969; Binghamton/SUNY, 1976-; Utica, 1977. A cofounder of the Tanager Gallery, NYC. **Commissions:** Mississippi State College for Women (cast concrete screen). **Awards:** Scholarship to Carnegie Institute of Technology; Traveling Fellowship (Italy), 1948-51; Ford Foundation Artist-in-Residence, Columbia, S.C./MA. **Address:** 92 Hester Street, NYC 10002. **One-man Exhibitions:** (first) Municipal Gallery Jackson, Miss., 1942; Tanager Gallery, NYC, 1953; Positano (Italy) Art Workshop, 1956; The Howard Wise Gallery, Cleveland, 1957, 59; The Howard Wise Gallery, NYC, 1960, 63; i Gallery, La Jolla, 1964; Kasha Heman, Chicago, 1964; Columbia, S.C./MA, 1965; Wooster Community Center, Danbury, Conn., 1966; Cornell U. (three-man), 1969; Roko Gallery, 1973; Landmark Gallery, NYC, 1982. **Group:** SRGM, Younger American Painters, 1954; Dallas/MFA, 1954; Walker, Vanguard, 1955; Cranbrook. 1958; Carnegie, 1961. **Collections:** Columbus; Cranbrook. **Bibliography:** Archives.

MITCHELL, JOAN. b. February 21, 1926, Chicago, Ill. **Studied:** Smith College, 1942-44; Columbia U.; Chicago Art Institute School, 1944-47, BFA; NYU, 1950, MFA. Resides in France. **Awards:** Hon. DFA, Miami U., 1971; Brandeis U., Creative Arts Award, 1974. **Address:** La Tour, Avenue Claude Monet, Vetheuil, 95510, France. **Dealer:** Xavier Fourcade, Inc., NYC. **One-man Exhibitions:** U. of Illinois, 1946 (two-man, with Richard Bowman); St. Paul Gallery, 1950; The New Gallery, NYC, 1952; The Stable Gallery, 1953, 54, 55, 57, 58, 61, 65; Galerie Neufville, Paris, 1960; B. C.

Holland Gallery, 1961; Dwan Gallery; Southern Illinois U.; Jacques Dubourg, Paris, 1962; Galerie Lawrence, Paris, 1962; Klipstein & Kornfeld, Berne, 1962; MIT, 1962; Galerie Fournier, Paris, 1967, 69, 71; Martha Jackson Gallery, 1968, 71, 72; Syracuse/Everson, 1972; Ruth S. Schaffner Gallery, Santa Barbara, 1974; Arts Club of Chicago, 1974; Galerie Jean Fournier, Paris, 1976, 78, 80, 83; Xavier Fourcade, Inc., NYC, 1976, 77, 80, 81, 83, 85; Ruth S. Schaffner Gallery, Los Angeles, 1978; Webb & Parsons, Bedford Village, N.Y., 1978; Paule Anglim Gallery, San Francisco, 1979; Richard Hines Gallery, Seattle, 1980; Gloria Luria Gallery, Bay Harbor Islands, Fla., 1981; Janie C. Lee Gallery, Houston, 1981; Paris/Moderne, 1982. **Retrospective:** WMAA, 1974. **Group:** U. of Illinois, 1950, 67; WMAA, 1950, 65-66, Annuals, 1967, 73; Chicago/AI; Walker, Vanguard, 1955; Corcoran; Arts Club of Chicago; U. of North Carolina; Minneapolis/Institute; PAFA, 1966; MOMA, Two Decades of American Painting, circ., Japan, India, Australia, 1967; U. of Illinois, 1967; Jewish Museum, 1967; Montclair/AM, The Recent Years, 1969; Carnegie, 1970; VMFA, 1970; MOMA, Younger Abstract Expressionists of the Fifties, 1971; Carnegie, Fresh Air School, circ., 1972; New York Cultural Center, Women Choose Women, 1973; WMAA, American Drawings, 1963-1973, 1973; Indianapolis, 1974; Corcoran, 1975; San Antonio/McNay, American Artist 76, 1976; Albright College, Reading, Pa., Perspecitve 78, 1978; Buffalo/Albright, American Painting of the 1970s, 1978; Hirshhorn, The Fifties: Aspects of Painting in New York, 1980; Corcoran Biennial, 1981; WMAA Biennial, 1983; Newport Harbor, Action/Precision, 1984; Fort Lauderdale, An American Renaissance: Painting and Sculpture Since 1940, 1986. **Collections:** Basel; Buffalo/Albright; Chase Manhattan Bank; Chicago/AI; Corcoran; First National Bank of Miami; Harvard U.; IBM; MOMA; Paris/Beaubourg; Phillips;

Rockefeller Institute; The Singer Company, Inc.; SRGM; Union Carbide Corp.; WMAA; Walker. **Bibliography:** Baur 5; Blesh 1; Downes, ed.; Friedman, ed.; Hunter 1; Hunter, ed.; Johnson, Ellen H.; **Joan Mitchell;** McCoubrey 1; *Metro;* Nordness, ed.; O'Hara 1; Plous; Read 2; Sandler 1; Seuphor 1.

MOHOLY-NAGY, LASZLO. b. July 20, 1895, Bacsbarsod, Hungary; **d.** November 24, 1946, Chicago, Ill. **Studied:** U. of Budapest, 1913-14, LL.B. **Taught:** Staatliches Bauhaus, Berlin, 1922; a founding collaborator with Gyorgy Kepes and Robert Wolff of the Institute of Design, Chicago, 1938-42; director of the New Bauhaus, Chicago. Designed for State Opera and the Piscator Theatre, Berlin, 1928. Traveled Europe extensively. To England, 1935, where he produced three volumes of photo documents and a film, *Life of the Lobster.* To USA, 1937. **One-man Exhibitions:** Amsterdam/Stedelijk; Brno, Czechoslovakia; Hamburg; Mannheim; Cologne; Budapest/National; Stockholm/National; A.F.A.; The London Gallery, London, 1937; Houston/Contemporary, 1948; Harvard U., 1950; Rose Fried Gallery, 1950; Colorado Springs/FA, 1950; Zurich, 1953; Kunst Kabinett Klihm, 1956, 59, 62, 66, 71; Kleeman Gallery, NYC, 1957; New London Gallery, London, 1961; Dusseldorf, 1961; Eindhoven, 1967, 72; Brandeis U., 1968; The Howard Wise Gallery, NYC, 1970; Galerie Rudolf Zwirner, 1971; Bauhaus-Archiv, Berlin, 1972; Ileana Sonnabend Gallery, NYC, 1973; Stephen Wirtz Gallery, San Francisco, 1978; Bronx Museum, 1983. **Retrospectives:** SRGM, 1947; Chicago/AI, 1969; Chicago/Contemporary, circ., 1969; Stuttgart/WK, 1974. **Group:** WMAA; SRGM; Yale U.; Harvard U.; MOMA, The Machine as Seen at the End of the Mechanical Age, 1968, and others. **Collections:** Chicago/AI; Dayton/AI; Detroit/Institute; Jacksonville/AM; Los Angeles/County MA;

MOMA; SFMA; SRGM. **Bibliography:** Barr 1; Battcock, ed.; Bihalji-Merin; Blanchard; Calas, N. and E.; Cassou; Craven, W.; Davis, D.; Frost; Giedion-Welcker 2; Goodrich and Baur 1; Hulten; Huyghe; Janis and Blesh 1; Janis S.; **Kostelanetz;** Krauss 3; Lane and Larsen; Langui; Licht, F.; MacAgy 2; **Moholy-Nagy, L. 1, 2; Moholy-Nagy, S. 1, 2;** Morris; Motherwell 1; Murken-Altrogge; Ramsden 1; Read 3; Roters; Rowell; Selz, J.; Seuphor 3; Tomkins; Trier 1; Valentine 2; **Weitemeir;** Weller; Wingler, ed. Archives.

MOLLER, HANS. b. March 20, 1905, Wuppertal-Barmen, Germany. **Studied:** Art School, Barmen, 1919-27; Academy of Fine Arts, Berlin, 1927-28; To USA, 1928; US Citizen, 1944. **Taught:** Cooper Union, 1944-56. **Member:** Federation of Modern Painters and Sculptors. **Commissions:** William Douglas McAdams, Inc., NYC (mural); Percival Goodman, Architect; tapestry design for synagogue ark curtains; A.F.A./Stained Glass Industry (stained-glass window); Christ Church, Washington, D.C. (stained-glass windows), 1968. **Awards:** Art Directors Club, NYC, Distinctive Merit Award, 1944, 55, 56; Corcoran, Hon. Men., 1949; American Institute of Graphic Art, Certificate of Excellence, 1949 (2), 51; National Religious Art Exhibition, Detroit, First Prize, 1964; Audubon Artists Annual, Salmagundi Club Award, 1967; NAD, Edwin Palmer Memorial Prize, 1968, 1980; NAD, Samuel F.B. Morse Gold Medal, 1969; Audubon Artists, Murray Kupferman Prize, 1973; NAD, Andrew Carnegie Prize, 1974; AAAL, Childe Hassam Fund, 1976; Youngstown/Butler, 1st Prize, 1978; NAD, Andrew Carnegie Prize, 1985. **Address:** 2207 Allen Street, Allentown, PA 18104; summer: Monhegan, ME 04852. **Dealer:** The Midtown Galleries. **One-man Exhibitions:** (first) Bonestell Gallery, NYC, 1942, also 1943; Arts Club of Chicago, 1945; U. of Michigan, 1945; Kleeman Gallery, NYC, 1945, 47,

49, 50; Pen and· Palette Gallery, St. Louis, 1949; Macon, Ga. 1949; Atlanta/AA, 1950; Grace Borgenicht Gallery, NYC, 1951; 53, 54, 56; Fine Arts Associates, NYC, 1957, 60; Albert Landry, NYC, 1962; The Midtown Galleries, NYC, 1964, 67, 70, 73, 76, 79, 81, 84; Philadelphia Art Alliance, 1968; Allentown/AM, 1969; Norfolk, 1970; Muhlenberg College, 1977; Hunterdon Art Center, Clinton, N.J., 1978; Northeastern Pennsylvania Art Alliance, 1980. **Retrospectives:** The Olsen Foundation Inc., Leetes Island, Conn., Hans Moller, 1926-56, circ., 1956-64; Lehigh U., 1977. **Group:** MMA; Brooklyn Museum; PAFA; Chicago/AI; The Print Club, Philadelphia; Des Moines; Detroit/Institute; Corcoran; U. of Illinois; Walker; Buffalo/Albright; SFMA; Colby College, 100 Artists of the 20th Century, 1964; WMAA Annual, 1965 and others; NAD Annuals, 1965, 67, 68, 69; Federation of Modern Painters and Sculptors, 1966, 67; NIAL, 1969. **Collections:** Allentown/AM; Bennington College; Brooklyn Museum; Container Corp. of America; Detroit/Institute; U. of Georgia; IBM; MOMA; Melbourne/National; Meta-Mold Aluminum Co.; NYPL; Norfolk; PAFA; Phillips; Princeton U.; Sacred Heart Seminary; Society of the Four Arts; Spelman College; U. of Texas; USIA; U.S. Rubber Co.; WMAA; Walker; Washington U.; Wuppertal; Yellowstone Art Center; Youngstown/Butler. **Bibliography:** Baur 5; Genauer.

MOORE, JOHN. b. April 25, 1941, St. Louis, Missouri. **Studied:** Washington U., 1962-66, BFA, with A. Osver, E. Boccia, B. Schactman; Yale U., 1966-68; MFA, with B. Chaet, J. Tworkov, L. Anderson. Traveled France, Spain, Italy. **Taught:** Tyler School of Art, Philadelphia, 1968-80, 83-86; Skowhegan School, 1974, 80, 84; U. of California, Berkeley, 1981-82. **Commissions:** Poster for Lincoln Center, NYC, 1977; John Hancock Building, Boston, 1985;

Smith Kline Co., Philadelphia, 1986; Becton-Dickson, N.J., 1986. **Awards:** National Endowment for the Arts, grant, 1966; John F. Milliken Foreign Travel Fellowship, 1968; Schless Memorial Prize, Yale U., 1968; AAAL, Hassam Award, 1973; National Endowment for the Arts, 1982. **Address:** 111 Woodland Road, Wyncote, Pa. 19095. **Dealer:** Hirschl & Adler Modern, NYC. **One-man Exhibitions:** Princeton U., 1970; Fischbach Gallery, NYC, 1973, 75, 78, 80; PAFA, 1973; David Gallery, Pittsfield, N.Y., 1974; Vick Gallery, Philadelphia, 1974; Alpha Gallery, Boston, 1974; Dart Gallery, Chicago, 1977; Vick, Klaus, Rosen Gallery, Philadelphia, 1977; U. of Missouri, 1978; Marion Locks Gallery, Philadelphia, 1979; College of William and Mary, 1981; Capricorn Gallery, Washington, D.C., 1981; Niagara U., 1983; Hirschl & Adler Modern, 1983, 85. **Group:** U. of Rhode Island, From Life, 1971; Potsdam/SUNY, New Realism, 1971; U. of Illinois, 1974; Queens Museum, New Images in American Painting, 1974; Minnesota/MA, Drawings U.S.A., '75, 1975; Akron/AI, Contemporary Images in Watercolor, 1976; U. of North Carolina, Art on Paper, 1976; Chicago/AI, Drawings of the 70s, 1977; William and Mary College, American Realism, 1978; Kent State U., Still Life, 1980; Tulsa/Philbrook, Realism/Photorealism, 1980; PAFA, Contemporary American Realism Since 1960, 1981; San Antonio/MA, Real, Really Real, Super Real, circ., 1981; MMA, Aspects of the City, 1984; Isetan Museum of Art, Tokyo, American Realism: The Precise Image, 1985. **Collections:** American Can Corp.; Arizona State U.; AT&T; Chase Manhattan Bank, NYC; Commerce Bank of Kansas City; Dartmouth College; First National Bank, Houston; IBM Corp.; Lehman Brothers, NYC; MMA; U. of Massachusetts; Minnesota/MA; PAFA; PMA; Purchase/SUNY; RISD; San Antonio/McNay; Smith College; Yale U. **Bibliography:** Arthur 3.

MORLEY, MALCOLM. b. 1931, London, England. **Studied:** Camberwell School of Arts and Crafts, London, 1953; Royal College of Art, London, 1957; Yale U., MFA. **Taught:** Ohio State U., 1965, 66; School of Visual Arts, NYC, 1967-69; Stony Brook/SUNY, 1971. **Awards:** Tate Gallery, Turner Prize, 1984. **Address:** 2 Spring Street, NYC 10012. **Dealer:** The Pace Gallery, NYC. **One-man Exhibitions:** The Kornblee Gallery, 1967, 69; Stefanotty Gallery, NYC, 1973; Galerie Gerald Piltzer, Paris, 1973; Stefanotty Gallery, NYC, 1974; The Clocktower, NYC, 1976, 79; Galerie Jurka, Amsterdam, 1977; Nancy Hoffman Gallery, NYC, 1979; Susanne Hilberry Gallery, Birmingham, Mich., 1979; Hartford/Wadsworth, 1980; Xavier Fourcade, Inc., NYC, 1981, 82, 84; Akron/AM, 1981; Ponova Gallery, Inc., Toronto, 1984; Galerie Nicoline Pon, Zurich, 1984; Fabian Carlsson Gallery, London, 1985; Carnegie, 1985. **Retrospective:** Whitechapel, London, circ., 1983. **Group:** SRGM, The Photographic Image, 1966; IX Sao Paulo Biennial, 1967; Vassar College, Realism Now, 1968; Akron/AI, Directions 2; Aspects of a New Realism, 1969; Riverside Museum, NYC, Paintings from the Photo, 1969; WMAA, 22 Realists, 1970; Princeton U., American Art since 1960, 1970; Documenta V, Kassel, 1972; Wurttembergischer Kunstverein, Amerikanischer Fotorealismus, 1972; Serpentine Gallery, London, Photo-Realism, 1973; Akademie der Kunste, Berlin, SoHo, 1976; Royal Academy of Arts, London, British Painting 1952-1977, 1977; Documenta 6, Kassel, 1977; Zurich, Painting in the Age of Photography, 1977; Canberra/National, Illusion of Reality, 1977; Oklahoma, Cityscape, 78, 1978; Royal Academy, London, A New Spirit in Painting, 1981; Akron/AM, The Image in American Painting and Sculpture, 1981; Indianapolis, 1982; Internationale Kunstausstellung Berlin, 1982; Houston/Contemporary, American Still Life, 1945-1983, 1983; Tate Gallery, New Art, 1983; MOMA, International Survey of Painting and Sculpture, 1984. **Collections:** Aachen/NG; Chicago/Contemporary; Cologne/NG; Detroit/Institute; Fordham U.; Hartford/Wadsworth; Hirshhorn; Humlebaek/Louisiana; MMA; MOMA; The Ohio State U.; Paris/Moderne; Utica; Utrecht; Victoria and Albert Museum. **Bibliography:** Alloway, 4; *Amerikanischer Fotorealismus*; Honisch and Jensen, eds.; Joachimides and Rosenthal; Johnson, Ellen H.; *Kunst um 1970*; Lindy; Lucie-Smith; Murken-Altrogge; Sager.

MORRIS, CARL. b. May 12, 1911, Yorba Linda, Calif. **Studied:** Fullerton Junior College, 1930-31; Chicago Art Institute School; Kunstgewerbeschule, Vienna, 1933-34; Academy of Fine Arts, Vienna, 1933-34. Traveled Italy. **Taught:** ASL, 1937-38; privately 1940-41; U. of Colorado, summer, 1957. Federal A.P.: Director at Spokane, Wash., 1938-39. **Commissions** (murals): US Post Office, Eugene, Ore., 1941-42; Hall of Religion, Oregon Centennial Exposition, Portland, 1959. **Awards:** Austro-American Scholarship, 1935; Institute of International Education Fellowship (Paris), 1935-36; Werkbund Scholarship, 1939, Seattle/AM, Hon. Men., 1939, 46, 47; Seattle/AM, Second Prize, 1943; Denver/AM, **P.P.**, 1946; Seattle/AM, Margaret E. Fuller Award, 1946; SFMA, Anne Bremer Memorial Prize, 1946; Pepsi-Cola Bronze Medal, 1948; SFMA, James D. Phelan Award, 1950; U. of Illinois, **P.P.**, 1958. **Address:** 919 N.W. Skyline Boulevard, Portland, OR 97229. **Dealers:** Kraushaar Galleries; Triangle Art Gallery; Gordon Woodside Gallery; Fountain Gallery. **One-man Exhibitions:** (first) Fondation des Etats-Unis, Paris, 1935; Paul Elder Gallery, San Francisco, 1937; Seattle/AM, 1940; Portland, Ore./AM, 1946, 52, 55; California Palace, 1947; U. of Oregon, 1947; Opportunity Gallery, NYC, 1948; Santa Barbara/MA, 1956; Zivile Gallery, Los Angeles, 1956; Mills College, 1956; Rotunda Gallery, San Francisco, 1956; Kraushaar Galleries, 1956, 57, 58, 61, 64, 67, 73; Reed College, 1959, 69 (two-man, with Hilda Morris), 1972; U. of Colorado, 1957; Fountain Gallery, 1963, 64, 65, 69, 71, 75; Feingarten Gallery, San Francisco, 1965; Triangle Art Gallery, 1966, 68, 70, 73; Gordon Woodside Gallery, 1966, 69, 73. **Retrospective:** A.F.A./Ford Foundation, circ., 1960. **Group:** Chicago/AI; Carnegie; Corcoran; MMA; WMAA; SRGM; Younger American Painters, 1954; III Sao Paulo Biennial, 1955; Colorado Springs/FA, 1965; Denver/AM, 1965; Art in the USA, 1965; Tamarind Lithography Workshop, 1967; PAFA, 1969; SFMA, Tamarind, 1969; MOMA, Tamarind: Homage to Lithography, 1969; Minnesota/MA, Drawings USA, 1971; NCFA, Art of the Pacific Northwest, 1974; NAD, 1974; Seattle/AM, Northwest Traditions, 1978. **Collections:** Allentown/AM; Buffalo/Albright; California Palace; Chicago/AI; Colorado Springs/FA; U. of Colorado; Columbus; Corcoran; Dayton/AI; Denver/AM; Eastern Oregon College; Hartford/Wadsworth; Houston/MFA; Hirshhorn; U. of Illinois; Kansas City/Nelson; MMA; Mead Corporation; Michigan State U.; Mills College; Minnesota/MA; NCFA; Norfolk/Chrysler; U. of Oregon; City of Portland, Ore.; Portland, Ore./AM; Portland State College; Reed College; U. of Rochester; SFMA; SRGM; Santa Barbara/MA; Sao Paulo; Seattle/AM; Southern Oregon College; Stanford U.; U. of Texas; Toronto; Utica; WMAA; Walker; Wichita. **Bibliography:** *Art of the Pacific Northwest*; Monte and Tucker; Nordness, ed.; *Northwest Traditions*; Pousette-Dart, ed.; Read 2.

MORRIS, GEORGE L.K. b. November 14, 1905, NYC; **d.** June 26, 1975, Stockbridge, Mass. **Studied:** Groton School, 1924; Yale U., 1928, BA; ASL, with John Sloan, Kenneth Hayes Miller; Academie Moderne, Paris, with F. Leger,

Amedee Ozenfant. Traveled around the world and spent much time in Paris. **Taught:** ASL, 1943-44; St. John's College, Annapolis, Md., 1950-61. Editor: Yale Literary Magazine, 1928; *The Miscellany*, 1929-31; *Plastique*, Paris, 1937-39; *Partisan Review*, 1937-43. **Member:** American Abstract Artists (a founder, 1936, and president, 1948-50); Federation of Modern Painters and Sculptors; NAD, Saltus Gold Medal, 1973. **Commissions:** Lenox (Mass.) Elementary School (mosaic). **Awards:** Pepsi-Cola, 1948; Pittsfield/Berkshire, Berkshire Hills Award, 1963; PAFA, Joseph E. Temple Gold Medal, 1965. **One-man Exhibitions:** (first) Valentine Dudensing Gallery, 1933; Pittsfield/Berkshire, 1933; Museum of Living Art, NYC, 1935; Passedoit Gallery, NYC, 1938; The Downtown Gallery, 1943, 44, 50, 64, 67; Galerie Colette Allendy, Paris, 1946; The Alan Gallery, NYC, 1955; Montclair/AM, 1971; Jacksonville/Cummer, 1973; Chattanooga/AA, 1973; Charleston/Carolina, 1973; Hirschl & Adler Galleries, 1974, 79; Daytona Beach, 1973; NIAL, 1975. **Retrospectives:** ICA, Washington, D.C., 1958; Sharon (Conn.) Creative Arts Foundation; Century Association; Corcoran; Pittsfield/Berkshire; Hirschl & Adler Galleries, 1971. **Group:** WMAA; American Abstract Artists, annually; Salon des Realites Nouvelles, Paris; MOMA; SRGM; Chicago/AI; SFMA; Rome/Nazionale. **Collections:** Brandeis U.; Brooklyn Museum; Chattanooga/AA; Corcoran; Dallas/MFA; Darmstadt/Kunsthalle; U. of Georgia; High Museum; Honolulu Academy; U. of Illinois; MMA; Madison Square Garden; U. of Michigan; Montclair/AM; U. of Oklahoma; PAFA; PMA; Phillips; Pittsfield/Berkshire; Portland, Ore./AM; Raleigh/NCMA; Syracuse U.; Utica; WMAA; Wichita/AM; Yale U. **Bibliography:** American Abstract Artists, ed.; Arp; Baur 7; Biederman 1; Blanchard; Blesh 1; Cheney; Flanagan; Frost; Kootz 2; Lane and Larsen; Marter, Tarbell, and

Wechsler; McCurdy, ed.; **Morris;** Newmeyer; Pagano; Pearson 2; Pousette-Dart, ed.; Read 2; Ritchie 1; Rose, B., 1, 4; Seuphor 1, 3; "What Abstract Art Means to Me." Archives.

MORRIS, ROBERT. b. February 9, 1931, Kansas City, Mo. **Studied:** Kansas City Junior College; Kansas City Art Institute, 1948-50; U. of Kansas City; San Francisco Art Institute; Reed College, 1953-55; Hunter College, MA, 1966. US Army Engineers, 1951-52. Traveled USA, Orient, Europe. **Taught:** Hunter College, 1967-. **Commissions:** National Planning Commission, Ottawa, Earth Project. **Awards:** National Council on the Arts, **P.P.;** Chicago/AI, 1966; SRGM, 1967; Torcuato di Tella, Buenos Aires, 1967; Guggenheim Foundation Fellowship, 1969; Skowhegan Medal of Progress and Environment, 1978. **Address:** No. Mountain Road, Gardiner, NY 12525. **Dealer:** Leo Castelli Inc., NYC; Sonnabend Gallery, NYC. **One-man Exhibitions:** (first) Dilexi Gallery, San Francisco, 1957, also 1958; Green Gallery, NYC, 1963, 64, 65; Galerie Schmela, 1964; Dwan Gallery, Los Angeles, 1966; Leo Castelli Inc., 1967, 68, 69, 70, 72, 74, 76 (two-man); 79, 80, 83, 85; Eindhoven, 1968; Ileana Sonnabend Gallery, Paris, 1968, 71, 73, 77, NYC, 1974, 76, 79, 83, 85; Corcoran, 1969, 77; Gian Enzo Sperone, Turin, 1969; Irving Blum Gallery, Los Angeles, 1969, 70; Tate, 1971; Konrad Fischer Gallery, Dusseldorf, 1973; Max Protetch Gallery, Washington, D.C., 1973; Galleria Forma, Genoa, 1973; Modern Art Agency, Naples, 1973; ICA, U. of Pennsylvania, 1974; Galerie Art in Progress, Munich, 1974; Belknap Park, Grand Rapids, 1974; Alessandro Ferranti Gallery, Rome, 1975; Humlebaek/Louisiana, 1977; Williams College, 1977; Portland (Ore.) Center for the Visual Arts, 1977; Amsterdam/Stedelijk, 1977; Galerie Art in Progress, Dusseldorf, 1977; Swarthmore College, 1978; Beaver College, 1978;

Robert Morris   *Untitled*   1955–83

Ferrara/Moderna, 1978; Wright State U., 1979; Chicago/AI, 1980; Richard Hines Gallery, Seattle, 1980; Waddington Gallery, London, 1980; Houston/Contemporary, 1981, 84; Williamstown/Clark, circ., 1982; U. of Illinois, 1983; Galerie Daniel Templon, Paris, 1983; Malmo, 1984; Galerie Nordenhake, Malmo, 1984; Padiglione d'Arte Contemporanea, Milano, 1984; Portland (Ore.) Center for the Visual Arts, 1984. **Retrospective:** WMAA, 1970; Detroit/Institute, 1970. **Group:** Hartford/Wadsworth, Black, White and Gray, 1964; WMAA, Young America, 1965; ICA, U. of Pennsylvania, The Other Tradition, 1966; Jewish Museum, Primary Structures, 1966; WMAA, Contemporary American Sculpture, Selection I, 1966; Chicago/AI, 1966; Walker, 1966; WMAA Sculpture Annuals, 1966, 68, 70; Detroit/Institute, Color, Image and Form, 1967; Los Angeles/County MA and PMA, American Sculpture of the Sixties, 1967; MOMA, The 1960's, 1967; Torcuato di Tella, Buenos Aires, 1967; Eindhoven, 1967; SRGM, Guggenheim International, 1967, 71; Buffalo/Albright, 1968; The Hague, Minimal Art, 1968; Foundation Maeght, 1968; MOMA, The Art of the Real, 1968; PMA, 1968; ICA, U. of Pennsylvania, 1969; Berne, When Attitudes Become Form, 1969; Walker, 14 Sculptors: The Industrial Edge, 1969; Indianapolis, 1969; WMAA, Anti-Illusion: Procedures/Materials, 1969; Hayward Gallery, London, Pop Art, 1969; MOMA, Spaces, 1969; MMA, New York Painting and Sculpture,

1940-1970, 1969-70; New School for Social Research, American Drawings of the Sixties, 1970; Boston U., American Artists of the Nineteen Sixties, 1970; Cornell U., Earth Art, 1970; Cincinnati/Contemporary, Monumental Art, 1970; ICA, U. of Pennsylvania, Against Order: Chance and Art, 1970; MOMA, Information, 1971; Kunsthalle, Nurnberg, Artist-Theory-Work, 1971; Buffalo/Albright, Kid Stuff, 1971; Dusseldorf/Kunsthalle, Prospect '71, 1971; Dublin/Municipal, International Quadriennial (ROSC), 1971; Chicago/Contemporary, Six Sculptors, 1971; Los Angeles/County MA, Art & Technology, 1971; Rijksmuseum Kroller-Muller, Diagrams and Drawings, 1972; New York Cultural Center, 3D into 2D, 1973; Parcheggio di Villa Borghese, Rome, Contemporanea, 1974; Princeton U., Line as Language, 1974; MIT, Interventions in Landscapes, 1974; Cologne/Kunstverein, Kunst uber Kunst, 1974; CNAC, Art/Voir, 1974; Dusseldorf/Kunsthalle, Surrealist-Bildrealitat: 1924-1974, 1974; Ackland, Light/Sculpture, 1975; Leverkusen, Drawings 3; American Drawings, 1975; MOMA, Drawings Now, 1976; ICA, U. of Pennsylvania, Improbable Furniture, 1977; Chicago/AI, Drawings of the 70's, 1977; U. of Chicago, Ideas in Sculpture, 1977; Kansas City/AI, Project Drawings, 1978; Ontario, Structures for Behaviour, 1978; WMAA, Art About Art, 1978; Dusseldorf/Kunsthalle, About the Strange Nature of Money, circ., 1978; ICA, Boston, The Reductive Object, 1979; Milwaukee, Emergency & Progression, circ., 1979; U. of North Carolina, Drawings about Drawing Today, 1979; P.S. 1, NYC, A Great Big Drawing Show, 1979; Brooklyn Museum, American Drawing in Black and White: 1970-1979, 1980; Exposition Société des Artistes Indépendents, Paris, 1980; ICA, Boston, Drawing/Structures, 1980; ICA, U. of Pennsylvania, Drawings: The Pluralist Decade, 1980; Purchase/SUNY, Hidden Desires, 1980; XXXIX Venice Biennial, 1980; AAIAL, 1981; Hirshhorn, Metaphor, New Projects by Contemporary Sculptors, 1981; Purchase/SUNY, Soundings, 1981; Centre d'Arts Plastiques Contemporains, Bordeaux, Art Povera, Antiform: Sculptures 1966-69, 1982; Internationale Kunstausstelung Berlin, 1982; Tate Gallery, New Art, 1983; WMAA, Twentieth Century Sculpture: Process and Presence, 1983; Hirshhorn, Content: A Contemporary Focus, 1974-1984, 1984; Hirshhorn, Dreams and Nightmares, 1984; WMAA, Blam!, 1984; MOMA, New Work on Paper 3, 1985. **Collections:** Dallas/MFA; Detroit/Institute; Hartford/Wadsworth; Melbourne/National; Milwaukee; National Gallery of Victoria, Melbourne; Oberlin College; Ottawa/National; Pasadena/AM; Stockholm/National; Tate; WMAA; Walker. **Bibliography:** *Art Now 74;* Alloway 4; Battcock, ed.; Calas, N. and E.; Celant; *Contemporanea;* Danto; Davis, D.; *Drawings: The Pluralist Decade;* De Vries, ed.; De Wilde 2; Friedman, M. 2; Friedman and van der Marck; Fry and Kuspit; Gablik; Goossen 1; *Happening & Fluxus;* Haskell 5; Honisch and Jensen, eds.; Honnef; Hunter, ed.; Joachimides and Rosenthal; Johnson, Ellen H.; Krauss 2, 3; Kozloff 3; *Kunst um 1970;* Lippard 3, 4, 5; Lippard, ed.; Lucie-Smith; Meyer; Muller; *Report;* Rowell; Russell and Gablik; Trier 1; Sandler 1; Trier 1; Tuchman 1; *When Attitudes Become Form.* Archives.

MOSKOWITZ, ROBERT. b. 1935, NYC. **Studied:** Pratt Institute, NYC. **Address:** 81 Leonard Street, NYC 10013. **Dealer:** Blum Helman Gallery, NYC. **One-man Exhibitions:** Leo Castelli Inc., NYC, 1962; French & Co., NYC, 1970; MIT, 1971; Nancy Hoffman Gallery, NYC, 1973, 74; The Clocktower, NYC, 1977; Daniel Weinberg Gallery, San Francisco, 1979, 80; Margo Leavin Gallery, Los Angeles, 1979, 80; Walker, 1981; Basel/Kunsthalle, 1981; Blum Helman Gallery, NYC, 1983; Portland (Ore.)

Center for the Visual Arts, 1983; MIT (two-man), 1985. **Group:** MOMA, The Art of Assemblage, circ., 1961; Buffalo/Albright, Mixed Media and Pop Art, 1963; Brandeis U., New Directions in American Painting, 1963; Oakland/AM, Pop Art USA, 1963; Hartford/Wadsworth, Black, White and Grey, 1964; WMAA, A Decade of American Drawings, 1955-1965, 1965; WMAA, Artists under Forty, 1968; WMAA Annual, 1969; WMAA Biennials, 1973, 79, 81; WMAA, New Image Painting, 1978; Buffalo/Albright, American Painting of the 1970s, circ., 1978; U. of Chicago, Visionary Images, 1979; NYU, American Painting: The Eighties, 1979; XXXIX Venice Bienniale, 1980; Indianapolis, 1980; MIT, Great Big Drawings, 1982; Chicago/AI, American, 1982; Palacio de Velazquez, Madrid, Tendencias en Nueva York, circ., 1983; MOMA, International Survey of Recent Painting and Sculpture, 1984; Hirshhorn, Content, 1984. **Collections:** Bennington College; Buffalo/Albright; U. of California, Berkeley; La Jolla; MOMA; Omaha/Joslyn; PMA; Seattle/AM; WMAA. **Bibliography:** Hiromoto.

MOTHERWELL, ROBERT. b. January 24, 1915, Aberdeen, Wash. **Studied:** Stanford U., 1932-37, AB (philosophy); California School of Fine Arts, ca. 1935; Harvard U., 1937-38; U. of Grenoble, summer, 1938; Columbia U., 1940-41; primarily self-taught in art. Traveled extensively, USA, Europe, Mexico. **Taught:** Hunter College, 1951-57; Columbia U., 1964-65; lectures extensively in American universities and museums. Series of paintings *Elegy to Spanish Republic* began 1947. Cofounder of a school, "Subject of the Artist," with William Baziotes, Barnett Newman, and Mark Rothko, NYC, 1948. Art Director, *Partisan Review*, 1962-65. Director, *Documents of Modern Art*, NYC, and *Documents of 20th Century Art*. **Member:** NIAL. **Commissions:** John F. Kennedy Federal Office Building, Boston, 1966; Stanford U., 1975; U. of Iowa; National Gallery, mural, 1978. **Awards:** IV Guggenheim International, 1964 ($2,500); Grande Medaille de Vermeil de la Ville de Paris, 1978; PAFA, Gold Medal of Honor, 1979; Skowhegan School, Medal for Printmaking, 1981; National Arts Club, Gold Medal of Honor, 1983; MacDowell Colony Medal, 1985. **Address:** 909 North Street, Greenwich, CT 06830. **Dealer:** M. Knoedler & Co., Inc., NYC. **One-man Exhibitions:** (first) Raymond Duncan Gallery, Paris, 1939; Art of This Century, NYC, 1944; Arts Club of Chicago, 1946; The Kootz Gallery, NYC, 1946, 47, 49, 52; SFMA, 1946, 67; New London, 1953; Sidney Janis Gallery, 1957, 59, 61, 62; Bennington College, 1959; John Berggruen Gallery, Paris, 1961, San Francisco, 1973; Sao Paulo, 1961; Pasadena/AM, 1962; Galleria Odyssia, Rome, 1962; Galerie der Spiegel, Cologne, 1962; Smith College, 1963; MIT, 1963; Galerie Schmela (two-man, with Conrad Marca-Relli); Duke U., 1965; Walker, 1965, 72, 74; College of St. Benedict, 1965; U. of Utah, 1966; Witte, 1966; U. of South Florida, 1966; Baltimore/MA, 1966; Indiana U., 1966; Amsterdam/Stedelijk, 1966; Whitechapel Art Gallery, London, 1966; Essen, 1966; Turin/Civico, 1966; WMAA, 1968; VMFA, 1969; Toledo/MA, 1969; Marlborough-Gerson Gallery Inc., 1969; David Mirvish Gallery, 1970, 73; Gallerie im Erker, St. Gallen, Switzerland, 1971; Kunstverein, Freiburg, 1971; Dayton's Gallery 12, Minneapolis, 1972; Lawrence Rubin Gallery, NYC, 1972, 73; MMA, 1972; U. of Iowa, 1972; Fendrick Gallery, 1972; Houston/MFA, 1972; Gertrude Kasle Gallery, 1972; Cleveland/MA, 1973; Princeton U., 1973; Current Editions, Seattle, 1973; Hartford/Wadsworth, 1973; Knoedler Contemporary Art, 1974, 75; Brooke Alexander, 1974, 76, 79; Otis Art Institute, 1974; Museum of Modern Art, Mexico City, 1975; Knoedler Contemporary Art, 1976, 78, 80; Janie C. Lee Gallery, Houston, 1976, 79; Watson/De

Nagy, Houston, 1977, 79; Galerie Andre Emmerich, Zurich, 1977; Diane Gilson Gallery, Seattle, Seattle, 1977, 79; Graphics 1 & Graphics 2, Boston, 1977; Hanson-Cowles Gallery, Minneapolis, 1977; Knoedler Gallery, London, 1978; Douglas Drake Gallery, Kansas City, Mo., 1978; Alice Simsar Gallery, Ann Arbor, 1978; U. of Connecticut, 1979; Ehrlich Gallery, NYC, 1979; Wichita State U., 1979; Galerie Veith Turske, Cologne, 1979; 2RC, Rome, 1979; U. of Missouri, 1979; Galerie Ponce, Mexico City, 1979; Gump's Gallery, San Francisco, 1979; Peter M. David Gallery, Minneapolis, 1979; West Coast Gallery, Newport Beach, 1979; Centre Cultural de la Caixa de Pensions, Barcelona, 1980; M. Knoedler & Co., Inc., 1981, 82, 83, 86; Turske Fine Art, Cologne, 1981; M. Knoedler, Zurich, 1983; Albany/SUNY, 1984; L. A. Louver Gallery, Los Angeles, 1984; Harcourts Gallery, San Francisco, 1984; Dolan/Maxwell Gallery, Philadelphia, 1984; Marianne Friedland Gallery, Toronto, 1985; Fort Worth, 1985; The Century Association, 1987. **Retrospectives:** Dusseldorf/Kunsthalle, circ., 1976, prints, circ., 1977; Phillips, 1965; MOMA, 1965-66; U. of Connecticut, 1979; MOMA & AFA, circ., 1980; Buffalo/Albright, circ., 1983. **Group:** Venice Biennial, Sao Paulo Biennial; WMAA Annuals; Brussels World's Fair, 1958; American Painting and Sculpture, Moscow, 1959; Documenta II & III, Kassel, 1959, 64; Tate, Dunn International, 1964; Tate, Gulbenkian International, 1964; U. of Illinois, 1967; Winnipeg Art Gallery, 1967; Chicago/AI Annuals; Boston Arts Festival; ICA, Boston, 1968; Carnegie, 1968, and others; MOMA, The New American Painting and Sculpture, 1969; Edmonton Art Gallery, Alberta, Masters of the Sixties, 1972; VMFA, Twelve American Painters, 1974; Corcoran Biennial, 1975; Minnesota/MA, American Drawings, 1927-1977, circ., 1977; National Gallery, American Art at Mid-Century, 1978; Cornell U., Abstract Expressionism:

The Formative Years, 1978; Montclair College, American Masters, 1979; Claremont College, Black and White Are Colors, 1979; Corcoran, Gesture on Paper, 1980; Brooklyn Museum, American Drawings in Black and White, 1970-1979, 1980; Hirshhorn, The Fifties: Aspects of Painting in New York, 1980; Nassau County Museum, The Abstract Expressionists and Their Precursors, 1981; Scottish Arts Council & International Council of MOMA, American Abstract Expressionists, 1981; SRGM, The New York School: Four Decades, 1982; Youngstown/Butler, Midyear Show, 1983; IEF, Twentieth Century American Drawings: The Figure in Context, circ., 1984. **Collections:** Amsterdam/Stedelijk; Andover/Phillips; Baltimore/MA; Bennington College; Brooklyn Museum; Brown U.; Buffalo/Albright; Chicago/AI; Cleveland/MA; Dallas/MFA; Dayton/AI; Fort Dodge/Blanden; Harvard U.; Hirshhorn; Houston/MFA; U. of Illinois; Kultusministerium Baden-Wurttemberg; Kunsthalle Stuttgart; Los Angeles/County MA; MMA; MOMA; U. of Minnesota; NYU; National Gallery; U. of Nebraska; PAFA; Paris/Moderne; Pasadena/AM; Phillips; Provincetown/Chrysler; Raleigh/NCMA; Rio de Janeiro; SFMA; SRGM; Smith College; Smithsonian; Society of the Four Arts; South Mall, Albany; Tel Aviv; Toronto; WMAA; Walker; Washington U.; U. of Washington; Yale U. **Bibliography:** Alloway 4; Ashton 3, 5; Baur 7; Biederman 1; Bihalji-Merin; *Black and White Are Colors*; Blanchard; Blesh 1; Danto; Carmean, Rathbone, and Hess; Chipp; Downes, ed.; Eliot; Finkelstein; Flanagan; Goldman 1; Goodrich and Baur 1; *The Great Decade*; Greenberg 1; Haftman; Henning; Hess, T.B., 1; Hunter 1, 6; Honisch and Jensen, eds.; Hunter, ed.; Janis and Blesh 1; Janis, S.; Kozloff 3; McCoubrey 1; McCurdy, ed.; Mendelowitz; *Metro*; Miller, ed. 2; **Motherwell 1, 2; Motherwell, ed.; Motherwell and Reinhardt, eds.;** Murken-Altrogge; Nordness, ed.;

O'Hara; Paalen; Plous; Ponente; Pous-ette-Dart, ed.; Read 2; Ritchie 1; Rose, B., 1, 4; Rubin 1; Sandler 1; Seitz 1, 3; Seuphor 1; Soby 5; Terentio; Tomkins 2; Tuchman, ed.; Weller; "What Abstract Art Means to Me." Archives.

MOY, SEONG. b. October 20, 1921, Canton, China. To USA, 1931. **Stud-ied:** Federal Art Project School, with Ben Swanson; St. Paul School of Art, 1936-40, with Cameron Booth; ASL, with Vaclav Vytlacil; Hofmann School, 1941-42, with Hans Hofmann; Atelier 17, NYC, 1948-50. US Air Force, 1943-46. **Taught:** U. of Minnesota, 1951; Indiana U., 1953; Smith College, 1954; Vassar College, 1955; Cooper Union, 1957-; Columbia U., 1959-; ASL, 1963-; Moy Summer School, Province-town; City College of New York, 1970-. Federal A.P.: Assistant in graphic shop. **Member:** Artists Equity; SAGA; Au-dubon Society. **Commissions:** Interna-tional Graphic Arts Society (3 editions); New York Hilton Hotel; Fourth Na-tional Bank and Trust, Wichita (2 mu-rals). **Awards:** Minneapolis/Institute, First Prize, 1939; The Print Club, Phila-delphia, First Prize, 1948; John Hay Whitney Fellowship, 1950; Brooklyn Museum, **P.P.,** 1953; Guggenheim Foundation Fellowship, 1955. **Ad-dress:** 100 La Salle Street, NYC 10027; studio; 2231 Broadway, NYC 10024. **One-man Exhibitions:** (first) Carmel (Calif.) Art Association, 1943; Ashby Gallery, NYC, 1947; Carlebach Gallery, NYC, 1949; Springfield, Ill./State, 1949; Hacker Gallery, NYC, 1950; Dubin Gal-lery, Philadelphia, 1950; U. of Min-nesota, 1951; The New Gallery, NYC, 1951, 52, 54; Boris Mirski Gallery, Boston, 1955; The Contemporaries, NYC, 1955; The Howard Wise Gallery, Cleveland, 1958; Grand Central Mod-erns, NYC, 1959; Yamada Gallery, Kyoto, 1959; The Miller Gallery, Cin-cinnati, 1974. **Group:** MMA, 1950; U. of Illinois, 1951, 53, 54; Carnegie, 1955; U. of Minnesota; Brooklyn Museum; Chicago/AI; MOMA; PAFA; Library of Congress; New York World's Fair, 1964-65. **Collections:** Abbott Laborato-ries; Andover/Phillips; Bibliotheque Nationale; Boston/MFA; Brooklyn Mu-seum; Indiana U.; Library of Congress; MMA; MOMA; Memphis/Brooks; U. of Minnesota; NYPL; PAFA; PMA; Smith College; Smithsonian; Tel Aviv; Victoria and Albert Museum; WMAA; Walker; Worcester/AM. **Bibliography:** Ar-chives.

MOYER, ROY. b. August 20, 1921, Al-lentown, Pa. **Studied:** Columbia U., BA, MA; U. of Oslo; self-taught in art. Traveled extensively; resided in Europe (mainly Greece), four years. **Taught:** U. of Salonica, Greece, 1948-51; U. of Toronto, 1953-55. Director, American Federation of Arts, 1963-72; retired art officer for UNICEF. **Member:** Presi-dent, American Society of Contempo-rary Artists. **Awards:** Audubon Artists, Jane Peterson Award, 1969, 72; Youngstown/Butler, First Prize for Painting, 1973; NAD, Emil and Dines Carlsen Award, 1977. **Address:** 440 Riverside Drive, NYC 10027. **Dealer:** Sneed-Hillman Gallery, Rockford, Ill. **One-man Exhibitions:** (first) Salonica, Greece, 1949; The Contemporaries, NYC, 1958, 59, 61, 62, 65; The Mid-town Galleries, 1967; Rockford/Burpee 1969; Sneed-Hillman Gallery, 1969; Rolly-Michaux, NYC, 1974, Boston, 1975; Kendall Gallery, Wellfleet Mass., 1975; Carl Battaglia Galleries Ltd., NYC, 1981; Fordham U., at Lincoln Center, NYC, 1981; Rolly-Michaux, Boston, 1981. **Retrospective:** Sneed-Hillman Gallery, Rockford, Ill., 1979. **Group:** U. of Illinois, 1959; WMAA Annual, 1960; Washington U., 1967; Colorado Springs/FA, 1967; Louis-ville/Speed, 1967; Akron/AI, 1968; U. of Georgia, 1968; and others. **Collections:** Brandeis U.; Fordham U.; NMAA; Sara Roby Foundation; U. of Rochester; Rock-ford Art Association; Rockford/Burpee; Wichita/AM; Youngstown/Butler.

MULLER, JAN. b. December 27, 1922, Hamburg, Germany; d. January 29, 1958, NYC. Traveled Czechoslovakia, Switzerland, Holland, southern France, 1933-41. To USA, 1941. **Studied:** Hofmann School, 1945-50. Cofounder of Hansa Gallery, NYC, 1952. **One-man Exhibitions:** (first) Hansa Gallery, NYC, 1953, also 1954, 55, 56, 57, 58; Sun Gallery, Provincetown 1955, 56; U. of Minnesota, 1960; The Zabriskie Gallery, 1961; Noah Goldowsky, 1970, 71, 72; Gruenebaum Gallery, NYC, 1976, 77; Rosa Esman Gallery, NYC, 1980; Oil and Steel, Long Island City, N.Y., 1985. **Retrospective:** Hansa Gallery, NYC, 1959; SRGM, 1962. **Group:** 813 Broadway (Gallery) NYC, 1952; Chicago/AI, 1953; U. of Minnesota, 1955; The Stable Gallery Annual, 1956; Jewish Museum, The New York School, Second Generation, 1957; WMAA, Young America, 1957; Carnegie, 1958; Festival of Two Worlds, Spoleto, 1958; ICA, Boston, 1958, 59; MOMA, New Images of Man, 1959; A.F.A., The Figure circ., 1960. **Collections:** Charlotte/Mint; MOMA; Newark Museum. **Bibliography: Messer;** Sandler 1.

MULLICAN, LEE. b. December 2, 1919, Chickasha, Okla. **Studied:** Abilene Christian College, 1937; U. of Oklahoma, 1939; Kansas City Art Institute and School of Design, 1941, with Fletcher Martin. Corps of Army Engineers, 1942-46. Traveled Europe, South America, Asia. **Taught:** UCLA, 1962-86; U. of Chile, Artist-in-Residence Exchange Program, 1968. **Awards:** Guggenheim Foundation Fellowship, 1959; U. of California, Creative Arts Grant, 1964; Tamarind Fellowship, 1964-65. **Address:** 370 Mesa Road, Santa Monica, Calif. **Dealer:** Herbert B. Palmer Gallery, Los Angeles. **One-man Exhibitions:** SFMA, 1949; The Swetzoff Gallery, Boston, 1950; The Willard Gallery, 1950, 52, 53, 59, 61, 67; Dynation Exhibition, San Francisco, 1951; Oklahoma, 1951, 67;

Paul Kantor Gallery, Beverly Hills, Calif., 1952, 53, 56; The Rose Rabow Gallery, San Francisco, 1955, 74; Santa Barbara/MA, 1958; Silvan Simone Gallery, 1965-67; Santiago, Chile, 1968; UCLA, 1969; Jodi Scully Gallery, 1973; Contemporary Art Gallery, Santa Fe, 1973; Paule Ánglim Gallery, San Francisco, 1979; Schreiner Gallery, NYC, 1981; Stables Gallery, Taos, N.M., 1977; Artists Space, NYC, 1986. **Retrospective:** Santa Barbara/MA, 1973. **Group:** Corcoran, 1948; Denver/AM Annuals, 1950, 55, 56, 57; Chicago/AI, 1951, 54; Carnegie, 1951, 64, 66; WMAA Annuals, 1952, 56; U. of Nebraska, 1953; U. of Illinois, 1953, 55, 57; MMA, 1954; Sao Paulo, 1955; Santa Barbara/MA, 1957; MOMA, 1957; PAFA, 1958, 67; Rome-New York Foundation, Rome, 1960; Pasadena/AM, 1961; Newport Harbor, The Artist Collects, 1975; Los Angeles/County MA, 5 Footnotes to Art History, 1977. **Collections:** U. of California; Amon Carter Museum; Colorado Springs/FA; Denver/AM; Detroit/Institute; La Jolla; Los Angeles/County MA; MOMA; New Orleans/Delgado; U. of North Carolina; Oakland/AM; Oklahoma; Paris/Moderne; Pasadena/AM; Phillips; Roswell; SFMA; San Francisco Municipal Art Commission; Santa Barbara/MA; Santa Fe, N.M.; Santiago, Chile; Smith College; Syracuse U.; Tulsa/Philbrook; Wichita State U. **Bibliography:** Pousette-Dart, ed.; Richardson, E.P.; Tuchman 3. Archives.

MURCH, WALTER TANDY. b. August 17, 1907, Toronto, Canada; d. December 11, 1967, NYC. **Studied:** Ontario College of Art, 1924-27, with Arthur Lismer, L. Harris; ASL, 1929-30, with Kenneth Hayes Miller, William Von Schlegell; Grand Central School, NYC, 1930, with Arshile Gorsky; and privately, with Gorky, 1931-32. US citizen, 1948. Traveled Mexico, Canada, France. **Taught:** Pratt Institute, 1952-61; NYU, 1961; Boston U., 1961-67; Columbia U., 1964. **Commis-**

sions: *Scientific American; Fortune* magazine. **Awards:** U. of Illinois, **P.P.**, 1949; NIAL, Grant, 1961; Ford Foundation, **P.P.** (2). **One-man Exhibitions:** (first) Wakefield Gallery, NYC, 1941; Mortimer Brandt, NYC, 1946; Betty Parsons Gallery, 1947, 49, 51, 54, 57, 59, 62, 66, 70, 71, 83; St. Louis Art Center, 1949; Allan Frumkin Gallery, Chicago, 1953; Worth Avenue Gallery, Palm Beach, Fla., 1955; Choate School, Wallingford, Conn., 1959; Hampton Gallery, Huntington, W. Va., 1964; Lehigh U., 1966; Galerie Jan Krugier, Geneva, 1976; Montclair/AM, 1978; Long Island U., Greenvale, circ., 1986. **Retrospective:** RISD, 1966. **Group:** Andover/Phillips, 1945; Corcoran, 1945, 56, 52-55, 58, 61, 64; Chicago/AI, 1945, 46, 53, 54, 55, 57, 59, 60, 63, 64; WMAA Annuals, 1945-64; Worcester/AM, 1947; U. of Illinois, 1951, 52, 54, 61, 63; Contemporary American Painting, Tokyo, 1952; Detroit/Institute, 1952, 57; MMA, Edward Root Collection, 1953; PMA, 1954; Indianapolis/Herron, 1954; WMAA, The New Decade, 1954-55; Walker, 1955; A.F.A., World at Work, 1955; ICA, London, American Painting; XXVIII Venice Biennial, 1956; Minneapolis/Institute, American Painting, 1945-57, 1957; ART: USA: 59, NYC, 1959; A.F.A., Private Worlds, 1960; Milwaukee, American Painting, 1760-1960, 1960; NIAL, 1961; New School for Social Research, The Creative Process, 1961; Carnegie, 1964; U. of Rochester, In Focus, 1964; New York World's Fair, 1964-65; Detroit/Institute, 40 Key Artists of the Mid-20th Century, 1965; WMAA, A Decade of American Drawings, 1965; RISD, Recent Still Life, 1966. **Collections:** Andover/Phillips; Barnes Foundation; Brooklyn Museum; Buffalo/Albright; Carnegie; Chase Manhattan Bank; Corcoran; First National City Bank; Hallmark Collection; Hartford/Wadsworth; IBM; U. of Illinois; Jay Mfg. Co.; Kalamazoo/Institute; Lane Foundation; MMA; MOMA; NCFA; Newark Museum; Omaha/Joslyn; PAFA; Scientific American Inc.; Toledo/MA; Union Carbide Corp.; Upjohn Co.; Utica; WGMA; WMAA; Westmoreland County/MA. **Bibliography:** Baur 7; Cummings 3; Flanagan; *From Foreign Shores:* Goodrich and Baur 1; Nordness, ed.; Pousette-Dart, ed.; **Robbins;** Soby 5. Archives.

MURPHY, CATHERINE. b. January 22, 1946, Cambridge, Mass. **Studied:** Pratt Institute, BFA, 1967; Skowhegan School of Painting and Sculpture, with Elmer Bischoff, 1966. **Awards:** National Endowment for the Arts, 1979; Guggenheim Foundation Fellowship, 1982. **m.** Harry Roseman. **Address:** Rt. 1, Box 47, E. Dorsey Lane, Poughkeepsie, N.Y. 12601. **Dealer:** Xavier Fourcade, Inc., NYC. **One-man Exhibitions:** Piper Gallery, Mass., 1972; First Street Gallery, NYC, 1972; Fourcade Droll, Inc., NYC, 1975; Xavier Fourcade, Inc., NYC, 1975, 79, 85; **Retrospective:** Phillips, 1976. **Group:** WMAA Annuals, 1972, 73; Sheldon Memorial Art Gallery, Poughkeepsie, A Sense of Place, 1973; Storm King Art Center, Painting and Sculpture, 1973— The Emerging Real, 1973; Museum of the Philadelphia Civic Center, Woman's Work, 1974; U. of North Carolina, Art on Paper, 1974; PMA, In Her Own Image, 1974; Lincoln, Mass./De Cordova, Candid Painting; American Genre 1950-1975, 1975; Albright College, Perspective 78, 1978; AAIAL, 1980; Brooklyn Museum, American Drawings in Black and White: 1970-1979, 1980; Akron/AM, The Image in American Painting and Sculpture, 1950-1980, 1981; Houston/Contemporary, Americans: The Landscape, 1981; PAFA, Contemporary American Realism Since 1960, 1981; Houston/Contemporary, American Still Life, 1945-1983, 1983; U. of North Carolina, Art on Paper, 1985; SFMA, American Realism (Janss), circ., 1985. **Collections:** Chase Manhattan Bank, NYC; Exxon Corp.; Hirshhorn; Newark Museum; U. of North Carolina; Phillips; Security Pacific National Bank, Los

Catherine Murphy *Cellar Light* 1985

Angeles; Trenton/State; WMAA. **Bibliography:** Arthur 2, 3.

MURRAY, ELIZABETH. b. June 9, 1940, Chicago, Ill. **Studied:** Chicago Art Institute School, BFA, 1962; Miles College, Oakland, MFA, 1964. **Taught:** Bard College, 1974-75, 76-77; Wayne State U., 1975; California Institute of the Arts, 1975-76; Chicago Art Institute School, 1975-76; Princeton U., 1977; Yale U., 1978-79. **Awards:** Chicago/AI, Walter M. Campana Award, 1982; AAIAL, 1984; Skowhegan School, Medal for Painting, 1986. **Address:** 17 White Street, NYC 10013. **Dealer:** Paula Cooper Gallery, NYC. **One-man Exhibitions:** Jacobs Ladder Gallery, Washington, D.C. (two-man), 1974; Paula Cooper Gallery, NYC (two-man) 1975, 76, 78, 81, 83, 84; Jared Sable Gal-

lery, Toronto, 1975; Ohio State U., 1978; Phyllis Kind Gallery, Chicago, 1978; Galerie Mukai, Tokyo, 1980; Susanne Hilberry Gallery, Birmingham, Mich., 1980; Smith College, 1982; Daniel Weinberg Gallery, Los Angeles, 1982; Portland (Ore.) Center for the Visual Arts, 1983; Knight Gallery, Charlotte, N.C., 1984; Brooke Alexander, 1984; U. of New Mexico, 1985. **Retrospective:** Dallas/MFA, circ., 1987. **Group:** WMAA Annuals, 1972, 73, 77, 79; WMAA, Contemporary American Drawings, 1973; California State U., Los Angeles, New Work/New York, 1976; SRGM, Nine Artists; Theodoron Awards, 1977; RISD, Space Window, 1977; Syracuse U., Critics' Choice, 1977; New Museum, NYC, Early Work by Five Contemporary Artists, 1977; Chicago/Contemporary, Ten Years, 1977; ICA, U. of Pennsylvania,

Elizabeth Murray   *Slip Away*   1986

Eight Abstract Painters, 1978; Tampa Bay Art Center, Two Decades of Abstraction, 1978; Hayward Gallery, London, New Painting, New York, 1979; U. of North Carolina, Art on Paper, 1979; Brooklyn Museum, American Drawing in Black and White: 1970-1979; 1980; Haus der Kunst, Munich, Amerikanische Malerie: 1930-1980, 1981; (change: WMAA Annual, 1972; WMAA Biennials, 1973, 77, 79) WMAA Biennials, 81, 85; Chicago/AI, 74th American Exhibition, 1982; High Museum, Art in our Time, 1982; Jacksonville/AM, Currents: A New Mannerism, circ., 1982; MIT, Great Big Drawings, 1982; WMAA, Abstract Drawings, 1911-1981, 1982; Brooklyn Museum, The American Artist as Printmaker, 1983; Hirshhorn, Directions, 1983; Cranbrook, Viewpoint '84, 1984; MOMA, International Survey of Recent Painting and Sculpture, 1984; WMAA, Five Painters in New York, 1984; MOMA, Large Drawings, 1985; Fort Lauderdale, An American Renaissance: Painting and Sculpture Since 1940, 1986. **Collections:** Ackland;

Boston/MFA; Chicago/AI; Cincinnati/AM; Dallas/MFA; Detroit/Institute; High Museum; Hirshhorn; MIT; MOMA; Memphis/Brooks; Milwaukee; Ohio State U.; PMA; RISD; SRGM; St. Louis/City; Walker; WMAA; Yale U. **Bibliography:** Armstrong and Marshall.

MURRAY, ROBERT. b. March 2, 1936, Vancouver (B.C.), Canada. **Studied:** School of Art, U. of Saskatchewan (with Arthur McKay, Roy Kiyooka, Kenneth Lochhead, R. Simmons), 1956-58; Emma Lake Artist's Workshops, U. of Saskatchewan, with Will Barnet, 1957, Barnett Newman, 1959, John Ferren, 1960, Clement Greenberg, 1962, Jack Shadbolt. Traveled Western Hemisphere, Royal Canadian Air Force (auxiliary). **Taught:** U. of Saskatchewan; Hunter College; Yale U.; U. of Oklahoma; School of Visual Arts, NYC. **Commissions:** Saskatoon City Hall, 1959-60; Long Beach State College, 1965; Expo '67, Montreal, 1967; Vancouver International Airport, 1967; Juneau Court Office Building, Juneau, Alaska, 1978. **Awards:** Canada Arts Council Scholarship, 1960, Grant, 1969; National Council on the Arts, 1968; National Endowment for the Arts, grant, 1969; Sao Paulo Biennial, Second Prize, 1969. **Address:** 66 Greene Street, NYC 10013. **Dealers:** Richard Green Gallery, NYC; Klonaridis, Inc., Toronto. **One-man Exhibitions:** (first in US) Betty Parsons Gallery, 1965, also 1966, 68; Jewish Museum, 1967; David Mirvish Gallery, 1967, 68, 70, 72, 74, 75; Vancouver (two-man), 1969 and 1970; Battery Park, NYC; Dag Hammarskjold Plaza, NYC, 1971; Paula Cooper Gallery, 1974; Janie C. Lee Gallery, Houston, 1977; Hamilton Gallery of Contemporary Art, NYC, 1977, 79, 80; Rice U., 1978; Klonaridis, Inc., Toronto, 1979, 81; Phillips Exeter Academy, 1983; Richard Green Gallery, 1986; Gallery 291, Atlanta 1986; Gallery One, Toronto, 1986; Centro Culturale Canadese, Rome, 1985. **Group:** Ottawa/National, Outdoor Sculpture Exhibition, 1962; Hart House, U. of Toronto, 1964; Finch College, NYC, Artists Select, 1964; U. of Toronto Sculpture Annuals, 1964, 67; WMAA Sculpture Annuals, 1964, 66, 68, 70, 73; WMAA, Young America, 1965; Toronto, 1965; Musée Cantonal des Beaux-Arts, Lausanne, II Salon International de Galeries Pilotes, 1966; Los Angeles/County MA, American Sculpture of the Sixties, circ., 1967; Expo '67, Montreal, 1967; ICA, Boston, Nine Canadians, 1967; SRGM, Guggenheim International, 1967; WMAA, 1967; Paris/Moderne, Canada; Art d'Aujourd'hui, 1968; Walker, 14 Sculptors; The Industrial Edge, 1969; X Sao Paulo Biennial, 1969; Grand Rapids, 1969; Cincinnati/Contemporary, Monumental Art, 1970; Chicago/Contemporary, 49th Parallel; New Canadian Art, 1971; Middelheim Park, Antwerp, XI Sculpture Biennial, 1971; Grand Rapids, Sculpture off the Pedestal, 1973; Newport, R.I., Monumenta, 1974; Akron/AI, Project; New Urban Monuments, 1977. **Collections:** U. of Alberta; Allied Chemical Building, Houston; City of Saskatoon; Columbus; Dayton/AI; Fredonia/SUNY; Hirshhorn; Honeywell, Inc., Minneapolis; Long Beach State College; Melbourne/National; MMA; Montreal/MFA; New Brunswick Museum; Ottawa/National; St. John, N.B.; Seagram Collection; Storm King Art Center; Swarthmore College; U. of Sydney; Syracuse/Everson; Toronto; Vancouver; WMAA; Walker; Wayne State U. **Bibliography:** Davies; Friedman, M., *Monumenta*; Tuchman 1.

N

NADELMAN, ELIE. b. February 20, 1882, Warsaw, Poland; **d.** December 28, 1946, NYC. **Studied:** Art Academy, Warsaw, 1901; Academie Colarossi, Paris, 1904; privately with Konstantin Lazczka, 1902. Imperial Russian Army, 1900. Traveled Russia, Europe, U.S.A. To USA, 1914. **Awards:** Sztuka Prize, 1902. **One-man Exhibitions:** (first) Galerie Drouant, Paris, 1909, also 1913; Photo-Secession, NYC, 1915; Scott and Fowles Gallery, NYC, 1917, 25; M. Knoedler & Co., NYC, 1919, 27; Galerie Bernheim Jeune, Paris, 1920, 27; Arts Club of Chicago; MOMA, 1948; The Zabriskie Gallery, 1967, 80, 82; Stanford U., 1968; Galerie Zabriskie, Paris, 1982; Hamiilton College, 1984; Fairweather-Hardin Gallery, 1985; Edward Thorp Gallery, NYC, 1986. **Retrospective:** WMAA, 1975. **Group:** Salon des Artistes Independants, Paris, 1905-08; Salon d'Automne, Paris, 1905-08; Non-Jury Salon, Berlin, 1913; The Armory Show, 1913; Photo-Secession, NYC, 1915; Carnegie, 1938; WMAA; MOMA; MMA. **Collections:** MOMA; Newark Museum; Utica; WMAA. **Bibliography:** *Avant-Garde Painting and Sculpture in America 1910-25;* **Baur 7; Biddle 4;** Birnbaum; Blesh 1; Brumme; Cherry; Craven, W.; *From Foreign Shores;* Goodrich and Baur 1; Hunter 6; Huyghe; *Index of 20th Century Artists;* **Kirstein 1, 2, 4;** Licht, F.; Marter, Tarbell, and Webster; McCurdy, ed.; Mendelowitz; Motherwell 1; **Murrell 2;** Richardson, E.P.; Ringel, ed.; Rose, B. 1; Selz, J.; Schwartz 2; Strachan. Archives.

NAKIAN, REUBEN. b. August 10, 1897, College Point, N.Y. **d.** December 4, 1986, Stamford Conn. **Studied:** Robert Henri School, with Homer Boss, A. S. Baylinson; ASL, 1912; apprenticed to Paul Manship, 1917-20, and Gaston Lachaise. Traveled Italy, France. **Taught:** Newark Fine Arts and Industrial Arts College; Pratt Institute, 1949. **Commissions:** NYU, 1960 (sculpture). **Awards:** Guggenheim Foundation Fellowship, 1930; Ford Foundation Grant, 1959 ($10,000); Sao Paulo, 1960; RISD, Athena Award, 1979. **One-man Exhibitions:** (first) The Downtown Gallery, 1933, also 1935; Charles Egan Gallery, NYC, 1949, 50, 52, 63, 64, 65, 68, 70; Stewart-Marean Gallery, NYC, 1958; Sao Paulo, 1961; Los Angeles/County MA, 1962; WGMA, 1963; Felix Landau Gallery, 1967; U. of Bridgeport, 1972; New York Studio School, Paris, 1974; The Graham Gallery, 1974; Gruenebaum Gallery, NYC, 1979. **Retrospective:** MOMA, 1966. **Group:** Salons of America, NYC, 1922; Whitney Studio Club, NYC; WMAA; Chicago/AI; PAFA; XXXIV Venice Biennial, 1968; MOMA, The New American Painting and Sculpture, 1969; WMAA, The Third Dimension, 1984. **Collections:** MOMA; NYU. **Bibliography:** Cahill and Barr, eds.; Cheney; Craven, W.; Downes, ed.; Geske; Hunter, ed.; **O'Hara 1, 5;** *New in the Seventies;* Phillips, Lisa; Rose, B., 1; Tuchman 1.

NATKIN, ROBERT. b. November 7, 1930, Chicago, Ill. **Studied:** Chicago/AI School, 1952. Designed backdrop for Paul Sanasardo Dance Co., NYC, 1974. **Address:** 24 Mark Twain Lane, West Redding, CT 06896. **Dealer:** Gimpel & Weitzenhoffer, Ltd., NYC. **One-man**

Robert Natkin   *Hitchcock Series*   1984

Exhibition: Wells Street Gallery, Chicago, 1957, 58; Poindexter Gallery, 1959, 61, 63, 65, 67, 68; Ferus Gallery, Los Angeles, 1960; Fairweather-Hardin Gallery, Chicago, 1963, 64, 66, 68, 73, 75; Gertrude Kasle Gallery, Detroit, 1966, 68, 74, 75; Meredith Long Gallery, 1968; Andre Emmerich Gallery, NYC, 1970, 73, 74, 76, 78; Zurich, 1974; The Pennsylvania State U. (two-man), 1973; Jack Glenn Gallery, Corona del Mar, 1973; Makler Gallery, Philadelphia, 1974, 75; Holburne of Menstrie Museum and Festival, Bath, England, 1974; William Sawyer Gallery, San Francisco, 1974, 75; Galerie Merian Edition, Krefeld, 1974; II Cerhio, Milan, 1974; Galleria Venezia, Venice, 1974; Chicago/AI, 1975; Hokin Gallery, Chicago, 1975, 79; Hokin Gallery, Palm Beach, 1975; Linda Farris Gallery, Seattle, 1975; Douglas Drake Gallery, Kansas City, 1976, 78; Andre Emmerich Gallery, Zurich, 1977; Gimpel Fils, London, 1977, 80, 81, 84; Hoshour Gallery, Albuquerque, 1978, 81, 84; Galerie Pudelko, Bonn; Thomas Segal Gallery, Boston, 1979; Gimpel & Weitzenhoffer, Ltd., 1979, 80, 82, 84, 85; Galerie Brusberg, Hannover, 1979; Tortue Gallery, Santa Monica, 1979; ABCD Gallery, Paris, 1979; Ivory/Kimpton Gallery, San Francisco, 1981; GMB, Detroit, 1981; Douglas Drake Gallery, Kansas City, 1981; Gloria Luria Gallery, Bay Harbor Islands, Fla., 1981, 84; Tortue Gallery, Santa Monica, 1981, 84; Hirshhorn, 1981; Gimpel-Hanover, Zurich, 1981; Ridgefield/Aldrich, 1982; Rosenberg Gallery, Toronto, 1982; Ginza Art Center, Tokyo, 1983; Nagoya Art Center, 1983; Columbus, 1983; Helander-Rubenstein Gallery, Palm Beach, 1985; Brenda Kroos Gallery, Columbus, 1985; Klonarides Gallery, Toronto, 1985. **Retrospective:** SFMA, 1969; Kansas City Art Institute, 1976; Moore College of Art, Philadelphia, 1976; Manus Presse Gmbh; Stuttgart, 1980. **Group:** Chicago/AI, Exhibition Momentum, 1950, 56, 57, also 1955, 57, 59, 62; WMAA, Young America, 1960; Carnegie, 1961; ICA, Boston, 1961; WGMA, Lyricism in Abstract Art, 1962; International Mitsubishi, Tokyo and other Japanese cities, 1963; WMAA Annuals, 1966, 68; Galerie Paul Facchetti, 1968; SFMA, 1969; WMAA Annual, 1969; SRGM, 1970, 74; Festival of Two Worlds, Spoleto, 1972. **Collections:** Akron/AI; Brandeis U.; Brooklyn Museum; Buffalo/Albright; Carnegie; Charlotte/Mint; City of Oakland; Columbus; Duke U.; Hartford/Wadsworth; Hirshhorn; Houston/MFA; ICA, Boston; U. of Illinois; Los Angeles/County MA; MOMA; Milwaukee; NYU; U. of Oklahoma; Paris/Beaubourg; The Pennsylvania State U.; RISD; SFMA; SRGM; WMAA; Worcester/AM.

NAUMAN, BRUCE. b. December 6, 1941, Fort Worth, Ind. **Studied:** U. of Wisconsin, BS, 1960-64, with Italo Scanga; U. of California, Davis, 1965, MA. **Taught:** U. of California, Irvine, 1970. **Awards:** National Endowment for the Arts, grant, 1968; Aspen Institute, 1970. **Address:** 4630 Rising Hill Road, Altadena, CA 91001. **Dealers:** Leo Castelli, Inc., NYC; Sperone Westwater, Inc., NYC. **One-man Exhibitions:** Nicholas Wilder Gallery, 1966, 69, 70, 77; Leo Castelli, Inc., NYC, 1968, 69, 71, 73, 75, 76, 78, 80, 82, 84; Konrad Fischer Gallery, Dusseldorf, 1968, 70, 71, 74, 75, 78, 81; Sacramento State College, 1968; Ileana Sonnabend Gallery, Paris, 1969, 72, 76; Gian Enzo Sperone, Turin, 1970; ACE Gallery, Vancouver, 1971, 76, 78; Joseph Helman Gallery, St. Louis, 1971; Francoise Lambert, Milan, 1971; U. of California, Irvine, 1973; Eindhoven, 1973; Galerie Art in Progress, Munich, 1974; Wide White Space Gallery, Antwerp, 1974; Cirrus Editions, Ltd., 1974; Buffalo/Albright, 1975; U. of Nevada, 1976; Sperone Westwater Fischer, Inc., NYC, 1976; Minneapolis, 1978; INK, Zurich, 1978, 81; Galerie Schmela, Dusseldorf, 1979; Deson-Zaks Gallery, Chicago, 1979; Portland (Ore.) Center for the Visual Arts, 1979; Hester van Royen Gallery, London, 1979; Hills Gallery, Santa Fe, 1980; Konrad Fischer Gallery, Dusseldorf, 1980, 83; Carol Taylor Gallery, Dallas, 1980; Nigel Greenwood Gallery, London, 1981; Rijksmuseum Kroller-Muller, circ., 1981; Young Hoffman Gallery, Chicago, 1981; Maude Boreel Print Art, The Hague, 1981; Albuquerque Museum, 1981; Sperone Westwater, Inc., NYC, 1982, 84; Baltimore/MA, 1982; Museum Haus Esters, Krefeld, 1983; Daniel Weinberg Gallery, Los Angeles, 1984. **Retrospectives:** Dusseldorf/Kunsthalle, 1973; Los Angeles/County MA, 1973. **Group:** SFMA, New Directions, 1966; Los Angeles/County MA, American Sculpture of the Sixties, circ., 1967; Documenta IV, Kassel, 1968; Oberlin College, Three Young Americans, 1968; A.F.A., Soft Sculpture, 1968; Corcoran, 1969; Berne, When Attitudes Become Form, 1969; WMAA, Anti-Illusion; Procedures/Materials, 1969; SRGM, 1969; Chicago/Contemporary, Holograms and Lasers, 1970; ICA, U. of Pennsylvania, Against Order; Chance and Art, 1970; WMAA, 1970; Dusseldorf/Kunsthalle, Prospect '71, 1971; MOMA, Information, 1971; Hayward Gallery, London, 11 Los Angeles Artists, 1971; Rijksmuseum Kroller-Muller, Diagrams and Drawings, 1972; Hamburg/Kunstverein, USA: West Coast, circ., 1972; New York Cultural Center, 3D into 2D, 1973; Seattle/AM, American Art—Third Quarter Century, 1973; Parcheggio di Villa Borghese, Rome, Contemporanea, 1974; Chicago/AI, Idea and Image in Recent Art, 1974; Indianapolis, 1974; CNAC, Art/Voir, 1974; MOMA, Drawing Now, 1975; Chicago/AI, 1976; WMAA, 200 Years of American Sculpture, 1976; Detroit/Institute, American Artists: A New Decade, 1976; U. of Chicago, Ideas on Paper 1970-76, 1976; WMAA Biennials 1977, 85; The U. of Chicago, Ideas in Sculpture, 1965-1977, 1977; Williamstown/Clark, The Dada/Surrealist Heritage, 1977; SFMA, Painting and Sculpture in California: The Modern Era, 1976; Madison Art Center, Works on Paper by American Artists, 1977; Amsterdam/Stedelijk, Made by Sculptors, 1978; Krefeld/Haus Lange, The Broadening of the Concept of Reality in the Art of the Sixties and Seventies, 1979; Aspen Center for the Visual Arts, American Portraits of the 60s and 70s, 1979; Franklin Institute, New Spaces: The Holographer's Vision, 1979; U. of Hartford, Conn., Southern California Drawings, 1980; Hayward Gallery, London, Pier & Ocean, 1980; Purchase/SUNY, Soundings, 1981; Documenta VII, Kassel, 1982; MOMA, A Century of Modern Drawings, circ., 1982. **Collections:** Aachen/Kunstverein; Amsterdam/Stedelijk; Buffalo/Albright; Canberra/National; Chicago/AI; Cologne; Harvard U.; Krefeld/Hans Lange; MOMA; Rijksmuseum Kroller-Muller; Rotterdam; Southwestern College, Chula Vista; SRGM; St. Louis/City; WMAA. **Bibliography:** *Art Now 74; Bruce Nauman;* Celant; *Contemporanea;* Davis, D.; De Wilde 2; Honisch and Jensen, eds.; Hunter, ed., 2; Johnson, Ellen H.; Krauss 2, 3; Kren; *Kunst um 1970;* Lippard, ed.; Lippard 3; Livingston and Tucker; Meyer; Muller; Pincus-Witten;

Report; Tuchman 3; *USA West Coast; When Attitudes Become Form.*

NEAL, REGINALD. b. May 20, 1909, Leicester, England. **Studied:** Yale U., 1929-30; Bradley U., BA, 1932; State U. of Iowa, summer, 1936; The U. of Chicago, MA (art history), 1939; Colorado Springs Fine Arts Center, summer, 1941. **Taught:** Millikin U., 1940-46; Escuela de Bellas Artes, San Miguel de Allende, Mexico, summer, 1944; U. of Mississippi, 1951-57; The Contemporaries Graphic Center, NYC, summer, 1956; New Paltz/SUNY, 1957-58; Southern Illinois U., 1958-59, 1966, 67; Douglass College, Rutgers, 1959-77; Yale U., 1966. **Commissions:** A.A.A. Gallery, NYC (two editions of lithographs). **Awards:** Film Council of America, Golden Reel Award, 1956 (American Film Festival, Chicago), for a 30-min. color film, *Color Lithography—An Art Medium.* **Address:** Circle Drive, RD 1, Lebanon, NJ 08833. **Dealers:** Princeton Gallery of Fine Arts, Princeton, N.J.; Haslem Fine Arts, Inc., Washington, D.C. **One-man Exhibitions:** Decatur, 1944; Davenport/Municipal, 1945, 51; South Bend (Ind.) Art Center 1950; A.A.A. Gallery, Chicago, 1950; U. of Mississippi, 1951, 55; The Salpeter Gallery, NYC, 1953; New Paltz/SUNY, 1953; Pratt-Contemporaries, NYC, 1960; Allan Stone Gallery, 1962; Primus-Stuart Gallery, Los Angeles, 1962; Rutgers U., 1965; A.M. Sachs Gallery, 1968; Rutgers U. 1965, 79; Haslem Fine Arts, Inc., Washington, D.C., 1973; Princeton Gallery of Fine Arts, Princeton, N.J., 1973; Rider College, Lawrenceville, N.J., 1984. **Retrospectives:** Somerset (N.J.) Art Association, 1975; Rutgers U., 1975, 86. **Group:** MMA; Cincinnati/AM, 1954, 56, 58; Brooklyn Museum; Library of Congress; Houston/MFA, 1956; Oakland/AM; Riverside Museum; Gallery of Modern Art, Ljubljana, Yugoslavia, III & IV International Exhibitions of Prints, 1959, 61; Albany/Institute, 1965; U. of North Car-

olina, 1965; Trenton State, 1965, 67, 68, 71, 72; Newark Museum, 1966, 68, 69, 72, 77. **Collections:** Allentown/AM; American Republic Insurance Co.; Atlanta/AA; Cincinnati/AM; Davenport/Municipal; Decatur; Des Moines; Grenchen; Hartford/Wadsworth; Library of Congress; MOMA; U. of Massachusetts; Memphis/Brooks; National Gallery; Philip Morris Collection; Newark Museum; Princeton U.; Queens U.; U. of Rochester; Rutgers U.; Southern Illinois U.; Trenton/State; WGMA. **Bibliography:** Bijalji-Merin; Reese.

NEPOTE, ALEXANDER. b. November 6, 1913, Valley Home, Calif. **Studied:** California College of Arts and Crafts, BA; Mills College; U. of California, MA. Traveled Europe. **Taught:** California College of Arts and Crafts, 1945-50; San Francisco State College, 1950-77. **Awards:** SFMA, James D. Phelan Award, 1941, 42; Oakland/AM, 1947, 48, **P.P.**, 1955, Silver Medal, 1957; San Francisco Art Festival, 1951, 53, 59, 60; San Mateo County Fair, 1954, 57; Pasadena/AM, **P.P.**, 1957; California State Fair, 1957, 58; California Palace, 1958; California Watercolor Society, First Award, 1965; Northern California Artists, First Award, 1965; Rio Hondo College Invitational, First Award, 1968; San Mateo Art Fiesta, First Award, 1969. **Address:** 410 Taylor Boulevard, Millbrae, CA 94030. **Dealer:** Suzanne Brown Gallery, Scottsdale, Ariz. **One-man Exhibitions:** Quay Gallery, 1966; Kramer Gallery, San Francisco, 1968; Richard White Gallery, Seattle, 1968; Emerson Art Gallery, Sacramento, 1969; St. Mary's College, Moraga, Calif., 1969; College of Idaho, 1970; Suzanne Brown Gallery, Scottsdale, Ariz., 1978, 80; Fresno Arts Center, Fresno, Calif., 1980. **Retrospective:** Redwood City Municipal Gallery, 1974. **Group:** United Nations Conference Exhibition, San Francisco, 1945; California Palace, 1947, 48, 52, 59, 60, 61; Grand Central, NYC, 1948; WMAA, 1951; U. of Illinois, 1951, 52; A.F.A.; MMA,

1952; Sao Paulo, 1955; SFMA, 1955; a gallery in Provincetown, Mass., 1958; ART: USA:58, NYC, 1958; VMFA, American Painting, 1962; Expo '70, Osaka, 1970; Auckland, Art of the Pacific Basin, 1971; National Watercolor Society Annuals, 1973, 74. **Collections:** California Palace; Chico State College; Denver/AM; Los Angeles/County MA; MMA; U. of Michigan; Mills College; Oakland/AM; Pasadena/AM; Rio Hondo College; SFMA; Sacramento/Crocker; San Francisco Municipal Art Commission; Southern Idaho College; Utah State U.; Walnut Creek Municipal Collection.

NERI, MANUEL. b. April 13, 1930, Sanger, Calif. **Studied:** San Francisco City College, 1949-50; U. of California, Berkeley, 1951-52; California School of Arts and Crafts, Oakland, 1952-57; California School of Fine Arts, San Francisco, 1957-59, with Elmer Bischoff. **Taught:** California School of Fine Arts, San Francisco, 1959-64; U. of

Manuel Neri   *Mujer Pegada Series No. 3*   1985

California, Davis, 1964-. **Commission:** Bateson Building, Sacramento, Calif., 1982. **Awards:** Oakland/AM, first award in sculpture, 1953; Oakland/AM, **P.P.** in painting, 1957; Nellie Sullivan Award, 1959; National Art Foundation award, 1965; Guggenheim Foundation Fellowship, 1979; National Endowment for the Arts grant, 1980; AAIAL, 1985. **Address:** % Dealer. **Dealer:** John Berggruen Gallery, San Francisco; Charles Cowles Gallery, NYC. **One-man Exhibitions:** Six Gallery, San Francisco, 1957; Spatsa Gallery, San Francisco, 1959; Dilexi Gallery, San Francisco, 1960, New Mission Gallery, San Francisco, 1963; Berkeley Gallery, Berkeley, 1964; Quay Gallery, San Francisco, 1966, 68, 71, 75; Louisiana State U., 1969; St. Mary's College, Moraga, Calif., 1970; SFMA, 1971; Sacramento State College, 1972; Davis Art Center, Calif., 1972; San Jose State U., 1974; Braunstein Quay Gallery, NYC, 1976; 60 Langton St., San Francisco, 1976; Oakland/AM, 1976; Sacramento/Crocker, 1977; Gallery Paule Anglim, San Francisco, 1979; Whitman College, 1980; Richmond (Calif.) Art Center, 1980; Grossmont College, 1980; The Mexican Museum, San Francisco, 1981; Seattle/AM, 1981; Charles Cowles Gallery, NYC, 1981, 82, 86; John Berggruen Gallery, 1981, 84; Middendorf/Lane Gallery, Washington, D.C., 1983; California State U., Chico, 1984; Galerie Andre Emmerich, Zurich, 1984; Gimpel-Hanover & Middendorf Gallery, Washington, D.C., 1984; California State U., Sacramento, 1985. **Group:** Oakland/AM Annuals, 1955, 57; SFMA, four-man show, 1959; California Palace, San Francisco, The Nude, 1962; Stanford U., Some Points of View, 1962; Oakland/AM, Sculpture Today, 1963; Stanford U., Current Painting and Sculpture of the Bay Area, 1964; U. of California, Irvine, Abstract Expressionist Ceramics, 1966; U. of California, Berkeley, Funk Art, 1967; SFMA, On Looking Back: Bay Area 1945-1962, 1969; WMAA Annual, 1970; U. of California, Berkeley, The

Eighties, 1970; SFAI, two-man show, 1970; U. of Nevada, two-man show, 1971; Sacramento/Crocker, Sacramento Sampler I, 1972; SFMA, A Third World Painting and Sculpture Exhibition, 1974; De Anza College, Survey of Sculptural Directions in the Bay Area, 1975; Sydney/AG, Biennial, 1976; SFMA, California Painting and Sculpture: The Modern Era, 1976; Santa Barbara/MA, The Handmade Paper Object, 1976; Syracuse/Everson, A Century of Ceramics in the U.S. 1878-1978, 1978; San Diego, Sculpture in California 1975-1980; SFMA, 20 American Artists, 1980; Oakland/AM, 100 Years of California Sculpture, 1982; California State U., Long Beach, Figurative Sculpture: Ten Artists/Two Decades, 1984; Hirshhorn, Drawings 1974-1984, 1984; Oakland/AM, Dilexi: The Dilexi Years, 1958-1970, 1984; Seattle/AM, American Sculpture: Three Decades, 1984; U. of Southern California, California Sculpture Show, circ., 1984; U. of Nebraska, Contemporary Bronze: Six in the Figurative Tradition, circ., 1985; Oakland/AM, Art in the San Francisco Bay Area, 1945-1980, 1985. **Collections:** U. of California, Davis; Chattanooga/Hunter; U. of Colorado; Des Moines; Honolulu Academy; U. of Nebraska; The Mexican Museum, San Francisco; Oakland/AM; SFMA; Sacramento/Crocker; Seattle/AM. **Bibliography: California Sculpture Show;** Gettings. Archives.

NESBITT, LOWELL. b. October 4, 1933, Baltimore, Md. **Studied:** Temple U., BFA, 1950-55; Royal College of Art, London, 1955-56. US Army, 1957-58. Traveled Europe. **Taught:** Baltimore/MA; Towson State Teachers College; Morgan State College; School of Visual Arts, NYC. **Commissions:** National Aeronautics & Space Administration. **Address:** 69 Wooster Street, NYC 10012. **Dealer:** DiLaurenti Gallery, NYC. **One-man Exhibitions:** (first) Baltimore/MA 1958, also 1959-69; Bader Gallery, Washington, DC, 1963;

Corcoran, 1964; Rolf Nelson Gallery, Los Angeles, 1966; Henri Gallery 1965-67, 1969; The Howard Wise Gallery, NYC, 1965, 66; Gertrude Kasle Gallery, 1966-69, 1970, 72, 74; Jefferson Gallery, 1967; Temple U., 1967; Galleria Sperone, Turin, 1967 (two-man, with Joseph Raffael); The Stable Gallery, NYC, 1968, 69; U. of Richmond; M. E. Thelen Gallery, Cologne, 1969, 70, 72; Gimpel Fils, 1970, 74; Gimpel & Weitzenhoffer Ltd., 1971, 73; Pyramid Art Galleries, 1971, 75; Hansen-Fuller Gallery, 1972; Gimpel & Hanover, 1972; Gallerie Fabian Carlson, Goteborg, 1972; Corcoran and Corcoran, Coral Gables, 1972; Gallerie Ostergren, Malmo, 1972; Kunstverein, Freiburg, 1972; Galerie Arnesen, Copenhagen, 1972, 74; Galerie Aronowitsch, Stockholm, 1972; Marion Locks Gallery, Philadelphia, 1973, Galerie Craven, Paris, 1973; Corcoran, 1973; Stefanotty Gallery, NYC, 1973, 74; Fendrick Gallery, 1974; Brooke Alexander, 1974; Walton Gallery, San Francisco, 1974; H.M., Brussels, 1974, 76; Museo de Bellas Artes, San Juan, 1974; U. of Rochester, 1975; City Center, NYC, 1975; Hokin Gallery, Palm Beach, 1976; Hokin Gallery, Chicago 1976; Gump's Gallery, San Francisco, 1977; Andrew Crispo Gallery, 1977, 78, 79; Wichita/Ulrich, 1977; Janus Gallerie, Venice; Cleveland, 1977; Arte/Contacto, Caracas, 1977, 80; Strong's Gallerie, Cleveland, 1978; Kent State.; B.R. Kornblatt Gallery, Baltimore, 1978; The Art Contact, Miami, 1978; San Antonio/McNay, 1980; Ridgefield/Aldrich, 1980; DiLaurenti Gallery, 1986. **Group:** Pan-American Union, Washington, D.C., circ., Latin America, 1964-66; New York World's Fair, 1964-65; Ridgefield/Aldrich, 1965; Flint/Institute, Realism Revisited, 1966; U. of Illinois, 1967; Milan, 1967; Los Angeles/County MA, 1967; International Biennial of Paintings, Tokyo, 1967; IX Sao Paulo Biennial, 1967; ICA, London, 1968; WMAA Annual, 1967; Milwaukee Aspects of a New Realism, 1969; Sweden/Goteborgs, Warmwind, 1970; Cologne, Target Moon, 1971;

Brooklyn Museum, Print Exhibition, 1972; Galerie des 4 Mouvements, Paris, Hyperrealistes Americans, 1972; Bibliotheque Nationale, L'Estampe Contemporaine, 1973; Tokyo Biennial, 1974; Paris/Moderne, 1974; West Palm Beach/Norton, Imagist Realism, 1975; U. of Redlands, Handcolored Prints, circ., 1975; US Department of the Interior, America 1976, circ., 1976; Brooklyn Museum, Thirty Years of American Printmaking, 1977; Museum of Contemporary Crafts, NYC, The Great American Foot, 1978-80. **Collections:** Aachen/NG; Amerada Hess Corp; AT&T; Baltimore/MA; The Bank of New York; Bibliotheque Nationale; CNAC; Chase Manhattan Bank; Chicago/AI; Cleveland/MA; Corcoran; Dallas/MFA; Detroit/Institute; F.T.D. Association; Ford Motor Company; Fort Worth; General Mills, Minneapolis; Goucher College; International Monetary Fund; La Jolla; Library of Congress; Milwaukee; MIT; MOMA; U. of Maryland; NCFA; National Art Gallery; Newark; Oberlin College; J. C. Penney Corp.; Phillips; PMA; Ponce; Prudential Insurance Co. of America; U. of Rochester; Saginaw; Temple U.; U. of Virginia; Wellington, N.F.; Wells, Rich, Greene, Inc., NYC; Worcester/AM; Yale U. **Bibliography:** *America 1976;* Arthur 1; Arthur 2; Davis, D.; Honisch and Jensen, eds.; *Kunst um 1970;* Sager.

NEUMAN, ROBERT S. b. September 9, 1926, Kellogg, Ida. **Studied:** California School of Fine Arts; Mills College, with Max Beckmann; U. of Idaho; Academy of Fine Arts, Stuttgart, with Willi Baumeister. Traveled Europe, USA. **Taught:** California College of Arts and Crafts, 1951-53; California School of Fine Arts, 1952-53; SUNY, 1954-56; Massachusetts College of Art, 1957-62; Brown U., 1962-63; Harvard U., 1963-72; Keene (N.H.) State College, 1972-. **Awards:** Fulbright Fellowship, 1953; Guggenheim Foundation Fellowship, 1956-57; Boston Arts

Festival, Grand Prize, 1961; Brown U.; Howard Foundation Grant for Painting, 1967. **Address:** 135 Cambridge Street, Winchester, Mass. 01890. **Dealer:** Wingspread Gallery, Northeast Harbor, Me. **One-man Exhibitions:** Gump's Gallery, 1952; Felix Landau Gallery, 1954; La Escondida, Taos, N.M., 1956; Sala Vayreda, Barcelona, 1956; Galleria del Cavallino, Venice, 1957, 60; The Swetzoff Gallery, Boston, 1957, 58; Allan Stone Gallery, Harrison, N.Y., 1959; Gres Gallery, Washington, D.C., 1959; The Pace Gallery, Boston, 1960, 62; Lincoln, Mass./De Cordova, 1963; Allan Stone Gallery, NYC, 1966, 72; Ward-Nasse Gallery, Boston, 1966, 67; Exeter, 1967; Waitsfield/Bundy, 1968; Michael Walls Gallery, 1968; Bristol (R.I.) Museum of Art, 1968 (two-man, with Hugh Townley); U. of Idaho, 1969; Brockton (Mass.) Art Center, 1971; Keene State College, 1972; BAAK Gallery, Cambridge, Mass., 1976; Sunne Savage Gallery, Boston, 1979; Wingspread Gallery, 1980, 82, 83, 85. **Group:** California Palace, 1951; SFMA, 1951-53; Denver/AM, 1952; MMA, 1952; WMAA, 1952, 58; U. of Illinois, 1952, 61; PAFA, 1953; Colorado Springs/FA, 1953; Kyoto, Japan, 1956; ICA, Boston, 1958-60; Carnegie, 1961; Seattle World's Fair, 1962; M. Knoedler & Co., Art across America, circ., 1965-67; New School for Social Research, 1966; State U. of Iowa, 1968; Lincoln, Mass./De Cordova, New England Drawings, 1974; Silvermine, Annual, 1976; Worcester/AM, Recent Acquisitions, 1977. **Collections:** American Broadcasting Co.; Andover/Phillips; Boston/MFA; Boston U.; Brandeis U.; Carnegie; Commercial Union Assurance Co., Boston; Dartmouth College; ICA, Boston; Lincoln, Mass./De Cordova; MOMA; U. of Massachusetts; SFMA; Worcester/AM; Yale U.

NEVELSON, LOUISE. b. 1900, Kiev, Russia. To USA, 1905. **Studied:** ASL, 1929-30, with Kenneth Hayes Miller;

Hofmann School, Munich, 1931; assistant to Diego Rivera in Mexico City, 1932-33. Legion Memorial Square, in the Wall Street area of Manhattan, was renamed Louise Nevelson Plaza, 1978. *Shadows and Flags*, seven large metal sculptures, are installed there. Traveled Europe, Central and South America. **Taught:** Educational Alliance, NYC; Great Neck (N.Y.) Adult Education Program; New York School for the Deaf. **Member:** Artists Equity (President); Sculpture Guild (Vice-President); Federation of Modern Painters and Sculptors (Vice-President). Federal A.P.: Easel painting; AAAL, 1979. **Commissions:** Princeton U., 1969; Temple Beth-El, Great Neck, N.Y., 1970; Temple Israel, Boston, 1973; City of Scottsdale, 1973; City of Binghamton, N.Y., 1973; Federal Courthouse, Philadelphia, 1975; MIT; St. Peter's Lutheran Church, NYC; World Trade Center, NYC; City of Jackson, Mich.; Embarcadero Center Plaza, San Francisco; Pepsico Co., Purchase, N.Y.; Bendix Corp., Southfield, Mich.; Federated Department Stores, Cincinnati, Ohio; Hallmark Center, Kansas City, 1980; U. of Iowa, 1980. **Awards:** ART: USA:59, NYC, Grand Prize, 1959; Chicago/AI, The Mr. & Mrs. Frank G. Logan Prize, 1960; Tamarind Fellowship, 1963; MacDowell Colony Medal, 1969; Hamline U., Honorary Doctor of Humanities; Brandeis U., Creative Arts Award, 1971; Hobart and William Smith College, Honorary Doctor of Humane Letters, 1971; Hon. DFA, Smith College, 1973; President's Medal of the Municipal Art Society of New York; Hon. DFA, Columbia U., 1978; Hon. DFA, Boston U.; AAIAL, Gold Medal for Sculpture, 1983; National Medal of the Arts, 1985; Chevalier de la Légion d'Honneur, Paris, 1986. **Address:** 29 Spring Street, NYC 10012. **Dealer:** The Pace Gallery. **One-man Exhibitions:** (first) Karl Nierendorf Gallery, NYC, 1941, also 1943, 44, 46; Norlyst Gallery, NYC, 1941, 43; Lotte Jacobi Gallery, NYC, 1950; Grand Central Moderns, NYC, 1951, 54, 56, 57, 58; Esther Stuttman Gallery, NYC, 1958; Martha Jackson Gallery, 1959, 61, 70; Daniel Cordier, Paris, 1960; David Herbert Gallery, NYC, 1960; Devorah Sherman Gallery, 1960; The Pace Gallery, Boston, 1960, 64, NYC, 1965, 66, 69, 72, 74, 76, 78, 80, 83, 85; Sidney Janis Gallery, 1963; Hanover Gallery, 1963; Gimpel & Hanover Galerie, Zurich, 1964; Berne, 1964; Galleria d'Arte Contemporanea, Turin, 1964; David Mirvish Gallery, 1965; Galerie Schmela, 1965; Ferus/Pace Gallery, Los Angeles, 1966; Arts Club of Chicago, 1968; Turin/Civico, 1969; Harcus-Krakow Gallery, 1969; Galerie Jeanne Bucher, Paris, 1969; the Pace Gallery, Columbus, 1969, 74, 78, 81; Houston/MFA, 1969; Rijksmuseum Kroller-Muller, 1969; U. of Texas, 1970; WMAA, 1970; Makler Gallery, 1971, 74, 76, 78; Dunkelman Gallery, Toronto, 1972; Parker Street 470 Gallery, Boston, 1972; Studio Marconi, Milan, 1973; Stockholm/National, 1973; Brussels/Beaux-Arts, 1974; Paris/Moderne, 1974; Berlin/National, 1974; Minami Gallery, 1975; Galleria d'Arte Spagnoli, Florence, Italy, 1975; Harcus Krakow Rosen Sonnabend, Boston, 1975; Purchase/SUNY, 1977; Richard Gray Gallery, Chicago, 1978, 82; Linda Farris Gallery, Seattle, 1978; Rockland, Maine, 1979; West Palm Beach/Norton, 1979; Jacksonville/AM, 1979; Wildenstein & Co., NYC, 1980; Scottsdale Center for the Arts, 1980; Phoenix/AM, 1980; Seattle/AM, 1980; Winnipeg Art Gallery, Ontario, Canada, 1980; U. of Iowa, 1980; Dayton/AI; 1980; WMAA, 1980; Wildenstein & Co., London, 1981; Galerie de France, Paris, 1981; Harcus Krakow Gallery, Boston, 1982; Wildenstein & Co., Tokyo, 1982; NYU, 1983; Barbara Krakow Gallery, Boston, 1984; Hokin Gallery, Bay Harbor Islands, Fla., 1984, 85; Makler Gallery, Philadelphia, 1984; Storm King Art Center, 1984; Buffalo/SUNY, Burchfield Center, 1984; Rockland/Farnsworth, 1985; Galerie Claude Bernard, Paris, 1986; Galerie Alice Pauli, Lausanne, Switzerland, 1986.

Retrospectives: WMAA, 1966; Walker, circ., 1973; WMAA, 1980. **Group:** Sezession Gallery (Europe), 1933-38; Contemporary Arts Gallery, NYC; Jacobsen Gallery, NYC; Society of Independent Artists, NYC; Brooklyn Museum; ACA Gallery; Federal Art Project Gallery, NYC, 1933-38; PAFA, 1944; VMFA, 1957; Riverside Museum, Directions in Sculpture, 1957; A.F.A., Art and the Found Object, circ., 1959; Jeanne Bucher, Paris (three-man), 1958; MOMA, Sixteen Americans, circ., 1959; ART:USA:59, NYC, 1959; Rome-New York Foundation, Rome, Ciphers, 1960; Utica, Art Across America, 1960; A.F.A., Unique Impressions, 1960; XXXI Venice Biennial, 1962; WMAA Annuals, 1947, 57, 61, 64, 66, 69; Federation of Modern Painters and Sculptors Annuals, 1955, 56, 57, 59; A.F.A., Contemporary Trends, circ., 1955-56; American Abstract Artists Annuals, 1956, 57, 59, 60; Documenta III, Kassel, 1964; MOMA, Contemporary Painters and Sculptors as Printmakers, 1964; Dallas/MFA, 1965; WMAA, Art of the U.S. 1670-1966, 1966; Chicago/AI, 1966, 67; Los Angeles/County MA, American Sculpture of the Sixties, 1967; SRGM, 1967; Jewish Museum, 1968; WMAA, 1969, 73; MOMA, Tamarind; Homage to Lithography, 1969; Princeton U., American Art since 1960, 1970; Expo '70, Osaka, 1970; Carnegie, 1970; Society of the Four Arts, Calder/Nevelson/David Smith, 1971; Seattle/AM, American Art—Third Quarter Century, 1973; National Gallery, American Art at Mid-Century, 1973; Newport, R.I., Monumenta, 1974; WMAA, The 20th Century: 35 Artists, 1974. **Collections:** Allentown/AM; Arts Club of Chicago; Birmingham, Ala./MA; Brandeis U.; Buffalo/Albright; Brooklyn Museum; Carnegie; Chicago/AI; Chicago/Contemporary; Cleveland/MA; Corcoran; Dallas/MFA; Detroit/Institute; Edinburgh/Modern; Fairmount Park Association; Grenoble; High Museum; Hirshhorn; Hospital Corp. of America; Houston/MFA; U. of Illinois; Indiana U.; Israel Museum; Jewish Museum; Julliard; Kansas City/Nelson; Los Angeles/County MA; MMA; MOMA; Montreal/MFA; NYU; U. of Nebraska; Newark Museum; New Orleans Museum; Norfolk/Chrysler; PAFA; Paris/Moderne; Pasadena/AM; Phoenix; Princeton U.; Queens College; Rijksmuseum Kroller-Muller; Sara Roby Foundation; Rockland/Farnsworth; Rotterdam; SRGM; St. Louis/City; South Mall, Albany; Tate Gallery; WMAA; Walker; Wilmington; Yale U. **Bibliography:** Baur 5; Calas, N. and E.; Craven; W.; Diamonstein; Davies; **Friedman, M., 3;** *From Foreign Shores;* **Glimcher;** Goodrich and Baur 1; **Gordon 4;** Honisch and Jensen, eds.; Hunter, ed.; *Louise Nevelson: Atmosphere and Environments;* Janis and Blesh 1; Licht, F.; Marter, Tarbell, and Wechsler; *Metro; Monumenta;* Nemser; Moser 1; Neumeyer; Phillips, Lisa; Rickey; Rose, B., 1; Rowell; Seitz 3; Selz, J.; Seuphor 3; Strachan; Toher, ed.; Trier 1; Tuchman 1. Archives.

NEVELSON, MIKE. b. February 23, 1922, NYC. **Studied:** NYU; self-taught in art. Traveled Europe, Mediterranean, Africa, Central and South America. **Taught:** Wooster Community Art Center, Danbury, Conn., 1965-68; Brookfield (Conn.) Craft Center, 1968; U. of New Mexico, 1969-70. **Member:** Artists Equity. **Awards:** Silvermine Guild, 1966. **Address:** 3 Milltown Road, New Fairfield, CT 06810. **One-man Exhibitions:** Roko Gallery, 1945; Rockland/Farnsworth, 1953; U. of Maine, 1953; Haystack Mountain School of Crafts, 1956; Carl Seimbab Gallery, 1959; Staempfli Gallery, 1961; The Amel Gallery, NYC, 1964; Wooster Community Art Center, Danbury, 1966; Dartmouth College, 1966; Grand Central Moderns, NYC, 1967; Expo '67, Montreal, 1967; Sachs New York, Inc., NYC, 1969; A.A.A. Gallery, NYC (two-man), 1970; Christ-Janer Gallery, New Canaan, Conn. (two-man), 1975. **Group:** Portland, Me./MA, 1956;

Boston Arts Festival, 1959; Norfolk Art Festival, Va., 1959; Carnegie, 1961; Houston/Contemporary, 1961; U. of Illinois, 1961; WMAA, 1962, 64; Hartford/Wadsworth, 1963; Silvermine Guild, 1964, 68, 69; Lincoln, Mass./De Cordova, 1964; Four Seasons Restaurant, Pop Exhibition, 1965; U. of Connecticut, 1965; Brooklyn Museum, 1972; Potsdam/SUNY, 1973; Norske Internasjonale Grafikk Biennale, Fredrikstad, Norway, 1974. **Collections:** Colby College; Hartford/Wadsworth; Housatonic Community College; Slater, Stratford College; WMAA; Youngstown/Butler. **Bibliography:** Archives.

NEWMAN, BARNETT. b. January 29, 1905, NYC; **d.** July 4, 1970, NYC. **Studied:** Cornell U., 1922-26; City College of New York, BA, 1927; ASL, with Duncan Smith, John Sloan, William Von Schlegell. Traveled USA, Canada, Europe. **Taught:** U. of Saskatchewan, 1959; U. of Pennsylvania, 1962-64. Cofounder of a school, "Subject of the Artist," with William Baziotes, Robert Motherwell, and Mark Rothko, NYC, 1948. **One-man Exhibitions:** (first) Betty Parsons Gallery, 1950, also 1951; Bennington College, 1958; French & Co., Inc., NYC, 1959; Allan Stone Gallery (two-man), 1962; SRGM, 1966; M. Knoedler & Co., 1969; Irving Blum Gallery, Los Angeles, 1970; Kammerkunsthalle, Berlin, 1970; U. of Washington, 1971; Baltimore/AM, circ., 1980; U. of Massachusetts, 1983. **Retrospectives:** Pasadena/AM, 1970; MOMA, 1971; Tate, 1972; Baltimore/MA, 1979. **Group:** Chicago/AI, Abstract and Surrealist Art, 1948; Minneapolis/Institute, American Painting, 1945-57, 1957; MOMA, The New American Painting, circ., Europe, 1958-59; Documenta II, Kassel, 1959; Kimura Gallery, Tokyo, 1959; SRGM, Abstract Expressionists and Imagists, 1961; SRGM/USIA, American Vanguard, circ., Europe, 1961-62; Seattle World's Fair, 1962; WMAA Annual, 1963; Brandeis U., New Directions in American Painting, 1963; Jewish Museum, Black and White, 1963; Tate, Dunn International, 1964; Chicago/AI Annual, 1964; SRGM, Guggenheim International, 1964; Kunsthalle, Basel, International Painting since 1950, 1964; MOMA, The New American Painting and Sculpture, 1969. **Collections:** Amsterdam/Stedelijk; Basel; Kunsthalle, Basel; MOMA; Stockholm/National. **Bibliography:** Alloway 4; Battcock, ed.; Calas, N. and E.; Carmean, Rathbone, and Hess; Chipp; Danto; De Vries, ed.; De Wilde 1, 2; *The Great Decade;* Goossen 1; Greenberg 1; Haftman; **Hess, T. B., 2, 3;** Hobbs and Levin; Honisch and Jensen, eds.; Hunter, ed.; Hunter 1; Johnson, Ellen H.; Kozloff 3; Lippard 5; *Metro; Monumenta;* Motherwell and Reinhardt, eds.; Murken-Altrogge; Richardson 1; Rickey; Rose, B., 1, 4; Rosenblum 2; Rubin 1; Sandler; Sandler 1; Schneider; Seuphor 1; Tomkins 2; Tuckman, ed.; Tuchman 3. Archives.

NICE, DON. b. June 26, 1932, Visalia, Calif. **Studied:** U. of Southern California, 1959-64, BFA; Yale U., 1962-64, MFA. **Taught:** Minneapolis School of Art, 1960-62; School of Visual Arts, NYC, 1963-; Dartmouth College, 1982. **Address:** Indian Brook Road, Garrison, N.Y. 10524. **Dealer:** Nancy Hoffman Gallery, NYC. **One-man Exhibitions:** Richard Feigen Gallery, Chicago, 1963; Allan Stone Gallery, NYC, 1967, 69, 71, 74; Galerie Alexandra Monett, Brussels, 1973, 75; Gallery A, Sydney, Australia, 1983; U. of Rochester, 1974; Arnhem 1974; Nancy Hoffman Gallery, 1975, 77, 79, 80, 81, 83, 84; D. M. Gallery, London, 1975; Dorry Gates Gallery, Kansas City, 1977; Thomas Segal Gallery, Boston, 1979; Brandeis U., circ., 1979; Gallery Moos, Toronto, 1980; U. of Michigan, 1982; Pace Editions, NYC, 1982; Dartmouth College, 1982; Palm Springs Desert Museum, 1983; Joe Chowning Gallery, San Francisco, 1983; John Berggruen Gallery, San Francisco, 1983; Lincoln Center Art Gallery, NYC, 1983; Images Gallery, Toledo, 1983. **Retrospective:** Fine Arts Museum of Long Island, 1985. **Group:** Vassar College, Realism Now, 1968; Indianapolis, 1974; Brooklyn Museum, Print Biennial, 1976; US Dept. of Interior, America 1976, circ., 1976; Contemporary Crafts Museum, NYC, The Great American Foot, 1978; U. of Nebraska, Things Seen; San Antonio/MA, Real, Really Real, Super Real, 1981; PAFA, Contemporary American Realism Since 1960, circ., 1981; Utica, A Painters Appreciation of Realism, 1982. **Collections:** Arnhem; Canberra/National; Flint/Institute; MOMA; Miami U.; Minneapolis/Institute; Ottawa/National; WMAA; Walker; Wilmington.

NICK, GEORGE. b. 1927, Rochester, N.Y. **Studied:** Cleveland Institute of Art, 1948-51; Brooklyn Museum School, 1951-52, with Edwin Dickinson; Art Students League, 1957-58, with Edwin Dickinson; Yale U., 1961-63, BFA, MFA. **Taught:** Garland Jr. College, 1963-64; Carnegie, 1964-65; Maryland Institute, 1965-66; U. of Pennsylvania, 1966-69; Massachusetts State College of Art, 1969-. **Awards:** National Endowment for the Arts, 1976; AAIAL, Childe Hassam Fund Purchase, 1976, 80. **Address:** 86 Philip Farm Road, Concord, Mass. 01742. **Dealer:** Fischbach Gallery, NYC. **One-man Exhibitions:** Carnegie Institute, 1964; Robert Schoelkopf Gallery, NYC, 1965, 67; Richard Gray Gallery, Chicago, 1969, 72, 74, 77, 82; 100 Acres Gallery, NYC, 1971; Harcus Krakow Gallery, Boston, 1974, 79, 82; Tibor de Nagy Gallery, NYC, 1977, 78, 79, 80, 81, 82, 84, 85; Gross McCleaf Gallery, Philadelphia, 1984; The Harcus Gallery, Boston, 1984. **Group:** Omaha/Joslyn, A Sense of Place, 1973; US Department of the Interior, America 1976, circ., 1976; Youngstown/Butler, Midyear Show, 1977, 83; Flint/Institute, Art and the Automobile, 1976; U. of Nebraska, Things Seen, 1978; Tulsa/Philbrook, Real-

Gladys Nilsson *Forewarned* 1986

ism/Photorealism, 1980; PAFA, Contemporary American Realism Since 1960, 1981. **Collections:** Boston/MFA; Brandeis U.; Charlotte/Mint; Essen; Hirshhorn; ICA/Boston; Johannesberg/ Municipal; Lincoln/DeCordova; MMA; U. of North Carolina; Omaha/Joslyn.

NILSSON, GLADYS. b. 1940, Chicago. **Studied:** Chicago Art Institute School, 1962, BA. **Commissions:** ART Park, Lewiston, N.Y., 1979. **Awards:** Chicago/AI, Logan Medal, 1967; Chicago/AI, Bartels Prize, 1978; National Endowment for the Arts, Grant, 1974. **m.** Jim Nutt. **Address:** 1035 Greenwood, Wilmette, IL 60091. **Dealer:** Phyllis Kind Gallery, Chicago and NYC. **One-man Exhibitions:** SFAI, 1969; Candy Store Gallery, Folsom, Calif., 1971, 72, 73; WMAA, 1973; U. of Wisconsin, Madison, 1977; Phyllis Kind Gallery, Chicago, 1970, 73, 74, 77, 78, 81, 83; Phyllis Kind Gallery, NYC,

1975, 79, 82; Portland (Ore.) Center for Visual Arts, 1979; Wake Forest U., 1979; Randolph Street Gallery, Chicago, 1984. **Group:** Hyde Park Art Center, Chicago. The Hairy Who, 1966, 67, 68; Chicago/Contemporary, Don Baum Sez, "Chicago Needs Famous Artists," 1969; ICA, U. of Philadelphia, Spirit of the Comics, 1969; WMAA, Human Concern/Personal Torment, 1970; SFMA, Poetic Fantasy, 1971; Chicago/Contemporary, Chicago Imagist Art, 1972; Ottawa/Ontario, What They're Up to in Chicago, 1972; Sao Paulo, XII Biennial; Madison Art Center, Contemporary Figurative Painting in the Midwest, 1977; Sacramento/Crocker, The Chicago Connection, 1977; Chicago/AI, 100 Artists— 100 Years, 1979; U. of North Carolina, Some Recent Art from Chicago, 1980; Sunderland (Eng.) Art Centre, Who Chicago?, circ., 1980; Kansas City/AI, Chicago Imagists, 1982; Illinois Wesleyan U., Contemporary Chicago Images, 1983. **Collections:** Art Gallery of Western Australia; Chicago/AI; Chicago/Contemporary; Continental Bank, Chicago; MOMA; Museum des 20. Jahrhunderts, Vienna; NMAA; New Orleans Museum; PMA; Phoenix; U. of Rochester; WMAA. **Bibliography:** Adrian; *Who Chicago?*.

NIVOLA, CONSTANTINO. b. July 5, 1911, Orani, Sardinia. **Studied:** Istituto Superiore d'Arte, Monza, Italy, with Marino Marini, Marcello Nizzoli, 1930-36, MA, Art Director for Olivetti Company, 1936-39. Traveled Europe, USA. To USA, 1939. Art Director, *Interiors* magazine, 1941-45. **Taught:** Director, Design Workshop of Harvard U. Graduate School, 1953-57; Columbia U., 1961-63; Harvard U., 1970-73; International U. of Art, Florence, Italy, 1971; Dartmouth College, 1978; U. of California, Berkeley, 1978-79. **Member:** Artists Equity; Architectural League of New York; NIAL. **Commissions:** Milan Triennial, 1933 (mural, with S.R. Francello); Italian Pavilion, Paris

World's Fair, 1937; Olivetti Showroom, NYC, 1953-54 (mural); Four Chaplains Memorial Fountain, Falls Church, Va., 1955; 1025 Fifth Avenue, NYC, 1955 (gardens); William E. Grady Vocational High School, Brooklyn, N.Y., 1957; Mutual Insurance Co. of Hartford, Hartford, Conn., 1957 (facade); P.S. 46, Brooklyn, N.Y., 1959 (murals and sculptures for playground); McCormick Place, Exposition Hall, Chicago, 1960 (facade); Motorola Building, Chicago, 1960 (murals); Saarinen Dormitories, Yale U., 1962 (35 sculptures); designed a memorial plaza in Nuoro, Italy, 1966; P.S. 320, Brooklyn, N.Y., 1967 (sculpture); Mexico City/Nacional, 19th Olympiad, 1968 (sculpture). **Awards:** Philadelphia Decorators Club Award, 1959; Carborundum Major Abrasive Marketing Award, 1962; Municipal Art Society of New York, Certificate of Merit, 1962; Regional Exhibition of Figurative Art, Cagliari, Italy, Gold Medal; Federation of Graphic Arts, Diploma; Park Association of New York, NYC, Certificate of Commendation, 1965; American Institute of Architects, Fine Arts Medal, 1968. **Address:** 410 Stone Road, Springs, East Hampton, NY 11937. **Dealer:** Washburn Gallery, Inc., NYC. **One-man Exhibitions:** (first) Sassari Gallery, Sardinia, 1927 (paintings); Betty Parsons Gallery, 1940 (two-man, with Saul Steinberg); (first one-man in USA) Tibor de Nagy Gallery, 1950; The Peridot Gallery, 1954, 57; Harvard U., 1956; The Bertha Schaefer Gallery, 1958; Architectural League of New York, 1958; Galleria Il Milione, Milan, 1959; Arts Club of Chicago, 1959; A.F.A., circ., 1960; Galleria dell' Ariete, 1962; The Byron Gallery, 1964-67; Andrew-Morris Gallery, NYC; Marlborough Galleria d'Arte, Rome, 1973; The Willard Gallery, 1973; Cagliari U., Italy, 1973; ICA, Boston, 1974; Gallery Paule Anglim, San Francisco, 1978; Washburn Gallery, Inc., 1984. **Group:** Brooklyn Museum, 1947; American Abstract Artists, 1947; Rome National Art Quadriennial, 1950, 73; Riverside Museum, NYC, 1955;

WMAA, 1957, Carnegie, 1958; Museum of Contemporary Crafts, 1962; National Gold Medal Exhibition of the Building Arts, NYC, 1962; A.F.A., American Drawing, circ., 1964. MOMA. **Collections:** U. of California, Berkeley; Harvard U.; Hirshhorn; MOMA; PMA; Uffizi Gallery; WMAA. **Bibliography:** Giedion-Welcker 1; Licht, F.; *Metro*; Seuphor 3; Trier 1.

NOGUCHI, ISAMU. b. November 17, 1904, Los Angeles, Calif. Resided Japan, ages 2-14. **Studied:** Columbia U., 1923-25 (premedical); apprenticed briefly to Gutzon Borglum; Leonardo da Vinci Art School, NYC; East Side Art School, NYC; apprenticed to Constantin Brancusi, Paris, 1927-29. Traveled Mexico, USSR, the Orient, Europe, Israel, USA. Designed numerous stage sets for Martha Graham Dance Co. In May 1985, **The Isamu Noguchi Garden Museum** opened in Long Island City, N.Y. **Member:** National Sculpture Society. **Commissions:** Connecticut General Life Insurance Co. (gardens and sculpture); First National Bank of Fort Worth, Tex. (piazza and sculpture); John Hancock Building (fountain and sculpture); Chase Manhattan Bank, NYC (garden); Associated Press, NYC (relief), 1938; Yale U. Library of Precious Books; Keyo U., Japan (2 gardens); UNESCO, Paris (garden); International Business Machines, Armonk, N.Y.; Billy Rose Garden, Jerusalem; Detroit Civic Center Memorial Fountain, 1974; Pepsico, Purchase, N.Y., 1974; Horace E. Dodge & Son Memorial Fountain, and Philip A. Hart Plaza, Detroit, Mich., 1973-79; stepped garden for Sogetsu School of Flower Arrangement, Tokyo, 1977-78. **Awards:** Guggenheim Foundation Fellowship, 1927; Bollingen Foundation Fellowship, 1950; Chicago/AI, The Mr. & Mrs. Frank G. Logan Medal; Hon. DFA, New School for Social Research, 1974; Hon. DFA, Columbia U., 1984; New York State Council on the Arts, Governor's Arts Award, 1984; Israel Museum Fellowship, 1985; Municipal Arts Society, NYC, President's Medal, 1985. **Address:** 32-37 Vernon Blvd., Long Island City, N.Y. 11106. **Dealer:** The Pace Gallery, NYC. **One-man Exhibitions:** (first) Eugene Schoen Gallery, NYC, 1929; Marie Sterner Gallery, NYC, 1930; Harvard Society for Contemporary Art, 1930; Arts Club of Chicago, 1930; Buffalo/Albright, 1930; Reinhardt Galleries, NYC, 1932; Demotte Gallery, NYC, 1932; Mellon Galleries, Philadelphia, 1933; Marie Harriman Gallery, NYC, 1934; Sidney Burney Gallery, London, 1934; Western Association of Art Museum Directors, circ., 1934; Honolulu Academy, 1934, 39; John Becker (Gallery), NYC, 1939, 42; SFMA, 1942; Charles Egan Gallery, 1948; Daniel Cordier, Paris; Cordier & Ekstrom, Inc., 1963, 65, 67-69, 70; Gimpel & Hanover, 1968, 72; Gimpel Fils, 1968, 72; Minami Gallery, 1973; The Pace Gallery, NYC, 1975, 80, 83; MOMA, 1977; Walker, circ., 1978-79; Andre Emmerich Gallery, NYC, 1980; WMAA, 1980; Galerie Maeght, Paris, 1981; Gemini G.E.L., Los Angeles, 1982; Richard Gray Gallery, Chicago; XLII Venice Biennial, 1986. **Retrospective:** WMAA, 1968. **Group:** MOMA, Fantastic Art, Dada, Surrealism, 1936; Musée du Jeu de Paume, Trois Siecles d'Art aux Etats-Unis, 1938; MOMA, Art in Our Time, 1939; MOMA, 14 Americans, 1946; MOMA, Abstract Painting and Sculpture in America, 1951; WMAA, Nature and Abstraction, 1958; Documenta II & III, Kassel, 1959, 64; WMAA, American Art of Our Century, 1961; Seattle World's Fair, 1962; Los Angeles/County MA, American Sculpture of the Sixties, circ., 1967; WMAA, 1970; Carnegie, 1970; Venice Biennial, 1972; SRGM, Masters of Modern Sculpture, 1974; WMAA, 200 Years of American Sculpture, 1976; WMAA, The Third Dimension, 1984. **Collections:** Art Gallery of Ontario, Toronto; Brooklyn Museum; Buffalo/Albright; Chicago/AI; Cleveland/MA; Des Moines; Hartford/Wadsworth; Hirshhorn; Honolulu Academy; Jerusalem/National; Kamakura; Los Angeles/County MA; MMA; MOMA; U.

of Nebraska; New School for Social Research; Princeton U.; Rijksmuseum Kroller-Muller; SFMA; SRGM; Society of Four Arts; Tate; Toledo/MA; Toronto; WMAA; Walker; West Palm Beach/Norton. **Bibliography:** Baur 5, 7; Biddle 4; Blesh 1; Breton 3; Brumme; Cahill and Barr, eds.; Calas; Cheney; Craven, W.; Cummings 1; Downes, ed.; Flanagan; Giedion-Welcker 1; Goodrich and Baur 1; **Gordon 2;** Hunter 6; *Index of 20th Century Artists;* **Isamu Noguchi; Isamu 2;** Krauss 2; Kuh 2; Lane and Larsen; Licht, F.; McCurdy, ed.; Marter, Tarbell, and Wechsler; Mendelowitz; *Metro;* Miller, ed. 2; Neumeyer; **Noguchi;** Phillips, Lisa; Read 3; Ritchie 1, 3; Rose, B., 1; Rowell; Rubin 1; Seuphor 3; Seymour; Strachan; **Takiguchi;** Trier 1; Tuchman 1. Archives.

NOLAND, KENNETH. b. April 10, 1924, Asheville, N.C. **Studied:** Black Mountain College, 1946, with Ilya Bolotowsky; Zadkine School of Sculpture, Paris, 1948-49. US Air Force, 1942-46. **Taught:** The Catholic U. of America; ICA, Washington, D.C.; Emma Lake Artist's Workshops, U. of Saskatchewan; Bennington College; Bard College, 1985. Designed sets for *Futurities*, a Steve Lacy/Robert Creeley ballet. **Awards:** Corcoran, 1967. **Member:** AAAL. **Address:** 125-A Kitchawan Road, South Salem, N.Y. 10590. **Dealer:** Andre Emmerich Gallery, NYC and Zurich. **One-man Exhibitions:** (first) Galerie Creuze, Paris, 1949; French & Co. Inc., NYC, 1959; Galleria dell'Ariete, 1960; Galerie Lawrence, Paris, 1961; Bennington College, 1961; Andre Emmerich Gallery, NYC, 1961-64, 1966, 67, 71, 73, 75, 77, 80, 81, 82, 83, 84, 85, 86; Galerie Charles Leinhard, Zurich, 1962; Galerie Schmela, 1962, 64; Kasmin Ltd., 1963, 65, 68; David Mirvish Gallery, 1965, 74, 76; Harvard U., Three American Painters (with Jules Olitski, Frank Stella), circ., Pasadena, 1965; St. John, N.B., 1966 (three-man, with Helen Frankenthaler, Jules Olitski); MMA, 1968

(three-man, with Morris Louis, Anthony Caro); Lawrence Rubin Gallery, 1969; Dayton's Gallery 12, Minneapolis, 1969 (three-man, with Anthony Caro, Frank Stella); Galerie Mikro, Berlin, 1972; Waddington Galleries, London, 1973; Jack Glenn Gallery, Corona del Mar, 1974; Janie C. Lee Gallery, Houston, 1974; Rutland Gallery, London, 1974; School of Visual Arts, NYC, 1975; Watson/De Nagy, Houston, 1975; Leo Castelli Inc., NYC, 1976, 79, 80; Galerie Wentzel, Hamburg, 1977; Thomas Segal Gallery, Boston, 1977, 79; Waddington Galleries, London, 1973, 78; Medici II Gallery, Bay Harbor Islands, Fla., 1978; Waddington Gallery, Montreal, 1979; Waddington Gallery, Toronto, 1979; Katonah (N.Y.) Art Gallery, Katona, 1979; Hokin Gallery, Palm Beach, 1979; Waddington Galleries, London, 1979; Ridgefield/Aldrich, 1980; Wichita State U., 1980; Waddington Galleries, London, 81; Sandra K. Bertsch Gallery, Oyster Bay, N.Y., 1982; Gimpel-Hanover & Andre Emmerich Gallerien, Zurich, 1982; Thomas Segal Gallery, Boston, 1982; Galerie Wentzel, Cologne, 1982, 84; Hokin Gallery, Bay Harbor Island, Fla., 1983; Mexico City/Moderno, 1983; Galeria Joan Prats, Barcelona, 1983, 85; U. of California, Berkeley, 1984; Galerie de France, Paris, 1984; Makler Gallery, Philadelphia, 1984; Mixografia Gallery, Los Angeles, 1984; Galerie Onnasch, Berlin, 1984; Galeria Joan Prats, NYC, 1984; Stadtische Galerie Villa Zanders, Bergisch Gladbach, 1984; Waddington & Shiell Galleries, Toronto, 1984; Diputacio De Valencia, Spain, 1985; Museu Provincial de Bellas Artes, Bilbao, 1985. **Retrospectives:** The Jewish Museum, 1964; SRGM, circ., 1977. **Group:** The Kootz Gallery, NYC, New Talent, 1954; Corcoran, 1958, 63, 67; SRGM, Abstract Expressionists and Imagists, 1961; Seattle World's Fair, 1962; WMAA, Geometric Abstraction in America, circ., 1962; Jewish Museum, Toward a New Abstraction, 1963; XX-XII Venice Biennial, 1964; Los Angeles/County, MA, New Abstraction,

1964; Tate, Gulbenkian International, 1964; Carnegie, 1964-65, 67; Detroit/Institute, Color, Image and Form, 1967; Expo '67, Montreal, 1967; Dublin/Municipal, I International Quadrennial (ROSC), 1967; International Biennial Exhibition of Paintings, Tokyo; Documenta IV, Kassel, 1968; MOMA, The Art of the Real, 1968; Pasadena/AM, Serial Imagery, 1968; Washington U., The Development of Modernist Painting, 1969; U. of California, Irvine, New York: The Second Breakthrough, 1959-1964, 1969; MMA, New York Painting and Sculpture: 1940-1970, 1969-70; Buffalo/Albright, Color and Field: 1890-1970, 1970; WMAA, The Structure of Color, 1971; Carnegie, 1971; Boston/MFA, Abstract Painting in the '70s, 1972; Houston/MFA, The Great Decade of American Abstraction: Modernist Art 1960-1970, 1974; Corcoran Biennial, 1975; MIT, Paper Forms: Handmade Paper Projects, 1977; Chicago/Contemporary, A View of a Decade, 1977; Indianapolis, 1976; Syracuse/Everson, A Century of Ceramics in the United States, 1878-1978, 1979; Montreal/Contemporain, Artistes Americains Contemporains, 1978; Buffalo/Albright, American Painting of the 1970s, 1978; U. of Illinois, 1978; Tokyo/Modern, Print Biennial, 1979; Brockton (Mass.)/Art Center, Aspects of the '70s,: Painterly Abstraction, 1980; Grand Palais, Paris, L'Amerique aux Independants, 1980; Walker, Artist & Printer, 1980; Cologne, Westkunst, 1981; Haus der Kunst, Munich, Amerikanische Malerie, 1930-1980, 1981; Edmonton Art Gallery, The Threshold of Color, 1982; SRGM, The New York School, 1982; Brooklyn Museum, The American Artist as Printmaker, 1984; Cleveland Center for Contemporary Art, Artists + Architects, Challenges in Collaboration, 1985; MOMA, Contrasts of Form: Geometric Abstract Art 1910-1980, 1985; Fort Lauderdale, An American Renaissance: Painting and Sculpture Since 1940, 1986. **Collections:** Adelaide; Baltimore/MA; Basel; Boston/MFA; Brandeis U.; Buf-falo/Albright; Canberra/National; Chicago/AI; Columbus; Corcoran; Des Moines; Detroit/Institute; Dusseldorf/KN-W; Harvard U.; Hirshhorn; Honolulu Academy; Humleback/ Louisiana; Los Angeles/County MA; MMA; MOMA; Milwaukee; National Gallery; Paris/Beaubourg; Pasadena/ AM; Phillips; SRGM; St. Louis/City; Tate Gallery; WMAA; Walker; Zurich. **Bibliography:** Alloway 3, 4; Battcock, ed.; Bihalji-Merin; Calas, N. and E.; *Contemporanea;* Coplans 3; Cummings 1; De Vries, ed.; Gablik; *The Great Decade;* Goossen 1; Honisch and Jensen, eds.; Hunter, ed.; Kozloff 3; Lippard 5; Lynton; *Metro;* Murken-Altrogge; Rickey; Rose, B., 1; Sandler 1; Tomkins 2; Waldman 4; Weller. Archives.

NOVROS, DAVID. b. August 8, 1941, Los Angeles, Calif. **Address:** 433 Broome Street, NYC, 10013. **Dealer:** Jon Leon Gallery, NYC. **One-man Exhibitions:** Dwan Gallery, Los Angeles, 1966, NYC, 1967; Galerie Muller, Stuttgart, 1967; Bykert Gallery, 1968, 69, 73, 74; Mizuno Gallery, 1969, 70; The Texas Gallery, 1973, 75; Weinberg Gallery, San Francisco, 1973; Rosa Esman Gallery, 1973; Sperone Westwater Fischer Inc., NYC, 1976, 78; Jon Leon Gallery, 1983. **Group:** SRGM, Systemic Painting, 1966; Kansas City/Nelson, Sound, Light, Silence, 1966; ICA, U. of Pennsylvania, A Romantic Minimalism, 1967; A.F.A., Rejective Art, 1967; WMAA, 1967, 69, 73; Washington U., The Development of Modernist Painting, 1969; Buffalo/ Albright, Modular Painting, 1970; WMAA, The Structure of Color, 1971; Corcoran Biennial, 1971; Chicago/ Contemporary, White on White, 1971-72; Chicago/AI, 1972; Chicago/Contemporary, Five Artists: A Logic of Vision, 1974. **Bibliography:** Murdock 1; *New in the Seventies.*

NOWACK, WAYNE K. b. May 7, 1923, Des Moines, Iowa. **Studied:** Drake U., 1943-45; State U. of Iowa, with Maurico Lasansky, James Lechay, Stuart Edie, 1945-57, BA, PBK, 1948, MA (art history), 1950, MFA (painting). Traveled

Mexico. **Awards:** Des Moines, First Prize, 1950; Danforth Foundation Grant, 1962; National Endowment for the Arts Grant, 1973. **Address:**R.D. 1, Box #346, Spencer, N.Y. 14883. **Dealer:** Allan Stone Gallery. **One-man Exhibitions:** (first) Des Moines, 1950, also 1957; Union College (N.Y.), 1957; Albany/Institute, 1961; Schenectady Museum Association, 1961; Allan Stone Gallery, 1967, 70, 74. **Group:** Omaha/Joslyn Annuals, 1947, 50; Denver/AM, 1948; Library of Congress Print Annual, 1948; Des Moines, 1948, 50-53; Silvermine Guild, 1954; Utica, 1961; Skidmore College, 1961; Brandeis U., Recent American Drawings, 1964; New School for Social Research, Albert List Collection, 1965; WMAA, Human Concern/Personal Torment, 1969; Minnesota/MA, American Drawings 1927-1977, 1977; Purchase/SUNY, The Private Eye, 1984. **Collections:** Des Moines; Drake U.; Fort Worth; Hirshhorn; State U. of Iowa; Skidmore College; Union College (N.Y.); Williams College.

NUTT, JIM. b. 1938, Pittsfield, Mass. **Studied:** Chicago Art Institute School, 1960-65, BFA. **m.** Gladys Nilsson. **Address:** 1035 Greenwood, Wilmette, IL 60091. **Dealer:** Phyllis Kind Gallery, Chicago and NYC. **One-man Exhibitions:** Candy Store Gallery, Folsom, Calif., 1971, 72, 73; Chicago/Contemporary, 1974; Walker, 1974; SFAI, 1975; Portland (Ore.) Center for Visual Arts, 1975; Phyllis Kind Gallery, Chicago, 1970, 72, 75, 77, 79, 82; Phyllis Kind Gallery, NYC, 1976, 77, 80, 84; James Mayor Gallery, London, 1983. **Retrospective:** Rotterdam, Kunstichting, 1980. **Group:** Hyde Park Art Center, Chicago, The Hairy Who, 1966, 67, 68; School of Visual Arts, NYC, The Hairy Who, 1969; Chicago/Contemporary, Don Baum Sez, "Chicago Needs Famous Artists," 1969; ICA, U. of Pennsylvania, Spirit of the Comics, 1969; WMAA, Human Concern/Personal Torment, 1970; SFAI, Surplus Slop from the Windy City, 1970; Chicago/Contemporary, Chicago

Jim Nutt *What I've Got is Much Worse!* 1984

Imagist Art, 1972; Sacramento/Crocker, Sacramento Sampler, 1972; Venice Biennial, 1972; WMAA, American Drawings, 1963-73, 1973; Sao Paulo Biennial, 1974; Chicago/AI, Annual, 1976; U. of Illinois, 1974; WMAA Biennials, 1973, 77; U. of Texas, Austin, New in the Seventies, 1977; Chicago/AI, Drawings of the 70s, 1977; Chicago/Contemporary, View of a Decade, 1977; Brooklyn Museum, American Drawings in Black and White, 1970-1979, 1980; Norfolk/Chrysler, American Figure Painting, 1980; WMAA, The Figurative Tradition and the WMAA, 1980; Sunderland (Eng.) Arts Centre, Who Chicago?, circ., 1980; Munich, Haus der Kunst, Amerikanische Malerie, 1930-1980, 1981; WMAA, Focus on the Figure, 1982; Milwaukee, American Prints, 1982; Illinois Wesleyan U., Contemporary Chicago Imagists, 1983; IEF, Twentieth Century American Drawings: The Figure in Context, circ., 1984; Hirshhorn, Contemporary Focus, 1984. **Collections:** Chicago/AI; Chicago/Contemporary; Glasgow/AGM; MMA; MOMA; Memphis/Brooks;Museum des 20. Jahrhunderts, Vienna; NMAA; New Orleans; U. of North Carolina; PMA; U. of Rochester; WMAA. **Bibliography:** Adrian; *The Chicago Connection; New in the Seventies; Who Chicago?.*

O

OHLSON, DOUG. b. November 18, 1936, Cherokee, Iowa. **Studied:** U. of Minnesota, 1959-61, BA. US Marine Corps, 1955-58. **Taught:** Hunter College, 1964-. **Awards:** Guggenheim Foundation Fellowship, 1969; CAPS Grant, 1974; National Endowment for the Arts, grant, 1976. **Member:** Board of Governors, Skowhegan School. **Address:** 35 Bond Street, NYC 10012. **Dealer:** Ruth Siegel, Ltd., NYC. **One-man Exhibitions:** Fischbach Gallery, 1964, 66, 67, 68, 69, 70, 72; Susan Caldwell Inc., 1974, 76, 77, 79, 81, 82, 83; Portland (Ore.) Center for the Visual Arts, 1977; Andre Zarre Gallery, NYC, 1985; Ruth Siegel, Ltd., 1985; Gallery 99, Bay Harbor Island, Fla., 1986; Nina Freudenheim, 1986. **Retrospective:** Bennington College, 1983. **Group:** Detroit/Institute, Color, Image and Form, 1967; MOMA, The Art of the Real, 1968; WMAA, The Structure of Color, 1971; Corcoran, 1975; UCLA, Fourteen Abstract Painters, 1975; NYU, Project Rebuild, 1976; Old Westbury/SUNY, Transitions I, 1979; P.S. 1, Long Island City, Abstract Painting: 1960-69, 1983; Frankfurt/Moderne, Bilder für Frankfurt, 1985. **Collections:** AT&T; Brooklyn Museum; Coudert Brothers, NYC; Corcoran; Dallas/MFA; Frankfurt/Moderne; U. of Iowa; Isham, Lincoln & Beale, Chicago; MMA; Minneapolis/Institute; National Gallery; U. of North Carolina; Utah; Security Pacific National Bank. **Bibliography:** Murdock 1.

OKADA, KENZO. b. September 28, 1902, Yokohama, Japan. **d.** July 25, 1982, Tokyo. **Studied:** Meijigakuin

Doug Ohlson *Lady X* 1985

Middle School; Tokyo U. of Arts, three semesters; in Paris, 1924-27. **Taught:** Nippon Art College, 1940-42; Musashino Art Institute, 1947-50; Tama College of Fine Arts, Tokyo, 1949-50. To USA, 1950; citizen, 1960. **Member:** Nikakai (Group), Japan, 1938-82. **Awards:** Nikakai (Group), Japan 1936; Showa Shorei, 1938; Yomiuri Press, 1947; Chicago/AI, 1954, 57; Carnegie, 1955; Columbia, S.C./MA, First Prize, 1957; XXIX Venice Biennial, 1958; Tate, Dunn International Prize, 1964; Mainichi Art Award, 1966; AAAL, Marjorie Peabody Waite Award, 1977. **One-man Exhibitions:** Nichido Gallery, Tokyo, 1929-35; Hokuso Gallery, 1948, 50; US Army Education Center, Yokohama, 1950; Betty Parsons Gallery, 1953, 55, 56, 59, 62-64, 67, 69, 71, 73, 76, 78; Corcoran, 1955; Sao Paulo, 1955; Fairweather-Hardin Gallery, 1956; Myrtle Todes Gallery, Glencoe, Ill., 1957; Venice/Contemporaneo, 1958; Ferus Gallery, Los Angeles, 1959; MIT, 1963; Buffalo/Albright, 1965; Columbus Gallery, 1979; U. of Texas, 1979; Indianapolis, 1979; Phillips, 1979; Marisa del Re Gallery, NYC, 1984, 86. **Retrospectives:** Traveling Exhibition, 1966-67, circ., Tokyo, Kyoto, Honolulu, San Francisco, and Austin, Tex.; Seibu Museum of Art, 1982. **Group:** Salon d'Automne, Paris, 1924-27; Nikakai (Group), Japan, 1938-82; WMAA; Chicago/AI; U. of Illinois; III Sao Paulo Biennial, 1955; Corcoran; MOMA; XXIX Venice Biennial, 1958; Tate, Dunn International, 1964. **Collections:** Baltimore/MA; Boston/MFA; Brooklyn Museum; Buffalo/Albright; Carnegie; Chase Manhattan Bank; Chicago/AI; U. of Colorado; Columbia, S.C./MA; Denver/AM; Equitable Life Assurance Society; Hartford/Wadsworth; Honolulu Academy; Indianapolis; Lincoln Center; MMA; MOMA; Memphis/Brooks; Phillips; Portland, Ore./AM; Purchase/SUNY; Reynolds Metals Co.; Rockefeller Institute; Rome/Nazionale; SFMA; SRGM; St. Lawrence U.; St. Louis/City; Santa Barbara/MA; Tokyo/Modern; Toldeo/MA; Tougaloo College; Utica; WMAA; Yale U. **Bibliography:** Baur 5; Hunter, ed.; Goodrich and Baur 1; Nordness, ed.; Ponente; Read 2; Rodman 1.

OKAMURA, ARTHUR. b. February 24, 1932, Long Beach, Calif. **Studied:** Chicago Art Institute School, with Paul Wieghardt, 1950-54; The U. of Chicago, 1951, 53, 57; Yale U., 1954. US Army, 1954. Traveled France, Spain, North Africa, Japan, Bali, Indonesia; resided Mallorca for a year. **Taught:** Central YMCA College, Chicago, 1956-57; Evanston (Ill.) Art Center, 1956-57; Northshore Art League, Winnetka, Ill., 1957; Academy of Art, San Francisco, 1957; Chicago Art Institute School, 1957; California School of Fine Arts, 1958; California College of Arts and Crafts, 1958-59, 1966-69; Saugatuck Summer School of Painting, 1959, 62; U. of

Utah, 1964. **Awards:** The U. of Chicago, Religious Arts, 1953; four-year scholarship to the Chicago Art Institute School; Edward L. Ryerson Traveling Fellowship, 1954; Chicago/AI, Martin B. Cahn Award, 1957; U. of Illinois, **P.P.,** 1960; WMAA, Neysa McMein **P.P.,** 1960; NIAL, **P.P.;** SFMA, Schwabacher-Frey Award, 1960. **Address:** P.O. Box 367, Bolinas, Calif. 94924. **Dealers:** Ruth Braunstein Gallery, San Francisco. **One-man Exhibitions:** (first) Frank Ryan Gallery, Chicago, 1953; La Boutique, Chicago, 1953, 54; Feingarten Gallery, Chicago, NYC, San Francisco, and Los Angeles, 1956-64, 69, 71, 73, 75, 77, 80; Santa Barbara/MA, 1958; Oakland/AM, 1959; California Palace, 1961; Dallas/MFA, 1962; La Jolla, 1963; U. of Utah, 1964; Hansen Gallery, San Francisco, 1964, 65, 66, 68, 71, 74; M. Knoedler & Co., 1965; College of the Holy Names, Oakland, Calif., 1966; SFMA, 1968; California College of Arts and Crafts, 1972; Southern Idaho College, 1972; Kent State U., 1973; Honolulu Academy, 1973; Hansen-Fuller Gallery, San Francisco, 1974; Walnut Creek Art Center (two-man), 1975; Ruth Braunstein Gallery, 1981, 82, 84, 86. **Group:** Chicago/AI Annuals, 1951-54; U. of Illinois, 1955, 59; Ravinia Festival, Highland Park, Ill., 1956, 64; Los Angeles/County MA, Contemporary Americans, 1957; SFMA, Art in Asia and the West, 1957; PAFA, 1954; de Young, Fresh Paint, 1958; U. of Nebraska, 1958; Denver/AM, 1958; USIA, Drawings from California, circ. Europe, 1958-59; A.F.A., New Talent, circ., 1959; Dallas/MFA, 1959; California Palace, 1959, Painters behind Painters, 1967; WMAA, 1960; Forty Artists under Forty, circ., 1962, Annuals, 1962, 63, 64; Friends of the Whitney, 1964; SFMA, Sculpture and Drawings, 1961, 1966; Sacramento/Crocker, 1966; Carnegie, 1967; Expo '70, Osaka, 1970; Scripps College, Lyric View, 1973. **Collections:** Achenbach Foundation; Borg-Warner International Corporation; California College of Arts and Crafts; California Palace; Chicago/AI; The U. of Chicago; Cincinnati/AM; Container Corp. of America; Corcoran; Hirshhorn; Illinois Bell Telephone Company; Illinois State Normal U.; U. of Illinois; Kalamazoo/Institute; Miles Laboratories Inc.; NCFA; NIAL; Oakland/AM; Phoenix; SFMA; Santa Barbara/MA; Southern Idaho College; Stanford U.; Steel Service Institute; WMAA. **Bibliography:** Nordness, ed.

O'KEEFFE, GEORGIA. b. November 15, 1887, Sun Prairie, Wisc. **d.** March 6, 1986, Santa Fe, N.M. **Studied:** Chatham Episcopal Institute (Va.), 1901; Chicago Art Institute School, 1904-05, with John Vanderpoel; ASL, 1907-08, with William M. Chase; Columbia U., 1916, with Arthur Dow, Alan Bement. Traveled Europe, Mexico, USA, Peru, Japan. **Taught:** U. of Virginia; Supervisor of Art in public schools, Amarillo, Tex., 1912-16; Columbia College (S.C.); West Texas Normal College. **Awards:** Hon. DFA, College of William and Mary, 1939; Hon. Litt.D., U. of Wisconsin, 1942; elected to the NIAL, 1947, AAAL, 1962; Brandeis U., Creative Arts Award, 1963; Hon. DFA, Randolph-Macon Woman's College, 1966; NIAL, gold medal, 1970; Hon. DHL, Columbia U., 1971; Hon. DFA, Brown U., 1971; Bryn Mawr College, M. Carey Thomas Prize, 1971; Hon. DFA, Minneapolis College of Art & Design, 1972; Edward MacDowell Medal, 1972; Skowhegan School of Painting and Sculpture, medal for Painting and gold medal, 1973; Hon. DFA, Harvard U., 1973; Governors' Award (New Mexico), 1974; Presidential Medal of Freedom, 1977; Hon. D. of Visual Arts, College of Santa Fe, 1977; Medal of Freedom, 1979. **m.** Alfred Stieglitz (1924). **One-man Exhibitions:** (first) "291," NYC, 1917, also 1926; Anderson Galleries, NYC, 1924; Stieglitz's Intimate Gallery, NYC, 1927, 29; An American Place (Gallery), NYC, 1931, 32, 35-42, 44-46, 50; U. of Minnesota, 1937; The Down-

town Gallery, 1937, 52, 55, 58, 61; College of William and Mary, 1938; La Escondida, Taos, N.M. 1951; Dallas/MFA, 1953; Mayo Hill, Delray Beach, Fla., 1953; Gibbs Art Gallery, Charleston, S.C., 1955; Pomona College, 1958; Milton College, 1965; U. of New Mexico, 1966; SFMA, 1971; Bryn Mawr College, 1971; Santa Fe, 1985. **Retrospectives:** Anderson Galleries, NYC, 1923; Chicago/AI, 1943; MOMA, 1946; Dallas/MFA, 1953; Worcester/AM, 1960; Amon Carter Museum, 1966; WMAA, 1970. **Group:** "291," NYC, 1916; MOMA, Paintings by 19 Living Americans, 1929; U. of Minnesota, 5 Painters, 1937; U. of Illinois, 1955, 57, 59, 69; Pomona College, Stieglitz Circle, 1958; MMA, 14 American Masters, 1958. **Collections:** Amon Carter Museum; Andover/Phillips; Arizona State College; U. of Arizona; Auburn U.; Baltimore/MA; Brooklyn Museum; Bryn Mawr College; Buffalo/Albright; Chicago/AI; Cleveland/MA; Colorado Springs/FA; Currier; Dallas/MFA; Detroit/Institute; Fisk U.; Fort Worth; U. of Georgia; IBM; Indianapolis/Herron; MMA; MOMA; The Miller Co.; Milwaukee; U. of Minnesota; NCFA; National Gallery; U. of Nebraska; Newark Museum; U. of Oklahoma; Omaha/Joslyn; PMA; Phillips; Randolph-Macon Woman's College; Reed College; U. of Rochester; Roswell; SFMA; St. Louis/City; Santa Barbara/MA; Shelburne; Smith College; Springfield, Mass./MFA; Tate; Texas Technological College; Toledo/MA; Utica; Valparaiso U. (Ind.); WMAA; Walker; Wellesley College; Westminster Academy; West Palm Beach/Norton; Wichita/AM; Wilmington. **Bibliography:** *Avant-Garde Painting and Sculpture in America, 1910-1925;* Barker 1; Baur 5, 7; Bazin; Bethers; Biddle 4; Blanchard; Blesh 1; Boswell 1; Brown 2; Bulliet 1; Cahill and Barr, eds.; Cheney; Christensen; Coke 2; Craven, T., 1; Downes, ed.; Flanagan; Frank, ed.; Frost; *Forerunners;* Goodrich and Baur 1; Goossen 1; Haftman; Hall; Hunter 6;

Huyghe; *Index of 20th Century Artists;* Janis, S.; Jewell 2; Kootz 1; Kozloff 3; Kuh 1, 2, 3; Lane; Lee and Burchwood; Lisle; Johnson, Ellen H.; Levin 2; Lippard 3; Mather 1; McCoubrey 1; McCurdy, ed.; Mellquist; Mendelowitz; Murken-Altrogge; Neuhaus; Newmeyer; Nordness, ed.; Pearson 1; Phillips 1, 2; Poore; Pousette-Dart, ed.; **Rich 1, 2;** Richardson, E.P.; Ringel, ed.; Ritchie 1; Rose, B., 1, 4; Rosenblum 2; Schwartz 2; Smith, S.C.K.; Soby 6; Sutton; Tuchman 3; Weller. Archives.

OKULICK, JOHN. b. March 3, 1947, NYC. **Studied:** U. of California, Santa Barbara, 1969, BA; U. of California, Irvine, 1974, MFA, with Barbara Rose, Frank Stella, Robert Morris. **Taught:** U. of California, Irvine, 1973-. **Address:** 604 Hampton Drive, Venice, Calif. 90291. **Dealer:** Nancy Hoffman Gallery, NYC; John Berggruen Gallery, San Francisco; Asher/Faure Gallery, Los Angeles; Richard Gray Gallery, Chicago. **One-man Exhibitions:** (first) Jack Glenn Gallery, Corona Del Mar, 1972, 74; California State U., Long Beach, 1973; Nancy Hoffman Gallery, 1973; Palomar College, 1975; Phyllis Kind Gallery, Chicago, 1976; California State U., Fullerton, 1977; ICA, Los Angeles, 1977; Grapestake Gallery, San Francisco, 1978, 79; Union College, 1979; Asher/Faure Gallery, 1980, 81, 83, 85; Santa Barbara (Calif.) Contemporary Arts Forum, 1982; John

Berggruen Gallery, 1983, 85; Richard Gray Gallery, 1986. **Group:** Cincinnati/Contemporary, Options, 73/30, 1973; Indianapolis, 1974, 76; San Diego, Sculpture in California, 1975-80, 1980; Laguna Beach Museum of Art, Southern California Artists, 1940-80, 1981; Sacramento/Crocker, Contemporary American Wood Sculpture, 1984. **Collections:** Chattanooga/Hunter; Harvard U.; Hirshhorn; Los Angeles/County MA; Newport Harbor; Oakland/AM; Phoenix; SFMA; U. of Sydney; VMFA.

OLDENBURG, CLAES THURE. b. January 28, 1929, Stockholm, Sweden. **Studied:** Yale U., 1950, BA; Chicago Art Institute School, 1952-55, with Paul Wieghardt. Traveled USA, Europe, Japan. Apprentice reporter, City News Bureau, Chicago, 1950-52. Films: *Colossal Keepsake No. 1,* 1969; *Sort of a Commercial for an Icebag,* 1969; *The Great Ice Cream Robbery,* 1970; *Birth of the Flag, Part One and Two,* 1965-74; *Ray Gun Theater,* 1962-75. **Member:** NIAL; AAIAL. **Commissions:** Oberlin College, 1970; Southern Methodist U., 1970; St. Louis/City, 1971; Rijksmuseum Kroller-Muller, 1971; Morse College, Yale U., 1974; Walker, 1974; South Mall, Albany, 1975; Hirshhorn, 1975; GSA, Social Security Administration, Chicago, 1975-77; City of Munster, 1976-77; Oberlin College, 1975-80; U. of Nevada, 1978-80; Salinas Community Center, Salinas, Calif., 1978-80; Civic

Claes Oldenburg   *Proposal for a Monument to the Survival of the University of El Salvador: Blasted Pencil (Which Still Writes)*   Model, 1983

Center, Des Moines, Iowa, 1978-79; Rotterdam, 1977-80. **Awards:** Brandeis U., Creative Arts Award; Skowhegan School Medal; Fellow of Morse College, Yale U.; Honorary Degrees: Oberlin College, 1973; Minneapolis College of Art and Design, 1974; Moore College of Art, Philadelphia, 1974. **Address:** 556 Broome Street, NYC 10013. **Dealer:** Leo Castelli, Inc., NYC. **One-man Exhibitions:** (first) Judson Gallery, NYC, 1959 (sculpture, drawings, poems); Judson Gallery, NYC (two-man, with Jim Dine), 1959; Reuben Gallery, NYC, 1960; Green Gallery, NYC, 1962; Dwan Gallery, 1963; Sidney Janis Gallery, 1964-67, 69, 70; The Pace Gallery, Boston, 1964; Ileana Sonnabend Gallery, Paris, 1964; Stockholm/National; 1966; Robert Fraser Gallery, 1966; U. of Illinois, 1967; Toronto, 1967 (three-man, with Jim Dine, George Segal); Chicago/Contemporary, 1967; Irving Blum Gallery, 1968; Richard Feigen Gallery, Chicago, 1969; UCLA, 1970, 77; Margo Leavin Gallery, 1971, 75; Kansas City/Nelson, 1972; Fort Worth, 1972; Des Moines, 1972; PMA, 1972; Chicago/AI, 1973; Minami Gallery, 1973; Leo Castelli, Inc., NYC, 1974, 80; Yale U., 1974; Lo Spazio, Rome, 1974; Kunsthalle, Tubingen, circ., 1975; Margo Leavin Gallery, Los Angeles, 1975, 76, 78, 83; F. H. Mayor Gallery, London, 1975; Walker, circ., 1975; Krefeld/Haus Lange, 1975; Petersburg Press, NYC, 1975; Jered Sable Gallery, Toronto, 1976; Multiples, Inc., NYC, 1976; John Berggruen Gallery, San Francisco, 1976; Hannover K-G, 1976; Leo Castelli, Inc., NYC, 1976, 80, 86; Amsterdam/Stedelijk, 1977; Richard Gray Gallery, Chicago, 1977; Akron/AI, 1977; Chicago/Contemporary, circ., 1977; Cologne/Ludwig, 1980; Salinas (Calif.) Community Center, 1982; Galerie Schmela, Dusseldorf, 1982; Wave Hill, 1984; Campo di Arsenale, Venice, 1985; SRGM, 1986. **Environments:** Judson Gallery, NYC, Ray Gun Street, 1960; Ray Gun Mfg. Co., The Store, 1961; Sidney Janis Gallery, Bedroom Ensemble, 1964. **Happenings:** Judson Gallery, NYC, Snapshots from the City, 1960; Reuben Gallery, NYC, Ironworks and Fotodeath, 1961; Dallas/MFA, Injun, 1962; Ray Gun Mfg. Co., Ray Gun Theater, 1962; The U. of Chicago, Gayety, 1963; WGMA, Stars, 1963; Los Angeles/County MA, Autobodys, 1963; Al Roon's Health Club, NYC, Washes, 1965; Film Maker's Cinematheque, NYC, Moviehouse, 1965; Stockholm/National, Massage 1966; Esquire Magazine, The Typewriter, 1969. **Retrospectives:** MOMA, 1969; Pasadena/AM, 1971; Walker, circ., 1975; Kunsthalle, Tubingen, circ., 1975. **Group:** Buffalo/Albright, Mixed Media and Pop Art, 1963; Oberlin College, 3 Young Painters, 1963; Chicago/AI, 1962, 63; Brandeis U., New Directions in American Painting, 1963; Cincinnati/AM, An American Viewpoint, 1963; Dallas/MFA; Tate, Dunn International, 1964; ICA, London, The Popular Image, 1963; Martha Jackson Gallery, New Media—New Forms, I & II, 1960, 61; Stockholm/National, American Pop Art, 1964; MOMA, Americans 1963, circ., 1963-64; Oakland/AM, Pop Art USA, 1963; Hartford/Wadsworth, Continuity and Change, 1962; WGMA, The Popular Image, 1963; Philadelphia YM-YWHA Arts Council, Art, A New Vocabulary, 1962; Sidney Janis Gallery, The New Realists, 1962; XXXII Venice Biennial, 1964; Akademie der Kunst, Berlin, Neue Realism und Pop Art, 1965; WMAA, A Decade of American Drawings, 1965; Musée Rodin, Paris, Sculpture of the 20th Century, 1965; WMAA Annuals, 1965, 68, 69; RISD, Recent Still Life, 1966; Walker, Eight Sculptors, 1966; Los Angeles/County MA, American Sculpture of the Sixties, 1967; IX Sao Paulo Biennial, 1967; SRGM, 1967; Carnegie, 1967; Expo '67, Montreal, US Pavilion, 1967; Moore College of Art, American Drawing, 1968; ICA, London, The Obsessive Image, 1968; Documenta IV, Kassel, 1968; Hayward Gallery, London, Pop Art, 1969; Berne, When Attitudes Become Form, 1969; MMA, 1969; MOMA, Technics and Creativity; Gemini GEL., 1971; Los Angeles/County MA, Art & Technology, 1971; Arnhem, Sonsbeek '71, 1971; Expo '70, Osaka, 1970; Foundation Maeght, 1970; Documenta V, Kassel, 1972; Seattle/AM, American Art—Third Quarter Century, 1973; WMAA, American Pop Art, 1974; Newport, R.I., Monumenta, 1974; Moore College of Art, Philadelphia, North, East, West, South and Middle, 1975; U. of Massachusetts, Artists and Fabricators, 1975; NCFA, Sculpture: American Directions, 1945-57, 1975; MOMA, Drawing Now, circ., 1976; SRGM, 20th Century American Drawings, 1976; Chicago/AI Annual, 1976; Akron/AI, Contemporary Images in Watercolor, 1976; WMAA, 200 Years of American Sculpture, 1976; Indianapolis, 1976; U. of Chicago, Ideas in Sculpture, 1976; Indianapolis, 1976; U. of Chicago, Ideas in Sculpture, 1965-1977, 1977; ICA, Philadelphia, Improbable Furniture, 1977; Cambridge, Jubilation, 1977; Minnesota/MA, American Drawing 1927-1977, circ., 1977; Flint/Institute, Art and the Automobile, 1978; WMAA, Art about Art, 1978; Nassau County Museum, Syosset, Monuments and Monoliths: A Metamorphosis, 1978; WMAA (downtown), Auto-Icons, 1979; Aspen Center for the Visual Arts, American Portraits of the Sixties & Seventies, 1979; U. of North Carolina, Drawings about Drawing Today, 1979; MOMA, Printed Art, 1980; WMAA, American Sculpture, 1980; Purchase/SUNY, Hidden Desires, 1980; Zurich, Reliefs, 1980; Brooklyn Museum, American Drawings in Black and White: 1970-1979, 1980; ICA, U. of Pennsylvania, Urban Encounters, 1980; Ridgefield/Aldrich, New Dimensions in Drawing, 1950-1980, 1981; Cologne/Stadt, Westkunst, 1981; WMAA, American Prints: Process and Proofs, 1981; Documenta VII, Kassel, 1982; Houston/Contemporary, The Americans: The Collage, 1982; Houston/MFA, A Century of Modern Sculpture, 1882-1982, 1983; Sunderland (Eng.) Arts Centre, Drawing in Air, 1983; Houston/Contemporary, American Still Life, 1945-1983, 1983; Boston/MFA, 10 Painters and Sculptors Draw, 1984; WMAA, Blam!, 1984; Sydney/AG, Pop Art 1955-1970, 1985; Fort Lauderdale, An American Renaissance: Painting and Sculpture Since 1940, 1985; Paris/Beaubourg, Livres d'Artistes. **Collections:** Amsterdam/Stedelijk; Baltimore/MA; Basel; Brandeis U.; Brussels/Beaux-Arts; Buffalo/Albright; Chicago/AI; Cologne; Des Moines; Fort Worth; Houston/MFA; U. of Illinois; Kansas City/Nelson; Los Angeles/County MA; MOMA; Milwaukee; Norfolk/Chrysler; Oberlin College; Paris/Beaubourg; Pasadena/AM; Rijksmuseum Kroller-Muller; SFAI; St. Louis/City; Southern Methodist U.; Stockholm/National; Tate Gallery; Toronto; Vancouver; Victoria & Albert Museum; WMAA; Walker. **Bibliography: Adriani, Koepplin, and Rose;** Alloway 4; Alloway 1; Battcock, ed.; Becker and Vostell; Bihalji-Merin; Callas, W.; Danto; Davies; Davis, D.; De Vries, ed.; De Wilde 2; Dienst 1; Finch; Friedman and van der Marck; *From Foreign Shores;* Gettings; Goldman 1; Hansen; *Happening & Fluxus;* **Haskell 2, 5;** Honisch and Jensen, eds.; Hunter, ed.; Janis and Blesh 1; Johnson, Ellen H.; Kaprow; Kirby; Kozloff 3; Krauss 2; Lippard 3; Lippard 5; Lippard, ed.; Lucie-Smith; *Metro; Monumenta;* **Oldenburg 1, 2, 3;** *Oldenburg; Report;* **Rose, B., 1, 2, 4;** Rowell; Rubin 1; Rublowsky; Russell and Gablik; Sandler 1; *Six Themes;* Strachan; Sontag; Tomkins and Time-Life Books; Tomkins 2; Trier 1; Tuchman 1; Van Briggen and Oldenburg; Warhol and Haskell; Weller; *When Attitudes Become Form.* Archives.

OLITSKI, JULES. b. March 27, 1922, Snovsk, USSR. **Studied:** NAD, with Sidney Dickinson, 1939-42; Beaux-Arts Institute of Design, NYC, 1940-47; Zadkine School of Sculpture, Paris, 1949; Academie de la Grande Chaumiere, 1949-50; NYU, BA, 1952; MA (Art Education), 1954; and privately with Chaim Gross. Traveled USA, Europe, Mexico. **Taught:** New Paltz/SUNY, 1954-55; C. W. Post College of Long Island U., Chairman of Fine Arts, 1956-63; Bennington College, 1963-67. Curator, NYU Art Education Gallery, 1955-56. **Awards:** Carnegie Second Prize, 1961; Ford Foundation, **P.P.**, 1964; Corcoran, 1967. **Address:** 827 Broadway, NYC 10003; summer: RD #1, Lovejoy Sands Road, Meredith, NH 03253. **Dealer:** Knoedler Contemporary Art; Andre Emmerich Gallery, NYC. **One-man Exhibitions:** (first) Galerie Huit, Paris, 1950; Alexandre Iolas Gallery, 1958; French & Co. Inc., NYC, 1959-61; Poindexter Gallery, 1961-65, 1968; Bennington College, 1962; Galleria Santa Croce, Florence, Italy, 1963; Galleria Trastevere, Rome, 1963; Galleria Toninelli, Milan, 1963; Richard Gray Gallery, 1964; David Mirvish Gallery, Toronto, 1964-75, 78; Kasmin Ltd., 1964-66, 1968-70, 1972; Galerie Lawrence, Paris, 1964; Harvard U. (three-man with Kenneth Noland, Frank Stella), 1965; St. John, N.B., 1966; Nicholas Wilder Gallery, 1966, 73; Andre Emmerich Gallery, NYC, 1966-68, 77, 80, 82, 84, 86; Zurich, 1973, 79; ICA, U. of Pennsylvania, 1968; MIT, 1968; MMA, 1969; Lawrence Rubin Gallery, NYC, 1969-73; Knoedler Contemporary Art, 1973, 75, 76, 77, 79; Galerie Wentzel, Hamburg, 1975, 77; Dart Gallery, Inc., Chicago, 1975; Watson/DeNagy, Houston, 1976; Boston/MFA, 1977; Hirshhorn, 1977; Amerika Haus, Berlin, 1977; David Mirvish Gallery, Toronto, 1978; Knoedler Gallery, London, 1978, 81; Edmonton Art Gallery, Edmonton, 1979; Downstairs Gallery, Edmonton, 1980; Galerie Daniel Templon, Paris, 1980, 84; Waddington Galleries, Toronto, 1980; Gallery One, Toronto, 1981, 82, 83, 84; Harcus-Krakow Gallery, Boston, 1981, 82; Janus Gallery, Venice, Calif., 1981; M. Knoedler & Co., NYC, 1981, 83, 85; Meredith Long Gallery, Houston, 1981, 82; Martha White Gallery, Louisville,

1982; Harcus Gallery, Boston, 1983; Fondation du Château de Jau, France, 1984; Yares Gallery, Scottsdale, 1984, 86; Exeter, 1985; Musée des Beaux-Arts, Valance, France, 1985. **Retrospectives:** Corcoran, circ., 1967; Boston/MFA, circ., 1973. **Group:** Carnegie, 1961, 64; WMAA Annuals, 1962, 68, 69, 70, 72; WGMA, The Formalists, 1963; Festival of Two Worlds, Spoleto, 1963; SFMA, Directions: American Painting, 1963; MOMA, Recent Acquisitions, 1963; Worcester/AM, 1963; IV International Art Biennial, San Marino, 1963; Chicago/AI Annuals, 1964, 69; ICA, U. of Pennsylvania, The Atmosphere of 1964, 1964; Los Angeles/County MA, Post Painterly Abstraction, 1964; SRGM, American Drawings, 1964; Chicago/AI, 67th American Exhibition, 1967; Kunsthalle, Basel, Austellung Signale, 1965; XXXIII Venice Biennial, 1966; Corcoran, 1967; Detroit/Institute, Color, Image and Form, 1967; Tokyo Biennial, 1967; Trenton/State, Focus on Light, 1967; Jewish Museum, Large Scale American Paintings, 1967; Honolulu Academy, 1967; Documenta IV, Kassel, 1968; MMA, New York Painting and Sculpture: 1940-1970, 1969-70; Pasadena/AM, Painting in New York: 1944 to 1969, 1969; Chicago/AI, 69th American Exhibition, 1969; Buffalo/Albright, Color and Field, 1890-1970, 1970; ICA, U. of Pennsylvania, Two Generations of Color Painting, 1970; Boston U., American Artists of the 1960s, 1970; Youngstown/Butler Annual, 1970; WMAA, The Structure of Color, 1971; Boston/MFA, Abstract Painting in the '70s, 1972; Dusseldorf/Kunsthalle, Prospect '73, 1973; Montreal/Contemporain, 11 Artistes Americains, 1973; Houston/MFA, The Great Decade of American Abstraction: Modernist Art 1960-1970, 1974; Indianapolis, 1974; Monumenta, Newport, R.I., 1974, Biennial, 1975; Caracas, El Lenguaje del Color, 1975; Syracuse/Everson, New Works in Clay, Contemporary Painting and Sculpture, 1976; Indianapolis, 1976; Chicago/AI,

Drawings of the 70's, 1977; U. of Nebraska, Expressionism in the Seventies, 1978; Buffalo/Albright, American Painting of the 1970s, circ., 1979; Boston/MFA, Monumental Abstractions, 1979; Grand Palais, Paris, L'Amerique aux Indépendants, 1980; Syracuse/Everson, A Century of Ceramics in the United States, circ., 1980; Haus der Kunst, Munich, Amerikanische Malerie: 1930-1980, 1981; Houston/MFA, Miró in America, 1982; St. Lawrence U., Pre-Postmodern, 1985; Fort Lauderdale, An American Renaissance: Painting and Sculpture Since 1940, 1986. **Collections:** Boston/MFA; Brooklyn Museum; Buffalo/Albright; Canberra/National; Cleveland/MA; Chicago/AI; U. of Chicago; Corcoran; Dallas/MFA; Dayton/AI; Detroit/Institute; Edmonton Art Gallery; Harvard U.; Hirshhorn; Houston/MFA; U. of Illinois; Jerusalem/National; Milwaukee; MIT; MMA; MOMA; NGA; Norfolk/Chrysler; Ottawa/National; Pasadena/AM; Princeton U.; Regina/MacKenzie; SRGM; St. Louis/City; U. of Saskatchewan; Seattle National Bank; Syracuse/Everson; Tel Aviv; Toronto; WMAA. **Bibliography:** Alloway 4; Battcock, ed.; Calas, N. and E.; De Vries, ed.; *From Foreign Shores; The Great Decade;* Honisch and Jensen, eds; Hunter, ed.; Kozloff 3; Krauss; Moffett; *Monumenta;* Murken-Altrogge; Report; Rose, B., 4; Sandler 1.

OLIVEIRA, NATHAN. b. December 19, 1928, Oakland, Calif. **Studied:** Mills College, California College of Arts and Crafts (MFA, 1952). US Army, 1953-55. Traveled Europe. **Taught:** San Francisco Art Institute; California College of Arts and Crafts, 1955-56; U. of Illinois, 1961-62; UCLA, 1963-64; Cornell U., 1964; Stanford U., 1964-79; U. of Colorado, 1965; U. of Hawaii, 1971; Cranbrook, 1972; Baltimore Art Institute, 1972; Indianapolis/Herron, 1972; Kent State U., 1973. **Member:** NAD. **Awards:** L.C. Tiffany Grant, 1957;

Guggenheim Foundation Fellowship, 1958; Chicago/AI, Norman Wait Harris Bronze Medal, 1960; El Retiro Parquet, Madrid, Arte de America y Espana, Special Prize, 1963; Tamarind Fellowship, 1964; National Endowment for the Arts, 1974; AAIAL, 1984. **Address:** 785 Santa Mari Avenue, Stanford, CA 94305. **Dealers:** John Berggruen Gallery, San Francisco; Richard Gray Gallery, Chicago. **One-man Exhibitions:** (first) The Alan Gallery, NYC, 1958, also 1959, 60, 63, 65; Paul Kantor Gallery, Beverly Hills, Calif., 1959, 60, 62, 63; U. of Illinois, 1961; Walker, 1961; Felix Landau Gallery, 1965, 68; The Landau-Alan Gallery, NYC, 1967; Gump's Gallery, 1968; Galerie Bleue, Stockholm, 1968; Stanford U., 1968; SFMA, 1969; Martha Jackson Gallery, 1969; Wisconsin State U., Oshkosh, 1970; Terry Dintenfass, Inc., 1971; Michael Smith Gallery, Los Angeles, 1971; Smith Anderson Gallery, Palo Alto, 1971, 74, 76; Charles Campbell Gallery, 1972, 75, 77, 79; Jack Glenn Gallery, Corona del Mar, 1973; Fullerton Junior College, 1973; U. of California, Santa Cruz, 1976; Galerie Veith Turske, Cologne, 1978, 79; Harvard U., 1978; Dorsky Gallery, NYC, 1978; John Berggruen Gallery, San Francisco, 1977, 79; Wichita State U., 1976; U. of Connecticut, 1976; Charles Cowles Gallery, 1980, 83; Arts Club of Chicago, 1981; John Berggruen Gallery, 1982, 83; Honolulu Academy, 1983, 85. **Retrospectives:** UCLA, circ., 1963; Oakland/AM, circ., 1973; California State U., Long Beach, 1980; SFMA, circ., 1985. **Group:** SFMA, 1954; Denver/AM, 1956; Carnegie, 1958; Mexico City, I Inter-American Paints and Prints Biennial, 1958; WMAA Annuals, 1958-61, 67; I Paris Biennial, 1959; MOMA, New Images of Man, 1959; U. of Illinois, 1961, 63, 67, 69, 74; SRGM, 1961; Amon Carter Museum, The Artist's Environment: West Coast, 1962; Chicago/AI, 1962; MOMA, Recent Painting USA: The Figure, circ., 1962; Seattle World's Fair, 1962; WMAA, Fifty California Artists, circ., 1962;

MOMA, Contemporary Painters and Sculptors as Printmakers, 1964; PAFA, 1966; California Palace, Painters behind Painters, 1967; U. of Oklahoma, East Coast—West Coast Paintings, 1968; Brooklyn Museum, Two Decades of American Prints, 1969; Corcoran, 1970; Los Angeles, Crocker-Citizens National Bank, A Century of California Painting 1870-1970, 1970; La Jolla, Continuing Art, 1971; SFMA, California Painting and Sculpture: The Modern Era, 1976; Brooklyn Museum, Thirty Years of American Printmaking, 1977; Indianapolis, Perceptions of the Spirit in 20th Century American Art, 1977; MMA, The Painterly Print, 1980; WMAA, American Prints: Process and Proofs, 1981; Rutgers U., Realism and Realities, 1982; NYU, The Figurative Mode: Bay Area Painting, 1956-1966, 1984; Oakland/AM, Art in the San Francisco Bay Area, 1945-1980, 1985. **Collections:** Brooklyn Museum; U. of California; Chicago/AI; Cleveland/MA; Dallas/MFA; Hirshhorn; Illinois Wesleyan U.; Lytton Savings and Loan Association; MOMA; U. of Michigan; NCFA; Oakland/AM; PMA; Ridgefield/Aldrich; SFMA; SRGM; Stanford U.; UCLA; Walker; Youngstown/Butler. **Bibliography:** Goldman 1; *Nathan Oliveira: Survey; New in the Seventies;* Nordness, ed.; Weller; **Wight 4.** Archives.

ONSLOW-FORD, GORDON. b. December 26, 1912, Wendover, England. **Studied:** Dragon School, Oxford, England; Royal Naval College, Dartmouth and Greenwich; self-taught in art; frequent visits to the studio of Fernand Leger. Traveled Europe, the Orient, and most of the world; resided in Paris, 1936-39, and Mexico, 1941-47. **Taught:** Series of lectures, New School for Social Research, 1940-41; California College of Arts and Crafts, 1956-58. **Address:** Inverness, CA 94937. **One-man Exhibitions:** N.S.F.S.R., NYC, 1940; Karl Nierendorf Gallery, NYC, 1946; SFMA (three-man, with Wolf-gang Paalen, Lee Mullican), 1950; SFMA (two-man, with Richard Bowman), 1959; The Rose Rabow Gallery, San Francisco, 1956, 64, 72; Galerie Samy Kinge, Paris, 1985. **Retrospectives:** SFMA; de Young; Victoria (B.C.), 1971; Oakland/AM, 1977. **Group:** SFMA, 1948, 60; de Young, 1962; Artists Space, NYC, Moderns in Mind, 1986; Los Angeles/County MA, The Spiritual in Art, 1986; Newport Harbor, The Interpretive Link, circ., 1986. **Collections:** Boston/MFA; U. of California; de Young; Harvard U.; Honolulu Academy; MOMA; Oakland/AM; SFMA; SRGM; Tate; WMAA. **Bibliography:** *Black and White Are Colors;* Breton 2; **Gordon Onslow-Ford;** Paalen; Ragon 1; Rubin 1; Tuchman 3; Weller. Archives.

OPPENHEIM, DENNIS. b. September 6, 1938, Electric City, Wash. **Studied:** Stanford U., BA, MA; California College of Arts and Crafts, with Norman Kantor. Traveled Europe, 1969-75. Produced films, 1969-75 and videotapes, 1969-74. **Taught:** Yale U.; Chicago/AI; Stony Brook/SUNY. **Awards:** Guggenheim Foundation Fellowship, 1972, 79; National Endowment for the Arts, 1974, 81. **Address:** 54 Franklin Street, NYC 10013. **Dealer:** Yvon Lambert, Paris. **One-man Exhibitions:** John Gibson Gallery, 1968, 69, 70, 74, 77; Yvon Lambert, 1969, 71, 75; MOMA, 1969; Reese Palley Gallery, San Francisco, 1970; Gallery 20, Amsterdam 1971; Harcus-Krakow Gallery, 1971; Francoise Lambert, Milan, 1971, 75; Gallery D. Brussels, 1972, 73, 74; Galleria l'Attico, Rome, 1972; Tate, 1972; Mathias Fels & Cie, Paris, 1972; Nova Scotia College of Art and Design, Halifax, 1972; Ileana Sonnabend Gallery, NYC, 1972, 73, Paris, 1973; M.O.C.A., San Francisco, 1973; F.H. Mayor Gallery, London, 1973; Galleria Forma, Genoa, 1973, 74; Rivkin Gallery, Washington, D.C., 1973; Paolo Barrozzi, Milan, 1974; Amsterdam/Stedelijk, 1974; Galleria A. Castelli, Milan, 1975; School of Visual

Arts, NYC, 1979; Multiples, NYC, 1977, 78; Deson Gallery, Chicago, 1978; d'Arc Gallery, NYC, 1976, 77; Robert Self Gallery, Newcastle-upon-Tyne, 1976; Akira Ikeda Gallery, Tokyo, 1983; Flow Ace Gallery, Venice, Calif., 1983; Galerie Schum, Stuttgart, 1983; Felicie Gallery, NYC, 1983; WMAA, 1983; SFMA, 1984; Grand Rapids, 1985. **Retrospectives:** Brussels/Beaux-Arts, 1975; Rotterdam, 1975. **Group:** WMAA Annuals, 1968, 70; Seattle/AM, 557, 087, 1969; Berne, When Attitudes Become Form 1969; Amsterdam/Stedelijk, Op Losse Schroeven, 1969; MOMA, New Media; New Methods, circ., 1969; ICA, U. of Pennsylvania, Against Order: Chance and Art, 1970; Turin/Civico, Conceptual Art, Arte Povera, Land Art, 1970; New York Cultural Center, Conceptual Art and Conceptual Aspects, 1970; Finch College, NYC, Artist/Videotape/Performance, 1971; VII Paris Biennial, 1971; Dusseldorf/Kunsthalle, Prospect '71, 1971; Documenta V, Kassel, 1972; WMAA, American Drawings, 1963-73, 1973; Cologne, Project '74, 1974; MIT, Interventions in Landscape, 1974; Venice, Biennale, 1974; Berlin/ National, Kunst mit Fotographi, 1983; WMAA Biennial, 1981; Hirshhorn, Metaphor, New Projects by Contemporary Sculptors, 1981. **Collections:** Akron/AM; Amsterdam/Stedelijk; Art Gallery of Ontario; Art Gallery of Winnipeg; Bordeaux/Contemporain; U. of California, Berkeley; Chicago/AI; Chicago/Contemporary; Corcoran; Cornell U.; Cranbrook; Denver/AM; Detroit/Institute; Edmonton Art Gallery; Geneva; The Hague; Humlebaek/ Louisiana; Israel Museum; La Jolla; Los Angeles/County MA; MOMA; Milwaukee; Monchengladbach; U. of New Mexico; Newport Harbor; Oakland Museum; PAFA; PMA; Paris/Beaubourg; Paris/Moderne; Potsdam/SUNY; Purchase/SUNY; Rijksmuseum Kroller-Muller; Rotterdam; SFMA; Stuttgart;

John Opper   *Color Series 8-72*   1972

Syracuse/Everson; Tate Gallery; Toulon; Utica; WMAA; Worcester/AM; Zurich. **Bibliography:** Alloway 4; *Art Now 74;* Celant; *Contemporanea;* De Wilde 2; Honisch and Jensen, eds.; Honnef; Hunter, ed.; Johnson, Ellen H.; Lippard, ed.; Lippard 3; Lucie-Smith; Meyer.

OPPER, JOHN. b. October 29, 1908, Chicago, Ill. **Studied:** Cleveland Institute of Art, 1926-28; Chicago Art Institute School, 1928-29; Western Reserve U., BS, 1931; Hofmann School, 1936; Columbia U., MA, 1942, Ed.D., 1952. Traveled Europe. **Taught:** U. of Wyoming, 1945-49; U. of North Carolina, 1952-57; Columbia U.; NYU, 1957-74. **Member:** American Abstract Artists, since 1936. Federal A.P.: Easel painting. **Awards:** Guggenheim Foundation Fellowship, 1969-70; National Endowment for the Arts, 1974. **Address:** Box 347, Amagansett, NY 11930. **Dealer:** Grace Borgenicht Gallery, Inc., NYC. **One-man Exhibitions:** (first) Artists' Gallery, NYC, 1938, also 1940; SFMA, 1939; San Diego, 1939; Charles Egan Gallery, 1955; The Stable Gallery, 1959, 60, 61, 62; Drew U., 1966; Grace Borgenicht Gallery, Inc., 1966, 68, 69, 71, 73, 75, 77, 79; Benson Gallery, 1967, 74; Guild Hall, 1973. **Retrospective:** Drew U. 1976; Montclair/AM, 1978. **Group:** Carnegie; MOMA; MMA; Brooklyn Museum; Chicago/AI; Baltimore/MA; Santa Barbara/MA, 1964. **Collections:** Amstar Corp., NYC; Atlantic Richfield Oil Co., NYC; Chase Manhattan Bank; First National City Bank, NYC; Harcourt Brace Jovanovich Inc., High Museum; Inmont Corp, NYC; Marine Midland Bank, Buffalo, N.Y.; MOMA; Montclair/AM; NYU; U. of North Carolina; Prudential Insurance Co. of America, Newark; U. of Texas; Union Carbide Corp. **Bibliography:** Archives.

ORTMAN, GEORGE. b. October 17, 1926, Oakland, Calif. **Studied:** California College of Arts and Crafts, 1947-48; Atelier 17, NYC, 1949, with S.W. Hayter; Academie Andre Lhote, Paris, 1950; Hofmann School, 1950-51. Traveled Europe, North America. **Taught:** School of Visual Arts, NYC, 1960-65; NYU, 1963-65; Fairleigh Dickinson College, summer, 1964; Princeton U., 1966-69; Honolulu Academy, 1969-70; Cranbrook, 1970-. **Awards:** Birmingham, Ala./MA 1966; Trenton/State, 1967; Guggenheim Foundation Fellowship; Ford Foundation Grant. **m.** Constance Whidden. **Address:** 45 Academy Way, Bloomfield Hills, MI 48013; summer: Box 192, Castine, ME 04421. **One-man Exhibitions:** (first) Tanager Gallery, NYC, 1953; Wittenborn Gallery, NYC, 1956; The Stable Gallery, 1957, 60; The Swetzoff Gallery, Boston, 1961, 62; The Howard Wise Gallery, NYC, 1962, 63, 64, 67, 69; Fairleigh Dickinson U., 1962; David Mirvish Gallery, 1964; Container Corp. of America, 1965; Walker, 1965; Milwaukee, 1966; Dallas/MFA, 1966; Akron/AI, 1966; Portland, Me./MA, 1966; Harcus-Krakow Gallery, 1966; David Stuart Gallery, 1966; The U. of Chicago, 1967; Galeria Van der Voort, 1967-69; Princeton U., 1967; Temple U., 1968; Middlebury College, 1969; Reed College, 1970; Cranbrook, 1970; J.L. Hudson Art Gallery, Detroit, 1971; Indianapolis, 1971; Western Michigan U., 1972; Gimpel & Weitzenhoffer, Ltd., 1972; Gertrude Kasle Gallery, Detroit, 1976; Cranbrook, 1981. **Retrospective:** Fairleigh Dickinson U., 1963; Walker, 1965; Princeton U., 1967. **Group:** Salon du Mai, Paris, 1950; SFMA Annual, 1952; Martha Jackson Gallery, New Media—New Forms I, 1960; Claude Bernard, Paris, 1960; WMAA, Young America, 1960; Carnegie, 1960, 64, 67, 70; Chicago/AI Annuals, 1961, 62; WMAA, Geometric Abstraction in America, circ., 1962; Seattle World's Fair, 1962; MOMA, Hans Hofmann and His Students, circ., 1963-64; Amsterdam/Stedelijk, 1963; Jewish Museum, Toward a New Abstraction, 1963; SFMA, Directions—Painting U.S.A., 1963; WMAA Annuals 1962-67; A.F.A., Contemporary Wall Sculpture, circ., 1963-64; A.F.A., Decade of New Talent, circ., 1964; International Biennial Exhibition of Paintings, Tokyo; WMAA, A Decade of American Drawings, 1965; U. of Illinois, 1965; WMAA, Art of the U.S. 1670-1966, 1966; Finch College, NYC, Holograms, 1971. **Collections:** Allentown/AM; American Republic; U. of California; Christian Theological Seminary; Des Moines; Lincoln, Mass./De Cordova; MOMA; Manufacturers Hanover Trust Co.; U. of Massachusetts; Milwaukee; NYPL; NYU; Omaha/Joslyn; P.S. 144, NYC; Portland, Me./MA; St. George's Episcopal Church, Princeton, N.J.; WMAA; Walker; Worcester/AM. **Bibliography:** Calas, N. and E.; Honisch and Jensen, eds.; Janis and Blesh 1; Moser 1; Sandler 1; Weller. Archives.

OSSORIO, ALFONSO. b. August 2, 1916, Manila, Philippine Islands. **Studied:** in England, 1924; Harvard U., BA, 1938; RISD, 1938-39. To USA, 1929. US Army, 1943-46. **Address:** P.O. Box 70, Wainscott, NY 11975. **Dealer:** Oscarsson Siegeltuch & Co., NYC. **One-man Exhibitions:** (first) Wakefield Gallery, NYC, 1941, also 1943; Mortimer Brandt, NYC, 1945; Galerie Paul Facchetti, 1951; Betty Parsons Gallery, 1951, 53, 56, 58, 59, 61; Galerie Stadler, Paris, 1960, 61; Cordier & Ekstrom, Inc., 1961, 64, 65, 67, 68, 69, 72; Yale U., 1974; Guild Hall, 1980; Oscarsson Hood Gallery, NYC, 1982, 84; Carl Hammer Gallery, Chicago, 1985; Oscarsson Siegeltuch & Co., 1986. **Group:** WMAA Annuals, 1953-; The Downtown Gallery, 1954; The Stable Gallery Annuals, 1955, 56; Rome-New York Foundation, Rome, 1957-59; Galerie Beyeler, Basel; Turin Art Festival, 1959; Martha Jackson Gallery, New Media—New Forms; Osaka (Japan) Art Festival; Gutai Sky Festival, Osaka, Carnegie; MOMA; The Art of Assemblage,

Alfonso Ossorio *Sunt Lacrimae Rerum* 1982

circ., 1961; SRGM/USIA, American Vanguard, circ., Europe, 1961-62; Musée Cantonal des Beaux-Arts, Lausanne, I Salon International de Galeries Pilotes, 1963; St.-Etienne, 1964; Documenta III, Kassel, 1964; Intuitiones y Realizaciones Formales, Buenos Aires, 1964; U. of Illinois, 1965; Chicago/AI, 1966; WMAA, Art of the U.S. 1670-1966, 1966; MOMA, The 1960s, 1967; Munich/Modern, New Art: USA, 1968; MOMA, Dada, Surrealism and Their Heritage, 1968; MOMA, The New American Painting and Sculpture, 1969; WMAA, Human Concern/Personal Torment, 1969; NCFA, The Object as a Poet, 1977; Guild Hall, Poets and Artists, 1982; Hofstra U.,

Androgyny in Art, 1982; U. of North Carolina, Art on Paper, 1983; IEF, Twentieth Century American Drawings: The Figure in Context, circ., 1984; XLII Venice Biennial, 1986. **Collections:** Brandeis U.; Cuenca; Hartford/Wadsworth; International Institute for Aesthetic Research; MMA; Manila; NYU; PMA; WMAA; Yale U. **Bibliography:** Calas, N. and E.; **Friedman, B.H., 1;** *From Foreign Shores;* Hunter, ed.; Seitz, 3; **Tapie** 1, **2.** Archives.

OSVER, ARTHUR. b. July 26, 1912, Chicago, Ill. **Studied:** Northwestern U., 1930-31; Chicago Art Institute School, with Boris Anisfeld. Traveled Europe; resided in France and Italy for several years. **Taught:** Brooklyn Museum School, 1947; Columbia U., 1950-51; U. of Florida, 1954; Cooper Union, 1955, 58; Yale U., 1956-57; American Academy, Rome, 1957-58; Washington U., 1960-81. **Member:** Artists Equity; Audubon Artists. Federal A.P.: teaching, painting. **Commissions:** *Fortune* magazine, 1960 (cover). **Awards:** Chicago/AI, James Nelson Raymond Traveling Fellowship ($2,000), 1936; VMFA, John Barton Payne Medal; Pepsi-Cola $500 Award, 1947; PAFA, Joseph E. Temple Gold Medal, 1947; Guggenheim Foundation Fellowship, 1948; renewed 1949; U. of Illinois, **P.P.,** 1949; Prix de Rome, 1952; renewed 1953; Audubon Artists, Emily Lowe Prize, 1961; Art Directors Club, Chicago, Medal, 1961; PAFA, J. Henry Schiedt Memorial Prize, 1966; National Council on the Arts, Sabbatical Leave Grant ($7,500), 1966; AAAL, **P.P.,** 1974. **Address:** 465 Foote Avenue, St. Louis, MO 63119. **Dealer:** Fairweather-Hardin Gallery, Chicago. **One-man Exhibitions:** (first) Mortimer Brandt, NYC, 1943; Grand Central Moderns, NYC, 1947, 49, 51, 57; Hamline U., 1950; U. of Florida, 1951, 55; Fairweather-Garnett Gallery, Evanston, 1955; Fairweather-Hardin Gallery, 1955, 57, 62, 64, 66, 82; U. of Chattanooga, 1958;

Syracuse U., 1959; Philadelphia Art Alliance, 1959; Milton College, 1964; Maryville College (Mo.), 1966; Martin Schweig Gallery, 1966; Coe College, 1966; Iowa State U., 1968; Webster College, 1968; Iowa State U., 1968; Terry Moore Gallery, St. Louis, 1975, 77; Timothy Burns Gallery, St. Louis, 1981, 84. **Retrospective:** St. Louis Artists' Guild, 1964. **Group:** Chicago/AI; PAFA; MMA; PMA; WMAA; MOMA; Carnegie; Corcoran; Phillips; Detroit/Institute; Brooklyn Museum; VMFA; Des Moines; Walker; Venice Biennial; Tokyo/Modern. **Collections:** Abbott Laboratories; Brooklyn Museum; Carnegie; Cincinnati/AM; Colorado Springs/FA; Corcoran; Davenport/Municipal; Des Moines; Detroit/Institute; U. of Georgia; Houston/MFA; IBM; U. of Illinois; Inland Steel Co.; S. C. Johnson & Son, Inc.; MMA; MOMA; U. of Michigan; Montclair/AM/U. of Nebraska; New Orleans/Delgado; PAFA; PMA; Peabody Museum; Phillips; Rio de Janeiro; U. of Rochester; St. Louis/City; Syracuse/Everson; Tokyo/Modern; Toledo/MA; WMAA; Walker; Washington U.; Wilmington. **Bibliography:** Bethers; Nordness, ed. Archives.

OTT, JERRY. b. July 31, 1947, Albert Lea, Minn. **Studied:** Mankato State College; U. of Minnesota. **Address:** 331 West 6th, Mankato, Minn. 56001. **One-man Exhibitions:** Mankato State College, 1967; One Hundred and Eighteen Gallery, Minneapolis, 1973; Louis K. Meisel Gallery, NYC, 1973, 75, 79; Smith Fine Art, Monte Carlo, Monaco, 1974; Morgan Gallery, Shawnee Mission, Kansas, 1977, 79; Hanson-Cowles Gallery, Minneapolis, 1978; St. Cloud State U., 1978. **Group:** Minnesota/MA, Drawings USA, 1971; Recklinghausen, Mit Camera, Penzil und Spritzpistol, 1973; Indianapolis, 1974; Tokyo, Bienniale, 1974; New York Cultural Center, Three Centuries of the American Nude, 1975; Christchurch, New Zealand, Photo Realism, American Paintings and Prints, circ., 1975; Potsdam/SUNY, The Presence and Absence of Realism, 1976; Madison Art Center, Figurative Painting in the Midwest, 1977; U. of Kansas, Artists Look at Art, 1978; Minneapolis/Institute, Five Realist Painters, 1979. **Collections:** Federal Reserve Bank, Minneapolis; U. of Georgia; U. of Kansas; Minneapolis/Institute; Tokyo/Contemporary; Walker.

P

PACE, STEPHEN. b. 1918, Charleston, Mo. **Studied:** Evansville Museum School, 1937-41, with Robert Lahr; Escuela de Bellas Artes, San Miguel de Allende, Mexico, 1945-46; ASL, 1948-49, with Cameron Booth, Morris Kantor; Academie de la Grande Chaumiere, 1950; Academy of Fine Arts, Florence, Italy, 1951; Hofmann School, 1951. US Army, 1943-46. Traveled Mexico, Europe, Canada, USA. **Taught:** Washington U., 1959; Pratt Institute, 1962-69; U. of California, Berkeley, 1968; Bard College, 1969-71; Des Moines, 1970; Kansas City/AI, 1973; Syracuse U., 1975. **Awards:** Dolia Laurian Fund Award, 1954; Hallmark International Competition, 1961; CAPS Grant, 1974. **Address:** 164 Seventh Avenue, NYC 10011. **One-man Exhibitions:** (first) Evansville, 1946; Hendler Gallery, Philadelphia, 1953; Artists' Gallery, NYC, 1954; Poindexter Gallery, 1956, 57; HCE Gallery, Provincetown, Mass., 1956-59, 62-66; Washington U., 1959; Dilexi Gallery, San Francisco, 1960; Holland-Goldowsky Gallery, Chicago, 1960; The Howard Wise Gallery, Cleveland, 1960, NYC, 1960, 61, 63, 64; Dwan Gallery, 1961; MIT, 1961; Ridley Gallery, Evansville, Inc., 1966; U. of California, 1968; The Graham Gallery, 1969; Walker, 1962; Columbus, 1962; Kalamazoo/Institute, 1962; Des Moines, 1970; U. of Texas, 1970; Kansas City/AI, 1973; A. M. Sachs Gallery, 1974, 76, 78, 79; Drew U., 1975; Robert Polo Gallery, Washington, D.C., 1976; New Harmony, New Harmony, Ind., 1977; Spook Farm Gallery, Far Hills, N.J., 1978; Barbara Fiedler, Washington, D.C., 1980; Chastenet Fine Arts Gallery, London, 1980; A.M. Sachs Gallery, NYC, 1983, 85; Leighton Gallery, Blue Hill, Me., 1985. **Retrospective:** Bard College, 1975; American U., 1976. **Group:** Brooklyn Museum, 1953, 55; WMAA Annuals, 1953, 54, 56, 57, 58, 61; PAFA, 1954; Carnegie, 1955; Walker, Vanguard, 1955; International Biennial Exhibition of Paintings, Tokyo; Walker, 60 American Painters, 1960; Cleveland/MA, Paths of Abstract Art, 1960; Hallmark Art Award, 1960 Brandeis U. (two-man), circ., 1961; USIA, American Paintings, circ., Latin America, 1961; Corcoran, 1963; MOMA, Hans Hofmann and His Students, circ., 1963-64; U. of Texas, Recent American Painting, 1964; MOMA, circ., Europe, Asia, Australia, 1964-66; Chicago/AI, 1966; AAA, Childe Hassam Purchase Exhibition, 1977; U. of North Carolina, Art on Paper, 1978-79; Syracuse/Everson, Provincetown Painting, 1890s—1970s, 1977; MMA, Hans Hofmann as Teacher, 1979; Corcoran, Ten Plus Ten Plus Ten, 1982; Corcoran, Washington Watercolors, 1984. **Collections:** American U.; Boston/MFA; U. of California; Chase Manhattan Bank; Ciba-Geigy Corp.; Corcoran; Des Moines; Evansville; MMA; Norfolk; Norfolk/Chrysler; U. of North Carolina; Phillips; Prudential Insurance Co. of America; Southern Illinois U.; U. of Texas; Utica; WMAA; Waitsfield/Bundy; Walker. **Bibliography:** Archives.

PADOVANO, ANTHONY. b. July 19, 1933, NYC. **Studied:** Brooklyn Museum School; Pratt Institute, with Alexander Kostellow; Columbia U., with

Oronzio Maldarelli, 1957, BFA; Carnegie Institute of Technology. US Army, 1957-59. Traveled Italy, Switzerland; resided Rome, two years. **Taught:** U. of Connecticut, 1962-64; Columbia U., 1964-70; Queens College, 1971-73; Sarah Lawrence College, 1974-79; Westchester County Center, 1973-75; 1974-79; Columbia Greene Community College, 1976-79; Kingsborough Community College, 1978-86. Subject of *Anthony Padovano, Sculptor,* by National Educational Television. **Member:** Silvermine Guild; American Association of University Professors; Sculptors Guild (vice-president). **Commissions:** World Trade Center, NYC, 1971; U. of Northern Iowa, 1972. **Awards:** Prix de Rome, 1960-62; III International Exhibition of Figurative Art, Rome, First Prize, 1962; Silvermine Guild, Olivetti Prize for Sculpture, 1963, 64; Guggenheim Foundation Fellowship, 1964; Ford Foundation, **P.P.,** 1964; AAAL, 1976; NAD, Gold Medal for Sculpture, 1983. **Address:** R.D. #1, Box 64, Putnam Valley, N.Y. 10579. **Dealer:** Forum Gallery, NYC. **One-man Exhibitions:** Lincoln, Mass./De Cordova, 1954 (drawings); Geejon Gallery, NYC, 1957; Sculptors Studio, Washington, D.C., 1958; Galleria George Lester, Rome, 1962; Ruth White Gallery, 1962; U. of Connecticut, 1962; 63; Richard Feigen Gallery, NYC, 1964; The Bertha Schaefer Gallery, 1968, 70; The Graham Gallery, N.Y., 1972, 75; 78, 81; IFA Gallery, Washington, D.C., 1975, 76; Alwin Gallery, London, 1978. **Group:** Carnegie, 1952; Portland, Me./MA, 1959; American Academy, Rome, 1960, 61, 62; Palazzo dell'Esposizione, Rome, 1961, 62; WMAA Annual, 1962; Baltimore/MA, 1963; Waitsfield/Bundy, Bundy Sculpture Competition, 1963; Lincoln, Mass./De Cordova, New England Sculpture, 1964, 66, 68, 72, 75, 76; Finch College, 1964; HemisFair '68, San Antonio, Tex., 1968. **Collections:** American Academy, Rome; U. of Delaware; First National City Bank, Chicago; U. of Illinois; Indianapolis/Herron; Kingsborough Community College; U. of Missouri; NCFA; U. of Nebraska; U. of Northern Iowa; Port Authority of New York & New Jersey; Ridgefield/Aldrich; Rutgers U.; St. Lawrence U.; Silvermine Guild; Trenton/State; Wichita/AM; WMAA; Worcester/AM.

PAIK, NAM JUNE. b. 1932, Seoul, Korea. **Studied:** U. of Tokyo, 1965, BA; U. of Munich; Conservatory of Music, Freiburg. To Germany, 1956; to USA, 1964. Composer/performer; Fluxus artist; TV, video, and film manipulator. **Awards:** JDR 3rd Fund Grant, 1965; Rockefeller Foundation Grant, 1967. **Address:** 110 Mercer Street, NYC 10012. **Dealer:** Holly Solomon Gallery, NYC; Carl Solway Gallery, Cincinnati. **One-man Exhibitions:** (first) Galerie Parnass, Wuppertal, 1963; New School, 1965; Galerie Bonino, NYC, 1965, 68; Syracuse/Everson, 1974; Rene Block Gallery, NYC, 1975; Cologne/Kunstverein, 1976; MOMA, 1977; Paris/Beaubourg, 1978; Berlin, Kunstverein, 1981; Holly Solomon Gallery, 1986. **Retrospective:** WMAA, circ., 1980. **Group:** ICA, Boston, Art Turned On, 1965; Walker, Light, Motion, Space, 1967; MOMA, The Machine, 1968; Brandeis U., Vision and Television, 1969; WMAA, Videoshow, 1971; Documenta VI, Kassel, 1972; WMAA Biennials, 1981, 87. **Collections:** Amsterdam/Stedelijk; Cologne/Ludwig; Humlebaek/Louisiana; Los Angeles/County MA; Paris/Beaubourg; Vienna/Moderner; WMAA.

PALMER, WILLIAM C. b. January 20, 1906, Des Moines, Iowa. **Studied:** ASL, 1924-26, with Boardman Robinson, Henry Schnakenberg, A. Tucker, Thomas Hart Benton, Kenneth Hayes Miller, and privately with Miller, 1928-29; Ecole des Beaux-Arts, Fontainebleau, with M. Baudoin. US Army, 1943-45. **Taught:** ASL, 1936-40; Hamilton College, 1941-47; Munson-

Williams-Proctor Institute, Utica, N.Y., 1941-73. Federal A.P.: Mural painter and supervisor, 1933-39; murals for: Queens General Hospital, Jamaica, N.Y., 1934-36; US Post Office Department Building, Washington, D.C., 1936; US Post Offices at Monticello, Iowa, 1935, and Arlington, Mass., 1938. **Member:** NAD; National Society of Mural Painters. **Commissions** (murals): First National City Bank, Socony Building, NYC; Homestead Savings and Loan Association, Utica, N.Y., 1957. **Awards:** Paris Salon Medal, 1937; NAD, 1946, elected National Academician, 1965; Audubon Artists, 1947; AAAL Grant, 1953; NAD, Andrew Carnegie Prize, 1980. **Address:** Butternut Hill, Chestnut Street, Clinton, NY 13323. **Dealer:** The Midtown Galleries. **One-man Exhibitions:** (first) The Midtown Galleries, 1932, also 1937, 40, 44, 50, 52, 54, 57, 59, 62, 67, 68, 69, 74, 77, 81, 82, 84, 85; Des Moines, 1948, 49, 79; Cazenovia Junior College, 1949; Utica, 1956; Syracuse U.; Skidmore College; Kansas City/Nelson; Colgate U.; St. Lawrence U.; Jacksonville/Cummer, 1972. **Retrospectives:** Utica, 1971; Wichita/AM, 1986. **Group:** Corcoran; VMFA; Carnegie, 1936; Brooklyn Museum; Chicago/AI; Toledo/MA; WMAA; New York World's Fair, 1939; MOMA; Kansas City/Nelson; Audubon Artists. **Collections:** AAAL; Allentown/AM; Andover/Phillips; Atlanta U.; Baltimore/MA; Britannica; Columbia S.C./MA; Columbus; Columbus, Ga.; Continental Grain Company; Cranbrook; Dallas/MFA; Des Moines; MMA; Phoenix; U. of Rochester; St. Lawrence U.; Syracuse U.; Transamerica Corp.; Trenton/State; Upjohn Co.; Utica; WMAA; The White House, Washington, D.C. **Bibliography:** Boswell 1; Bruce and Watson; Palmer; Watson, E.W., 2. Archives.

PAONE, PETER. b. October 2, 1936, Philadelphia, Pa. **Studied:** Barnes Foundation, 1953-54; Philadelphia Museum School, 1953, BA. Traveled Europe; resided London, two years. **Taught:** Pratt Institute, 1956-66, 1970-72; Philadelphia Museum School, 1958-59; Samuel S. Fleisher Art Memorial, Philadelphia, 1958-65; Positano (Italy) Art Workshop, 1961; U. of New Mexico, 1974; PAFA, 1979-80. **Member:** SAGA; NAD. **Awards:** PMA, **P.P.,** 1959; Library of Congress; Pennell **P.P.,** 1962; L.C. Tiffany Grants, 1962, 64; The Print Club, Philadelphia, **P.P.,** 1963; Syracuse U., **P.P.,** 1964; Pennsylvania Council on the Visual Arts, 1985. **Address:** 1027 Westview Street, Philadephia, PA 19119. **Dealer:** Hooks-Epstein Gallery Inc., Houston. **One-man Exhibitions:** (first) Dubin Gallery, Philadelphia, 1957; The Print Club, Philadelphia, 1958, 61, 62, 83; Gallery Ten, New Hope, Pa., 1959; Grippi Gallery, NYC, 1959-62; Fort Worth, 1964; The Forum Gallery, 1965; Jessop Gallery, London, 1967; Benson Gallery, 1967; David Gallery, 1968; Roswell, 1977; Amarillo Art Center; Art Center, Waco; Hooks Epstein Gallery, Houston, 1978; PAFA, 1983; Hooks-Epstein Gallery Inc., 1983, 85, 86. **Group:** PMA, 1959, 62; Brooklyn Museum, 1962, and Print Biennials; Escuela Nacional de Artes Plasticas, Mexico City, 1963; III Paris Biennial, 1963; Dallas/MFA, Four Young Artists, 1964; Syracuse/Everson, American Printmakers, 1964; New York World's Fair, 1964-65; Otis Art Institute. **Collections:** British Museum; Chicago/AI; Fort Worth; Free Library of Philadelphia; General Mills Inc.; U. of Kansas; Lehigh U.; Library of Congress; MOMA; U. of Massachusetts; National Gallery; PAFA; PMA; Princeton U.; The Print Club, Philadelphia; Carl Sandburg Memorial Library; Southern Nevada U.; Syracuse U.; Trenton/State; U. of Utah; Victoria and Albert Museum; Youngstown/Butler. **Bibliography:** Rodman 3.

PARIS, HOWARD P. b. August 16, 1925, Edgemere, N.Y.; **d.** 1979, Oakland, Calif. **Studied:** Atelier 17,

NYC, 1949; Creative Workshop, NYC, 1951-52; Academy of Fine Arts, Munich, 1953-56. Traveled Europe. **Taught:** U. of California, Berkeley. **Awards:** L. C. Tiffany Grant, 1949; Guggenheim Foundation Fellowship, 1953; Fulbright Fellowship (Germany), 1953; U. of California, Creative Arts Award and Institute Fellowship, 1967-68. **One-man Exhibitions:** (first) Argent Gallery, NYC, 1951; Philadelphia Art Alliance, 1951; Village Art Center, NYC, 1952; Wittenborn Gallery, NYC, 1952; Galerie Moderne, NYC, 1953; Esther Stuttman Gallery, NYC, 1960; Tulane U., 1960; Pratt Graphic Art Center, 1960; Silvan Simone Gallery, 1960; U. of California, Berkeley, 1961; Paul Kantor Gallery, Beverly Hills, Calif., 1961; Bolles Gallery, 1962 (two-man, with Angelo Ippolito); Humboldt State College, 1963; Hansen Gallery, San Francisco, 1965, 67; Mills College, 1967; Reed College, 1967; Sally Judd Gallery, Portland, Ore., 1968; Michael Smith Gallery, Los Angeles, 1972; Smith-Andersen Gallery, San Francisco, 1975, 76, 77; Stephen Wirtz Gallery, San Francisco, 1979, 84. **Group:** MMA; Boston/MFA; Vienna Sezession; The Hague; Amerika Haus, Munich; California Palace; Baltimore/MA; Smithsonian; New Orleans/Delgado; Pasadena/AM; Brooklyn Museum, 1948, 49, 50, 52, 54; PAFA, 1949, 50, 52, 54; Galerie Kunst der Gegenwart, Salzburg, 1952; MOMA, 1953; PMA, 1953-56, 1959, 64; SFMA, 1953, 1960-65, Annual, 1963; III Biennial of Spanish-American Art, Barcelona, 1955; Ottawa/National, 1956; WMAA, 1956, Sculpture Annual, 1964; Salon de la Jeune Sculpture, Paris, 1958; Stanford U., Some Points of View for '62, 1961; Museum of Contemporary Crafts, 1963, 66; U. of California, circ., 1963-64; France/National, 1964; San Francisco Art Institute, 1964; New School for Social Research, 1964; La Jolla, 1965; The Pennsylvania State U., 1965; Newport Harbor Art Museum, Balboa, Calif., 1965; M. Knoedler & Co., Art across America, circ., 1965-67;

Los Angeles/County MA, 1966. **Collections:** California Palace; U. of California; Chicago/AI; U. of Delaware; Goddard College; La Jolla; Library of Congress; MOMA; Memphis/Brooks; NYPL; U. of North Dakota; Oakland/AM; Ottawa/National; PMA; SFMA; WMAA; U. of Wisconsin. **Bibliography:** Selz, P. 2; Tuchman 1.

PARK, DAVID. b. March 17, 1911, Boston, Mass.; **d.** September 20, 1960, Berkeley, Calif. **Studied:** Otis Art Institute, Los Angeles, 1928; assistant to Ralph Stackpole, 1929. **Taught:** Various private schools, San Francisco, 1931-36; Winsor School, Boston, 1936-41; California School of Fine Arts, 1943-52; U. of California, Berkeley, 1955-60. Designed sets and costumes for the U. of California, Berkeley, production of the opera *The Sorrows of Orpheus,* by Darius Milhaud, 1958. Federal A.P.: Mural painting, San Francisco. **Awards:** SFMA, 1935, 51, 53, 55, 57; Oakland/AM, Gold Medal, 1957; PAFA, Walter Lippincott Prize, 1960. **One-man Exhibitions:** SFMA, 1935, 40; Delphic Studios, NYC, 1936; New Gallery, Boston, 1939; Albany/Institute (two-man, with Dorothy Dehner), ca. 1944; California Palace, 1946; Paul Kantor Gallery, Beverly Hills, Calif., 1954; RAC, 1955; U. of California, College of Architecture, 1956; Oakland/AM, 1957; de Young, 1959; Staempfli Gallery, 1959, 61, 63, 65; U. of California, Berkeley, circ., 1964; Santa Barbara/MA, 1968; Maxwell Galleries, Ltd., San Francisco, 1970; Salander-O'Reilly Galleries, NYC, 1983, 85. **Retrospective:** Oakland/AM, 1977. **Group:** PAFA, 1950; U. of Illinois, 1952, 57, 59, 61; III Sao Paulo Biennial, 1955; ART:USA:58 and ART:USA:59, NYC, 1958, 59; WMAA Annual, 1959; Indiana U., New Imagery in American Painting, 1959; A.F.A., The Figure, circ., 1960; Chicago/AI; Corcoran; SRGM/USIA, American Vanguard, circ., Europe, 1961-62; J.L. Hudson Art Gallery, Detroit, Four California Painters, 1966. **Collections:** U. of California, Berkeley; ICA, Boston; U. of Illinois; Indian Head Mills, Inc.; Oakland/AM; SFMA; WMAA. **Bibliography:** Goodrich and Baur 1; Sandler 1. Archives.

PARKER, RAYMOND. b. August 22, 1922, Beresford, S.D. **Studied:** U. of Iowa, 1946, BA, 1948, MFA. **Taught:** Hunter College, 1955-; U. of Southern California, summer, 1959; State U. of Iowa; U. of Minnesota; Columbia U., 1970-71. **Awards:** Ford Foundation, **P.P.,** 1963; Ford Foundation/A.F.A. Artist-in-Residence Grant, 1965; National Council on the Arts, 1967; Guggenheim Foundation Fellowship, 1967. **Address:** 52 Carmine Street, NYC. **One-man Exhibitions:** Walker, 1950; Memphis/Brooks, 1953; Paul Kantor Gallery, Beverly Hills, Calif., 1953, 56; Louisville/Speed, 1954; Union College (N.Y.), 1955; Widdifield Gallery, NYC, 1957, 59; U. of Southern California, 1959; Dwan Gallery, 1960, 62; Galerie Lawrence, Paris, 1960; The Kootz Gallery, NYC, 1960-64; Galleria dell'Ariete, 1961; SRGM, 1961; Bennington College, 1961; Des Moines, 1962 (three-man); Gertrude Kasle Gallery, 1966, 70; U. of New Mexico, 1967; Galerie Muller, 1967; Simone Sterne Gallery, New Orleans (two-man), 1968; Molly Barnes Gallery, Los Angeles, 1968, 70; Quay Gallery, 1970, 72, 74; Fischbach Gallery, 1971, 73, 74; Arts Club of Chicago, 1971; Miami-Dade, 1971; Michael Berger Gallery, Pittsburgh, 1974; Portland (Ore.) Center for the Visual Arts, 1974; Benson Gallery, 1974; Berenson Gallery, Miami, 1974; American U., 1975; Susan Caldwell Gallery, NYC, 1976, 77; U. of Maryland, 1977; U. of Texas, Austin, 1977; The Billiard Room Gallery, Cambridge, Mass., 1979; Betty Cuningham, NYC, 1979, 80; Phillips, 1979; Susan Caldwell Gallery, NYC, 1980. **Retrospectives:** Dayton/AI, 1965; WGMA, 1966; SFMA, 1967; School of Visual Arts, NYC, 1971. **Group:** Minnesota State Historical Society, St. Paul, Centennial Minnesota; Walker Biennials, 1949, 51; MOMA, New Talent; MMA, American Paintings Today, 1950; WMAA Annuals, 1950, 52, 58, 67, 79, 72, 73; Oberlin College, 1951; Walker, Vanguard, 1955; Tokyo/Modern, 1957; Walker, 60 American Painters, 1960; II Inter-American Paintings and Prints Biennial, Mexico City, 1960; SRGM, Abstract Expressionists and Imagists, 1961; U. of Illinois, 1961, 62; Seattle World's Fair, 1962; Corcoran, 1963; Jewish Museum, Toward a New Abstraction, 1963; Hartford/Wadsworth, Black, White, and Gray, 1964; Chicago/AI, 1964; Los Angeles/County MA, Post Painterly Abstraction, 1964; Tate, Painting and Sculpture of a Decade, 1954-64, 1964; XXXII Venice Biennial, 1964; Cambridge, 1964, 65; MOMA, The Art of the Real, 1968; MOMA, Younger Abstract Expressionists of the Fifties, 1971; U. of Texas, Color Forum, 1972. **Collections:** AAAL; Akron/AI, Allentown/AM; Brandeis U.; Buffalo/Albright; Chicago/AI; Ciba-Geigy Corp.; Cleveland/MA; Commerce Bank of Kansas City; Dayton/AI; Des Moines; Fort Worth; Hartford/Wadsworth; International Minerals & Chemicals Corp.; State U. of Iowa; Los Angeles/County/MA; MIT; MMA; MOMA; Miami-Dade; Minneapolis/Institute; Minnesota State Historical Society; U. of New Mexico; New Orleans/Delgado; PMA; Portland, Ore./AM; Phillips; Princeton U.; Ridgefield/Aldrich; SFMA; SRGM; Tate; U. of Texas; Vassar College; WMAA; Walker. **Bibliography:** Friedman, ed.; Goossen 1; McChesney; *New in the Seventies; Metro;* Rickey; Sandler; Weller.

PARKER, ROBERT ANDREW. b. May 14, 1927, Norfolk, Va. **Studied:** Chicago Art Institute School, with Paul Wieghardt, Rudolph Pen, Max Kahn, 1948-52, B.A. Ed.; Atelier 17, NYC, 1952-53, with Peter Grippe. US Army Air Force, 1945-46. Traveled Europe, Africa, Central and South America.

Taught: New York School for the Deaf, 1952-55; School of Visual Arts, NYC, 1959-63; RISD; Syracuse U.; Parsons School of Design, NYC. **Member:** American Federation of Musicians; NAD. Worked on film *The Days of Wilfred Owen*, with Richard Burton. **Commissions:** Illustrated 8 Poems by Marianne Moore (MOMA, 1962); sets for the MOMA production of *The Mighty Casey*, opera by William Schuman; New York World's Fair, 1964-65. **Awards:** Chicago/AI, 1952; Skowhegan School, 1952; Chicago/AI, Maurice L. Rothschild Scholarship, 1962; NIAL, Richard and Hinda Rosenthal Foundation Award, 1962; Tamarind Fellowship, 1967; Guggenheim Foundation Fellowship, 1969. **Address:** River Road, W. Cornwall, Ct. 06796. **Dealer:** Terry Dintenfass, Inc. **One-man Exhibitions:** (first) The Little Gallery, Chicago, 1949; Roko Gallery, NYC, 1953, 54, 57, 58, 59; Palmer House Galleries, Chicago, 1957; Nexus Gallery, Boston, 1957; Katonah (N.Y.) Library, 1957, 63; Felix Landau Gallery, 1961; St. Paul Gallery, 1961; Nashville, 1961; World House Galleries, NYC, 1961, 62, 64; Raymond Burr Gallery, Los Angeles, 1962; Obelisk Gallery, Washington, D.C., 1963; J. L. Hudson Art Gallery, Detroit, 1963, 69; Terry Dintenfass, Inc., 1966, 67, 69, 70, 71, 72, 78, 79, 82; The Schuman Gallery, Rochester, N.Y., 1967; Lehigh U., 1969; U. of Connecticut, 1971; Achim Moeller Ltd., London, 1973; Martin Sumers Graphics, NYC, 1978; Bethel (Conn.) Art Gallery, 1978; Moravian College, 1978; Pennsylvania State U., 1981; Brooklyn Museum, 1982; Rossi Gallery, Morristown, N.J., 1982. **Group:** MMA, American Watercolors, Drawings and Prints, 1952; MOMA, Young American Printmakers, 1953; WMAA Annuals, 1955, 56, 59; A.F.A., New Talent, circ., 1956; La Napoule, France, 5 Masters of Line, 1957; WMAA, Young America, 1957; USIA, Contemporary Graphic Art in the USA, circ., Europe and Asia, 1957-59; WMAA, Forty Americans under Forty, circ., 1962; Brooklyn Mu-

seum, 1963, 1968-69; MOMA, 1966; PAFA Annuals, 1966, 67; Indianapolis/Herron, 1967, 68; Brooklyn Museum Print Biennials, 1968, 69; U. of North Carolina, 1969, 71; New School for Social Research, Humor, Satire, and Irony, 1972; NAD Annual, 1977; Indiana U., Contemporary Pastel and Watercolors, 1977; Potsdam/SUNY, Off the Beaten Path, 1977; NAD, Ward Ranger Annual Exhibition, 1979. **Collections:** Amerada Hess Corp.; U. of Arkansas; Brooklyn Museum; Dublin/Municipal; Hirshhorn; Kalamazoo/Institute; Los Angeles/County MA; MOMA; U. of Massachusetts; U. of Michigan; Minnesota/MA; Montclair/AM; The Morgan Library; NAD; Nashville; Newark Museum; Pasadena/AM; Phoenix; NAD; Nashville; Newark Museum; Pasadena/AM; Phoenix; Raleigh/NCMA; Smith College; Tacoma; WMAA.

PARRISH, DAVID. b. June 19, 1939, Birmingham, Ala. **Studied:** U. of Alabama, BFA. **Address:** 700 Cleermont Drive, S.E., Huntsville, Ala. 35801. **Dealer:** Nancy Hoffman Gallery, NYC. **One-man Exhibitions:** Memphis/Brooks, 1971; Sherry French Gallery, NYC, 1972; Galerie Petit, Paris, 1973; Sidney Janis Gallery, NYC, 1975; Huntsville, 1977; Birmingham, Ala./MA, circ., 1981; Nancy Hoffman Gallery, 1981. **Group:** U. of North Carolina, Art on Paper, 1968; Youngstown/Butler, Mid-year Show, 1969; Indianapolis, 1972, 78; Baltimore/MA, Super Realism, 1975; U. of Nebraska, Things Seen, circ., 1978; San Antonio/MA, Real, Really Real, Super Real, circ., 1981; PAFA, Contemporary American Realism Since 1960, 1981; SFMA, American Realism (Janss), circ., 1985. **Collections:** Birmingham, Ala./MA; Memphis/Brooks; Flint; Huntsville; Montgomery Museum; Brandeis U.; Nashville; Hartford/Wadsworth.

Ed Paschke *Joeski* 1986

PASCHKE, ED. b. June 22, 1939, Chicago. **Studied:** Chicago Art Institute School, BFA, MA. US Army, 1962-64. **Taught:** Meramac College, St. Louis, 1970-71; Chicago Art Institute School, 1973; Barat College, Lake Forest, 1971-77; Northwestern U., 1978-. **Address:** 6129 North Kilbourn, Chicago, Ill. 60646. **Dealers:** Phyllis Kind Gallery, NYC, Chicago; Galerie Darthea Speyer, Paris. **One-man Exhibitions:** Deson Zaks Gallery, Chicago, 1970, 72, 73, 75; Richard DeMarco Gallery, Edinburgh, 1973; Cincinnati/Contemporary, 1974; Hundred Acres Gallery, NYC, 1971, 74; Pyramid Gallery, Washington, D.C., 1975; Marion Locks Gallery, Philadelphia, 1976; Galerie Darthea Speyer, Paris, 1974, 76, 78, 81, 83, 85; Phyllis Kind Gallery, Chicago, 1977, 79, 83; Phyllis Kind Gallery, NYC, 1978, 79, 80, 82, 83, 84, 85; Galerie Bonnier, Geneva, 1984; Fuller Goldeen San Francisco, 1984. **Retrospective:** U. of Chicago, circ., 1981. **Group:** Chicago/Contemporary, Don Baum Sez, "Chicago Needs Famous Artists," 1969; Chicago/AI, Chicago and Vicinity, 1962, 67, 73; Chicago/Contemporary, Chicago Imagist Art, 1972; Ottawa/Ontario, What They're Up to in Chicago, 1972; WMAA Biennial, 1973; Chicago Art Institute School, Former Famous Alumni, 1976; Sacramento/Crocker, The Chicago Connection, 1977; U. of Texas, New in the Seventies, 1977; Grand Palais, Paris, Salon de Mai, 1978; Sunderland (Eng.) Arts Centre, Who Chicago?, circ., 1980; Haus der Kunst, Munich, Amerikanische Malerie, 1930-1980, 1981; WMAA Biennial, 1981, 85; Kansas City/AI, Chicago Imagists, 1982; Indianapolis, 1982; Hirshhorn, Correspondances: New York Choice '84, 1984; MOMA, International Survey of Recent Painting and Sculpture, 1984; Corcoran Biennial, 1985. **Collections:** Brooklyn Museum; Baltimore/MA; Chicago/AI; Chicago/Contemporary; Jacksonville/ AM; Kalamazoo/Institute; MMA; Museum des 20. Jahrhunderts, Vienna; NMAA; Paris/Beaubourg; Paris/ Moderne; Phoenix; Rotterdam; Vienna/ Moderner; WMAA. **Bibliography:** Adrian; *The Chicago Connection; New in the Seventies; Who Chicago?.*

PEARLSTEIN, PHILIP. b. May 24, 1924, Pittsburgh, Pa. **Studied:** Carnegie Institute of Technology, with Sam Rosenberg, Robert Lepper, Balcomb Greene; NYU, BA, MFA. **Taught:** Pratt Institute, 1959-63; Brooklyn College, 1963-. **Member:** Tanager Gallery, NYC; AAIAL; Century Association. **Awards:** Fulbright Fellowship (Italy), 1958; National Council on the Arts Grant, 1969, AAAL, **P.P.,** 1973; American Academy, Rome, Artist in Residence, 1982; Skowhegan School, Gold Medal, 1985. Subject of video, *Philip Pearlstein Draws the Artist's Model*, 1985, produced by Interactive Media Corp., NYC. **Address:** 163 West 88 Street, NYC 10024. **Dealer:** Hirschl & Adler Modern, NYC. **One-man Exhibitions:** (first) Tanager Gallery, NYC, 1955, 59; The Periodot Gallery, NYC, 1956, 57, 59; Allan Frumkin Gallery, Chicago, 1960, 65, 69, 73, 75; Allan Frumkin Gallery, NYC, 1961-67, 69, 72, 74, 76, 78, 80, 82; Kansas City/Nelson, 1962; Reed College, 1965, 79; Ceeje Galleries, Los Angeles, 1965, 66; Bradford Junior College, 1967; Carnegie, 1968; U. of South Florida, 1969; Chatham College, Pittsburgh, 1970; Graphics I & Graphics II, Boston, 1971, 81; M.E. Thelen Gallery, Cologne, 1972; Galleri Ostergren, Malmo, 1972; Galerie Kornfeld, Zurich, 1972; Berlin, 1972; Donald Morris Gal-

Philip Pearlstein *Two Nudes on Bedouin Carpet* 1987

lery, 1972, 76, 80, 82; Parker Street 470 Gallery, Boston, 1973; Galerie La Tortue, Paris, 1973; Finch College, NYC, circ., 1974; Purchase/SUNY, 1975; Friedland Gallery, Toronto, 1975, 81, 84; John Berger Gallery, Pittsburgh, 1975; Fendrick Gallery, Washington, D.C., 1976; Harcus-Krakow Gallery, Boston, 1978; Carnegie-Mellon U., 1979; Gimpel Fils, London, 1979; Jollembeck, Cologne, 1979; Plattsburgh/SUNY, 1979; Wesleyan U., 1979; Associated American Artists, NYC, 1980; Brooke Alexander, Inc., 1981; Columbus College, 1981; U. of North Carolina, 1981; North Dakota State U., 1981; Reynolds/Minor Gallery, Richmond, Va., 1981; Ringling, 1981; Springfield, Mo./AM; 1981; Summit (N.J.) Art Center, 1982; Michael Berger Gallery, Pittsburgh, 1983; American Academy, Rome, 1983; Galleria Il Ponte, Rome, 1983; U. of Northern Iowa, 1983; Fay Gold Gallery, Atlanta, 1984; Richmond U., 1984; Hirschl & Adler Modern, 1985; James Madison

U., 1986; Palace Theatre of the Arts, Stamford, Ct., 1986. **Retrospectives:** U. of Georgia, 1970; Springfield, Mass./MFA, 1978; Milwaukee, circ., 1983. **Group:** The Kootz Gallery, NYC, New Talent, 1954; The Stable Gallery Annuals, 1955-57; Carnegie, 1955, 66; 73; U. of Nebraska, 1956, 57; Walker, Expressionism, 1900-1955, 1956, also 1958; Chicago/AI, 1959, 62; Kansas City/Nelson, 1962; U. of Colorado, 1962, 67; SFMA, Directions—Painting U.S.A., 1963, also 1968; Boston U., 1964; U. of Illinois, 1965, 67, 69; U. of Texas, 1966; Corcoran, 1967; Harvard U., 1967; Trenton/State, Focus on Light, 1967; Torcuato di Tella, Buenos Aires; Vassar College, 1968; Smithsonian, circ., Latin America, 1968-70; Milwaukee, Aspects of a New Realism, 1969; WMAA, 22 Realists, 1970; MIT, Leslie Pearlstein, Thiebaud, 1971; Indianapolis, 1972; A.F.A., Realist Revival, 1972; WMAA, American Drawings, 1963-1973, 1973; Yale U., American Drawing: 1970-1973, 1973; Hofstra U., The Male Nude, 1973; Ars 74, Helsinki, 1974; VMFA, Twelve American Painters, 1974; Westminster College, The Figure in Recent American Painting, 1974; Cleveland/MA, Aspects of the Figure, 1974; Yale U., Seven Realists, 1973; Corcoran Biennial, 1975; Lincoln, Mass./De Cordova, Candid Painting; American Genre 1950-1975, 1975; PAFA, Eight Contemporary Realists, 1977; Darmstadt/Kunsthalle, Realism and Reality, 1975, U. of Colorado, Six Painters of the Figure, 1979; US Dept. of the Interior, America 1976, circ., 1976; WMAA Biennial, 1979; Corcoran, The Human Form, 1980; NPG, American Portrait Drawings, 1980; Brooklyn Museum, American Drawing in Black and White, 1970-1979, 1980; Akron/AM, The Image in American Painting and Sculpture, 1950-1980, 1981; San Antonio/MA, Real, Really Real, Super Real, circ., 1981; Haus der Kunst, Munich, Amerikanische Malerie, 1930-1980, 1981; PAFA, Contemporary American Realism Since 1960, circ., 1982; Isetan Museum of Art, Tokyo, American Realism, The Pre-

cise Image, 1985; Fort Lauderdale, An American Renaissance: Painting and Sculpture Since 1940, 1986. **Collections:** Akron/AM; Boston/MFA; Brandeis U.; Brooklyn College; Brooklyn Museum; Brown U.; Canton Art Institute; Carnegie; Cleveland/MA; Cornell U.; Chicago/AI; Chicago/Contemporary; U. of Chicago; Colgate U.; Colorado Springs/FA; Corcoran; Des Moines; Hirshhorn; Hunter College; U. of Indiana; Louisville/Speed; MMA; MOMA; Milwaukee; NYU; U. of Nebraska; Newark Museum; U. of North Carolina; PMA; Princeton U.; RISD; Reed College; Rensselaer Polytechnic Institute; Ringling; Syracuse U.; Toledo/MA; Trenton/State; Vassar College; WMAA; Yale U. **Bibliography:** Adrian; *America 1976*; Arthur 1, 2, 3; Cummings 1; Goldman 1; Goodyear; Honisch and Jensen, eds.; *Kunst um 1970*; Murken-Altrogge; Nochlin; Rubin 1; Sandler 1; Sager; Strand, ed.; Weller. Archives.

PEARSON, HENRY CHARLES. b. October 8, 1914, Kinston, N.C. **Studied:** U. of North Carolina; Yale U., BA, MFA; ASL, 1953-55, with Reginald Marsh, Will Barnet, Robert Hale. US Army and Air Force, 1942-53. Traveled USA, the Orient. The biographer of Seamus Heaney. **Taught:** Boston Museum School; New School for Social Research; U. of Minnesota, Duluth; Ball State U.; PAFA; and privately. **Member:** American Abstract Artists; Century Association. **Awards:** Raleigh/NCMA, 1957; Tamarind Fellowship, 1964; Corcoran, **P.P.,** 1965; PAFA, J. Henry Schiedt Memorial Prize, 1968; North Carolina Governor's Arts Medal, 1969. **Address:** 58 West 58th Street, NYC 10019; 1601 Cambridge Drive, Kinston, NC 28501. **Dealer:** Marilyn Pearl Gallery, NYC. **One-man Exhibitions:** (first) Workshop Gallery, NYC, 1958; Stephen Radich Gallery, NYC, 1961, 62, 66, 69; Ball State U., 1965; U. of Minnesota, 1965;

Parsons-Truman Gallery, NYC, 1975, 77; Marilyn Pearl Gallery, NYC, 1980, 83, 86; Century Association, 1982. **Retrospective:** Raleigh/NCMA, 1969. **Group:** Scranton/Everhart, Contemporary Americans, 1956; PAFA, 1956, 64; American Abstract Artists Annuals, 1958-64; A.F.A., Purist Painting, circ., 1960-61; A.F.A., Drawings from the WMAA Annual 1960, circ., 1961-62; WMAA, Geometric Abstraction in America, circ., 1962; MOMA, Contemporary Painters and Sculptors as Printmakers, 1964, The Responsive Eye, 1965, also 1969; Corcoran Biennial, 1965; Chicago/AI, 1965; Gallery of Modern Art, NYC, 1965; WMAA Annuals, 1965, 66, 68; Brooklyn Museum, Print Biennial; Grolier Club, 1966; Gallery of Modern Art, Ljubljana, Yugoslavia, VII International Exhibition of Prints, 1967; Utica, 1968; WMAA, Twentieth-Century Drawings from the Whitney Museum of American Art, circ., 1979-81; U. of North Carolina, Art on Paper, 1980; Bard College, White & Black, 1983. **Collections:** Ackland; Allentown/AM; Buffalo/Albright; Burlington Mills Collection; Chase Manhattan Bank; Chicago/AI; Ciba-Geigy Corp.; Cincinnati/AM; Columbia Broadcasting System; Corcoran; Hirshhorn; Housatonic Community College; Kansas City/Nelson; MMA; MOMA; Malmo; U. of Massachusetts; Minneapolis/Institute; Minnesota/MA; U. of Minnesota; NYPL; National Gallery; U. of Nebraska; Newark Museum; U. of North Carolina; Oslo/National, Raleigh/NCMA; St. Louis/City; The Singer Company, Inc.; Southern Illinois U.; SRGM; Trinity College, Dublin; U.S. Steel Corp.; Union Carbide Corp.; WMAA; Wells College. **Bibliography:** Archives.

PEIRCE, WALDO. b. December 17, 1884, Bangor, Me.; **d.** March 8, 1970, Newburyport, Mass. **Studied:** Phillips Academy; Harvard U., 1908, A.B.; Academie Julian, Paris, 1911. Traveled Europe, North Africa, Spain. **Commis-**sions (murals): US Post Offices, Westbrooke, Me., Troy, N.Y., and Peabody, Mass.; Field Service Building, NYC, 1961. **Awards:** Pomona College, 1939; Pepsi-Cola, 1944; Carnegie, First Hon. Men., 1944. **One-man Exhibitions:** (first) Wildenstein & Co., NYC, 1926, 41 (two-man); The Midtown Galleries, 1939, 41, 44, 45, 49, 60, 68, 72. **Retrospective:** Rockland/Farnsworth, 1950. **Group:** Salon du Mai, Paris, 1912, 13, 14; Salon d' Automne, Paris, 1922. **Collections:** Andover/Phillips; Arizona State U.; U. of Arizona; Augusta, Me./State; Bangor Public Library; Britannica; Brooklyn Museum; Carnegie; Colby College; Columbus; Harvard U.; MMA; U. of Maine; U. of Nebraska; PAFA; Pepsi-Cola Co.; Rockland/Farnsworth; Upjohn Co.; WMAA; Youngstown/Butler.   **Bibliography:** American Artists Group Inc. 3; Baur 7; Bazin; Bethers; Boswell 1; Eliot; **Hale;** Hall; Mellquist; **Peirce;** 7 *Decades;* **Varga.** Archives.

PENNEY, JAMES. b. September 6, 1910, St. Joseph, Mo. **d.** August 1, 1982, Utica, N.Y. **Studied:** U. of Kansas, with Albert Bloch, Karl Mattern, R. J. Eastwood, 1931, BFA; ASL, 1931-34, with George Grosz, Charles Locke, William Von Schlegell, Thomas Hart Benton, John Sloan. Traveled USA, Mexico, Europe, Canada. **Taught:** U. of Kansas, 1938-39; Hunter College, 1941-42; Bennett College (N.Y.), 1945-46; Bennington College, 1946-47; School for Art Studies, NYC, 1947; Munson-Williams-Proctor Institute, Utica, N.Y., 1948-55; Hamilton College, 1948-76; Kansas State U., summer, 1955; Vassar College, 1955-56; California College of Arts and Crafts, summer, 1960. **Member:** ASL; National Society of Mural Painters; Audubon Artists; NAD. **Commissions:** Federal A.P. (murals): Greenpoint Hospital, Brooklyn, N.Y. (with Moses Soyer); Flushing (N.Y.) High School, P.S. 231, NYC; Far Rockaway (N.Y.) High School; New York World's Fair, 1939;

Section of Fine Arts, Washington, D.C., 1939; Bristol Center, Hamilton College, 1959; Nebraska State Capitol, 1962-63(3); US Post Offices, Union, Mo., and Palmyra, Mo.; Omaha National Bank Centennial, 1966. **Awards:** Kansas City/Nelson, Medal, 1931; Section of Fine Arts, 1939, 40, 41; Pepsi-Cola, Award and Medal, 1948; Western New York Printmakers Annual, First Prize, 1950; Kansas State U., **P.P.,** 1951, 53, 57; AAAL, Childe Hassam Award, 1953; Utica, **P.P.,** 1955, 57; Yaddo Fellowship, 1956, 61; Our Town Competition, 1958; Audubon Artists Award, 1967; Audubon Artists Annual, Sterne Award, 1977. **One-man Exhibitions:** U. of Kansas, 1934, 37; Eighth Street Playhouse, NYC, 1936; Mulvane Art Museum, 1937; Hudson D. Walker Gallery, NYC, 1939; Bennington College, 1946; Kraushaar Galleries, 1950, 54, 57, 61, 65, 69, 74, 84; Utica, 1951, 74; Colgate U., 1952, 54; Wells College, 1953; Union College (N.Y.), 1955; Kansas State College, 1955; Wichita/AM, 1955; Vassar College, 1956; Syracuse U., 1957; Cazenovia Junior College, 1962; Kirkland Art Center, Clinton, N.Y., 1964; Omaha/Joslyn, 1966; Hamilton College, 1967, 71, 76, 83; Upstairs Gallery, Ithaca, N.Y., 1967-68; Cooperstown (N.Y.) Art Association, 1969; Rome (N.Y.) Art and Community Center, 1978. **Retrospectives:** Utica, 1955; Hamilton College, 1962; Utica College, 1972. **Group:** Carnegie; Brooklyn Museum; PAFA; American Watercolor Society; New York World's Fair, 1939; Pepsi-Cola; Audubon Artists; U. of Illinois; Chicago/AI; WMAA Annuals; California Palace; Kansas City/Nelson; Cleveland/MA; National Gallery; Newark Museum; Walker; Fort Worth; Colby College; Toledo/MA; Atlanta/AA; NIAL; New York State Fair, Syracuse, 1966; NAD, 1973, 74, 75; Syracuse U., Art in Crisis, 1974; AAAL, 1973. **Collections:** Clearwater/Gulf Coast; Columbus; Continental Grain Company; Des Moines; Exeter; Fort Worth; Hamilton College; Hirshhorn; Howard U.; Kansas City/Nelson; Kan-

sas State College; Lehigh U.; Lincoln Life Insurance Co.; Lincoln-Rochester Trust Co.; U. of Minnesota; Montreal/MFA; Mount Holyoke College; NAD; NCFA; U. of Nebraska; New Britain; Ohio Oil Co., NYC; Omaha/Joslyn; St. Joseph/Albrecht; Springfield, Mass./MFA; Syracuse U.; Upjohn Co.; Utica; Wichita/AM. **Bibliography:** Baur 5. Archives.

PEPPER, BEVERLY. b. December 20, 1924, Brooklyn. **Studied:** Pratt Institute, 1939-41, BA; Art Students League, 1946; Academie de la Grande Chaumiere, Paris; Atelier Andre l'Hote, 1948, and Atelier Fernand Leger. Painted from 1949-60, then began sculpture. Advertising art director, 1942-48. Traveled Europe, North Africa, Israel, Orient; since 1949 has lived in Italy. **Commissions:** Festival di Due Mondi, Spoleto, 1962; U.S. Plywood Building, NYC, 1963; Weizmann Institute, Rehovoth, Israel, 1964; Southland Mall, Memphis, 1966; Government Center, Boston, 1971; North Park Shopping Mall, Dallas, 1971; Albany (N.Y.) Mall, 1973; Federal Reserve Bank, Philadelphia, 1974; San Diego Federal Building, 1975; AT&T, Long Lines Building, Bedminster, N.J., 1974; Dartmouth College, 1975; The Carborundum Co., Niagara Falls, 1978; City Hall, Toledo, Ohio, 1979; Physiocontrol Co., Seattle, 1979; City of Niagara Falls, 1979; Todi, Italy, 1979; Toledo (O.) Civic Center, 1979; Buffalo (N.Y.) Convention Center, 1979; Richard J. Hughes Justice Complex, Trenton, N.J., 1981; Four-Leaf Towers, Houston, 1982; Phoenix Center, Pontiac, Mich., 1982; Laumeier Sculpture Park, 1983; Johns Hopkins Hospital, Baltimore, 1983; Buffalo/SUNY, 1983. **Awards:** Hon. DFA, Pratt Institute, 1982; Hon. DFA, Maryland Institute, 1983. **Address:** Torre Gentile di Todi, Perugia 06059, Italy; 86 Thomas Street, NYC 10013. **Dealer:** Andre Emmerich Gallery, NYC. **One-man Exhibitions:** (first) Galleria dello Zodiaco, Rome,

1952; Barone, NYC, 1954, 56, 68; Obelisk Gallery, Washington, D.C., 1955; Galleria d'Arte l'Obelisco, Rome, 1959; Galleria Pogliani, Rome, 1961; Thibaut Gallery, NYC, 1961; Marlborough Galleria d'Arte, Rome, 1965, 68, 72; McCormick Place-on-the-Lake, Chicago, 1966; Galleria d'Arte La Bussola, Turin, 1968; Paola Barozzi, Venice, 1968; Marlborough Gallery, NYC, 1969; Chicago/Contemporary, 1969; MIT, 1969; Buffalo/Albright, 1969; Syracuse/Everson, 1970; Piazza della Rotonda, Milan, 1970; Studio Marconi, Milan, 1971; Galerie Hella Nebelung, Dusseldorf, 1971; Piazza Margana, Rome, 1971; Parker Street 470 Gallery, Boston, 1971; Qui Arte Contemporanea, Rome, 1972; Tyler School, Temple U.; Rome, 1973; Hammarskjold Plaza, NYC, 1975; Andre Emmerich Gallery, NYC, 1975, 77, 79, 82, 83, 84; SFMA, 1976; Seattle/AM, 1977; Indianapolis, 1977, 78; Dartmouth College, 1977; Princeton U., 1978; Hofstra U., 1979; Thomas Segal Gallery, Boston, 1980; Andre Emmerich Gallery, Zurich, 1980; Nina Freudenheim Gallery, Buffalo, 1980; Makler Gallery, Philadelphia, 1981; Linda Farris Gallery, Seattle, 1981; Davenport, 1981; Hansen Fuller Goldeen Gallery, San Francisco, 1981; Laumeier International Sculpture Park, 1982; Yares Gallery, Scottsdale, 1982; Galleria Il Ponte, Rome, 1982; Gimpel-Hanover & Galerie Andre Emmerich, Zurich, 1983; Huntington Galleries, 1983; John Berggruen Gallery, San Francisco, 1983, 85. **Group:** Rome-New York Foundation, Rome, The Quest and the Quarry, 1961; Buffalo/Albright, Plus by Minus, 1968; Indianapolis, 1970; Venice, Biennale, 1972; Philadelphia Civic Center, Women's Work: American Art, 1974, 1974; Quandrienniale, 1977; Documenta 6, Kassel, 1977; GSA, Washington, D.C., Drawings for Outdoor Sculpture: 1946-1977, 1978; NCFA, Across the Nation, circ., 1980; Nassau County Museum of Fine Art, Sculpture: The Tradition in Steel, 1983; Seattle/AM, American Sculpture, Three

Decades, 1984; Sonoma State U., Works in Bronze, circ., 1984. **Collections:** AT&T; Buffalo/Albright; Dartmouth College; Fidelity Union Life Insurance Co.; Florence (Italy)/Modern; Graphische Sammlung Albertina; Harvard U.; Hirshhorn; Indianapolis; Instituto Italiano di Cultura, Stockholm; Jacksonville/AM; MIT; MMA; Milwaukee; Mount Holyoke College; Parkersburg (W. Va.) Art Center; U. of Rochester; Rutgers U.; Syracuse/Everson; Turin/Civico; Vassar College; Walker; Worcester/AM.

PEREIRA, I. RICE. b. August 5, 1901, Boston, Mass.; d. January 11, 1971, Marbella, Spain. **Studied:** ASL, with Richard Lahey, Jan Matulka. Traveled Europe, North Africa, resided London, Paris. **Taught:** Pratt Institute. Federal A.P.: Easel painting, teaching. **Awards:** Pepsi-Cola, 1943. **One-man Exhibitions:** ACA Gallery, 1933, also 1934, 35, 46, 49; Howard U., 1938; East River Gallery, NYC, 1939; Julien Levy Galleries, NYC, 1939; Art of This Century, NYC, 1944; Arts Club of Chicago, 1945; SFMA, 1947; Barnett Aden Gallery, Washington, D.C., 1948; Andover/Phillips, 1949; Santa Barbara/MA, 1950; Portland, Ore./AM, 1950; de Young, 1950; Syracuse U., 1951; Baltimore/MA, 1951; Ball State Teachers College, 1951; Durlacher Brothers, NYC, 1951; Phillips, 1952; Dayton/AI, 1952; Adele Lawson Gallery, Chicago, 1954; Hofstra College, 1954; U. of Michigan, 1954; Philadelphia Art Alliance, 1955; Corcoran, 1956; Adele Lawson Gallery, NYC, 1956; Lee Nordness Gallery, NYC, 1958, 59, 61; Rome—New York Foundation, Rome, 1960; A.A.A. Gallery, Washington, D.C., 1961; The Amel Gallery, NYC, 1961; Galerie Internationale, NYC, 1964; Agra Gallery, 1965; Distelheim Gallery, 1965; Wilmington College (N.C.), 1968; U. of North Carolina, 1968; Charlotte/Mint, 1968; Andre Zarre Gallery, NYC, 1974, 78, 79, 81, 84, 85; Andrew Crispo Gallery, NYC,

1976; Andre Zarre Gallery, NYC, 1978, 79. **Retrospective:** WMAA, circ., 1953. **Group:** Venice Biennial; Tate; ICA, London; MOMA, Fourteen Americans, circ., 1946; Darmstadt/Kunsthalle; Lille; Internationale Kunstausstellung, Berlin, 1951; Chicago/AI Annuals; PAFA; Carnegie; I Sao Paulo Biennial, 1951; USIA, 20th Century Highlights, circ., 1957-58; WMAA, 1966-68; Corcoran, 1969. **Collections:** Allentown/AM; Andover/Phillips; Arizona State College; U. of Arizona; Atlanta U.; Ball State U.; Baltimore/MA; Boston/MFA; Boston U.; Brandeis U.; The Catholic U. of America; Chicago/AI; Connecticut College; Dallas/MFA; Detroit/Institute; Goucher College; Hartford/Wadsworth; Harvard U.; Howard U.; State U. of Iowa; Kansas City/Nelson; MMA; MOMA; The Miller Co.; U. of Minnesota; NCFA; Newark Museum; New London; New Orleans/Delgado; New Paltz/SUNY; Norfolk; Phillips; Phoenix; SFMA; SRGM; Smith College; Syracuse U.; Toledo/MA; Utica; Vassar College; WMAA; Walker; Worcester/AM; Youngstown/Butler. **Bibliography:** **Baur 4,** 5, 7; Bazin; Flanagan; Genauer; Goodrich and Baur 1; Janis, S.; Kootz 2; Lane and Larsen; Mendelowitz; Miller, ed. 2; Nordness, ed.; Pearson 2; Pousette-Dart, ed.; Read 2; Richardson, E.P.; Ritchie 1; Soby 5, 6; Wight 2. Archives.

PERLIN, BERNARD. b. November 21, 1918, Richmond, Va. **Studied:** New York School of Design, 1934-36; NAD, 1936-37, with Leon Kroll; ASL, 1936-37, with Isabel Bishop, William Palmer, Harry Sternberg. Traveled Europe, Mediterranean, the Orient; resided Italy, 1948-54. **Taught:** Brooklyn Museum School, 1947-48; Wooster Community Art Center, Danbury, Conn., 1967-69. **Commissions:** US Treasury Department; US Post Office Department, 1940. **Awards:** Kosciuszko Foundation, 1938; Chaloner Prize Foundation Award, 1948; Fulbright Fel-

lowship, 1950; Guggenheim Foundation Fellowship, 1954, 59; NIAL, 1964. **Address:** 56 Shadow Lake Road, Ridgefield, CT 06877. **One-man Exhibitions:** M. Knoedler & Co., 1948; Catherine Viviano Gallery, 1955, 58, 63, 66, 70; Wooster School, Danbury, Conn., 1968. **Retrospective:** U. of Bridgeport, 1969. **Group:** Chicago/AI Annuals, 1948, 54, 59; Carnegie, 1949, 52; MMA, 1950; Palazzo di Venezia, Rome, 1950; ICA, London, 1950; WMAA Annuals, 1951, 55; Corcoran, 1953, 59; WMAA, The New Decade, 1954-55; U. of Illinois, 1955, 59; XXVIII Venice Biennial, 1956; Brussels World's Fair, 1958; Cincinnati/AM, 1958; Detroit/Institute, 1960; PAFA, 1960. **Collections:** California Palace; Chicago/AI; Denver/AM; Detroit/Institute; Kansas City/Nelson; MOMA; NCFA; Princeton U.; Springfield, Mass./MFA; Tate; WMAA. **Bibliography:** Baur 7; Eliot; Goodrich and Baur 1; McCurdy, ed.; Mendelowitz; Pousette-Dart, ed.; Rodman 1, 2. Archives.

PERLMAN, JOEL. b. June 12, 1943, NYC. **Studied:** Cornell U., 1965, BFA, with Jack Squier; U. of California, Berkeley, 1968, MA; Central School of Art, London, with Brian Wall. Resided England, 1964-69, excluding 1968. **Member:** Sculptors Guild. **Taught:** Central School, London, 1967-68; U. of Rhode Island, 1968; Winchester College, 1968-69; Bennington College, 1969-72; Middlebury College, 1972; School of Visual Arts, 1973-; Fordham U., 1974-80. **Awards:** Guggenheim Foundation Fellowship, 1974; National Endowment for the Arts, 1979. **Address:** 250 West Broadway, NYC 10013. **Dealer:** Andre Emmerich Gallery, NYC. **One-man Exhibitions:** (first) Axiom Gallery, London, 1969; Bennington College, 1970; Andre Emmerich Gallery, NYC, 1973, 76, 78, 80, 82, 85; Galerie Andre Emmerich, Zurich, 1977; Galerie Pudelko, Bonn, 1978; Roy Boyd Gallery, Chicago, 1978, 80, 81, 83, 86; Ehrlich Gallery, NYC,

Gabor Peterdi *Werland Gold* 1978–79

1980; Gloria Luria Gallery, Bay Harbor Island, Fla., 1983. **Group:** WMAA Biennial, 1973; Cornell U., Cornell Then, Sculpture Now, 1978; Indianapolis, 1979; Lake George Arts Project, Lake George, N.Y., Prospect Mountain Sculpture Exhibition: An Hommage to David Smith, 1979; Sonoma State U., Works in Bronze, A Modern Survey, circ., 1984. **Collections:** Brooklyn Museum; Cornell U.; Guild Hall; Hirshhorn; MMA; U. of Miami; Niagara U.; Ridgefield/Aldrich; Storm King Art Center.

PETERDI, GABOR. b. September 17, 1915, Budapest, Hungary. **Studied:** Academy of Fine Arts, Budapest, 1929; Academie Julian, Paris, 1931; Academie Scandinave, Paris, 1932; Academy of Fine Arts, Rome, 1930; Atelier 17, Paris, 1935. **Taught:** Brooklyn Museum School, 1948-53; Yale U., 1954-; Hunter College, 1960-. **Member:** Silvermine Guild. **Awards:** Prix de Rome, 1930; Paris World's Fair, 1937, Gold Medal (jointly with Lurcat); Brooklyn Museum, 1950, 52, 60; American Color Print Society, 1951; Oakland/AM, 1957, 60; PAFA, Gold Medal, 1957; Boston Printmakers, 1959; Seattle/AM, **P.P.**, 1960; Pasadena/AM, **P.P.**, 1960; Bay Printmakers Society, Oakland, Adell Hyde Morrison Memorial Medal, 1960; Ford Foundation Grant, 1960; PAFA, Pennell Memorial Medal, 1961; IV International Biennial Exhibition of Prints, Tokyo, Museum of Western Art Prize, 1964; Guggenheim Foundation Fellowship, 1964-65. **Address:** 108 Highland Avenue, Rowayton, CT 06853. **Dealers:** Grace Borgenicht Gallery, Inc., NYC; Haslem Fine Arts, Inc., Washington, D.C.; Nielsen Gallery, Boston. **One-man Exhibitions:** (first) Ernst Museum, Budapest, 1930, also 1934; Bratislava, Czechoslovakia, 1930; Prague/National, 1930; Rome/Nazionale, 1930; Jeanne Bucher, Paris, 1936; Julien Levy Galleries, NYC, 1939; Norlyst Gallery, NYC, 1943, 44; Laurel Gallery, NYC, 1948, 49; Philadelphia Art Alliance, 1950, 55; Smithsonian, 1951; Silvermine Guild, 1952; Grace Borgenicht Gallery, Inc., 1952, 55, 59, 61, 66, 74, 79; Kanegis Gallery, 1956, 57, 59, 61; St. George's Gallery, London, 1958; The Howard Wise Gallery, Cleveland, 1959; Boston/MFA, 1959; Achenbach Foundation, 1960; Lincoln, Mass./De Cordova, 1964; Corcoran, 1964; Michigan State U., 1964; Yale U., 1964; Atlanta/AA, 1965; Ridgefield/Aldrich, 1965; Honolulu Academy, 1968, 72; U. of Connecticut, 1974. **Group:** Salon des Surindependants, Paris, 1936, 38; Library of Congress, 1943, 47; The Print Club, Philadelphia, 1948; Brooklyn Museum, 1948, 49, 64; WMAA, 1949; MOMA, 1949; Yale U., 1949; Corcoran, 1949; PAFA, 1949, 61; Silvermine Guild; NYPL; Chicago/AI; Achenbach Foundation; U. of Nebraska; Minneapolis/Institute; Oakland/AM; U. of Illinois. **Collections:** Abilene Christian College; Achenbach Foundation; Albion College; Andover/Phillips; Baltimore/MA; Beloit College; Berea College; Boston/MFA; Brandeis U.; Brooklyn Museum; Brown U.; Budapest/National; Buffalo/Albright; Chicago/AI; Clearwater/Gulf Coast; Cleveland/MA; Columbia, S.C./MA; Corcoran; Cranbrook; Currier; Dartmouth College; U. of Georgia; Hartford/Wadsworth; Honolulu Academy; Illinois Wesleyan U.; U. of Illinois; Indiana U.; MMA; MOMA; Memphis/Brooks; Michigan State U.; U. of Michigan; Minneapolis/Institute; NYPL; U. of Nebraska; Northwestern U.; Oakland/AM; U. of Oklahoma; Oregon State U.; PAFA; PMA; Pasadena/AM; Prague/National; Princeton U.; RISD; Rome/Nazionale; Rutgers U.; Sao Paulo; Seattle/AM; Smith College; Smithsonian; Texas Wesleyan College; Vassar College; WMAA; Walker. **Bibliography:** Baur 5; Chaet; Goodrich and Baur 1; Hayter 1; **Johnson 1; Peterdi.** Archives.

PETERSEN, ROLAND CONRAD. b. March 31, 1926, Endelave, Horsens,

Denmark. **Studied:** With Glenn Wessels, Chiura Obata, Erle Loran, John Haley, Worth Ryder, James McCray, U. of the Pacific and U. of California, AB, 1949, MA, 1950; Hofmann School, 1950-51; Atelier 17, Paris, 1950, and with S. W. Hayter, Paris, 1963, 70; California School of Fine Arts, 1954. To USA, 1928. US Navy, 1943-45. Traveled Europe. **Taught:** Washington State U.; 1952-56; U. of California, 1956-. **Awards:** Sigmund Martin Heller Traveling Fellowship, 1950; SFMA, Anne Bremer Memorial Prize, 1950; Oakland/AM, First Prize, Gold Medal, 1953; California State Fair. **P.P.,** 1957, 60; Guggenheim Foundation Fellowship, 1963; U. of the Pacific, **P.P.,** 1969; Fulbright Fellowship, 1970; U. of California Regents Fellow, 1977; Accademia Italia dell'Arte e del Lavoro, Terme, Gold Medal, 1985. **Address:** 6 Lanai Way, P.O. Box 1, Dillon Beach, Calif. 94929. **Dealer:** Rorick Gallery, San Francisco. **One-man Exhibitions:** (first) Oakland/AM, 1954; Spokane Art Center of Washington State U., 1954, 55, 57; Boise (Idaho) Art Association, 1954; Esther Robles Gallery, 1961; City Library, Sacramento, Calif., 1961; California Palace, 1961; Gump's Gallery, 1962; Staempfli Gallery, 1963, 65, 67; Sacramento/Crocker, 1966; Adele Bednarz Gallery, 1966, 69, 72, 73, 75, 76; Chico State College, 1966; de Young, 1968; Western Association of Art Museum Directors, circ., 1968-69; Phoenix, 1972; Santa Barbara/MA, 1973; Whitman College, 1974; Solano Community College, Solano, 1975; U. of California, Davis, 1976; American River College, 1976; College of Siskiyous, 1977; Artists Cooperative Gallery, Sacramento, 1977; California State College, Stanislaus, 1978; Shasta College, Redding, 1978; Brubacher Gallery, Sarasota, Fla., 1979; U. of Nevada, 1980; U. of Reading (England), 1980; Davis (Calif.) Art Center, 1981, 84; The Print Mint, Chicago, 1981; Rorick Gallery, 1981, 82, 83, 84, 85; Rara Avis Gallery, Sacramento, 1982; University Club, Chicago, 1982; Cunningham Memorial Art Gallery,

Bakersfield, Calif., 1983; Art Works, Fair Oaks, Calif., 1984, 85; Smith Anderson Gallery, Palo Alto, 1984; Sacramento, State Capital, 1984. **Retrospectives:** Chico State College (15-year, 1950-65), 1966; de Young (5-year, 1963-68), 1968; U. of California, Davis, 1978; Washington State U., Pullman, 1976. **Group:** Pasadena/AM, Pacific Profile, 1961; Poindexter Gallery, 1961; U. of Illinois, 1961, 63, 69; Santa Barbara/MA, 1962; Carnegie, 1964; Chicago/AI Annual, 1965; VMFA, American Painting, 1966; New School for Social Research, Humanist Tradition, 1968; Oakland/AM, California Landscape, 1975; U. of Wisconsin, Madison, Atelier 17, 1977. **Collections:** Achenbach Foundation; CSCS; U. of California, Davis; Chase Manhattan Bank; De Beers Collection; de Young; Illinois Wesleyan U.; La Jolla; Long Beach/MA;

MOMA; U. of Miami; Musée Municipal, Brest; NCFA; U. of North Carolina; Oakland/AM; Oakland Public Library; Ohio U.; PMA; U. of the Pacific; Phoenix; Sacramento/Crocker; San Diego; Santa Barbara/MA; Shasta College; Spokane Coliseum; VMFA; WMAA; Washington State U. **Bibliography:** Hager 1.

PETLIN, IRVING. b. December 17, 1934, Chicago, Ill. **Studied:** Chicago/AI, 1952-56, BFA; Yale U., 1959, MFA, with Josef Albers. US Army, 1957-59. Traveled USA; resided France, 1959-63. **Taught:** UCLA, 1963-66; RISD, 1978; Cooper Union, NYC, 1977-80. **Commission:** Sets for the opera, *The Double Life of Amphibians* by Morton Subotnik, 1984. **Awards:** Ryerson Fellowship, 1956; Copley Foundation

Irving Petlin *On the Beach . . . in the Spirit of Evaporation* 1985

Grant, 1961; Guggenheim Foundation Fellowship, 1971. **Address:** 257 West 11th Street, NYC 10014. **Dealer:** Kent Fine Art Inc., NYC. **One-man Exhibitions:** (first) Dilexi Gallery, San Francisco, 1958; Cliffdweller Gallery, Chicago, 1956; Galerie du Dragon, Paris, 1960, 62, 63, 64, 68; Galatea, Turin, 1962; Hanover Gallery, London, 1964; Palais des Beaux-Arts, Paris, 1965; Rolf Nelson Gallery, Los Angeles, 1966; Odyssia Gallery, NYC, 1967, 68, 69, 70, 79; Galleria Odyssia, Rome, 1969, 71, 76; Galleria il Fante di Spade, Rome, 1968; Galleria Bergamini, Turin, 1974; Documenta, Turin, 1974; Rebecca Cooper Gallery, Washington, D.C., 1976; Galleria Bergamini, Milan, 1977; Purchase/SUNY, 1978; Arts Club, Chicago, 1978; Gallerie Nina Dausset, Paris, 1980; Odyssia Gallery, NYC, 1981, 83; Dart Gallery, Chicago, 1983; Dartmouth College, 1983; Marlborough Gallery, Inc., NYC, 86. **Retrospective:** Brussels/Beaux-Arts, 1965. **Group:** Chicago/AI, 1953, 56, 72; Paris/Moderne, 1961-66; WMAA, 1973; Chicago/Contemporary, Chicago Imagist Art, 1972; Chicago Art Institute School, Visions, 1976; Chicago/AI, American Drawings of the '70s, 1977; Jewish Museum, Jewish Themes/Contemporary American Artists, 1982; IEF, Twentieth Century American Drawings: The Figure in Context, circ., 1984. **Collections:** Amsterdam/Stedelijk; U. of Arkansas; Chicago/AI; Chicago/Contemporary; Des Moines; Jewish Museum; MMA; MOMA; Paris/Beaubourg; Paris/Moderne; Recklinghausen. **Bibliography:** Schulze.

PETTET, WILLIAM. b. October 10, 1942, Whittier, Calif. **Studied:** California Institute of the Arts, Valencia; Chouinard Art Institute, 1965, BFA. Traveled Canada, Europe, Mexico. **Taught:** Skowhegan School, 1972; Empire State College, N.Y., 1977. **Awards:** Tamarind Fellowship, 1970. **Address:** 14 Beach 213th St., Breezy Point, NY 11697. **One-man Exhibitions:** (first)

Nicholas Wilder Gallery, 1966, 68, 70; Robert Elkon Gallery, 1968, 69; David Whitney Gallery, NYC, 1970, 71; Dunkelman Gallery, Toronto, 1971, 73; The Willard Gallery, 1973, 74, 75; S. & G. Mathews Gallery, San Antonio, 1978, 79. **Group:** Trenton/State, Focus on Light, 1967; WMAA Annuals, 1967, 69, 73; Corcoran, 1969; Washington U., Here and Now, 1969; Ridgefield/Aldrich, Lyrical Abstraction, 1970; ICA, U. of Pennsylvania, Two Generations of Color Painting, 1970; Santa Barbara/MA, Spray, 1971; WMAA, Lyrical Abstraction, 1971; Hamburg/Kunstverein, USA: West Coast, circ., 1972; WMAA, 35 American Artists, 1974; MOMA, 60s and 70s, 1974; U. of Texas, Austin, New in the Seventies, 1977. **Collections:** Hirshhorn; MOMA; WMAA. **Bibliography:** *New in the Seventies; USA West Coast.*

PFRIEM, BERNARD. b. September 7, 1916, Cleveland, Ohio. **Studied:** John Huntington Polytechnical Institute, 1934-36; Cleveland Institute of Art, 1936-40. US Air Force, 1942-46. Traveled Europe, Mediterranean; resided Mexico, 1940-42, Paris, 1952-63. **Taught:** Cleveland Institute of Art School, 1938-40; Peoples Art Center (MOMA), 1946-51; Cooper Union, 1963-71; Sarah Lawrence College, 1969-76; US Army Air Force, 1942-46. Assistant to Jose Clemente Orozco on frescoes, Jiquilpan (Michoacan), Mexico, and to Julio Castellanos on murals, Mexico City, Chief Designer, US Government exhibitions and pavilions in Europe, 1953-56. **Awards:** Agnes Gund and Mary S. Ranney Traveling Fellowship, 1940; Copley Foundation Grant, 1959. **Member:** Century Association; Chelsea Arts Club, London. Designer for Tibor deNagy Marionette Co., 1946-50. **Address:** 115 Spring Street, NYC 10012. **Dealer:** Staempfli Gallery, NYC. **One-man Exhibitions:** (first) Hugo Gallery, NYC, 1951; US Cultural Center, Paris, 1954; Galerie du

Dragon, 1960; Alexandre Iolas Gallery, NYC, 1961, 63; Obelisk Gallery, Washington, D.C., 1963; International Gallery, Baltimore, 1965; Wooster Community Art Center, Danbury, 1965; Richard Feigen Gallery, Chicago, 1966; Sarah Lawrence College, 1969; U. of Arkansas, 1970; Midtown Gallery, Atlanta, 1971. **Retrospective:** Cleveland Institute of Art, 1963. **Group:** Cleveland/MA, 1939-41; Youngstown/Butler, 1941; Columbus, 1942; Carnegie, 1942; Hugo Gallery, NYC, 1948, 49, 50; WMAA Annual, 1951; Smithsonian, circ., American Drawings, circ., 1965; WMAA, A Decade of American Drawings, 1955-1965, 1965; American Drawing Society, 1970; Cleveland Institute of Art, 1973; The Pennsylvania State U., 1974. **Collections:** U. of Arkansas; Brooklyn Museum; Chase Manhattan Bank; Chicago/AI; Columbia Banking, Savings and Loan Association; Corcoran; MMA; MOMA; Minnesota/MA; Utah; Worcester/AM. **Bibliography: Waldberg 1, 2.**

PHILLIPS, MATT. b. 1927, NYC. **Studied:** Barnes Foundation, 1950-52; U. of Chicago, 1952, MA; Stanford U., 1952-54; Atelier 17, Paris. **Taught:** The Pennsylvania State U., 1956-62; American College in Paris, 1962-64; Bard College, 1964-. **Awards:** Guggenheim Foundation Fellowship, 1974; National Endowment for the Arts, 1975. **Address:** Bard College, Annandale-on-Hudson, N.Y. 12004. **Dealer:** Marilyn Pearl Gallery, NYC. **One-man Exhibitions:** Peter Deitsch Gallery, NYC, 1962, 65; Makler Gallery, Philadelphia, 1962; Bernheim-Jeune Gallery, Paris, 1962; Bard College, 1964, 69; The Print Club, 1966, William Zierler Inc., NYC, 1973, 74, 76; Vassar College, 1976; Marilyn Pearl Gallery, 1977, 79, 80, 81, 83, 84; Middendorf-Lane Gallery, Washington, D.C., 1978; Des Moines, 1978; William Sawyer Gallery, San Francisco, 1978; Phillips, 1978; Donald Morris Gallery, Detroit, 1978, 81; Marianne

Friedland Gallery, Toronto, 1979; A.A.A., NYC, 1979; A.A.A., Philadelphia, 1982; Dolly Fiterman Gallery, Minneapolis, 1982; Smith-Anderson Gallery, Palo Alto, 1982; Michael Berger Gallery, Pittsburgh, 1983; Addison Ripley Gallery, Washington, D.C., 1983; Keny and Johnson Gallery, Columbus, Ohio, 1984. **Retrospective:** Baltimore/MA, 1976. **Group:** Indianapolis, 1972; Smithsonian, New American Monotypes, circ., 1978; MMA, The Painterly Print, 1980. **Collections:** Achenbach Foundation; Akron/AM; U. of Arizona; Bard College; Chicago/AI; Des Moines; High Museum; Hirshhorn; Huntsville Museum; Indianapolis; Library of Congress; MMA; NYPL; U. of Nebraska; New Britain/American; PMA; Philadelphia Free Library; Phillips; Toledo; WMAA; U. of Wisconsin.

PINEDA, MARIANNA. b. May 10, 1925, Evanston, Ill. **Studied:** Cranbrook, with Carl Milles, 1942; Bennington College, 1942-43; U. of California, Berkeley, with Raymond Puccinelli, 1943-45; Columbia U., with Oronzio Maldarelli, 1945-46; with George Stanley, Los Angeles (sculpture); with Ossip Zadkine, Paris, 1949-50; Scholar, Radcliffe Institute for Independent Study, 1962-64. Resided Paris, 1949-51, Florence, 1954-57, Rome, 1966. **Taught:** Newton College, Mass., 1972-75; Boston U., 1974-78; Boston College, 1975-77. **Member:** Artists Equity; Sculptors Guild; Boston Visual Artists Union. **Commissions:** Boston Conservatory of Music, Jan Veen Memorial Medal; State Capitol, Honolulu, 1980. **Awards:** Buffalo/Albright, 1948; Walker, **P.P.,** 1951; Boston Arts Festival, 1957, 60; San Francisco Art Association, First Prize for Sculpture, 1955; Chicago/AI, 1957. **m.** Harold Tovish. **Address:** 380 Marlborough Street, Boston, MA 02115. **One-man Exhibitions:** (first) Slaughter Gallery, San Francisco, 1951; Walker, 1952; The Swetzoff Gallery, Boston,

1953, 64; Lincoln, Mass./De Cordova, 1954; Premier Gallery, Minneapolis, 1963; Alpha Gallery, 1972; Bumpus Gallery, Duxbury, 1974. **Group:** Buffalo/Albright, 1948; WMAA, 1953, 54, 57, 59; MMA, 1957; U. of Illinois, 1957; Chicago/AI, 1957, 60; Boston Arts Festival, 1957, 58, 60; Carnegie, 1958; MOMA, 1959; Waitsfield/Bundy, 1963; New York World's Fair, 1964-65; Lincoln, Mass./De Cordova, Sculpture in the Park, 1972; The Pennsylvania State U., Contemporary Artists and the Figure, 1974; Lincoln, Mass./De Cordova, New England Women, 1975; Los Angeles/County MA, Women Artists 1550-1950, 1976; Brockton/Fuller, Artists in Boston, 1978. **Retrospectives:** Honolulu Academy, 1970; Newton College, 1972. **Collections:** Andover/Phillips; Boston/MFA; Boston Public Library; Bowdoin College; Dartmouth College; Hartford/Wadsworth; Harvard U.; U. of Massachusetts; Mount Holyoke College; Radcliffe College; State of Hawaii; Utica; Walker; Williams College.

PINTO, JODY. b. August 4, 1942, NYC. **Studied:** PAFA, 1964-68; Philadelphia College of Art, 1971-73, BFA. Traveled Europe. **Taught:** U. of Guelph, 1977; Wright State U., 1978; PAFA, 1980-; RISD, 1980-. **Awards:** PAFA, Cresson Fellowship, 1967; National Endowment for the Arts, 1979; Pennsylvania Council on the Arts Grant, 1980; N.J. Council on the Arts Grant, 1982. **Commission:** Fairmont Park, Philadelphia, 1986. Designed sets and costumes for South Street Dance Co., Philadelphia, and Theatre for the New City, NYC, 1985. **Address:** 124 Chambers Street, NYC 10007. **Dealer:** Hal Bromm Gallery, NYC. **One-man Exhibitions:** (first) Nexus Gallery, Philadelphia, 1977; Hal Bromm Gallery, 1978, 79, 80, 81, 83, 85; 112 Greene Street, NYC, 1979; Richard Demarco Gallery, Edinburgh, 1979; Marion Locks Gallery, Philadelphia, 1980; California State U., Northridge, 1980;

PAFA, 1980; Wilkes College, 1980; Kutztown State College, 1981; ICA, U. of Pennsylvania, 1984; Roger Ramsay Gallery, Chicago, 1985; Bucks County Community College, 1985. **Group:** ICA, U. of Pennsylvania, Dwellings, 1978; ICA, U. of Pennsylvania, Material Pleasures, 1979; PMA, Contemporary Drawing: Philadelphia II, 1979; WMAA Biennial, 1979; XXXIX Venice Biennial, 1980; PAFA, Form and Function, 1982; Bard College, Landmarks, 1984; IEF, 20th Century American Drawings: The Figure in Context, circ., 1984. **Collections:** Des Moines; PAFA; PMA; Prudential Insurance Co. of America; SRGM; WMAA; Wake Forest U.

PLAGENS, PETER. b. March, 1, 1941, Dayton, Ohio. **Studied:** Syracuse U., MFA, 1964; U. of Southern California, MFA, magna cum laude, 1962. **Taught:** U. of Texas, Austin, 1966-69; California State U., Northridge, 1969-78; U. of Southern California, 1978-80, 84-85; U. of North Carolina, 1980-84; California State U., Long Beach, 1985; Columbia U., 1985-86; Hofstra U., 1985-86; Princeton U., 1985-86. Contributing editor, *Artforum*, 1966-76. **Member:** Chairman, Board of Directors, ICA, Los Angeles, 1977-79. **Awards:** Guggenheim Foundation Fellowship, 1972; National Endowment for the Arts, Grant in Criticism, 1973; National Endowment for the Arts, Grant, Painting, 1977, 85. **Address:** 56 Lispenard Street, NYC 10013. **Dealers:** Nancy Hoffman Gallery, NYC; Jan Baum Gallery, Los Angeles. **One-man Exhibitions:** Riko Mizuno, Los Angeles, 1971; Reese Palley Gallery, NYC, 1971; Reese Palley Gallery, San Francisco, 1972; SFAI, 1972; U. of Oklahoma, 1973; Texas Gallery, Houston, 1973, 75; Leslie Collins Art Works, Dallas, 1973; John Berggruen Gallery, San Francisco, 1974, 77; California State U., San Jose, 1974; Betty Gold Gallery, Los Angeles, 1974; Dootson-Calderhead, Seattle, 1975; Nancy Hoffman Gallery, NYC, 1975, 76, 77, 80, 81, 84; Galerie Doyle, Paris,

1975; Hirshhorn, 1976; Baum/Silverman Gallery, Los Angeles, 1977; Marianne Deson Gallery, Chicago, 1978; ICA, Los Angeles, 1979; Baum-Silverman Gallery, Los Angeles, 1980; Lincoln Center, 1983; Jan Cicero Gallery, Chicago, 1983, 85; Southeast Center for Contemporary Art, Winston-Salem, N.C., 1984; California State U., Long Beach, 1985. **Group:** Oakland/AM, Contemporary American Drawings and Prints, 1969; LA/County MA, 24 Young Los Angeles Artists, 1971; Oakland/AM, Off the Stretcher, 1972; Scripps College, Painting: Color, Form, Surface, 1974; Utrecht, Young Americans, 1975; Potsdam/SUNY, New Directions in Abstraction, 1975; Fort Wayne, Hue and Far Cry of Color, 1976; Youngstown/Butler, 1976; SFMA, Painting and Sculpture in California: The Modern Era, 1977; ICA, Los Angeles, 100 +, 1977; ICA, Los Angeles, Unstretched, 1977; U. of Southern California, Sunshine and Shadow, 1985. **Collections:** Baltimore/MA; Buffalo/Albright; Continental Grain Corp., NYC; Dechert, Price and Rhodes, Philadelphia Harris Bank, Chicago; Hirshhorn; Miami-Dade Community College; Newark Museum; U. of North Carolina; Owens-Corning Fiberglas Corp.; Prudential Insurance Co. of America; Toledo.

POLLACK, REGINALD. b. July 29, 1924, Middle Village, N.Y. **Studied:** ASL, with Wallace Harrison, Moses Soyer, Boardman Robinson. US Navy, 1941-45. Resided France, 1948-59, 1960-61. Traveled France, Italy, Caribbean Islands. **Taught:** Yale U., 1962-63; Cooper Union, 1963-64. **Member:** board, WPA, Washington, D.C., 1975-79. **Commissions:** Seagram Corporation; Container Corp. of America; New York State Telephone System; original film using his painting on the theme of riots, segregation, and war, commissioned by Zubin Mehta for the Los Angeles Philharmonic Orchestra; Washington Cathedral, 1974. **Awards:**

Prix Neumann, Paris, 1952; Prix Othon Friesz, Paris, Menton, 1954, 57; Paris/Moderne, Prix de Peintres Etrangers, Second Prize, 1958; Ingram Merrill Foundation Grant, 1964, 70, 71. **Address:** 205 River Bend Road, Great Falls, Va. 22066. **One-man Exhibitions:** (first) Charles Fourth Gallery, NYC, 1948; The Peridot Gallery, 1949, 52, 55, 56, 57, 59, 61, 63, 65, 67, 69; Galerie Saint-Placide, Paris, 1952; Dwan Gallery, 1960; Goldwach Gallery, Chicago, 1964-66; Felix Landau Gallery, 1964, 66; Original Graphics Ltd., Los Angeles, 1968; Olson-Resnick Gallery, Los Angeles, 1968; Jefferson Gallery, Los Angeles, 1969; Gallery Z, Beverly Hills, 1973, 75; Jack Rasmussen Gallery, Washington, D.C. 1978, 80, 81, 82; Tartt Gallery, Washington, D.C., 1986. **Retrospective:** WPA, Washington, D.C., 1977. **Group:** WMAA, 1953, 55, 56, 58, 63; U. of Nebraska, 1957; Chicago/AI; Carnegie; NIAL; PAFA, 1962, 66; Salon du Mai, Paris; U. of Illinois, 1964; Salon des Artistes Independants, Paris, 1952, 53, 54; Corcoran, 1963; Newark Museum, 1964; New School for Social Research, 1964; Lytton Art Center, Los Angeles, 1967; Long Beach/MA, circ.; Smithsonian, circ., 1968-69. **Collections:** Bezalel Museum; Brooklyn Museum; Collection de l'Etat; Fort Lauderdale; U. of Glasgow; Haifa; MOMA; U. of Miami; NMAA; U. of Nebraska; Newark Museum; New York Hilton Hotel; Purchase/SUNY; Rockefeller Institute; Southern Illinois U.; Tel Aviv; WMAA; Worcester/AM; Yale U. **Bibliography:** Tomkins. Archives.

POLLOCK, JACKSON. b. January 28, 1912, Cody, Wyo.; **d.** August 11, 1956, Southampton, N.Y. **Studied:** ASL, 1929-31, with Thomas Hart Benton. Federal A.P.: Easel painting, 1938-42. **m.** Lee Krasner (1944). Subject and narrator of a 1951 film, *Jackson Pollock*, produced by Hans Namuth and Paul Falkenberg. **One-man Exhibitions:** (first) Art of This Century, NYC, 1943, also 1946, 47; Arts Club of Chicago,

Jackson Pollock *Untitled Drawing* 1944

1945, 51; Museo Civico Correr, Venice; Galleria d'Arte del Naviglio, Milan, 1950; Galerie Paul Facchetti, 1952; Sidney Janis Gallery, 1952, 54, 55, 57; Zurich, 1953; IV Sao Paulo Biennial, 1957; Marlborough Galleria d'Arte, Rome, 1962; Marlborough-Gerson Gallery, Inc., NYC, 1964, 69; Marlborough Fine Art Ltd., London, 1965; WMAA, 1970; Berry-Hill Galleries, NYC, 1977; Yale U., 1978; American Cultural Center, Paris, 1979; Paris/Moderne, 1979; Betty Parsons Gallery, NYC, 1983; Jason McCoy Inc., NYC, 1987. **Retrospectives:** MOMA, 1956, 67, 80; Guild Hall, 1981; Paris/Beaubourg, 1982. **Group:** XXIV, XXV, and XXVIII Venice Biennials, 1948, 50, 56; I Sao Paulo Biennial, 1951; MOMA, Fifteen Americans, circ., 1952; Galerie de France, Paris, American Vanguard, 1952; MOMA, 12 Modern American Painters and Sculptors, circ., Europe, 1953-55; WMAA, The New Decade, 1954-55; SRGM, 75 Paintings from The Solomon R. Guggenheim Museum, circ., Europe, 1957; PAFA; Chicago/AI; Brooklyn Museum; Buffalo/Albright; MOMA, The New American Painting

and Sculpture, 1969. **Collections:** Andover/Phillips; Baltimore/MA; Brooklyn Museum; Buffalo/Albright; Canberra/National; Carnegie; Chicago/AI; Dallas/MFA; Dusseldorf/KNW; Hartford/Wadsworth; State U. of Iowa; Los Angeles/County MA; MMA; MOMA; Ohara Art Museum; Omaha/Joslyn; Ottawa/National; Rio de Janeiro; SFMA; SRGM; Stuttgart; Utica; WMAA; Washington U.; West Palm Beach/Norton; Yale U. **Bibliography:** Alloway 4; Ashton 5; Barr 3; Battcock, ed.; Baur 5, 7; Bazin; Beekman; Biddle 4; Bihalji-Merin; *Black and White Are Colors*; Blesh 1; Brion 1; Carmean, Rathbone, and Hess; Calas, N. and E.; Canaday; Chipp; Christensen; Danto; Davis, D.; De Vries, ed.; De Wilde 1; Downes, ed.; Eliot; Elsen 2; Finch; Flanagan; **Friedman, B. H., 2;** Gablik; Gaunt; Goodrich and Baur 1; Goossen 1; Greenberg 1; Greengood; Haftman; Henning; Hess, T. B., 1; Hobbs and Levin; Honisch & Jensen, eds.; Hunter 1, 6; Hunter, ed.; Janis and Blesh 1; **Jackson Pollock;** Janis, S.; Johnson, Ellen H.; **Kligman;** Kozloff 3; Krauss 2, 3; Kuh 3; Langui; Leepa; Lippard 3; Lowry; Lynton; McCoubrey 1; McCurdy, ed.; Mendelowitz; Moser 1; Motherwell, ed.; Murken-Altrogge; Neff, ed.; Neumeyer; O'Doherty; **O'Hara** 1, **4;** Paalen; Ponente; Potter; Pousette-Dart, ed.; Ragon 1, 2; Read 2, 3, 6; Restany 2; Richardson, E.P.; Rickey; Ritchie 1; **Robertson 2;** Rodman 1, 2, 3; Rose, B., 1, 4; **Rose, Bernice;** Rosenblum 2; Rubin 1; Sandler 1; Seuphor 1; Soby 5; Tapie 1; Tomkins 2; Tomkins and Time-Life Books; Tuchman, ed.; Tuchman 3; Weller. Archives.

PONCE DE LEON, MICHAEL. b. July 4, 1922, Miami, Fla. **Studied:** NAD; ASL, with Cameron Booth, Vaclav Vytlacil, Will Barnet, Harry Sternberg; PAFA; Brooklyn Museum, with Ben Shahn, Gabor Peterdi, John Ferren; U. of Mexico City, BA. US Air Force, three years. Traveled Mexico, Norway, Europe (extensively), Pakistan, India.

Taught: Vassar College; Cooper Union; Pratt Graphic Art Center; Hunter College; in India and Pakistan, 1967-68; NYU, 1977; Pratt Institute, 1978; ASL, 1978. **Member:** SAGA. **Commissions:** US Post Office Department (design for fine-arts commemorative stamp). **Awards:** L.C. Tiffany Grant, 1953, 55; Bradley U., **P.P.,** 1954; Dallas/MFA, **P.P.,** 1954; SAGA, Gold Medal, 1954; U. of Nebraska; Oakland/AM, Gold Medal; Fulbright Fellowship, 1956, 57; The Print Club, Phildelphia, 1958; Audubon Artists, Gold Medal of Honor; Guggenheim Foundation Fellowship, 1967. **Address:** 463 West Street, NYC 10014. **One-man Exhibitions:** (first) Galeria Proteo, Mexico City, 1954; Oslo/National; Oakland/AM; Corcoran, 1967; Cynthia Comsky Gallery, 1970. **Retrospective:** Pioneer-Moss Gallery, NYC, 1975. **Group:** MMA; MOMA; Brooklyn Museum; Walker; Victoria and Albert Museum; PAFA; SAGA; Portland, Me./MA; Audubon Artists; Denver/AM; Bradley U.; Chicago/AI; I Inter-American Paintings and Prints Biennial, Mexico City, 1958; NAD; Boston/MFA; U. of Illinois. **Collections:** Achenbach Foundation, Brooklyn Museum; Cincinnati/AM; Columbia, S.C./MA; Dallas/MFA; U. of Florida; U. of Illinois; Indiana U.; Jacksonville/AM; Library of Congress; MOMA; Melbourne/National; Mexico City/Nacional; NYPL; NYU; National Gallery; U. of Nebraska; Oslo/National; PAFA; PMA; Paris/Moderne; SFMA; US State Department; United Nations; Victoria and Albert Museum; Walker. **Bibliography:** Archives.

POND, CLAYTON. b. June 10, 1941, Bayside, N.Y. **Studied:** Hiram College, 1959-61; Carnegie Tech, BFA, 1964; Pratt Institute, MFA, 1964-66. Traveled Europe, Africa, Japan. **Taught:** Junior High School, Palm Beach, Fla., 1964; C. W. Post College, 1966-68; School of Visual Arts, NYC, 1968-70; U. of Wisconsin, Madison, 1972. **Member:** Boston Printmakers; The Print Club, Philadel-

phia. **Commissions:** New York State Council on the Arts, 1967. **Awards:** Bradley U., Print Annual, **P.P.,** 1966; Kalamazoo/Institute, **P.P.,** 1966; Arden Prize, 1966; US State Department Grant, 1967; Albion College, **P.P.,** 1968; Boston Printmakers, **P.P.,** 1968; Dulin Gallery Fifth National Print and Drawing Exhibition, **P.P.,** 1969. **Address:** 130 Greene Street, NYC 10012; Turnbridge, VT 05077. **One-man Exhibitions:** (first) Pratt Institute, 1966; Dartmouth College, 1966; C.W. Post College (two-man), 1966; Gordon Craig Gallery, Miami, Fla., 1968; WGMA, 1968; Princeton U. (2-man), 1968; Martha Jackson Gallery, 1968, 72, 73, 75; Port Washington (N.Y.) Public Library, 1968, 72; Kalamazoo/Institute, 1969; The Print Club, Philadelphia, 1969; Nassau Community College, Garden City, N.Y., 1969; Upstairs Gallery, Ithaca, 1970; Gallery 2, Woodstock, Vt., 1970; Van Staaten Gallery, 1971, 73; Images Gallery, Toledo, 1971; Lincoln, Mass./De Cordova, 1972; Madison Art Center, 1972; Arts & Crafts Center of Pittsburgh, 1972; Langman Gallery, Jenkintown, Pa., 1973; Graphics I & Graphics II, Boston, 1973, 75; Montgomery Museum, 1973; U. of Florida, Gainsville, 1973; U. of Nebraska, 1974; Phoenix, 1974; Yumi Gallery, Tokyo, 1975; Roanoke Art Center, 1976; Martha Jackson Gallery, NYC, 1977, Editions Limited Gallery, Indianapolis, 1977; Graphic Eye Gallery, Port Washington, N.Y., 1977; Jack Gallery, NYC, 1979; Schenectady, 1983. **Group:** San Francisco Art Institute Annual, 1965; Brooklyn Museum, Print Biennial; NAD, 1966; Pratt Institute, 1966; Pacific Print Invitational, 1966-67; WMAA Sculpture Annual, 1966; Boston/MFA, 1967-69; Gallery of Modern Art, Ljubljana, Yugoslavia, VII International Exhibition of Prints, 1967; Seattle Civic Center, 1968; Library of Congress Print Annual, 1969; Boston/MFA, Boston Printmakers, 1969; Expo '70, Osaka, 1970; Paris/Moderne, International Exhibition of Colored Prints, 1970; USIA,

Vienna, New American Prints, circ., 1971; City Museum and Art Gallery, Hong Kong, Graphics Now! USA, 1972; NCFA, XXIII Library of Congress Exhibition, 1973. **Collections:** AT&T; Albany/SUNY; Albion College; American Republic Insurance Co.; The Bank of New York; Bezalel Museum; Boston/MFA; Bradley U.; Buffalo/Albright; U. of California; Amon Carter Museum; Chase Manhattan Bank; Chicago/AI; Colgate U.; College of St. Benedict; Columbus, Ga.; Dartmouth College; Dulin Gallery; First National Bank of Chicago; Fort Worth; Grunwald Foundation; Indiana U.; Indianapolis/Herron; Kalamazoo/Institute; Library of Congress; Los Angeles/County MA; MOMA; Manufacturers Hanover Trust Co.; Minneapolis/Institute; NCFA; PMA; Pasadena/AM; Potsdam/SUNY; Princeton U.; Quaker Oats Co.; U. of Tennessee; Toledo/MA; US State Department; *Washington Post;* Western Michigan U.; U. of Wisconsin.

POONS, LARRY. b. October 1, 1937, Tokyo, Japan. **Studied:** New England Conservatory of Music, 1955-57; Boston Museum School, 1958. **Address:** 831 Broadway, NYC 10013. **Dealer:** Andre Emmerich Gallery, NYC. **One-man Exhibitions:** (first) Green Gallery, NYC, 1963, also 1964, 65; Leo Castelli, Inc., 1967, 68, 69; Kasmin Ltd., 1968, 71; Lawrence Rubin Gallery, NYC, 1969, 70, 72; David Mirvish Gallery, 1970, 76; ACE Gallery, Los Angeles, 1975, 77; Galerie Andre Emmerich, Zurich, 1975; Knoedler Contemporary Art, NYC, 1975, 76, 77; Daniel Templon, Paris, 1976; Watson/De Nagy, Houston, 1977; Galerie 99, Bay Harbor Islands, Fla., 1978; Andre Emmerich Gallery, NYC, 1979, 81, 82, 83, 85; Hett Gallery, Edmonton, 1980; Galerie Ulysses, Vienna, 1980; Waddington Gallery, Toronto, 1980, 82; Galerie Artline, The Hague, 1981; Galerie Ninety-Nine, Bay Harbor Islands, Fla., 1981; Gallery One, Toronto, 1981, 82, 84; Meredith Long &

Co., Houston, 1982. **Retrospective:** Boston/MFA, circ., 1981. **Group:** WGMA, 1963; Sidney Janis Gallery, The Classic Spirit, 1964; SRGM, American Drawings, 1964, Systemic Painting, 1966; MOMA, The Responsive Eye, 1965; Smithsonian, 1965; VIII Sao Paulo Biennial, 1965; WMAA Annuals, 1965, 67, also Young America, 1965; Chicago/AI, 1966; Corcoran, 1967; Carnegie, 1967; Documenta IV, Kassel, 1968; WMAA Annual, 1969; MMA, New York Painting and Sculpture, 1940-1970, 1969; Washington U., The Development of Modernist Painting; Jackson Pollock to the Present, 1969; Pasadena/AM, Painting in New York: 1944-1969, 1969; Buffalo/Albright, Color and Field, 1890-1970, 1970; WMAA, The Structure of Color, 1971; Buffalo/Albright, Six Painters, 1971; Boston/MFA, Abstract Painting in the '70s, 1972; Kansas City/Nelson, Color Field Painting to Post Color Field Abstraction, 1972; Houston/MFA, The Great Decade of American Abstraction: Modernist Art, 1960-1970, 1974; U. of Miami (Fla.), Less Is More: The Influence of the Bauhaus on American Art, 1974; Caracas, El Lenguaje del Color, 1974; Corcoran Biennial, 1975; Syracuse/Everson, New Works in Clay by Contemporary Painters and Sculptors, 1976; Everson/Syracuse, A Century of Ceramics in the U.S., 1878-1978, 1979; Syracuse/Everson, A Century of Ceramics in the U.S., 1878-1978, 1979; Grand Palais, Paris, L'Amerique aux Indépendants, 1980; Houston/MFA, Miró in America, 1982; St. Lawrence U., Pre-Postmodern, 1985. **Collections:** Boston/MFA; Buffalo/Albright; Cleveland/MA; Denver/AM; Eindhoven; Hirshhorn; MMA; Milwaukee; MOMA; Oberlin College; PMA; Tate; WMAA. **Bibliography:** Alloway 3; Battcock, ed.; Calas, N. and E.; Goossen 1; *The Great Decade;* Hansen; Haskell 5; Hunter, ed.; Johnson, Ellen H.; Kozloff 3; Lippard 2, 5; MacAgy 2; Murken-Altrogge; Rickey; Rose, B., 1; Wood.

POOR, HENRY VARNUM. b. September 30, 1888, Chapman, Kans.; **d.** December 8, 1970, NYC. **Studied:** Stanford U., AB, **PBK,** 1910; U. of London, Slade School, 1910, with Walter Sickert; Academie Julian, Paris, 1911, with Jean Paul Laurens. US Army, 1918. **Taught:** Stanford U.; Mark Hopkins Art School, 1917; Colorado Springs Fine Arts Center, 1937; Skowhegan School. Active 1920-30 only as a potter; there are no paintings from this period. **Commissions** (murals): Justice Department, Washington, D.C., 1935; Interior Department, Washington, D.C., 1937; Penn State College, 1940; Deerfield (Mass.) Academy; Mt. Sinai Hospital, NYC. **Awards:** Chicago/AI, Norman Wait Harris Silver Medal, 1932; Carnegie, Third Prize, 1933; Syracuse/Everson, First Prize, 1937; Architectural League of New York, Gold Medal of Honor, 1938. **One-man Exhibitions:** (first) H. Kevorkian, NYC, 1920; Montross Gallery, NYC, 1921-31; Rehn Galleries, 1933-70. **Retrospective:** The Pennsylvania State U., 1983. **Group:** WMAA; Carnegie; Chicago/AI; U. of Illinois. **Collections:** Andover/Phillips; Brooklyn Museum; Cleveland/MA; Columbus; U. of Kansas; MMA; U. of Nebraska; Newark Museum; SFMA; San Diego; WMAA; Wichita/AM. **Bibliography:** Baur 7; Biddle 4; **Boswell 1, 2;** Bruce and Watson; Cahill and Barr, eds.; Cheney; Genauer; Goodrich and Baur 1; Hall; Kent, N.; Mellquist; Nordmark; **Poor 1, 2;** Richardson, E.P.; Soyer, R. 1. Archives.

PORTER, DAVID. b. May 18, 1912, Chicago Art Institute School, briefly. Traveled USA, Mexico, Italy, France, Switzerland. **Taught:** Privately, 1952-57; Ogunquit, 1964; Dartmouth College, 1964; Cooper Union, 1968. Co-author of the Broadway play *Mrs. Patterson.* Operated the David Porter Gallery, Washington, D.C., 1942-46. Publisher, *Cosmopolitan* magazine, 1954-55; Guild Hall, East Hampton, 1974-79.

Awards: Guild Hall, Hon. Men., 1951; Provincetown Arts Festival, First Prize, 1958; Sassoferrato (Italy) International, Second Gold Medal, 1960, and First Prize, Gold Medal of President Gronchi, 1961; Guild Hall, First Prize, 1964; NIAL, Grant, 1970. **Address:** Box 711, Wainscott, NY 11975. **One-man Exhibitions:** (first) Hugo Gallery, NYC, 1952; Deerfield (Mass.) Academy, 1953; Galerie Hervé, NYC, 1955; The New Gallery, NYC, 1957; Obelisk Gallery, Washington, D.C., 1958; Tirca Karlis Gallery, 1959; Galleria L'Incontro, Rome, 1960; Modern Art Gallery, Palermo, Sicily, 1960; Ann Ross Gallery, White Plains, N. Y., 1961, 62; Southampton/Parrish, 1962; Alan Auslander Gallery, NYC, 1962; Ferrill Galleries, Santa Fe, N. M., 1963; Royal Athena II, NYC, 1964; Mickelson's Gallery, Washington, D. C., 1964, 68; Dartmouth College, 1964; NYPL, 1966; American Institute of Architects, N. Y. Chapter, 1969; Guild Hall, East Hampton, 1970; Benson Gallery, Southampton, N.Y., 1986. **Retrospective:** Nassau Community College, Garden City, 1983. **Group:** Ninth Street Exhibition, NYC, 1951; WMAA Annual, 1951; Guild Hall, 1951, 54, 55, 56, 58, 64; Chicago/AI, 1952; U. of Illinois, 1952, 53; Carnegie, 1958; Corcoran, 1959; Dayton/AI, Modern Americans, 1959; Lincoln, Mass./De Cordova, 1965; Huntington, N. Y./Heckscher, Artists of Suffolk County, Part III; Figurative Traditions, 1971. **Collections:** American Airlines; Brown U.; Chase Manhattan Bank, NYC; Dartmouth College; Dayton/AI; Guild Hall; Hempstead Bank; Miami/Modern; NYU; Norfolk; Norfolk/Chrysler; Southampton/Parrish; Union Carbide Corp.; WMAA. **Bibliography:** Janis and Blesh 1. Archives.

PORTER, FAIRFIELD. b. June 10, 1907, Winnetka, Ill.; **d.** September 18, 1975, Southampton, N. Y. **Studied:** Harvard U.; ASL, with Boardman Robinson, Thomas Hart Benton. Traveled Europe, USSR, Scandinavia, USA, Canada. **Taught:** Long Island U., Southampton College, 1965-66; Queens College, 1968; Amherst College, 1969-70; School of Visual Arts, NYC, 1974-75. Editorial associate, *Art News* magazine, 1951-58; art critic, *The Nation* magazine, 1959-60. **Awards:** Longview Foundation (for art criticism), 1959; Purdue U., **P.P.**, 1966; NAD, **P.P. One-man Exhibitions:** (first) Community House, Winnetka, Ill., 1939; Tibor de Nagy Gallery, 1951-70; RISD, 1959; U. of Alabama, 1963; Reed College, 1965; Trinity College (Conn.), 1966; Kent State U., 1967; Swarthmore College, 1967; Hirschl & Adler Galleries, 1972, 74, 76, 79; Southampton/Parrish, 1971, 76; Maryland Institute, 1973; Brooke Alexander, 1975; U. of Connecticut, 1975; Hirschl & Adler Galleries, 1976, 79, 85; Alpha Gallery, Boston, 1977; Colby College, 1977; Harbor Gallery, Cold Spring Harbor, N.Y., 1977; Southampton/Parrish, 1977; Gross-McCleaf Gallery, Philadelphia, 1978, 79; Esther Robles Gallery, Los Angeles, 1978; Artists Choice Museum, NYC, 1979; Barridoff Galleries, Portland, Me., 1979; Hull Gallery, Washington, D.C., 1979; Mickelson Gallery, Washington, D.C., 1979; WMAA (Fairfield County), 1984. **Retrospectives:** Cleveland/MA, 1966; Huntington, N.Y./Heckscher, circ., 1974; Boston/MFA, circ., 1982. **Group:** Dayton/AI, 1961; MOMA, 1961; Yale U., 1961-62; WMAA Annuals, 1961-66; PAFA, 1962; NIAL, 1962; U. of Nebraska, 1963; Colby College, Maine and Its Artists, 1963; Chicago/AI; Venice Biennial; New York World's Fair, 1964-65; Gallery of Modern Art, NYC, 1965; Purdue U., 1966; Akron/AI, 1967; Flint/Institute, 1967; US Dept. of the Interior, America 1976, 1976; PAFA, Contemporary Realism Since 1960, circ., 1981; Guild Hall, Art and Friendship: A Tribute to Fairfield Porter, 1984; Southampton/Parrish, Painting Naturally: Fairfield Porter and His Influences, 1984. **Collections:** Boston/MFA; Brooklyn Museum; Chase Manhattan Bank; Cleveland/MA; Corcoran; Dayton/AI; Hartford/Wadsworth; Hirshhorn; MMA; MOMA; U. of Nebraska; U. of North Carolina; Purdue U.; Santa Fe, N. M.; Toledo, MA; WMAA: Woodward Foundation. **Bibliography:** *America 1976*; Arthur 1; **Ashbery and Moffett;** Cummings 1; Downes, ed.; Geske; Lindman; McCoubrey 1; **Porter;** Sandler 1. Archives.

PORTER, KATHERINE. b. 1941, Cedar Rapids, Iowa. **Studied:** Colorado College, BA, 1959-1963; Boston U., 1962. **Awards:** Hon. DFA, Colby College, 1982. **Address:** 610 Cathedral Parkway, NYC 10025. **Dealer:** Sidney Janis Gallery, NYC. **One-man Exhibitions:** Parker 470 Gallery, Boston 1971, 72; U. of Rhode Island, 1971; Henri Gallery, Washington, D.C., 1972; Worcester, 1973; MIT, 1974; David McKee, Inc., NYC, 1975, 78, 79, 82, 84; Harcus-Krakow Gallery, Boston, 1976; Alpha Gallery, Boston (two-man), 1979; San Francisco/Achenbach, 1980; Dartmouth College, 1981; Arts Club of Chicago, 1984; Brandeis U., 1985; Sidney Janis Gallery, 1987. **Group:** WMAA Annuals, 1969, 73; MIT, Six Artists, 1970; ICA, Boston, Drawings Re-examined, 1970; ICA, U. of Pennsylvania, Six Visions, 1973; SRGM, Theodoron Awards, 1977; Brandeis U., From Women's Eyes, 1977; Otis Art Institute, Los Angeles, New York: A Selection from the Last 10 Years, 1979; Winter Olympics, Lake Placid, NY, 1980; WMAA Biennial, 1981; Chicago/AI, 74th American Exhibition, 1982; MOMA, International Survey of Recent Painting and Sculpture, 1984; Fort Lauderdale, An American Renaissance: Painting and Sculpture Since 1940, 1986. **Collections:** Andover/Phillips; Brandeis U.; Carnegie; Chase Manhattan Bank, NYC; Colby College; Currier; Denver/AM; Harvard U.; High Museum; MOMA; PMA; Portland, Me./MA; Prudential Insurance Co. of America, Newark; SRGM; San Francisco/Achenbach; WMAA; Worcester/AM. **Bibliograpy:** Lucie-Smith.

PORTER, LILIANA. b. October 6, 1941, Buenos Aires, Argentina. **Studied:** National School of Fine Arts, Buenos Aires, 1954-57; Universidad Iberoamericana, Mexico City, 1958-60; School of Fine Arts, Buenos Aires, 1961-63. Traveled Mexico, Europe, South America. **Taught:** New York Graphic Workshop, 1965-70; Old Westbury/SUNY, 1974-76. **Member:** Artists Equity. **Awards:** Salon de Otono, Buenos Aires, first prize, 1962; Salon Artes Plasticas Hebraica Argentina, first prize, 1962; San Juan, first prize, 1st Latin American Biennial of Prints, 1970; Museum of Fine Arts, Buenos Aires, first prize, 1978; Guggenheim Foundation Fellowship, 1980; Montevideo, First Iberoamerican Graphics Biennial, 1st prize, 1983; New York Foundation for the Arts, 1985. **Address:** 178 Franklin Street, NYC 10013. **Dealers:** Barbara Toll Fine Arts, NYC; Dolan/Maxwell Gallery, Philadelphia. **One-man Exhibitions:** (first) Galeria Proteo, Mexico City, 1959; Galeria Municipal de Veracruz, Mexico, 1960; Galeria Galatea, Buenos Aires, 1961; Galeria Nice, Buenos Aires, 1962; Galeria Plasticas de Mexico, Mexico City, 1963; Prints International, Toronto, 1963; Galeria Lirolay, Buenos Aires, 1963, 66; Van Bovenkamp Gallery, NYC, 1964; Galeria Amigos del Arte, Montevideo, 1966; Caracas, 1969; A.A.A. Gallery, NYC, 1969; Santiago, Chile, 1969; Instituto Torcuato Di Tella, Buenos Aires, 1969; Galleria Diagramma, Milan, 1972; Hundred Acres Gallery (two-man), 1973, 75, 77; MOMA, 1973; Galleria Conz, Venice, 1973; Galeria Colibri, San Juan, 1974; Galeria Conkright, Caracas, 1974; Galerie Stamps, Basel, 1974; Museo de Arte Moderno, Bogota, 1974; Galeria Belarca, Bogota, 1975; Galleria della Villa Schifanoia, Florence, 1976; Galeria Artemultiple, Buenos Aires, 1977, 78; Barbara Toll Fine Arts, NYC, 1979, 80, 82, 84; Museo de Arte Moderno, Cali, 1978, 83; Galerie Arte Nuevo, Buenos Aires, 1980; Center for Interamerican Relations, NYC, 1980; Galeria Garces-Valesquez, Bogota, 1982, 84; Galerie Jolliet, Montreal, 1983; Galeria Taller, 1983; U. of Alberta, 1984; Centro de Arte Actual, Pereira, Colombia, 1984; Panama City, Museo de Arte Contemporaneo, 1984; Dolan/Maxwell Gallery, 1985. **Retrospectives:** School of Architecture, Caracas, 1969; Galerie Arte Nuevo, Buenos Aires, Center for Inter-American Relations, NYC, 1980. **Group:** Jewish Museum, NYC, 100 Contemporary Prints, 1965; Ljubljana Biennials, 1965, 73, 75, 77, 79; NYU, Art in Editions, 1968; Krakow, print biennials, 1968, 70, 74; ICA, London, Printmaking in America, 1969; San Juan, print biennials, 1970, 72; MOMA, Information, 1970; Paris/Bibliotheque Nationale, L'Estampe Contemporaine, 1973; U. of California, Berkeley, Books Made by Artists, 1973; Segovia, print biennial, 1974; Bradford (England) print biennials, 1974, 76, 79; Canberra/National, Illusion and Reality, 1977; William Paterson College, Works on the Wall, 1979; Syracuse/Everson, Roots-Visions, 1979; Jackson/MMA, Collage and Assemblage, circ., 1981; U. of North Carolina, Art on Paper, 1982; Queens College, Latin American Artists in the US 1950-1970, 1983; SFMA, World Print Four, 1983; 1st Bienal de la Habana, Cuba, 1984. **Collections:** Caracas; Chase Manhattan Bank, NYC; Chattanooga/Hunter; Columbia U.; Lodz; Montreal/Contemporain; MOMA; Musée del Grabado, Buenos Aires; Museo de Arte Contemporaneo "La Tertulia"; Museo Universitario, Mexico City; NYPL; Paris/Bibliotheque Nationale; PMA; Santiago, Chile; R.C.A. Corp., NYC; U. of Texas.

PORTNOW, MARJORIE. b. September 30, 1942, NYC. **Studied:** Case Western Reserve U., 1960-64, BA, Art History, magna cum laude, with Dr. Sherman E. Lee; Pratt Institute, 1964, with Alex Katz, Gabriel Laderman; Skowhegan School, 1965, with Lennart Anderson, Alfred Leslie, John Button; Brooklyn College, 1970-72, MFA, summa cum laude, with Alfred Russell, Joe Groell, Philip Pearlstein, Larry Campbell. Traveled USA. **Taught:** Queens College, 1973-74; Boston Museum School, 1974-75; Virginia Polytechnic Institute, 1982, 84. **Awards:** L.C. Tiffany Grant, 1972, 78; Ingram Merrill Foundation Grant, 1975; National Endowment for the Arts, 1980; CAPS, 1981. Designed sets and multimedia works for poet Bob Holman. **Address:** 67 Vestry Street, NYC 10013. **Dealer:** Fischbach Gallery, NYC; Harcus Gallery, Boston. **One-man Exhibitions:** First Street Gallery, NYC, 1972; The Kornblee Gallery, 1974; Harcus-Krakow Gallery, Boston, 1978, 83; Odyssia Gallery, 1983; Fischbach Gallery, 1985. **Group:** Colgate U., Painters of the Land and Sky, 1972; Corcoran, The Delaware Water Gap, 1975; Bronx Museum, Personal Visions, 1978; NAD, 1981; Albany/Institute, The New Response, 1985. **Collections:** Amherst College; Chase Manhattan Bank; The Commerce Bancshares of Kansas City; MMA; U. of Nebraska.

POSEN, STEPHEN. b. September 27, 1939, St. Louis, Mo. **Studied:** Washington U., 1962, BFA; Yale U., 1964, MFA. US Army, 1957. Traveled Europe. **Taught:** Cooper Union. **Awards:** Fulbright Fellowship, 1964-66; Milliken Traveling Scholarship, 1964; CAPS, 1973. **Address:** 115 Spring Street, NYC 10012. **One-man Exhibitions:** OK Harris Works of Art, 1971, 74; Robert Miller Gallery, Inc., NYC, 1978. **Group:** Chicago/Contemporary, Radical Realism, 1971; Eindhoven, Relativerend Realisme, 1972; WMAA Annual, 1972; Documenta V, Kassel, 1972; Cleveland/MA, 32 Realists, 1972; Yale U., 7 Realists, 1973; Chicago/AI, New Realism, 1973; Lunds Konsthall, Sweden, Amerikansk Realism, 1974; Tokyo Biennial, 1974; Chicago/AI, 71st American Exhibition, 1974; Potsdam/SUNY, New Realism Revisited, 1974; Taft Museum, Tromp L'Oeil, 1975, Canberra/National, Illusion and Reality, circ., 1977-78; PAFA, Eight Contempo-

rary American Realists, 1977. **Collections:** Chase Manhattan Bank; PAFA; RAC. **Bibliography:** Arthur 1, 2; Goodyear; Hunter, ed.; Lucie-Smith; Sager.

POUSETTE-DART, RICHARD. b. June 8, 1916, St. Paul, Minn. **Studied:** Bard College, 1936. Traveled France. **Taught:** New School for Social Research, 1959-61; School of Visual Arts, NYC, 1965; Columbia U., 1968-69; Sarah Lawrence College, 1970-74; Art Students League, 1980-81; Bard College, 1983. **Awards:** Guggenheim Foundation Fellowship, 1951; Ford Foundation Grant, 1959; Corcoran Biennial, Silver Medal, 1965; Honorary Doctor of Humane Letters, Bard College, 1965; National Endowment for the Arts Grant, 1967; L. C. Tiffany Foundation, Distinguished Lifetime in Art Award, 1981. **Address:** 286 Haverstraw Road, Suffern, NY 10901. **Dealer:** Marisa del Re Gallery, NYC. **One-man Exhibitions:** (first) Artists Gallery, NYC, 1941; The Willard Gallery, 1943, 45, 56; Art of This Century, NYC, 1947; Betty Parsons Gallery, 1948-51, 1953, 55, 58, 59, 61, 64, 67; Katonah (N.Y.) Art Gallery, 1967; Washington U., 1969; Obelisk Gallery, 1969; Andrew Crispo Gallery, 1974, 76, 78; MOMA, circ., 1969-70; Allentown/AM, 1975; Wichita State U., 1975; Arts Club of Chicago, 1978; Marisa del Re Gallery, 1981, 82, 83; Schwartz-Galdo Gallery, Birmingham, Mich., 1983; Makler Gallery, Philadelphia, 1983. **Retrospectives:** WMAA, 1963, 74. **Group:** Chicago/AI, Abstract and Surrealist Art, 1948; WMAA Annuals, 1949, 51, 53, 1955-59, 1961, 72, 73; MOMA, Abstract Painting and Sculpture in America, 1951; U. of Illinois, 1951-53; Buffalo/Albright, Expressionism in American Painting, 1952; WMAA, The New Decade, 1954-55; WMAA, Nature in Abstraction, 1958; I Inter-American Painting and Prints Biennial, Mexico City, 1958; Carnegie, 1958, 61; Documenta II, Kassel, 1959; SRGM, Abstract Expressionists and Imagists, 1961;

MOMA, The Art of Assemblage, circ., 1961; Hartford/Wadsworth, Continuity and Change, 1962; MOMA, The New American Painting and Sculpture, 1969; National Gallery, American Art at Mid-Century, 1973; Philadelphia College of Art, Private Notations: Artists' Sketchbooks, 1976; Bronx Museum of the Arts, The Magic Circle, 1977; Indianapolis, Perceptions of the Spirit in 20th Century American Art, circ., 1977; Cornell U., Abstract Expressionists: Formative Years, 1978; Chicago/Terra, Solitude: Inner Visions in American Art, 1982; Haus der Kunst, Munich, Amerikanische Malerie: 1930-1980, 1982; XL Venice Biennial, 1982. **Collections:** Andover/Phillips; Buffalo/Albright; Chase Manhattan Bank; Ciba-Geigy Corp., Ardsley; Corcoran; Cornell U.; Equitable Life Assurance Society; Hirshhorn; U. of Iowa; MMA; MOMA; U. of Nebraska; NCFA; NMAA; Newark Museum; North Central Bronx Hospital; Oklahoma; PMA; Pasadena/AM; Ringling; The Singer Company, Inc.; SRGM; Uffizi Gallery; Union Carbide Corp.; Upjohn Co.; WMAA; Washington U.; Wichita State U. **Bibliography:** Baur 5; Blesh 1; Goodrich and Baur 1; Janis and Blesh 1; Motherwell and Reinhardt, eds.; Nordness, ed.; Pousette-Dart, ed.; Ragon 2; Ritchie 1; Seitz 3; Tuchman, ed.; Tuchman 3. Archives.

POZZATTI, RUDY. b. January 14, 1926, Telluride, Colo. **Studied:** U. of Colorado, with Wendell Black, Ben Shahn, Max Beckmann, 1948, BFA, 1950, MFA. US Army, 1943-46. Traveled Europe, USSR, Mexico, South America; resided Italy. **Taught:** U. of Colorado, 1948-50, summers, 1951, 54; U. of Nebraska, 1950-56; Cooper Union, summer, 1955; Indiana U., 1956-; Yale-Norfolk Summer Art School, 1957; The Ohio State U., summer, 1959; Florence, Italy, Print Workshop, summer, 1967; Honolulu Academy, 1971; Instituto d'Arte, Massa, Italy, 1974. **Member:** SAGA; Board of Directors, College Art Association, 1974-78. NAD. Subject of *Artists in America*, half-hour TV color film, N.E.T., 1971; Academia Italia della Arte e del Lavoro. **Commissions:** International Graphic Arts Society (3 editions); Print Club of Cleveland; New York Hilton Hotel. **Awards:** U. of Illinois, Graphic Art Exhibition, First Prize, 1949; Walker, **P.P.,** 1951; Youngstown/Butler, **P.P.,** 1951, 52; St. Louis/City, Vladimir Golschmann Prize, 1952; Fulbright Fellowship (Italy), 1952-53; St. Louis/City, Henry V. Putzell Prize, 1955; The Print Club, Philadelphia, Mildred Boericke Award, 1955, also 1969; PAFA, Alice McFadden Eyre Medal, 1957; Library of Congress, Pennell **P.P.,** 1958; Boston Printmakers, Paul J. Sachs Award 1958, 61; PAFA, **P.P.,** 1959 (2); AAAL, **P.P.,** 1960; SAGA, 100 Prints of the Year, First Prize, 1963; Guggenheim Foundation Fellowship, 1963-64; Ford Foundation Grant; US State Department Cultural Exchange Grant, 1965; Flint/Institute, 1965; American Color Print Society, **P.P.,** 1968; III Annual 500 Mile Race Art Exhibit, Indianapolis, First Prize, ($1,000), 1968; U. of Colorado, George Norlin Silver Medal for Distinguished Achievements in Chosen Profession, 1972; Honorary Doctor of Humane Letters, U. of Colorado, 1973; and many others; Carl Zigrosser Memorial Award, American Color Print Society, 1979. **Address:** 117 South Meadowbrook, Bloomington, IN 47401. **Dealer:** Haslem Fine Arts, Inc. **One-man Exhibitions:** (first) Chicago/AI, 1953; Philadelphia Art Alliance, 1953; Martha Jackson Gallery, 1954; Cleveland/MA, 1955; Kansas City/Nelson, 1955; U. of Maine, 1956; U. of Nebraska, 1956; Gump's Gallery, 1956, 60; Weyhe Gallery, 1957; Clarke College, 1957; Carleton College, 1957; U. of Minnesota, 1958; Louisville/Speed, 1958; Ohio U., 1960; Walker, 1960; J. Seligmann and Co., 1961; U. of Louisville, 1963; Jane Haslem Gallery, Durham, N.C., 1963; Kalamazoo/Institute, 1967; Merida Gallery, Inc., 1967; Daberkow Gallery, Frankfort, 1969; Karlsruhe, 1969; Honolulu Academy, 1971; Louisville/Speed, 1973; Institute of Fine Arts, Salvadore, Brazil, 1974; Institute of Fine Arts, Sao Paulo, 1974; I.B.E.U., Rio de Janeiro, 1974; US Embassy, Ankara (two-man), 1975; Terre Haute/Swope, 1979; Cushing Gallery, Dallas, 1977; Roswell, 1980; Terre Haute/Swope, 1979, 81; Roswell, 1980; Heath Gallery, Atlanta, 1982; U. of Tennessee, 1982; U. of West Virginia, 1982; Evansville, 1983; Lake Erie College, 1983; American Embassy, Belgrade, 1984; U. of Arkansas, 1985; Centre College, 1985. **Retrospectives:** U. of Nebraska, 1971; Southern Illinois U., circ., 1982. **Group:** The Print Club, Philadelphia, 1954; U. of Oklahoma, 1956; WMAA, Fulbright Artists, 1958; U. of Michigan, 1959; The Pennsylvania State U., 10 American Printmakers, 1959; WMAA, Young America, 1960; Syracuse U., 1962; PCA, American Prints Today, circ., 1962; U. of Kentucky, Graphics IV, 1962; IBM Gallery of Arts and Sciences, NYC, 30 American Printmakers, circ., 1974. **Collections:** Achenbach Foundation; Albion College; Allegheny College; Alverthrope Gallery; Anchorage; Ashland Oil Inc.; Ball State U.; Baltimore/MA; Bibliotheque Nationale; Boston/MFA; Bradley U.; Brooklyn Museum; U. of California, Berkeley; Cleveland/MA; U. of Colorado; Concordia Teachers College (Neb.); Davidson, N.C.; Dayton/AI; U. of Delaware; De Pauw U.; Duke U.; Eastern Michigan U.; Hamline U.; Harvard U.; Indiana U.; Indianapolis/Herron; State College of Iowa; Jacksonville/AM; Kansas City/Nelson; Kansas State College; Kemper Insurance Co.; La Jolla; Library of Congress; Los Angeles/County MA; Louisville/Speed; U. of Louisville; MMA; MOMA; U. of Maine; Malmo; Marshall U.; U. of Michigan; National Gallery; Nebraska State Teachers College; U. of Nebraska; Newark Museum; Oakland/AM; Oberlin College; The Ohio State U.; Oklahoma City U.; U. of Oklahoma; Omaha/Joslyn; PAFA;

PMA; U. of Puerto Rico; SFMA; St. Cloud State College; St. Lawrence U.; St. Louis/City; St. Mary's College (Ind.); San Jose State College; Seattle/AM; Sioux City Art Center; Springfield, Mo./AM; Syracuse U.; Texas Western College, Toronto; Texas Tech U.; US State Department; Utica; Victoria and Albert Museum; Walker; Washburn U. of Topeka; Wichita/AM; College of William and Mary; U. of Wisconsin; Yale U.; Youngstown/Butler; Youngstown U. **Bibliography:** Chaet; **Print Club of Cleveland.**

PRESTOPINO, GREGORIO. b. June 21, 1907, NYC. **d.** December 19, 1984, Princeton, N.J. **Studied:** NAD, with C. W. Hawthorne. Traveled Europe, southwestern USA, Mexico. **Taught:** Veterans Art Center, MOMA, 1946-48; Brooklyn Museum School, 1946-59; New School for Social Research, 1949-56, 57, 65; American Academy, Rome, 1968-69. Federal A.P.: Easel painting. **Awards:** PAFA, Joseph E. Temple Gold Medal, 1946; Pepsi-Cola, Third Prize, 1946; Youngstown/Butler, First Prize, 1958; Cannes Film Festival, First Prize (for the art film *Harlem Wednesday*), 1958; NIAL Grant, 1961; NAD, Benjamin Altman Prize, 1972; NAD, Emily Goldsmith Award, 1977; NAD, Benjamin Altman (Figure) Prize, 1984. **One-man Exhibitions:** (first) ACA Gallery, 1943, also 1946, 48, 50, 51, 53, 54, 57; Lee Nordness Gallery, NYC, 1959, 60, 61, 62, 64; Rex Evans Gallery, 1961; White; Terry Dintenfass, Inc., 1966, 68, 71, 74; Virginia Union U., 1967; Keene (N.H.) State College, 1974; Pine Public Library, Fairlawn, N.J., 1979; Midtown Galleries, 1983, 85; Sheraton Arts Center, Sharon, N.H., 1985. **Retrospectives:** Michigan State U.; Fort Lauderdale, 1980. **Group:** WMAA annuals; MOMA; Corcoran; New York World's Fair, 1939; Golden Gate International Exposition, San Francisco, 1939; Chicago/AI; Venice Biennial; USIA; PAFA Annual, 1967; and others. **Collections:** U. of Alabama; Andover/Phillips; Brandeis U.; Chicago/AI; Currier; U. of Hawaii; IBM; U. of Illinois; MOMA; Martha Washington U.; Mary Washington College; Montclair/AM; NCFA; U. of Nebraska; U. of Notre Dame; U. of Oklahoma; Phillips; U. of Rochester; Southern Methodist U.; U. of Texas; Trenton/State; WMAA; Walker; Youngstown/Butler. **Bibliography:** Genauer; Nordness, ed.; Pousette-Dart, ed. Archives.

PRICE, KENNETH. b. 1935, Los Angeles, Calif. **Studied:** U. of California; Otis Art Institute; Chouinard Art Institute; U. of Southern California, BFA, 1956; Alfred/SUNY, MFA, 1958. **Awards:** Tamarind Fellowship, 1968. **Address:** P.O. Box 1356, Taos, N.M. 87571. **One-man Exhibitions:** U. of California, 1956; Ferus Gallery, Los Angeles, 1960, 61, 64; Los Angeles/County MA (two-man), 1966, 78; Kasmin Ltd., 1968, 70; WMAA, 1969; Mizuno Gallery, 1969, 71; David Whitney Gallery, NYC, 1971; Galerie Hans R. Neuendorf, Cologne, 1971, Hamburg, 1971; D.M. Gallery, London, 1972; Nicholas Wilder Gallery, 1973; Felicity Samuel Gallery, London, 1974; The Willard Gallery, NYC, 1974, 79, 82, 83, 85; Ronald Greenberg Gallery, St. Louis, 1976; James Corcoran Galleries, Los Angeles, 1976; Los Angeles/County MA, 1978; Gallery of Contemporary Arts, Taos, 1978; The Texas Gallery, Houston, 1979, 80, 84; Hansen Fuller Goldeen Gallery, San Francisco, 1979; School of Visual Arts, NYC, 1980; James Corcoran Gallery, Los Angeles, 1980, 82; Houston/Contemporary, 1980; Betsy Rosenfield Gallery, Chicago, 1980, 84; Leo Castelli Gallery, Inc., NYC, 1983;

Harcus Gallery, Boston, 1984; Jane Beggs Fine Arts, Aspen, Col., 1985. **Group:** SFMA, Fifty California Artists, circ., 1962; Pasadena/AM, New American Sculpture, 1964; Seattle/AM, Ten from Los Angeles, 1966; U. of California, Irvine, Abstract Expressionist Ceramics, 1966; Los Angeles/County MA, American Sculpture of the Sixties, 1967; MOMA, Tamarind; Homage to Lithography, 1969; Fort Worth Drawings, 1969; Pasadena/AM, West Coast: 1945-69, 1969; Eindhoven, Kompas IV, 1969-70; WMAA Biennial, 1970; Brooklyn Museum, Print Annual, 1980; Hayward Gallery, London, Eleven Los Angeles Artists, 1971; MOMA, Technics and Creativity: Gemini: G.E.L. 1971; Cologne/Kunstverein, USA, West Coast, 1972; Rotterdam (three-man exhibition), 1972; NCFA, Sculpture: American Directions, 1945-1975, 1975; WMAA, 200 Years of American Sculpture, 1976; Brooklyn Museum, 30 Years of American Printmaking, 1976; Syracuse/Everson, New Works in Clay by Contemporary Painters and Sculptors, 1976; Syracuse/Everson, A Century of Ceramics in the U.S., 1878-1978, 1979; WMAA Biennial, 1979; WMAA Biennial, 1981; WMAA, Ceramic Sculpture: Six Artists, 1981; Indianapolis, 1982; Dusseldorf/Kunsthalle, A Different Climate, 1984; MOMA, International Survey of Recent Painting and Sculpture, 1984; American Craft Museum, Craft Today: Poetry of the Physical, 1986. **Collections:** Chicago/AI; Eindhoven; Denver; Hirshhorn; Los Angeles/County MA; MOMA; Pasadena/AM; Art Museum of South Texas; SFMA; Victoria and Albert; WMAA. **Bibliography:** Selz, P., 2; *The State of California Painting; USA West Coast.*

QUAYTMAN, HARVEY. b. April 20, 1937, Far Rockaway, N.Y. **Studied:** Syracuse U., 1955-57; Skowhegan School, 1957; Boston Museum School, with Jan Cox, 1957-60; Tufts U., 1957-60, BFA; Royal College of Art, London, 1961-62. **Taught:** Tufts U., 1959; Boston Museum School, 1960, 1962-63; Middlebury College, 1961; Newton Creative Arts Center, 1961, 63, 64; Roxbury (Mass.) Latin School, 1962-63; Harvard U., 1961, 64, 65; School of Visual Arts, NYC, 1969-71; Cooper Union, 1972-77; Syracuse U., 1977; Parsons School of Design, 1978. **Awards:** New York Board of Regents Scholarship, 1955-57; Boston/MFA; James William Paige Traveling Fellowship, 1960; CAPS, 1973; Guggenheim Foundation Fellowship, 1979, 85; National Endowment for the Arts, 1983. **Address:** 231 Bowery, NYC 10002. **Dealer:** David McKee Gallery. **One-man Exhibitions:** A.I.A. Gallery, London, 1962; Ward-Nasse Gallery, Boston, 1964; Royal Marks Gallery, 1966; Ohio State U., 1967; Houston/Contemporary, 1967, 73; Paula Cooper Gallery, 1967, 71; U. of Rochester, 1972; Galerie Onnasch, Cologne, 1971; Galerie Mikro, Berlin, 1971; Galleri Ostergren, Malmo, 1973; Henri 2, Washington, D.C., 1973; Cunningham-Ward Gallery, 1974; David McKee Gallery, 1975, 77, 78, 80, 82, 84, 85; Nielsen Gallery, Boston, 1976, 78, 80, 83; Charles Casat Gallery, La Jolla, 1977; Galerie Arnseen, Copenhagen, 1981; Galerie Nordenhake, Malmo, 1982, 86; Harvard U., 1983; Storrer Gallery, Zurich, 1983; Galleria Katarina, Helsinki, 1984. **Group:** ICA, Boston, Painting without a Brush, 1965; U. of Illinois, 1967; WMAA Annuals, 1969, 71, 73; Indianapolis, 1970; Jewish Museum, Beautiful Painting & Sculpture, 1970; Foundation Maeght, 1970; WMAA, The Structure of Color, 1971; UCLA, Fourteen Abstract Painters, 1975; ICA, Boston, Contemporary Painters, 1975; High Museum, The New Image, 1975; Rice U., Drawing Today in New York, 1976; U. of Texas, Austin, New Painting in New York, 1977; Rutgers U., Contemporary American Abstractionists, 1979; Buffalo/Albright, Contructivism and the Geometric Tradition, 1979; Grand Palais, Paris, L'Amerique aux Indépendants, 1980; Denver/AM, Constructivism in the Geometric Tradition, 1982; Long Island U., Abstract Painting as Surface and Object, 1985. **Collections:** Boston/MFA; Brandeis U.; Canberra/National; Carnegie; Chase Manhattan Bank; Corcoran; Cornell U.; Dartmouth College; Emory U.; Harvard U.; Houston/MFA; Humlebaek/Louisiana; Israel Museum; Kent State U.; U. of Massachusetts; MIT; MOMA; Malmo; McCrory Corp.; NYC; Middlebury College; U. of Minnesota, Duluth; NYU; Oberlin College; Pasadena/AM; Port Authority of New York & New Jersey; Prudential Insurance Co. of America; Purchase/SUNY; Rutgers U.; Satakumman Museo; U. of Sydney; Tate Gallery; Tel Aviv; Trenton/State; VMFA; Wellington/National Gallery; WMAA; Worcester/AM; Wright State U. **Bibliography:** *New in the Seventies.*

QUISGARD, LIZ WHITNEY. b. October 23, 1929, Philadelphia, Pa. **Stud-**

ied: Johns Hopkins U.; U. of Baltimore; Maryland Institute, 1947-49, MFA, 1966; privately with Morris Louis, 1957-60. Traveled Europe, North America. **Taught:** Baltimore Hebrew Congregation, 1962-78; Maryland Institute, 1965-76; Goucher College, 1966-68; U. of Maryland, 1970-71; Baltimore Jewish Community Center, 1974-78; Villa Julia College, 1978-81. Art critic, *Baltimore Sun,* 1968-70. Set designer for theater productions at Goucher College, Center Stage, and Theater Hopkins, 1966-; Villa Julia College, Stevenson, Md.; Beth El Congregation, Baltimore. **Commission:** William Fell School, Baltimore, mural. **Awards:** Baltimore/MA, Second Prize, 1958; Maryland Institute, Fellow of the Rinehart School of Sculpture, 1964-65; National Scholastic Art Awards Scholarship; E. M. Reed Scholarship; Maryland Arts Council, Grant, 1979. **Address:** 145 Reade Street, NYC 10013. **Dealers:** Elaine Starkman Gallery, NYC; Henri Gallery, Washington, D.C.; Campanile Gallery, Chicago. **One-man Exhibitions:** (first) Ef Gallery, Baltimore, 1954; Main Gallery, Maryland Institute, 1955; Martick's Gallery, Baltimore, 1956, 58; Johns Hopkins U., 1958; Jefferson Place Gallery, 1961; Key Gallery, NYC, 1961; Andre Emmerich Gallery, NYC, 1962; Arts and Science Center, Nashua, N.J., 1975; Gannon College, Erie, Pa., 1978; Mechanics Gallery, Baltimore, 1978; Fells Point Gallery, Baltimore, 1980; Marymount Manhattan College, 1983; Mussavi Arts Center, NYC, 1984; Elaine Starkman Gallery, 1984; Fordham U., 1985; Art Institute of Pittsburgh, 1987; Henri Gallery, 1987. **Group:** Peale Museum, Baltimore, 1947, 50; Baltimore/MA, 1951, 52, 53, 58; Youngstown/Butler, 1956; Corcoran, 1957, 64; PAFA Annual, 1964. **Collections:** U. of Arizona; U. of Baltimore; Hampton School; Johns Hopkins U.

R

RABKIN, LEO. b. July 21, 1919, Cincinnati, Ohio. **Studied:** U. of Cincinnati, BA, B. Ed.; Art Academy of Cincinnati; NYU, with Robert Iglehart, Hale Woodruff, Tony Smith, William Baziotes, MA. Traveled Mexico, Europe, Guatemala. **Taught:** NYC public school system. **Member:** American Abstract Artists (past president). **Awards:** MOMA, Larry Aldrich **P.P.,** 1959; Ford Foundation, **P.P.,** 1961; Silvermine Guild, Watercolor Award, 1961, 64. **Address:** 218 West 20th Street, NYC 10011. **Dealer:** Marilyn Pearl Gallery, NYC. **One-man Exhibitions:** (first) Stairway Gallery, NYC, 1954; Muriel Latow Gallery, NYC, 1961; Gotham Gallery, New Hope, Pa., 1961; Louis Alexander Gallery, NYC, 1962, 63; Gertrude Kasle Gallery, 1965; Richard Feigen Gallery, 1965, 67; Drew U., 1966; Benson Gallery, 1970; Fairleigh Dickinson U., 1971; Allentown/AM, 1977; Truman Gallery, NYC, 1978, 79; Parsons-Dreyfuss Gallery, NYC, 1980; Hal Bromm Gallery, NYC, 1980; La Jolla, 1981; Marilyn Pearl Gallery, 1981, 83, 84; Deicas Art Gallery, La Jolla, 1982. **Retrospective:** Storm King Art Center, 1970. **Group:** Brooklyn Museum, Watercolor Biennial; Hirschl & Adler Galleries, Inc., NYC, Experiences in Art, I & II, 1959, 60; MOMA, New Talent; WMAA Annual, 1959; Martha Jackson Gallery, New Media—New Forms, I & II, 1960, 61; MOMA, Abstract American Drawings and Watercolors, circ., Latin America, 1961-63; A.F.A., Affinities, circ., 1962; SRGM, 1962, 65; American Abstract Artists Annuals, 1963, 64, 66, 68, 70; WMAA, 1959, 60, 61, 64, 66, 68, 69; Eindhoven, 1966; Walker, Light Motion Space, 1967; Smithsonian, 1967; Trenton/State, Focus on Light, 1967; Brooklyn Museum Print Exhibitions; Finch College, NYC, Destructionists, 1968; Milwaukee, A Plastic Presence, circ., 1969; Honolulu Academy, 1971; Sculptors Guild, 1972, 74; Brooklyn Museum, Print Exhibition, 1972; Drew U., Reality in Art, 1978; Betty Parsons Gallery, NYC, American Abstract Artists, 1979; Albright College, Small Is Beautiful, 1979; U. of North Carolina, American Abstract Artists, 1983. **Collections:** Brooklyn Museum; U. of California, Berkeley; Chase Manhattan Bank; Ciba-Geigy Corp.; La Jolla; MOMA; Mc Crory Corporation; NYU; Purchase/SUNY; Raleigh/NCMA; Randolph-Macon College; SRGM; Savings Bank Association of New York State; The Singer Company, Inc.; Smithsonian; Storm King Art Center; Virginia Commonwealth U.; WMAA; Woodward Foundation. **Bibliography:** Toher, ed. Archives.

RACZ, ANDRE. b. November 21, 1916, Cluj, Rumania. **Studied:** U. of Bucharest, 1935, BA; Atelier 17, NYC, 1943-45; New School for Social Research, 1943-45. To USA, 1939; citizen, 1948. Traveled Europe, Latin America, Mexico. **Taught:** U. of Chile, 1957; Columbia U., 1951-83; U. of Kentucky, 1960. **Member:** American Association of University Professors; SAGA. **Awards:** SAGA, Mrs. A. W. Erickson Prize, 1953; Noyes Memorial Prize, 1955; Guggenheim Foundation Fellowship, 1956; Fulbright Research Scholar (Chile), 1957; U. of Kentucky, **P.P.,** 1959; Ford Foundation, **P.P.,** 1962; Columbia U., Bankroft Award for Distinguished Teacher, 1983. **Address:**

P.O. Box 43, Demarest, NJ 07627. **One-man Exhibitions:** (first) New School for Social Research, 1942; A.F.A., circ., 1948-51; Columbia U., 1983; and exhibits in NYC nearly every year. **Retrospective:** NYPL, 1954; Museo de Bellas Artes, Santiago, Chile, 1957; U. of Kentucky, 1960. **Group:** MOMA; WMAA Annuals; Brooklyn Museum; Corcoran; Library of Congress; MOMA, 50 Years of American Art, circ., Europe, 1955; I Inter-American Paintings and Prints Biennial, Mexico City, 1958; I International Religious Art Biennial, Salzburg, 1958; MOMA, American Prints, 1913-1963, 1974-75; Rutgers U., Surrealism and American Art, 1977; U. of Wisconsin, Atelier 17, 1977. **Collections:** Bibliotheque Nationale; Brooklyn Museum; Columbia U.; Cordoba/Provincial; George Washington U.; U. of Kentucky; Library of Congress; MMA; MOMA; Melbourne/National; U. of Minnesota; NYPL; National Gallery; Oslo/National; PMA; SFMA; Salzburg; Smith College; Smithsonian; WMAA; Youngstown/Butler. **Bibliography:** Baur 7; Hayter 2; Janis, S.; Moser 1.

RAFFAEL, JOSEPH. b. February 22, 1933, Brooklyn, N.Y. **Studied:** Cooper Union, 1951-54, with Sidney Delevante, Leo Manso; Yale U., with Josef Albers, James Brooks, BFA. Traveled Europe, Hawaiian Islands; resided Rome and Florence, 1958-60. **Taught:** U. of California, Davis, 1966, Berkeley, summer, 1969; School of Visual Arts, NYC, 1967-69; California State U., Sacramento, 1969-74. **Awards:** Yale-Norfolk Summer Art School Fellowship, 1954, 55; Fulbright Fellowship, 1958; L.C. Tiffany Grant, 1961; Tokyo Biennial, First Prize, Figurative Painting, 1974. **Address:** % Dealer. **Dealer:** Nancy Hoffman Gallery; John Berggruen, San Francisco; Fendrick Gallery, Washington, D.C. **One-man Exhibitions:** (first) Kanegis Gallery, 1958; Numero Galleria d'Arte, Florence, Italy, 1959; D'Arcy Gallery, NYC, 1962, 63;

Joseph Raffael *Haven* 1986

The Stable Gallery, 1965, 66, 68; Galleria Sperone, Turin, 1967 (two-man, with Lowell Nesbitt); Berkeley Gallery, San Francisco, 1968; Sacramento State U., 1969; U. of California, Berkeley, 1969, 73; Wichita/AM, 1970; Reese Palley Gallery, San Francisco, 1970, 72; U. of California, San Diego, 1971; Nancy Hoffman Gallery, NYC, 1972, 73, 74, 76, 79, 80, 82, 83, 84, 86; Chicago/Contemporary, 1973; Worcester/AM (three-man), 1974; de Young, 1975; Barbara Okum Gallery, St. Louis, 1974; U. of Saskatchewan, 1975; U. of Nevada, Las Vegas, 1975; Quay Gallery, San Francisco, 1976; Roy Boyd Gallery, Chicago, 1977; Arco Center for Visual Arts, Los Angeles, 1977; Museum of Fine Arts, St. Petersburg, Fla., 1977; Fendrick Gallery, Washington, D.C., 1978; Valparaiso U., 1971; John Berggruen Gallery, San Francisco, 1978; Columbus, Ga., 1980; Wake Forest U., 1980; John Berggruen Gallery, 81, 82; U. of Connecticut, 1981; U. of Wisconsin, 1981; Allport Assoc. Gallery, Larkspur, Calif., 1982; Jacksonville/AM, 1982; Saddleback Community College, 1982; Santa Ana Community College, 1982; Richard Gray Gallery, 1983; U. of Texas, 1983; Gibbes Art Gallery, Charleston, N.C., 1985; New York Academy of Sciences, 1985; Salt Lake City Art Center, 1985; Woltjen/Udell Gallery, Edmonton, 1986. **Retrospective:** SFMA, circ., 1978-79. **Group:** Brooklyn Museum; Chicago/AI, 1965; Corcoran, 1966; MOMA, Art in the Mirror, 1966, and others; ICA, U. of Pennsylvania, The Other Tradition, 1966; IX Sao Paulo Biennial, 1967; Los Angeles/County MA, 1967; U. of Illinois, 1967; U. of Miami, 1968; ICA, London, The Obsessive Image, 1968; Indianapolis/Herron, 1969; WMAA, Human Concern/Personal Torment, 1969; VMFA, American Painting, 1970; Darmstadt Biennial, 1970; U. of Miami, Phases of New Realism, 1972; Chicago/AI, 1972, 74; WMAA Annual, 1973; Cincinnati/Contemporary, Options, 70/30, 1973; Los Angeles Municipal Art Gallery, Separate Realities, 1973; Hartford/Wadsworth, New/Photo Realism, 1974; Indianapolis, 1974; U. of Illinois, 1974; Oklahoma, Contemporary American Landscape, 1974; Rutgers U., A Response to the Environment, 1975; Akron/AI, Contemporary Images in Watercolor, 1976; SFMA, California Painting and Sculpture: The Modern Era, 1976; Fort Wayne/AM, Hue and Far Cry of Color, 1976; PAFA, 8 Contemporary American Realists, 1977; U. of Missouri; St. Louis, West Coast Art 1970-76, 1977; Chicago/AI, Drawings of the '70's, 1977; Huntsville Museum of Art, Ala., The Modern Era: Bay Area Update, 1977; US Department of the Interior, America 1976, 1976; Sydney, Australia, Gallery Directors Council, Illusions and Reality, 1976; Indianapolis, Perceptions of the Spirit in 20th Century American Art, 1977; Creighton U., A Century of Master Drawings, 1978; Smithsonian, New American Monotypes, circ., 1978-80; Santa Barbara, Photo-realist Painting in California: A Survey, 1980; Montclair/AM, Josef Al-

bers: His Influence, 1981; PAFA, Contemporary American Realism Since 1960, circ., 1981; San Antonio/MA, Real, Really Real, Super Real, circ., 1981; Brooklyn Museum, The American Artist as Printmaker, 1983; Laguna Beach Museum of Art, West Coast Realism, 1983; Gallery Association of N.Y. State, Hamilton, Twentieth-Century American Watercolor, 1984; U. of Nebraska, San Francisco Bay Area Painting, 1984; WMAA, Reflections of Nature, 1984; Oakland/AM, Art in the San Francisco Bay Area, 1945-1980, 1985; SFMA, American Realism (Janss), 1985; Hudson River Museum, Form or Formula: Drawing and Drawings, 1986. **Collections:** Brooklyn Museum; U. of California, Berkeley; Charlotte/Mint; Chicago/AI; Chicago/Contemporary; Cleveland/MA; U. of Connecticut; Delaware Art Museum; Des Moines; U. of Florida; Fort Worth; U. of Georgia; Hagerstown/County MFA; Hirshhorn; U. of Illinois; Jacksonville/AM; Library of Congress; Long Beach/MA; Los Angeles/County MA; MMA; U. of Massachusetts; NCFA; U. of New Mexico; Oakland/AM; Omaha/Joslyn; PMA; SFMA; Sacramento/Crocker; St. Petersburg, Fla.; Santa Barbara/MA; Syracuse/Everson; Toledo/MA; Utah; VMFA; WMAA; Walker. **Bibliography:** *America 1976*; Arthur 1, 2, 4; Goodyear; Lindy; Lucie-Smith; *Three Realists*.

RAMBERG, CHRISTINA. b. 1946, Fort Campbell, Ky. **Studied:** Chicago Art Institute School, 1968, BA; 1973, MFA. **Address:** % Dealer. **Dealer:** Phyllis Kind Gallery, NYC & Chicago. **One-man Exhibitions:** Phyllis Kind Gallery, Chicago, 1974, 81; Phyllis Kind Gallery, NYC, 1977, 82. **Group:** Hyde Park Art Center, Chicago, False Image, 1968, 69; Chicago/Contemporary, Don Baum Sez, "Chicago Needs Famous Artists," 1969; ICA, U. of Pennsylvania, Spirit of the Comics, 1969; Chicago/Contemporary, Chicago Imagist Art, 1972; Ottawa/Ontario, What They're Up to in Chicago, 1972;

WMAA Biennials, 1972, 79; Sao Paulo, Biennale, 1973; Chicago Art Institute School, Former Famous Alumni, 1976; Sacramento/Crocker, The Chicago Connection, 1976; WMAA, The Figurative Tradition and the WMAA, 1980; Sunderland (Eng.) Arts Centre, Who Chicago?, circ., 1980; Kansas City/AI, Chicago Imagists, 1982; Chicago/Contemporary, Alternative Spaces: A History in Chicago, 1984. **Collections:** Ball State U.; Baltimore/MA; Baxter Laboratories, Chicago; Chase Manhattan Bank; Chicago/AI; Chicago/Contemporary; Elmhurst College; Museum des 20. Jahrhunderts, Vienna; NCFA; Phoenix; U. of Rochester; South Bend Art Center; Springfield, Ill./State; WMAA. **Bibliography:** *The Chicago Connection; Who Chicago?.*

RAMOS, MEL. b. July 24, 1935, Sacramento, Calif. **Studied:** San Jose State College, 1954-55; Sacramento State College, AB, MA, 1955-58. Traveled England, Spain, France, Italy, 1964, Hawaii, 1967, Africa. **Taught:** Mira Loma High School, Sacramento, Calif., 1960-66; California State College at Hayward, 1966-; Arizona State U., 1967. **Awards:** SFMA, **P.P.,** 1948; Oakland/AM, **P.P.,** 1959. **Address:** 5941 Ocean View Drive, Oakland, CA 94618; Moragrega 38, Horta de San Juan (Tarragone), Spain. **Dealer:** Louis K. Meisel Gallery, NYC. **One-man Exhibitions:** (first) The Bianchini Gallery, NYC, 1964, also 1965; David Stuart Gallery, Los Angeles, 1965, 67, 68, 74; Galerie Rolf Ricke, Kassel, 1966; Galerie Tobies-Silex, Cologne, 1967; Berkeley Gallery (two-man), 1967; SFMA, 1967; Galleries Reese Palley, 1969; Galerie Bischofberger, Zurich, 1971; Utah, 1972; Louis K. Meisel Gallery, NYC, 1974, 76, 81; Krefeld/Haus Lange, 1975; U. of Nevada, 1978; Galleria Cadaques, Spain, 1979; Morgan Gallery, Shawnee Mission, Mo., 1977; California State U., Chico, 1979; U. of Nevada, 1978; Galeria Plura, Milan, 1978. **Retrospec-**

tives: Krefeld/Kaiser Wilhelm, 1975; Oakland/MA, 1977; Brandeis U., 1980. **Group:** California Palace, 1959, 60, 61, Painters behind Painters, 1967; Houston/Contemporary, Pop Goes the Easel, 1963; Oakland/AM, Pop Art USA, 1963; Los Angeles/County MA, 1963; Buffalo/Albright, Mixed Media and Pop Art, 1963; ICA, London, The Popular Image, 1963; II American Art Biennial, Cordoba, Argentina, 1964; Akademie der Kunst, Berlin, 1965; Palais des Beaux-Arts, Brussels, 1965; Hamburg, 1965; Milwaukee, 1965; La Jolla, 1966; Portland, Ore./AM, 1968; WMAA, Human Concern/Personal Torment, 1969; Omaha/Joslyn, Looking West, 1970; WMAA, American Pop Art, 1974; U. of Illinois, 1974; New York Cultural Center, Three Centuries of the American Nude, 1975; SFMA, California Painting and Sculpture: The Modern Era, 1976; WMAA, Art about Art, 1978; Berlin/National, Aspekte der 60er Jahre, 1978; Indianapolis, 1980; Brooklyn Museum, American Drawings in Black and White: 1970-1979, 1980; WMAA (Downtown Branch), The Comic Art Show, 1983. **Collections:** Aachen; Indianapolis; Krefeld/Kaiser Wilhelm; Norfolk/Chrysler; Oakland/AM; SFMA; U.S. Pro Action, Inc., Reno. **Bibliography:** Alloway 1; Honisch and Jensen, eds.; *Kunst um 1970;* Lippard 5; Lucie-Smith; *Mel Ramos: Watercolors;* Murken-Altrogge; Sager.

RANDELL, RICHARD, K. b. 1929, Minneapolis, Minn. **Taught:** Assistant to John Rood, Minneapolis, 1954-57; Hamline U., 1954-61; Macalaster College, 1961; U. of Minnesota, 1961-65; Sacramento State College, 1966. **Awards:** Walker Biennial, **P.P.,** 1956, 62, 66; Minneapolis/Institute, First Prize and **P.P.,** 1957, Hon. Mention, 1959; St. Paul Gallery, **P.P.,** 1961. **Address:** % Dealer. **Dealer:** Smith-Anderson Gallery, Palo Alto, Calif. **One-man Exhibitions:** Walker, 1959, 64; Minneapolis/Institute, 1964; Royal

Marks Gallery, 1965, 66, 68, 69, 71. **Group:** Minneapolis/Institute, 1956, 57, 59, 61, 63; Walker Biennial, 1956, 58, 62, 66; PAFA Annual, 1959; Detroit/Institute, 1959; Chicago/AI Annual, 1961; St. Paul Gallery, 1961; Museum of Contemporary Crafts, 1963; M. Knoedler & Co., Art across America, circ., 1965-67; New York World's Fair, 1964-65; The Ohio State U., 1966; U. of Illinois, 1967; Los Angeles/County MA, American Sculpture of the Sixties, 1967; Southern Illinois U., 1967; Indianapolis/Herron, 1967. **Collections:** Minneapolis/Institute; Minnesota/MA; U. of Minnesota; Walker. **Bibliography:** Friedman, M., 2; Tuchman 1.

RATTNER, ABRAHAM. b. July 8, 1895, Poughkeepsie, N.Y.; **d.** February 14, 1978, New York. **Studied:** George Washington U.; The Corcoran School of Art; PAFA, 1916-17; Academie des Beaux-Arts, Paris; Academie Julian, Paris; Academie Ranson, Paris; Academie de la Grande Chaumiere, 1920. US Army, 1917-19. Traveled Europe, USA; resided New York and Paris. **Taught:** New School for Social Research, 1947-55; Yale U., 1949; Brooklyn Museum School, 1950-51; American Academy, Rome, 1951; U. of Illinois, 1952-54; ASL, 1954; PAFA, 1954; Sag Harbor Summer Art Center, 1956; Michigan State U., 1956-58. **Commissions:** St. Francis Monastery, Chicago, 1956; Fairmount Temple, Cleveland, 1957; Loop Synagogue, Chicago, 1958; Duluth (Minn.) Synagogue; De Waters Art Center, Flint, Mich., 1958; US Navy Department, Washington, D.C. **Awards:** PAFA, Cresson Fellowship, 1919; PAFA, Joseph E. Temple Gold Medal, 1945; Pepsi-Cola, Second Prize, 1946; La Tausca Competition, First Prize, 1947; Carnegie, Hon. Men., 1949; U. of Illinois. **P.P.,** 1950; Corcoran, First Prize, 1953; NIAL, 1958. **One-man Exhibitions:** (first) Galerie Bonjean, Paris, 1935; Julien Levy Galleries, NYC, 1936-41; Courvoisier Gallery, San Francisco, 1940; Arts Club of Chicago, 1940; P. Rosenberg and Co., 1943, 44, 46, 48, 50, 52, 56; Stendahl Gallery, Los Angeles, 1943; Santa Barbara/MA, 1943; Philadelphia Art Alliance, 1945; Arts and Crafts Club, New Orleans, 1952; Chicago/AI, 1955; Renaissance Society, 1957; The Downtown Gallery, 1957, 58, 60, 66; Corcoran, 1958; North Shore Congregation Israel, Chicago, 1958; WMAA, 1959 (four-man); Galerie Internationale, NYC, 1961; The Contemporaries, NYC, 1967; Kennedy Gallery, 1969, 70, 72, 74, 75, 78, 79, 81; New School for Social Research, 1970; NCFA, 1976. **Retrospectives:** Baltimore/MA, 1946; Vassar College, 1948; U. of Illinois, 1952; A.F.A., circ., 1960. **Group:** PAFA; Corcoran; Chicago/AI; U. of Illinois; Carnegie; MMA; WMAA; Buffalo/Albright; Baltimore/MA; Detroit/Institute; Des Moines; New School for Social Research. **Collections:** Arizona State College; Ball State U.; Buffalo/Albright; CIT Corporation; Chicago/AI; Cornell U.; Dartmouth College; Des Moines; Detroit/Institute; Fort Worth; Hartford/Wadsworth; U. of Illinois; Jewish Museum; Johnson College; MMA; Manufacturers Hanover Trust Co.; Marquette U.; Michigan State U.; Musée du Jeu de Paume; U. of Nebraska; Newark Museum; New School for Social Research; U. of Oklahoma; PAFA; PMA; Phillips; St. Louis/City; Santa Barbara/MA; Vassar College; WMAA; Walker; Washington U.; Williams College; Yale U.; Youngstown/Butler. **Bibliography:** Baur 5, 7; Biddle 4; Eliot; Frost; Genauer; Getlein 2; **Goodrich and Baur** 1, **2;** Hayter 1, 2; Janis, S.; Kootz 2; Leepa; Mendelowitz; Moser 1, Newtown 1; Nordness ed.; Pagano; Pearson 2; Pousette-Dart, ed.; Read 2; Richardson, E.P.; Weller, Wight 2. Archives.

RAUSCHENBERG, ROBERT. b. October 22, 1925, Port Arthur, Tex. **Studied:** Kansas City Art Institute and School of Design, 1946-47; Academie

Robert Rauschenberg *Tatoo (Spread)* 1981

Julian, Paris, 1947; Black Mountain College, 1948-49, with Josef Albers; ASL, 1949-50, with Vaclav Vytlacil, Morris Kantor. US Navy. Traveled Italy, North Africa, 1952-53. **Taught:** Black Mountain College, 1952. Designs stage sets and costumes for the Merce Cunningham Dance Co. (since 1955); technical director since early 1960s. **Awards:** Gallery of Modern Art, Ljubljana, Yugoslavia, V International Exhibition of Prints, First Prize, 1963; XXXII Venice Biennial, First Prize, 1964; Corcoran, First Prize, 1965; New York City Mayor's Award of Honor in Arts and Culture, 1977; RISD, President's Fellow Award, 1978; Skowhegan School, Medal for Painting, 1982; Officier des Arts et Lettres, France, 1981; Royal Academy of Fine Arts, Sweden, elected foreign member. **Address:** 381 Lafayette Street, NYC 10003. **Dealer:** Leo Castelli, Inc. **One-man Exhibitions:** Betty Parsons Gallery, 1951; The Stable Gallery, 1953; Gallerie d'Arte Contemporanea, Florence, Italy, 1953; Charles Egan Gallery, 1955; Leo Castelli, Inc., NYC, 1958-61, 63, 65, 67-69, 70, 71, 73, 74, 75, 77, 79, 80, 82, 83, 84; La Tartaruga, Rome, 1959; Galerie 22, Dusseldorf, 1959; Daniel Cordier, Paris, 1961; Galleria dell'Ariete, 1961; Dwan Gallery, 1962; L'Obelisco, Rome, 1963; Ileana Sonnabend Gallery, Paris, 1963, 64, 71, 72, 73, 75, 77, NYC, 1974, 77, 79, 81, 82, 83, 84; Galleria Civica d'Arte Moderna, Turin, 1964; Amerika Haus, Berlin, 1965; Contemporary Arts Society, Houston, 1965; Walker, 1965; Stockholm/National, 1965; MOMA, 1966, 68; Douglas Gallery, Vancouver, 1967, 69; Amsterdam/Stedelijk, 1968; Peale House, Philadelphia, 1968; Cologne/Kunstverein, 1968;

Paris/Moderne, 1968; Fort Worth, 1969; Newport Harbor, 1969; Phoenix, 1970; Seattle/AM, 1970; ICA, U. of Pennsylvania, 1970, 71, 75; Automation House, NYC, 1970; New York Cultural Center, 1970; Minneapolis/Institute, 1970; Hannover/Kunstverein, 1970; Chicago/Contemporary, 1970; Fort Worth, 1970; Galerie Rene Ziegler, Zurich, 1970; Visual Arts Gallery, NYC, 1970; Chicago/AI, 1971; Centro C., Caracas, 1971; Galerie Buren, Stockholm, 1972; F. H. Mayor Gallery, London, 1973, 78; ACE Gallery, Venice, Calif., 1973, 74, 77, 79; Jack Glenn Gallery, San Diego, 1973; Galerie Mikro, Berlin, 1974; Jerusalem National, 1974; Modern Art Agency, Naples, 1974; Galerie Sonnabend, Geneva, 1974; Jared Sable Gallery, Toronto, 1974; Margo Leavin Gallery, Los Angeles, 1975, 76; Galerie de Gestlo, Hamburg, 1975; ACE Gallery, Vancouver, 1973, 75; Galerie Tanit, Munich, 1975, 79; Museo d'Arte Radema, Venice, 1975; Greenberg Gallery, St. Louis, 1976; H.M., Brussels, 1976; Alberta College, 1976; Robinson Galleries, Houston, 1977; Galerie Rudolf Zwirner, Cologne, 1977; Linda Farris Gallery, Seattle, 1977; Janie C. Lee Gallery, Houston, 1977; Vancouver Art Gallery, 1978; Richard Gray Gallery, Chicago, 1979; Richard Hines Gallery, Seattle, 1979; Portland (Ore.) Center for the Visual Arts, 1979; Kunsthalle, Tubingen, 1979; Musée d'Art, Toulon, France, 1979; Tucson/MA, 1979; Palm Springs Desert Museum, 1979; Galerie Mathilde, Amsterdam, 1979; Ohio State U., 1980; West Coast Gallery, Newport Beach, 1980; Ace Gallery, Vancouver, 1980; Baltimore/MA, 1980; Cranbrook, 1980; Galleriet Kungsgatan, Lund, Sweden, 1980; Mat tingly Baker Gallery, Dallas, 1980; School of Visual Arts, NYC, 1980; Galerie im Lenbachhaus, Munich, 1981; Gibbes Art Gallery, Charleston, N.C., 1981; C. Grimaldis Gallery, Baltimore, 1981; ICA, Boston, 1981; Magnuson-Lee Gallery, Boston, 1981; The New Gallery, Cleveland, 1981; Paris/Beaubourg, 1981; Galerie Watari,

Tokyo, 1981; Rosamund Felsen Gallery, Los Angeles, 1982; Flow Ace Gallery, Paris, 1982; Hara Museum, Tokyo, 1982; Long Beach/MA, 1982; MOMA, 1982; Van Straaten Gallery, Chicago, 1982; Thomas Babeor Gallery, La Jolla, Calif., 1983; Canberra/National, 1983; Cooper Union, 1983; G. H. Dalsheimer, Baltimore, 1983; Flow Ace Gallery, Los Angeles, 1983; Susanne Hilberry Gallery, Birmingham, Mich., 1983; Galerie Beyeler, Basel, 1984; Foundation Maeght, 1984; Fay Gold Gallery, Atlanta, 1984; Helland Thorden Wetterling Galleries, Stockholm, 1984; Houston/Contemporary, 1984. **Retrospectives:** Jewish Museum, 1963; Whitechapel Art Gallery, London, 1964; NCFA, circ., 1976; Berlin, circ., 1980; Tate Gallery, 1981. **Group:** The Stable Gallery Annuals, 1951-56; Jewish Museum, The New York School, Second Generation, 1957; A.F.A., Collage in America, circ., 1957-58; Houston/MFA, Collage International, 1958; Carnegie, 1958, 61, 64, 67; A.F.A., Art and Found Object, circ., 1959; I Paris Biennial, 1959; Daniel Cordier, Paris, Exposition Internationale de Surrealisme, 1959; MOMA, Sixteen Americans, circ., 1959; V & IX Sao Paulo Biennials, 1959, 67; Documenta II & IV, Kassel, 1959, 68; A.F.A., School of New York—Some Younger American Painters, 1960; Martha Jackson Gallery, New Media—New Forms, I & II, 1960, 61; Des Moines, Six Decades of American Painting, 1961; MOMA, The Art of Assemblage, circ., 1961; SRGM, Abstract Expressionists and Imagists, 1961; Galerie Rive Droite, Paris, Le Nouveau Realisme, 1961; MOMA, Abstract Watercolors and Drawings: USA, circ., Latin America and Europe, 1961-62; SRGM/USIA, American Vanguard, circ., Europe, 1961-62; Stockholm/National, 4 Americans, circ., 1962; Salon du Mai, Paris, 1962; Seattle World's Fair, 1962; III International Biennial Exhibition of Prints, Tokyo, 1962; Art: USA: Now, circ., 1962-67; SRGM, Six Painters and the Object, circ., 1963; WGMA, The Popular Image, 1963, Musée Cantonal des Beaux-Arts, Lausanne, I Salon International de Galeries Pilotes, 1963; ICA, London, The Popular Image, 1963; El Retiro Parquet, Madrid, Arte de America y Espana, 1963; Gallery of Modern Art, Ljubljana, Yugoslavia, V International Exhibition of Prints, 1963; Brandeis U., New Directions in American Painting, 1963; Jewish Museum, Black and White, 1963; Corcoran, 1963, 65; Chicago/AI, 1963, 66; Tate, Dunn International, 1964; Hartford/Wadsworth, Black, White, and Gray, 1964; New York State Pavilion, New York World's Fair, 1964-65; SRGM, 1964, 65; Kunstverein in Hamburg, 1965; U. of Texas, 1965; Cincinnati/Contemporary, 1965; Kansas City/Nelson, Sound, Light, Silence, 1966; Flint/Institute, I Flint Invitational, 1966; Expo '67, Montreal, 1967; MOMA, The 1960's, 1967; Eindhoven, 1967; Foundation Maeght, L'Art Vivant, circ., French museums, 1968; MOMA, Dada, Surrealism and Their Heritage, 1968; Milwaukee, Directions I: Options, circ., 1968; Jewish Museum, 1968; Vancouver, 1968; U. of California, Irvine, 1968; Arts Council of Great Britain, 1968; MMA, New York Painting and Sculpture: 1940-1970, 1969-70; Expo '70, Osaka, 1970; Los Angeles/County MA, Art & Technology, 1971; WMAA, 1973; Parcheggio di Villa Borghese, Rome, Contemporanea, 1974; Chicago/AI, Idea and Image in Recent Art, 1974; WMAA, American Pop Art, 1974; MOMA, Drawing Now, 1976; WMAA, 200 Years of American Sculpture, 1976; WMAA, New York on Paper, 1977; Williamstown/Clark, The Dada/Surrealist Heritage, 1977; Cambridge, Jubilation, 1977; Minnesota/MA, American Drawings, 1927-1977, 1977; NCFA, New Ways with Paper, 1978; WMAA, Art about Art, 1978; MOMA, Artists and Writers, 1978; Buffalo/Albright, American Painting of the 1970s, circ., 1978; Corcoran Biennial, 1979; Denver/AM, Poets and Painters, 1979; Brooklyn Museum, American Drawings in Black and White: 1970-1979,

1980; Grand Palais, Paris, Exposition des Artistes Indépendents, 1980; Hirshhorn, The Fifties: Aspects of Painting in New York, 1980; Purchase/SUNY, Hidden Desires, 1980; Akron/AM, The Image in American Painting and Sculpture 1950-1980, 1981; Purchase/SUNY, Soundings, 1981; Amsterdam/Stedelijk, '60-'80: Attitudes/Concepts/Images, 1982; Houston/Contemporary, The Americans: The Collage, 1982; ICA, U. of Pennsylvania, Connections, 1983; Boston/MFA, 10 Painters and Sculptors Draw, 1984; WMAA, Blam!, 1984. **Collections:** Aachen/Ludwig; Amsterdam/Stedelijk; Baltimore/MA; Buffalo/Albright; Chicago/Contemporary; Cologne; Cornell U.; Dusseldorf; Goucher College; Hartford/Wadsworth; Hirshhorn; Minneapolis/Institute; NCFA; Aachen/NG; PMA; Pasadena/AM; The Singer Company, Inc.; Stockholm/National; Tate; WMAA. **Bibliography:** Alloway 4, *Art Now 74;* Ashton 5; Atkinson; Battcock, ed.; Becker and Vostell; Bihalji-Merin; Callas, N. and E.; *Contemporanea;* Danto; Davis, D.; De Vries, ed.; De Wilde 2; Diamonstein; Dienst 1; Downes, ed.; Elsen 2; Finch; Friedman, ed.; Gablick; *Happening & Fluxus;* Haskell 5; Honisch and Jensen, eds.; Hulten; Hunter, ed.; Janis and Blesh 1; Johnson, Ellen H.; Kaprow; Kozloff 3; Kramer 2; *Kunst um 1970;* Licht, F.; Lippard 5; Lynton; *Metro;* Murken-Altrogge; Newmeyer; Nordness, ed.; O'Doherty; *Poets & Painters;* Read 3; *Report;* Rickey; Robert Rauschenberg; Rodman 3; Rose B., 1, 4; Rubin 1; Russell and Gablik; Sager; Sandler 1; Sontag; Tomkins and Time-Life Books; Tuchman 1; Warhol and Hackett; Weller.

REDER, BERNARD. b. June 29, 1897, Czernowitz, Bukovina, Austria; **d.** September 7, 1963, NYC. Austrian Army, 1914-18. **Studied:** Academy of Fine Arts, Prague, 1919, with Peter Bromse, Jan Stursa. Traveled Cuba, USA, Europe extensively. To USA, 1943; citizen,

1948. **Awards:** International architectural competition to house the monument to Christopher Columbus in Santo Domingo, 1927; Ford Foundation Grant, Program in Humanities and the Arts ($10,000), 1960. **One-man Exhibitions:** (first) The Rudolphinium, Prague, 1928 (watercolors); Manes Gallery, Prague, 1935; Galerie de Berri, Paris, 1940; Lyceum Gallery, Havana, 1942; U. of Ravenna, 1942; Weyhe Gallery, 1943; Philadelphia Art Alliance, 1950; Bezalel Museum, 1950; The Print Club, Philadelphia, 1950; Tel Aviv, 1950, 63; Grace Borgenicht Gallery, Inc., 1951, 52, 53; Dominion Gallery, Montreal, 1953; Chicago/AI, 1953; Galleria d'Arte Moderna L'Indiano, Florence, Italy, 1956, 57; The Contemporaries, NYC, 1956; Palazzo Torrigiani, Florence, Italy, 1957; World House Galleries, NYC, 1951, 61. **Retrospective:** WMAA, 1961. **Group:** WMAA, European Artists in America, 1945; Chicago/AI; PMA, 1949; MOMA, 1949, 51; U. of Illinois, 1953. **Collections:** Baltimore/MA; Brooklyn Museum; Chicago/AI; Harvard U.; Jewish Museum; MMA; MOMA; NYPI; National Gallery; PMA; Sao Paulo. **Bibliography: Bernard Reder;** Goodrich and Baur 1; Licht, F. Archives.

REICHEK, JESSE. b. August 16, 1916, Brooklyn, N.Y. **Studied:** Institute of Design, Chicago, 1941-42; Academie Julian, Paris (diploma), 1947-51. US Army Engineers, 1942-46. Traveled Europe, India, the Orient; resided Paris, India. **Taught:** U. of Michigan, 1946-47; Illinois Institute of Technology, 1951-53; U. of California, Berkeley, 1953-; American Academy, Rome, 1971. **Awards:** Graham Foundation Grant, 1962; Tamarind Fellowship, 1966. **Address:** 5925 Red Hill Road, Petaluma, CA 94952. **One-man Exhibitons:** (first) Galerie des Cahiers d'Art, 1951, also 1959; U. of California, 1954; Betty Parsons Gallery, 1958-60, 63, 65, 67, 68, 70; Wittenborn Gallery, NYC, 1962; Molton Gallery, London,

1962; Bennington College, 1963; American Cultural Center, Florence, Italy, 1964; U. of New Mexico, 1966; Axiom Gallery, London, 1968; Yoseido Gallery, Tokyo, 1968; Galeria Van der Voort, 1969; Los Angeles/County MA, 1971. **Retrospective:** U. of Southern California, 1967. **Group:** Brooklyn Museum, 1959; MOMA, 1962; Buffalo/Albright, 1965; Cincinnati/AM, 1966; Arts Club of Chicago, 1966; Cranbrook, 1967; Finch College, 1967; Caracas, 1969; Foundation Maeght, 1971. **Collections:** Bibliotheque Nationale; U. of California; Amon Carter Museum; Chicago/AI; Grunwald Foundation; La Jolla; Los Angeles/County MA; MOMA; U. of New Mexico; Pasadena/AM; San Diego; Victoria and Albert. **Bibliography:** *Report.*

REINHARDT, AD. b. December 24, 1913, Buffalo, N.Y.; **d.** August 30, 1967, NYC. **Studied:** Columbia U., with Meyer Schapiro, 1931-35, BA, 1936-37; NAD, 1936-37, with Francis Criss, Carl Holty; NYU, Institute of Fine Arts, 1945-51, with Alfred Salmony. US Navy photographer, 1944-45. Traveled Europe and Asia extensively. **Taught:** Brooklyn College, 1947-67; California School of Fine Arts, 1950; U. of Wyoming, 1951; Yale U., 1952-53; Syracuse U., 1957; Hunter College, 1959-67. Worked for *PM* (newspaper), NYC, 1944-47. Articles in *Art International, Art News, College Art Journal, It Is* (magazines). **Member:** American Abstract Artists, 1937-47; Asia Society; Chinese Art Society. Federal A.P.: Easel painting, 1936-39. **One-man Exhibitions:** (first) Columbia U., 1943; Artists Gallery, NYC, 1944; Mortimer Brandt, NYC, 1945; Brooklyn Museum School, 1946; Betty Parsons Gallery, 1946-53, 55, 56, 59, 60; Syracuse U., 1957; Leverkusen, 1961; Dwan Gallery, 1961, 63; Iris Clert Gallery, 1963; ICA, London, 1964; Marlborough Gallery Inc., NYC, 1970, 74, 77, 80; Irving Blum Gallery, Los Angeles, 1970; Richard Feigen Gallery, 1970; Dusseldorf/Kunsthalle,

1972; Eindhoven, 1973; Marlborough Galerie AG, Zurich, 1974; The Pace Gallery, NYC, 1976, 82; Truman Gallery, 1976; WMAA, 1980; SRGM, 1980; Margo Leavin Gallery, Los Angeles, 1984; Galerie Karstein Greve, Cologne, 1985; Staatsgalerie, Stuttgart, 1985. **Retrospective:** Jewish Museum, 1967. **Group:** New York World's Fair, 1939; American Abstract Artists Annuals; MOMA, Abstract Painting and Sculpture in America, 1951; WMAA, The New Decade, 1954-55, and others; Brussels World's Fair, 1958; SRGM, Abstract Expressionists and Imagists, 1961; Seattle World's Fair, 1962; MOMA, Americans 1963, circ., 1963-64; Tate, 1964; WMAA, The 1930's, 1968; MOMA, The New American Painting and Sculpture, 1969; Buffalo/Albright, Color and Field: 1890-1970, 1970; Milwaukee, Color Renaissance, 1974. **Collections:** Baltimore/MA; Buffalo/Albright; Dayton/AI; Leverkusen; Los Angeles/County MA; MOMA; U. of Nebraska; Oslo/National; PMA; SFMA; Toledo/MA; WMAA; Yale U. **Bibliography:** Alloway 4; Battcock, ed.; Blesh 1; Calas, N. and E.; *Contemporanea;* Coplans 3; Danto; De Vries, ed.; Downes, ed.; Goossen 1; Hess, T.B., 1; Hobbs and Levin; Honisch and Jensen, eds.; Janis and Blesh 1; Janis, S.; Lane and Larsen; Lippard 1, 3, **7;** MacAgy 2; McChesney; **Motherwell and Reinhardt, eds.;** Murken-Altrogge; Rickey; Ritchie 1; Rodman 1; Rose, B., 1, 4; Rose, ed.; Sandler; Sandler 1; Tomkins 2; Tuchman, ed.; Tuchman 3; Weller. Archives.

REINHARDT, SIEGFRIED GERHARD. b. July 31, 1925, Eydkuhnen, Germany. To USA, 1928; citizen, 1936. **Studied:** Washington U., AB. **Taught:** Washington U., 1955-70. **Commissions:** (murals) St. Louis Airport; Fabick Tractor Co. US Army, 1944-46. **Awards:** Scholarship, John Herron Art Institute, 1943; 20th Century Book Club Award, 1945; St. Louis Artists' Guild, 1951, 53, 54, 55, 57, 58; St. Louis/City, 1951, 53, 55, 56; Cincinnati/AM, 1958; International Novara, Trieste, 1961; Hon. DFA, London Institute for Applied Research, 1973; Doctor of Humanities, Occidental U., 1977; DFA and Humanities, Concordia Seminary, 1977. **Address:** 635 Craig Woods Drive, Kirkwood 22, MO 63122. **Dealer:** The Midtown Galleries. **One-man Exhibitions:** Eleanor Smith Gallery, St. Louis, 1942, 43, 47; Southern Illinois U., 1951, 52, 69; St. Louis Artists' Guild, 1951, 58; Stevens-Gross Gallery, Chicago, 1952; Art Mart, Clayton, Mo., 1953; Texas Western College, 1954; Illinois State Normal U., Normal, Ill., 1954; Martin Schweig Gallery, 1956; Hewitt Gallery, NYC, 1957; The Midtown Galleries, 1961, 66; St. Louis Artists Guild, 1958, 65; Chase Park Plaza Hotel, St. Louis, 1967; U. of Miami, 1968; Tulsa/Philbrook, 1969; Southern Illinois, The School of the Ozarks, 1969; Jack O'Grady Galleries, Chicago, 1977. **Group:** St. Louis/City 1943, 45, 47, 49, 51, 53, 58, 61; Chicago/AI, 1947, 54; Washington U., 1950; MMA, 1950; Los Angeles/County MA, 1951, 55; WMAA, 1951-55, 1960; Walker, 1954; Dallas/MFA, 1954; Beloit College, 1954; A.F.A. (stained glass), circ.; Cincinnati/AM, 1955, 58, 61; ICA, Boston, 1958; PAFA, 1958, ART:USA:58, NYC, 1958; Kansas State College, 1958; USIA, circ., Europe, 1959; Boston/MFA, 1960, 61; Columbus, 1961; Trieste, 1961; NAD, 1977. **Collections:** AAAL; Abbott Laboratories; Beloit College; Cincinnati/AM; Concordia Teachers College (Neb.); Jacksonville/Cummer; Kansas City/Nelson; Newark Museum; RISD; St. Louis/City; Southern Illinois U.; WMAA. **Bibliography:** Nordness, ed.; Pousette-Dart, ed.

REMINGTON, DEBORAH. b. June 25, 1930, Haddonfield, N.J. **Studied:** California School of Fine Arts, 1949-52; San Francisco Art Institute, BFA, 1955. Traveled Asia, 1955-58, Europe,

1967-68. **Taught:** San Francisco Art Institute, 1958-65, 66, 68; U. of California, Davis, 1962; San Francisco State College, 1965; Cooper Union, 1970-. **Awards:** Tamarind Fellowship, 1973; National Endowment for the Arts, fellowship, 1979; Guggenheim Foundation Fellowship, 1984. **Address:** 309 West Broadway, NYC 10013. **Dealer:** Jack Shainman, NYC. **One-man Exhibitions:** SFMA, 1964; Dilexi Gallery, San Francisco, 1962, 63, 65; Bykert Gallery, 1967, 69, 72, 74; Darthea Speyer Gallery, 1968, 71, 73; Obelisk Gallery, 1971; Pyramid Art Galleries, Washington, D.C., 1973, 76; Michael Berger Gallery, Pittsburgh, 1974, 79; Brooke Alexander, 1974; Zolla-Lieberman, Chicago, 1976; Hamilton Gallery of Contemporary Art, NYC, 1977; Portland (Ore.) Center for the Visual Arts, 1977; U. of Missouri, Kansas, 1977; Miami Dade Community College, 1978; Bonfoey Gallery, Cleveland, 1980; Mary Ryan Gallery, NYC, 1982; Ramon Osuna Gallery, Washington, D.C., 1983; Adams-Middleton Gallery, 1984; Paule Anglim Associates, San Francisco, 1984; Ianuzzi Gallery, Phoenix, 1985; Southern Methodist U., 1987. **Retrospectives:** Newport Harbor, 1983; Oakland/AM, 1984. **Group:** WMAA Annuals, 1965, 67, Recent Acquisitions, 1966; Musée Cantonal des Beaux-Arts, Lausanne, II Salon International de Galeries Pilotes, 1966; U. of Illinois Biennial, 1967; Smithsonian, The Art of Organic Forms, 1968; Foundation Maeght, l'Art Vivant, circ., French museums, 1968; U. of North Carolina, Works on Paper, 1968; Foundation Maeght, 1970; VMFA, American Painting, 1970; Oakland/AM, A Period of Exploration, 1973; PMA/Museum of the Philadelphia Center, Focus, 1974; Chicago/AI, 71st American Exhibiton, 1974; Toledo/MA, Image, Color and Form, 1975; ICA, Boston, Painting Endures, 1975; San Antonio/McNay, American Artists, '76: A Celebration, 1976; SFMA, Painting and Sculpture in California: The Modern Era, 1976; North Texas State U., Three Artists,

Three Viewpoints, 1976; Chicago/AI, Drawings of the '70's, 1977; U. of Texas, Austin, New in the Seventies, 1977; Oakland/AM, Dilexi: The Dilexi Years: 1958-1970, 1984. **Collections:** Achenbach Foundation; Andover/Phillips; Auckland; CNAC; CSCS; California Palace; U. of California, Berkeley; Crown Zellerbach Foundation; Hartford/Wadsworth; Indianapolis; Milwaukee; NMAA; U. of New Mexico; Newport Harbor; Oakland/AM; Phoenix; Rotterdam; SFMA; Toledo/MA; WMAA. **Bibliography:** *Art: A Woman's Sensibility*; McChesney; *New in the Seventies*. Archives.

RENOUF, EDDA. b. June 17, 1943, Mexico City. **Studied:** Putney School, 1957-61; Sarah Lawrence College, BA, 1961-65; Institut d'art et d'archeologie, Paris, 1963-64; Academie Julian, Paris, 1963-64; Atelier Geitlinger, Munich, 1966-67; ASL, 1967-68; Columbia U., MFA, 1968-71; Akademie der Bildenden Kunste, Munich, 1969-70. Traveled Mexico, Iran, Turkey, India; resided in Paris, 1963-64, 71-75; Munich, 1966-67, 69-70. **Taught:** Sarah Lawrence College, Paris, 1974. **Awards:** National Endowment for the Arts, 1978. **Address:** 20 West 30th Street, NYC 10001. **Dealer:** Blum Helman Gallery, NYC; Yvon Lambert, Paris. **One-man Exhibitions:** (first) Yvon Lambert, Paris, 1972, 74, 75, 78, 84; Francoise Lambert, Milan, 1973, 75, 76, 78, 83; Konrad Fischer Gallery, Dusseldorf, 1974, 79; Galerie MTL, Brussels, 1974, 77; Galleria Marilena Bonomo, Bari, 1975; Rolf Preisig Gallery, Basel, 1976; Allesandro Ferranti, Rome, 1976; Julian Pretto and Co., New York, 1976; Weinberg Gallery, San Francisco, 1977, 79; Kathryn Markel Fine Arts, Inc., New York, 1977; Hartford/Wadsworth, 1978; Blum Helman Gallery, NYC, 1978, 79, 80, 82, 85; Ugo Ferranti, Rome, 1978; Graeme Murray Gallery, Edinburgh, 1978, 81; Margo Leavin Gallery, Los Angeles, 1978;

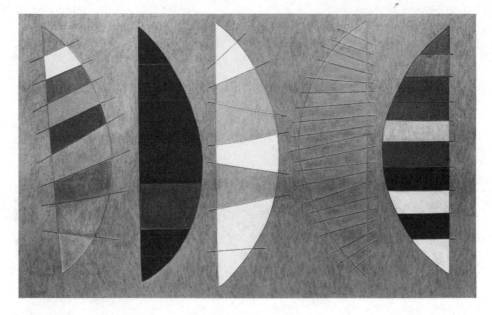

Edda Renouf *Gongs* 1985

Young-Hoffman Gallery, Chicago, 1978; Ronald Greenberg Gallery, St. Louis, 1980; Carol Taylor Gallery, Dallas, 1982. **Group:** VIII Paris Biennale, 1973; Dusseldorf, Prospekt, 1973; Rome, Contemporanea, 1973; Amsterdam/Stedelijk, Fundamental Painting, 1975; Paris/Moderne, Tendances actuelles de la nouvelle peinture americaine, 1975; MOMA, Extraordinary Women, 1977; U. of California, Santa Barbara, Contemporary Drawing/New York, 1978; WMAA Biennial, 1979; Paris/Beaubourg, Livres d'Artistes, 1985; WMAA, Drawing Acquisitions 1981-85, 1985. **Collections:** Canberra/National; Chicago/AI; Cincinnati/AM; Dallas/MFA; Detroit/Institute; Grenoble; MMA; MOMA; McCrory Corp.; NYPL; PMA; Paris/Beaubourg; Purchase/SUNY; St. Louis/City; WMAA; Yale U. **Bibliography:** *Fundamentele Schilderkunst.*

RESIKA, PAUL. b. August 15, 1928, NYC. **Studied:** Privately in NYC with Sol Wilson, 1940-44, and Hans Hofmann, 1945-47. Traveled France, Italy. **Taught:** U. of Oregon, 1965; ASL, 1968-69; Cooper Union, 1966-77; Dartmouth College, 1972; Skowhegan School, 1973; U. of Pennsylvania, 1974; Purchase/SUNY, 1977. **Awards:** Bordighera, Americans in Europe, **P.P.,** 1952; L. C. Tiffany Grant, 1959; NAD, Ranger Fund **P.P.,** 1961; Ingram Merrill Grant, 1969; AAAL, Childe Hassam **Fund P.P.,** 1970; AAAL, 1977; NAD, Benjamin Altman Prize for Landscape, 1982; Guggenheim Foundation Fellowship, 1984. **Address:** 114 East 84th Street, NYC 10028. **Dealer:** Graham Gallery, NYC. **One-man Exhibitions:** (first) George Dix Gallery, NYC, 1948; The Peridot Gallery, 1964, 65, 67-69, 1970; Washburn Gallery, Inc., 1971-73; Dartmouth College, 1972; Swain School of Design, New Bedford, Mass., 1974; Carlton Gallery, NYC, 1975; Graham Gallery, 1976, 81, 83, 85, 86; Century Association, 1982; Long Point Gallery, Provincetown, Mass., 1984; Crane Kalman Gallery, London, 1986; Kornbluth Gallery, Fairlawn, N.J., 1986. **Retrospective:** Artists' Choice Museum,

Paul Resika   *Horseleech Pond, Grey*   1984

NYC, 1985. **Group:** American Painters in Venice, 1952; Hartford/Wadsworth, Figures, 1964; Swarthmore College, 1968; Rijksakademie Amsterdam, 1968; State University of New York, 1969; AAAL, 1969, 70, 71, 75; A.F.A., Realism and Surrealism in American Art, 1971; NAD, 1972, 83, 84, 85; Omaha/Joslyn, A Sense of Place, 1973; Queens Museum, New Images, 1974; AAAL, Childe Hassam Fund Exhibition, 1976; Parsons School of Design, NYC, In Praise of Space, 1976; NAD Annual, 1977. **Collections:** Bordighera; Chase Manhattan Bank; Colby College; Dartmouth College; Goddard Art Center; Hirshhorn; Indianapolis/Herron; Lenox School; Memorial Sloan-Kettering Cancer Center, NYC; NAD; U. of Nebraska.

RESNICK, MILTON. b. January 8, 1917, Bratslov, Russia. **Studied:** Pratt Institute, 1935; American Artists School, 1936-37. US Army, 1940-45. Resided Paris, 1946-48. **Taught:** Pratt Institute, 1954-55; U. of California, Berkeley, 1955-56. Federal A.P.: Teacher. **Address:** 80 Forsyth Street, NYC 10002. **Dealers:** Robert Miller Gallery, Inc. NYC; Gruenebaum Gallery, NYC. **One-man Exhibitions:** (first) Poindexter Gallery, 1955, also, 1957, 59; de Young, 1955; Ellison Gallery, Fort Worth, 1959; Holland-Goldowsky Gallery, Chicago, 1959; The Howard Wise Gallery, Cleveland, 1960; The Howard Wise Gallery, NYC, 1960, 61, 64; Feiner Gallery, NYC, 1964; Anderson Gallery, Edgartown, Mass., 1969; Fort Worth, 1971; Max Hutchinson Gallery, NYC, 1972, 77, 79, 80, 82; Robert Miller Gallery, 1979, 85; Gruenebaum Gallery, 1983; San Jose State U., 1983; Hand in Hand Galleries, NYC, 1985. **Retrospective:** Houston/Contemporary, 1985. **Group:** WMAA Annuals, 1957,

Milton Resnick *Straws in the Wind #1* 1981

59, 61, 63; Carnegie, 1958; Walker, 60 American Painters, 1960; SRGM, Abstract Expressionists and Imagists, 1961; USIA, Contemporary American Prints, circ., Latin America, 1961-62; Chicago/AI Annual, 1962; PAFA Annual, 1962; Seattle World's Fair, 1962; SFMA, Directions—Painting U.S.A., 1963; MOMA, The New American Painting and Sculpture, 1969; U. of California, Santa Barbara, 5 American Painters, 1974; WMAA, Frank O'Hara, A Poet among Painters, 1974; Milwaukee, From Foreign Shores, 1976; Buffalo/Albright, American Painting of the 1970s, circ., 1978. **Collections:** Akron/AI; U. of California, Berkeley; Canberra/National; Ciba-Geigy Corp.; Cleveland/MA; Dartmouth College; Fort Worth; Hartford/Wadsworth; Honolulu Academy; Milwaukee; MOMA; National Gallery; U. of North Carolina; NYU; Ottawa/National; Reed College; Roswell; Skidmore, Owings & Merrill, NYC; WMAA; Waitsfield/Bundy. **Bibliography: Cathcart;** *From Foreign*

Shores; Goodrich and Baur 1; Hunter 1; Nordness, ed.; Passloff; Plous; Sandler 1. Archives.

RICHARDSON, SAM. b. July 19, 1934, Oakland, Calif. **Studied:** California College of Arts and Crafts, 1956, BA, 1960, MFA. **Taught:** Oakland City College, 1959-60; San Jose State College, 1963-. Art Director, Museum of Contemporary Crafts, 1960-63. **Address:** 4121 Sequoyah Road, Oakland, CA 94605. **Dealer:** Fuller Goldeen, San Francisco. **One-man Exhibitions:** Hansen Gallery, San Francisco, 1961, 66, 68, 69; Humboldt (Calif.) State College, 1967; Esther Robles Gallery, 1968; California State U., Fullerton, 1968, 77; U. of Nebraska, 1968; Martha Jackson Gallery, 1969, 70, 73, 74, 75, 76; Hansen-Fuller Gallery, 1971, 74, 75; Akron/AI, 1972; Contemporary Arts Center, Cincinnati, 1972; Mills College, 1973; Cranbrook, 1973; St. Mary's College, Moraga, Calif., 1975; Rutgers U., 1975; Dallas/MFA, 1976; Richard Gray Gallery, Chicago, 1976; Oakland/AM, 1976; U. of California, Davis, 1978; San Jose Museum of Art, 1969, 78, 82; Oakland/AM, 78; Hansen Fuller Goldeen Gallery, San Francisco, 1979, 80; Palomar College, 1979; Woodworks Gallery, San Jose, 1979; Janus Gallery, Los Angeles, 1980; Santa Barbara/MA, 1981; Klein Gallery, Chicago, 1982, 84; Fuller Goldeen, 1983, 85. **Group:** California Palace, Winter Invitational, 1961; SFMA, 1965, 66; California Palace, Painters behind Painters, 1967; U. of Illinois, 1967, 69; Sacramento/Crocker, West Coast '68, 1968; Museum of Contemporary Crafts, Plastic as Plastic, 1968; WMAA, 1968; ICA, U. of Pennsylvania, Plastics and New Art, 1969; MOMA, New Media, New Methods, circ., 1969; Occidental College, Los Angeles, Four Directions, 1969; WMAA, Contemporary American Sculpture, 1968-69; Milwaukee, A Plastic Presence, circ., 1969; SFAI, Centennial Exhibition, 1971; Chicago/Contemporary, White on White,

1971-72; Stanford U., Sculpture '72, 1972; Vassar College, New American Landscapes, 1972; Museum of Contemporary Crafts, Creative Casting, 1973; Rutgers U., Response to the Environment, 1975; Oakland/AM, California Landscape, 1975; SFMA, California Painting and Sculpture: The Modern Era, 1976; Cornell U., Landscape: New Views, 1978; Honolulu Academy, California 3×8 Twice, 1978; Palm Springs Desert Museum, The West as Art, 1982; Oakland/AM, 100 Years of California Sculpture, 1982; Fresno Art Center, Forgotten Dimension, 1982; U. of Southern California, California Sculpture Show, circ., 1984; Oakland/AM, Art in the San Francisco Bay Area, 1945-1980, 1985. **Collections:** Dallas/MFA; Denver/AM; de Young; Fort Worth; Hirshhorn; Milwaukee; NMAA; U. of Nebraska; Oakland Museum; Palomar College; SFMA; Sacramento/Crocker; San Jose Museum of Art; U. of Sydney; WMAA; U. of Wisconsin. **Bibliography:** *California Sculpture Show.*

RICHENBURG, ROBERT B. b. July 14, 1917, Boston, Mass. **Studied:** Boston Museum School; George Washington U.; Boston U.; The Corcoran School of Art; Ozenfant School of Art, NYC; Hofmann School; ASL, with Reginald Marsh, George Grosz. US Army, 1942-45. **Taught:** Schrivenham American U.; Brooklyn-Queens Central YMCA, 1947-51; City College of New York, 1947-52; Pratt Institute, 1951-64; Cooper Union, 1954-55; NYU, 1960-61; Cornell U., 1964-67; Hunter College, 1967-70; Ithaca College, 1970-83. **Awards:** Boston Museum School, Scholarship; *Art in America* (magazine), New Talent. **Address:** 1006 Springs Fireplace Road, East Hampton, N.Y. 11307. **One-man Exhibitions:** (first) Hendler Gallery, Philadelphia, 1954; Artists' Gallery, NYC, 1957; Artists' Gallery, Provincetown, 1958; Hansa Gallery, NYC, 1958; Tibor de Nagy Gallery, 1959-64; Dwan Gallery, 1960;

RISD, 1960 (four-man); Santa Barbara/MA, 1961; Dayton/AI, 1962; Cornell U., 1964, 82; Colgate U., 1970; Ithaca College, 1971; Upstairs Gallery, Ithaca, N.Y., 1976, 81; Benson Gallery, Southampton, N.Y., 1986. **Retrospectives:** Colgate U., 1970; Ithaca College, 1971. **Group:** SRGM, 1949; Eighth Street Exhibition, NYC; Ninth Street Exhibition, NYC; MOMA, The Art of Assemblage, circ., 1961; SRGM, Abstract Expressionists and Imagists, 1961; Baltimore/MA, 1961; WMAA Annuals, 1961, 64, 68, Sculpture Annuals, 1966-69; Dayton/AI, 1962; Kansas City/Nelson, 1962; U. of Illinois, 1963; Corcoran, 1963; MOMA, Hans Hofmann and His Students, circ., 1963-64; U. of Nebraska; A.F.A., New Talent, circ., 1964, also 1968-69; Seattle/AM, 1965; Hamilton College, 1965; A.F.A., The Square in Painting, 1968; WMAA Annual, 1968. **Collections:** Allentown/AM; U. of California; Hirshhorn; Ithaca College; MOMA; Norfolk; Norfolk/Chrysler; PMA; Pasadena/AM; Ridgefield/Aldrich; U. of Texas; WMAA; College of William and Mary. **Bibliography:** Seitz 3.

RICKEY, GEORGE. b. June 6, 1907, South Bend, Ind. To Scotland, 1913. **Studied:** Trinity College, Glenalmond, Scotland, 1921-26; Balliol College, Oxford, 1926-29, BA, 1941, MA with honors; Ruskin School of Drawing and of Fine Art, Oxford, 1928-29; Academie Andre Lhote and Academie Moderne, Paris, 1929-30; NYU, 1945-46; State U. of Iowa, 1947, with Maurico Lasansky; Institute of Design, Chicago, 1948-49. Traveled Europe and Mexico extensively; resided Paris, 1933-34. US Army Air Corps, 1941-45. **Taught:** Groton School, 1930-33 (history department); Knox College, 1940-41; Muhlenberg College, 1941, 1946-48; U. of Washington, 1948; Indiana U., 1949-55; Tulane U., 1955-62; U. of California, Santa Barbara, 1960; Rensselaer Polytechnic Institute, 1961-65. Editorial department, *Newsweek* magazine, 1936. Director,

George Rickey *Two Open Triangles*
Up 1983

The Kalamazoo Institute of Arts,
1939-40. Shifted emphasis from painting to sculpture, 1950. **Member:** NIAL.
Commissions: (murals) Olivet Col-
lege, 1938-39; US Post Office, Se-
linsgrove, Pa., 1938; Knox College,
1940-41; (sculpture), Belle Boas Memorial Library, Baltimore Museum, 1955;
Union Carbide Corp., Toronto, 1960;
The Joseph H. Hirshhorn Collection,
NYC, 1962; Hamburger Kunsthalle,
1963; Westland Center, Detroit, 1964;
Keene Teachers College, 1964; Lytton
Savings and Loan Association,
Oakland, Calif., 1964; The Singer Com-
pany, Inc., 1964; Hood College, 1964;
Berlin/National; Rijksmuseum Kroller-
Muller; Oakland/AM; Siemens Re-
search Center, Erlangen, Germany;
Henkel GMBH, Germany; NCFA; Nord-
park, Dusseldorf, 1965; State Employ-
ment Building, Albany, 1966; Omaha
National Bank, 1967; Berlin/National,
1969; High Museum, 1969; The Free
University, Berlin, 1969; Neue Heimat
Bayern, Munich, 1969; U. of Glasgow,
1971; U. of Heidelberg, 1972; Fort
Worth City Hall, 1974; US Federal

Courthouse, Honolulu, 1975; Univer-
sitatsbauamt, Ulm, 1977; Ruhr U.,
1978; K & B Plaza, New Orleans, 1978;
Peoria Airport, 1978; Pasadena/AM,
1978; Central Trust Co., Cincinnati,
1979; Oliver Tyrone Corp., Cleveland,
1980; Jackson Hospital, Miami, 1980.
Awards: Guggenheim Foundation Fel-
lowship, 1960, 61; Hon. DFA, Knox
College, 1970; American Institute of Ar-
chitects, Fine Arts Honor Award, 1972;
Hon. DFA, Williams College, 1972;
Skowhegan School, Medal for Sculpture, 1973; Union College, 1973; Hon.
DFA, Indiana U., 1974; Hon. Degree,
Kalamazoo College, 1977; Hon. Doctor
of Letters, York U., 1978; Brandeis U.,
Creative Arts Award, 1979; Hon. DFA,
Tulane U., 1983. **Address:** RD #2, East
Chatham, N.Y. **Dealers:** The Zabriskie
Gallery, NYC; Maxwell Davidson Gal-
lery, NYC. **One-man Exhibitions:**
(first) Caz-Delbo Gallery, NYC, 1933;
Denver/AM, 1935, 43, 45, 48; Indi-
anapolis/Herron, 1953 (first sculpture
shown); The Little Gallery, Louisville,
1954; Kraushaar Galleries, 1955, 59, 61;
New Orleans/Delgado, 1956; Amerika
Haus, Hamburg, 1957; Orleans Gallery,
New Orleans, 1960; Santa Barbara/MA,
1960; U. of Oklahoma, 1961; Phoenix,
1961; Primus-Stuart Gallery, Los An-
geles, 1962; Galerie Springer, Berlin,
1962; Grand Rapids, 1962; Hyde Park
Art Center, Chicago, 1963; Williams
College, 1963; U. of Rochester, 1963;
Dartmouth College, 1963; ICA, Boston,
1964; David Stuart Gallery, 1964; Kala-
mazoo/Institute, 1964 (two-man, with
Ulfert Wilke); Staempfli Gallery, 1964,
67, 71, 75; Skidmore College, 1965;
Walker, 1967; Haus am Waldsee,
Berlin, circ., 1969; Kunsthalle,
Nurnberg, 1969; Trenton/State, 1969;
Whatcom, 1970; U. of Washington,
1970; Indiana U., (three-man), 1970; U.
of Iowa, 1972; Hannover/K-G, 1973;
Berlin/National, 1973; Galerie
Buchholz, Munich, 1974; Galerie Es-
pace, Amsterdam, 1974; Gimpel &
Hanover, Zurich, 1975, 78; Gimpel Fils,
1975; Fordham U., 1975; Bielefeld,
1976; Frankfurt am Main, 1977; Gallery

Kasahara, Osaka, 1978; Amerika Haus, Berlin, 1979; Ministry of Cultural Affairs, Montreal, 1980; John Berggruen Gallery, San Francisco, 1982; The Zabriskie Gallery, 1986. **Retrospectives:** Corcoran, 1966; SRGM, 1979; UCLA, circ., 1971; U. of Notre Dame, 1985. **Group:** Salon des Artistes Independents, Paris, 1930; MMA, National Sculpture Exhibition, 1951; WMAA, 1952, 53, 66, 68-69, Annual, 1964; PAFA, 1953, 54; Chicago/AI, Exhibition Momentum, 1954, 55; U. of Nebraska, 1955; U. of Minnesota, 1955; MOMA, Recent Sculpture, USA, 1959; Santa Barbara/MA, 1960; Amsterdam/Stedelijk, Art in Motion, circ., Europe, 1961-62; Battersea Park, London, International Sculpture Exhibition, 1963; Documenta III & IV, Kassel, 1964, 68; Berne, 1965; Palais des Beaux-Arts, Brussels, 1965; Staatliche Kunsthalle, Baden-Baden, 1965; St. Louis Bicentennial Sculpture Exhibition, 1965; Park Sonsbeek, Holland, 1966; Los Angeles/County MA, 1967; Carnegie, 1967; XXXIV Venice Biennial, 1968; Denver/AM, Report on the Sixties, 1969; Hayward Gallery, London, Kinetics, 1970; U. of Nebraska, American Sculpture, 1970; Katonah (N.Y.) Art Gallery, Drawing in Space, 1972; Newport, R.I., Monumenta, 1974; Documenta IV, Kassel, 1968; Antwerp Biennial, 1971; Hayward Gallery, London, Pier and Ocean, 1980. **Collections:** Allentown/AM; Andover/Phillips; Atlanta/AA; Ball State U.; Baltimore/MA; Bethlehem Steel Corp.; Bochum/Museum Bochum; Boston/MFA; Buffalo/Albright; Cincinnati/AM; Columbus; Corcoran; Dallas/MFA; Dartmouth College; Denver/AM; Detroit/Institute; Flint/Institute; U. of Glasgow; Hamburg; High Museum; Hirshhorn; Honolulu Academy; Humlebaek/Louisiana; Indiana U.; U. of Iowa; Jackson Hospital, Miami; Kalamazoo/Institute; Kansas City/Nelson; Long Beach/MA; MOMA; Max Planck Institute; Freiburg; Memphis/Brooks; Minnesota/MA; Raleigh/NCMA; NCFA;

Newark Museum; U. of North Carolina; Oakland/MA; Princeton U.; Ruhr U.; Santa Barbara/MA; The Singer Company, Inc., NYC; SRGM; Storm King Art Center; Syntex Research Center, Palo Alto; Tate, Toronto; Trenton/State; Ulm U.; Union Carbide Corp.; WMAA; Walker; Yale U.; York U. **Bibliography:** Battcock, ed.; Calas, N. and E.; Chipp; Craven, W.; Davis, D.; **George Rickey;** MacAgy 2; *Monumenta;* Read 3; **Rickey;** Rodman 1; Selz, P., 1; Trier 1; Tuchman 1. Archives.

RIVERS, LARRY. b. August 17, 1923, Bronx, NY. US Army Air Corps, 1942-43. **Studied:** Julliard School of Music, NYC, 1944-45; Hofmann School; NYU, 1947-48. Traveled Europe, USA, USSR, Africa. Active as a professional jazz musician. Began sculpture 1953. Appeared on "$64,000 Question" (CBS-TV) as an art expert and ran his winnings to $32,000 on "$64,000 Challenge," 1957-58. **Commissions:** Outdoor billboard for First New York Film Festival, 1963. **Awards:** Corcoran, Third Prize, 1954. **Address:** 92 Little Plains Road, Southhampton, NY 11968. **Dealer:** Marlborough Gallery, Inc., NYC; Robert Miller Gallery, NYC. **One-man Exhibitions:** (first) Jane Street Gallery, NYC, 1949; Tibor de Nagy Gallery, 1951-54, 1957-60, 1962; The Stable Gallery, 1954 (sculpture); Martha Jackson Gallery, 1960 (sculpture); Dwan Gallery, 1960; Galerie Rive Droite, 1962; Gimpel Fils, London, 1962, 64, 76; Marlborough Gallery, Inc., 1970, 71, 73, 75, 77, 79, 81; Brandeis U.; Chicago/AI, circ., 1970; Quay Gallery, 1972; Tower Gallery, Southampton, 1973; Olympia Galleries, Glenside, Pa., 1975; Robert Miller Gallery, NYC, 1977; Hokin Gallery, Chicago, 1977; ACA Gallery, NYC, 1977; Marlborough Gallery, London, 1981; Ridgefield/Aldrich, 1983; Guild Hall, 1983; Hirshhorn, 1984; Kouros Gallery, NYC, 1984. **Retrospectives:** Caracas/Contemporaneo, 1980; Hannover/K-G, circ., 1980. **Group:** WMAA Annuals, 1954, 58, 60, 61, 63, 66; MOMA, Twelve Americans, circ., 1956; Sao Paulo, 1957; Carnegie, 1958, 61; WMAA, Business Buys American Art, 1960; II Inter-American Paintings and Prints Biennial, Mexico City, 1960; Seattle World's Fair, 1962; PAFA, 1963; WMAA, Between the Fairs, 1964; WMAA, Art of the U.S. 1670-1966, 1966; Flint/Institute, I Flint Invitational, 1966; Indianapolis/Herron, 1966; SFMA, 1966; MOMA, Two Decades of American Painting, circ., Japan, India, Australia, 1967; U. of Illinois, 1967; Documenta IV, Kassel, 1968; Hirshhorn, Drawings, 1974-1984, 1984. **Collections:** Allentown/AM; Baltimore/MA; Brandeis U.; Brooklyn Museum; Buffalo/Albright; Caracas/Contemporaneo; Chicago/AI; Container Corp. of America; Corcoran; Dallas/MFA; Fort Wayne/AM; Hirshhorn; Kansas City/AI; Kansas City/Nelson; Los Angeles/County MA; MMA; MOMA; Mexico City/Tamayo; Minneapolis/Institute; National Gallery; New England Merchants National Bank, Boston; New Paltz/SUNY; Norfolk/Chrysler; U. of North Carolina; RISD; Raleigh/NCMA; SFMA; Seagram Collection; Southampton/Parrish; Stockholm/SFK; Tate; Utica; Victoria and Albert Museum; WMAA. **Bibliography:** Alloway 1; Calas, N. and E.; Dienst 1; Diamonstein; Friedman, ed.; Gaunt; Gettings; Goldman 1; **Harrison;** Honisch and Jensen, eds.; **Hunter 5;** Hunter, ed.; Lippard 5; McCurdy ed.; *Metro;* Murken-Altrogge; Nordness, ed.; O'Hara 1; *Poets & Painters;* Rivers with Brightman; Rodman 1; Russell and Gablik; Sandler 1; Soby 6; Tomkins 2; Warhol and Hackett; Weller. Archives.

ROBINSON, BOARDMAN. b. September 6, 1876, Somerset (Nova Scotia), Canada; **d.** September 6, 1952. Colorado Springs, Colo. To USA, 1894. **Studied:** Academie Colarossi, Academie des Beaux-Arts, and Academie Julian, Paris, 1898-1900; Boston Normal Art School, 1894-97, with E. W. Hamilton. Traveled the world extensively. **Taught:** ASL, 1919-22, 1924-26; Fountain Valley School, Colorado Springs, 1930-44; Colorado Springs Fine Arts Center, 1937-39; Michigan State College, 1945. Illustrated many editions of classics, as well as popular books. Drew cartoons for the *Morning Telegraph,* 1907-1910, and the *New York Tribune* (four years). **Commissions:** (murals) Kaufmann Department Store, Pittsburgh, 1928-29; Colorado Springs/FA, 1936; Justice Department Building, Washington, D.C., 1937 (18); US Post Office, Englewood, Colo., 1940. **One-man Exhibitions:** Thumb Box Gallery, NYC, 1916; M. Knoedler & Co., 1919; Weyhe Gallery, 1924; ASL, 1929; Delphic Studios, NYC, 1930; Hudson D. Walker Gallery, NYC, 1940; Chicago/AI, 1942; Forum Gallery, NYC, 1979; NCFA, 1979. **Retrospectives:** Colorado Springs/FA, 1943; Dallas/MFA, 1946; Kraushaar Galleries, 1946. **Group:** WMAA; Chicago/AI; Colorado Springs/FA; Cleveland/MA; Los Angeles/County MA; MMA; NAD. **Collections:** AAAL; U. of Arizona; Chicago/AI; Cleveland/MA; Colorado Springs/FA; Cranbrook; Dallas/MFA; Denver/AM; U. of Georgia; Harvard U.; IBM; Los Angeles/County MA; MMA; Minneapolis/Institute; NYPL; NYU; U. of Nebraska; Newark Museum; New Britain; PMA; U. of Vermont; WMAA; Wichita/AM. **Bibliography:** Baur 7, **Biddle 2, 4;** Brown; Bruce and Watson; Cahill and Barr, eds.; Cheney; **Christ-Janer;** Gallatin 2; Genauer; *Index of 20th Century Artists;* Mather 1; Mellquist; Poore; Richardson, E.P.; Rose, B., 1.

ROBUS, HUGO. b. May 10, 1885, Cleveland, Ohio; **d.** January 14, 1964, NYC. **Studied;** Cleveland Institute of Art, 1904-08; NAD, 1910-11; Academie de la Grand Chaumiere, 1912-14, with Antoine Bourdelle. **Taught:** Myra Carr Art School, ca. 1915-17; Columbia U., summers, 1942, 43, 46, 48, 50, 52, 53, 55, 56; Munson-Williams-Proctor Institute, Utica, N.Y., 1948; Hunter College, 1950-58; Brooklyn Museum School, 1955-56. Changed from painting to sculpture, 1920. Federal A.P.: 1937-39. **Awards:** MMA, Artists for Victory, Second Prize, 1942; PAFA, George D. Widener, Memorial Gold Medal, 1950; PAFA, Alfred G. B. Steel Memorial Prize, 1953; NIAL, Citation and Grant, 1957. **One-man Exhibitions:** (first) Grand Central, NYC, 1946, also 1948; Utica, 1948; Corcoran, 1958; The Forum Gallery, 1963, 66, 74, 79; NCFA, 1979. **Retrospective:** A.F.A./Ford Foundation, 1961. **Group:** WMAA; PAFA; MMA; Corcoran. **Collections:** Brooklyn Museum; Cleveland/MA; Corcoran; Fairleigh Dickinson U.; IBM; Israel Museum; MMA; MOMA; NMAA; SRGM; Utica; WMAA; Walker. **Bibliography:** *Avant-Garde Painting and Sculpture in America 1910-25;* Baur 7; Brumme; Craven, W.; Goodrich and Baur 1; Mendelowitz; Marter, Tarbell, and Wechsler; Pearson 2. Archives.

ROCKBURNE, DOROTHEA. b. 1929, Verdun, Quebec, Canada. **Studied:** Ecole des Beaux-Arts, Paris, 1947-50; Black Mountain College, 1951-56. Traveled Europe, South America, Egypt. **Taught:** School of Visual Arts, NYC; Bard College. **Award:** Brandeis U., Creative Arts Award, 1985. **Address:** 140 Grand Street, NYC 10013. **One-man Exhibitions:** (first) Bykert Gallery, NYC, 1970, 72, 73; Ileana Sonnabend Gallery, Paris, 1971; New Gallery, Cleveland, 1972; U. of Rochester, 1972; Galleria Toselli, Milan, 1972, 73, 74; Hartford College of Art, 1983; Lisson Gallery, London, 1973; Galleria Schema, Florence, 1973, 75; Daniel

Dorothea Rockburne   *Narcissus*   1984

Weinberg Gallery, San Francisco, 1973; Galerie Charles Kriwin, Brussels, 1975; John Weber Gallery, NYC, 1976, 78; Texas Gallery, Houston, 1979, 81; David Bellman Gallery, Toronto, 1981; Xavier Fourcade, Inc., 1981 82, 85; Galleriet, Lund, Sweden, 1982; Margo Leavin Gallery, 1982, 83. **Group:** WMAA, Annuals, 1970, 72, 73; Chicago/AI, 1972, 76; Chicago/Contemporary, White on White, 1972; Festival of Two Worlds, Spoleto, 1972; Documenta V & VI, Kassel, 1972, 77; New York Cultural Center, 3D into 2D, 1973; WMAA, American Drawings: 1963-1973, 1973; MOMA, Eight Contemporary Artists, 1974; Corcoran, 1975; Houston/MFA, Modern Painting, 1900 to the Present, 1975; Paris/Moderne, Tendances actuelles de la peinture americaine, 1975; MOMA, Drawing Now, 1976; MOMA, Extraordinary Women, 1977; WMAA Biennials, 1977, 79; U. of California, Santa Barbara, Contemporary Drawing/New York, 1978; U. of North Carolina, Drawings about Drawing Today, 1979; New Museum, The 1970s: New American Painting, 1979; Brooklyn Museum, American Drawings in Black and White: 1970-1979, 1980; XXXIX Venice Biennial, 1980; MOMA, A Century of Modern Drawing, 1982; WMAA, Abstract Drawings, 1911-1981, 1982; New Museum, Language, Drama Source & Vision, 1983; U. of North Carolina, Art on Paper, 1984; Fort Lauderdale, An American Renaissance: Painting and Sculpture Since 1940, 1986. **Collections:** Aachen/Ludwig; Harvard U.; High Museum; MMA; MOMA; U. of Michigan; Minneapolis/Institute; Ohio State U.; WMAA. **Bibliography:** Tuchman 3.

ROCKLIN, RAYMOND. b. August 18, 1922, Moodus, Conn. **Studied:** MOMA School, 1940; Cooper Union, 1951, with Milton Hebald, John Hovannes, Warren Wheelock; Educational Alliance, NYC, with Abbo Ostrowsky; Temple U., 1942; Cooper Union, BFA, 1977.

Traveled Europe, USA, Middle East. **Taught:** American U., 1956; U. of California, Berkeley, 1959-60; Scarsdale Studio Workshop, 1960-; Ball State Teachers College, 1964; YMHA, Essex County, N.J., 1971-74; Manhattan Community College, 1977-. **Member:** Sculptors Guild. **Awards:** Fulbright Fellowship (Italy), 1952; Yaddo Fellowship, 1956. **Address:** 232B Watch Hill Road, Peekskill, NY 10566. **One-man Exhibitions:** (first) Tanager Gallery, NYC, 1956; American U., 1956; Oakland/AM, 1956; U. of California, Berkeley, 1959; Pomona College, 1960; Santa Barbara/MA, 1960; Dilexi Gallery, San Francisco, 1960; The Bertha Schaefer Gallery, 1960 (two-man); Ball State Teachers College, 1964; Briarcliff College, 1973. **Group:** WMAA, Young America; WMAA, New Talent, 1957; U. of Illinois, 1959; WMAA Annual, 1960; Claude Bernard, Paris, 1960; American Abstract Artists Annuals; U. of Nebraska, 1960. **Collections:** Norfolk/Chrysler; Skowhegan School; Temple Israel, St. Louis; WMAA. **Bibliography:** Seuphor 3.

ROHM, ROBERT. b. February 6, 1934, Cincinnati, Ohio. **Studied:** Pratt Institute, B. Industrial Design, 1956; Cranbrook Academy of Art (with Bethold Schweitz), MFA, 1960. Traveled USA, England; resided Mexico, 1964; traveled around the world, 1980. **Taught:** Columbus College of Art and Design, 1956-59; Pratt Institute, 1960-65; U. of Rhode Island, 1965-; Stourbridge (Eng.) College of Art, 1974. **Member:** Sculptors Guild. **Awards:** PAFA, Hon. Men., 1959; Columbus, Sculpture Prize, 1957, 59; Guggenheim Foundation Fellowship, 1964; U. of Rhode Island Research Grant-in-Aid, 1965, 66, 69; Cassandra Foundation, 1966; Rhode Island State Council on the Arts Grant, 1973, 82; National Endowment for the Arts, 1974. **Address:** 26 Lake Street, Wakefield, RI 02879. **Dealers:** OK Harris Works of Art, NYC; Nielsen Gallery, Boston. **One-**

Robert Rohm   *Untitled (Post)* 1986

man Exhibitions: Columbus (two-man), 1958; Aspen, (Colo.) Art Gallery, 1963; Royal Marks Gallery, 1964; U. of Rhode Island, 1966, 72; U. of Maine (two-man), 1969; Nova Scotia College of Art and Design, Halifax, 1969; Massachusetts College of Art, Boston, 1970; Parker Street 470 Gallery, Boston, 1970, 72; OK Harris Works of Art, NYC, 1970, 72, 73, 76, 77, 80, 82, 84, 86; U. of Rochester, 1971; Hobart and William Smith College, 1973; Boston/MFA (two-man), 1974; Suzette Schochett Gallery, Newport, R.I., 1978; Worcester/AM, 1979; Nielsen Gallery, 1985; La Jolla, 1985; U. of Rhode Island, 1981. **Group:** PAFA, 1961; Silvermine Guild, 1962; Aspen (Colo.) Art Gallery, 1963; Waitsfield/Bundy, Bundy Sculpture Competition, 1963; WMAA Annual, 1963, 64; Tufts U., 1968; The Pennsylvania State U., 1968; WMAA, 1969; Lincoln, Mass./De Cordova, 1969; Trenton/State, Soft Art, 1969; WMAA, Anti-Illusion: Procedures/Materials, 1969; Seattle/AM, 557,087, 1969; Indi-

anapolis, 1970; MIT, Six Artists, 1970; ICA, Boston, Art on Paper, 1970; WMAA Annuals, 1970, 73; New Delhi, Second World Triennial, 1971; Harvard U., Recent Abstract Art, 1971; U. of Rochester, N.Y., Drawings and Prints—New York, 1977; WMAA, The Sculptor as Draftsman, circ., 1983. **Collections:** Brandeis U.; Columbus; Federal Reserve Bank, NYC; Fontana-Hollywood Corp.; MMA; MOMA; Oberlin College; U. of New Mexico; The Pennsylvania State U.; St. Lawrence U.; Sarah Lawrence College; VMFA; Waitsfield/Bundy; Worcester/AM; WMAA; Zurich. **Bibliography:** Mônte and Tucker.

ROSATI, JAMES. b. 1912, Washington, Pa. Violinist with the Pittsburgh Symphony for two years. **Taught:** Cooper Union; Pratt Institute; Yale U., 1960-73; U. of Pennsylvania, 1977-79; Dartmouth College, 1960-73; Federal A.P.: Sculptor. **Commissions:** St. John's Abbey, Collegeville, Minn. (sculpture). **Awards:** Brandeis U., Creative Arts Award, 1960; Chicago/AI, The Mr. & Mrs. Frank G. Logan Medal and Prize, 1962; Carborundum Major Abrasive Marketing Award, 1963; Guggenheim Foundation Fellowship, 1964; National Council on the Arts Grant, 1968; Design in Steel Award, American Iron and Steel Institute, 1973. **Address:** 56 Seventh Avenue, NYC, 10014. **Dealer:** Marlborough Gallery, Inc., NYC. **One-man Exhibitions:** (first) The Peridot Gallery, 1954; Otto Gerson Gallery, NYC, 1959, 62; Dartmouth College, 1963; Colgate U., 1968; Brandeis U., 1969; Buffalo/Albright, 1970; Yale U., 1970; Marlborough Gallery Inc., NYC, 1970, 77, 81; Gibbes Art Gallery, Charleston, S.C., 1981. **Group:** Ninth Street Exhibition, NYC, 1951; WMAA Annuals, 1952, 53, 54, 60, 62, 66; Carnegie, 1958, 61, 64; Claude Bernard, Paris, 1960; A.F.A., Contemporary Sculpture, 1960; International Outdoor Sculpture Exhibitions, Otterlo, Holland, 1961; Chicago/AI, 1961, 62; Seattle World's Fair, 1962; WMAA, First Five Years, 1962; Festival of Two Worlds, Spoleto, 1962; Battersea Park, London, International Sculpture Exhibition, 1963; New York World's Fair, 1964-65; Flint/Institute, 1 Flint Invitational, 1966; Colby College, 1967; Museum of Contemporary Crafts, circ., 1967-68; HemisFair, San Antonio, 1968; Grand Rapids, Sculpture of the 60s, 1969; Foundation Maeght, l'Art Vivant Aux Etats Unis, 1979; U. of Nebraska, American Sculpture, 1970; Baltimore/MA, The Partial Figure in Modern Sculpture, 1970; Antwerp, Biennial Middleheim, 1971; Newport, R.I., Monumenta, 1974; U. of Massachusetts, Artist and Fabricator, 1975; Stamford Museum, The American Salon des Refuses, 1976. **Collections:** Atlantic Richfield Oil Co., Los Angeles; Bank of Oklahoma, Tulsa; Buffalo/Albright; Brandeis U.; Carnegie; Ciba-Geigy Corp.; Colby College; Dartmouth College; Davenport/Municipal; Drake U.; Edmonton Art Gallery; Hirshhorn; Honolulu Academy; The Hubert Humphrey Building, Washington, D.C.; Mexico City/Tamayo; MOMA; National Gallery; Spencer Museum of Art/Lawrence, Kans.; NYU; Newark Museum; Park Hilton Hotel, Seattle; Prudential Insurance Co. of America; Rockefeller University; WMAA; World Trade Center; Yale U. **Bibliography:** Davies; *Monumenta;* Read 3; Selz, J.; Seuphor 3.

ROSEMAN, HARRY. b. May 10, 1945, Brooklyn, N.Y. **Studied:** Pratt Institute, 1963-67, BFA. **Taught:** Queens College, 1973-75; Brooklyn College, 1974; Philadelphia College of Art, 1974-75; Jersey City State College, 1975-77; Vassar College, 1981-. **Awards:** CAPS, 1982; Vassar College, Mellon Grant, 1985. **m.** Catherine Murphy. **Address:** Rt. 1, Box 47, East Dorsey Lane, Poughkeepsie, N.Y. 12601. **Dealer:** Davis & Langdale Co., Inc., NYC. **One-man Exhibitions:** Piper Gallery, Lexington, Mass, 1969; Davis and Long Company, NYC, 1979; Daniel Weinberg Gallery,

San Francisco, 1982, 83; U. of California, Santa Barbara, 1983; Barbara Mathes Gallery, NYC, 1984; Dart Gallery, Chicago, 1985; Davis & Langdale Co., Inc., 1986. **Group:** Walker, Scale and Environment, 1977; NAD, 1981; RISD, Metals: Cast-Cut-Coiled, 1982; Houston/Contemporary, American Still Life, 1945-1983, 1983. **Collections:** Cincinnati/AM; La Jolla; Levi-Strauss Corp., San Francisco; RISD; Walker.

ROSENQUIST, JAMES. b. November 29, 1933, Grand Forks, N.D. **Studied:** U. of Minnesota, AA, 1954. **Commission:** Florida State Capitol, Tallahassee, 1978 (Mural). **Awards:** Torcuato di Tella, Buenos Aires, International Prize, 1965. **Address:** Box 4, Aripeka, FL 33502; 162 Chambers Street, NYC 10007. **Dealer:** Leo Castelli, Inc. **One-man Exhibitions:** (first) Green Gallery, NYC, 1962, also 1964; Dwan Gallery, 1964; Ileana Sonnabend Gallery, Paris, 1964, 65, 68, 79; Galleria d'Arte Contemporaneo, Turin, 1965; Leo Castelli, Inc., 1965, 66, 69, 70, 73, 75, 77, 81; Stockholm/National, 1966; Amsterdam/Stedelijk, 1966, 73; Berne, 1966; Humlebaek/Louisiana, 1966; Staatliche Kunsthalle, Baden-Baden, 1966; Ottawa/National, 1968; Galleria Sperone,

James Rosenquist *Mute Transformations II* 1985-86

Turin, 1968; MMA, 1968; Galerie Rolf Ricke, 1970; Cologne, 1972; Margo Leavin Gallery, 1972, 74; Chicago/Contemporary, 1972; Courtney Sales Gallery, Dallas, 1973; Jack Glenn Gallery, Corona del Mar, 1973; Portland (Ore.) Center for the Visual Arts, 1973; Max Protetch Gallery, Washington, D.C., 1974; Jared Sable Gallery, Toronto, 1974; Galerie Michael Pabst, Vienna, 1974; Gallery A, Sydney, Australia, 1976; The Berenson Gallery, Bay Harbor Islands, Miami Beach, Fla., 1976; Corcoran & Greenberg Inc., Coral Gables, Fla., 1976; F.H. Mayor Gallery, London, 1976, 78; Paule Anglim Associates, San Francisco, 1976; Ronald Greenberg Gallery, St. Louis, 1976; Sable-Castelli Gallery, Ltd., Toronto, 1977; National Gallery of Victoria, Melbourne, Australia, 1977; Institute of Modern Art, Brisbane, 1977; Ringling, 1979; The Plains Art Museum, Moorhead, Minn, 1979; Multiples, NYC, 1978; Buffalo/Albright, 1979; Castelli Feigen Corcoran, NYC, 1980, 82; Texas Gallery, Houston, 1980; Castelli-Goodman-Solomon, East Hampton, N.Y., 1981; Dolly Fiterman Gallery, Minneapolis, 1981; Colorado State U., 1982; Barbara Gillman Gallery, Miami, 1982; Mayor Gallery, London, 1982; Thorden Wetterling Galleries, Goteborg, 1983, 84; Van Straaten Gallery, Chicago, 1983; U. of Southern Florida, 1984. **Retrospective:** Denver/AM, circ., 1985. **Group:** Hartford/Wadsworth, 1962; Dallas/MFA, 1962; WGMA, The Popular Image, 1962; Chicago/AI, 1962, 66; SRGM, Six Painters and the Object, 1963; Buffalo/Albright, Mixed Media and Pop Art, 1963; ICA, U. of Pennsylvania, The Atmosphere of '64, 1964; Salon du mai, Paris, 1964; Tate, Dunn International, 1964; Amsterdam/Stedelijk, American Pop Art, 1964; New York State Pavilion, New York World's Fair, 1964-65; Worcester/AM, 1965; Palais des Beaux-Arts, Brussels, 1965; Torcuato di Tella, Buenos Aires, 1965; Hamburger Kunstkabinett, 1965; MOMA, Around the Automobile, 1965; Kansas City/Nelson, Sound, Light, Silence, 1966; Flint/Institute, 1 Flint Invitational, 1966; Expo '67, Montreal, 1967; IX Sao Paulo Biennial, 1967; MOMA, The 1960's, 1967; Eindhoven, 1967; Palazzo Grassi, Venice, 1967; WMAA Annual 1967; Documenta IV, Kassel, 1968; Vancouver, 1969; U. of California, Irvine, New York: The Second Breakthrough 1959-1964, 1969; Hayward Gallery, London, Pop Art, 1969; MMA, Prints by Four New York Painters, 1969, New York Painting and Sculpture: 1940-1970, 1969-70; VMFA, American Painting, 1970; Foundation Maeght, 1970; Indiana U., American Scene: 1900-1970, 1970; Buffalo/Albright, Kid Stuff, 1971; Los Angeles/County MA, Art & Technology, 1971; Musee Galleria, Paris, Festival d'Automne, 1973; Yale U., American Art—Third Quarter Century, 1973; WMAA, American Pop Art, 1974; MOMA, Works from Change, 1974; MMA, Contemporary American Prints, 1976; Williamstown/Clark, The Dada/Surrealist Heritage, 1977; Cambridge, Jubiliation, 1977; Venice Biennial, 1978; Flint/Institute, Art and the Automobile, 1978; Buffalo/Albright, American Painting of the 1970s, circ., 1978; Scripps College, Black and White Are Colors: Paintings of the 1950s-1970s, 1979; Brooklyn Museum, American Drawings in Black and White: 1970-1979, 1980; Istituto di Cultura di Palazzo Grassi, Venice, Pop Art: Evolution of a Generation, 1980; Norfolk/Chrysler, American Figurative Painting, 1950-1980, 1980; Purchase/SUNY, Hidden Desires, 1980; Walker, Artist and Printer, 1980; Akron/AM, The Image in American Painting and Sculpture, 1950-1980, 1981; WMAA, American Prints: Process and Proofs, 1981; WMAA Biennial, 1981; Houston/Contemporary, The Americans: Collage, 1982; Krefeld/Haus Lange, Sweet Dreams Baby!: American Pop Graphics, 1983; Boston/MFA, 10 Painters and Sculptors Draw, 1984; WMAA, Blam!, 1984. **Collections:** Aachen; Brandeis U.; Buffalo/Albright; Chicago/Contemporary; Dallas/MFA; Hirshhorn; MMA; MOMA; Nagaoka, Japan; Norfolk/Chrysler; Oberlin College; Ottawa/National; Paris/Beaubourg; Pasadena/AM; Stockholm/National; Purchase/SUNY; Toronto; Tate; WMAA. **Bibliography:** Alloway 1; Becker and Vostell; Bihalji-Merin; *Black and White Are Colors;* Danto; Goldman 1; **Goldman 2;** Haskell 5; Honisch and Jensen, eds.; Hulten; Hunter, ed.; Johnson, Ellen H.; Kozloff 3; Lippard 2; *Metro;* Murken-Altrogge; Pincus-Witten; *Report;* Rose, B., 1; Rublowsky; Russell and Gablik; Sandler 1; Tomkins 2; Tomkins and Time-Life Books; Warhol and Hackett; Weller.

ROSENTHAL, BERNARD (TONY). b. August 9, 1914, Highland Park, Ill. **Studied:** U. of Michigan, 1936, BA; Chicago Art Institute School; Cranbrook Academy of Art, with Carl Milles. Corps of Army Engineers, 1942-46. Traveled Mexico, Europe, USA, France. **Taught:** California School of Art, 1947-48; UCLA, 1953. Federal A.P.: U.S. Post Office, Nakomis, Ill. (relief). **Commissions:** Elgin Watch Building, New York World's Fair, 1939; Museum of Science and Industry, Chicago, 1941; General Petroleum Building, Los Angeles, 1949; 260 Beverly Drive, Beverly Hills, 1950 (bronze reliefs, 3 storeys high); Bullock's Westwood, Los Angeles, 1951; RKO Studios, Hollywood, 1952; UCLA Elementary School, 1952; J. W. Robinson Department Store, Beverly Hills, 1952; Capri Theatre, San Diego, 1954; 1000 Lake Shore Drive, Chicago, 1954 (30-ft. relief); Beverly Hilton Hotel, Beverly Hills, 1955; Temple Emanuel, Beverly Hills, 1955; Century City (Alcoa Development), 1963; U. of Michigan, 1968; CSCS, Fullerton, 1969; NYC Department of Parks for Astor Place, 1967; City of New York, Police Headquarters, 1971; to design and execute a sculpture park in NYC, 1980; Temple Beth-El, Birmingham, Michigan, 1973;

Cranbrook, 1980. **Awards:** SFMA, Sculpture Award, 1950; Los Angeles/County MA, **P.P.,** 1950; Los Angeles All-City Show, Sculpture Prize, 1951; Audubon Artists, Sculpture Award, 1953; PAFA, Hon. Men., 1954; Los Angeles/County MA, Sculpture Award, 1957; American Institute of Architects, Southern California Chapter, Honor Award, 1959; Ford Foundation, **P.P.,** 1963; Tamarind Fellowship, 1964; U. of Michigan, Outstanding Achievement Award, 1967; Carborundum Major Abrasive Marketing Award, 1969; American Iron and Steel Instrument, Design in Steel Award, 1975. **Address:** 173 East 73rd Street, NYC 10021. **Dealer:** Knoedler Contemporary Art. **One-man Exhibitions:** (first) Pat Wall Gallery, Monterey, 1947; A.A.A. Gallery, Chicago, 1947; Scripps College, 1948; SFMA, 1950; A.A.A. Gallery, NYC, 1950; Santa Barbara/MA, 1952; Long Beach/MA, 1952; Catherine Viviano Gallery, 1954, 58, 59; Carnegie, 1959; The Kootz Gallery, NYC, 1961, 63, 66; M. Knoedler & Co. 1968, 77; Gertrude Kasle Gallery, 1973; Hammarskjold Sculpture Plaza, NYC, 1977; Federal Plaza, NYC, 1977; Cranbrook, 1980. **Group:** MMA; MOMA; Sao Paulo Biennial; Brussels World's Fair, 1958; Chicago/AI; PAFA; Sculptors Guild; Audubon Artists; Walker; ICA, Boston; Yale U.; WMAA, 1964, 66, 68; Buffalo// Albright, 1965; Boston/MFA, 1966; Sculpture in Environment, New York Citywide Exhibition, 1967; HemisFair '68, San Antonio, Tex., 1968; Grand Rapids, 1969; Grand Rapids, Sculpture of the 60s, 1969; Cincinnati/Contemporary, Monumental Art, 1970; Indianapolis, Seven Outside, 1971; U. of Illinois, 1971; Newport, R.I., Monumenta, 1974; Stamford Museum, The American Salon des Refuses, 1976; P.S. 1, NYC, A Great Big Drawing Show, 1979. **Collections:** Antwerp/Middelheim; Arizona State College; Astor Place, NYC; Baltimore/MA; Buffalo/Albright; Calcutta; Carborundum Company; Connecticut College; U. of Illinois; Indianapolis; Indianapolis/Herron; Jerusalem/National; Lincoln, Mass./De Cordova; Long Beach/MA; Los Angeles/County MA; Lytton Savings and Loan Association; MOMA; U. of Michigan; Milwaukee; NCFA; NYU; New School; Newark Museum; Norfolk/Chrysler; Princeton U.; Ridgefield/Aldrich; SRGM; San Diego; Santa Barbara/MA; South Mall, Albany; Springfield, Ill./State; Stony Brook/SUNY; UCLA; Yale U.; WMAA; Xerox Corp. **Bibliography:** Hunter 8; *Monumenta*; Read 3; Rodman 2; Trier 1. Archives.

ROSS, CHARLES. b. December 17, 1937, Philadelphia, Pa. **Studied:** U. of California, AB, 1960, MA, 1962. **Taught:** U. of California, 1962, 65; Cornell U., 1964; U. of Kentucky, Artist-in-Residence, 1965; School of Visual Arts, NYC, 1967, 70-71; Herbert H. Lehman College, Bronx, N.Y., 1968; U. of Utah, 1972-74; MIT, 1977. Codirector and collaborator, Dancers Workshop Company, San Francisco, 1964-66. Films: *Sunlight Dispersion*, 16 mm, 1972; *Arisaig, July 10, 1972*, 16 mm, 1972. **Commissions:** Temple of Porat Yeshivat Joseph, Jerusalem, 1972; GSA, Federal Building, Lincoln, Neb., 1975; U. of Pennsylvania, 1977; Prestonwood Town Center, Dallas, 1978; Dietrich Foundation, Phila., 1978; Lincoln Court Building, Denver, 1980; Grand Rapids, 1982; Towson State U., 1983; Plaza of the Americas, Dallas, 1985; Wells Fargo Bldg., San Diego, 1986. **Awards:** U. of California, James D. Phelan Traveling Scholarship, 1962; National Endowment for the Arts, grant, 1976. **Address:** 383 West Broadway, NYC 10012. **Dealer:** Joyce Schwartz Ltd., NYC. **One-man Exhibitions:** (first) Dilexi Gallery, San Francisco, 1961, also 1965, 66, 68; RAC, 1962; Cornell U., 1964; U. of Kentucky, 1965; Dwan Gallery, 1968, 69, 71; Dayton's Gallery 12, Minneapolis, 1968; John Weber Gallery, 1972, 79, 81; The Clocktower, NYC, 1974; Utah, 1975; La Jolla, 1976; Chicago/Contemporary, 1977; John

Weber Gallery and Susan Caldwell Inc., 1977; MIT, 1977; Portland (Ore.) Center for the Visual Arts, 1981; Heydt-Blair Gallery, Santa Fe, 1982; BMW-Museum, Munich, 1983; Bard College, 1984; School of Visual Arts, NYC, 1985. **Group:** Dance theater; Judson Dance Theater, NYC, A Collaborative Event (with the Judson Dancers), 1963; Musée Cantonal des Beaux-Arts, Lausanne, II Salon International de Galeries Pilotes, 1966; Paris Biennial; Architectural League of New York, 1967; A.F.A., 1967; Finch College, 1967; Ridgefield/Aldrich, 1967; Kansas City/Nelson, The Magic Theatre, 1968; Newark Museum, 1968; Milwaukee, Directions I: Options, circ., 1968; Prospect '68, Dusseldorf, 1968; ICA, U. of Pennsylvania, WMAA Sculpture Annual, 1969; Toronto, New Alchemy: Elements, Systems, Forces, 1969; Dusseldorf/Kunsthalle, Prospect '69, '71, 1969, 71; Finch College, NYC, Projected Art, 1971; U. of Wisconsin, Earth, Air, Fire, Water, 1974; Indianapolis, 1974; Leverkusen, Drawings 3: American Drawings, 1975; U. of Colorado, Locate, Order, Measure, 1975; Philadelphia College of Art, Time, 1977; Museum of Natural History, NYC, Maps: Their Science and Their Art, 1977; Hirshhorn, Probing the Earth, 1977; Worcester, Two Decades of American Printmakers, 1957-1977, 1978; Taft Museum, Galaxies, 1978. **Collections:** U. of California, Berkeley; Indianapolis; Kansas City/Nelson; WMAA. **Bibliography:** Atkinson.

ROSSI, BARBARA. b. September 20, 1940, Chicago. **Studied:** Chicago Art Institute School, 1968-70, MFA, with Ray Yoshida and Whitney Halsted. Traveled India, Western Europe. **Taught:** Chicago Art Institute School, 1971-. **Awards:** National Endowment for the Arts, 1971, 85; Indo-US Subcommission on Education and Culture Research, fellowship, 1985. **Address:** 1420 Newcastle, Westchester, Ill. 60153. **Dealer:** Phyllis Kind Gallery,

Barbara Rossi *Day for Divers* 1982

Chicago and NYC. **One-man Exhibitions:** Phyllis Kind Gallery, NYC, 1975, 76, 78, 82; Phyllis Kind Gallery, Chicago, 1980, 83. **Group:** Chicago//Contemporary, Dan Baum Sez, "Chicago Needs Famous Artists," 1969; ICA, U. of Pennsylvania, Spirit of the Comics, 1969; Chicago/Contemporary, Chicago Imagist Art, 1972; Ottawa/Ontario, What They're Up to in Chicago, 1972; WMAA, American Drawings, 1963-1973, 1973; Sao Paulo, Biennial, 1973; WMAA Biennial, 1975; Chicago Art Institute School, Former Famous Alumni, 1976; Sacramento/Crocker, The Chicago Connection, 1977; U. of Texas, New in the Seventies, 1977; Hirshhorn, Directions, 1979; Ridgefield/Aldrich, New Dimensions in Drawing, 1981; Sunderland (Eng.) Arts Centre, Who Chicago?, circ., 1980; Kansas City/AI, Chicago Imagists,

1982; Illinois Wesleyan U., Contemporary Chicago Imagists, 1983. **Collections:** Ball State U.; Baltimore/MA; Chase Manhattan Bank; Chicago/AI; Chicago/Contemporary; Harvard U.; Indianapolis; Mid-America Club, Chicago; Museum des 20. Jahrhunderts, Vienna; NMAA; U. of North Carolina; Northwestern U. **Bibliography:** Adrian; *The Chicago Connection; New in the Seventies; Who Chicago?.*

ROSZAK, THEODORE. b. May 1, 1907, Pozman, Poland; **d.** Sept. 2, 1981, New York City. **Studied:** Columbia U., 1925-26; Chicago Art Institute School, 1922-29, with John W. Norton, Boris Anisfeld; NAD, 1925-26, with C. W. Hawthorne. Traveled Latin America, Europe extensively. **Taught:** Chicago Art Institute School, 1927-29; Design

Theodore Roszak *White and Steel Polars* 1945

Laboratory, NYC, 1938-40; Sarah Lawrence College, 1940-56; Columbia U., 1970-72; lectured at many museums and universities. Began abstract constructions, 1936, free-form sculpture, 1946. **Member:** Commission of Fine Arts, Washington, D.C. (appointed for 1963-67); Advisory Committee on the Arts, US State Department (appointed for 1963-67); National Council on Art and Government. Federal A.P.: Easel painting; New York City Art

Commission, 1969-75; NIAL. **Commissions:** Yale & Towne, Inc.; MIT (spire and bell tower); Reynolds Metals Co. (aluminum sculpture memorial); American Embassy, London; Maremont Building, Chicago; New York World's Fair, 1964-65; New Public Health Laboratory, NYC (outdoor sculpture), 1968; Lafayette Square, Washington, D.C.; Court of Claims, NYC. **Awards:** World's Fair, Poland, 1929, Silver Medal; Chicago/AI, Joseph N. Eisendrath Prize, 1934; Chicago/AI, The Mr. & Mrs. Frank G. Logan Medal, 1947, 51; I Sao Paulo Biennial, 1951; ICA, London/Tate, International Unknown Political Prisoner Competition, 1953; PAFA, George D. Widener Memorial Gold Medal, 1958; Chicago/AI, Campana Prize, 1961; Ball State Teachers College, Griner Award, 1962; elected to the NIAL; Century Association, Medal for Sculpture. **One-man Exhibitons:** (first) Allerton Galleries, Chicago, 1928; Nicholas Roerich Museum, 1935; Albany/Institute, 1936; Artists' Gallery, NYC, 1941; Julien Levy Galleries, NYC, 1941; Pierre Matisse Gallery, 1957, 62, 74, 76; ICA, Boston, circ., 1959; XXX Venice Biennial, 1960; Century Association, 1971; Harold Ernst Gallery, 1973; Arts Club of Chicago, 1977; Fairweather-Hardin Gallery, Chicago, 1977; Zabriskie Gallery, NYC, 1978, 85; MIT, 1979; Fort Lauderdale, 1981; WMAA, 1984; SFMA, 1984. **Retrospective:** WMAA, circ., 1956. **Group:** Chicago/AI Annuals, 1931, 32, 35, 37, 38, 41; WMAA Annuals, 1932-38, 1941, 57, 58, 59, 62, 1964-68; A Century of Progress, Chicago, 1933-34; MOMA, Fourteen Americans, circ., 1946; PAFA, 1946, 64; A.F.A., Tradition and Experiment in Modern Sculpture, circ., 1950-51; Documenta I & II, Kassel, 1955, 59; Brussels World's Fair, 1958; Carnegie, 1958; NIAL, 1958, 59; Tate, 1959; American Painting and Sculpture, Moscow, 1959; Seattle World's Fair, 1962; Silvermine Guild, 1962; Museum des 20. Jahrhunderts, 1962; MOMA, 1963; Cleveland/MA, 1964; MOMA, The New American

Painting and Sculpture, 1969; WMAA, Third Dimension, 1984; Sarah Lawrence College, Sculptural Expressions, 1985; WMAA, Drawing Acquisitions 1981-85, 1985. **Collections:** Akron/AI; U. of Arizona; Baltimore/MA; Chicago/AI; Cleveland/MA; U. of Colorado; Hirshhorn; Houston/MFA; U. of Illinois; Industrial Museum, Barcelona; U. of Iowa; MIT; MOMA; U. of Michigan; Newark/Museum; U. of North Carolina; PAFA; SRGM; Purchase/SUNY; St. Joseph/Albrecht; Sao Paulo; Smithsonian; Tate; Trenton/State; WMAA; Walker; West Palm Beach/Norton; Wichita/Ulrich; U. of Wisconsin; Worcester/AM; Yale U. **Bibliography: Arnason 5;** Baur 7; Blesh 1; Brumme; Chipp; Craven, W.; *From Foreign Shores;* Gertz; Giedion-Welcker 1; Goodrich and Baur 1; Hunter 6; Kepes 2; Kuh 1, 3; Lane and Larsen; Langui; Licht, F.; Marter, Tarbell, and Wechsler; McCurdy, ed.; Mendelowitz; *Metro;* Miller, ed., 2; Myers 2; Phillips, Lisa; Neumeyer; Read 3; Ritchie 1, 3; Rodman 3; Seuphor 3; Seymour; Toher, ed.; Trier 1; Weller. Archives.

ROTH, FRANK. b. February 22, 1936, Boston, Mass. **Studied:** Cooper Union, 1954; Hofmann School, 1955. Traveled Europe, Mexico. **Taught:** School of Visual Arts, NYC, 1963-79; State U. of Iowa, 1964; U. of California, Berkeley, 1968, Irvine, 1971-73. **Awards:** Chaloner Prize Foundation Award, 1961; Guggenheim Foundation Fellowship, 1964; Ford Foundation Artist-in-Residence, 1966; IV International Young Artists Exhibit, America-Japan, Tokyo, Minister of Foreign Affairs Award, 1967; National Endowment for the Arts, Grant, 1977. **Address:** 135 Wooster Street, NYC 10012; 120 Acabonac Road, East Hampton, NY 11973. **Dealer:** Louis K, Meisel Gallery, NYC. **One-man Exhibitions:** (first) Artists' Gallery, NYC, 1958; Grace Borgenicht Gallery, Inc., 1960, 1962-65; The American Gallery, NYC, 1962; Galerie Anderson-Mayer, Paris, 1964;

American Embassy, London, 1965; Hamilton Galleries, London, 1965, 67; U. of Utah, 1967; Martha Jackson Gallery, 1967, 68, 70, 71; Molly Barnes Gallery, Los Angeles, 1968; Galerie Paul Facchetti, 1968; Obelisk Gallery, 1969; Gimpel & Weitzenhoffer Ltd., 1974; OK Harris Works of Art, NYC, 1975; Oklahoma, 1981; Louis K. Meisel Gallery, 1981, 82, 84; Martha White Gallery, Louisville, 1981. **Group:** Buffalo/Albright, 1958; WMAA Annuals, 1958; WMAA, Young America, 1960; Walker, 60 American Painters, 1960; Corcoran, 1962; Flint/Institute, 1963; Tate, 1965; U. of Illinois, 1965; M. Knoedler & Co., Art across America, circ., 1965-67; IV International Young Artists Exhibit, America-Japan, Tokyo, 1967; RISD, 1967; Kent State U., 1968; A.F.A., 1968; Moore College of Art, Science, and Industry, 1969; Philadelphia Art Alliance, 1969; VMFA, American Painting, 1970; Foundation Maeght, 1970; Indianapolis, 1970; Amherst College, Color Painting, 1972; Lehigh U., Contemporary American Painting, 1972. **Collections:** American Republic Insurance Co.; Baltimore/MA; Bellevue Hospital; Buffalo/Albright; Chase Manhattan Bank; Colonial Bank & Trust Co.; Cornell U.; Des Moines; Hirshhorn; Leicester Education Committee; MOMA; Manufacturers Hanover Trust Co.; McDonald & Company; Mead Corporation; Michigan State U.; NYU; U. of Oklahoma; Pasadena/AM; Prudential Insurance Co. of America; RISD; Ringling; Santa Barbara/MA; Schiedam/Stedelijk; Tate; U. of Utah; WMAA; Walker. **Bibliography:** Gerdts.

ROTHENBERG, SUSAN. b. January 20, 1945, Buffalo, N.Y. **Studied:** Cornell U., 1967, BFA. **Awards:** CPAD, 1976; National Endowment for the Arts, 1979; Guggenheim Foundation Fellowship, 1980; AAIAL, 1983; Ljubliana (Yugoslavia) Biennial, Grand Prize for Prints, 1985. **Address:** % Dealer. **Dealer:** Sperone Westwater,

Inc., NYC. **One-man Exhibitions:** (first) 112 Greene Street, 1974; The Willard Gallery, 1976, 77, 79, 81, 83, 85; U. of California, Berkeley, 1978; Greenberg Gallery, 1978; Walker, 1978; Mayor Gallery, London, 1980; Galerie Rudolf Zwirner, 1980; Akron/AM, 1981; Amsterdam/Stedelijk, 1982; Los Angeles/County MA, circ., 1983; Barbara Krakow Gallery, Boston, 1984; Wesleyan U., 1984; Bank of America, San Francisco, 1985; U. of California, Long Beach, 1985; Des Moines, 1985; A.P. Giannini Gallery, San Francisco, 1985; Phillips, 1985; Portland (Ore.) Visual Arts Center, 1985. **Group:** MOMA, American Drawn and Matched, 1977; MOMA, Extraordinary Women, 1977; Buffalo/Albright, American Paintings of the 1970s, circ., 1978; Cleveland/MA, Seven Artists: Contemporary Drawings, 1978; WMAA, New Image Painting, 1978; U. of Chicago, Visionary Images, 1979; NYU, American Painting: The Eighties, 1979; Indianapolis, 1980; XXXIX Venice Biennial, 1980; Akron/AM, The Image in American Painting and Sculpture, 1981; U. of California, Santa Barbara, Contemporary Drawings: In Search of an Image, 1981; Internationale Kunstausstellung, Berlin, 1982; Chicago/AI, 74th American Exhibition, 1982; Milwaukee, New Figuration in America, 1982; WMAA, American Prints: Process and Proofs, 1982; AAIAL, 1983, 85; ARS 83, Helsinki, 1983; Bonn, Back to the USA, circ., 1983; MOMA, Prints from Blocks: Gauguin to Now, 1983; Palacio de Velasquez, Madrid, Tendencias en Nueva York, circ., 1983; Pall Mall Canada Ltd., American Accents, circ., 1983; Youngstown/Butler, 1983; Hirshhorn, Content: A Contemporary Focus, 1974-1984, 1984; MOMA, International Survey of Recent Painting and Sculpture, 1984; Potsdam/SUNY, Pressures of the Hand, 1984; Walker, Images and Impressions: Painters Who Print, 1984; Carnegie, International, 1985; WMAA, Three Printmakers, 1986. **Collections:** Akron/AM; Amsterdam/Stedelijk; Art Museum of South

Texas; Buffalo/Albright; Carnegie; Dallas/MFA; Des Moines; High Museum; Houston/MFA; Israel Museum; Kansas City/Nelson; Los Angeles/County MA; MOMA; Milwaukee; National Gallery; Purchase/SUNY; St. Louis/City; Seattle/AM; Utica; WMAA; Walker. **Bibliography:** *Back to the USA;* Hiromoto; Joachimides and Rosenthal; Murken-Altrogge.

ROTHKO, MARK. b. September 25, 1903, Dvinska, Russia; **d.** February 25, 1970, NYC. To USA, 1913. **Studied:** Yale U., 1921-23; ASL, 1925, with Max Weber. Traveled Europe, USA. **Taught:** Center Academy, Brooklyn, N.Y., 1929-52; California School of Fine Arts, summers, 1947, 49; Brooklyn College, 1951-54; U. of Colorado, 1955; Tulane U., 1956. A cofounder of the Expressionist group The Ten, 1935. Cofounder of a school, "Subject of the Artist," with William Baziotes, Robert Motherwell, and Barnett Newman, NYC, 1948. Federal A.P.: 1936-37. **Awards:** Hon. DFA, Yale U., 1969. **One-man Exhibitions:** (first) Contemporary Arts Gallery, NYC, 1933; Portland, Ore./AM, 1933; Art of This Century, NYC, 1945; Santa Barbara/MA, 1946; Betty Parsons Gallery, 1946-51; RISD, 1954; Chicago/AI, 1954; Sidney Janis Gallery, 1955, 58; Houston/MFA, 1957; XXIX Venice Biennial, 1958; Phillips, 1960; MOMA, 1961; Whitechapel Art Gallery, London, 1961; Amsterdam/Stedelijk, 1961; Palais des Beaux-Arts, Brussels, 1962; Kunsthalle, Basel, 1962; Paris/Moderne, 1962, 72; Marlborough Fine Art Ltd., London, 1964, 70; Marlborough Gallery, Inc., NYC, 1970, Zurich, 1971; Berlin/National, 1971; Newport Harbor, 1974; The Pace Gallery, NYC, 1978; Mantova (Italy), 1977; SFMA, 1983; Walker, 1983; National Gallery, circ., 1984; Tate Gallery, 1986. **Retrospective:** SRGM, 1978. **Group:** PAFA, 1940; WMAA, 1945-50; XXIV Venice Biennial, 1948; MOMA, Abstract Painting and Sculpture in Amer ica, 1951; MOMA, Fifteen Americans, circ., 1952; 10th Inter-American Conference, Caracas, 1954; 3rd International Contemporary Art Exhibition, New Delhi, 1957; Carnegie, 1958, 61; MOMA, The New American Painting, circ., Europe, 1958-59; Documenta II, Kassel, 1959; Federation of Modern Painters and Sculptors Annuals; Walker, 60 American Painters, 1960; Cleveland/MA, 1966; MOMA, The New American Painting and Sculpture, 1969; MMA, New York Painting and Sculpture; 1940-1970, 1969-70; Venice Biennial, 1974; SRGM, 20th Century American Drawing: Three Avant-Garde Generations, 1976. **Collections:** U. of Arizona; Baltimore/MA; Brooklyn Museum; Buffalo/Albright; Chicago/AI;   Dusseldorf/KN-W; Kansas City/Nelson; MMA; MOMA; Paris/Moderne; Phillips; Rio de Janeiro; SFMA; Tate Gallery; Utica; Vassar College; WMAA. **Bibliography:** Alloway 4; Ashton 3, 5; Barker 1; Barr 3; Battcock, ed.; Baur 7; Bihalji-Merin; Blesh 1; Calas, N. and E.; Carmean, Rathbone, and Hess; Chipp; Clearwater; De Wilde 1; Downes, ed.; Eliot; Elsen 2; *From Foreign Shores;* Goodrich and Baur 1; Goossen 1; *The Great Decade;* Greenberg 1; Haftman; Henning; Hess, T.B., 1; Hobbs and Levin; Honisch and Jensen, eds.; Hunter 1, 6; Hunter, ed.; Janis and Blesh 1; Janis, S.; Johnson, Ellen H.; Kozloff 3; Lucie-Smith; Lynton; McChesney; McCoubrey 1; McCurdy, ed.; *Metro;* Motherwell,   ed.;   Murken-Altrogge; O'Doherty; Ponente; Read 2; Restany 2; Richardson, E.P.; Rickey; Ritchie 1; Rodman 1, Rose, B., 1, 4; Rosenblum 2; Rubin 1; Sandler; Sandler 1; Seitz 1; **Selz, P., 4;** Seuphor 1; Soby 5; Tomkins 2; Tuchman, ed.; Tuchman 3; Waldman 5; Weller. Archives.

ROTTERDAM, PAUL Z. (Werner Paul Zwietnig-Rotterdam) **b.** February 12, 1939, Neustadt, near Vienna. **Studied:** Academy of Fine and Applied Arts, Vienna, 1959-60; U. of Vienna. Resided Paris, Rome, Vienna, 1961; to USA, 1968; to NYC, 1973. **Taught:** Harvard U., 1968; Cooper Union, NYC, 1974. **Awards:** Premio internazionale d'art grafica, Livorno, 1965; Ancona, prize, prints, 1968. **Address:** 115 West Broadway, NYC 10013. **Dealer:** Galerie Maeght Lelong, NYC; Adams-Middleton Gallery, Dallas; Galerie Maeght, Paris. **One-man Exhibitions:** (first) Numero Gallery, Florence, 1961; Lincoln, Mass./De Cordova, 1970; Kunstverein, Freiburg, 1971; Graz/Johanneum, 1971; Nielsen Gallery, Boston, 1973, 76, 81, 85; Susan Caldwell Inc., NYC, 1975, 76, 78, 81; Musée l'Abbaye, St. Croix, Les Sables d'Olonne, France, 1976; Galerie Parallele,   Geneva,   1976;   Galerie Maeght, Paris, 1979, 82; Nice/Municipa, 1976; Annely Juda Fine Art, London, 1978; Galerie Charles Kriwin, Brussels, 1980; Nantenshi Gallery, Tokyo, 1982, 85; Adams-Middleton Gallery, 1983, 84; Galerie Maeght Lelong, NYC, 1984; Storrer Gallery, Zurich, 1985. **Group:** Vienna/Stadt, Oesterreichische Kunst seit 1960. 1963; Biennial, Tokyo/Modern, 1965; Biennial of Young Artists, Paris, 1965; WMAA Biennial, 1975; Hirshhorn, The Golden Door: Immigrant Artists of America, 1876-1976, 1976; Tulane U., Drawing Today in New York, 1976; Brooklyn Museum, American Drawings in Black and White: 1970-1979, 1980. **Collections:** Birmingham (Mich.) Museum of Art; Brooklyn Museum; Busch-Reisinger Museum; Des Moines; Graphische Sammlung Albertina; Graz Johanneum;   Little   Rock/MFA;   MMA; MOMA; Milwaukee; Museum der Stadt Leoben, Austria; Nice; Osaka/National; Paris/Beaubourg; Portland, Ore./AM; SRGM; U. of Sydney; Vassar College.

RUBEN, RICHARDS. b. November 29, 1925, Los Angeles, Calif. **Studied:** Chouinard   Art   Institute,   1944-46; Bradley U., BFA, 1951. US Army, 1942-44. **Taught:** Arts and Crafts Center, Pittsburgh, 1949; Chouinard Art Institute, 1954-61; Pomona College, 1958-59; Pasadena Museum School; UCLA, 1958-62; Cooper Union, 1962-64; Otis Art Institute; NYU, 1963-. **Awards:** International Arts Festival, Newport, R.I., First Prize, 1951; Bradley U., **P.P.**, 1952; Brooklyn Museum, First Prize, 1953, 54; SFMA, Anne Bremer Memorial Prize, 1954; L.C. Tiffany Grant, 1954. **Address:** 85 Mercer Street, NYC 10012. **One-man Exhibitions:** Felix Landau Gallery, 1952, 54; Pasadena/AM, 1954, 55, 61; Oakland/AM, 1957; Paul Kantor Gallery, Beverly Hills, Calif., 1958; Grand Central Moderns, NYC, 1958; Ferus Gallery, Los Angeles, 1960, 61, 63; California Palace, 1961; Poindexter Gallery, 1962, 64, 69; SFMA, 1970; Ericson Gallery, NYC, 1979; Purchase/SUNY, 1977, Cornell U., 1976; Peter Rose Gallery, NYC, 1977. **Group:** Los Angeles/County MA, 1948, 53, 55, 57; Bradley U., 1952; U. of Illinois, 1952, 56; Dallas/MFA, 1953; Corcoran, 1953; PAFA, 1954; SRGM, Younger American Painters, 1954; Sao Paulo, 1955; Carnegie, 1955; Santa Barbara/MA, 1955, 58; Brooklyn Museum, 1957, 59; I Paris Biennial, 1959; WMAA, Fifty California Artists, 1962-63; El Retiro Parquet, Madrid, Arte de America y Espana, 1963; WMAA, 1964. **Collections:** Boston/MFA; Bradley U.; Brooklyn Museum; Los Angeles/County MA; Oakland/AM; Pasadena/AM; Raleigh/NCMA; W. & J. Sloane, Inc.; U. of Southern California; Stanford U.

RUDA, EDWIN. b. May 15, 1922, NYC. **Studied:** ASL, 1940-41; Cornell U., 1947, BS; New School for Social Research, 1948; Columbia U., 1949, MA; School of Painting and Sculpture, Mexico City, 1949-51; U. of Illinois, 1956, MFA. Traveled Mexico, Europe, Southwest Pacific, Australia. US Naval Reserve, 1943-46. **Taught:** School of Visual Arts, NYC; Pratt Institute; U. of Texas; Syracuse U., 1978; Ohio State U., 1978; Tyler School of Art, Philadelphia, 1979. **Awards:** CAPS, 1978. **Address:** 44 Walker Street, NYC 10013.

One-man Exhibitions: (first) Globe Gallery, NYC, 1961; Feiner Gallery, NYC, 1963; Park Place Gallery, NYC, 1966-67; Paula Cooper Gallery, 1969, 71, 73, 75; Gallery A, Sydney, 1973; Tyler School of Art, Philadelphia, 1974, 79; Max Hutchinson Gallery, NYC, 1978-79; Ohio State U., 1978. **Group:** New York World's Fair, 1965; SRGM, Systemic Painting, 1966; U. of Illinois, 1967, 74; ICA, U. of Pennsylvania, Art in the City, 1967; Newark Museum, Cool Art, 1968; Fort Worth Art Museum, Drawings, 1969; WMAA Annuals, 1969, 73; Indianapolis, 1970, 72; Chicago/AI, 1970; ICA, U. of Pennsylvania, Two Generations of Color Painting, 1970; U. of Texas, Color Forum, 1972; Cincinnati/Contemporary, Options, 73/70, 1973; WMAA Biennial, 1973; U. of Illinois, 1974; Buffalo/Albright, SoHo Scenes, 1975; Baltimore/MA, Drawing Exhibition, 1976. **Collections:** Allentown/AM; Canberra/National; Chase Manhattan Bank; U. of Connecticut; Cornell U.; Great Southwest Industrial Park; Greenville; Indianapolis; U. of North Carolina; South Mall, Albany.

RUSCHA, EDWARD. b. December 16, 1937, Omaha, Neb. **Studied:** Chouinard Art Institute (with Richards Ruben). Traveled Europe. **Taught:** U. of Arizona; U. of North Dakota; UCLA; Vancouver (B.C.) School of Art; SFAI. **Films:** *Premium*, 16 mm, 1970; *Miracle*, 16mm, 1974. **Commission:** Metropolitan Dade County, Fla., Art in Public Places (mural) 1985. **Awards:** National Council on the Arts, 1967; Guggenheim Foundation Fellowship, 1971; Ljubljana Biennial, **P.P.**, 1977; National Endowment for the Arts, 1978. **Address:** 1024¾ N. Western Avenue, Hollywood, CA 90029. **Dealer:** Leo Castelli Inc., NYC; James Corcoran Gallery, Los Angeles. **One-man Exhibitions:** (first) Ferus Gallery, Los Angeles, 1963, also 1964, 65; Alexandre Iolas Gallery, NYC, 1967, 70; Irving Blum Gallery, Los Angeles, 1968, 69;

Galerie Rudolf Zwirner, 1968; Pavilion Art Gallery, Newport Beach, Calif. (two-man), 1968; Galerie Heiner Friedrich, Munich, 1970; Nigel Greenwood Ltd., London, 1970; Contract Graphics Associates, Houston, 1971; Janie C. Lee Gallery, Dallas, 1972; Corcoran and Corcoran, Coral Gables, 1972; Minneapolis/Institute, 1972; D.M. Gallery, London, 1972; Leo Castelli, Inc., NYC, 1973, 74, 78, 80, 81, 82, 84, 86; John Berggruen Gallery, 1973; Projections: Ursula Wevers Gallery, Cologne, 1973; Ronald Greenberg Gallery, St. Louis, 1973; ACE Gallery, Los Angeles, 1973, 75, 77; Colgate U., 1973; Yvon Lambert, 1973; Francoise Lambert, Milan, 1973; The Texas Gallery, 1974; Galerie Rolf Ricke, Cologne, 1975, 78; Jared Sable Gallery, Toronto, 1975; U. of North Dakota, Grand Forks, 1975; Arts Council of Great Britain, circ., 1975; Northern Kentucky State College, Highland Heights, 1975; ACE Gallery, Vancouver, 1976, 78; ICA, Los Angeles, 1976; Hartford/Wadsworth, 1976; Amsterdam/Stedelijk, 1976; Dootson Calderhead Gallery, Seattle, 1976; ICA, London, 1976; Sable-Castelli Gallery, Toronto, 1976; U. of Lethbridge, Alberta, 1977; U. of Calgary, 1977; Fort Worth, 1977; Galerie MTL, Brussels, 1978; Rudiger Schottle, Munich, 1978; U. of Redlands, 1978; Auckland, 1978; Getler/Pall, NYC, 1978; Richard Hines Gallery, Seattle, 1979; The Texas Gallery, Houston, 1979; inK, Zurich, 1979; Portland (Ore.) Center for the Visual Arts, 1980; Ace Gallery, Venice, Calif., 1980; Foster-Goldstrom Fine Arts, San Francisco, 1980; ARCO Center for the Visual Arts, Los Angeles, 1981; Ace Gallery, Vancouver, 1981; Douglas Dean Courtenier Inc., East Hampton, N.Y., 1981; Castelli Feigen Corcoran, NYC, 1982; Flow Ace Gallery, Los Angeles, 1982; Jacobson/Hochman Gallery, NYC, 1982; Bernard Jacobson Ltd., Los Angeles, 1983; Route 66, Philadelphia, 1983; Gilbert Brownstone & Cie, Paris, 1985; Galerie Tanja Grunert, Cologne, 1985; Munster, 1986. **Retrospectives:** Buffalo/Albright, 1976; SFMA, circ., 1982; Musée St. Pierre,

1986. **Group:** Oklahoma, 1960; Pasadena/AM, New Paintings of Common Objects, 1962; Oakland/AM, Pop Art USA, 1963; SRGM, American Drawings, 1964; M. Knoedler & Co., Art across America, circ., 1965-67; SRGM, 1965; Seattle/AM, 1966; IX Sao Paulo Biennial, 1967; V Paris Biennial, 1967; WMAA Annual, 1967; Hayward Gallery, London, Pop Art, 1969; XXX Venice Biennial, 1970; Hayward Gallery, London, Eleven Los Angeles Artists, 1971; Akron/AI, Four Artists, 1972; Amerika Haus, Berlin, 1973; Yale U., American Drawings: 1970-1973, 1973; Oakland/AM, Cirrus Editions, 1974; WMAA, American Pop Art, 1974; VMFA, Works on Paper, 1974; Malmo, New Media I, 1975; Moore College of Art, Philadelphia, North, East, West, South, and Middle, 1975; Newport Harbor, The Last Time I Saw Ferus, 1976; SFMW, Painting and Sculpture in California: The Modern Era, 1976; The Image and the Myth, Beverly Hills, L.A. Art 2001, 1976; Brooklyn Museum, Twenty Years of American Printmaking, 1976; ICA, Los Angeles, 100+, Current Directions in Southern California Art, 1977; Laguna Gloria Art Museum, Austin, Texas; Joe Goode, Edward Ruscha, Drawings, 1977; Philadelphia College of Art, Time, 1977; Williamstown/Clark, The Dada/Surrealist Heritage, 1977; MOMA, Bookworks, 1977; Minnesota/AM, American Drawing, 1927-1977, circ., 1977; X Biennial de Paris, 1977; Honolulu Academy, California: 3 by 8 Twice, 1978; SFMA, Aesthetics of Graffiti, 1978; MOMA, Mirrors and Windows, 1978; U. of North Carolina, Drawings about Drawing Today, 1979; Buffalo/Albright, American Painting of the 1970s, circ., 1978-79; Museum Bochum, Words, circ., 1979; Albuquerque Museum, Reflections of Realism, 1979; Chicago/AI, 73rd American Exhibition, 1979; U. of North Carolina, Drawings About Drawing Today, 1979; Brooklyn Museum, American Drawings in Black and White: 1970-1979, 1980; MOMA, Printed Art: A View of Two Decades, 1980; Purchase/SUNY, Hidden Desires,

1980; Houston/Contemporary, Americans: The Landscape, 1981; Documenta VII, Kassel, 1982; Paris/Beaubourg, Livres d'Artistes, 1982; New Museum, Language, Drama Source & Vision, 1983; Sydney/AG, Pop Art 1955-1970, 1985; Fort Lauderdale, An American Renaissance: Painting and Sculpture Since 1940, 1986. **Collections:** Amsterdam/Stedelijk; Art Museum of South Texas; Auckland; U. of California, Berkeley; Chicago/AI; Fort Worth; Hirshhorn; Los Angeles/County MA; MOMA; U. of Massachusetts; Mead Paper Co.; Minneapolis/Institute; Musée St. Pierre; Oklahoma City; Pasadena/AM; Pomona College; Reynolda House, Winston-Salem; U. of Rochester; SFMA; VMFA; WMAA; Walker; Yale U. **Bibliography:** Alloway 1; *Contemporanea;* De Wilde 2; Finch; **Hickey and Plagens;** Honisch and Jensen, eds.; Hunter, ed.; Lippard 5; Lippard, ed.; Meyer; Murken-Altrogge; *The State of California Painting: USA West Coast.*

RUSSELL, MORGAN. b. January 25, 1886, NYC; **d.** 1953, Broomall, Pa. **Studied:** Privately with Robert Henri; ASL (with James E. Fraser). Traveled Europe; resided Paris, 1906-1946. Developed Synchromism, with Stanton Macdonald-Wright, in Paris, 1912. **One-man Exhibitions:** Galerie Bernheim-Jeune, Paris, 1013; Neue Kunstsalon, Munich, 1913; Carrol Gallery, NYC, 1914; Galerie la Licorne, Paris, 1923; Rose Fried Gallery, 1953; Walker, 1954; Washburn Gallery, NYC, 1978, 80; Flow Ace Gallery, Los Angeles, 1985; Salander-O'Reilly Galleries, 1985. **Group:** Salon d'Automne, Paris, 1910; Salon des Artistes Independants, Paris, 1913; The Armory Show, 1913; Anderson Galleries, NYC, Forum Exhibition, 1916; Dallas/Contemporary, 1960; WMAA, 1963; M. Knoedler & Co., 1965; Marlborough-Gerson Gallery Inc., 1967; U. of New Mexico, Cubism: Its Impact in the USA, 1967; WMAA, Synchromism and American Color Abstraction, 1978; Los Angeles/County MA, California: 5 Footnotes to Modern Art History, 1977. **Collections:** Evansville; Los Angeles/County MA; MOMA; NYU; Utica; WMAA. **Bibliography:** *Avant Garde Painting & Sculpture in America 1910-25;* Baur 7; Blesh 1; Brown; Brown 2; Canaday; Haftman; Hunter 6; Levin 2; Richardson, E.P.; Rickey; Rose, B., 1; Seuphor 1; Wright 2; Archives.

RUVOLO, FELIX. b. April 28, 1912, NYC. Throughout his youth, family resided in Italy, where he first attended art school (Catania). **Studied:** Chicago Art Institute School. Traveled Europe, Mexico, Canada, USA. **Taught:** Chicago Art Institute School, 1945-47; Mills College, summer, 1948; U. of California, Berkeley, 1950-; U. of Southern California, 1963. Federal A.P.: Easel painting. **Commissions:** Merchandise Mart, Chicago (murals). **Awards:** SFMA, Anne Bremer Memorial Prize, 1942; Chicago/AI, **P.P.,** 1942, 46, 47; California Palace, Gold Medal, 1946; Milwaukee, Kearney Memorial Prize, 1946; Pepsi-Cola, 1947, 48; Hallmark International Competition, 1949; U. of Illinois, **P.P.,** 1949; SFMA, **P.P.,** 1950; U. of California Institute for Creative Work in the Arts, Travel Fellowship, 1964; and some two dozen others. **Address:** 78 Strathmoor Drive, Berkeley, CA 94705. **Dealer:** Gruenebaum Gallery, NYC. **One-man Exhibitions:** (first) Durand-Ruel Gallery, NYC, 1946; Mills College, 1947; de Young, 1947, 58; Grand Central Moderns, NYC, 1948; Catherine Viviano Gallery, 1949, 50, 52, 54; Poindexter Gallery, 1957, 58; U. of Southern California, 1963; Galleria Van der Voort, 1970; Jason Avers Gallery, San Francisco, 1971; Gruenebaum Gallery, 1982. **Group:** U. of Illinois, 1947, 61; MOMA, Abstract Painting and Sculpture in America, 1951; Buffalo/Albright, Expressionism in American Painting, 1952; Walker, 60 American Painters, 1960; Chicago/AI Annuals; MMA; Corcoran; PAFA; WMAA.

Collections: Auckland; U. of California; Chicago/AI; Denison U.; Denver/AM; Des Moines; U. of Illinois; Mills College; SFMA; U. of Southern California; Tulsa/Philbrook; Walter. **Bibliography:** Genauer; Pousette-Dart, ed.; Ritchie 1.

RYMAN, ROBERT. b. May 30, 1930, Nashville, Tenn. **Studied:** Tennessee Polytechnic Institute, 1948-49; George Peabody College, 1949-50. US Army, 1950-52. **Member:** American Abstract Artists. **Awards:** Guggenheim Foundation Grant, 1973. **Address:** 17 West 16th Street, NYC 10003. **One-man Exhibitions:** Paul Bianchini Gallery, NYC, 1967; Konrad Fischer Gallery, Dusseldorf, 1968, 69, 73, 80; Galerie Heiner Friedrich, Munich, 1968, 69, 73; Fischbach Gallery, 1969, 70, 71; Francoise Lambert, Milan, 1969; Yvon Lambert, 1969; ACE Gallery, Los Angeles, 1969; Current Editions, Seattle, 1971, 72; Dwan Gallery, NYC, 1971; Galerie Heiner Friedrich, Cologne, 1971, 72; John Weber Gallery, NYC, 1972, 73, 74; 75; Galerie Annemarie Verna, Zurich, 1972; Galleria del Cortile, Rome, 1972; Lisson Gallery, 1972; Galleria San Fedele, Milan, 1973; Art & Project, Amsterdam, 1973; Brussels/Beaux-Arts, 1975; Basel, 1975; P.S. #1, L.I.C., 1977; Gian Enzo Sperone, Rome, 1977; Galerie Annemarie Verna, Zurich, 1977; Whitechapel Art Gallery, London, 1977; Galerie Charles Kriwin, Brussels, 1977; InK, Zurich, 1978, 80; Sidney Janis Gallery, NYC, 1979, 81; Kunstraum, Munich, 1980; Paris/Beaubourg, 1981; Young Hoffman Gallery, Chicago, 1982; Kunsthalle, Cologne, 1982; The Mayor Gallery, London, 1982; Galerie Maeght-Lelong, NYC, 1985, 86. **Retrospective:** SRGM, 1972. **Group:** New York World's Fair, 1964-65; American Abstract Artists, 1965; SRGM, Systemic Painting, 1966; A.F.A., Rejective Art, 1967; ICA, U. of

Pennsylvania, A Romantic Minimalism, 1967; A.F.A., The Square in Painting, 1968; Washington U., Here and Now, 1969; Berne, When Attitudes Become Form, 1969; WMAA, Anti-Illusion: Procedures/Materials, 1969; Seattle/AM, 557,087, 1969; Dusseldorf/Kunsthalle, Prospect '69, 1969; Fort Worth Art Museum, Drawings 1969; Amsterdam/Stedelijk, Op Losse Schroeven, 1969; Buffalo/Albright, Modular Painting, 1970; Cincinnati/Contemporary, Monumental Art, 1970; New Delhi, Second World Triennial, 1971; SRGM, Guggenheim International, 1971; Chicago/Contemporary, White on White, 1971-72; Chicago/AI, 1972; Documenta V, Kassel, 1972; Seattle/AM, American Art: Third Quarter Century, 1973; MOMA, U. of California, Santa Barbara, 1975; UCLA, Fourteen Abstract Painters, 1975; Amsterdam/Stedelijk, Fundamental Painting, 1975; MOMA, Drawing Now, 1976; Detroit/Institute, American Artists, A New Decade, 1976; WMAA, Biennial, 1977; Documenta 6, Kassel; Sarah Lawrence College, Ferra, Lichtenstein, Nevelson, Ryman, 1977; Worcester/AM, Two Decades of American Printmaking, 1957-1977; Chicago/AI, 1979; AAAL, Childe Hassam Fund Exhibition, 1979; ICA, Boston, The Reductive Object, 1979; Humlebaek/Louisiana, Andre, Dibbets, Long, Ryman, 1980; MOMA, Printed Art, 1980; XXXIX Venice Biennale, 1980; Royal Academy, London, A New Spirit in Painting, 1981. **Collections:** Amsterdam/Stedelijk; Dayton/AI; Hartford/Wadsworth; MOMA; Milwaukee; Minneapolis/Institute; WMAA. **Bibliography:** *Contemporanea;* Danto; De Wilde 1, 2; Diamonstein; *Fundamentele Schilderkunst;* Gablik; Honisch and Jensen, eds.; Lippard 3; Lippard, ed.; Murdock 1; Murken-Altrogge; *Robert Ryman; When Attitudes Become Form.* Archives.

SAGE, KAY. b. June 25, 1898, Albany, N.Y.; **d.** January 7, 1963, Woodbury, Conn. Self-taught. Resided Italy, 1900-14, 1919-37, Paris 1937-39. **m.** Yves Tanguy. **One-man Exhibitions:** (first) Galleria Il Milione, Milan, 1936; Pierre Matisse Gallery, 1940; SFMA, 1941; Julien Levy Galleries, NYC, 1944, 47; Catherine Viviano Gallery, 1950, 52, 56, 58; L'Obelisco, Rome, 1953; Galerie Nina Dausset, Paris, 1953; Hartford/Wadsworth, 1954 (two-man); Mattatuck Historical Society Museum, Waterbury, Conn., 1965; Cornell U., 1977. **Retrospective:** Catherine Viviano Gallery, 1960. **Group:** Salon des Surindependants, Paris, 1938; International Surrealist Exhibition, NYC, 1942; Chicago/AI, 1945, 47, 51; Carnegie, 1946-50; WMAA, 1946-55; Toledo/MA, 1947, 49; California Palace, 1949, 50; U. of Illinois, 1949, 51; Brussels World's Fair, 1958. **Collections:** California Palace; Chicago/AI; MMA; MOMA; SMFA; WMAA; Wesleyan U. **Bibliography:** Breton 3; Goodrich and Baur 1; Krieger; Pearson 2; Seitz 3; Tomkins and Time-Life Books; Waldberg 3. Archives.

SALEMME, ATTILIO. b. October 18, 1911, Boston, Mass.; **d.** January 24, 1955, NYC. Self-taught. US Marine Corps, 1927-28. Traveled USA. **Commissions** (murals): Moore-McCormack Lines, Inc., 1949; 200 East 66th Street, NYC 1950. **Awards:** Chicago/AI, Flora Mayer Witkowsky Prize, 1949; MMA, **P.P.,** 1950; William and Norma Copley Foundation Grant, 1954. **One-man Exhibitions:** (first) "67" Gallery, NYC, 1945; Carlebach Gallery, NYC, 1947; Passedoit Gallery, NYC, 1948; Saidenberg Gallery, 1950; Grace Borgenicht Gallery, Inc., 1953, 81, 82, 83; Duveen-Graham Gallery, NYC, 1955; ICA, Boston, 1958; Walker, 1958; Catherine Viviano Gallery, 1960; Staempfli Gallery, 1963; Terry Dintenfass, Inc., 1974. **Retrospectives:** WMAA, 1960; NCFA, 1978. **Group:** Carnegie; WMAA Annuals; Chicago/AI Annuals; U. of Illinois, 1955. **Collections:** Brooklyn Museum; MMA; MOMA; WMAA. **Bibliography:** Goodrich and Baur 1; Kent, N.; McCurdy, ed.; Newmeyer; Pousette-Dart, ed. Archives.

SALLE, DAVID. b. 1952, Norman, Ok. **Studied:** California Institute of Arts, 1973, BFA; 1975, MFA. **Address:** % Dealers. **Dealer:** Leo Castelli Inc., NYC; Mary Boone Gallery, NYC. **One-man Exhibitions:** Project Inc., Cambridge, Mass, 1975; Copley Gallery, Los Angeles, 1975; Fondation Corps de Garde, Groningen, 1976, 78; Artists Space, NYC, 1976; Foundation de Appel, Amsterdam, 1977, 79; The Kitchen, NYC, 1977, 79; Real Art Ways, Hartford, Ct., 1978; Nova Scotia College of Art and Design, 1979; Gagosian/Nosei-Weber Gallery, NYC, 1979; Annina Nosei Gallery, NYC, 1980; Galerie Bischofberger, Zurich, 1980, 84; Mary Boone Gallery, NYC, 1981, 82, 83, 85; Larry Gagosian Gallery, Los Angeles, 1981, 83; Lucio Amelio Gallery, Naples, 1981; Galleria Mario Diacono, Rome, 1982, 84; Anthony d'Offay Gallery, London, 1982; The Greenberg Gallery, St. Louis, 1983; Rotterdam, 1983; B. R. Kornblatt Gallery, Washington, D.C., 1983; Ascan Crone Gallery, Hamburg,

David Salle *Maid of Germany* 1986

1983; Gallerie Schellmann & Kluser, Munich, 1983; Leo Castelli Inc., 1982, 84; Texas Gallery, Houston, 1985; Galerie Daniel Templon, Paris, 1985; Andover/Phillips, 1983; Akira Ikeda, Tokyo, 1983; American Graffiti Gallery, Amsterdam, 1982; Chicago/Contemporary, 1985; Galerie Michael Werner, Cologne, 1985. **Retrospective:** ICA, U. of Pennsylvania, circ., 1986. **Group:** Grand Palais, Paris, L'Amerique aux Indépendants, 1980; Cologne/Stadt, Westkunst, 1981; Buffalo/Albright, Figures: Forms and Expressions, 1981; Documenta VII, Kassel, 1982; Internationale Kunstausstellung Berlin, 1982; Houston/Contemporary, The Americans: The Collage, 1982; Hirshhorn, Directions, 1983; WMAA, Biennials, 1983, 85; Bonn, Back to the USA, circ., 1983; Milwaukee, New Figuration in America, 1982; Hirshhorn, Content,

1984; Independent Curator Inc., NYC, Drawings: After Photography, 1984; XL Venice Biennial, 1982; ICA, U. of Pennsylvania, Image Scavengers, 1982; Sao Paulo Biennial, 1983; MOMA, International Survey of Contemporary Painting and Sculpture, 1984; SFMA, The Human Condition, 1984; Carnegie, International, 1985. **Collections:** Aachen/Ludwig; Chicago/AI; Chicago/Contemporary; Los Angeles/MOCA; MMA; MOMA; Milwaukee; Paris/Beaubourg; Tate Gallery. **Bibliography:** Haenlein; Hiromoto; Joachimides and Rosenthal; **Kardon 2;** Murken-Altrogge; Pincus-Witten 2.

SAMARAS, LUCAS. b. September 14, 1936, Kastoria, Macedonia, Greece. To USA, 1948; citizen, 1955. **Studied:** Rutgers U., 1955-59, BA; Columbia U. Graduate School, 1959-62; Stella Adler

Theatre Studio, NYC, 1960. **Taught:** Yale U., 1969; Brooklyn College, 1971-72. **Commissions:** GSA, for Hale Boggs Federal Courthouse, New Orleans, 1976. Traveled Europe, Near East, Japan. Completed film, *Self*, 22½ minutes, with Kim Levin, 1969. **Awards:** Woodrow Wilson Fellow, Columbia U. **Address:** 52 West 71st Street, NYC 10023. **Dealer:** The Pace Gallery, NYC. **One-man Exhibitions:** Rutgers U., 1955, 58; Reuben Gallery, NYC, 1959; Green Gallery, NYC, 1961, 64; Dwan Gallery, Los Angeles, 1964; The Pace Gallery, NYC, 1966, 68, 70, 71, 72, 74, 75, 76, 78, 80, 82, 84, 85; Hannover/Kunstverein, 1970; MOMA, 1975; Makler Gallery, Philadelphia, 1975; California State U., Long Beach, 1975; U. of North Dakota, 1976; Wright State U., 1976; ICA, Boston, 1976; Seattle, 1976; Alberta College, Calgary, 1976; Margo Leavin Gallery, Los Angeles, 1976, 80; Zabriskie Gallery, Paris, 1977; Walker, 1977; F.H. Mayor Gallery, London, 1978; Akron/AI, 1978; Richard Gray Gallery, Chicago, 1979; Galerie Watari, Tokyo, 1981; Jean Bernier Gallery, Athens, Greece, 1983; ICA, Boston, 1983; Paris/Beaubourg, 1983; ICP, circ., 1984; Pace-McGill Gallery, NYC, 1984; Reed College, 1985. **Retrospectives:** Chicago/Contemporary, 1971; WMAA, 1972; Denver/AM, circ., 1983; Polaroid Corp., Rochester, N.Y., circ., 1984. **Group:** Martha Jackson Gallery, New Media—New Forms, II, 1961; MOMA, The Art of Assemblage, circ., 1961; MOMA, Lettering by Hand, 1962; Corcoran, 1963; Brandeis U., Recent American Drawings, 1964; WMAA Annuals, 1964, 68, 70, Young America, 1965; SRGM, 1965; RISD, 1965, Recent Still Life, 1966; WMAA, Contemporary American Sculpture, Selection I, 1966; MOMA, 1966; Walker, 1966; Los Angeles/County MA, American Sculpture of the Sixties, 1967; Chicago/AI, 1967, 74; ICA, London, The Obsessive Image, 1968; MOMA, Dada, Surrealism and Their Heritage, 1968; Documenta IV & V, Kassel, 1968, 72; Monumenta,

Newport, R.I., 1974; Chicago/Century, Bodyworks, 1975; WMAA, 200 Years of American Sculpture, 1976; Documenta 6, Kassel, 1977; Williamstown/Clark, The Dada/Surrealist, Heritage, 1977; ICA, Philadelphia, The Decorative Impulse, 1979; XXXIX Venice Biennale, 1980; AAIAL, 1984; WMAA, Blam!, 1984; Hera Art Foundation, Cambridge, Mass., Offset: A Survey of Artists' Books, 1985. **Collections:** Buffalo/Albright; Canberra/National; Chicago/AI; Chicago/Contemporary; Dallas/MFA; Fort Worth; Hartford/Wadsworth; Harvard U.; Hirshhorn; Indiana U.; Los Angeles/County MA; Miami-Dade; Minneapolis/Institute; MMA; MOMA; New Orleans/Museum; PMA; Phoenix; Princeton U.; Prudential Insurance Co. of America; Ridgefield/Aldrich; RISD; SFMA; Seattle; SRGM; St. Louis/City; U. of St. Thomas (Tex.); WMAA; Walker. **Bibliography: Alloway 2,** 4; Battcock, ed.; Cummings 1; Diamonstein; Davies; *Drawings: The Pluralist Decade*; Finch; Friedman and van der Marck; *From Foreign Shores*; Hansen; *Happening & Fluxus*; Haskell 5; Hunter, ed.; Kozloff 3; Lippard 5; *Monumenta*; Pincus-Witten; Rickey; **Samaras, 2;** Schwartz 2; Seitz 3; Tuchman 1. Archives.

SANDBACK, FRED. b. 1943, Bronxville, N.Y. **Studied:** Williston Academy, 1957-61; Theodor Heuss Gymnasium, Heilbronn, 1961-62; Yale U., 1962-66; Yale School of Art and Architecture, 1966-69. **Awards:** CAPS Grant, 1972. **Address:** 561 Broadway, NYC 10012. **Dealer:** John Weber Gallery. **One-man Exhibitions:** (first) Konrad Fischer Gallery, Dusseldorf, 1968; Galerie Heiner Friedrich, Munich, 1968, 70, 72, 73, 74, 75, 76, 78; Dwan Gallery, NYC, 1969, 70; ACE Gallery, Los Angeles, 1969; Francoise Lambert, Milan, 1970; Yvon Lambert, 1970; Galerie Reckermann, Cologne, 1970, 72; Galerie Annemarie Verna, Zurich, 1971, 72; John Weber Gallery, 1972, 74,

76; Galerie Diogenes, Berlin, 1972; Galerie Nachst St. Stephen, Vienna, 1973; Galerie im Taxispalais, Innsbruck, 1973; Berne, 1973; Galleria Martano Due Torino, 1974; Galeria Milano, Milan, 1974; Galeria Piano Primo, Rome, 1974; Leverkusen, 1974; Galerie Heiner Friedrich, Cologne, 1974; Essen, 1974; Kunstraum, Munich, 1975; Darmstadt/Hessisches, 1975; Galerie d & c Mueller-Roth, Stuttgart, 1975; Galerie Dorothea Loehr, Frankfurt, 1975; Galerie Klein, Bonn, 1975; Brooke Alexander, Inc., NYC, 1976; Galerie Annemarie Verna, Zurich, 1976; Galleria Primo Piano, Rome, 1976; Galleria Durand-Dessert, Paris, 1976; Lisson Gallery, London, 1977; Hester Van Royen Gallery, London, 1977; Heiner Friedrich Gallery, NYC, 1978; P.S. 1, Long Island City, 1978; MOMA, 1978; Marion Goodman Gallery, NYC, 1985. **Group:** WMAA, 1968; Dusseldorf/Kunsthalle, Prospect '68, 1968; MOMA, New Media: New Methods, circ., 1969; Berne, When Attitudes Become Form, 1969; ICA, U. of Pennsylvania, Between Object and Environment, 1969; Arnhem, Sonsbeek '71, 1971; Neuer Berliner Kunstverein, Berlin, Multiples, 1974; MOMA, Drawing Now, 1976; Leverkusen, Drawings 3, 1975; Sydney, Biennale, 1976; Chicago/AI, Americans, 1979. **Collections:** Krefeld/Kaiser Wilhelm; MOMA; RISD; WMAA. **Bibliography:** Honisch and Jensen, eds.; Kren.

SANDER, LUDWIG. b. July 18, 1906, NYC; **d.** July 31, 1975, NYC. **Studied:** NYU, BA; Hofmann School, Munich, two semesters. Traveled Europe, 1927, 1931-32. US Army, World War II. **Taught:** Colorado College, summers, 1951, 52, 53; Bard College, 1956-58. **Member:** NIAL. **Awards:** Hallmark International Competition; Longview Foundation Grant; National Council on the Arts; Guggenheim Foundation Fellowship, 1968; AAAL, Childe Hassam Fund Purchase, 1973. **One-man Exhibitions:** (first) Morton Gallery, NYC,

1930; Hacker Gallery, NYC, 1952; Leo Castelli, Inc., 1959, 61; The Kootz Gallery, NYC, 1962, 64, 65; A. M. Sachs Gallery, 1967, 69; Lawrence Rubin Gallery, NYC, 1970, 71, 73; Waddington Galleries, London, 1972; Knoedler Contemporary Art, 1974, 75, 77, 79; The Berenson Gallery, Bay Harbor Islands, Miami, 1975; Rosa Esman Gallery, NYC, 1977; M. Knoedler & Co., NYC, 1982, 85. **Group:** Ninth Street Exhibition, NYC, 1951; SRGM, Abstract Expressionists and Imagists, 1961; Chicago/AI Annuals, 1961, 62; MOMA, Recent American Painting and Sculpture, circ., USA and Canada, 1961-62; WMAA, Geometric Abstraction in America, circ., 1962; Seattle World's Fair, 1962; Los Angeles/County MA, Post Painterly Abstraction, 1964; XXXII Venice Biennial, 1964; Toledo/MA, Form of Color, 1970; WMAA, 1973; SRGM, American Painters through Two Decades, 1973; U. of Miami, Less Is More; The Influence of the Bauhaus on American Art, 1974; Corcoran, 1975; Brooklyn Museum, American Drawings in Black and White: 1970-1979, 1980; MOMA, Contrasts of Form: Geometric Abstract Art 1910-1980, 1985. **Collections:** American Republic Insurance Co.; Baltimore/MA; Brandeis U.; Buffalo/Albright; Chase Manhattan Bank; Chicago/AI; Ciba-Geigy Corp; Columbia Broadcasting System; Corcoran; Fort Worth; International Minerals & Chemicals Corp.; MIT; MMA; Ridgefield/Aldrich; SFMA; SRGM; U. of Texas; Union Carbide Corp.; Uris Building Corp.; WMAA; Walker. **Bibliography:** MacAgy 2; Weller. Archives.

SANDOL, MAYNARD. b. 1930, Newark, N.J. **Studied:** Newark State Teachers College, 1952. Traveled Europe. **Taught:** Hackettstown (N.J.) High School, 1964-; Fairleigh Dickinson U., 1965-68. **Address:** Bunn Street, Box 364, R.R. 2, Clifton, NJ 07830. **One-man Exhibitions:** Suttman-Riley Gallery, NYC, 1958; Artists' Gallery, NYC,

1959; Castellane, NYC, 1960, 63; Castellane, Provincetown, 1962, 63; Athena Gallery, New Haven, 1963; Chapman Kelly Gallery, 1964; The Peridot Gallery, 1967, 68; Washburn Gallery Inc., 1971. **Group:** Newark Museum; Hartford/Wadsworth; MOMA; Corcoran; New York World's Fair, 1964-65; Trenton/State. **Collections:** Brandeis U.; Hartford/Wadsworth; Hirshhorn; Newark Museum; Princeton U. **Bibliography:** Gerdts.

SARET, ALAN. b. December 25, 1944, NYC. **Studied:** Cornell U., 1961-66, B. Arch; Hunter College, 1967-68. Traveled Europe, Mexico, North Africa; resided in India, 1971-73. **Taught:** U. of California, Irvine, 1979. **Awards:** Guggenheim Foundation Fellowship, 1969; National Endowment for the Arts, grant, 1975; CAPS, award, 1976. **Address:** 54 Leonard Street, NYC 10013. **Dealers:** Charles Cowles Gallery, NYC; Weinberg Gallery, San Francisco. **One-man Exhibitions:** Bykert Gallery, 1968, 70; The Clocktower, NYC, 1973; Seattle/AM, 1977, and/or, Seattle, 1977; U. of California, Berkeley, 1978; SITE, San Francisco, 1979; Weinberg Gallery, San Francisco, 1979; Charles Cowles Gallery, NYC, 1980; U. of California, Santa Barbara, 1984. **Group:** WMAA, 1968; Oberlin College, 1968; U. of North Carolina, 1969; Amsterdam/Stedelijk, Op Losse Schroeven, 1969; Berne, When Attitudes Become Form, 1969; MOMA, New Media; New Methods, circ., 1969; New Delhi, Second World Triennial, 1971; Akademie der Kunst, Berlin, SoHo, 1976; U. of Georgia, Open to New Ideas, 1977; Venice Biennial, 1980; ICA, Boston, Drawing/Structures, 1980; Wave Hill, NYC, Temporary Structures, 1980. **Collections:** Art Museum of South Texas; Chicago/Contemporary; Dallas/MFA; Detroit/Institute; U. of Georgia; Los Angeles/County MA; MOMA; SFMA; Society of the Four Arts; Toronto; WMAA. **Bibliography:** *Drawings: The*

Pluralist Decade; Johnson, Ellen H.; *When Attitudes Become Form.*

SARKISIAN, PAUL. b. 1928, Chicago, Ill. **Studied:** Chicago Art Institute School, 1945-48; Otis Art Institute, Los Angeles, 1953-54; Mexico City College, 1955-56. **Taught:** Pasadena/AM, 1965-69; U. of Southern California, Los Angeles, 1969; U. of California, Berkeley, 1970; U. of Oregon, 1971; U. of Southern Florida, 1972. **Address:** Cerrillos, NM 87010. **Dealer:** Nancy Hoffman Gallery, NYC. **One-man Exhibitions:** Nova Gallery, Boston, 1958; Aura Gallery, Pasadena, 1962; La Jolla, 1963; Pasadena/AM, 1968; Corcoran, 1970; Michael Walls Gallery, San Francisco, 1970; Santa Barbara/MA, 1970; Chicago/Contemporary, 1972; Michael Walls Gallery, Los Angeles, 1973; Houston/Contemporary, 1977; Nancy Hoffman Gallery, NYC, 1978, 80, 82; Arts Club, Chicago, 1979; Wright State U., 1980; ARCO Center for the Visual Arts, Los Angeles, 1981; Fendrick Gallery, Washington, D.C., 1981; Aspen Center for the Visual Arts, 1982; Union County College, Cranford, N.J., 1984. **Group:** Pasadena/AM, Annual, 1960; Pasadena/AM, 100 California Artists, 1963; Los Angeles/County MA, Late Fifties at the Ferus, 1968; WMAA Annual, 1969; Los Angeles Municipal Art Gallery, Separate Realities, 1973; Expo '74, Spokane, 1974; Chicago/AI, 71st American Exhibition, 1974; Corcoran Biennial, 1975; Indianapolis, 1976; SFMA, Painting and Sculpture in California: The Modern Era, 1976; Chicago/AI, Visions, 1976; Jacksonville/AM, New Realism, 1977; Zurich, Painting in the Age of Photography, 1977; Canberra/National, Illusions of Reality, 1977; Denver/AM, Biennial, 1979. **Collections:** Aachen; Albuquerque; Chicago/AI; Corcoran; Des Moines; U. of Georgia; Hirshhorn; Indianapolis; Little Rock/MFA; MMA; Milwaukee; Minneapolis/Institute; U. of Nebraska; U. of New Mexico; Oakland/AM; Pasadena/AM; Roswell;

Santa Barbara/MA; Santa Fe. **Bibliography:** Arthur 1.

SAUL, PETER. b. August 16, 1934, San Francisco, Calif. **Studied:** Stanford U.; California School of Fine Arts, 1950-52; Washington U., with Fred Conway, 1952-56, BFA. Traveled Europe. Resided Holland, 1956-58; Paris, 1958-62; Rome, 1962-64. **Awards:** *Art in America* (magazine), New Talent, 1962; William and Noma Copley Foundation Grant, 1962; National Endowment for the Arts, Grant, 1980. **Address:** 4106 Avenue B, Austin, Tx. 78751. **Dealer:** Allan Frumkin Gallery, NYC and Chicago. **One-man Exhibitions:** Allan Frumkin Gallery, Chicago, 1961, 63, 64, 66, 69, 72, 74, 77; NYC, 1962-64, 66, 68, 69, 71, 73, 75, 77, 78, 81, 84; Galerie Breteau, Paris, 1962, 63, 64, 67; La Tartaruga, Rome, 1963; Rolf Nelson Gallery, Los Angeles, 1963; Notizie Gallery, Turin, 1964; Galerie Anne Abels, Cologne, 1965; Contemporary Gallery, Kansas City, 1967; Palos Verdes Estates, Calif., 1967; Wanamaker Gallery, Philadel-

phia, 1967; San Francisco Art Institute, 1968; Reed College, 1968; California College of Arts and Crafts, 1968; Darthea Speyer Gallery, 1969, 72; Musée d'Art et d'Industrie, Paris, 1971; California State U., Sacramento, 1973; Housatonic Museum of Art, Bridgeport, Conn., 1976; Frumkin and Struve Gallery, Chicago, 1984. **Retrospective:** U. of Northern Illinois, circ., 1980. **Group:** Salon des Jeunes Peintres, Paris, 1959, 60; Dayton/AI, International Selection, 1961; U. of Colorado, 1962; Chicago/AI, 1962, 63, 64; SFMA, Directions—Painting U.S.A., 1963; U. of Michigan, 1963, 65; Musée Cantonal des Beaux-Arts, Lausanne, 1 Salon International de Galeries Pilotes, 1963; Abbey Saint-Pierre, Ghent, Forum, 1963; Brandeis U., Recent American Drawings, 1964; The Hague, New Realism, 1964; Des Moines, 1965; Indianapolis/Herron, 1966; U. of Kentucky, 1966; Carnegie, 1967; MOMA, circ., 1968; U. of Oklahoma, 1968; U. of Illinois, 1969; WMAA, Human Concern/Personal Torment, 1969; Corcoran, 1971; Chi-

Peter Saul *Self Portrait: Splithead ($10)* 1986

cago/AI, 1972; Paris/Beaubourg, Paris—New York, 1977; WMAA, Art about Art, 1978; Haus der Kunst, Munich, Amerikanische Malerie, 1930-1980, 1981. **Collections:** U. of California, Berkeley; Chicago/AI; U. of Illinois; MOMA; U. of Massachusetts; Oberlin College; WMAA. **Bibliography:** Adrian; Lucie-Smith.

SAUNDERS, RAYMOND. b. October 28, 1934, Homestead, Pa. **Studied:** U. of Pennsylvania, 1954-57; Barnes Foundation, 1953-55; PAFA, 1953-57; Carnegie Institute of Technology, 1959-60, BFA; California College of Arts and Crafts, 1960-61, MFA. Traveled Mexico, Europe, USA. **Taught:** RISD; California State U., Hayward, 1968-; Hunter College, 1981; U. of Texas, 1983. **Awards:** PAFA, Cresson Fellowship, 1956; AAAL Grant, 1963; Eakins Prize; Ford Foundation, **P.P.,** 1964; Prix de Rome, 1964, 65; Guggenheim Foundation Fellowship, 1976; National Endowment for the Arts, grant, 1977, 84. **Address:** 6007 Rock Ridge Boulevard, Oakland, CA 94618. **Dealer:** Stephen Wirtz Gallery, San Francisco. **One-man Exhibitions:** (first) Pittsburgh Playhouse Gallery, 1953, also 1955; Terry Dintenfass, Inc., NYC, 1962, 64, 66-69, 71, 73, 75, 86; Dartmouth College, 1969; Simpson College, Indianola, Iowa, 1969; Lehigh U., 1970; Miami-Dade, 1971; Spelman College, 1972; RISD, 1972; Carleton College, 1974; Peale House, Philadelphia (two-man), 1974; U. of California, Berkeley, 1975; U. of California, La Jolla, 1979; Baum/Silverman Gallery, Los Angeles, 1979; Stephen Wirtz Gallery, San Francisco, 1970, 80, 82, 83, 85, 87; Los Angeles Municipal Art Gallery, 1980; Santa Clara/Triton, 1980; Seattle/AM, 1981; Portland (Ore.) Museum School, 1981; Hunsaker/Schlesinger Gallery, Los Angeles, 1981, 85; Hunter College, 1981; Arizona State U., 1982; Miami-Dade Community College, 1982; U. of California, Santa Cruz, 1982; U. of Texas, 1983; Los Angeles/Municipal, 1984 Angles Gallery, Santa Monica,

1985; Thomas Babeor Gallery, La Jolla, 1985; Boise, 1985; St. Mary's College, 1986; U. of Idaho, 1986; Ohio State U., 1987; Cava Gallery, Philadelphia, 1987; Phillips/Andover, 1987. **Group:** PAFA Annuals, 1962-67; SFMA Annuals; New School for Social Research; WMAA, 1971, Annuals, 72, 73; NAD; UCLA, The Negro in American Art, 1966; A.F.A., 1966, 67; Dartmouth College, 1968; 30 Contemporary Black Artists, circ., 1968-69; Westmoreland County/MA, 1969; Boston/MFA, Black Artists: New York and Boston, 1970; Oakland/AM, Oakland Artists, 1974; VMFA, 1974; Cranbrook, Drawings by Contemporary American Artists, 1975; Skidmore College, Contemporary Drawings, 1975; Afro-American Art Pavilion, Expo 74, Spokane, 1974; Oakland/AM, 1979; Sacramento/Crocker, Aspects of Abstract Art, 1979; SFMA, Resource/Resevoir, 1982; Corcoran Biennial, 1983; SFMA, Biennial, 1984; Bucknell U., Harlem Renaissance, 1985; AAIAL, 1985; Sacramento/Crocker, Works of Art on Paper, 1986; Studio Museum of Harlem, Tradition and Conflict: Images of A Turbulent Decade, circ., 1985. **Collections:** Achenbach Foundation; Allentown/AM; Andover/Phillips; Arizona State U.; California College of Arts and Crafts; California State College, San Bernardino; U. of California, Berkeley; Carnegie; Dartmouth College; Fisk U.; Howard U.; Hunter College; MMA; Miami-Dade Community College; MOMA; Mount Holyoke College; NIAL; Oakland/AM; U. of North Carolina; PAFA; SFMA; St. Louis/City; Seattle/AM; U. of Texas; Tougaloo College; U. of Utah; WMAA; U. of Wisconsin.

SAUNDERS, WADE. b. 1949, Berkeley, Calif. **Studied:** Wesleyan U., 1971, BA; U. of California, San Diego, 1974, MFA. **Address:** 26 Bernon Street, Providence, R.I. 02908. **Dealer:** Diane Brown Gallery, NYC. **One-man Exhibitions:** Grossmont College, 1975; Pyra-

Wade Saunders *Breathe* 1986

mid Art Galleries Ltd., Washington, D.C., 1975, 77; Braunstein-Quay Gallery, San Francisco, 1976; Newspace, Los Angeles, 1977, 79, 81, 83, 85; PAFA, 1980; Diane Brown Gallery, Washington, D.C., 1981, 81; Charles Cowles Gallery, NYC, 1981, 82; Jeffrey Fuller Fine Art, Philadelphia, 1982; C. Grimaldis Gallery, Baltimore, 1983, 84; Helen Shlein Gallery, Boston, 1984; Linda Durham Gallery, Santa Fe, 1984; Lawrence Oliver Gallery, Philadelphia,

1984, 86; Diane Brown Gallery, NYC, 1984, 85; Quint Gallery, San Diego, 1985; San Diego State U., 1985; Portland (Ore.) Center for the Visual Arts, 1985. **Group:** Oakland/AM, Public Sculpture: Urban Environment, 1974; ICA, U. of Pennsylvania, Dwellings, 1978; San Diego, Sculpture in California, 1975-80, 1980; ICA, U. of Pennsylvania, Connections, 1983; ICA, U. of Pennsylvania, Made in Philadelphia, 1984. **Collections:** Andover/Phllips; Baltimore/MA; Best Products Corp.; Corcoran; MMA; Milwaukee; Newark Museum; U. of Nebraska; Newport Harbor; PMA; Seattle/AM.

SAVELLI, ANGELO. b. October 30, 1911, Pizzo Calabro, Italy. **Studied:** Liceo Artistico, Rome, 1930-32; Academy of Fine Arts, Rome, with Ferruccio Ferrazzi, Diploma di Decorazione, 1932-36. To USA, 1954. Traveled Europe, USA. A cofounder of The Art Club, Rome, with Gino Severini, Enrico Pramolini, Fazzini, and others, 1944. **Taught:** Collegio Nazionale, Rome, 1939-40; Liceo Artistico, Rome, 1940-43, 1948-54; Scarsdale Art Workshop, 1957-61; New School for Social Research, 1959-64; Positano (Italy) Art Workshop, 1960-62; U. of Pennsylvania, 1960-69, 76; Columbia U., 1966; Hunter College, 1968; U. of Minnesota, 1974; Cornell U., 1974; PAFA, 1975; U. of Arkansas, 1975; U. of Texas, Arlington, 1977-82. **Member:** Artists Equity. **Commissions:** Sora, Italy (church facade, fresco); F.A.U., Rome (mural); Italian Line (paintings for SS *Leonardo da Vinci* and SS *Michelangelo*); Lincoln Plaza, Syracuse, N.Y.; Audubon Art Center, New Haven, Conn. **Awards:** Fellowship from the Italian Ministry of Education, 1948; Bergamo, First Prize, 1941, 42; Battistoni, First Prize, 1958; XXXII Venice Biennial, 1964, Grand Prize for Graphics; Potsdam/SUNY, **P.P.,** 1965; Vancouver, **P.P.,** 1968; Tiffany Grant, 1976; Guggenheim Foundation Fellowship, 1979; AAAL, 1983. **Address:** 74 Grand

Street, NYC 10013. **Dealer:** Max Hutchinson Gallery, NYC; Galleria Lorenzelli, Milan. **One-man Exhibitions:** (first) Galleria Roma, Rome, 1941; La Spiga, Milan, 1942; Galleria Ritrove, Rome, 1943; Galleria San Marco, Rome, 1944, 51; Galleria Cronache, Bologna, Italy, 1946; Oblo Capri, 1946; Galleria d'Arte del Naviglio, Milan, 1947, 54, 61; Galleria Sandri, Venice, 1947; Centre d'Art Italien, Paris, 1952; Numero Galleria d'Arte, Florence, Italy, 1953; The Contemporaries, NYC, 1955; D'Amecourt Gallery, Washington, D.C., 1956; Leo Castelli, Inc., 1958; Galleria del Cavallino, Venice, 1958; Galleria Selecta, Rome, 1959; U. of Minnesota, 1960, 74; Peter H. Deitsch Gallery, 1962; D'Arcy Gallery, NYC, 1963; Philadelphia Art Alliance, 1963; XXXII Venice Biennial, 1964; Eastern Illinois U., 1964; Wellfleet Art Gallery, 1964; Contemporary Prints and Drawings, Chicago, 1966; Henri Gallery, 1969; Peale House, Philadelphia, 1969; Syracuse/Everson, 1972; Stout State U., Menomonie, Wisc., 1973; U. of Minnesota, Duluth, 1973; The Pennsylvania State U., 1975, 76; Max Hutchinson Gallery, NYC, 1978; Sculpture Now, NYC, 1978; Parsons-Dreyfuss Gallery, NYC, 1978; Galleria Lorenzelli, 1981; Arco d'Alibert, Rome, 1981; Gimpel-Hanover, Zurich, 1981; Studio Bonifacio, Genoa, 1986; Galleria Editalia, Rome, 1981. **Retrospectives:** Cantanzaro, Italy, 1954; Padiglione d'Arte Contemporanea, Milan, 1984. **Group:** Rome National Art Quadrennial, 1943-; Venice Biennial, 1948-; Rose Fried Gallery, International College Exhibition, 1956; Hartford/Wadsworth, Graphics, 1956; A.F.A., Collage in America, circ., 1957-58; Library of Congress, 1959; Brooklyn Museum, 1962, 63; Gallery of Modern Art, Ljubljana, Yugoslavia; A.F.A., Moods of Light, circ., 1963-64; Sidney Janis Gallery, 1964; WMAA Annuals, 1966, 67; PAFA Annual, 1963; Brooklyn Museum, 1968; Corcoran Biennial, 1969; Salon du Mai, Paris, 1969; Madrid/Nacional, II Biennial, 1969; Corcoran, 1969; Chi-

cago/Contemporary, White on White, 1971-72; Festival of Two Worlds, Charleston, N.C., 1978; Italian Cultural Institute, NYC, 1979. **Collections:** Brooklyn Museum; Chase Manhattan Bank; Cincinnati/AM; Corcoran; Eliat; Helsinki; High Museum; Kalamazoo/Institute; Library of Congress; MOMA; U. of Minnesota; National Gallery; NCFA; NYPL; Norfolk/Chrysler; PMA; U. of Pennsylvania; Phoenix; Rome/Nazionale; Syracuse/Everson; Turin/Civico; Vancouver; Victoria and Albert Museum; WMAA.

SCARPITTA, SALVATORE. b. March 23, 1919, NYC. To Italy to study, 1936; returned to NYC, 1959. Traveled Italy, Switzerland. **Studied:** Royal Academy of Fine Arts, Rome. **Taught:** Maryland Institute, 1965-. US Navy 1945; and underground in WWII, in Italy. Subject of award winning video, *Sal Is Racer*, 1986, at C.A.G.E. Video Festival, Cincinnati, 1986. **Address:** 307 East 84th Street, NYC 10028. **Dealer:** Leo Castelli Inc. **One-man Exhibitions:** Gaetano Chiurazzi, Rome, 1949; Galleria II Pincio, Rome, 1951; La Tartaruga, Rome, 1955, 57, 58, 76; Galleria d'Arte del Naviglio, Milan, 1956, 58; Leo Castelli Inc., 1959, 60, 63, 65, 75, 80, 82, 84; Leo Castelli Warehouse, 1969; Dwan Gallery, NYC, 1961; Galerie Schmela, 1963; Galleria dell'Ariete, 1963; Brussels/Royaux, 1964; Galleria Notizie, Turin, 1972; Galerie Jacques Benador, Geneva, 1973; L'Uomo e l'Arte, Milan, 1974; Robinson Galleries, Houston, 1978; Portland (Ore.) Center for the Visual Arts, 1978; Padiglione d'Arte Contemporanea, Milano, 1985. **Retrospective:** Houston/Contemporary, 1977. **Group:** Galleria Roma, Rome, 1944; Rome National Art Quadrennial, 1948; XXVI, XXVIII, and XXIX Venice Biennials, 1952, 56, 58; Columbus, 1960; Martha Jackson Gallery, New Media—New Forms I & II, 1960, 61; Houston/MFA, Ways and Means, 1961; Corcoran, 1963; Musée Cantonal

Salvatore Scarpitta   *Trolley Stop*   1979

des Beaux-Arts, Lausanne, I Salon International de Galeries Pilotes, 1963; Maryland Institute, 1964; Chicago/AI, 1964; U. of Illinois, 1965; ICA, U. of Pennsylvania, Highway, 1970; Hofstra U., Art around the Automobile, 1971; Rome, III Quadrennial, 1972; The Fine Arts Building, NYC, Personal Mythologies, 1976; Vassar College, Contemporary Primitivism, 1976; Queens Museum, Private Myths, 1978; The New Museum, NYC, Sustained Vision, 1979. **Collections:** Amsterdam/Stedelijk; Buffalo/Albright; Los Angeles/County MA; MOMA; Tel Aviv. **Bibliography:** Janis and Blesh 1; *Metro*; Weller. Archives.

SCHAPIRO, MIRIAM. b. 1923, Toronto, Canada. **Studied:** State U. of Iowa, 1945, BA; 1946, MA; 1949. **Taught:** State U. of Iowa, 1946-49; Scarsdale School of Art, 1965-66; Connecticut College for Women, 1966; Parsons School of Design, NYC, 1966-67; U. of California, 1967-69; California Institute of the Arts, Valencia, 1971-75; Nova Scotia College of Art and Design, Halifax, 1974; Bryn Mawr College, 1977; Tyler School of Art, Philadelphia, 1977-78; Amherst College, 1978. **Awards:** Tamarind Fellowship, 1963; National Endowment for the Arts, 1976, 85; Ford Foundation Grant, 1964; Hon. DFA, College of Wooster, 1983. **Member:** Board of Directors, College Art Association and Los Angeles Institute of Contemporary Art; ICA, Los Angeles, founding member, 1974-75; CAAA, board of directors, 1974-78; Women's Caucus for Art, Advisory Board, 1974-; Heresies Collective, founding member, 1976-; Feminist Art Institute, founding member, 1977. **Commissions:** Stained glass windows, Temple Shalom, Chicago, 1984. **m.** Paul Brach. **Address:** 393 W. Broadway, NYC 10012; Montauk Highway, East Hampton, NY 11037. **Dealer:** Bernice

Steinbaum Gallery, NYC. **One-man Exhibitions:** U. of Missouri, 1950; Illinois Wesleyan U., 1951; Andre Emmerich Gallery, NYC, 1958, 61, 63, 67, 69, 71, 73, 76, 77; Skidmore College, 1964; Franklin Siden Gallery, Detroit, 1965; Vassar College, 1973; Cynthia Comsky Gallery, 1974, 75; Douglass College Library, 1975; Benson Gallery, 1975; Mills College, 1975; College of St. Catherine, St. Paul, Minn., 1976; U. of Wisconsin, La Crosse, 1976; A.R.C. Gallery, Chicago, 1976; Douglas Drake Gallery, Kansas City, Kansas, 1976; Douglass College, New Brunswick, N.J., 1976; Oberlin College, 1977; State U. of Oregon, Corvallis, 1977; Reed College, 1978; Lerner Heller Gallery, NYC, 1979, 80; Gladstone/Villani Gallery, NYC, 1979; Barbara Gladstone, 1980, 81, 82; Dart Gallery, 1980, 84; Galerie Rudolf Zwirner, Cologne, 1981; Axiom Gallery, New South Wales, Australia, 1982; Douglas Drake Gallery, Kansas City, Kan., 1982; David Heath Gallery, Atlanta, 1982; Hodges Taylor Gallery, Charlotte, N.C., 1982; Yares Gallery, Scottsdale, 1982; Barbara Gilman Gallery, Miami, 1983; Kent State U., 1983; Koplin Gallery, Los Angeles, 1983; Marion Locks Gallery, Philadelphia, 1983; Thomas Segal Gallery, Boston, 1983; New Smyrna Beach, Fla., 1984; Brentwood Gallery, St. Louis, 1985, 86; Bernice Steinbaum Gallery, 1986. **Retrospectives:** New London, 1966; Newport Harbor and La Jolla, Paul Brach and Miriam Schapiro, 1969; U. of California, San Diego, 1975; College of Wooster, 1980. **Group:** MOMA, New Talent; U. of Nottingham (England), Abstract Impressionists, 1958; International Biennial Exhibition of Paintings, Tokyo; Carnegie, 1959; WMAA, 1959; MOMA, Abstract American Drawings and Watercolors, circ., Latin America, 1961-63; Jewish Museum, Toward a New Abstraction, 1963; SFMA, Directions—Painting U.S.A., 1963; Walker; Denver/AM; Brooklyn Museum; Chicago/AI; Brandeis U., New Directions in American Painting, 1963; PAFA 1963, 64; Day-

ton/AI, 1967; Fort Worth Art Museum, Drawings, 1969; Jewish Museum, Superlimited: Books, Boxes, and Things, 1969; Long Beach/MA, Invisible/Visible, Twenty-one Artists, 1972; Scripps College, California Women Artists, 1972; Womanhouse, Los Angeles, 1972; U. of North Dakota, 14 Women, 1973; Womanspace, Los Angeles, Female Sexuality/Female Identity, 1973; PMA/Museum of the Philadelphia Civic Center, Focus, 1974; Newport Harbor, The Audacious Years, 1974; Cerritos College Art Gallery, Norwalk, Calif., 16 Los Angeles Women Artists, 1974; Bronx Museum of Art, The Year of the Woman, 1975; San Antonio/McNay, American Artists, '76, 1976; Guild Hall, Artists of East Hampton, 1850-1975, 1976; West Palm Beach/Norton, Hi Mom, What's New?, 1977; The American Foundation for the Arts, Miami, Patterning and Decoration, 1977; Brussels/Beaux Arts, Pattern and Decoration, 1979; Aachen/Ludwig, Les Nouveaux Fauves-Die Neuen Wilden, 1980; Dublin/Municipal, International Quadriennale (ROSC), 1980; Indianapolis, 1980; Houston/Contemporary, The Americans: The Collage, 1982; Bonn, Back to the USA, circ., 1983; Boston/MFA, Brave New Works, 1983; Hudson River Museum, Ornamentalism, 1983; Pittsfield/Berkshire, New Decorative Art, 1983; San Antonio/McNay, The Artist and the Quilt, 1983. **Collections:** Aachen/Ludwig; Albion College; Amstar Corp.; Avco Corp.; Bank of America; Best Products Co., Ashland, Va.; Boston/MFA; Canberra/National; Hirshhorn; Illinois Wesleyan U.; IBM, Atlanta; U. of Iowa; La Jolla; Levin Townsend Computer Corp.; MOMA; Mills College; Minneapolis/Institute; Mulvane; NYU; National Gallery; Newport Harbor; Oberlin College; St. Louis/City; Security Pacific Bank; Southampton/Parrish; Stanford U.; Stephens College; Syracuse/Everson; Tougaloo College; United Nations; Williams College; WMA; Worcester/AM. **Bibliography:** *Art: A Woman's Sen-*

sibility; *Back to the USA*; Lippard 3; Lucie-Smith; **Miriam Schapiro.**

SCHMIDT, JULIUS. b. 1932, Stamford, Conn. **Studied:** Oklahoma A. and M. College, 1950-51; Cranbrook Academy of Art, 1952, BFA, 1955, MFA; Zadkine School of Sculpture, Paris, 1953; Academy of Fine Arts, Florence, Italy. Traveled Europe, USA, Mexico, Mediterranean. **Taught:** Silvermine Guild School of Art, summers, 1953, 54; Cleveland Institute of Art, 1957; Kansas City/AI, 1954-59; RISD, 1959-60; U. of California, Berkeley, 1961-62; Cranbrook, 1962-70; U. of Iowa, 1970-. **Commission:** Iowa State U., bronze sculpture, 1985. **Awards:** Mid-American Biennial, First Prize and **P.P.;** Guggenheim Foundation Fellowship, 1963. **Address:** U. of Iowa, Art Department, Iowa City, IA 52242. **One-man Exhibitions:** Silvermine Guild, 1953; Kansas City/AI, 1956, 1965-66; Santa Barbara/MA, 1961; Otto Gerson Gallery, NYC, 1961, 63; Franklin Siden Gallery, Detroit, 1964; Gertrude Kasle Gallery, 1965, 67, 72, 74; U. of Arkansas, 1966; Talladega College, 1966; Marlborough-Gerson Gallery Inc., 1966, 71; Rockford (Ill.) College Museum of Art, 1974; Terre Haute/Swope, 1980; Augusta College, 1981; Monmouth College, 1984; Terre Haute, 1985. **Retrospective:** U. of Iowa, 1974. **Group:** Detroit/Institute, 1958; PAFA, 1958, Annual, 1964; MOMA, Sixteen Americans, circ., 1959; Claude Bernard, Paris, Aspects of American Sculpture, 1960; Chicago/AI, 1960; WMAA Annuals, 1960-63; Carnegie, 1961; Dayton/AI, 1961; Boston Arts Festival, 1961; MOMA, American Painting and Sculpture, circ., 1961; New School for Social Research, Mechanism and Organism, 1961, also 1966; SFMA, 1962; SRGM, The Joseph H. Hirshhorn Collection, 1962; Battersea Park, London, International Sculpture Exhibition, 1963; Sao Paulo, 1963; Walker, Ten American Sculptors, 1964; Flint/Institute, 1965; WMAA, Contemporary American Sculpture, Selection I, 1966; U. of Illinois, 1967; PMA, American Sculpture of the Sixties, 1967; U. of California, 1968; U. of Wisconsin, 1975. **Collections:** American Republic Insurance Co.; Brenton Bank; Buffalo/Albright; Buffalo/SUNY; Chase Manhattan Bank; Chicago/AI; Cranbrook; Davenport/Municipal; Detroit/Institute; U. of Illinois; U. of Iowa; Iowa State U.; Kalamazoo/Institute; Kansas City/Nelson; MOMA; U. of Massachusetts; U. of Michigan; U. of Nebraska; Oswego/SUNY; Princeton U.; Santa Barbara/MA; WMAA; Walker; Washington U.; U. of Wisconsin. **Bibliography:** Read 3.

SCHNABEL, JULIAN. b. 1951, NYC. **Studied:** U. of Houston, 1969-72, BFA; WMAA, Independent Study Program, 1973-74. **Address:** 24 East 20th Street, NYC 10003. **Dealer:** The Pace Gallery, NYC. **One-man Exhibitions:** Houston/Contemporary, 1976; Galerie December, Dusseldorf, 1978; Mary Boone Gallery, NYC, 1979, 81, 82; Daniel Weinberg Gallery, San Francisco, 1979, 82; Gallerie Bischofberger, Zurich, 1980, 82, 83, 84, 85; Young Hoffman Gallery, Chicago, 1980; Anthony D'Offay Gallery, London, 1981; Amsterdam/Stedelijk, 1982; Margo Leavin Gallery, Los Angeles, 1982; Los Angeles/MOCA, 1982; U. of California, Berkeley, 1982; Tate Gallery, 1982; Leo Castelli Inc., NYC, 1981, 82; Akron/AM, 1983; Galleria Mario Diacono, Rome, 1983; Waddington Galleries, London, 1983, 85; Akira Ikeda, Nagoya, 1983; Akira Ikeda, Tokyo, 1984; The Pace Gallery, 1984; Gian Enzo Sperone, Rome, 1985. **Group:** WMAA, WISP, 1974; Grand Palais, Paris, L'Amerique aux Indépendants, 1980; XXXIX & XL Venice Biennials, 1980, 82; Indianapolis, 1980; The Royal Academy, London, A New Spirit in Painting, 1981; WMAA Biennials, 1981, 83; Cologne/Stadt, Westkunst, 1981; Amsterdam/Stedelijk, '60-'80: Attitude, Concepts, Images, 1982; Chicago/AI, 1982; Galeria Politi, Milan, Transavangarde International, 1982; Houston/Contemporary, The Americans: Collage, 1950-1982, 1982; Internationale Kunstausstellung Berlin, 1982; Hannover/KG, New York Now, circ., 1982; Milwaukee, New Figuration in America, 1982; Dublin/Municipal, International Quadriennial (ROSC), 1984; Carnegie, International, 1985. **Collections:** Amsterdam/Stedelijk; Basel; Carnegie; Chicago/AI; Harvard U.; Lannan Foundation; Los Angeles/MOCA; MMA; MOMA; Milwaukee; Ottawa/National;   Paris/Beaubourg; Tate Gallery; WMAA. **Bibliography:** *Back to the USA;* Danto; De Wilde 1; De Wilde 2; Haenlein; Hiromoto; Joachimides and Rosenthal; Murken-Altrogge; Pincus-Witten 2.

SCHNAKENBERG, HENRY. b. September 14, 1892, New Brighton (Staten Island), N.Y.; **d.** October 15, 1970, Newton, Conn. **Studied:** ASL, 1914, with Kenneth Hayes Miller. US Army, 1917-19, with Kenneth Hayes Miller. US Army, 1917-19. Traveled Mexico, Europe. **Taught:** ASL. **Commissions** (murals): US Post Offices, West New York, N.J., and Amsterdam, N.Y. **Awards:** Hon. DFA, U. of Vermont; elected to the NIAL, 1952. **One-man Exhibitions:** (first) Whitney Studio Club, NYC, 1921; Alfredo Valente Gallery, NYC, 1926; Hartford/Wadsworth (two-man), 1955; Kraushaar Galleries, 1929, 35, 37, 40, 41, 42, 46, 48, 50, 54, 56, 60, 63, 69. **Group:** MMA; WMAA; U. of Nebraska; Chicago/AI; Brooklyn Museum; Newark Museum. **Collections:** ASL; Andover/Phillips; Brooklyn Museum; California Palace; Chicago/AI; Dallas/MFA; Dartmouth College; Hartford (Conn.) State Library; Hartford/Wadsworth; MMA; Minneapolis/Institute;   Montclair/AM;   U. of Nebraska; Newark Museum; New Britain; PAFA; Princeton U.; SFMA; Scripps College; Springfield, Mass./MFA; U.S. Military Academy; U. of Vermont; WMAA; Wichita/AM; Yale U.

Bibliography: *America 1976;* Baur 7; Cheney; **Goodrich 6;** Goodrich and Baur 1; Hall; *Index of 20th Century Artists;* Kent, N.; Mellquist; Pearson 1; Richardson, E.P. Archives.

SCHOLDER, FRITZ. b. October 6, 1937, Breckenridge, Minn. **Studied:** Sacramento City College, 1958, AA, with Wayne Thiebaud; Sacramento State U., 1960, BA; U. of Arizona, MFA. Traveled USA. **Taught:** Institute of American Indian Arts, Santa Fe; Dartmouth College; U. of Southern Calif. **Awards:** John Hay Whitney Foundation, fellow, 1962-63; Ford Foundation, **P.P.,** 1962, Hon. DFA, Ripon College, 1984; Hon. DFA, U. of Arizona, 1985; Hon. DFA, Concordia College, 1986. **Subject of films:** *Fritz Scholder,* PBS, 1976; *Fritz Scholder/An American Portrait,* PBS, 1983. **Address:** Galisteo, New Mexico, 87540; 118 Cattle Track Road, Scottsdale, Ariz. 85253; and 260 West Broadway, NYC 10013. **Dealers:** ACA Gallery, NYC; Marilyn Butler Fine Arts, Scottsdale, Ariz. **One-man Exhibitions:** Sacramento City College, 1958; Artist's Cooperative Gallery, Sacramento, 1959; Sacramento/Crocker, 1959, 72; U. of Arizona, 1964; College of Santa Fe, 1967; Roswell, 1968; Lee Nordness Gallery, NYC, 1970; Esther Baer Gallery, Santa Barbara, Calif., 1971; Heard Museum, Phoenix, 1971; Jamison Galleries, Santa Fe, 1971; Talley Richards Gallery, Taos, N.M., 1981; Southwest Missouri State College, 1981; Art Wagon Galleries, Scottsdale, 1972; Cedar Rapids/AA, 1972; Cordier & Ekstrom Gallery, NYC, 1972, 74, 76, 78; Luther College, 1972; St. John's College, Santa Fe, 1972; Dartmouth College, 1973; MIT, 1973; U. of North Carolina, 1973; U. of Nebraska, 1973; Charles Russell Gallery, Great Falls, Mont., 1973; Yellowstone Art Center, 1973; Brigham Young U., 1974; Memphis/Brooks, 1974; Gallery Moos, Toronto, 1974; U. of Santa Clara, 1975; Bradley U., 1976; Fresno Art Center, 1976; Moody Gallery, Houston, 1976;

U. of New Mexico, 1976; U. of North Dakota, 1976; U. of Notre Dame, 1976; Gimpel & Weitzenhoffer, NYC, 1977; Oakland Museum, 1977; Smith-Andersen Gallery, Palo Alto, 1979, 84; El Paso Museum of Art, 1980, 82; U. of Minnesota, 1980; Plains Art Museum, Moorhead, Minn., 1980; Augsburg College, 1981; Marilyn Butler Fine Art, 1981, 83, 84, 85; Tucson Museum of Art, 1981; ACA Galleries, 1982, 84; U. of Texas, Odessa, 1984; U. of Arizona, 1985; Nimbus Gallery, Dallas, 1985. **Group:** Denver; Youngstown Butler; U. of North Carolina; NCFA; Brooklyn Museum; Museum of Contemporary Crafts, NYC; Corcoran; Grand Palais, Paris. **Collections:** Albuquerque Museum; Arizona State U.; U. of Arizona; Baltimore/MA; Bibliotheque Nationale, Paris; Boston/MFA; Brooklyn Museum; Buffalo/Albright; U. of California, Berkeley; Carnegie; Chicago/AI; Chicago/Contemporary; Cincinnati/AM; Corcoran; Dallas/MFA; Dartmouth U.; Denver/AM; El Paso Museum of Art; Flint/Institute; Fort Worth; Hartford/Wadsworth; Harvard U.; High Museum; Hirshhorn; Houston/MFA; Indianapolis; Kansas City/Nelson; Los Angeles/County MA; MOMA; Milwaukee; U. of Minnesota; NMAA; Omaha/Joslyn; PMA; Princeton U.; RISD; Roswell; Sacramento City College; Sacramento/Crocker; San Diego; Seattle/AM; Syracuse/Everson; U. of Texas; Toronto; Tucson; Utah; Walker; Wichita/AM; Worcester; Yale U.

SCHRAG, KARL. b. December 7, 1912, Karlsruhe, Germany. **Studied:** Humanistisches Gymnasium, Karlsruhe, 1930; Ecole des Beaux-Arts, Geneva, 1931; Atelier Lucien Simon, Paris; Academie Ranson, Paris, with Roger Bissiere; Academie de la Grande Chaumiere, 1931-35; ASL, with Harry Sternberg; Atelier 17, NYC, with S.W. Hayter. To USA, 1938; citizen, 1944. Traveled Europe, Mexico. **Taught:** Brooklyn College, 1953; Cooper Union 1954-68; Director of Atelier 17, NYC,

1950. **Member:** Artists Equity; SAGA; ASL; NAD. **Awards:** Brooklyn Museum Biennials, **P.P.,** 1947, 50; SAGA, **P.P.,** 1954; The Print Club, Philadelphia, Charles M. Lea Prize, 1954; American Color Print Society, 1958; Florence Tonner Prize, 1960, Sonia Wather Award, 1964; Ford Foundation Fellowship for work at Tamarind Lithography Workshop; Syracuse State Fair, Nelson Rockefeller Award, 1963; AAAL, 1966; Albion College, **P.P.,** 1968; AAAL, Childe Hassam Fund **P.P.,** 1969, 73; Ball State U., Drawings Prize, 1970; Davidson College, **P.P.,** 1974; SAGA, award, 1971; SAGA, James R. Marsh Memorial Award, 1977; NAD, Benjamin Altman (Landscape) Prize, 1981; NAD, Andrew Carnegie Prize, 1986. **Address:** 127 East 95th Street, NYC 10028. **Dealer:** Kraushaar Galleries, NYC; A.A.A. Gallery, NYC. **One-man Exhibitions:** (first) Galerie Arenberg, Brussels, 1938; Smithsonian, 1945; Kraushaar Galleries, 1947, 50, 52, 56, 59, 62, 64, 66, 68, 71, 75, 77, 79, 82, 84; U. of Alabama, 1949; Philadelphia Art Alliance, 1952; U. of Maine, 1953; State U. of New York, Oneonta, 1958; Gesellschaft der Freunde junger Kunst, Baden-Baden, Germany, 1958; Storm King Art Center, 1967; NCFA, 1972; A.A.A. Gallery, 1986; Bethesda (Md.) Art Gallery, 1977; Syracuse U., 1981; St. Mary's College, 1981. **Retrospectives:** A.F.A./Ford Foundation, circ., 1960-62; A.A.A. Gallery, 1972, 80; NCFA, 1972. **Group:** SAGA; PAFA; The Print Club, Philadelphia; Brooklyn Museum; Graphische Sammlung Albertina; SFMA, 1941, 45, 46; WMAA, 1943, 55, 57; Carnegie, 1944, 47; Musee du Petit Palais, Paris, 1949; Chicago/AI; Instituto Nacional de Bellas Artes, Mexico City, 1958; U. of Nebraska, 1973; MOMA, 1975; MOMA, American Prints 1913-1963, circ. internationally, 1976; MMA, Contemporary American Prints from the Singer Collection, 1976; Brooklyn Museum, 30 Years of American Printmaking, 1976. **Collections:** Achenbach Foundation; U. of Alabama; Atlanta U.; Bibliotheque Nationale;

Boston/MFA; Bradley U.; Brandeis U.; Brooklyn Museum; Chicago/AI; Cleveland/MA; Commerce Trust Co., Kansas City, Mo.; Dartmouth College; Detroit/Institute; Hartford/Wadsworth; Hirshhorn; U. of Illinois; Karlsruhe; Lehigh U.; Library of Congress; Lincoln Life Insurance Co.; Los Angeles/County MA; MMA; MOMA; U. of Maine; U. of Nebraska; NYPL; National Gallery; Newark Museum; Oakland/AM; Omaha/Joslyn; PMA; The Pennsylvania State U.; RISD; Smithsonian; Springfield, Mass./MFA; SRGM, Syracuse/Everson; Syracuse U.; U.S. Rubber Co.; Utica; Victoria and Albert Museum; WMAA; Yale U.; Youngstown/Butler.   **Bibliography: Gordon 3;** Hayter 1, 2; Moser; Reese. Archives.

SCHUCKER, CHARLES. b. January 19, 1908, Gap, Pa. **Studied:** Maryland Institute, 1928-34. **Taught:** NYU, 1947-54; Pratt Institute, 1956-; CCNY, 1955-56. **Member:** Yaddo Board of Directors. Federal A.P.: Easel painting in Chicago, 1938-42. **Awards:** Henry Walters Traveling Fellowship; Guggenheim Foundation Fellowship, 1953; Audubon Artists, Prize for Oil Painting; AAAL, Childe Hassam Fund, **P.P.,** 1952. **Address:** 33 Middagh Street, Brooklyn, NY 11201. **Dealers:** Gallery Camino Real, Boca Raton, Fla.; Katonah (N.Y.) Art Gallery. **One-man Exhibitions:** (first) Renaissance Society, Chicago; Albert Roullier Gallery, Chicago; Chicago/AI; The Chicago Artists Room; Macbeth Gallery, NYC, 1946, 49, 53; Passedoit Gallery, NYC, 1955, 58; Katonah (N.Y.) Art Gallery, 1955, 73, 78; The Howard Wise Gallery, NYC, 1963; Lincoln Center, 1968; WMAA, 1971; Max Hutchinson Gallery, 1972, 74, 75; Aaron Gallery, Washington, D.C., 1978; Gallery Camino Real, Boca Raton, Fla., 1980, 81, 84; Brooklyn Borough Hall, 1981; Peri/Renneth Gallery, Westhampton Beach, N.Y., 1983. **Group:** MOMA, Painting and Sculpture from 16 American Cities, 1933; Carnegie,

1949; Walker, Contemporary American Painting, 1950; MMA, American Paintings Today, 1950; PAFA, 1951, 52, 53; California Palace Annual, 1952; WMAA Annuals, 1952-57, 1960, 61, 63; Chicago/AI, 1954; SFMA, Art in the Twentieth Century, 1955; WMAA, Nature in Abstraction, 1958; Corcoran; Brooklyn Museum; Riverside Museum, NYC; Amherst College, Color Painting, 1972; Cincinnati/Contemporary, Options, 73/30, 1973; WMAA, 1973; Katonah (N.Y.) Art Gallery, 1973; Potsdam/SUNY, Abstraction Alive & Well, 1975; Brooklyn Museum, Great East River Bridge: 1883-1983, 1983. **Collections:** AAAL; Brooklyn Museum; Harcourt Brace Jovanovich Inc.; Newark Museum; New Britain; WMAA. **Bibliography:** Baur 5; Goodrich and Baur 1. Archives.

SCHUELER, JON. b. September 12, 1916, Milwaukee, Wisc. **Studied:** U. of Wisconsin, 1934-38, BA (economics), 1939-40, MA (English literature); Bread Loaf School of English, Middlebury, Vt., 1941; California School of Fine Arts, 1948-51, with David Park, Elmer Bischoff, Richard Diebenkorn, Hassel Smith, Clyfford Still, Clay Spohn. US Air Force, 1941-43. Traveled Europe, Great Britain, USA extensively. **Taught:** U. of San Francisco, 1947-49 (English literature); Yale U., 1960-62, and summer school, 1960, 61; Maryland Institute, 1963. **Member:** Artists Equity. Subject of film, *Jon Schueler: An Artist and His Vision.* **Commissions:** New York Hilton Hotel, 1962 (lithograph). **Awards:** National Endowment for the Arts, 1980. **Address:** 40 West 22nd Street, NYC, 10010; and Romasaig, Mallaig, Inverness, Scotland. **Dealers:** Katharine Rich Perlow Gallery, NYC; John Stoller & Co., Minneapolis; William Sawyer Gallery, San Francisco. **One-man Exhibitions:** (first) Metart Gallery, San Francisco, 1950; The Stable Gallery, NYC, 1954, 62, 64; Leo Castelli Inc., 1957, 59; B.C. Holland Gallery, 1960; Hirschl & Adler

Galleries, Inc., NYC, 1960; Cornell U., 1962; Columbia U. School of Architecture, 1962; Maryland Institute, 1962, 64; Richard Demarco Gallery, Edinburgh, 1973; Edinburgh College of Art, 1973; WMAA, 1975; Cleveland/MA (three-man), 1975; Landmark Gallery, NYC, 1977; House Gallery, London, 1978; John Stoller & Co., 1980; U. of Edinburgh, 1981; Dorry Gates Gallery, Kansas City, Mo., 1981, 86; Dorothy Rosenthal Gallery, Chicago, 1981, 84; A. M. Sachs Gallery, NYC, 1983, 84; William Sawyer Gallery, 1984; Katharine Rich Perlow Gallery, 1986. **Group:** Walker, 1955; WMAA Annuals, 1956, 59, 61, 63; Corcoran, 1958, 62; A.F.A., School of New York—Some Younger American Painters, 1960; Walker, 60 American Painters, 1960; WMAA, 50 Years of American Art, 1964; Cleveland/MA, Landscape, Interior, and Exterior, 1975; Edinburgh/Modern, Creation, Modern Art and Nature, 1984. **Collections:** U. of California, Santa Cruz; Cleveland/MA; Edinburgh/Modern; Glasgow/AGM; Greenville; Kirkaldy; New York Hilton Hotel; Purchase/SUNY; U. of Stirling; Union Carbide Corp.; WMAA. **Bibliography:** Baur 5; Friedman, ed.; Goodrich and Baur 1; McChesney.

SCULLY, SEAN. b. 1945, Dublin, Ireland. To USA, 1975. Citizen, 1983. **Studied:** Croyden College of Art, London, 1965-68; Newcastle U., 1968-71; Harvard U., 1972-73. **Taught:** Princeton U., 1977-83. **Awards:** Guggenheim Foundation Fellowship, 1983; National Endowment for the Arts, 1984. **Address:** 217 East 12th Street, NYC 10003. **Dealer:** David McKee Gallery, NYC. **One-man Exhibitions:** Rowan Gallery, London, 1973, 75, 77, 79; Tortue Gallery, Santa Monica, 1975, 76; Duffy-Gibbs Gallery, NYC, 1977; Nadin Gallery, NYC, 1977; The Clocktower, NYC, 1979; Susan Caldwell Gallery, NYC, 1980, 81; William Beadleston Gallery, NYC, 1982; David McKee Gallery, 1983, 85, 87; Juda

Rowan Gallery, London, 1984; Galerij S.65, Aalst, Belgium, 1984; Carnegie, circ., 1985; Barbara Krakow Gallery, Boston, 1985; Galerie Schmela, Düsseldorf, 1985. **Retrospective:** Ikon Gallery, Birmingham, England, circ., 1981. **Group:** Hayward Gallery, London, British Painting, 1983; MOMA, International Survey of Recent Painting and Sculpture, 1984; AAIAL, 1984; U. of North Carolina, Art on Paper, 1985. **Collections:** MMA; Mellon Bank, Pittsburgh; Philip Morris, Inc.; Walker.

SEERY, JOHN. b. October 29, 1941, Cincinnati, Ohio. **Studied:** Miami U., 1959-63; Cincinnati Art Academy, 1963; Ohio State U., 1963-64. Traveled Europe, Australia, Pacific Islands. **Taught:** Hunter College, 1973. **Address:** % Dealer. **Dealer:** Gruenebaum Gallery, NYC. **One-man Exhibitions:** Andre Emmerich Gallery, NYC, 1970, 72, 74, 77; Richard Gray Gallery, Chicago, 1971, 72, 75, 78, 81; New Gallery, Cleveland, 1971; Ohio State U., 1972; Gallery A, Sydney, 1974; Madison Art Center (two-man), 1974; Galerie Andre Emmerich, Zurich, 1975; Reed College, 1977; Berenson Gallery, Bay Harbor Islands, Miami, Fla., 1979; Max Hutchinson, Houston, 1979; Medici/Berenson Gallery, Miami, 1979, 82; Gruenebaum Gallery, NYC, 1981, 85; Peter Noser Gallery, Zurich, 1982; Hokin/Kaufman Gallery, Chicago, 1983; Elaine Horwitch Gallery, Scottsdale, 1983; Harvard U., 1984. **Group:** ICA, U. of Pennsylvania, Two Generations of Color Painting, 1970; Cincinnati/Contemporary, Young American Artists, 1970; Spoleto, Festival of Two Worlds, 1972; Glassboro State College, Paintings on Paper, 1972; U. of North Carolina, Six Painters of the 70s, 1973; WMAA Annual, 1973; Milwaukee, Art Works, 1976; Syracuse U., The Critics' Choice, 1977; Indianapolis, 1978. **Collections:** Baltimore/MA; Boston/MFA; Brooklyn Museum; Canberra/National; Chicago/AI; Cincinnati/Contemporary; Fort Lauderdale; Harvard U.; Hirshhorn; Houston/Contemporary; ICA, Boston; Louisville/Speed; Madison Art Center; NMAA; RISD; SRGM; Santa Barbara/MA; Toledo/MA; WMAA. **Bibliography:** *Poets and Painters*; Rowell.

SEGAL, GEORGE. b. November 26, 1924, NYC. **Studied:** NYU, 1950, BS; Rutgers U., 1963, MFA. **Taught:** New Jersey high schools, 1957-63. **Awards:** Walter K. Gutman Foundation Grant, 1962; Chicago/AI, First Prize, 1966; Hon. Ph.D., Rutgers U., 1970. **Address:** RFD #4, Box 323, North Brunswick, NJ 08902. **Dealer:** Sidney Janis Gallery. **One-man Exhibitions:** (first) Hansa Gallery, NYC, 1956, also 1957, 58, 59; Rutgers U., 1958; Green Gallery, NYC, 1960, 62, 64; Ileana Son-

nabend Gallery, Paris, 1963; Galerie Schmela, 1963; Sidney Janis Gallery, 1965, 67, 68, 70, 71, 73, 74, 77, 78, 80, 82, 84; Toronto (three-man, with Jim Dine, Claes Oldenburg); Chicago/Contemporary, 1968; Darthea Speyer Gallery, 1969, 71; Galerie der Spiegel, Cologne, 1970; Galerie Onnasch, Cologne, 1971; Zurich, circ., 1971, 73; Trenton/State (two-man), 1971; U. of Wisconsin, Milwaukee, 1973; Andre Emmerich Gallery, Zurich, 1975; Dartmouth College, 1975; ICA, U. of Pennsylvania, 1976; Nina Freudenheim Gallery, Buffalo, 1976; Newport (R.I.) Art Association, 1976; Suzette Schochett Gallery, Newport, R.I., 1976; Santa Barbara/MA, 1976; Greenwich (Conn.) Arts Council, 1977; Ohio U., 1978; Serge De Bloe Gallery, Brussels, 1979; Makler Gallery, Phila-

George Segal   *Nude on Coach (On Her Stomach)*   1985

delphia, 1979, 84; Akron/AM, 1980; Gatodo Gallery, Tokyo, 1980; Fay Gold Gallery, Atlanta, 1980; Gloria Luria Gallery, Bay Harbor Islands, Fla., 1980; Contemporary Sculpture Center, Tokyo, 1982; Ohara Museum of Art, Kurashiki, 1982; Museum of Modern Art, Toyama, 1982; Seibu Museum of Art, Tokyo, 1982; Takanawa Museum, Karuizawa, 1982; Jewish Museum, 1983, 85; U. of Miami, 1983; Osaka/National, 1983; Il Ponte Gallery, Rome, 1984; Galerie Esperanza, Montreal, 1985; Galerie Maeght, Paris, 1985; Youngstown/Butler, 1985. **Retrospectives:** California State U., Long Beach, circ., 1977-78; Walker, circ., 1978-79. **Group:** Boston Arts Festival, 1956; Jewish Museum, The New York School, Second Generation, 1957, Recent American Sculpture, 1964, also 1966; WMAA Annuals, 1960, 64, 68; A.F.A., The Figure, circ., 1960, also 1968; Sidney Janis Gallery, The New Realists, 1962; VII & IX Sao Paulo Biennials, 1963, 67; Stockholm/National, American Pop Art, 1964; Corcoran Biennial, 1965; Cordier & Ekstrom, Inc., 1965; Palais des Beaux-Arts, Brussels, 1965; WMAA, A Decade of American Drawings, 1965; SRGM, 1965, 67; RISD, Recent Still Life, 1966; Chicago/AI, 1966, 74; Walker, 1966; Los Angeles/County MA, American Sculpture of the Sixties, 1967; MOMA, The 1960's, 1967; Carnegie, 1967; II Internationale der Zeichnung, Darmstadt, 1967; Trenton/State, Focus on Light, 1967; Gelsenkirchen, 1967; Documenta IV, Kassel, 1968; St. Paul Gallery, 1968; ICA, London, The Obsessive Image, 1968; Fort Worth Art Museum, Drawings, 1969; Grand Rapids, Sculpture of the 60s, 1969; Boston U., American Artists of the Nineteen Sixties, 1970; Expo '70, Osaka, 1970; Indianapolis, 1970; Carnegie, 1970; WMAA, 1970; Walker, Figures/Environments, circ., 1970-71; Chicago/AI, Contemporary Drawings, 1971; Chicago/Contemporary, White on White, 1971-72; Utica, 1972; Harvard U., Recent Figure Sculpture, 1972; Cleveland/MA, Contempo-

rary American Artists, 1974; Chicago/Contemporary, 1974, 76; Darmstadt, Kunsthalle, Realism and Reality, 1975; New York Cultural Center, Three Centuries of the American Nude, 1975; NCFA, Sculpture: American Directions 1945-75, 1975; Philadelphia College of Art, Artists' Sketchbooks, 1976; Documenta, Kassel, 1977; WMAA, Art about Art, 1978; Purchase/SUNY, Hidden Desires, 1980; NAD, 1981; Newport Harbor, Inside Out, Self Beyond Likeness, 1981; PAFA, Contemporary American Realism Since 1960, 1981; AAIAL, 1982; San Antonio/MA Real, Really Real, Super Real, 1982; Houston/Contemporary, American Still Life, 1945-1983, circ., 1983; Ridgefield/Aldrich, A Second Talent, 1984; Williams College, Six on Bronze, circ., 1984; WMAA, Blam!, 1984. **Collections:** Aachen/NG; Akron/AI; Amsterdam/Stedelijk; Birmingham, Ala./MA; CNAC; Caracas; Carnegie; Charlotte/Mint; Chicago/AI; Cleveland/MA; Columbus; Dartmouth College; Des Moines; Detroit/Institute; Hartford/Wadsworth; Helsinki; Hirshhorn; Indiana U.; Israel Museum; Krefeld/Kaiser Wilhelm; MMA; MOMA; Mexico City/Tamayo; Milwaukee; Montreal/Contemporain; Munich/SG; NCFA; National Gallery; Newark Museum; U. of North Carolina; Omaha/Joslyn; Ottawa/National; PAFA; PMA; Paris/Beaubourg; Portland, Ore./AM; Purchase/SUNY; Rotterdam; SFMA; St. Louis/City; Seattle/AM; Schwebber Electronics; SRGM; Stockholm/National; Stuttgart; U. of Texas; Tokyo/Central; Toronto; Trenton/State; Vancouver; WMAA; Walker; Wuppertal; Zurich. **Bibliography:** Alloway 4; Battcock, ed.; Becker and Vostell; Bihalji-Merin; Calas, N. and E.; *Contemporanea*; Craven, W.; Diamonstein; Dienst 1; *Figures/Environments*; Finch; Friedman and van der Marck; Gerdts; Hansen; Haskell 5; Honisch and Jensen, eds.; Hunter, ed.; Johnson, Ellen H.; Kaprow; Kozloff 3; *Kunst um 1970*; Licht, F.; Lippart 5; *Recent Figure Sculpture*; Rowell; Sandler

1; Trier 1; Tuchman 1; Weller. Archives.

SELIGER, CHARLES. b. June 3, 1926, NYC. Self-taught in art. Traveled Switzerland, France. **Taught:** Mt. Vernon (N.Y.) Art Center, 1950-51. **Address:** 10 Lenox Avenue, Mount Vernon, NY 10552. **Dealer:** Gallery Schlesinger-Boisanté, NYC. **One-man Exhibitions:** (first) Art of This Century, NYC, 1945, also 1946; Carlebach Gallery, NYC, 1948, 49; de Young, 1949; Art Center School, Los Angeles, 1949; Willard Gallery, NYC, 1951, 53, 55, 57, 61, 62, 65, 66, 67, 78; Otto Seligman Gallery, 1955, 58, 65, 66; Haydon Calhoun Gallery, Dallas, 1962; Nassau Community College, Garden City, N.Y., 1966; Andrew Crispo Gallery, NYC, 1974, 76, 78, 79, 81, 83; Les Copains Art Ltd., Buffalo, N.Y., 1976; Makler Gallery, Philadelphia, 1979; Miami-Dade Community College, Miami, 1981; Jacksonville/AM, 1981; Gallery Schlesinger-Boisanté, 1985, 86; Galerie Lopes, Zurich, 1986. **Retrospectives:** Wooster Community Art Center, Danbury, Conn., 1969; SRGM, 1986. **Group:** VMFA, 1946; Chicago/AI, Abstract and Surrealist Art, 1948; XXIV Venice Biennial, 1948; WMAA Annuals, 1948, 49, 51, 52, 53, 54, 55, 56, 57, 58, 60; Guggenheim Colletion; Brooklyn Museum, 1949; Cornell U., Young Painters, 1951; MOMA, Abstract Painting and Sculpture in America, 1951; Chicago/AI, 1952; USIA, American Painting, circ., Europe, 1956; Utica, 1957; Rome-New York Foundation, Rome, 1960; Norfolk; St. Paul Gallery, 1966; AAAL, 1966, 68; The Willard Gallery, 1967; Smithsonian, The Art of Organic Forms, 1968; Skidmore College, Watercolors: Historical and Contemporary, 1976; Chicago/Terra, Solitude, Inner Visions in American Art, 1982. **Collections:** Andover/Phillips; Baltimore/MA; Brandeis U.; Carnegie; Chicago/AI; Chicago/Terra; The Hague; Hartford/Wadsworth; High Museum; Hirshhorn; Iowa State U.;

Jacksonville/AM; Jerusalem/National; Karlsruhe; MMA; MOMA; Newark Museum; Phillips; Seattle/AM; Southern Illinois U.; SRGM; Tel Aviv; US State Department; Utica; Vancouver; Vassar College; WMAA. **Bibliography:** Baur 7; Read 2, 4; Richardson, E.P.; Ritchie 1. Archives.

SELIGMANN, KURT. b. July 20, 1900, Basel, Switzerland; **d.** January 2, 1962, NYC. **Studied:** Ecole des Beaux-Arts, Geneva, 1920; Academy of Fine Arts, Florence, Italy, 1927. To USA, 1939; became a citizen. **Taught:** Brooklyn Museum School. Designed sets for modern dance and ballet groups. Authority on magic. **One-man Exhibitions:** Jeanne Bucher, Paris, 1932, 35; Zwemmer Gallery, London, 1933; Mitzowko-Shi, Tokyo, 1935; Wakefield Gallery, NYC; Karl Nierendorf Gallery, NYC, 1939, 41; New School for Social Research, 1940; Mexico City/Nacional, 1943; Durlacher Brothers, NYC, 1944, 46, 48, 50, 53; Arts Club of Chicago, 1946; Alexander Iolas Gallery, 1953; Walker, 1958; Fine Arts Associates, NYC, 1960; Ruth White Gallery, 1960, 61, 68; D'Arcy Gallery, NYC, 1964; Berne, 1967; Galerie Jacques Benador, Geneva, 1974; John Bernard Myers Gallery, NYC, 1974; Springfield, Mass./MFA, 1974; La Boetie, Inc., NYC, 1973, 76; Buffalo/Albright, 1983. **Retrospective:** La Boetie, NYC, 1973. **Group:** WMAA; MOMA; Chicago/AI; Detroit/Institute; U. of Illinois; MMA; NYPL; PAFA; Buffalo/Albright, Drawings and Watercolors, 1968. **Collections:** Aubusson; Bibliotheque Nationale; Brooklyn Museum; Buffalo/Albright; Chicago/AI; College des Musées Nationaux de France; U. of Illinois; Kunstkredit; Lodz; MMA; MOMA; Mexico City/Nacional; NYPL; PAFA; Smith College; WMAA. **Bibliography:** *Abstraction Création 1931-1936;* Blesh 1; Breton 2; Dorner; Flanagan; Frost; Goodrich and Baur 1; Huyghe; Jakovski; Janis and Blesh 1; Janis, S.; Kuh 1; Murken-Altrogge; Neff, ed.;

Pearson 1; Pousette-Dart, ed.; Richardson, E.P.; Rubin 1; Sachs; **Seligmann;** Tomkins and Time-Life Books; Waldberg, 4. Archives.

SENNHAUSER, JOHN. b. December 10, 1907, Rorschach, Switzerland; **d.** January 7, 1978, Escondido, Calif. **Studied:** Technical Institute, Treviso, Italy; Academy of Fine Arts, Venice; Cooper Union. Traveled Europe, USA. **Taught:** Leonardo da Vinci Art School, NYC, 1936-39; Contemporary School of Art, NYC, 1939-42. **Member:** American Abstract Artists; Federation of Modern Painters and Sculptors; International Institute of Arts and Letters. **Commissions:** Murals for banks and private buildings in NYC and other cities. **Awards:** WMAA, **P.P.,** 1951; Tulsa/Philbrook, **P.P.,** 1951; Mark Rothko Foundation Grant, 1971, 72. **One-man Exhibitions:** (first) Leonardo da Vinci Art School Gallery, NYC, 1936; Contemporary Arts Gallery, NYC, 1939; Theodore A. Kohn Gallery, NYC, 1942; Artists' Gallery, NYC, 1947, 50, 52; Brown U., 1954; U. of Maine, 1955; Black Mountain College, 1956; The Zabriskie Gallery, 1956, 57; Knapik Gallery, NYC, 1961; The Salpeter Gallery, NYC, 1964; Meierhans Art Galleries, Perkasie, Pa., 1963, 68; Lenox (Mass.) Library, 1972; San Diego Public Library, 1979; Martin Diamond Gallery, NYC, 1980. **Group:** Brunswick U.; Bennington College; Worcester/AM; Walker; Dallas/MFA; NAD; PAFA; Chicago/AI; Museum of Non-Objective Art, NYC; Corcoran; U. of Illinois; Brooklyn Museum; Baltimore/MA; Salon des Realites Nouvelles, Paris; A.F.A., Collage in America, 1958; A.F.A., Geometrical Abstraction of the 1930s, 1972. **Collections:** American Museum of Immigration; Calcutta; U. of Georgia; St. Lawrence U.; SRGM; Tulsa/Philbrook; Utica; Wichita State U.; WMAA. **Bibliography:** Lane and Larsen; Pousette-Dart, ed. Archives.

SERRA, RICHARD. b. November 2, 1938, San Francisco, Calif. **Studied:** U. of California, Berkeley and Santa Barbara, 1957-61, BA, MA; Yale U., 1961-64; BA and MA. Traveled Italy. **Commissions:** Western Washington U., Bellingham, 1978. **Awards:** Fulbright Fellowship, 1965-66; Skowhegan School Medal, 1975. **Address:** 319 Greenwich Street, NYC 10013. **Dealer:** Leo Castelli, Inc., NYC. **One-man Exhibitions:** Galleria la Salita, Rome, 1966; Galerie Rolf Ricke, 1968, 73; Galerie Lambert, Milan, 1969; Leo Castelli, Inc., NYC, 1970, 72, 74, 81, 82, 84; ACE Gallery, Los Angeles, 1970, 72, 74; U. of California, San Diego, 1970; Pasadena/AM, 1970; School of Visual Arts, NYC, 1974; ACE Gallery, Los Angeles, 1976; Portland (Ore.) Center for the Visual Arts, 1974; Galerie de Gestlo, Hamburg, 1975; ACE Gallery, Venice, Calif., 1976, 78; Galerie Daniel Templon, Paris, 1977; Galerie, Bochum-Weitmar, West Germany, 1977; Amsterdam/Stedelijk, circ., 1977; Blum Helman Gallery, NYC, 1976, 78, 81, 83; Oxford, England, MOMA, 1978; Richard Hines Gallery, Seattle, 1979; U. of California, Berkeley, 1979; KOH Gallery, Tokyo, 1979, 81; Galerie Schmela, Dusseldorf, 1979; Hudson River Museum, 1980; Rotterdam, 1980; Monchenhausmuseum, Goslar, West Germany, 1981; Gemini G.E.L., Los Angeles, 1982; St. Louis/City, 1982; Carol Taylor Gallery, Dallas, 1982; Akira Ikeda Gallery, Tokyo, 1983; Larry Gagosian Gallery, Los Angeles, 1983, 84; Galerie Nordenhake, Malmo, Sweden, 1983, 84; Richard Onnasch Gallery, Berlin, 1983; Galerie Daniel Templon, Paris, 1984; Galerie Maeght Lelong, NYC, 1985. **Group:** Yale U., Drawings, 1966; Ithaca College, Drawings 1967, 1967; A.F.A., Soft Sculpture, 1968; WMAA, 1968, 70, 73; MOMA, New Media: New Methods, circ., 1969; Seattle/AM, 557,087, 1969; Trenton/State, Soft Art, 1969; Berne, When Attitudes Become Form, 1969; WMAA, Anti-Illusion: Procedures/Materials,

1969; SRGM, Nine Young Artists, 1969; Chicago/Contemporary, Art by Telephone, 1969; U. of California, Irvine, Five Sculptors, 1969; Hannover/Kunstverein, Identifications, 1970; SRGM, Guggenheim International, 1971; Dusseldorf/Kunsthalle, Prospect '71, 1971; Los Angeles/County MA, Art & Technology, 1971; Arnhem, Sonsbeek '71, 1971; Documenta V, Kassel, 1972; Rijksmuseum Kroller-Muller, Diagrams and Drawings, 1972; Festival of Two Worlds, Spoleto, 1972; New York Cultural Center, 3D into 2D, 1973; Yale U., Options and Alternatives, 1973; Detroit/Institute, Art in Space, 1973; Yale U., American Drawings, 1970-1973, 1973; Parcheggio di Villa Borghese, Rome, Contemporanea, 1974; Princeton U., Line as Language, 1974; MIT, Interventions in Landscapes, 1974; CNAC, Art/Voir, 1974; Oakland/AM, Public Sculpture; Urban Environment, 1974; Baltimore/MA, Artists, 1975; Hayward Gallery, London, The Condition of Sculpture, 1975; WMAA, Projected Video, 1975; NCFA, Sculpture: American Directions, 1945-1975, 1975; MOMA, Drawing Now, 1976; WMAA, 200 Years of American Sculpture, 1976; Philadelphia College of Art, Private Notation: Artists' Sketchbooks II, 1976; Akademie der Kunst, Berlin, SoHo, 1976; Documenta 6, Kassel, 1977; WMAA Biennial, 1977; U. of Chicago, Ideas in Sculpture, 1977; Worcester/AM, Between Sculpture and Painting, 1978; Amsterdam/Stedelijk, Made by Sculptors, 1978; Krefeld/Haus Lange, The Broadening of the Concept of Reality in the Art of the 60s and 70s, 1979; P.S. 1, Long Island City, Great Big Drawing Show, 1979; Brooklyn Museum, American Drawings in Black and White: 1970-1979, 1980; Corcoran Biennial, 1981; Grand Palais, Paris, L'Amerique aux Indépendants, 1980; XXXIL Venice Biennale, 1980; Zurich, Reliefs, 1980; Amsterdam/Stedelijk, 60-'80: Attitudes/Concepts/Images, 1982; Centre d'Arts Plastiques Contemporains, Bordeaux, Art Povera, Anitiform: Sculp-

tures 1966-69, 1982; Documenta CII, Kassel, 1982; Dublin/Municipal, International Quadriennial (ROSC), 1984. **Collections:** Amsterdam/Stedelijk; Canberra/National; Cologne; Detroit/Institute; Krefeld/Haus Lange; Kyoto; La Jolla; Melbourne/National; MMA; MOMA; Oberlin College; Ontario; Ottawa/National; Pasadena/AM; Ridgefield/Aldrich; Rijksmuseum Kroller-Muller; SRGM; Stockholm/National; Tate; WMAA; Yale University. **Bibliography:** *Art Now 75;* Celant; *Contemporanea;* Danto; De Wilde 2; Gablik; Honisch and Jensen, eds.; Johnson, Ellen H.; Krauss 2, 3; *Kunst um 1970;* Lippard, 3; Lippard, ed.; Muller; *Options and Alternatives;* Pincus-Witten; *Report; When Attitudes Become Form.*

SHAHN, BEN. b. September 12, 1898, Kovno, Lithuania; **d.** May 14, 1969, NYC. To USA, 1906. **Studied:** NYU; City College of New York, 1919-22 (biology); NAD, 1922; ASL. Traveled Europe, Japan, North Africa, USA. Photographer and designer for Farm Security Administration, 1935-38. Designed posters for Office of War Information, 1942, and for CIO, 1944-46. Designed sets for *Ballets: USA* and for the Festival of Two Worlds, Spoleto, 1958. **Commissions:** Community Building, Roosevelt, N.J., 1938-39; US Post Offices, Bronx, N.Y., 1938-39 (with Bernarda Bryson), and Jamaica, N.Y., 1939; Social Security Building, Washington, D.C., 1940-42; William E. Grady Vocational High School, Brooklyn, N.Y., 1957 (mosaic). **Awards:** PAFA, Pennell Memorial Medal, 1939, 53, Alice McFadden Eyre Medal, 1952, Joseph E. Temple Gold Medal, 1956; *Look* magazine poll of "Ten Best Painters," 1948; II Sao Paulo Biennial, 1953; XXVII Venice Biennial, 1954; Harvard U., Medal, 1956; American Institute of Graphic Art, Medal, 1958; North Shore, Long Island, N.Y., Art Festival Annual Award, 1959. **One-man Exhibitions:** The Downtown Gallery, 1930, 32, 33, 44, 49, 51, 52, 55, 57, 59, 61; Julien Levy Galleries, NYC, 1940; MOMA, 1947; Arts Council of Great Britain, circ., 1947; Albright Art School, 1950; Perls Galleries, 1950; Arts Club of Chicago, 1951; Santa Barbara/MA, circ., 1952, also 1967; Houston/MFA, 1954; Detroit/Institute (three-man), 1954; Chicago/AI, 1954; XXVII Venice Biennial, 1954; Southern Illinois U., 1954; American Institute of Graphic Art, 1957; St. Mary's College (Ind.), 1958; Bucknell U., 1958; Katonah (N.Y.) Art Gallery, 1959; Leicester Gallery, London, 1959, 64; U. of Louisville, 1960; U. of Utah, 1960; Library of the New Haven (Conn.) Jewish Community Center, 1961; Institute of Modern Art, Boston, Documentary, 1957; Amsterdam/Stedelijk, 1961; Rome/Nazionale, 1962; MOMA, Ben Shahn, circ., Europe, 1962; Randolph-Macon Woman's College, 1966; PMA, 1967; Orlando, 1968; Kennedy Gallery, 1968-69, 1970, 71, 73; Nantenshi Gallery, Tokyo, 1970; Syracuse U., 1977; Nardin Gallery, NYC, 1979; Hooks-Epstein Galleries, Houston, 1983, 84; Terry Dintenfass Inc., NYC, 1987. **Retrospectives:** MOMA, 1947; ICA, Boston, 1948; Osaka Municipal, 1970; National Museum of Western Art, Tokyo, 1970; Jewish Museum, NYC, 1976; Fort Worth, 1977. **Group:** Corcoran; Carnegie; WMAA; Chicago/AI; U. of Nebraska; Brooklyn Museum; MOMA; Buffalo/Albright. **Collections:** Abbott Laboratories; Andover/Phillips; Arizona State College; U. of Arizona; Auburn U.; Baltimore/MA; Brandeis U.; Brooklyn Museum; Buffalo/Albright; California Palace; Carnegie; Chicago/AI; Container Corp. of America; Cranbrook; Dartmouth College; Des Moines; Detroit/Institute; Fort Wayne/AM; U. of Georgia; Grand Rapids; Hartford/Wadsworth; Harvard U.; U. of Illinois; Indiana U.; Inland Steel Co.; Jewish Museum; MMA; MOMA; Mary Washington College; U. of Michigan; Museum of the City of New York; U. of Nebraska; Newark Museum; U. of Oklahoma;

Omaha/Joslyn; PAFA; Phillips; Sara Roby Foundation; St. Louis/City; Santa Barbara/MA; Smith College; Springfield, Mo./AM; Syracuse U.; Terry Art Institute; VMFA; WMAA; Walker; Wellesley College; Wesleyan U.; Wichita/AM; Youngstown/Butler. **Bibliography:** Baigell 1; Barr 3; Baur 7; Bazin; Biddle 4; Bihalji-Merin; Blesh 1; **Bush 1;** Brown 2; Canaday; Christensen; *Cityscape 1919-39*; Eliot; Finkelstein; Flanagan; Flexner; *From Foreign Shores*; Gaunt; Gerdts; Goodrich and Baur 1; Greengood; Haftman; Honisch and Jensen, eds.; Hunter 6; Kepes 2; Kuh 1, 2; Langui; Lee and Burchwood; McCurdy, ed.; Mendelowitz; *Metro*; **Morse;** Munsterberg; Newmeyer; Newton 1; Nordness, ed.; Pearson 1, 2; Pousette-Dart, ed.; Read 2; Richardson, E.P.; Rodman 1, 2, 3; Sachs; **Shahn 1, 2; Shahan, B.B.;** Shapiro; **Soby 2, 3, 4, 5;** Sutton; Weller; Wight 2. Archives.

SHAPIRO, JOEL. b. September 27, 1941, New York City. **Studied:** NYU, 1964, BA; 1969, MA; with the Peace Corps in India, 1965-66. **Taught:** Princeton U., 1974-76; School of Visual Arts, 1977-82. **Awards:** National Endowment for the Arts, grant, 1975; Brandeis U., Creative Arts Award, 1984; Skowhegan School, Medal for Sculpture, 1986. **Address:** 284 Lafayette Street, NYC 10012. **Dealer:** Paula Cooper Gallery. **One-man Exhibitions:** (first) Paula Cooper Gallery, 1970, 72, 74, 75, 76, 77, 79, 80, 82, 83, 84; The Clocktower, NYC, 1973; Galerie Salvatore, Ala, Milan, 1974; Garage Gallery, London (two-man), 1975; Walter Kelly Gallery, Chicago, 1975; Chicago/Contemporary, 1976; Max Protetch Gallery, Washington, D.C., 1977; Buffalo/Albright, 1977; Susanne Hilberry Gallery, Detroit, 1977; Galerie Nancy Gillespie-Elisabeth de Laage, Paris, 1977, 79; Gallerie Aronowitsch, Stockholm, 1977; Greenberg Gallery, St. Louis, 1978; Galerie M. Bochum, West Germany, 1978; Akron/AI, 1979; Ohio State U., 1979; Whitechapel Art

Joel Shapiro *Untitled* 1986

Gallery, London, 1980; Galerie Aroniwitsch, Stockholm, 1980, 83, 84; Brown U., 1980; Israel Museum, 1981; Galerie Mukai, Tokyo, 1981; U. of North Carolina, 1981; John Stoller & Co., Inc., 1981; Young Hoffman Gallery, Chicago, 1981; Susanne Hilberry Gallery, Birmingham, Mich., 1982; Portland (Ore.) Center for the Visual Arts, 1982; Yarlow/Salzman Gallery, Toronto, 1982; Asher/Faure, 1983; Knoedler Kasmin Gallery, London, 1985. **Retrospectives:** WMAA, circ., 1982; Amsterdam/Stedelijk, circ., 1985. **Group:** WMAA, Anti-Illusion: Procedure/Material, 1969; MOMA, Paperworks, 1970; WMAA Annuals, 1970; WMAA, American Drawings, 1963-1973, 1973; Chicago/AI, 1974; U. of Massachusetts, Critical Perspectives in American Art, 1976; Venice Biennial, 1976; Akademie der Kunst, Berlin, SoHo, 1976; ICA, U. of Pennsylvania, Improbable Furniture, 1977; Documenta 6, Kassel, 1977; Walker, Scale and Environment, 1977; U. of Chicago,

33 Ideas in Sculpture, 1977; Vassar College, five-man show, 1978; Amsterdam/Stedelijk, Made by Sculptors, 1978; U. of North Carolina, Drawings about Drawings Today, 1979; WMAA Biennials, 1977, 79, 81; Hayward Gallery, London, Pier and Ocean, 1979; Lenbachhaus, Munich, Tendenies in American Drawings of the Late Seventies, 1979; U. of North Carolina, Drawings About Drawing Today, 1979; Brooklyn Museum, American Drawings in Black and White: 1970-1979, 1980; XXXIX Venice Biennial, 1980; Akron/AM, The Image in American Painting and Sculpture, 1950-1980, 1981; Rice U., Variants, 1981; Documenta VII, Kassel, 1982; MIT, Body Language, circ., 1982; MIT, Great Big Drawings, 1982; Milwaukee, American Prints, 1960-1980, 1982; ARS '83, Helsinki, 1983; Bonn, Back to the USA, 1983; Brooklyn Museum, The American Artist as Printmaker, 1983; Dublin/Municipal, International Quadriennial (ROSC), 1984; Hirshhorn, Drawings 1974-1984, 1984; MOMA, International Survey of Recent Painting and Sculpture, 1984; Newark Museum, American Bronze Sculpture, 1850 To The Present, 1984; Purchase/SUNY, Hidden Desire, 1984; Seattle/AM, American Sculpture: Three Decades, 1984; Hudson River Museum, A New Beginning, 1968-1978, 1985; U. of Nebraska, Contemporary Bronze: Six in the Figurative Tradition, 1985; Fort Lauderdale, An American Renaissance: Painting and Sculpture Since 1940, 1986; Frankfurter Kunstverein, Frankfurt, Vom Zeichen, 1986. **Collections:** Amsterdam/Stedelijk; Art Museum of South Texas, Corpus Christi; Buffalo/Albright; Canberra/National; Colgate U.; Dallas/MFA; Detroit/Institute; Des Moines; Fort Worth; Friuli, Italy/MOMA; MMA; Harvard U.; Jerusalem/National; La Jolla; McCrory Corporation, NYC; U. of North Carolina; Ohio State U.; R.S.M. Co., Cincinnati; Walker; Whitney Communications, NYC; WMAA; Zurich. **Bibliography:** *Drawings: The Pluralist Decade;*

Gettings; Kren; Lucie-Smith; Schwartz 2.

SHATTER, SUSAN. b. January 17, 1943, NYC. **Studied:** U. of Wisconsin; Skowhegan School, 1964, with John Button, Fairfield Porter; Pratt Institute, 1965, BFA, with Alex Katz, Gabriel Laderman, Philip Pearlstein; Boston U., 1972, MFA, with James Weeks. Traveled USA, Peru, Greece, Italy. **Taught:** Skowhegan School, 1977, 79; Bennington College, 1979; School of Visual Arts, NYC, 1979, 83, 84; U. of Pennsylvania, 1983-84; Tyler School of Art, 1985. **Awards:** Ingram Merrill Foundation Grant, 1976-77; National Endowment for the Arts, 1980; New York State Foundation for the Arts, grant, 1985. **Address:** 26 West 20th Street, NYC 10011. **Dealer:** Fischbach Gallery, NYC; Harcus Gallery, Boston; John Berggruen Gallery, San Francisco. **One-man Exhibitions:** (first) Fischbach Gallery, 1973, 76, 78, 80, 82, 84; Harcus Krakow Rosen Sonnabend, Boston, 1975; Harcus-Krakow Gallery, Boston, 1977, 79; Mattingly Baker Gallery, Dallas, 1981; Harcus Gallery, 1984; John Berggruen Gallery, 1986. **Group:** American Federation of the Arts, Painterly Realism, 1970; AAAIL, 1972; Omaha/Joslyn, A Sense of Place, 1973; Lincoln, Mass./De Cordova, New England Women, 1975; US Department of the Interior, America 1976, circ., 1976; PAFA, Contemporary American Realism Since 1960, 1981; SFMA, American Realism (Janss), circ., 1985. **Collections:** Boston/MFA; Boston Public Library; Currier; Dartmouth College; MIT; PMA; St. Joseph/Albrecht; Tufts U.; Utah.

SHAW, CHARLES. b. May 1, 1892, NYC; d. April 2, 1974, NYC. **Studied:** Yale U., Ph.D.; Columbia U. School of Architecture; ASL, with Thomas Hart Benton; and privately with George Luks. US Army, World War I. Traveled Europe extensively, Scandinavia, West Indies. Author of children's books, poetry, and articles for *Vanity Fair, The Bookman, Smart Set,* and other magazines. **Member:** American Abstract Artists; Federation of Modern Painters and Sculptors; Fellow of the International Institute of Arts and Letters. **Commissions:** *Vanity Fair* (magazine) (covers); Shell-Mex Ltd. (poster). **Awards:** Nantucket, First and Second Prizes; Century Association, Hon. Men., 1964. **One-man Exhibitions:** (first) Curt Valentine Gallery, NYC, 1934, also 1938; Museum of Living Art, NYC, 1935; SRGM, 1940; Passedoit Gallery, NYC, 1945, 46, 50, 51, 54, 1956-59; Nantucket, 1954-68; Albert Landry, NYC, 1960, 61; Art Association of Newport (R.I.), 1960, 62; U. of Louisville, 1963; Southampton East Gallery, Southampton, N.Y., 1963, 64; The Bertha Schaefer Gallery, 1963, 64, 66, 68, 71; Faure Gallery, La Jolla, 1964; Century Association, 1967, 75; Washburn Gallery, NYC, 1976, 79, 82, 83; Helander Gallery, Palm Beach, Fla., 1985. **Group:** WMAA Annuals; Chicago/AI; Carnegie; Walker; SFMA; U. of Illinois; Corcoran; American Abstract Artists, annually, 1936-68; Federation of Modern Painters and Sculptors, annually, 1940-68; PMA, "8×8," 1945; MOMA, Abstract Painting and Sculpture in America, 1951; International Association of Plastic Arts, Contemporary American Paintings, circ., Europe, 1956-57; WMAA, Geometric Abstraction in America, circ., 1962; PAFA, 1966; U. of Colorado, 1966. **Collections:** Atlanta U.; Baltimore/MA; Boston/MFA; Brandeis U.; Brooklyn Museum; California Palace; Chase Manhattan Bank; Chicago/AI; Cincinnati/AM; Cleveland/MA; Corcoran; Dayton/AI; Denver/MA; Detroit/Institute; Fort Worth; U. of Georgia; Hartford/Wadsworth; Los Angeles/County MA; U. of Louisville; MMA; MOMA; NYU; Nantucket; Newark Museum; Norfolk/Chrysler; U. of North Carolina; PMA; Paris/Moderne; Phillips; Pittsfield/Berkshire; RISD; Raleigh/NCMA; Rockefeller Institute;

SFMA; SRGM; WMAA; Walker; Wichita/AM; Williams College; Yale U. **Bibliography:** Baur 7; Cheney; Kootz 2; Lane and Larsen; Marter, Tarbell, and Wechsler; Pousette-Dart, ed.; Ritchie 1; Toher, ed. Archives.

SCHECHTER, LAURA. b. August 26, 1944, Brooklyn, N.Y. **Studied:** Brooklyn College, BFA, Magna cum laude, 1961-65, with Ad Reinhardt and Alfred Russell. **Taught:** Parsons School of Design, NYC, 1984; NAD, 1985, 86. **Awards:** CAPS, 1981, 82. **Member:** Artists Equity. **Address:** 429 4th Street, Brooklyn, N.Y. 11215. **Dealer:** Staempfli Gallery, NYC. **One-man Exhibitions:** (first) Green Mountain Gallery, NYC, 1971; Suffolk County Historical Museum, 1971; Larcada Gallery, NYC, 1972; The Forum Gallery, 1976, 80, 83; Capricorn Gallery, Bethesda, Md., 1977; Suffolk County Community College, 1978; Nicholas Roerrich Museum, 1981; Pucker Safrai Gallery, Boston, 1981; Greenville, 1982; U. of Wisconsin, 1982; Van Straaten Gallery, Chicago, 1983; Robert Schoelkopf Gallery, NYC, 1985. **Group:** St. Joseph/Albrecht, Drawing, America 1975, 1975; Westmoreland County/AM, New American Still Life, 1979; PAFA, Perspectives on Contemporary American Realism, 1983; Brooklyn Museum, Homer, Sargent and the American Watercolor Tradition, 1984; West Palm Beach/Norton, The Fine Line, 1985. **Collections:** Arizona State U.; Boston; Buffalo/Albright; Carnegie; Chicago/AI; Greenville; U. of Indiana; Indianapolis; Israel Museum; Jewish Museum; U. of Minnesota; NMAA; NYPL; Nicholas Roerich Museum; Rutgers U.; Tel Aviv.

SHEELER, CHARLES. b. July 16, 1883, Philadelphia, Pa.; **d.** May 7, 1965, Dobbs Ferry, N.Y. **Studied:** Pennsylvania School of Industrial Art, Philadelphia, 1900-03; PAFA, 1903-06, with William M. Chase. Traveled Europe, USA. **Taught:** Phillips Academy, 1946; Currier Gallery School, 1948. Collaborated with Paul Strand on the film *Mannhattana*. **Commissions:** Ford Motor Co., photographed the Ford Plant, 1927. **Awards:** Chicago/AI, Norman Wait Harris Medal, 1945; PAFA, Alumni Award, 1957; Hallmark International Competition, 1958 ($1,000); AAAL, Award of Merit Medal, 1962. **One-man Exhibitions:** (first) Modern Gallery, NYC, 1918 (photographs); De-Zayas Gallery, NYC, 1922; Whitney Studio Club, NYC, 1924; J. B. Neumann Gallery, NYC (two-man), 1926; Art Center, NYC, 1926; The Downtown Gallery, 1931, 38, 40, 41, 43, 46, 49, 51, 56, 58, 65, 66; Arts Club of Chicago, 1932; Harvard U. (three-man), 1934; Society of Arts and Crafts, Detroit, 1935; Cincinnati/AM (four-man), 1941; Dayton/AI, 1944; Andover/Phillips, 1946; Currier, 1948; Houston/MFA (two-man), 1951; Walker, 1952; Detroit/Institute (three-man), 1954; Katonah (N.Y.) Art Gallery, 1960; State U. of Iowa, 1963; NCFA, 1968; Terry Dintenfass, Inc., 1974, 80; WMAA, 1980; MMA, 1982; Chicago/Terra, 1985. **Retrospective:** MOMA, 1939; UCLA, circ., 1954; MIT, 1959; Allentown/AM, 1961; Cedar Rapids/AA, 1967; NCFA, 1968. **Group:** NAD, 1906; PAFA, 1907, 1908-10; The Armory Show, 1913; Anderson Galleries, NYC, Forum Exhibition, 1916; Society of Independent Artists, NYC, 1917; Brooklyn Museum, 1923, 25; Cincinnati/AM, 1924, 1927-31, 34, 35, 39; Whitney Studio Club Annuals, NYC, 1925, 27, 30; Cleveland/MA, 1926, 1927-29, 31, 32, 34; Royal Academy, London, 1930; St. Louis/City, 1931-34, 41, 42, 44, 45; Carnegie, 1931, 33, 35, 37, 40, 41, 43, 45, 48, 52; WMAA, 1932, 34, 36, 42; XVII & XXVIII Venice Biennials, 1934, 56; Chicago/AI, 1935, 37, 38, 41, 46, 48, 49, 51, 54. **Collections:** Albany/Institute; Andover/Phillips; Arizona State College; Boston/MFA; Britannica; Brooklyn Museum; Buffalo/Albright; California Palace; Chicago/AI; Cleveland/MA; Colonial Williamsburg; Columbus; Currier;

Detroit/Institute; General Motors Corp.; Harvard U.; Kansas City/Nelson; MMA; MOMA; The Miller Co.; Mount Holyoke College; U. of Nebraska; Newark Museum; New Britain; PAFA; PMA; Phillips; RISD; Sara Roby Foundation; Santa Barbara/MA; Smith College; Springfield, Mass./MFA; Tel Aviv; Toledo/MA; Utica; VMFA; WMAA; Walker; Wesleyan U.; West Palm Beach/Norton; Wichita/AM; Williams College; Worcester/AM; Yale U.; Youngstown/Butler. **Bibliography:** *Avant-Garde Painting and Sculpture in America, 1910-25;* Barker 1; Barr 3; Baur 7; Bazin; Beam; Biddle 4; Blesh 1; Born; Boswell 1; Brown 2; Bulliet 1; Cahill and Barr, eds.; **Charles Sheeler;** Cheney; Christensen; *Cityscape, 1919-39;* Dijkstra, ed.; **Dochterman;** Dorner; Eliot; Flanagan; Flexner; *Forerunners;* Frank, ed.; Frost; Goldwater and Treves, eds.; Goodrich and Baur 1; Haftman; Hall; Halpert; **Hirsch;** Hunter 7; Huyghe; *Index of 20th Century Artists;* Janis and Blesh 1; Janis, S.; Jewell 2; Kootz 1, 2; Kouvenhoven; Kuh 1; Levin 2; Mather 1; McCoubrey 1; McCurdy, ed.; Mellquist; Mendelowitz; Murken-Altrogge; Nauhaus; Newmeyer; Nordness, ed.; Pagano; Phillips 1, 2; Poore; Pousette-Dart, ed.; Rose, B., 1, 4; Rosenblum 1; **Rourke;** Sachs; Sager; Soby 5; Tashijan; Wight 2; **Williams, W. C.** Archives.

SHEETS, MILLARD. b. June 24, 1907, Pomona, Calif. **Studied:** Chouinard Art Institute, Los Angeles, 1925-29, with F.T. Chamberlain, Clarence Hinkle. Traveled Europe, Central America, Mexico, USA, Pacific, China, Russia, the Orient, Southeast Asia, West Africa. **Taught:** Chouinard Art Institute, 1928-35; Scripps College, 1932-54, 1955-72; Director, Los Angeles County Art Institute, 1953-60. **Member:** California Watercolor Society; NAD; American Watercolor Society; Society of Motion Picture Art Directors; Bohe-mian Club. President, Millard Sheets Designs, Inc.; architectural designer; Federal A.P.: Assistant Director with Merle Armitage, S. MacDonald-Wright. **Commissions** (murals): Pomona (Calif.) First Federal Savings and Loan Association; Our Lady of the Assumption Church, Ventura, Calif. (interior and exterior); over 100 murals and mosaics including San Jose Airport Terminal, 1977. **Awards:** Witte, Edgar B. Davis Prize; California Watercolor Society, 1927; Arizona State Fair, 1928, 29, 30; California State Fair, 1930, 32 (first prize), 33, 38; Los Angeles/County MA, First Prize, 1932, and 1945; Chicago/AI, 1938; Hon. LLD, U. of Notre Dame; American Watercolor Society, Dolphin Medal Award, 1986. **Address:** 35800 South Highway One, Gualala, Calif. 95445. **Dealer:** Kennedy Galleries, NYC. **One-man Exhibitions:** (first) Los Angeles, Calif. 1929; Los Angeles/County MA; California Palace; San Diego; Fort Worth, 1931, 34; Milwaukee; Baltimore/MA; Buffalo/Albright; Albany/Institute; Witte, 1931, 34; New Orleans/Delgado; Memphis/Brooks; Springfield, Mass./MFA; U. of Oklahoma; U. of Rochester; A. Tooth & Sons, London, 1964; Dalzell-Hatfield Gallery, Los Angeles, 1975; Kennedy Galleries, NYC, 1978, 80, 82, 85. **Retrospectives:** Scripps College, 1976; Laguna Beach Museum of Art, 1983; Ontario Museum of Art and History, 1985. **Group:** Chicago/AI, 1931-35; NAD Annuals, 1932-35; A Century of Progress, Chicago, 1933-34; Denver/AM, 1935; Sao Paulo, 1955; WMAA; Carnegie; Oakland/AM; Buffalo/Albright; Kansas City/Nelson; U. of Nebraska. **Collections:** Albany/Institute; Britannica; Brooklyn Museum; Carnegie; Cleveland/MA; Chicago/AI; Dayton-AI; de Young; Fort Worth; High Museum; Houston/MFA; Los Angeles/County MA; Los Angeles Public Library; MMA; MOMA; Montclair/AM; Montpelier; Muskegon/Hackley; U. of Oklahoma; RISD; SFMA; San Diego; Seattle/AM; WMAA; Witte. **Bibliogra-**

phy: Cheney; Hall; **Miller 2;** Pagano. Archives.

SHIELDS, ALAN. b. February 4, 1944, Lost Springs, Kansas. **Studied:** Kansas State U.; U. of Maine. **Award:** Guggenheim Foundation Fellowship, 1973. **Address:** P.O. Box 1554, Shelter Island, NY 11964. **Dealer:** Paula Cooper Gallery, NYC. **One-man Exhibitions:** Paula Cooper Gallery, 1969, 70, 72, 74, 76, 78; Janie C. Lee Gallery, Dallas, 1970, 71; New Gallery, Cleveland, 1971; Ileana Sonnabend Gallery, Paris, 1971; Galleria dell'Ariete, 1972; Hansen-Fuller Gallery, 1973; U. of Rhode Island, 1973; Madison Art Center, 1973; Galerie Aronowitsch, Stockholm, 1973; Richard Gray Gallery, 1974, 76; Phoenix Gallery, San Francisco, 1974; Barbara Okun Gallery, St. Louis, 1974, 77, 78; The Texas Gallery, 1974; U. of Kansas, 1975; E.G. Gallery, Kansas City, 1975; Dootson Calderhead Gallery, Seattle, 1975; Galerie Daniel Templon, Paris, 1975, 78; St. Etienne, 1976; Portland (Ore.) Center for the Visual Arts, 1976; Paula Cooper Gallery, NYC, 1976, 80, 82, 83, 84, 85, 86; Rio de Janeiro, 1976; Galerie Simone Stern, New Orleans, 1976; Moore College of Art, Philadelphia, 1977; Nina Freudenheim Gallery, Buffalo, 1977; Strasbourg/Moderne, 1977; Galerie Munro, Hamburg, 1978; P.S. 1, Long Island City, 1978; Galeria Luisa Strina, Sao Paulo, 1978; Thomas Segal Gallery, Boston, 1979; Gimpel & Hanover Gallery, Zurich, 1979; Andre Emmerich Gallery, Zurich, 1979; Williams College, 1979; Dorry Gates Gallery, Kansas City, 1980; Bowdoin College, 1981; Heath Gallery, Atlanta, 1981; Middlebury College, 1982; Mobile/FAMS, 1982; Purchase/SUNY, 1982; Stony Brook/SUNY, 1982; Memphis/Brooks, circ., 1983; Thomas Segal Gallery, Boston, 1983; Gallery Ueda, Tokyo, 1983; Galerie Andre Emmerich, Zurich, 1984; U. of Massachusetts, 1985. **Retrospectives:** Chicago/Contemporary, 1973; Houston/Contemporary, 1973.

Group: Trenton/State, Soft Art, 1969; WMAA, 1969, 72; Indianapolis, 1970; Chicago/AI, 1970, 72, 73; ICA, U. of Pennsylvania, Two Generations of Color Painting, 1970; U. of North Carolina, 1970; Corcoran, Depth and Presence, 1971; U. of Rochester, Aspects of Current Painting, 1971; SRGM, Contemporary Prints and Drawings, 1971; ICA, U. of Pennsylvania, Grids, 1972; U. of California, Berkeley, Eight New York Painters, 1972; Documenta V, Kassel, 1972; Detroit/Institute, 12 Statements, 1972; New York Cultural Center, Soft as Art, 1973; Seattle/AM, American Art: Third Quarter Century, 1973; VIII Paris Biennial, 1973; Indianapolis, 1974; MOMA, Printed, Folded, Cut and Torn, 1974; Corcoran Biennial, 1975; Toledo/MA, Image, Color and Form, 1975; Tyler School of Art, Philadelphia, Drawings, 1975; Akron/AI, Contemporary Images in Watercolor, 1976; Venice Biennial, 1976; Brooklyn Museum, 30 Years of American Printmaking, 1976; Chicago/AI, Drawings of the 70s, 1977; Ljubljana Biennial, 1977; Minnesota/MA, American Drawing 1927-1977, circ. 1977; The American Foundation for the Arts, Miami, Patterning and Decoration, 1970; WMAA, Recent Drawings by Younger Artists, 1978; Tampa Bay Art Center, Two Decades of Abstraction, 1978; Buffalo/Albright, American Painting in the 70s, 1978; Georgia State U., two-man, 1979; U. of North Carolina, Drawings about Drawings, 1979; U. of North Carolina, Art on Paper, 1979; ICA, U. of Pennsylvania, Masks, Tents, Vessels, Talismans, 1979; XXXIX Venice Biennial, 1980; Rice U., Variants, 1981; Houston/Contemporary, The Americans: The Collage, 1982; MOMA, Handmade Paper, 1982; WMAA, Block Prints, 1982; Arts Council of Great Britain, Paper as Image, circ., 1983; U. of North Carolina, Art on Paper, 1983; MOMA, About Paper, 1984. **Collections:** Akron/AI; Boston/MFA; Chase Manhattan Bank; Chicago/AI; Cleveland/MA; Commerce Bank, Kansas City; Dallas/MFA; First City National Bank, Houston; First National City Bank, NYC; Harvard U.; High Museum, Atlanta; Hirshhorn; MOMA; McCrory Corporation; Milwaukee; National Gallery; Oberlin College; U. of Pennsylvania; PMA; Prudential Insurance Co. of America, Newark; Ridgefield/Aldrich; RSM Co., Cincinnati; Rutgers U.; SRGM; Strasbourg/Moderne; Vassar College; Walker; Westinghouse Corp., Pittsburgh; WMAA. **Bibliography:** *Art Now 74.*

SHINN, EVERETT. **b.** November 6, 1876, Woodstown, N.J.; **d.** January 2, 1953, NYC. **Studied:** PAFA. Wrote and produced a number of melodramas in NYC. **Member:** The Eight. **Commissions** (murals): Trenton (N.J.) City Hall; Spring Garden Institute, Philadelphia. **Awards:** Chicago/AI, Watson F. Blair Prize, 1939; elected to the NIAL, 1951. **One-man Exhibitions:** M. Knoedler & Co. 1903, 69; 56th Street Gallery, NYC, 1930; Metropolitan Gallery, NYC, 1931; Morton Gallery, NYC, 1935; One-Ten Gallery, NYC, 1939; Ferargil Galleries, NYC, 1943; James Vigeveno Gallery, Los Angeles, 1945, 47, 48; American-British Art Center, NYC, 1945, 56, 49; The Graham Gallery, 1952, 58, 65; Davis Gallery, 1959; U. of Pennsylvania, 1959; Trenton/State, 1971. **Retrospective:** Trenton/State, 1973. **Group:** Macbeth Gallery, NYC, The Eight, 1908; The Armory Show, 1913; Brooklyn Museum, The Eight, 1943; PMA, 1945; Syracuse/Everson, The Eight 1958; U. of Pittsburgh, 1959. **Collections:** Boston/MFA; Brooklyn Museum; Buffalo/Albright; Chicago/AI; Detroit/Institute; MMA; New Britain; Phillips; WMAA. **Bibliography:** Baur 7, Biddle 4, Blesh 1; Brown; Brown 2; Canaday; Cheney; Eliot; Flanagan; Flexner; Gallatin 8; Gerdts; Glackens; Goodrich and Baur 1; Hartmann; Hunter 6; Kent, N.; McCoubrey 1; McCurdy, ed.; Mellquist; Mendelowitz; Neuhaus; Pagano; Perlman; Richardson, E.P.; Rose, B., 1; Sutton. Archives.

SIMON, SIDNEY. **b.** June 21, 1917, Pittsburgh, Pa. **Studied:** Carnegie Institute of Technology; PAFA; U. of Pennsylvania, with George Harding, BFA; Barnes Foundation. US Army artist, 1943-46. Traveled Austria, Italy, Morocco. **Taught:** Skowhegan School, 1946-58 (vice-president and director), 1975; Cooper Union, 1947-48; Brooklyn Museum School, 1950-52, 1954-56; Parsons School of Design, 1962-63; Salzburg Center for American Studies, 1971; ASL, 1973-; Castle Hill Art Center, 1973-74; U. of Pennsylvania, 1980. **Member:** Artists Equity (national director, treasurer, vice-president, 1946-60); Century Association; Architectural League of New York; vice-president, Sculptors Guild; New York City Art Commission, 1975-79; NAD. Federal A.P.: US Post Office, Fleminsburgh, Ky. (mural). **Commissions:** Fort Belvoir, Va., 1942 (3 murals); Temple Beth Abraham, Tarrytown, N.Y.; Walt Whitman Junior High School, Yonkers, N.Y.; stage set for NYC production of *Ulysses in Nighttown,* by James Joyce, 1959; Federation of Jewish Philanthropies; *The Family,* sculpture group for the film *David and Lisa,* 1962 (with Robert Cook and Dorothy Greenbaum); Protestant Council of New York (Family of Man Medal, presented to President John F. Kennedy, 1963); *The Circus,* sculpture for Woodland House, Hartford, Conn., 1963; Our Lady of the Angels Seminary, Glenmont, N.Y., 1965; Downstate Medical Center, Brooklyn, N.Y. 1967; Prospect Park Playground, 1968; 747 Third Avenue Building, NYC, 1973. **Awards:** PAFA, Cresson Fellowship; Edwin Austin Abbey Fellowship, 1940; Prix de Rome, Hon. Men., 1940; Chicago/AI, Posner Painting Prize; PAFA, Fellowship, 1960; Chautauqua Institute, Babcock Memorial Award, 1963; Century Association, Gold Medal for Sculpture, 1969; AAAL, Award, 1976; National Arts Club, Silver

Medal, 1978; NAD, Gold Medal, 1980. **Address:** 95 Bedford Street, NYC 10014. **Dealer:** Long Point Gallery, Provincetown. **One-man Exhibitions:** (first) PAFA, 1946; Niveau Gallery, NYC, 1949; Grand Central Moderns, NYC, 1951, 53; Rockland Foundation, 1955; Motel on the Mountain, 1959; Market Fair, Nyack, N.Y., 1960; Grippi Gallery, NYC, 1963 and others; Pittsburgh Plan for Art; Yale U., 1966; Wellfleet Art Gallery, 1966-67, 69, 71, 73; New School for Social Research, 1969; The Graham Gallery, 1970; Longpoint Gallery, Provincetown, Mass., 1977, 79; Sculpture Center, NYC, 1979. **Retrospective:** Sarah Lawrence College, 1971. **Group:** NAD Annuals, 1944-60; PAFA, 1948-53, 1962; MMA, American Painters under 35, 1950; WMAA, 1950, 52-55, 59, 62, 63; International Biennial Exhibition of Paintings, Tokyo; Brooklyn Museum, 1953; U. of Nebraska Annuals, 1954, 55; Corcoran, 1955; MOMA, The Art of Assemblage, circ., 1961; A.F.A., Educational Alliance Retrospective, 1963. **Collections:** ASL; Century Association; Chautauqua Institute; Colby College; Cornell U.; MMA; U. of North Carolina; The Pentagon; Sports Museum; Smith College; US State Department; Williams College. **Bibliography:** Seitz 3. Archives.

SIMONDS, CHARLES. b. November 14, 1945, New York City. **Studied:** U. of California, Berkeley, 1963-67, BA; Rutgers U., 1967-69; MFA. **Taught:** Newark State College, 1969-71. **Member:** Lower East Side Coalition for Human Housing. **Commissions:** Artpark, Lewiston, N.Y., 1974; Lannan Foundation, Palm Beach, 1981; WMAA, 1981; Zurich, 1981; Chicago/Contemporary, 1981. **Awards:** National Endowment for the Arts, grant, 1974; New York State Council on the Arts, grant, 1974. Also active as a filmmaker. **Address:** 26 East 22nd Street, NYC 10010. **Dealer:** Leo Castelli Inc., NYC. **One-man Exhibitions:** Paris, CNAC, 1975; Galleria Saman, Genoa, 1975;

MOMA, 1976; Buffalo/Albright, 1977; Munster/WK, circ., 1978; Cologne, circ., 1979; Dartmouth College, 1980; California State U., Los Angeles, 1980; Chicago/Contemporary, circ., 1981; Phoenix, 1983; Memphis/Brooks, 1983; SRMG, 1983; Leo Castelli Inc., 1984. **Group:** Biennale de Paris, 1973, 75; WMAA Biennials, 1975, 77; Vassar College, Primitive Presence in the 70s, 1975; Chicago/AI, Small Scale, 1975; XXXVII & XXXCIII Venice Biennials, 1976, 78; Walker, Scale and Environment, 1977; Hirshhorn, Probing the Earth, circ., 1977; Amsterdam/Stedelijk, Made by Sculptors, 1978; ICA/Philadelphia, Dwellings, 1978; Hayward Gallery, London, Pier & Ocean, 1980; Dublin/Municipal, International Quadriennial (ROSC), 1980; Zurich, Myth & Ritual, 1981; Palm Springs Desert Museum, Return of the Narrative, 1984. **Collections:** Adelaide; Chicago/Contemporary; Cologne; Des Moines; Israel Museum; MIT; MOMA; Oberlin College; Paris/Beaubourg; Paris/CNAC; Storm King Art Center; WMAA; Walker; Zurich. **Bibliography:** Lucie-Smith.

SIMPSON, DAVID. b. January 20, 1928, Pasadena, Calif. **Studied:** California School of Fine Arts, with Leonard Edmondson, Clyfford Still, 1956, BFA; San Francisco State College, 1958, MA. US Navy, 1945-46. Traveled Mexico, 1953, Western Europe, 1969. **Taught:** American River Junior College, 1959-61; Contra Costa College, 1961-65; U. of California, Berkeley, 1965-. **Address:** 565 Vistamont Avenue, Berkeley, CA 94708. **Dealer:** Modernism Gallery, San Francisco. **One-man Exhibitions:** (first) San Francisco Art Association, 1958; David Cole Gallery, Sausalito, Calif., 1959; Santa Barbara/MA, 1960; Esther Robles Gallery, 1960; de Young, 1961; Joachim Gallery, Chicago, 1961; Robert Elkon Gallery, 1961, 63, 64; David Stuart Gallery, 1963, 64, 66, 68; Henri Gallery, 1968; Galeria Van der Voort, 1969; Hank

Baum Gallery, San Francisco, 1972, 73, Los Angeles, 1972; Cheney Cowles Memorial Museum, Spokane, 1962; St. Mary's College, Moraga, Calif., 1974; Modernism Gallery, San Francisco, 1979, 80, 82, 84, 86; Los Angeles State U., 1980. **Retrospectives:** SFMA, 1967; Oakland, 1978. **Group:** Carnegie, 1961, 62, 67; Portland (Ore.)/AM, 1968; U. of Illinois, 1963, 69; Los Angeles/County MA, Post Painterly Abstraction, 1964; Chicago/AI; Walker; PAFA, 1967; U. of Illinois, 1969; Spokane World's Fair, 1974; SFMA, California, Painting and Sculpture: The Modern Era, 1976; U. of Santa Clara, Northern California Art of the Sixties, 1982; SFMA, On Reflection, 1982; U. of California, Davis, Directions in Bay Area Painting, 1983; Oakland/AM, Art in the San Francisco Bay Area, 1945-1980, 1985. **Collections:** Baltimore/MA; Central Research Corp.; Columbia Broadcasting System; Crown Zellerbach Foundation; First National Bank of Seattle; Golden Gateway Center; La Jolla; MOMA; NCFA; U. of Nebraska; Oakland/AM; PMA; Phoenix; SFMA; Seattle/AM; Stanford U.; Storm King Art Center.

SINGER, MICHAEL. b. 1945, Brooklyn, N.Y. **Studied:** Cornell U., 1963-67, BFA; Rutgers U., 1968; Yale U., Norfolk Program, 1968. **Address:** Box 682, Parsons Road, Wilmington, Vt. 05363. **Dealer:** Sperone Westwater Inc., NYC. **One-man Exhibitions:** Sperone Westwater Fischer Inc., NYC, 1975, 78, 81; Hartford/Wadsworth, 1976; Smith College, 1977; Corpus Christi, 1977; Purchase/SUNY, 1977; Greenburgh Nature Center, Scarsdale, N.Y., 1977; Portland (Ore.) Center for the Visual Arts, 1979; School of Visual Arts, NYC, 1979; U. of California, Berkeley, 1979; U. of Chicago, 1980; Galerie Zabriskie, Paris, 1981; J. Walter Thompson Art Gallery, NYC, 1983; SRGM, 1984; Sperone Westwater Inc., 1986. **Group:** SRGM, Ten Young Artists, 1971; SRGM, Museum Collection: Recent American Arts, 1975; Rice U.,

Drawing Today in New York, circ., 1977; Documenta VI, Kassel, 1977; WMAA Biennial, 1979; Wenken Park Riehen, Basel, Skulptur in 20. Jahrhundert, 1980; ICA, U. of Pennsylvania, Drawings: The Pluralist Decade, circ., 1980; Zurich, Myth & Ritual, 1981; Rice U., Variants, circ., 1981; Wesleyan U., Large Drawings, 1984; U. of North Carolina, Art on Paper, 1984; SRGM, Transformation in Sculpture, 1985. **Collections:** Buffalo/Albright; Canberra/National; Chase Manhattan Bank; Denver/AM; Fort Worth; Humlebaek/Louisiana; MMA; MOMA; PMA; Paine Webber Inc.; Prudential Insurance Co. of America; SRGM; Seagram Collection; Walker; Yale U.

SINTON, NELL. b. June 4, 1910, San Francisco, Calif. **Studied:** California School of Fine Arts, with Maurice Sterne, Spencer Mackay, Ralph Stackpole. Traveled Europe, India, the Orient, Africa, South America, Middle East, USA, Mexico. **Taught:** SFAI, 1970, 71; San Francisco Student League, 1973-75; Institute for Creative and Artistic Development, Oakland, 1974, 75. **Member:** San Francisco City Art Commission; Artists Committee, San Francisco Art Institute (Trustee). **Award:** San Francisco City Art Commission, Award of Honor, 1984. **Address:** 1020 Francisco Street, San Francisco, CA 94109. **Dealer:** Braunstein Gallery, San Francisco. **One-man Exhibitions:** (first) California Palace, 1949; Santa Barbara/MA, 1950; SFMA (two-man), 1957; Bolles Gallery, San Francisco and New York, 1962; SFMA (four-man), 1962; Quay Gallery, 1969, 71, 74; SFMA, 1970; Jacqueline Anhalt Gallery, 1972; U. of California, San Francisco, 1975; Louisiana State U., 1976; Oakland/AM, 1977; Temple Emanu-El, San Francisco, 1977; Braunstein-Quay Gallery, NYC, 1977, 78; U. of Illinois, 1978; Mills College, 1979; Braunstein Gallery, San Francisco, 1980, 81, 83, 86; U. of Illinois, 1982. **Retrospective:** Mills College, 1981.

Group: MMA, 1952; ART:USA:58, NYC, 1958; Vancouver, 1958; Denver/AM, 1958, 60; SFMA; de Young; California Palace; Oakland/AM, Scripps College, 1961; Los Angeles/County MA, 1961; A.F.A.; Stanford U.; U. of Nevada, 1969; Claremont College, 1973; SFAI, 1974; SFMA, California Painting and Sculpture: The Modern Era, 1976. **Collections:** AT&T; U. of California, Berkeley; Chase Manhattan Bank; Lytton Savings and Loan Association; Mills College; Oakland/AM; SMFA. **Bibliography:** Archives.

SIPORIN, MITCHELL. b. May 5, 1910, NYC; **d.** June 11, 1976, Newton, Mass. **Studied:** Crane Junior College; Chicago Art Institute School; privately with Todros Geller; American Academy, Rome, 1949-50. US Army, 1942-45. Traveled Mexico, Latin America, Africa, Europe. **Taught:** Boston Museum School, 1949; Columbia U., 1951; Brandeis U., 1957-76; American Academy, Rome, Artist-in-Residence, 1966-67. **Member:** Brandeis U. Creative Arts Award Commission; Fellow, American Academy, Rome. Federal A.P.: Mural painting. **Commissions:** Bloom Township High School, Chicago, 1938 (mural); US Post Offices, Decatur, Ill., 1940, and St. Louis, Mo. (with Edward Millman), 1940-42 (mural); Berlin Chapel, Brandeis U. (ark curtain). **Awards:** Chicago/AI, Bertha Aberle Florsheim Prize, 1942; Guggenheim Foundation Fellowship, 1945, 46; PAFA, Pennell Memorial Medal, 1946; Chicago/AI, The Mr. & Mrs. Frank G. Logan Medal, 1947; State U. of Iowa, First **P.P.**, 1947; Prix de Rome, 1949; Hallmark International Competition, Second Prize, 1949; Boston Arts Festival, Second Prize, 1954; and Third Prize, 1955; AAAL, 1955; Youngstown/Butler, First Prize for Watercolors, 1961; Fulbright Fellowship (Italy), 1966-67. **One-man Exhibitions:** The Downtown Gallery, 1940, 42, 46, 47, 57; Springfield, Mass./MFA; Chi-

cago/AI, 1947; Philadelphia Art Alliance, 1949; Boris Mirski Gallery, Boston, 1952; Jewish Community Center, Cleveland, 1953; The Alan Gallery, NYC, 1954; Lincoln Mass./De Cordova, 1955; U. of Vermont, 1956; Park Gallery, Detroit, 1960; Lee Nordness Gallery, NYC, 1960; U. of Oklahoma, 1980. **Retrospective:** Lincoln, Mass./De Cordova, 1954; Brandeis U., 1976. **Group:** A Century of Progress, 1933-34; MOMA, New Horizons in American Art, 1936; New York World's Fair, 1939; Golden Gate International Exposition, San Francisco, 1939; MOMA/USIA, Pintura Contemporanea Norteamericana, circ., Latin America, 1941; MOMA, Americans 1942, circ., 1942; Chicago/AI, 1942-46; WMAA, 1942-57; Carnegie, 1944-49; Paris/Moderne, 1946; ICA, Boston, American Painting in Our Century, circ., 1949; Contemporary American Drawings, circ. France, 1956; Art: USA: Now, circ., 1962-67; NCFA, After the Crash, 1980. **Collections:** Andover/Phillips; U. of Arizona; Auburn U.; Brandeis U.; Britannica; Chicago/AI; Cranbrook; U. of Georgia; Harvard U.; U. of Illinois; State U. of Iowa; MMA; MOMA; NCFA; NYPL; U. of Nebraska; Newark Museum; U. of New Mexico; PMA; Smith College; WMAA; Wichita/AM; Woodstock Art Association; Worcester/AM; Youngstown/Butler. **Bibliography:** Baur 7; Goodrich and Baur 1; Halpert; Miller, ed. 1; Nordness, ed.; Pagano; Pousette-Dart, ed.; Wight 2. Archives.

SLOAN, JOHN. b. August 2, 1871, Loch Haven, Pa.; **d.** September 7, 1951, Hanover, N.H. **Studied:** Spring Garden Institute, Philadelphia; PAFA, 1892, with Thomas Anshutz. **Taught:** ASL, 1914-26, 1935-37; Archipenko School of Art, 1932-33; George Luks School, 1934. Art Editor of *The Masses* (magazine), 1912-16. Organized a group called The Eight. **Member:** Society of Independent Artists, NYC (President, 1918-42); NIAL. **Awards:** Carnegie, Hon. Men., 1905; Panama-

Pacific Exposition, San Francisco, 1915, Medal; Philadelphia, Sesquicentennial, 1926, Medal; PAFA; Carol H. Beck Gold Medal, 1931; MMA, 1942 ($500); NIAL, Gold Medal, 1950. **One-man Exhibitions:** (first) Whitney Studio Club, NYC, 1916; Hudson Guild, NYC, 1916; Kraushaar Galleries, 1917, 26, 27, 30, 37, 39, 43, 48, 52, 60, 66; Corcoran, 1933; Montross Gallery, NYC, 1934; WMAA, 1936, 52; Carnegie, 1939; Currier, 1940; The U. of Chicago, 1942; PMA, 1948; Santa Fe, N.M., 1951; Wilmington, 1961; Bowdoin College, 1962; Kennedy Gallery, 1964 (twoman); U. of Connecticut, 1971; Harbor Gallery, Cold Spring, N.Y., 1972; WMAA, 1980; Salander-O'Reilly Galleries, Inc., NYC, 1980; Bowdoin College, 1981; Dartmouth College, 1981; NMAA, 1981; Mary Ryan Gallery, NYC, 1983; WMAA (Downtown Branch), 1983; Kennedy Galleries, NYC, 1984; Kraushaar Galleries, NYC, 1984; Queens Museum, 1985. **Retrospectives:** Wanamaker Gallery, Philadelphia, 1940; Dartmouth College, 1946; Andover/Phillips, 1946; National Gallery, 1971. **Group:** Macbeth Gallery, NYC, The Eight, 1908; The Armory Show, 1913; MMA; Brooklyn Museum, The Eight, 1943; PMA; Syracuse/Everson, The Eight, 1958; Chicago/AI; Detroit/Institute; PAFA; Carnegie; Corcoran; WMAA, The 1930's, 1968, and others. **Collections:** Barnes Foundation; Boston/MFA; Brooklyn Museum; Carnegie; Chicago/AI; Cincinnati/AM; Cleveland/MA; Corcoran; Detroit/Institute; Hartford/Wadsworth; IBM; MMA; NYPL; Newark Public Library; PMA; The Pennsylvania State U.; Phillips; U. of Rochester; San Diego; Santa Fe, N.M.; WMAA; Walker. **Bibliography:** Baur 7; Bazin; Beam; Blesh 1; Boswell 1; **Brooks;** Brown; Brown 2; Bryant, L.; Cahill and Barr, eds.; Canaday; Cheney; *Cityscape 1919-39;* Coke 2; Craven, T., 1, 2.; Downes, ed.; Du Bois 4; Eliot; Ely; Finkelstein; Flanagan; Flexner; **Gallatin 2, 5;** Gerdts; Glackens; **Goodrich 7;** Goodrich and Baur 1; Greengood;

Haftman; Hall; Hartmann; Hunter 6; Huyghe; *Index of 20th Century Artists;* Jackman; Jewell 2; Kent, N.; Kouvenhoven; Mather 1; McCoubrey 1; McCurdy, ed.; Mendelowitz; Newmeyer; Pach 1, 3; Pagano; Pearson 1; Perlman; Phillips 2; Poore; Pousette-Dart, ed.; Reese; Richardson, E.P.; Ringel, ed.; Rose, B., 1, 4; Sachs; **St. John; St. John, ed.; Sloan, H.F.; Sloan, ed.; Sloan, J., 1, 2, 3, 4, 5;** Smith, S.C.K.; Sutton; Wight 2. Archives.

SMITH, DAVID. b. 1906, Decatur, Ind.; **d.** May 24, 1965, Bennington, Vt. **Studied:** Ohio U., 1924: ASL, 1926-30, with John Sloan, Jan Matulka. Traveled Europe, USSR, 1935; resided Voltri and Spoleto, Italy, 1962. **Taught:** Sarah Lawrence College, 1948; U. of Arkansas, 1953; Indiana U., 1954; U. of Mississippi, 1955. Created a series of 15 bronze "Medals of Dishonor," 1937-40. **Awards:** Guggenheim Foundation Fellowship, 1950, 51; Brandeis U., Creative Arts Award, 1964. **One-man Exhibitions:** East River Gallery, NYC, 1938; Skidmore College, 1939, 43, 46; Neumann-Willard Gallery, NYC, 1940; The Willard Gallery, NYC, 1940, 43, 46, 47, 50, 51, 54, 55, 56; Kalamazoo/Institute, 1941; Walker, 1943, 48, 52; Buchholz Gallery, NYC, 1946; Cooling Gallery, London, 1946; Utica, 1947; Kleemann Gallery, NYC, 1952; Tulsa/Philbrook, 1953; The Kootz Gallery, NYC, 1953; Cincinnati/AM, 1954; MOMA, 1957; Fine Arts Associates, NYC, 1957; Otto Gerson Gallery, NYC, 1957, 61; French & Co., Inc., NYC, 1959, 60; MOMA, circ. only, 1960; Everett Ellin Gallery, Los Angeles, 1960; ICA, U. of Pennsylvania, 1964; Marlborough-Gerson Gallery Inc., 1964, 67, 68; Harvard U., 1966; Storm King Art Center, 1971; Glens Falls, N.Y., 1974; Dart Gallery, Chicago, 1975; Storm King Art Center, 1976; Knoedler Contemporary Art, NYC, 1974, 76, 77, 78, 80, 81, 82; Galerie Wentzel, Hamburg, 1979; Caracas, 1979; Hyde Collection, 1974; Hirshhorn, 1979; M. Knoedler Ltd., London, 1980; Mekler Gallery, Los Angeles, 1981; Janie C. Lee Gallery, Houston, 1982; Storm King Art Center, 1982; Arts Club of Chicago, 1983; Milwaukee, 1983; Washburn Gallery, Inc., 1983; Jeffrey Hoffeld & Co., NYC, 1984; Nielson Gallery, Boston, 1984; Klonaridis Inc., Toronto, 1981; American Academy, Rome, 1983; Rutgers U. (two-man), 1984; Anthony d'Offay Gallery, London, 1985. **Retrospectives:** Tate, 1966; SRGM, 1968; WMAA, circ., 1979; Edmonton Art Gallery, circ., 1982; National Gallery, 1982; Hirshhorn, circ., 1982; IEF, circ., 1986; Dusseldorf/KN-W, circ., 1986. **Group:** XXIX Venice Biennial, 1958; Sao Paulo, 1959; Documenta II & III, Kassel, 1959, 64; WMAA; Chicago/AI; Carnegie; MOMA, The New American Painting and Sculpture, 1969, and others; Houston/MFA, The Great Decade of American Abstraction, 1974; Edmonton Art Gallery, Sculpture in Steel, 1974; U. of California, Santa Barbara, Sculptors in the 1950s, Alberta, 1976; Syracuse/Everson, New Works in Clay, 1976; Norfolk/Chrysler, 300 Years of American Art, 1976; WMAA, 200 Years of American Sculpture, 1976; Brown U., Graham, Gorky, Smith, and Davis, 1977; Minnesota/MA, American Drawing, 1927-1977, 1977; National Gallery, American Art at Mid-Century: The Subjects of the Artists, 1978; Rutgers U., Vanguard American Sculpture, 1919-1939, 1979; Drawing Center, NYC, Sculptor's Drawings Over Six Centuries, 1981; Fondation Maeght, Sculpture of the 20th Century, 1981; Carnegie, Abstract Painting and Sculpture in America, 1927-44, circ., 1983; Houston/Contemporary, American Still Life, 1945-1983, 1983; MOMA, The Modern Drawing, 1983; Sunderland (Eng.) Arts Center, Drawing in Air, 1983; Seattle/AM, American Sculpture: Three Decades, 1984; SRGM, Transformations in Sculpture, 1985; Sarah Lawrence College, Sculptural Expressions, 1985; WMAA, The Third Dimension, 1985. **Collections:** Andover/Phillips;

Baltimore/MA; Boston/MFA; Brandeis U.; Brooklyn Museum; Buffalo/Albright; Carnegie; Chicago/AI; Cincinnati/AM; Cologne/Ludwig; Dallas/MFA; Des Moines; Detroit/Institute; Duisburg; Harvard U.; Hirshhorn; Houston/MFA; Israel Museum; Los Angeles/County MA; MMA; MOMA; U. of Michigan; U. of Minnesota; National Gallery; Norfolk/Chrysler; U. of North Carolina; Ottawa/National; PMA; Phillips; Rijksmuseum Kroller-Muller; SFMA; SRGM; St. Louis/City; Seattle/AM; Southern Methodist U.; Storm King Art Center; Tate Gallery; Utica; WMAA; Walker. **Bibliography:** Alloway 4; Battcock, ed.; Baur 5, 7; Blesh 1; Brumme; Calas, N. and E.; Carmean, Rathbone, and Hess; Chipp; **Cone 1;** Craven, W.; Cummings 2; *David Smith: The Prints;* Davis, D.; Downes, ed.; Fry; Gertz; Giedion-Welcker 1; Goodrich and Baur 1; Goossen 1; *Graham, Gorky, Smith & Davis in the Thirties; The Great Decade;* Greenberg 1; Henning; Honisch and Jensen, eds.; Hunter 6; Hunter, ed.; Janis and Blesh 1; Kozloff 3; **Kramer 1;** Krauss 2; Kuh 1, 2, 3; Lane and Larsen; Licht, F.; Lynton; Marten, Tarbell, and Wechsler; **McCoy;** McCurdy, ed.; Mendelowitz; **Merkert, ed.;** *Metro; Monumenta;* Moser 1; Motherwell, ed.; Motherwell and Reinhardt, eds.; Myers 2; **O'Hara** 1, 2; Passloff; Phillips, Lisa; Read 3; Rickey; Ritchie 1, 3; Rodman 1, 3; Rose, B. 1, 4; Rowell; Rubin 1; Sandler 1; Seitz 3; Selz, J.; Seuphor 3; Seymour; **Smith, D.;** Strachan; Trier 1; Tuchman 1. Archives.

SMITH, HASSEL W., Jr. b. April 24, 1915, Sturgis, Mich. **Studied:** Northwestern U., BS; California School of Fine Arts, with Maurice Sterne. Traveled Europe, USA, Mexico. **Taught:** California School of Fine Arts, 1945, 47, 48, 52; San Francisco State College, 1946; U. of Oregon, 1947-48; Presidio Hill School, San Francisco, 1952-55; U. of California, Berkeley, 1963-65, 77-80; UCLA, 1965-66; Bristol (Eng.) Polytechnic, 1966-; SFAI, 1978, 79, 80. **Awards:** Abraham Rosenberg Foundation Fellowship, 1941. **Address:** 19 Ashgrove Road, Bristol 6, England. **Dealer:** John Berggruen Gallery, San Francisco. **One-man Exhibitions:** (first) California Palace, 1947, also 1952; California School of Fine Arts, 1956; New Arts Gallery, Houston, 1960; 62; Ferus Gallery, Los Angeles, 1960; Gimpel Fils Ltd., 1961; Pasadena/AM, 1961; Andre Emmerich Gallery, NYC, 1961, 62, 63; Dilexi Gallery, San Francisco, 1962; U. of Minnesota, 1962; Galleria dell'Ariete, 1962; David Stuart Gallery, 1963, 68, 73; U. of California, Berkeley, 1964; Santa Barbara/MA, 1969; Suzanne Saxe Gallery, San Francisco, 1970, 73; City Art Gallery, Bristol, 1972; ARCO Center for Visual Art, Los Angeles, 1978; Tortue Gallery, Santa Monica, 1980; Gallery Paule Anglim, 1977, 78, 79; John Berggruen Gallery, 1986. **Retrospective:** San Francisco State College, 1964; SFMA, 1976. **Group:** California Palace; Pasadena/AM; WMAA Annuals; Los Angeles/County MA; Oakland/AM; SFMA; U. of California, Berkeley; Oakland/AM, A Period of Exploration, 1973; SFMA, 200 Years of California Painting, 1976. **Collections:** Buffalo/Albright; Corcoran; Dallas/MFA; Hirshhorn; Houston/MFA; Los Angeles/County MA; New Paltz/SUNY; Oakland/AM; Pasadena/AM; Phillips; SFMA; St. Louis/City; Tate; WMAA; Washington U. **Bibliography:** McChesney. Archives.

SMITH, LEON POLK. b. May 20, 1906, Chickasha, Okla. **Studied:** East Central State College, AB; Columbia U., MA. Traveled Mexico, Europe, Canada, USA, Venezuela. **Taught:** Oklahoma public schools, 1933-39; Georgia University System, Teachers College, 1939-41; State Supervisor, Delaware, 1941-43; Rollins College, 1949-51; Mills College of Education, 1951-58; Artist-in-Residence, Brandeis U., 1968, and U. of California, Davis, 1972; Philadelphia College of Art,

1982-83; Yale U., 1983. **Awards:** Guggenheim Foundation Fellowship, 1944; Longview Foundation Grant, 1959; National Council on the Arts; Tamarind Fellowship; AAIAI, **P.P.,** 1979. **Address:** 31 Union Square West, NYC 10003. **Dealer:** DiLaurenti Gallery, NYC. **One-man Exhibitions:** (first) Uptown Gallery, NYC, 1940; Savannah/Telfair, 1941; Rose Fried Gallery, 1942, 46, 49; Santa Fe, N.M., 1943; Charles Egan Gallery, 1945; Betty Parsons Gallery, 1957, 59; The Stable Gallery, 1960, 62; Caracas, 1962; Galerie Muller, 1964; Galerie Chalette, 1967, 68, 69, 70; Brandeis U., 1968; SFMA, 1968; Fort Worth Art Museum, 1968; Galerie Denise Rene, Paris, 1973, 75; Pelham-von Stoffler Gallery, Houston, 1977, 78; Old Westbury/SUNY, 1978; Susan Caldwell Inc., NYC 1979; ACE Gallery, Vancouver, 1979; ACE Gallery, Venice, Calif., 1979; Paule Anglim Associates, San Francisco, 1979; Washburn Gallery, Inc., NYC, 1981, 82, 84; Virginia Commonwealth U., 1980; Stony Brook/SUNY, 1981; U. of Nebraska, 1983; Nationalgalerie, Berlin, 1984; DiLaurenti Gallery, 1986. **Group:** WMAA, 1959; Helmhaus Gallery, Zurich, Konkrete Kunst, 1960; SRGM, Abstract Expressionists and Imagists, 1961; WMAA Annual, 1962; WMAA, Geometric Abstraction in America, circ., 1962; Chicago/AI, 1962; Dallas/MFA, "1961," 1962; Corcoran, 1963; Brandeis U., New Directions in American Painting, 1963; MOMA, American Collages, 1965; MOMA, The Responsive Eye, 1965; SFMA, Colorists 1950-1965, 1965; SRGM, Systemic Painting, 1966; Carnegie, 1967, 70; Buffalo/Albright, Plus by Minus, 1968; Chicago/Contemporary, Post-Mondrian Abstraction in America, 1973; Carnegie, Celebration, 1974-75; Paris/Moderne, Paris-New York, 1977; Claremont College, Black and White Are Colors, 1979; Yale U., Mondrian and Neoplasticism in America, 1979; Haus der Kunst, Munich, Amerikanische Malerie, 1930-1980, 1981; National Gallery and Yale U., The Folding

Image, 1984; XLII Venice Biennial, 1986. **Collections:** Aachen; Birmingham, Ala./MA; Brandeis U.; Buffalo/Albright; Carnegie; Cleveland/MA; Detroit/Institute; First National Bank of Chicago; Fort Worth; Hirshhorn; Indianapolis; Los Angeles/County MA; U. of Massachusetts; Milwaukee; MMA; MOMA; U. of Nebraska; Oklahoma State Art Collection; RISD; SFMA; SRGM; Springfield, Mass./MFA; U. of Sydney; WMAA. **Bibliography:** Alloway 3; *Black and White Are Colors*; American Artists Group Inc. 2; Battcock, ed.; Calas, N. and E.; *Kunst um 1970*; MacAgy 2; Rickey; Sandler 1; Seuphor 1.

SMITH, TONY. b. 1912, South Orange, N.J.; **d.** December 26, 1980, NYC. **Studied:** ASL, 1933-36; New Bauhaus, Chicago, 1937-38. Worked on new buildings designed by Frank Lloyd Wright, 1938-39. **Taught:** NYU, 1946-50; Cooper Union, 1950-53; Pratt Institute, 1950-53, 1957-58; Bennington College, 1958-61; Hunter College, 1962-74; Princeton U., 1975-78. **Member:** AAIAL, 1979. **Awards:** Longview Foundation Grant, 1966; National Council on the Arts, 1966; Guggenheim Foundation Fellowship, 1968; College Art Association, Distinguished Teaching of Art Award, 1974; Brandeis U., Creative Arts Award for Sculpture, 1974. **One-man Exhibitions:** Hartford/Wadsworth, 1966; ICA, U. of Pennsylvania, 1966; Walker, 1967; Galerie Muller, Stuttgart, 1967; Bryant Park, NYC, 1967; Galerie Rene Ziegler, 1968; Yvon Lambert, 1968; Donald Morris Gallery, Detroit, 1968; MOMA, circ., 1968; U. of Hawaii, 1969; Newark Museum, 1970; Montclair/AM, 1970; Princeton U., 1979; Trenton/State, 1970; Knoedler Contemporary Art, 1970; MOMA, 1970; U. of Maryland, 1974; Fourcade, Droll Gallery, NYC, 1976; Susanne Hilberry Gallery, Birmingham, Mich., 1977; The Pace Gallery, 1979, 83; Ace Gallery, Venice, Calif., 1980; Richard Gray Gallery, Chicago, 1980; Kean College, Union, N.J., 1981; Moira Kelly Fine Art, London, 1982; Hunter College, 1984; Paula Cooper Gallery, 1985; Margo Leavin Gallery, 1985; Xavier Fourcade, Inc., 1986. **Group:** Hartford/Wadsworth, Black, White, and Grey, 1964; Jewish Museum, Primary Structure Sculptures, 1966; WMAA, 1966, 71, 73; Detroit/Institute, Color, Image and Form, 1967; Chicago/AI, A Generation of Innovation, 1967; Los Angeles/County MA, American Sculpture of the Sixties, circ., 1967; Carnegie, 1967; Corcoran, Scale as Content, 1967; SRGM; Guggenheim International, 1967; A.F.A., Rejective Art, 1967; Finch College, NYC, Schemata 7, 1967; Documenta IV, Kassel, 1968; Buffalo/Albright, Plus by Minus, 1968; HemisFair '68, San Antonio, Tex., 1968; MMA, New York Painting and Sculpture; 1940-1970, 1969-70; Akademie der Kunst, Berlin, Minimal Art, 1969; Expo '70, Osaka, 1970; Cincinnati/Contemporary, Monumental Art, 1970; U. of Nebraska, American Sculpture, 1970; Los Angeles/County MA, Art & Technology, 1971; Foundation Maeght, 1971; Arnhem, Sonsbeek, '71, 1971; Indianapolis, 1974; NCFA, Sculpture: American Directions 1945-75, 1975; Indianapolis, 1976; WMAA, 200 Years of American Sculpture, 1976; AAIAL, 1978; SFMA, Twenty American Artists, 1980; Paris/Beaubourg, Qu'est Ce Que La Sculpture Moderne, 1986. **Collections:** Banque Lambert, Brussels; Buffalo/Albright; Case Western Reserve U.; Corcoran; Detroit/Institute; Hartford/Wadsworth; MOMA; Mutual Life Insurance Building, Chicago; U. of Nebraska; Newark Museum; Ottawa/National; U. of Pennsylvania; Princeton U.; Rice U.; Rijksmuseum Kroller-Muller; U. of Rochester; Trenton/State; Walker. **Bibliography:** Calas, N. and E.; Krauss 3; *Monumenta*; *Report*; Rowell; *Tony Smith*; Tuchman 3. Archives.

SMITHSON, ROBERT. b. January 2, 1938, Passaic, N.J.; **d.** July 20, 1973, Tecovas Lake, Tex. **Studied:** ASL, 1953, with John Groth; Brooklyn Museum School, 1956. US Army Reserve Forces, Special Services. Traveled USA, Mexico, London, Rome. **One-man Exhibitions:** (first) Artists' Gallery, NYC, 1959; Galleria George Lester, Rome, 1961; Dwan Gallery, NYC, 1966-69, 70; Konrad Fischer Gallery, Dusseldorf, 1968-69; Galleria l'Attico, Rome, 1969; ACE Gallery, Los Angeles and Vancouver, 1970; New York Cultural Center, circ., 1974; Kunstmuseum, Lucerne, circ., 1975; John Weber Gallery, NYC, 1976, 82, 83; Portland (Ore.) Center for Visual Arts, 1977; U. of Massachusetts, 1976; Centre d'Art Contemporain, Geneva, 1981; Humlebaek/Louisiana, 1984; Diane Brown Gallery, NYC, 1984, 85; Middendorf Gallery, Washington, D.C., 1985. **Retrospective:** Cornell U., 1980. **Group:** ICA, U. of Pennsylvania, Current Art, 1965; Jewish Museum, Primary Structure Sculptures, 1966; Finch College, NYC, 1966, 67; WMAA, 1966, 69, 70, Annual, 1969; Los Angeles/County MA, American Sculpture of the Sixties, 1967; Trenton/State, Focus on Light, 1967; The Hague, Minimal Art, 1968; MOMA, The Art of the Real, 1968; Buffalo/Albright, Plus by Minus, 1968; Dusseldorf/Kunsthalle, Prospect '68, '69, 1968, 69; Milwaukee, Directions 1: Options, circ., 1968; Amsterdam/Stedelijk, Op Losse Schroeven, 1969; Berne, When Attitudes Become Form, 1969; ICA, U. of Pennsylvania, Between Object and Environment, 1969; Chicago/Contemporary, Art by Telephone, 1969; Seattle/AM, 557,087, 1969; ICA, U. of Pennsylvania, Against Order: Chance and Art, 1970; Chicago/AI, 69th and 70th American Exhibitions, 1969, 72; MOMA, Information, 1971; Documenta V, Kassel, 1972; Rijksmuseum Kroller-Muller, Diagrams and Drawings, 1972; New York Cultural Center, 3D into 2D, 1973; MIT, Interventions in Landscape, 1974;

Neuer Berliner Kunstverein, Berlin, Multiples, 1974; Rutgers U., Response to the Environment, 1975; ICA, Boston, The Reductive Object, 1979; U. of North Carolina, Drawings About Drawing Today, 1979; Brooklyn Museum, American Drawings in Black & White: 1970-1979, 1980; Hayward Gallery, London, Pier & Ocean, 1980; XXXIX + XL Venice Biennials, 1980, 82; Rice U., Variants, 1981; MOMA, Primitivism in 20th Century Art, 1984; WMAA, The Sculptor as Draftsman, circ., 1984. **Collections:** Aachen/Ludwig; Chicago/AI; Chicago/Contemporary; Des Moines; Harvard U.; High Museum; Kingsborough Community College; Los Angeles/County MA; MMA; MOMA; Mexico City/Tamayo; Milwaukee; Ontario; Ottawa; Paris/Beaubourg; Rijksmuseum Kröller-Müller; Tate Gallery; WMAA; Walker. **Bibliography:** Alloway 4; Atkinson; Battcock, ed.; Calas, N. and E.; Celant; Cummings 1; De Vries, ed.; *Drawings: The Pluralist Decade*; Gablik; Goossen 1; Holt ed.; Honisch and Jensen, eds.; Johnson, Ellen H.; Krauss 2, 3; *Kunst um 1970*; Lippard 3, 4; Lippard, ed.; MacAgy 2; Muller; *Report*; Rowell; Tuchman 1; *When Attitudes Become Form.* Archives.

SNELGROVE, WALTER b. March 22, 1924, Seattle, Wash. **Studied:** U. of Washington; U. of California, Berkeley, with James McCray, M. O'Hagan, BA, MA; California School of Fine Arts, with Hassel Smith, Antonio Sotamayor, James Weeks. US Navy, 1941-46. Traveled Europe; resided Florence, Italy. **Taught:** U. of California, 1951-53. **Awards:** U. of California, James D. Phelan Traveling Scholarship, 1951; SFMA, M. Grumbacher Award, 1959; Oakland/AM, First Prize, 1962. **Address:** 2966 Adeline Street, Berkeley, Calif. 94903. **Dealer:** Gump's Gallery, San Francisco. **One-man Exhibitions:** (first) Oakland/AM, 1959; California Palace; Santa Barbara/MA; Gump's Gallery; Colorado Springs/FA;

Denver/AM. **Retrospective:** Foothill College, 1967. **Group:** de Young; SFMA; RAC; Oakland/AM, Contemporary Bay Area Figurative Painting, 1957; Los Angeles/County MA; WMAA, Fifty California Artists, 1962-63; VMFA; U. of Illinois, 1963; Carnegie, 1964; Denver/AM, 1964; U. of Washington; Des Moines. **Collections:** A.F.A.; California Palace; Colorado Springs/FA; Oakland/AM; Stanford U.; WMAA.

SNELSON, KENNETH b. June 29, 1927, Pendleton, Ore. **Studied:** U. of Oregon (with Jack Wilkinson); Black Mountain College (with Josef Albers, Buckminster Fuller, Willem de Kooning); Academie Montmartre, Paris (with Fernand Leger). US Naval Reserve, 1945-46. Traveled Europe, Near East, Far East. **Taught:** Cooper Union; Pratt Institute; School of Visual Arts, NYC; Southern Illinois U.; Yale U. **Member:** I.A.T.S.E. **Commission:** Reynolds Metals Co., Sculpture Award, 1974. **Awards:** Milan Triennial, Silver Medal, 1964; New York City Council on the Arts Award, 1971; DAAD Fellowship, Berlin, 1975, 76; National Endowment for the Arts, 1975; American Institute of Architects, Medal, 1981; Hon. DFA, Rensselaer Polytechnic Institute, 1985. **Address:** 140 Sullivan Street, NYC 10012. **Dealer:** The Zabriskie Gallery, NYC. **One-man Exhibitions:** (first) Pratt Institute, 1963; New York World's Fair, 1964-65; Dwan Gallery, NYC, 1966, 68; Dwan Gallery, Los Angeles, 1967; Bryant Park, NYC, 1968; Fort Worth, 1969; Rijksmuseum Kroller-Muller, 1969; Stadtische Kunsthalle, Dusseldorf, 1969; Hannover/Kunstverein, 1971; John Weber Gallery, 1972; Galeria van der Voort, Ibiza, 1972; Waterside Place, NYC, 1974; Galerie Buchholz, Munich, 1975; Berlin/National, 1977; Duisburg, 1977; Gallery de Gestlo, Hamburg, 1977; Maryland Academy of Science, Baltimore, 1978; Sonnabend Gallery, NYC, 1978, 80; The Zabriskie Gallery, 1979,

81, 84; Galerie Zabriskie, Paris, 1980, 84; Birmingham, Ala./AM, 1980; Tampa/AI, 1981; Hirshhorn, 1981; Construct, Chicago, 1981; Buffalo/Albright, 1981; U. of Houston, 1982; U. of Pittsburgh, 1982; Museum of Science and Industry, Tampa, 1982; North Carolina Museum of Life and Science, Durham, 1982; Fleet Space Theatre and Science Center, San Diego, 1983; The Schenectady Museum, 1983; Columbus, 1984; Lincoln, Mass./De Cordova, 1984; Taft Museum, 1985; Cleveland/MA, 1985.

Kenneth Snelson   *Model for Virlane Tower*   1980

Group: MOMA, 1959, 62; Milan Triennial, 1964; WMAA Sculpture Annual, 1966-69; Los Angeles/County MA, American Sculpture of the Sixties, 1967; CSCS, Los Angeles, 1967; Chicago/AI, 1967; Buffalo/Albright, Plus by Minus, 1968; Dusseldorf/Kunsthalle, Prospect '68, 1968; PMA, 1968; Grant Park, Chicago, Sculpture in the Park, 1974; AAAL, 1977; NYU, Panoramic Photography, 1977; Brooklyn Museum, Great East River Bridge, 1883-1983, 1983; MOMA, Big Pictures by Contemporary Photographers, 1983. **Collections:** Amsterdam/Stedelijk; City of Baltimore; Birmingham, Ala./AM; Buffalo/Albright; Bundeswehr; Canberra/National; Carnegie; Chattanooga/Hunter; Chicago/AI; Cleveland/MA; Columbus; Dallas/MFA; Duisburg; City of Hamburg; City of Hannover; Hirshhorn; City of Iowa; Japan Iron and Steel Federation, Osaka; Louisville/Speed; MMA; Milwaukee; MOMA; Portland, Ore./AM; Princeton U.; Rijksmuseum Kroller-Muller; City of San Diego; Stanford U.; Storm King Art Center; Trenton/State; WMAA. **Bibliography:** MacAgy 2; Tuchman 1.

SNYDER, JOAN. b. April 16, 1940, Highland Park, N.J. **Studied:** Douglass College, 1962, BA; Rutgers U., 1966, MFA. **Taught:** Princeton U., 1975-79; Yale U. **Awards:** National Endowment for the Arts, 1974; Guggenheim Foundation Fellowship, 1982. **Address:** 105 Mulberry Street, NYC 10017. **Dealer:** Hirschl & Adler Modern, NYC. **One-man Exhibitions:** Rutgers U., 1966; Little Gallery, New Brunswick, N.J., 1967; Pale & Lowe Inc., NYC, 1970, 71, 73; Michael Walls Gallery, San Francisco, 1971; Douglass College, 1972, 76; Parker Street 470 Gallery, Boston, 1972; Broxton Gallery, Los Angeles, 1976; ICA, Los Angeles, 1976; Portland (Ore.) Center for the Visual Arts, 1976; Reed College, 1976; Carl Solway Gallery, NYC, 1976; Wake Forest U., 1977; Hamilton Gallery of Contemporary Art, NYC, 1978, 79, 82; Purchase/SUNY, 1978; Women's Art Registry, Minneapolis, 1978; SFAI, 1979; Hartford/Wadsworth, 1981; Nielsen Gallery, Boston, 1981, 83. **Group:** U. of California, Berkeley, Eight New York Painters, 1972; Detroit/Institute, 12 Statements, 1972; GEDOK, Hamburg, American Woman Artist Show, 1972; ICA, U. of Pennsylvania, Grids, 1972; WMAA Annuals, 1972, 73; New York Cultural Center, Women Choose Women, 1973; Corcoran Biennial, 1975; UCLA, Fourteen Abstract Painters, 1975; Brooklyn Museum, Works on Paper—Women Artists, 1977. **Collections:** Dallas/MFA; High Museum; Louisville/Speed; MMA; MOMA; Oberlin College; WMAA.

SOLOMON, HYDE. b. May 3, 1911, NYC. **Studied:** Columbia U., with Meyer Shapiro; American Artists School, NYC, 1938; Pratt Institute; ASL, 1943, with Ossip Zadkine. Traveled Europe. **Taught:** Princeton U., 1959-62; Goddard College, summers, 1954, 55. **Member:** American Abstract Artists. **Awards:** MacDowell Colony Fellowship, 1949, 50, 51, 52; Yaddo Fellowship, 1951, 56, 57, 58, 59, 62, 63, 64; AAAL, **P.P.,** 1971; Mark Rothko Foundation, 1973; Wurlitzer Foundation Grant, 1974; Rothko Foundation Grant, 1973; Gottlieb Foundation Grant, 1978. **Address:** P.O. Box 2538, Taos, NM 87571. **Dealers:** Stables Gallery, Taos; Ledoux Gallery, Taos. **One-man Exhibitions:** (first) Vendome Galleries, NYC, 1941; Jane Street Gallery, NYC, 1945, 48; The Peridot Gallery, 1954, 55, 56; Poindexter Gallery, 1956, 58, 60, 63, 65, 67, 69, 70, 71, 73; Princeton U., 1959; Rutgers U., 1961; Skidmore College, 1962; Ledoux Gallery, Taos, 1979; Stables Gallery, Taos, 1980. **Group:** MOMA; Walker; Brooklyn Museum; Newark Museum; Yale U.; Hartford/Wadsworth; PMA; The Kootz Gallery, NYC, New Talent, 1950; WMAA, Nature in Abstraction, 1958; Annual, 1965, and others; Carnegie, 1964, 67;

VMFA, American Painting, 1966; New School for Social Research, Humanist Tradition, 1968; Allentown/AM, Monhegan Island Painters, 1974; NAD, 1977, 78. **Collections:** Brandeis U.; U. of California, Berkeley; Chase Manhattan Bank; Ciba-Geigy Corp.; Ford Foundation; Hartford/Wadsworth; Mitsui Bank of Japan; Newark Museum; Reader's Digest; Utica; WMAA; Walker; Westinghouse. **Bibliography:** Archives.

SONENBERG, JACK. b. December 28, 1925, Toronto, Canada. **Studied:** NYU; Washington U., BFA, 1951, with Paul Burlin; Farnham School of Art, England, 1945-56; Ontario College of Art, 1942. **Taught:** School of Visual Arts, NYC, 1962-74; Pratt Institute, 1967-80; Brooklyn College, 1972; U. of New Mexico, 1970. **Commissions:** International Graphic Arts Society; New York Hilton Hotel. **Awards:** L. C. Tiffany Grant (printmaking), 1962; Silvermine Guild, First Prize, 1962; St. Paul Gallery, Drawing USA, **P.P.**, Bradley U., Print Annual, **P.P.;** Ford Foundation/A.F.A., Artist-in-Residence, 1966; Guggenheim Foundation Fellowship, 1973; CAPS, New York State Council of the Arts, 1973, 76; National Endowment for the Arts, 1984. **Address:** 217 East 23rd Street, NYC 10010. **One-man Exhibitions:** (first) Washington Irving Gallery, NYC, 1958; Carl Siembab Gallery, Boston, 1959; Roko Gallery, NYC, 1961; Feingarten Gallery, Los Angeles, 1962, NYC, 1963; Des Moines, 1964; The Byron Gallery, 1965, 68; Hampton Institute, 1966; Grand Rapids, 1968; U. of Iowa, 1969; Flint/Institute, 1973; Fischbach Gallery, 1973; 55 Mercer Street, NYC, 1980. **Group:** Brooklyn Museum, Print Biennials; Chicago/AI; Silvermine Guild; SRGM; Des Moines; WMAA, American Prints Today, 1959, Annual, 1968; Youngstown/Butler, 1961; U. of Illinois, 1963; New York World's Fair, 1964-65; Finch College, 1965; PAFA, 1969; WMAA, 1973; MOMA, Printed, Folded, Cut and

Torn, 1974; Kent State U., Blossom Festival, 1978; NCFA, New Ways with Paper, 1978; National Gallery, Contemporary American Prints and Drawings, 1940-1980, 1981; Pratt Manhattan Center, Exceptions 3: Paperworks, 1985. **Collections:** Bradley U.; Brandeis U.; Grand Rapids; Hampton Institute; MMA; MOMA; Minnesota/MA; NYPL; PMA; Purchase/SUNY; SRGM; Syracuse U.; WMAA; Washington U.

SONFIST, ALAN. b. May 26, 1946, New York City. **Studied:** ASL, 1963; Pratt Institute, 1965, 66; Western Illinois U., 1964-67, BA; Hunter College, 1969; Ohio State U., 1968. **Taught:** Lombard (Ill.) H.S., 1967; Ohio State U., 1968; MIT, 1967-76; Philadelphia College of Art, 1975-76. Editor, *Art in the Land*, published by E.P. Dutton. **Commissions:** Airco Industries, Mountainville, N.J.; Chase Manhattan Bank, NYC; Ponderosa Inc., Dayton; Best Products, Inc., Richmond, Va.; Brooklyn Planning Board, NYC; Sunforest Medical Center, Toledo. **Awards:** National Endowment for the Arts, grant, 1975, 78; Citibank Foundation grant; Gilman Foundation grant; CAPS, 1977; Graham Foundation grant, 1972; Australian Council for the Arts, travel grant, 1981; National Endowment for the Arts, 1981. **Address:** 205 Mulberry Street, NYC 10012. **One-man Exhibitions:** Reese Palley Gallery, NYC, 1970; Harcus-Krakow Gallery, Boston, 1971; Deson Zaks Gallery, Chicago, 1971; Finch College, NYC, 1971; ICA, London, 1972; Automation House, NYC, 1972; Akron/AI, 1972; Paley & Lowe Gallery, NYC, 1977; Solway Gallery, Cincinnati, 1974, 77; Galerie Thelen, Cologne, 1974; Stefanotty Gallery, NYC, 1975; Cornell U., 1975; Adiene Gallery, NYC, 1975; Galeria Massimo Valsecchi, Milan, 1976; Galleria Cavellino, Venice, 1976; Purchase/SUNY, 1978; Leo Castelli Gallery, NYC, 1978; Marian Goodman Gallery, NYC, 1981; Louisville/Speed, 1981; Melbourne/National, 1981; U. of

Miami, 1982; Carl Solway Gallery, Cincinnati, 1982; Cavallino Gallery, Venice, 1984; Corcoran, 1984; Auckland, 1985; Kansas City/Nelson, 1985; Celle Art Spaces, Celle, Italy, 1986; First Street Forum, St. Louis, Mo., 1986. **Group:** Indianapolis, 1972; Cologne, Projects 74, 1974; Venice, Biennale, 1976; Paris, Biennale, 1975; Aachen, 1975; Boston/MFA, 1977; Kassel, Documenta, 1977; U. of Colorado, Boulder, and Independent Curators, NYC, Mapped Art, 1982. **Collections:** Aachen/Ludwig; Akron/AM; Boston/MFA; Brandeis U.; Brooklyn Museum; Buffalo/Albright; U. of California, Berkeley; Canberra/National; Chicago/Contemporary; Cologne; Dallas/MFA; Des Moines; Hartford/Wadsworth; High Museum; Houston/MFA; Los Angeles/County MA; Los Angeles/MOCA; Louisville/Speed; MOMA; U. of Miami; Oberlin College; Paris/Moderne; Princeton U.; Queens Museum; Rutgers U.; U. of Sydney; Toronto; Trenton/State. **Bibliography:** Lucie-Smith.

SONNIER, KEITH. b. 1941, Mamou, La. **Studied:** U. of Southwestern Louisiana, 1959-63, BA; Rutgers U., 1965-66, MFA. Resided France, 1963-64. **Awards:** Tokyo Print Biennial, First Prize, 1974; Guggenheim Foundation Fellowship, 1974. **Address:** 33 Rector Street, NYC 10006. **Dealer:** Leo Castelli, Inc., NYC. **One-man Exhibitions:** Douglass College, New Brunswick, N.J., 1966; Galerie Rolf Ricke, 1968, 71, 72, 75, 78; Leo Castelli, Inc., NYC, 1970, 72, 74, 75, 76, 78, 79, 82, 84, 85; ACE Gallery, Los Angeles, 1970, 75, 77; Eindhoven, 1970; MOMA, 1971; Seder/Creigh Gallery, Coronado, 1974, 76; Rosamund Felson Gallery, Los Angeles, 1978; The Clocktower, NYC, 1978; Krefeld, 1979; Galerie Michele Lachowsky, Brussels, 1979; Eric Fabre Gallery, Paris, 1979; Paris/Beaubourg, 1979; Galerie France Morin, Montreal, 1980; Tony Shafrazi Gallery, 1980; David Bellman Gallery, Toronto, 1981; Michele Lachowsky Gallery, Antwerp, 1981; Galerie Ricke, Cologne, 81, 84; Portland (Ore.) Center for the Visual Arts, 1981; Galerie Eric Fabre, Paris, 1982; Rosamund Felson Gallery, Los Angeles, 1982, 85; P.S. 1, Long Island City, 1983; Hara Museum, Tokyo, 1984; Galeria Schema, Florence, 1984; Carol Taylor Art Gallery, Dallas, 1984; Virginia Polytechnic Institute, 1984; Susanna Hilberry Gallery, Birmingham, Mich., 1985. **Group:** A.F.A., Soft Sculpture, 1968; American Abstract Artists, 1968; Trenton/State, Soft Art, 1969; Washington U., Here and Now, 1969; Berne, When Attitudes Become Form, 1969; WMAA, Anti-Illusion: Procedures/Materials, 1969; Chicago/AI, 1970; ICA, U. of Pennsylvania, Against Order: Chance and Art, 1970; WMAA, 1970; MOMA, Information, 1971; Dusseldorf/Kunsthalle, Prospect '71, 1971; New Delhi, Second World Triennial, 1971; Humlebaek/Louisiana, American Art, 1950-1970, 1971; Venice Biennial, 1972; Festival of Two Worlds, Spoleto, 1972; Yale U., Options and Alternatives, 1973; New York Cultural Center, 3D into 2D, 1973; Parcheggio di Villa Borghese, Rome, Contemporanea, 1974; WMAA, 1973; Seattle/AM, American Art—Third Quarter Century, 1973; CNAC, Art/Voir, 1974; WMAA, Projected Video, 1975; NCFA, Sculpture; American Directions 1945-1975, 1975; WMAA, 200 Years of American Sculpture, 1976; Fort Worth, American Artists: A New Decade, 1976; New Orleans Museum, Five From Louisiana, 1977; Rutgers U., Twelve From Rutgers, 1977; Aspen Center for the Visual Arts, American Portraits of the Sixties and Seventies, 1970; Aspen Center for the Visual Arts, American Portraits of the Sixties and Seventies, 1979; Basel/Kunsthalle, Amerikanische Zeichnungen der Siebziger Jahre, 1981; XL Venice Biennial, 1982; MOMA, Made in India: Fall 1985, 1986. **Collections:** Aachen; Canberra/National; Cologne; Harvard U.; MOMA; U. of North Carolina; Stockholm/National;

WMAA. **Bibliography:** *Art Now 74;* Celant; *Contemporanea;* Davis, D.; Kren; *Kunst um 1970;* Lippard, ed.; Muller; *Options and Alternatives;* Honisch and Jensen, eds.; Pincus-Witten; *When Attitudes Become Form.* Archives.

SOYER, MOSES. b. December 25, 1899, Tombov, Russia; **d.** September 2, 1974, NYC. To USA, 1913; citizen, 1925. **Studied:** Cooper Union; NAD; Educational Alliance, NYC; Ferrer School, San Francisco, with Robert Henri, George Bellows. Traveled Europe, Russia. **Taught:** Contemporary School of Art, NYC; New School for Social Research; Educational Alliance, NYC; and elsewhere. **Member:** NAD; Artists Equity; Audubon Artists; NIAL. Federal A.P.; US Post Office, Philadelphia, Pa.; Greenpoint Hospital, Brooklyn, N.Y. (mural, with James Penney); 10 portable murals for libraries. **Awards:** AAAL, Childe Hassam Award (2); NAD, Annual, Andrew Carnegie Prize. **One-man Exhibitions:** (first) J. B. Neumann's New Art Circle, NYC, 1928; Kleeman Gallery, NYC, 1935; Macbeth Gallery, NYC, 1940; 41, 43; Boyer Gallery, NYC; ACA Gallery, 1944, 47, 70, 72, 77; Guild Hall, 1972. **Retrospective:** U. of North Carolina, 1972. **Group:** MMA; WMAA; Brooklyn Museum; Detroit/Institute; Youngstown/Butler; NAD. **Collections:** AAAL; Birmingham, Ala./MA; Brooklyn Museum; Detroit/Institute; Hartford/Wadsworth; U. of Kansas; Library of Congress; MMA; MOMA; NAD; Newark Museum; PMA; Phillips; Toledo/MA; WMAA; Youngstown/Butler. **Bibliography:** Brown 2; Cheney; Finkelstein; Mendelowitz; **Smith, B.; Soyer, M.; Soyer, R., 1; Wheeler; Willard.** Archives.

SOYER, RAPHAEL. b. December 25, 1899, Tombov, Russia. To USA, 1912. **Studied:** Cooper Union; NAD, 1919-21; ASL, with Guy DuBois. **Taught:** ASL; American Art School, NYC; New

Raphael Soyer   *Elissa*

School for Social Research; NAD, 1965-67. **Member:** NIAL; NAD. Federal A.P.: Easel painting. **Commissions:** US Post Office, Kingsessing. **Awards:** Carnegie, Hon. Men. (3); Chicago/AI, The M. V. Kohnstamm Prize, 1932; Chicago/AI, Norman Wait Harris Gold Medal, 1932; PAFA, Carol H. Beck Gold Medal, 1934; Chicago/AI, Norman Wait Harris Bronze Medal, 1940; PAFA, Joseph E. Temple Gold Medal, 1943; PAFA, Walter Lippincott Prize, 1946; Corcoran, William A. Black Prize and Corcoran Gold Medal, 1951; ART:USA:59, NYC, $1,000 Prize, 1959. **Address:** 88 Central Park West, NYC 10023. **Dealer:** The Forum Gallery. **One-man Exhibitions:** The Daniel Gallery, NYC, 1929; L'Elan Gallery, NYC, 1932; Curt Valentine Gallery, NYC, 1933, 34, 35, 37, 38; Frank K.M. Rehn Gallery, NYC, 1939; Treasury Section, Fine Arts Division, 1939; A.A.A. Gallery, NYC, 1940, 41, 48, 53, 55; Weyhe Gallery, 1944; Philadelphia Art Alliance, 1949; ACA Gallery, 1960; Alfredo Valente Gallery, NYC, 1961; Bernard Crystal Gallery, NYC, 1962; The Forum Gallery, 1964, 66, 67, 72, 77, 81; The Margo Feiden Galleries, NYC, 1972; Galerie Albert Loeb, Paris, 1980. **Retrospectives:** WMAA, circ., 1967; Hirshhorn, 1982. **Group:** Salons of America, NYC, 1926; WMAA Annuals, 1932-; PAFA, 1934, 43, 46; Corcoran, 1937, 51; VMFA, 1938; Chicago/AI, 1940; Brooklyn Museum, 1941; Carnegie, 1944; Phillips, 1944; Dallas/MFA, 1945; California Palace; 1945; MOMA, 1946; NAD, 1951, 52; A.F.A., 1967; NAD, American Portrait Drawings, 1980; Trenton/State, American Art of the 1930's, 1979; Akademie der Kunst, Berlin, American Art: 1920-1940, 1980. **Collections:** Andover/Phillips; U. of Arizona; Boston/MFA; Brooklyn Museum; Buffalo/Albright; Columbus; Corcoran; Detroit/Institute; Hartford/Wadsworth; MMA; MOMA; Montclair/AM; U. of Nebraska; Newark Museum; Norfolk/Chrysler; Oslo/National; Phillips; WMAA. **Bibliography:** American Artists Congress, Inc.; American Artists Group Inc. 3; Bazin; Biddle 4; Boswell 1; Brown 2; Cheney; Finkelstein; **Foster;** *From Foreign Shores;* **Goodrich 10;** Goodrich and Baur 1; **Gutman;** Hall; Kent, N.; Mellquist; Mendelowitz; Nordness, ed.; Pagano; Reese; **Soyer, R., 1, 2, 3;** Wheeler; Zigrosser 1. Archives.

SPEICHER, EUGENE. b. April, 5, 1883, Buffalo, N.Y.; **d.** 1962. **Studied:** Buffalo Fine Arts Academy, 1902-06; ASL, 1907-08, with Frank V. DuMond, William M. Chase; Robert Henri School, 1909, with Robert Henri. Traveled Europe extensively. **Member:** NIAL; NAD; National Arts Club. **Awards:** ASL, Kelley Prize, 1907; NAD, Thomas R. Proctor Prize, 1911; Salmagundi Club, Jose S. Isadora Prize, 1913; NAD, Hallgarten Prize, 1914, 15; Panama-Pacific Exposition, San Francisco, 1915, Silver Medal; PAFA, Carol H. Beck Gold Medal, 1920; Carnegie, Third Prize, 1921, Second Prize, 1923;

Chicago/AI, Potter Palmer Gold Medal, 1926; Corcoran, Second William A. Clark Prize, 1928; Corcoran, First Prize; VMFA, **P.P.;** Hon. DFA, Syracuse U., 1945. **One-man Exhibitions:** Montross Gallery, NYC, 1918; M. Knoedler & Co., 1920; Carnegie, 1924; Boston Arts Club, 1925; Rehn Galleries, 1925, 29, 34, 41, 43; Des Moines, 1926; Denver/AM, 1948; Wildenstein & Co., NYC, 1954; AAAL, Memorial Exhibition, 1963; ACA Gallery, 1965; Salander-O'Reilly Galleries, NYC, 1981. **Retrospective:** Buffalo/Albright, 1950. **Group:** WMAA; PAFA; Carnegie; Century Association, Robert Henri and Five Pupils, 1946; MOMA; Chicago/AI. **Collections:** ASL; Andover/Phillips; Boston/MFA; Britannica; Brooklyn Museum; Buffalo/Albright; Cincinnati/AM; Cleveland/MA; Corcoran; Decatur; Des Moines; Detroit/Institute; Galveston; Harvard U.; IBM; Indianapolis/Herron; Kansas City/Nelson; Los Angeles/County MA; MMA; MOMA; Minneapolis/Institute; Phillips; RISD; St. Louis/City; Toledo/MA; VMFA; WMAA; West Palm Beach/Norton; Worcester/AM; Yale U. **Bibliography:** Baur 7; Bazin; Biddle 4; Blesh 1; Boswell 1; Brown; Bryant, L.; Burchfield 3; Cahill and Barr, eds.; Cheney; Elliot; Goodrich and Baur 1; Hall; *Index of 20th Century Artists;* Jackson; Jewell 2; Kent N.; **Mather 1, 2;** McCurdy, ed.; Mellquist; Mendelowitz; Narodny; Neuhaus; Pagano; Phillip 2; Poore; Richardson, E.P.; Sachs; Smith, S.C.K.; **Speicher;** Watson, E.W. 1; *Woodstock: An American Art Colony, 1902-1977;* Zaidenberg, ed. Archives.

SPENCER, NILES. b. May 16, 1893, Pawtucket, R.I.; **d.** May 15, 1952, Dingman's Ferry, Pa. **Studied:** RISD, 1913-15; Ferrer School, NYC (with Robert Henri, George Bellows), 1915; ASL (with Kenneth Hayes Miller), 1915. Traveled Europe, 1921-22, 1928-29. **Taught:** RISD, 1915. **Awards:** Carnegie, Hon. Mention, 1930; MMA, **P.P.,** 1942. **One-man Exhibitions:**

(first) The Daniel Gallery, NYC, 1925, also 1928; The Downtown Gallery, 1947, 52; Washburn Gallery Inc., 1972. **Retrospective:** Downtown Gallery, 1947, 52; MOMA, 1954; U. of Kentucky, 1965. **Group:** Whitney Studio Club, NYC, from 1923; MOMA, Paintings by 19 Living Americans, 1929; Cincinnati/AM, A New Realism, 1941; Providence (R.I.) Art Club; Carnegie; MMA, Artists for Victory, 1942; Walker, The Precisionist View, 1960; WMAA, 1966; U. of New Mexico, Cubism: Its Impact in the USA, 1967. **Collections:** Andover/Phillips; Arizona State College; U. of Arizona; Buffalo/Albright; Columbus; Cornell U.; Illinois Wesleyan U.; MMA; MOMA; U. of Michigan; U. of Nebraska; Newark Museum; Phillips; RISD; SFMA; San Francisco Art Institute; Santa Barbara/MA; WMAA; Walker; Wichita/AM; Youngstown/Butler. **Bibliography:** Baur 7; Brown 2; Hunter 6; *Cityscape 1919-39; Index of 20th Century Artists;* Kootz 1, 2; Pousette-Dart, ed. Archives.

SQUIER, JACK. b. February 27, 1927, Dixon, Ill. **Studied:** Oberlin College; Indiana U., with Robert Laurent, Leo Steppat, 1950, BS; Cornell U., with John Hartell, 1952, MFA. Traveled Central and South America, Europe, Middle East, the Orient, Russia. **Taught:** Cornell U., 1952-. **Address:** 221 Berkshire Road, Ithaca, NY 14850. **One-man Exhibitions:** (first) The Alan Gallery, NYC, 1956, also 1959, 62, 64, 66, 68; Cornell U., 1959, 64, 68; Lima, Peru, 1963. **Group:** WMAA; MOMA; Houston-MFA; Andover/Phillips; Boston/MFA; Brussels World's Fair, 1958; U. of Illinois; Chicago/AI; Boston Arts Festival; Carnegie; Claude Bernard, Paris; Buffalo/Albright. **Collections:** Cornell U.; Hirshhorn; Ithaca College; Lima, Peru; MOMA; St. Lawrence U.; Potsdam/SUNY; Stanford U.; Syracuse/Everson; WMAA. **Bibliography:** Weller.

STAMOS, THEODOROS. b. December 31, 1922, NYC. **Studied:** American Artists School, NYC, with Simon Kennedy, Joseph Konzal. Traveled Europe, Near East, Greece. **Taught:** Black Mountain College; Cummington School of Fine Arts; ASL, 1958-75; Brandeis U. **Commissions:** Moore McCormack Lines Inc., SS *Argentina* (mural). **Awards:** L.C. Tiffany Grant, 1951; NIAL, 1956; Brandeis U., Creative Arts Award 1959; National Arts Foundation, 1967. **Address:** Plateia Hrwon, Paralia 6, Lefkada, Greece; 37 West 83rd Street, NYC 10024. **Dealer:** Kouros Gallery, NYC. **One-man Exhibitions:** (first) Wakefield Gallery, NYC, 1940; Mortimer Brandt, NYC, 1945; Betty Parsons Gallery, 1947, 56; Phillips, 1950, 54; Philadelphia Art Alliance, 1957; Andre Emmerich Gallery, NYC, 1958, 59, 60, 63, 66, 68; San Antonio/McNay, 1960; Gimpel Fils Ltd., 1960; Galleria d'Arte del Naviglio, Milan, 1961; Brandeis U., 1967; Waddington Fine Arts Ltd., Montreal, 1968; Marlborough Gallery, Inc., NYC, 1970; Omaha/Joslyn, 1973; Athens Gallery, 1974; Louis K. Meisel Gallery, NYC, 1977, 79, 81; Galerie Le Portail, Heidelberg, 1977; Morgan Art Gallery, Shawnee Mission, 1977; Union College, 1978; Hokin Gallery, Palm Beach, 1978; Wichita State U., 1979; Utica, 1980; Hokin Gallery, Chicago, 1980; Turske Fine Art, Cologne, 1980; Bernier Gallery, Athens, 1982; Knoedler & Co., Inc., Zurich, 1984; Ericson Gallery, NYC, 1985; Harcourts Gallery, San Francisco, 1985, 86; Kouros Gallery, 1985, 86; Turske & Turske Gallery, Zurich, 1985; Wurthle Gallery, Vienna, 1985; Hokin Gallery, Bay Harbor Islands, Fla., 1986. **Retrospectives:** Corcoran, 1959; New Paltz/SUNY, 1980. **Group:** Carnegie, 1955, 58, 61, 64; International Biennial Exhibition of Paintings, Tokyo; MOMA, The New American Painting, circ., Europe, 1958-59; WMAA, Nature in Abstraction, 1958, Annual, 1963; Venice Biennial; Documenta II, Kassel, 1959; SRGM, Abstract Expressionists and Imagists, 1961;

MMA, 1965; WMAA, Art of the U.S. 1670-1966, 1966; Corcoran Biennial, 1967; MOMA, Dada, Surrealism and Their Heritage, 1968; MOMA, The New American Painting and Sculpture, 1969; Cornell U., Abstract Expressionism, The Formative Years, 1978. **Collections:** Andover/Phillips; U. of Arizona; Baltimore/MA; Brandeis U.; Buffalo/Albright; California Palace; Case Institute; Chase Manhattan Bank; Chicago/AI; Ciba-Geigy Corp.; Colorado Springs/FA; Columbus; Corcoran; Cornell U.; Des Moines; Detroit/Institute; Greece/National; Hartford/Wadsworth; Hirshhorn; U. of Illinois; State U. of Iowa; La Jolla; MIT; MMA; MOMA; Memphis/Brooks; Michigan State U.; U. of Michigan; Montclair/AM; NMAA; NYU; U. of Nebraska; U. of North Carolina; Notre Dame U.; Phillips; Phoenix; Rio de Janeiro; SFMA; SRGM; San Antonio/McNay; Smith College; Tel Aviv; Toronto; Trenton/State; Utica; Vassar College; Vienna/Moderner; WGMA; WMAA; Walker; Wellesley College; Yale U.; Youngstown/Butler. **Bibliography:** Alloway 4; Barker 1; Baur 5, 7; Biddle 4; Blesh 1; Eliot; Goodrich and Baur 1; Haftman; Hobbs and Levin; Janis and Blesh 1; McCurdy, ed.; Mendelowitz; Nordness, ed.; **Pomeroy;** Pousette-Dart, ed.; Read 2; Richardson, E.P.; Ritchie 1; Rubin 1; Sandler; Seuphor 1; Soby 5. Archives.

STANCZAK, JULIAN. b. November 5, 1928, Borownica, Poland. To USA, 1950; citizen, 1956. **Studied:** Borough Polytechnic, London, 1949-50; Cleveland Institute of Art, BFA, 1950-54; Yale U. (with Josef Albers, Conrad Marca Relli), MFA, 1954-56. Traveled Poland, Russia, Persia, India, East Africa, England, Western Europe. **Taught:** Art Academy of Cincinnati, 1957-64; Cleveland Institute of Art, 1964-; Dartmouth College, Artist-in-Residence, 1968. **Member:** American Abstract Artists. **Commissions:** First National Bank, Dayton, Ohio, 1972; National City Bank, Dayton, Ohio,

1973; Cleveland Area Arts Council, 1974; Ohio Building Authority, Columbus, 1974; Rotweil, West Germany (flag design), 1974; Ohio Arts Council, 1975; Cleveland Public Library, 1979. **Awards:** Ohio State Council on the Arts Award, 1972. **Address:** 6229 Cabrini Lane, Seven Hills, OH 44131. **One-man Exhibitions:** (first) Dayton/AI, 1964; Martha Jackson Gallery, 1964, 65, 68, 71, 72, 73, 75, 79; Miami U., 1965; U. of Wisconsin, 1965; Feingarten Gallery, 1966; Kent State U., 1968; Dartmouth College, 1968; Makler Gallery, Philadelphia, 1969; London Arts, Detroit, 1969, 72, London, 1971; Akron/AI, 1970; Women's City Club, Cleveland, 1970; The Packard Gallery, Akron, 1970; Images Gallery, Toledo, 1971, 72; Carl Solway Gallery, Cincinnati, 1972; Corcoran, 1972; Cincinnati/AM, 1972; New Gallery, Cleveland, 1972, 76; Haslem Fine Arts, Inc., 1972; Phoenix Gallery, San Francisco, 1974; Canton Art Institute, 1974; Pollock Gallery, Toronto, 1975; Lakeland College, 1975; Alice Simsar Inc., Ann Arbor, 1975; Marjorie Kauffman Graphics, Los Angeles, 1976; Kingpitcher Gallery, Pittsburgh, 1976; Ohio State U., 1976; The Miller Gallery, Cincinnati, 1978; A.S.A. Gallery, Oak Ridge, 1978; Kauffman Fine Arts, Houston, 1978; International Monetary Fund, Washington, D.C., 1978; Youngstown/Butler, 1980; Carl Solway Gallery, Cincinnati, 1980; Alice Simsar Gallery, Ann Arbor, 1981, 82; Sandusky Area Cultural Center, 1981; Warsaw/National; Brubaker Gallery, Sarasota, Fla., 1983; New Gallery, Cleveland, 1983; Charles Foley Gallery, Columbus, Ohio, 1984; Walker Gallery, Chicago, 1986; Jane Haslem Gallery, Washington, D.C., 1986. **Retrospectives:** Cleveland Institute of Art, 1971; Lakeland College, Sheboygan, Wis., 1975. **Group:** MOMA, The Responsive Eye, 1965; Buffalo/Albright, 1965, Plus by Minus, 1968; Riverside Museum; Detroit/Institute; U. of Illinois, 1965, 69; WMAA Annual, 1967; Carnegie, 1967; Indianapolis/Herron, 1969; U. of

Illinois, 1969, 74; Flint/Institute International, 1969; Carnegie, 1970; NCFA, Black and White, 1970-72; Amherst College, Color Painting, 1972; Mansfield Art Center, Stanczak-Anuszkiewicz, 1973; Minnesota/MA, Drawings USA, 1973; U. of Miami, Less Is More: The Influence of the Bauhaus on American Art, 1974; Akron, Forms of Color, 1975; Indianapolis, 1976; Brooklyn, Thirty Years of American Printmaking, 1976; Cleveland Institute of Art, Visual Logic, 1979; Brooklyn Museum, American Drawings in Black and White, 1970-1979, 1980; Montclair/AM, Josef Albers: His Influence, 1982. **Collections:** Akron/AI; American Republic Insurance Co.; Baltimore/MA; Buffalo/Albright; Canton Art Institute; Carnegie; Cincinnati/AM; Cleveland/MA; Columbus; Corcoran; Dartmouth College; Dayton/AI; Hirshhorn; Houston/Contemporary; Indianapolis/Herron; Kalamazoo; Metropolitan Museum & Art Center; Mexico City/Tamayo; U. of Miami; Miami-Dade; Milwaukee; National Gallery; Oklahoma; PAFA; Ridgefield/Aldrich; SFMA; Trade Bank and Trust Company, NYC; Tulsa/Philbrook; Youngstown/Butler. **Bibliography:** MacAgy 2; Weller. Archives.

STANKIEWICZ, RICHARD P. b. October 18, 1922, Philadelphia, PA. **d.** March 27, 1983, Worthington, Mass. **Studied:** Hofmann School, 1948-49, with Hans Hofmann; Atelier Fernand Leger, Paris, 1950-51; Zadkine School of Sculpture, Paris, 1950-51. **Taught:** Albany/SUNY, 1967-. Traveled Europe, Australia, USA. An organizer of Hansa Gallery, NYC, 1952. US Navy, 1941-47. **Member:** International Institute of Arts and Letters; NIAL; Century Association. **Awards:** Brandeis U.; National Academy of Arts and Sciences; Ford Foundation Grant. **One-man Exhibitions:** (first) Hansa Gallery, NYC, 1953, also 1954-58; The Stable Gallery, 1959-63; Galerie Neufville, Paris, 1960; The Pace Gallery, Boston, 1961;

Richard Stankiewicz *1972–1* 1972

Walker, 1963 (two-man, with Robert Indiana); Daniel Cordier, Paris, 1964; Tampa/AI, 1965; Frank Watters Gallery, 1969; Melbourne/National, 1969; The Zabriskie Gallery, 1972, 73, 75, 77, 79, 81, 83, 84. **Retrospective:** Albany/SUNY, 1979. **Group:** PAFA, 1954; WMAA, 1956, 60, 62, Young America, 1957; Houston/MFA, Irons in the Fire, 1957; XXIX Venice Biennial, 1958; Carnegie, 1958, 61; A.F.A., Recent Sculpture, USA, 1959; MOMA, Sixteen Americans, circ., 1959; Claude Bernard, Paris, Aspects of American Sculpture, 1960; Amsterdam/Stedelijk, 1961; Chicago/AI, 1961, 62; VI Sao Paulo Biennial, 1961; MOMA, The Art of Assemblage, circ., 1961; Stock-holm/National, 4 Americans, circ., 1962; Seattle World's Fair, 1962; SRGM, The Joseph H. Hirshhorn Collection, 1962; WMAA, Forty Artists under Forty, circ., 1962; Amsterdam/Stedelijk, Four Americans, 1962; MOMA, Hans Hofmann and His Students, circ., 1963-64; Battersea Park, London, International Sculpture Exhibition, 1963; Jewish Museum, Recent American Sculptors, 1964; MOMA, The Machine, 1968; Dallas/AM, Poets of the Cities, circ., 1974; U. of California, Santa Barbara, Sculptors in the 1950s, 1976; Storm King Art Center, Sculpture: A Study in Materials, 1978; WMAA, The Third Dimension, 1984. **Collections:** Akron/AI; Buffalo/Albright; Chicago/AI; Dayton/AI; Fredonia/SUNY; Hirshhorn; Houston/MFA; MOMA; NMAA; Newark Museum; Paris/Beaubourg; PAFA; PMA; Portland, Ore./AM; Smith College; SRGM; Stockholm/National; Storm King Art Center; Springfield, Mass./MFA; Tel Aviv; WMAA; Walker. **Bibliography:** Blesh 1; Chipp; Craven, W.; Downer, ed.; Friedman, ed; Goodrich and Baur 1; Hulten; Hunter, ed.; Janis and Blesh 1; Kuh 3; Licht, F.; Lowry; *Metro;* Phillips, Lisa; Read 3; Rowell; Sandler 1; Seitz 3; Seuphor 3; Weller. Archives.

STANLEY, ROBERT. b. January 3, 1932, Yonkers, N.Y. **Studied:** Oglethorpe U. (with Marion O'Donnell, Wendell Brown), BA, 1953; ASL, 1953; Brooklyn Museum School (with Yonia Fain, William King), 1954-56. Traveled USA, Holland, Germany, Caribbean. **Taught:** School of Visual Arts, NYC, 1970-72, 84-; Louisiana State U., 1976; Syracuse U., 1978; Princeton U., 1979-80. **Awards:** Cassandra Foundation, 1969. **Address:** 3 Crosby Street, NYC 10013. **Dealers:** John Nichols, NYC; Joe Fawbush Editions, NYC. **One-man Exhibitions:** (first) The Bianchini Gallery, NYC, 1965, also 1966; Orez International Gallery, The Hague, 1966; Cincinnati/Contemporary, 1966; Galerie Rolf Ricke, Kassel, 1966, 67; Galerie Kuckels, Bochum, Germany, 1967; Kleine Galerie, Frankfurt, 1968; Gegenverkehr, Aachen, 1969; On First, NYC, 1969; Warren Benedek Gallery, NYC, 1972; New York Cultural Center, 1974;

Louisiana State U., 1976; P.S. 1, Long Island City (two-man), 1977; Hal Bromm Gallery, NYC, 1978; Elizabeth Weiner Gallery, NYC, 1978; St. Thomas Aquinas College, 1978; Bucklew-Goehring Gallery, Tampa, 1983; Centre d'Art Contemporain, Dijon, France. **Retrospective:** Holly Keenberg Contemporary Art, Winnipeg, 1980. **Group:** Van Bovenkamp Gallery, NYC, 1965; Chicago/AI, 1965-69; Indianapolis/Herron, 1967; WMAA Annual, 1967; Documenta IV, Kassel, 1968; ICA, London, The Obsessive Image, 1968; Milwaukee, Aspects of a New Realism, 1969; David Stuart Gallery, 1969; Chicago/AI, 1969; Cincinnati/Contemporary, Monumental Art, 1970; WMAA, 1972, 73; Eindhoven, Relativerend Realisme, 1972; U. of North Carolina, 1973; New York Cultural Center, Three Centuries of the American Nude, 1975; P.S. 1, Long Island City, Another Aspect of Pop, 1978; AAIAL, 1982. **Collections:** American Republic Insurance Co., Cincinnati/Contemporary; Cologne; Corcoran; Des Moines; Donaldson, Lufkin, & Jenrette, Inc.; Fort Worth; Harvard U.; Housatonic Community College; MMA; Madison Art Center; McCrory Corporation; Milwaukee; Norfolk/Chrysler; Rutgers U.; Time Inc.; WMAA; Washington U. (St. Louis); Westport Art Education Society; Yeshiva U. **Bibliography:** Honisch and Jensen, eds.; Lippard 5.

STASIK, ANDREW. b. March 16, 1932, New Brunswick, N.J. **Studied:** NYU; Columbia U., BA; State U. of Iowa; Ohio U., MFA. **Taught:** New School for Social Research; Ohio U.; Ball State Teachers College; Pratt Graphic Art Center; Pratt Institute; Yale U.; U. of Calgary, Editorial Staff, *Artist's Proof* magazine. Traveled Europe, Scandinavia, Orient. Director, Pratt Graphics Center, 1966-85; Founder & Editor, *Print Review*, 1972-76; Gallery Director, Silvermine (Conn.) Galleries; Director, International Graphic Arts Foundation, NYC. **Awards:** Cleveland/MA, First Prize in Lithography, 1958; Bay Printmakers Society, Oakland, **P.P.,** 1958; Cleveland/MA, First Prize in Serigraphy, 1958; Pasadena/AM, **P.P.,** 1958; Gallery of Modern Art, Ljubljana, Yugoslavia, III International Exhibition of Prints, 1959, Le Prix Internationale de 100,000 dn; Achenbach Foundation, Open Award for All Media, 1961; The Print Club, Philadelphia, Collins Prize; L.C. Tiffany Grant, 1966; Audubon Artists Medal, 1969; Silvermine Guild, **P.P.,** 1974; Texas Tech U., **P.P.,** Colorprint USA, 1974. **Address:** 395 West Avenue, Darien, Conn. 06840. **One-man Exhibitions:** Ohio U., 1956; Avant Garde, NYC, 1958; Ball State Teachers College, 1959; Ross Widen Gallery, Cleveland, 1960; Miami/Modern, 1960; Samuel S. Fleisher Art Memorial, Philadelphia, 1961; Yoseido Gallery, Tokyo, 1961; Castagno Gallery, NYC, 1966; Gallery of Graphic Arts, NYC, 1967; Pollock Gallery, Toronto, 1968; Museu de Arte, Rio Grande do Sul, Brazil, 1968; Union of Plastic Gallery, Krakow, 1968; Centar Gallery, Zagreb, 1968; Galeria Colibri, San Juan, Puerto Rico, 1968; U. of Calgary, 1969; Mala Gallery, Ljubljana, Yugoslavia, 1969; Bader Gallery, Washington, D.C. (two-man), 1969; Secession Gallery, Vienna, 1970; Spectrum Gallery, NYC, 1971; A.A.A. Gallery, 1971; Graphics Gallery, 1971; Molloy College, Rockville Centre, N.Y., 1971; Jacques Baruch Gallery, 1973; Montclair State College (two-man), 1974; J. Fields Gallery, NYC, 1982; Ana Sklar Gallery, Miami, 1985; Galerie Vivant, Tokyo, 1985. **Group:** Cincinnati/AM Biennials, 1956, 58, 60, 62, 68; PCA, American Prints Today, circ. 1959-62; Gallery of Modern Art, Ljubljana, Yugoslavia, III, IV, VI, VII & VIII International Exhibition of Prints, 1959, 61, 65, 67, 69; A.F.A., Prints of the World, 1962; The Print Club, Philadelphia, 1962; Library of Congress; MOMA, Prize-Winning American Prints, circ., Canada; Krakow Print Biennials, 1968, 70, 72; U. of Washing-

ton, 1969; International Print Biennials, Ljubljana, Yugoslavia, 1969, 71, 73; U. of Washington, Prints/Multiples, 1970; IV American Biennial, Santiago, 1970; Taipei, Taiwan, International Print Exhibition, 1983, 85. **Collections:** Amsterdam/Stedelijk; Ball State U.; Budapest/National; California Palace; Cincinnati/AM; Library of Congress; MMA; MOMA; NCFA; NYPL; NYU; National Gallery; U. of Nebraska; Oakland/AM; PMA; Pasadena/AM; Rockefeller Brothers Fund; Warsaw/National.

STEFANELLI, JOSEPH. b. March 20, 1921, Philadephia, Pa. **Studied:** Philadelphia Museum School, 1938-40; PAFA, 1941-42; ASL, 1946-48; Hofmann School, 1948-49. Traveled Europe, Middle East. **Taught:** U. of California, Berkeley, 1960, 63; Princeton U., 1963-66; Columbia U., 1966-74; Princeton U., 1963-66; Brooklyn College, 1974-77; New School for Social Research, 1966; NYU, 1979-80. Artist for *Yank* magazine, 1942-46 (field drawings made during World War II are in the permanent collection of the War Archives Building, Washington, D.C.). **Awards:** Fulbright Fellowship (Rome), 1958-59; New York State Council on the Arts Grant, 1971. **Address:** 463 West Street, NYC 10014. **Dealer:** Ingber Art Gallery, Ltd., NYC. **One-man Exhibitions:** Artists' Gallery, NYC, 1950, 54; The New Gallery, NYC, 1952; Hendler Gallery, Philadelphia, 1953; Ganymede Gallery, NYC, 1956; Poindexter Gallery, 1957, 58, 60; Hacker Gallery, NYC, 1962; Thibaut Gallery, NYC, 1963; Princeton U., 1964; U. of Arkansas, 1965; Westbeth Gallery, NYC, 1971; New School for Social Research, 1972; The New Bertha Schaefer Gallery, 1973, 74; Terry Dintenfass Gallery, NYC, 1974; Andre Zarre, 1977; Temple U., Rome, 1978; Landmark Gallery, NYC, 1980; Benson Gallery, Southampton, N.Y., 1981; New School for Social Research, 1982; Ingber Art Gallery, Ltd., 1986. **Group:** Ninth Street

Exhibition, NYC, 1951; PAFA; WMAA; Corcoran; Carnegie; U. of Illinois; Buffalo/Albright; Walker; Chicago/AI; MOMA. **Collections:** Baltimore/MA; U. of California, Berkeley; Chase Manhattan Bank; Chicago/AI; Cornell U.; U. of Massachusetts; U. of Montana; NYU; Norfolk; Norfolk/Chrysler; Sarah Lawrence College; Union Carbide Corp.; WMAA; Walker. **Bibliography:** Sandler 1.

STEG, J. L. b. February 6, 1922, Alexandria, Va. **Studied:** Rochester Institute of Technology; State U. of Iowa, BFA, MFA. Traveled Europe, Mexico, Spain. **Taught:** Cornell U., 1949-51; Tulane U., 1951. **Member:** SAGA. **Awards:** Carnegie Exchange Fellowship (Italy); VIII Lugano Drawing and Print Show, 1,000 Franc Award; Brooklyn Museum, **P.P.;** Seattle/AM, **P.P.;** Dallas/MFA, **P.P.;** Birmingham, Ala./MA, **P.P.;** U. of Minnesota, **P.P.,** Syracuse State Fair, **P.P.;** The Print Club, Philadelphia, **P.P.;** Minnesota/MA, **P.P.,** 1980. **Address:** 7919 Spruce Street, New Orleans, LA 70118. **Dealer:** A.A.A. Gallery, NYC. **One-man Exhibitions:** (first) Weyhe Gallery, 1945; Utica, 1951; Philadelphia Art Alliance, 1957; Davenport/Municipal, 1958; Dallas/MFA; Orleans Gallery, New Orleans; A.A.A. Gallery, NYC; U. of South Florida; Baton Rouge; Studio-Craft Gallery, Miami; Bienville Gallery, 1970; The Ohio State U., 1971; Tulane U., 1972, 74; USIS, Ankara, 1975; Newcomb College, 1975; Circle Gallery Ltd., NYC, 1976, 78; USIA, Cultural Center, Ankara, Turkey, 1977; U. of Mississippi, Oxford, 1978. **Retrospective:** New Orleans Museum, circ., 1978. **Group:** ART:USA, NYC; New York World's Fair, 1964-65; Oakland/AM; USIA; Philadelphia Art Alliance, 50th Anniversary, 1968; U. of Pittsburgh; Oneonta/SUNY, 1969; Smithsonian Exhibition, American Drawings II, circ., 1965; Trenton State, National Drawings, 1979. **Collections:** Albion College; Bezalel Museum; Bowling Green

state U.; Brooklyn Museum; Carnegie; Cleveland/MA; Colgate U.; Dallas/MFA; U. of Delaware; George Washington U.; Georgia State U.; Harvard U.; IBM; Library of Congress; MOMA; Malmo; U. of Minnesota; NYPL; U. of Nebraska; New Orleans/Delgado; The Ohio State U.; Oklahoma; Oslo/National; PMA; Princeton Print Club; The Print Club, Philadelphia; Print Club of Rochester; Randolph-Macon College; Remington-Rand Corp.; Roanoke; Sao Paulo; San Antonio/McNay; Seattle/AM; Smithsonian; Southern Illinois U.; USIA; US State Department; Utica; Worcester/AM.

STEINBERG, SAUL. b. June 15, 1914, Ramnicul-Sarat, Rumania. **Studied:** U. of Milan, 1932-40. To USA, 1942; citizen, 1943. US Navy, 1943-46. **Commissions:** Terrace Plaza Hotel, Cincinnati, 1948 (mural); Decor for *Count Ory* by Rossini at Juilliard School of Music, NYC, 1958. **Address:** Amagansett, NY 11930. **Dealer:** The Pace Gallery, NYC. **One-man Exhibitions:** (first) Wakefield Gallery, NYC, 1943; Young Brooks, Inc., NYC, 1945; Institute of Design, Chicago, 1948; Betty Parsons Gallery, NYC, 1950, 52, 66, 69, 73, 76; RISD, 1950; Galleria l'Obelisco, Rome, 1951, 52; Galeria de Arte, Sao Paulo, 1952; Sao Paulo, 1952; ICA, London, 1952, 57; Sidney Janis Gallery, 1952, 66, 69, 73, 76; Leopold-Hoesch-Museum, Duren, 1952; Frank Perls Gallery, Los Angeles, 1952; Wuppertal, 1952; Amsterdam/Stedelijk, 1953; Arts Club of Chicago, 1953; Galerie Blanche, Stockholm, 1953; Galerie Maeght, Paris, 1953, 66, 71, 74, 76; VMFA, 1953; Basel, 1954; Corcoran, 1954; Dallas/MFA, 1954; Dortmund, 1954; Frankfurt am Main, 1954; Santa Barbara/MA, 1954; Harvard U., 1955; Allan Frumkin Gallery, Chicago, 1956; Brussels/Moderne, 1969, 67; U. of California, Santa Barbara, 1962; Wesleyan U., 1965; Cologne, 1966; B.C. Holland Gallery, Chicago, 1967; Rotterdam, 1967; Caracas, 1968; Hamburg, 1968; Stockholm/National, 1968; Felix Landau Gallery, Los Angeles, 1970; Richard Gray Gallery, Chicago, 1971, 82; NCFA, 1973; ICA, Boston, 1974; The Pace Gallery, 1982; U. of Bridgeport, 1983; Gemini G.E.L., Los Angeles, 1983; Harvard U., 1985. **Retrospectives:** Cologne/Kunstverein, circ., 1974-75; WMAA, circ., 1978. **Group:** MOMA, Fourteen Americans, circ., 1946; Chicago/AI, 1949; L'Obelisco, Rome, 1951; ICA, London, 1952; Brussels World's Fair, 1958; Salon du Mai, Paris, 1966; Carnegie, 1970; Foundation Maeght, L'Art Vivant, 1970; Chicago/AI, 1971; Bibliotheque Nationale, Paris, Les Dessins d'humor, 1971; Recklinghausen, Zeitgenossische Karikaturen Zeitgenossen, 1972; Yale U., American Drawing, 1970-1973, 1973; Akron/AI, Contemporary Images in Watercolor, 1976; Documenta 6, Kassel, 1977; Renwick Gallery, Washington, D.C., The Object as Poet, 1977; Minneapolis/MA, American Drawings 1927-1977, 1977. **Collections:** Buffalo/Albright; Detroit/Institute; Harvard U.; MMA; MOMA; Utica; Victoria and Albert Museum; WMAA. **Bibliography: Baudson;** Baur 7; Biddle 4; Kepes 2; *From Foreign Shores;* Kepes 2; *Metro;* Miller, ed. 2; Richardson, E.P.; Rodman 1; Rosenberg 3; Sachs; Schneider; **Steinberg, S., 1, 2, 3.** Archives.

STEINER, MICHAEL. b. 1945, NYC. **Studied:** ASL, with Stephen Green. **Awards:** Guggenheim Foundation Fellowship, 1971. **Address:** 704 Broadway, NYC 10003. **Dealer:** Andre Emmerich Gallery, NYC. **One-man Exhibitions:** (first) Fischbach Gallery, 1964; Dwan Gallery, NYC, 1966, 68; U. of Saskatchewan, Regina, 1970; Marlborough Gallery, Inc., NYC, 1970, 72, 74; Mackler Gallery, 1970; David Mirvish Gallery, 1970, Toronto 1976, 78; U. of Toronto, 1971; Noah Goldowsky/Richard Bellamy, NYC, 1972; Boston/MFA, 1974; Andre Emmerich Gallery, NYC, 1976, 78, 79, 80, 81, 82,

83, 85; Galerie Wentzel, Hamburg, 1976, 79; Bielefeld/Kunsthalle, 1977; Watson/deNagy, Houston, 1977; Galerie Andre Emmerich, Zurich, 1977; Harcus-Krakow Gallery, Boston, 1977, 79; Galerie Gerard Piltzer, Paris, 1978; Kunst-und-Museumsverein, Wuppertal, 1978; America House, Berlin, 1979; Amerika Haus, Hannover, 1979; Gallery Ninety-Nine, Bay Harbor Islands, Fla., 1980; Meredith Long Gallery, Houston, 1980, 81; Gallery One, Toronto, 1981; Galerie Wentzel, Hamburg, 1981, 82; Barbara Balkin Gallery, Chicago, 1982; Harcus-Krakow Gallery, Boston, 1982; The Hett Gallery Ltd., Edmonton, 1982; Martha White Gallery, Louisville, 1983; Douglas Drake Gallery, Kansas City, 1985; Elca London Gallery, Montreal, 1985. **Group:** Ridgefield/Aldrich, 1968; The Hague, 1968; Wellesley College, 1970; Toledo/MA, The Form of Color, 1970; WMAA, 1970, 72; Akron/AI, 20th Century Sculpture, 1971; Edmonton Art Gallery, Alberta, Masters of the Sixties, 1972; Montreal/Contemporain, 11 Artists Americains, 1973; NIAL, 1975; Syracuse/Everson, New Works in Clay, 1976; Wuppertal, Skulpturen und Gemalde aus New York, 1978; Syracuse/Everson, A Century of Ceramics in the United States, 1878-1978, 1979; Grand Palais, Paris, L'Amerique aux Indépendants, 1980; Sonoma State U., Works in Bronze, A Modern Survey, circ., 1984; St. Lawrence U., Pre-Postmodern: Good in the Art of Our Time, 1985. **Collections:** Art Gallery of Hamilton; Bielefeld; Boston/MFA; Denver/AM; Des Moines; Duisburg; Edmonton Art Gallery; Hirshhorn; Houston/MFA; Laumeier Sculpture Park, St. Louis; Louisville/Speed; MIT; MOMA; Paris/Beaubourg; SRGM; Storm King Art Center; U. of Sydney; Syracuse/Everson; Walker; Wellesley College.

STELLA, FRANK. b. May, 1936, Malden, Mass. **Studied:** Phillips Academy, with Patrick Morgan; Princeton U., with William Seitz, Stephen Greene. **Taught:** Dartmouth College, 1963; Brandeis U., 1969. **Awards:** International Biennial Exhibition of Paintings, Tokyo, First Prize, 1967. Skowhegan School, Medal for Painting, 1981. **Address:** 17 Jones Street, NYC 10013. **Dealers:** Leo Castelli, Inc., NYC; M. Knoedler & Co., NYC. **One-man Exhibitions:** Leo Castelli Inc., 1960, 62, 64, 66, 67, 69, 70, 73, 75, 79, 82; and two-man, 1962; Galerie Lawrence, Paris, 1961, 64; Ferus Gallery, Los Angeles, 1963, 65; Kasmin Ltd., 1964, 66, 68, 71; Harvard U., Three American Painters (three-man, with Kenneth Noland, Jules Olitski), circ., Pasadena, 1965; Pasadena/AM, 1966, 71; David Mirvish Gallery, 1966, 68, 71; Seattle/AM, 1967; Galerie Bischofberger, Zurich, 1967; Douglas Gallery, Vancouver, 1967; WGMA, 1968; Irving Blum Gallery, Los Angeles, 1968, 69, 70, 72; Bennington College, 1968; U. of Puerto Rico, 1969; Brandeis U., 1969; MOMA, 1970; Lawrence Rubin Gallery, NYC, 1970, 71; Galerie Rene Ziegler, 1970; Hayward Gallery, London, 1970; Amsterdam/Stedelijk, 1970; Joseph Helman Gallery, St. Louis, 1970; Toronto, 1971; Hansen-Fuller Gallery, 1971; John Berggruen Gallery, 1971; Knoedler Contemporary Art, 1973; Portland (Ore.) Center for the Visual Arts, 1974; U. of Washington, Seattle, 1974; ACE Gallery, Vancouver, 1974, Venice, Calif., 1975; Galerie Daniel Templon, Paris, 1975; Janie C. Lee Gallery, Houston, 1975; Galerie Andre Emmerich, Zurich, 1976; Basel, 1976; Sears Bank, Chicago, 1976; Knoedler Contemporary Art, NYC, 1976; David Mirvish Gallery, Toronto, 1976; B. R. Kornblatt Gallery, Baltimore, 1976; Galerie M., Bochum, 1977; Baltimore/MA, 1977; Bielefeld, 1977; Museum of Modern Art, Oxford, 1977; Linda Farris Gallery, Seattle, 1977; Knoedler Ltd., London, 1977; School of Visual Arts, NYC, 1978; MOMA, 1979; Brandeis U., 1979; Galerie Valeur, Nagoya, 1979; Galerie 99, Bay Harbor Islands, Fla., 1980;

Akira Ikeda Gallery, Nagoya, Japan, 1980, 81, 82, 83, 84, 85; Basel, 1980; Centre d'Arts, Bordeaux, 1980; Knoedler Kasmin Ltd., London, 1980; Koh Gallery, Tokyo, 1980; Galerie Valeur, Nagoya, Japan, 1980; M. Knoedler & Co., 81, 85; Hans Strelow Gallery, Dusseldorf, 1981; Galerie Daniel Templon, Paris, 1981; Albert White Gallery, Toronto, 1981; Andover/Phillips, 1982; Larry Gagosian Gallery, Los Angeles, 1982; Hamilton/AG, 1982; Kitakushu (Japan) City Museum of Art, 1982; MOMA, 1982; Harcus Gallery, Boston, 1983; Jacksonville/AM, 1983; Jewish Museum, 1983, 85; Knoedler Gallery, Zurich, 1983; Princeton U., 1983; SFMA, 1983; Cleveland/AM, 1984; Fort Worth, 1984; Galerie Wurthle, Wien, Switzerland, 1984; Bordeaux/Contemporaine, 1985; Richard Gray Gallery, Chicago, 1985; L. A. Louver Gallery, Venice, Calif., 1985; ICA, London, 1985. **Retrospectives:** Fort Worth, circ., 1978; U. of Michigan, circ., 1982. **Group:** Oberlin College, 3 Young Painters, 1959; MOMA, Sixteen Americans, circ., 1959; SRGM, Abstract Expressionists and Imagists, 1961; Houston/MFA, Ways and Means, 1961; A.F.A., Explorers of Space, circ., 1961-62; Seattle World's Fair, 1962; WMAA, Geometric Abstraction in America, circ., 1962; Chicago/AI, 1963, 65; Corcoran, 1963; Biennial, 1967; WGMA, The Formalists, 1963; Jewish Museum, Toward a New Abstraction, 1963; Musee Cantonal des Beaux-Arts, Lausanne, 1 Salon International de Galleries Pilotes, 1963; Brandeis U., New Directions in American Painting, 1963; Jewish Museum, Black and White, 1963; Hartford/Wadsworth, Black, White and Gray, 1964; Los Angeles/County MA, Post Painterly Abstraction, 1964; XXXII Venice Biennial, 1964; WMAA Annuals, 1964, 67; MOMA, The Responsive Eye, 1965; VII Sao Paulo Biennial, 1965; SRGM, Systemic Painting, 1966; Kansas City/Nelson, Sound, Light, Silence, 1966; Amsterdam/Stedelijk, New Shapes of Color, 1966; Expo '67,

Montreal, 1967; International Quadriennial (ROSC), 1971; High Museum, The Modern Image, 1972; Kansas City/Nelson, Color Field Painting to Post Color Field Abstraction, 1972; Houston/MFA, The Great Decade of American Abstraction: Modernist Art 1960-1970, 1974; U. of Miami, Less Is More: The Influence of the Bauhaus on American Art, 1974; VMFA, Twelve American Painters, 1974; High Museum, The New Image, 1975; SRGM, 20th Century American Drawing, 1976; Cambridge U., Jubilation, 1977; Museum of the American Foundation for the Arts, Miami, Pattern & Decorative Painting, 1977; NCFA, New Ways with Paper, 1977; Flint/Institute, Art and the Automobile, 1976; Worcester/AM, Between Sculpture & Painting, 1978; WMAA, Art about Art, 1978; Buffalo/Albright, American Painting of the 1970s, 1978; Pomona College, Black and White Are Colors, 1979; ICA, Boston, The Reductive Object, 1979; P.S. 1, Long Island City, A Great Big Drawing Show, 1979; WMAA Biennial, 1979; School of Visual Arts, NYC, Shaped Paintings, 1979; Lincoln/De Cordova, Born in Boston, 1979; ICA, U. of Pennsylvania, The Decorative Impulse, 1979; ICA, U. of Pennsylvania, Drawings: The Pluralist Decade, 1980; MOMA, Printed Art, 1980; Montgomery Museum, American Painting of the 60's and 70's, 1980; Purchase/SUNY, Hidden Desires, 1980; SFMA, Twenty American Artists, 1980; XXXIX Venice Biennial, 1980; Zurich, Reliefs, 1980; Corcoran Biennial, 1981; Royal Academy, London, A New Spirit in Painting, 1981; Amsterdam/Stedelijk, '60-'80: Attitudes/Concepts/Images, 1982; Houston/Contemporary, The Americans: The Collage, 1982; Internationale Kunstausstellung Berlin, 1982; Brooklyn Museum, The American Artist as Printmaker, 1983; WMAA Biennial, 1983; Bordeaux/Contemporaine, Art Minimal I, 1985. **Collections:** Amsterdam/Stedelijk; Baltimore/MA; Basel; Brooklyn Museum; Buffalo/Albright; Chicago/AI; Cologne;

Des Moines; Detroit/Institute; Fort Worth; Hirshhorn; Houston/MFA; Los Angeles/County MA; MOMA; NCFA; Nagoya Museum, Japan; PMA; Pasadena/AM; SFMA; Tate; WMAA; Walker. **Bibliography:** Alloway 3, 4; Axom; Battcock, ed.; Bihalji-Merin; *Black and White Are Colors;* Calas, N. and E.; *Contemporanea;* Coplans 2; De Wilde 1, 2; De Vries, ed.; *Drawings: The Pluralist Decade;* Gablik; Goldman, 1; Gooseen 3; *The Great Decade;* Haskell 5; Honisch and Jensen, eds.; Hunter, ed.; Joachimides and Rosenthal; Johnson, Ellen H.; Krauss 2; Kozloff 3; Lippard 5; Lucie-Smith; MacAgy 2; Murken-Altrogge; Rickey; Rose, B., 1, 4; **Rubin, Lawrence; Rubin 2;** Sandler 1; *7 Decades;* Tomkins, 2; Warhol and Hackett.

STELLA, JOSEPH, b. June 13, 1877, Muro Lucano, Italy; **d.** November 5, 1946, NYC. To USA, 1896; citizen, 1923. **Studied** medicine and pharmacology, 1896; ASL, 1897; New York School of Art, 1898-1900, with William M. Chase. Traveled Europe, USA. **Member:** Societe Anonyme. **Awards:** One-year scholarship to New York School of Art, 1899. **One-man Exhibitions:** (first) Carnegie, 1910; Italian National Club, NYC, 1913; Bourgeois Gallery, NYC, 1920; Societe Anonyme, NYC; Dudensing Gallery, NYC, 1924; The New Gallery, NYC, 1926; Des Moines Art Association, 1926; Curt Valentine Gallery, NYC, 1926, 28, 31, 35; Angiporto Galleria, Naples, 1929; Galerie Sloden, Paris, 1930; Washington Place, Paris, 1932; Cooperative Gallery, Newark 1937; A.A.A. Gallery, NYC, 1941; M. Knoedler & Co., NYC, 1942; ACA Gallery, 1943; The Zabriskie Gallery, 1958, 59, 60, 61; MOMA, circ., 1960 (drawings); Robert Schoelkopf Gallery, NYC, 1963, 64, 66, 70, 77, 79, 81, 84; U. of Maryland, 1968; Rutgers U., 1970; Hirshhorn, 1983. **Retrospective:** Newark Museum, 1939; WMAA, 1963. **Collections:** Indiana State College; Iowa State Education Association; MMA; MOMA; U. of Nebraska; Newark Museum; WMAA; Walker; Yale U. **Bibliography:** *Arthur Dove: The Years of Collage; Avant-Garde Painting and Sculpture in America, 1910-25;* **Baur 3,** 5, 7; Bethers; Biddle 4; Blanchard; Blesh 1; Brown 2; Cahill and Barr, eds.; Christensen; Dreier 2; Eliot; Elsen 2; Flanagan; *Forerunners; From Foreign Shores;* Frost; Gerdts; Goodrich and Baur 1; Haftman; Hess, T.B., 1; Hulten; Hunter 6; Janis and Blesh 1; Janis, S.; Kozloff 3; Kuh 1; Levin 2; McCoubrey 1; McCurdy, ed.; Mellquist, Mendelowitz; Poore; Richardson, E.P.; Ritchie 1; Rose, B., 1, 4; Rosenblum 1; Rubin 1; Seitz, 3; Soby 5; Tashijian; Tomkins and Time-Life Books. Archives.

STEPHAN, GARY. b. December 24, 1942, Brooklyn, N.Y. **Studied:** Parsons School of Design, NYC, 1960-61; ASL, 1961; Pratt Institute, 1961-64; San Francisco Art Institute, 1964-67, MFA. Traveled France, Italy. **Taught:** School of Visual Arts, NYC, 1973. **Address:** 530 Canal Street, NYC 10013. **Dealer:** Mary Boone Gallery, NYC. **One-man Exhibitions:** (first) David Whitney Gallery, NYC, 1969, 70, 71; Quay Gallery, San Francisco, 1971; Galleri Hans R. Neu-

endorf, Cologne, 1972; Galleri Hans R. Neuendorf, Hamburg, 1972; The Texas Gallery, Houston 1973, 75, 76, 78; Galleri Ostergren, Malmo, 1973; Galleri Fabian Carlson, Goteborg, 1973; Weinberg Gallery, San Francisco, 1973, 75, 77; Alfred/SUNY, 1974; Bykert Gallery, NYC, 1974, 75, 76; Mary Boone Gallery, NYC, 1978, 79, 80, 81, 82, 83; Arnold Gallery, Atlanta, 1978; Margo Leavin Gallery, Los Angeles, 1979, 80, 81, 83; Mattingly-Baker Gallery, Dallas, 1981; The Greenberg Gallery, St. Louis, 1982; Daniel Weinberg Gallery, San Francisco, 1982; Texas Gallery, Houston, 1983; Marlborough Gallery, NYC, 1984; Portico Row Gallery, Philadelphia, 1984; U. of Rhode Island, 1984. **Group:** WMAA Biennials, 1969, 71, 73; Pratt Institute, NYC, Recent Abstract Paintings, 1973; P.S. 1, Long Island City, The Altered Photograph/20 Walls, 20 Curators, 1979; NYU, American Painting: The Eighties, 1979; MIT, Great Big Drawings, 1982; WMAA, Five Painters in New York, 1984; MOMA, International Survey of Painting and Sculpture, 1984; Milwaukee, Currents 6, 1984. **Bibliography:** Pincus-Witten 2.

Gary Stephan   *Madame As Recamier*   1986

STERNBERG, HARRY. b. July 19, 1904, NYC. **Studied:** ASL; and privately with Harry Wickey. Traveled Mexico, Canada, Great Britain. **Taught:** ASL, 1933-68; New School for Social Research, 1942-45, 1950-51; Brigham Young U., 1958; U. of Southern California, 1959-69; Palomar College, 1974. Directed and produced a film, *The Many Worlds of Art*, 1960. Federal A.P. (murals): US Post Offices, Sellersville, Pa., and Chester, Pa. (1935-37); advisor on graphic project. **Commission:** Mural, Escondido, Calif. Community Clinic, 1979. **Awards:** Fifty Prints of the Year, 1930; Fine Prints of the Year, 1932, 33, 34; Guggenheim Foundation Fellowship, 1936; 100 Prints of the Year, 1938; The Print Club, Philadelphia, 1942; Audubon Artists, 1955; AAAL, **P.P.,** 1972. **Address:** 1606 Conway Drive, Escondido, CA 92027. **Dealer:** Mary Ryan Gallery, NYC. **One-man Exhibitions:** Keppel & Co., NYC, 1937; Weyhe Gallery, 1941; ACA Gallery, 1947, 50, 56, 58, 61, 62, 64, 66, 68, 70, 72, 74; U. of Minnesota, 1957; Garelick's Gallery, Detroit, 1958; Brigham Young U., 1958; Idyllwild Art School, 1958; Gallery Eight, Santa Barbara, 1961; Salt Lake Art Center, Salt Lake City, 1961; Art and Design Gallery, Nonsall, Calif., 1976; Tobey C. Moss Gallery, Los Angeles, 1986; San Diego Print Club, 1986. **Group:** WMAA; Chicago/AI; Walker; U. of Minnesota; de Young; Brooklyn Museum; MOMA; 100th Anniversary Exhibition of ASL, NYC, 1976. **Collections:** ASL; Andover/Phillips; Auckland; Bibliotheque Nationale; Brooklyn Museum; Chicago/AI; City College, NYC; Cleveland/MA, de Young; Harvard U.; Library of Congress; MMA; MOMA; U. of Minnesota; NYPL; Phillips; U. of Southern California; Syracuse U.; Tel Aviv; Victoria and Albert Museum; WMAA; Walker. **Bibliography:** American Artists Congress, Inc.; American Artists Group Inc. 3; Hayter 1; *Index of 20th Century Artists;* Mellquist; Reese; **Smith, A.; Sternberg, 1, 2;** Zigrosser 1. Archives.

STERNE, MAURICE. b. 1878, Libau, on the Baltic; **d.** 1957, NYC. To USA, 1889. **Studied:** Cooper Union, 1892; NAD, 1894-99, with Thomas Eakins. Traveled Europe, India, Burma, Java, Egypt. **Member:** National Fine Arts Commission, 1945-51. **Commissions:** Justice Department, Washington, D.C. (mural); Fairmount Park, Philadelphia (monument); Rogers-Kennedy Memorial, Worcester, Mass., 1926. **Awards:** Mooney Traveling Scholarship, 1904; Chicago/AI, The Mr. & Mrs. Frank G. Logan Prize, 1928; Corcoran, William A. Clark Prize and Corcoran Gold Medal, 1930; Carnegie, Hon. Men., 1930; Golden Gate International Exposition, San Francisco, 1939; NAD Annual, Andrew Carnegie Prize, 1959. **One-man Exhibitions:** Paul Cassirer Gallery, Berlin, 1910; Berlin Photograph Co., NYC, 1910, 15; Chicago/AI, 1917; Bourgeois Gallery, NYC, 1917, 22; Boston Arts Club, 1919; Scott and Fowles Gallery, NYC, 1926; Reinhardt Galleries, NYC, 1928, 30; SFMA, 1936, 38; Honolulu Academy, 1939; The Milch Gallery, 1962. **Retrospective:** MOMA, 1933; Phillips, 1952; Hirschl & Adler Galleries, Inc., NYC, 1962. **Group:** Rome National Art Quadrennial, 1925; Chicago/AI; Corcoran; WMAA; SFMA; Brooklyn Museum; Newark Museum. **Collections:** Carnegie; Chicago/AI; Cleveland/MA; Cologne; Corcoran; Detroit/Institute; MMA; Phillips; RISD; San Diego; Yale U. **Bibliography:** Baur 7; Biddle 4; Birnbaum; Blesh 1; Brown; Cahill and Barr, eds.; Cheney; Coke 2; Eliot; Genauer; Goodrich and Baur 1; Hall; *Index of 20th Century Artists;* Jackman; Jewell 2; **Kallem;** Kent, N.; Kootz 1; Mather 1; Mayerson, ed.; McCurdy, ed.; Mendelowitz; Neuhaus; Parkes; Phillips 2; Richardson, E.P.; Ringel, ed.; Rose, B., 1; Sachs. Archives.

STEVENSON, HAROLD. b. March 11, 1929, Idabel, Okla. **Studied:** U. of Oklahoma; U. of Mexico; ASL. Traveled Europe, Mexico, USA; resided

Paris ten years. Subject of the Andy Warhol film *Harold*, 1964. Designed the Tennessee Williams gold medallion for National Committee for the Literary Arts, 1981. **Taught:** Austin College, Artist-in-Residence. **Address:** 302 Southeast Adams, Isabel, OK 74745; and 21-14 45th Avenue, Long Island City, N.Y. 11101. **Dealer:** Keith Green Gallery, NYC. **One-man Exhibitions:** (first) Alexandre Iolas Gallery, NYC, 1956, also 1958, 65, 72, 73, 74; Galerie la Cour d'Ingres, Paris, 1960; Iris Clert Gallery, 1962, 63, 68; Robert Fraser Gallery, 1962; Richard Feigen Gallery, Chicago, Los Angeles, and NYC, 1964; Galerie Svensk-Franska, Stockholm, 1965; American Embassy, Paris, 1969; Knoedler & Co., Paris, 1970; Galeria Blu, Milan, 1971; La Medusa Gallery, Rome, 1970, 73; Alexandre Iolas Gallery, Paris, 1973; Galeria Zoumbulaskis, Athens, 1973; Brooks Jackson Iolas Gallery, NYC, 1976, 77, 82, 84; Galerie Iris Clert, Paris, 1979; Keith Green Gallery, 1986. **Group:** Salon du Mai, Paris, 1962; WMAA Annual, 1964; Musée de la Haye, Amsterdam, 1964; Palais des Beaux-Arts, Brussels, 1965; Galerie Svensk-Franska, Stockholm, 1965; ICA, London, The Obsessive Image, 1968; Dusseldorf/Kunsthalle, Prospect '68, 1968; HemisFair '68, San Antonio, Tex., 1968; Musée du Louvre, Paris, Comparaisons, 1969; CNAC, L'Image en Question, 1971; Paris, Salon d-Automne, 1971; Musée du Louvre, La famille des portraits, 1980; Paris/Beaubourg, Americans in Paris, 1979; IEF, Twentieth Century American Drawings: The Figure in Context, circ., 1984. **Bibliography:** Lippard 5. Archives.

STILL, CLYFFORD. b. November 30, 1904, Grandin, N.D.; **d.** June 23, 1980, Baltimore, Md. **Studied:** Spokane U., 1933, BA; Washington State College, MA. **Taught:** Yaddo, 1934, 35; Washington State College, 1935-45; College of William and Mary, 1944; California School of Fine Arts 1946-50; "Subject of the Artist," NYC, 1947-48; Hunter College, 1952; Brooklyn Museum School, 1952; U. of Pennsylvania, 1963; Encouraged California students to form a group, which became the Metart Gallery. **Awards:** Skowhegan School, Medal for Painting, 1975; AAAL, award of merit medal for painting, 1972; Hon. DFA, North Dakota U., 1972; Hon. DFA, SFAI, 1976. **One-man Exhibitions:** (first) SFMA, 1943; Art of This Century, NYC, 1946; Metart Gallery, San Francisco, 1950; ICA, U. of Pennsylvania, 1964; Marlborough-Gerson Gallery Inc., 1969, 71; Buffalo/Albright, 1980. **Retrospective:** Buffalo/Albright, 1959; MMA, 1979. **Group:** MOMA, Fifteen Americans, circ., 1952; MOMA, The New American Painting, circ. Europe, 1958-59; Documenta II, Kassel, 1959; MOMA, The New American Painting and Sculpture, 1969; Corcoran Biennial, 1971; Carnegie, International, 1978. **Collections:** Baltimore/MA; Buffalo/Albright; MOMA; Phillips; SFMA; WMAA. **Bibliography:** Alloway 4; Ashton 5; Battcock, ed.; Blesh 1; Chipp; **Clyfford Still;** Downes, ed.; Finkelstein; Flanagan; Gaunt; Goosen 1; *The Great Decade;* Greenberg 1; Haftman; Hess, T.B., 1; Hobbs and Levin; Honisch and Jensen, eds.; Hunter 1, 6; Hunter, ed.; O'Neill, ed.; McChesney; McCurdy, ed.; *Metro;* Murken-Altrogge; Ponente; Read 2; Richardson, E.P.; Rickey; Rose, B., 1; Rosenblum 2; Rubin 1; Sandler 1; Seuphor 1; Tomkins 2; Tuchman, ed. Archives.

STONE, SYLVIA. b. June 18, 1928, Toronto, Canada. **Studied:** ASL, 1950-52, with Vaclav Vytlacil and Morris Kantor. Traveled Europe, Central America, Morocco. **Taught:** Brooklyn College, 1968-. **Commissions:** Xerox Corp., NYC, 1969; Sunrise Mall, Massapequa, N.Y., 1972; GSA, Federal Court House, Ft. Lauderdale, 1979. **Awards:** CAPS, 1971; National Endowment for the Arts, grant; City University of New York, research grant, 1977.

Address: 519 Broadway, NYC 10012. **Dealer:** Andre Emmerich Gallery, NYC. **One-man Exhibitions:** Brata Gallery, NYC (two-man), 1959; Tibor de Nagy, NYC, 1967, 68, 69; Andre Emmerich Gallery, NYC, 1972, 75, 78, 79, 80; Bennington College, 1978. **Group:** Newark Museum, Cool Art, 1968; Walker, 14 Sculptors: The Industrial Edge, 1969; WMAA, 1969, 71, 73; ICA, U. of Pennsylvania, Plastics and New Art, 1969; Milwaukee, A Plastic Presence, circ., 1969; WMAA Biennials, 1970, 73; U. of North Carolina, Works on Paper, 1971; Indianapolis, 1974; Hayward, London, The Condition of Sculpture, 1975; WMAA, 200 Years of American Sculpture, 1976; Albright College, Perspective 1976, 1976. **Collections:** Buffalo/Albright; Hartford/Wadsworth; The New Museum, NYC; University of North Carolina; Omni Corp., NYC; Ridgefield/Aldrich; WMAA; Walker. **Bibliography:** Friedman, M., 2.

STOUT, MYRON. b. December 5, 1908, Denton, Tex. **Studied:** North Texas State U., 1930, BS; Columbia U., with C. J. Martin, MA; Academia San Carlos, Mexico City, 1933; Hofmann School. US Army and Air Force, 1943-45. Traveled France, Italy, Mexico, Greece, Turkey. **Taught:** Fine Arts Work Center, Provincetown, Mass., Artist-in-Residence, 1968; Kamehameha Schools, Honolulu, 1938-45, 46-49. **Awards:** National Council on the Arts, 1966; J. S. Guggenheim Fellowship, 1969; AAIAL, Award of Merit, 1982. **Address:** 4 Brewster Street, Provincetown, MA 02657; 716 Ector, Denton, TX 76201. **Dealer:** Oil and Steel Gallery, Long Island City, N.Y. **One-man Exhibitions:** (first) The Stable Gallery, NYC, 1954, Hansa Gallery, NYC, 1957, 58, (three-man); Houston/Contemporary, 1977. **Retrospective:** WMAA, 1980. **Group:** WMAA Annual, 1958; Carnegie, 1959; ICA, Boston, 100 Works on Paper, circ., Europe, 1959; ICA, Boston, Paint-

ings, USA, 1959; A.F.A., New Talent, circ., 1960; WMAA, Geometric Abstraction in America, circ., 1962; Jewish Museum, 1964; SRGM, American Drawings, 1964; Corcoran Biennial; Buffalo/Albright, Plus by Minus, 1968; WMAA, American Drawings: 1963-1973, 1973. **Collections:** Brooklyn Museum; Buffalo/Albright; Carnegie; Chicago/AI; Hirshhorn; MOMA; McCrory Corp., NYC; NYU; National Gallery; Portland, Me./MA; SRGM; WMAA; Woodward Foundation. **Bibliography:** MacAgy 2.; Sandler 1; Schwartz 1, 2. Archives.

STROUD, PETER ANTHONY. b. May 23, 1921, London, England. **Studied:** London University; Central School of Arts and Crafts, London, 1950, BFA, 1952, BA. Ed., 1953, MFA. British Army, 1939-45. Traveled Europe, Near East. **Taught:** Maidstone College of Art, 1962-63; Bennington College, 1963-64, 1966-68; Hunter College, 1965-66; Maryland Institute, 1968; Rutgers U., 1968-. **Commissions:** Royal Festival Hall, London, "Groupe Espace" Project, 1958; International Union of Architects, London (mural), 1961; State School, Leverkusen, Germany (mural), 1963; Manufacturers Hanover Trust Co., NYC (mural), 1969; Watertown (N.Y.) State Office Building, 1970. **Address:** % Art Dept., Rutgers U., New Brunswick, N.J. 08903. **One-man Exhibitions:** ICA, London, 1961; Bennington College, 1964; U. of Vermont, 1966; Marlborough-Gerson Gallery Inc., 1966; Nicholas Wilder Gallery, 1967; Axiom Gallery, London, 1968; Galerie Muller, 1969; Gertrude Kasle Gallery, 1969; Rutgers U., 1969; Max Hutchinson Gallery, 1970, 72, 73; Bernard Jacobson Gallery, London, 1971; Hoya Gallery, London, 1974; Annely Juda Fine Art, London, 1977; Union College, N.J., 1978. **Group:** Groupe Espace, London and Paris, 1957; New Vision Centre, London, Form and Experiment, 1957; Drian Gallery, London, Construction

Great Britain: 1950-60, 1960; Carnegie, 1961, 64; Leverkusen, Construction 1962, 1962; Kunsthalle, Basel, Seven Young British Painters, 1963; MOMA, The Responsive Eye, 1965; Jewish Museum, European Painters Today, 1968; Museum of Modern Art, Oxford, Painters of the Sixties, 1969; Melbourne/National, Form and Structure, 1970; U. of California, Santa Barbara, Constructivist Tendencies, circ., 1970; Ulster Museum, From Sickert to Conceptual Art, 1971; Finch College, NYC, The Constructivist Tradition, 1972. **Collections:** Detroit/Institute; Leverkusen; Los Angeles/County MA; Newark Museum; Pasadena/AM; SRGM; San Diego; Tate; Trenton/State; U. of Vermont; Whitworth.

SUGARMAN, GEORGE. b. May 11, 1912, NYC. **Studied:** Zadkine School of Sculpture, Paris, 1955-56. Traveled Mexico, USA, Europe; resided Paris, 1951-55. **Taught:** Hunter College, 1960-; Yale U., 1967-68. **Commissions:** Geigy Chemical Corp. (wall structure); Xerox Data Systems, El Segundo, Calif.; First National Bank of St. Paul, Minn.; Albert M. Greenfield School, Philadelphia; City of Leverkusen, West Germany; South Mall, Albany; Brussels World Trade Center; Garmatz Federal Building, Baltimore; International Building, Miami, Fla., Airport, 1977; Federal Court House and Office Building, Baltimore, 1976-78; Detroit General Hospital, 1980. **Awards:** Longview Foundation Grant, 1960, 61, 63; Carnegie, Second Prize, 1961; Ford Foundation, 1965; National Council on the Arts, 1966; AAIAL, 1985. **Address:** 21 Bond Street, NYC 10012. **Dealer:** Robert Miller Gallery, NYC. **One-man Exhibitions:** Union Dime Savings, NYC,

George Sugarman *For Watteau* 1984

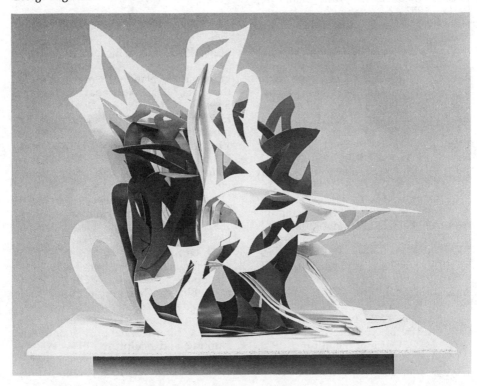

1958; Widdifield Gallery, NYC, 1960; Stephen Radich Gallery, 1961, 64, 65, 66; Philadelphia Art Alliance, 1965; Dayton's Gallery 12, Minneapolis, 1966; Fischbach Gallery, 1966-69; Galerie Schmela, 1967; Ziegler Gallery, 1967; Kunsthalle, Basel, 1969; Krefeld/Kaiser Wilhelm, 1969; One Hundred and Eighteen: An Art Gallery, Minneapolis, 1971; Dag Hammarskjold Plaza, NYC, 1974; The Zabriskie Gallery, 1974; Robert Miller Gallery, NYC, 1978, 79, 80, 82, 85; Galerie Liatowitach, Basel, 1979; Galerie Rudolf Zwirner, Cologne, 1980; Smith-Andersen Gallery, Palo Alto, 1981; Springfield, Mass./MFA, 1981; Galerie Ziegler, Zurich, 1981; San Jose State U., 1982; Fuller Goldeen Gallery, San Francisco, 1984. **Retrospectives:** Kunsthalle, Basel, circ., Amsterdam, West Germany, 1969; Omaha/Joslyn, circ., 1981; WMAA, 1985. **Group:** A.F.A., Sculpture in Wood, circ., 1941-42; Salon de la Jeune Sculpture, Paris, 1952, 54; Salon des Realites Nouvelles, Paris, 1954; Silvermine Guild, 1958; Claude Bernard, Paris, 1960; Carnegie, 1961; Seattle World's Fair, 1962; Hartford/Wadsworth, 1962; A.F.A., Sculpture for the Home, circ., 1962; Chicago/AI, 1962, 66; VII Sao Paulo Biennial, 1963; Walker, Ten American Sculptors, 1964; Jewish Museum, Recent American Sculpture, 1964; ICA, U. of Pennsylvania, 1964; New York World's Fair, 1964-65; NYU, 1965; Flint/Institute, 1965; WMAA, Art of the U.S., 1670-1966, 1966; Los Angeles/County MA, American Sculpture of the Sixties, 1967; WMAA Sculpture Annuals, 1967, 69; Foundation Maeght, L'Art Vivant, circ., French museums, 1968; XXXIV Venice Biennial, 1968; MOMA, 1969; Foundation Maeght, L'Art Vivant, 1970; U. of Nebraska, American Sculpture, 1970; WMAA, 1970, 73; Cincinnati/Contemporary, Monumental Art, 1970; Middelheim Park, Antwerp, XI Sculpture Biennial, 1971; MIT, Outdoor Sculpture, 1972; WMAA, American Drawings: 1963-1973, 1973; Newport, R. I., Monu-

menta, 1974; NCFA, Sculpture: American Directions, 1945-1975, 1975; WMAA, 200 Years of American Sculpture, 1976; ICA, U. of Pennsylvania, The Decorative Impulse, circ., 1979; Buffalo/Albright; ICA, U. of Pennsylvania; NCFA, Across the Nation, 1980; Rice U., Variants, 1981; Houston/Contemporary, The Americans: The Collage, 1982; Pittsfield/Berkshire, New Decorative Art, 1983; WMAA, The Third Dimension, 1984. **Collections:** Basel; Buffalo/Albright; Chicago/AI; Ciba-Geigy Corp.; Kalamazoo/Institute; Krefeld/Haus Lange; MMA; MIT; MOMA; Museum Schloss Marberg; NCFA; NYU; St. Louis/City; The Singer Company, Inc.; Torrington Mfg. Corp.; WMAA; Walker; Wuppertal. **Bibliography:** Battcock, ed.; Calas, N. and E.; Danto; Davies; Day; Janis and Blesh 1; *Monumenta*; Phillips, Lisa; Rickey; Sandler 1; Tuchman 1. Archives.

SULTAN, DONALD. b. 1951, Asheville, N.C. **Studied:** U. of North Carolina, 1973, BFA; Chicago Art Institute School, 1975, MFA. **Awards:** CAPS grant, 1978; National Endowment for the Arts, 1980. **Address:** 54 Leonard Street, NYC 10013. **Dealer:** Blum Helman Gallery, NYC. **One-man Exhibitions:** N.A.M.E. Gallery, Chicago, 1976; Artists Space, NYC, 1977; P.S. 1, Long Island City, 1977; The Willard Gallery, NYC, 1979, 80; Young Hoffman Gallery, Chicago, 1979; Daniel Weinberg Gallery, San Francisco, 1981; Blum Helman Gallery, 1982, 84, 85; Gallerie Hans Strelow, Düsseldorf, 1982; Akira Ikeda, Tokyo, 1983. **Group:** WMAA Biennial, 1979; U. of Chicago, Visionary Images, 1979; Indianapolis, 1980, 82; MOMA, Prints from Blocks: Gauguin to Now, 1983; Palacio de Velazquez, Madrid, Tendencias en Nueva York, circ., 1983; MOMA, International Survey of Recent Painting and Sculpture, 1984; Walker, Images and Impressions: Painters Who Print, 1984. **Collections:** An-

Donald Sultan   *Five Lemons and Tangerine,*
April 21, 1986   1986

dover/Phillips;   Boston/MFA;   Buffalo/Albright;   Canberra/National;
Chicago/AI;   Dallas/MFA;   Des
Moines; High Museum; Kitakyushu
Museum; La Jolla; MMA; MOMA;
Purchase/SUNY;   SFMA;   SRGM;
Toledo/MA; Walker. **Bibliography:**
Hiromoto.

SUMMERS, CAROL. b. December 26,
1925, Kingston, N.Y. **Studied:** Bard
College, with Stefan Hirsch, Louis
Schanker, 1951, BA. US Marine Corps,
1944-48. Traveled the Orient, Italy,
France, Czechoslovakia, Central America, India, Nepal. **Taught:** Hunter College,   1963-64;   Brooklyn   Museum
School; School of Visual Arts, NYC;
Pratt Graphics Center, NYC; Columbia
U.; Haystack Mountain School of
Crafts; U. of Pennsylvania; SFAI, 1973.
Awards: Italian Government Travel
Grant, 1955; L. C. Tiffany Grant, 1955,
61; J. S. Guggenheim Fellowship, 1959;
Fulbright Fellowship (Italy), 1961. **Address:** 131 Prospect Court, Santa Cruz,
CA 95065. **Dealer:** Christie's Contemporary, NYC. **One-man Exhibitions:**
(first) The Contemporaries, NYC, 1954,
also 1961; MOMA, circ., 1964-66;
A.A.A. Gallery, NYC, 1967, 80; Bard

College, 1968; ADI Gallery, San Francisco, 1980; Beck Gallery, Boston, 1986;
Christie's Contemporary, NYC, 1986.
Retrospective: SFMA, 1967; Brooklyn
Museum, 1977. **Group:** Major national
print exhibitions. **Collections:** Baltimore/MA; Bibliotheque Nationale;
Boston/MFA; Bradley U.; Brooklyn Museum;   Chicago/AI;   Cincinnati/AM;
Cornell U.; Free Library of Philadelphia; U. of Kentucky; Library of Congress;   Los   Angeles/County   MA;
Lugano; MMA; MOMA; Milwaukee-Downer College; U. of Minnesota;
NYPL;   National   Gallery;   U.   of
Nebraska; New Britain; Ohio U.; PMA;
Seattle/AM; U. of Tennessee; U. of
Utah; Victoria and Albert Museum;
Walker. **Bibliography:** *Carol Summers.*
Woodcuts 1950-1967. Archives.

SUTTMAN, PAUL. b. July 16, 1933,
Enid, Okla. **Studied:** Adelphi College,
with Robert Cronbach; U. of New Mexico, with Adja Yunkers, Robert Mallory, 1956, BFA; Cranbrook, with Tex
Schwetz, Maija Groten, 1958, MFA;
with Giacomo Manzu, 1960. Traveled
Europe, Latin America; resided Mexico, Italy. **Taught:** U. of Michigan,
1958-62; Dartmouth College, 1973.
Commissions: Roswell (N.M.) Museum and Art Center (bronze relief for
facade); National Educational Television, 1961 ("The Bronze Man," a film
illustrating   casting   techniques);
Hughes, Hatcher & Suffrin Building,
Detroit, 1964; U. of Michigan, 1967.
Awards: Cranbrook, Horace H. Rackham Research Grant (Florence, Italy),
1960; Fulbright Fellowship (Paris),
1963; Prix de Rome, 1965, 66, 67; Ingram Merrill Foundation Grant, 1972.
One-man Exhibitions: Roswell, 1959;
Park Gallery, Detroit, 1959, 62; Donald
Morris Gallery, 1959, 62, 65, 67, 69; U.
of Michigan, 1962; Terry Dintenfass,
Inc., 1962, 64, 65, 67, 69, 71, 73; Felix
Landau   Gallery,   1970;   Robinson
Galleries, 1971; Galleria Nuovo Carpine, Sardinia, 1972; Dartmouth College, 1973. **Group:** Youngstown/Butler;

Detroit/Institute; U. of Michigan; Santa Barbara/MA; de Young; U. of New Mexico; American Academy, Rome, 1966-68; Musee Rodin, Paris, International Sculpture, 1968; Indianapolis/Herron, 1969; PAFA Annual, 1969; USIS, Rome, 1969, 70, 72; Colorado Springs Fine Arts Center, Ten Take Ten, 1977. **Collections:** Detroit/Institute; First National Bank of Chicago; Kalamazoo/Institute; Layton School of Art; MOMA; Macomb County Community College; U. of Michigan; Roswell. **Bibliography:** Walker. Archives.

SUZUKI, JAMES HIROSHI. b. September 19, 1933, Yokohama, Japan. **Studied:** Privately with Yoshio Markino; Portland (Me.) School of Fine and Applied Art, 1952; The Corcoran School of Art, 1953-54. To USA, 1952. Traveled USA. Japan. **Taught:** U. of California, Berkeley, 1962-63; U. of Kentucky, 1966-68. **Awards:** Corcoran, Eugene Weiss Scholarship, 1954; John Hay Whitney Fellowship, 1958; Silvermine Guild, Larry Aldrich Prize, 1959. **Address:** 2021 E. 29th Street, Oakland, CA 94606. **Dealer:** Braunstein Quay Gallery, San Francisco. **One-man Exhibitions:** (first) The Graham Gallery, 1957, also 1958, 59, 61, 62; U. of California, Berkeley, 1963; Nihonbashi Gallery, Tokyo, 1963; Seido (Gallery), Kyoto, 1963; Comara Gallery, 1970; Palos Verdes, 1970; Quay Gallery, 1973; Braunstein Quay Gallery, 1976, 78; Sacramento State U., 1978. **Group:** Corcoran, 1956, 58, 60; WMAA; Baltimore/MA; ICA, Boston, Contemporary Painters of Japanese Origin in America; Cincinnati/AM; Des Moines; A.F.A., Cross-Currents, circ., 1957-58; Syracuse/Everson, 1958; Silvermine Guild, 1959; Hartford/Wadsworth, 1959; Houston/MFA, Waning Moon and Rising Sun, 1959; U. of Nebraska, 1960; SFMA, 1963, 64; Tokyo/Modern, 1964; SFMA, Aesthetics of Graffiti, 1978. **Collections:** Corcoran; Hartford/Wadsworth; Kamakura; McDonnell & Co. Inc.; Rockefeller Institute; Tokyo/Modern; Toldeo/MA.

SWAIN, ROBERT. b. December 7, 1940, Austin, Texas. **Studied:** American U., Washington, D.C., BA, 1964. Traveled Central America, Europe. **Taught:** Hunter College, 1968. **Awards:** Guggenheim Foundation Fellowship, 1969; National Endowment for the Arts, grant, 1976; CAPS, 1982. **Address:** 57 Leonard Street, NYC 10013. **One-man Exhibitions:** (first) The Thenen Gallery, NYC, 1965; Fischbach Gallery, NYC, 1968, 69; Syracuse/Everson, 1974; Susan Caldwell Inc., NYC, 1974, 75, 78, 81; The Texas Gallery, Houston, 1975; Columbus, 1975; Lockwood-Matthews Mansion Museum, Norwalk, Conn., 1978; Darien, Conn., Library, 1978; Nina Freudenheim Gallery, Buffalo, 1978; Toni Birckhead Gallery, Cincinnati, 1980. **Group:** MOMA, The Art of the Real, circ., 1968; Corcoran Biennial, 1968; U. of North Carolina, Art on Paper, 1968; WMAA, The Structure of Color, 1971; Indianapolis, 1974; MOMA, Color as Language, circ., 1974; UCLA, Fourteen Abstract Painters, 1975; Hunter College, Repetitions, 1985. **Collections:** Amerada Hess Corp.; American Republic Insurance Co.; Ardsley; Ball State U.; Buffalo/Albright; Chase Manhattan Bank; Ciba-Geigy Corp.; Columbus; Corcoran; Denver/AM; Detroit/Institute; The Harris Bank; Lehman Brothers; MMA; McCrory Corp.; Milwaukee; Mobil Oil Co.; Prudential Insurance Co. of America; Syracuse/Everson; Travenol Laboratories; Trina Inc.; VMFA; Walker.

T

TAKAL, PETER. b. December 8, 1905, Bucharest, Rumania. **Studied:** Paris, Berlin. To USA, 1939; citizen, 1944. Traveled Europe, Africa, North and South America, Mexico. **Taught:** Beloit College, 1965; Central College, Iowa, 1968. **Member:** Artists Equity; Color Print Society, SAGA. **Commissions** (graphic art): International Graphic Arts Society, 1956, 59, 63; Print Club of Cleveland, 1956, 57; The Contemporaries, NYC, 1957; A.A.A. Gallery, NYC, 1958. **Awards:** The Print Club, Philadelphia, Max Katzman Award, 1957; Silvermine Guild, Nancy A. Fuller Award, 1959; Yaddo Fellowship, 1961; Pasadena/AM Annual, **P.P.**, 1962; Tamarind Fellowship, 1963-64; Ford Foundation/A.F.A., Artist-in-Residence, 1965. **Address:** Saylorsburg, PA 18353; 116 East 68th Street, NYC 10021; 40 rue du Mole, CH 1201, Geneva, Switzerland. **Dealers:** Weyhe Gallery; A.A.A. Gallery, NYC; Gallerie Benador, Geneva. **One-man Exhibitions:** (first) Gallery Gurlitt, Berlin, 1932; Galerie Zak, Paris, 1933; Galerie Jeanne Castel, Paris, 1935, 37; Galerie Derche, Casablanca, 1937; Katherine Kuh Gallery, Chicago, 1937, 39, 41; Galerie Charpentier, Paris, 1939; Chauvin Gallery, Algiers, 1939; Carstairs Gallery, NYC, 1940; Santa Barbara/MA, 1941, 57; de Young, 1942; Karl Nierendorf Gallery, NYC, 1942; Artists' Gallery, NYC, 1954; Duveen/Graham Gallery, NYC, 1955, 58, 1957-58 (circ., American museums and colleges); Wittenborn Gallery, NYC, 1956; Pasadena/AM, 1956; Minneapolis/Institute, 1957; Los Angeles/County MA, 1957; Dallas/MFA, 1957; La Jolla, 1957; Carnegie College of Art, 1957; Mills College, 1957; The Print Club of Philadelphia, 1958; Kansas City/Nelson, 1958; Cleveland/MA, 1959; Memphis/Brooks, 1959; Galeria de Arte Mexicano, Mexico City, 1959; Smithsonian, circ., USA, 1959-60; Cushing Galleries, Dallas, 1959-60, 1966; The Contemporaries, NYC, 1959, 60, 62, 66; Palazzo Strozzi, Florence, Italy, 1960; Sabersky Gallery, Los Angeles, 1961; Kestner-Museum, circ., Germany, 1961-62; Philadelphia Art Alliance, 1962; Mary Harriman Gallery, Inc., Boston, 1964; Weyhe Gallery, 1964, 65, 68, 72; Beloit College, 1965; Scranton/Everhart, 1967; Central College, 1968; Carnegie/Mellon U., 1969; Hunt Botanical Library, Pittsburgh, 1969; Galerie Benador, Geneva, 1977. **Retrospective:** Galerie du Grand-Mezel, Geneva, 1970. **Group:** Salon d'Automne, Paris, 1933-35; A.F.A.; PAFA, 1953, 59, 60, 63, 65, 67, 69; Brooklyn Museum, Print Biennials, 1955-64; WMAA Annuals, 1955-60, 1962-64; Library of Congress Print Annuals, 1955, 58, 59, 60, 62; MOMA, Recent Drawings USA, 1956; The Print Club, Philadelphia, 1956-58, 1961-63; Boston Printmakers, 1956-59, 1962, 63, 64; ICA, Boston, 100 Works on Paper, circ., Europe, 1959; PCA, American Prints Today, circ., 1959-62; Gallery of Modern Art, Ljubljana, Yugoslavia, IV International Exhibition of Prints, 1961; MOMA, circ., Europe and Far East, 1961 (drawings); St. Paul Gallery, Drawings, USA, 1963; SAGA Annual, 1963, 65; Minnesota/MA, 1963; 1966-68, 1971-73; The Japan Print Association, Tokyo, 1967; WMAA, 1968, 69; MOMA, Tamarind: Homage to Lithography, 1969; SAGA, 1979. **Col-**

lections: Achenbach Foundation; Alboin College; Andover/Phillips; Baltimore/MA; Beloit College; Berlin/National; Bibliotheque Nationale; Brandeis U.; Bremen; Brooklyn Museum; U. of California, Berkeley; Carnegie; Chicago/AI; Cincinnati/AM; Cleveland/MA; Copenhagen; Dallas/MFA; Darmstadt/Hessisches; de Young; Exeter; Fort Worth; Graphische Sammlung der E.T.H.; Grenoble; Hamburg; Indianapolis/Herron; Karlsruhe; Kassel; Kestner-Museum; Kupferstichkabinett; La Jolla; Library of Congress; Lincoln, Mass./De Cordova; Los Angeles/County MA; MMA; MOMA; U. of Maine; Mills College; U. of Minnesota; Minnesota/MA; Montreal/MFA; NYPL; NYU; National Gallery; Omaha/Joslyn; Oran; PAFA; PMA; Paris/Moderne; Paris/Outre-Mer; Pasadena/MA; RISD; Recklinghausen; Saarlandmuseum; Stockholm/National; Stuttgart; Stuttgart/WK; U. of Texas; Topeka Public Library; UCLA; USIA; US State Department; Uffizi Gallery; Victoria and Albert Museum; WMAA; Walker; U. of Wisconsin; Wuppertal; Yale U. **Bibliography:** Kent, N.

TAM, REUBEN. b. January 17, 1916, Kapaa, Hawaii. **Studied:** U. of Hawaii, 1933-37, with Huc Luquiens and Henry Rempel, BA; graduate study, 1937-38; California School of Fine Arts, 1940; Columbia U.; New School for Social Research, NYC, 1943-45, with Erwin Edman, Meyer Schapiro, Maurice Wertheimer, Rudolf Arnheim; ASL, 1941; Hans Hoffmann, 1941. **Taught:** Brooklyn Museum School, 1948-; Oregon State U., 1966; Queens College, 1973. **Awards:** Guggenheim Foundation Fellowship, 1948; Golden Gate International Exposition, San Francisco, 1939, First Prize; U. of Illinois, **P.P.;** Honolulu Academy, First Prize, 1939, 40; Brooklyn Museum, First Prize, 1952, 58; NAD, Landscape Prize, 1974; NAD, first prize, 1974, 77; AAIAL, award, 1978. **Address:** P.O. Box 831, Kapaa, Hi. 96746. **Dealer:** A

Thing of Beauty, Gallery at Waiohai, Kauai, Hi. **One-man Exhibitions:** (first) California Palace, 1940; Sacramento/Crocker, 1941; Honolulu Academy, 1941, 67; The Downtown Gallery, 1945, 46, 49, 52; U. of Illinois, 1949, 51, 53, 55, 59; Philadelphia Art Alliance, 1954; The Alan Gallery, NYC, 1955, 57, 59, 61, 64; Portland, Ore./AM, 1966; Oregon State U., 1966; The Landau-Alan Gallery, NYC, 1967; Coe Kerr Gallery, NYC, 1971, 75, 79; Wichita Art Association, 1971; Molloy College, Rockville Centre, N.Y., 1973; Joe de Mers Gallery, Hilton Head, 1974, 76; U. of Nebraska, 1976; Savannah, Telfair, 1976; Palm Beach Galleries, 1978; El Paso Museum, 1978; Honolulu Academy, 1984; Kauai Museum, 1984. **Group:** Carnegie; Brooklyn Museum, Watercolor Biennials; PAFA; Corcoran; Chicago/AI Annuals; VMFA; Walker; WMAA Annuals; WMAA, Artists of Maine; MMA, American Paintings Today, 1950; MMA, American Painting, 1953; MOMA, Recent Drawings USA, 1956; U. of Illinois, 1961, 65, 69; Smithsonian, 1969; Omaha/Joslyn, A Sense of Place, 1973; AAAL, 1973; U. of Iowa, 1974; NAD, 1974, 75; NAD, 1975, 76, 77, 78, 79, 80; ICA, Boston, Bicentennial Exhibit, 1976. **Collections:** AAAL; Andover/Phillips; Berea College; Bowdoin College; Brooklyn Museum; Colby College; Corcoran; Dallas/MFA; Des Moines; Endicott, N.Y.; Fort Worth; U. of Georgia; Hawaii State Foundation; Hirshhorn; IBM; U. of Illinois; MMA; MOMA; U. of Maine; U. of Michigan; Montclair/AM; NCFA; NYPL; U. of Nebraska; Newark Museum; U. of North Carolina; The Pennsylvania State U.; Tel Aviv; Temple U.; Utica; WMAA; Wichita/AM; Youngstown/Butler. **Bibliography:** Archives.

TANGUY, YVES. b. January 5, 1900, Paris, France; **d.** January 15, 1955, Woodbury, Conn. French Army, 1920-22. Traveled Africa, USA. To USA, 1939; citizen, 1948. **m.** Kay Sage.

Subject of film, *Esquisse Tanguy*, 1981, 90 minutes, produced by José Pierre and Fabrice Maze. **One-man Exhibitions:** (first) Galerie Surrealiste, Paris, 1928; Galerie des Cahiers d'Art, Paris, 1935, 47; Stanley Rose Gallery, Hollywood, 1935; Julien Levy Galleries, NYC, 1936; Howard Putzell Gallery, Hollywood 1936; Palais des Beaux-Arts, Brussels (three-man), 1937; Bucher-Myrbor Galerie, Paris, 1938; Guggenheim Jeune Gallery, London, 1938; Hartford/Wadsworth, 1939; Pierre Matisse Gallery, 1939, 42, 43, 45, 46, 50, 63; Arts Club of Chicago, 1940; "G" Place Gallery, Washington, D.C., 1943; SFMA, 1946; Musée du Luxembourg, Paris, 1947; Galerie Maeght, 1947; Copley Gallery, Hollywood, 1948; Galerie Nin Dausset, Paris, 1949; ICA, Washington, D.C., 1952; Kunsthalle, Basel, 1952; L'Obelisco, Rome, 1953; Hartford/Wadsworth, 1954 (two-man); MIT (two-man); Bodley Gallery, NYC, 1960; Petit Galerie, Paris, 1961, 77; Galatea Galleria d'Arte, Turin, 1971; Acquavella Gallery, NYC, 1974; Kunsthandel, Dusseldorf, 1976. **Retrospectives:** MOMA, 1955; Paris/Beaubourg, circ., 1982; SRGM, 1983. **Group:** Chicago/AI; Hartford/Wadsworth; WMAA; MOMA; Fantastic Art, DADA, Surrealism, 1936; Palais des Beaux-Arts, Brussels, 6 Surrealist Painters, 1967; MOMA, Dada, Surrealism and Their Heritage, 1968; Paris/Beaubourg, Paris-New York, 1977; MOMA, Art of the Twenties, 1979. **Collections:** Buffalo/Albright; Chicago/AI; Hartford/Wadsworth; U. of Illinois; MMA; MOMA; PMA; WMAA; Washington U. **Bibliography:** Battcock, ed.; Baur 7; Blanchard; Blesh 1; **Breton** 1, 2, 3, **4;** Canaday; Christensen; Flanagan; Ford; Gascoyne; Genauer; Goodrich and Baur 1; Guggenheim, ed.; Haftman; Hunter 6; Hunter, ed.; Janis, S.; Kozloff 3; Kuh 1; Langui; McCurdy, ed.; Mendelowitz; Murken-Altrogge; Neff, ed.; Pearson 2; Pousette-Dart, ed.; Ramsden 1; Raynal 3; Read 5; Richardson, E.P.; Rosenblum 2; Rubin 1; Sachs; Seitz 3; **Soby** 1, **8;**

Tanguy; Tomkins and Time-Life Books; Waldberg 3, 4; **Yves Tanguy: Retrospective 1925-1955;** Zervos. Archives.

TANSEY, MARK. b. 1949, San Jose, Calif. **Studied:** Art Center College of Design, 1969, BFA; Harvard U., summer, 1974; Hunter College, 1975-78. **Address:** 90 Warren Street, NYC 10007. **Dealer:** Curt Marcus Gallery, NYC. **One-man Exhibitions:** Grace Borgenicht Gallery, NYC, 1982, 84; John Berggruen Gallery, San Francisco, 1984; Houston/Contemporary, 1984; Curt Marcus Gallery, 1986. **Group:** New Museum, Not Just for Laughs; The Art of Subversion, 1981; Drawing Center, NYC, New Drawing in America, 1982; Indianapolis, 1982; WMAA Biennial, 1983; Los Angeles/MOCA, Automobile and Culture, 1984; MOMA, International Survey of Recent Painting and Sculpture, 1984; MMA, Figurative American Art of the 20th Century, 1985; XLII Venice Biennial, 1986. **Collections:** Carnegie; Indianapolis; MMA; Montreal/MFA; MOMA; SFMA; WMAA.

TAUBES, FREDERIC. b. April 15, 1900, Lwow, Poland; **d.** June 20, 1981, Nyack, N.Y. **Studied:** Academy of Fine Arts, Munich, 1918-20, with Franz von Stuck, Max Doerner; Bauhaus, Weimar, 1920-21, with Josef Itten; and in Berlin and Italy. Traveled Europe extensively, USA, Africa, Near East, Far East. To USA, 1930. **Taught:** Mills College, 1938; U. of Hawaii, 1939; U. of Illinois, 1940-41; Cooper Union, 1943; U. of Wisconsin, 1943; U. of Oklahoma; London U.; Oxford; Royal College of Art; contributing editor, *American Artist* magazine, 1943-62; columnist and American editor, *Artist* magazine; U. of Alberta. **Member:** Fellow, Royal Society of Arts; International Society of Arts and Letters; formulator of Taubes varnishes and Copal painting media, manufactured by Permanent Pigments Co. **One-man Exhibitions:** (first)

Vienna/Stadt, 1921; The Midtown Galleries; San Diego; Los Angeles/County MA; SFMA; Sacramento/Crocker; Honolulu Academy; U. of Nebraska; Kansas City/Nelson; Mills College; Seattle/AM. **Group:** PAFA, 1935-44; Chicago/AI, 1935-46; Carnegie, 1936-46; Corcoran, 1936-46; VMFA, 1938-46; Memphis/Brooks. **Collections:** American Locomotive Co.; Atlanta/AA; Britannica; de Young; IBM; Indiana U.; Kansas City/Nelson; MMA; Mills College; SFMA; San Diego; Santa Barbara/MA; Standard Oil Co.; Stony Brook/SUNY. **Bibliography:** Allen, C.C., ed.; Bowell 1; **Boswell, ed.;** Kent, N.; **Taubes 1, 2, 3, 4, 5, 6, 7, 8, 9, 10, 11, 12, 13;** Watson, E. W., 2.

TCHELITCHEW, PAVEL. b. September 21, 1898, District of Kaluga, near Moscow, Russia; **d.** July 31, 1957, Grotta Ferrata, Italy. **Studied:** U. of Moscow; Kiev Academy, 1918-20. Traveled Europe, USA, North Africa, USSR. To USA, 1934; citizen, 1952. Designed sets and costumes for ballets by Balanchine, Massine, and others. **One-man Exhibitions:** (first) Claridge Gallery, London, 1928; A. Tooth & Sons, London, 1933, 35, 38; Julien Levy Galleries, NYC, 1934, 37, 38; Arts Club of Chicago, 1935, 38; Durlacher Brothers, NYC, 1942, 45, 51; Hanover Gallery, 1949; Institute of Modern Art, Buenos Aires, 1949; Detroit/Institute, 1952; Galerie Rive Gauche, Paris, 1954, 56; Galleria d'Arte del Naviglio, Milan, 1955; Catherine Viviano Gallery, 1964, 67; Galerie Lucie Weile, Paris, 1966; MOMA, 1972; Alpine Club London, 1972, 74, 76. **Retrospective:** Durlacher Brothers, NYC, 1948; Gallery of Modern Art, NYC, 1964. **Group:** Many national and international exhibitions. **Collections:** Hartford/Wadsworth; Kansas City/Nelson; MMA; MOMA; U. of Michigan; Santa Barbara/MA; Tretyakov Art Gallery, Yale U. **Bibliography:** Bazin; Canaday; Flanagan; Ford; Frost; Holme 1; Huyghe; **Kirstein 3; Kirstein, ed.;** Kuh 1; McCurdy, ed.;

Mendelowitz; Neff, ed.; Pousette-Dart, ed.; Richardson, E.P.; **Soby 1, 7; Tyler, P., 1;** Wight 2.

THEK, PAUL. b. November 2, 1933, Brooklyn, N.Y. **Studied:** Cooper Union, ASL, Pratt Institute, 1951-54. Traveled Europe; resided Rome, 1967-75. **Taught:** Cooper Union. **Commissions:** Nederlands Dans Theater, sets and costumes for the ballet *Arena*, by Glen Tetley, 1969. **Awards:** Fulbright Fellowship, 1967-70; National Endowment for the Arts, 1975; CAPS Grant, 1976. **Address:** 58 East 3rd Street, NYC 10003. **One-man Exhibitions:** Mirell Gallery, Miami, Fla., 1957; Galleria 88, Rome, 1963; The Pace Gallery, NYC, 1966; The Stable Gallery, 1964, 67, 69, 70; M. E. Thelen Gallery, Cologne, 1968, 72; Loernerscuit Gallery, Amsterdam, 1968, 69; Amsterdam/Stedelijk, 1969; Stockholm/National, 1969, 71; Galerie 20, Amsterdam (two-man), 1969; Alexandre Iolas Gallery, NYC, 1975; Loernerscuit Gallery, Amsterdam (two-man), 1969; Lucerne, 1973; Gallerie Stahli, Lucerne, 1973; Duisburg, 1973; Galerie Alexandre Iolas, Paris, 1976; Il Fante di Spade, Rome, 1977; Brooks Jackson Gallery Iolas, NYC, 1977, 80, 81, 83; Serpentine Gallery, London, 1981; Galerie Samy Kinge, Paris, 1982; Barbara Gladstone Gallery, NYC, 1984. **Retrospective:** ICA, U. of Pennsylvania. **Group:** Carnegie, 1967; ICA, London, The Obsessive Image, 1968; Documenta 4, Kassel, 1968; Walker, 1968; Cologne, 1969; MOMA, Art in the Mirror, 1966; ICA, U. of Pennsylvania, The Other Tradition, 1966; Carnegie, 1967; ICA, U. of Pennsylvania, The Obsessive Image, 1968; Indianapolis, 1968; WMAA, Human Concern/Personal Torment, 1969; Walker, Figures/Environments, circ., 1970-71; La Jolla, Continuing Art, 1971; Documenta 5, Kassel, 1972; Venice Biennials, 1976, 80; ICA, U. of Pennsylvania, Processions, 1977; XXXIX Venice Biennial, 1980; Basel/Kunsthalle, Amerikanische Zeichnungen der siebziger Jahre, 1981; Sao Paulo Biennial, 1985. **Collections:** CNAC; Cologne. **Bibliography:** *Figures/Environments;* Kren; Lucie-Smith.

THIEBAUD, WAYNE. b. November 15, 1920, Mesa, Ariz. **Studied:** San Jose State College; Sacramento State College, BA, MA. US Army Air Force, 1942-45. Traveled Europe, Mexico, USA. **Taught:** Sacramento City College, 1951-60; Sacramento State College, 1954-55; California School of Fine Arts, 1958; U. of California, Davis, 1960-; Cornell U., summer, 1967. Produced 11 educational motion pictures; 22-minute color film produced by Carr Films, 1971, covers 9 years of work. **Commissions:** California State Fair, 1950, 52, 55; Sacramento (Calif.) Municipal Utility Building, 1959 (mosaic mural). **Awards:** California State Fair, Art Film Festival, First Prize, 1956; Film Council of America, Golden Reel Award, 1956 (American Film Festival, Chicago); Columbia Records Award, 1959 ($6,000); Scholastic Art Awards for the films *Space* and *Design*, 1961; Creative Research Foundation, $1,000 Grant, 1961. **Address:** 1617 7th Ave., Sacramento, CA 95817. **Dealers:** Allan Stone Gallery; John Berggruen, San Francisco. **One-man Exhibitions:** (first) Sacramento/Crocker, 1951, 69; Artists Co-op Gallery, Sacramento, 1957, 58; SFMA, 1961, 78; de Young, 1962; Allan Stone Gallery, 1962-67, 77, 78, 79, 80; Galleria Schwarz; Stanford U., 1965; Albright Museum, Kansas City, Mo., 1966; Pasadena/AM; WMAA, 1971; John Berggruen, San Francisco, 1980, Denver, 1975; U. of California, Santa Cruz, 1976; U. of California, Davis, 1977; Diablo Valley College, 1977. **Retrospectives:** Walker, 1979; Phoenix, 1976; Newport Harbor, 1986. **Group:** SFMA Annual; Chicago/AI Annual; WMAA Annual; Los Angeles/County MA; California Palace; Denver/AM; ICA, London; Pasadena/AM, New Paintings of Common

Objects, 1962; Houston-Contemporary, Pop Goes the Easel, 1963; IX Sao Paulo Biennial, 1967; Documenta V, Kassel, 1972; and print exhibitions abroad. **Collections:** Achenbach Foundation; American Broadcasting Co.; Brandeis U.; Bryn Mawr College; Buffalo/Albright; California State Library; Chicago/AI; Corcoran; Dallas/MFA; Hartford/Wadsworth; Harvard U.; Houston/MFA; Immaculate Heart College; Kansas City/Nelson; Library of Congress; MMA; MOMA; U. of Miami; Milwaukee; U. of Nebraska; Newark Museum; Oakland/AM; PMA; RISD; SFMA; Sacramento/Crocker; Sacramento State College; San Jose State College; Shasta College; Southern Illinois U.; Stanford U.; Time Inc.; Utah; WGMA; WMAA. **Bibliography:** Alloway 4; *America 1976;* Arthur 1, 2, 4; Gettings; Hunter, ed.; Lippard 5; Murken-Altrogge; *New in the Seventies;* Sager; Strand, ed.; *The State of California Painting;* **Tsujimoto;** Weller.

THOMPSON, BOB. b. June 26, 1937, Louisville, Ky.; **d.** May 30, 1966, Rome, Italy. **Studied:** Boston Museum School, 1955; U. of Louisville, 1955-58. Traveled Europe, North Africa; resided Paris, Ibiza, NYC, Rome. **Awards:** Walter K. Gutman Foundation Grant, 1961; John Hay Whitney Fellowship, 1962-63. **One-man Exhibitions:** Delancey Street Museum, NYC, 1960; Superior Street Gallery, Chicago, 1961; Martha Jackson Gallery, 1963, 65, 68; El Cosario Gallery, Ibiza, Spain, 1963; The Drawing Shop, NYC, 1963-64; Richard Gray Gallery, 1964, 65; Paula Johnson Gallery, NYC, 1964; Donald Morris Gallery, 1965, 70; East End Gallery, Provincetown, 1965; Louisville/Speed, 1971; U. of Massachusetts, 1974; PAFA, 1976; Vanderwoude Tananbaum Gallery, NYC, 1983, 86; Miami-Dade Community College (two-man), circ., 1985; Hartford/Wadsworth, 1986. **Retrospective:** New School for Social Research, 1969; Studio Museum in Harlem, NYC, 1978. **Group:** Martha

Jackson Gallery, 1964; Dayton/AI, International Selection, 1964; Yale U., 1964; New School for Social Research, 1965; Gallery 12 St. Marks, NYC, 1967; Star Turtle Gallery, NYC, The Tenants of Sam Wapnowitz, 1969; Brooklyn Museum, Eight Afro-American Artists, 1971; Bucknell U., Since The Harlem Renaissance: Fifty Years of Afro-American Art, circ., 1983; Bergen Museum of Science and Art, Transitions: The Afro-American Artists, 1986. **Collections:** A.F.A.; American Republic Insurance Co.; Buffalo/Albright; Charlotte/Mint; Dayton/AI; Jay Dorf, Inc.; Miles College; Norfolk/Chrysler.

TING, WALASSE. b. October 13, 1929, Shanghai, China. To USA; citizen, 1970. Resided Paris, 1950-60. **Awards:** Guggenheim Foundation Fellowship, 1970. **Address:** 463 West Street, NYC 10014. **One-man Exhibitions:** Hong Kong, 1952; Paul Facchetti Gallery, Paris, 1954; Martha Jackson Gallery, NYC, 1959, 60; Lefebre Gallery, NYC, 1963, 66, 67, 68, 69, 70, 71, 72, 80; Gallerie Birch, Copenhagen, 1963, 70, 75; Galerie de France, Paris, 1968; Galerie Adrien Maeght, Paris, 1974, 77. **Group:** Salon de Mai, Paris, 1964, 65, 66, 67, 68; Carnegie, International, 1961, 64, 67, 70. **Collections:** Amsterdam/Stedelijk; Chicago/AI; Detroit/Institute; SRGM; MOMA; Rockefeller U.; Buffalo/Albright; Norfolk/Chrysler.

TOBEY, MARK. b. December 11, 1890, Centerville, Wisc.; **d.** April 24, 1976, Basel, Switzerland. **Studied:** Chicago Art Institute School, 1908, with Frank Zimmerer, Prof. Reynolds. Traveled Europe, Mexico, USA, the Orient, extensively. **Taught:** Cornish School, Seattle, intermittently, 1923-29; Dartington Hall, Devonshire, England, 1931-38. Federal A.P.: Easel painting, 1938. **Awards:** Seattle/AM, Katherine Baker Memorial Award, 1940; MMA, Artists for Victory, $500 Prize, 1942;

Portrait of America, Fourth Prize, 1945; NIAL, 1956; Guggenheim International, $1,000 Award, 1956; American Institute of Architects, Fine Arts Medal, 1957; XXIX Venice Biennial, 1958, First Prize of the Commune of Venice; *Art in America* magazine, 1958 ($1,000); elected to American Academy of Arts and Sciences, 1960 (fails to accept election); Skowhegan School, Painting Award, 1971. **One-man Exhibitions:** (first) M. Knoedler & Co., NYC, 1917; Arts Club of Chicago, 1928, 40; Romany Marie's Cafe Gallery, NYC, 1929; Cornish School, Seattle, 1930; Contemporary Arts Gallery, NYC, 1931; Paul Elder Gallery, San Francisco, 1934; Beaux Arts Gallery, London, 1934; Stanley Rose Gallery, Hollywood, 1935; Seattle/AM, 1942; The Willard Gallery, 1944, 45, 47, 49, 50, 51, 53, 54, 57, 71, 74; Margaret Brown Gallery, Boston, 1949, 54, 56; Portland, Ore./AM, 1950 (three-man); California Palace, circ., 1951; The U. of Chicago, 1952; Zoe Dusanne Gallery, Seattle, 1952; Otto Seligman Gallery, 1954, 57, 62; Chicago/AI, 1955; Gump's Gallery, 1955; Jeanne Bucher, Paris, 1955, 59, 68, 77; Paul Kantor Gallery, Beverly Hills, Calif., 1955; ICA, London, 1955; Victoria (B.C.), 1957; Galerie Stadler, Paris, 1958; St. Albans School, Washington, D.C., 1959; Frederic Hobbs Fine Art Center, San Francisco, 1960; Mannheim, 1960; Galerie Beyeler, Basel, 1961, 70, 71; Royal Marks Gallery, 1961; Seattle World's Fair, 1962; Phillips, 1962; Hanover Gallery, 1968; Bon Marche, Seattle, 1969; PAFA, 1969; Baukunst Galerie, Cologne, 1971; WMAA, 1971; Galleria dell'Ariete, 1971; Tacoma, 1972; Cincinnati/AM, 1972; Galerie Biedermann, Munich, 1973; NCFA, 1974; Krefeld/Haus Lange, 1975; Foster White Gallery, Seattle, 1980; Alex Rosenberg Gallery, NYC, 1979; Haslem Fine Arts, Inc., Washington, D.C., 1979; Elaine Granz Gallery, San Francisco, 1976; George Belcher Gallery, San Francisco, 1978; La Boetie Inc., NYC, 1986. **Retrospectives:** Seattle/AM, circ.,

1959, 70; Musee des Arts Decoratifs, 1961; MOMA, 1962; Kunstverein, Dusseldorf, 1966; Berne, 1966; Hannover/K-G, 1966; Amsterdam/Stedelijk, 1966; Dallas/MFA, 1968; National Gallery, 1984. **Group:** MOMA, Paintings by 19 Living Americans, 1929; New York World's Fair, 1939; Chicago/AI, 1940, 45, 47, 48, 51; MMA, 1942, 44, 45; MOMA, Romantic Painting in America, 1943; Brooklyn Museum, 1945, 51; Seattle/AM, 1945, 50, 51, 52, 53, 55, 56, 58; WMAA, 1945, 46, 47, 49, 62; Tate, 1946; MOMA, Fourteen Americans, circ., 1946; Utica, circ., 1947; XXIV, XXVIII & XXIX Venice Biennials, 1948, 56, 58; U. of Illinois, 1949, 50, 51, 55, 59; SFMA, 1949; Walker, Contemporary American Painting, 1950; MMA, American Paintings Today, 1950; MOMA, Abstract Painting and Sculpture in America, 1951; Ueno Art Gallery, Tokyo, 1951; U. of Minnesota, 40 American Painters, 1940-50, 1951; I & III Sao Paulo Biennials, 1951, 55; Carnegie, 1952, 55, 58, 61; International Biennial Exhibition of Paintings, Tokyo; Pavillion, Vendome, Aix-en-Provence, 1954; France/National, 50 ans d'art aux Etats-Unis, circ., Europe, 1955; Darmstadt/Kunsthalle, circ., 1956; III International Contemporary Art Exhibition, New Delhi, 1957; USIA, Eight American Artists, circ., Europe and Asia, 1957-58; WMAA, Nature in Abstraction, 1958; Brussels World's Fair, 1958; American Painting and Sculpture, Moscow, 1959; Documenta II, Kassel, 1959; Walker, 60 American Painters, 1960; Seattle World's Fair, 1962; National Gallery, American Art at Mid-Century, 1973; NCFA, Art of the Pacific Northwest, 1974. **Collections:** Andover/Phillips; Baltimore/MA; Boston/MFA; Brooklyn Museum; Buffalo/Albright; Carnegie; Chicago/AI; Detroit/Institute; Hartford/Wadsworth; MMA; MOMA; Milwaukee; Phillips; Portland; Ore./AM; SFMA; St. Louis/City; Seattle/AM; Utica; WMAA; West Palm Beach/Norton. **Bibliography: Alvard;** *Art of the Pacific Northwest;* Ashton 5; Baur 5, 7; Beekman; Biddle 4; Bihalji-Merin; Blesh 1; Eliot; Clark and Cowles; Gaunt; Goodrich and Baur 1; Haftman; Henning; Hess, T.B., 1; Honisch and Jensen, eds.; Hulten; Hunter 1, 6; Hunter, ed.; Janis, S.; Kuh 2, 3; Langui; Leepa; Lynton; McCurdy, ed.; *Mark Tobey;* Mendelowitz; *Metro;* Miller, ed. 2; Murken-Altrogge; Neumeyer; Nordness ed.; *Northwest Traditions;* Ponente; Pousette-Dart, ed.; Ragon 1, 2; Read 2; Restany 2; Richardson, E.P.; Rickey, Ritchie 1; **Roberts;** Rodman 1, 3; Rose, B., 1; **Seitz** 1, **5;** Seuphor 1; Soby 5; Tapie 1; **Thomas; Tobey;** Tuchman 3; Weller. Archives.

TODD, MICHAEL. b. June 20, 1935, Omaha, Neb. **Studied:** U. of Notre Dame, 1957, BFA, magna cum laude; UCLA, 1959, MA. **Taught:** UCLA, 1959-61, San Diego, 1968-; Bennington College, 1966-68; San Diego, 1968-76; California Institute of Arts, 1977; Otis Art Institute, 1978. **Member:** Artists Equity, Sculptors Guild. **Awards:** Woodrow Wilson Fellowship, 1957-59; Fulbright Fellowship (Paris), 1961-63; National Endowment for the Arts, 1974. **Address:** 2817 Clearwater Street, Los Angeles, Calif. 90039. **Dealers:** Charles Cowles Gallery, NYC, Kornblatt Gallery, Washington, D.C.; Tortue Gallery, Los Angeles; Gallery Paule Anglim, San Francisco. **One-man Exhibitions:** Hanover Gallery, 1964; The Pace Gallery, NYC, 1964; Henri Gallery, 1965, 68; Gertrude Kasle Gallery, 1968; Salk Institute, La Jolla, 1969; Reese Palley Gallery, NYC, 1971; California State U., Fullerton, 1972; U. of Notre Dame, 1972; Palo Alto Square, 1973, 74; The Zabriskie Gallery, 1974, 76; Seder/Creigh Gallery, Coronado, Calif., 1975; Hammarskjold Plaza, NYC, 1976; Nicholas Wilder Gallery, Los Angeles, 1976; Charles Casat Gallery, La Jolla, 1978; Oakland/AM, 1978; Paule Anglim Gallery, San Francisco, 1978; Tortue Gallery, Los Angeles, 1978; Diane Brown Gallery, Washington, D.C., 1978; Arco Center for Visual Arts, Los Angeles, 1979; Betty

Michael Todd   *Shiva's Dance IV*   1986

Cuningham, NYC, 1979; Paule Anglim Associates, 1980, 82, 84; Claremont College, 1980; Tortue Gallery, Santa Monica, 1980, 82, 84; Diane Brown Gallery, Washington, D.C., 1981; Charles Cowles Gallery, 1981, 83, 85; Paul Klein Gallery, Chicago, 1983, 85; Kornblatt Gallery, 1983, 85; Bemis Project Gallery, Omaha, 1986; Peter Sremmel Gallery, Reno, 1986; Triton Museum, Monterey, Calif., 1986; Honolulu Academy, 1987; Milwaukee, 1987; U. of Nebraska, 1987. **Group:** American Cultural Center, Paris, 1962; WMAA, 1965, 67, 68, 70; WMAA, Young America, 1965; Jewish Museum, Primary Structure Sculptures, 1966; Los Angeles/County MA, American Sculpture of the Sixties, circ., 1967; Corcoran, 1968; Maeght Foundation, 1970; San Diego, 1974; SFMA, California Painting and Sculpture: The Modern Era, 1976; Oakland Museum, One Hundred Years of California Sculpture, 1982; SFMA, Twenty American Artists, 1982; U. of Southern California, California Sculpture Show, circ., 1984. **Collections:** California State U.; Hirshhorn; La Jolla; Los Angeles/County MA; MMA; U. of Notre Dame; Oakland/AM; Palomar College; Pasadena/AM; Portland, Ore./AM; SFMA; Southwestern Community College; Storm King Art Center; WMAA; Wayne State U. **Bibliography:** *California Sculpture Show.*

TOMLIN, BRADLEY WALKER. b. August 19, 1899, Syracuse, N.Y.; **d.** May 11, 1953, NYC. **Studied:** Studio of Hugo Gari Wagner, 1913; Syracuse U., 1917-21; Academie Colarossi, Paris, and Academie de la Grande Chaumiere, 1923. Traveled Europe. **Taught:** Buckley School, 1932-33; Sarah Lawrence College, 1932-41; Dalton Schools, NYC, 1933-34. **Member:** Federation of Modern Painters and Sculptors; Whitney Studio Club, NYC; Woodstock Artists Association. **Awards:** Scholarship to Wagner Studio, 1913; Syracuse U., Hiram Gee Fellowship; Scholarship to L. C. Tiffany Foundation, Oyster Bay, N.Y.; Carnegie, Hon. Men., 1946; U. of Illinois, **P.P.**, 1949. **One-man Exhibitions:** Skaneateles and Cazenovia, N.Y., 1922; Anderson Galleries, NYC, 1923; Montross Gallery, NYC, 1926, 27; Frank K. M. Rehn Gallery, NYC, 1931, 44; Betty Parsons Gallery, 1950, 53; Phillips, 1955; Buffalo/Albright, 1975. **Retrospective:** WMAA, circ., 1957; Hofstra U., 1975 **Group:** U. of Illinois, 1949, 51; MOMA, Abstract Painting and Sculpture in America, 1951; U. of Minnesota, 1951; MOMA, Fifteen Americans, circ., 1952; MMA, 1953; WMAA, The New Decade, 1954-55; France/National, 1955; MOMA, The New American Painting and Sculpture, 1969. **Collections:** Andover/Phillips; Cranbrook; U. of Illinois; MMA; Phillips; Utica; WMAA. **Bibliography:** Baur 7; Blesh 1; Flanagan; Goodrich and Baur 1; Haftman; Hess, T. B., 1; Hobby and Levin; Hunter 1, 6; Hunter, ed.; McCoubrey 1; McCurdy, ed.; Mendelowitz; Motherwell and Reinhardt, eds.; Pagano; Ponente; Pousette-Dart, ed.; Read 2; Ritchie 1; Rose, B., 1; Sandler; Seuphor 1; Tuchman, ed.; Weller; *Woodstock: An American Art Colony, 1902-1977.* Archives.

TOOKER, GEORGE. b. August 5, 1920, NYC. **Studied:** Phillips Academy, 1936-38; Harvard U., AB, 1942; ASL, with Reginald Marsh, Paul Cadmus, Kenneth Hayes Miller, Harry Sternberg. US Marine Corps, 1942-43. Traveled France, Italy, Great Britain. **Taught:** ASL, 1965-68. **Member:** AAIAL; NAD. **Commissions:** St. Francis of Assisi Church, Windsor, Vt., 1981. **Awards:** NIAL Grant, 1960. **Address:** Hartland, Vt. **Dealer:** Marisa del Re Gallery, NYC. **One-man Exhibitions:** (first) Hewitt Gallery, NYC, 1951, also 1955; Robert Isaacson Gallery, NYC, 1960, 62; Durlacher Brothers, NYC, 1964, 67; Dartmouth College, 1960, 62, 67; Marisa del Re Gallery, 1985. **Retrospective:** WMAA, 1974. **Group:** WMAA; MOMA; MMA, 1950, 52; Chicago/AI, 1951; Corcoran, 1951; ICA, London; PAFA, 1952; XXVIII Venice Biennial, 1956; Carnegie, 1958; Festival of Two Worlds, Spoleto, 1958; Ridgefield/Aldrich, Homo Sapiens, 1982; Hirshhorn, Dreams and Nightmares, 1983. **Collections:** Chicago/AI; Dartmouth College; MMA; MOMA; NAD; NCFA; NMAA; Sara Roby Foundation; WMAA; Walker. **Bibliography:** Garver 1, 2; Goodrich and Baur 1; Mendelowitz; Newmeyer; Nordness, ed.; Pousette-Dart, ed.; Rodman 1; Weller. Archives.

TOVISH, HAROLD. b. July 31, 1921, NYC. **Studied:** WPA Art Project, with Andrew Berger; Columbia U., 1940-43, with Oronzio Maldarelli; Zadkine School of Sculpture, Paris, 1949-50; Academie de la Grande Chaumiere, 1950-51. Traveled France, Italy, Japan, Indonesia, Nepal, Iran, Turkey. **Taught:** New York State College of Ceramics, 1947-49; U. of Minnesota, 1951-54; Boston Museum School, 1957-66; U. of Hawaii, 1969-70; Boston U., 1971-. **Member:** Artists Equity; Boston Visual Artists Union. **Awards:** Minneapolis/Institute, First Prize, Sculpture, 1954; Boston Arts Festival, First Prize for Drawing, 1958, First

Prize for Sculpture, 1959; NIAL Grant, 1971. **m.** Marianna Pineda. **Address:** 380 Marlborough Street, Boston, MA 02115. **Dealer:** Terry Dintenfass, Inc., NYC; Alpha Gallery, Boston. **One-man Exhibitions:** (first) Walker, 1953; The Swetzoff Gallery, Boston, 1957, 60, 65; Fairweather-Hardin Gallery, 1960; Terry Dintenfass, Inc., 1965, 73, 80; Andover/Phillips, 1965; Alpha Gallery, 1968, 73; Boston U., 1980. **Retrospective:** Wheaton College, 1967; SRGM, 1968. **Group:** MMA, Artists for Victory, 1942; Toledo/MA, Sculpture Today, 1947; Walker, 1951; SFMA, 1952; Minneapolis/Institute, 1952, 54; WMAA, 1952, 54, 57, 60, 64, 67; Denver/AM, 1955; Carnegie, 1958; Chicago/AI, 1959; MOMA, Recent Sculpture USA, 1959; Venice Biennial; SRGM, The Joseph H. Hirshhorn Collection, 1962; Lincoln, Mass./De Cordova, 1964; U. of Illinois, 1964, 67, 68, 69; PAFA Annual, 1967; HemisFair '68, San Antonio, Tex., 1968; U. of Illinois, 1967, 69. **Collections:** Andover/Phillips; Boston/MFA; Boston Public Library; Chicago/AI; U. of Hawaii; Hirshhorn; MMA; MOMA; Minneapolis/Institute; U. of Minnesota; PMA; SRGM; WMAA; Walker; Worcester/AM. **Bibliography:** Weller.

TOWNLEY, HUGH. b. February 6, 1923, West Lafayette, Ind. **Studied:** U. of Wisconsin, 1946-48; privately with Ossip Zadkine, Paris, 1948-49; Central School of Arts and Crafts, London, 1949-50, with Victor Passmore. Traveled France, Great Britain, Holland, Brazil, Peru. **Taught:** Layton School of Art, 1951-56; Beloit College, 1956-57; Boston U., 1957-61; U. of California, Berkeley, 1961, Santa Barbara, 1968; Harvard U., 1967; Brown U., 1961-. **Member:** Artists Equity, Boston, 1961. **Commissions:** YMCA, Milwaukee, 1956; Sobin Chemical Co., Boston, 1963. **Awards:** SFMA Annual, 1952; Chicago/AI, Exhibition Momentum, 1952, 53; MIT, Summer Fellowship, 1956; ICA, Boston, Selections, 1961; Berkshire Art Association Annual,

1961, 63; Hon. MFA, Brown U., 1962; Rhode Island Arts Festival, 1962, 63; Silvermine Guild, 1963; Yaddo Fellowship, 1964; Kalamazoo Art Center, Lithographic Workshop, Fellowship, 1964; NIAL, 1967; Tamarind Fellowship, 1969; Rhode Island, Governor's Arts Award, 1972. **Address:** 131 Hope Street, Bristol, RI 02809. **One-man Exhibitions:** Studio 40, The Hague, 1950 (two-man); Gallerie Apollinaire, London, 1951; U. of Wisconsin, 1955, 68; Beloit College, 1956 (two-man); Milwaukee, 1957; Arts Council of Winston-Salem (N.C.), 1958; The Swetzoff Gallery, Boston, 1958, 59; Connecticut College, 1960; The Pace Gallery, Boston, 1960, 64, NYC, 1964; U. of Connecticut, 1964; Valparaiso U. (Ind.), 1965; Mitchem Gallery, Milwaukee, 1965; U. of New Hampshire, 1965; Temple U., 1966; Eleanor Rigelhaupt Gallery, Boston, 1966; Exeter, 1966; Yale U., 1966; Bristol (R.I.) Museum of Art, 1968 (two-man, with Robert S. Neuman); Michael Walls Gallery, 1968 (two-man); Lincoln, Mass./De Cordova, 1969; Graphics Gallery, 1969; Bradley Galleries, Milwaukee, 1970; Brockton/Fuller (two-man), 1971; Brown U., 1972; Tyler School, Philadelphia, 1972; U. of Oregon, 1976; Suzette Schochett Gallery, Newport, R.I., 1977; Western Carolina U., 1978; Worcester/AM, 1980; General Electric Co., Schenectady, 1983; Newport Harbor, 1984. **Group:** USIA, Americans in Paris, circ., Europe, 1949; SFMA Annual, 1952; MOMA, New Talent; Chicago/AI, Exhibition Momentum, 1952, 53, 56, 57, also 1964; Walker, 1956; WMAA, Young America, 1957, Annual, 1962; Carnegie, 1958; Boston Arts Festival, 1958, 61, 64; Silvermine Guild, 1959, 60, 62, 63, 64, 66; ICA, Boston, View, 1960, Selections, 1961; U. of Illinois, 1961, 63; Hartford/Wadsworth, Eleven New England Sculptors, 1963; Lincoln, Mass./De Cordova, 1964; M. Knoedler & Co., Art across America, circ., 1965-67; Andover/Phillips, 1966; Birmingham, Mich., Art Museum, 1966;

U. of North Carolina, 1966; Flint/Institute, I Flint Invitational, 1966; NIAL, 1967; Oakland/AM, 1969; Utica, 1970; Newport, R.I., Monumenta, 1974; Portland, Ore./AM, 1976. **Collections:** Andover/Phillips; Boston/MFA; Brandeis U.; Brown U.; Chicago/AI; Colby College; First National Bank of Boston; First National Bank, St. Paul; Harvard U.; Kalamazoo/Institute; Lincoln, Mass./De Cordova; Los Angeles/County MA; MOMA; Mead Corporation; Milwaukee; Princeton U.; U. of Rhode Island; RISD: SFMA; Utica, WMAA; Williams College; Wrexham Foundation. **Bibliography:** *Monumenta.*

TREIMAN, JOYCE. b. May 29, 1922, Evanston, Ill. **Studied:** Stephens College, 1941, AA; State U. of Iowa, with Philip Guston, Lester Longman, 1943, BFA. Traveled Europe, Mediterranean, Middle East. **Taught:** U. of Illinois, 1958-60; San Fernando Valley State College, 1968; UCLA, 1969-70; Art Center School, Los Angeles, 1968; California State U., Long Beach, 1977. **Awards:** Graduate Fellowship to State U. of Iowa, 1943; L. C. Tiffany Grant, 1947; Denver/AM, **P.P.,** 1948; Springfield, Ill./State; Chicago/AI, Mr. & Mrs. Frank H. Armstrong Prize, 1949; Chicago/AI, The Mr. & Mrs. Frank G. Logan Prize, 1951; Chicago/AI, Pauline Palmer Prize, 1953; Tupperware Art Fund, 1955; Chicago/AI, Martin B. Cahn Award, 1949, 60; Ford Foundation, **P.P.,** 1960; Pasadena/AM, 1962; La Jolla, 1962; Tamarind Fellowship, 1962; Ford Foundation/A.F.A. Artist-in-Residence, 1963; Los Angeles, All-City Show, **P.P.,** 1964, Sculpture Prize, 1966; Los Angeles Times, Woman of the Year for Art, 1965. **Address:** 712 Amalfi Drive, Pacific Palisades, CA 90272. **Dealers:** Schmidt-Bingham Gallery, NYC; Fairweather-Hardin Gallery; Tortue Gallery, Los Angeles. **One-man Exhibitions:** (first) Paul Theobald Gallery, Chicago, 1942; John Snowden Gallery, Chicago, 1945; Chicago/AI: The Chicago Artists Room, 1947; Fair-

Joyce Treiman *Sailing Away* 1985–86

weather-Garnett Gallery, Evanston, Ill., 1950; Hewitt Gallery, NYC, 1950; Palmer House Galleries, Chicago, 1952; Elizabeth Nelson Gallery, Chicago, 1953; Feingarten Gallery, Chicago, 1955; Cliff Dwellers Club, Chicago, 1955; Fairweather-Hardin Gallery, 1955, 58, 62, 64, 73, 78, 82, 86; The Willard Gallery, 1960; Felix Landau Gallery, 1961, 64; The Forum Gallery, NYC, 1963, 66, 71, 75, 81; Adele Bednarz Gallery, Los Angeles, 1969, 71, 74, 76; Palos Verdes Art Center, circ., 1976; Tortue Gallery, Santa Monica, 1978, 79, 81, 83, 84; Chicago/AI, 1979; UCLA, 1979; California State U., 1982; Portland, Ore./AM, 1982; Santa Barbara/MA, 1985; Schmidt-Bingham Gallery, 1986. **Retrospective:** La Jolla, 1972; Municipal Art Gallery, Los Angeles, 1978. **Group:** Denver/AM, 1943, 48, 55, 58, 60, 64; Chicago/AI Annuals, 1945-59, Directions in American Painting, 1946, 51, 54, 56, 59, 60, also 1964, 68; MMA, American Painters under 35, 1950; U. of Illinois, 1950, 51, 52, 56, 61, 63; WMAA Annuals, 1951, 52, 53, 58, Young America, 1957; Library of Congress, 1954; Carnegie, 1955, 57; Corcoran, 1957; U. of Nebraska, 1957; PAFA, 1958; MOMA, Recent Painting USA: The Figure, circ., 1962-63; WMAA, Fifty California Artists, 1962-63; Ravinia Festival, Highland Park, Ill.; U. of Illinois, 1965, 67, 69, 71, 74; NAD, 1972, 73; AAAL, 1974; Chicago/AI, Visions, 1976; ICA, Los Angeles, Current Directions in Southern California Art, 1978; Smithsonian, New American Monotypes, circ., 1978-80; NPG, American Portrait Drawings, 1979; Chicago/AI, 100 Artists-100 Years, 1980; Laguna Beach Museum of Art, Southern California Artists, 1981; Long Beach/MA, Drawings by Painters, 1982; IEF, Twentieth Century American Drawings: The Figure in Context, circ., 1984; MMA, Figurative American Art of the 20th Century, 1985. **Collections:** Abbott Laboratories; Ball State U.; U. of California, Santa Cruz; Chicago/AI; Denver/AM; Loan Association, Los Angeles; Illinois State U.; U. of Illinois; International Minerals & Chemicals Corp.; State U. of Iowa; Little Rock/MFA; Long Beach/MA; Los Angeles/County MA; MMA; MOMA; National Gallery; Oakland Museum; Oberlin College; U. of Oregon; Orlando; Pasadena/AM; Portland, Ore./AM; San Fernando Valley State U.; Springfield, Ill./State; Santa Barbara/MA; Tulsa/Philbrook; Tupperware Museum; UCLA; Utah State U.; WMAA. **Bibliography:** Pousette-Dart, ed. Archives.

TROVA, ERNEST. b. February 19, 1927, St. Louis, Mo. Self-taught in art. **Address:** Trova Foundation, 8112 Maryland Avenue, Suite 2000, St. Louis, MO 63105. **Dealer:** Philip Samuels Fine Art. **One-man Exhibitions:** Image Gallery, St. Louis, 1959, 61; H. Balaban Carp Gallery, St. Louis, 1963; The Pace Gallery, Boston, 1963, NYC, 1963, 65, 67, 69, 70,

71, 73, 75, 76, 80; Hanover Gallery, 1964, 66, 68, 70; Famous-Barr Co., St. Louis Bicentennial, 1964; MIT; Container Corp. of America, Chicago and NYC, 1965; The Pace Gallery, Columbus, 1966, 70, 75, 76; J. L. Hudson Art Gallery, Detroit, 1967; Harcus-Krakow Gallery, 1968; Dunkelman Gallery, Toronto, 1969; Gimpel & Hanover, 1970; Galerie der Spiegel, Cologne, 1970; Rene Block Gallery Ltd., 1970; Galerie Dieter Brusberg, Hanover, 1970; Fundacion Eugenio Mendoza, Caracas, 1971; Jerusalem/National, 1971; Makler Gallery, 1972; Galerie Charles Kriwin, Brussels, 1972; Elizabeth Stein Gallery, St. Louis, 1973; Phoenix, 1974; Hokin Gallery, Palm Beach, 1975; Hanover Gallery, London, 1979; Kingpitcher Gallery, Pittsburgh, 1975; Lakeview Center for the Arts & Sciences, Peoria, 1975; Hokin Gallery, Chicago, 1978; Medici/Berenson Gallery, Miami, 1979; Arte/Contacto, Caracas, 1979. **Group:** Oakland/AM, Pop Art USA, 1963; Chi-

cago/AI Annual, 1964, 67; SRGM, American Drawings, 1964; Dallas/MFA, 1965; SRGM, 1965-66; Walker, 1966; SFMA, 1966; WMAA, Art of the U.S. 1670-1966, 1966; WMAA Sculpture Annual, 1966, 68; VMFA, American Painting, 1966; U. of Illinois, 1967; SRGM, Sculpture International, 1967; MOMA, Dada, Surrealism and Their Heritage, 1968; Documenta IV, Kassel, 1968; WMAA, Human Concern/Personal Torment, 1969; ICA, U. of Pennsylvania, Highway, 1970; Cincinnati/Contemporary, Monumental Art, 1970; Museo de Arte Contemporaneo, Cali, Colombia, S.A., Bienal Graficas, 1973; V International Poster Biennial, Warsaw, 1974; Hirshhorn, Inaugural Exhibition, 1974. **Collections:** Brandeis U.; Buffalo/Albright; Baltimore/MA; Des Moines; High Museum; Houston/MFA; Indiana U.; Indianapolis; Kansas City/Nelson; Los Angeles/County MA; MMA; MOMA; NYU; New Orleans Museum; Phoenix; RISD; Ridgefield/Aldrich; Raleigh/

David True   *Promises Kept*   1986

NCMA; Society of the Four Arts; Springfield, Mass./MFA; SRGM; St. Louis/City; Syracuse/Everson; Tate; VMFA; WMAA; Walker; Wichita State U.; Worcester/AM; Yale U. **Bibliography:** Finch; Friedman and van der Marck; Lippard 5; Rubin 1; Trier 1; Tuchman 1; Weller. Archives.

TRUE, DAVID F. b. February 24, 1942, Marietta, Ohio. **Studied:** Ohio U., 1966, BFA, 1967, MFA. Traveled Europe, USA. **Taught:** New Lincoln School, 1967-74. **Award:** National Endowment for the Arts, 1982. **Address:** 457 Broome Street, NYC, 10013. **Dealer:** Blum Helman Gallery, NYC; Crown Point Press, NYC. **One-man Exhibitions:** (first) Michael Walls Gallery, NYC, 1974; Edward Thorp Gallery, NYC, 1977, 81, 82, 85; Barbara Krakow Gallery, Boston, 1986. **Retrospective:** VMFA, 1984. **Group:** WMAA Biennial, 1977; WMAA, New Image Painting, 1979; Indianapolis, 1980; Norfolk/Chrysler, Reallegory, 1983; Hudson River Museum, New Vistas, 1984; MOMA, International Survey of Recent Painting and Sculpture, 1984; XLI Venice Biennale, 1984. **Collections:** MMA; MOMA; Utica; VMFA; WMAA; Walker.

TRUITT, ANNE. b. March 16, 1921, Baltimore, Md. **Studied:** Bryn Mawr College, 1943, BA; ICA, Washington, D.C., 1948-49; Dallas/MFA, 1950. **Taught:** U. of Maryland, 1975-. **Awards:** Guggenheim Foundation Fellowship, 1971; National Endowment for the Arts, 1972, 77, commission for sculpture, 78; Yaddo Fellowship, 1974, 75, 78; Australia Council for the Arts, fellowship, 1981. **Address:** % Dealer. **Dealers:** Andre Emmerich Gallery, NYC; Pyramid Art Galleries Ltd. **One-man Exhibitions:** Andre Emmerich Gallery, NYC, 1963, 65, 69, 75, 80, 86; Minami Gallery, 1964, 67; Baltimore/MA, 1969, 74; Pyramid Art Galleries Ltd., 1971, 73, 75, 77; WMAA,

1973; Corcoran, 1974; Bayley Museum, Charlottesville, 1975; U. of Virginia, 1976; Osuna Gallery, Washington, D.C., 1979; Osuna Gallery, Washington, D.C., 1981; James Madison U., 1983; Artemesia Gallery, Chicago, 1983. **Group:** Pan American Union, Washington, D.C., Artists of the United States in Latin America, 1955; Hartford/Wadsworth, Black, White, and Grey, 1964; ICA, U. of Pennsylvania, 7 Sculptors, 1965; Jewish Museum, Primary Structure Sculptures, 1966; Los Angeles/County MA, American Sculpture of the Sixties, circ., 1967; Hemis-Fair '68, San Antonio, Tex., 1968; WMAA, 1968, 70, 72; Chicago/Contemporary, Five Artists: A Logic of Vision, 1974; Corcoran Biennial, 1975; NCFA, Sculpture: American Directions, 1945-75, 1975; WMAA, 200 Years of American Sculpture, 1976; AAIAL, 1979; Brooklyn Museum, American Drawings in Black and White: 1970-1979, 1980; Milwaukee, Washington Color Painters, 1980; U. of Maryland, U. of Maryland Artists, 1983. **Collections:** U. of Arizona; Baltimore/MA; Buffalo/Albright; Charlotte/Mint; Corcoran; Hirshhorn; Houston/MFA; MMA; MOMA; NCFA; NMAA; NMWA; National Gallery; New Orleans Museum; St. Louis/City; Vassar College; WMAA; Walker.

TSUTAKAWA, GEORGE. b. February 22, 1910, Seattle, Wash. **Studied:** U. of Washington, 1937, BA, MFA, 1950. US Army, 1942-46. Traveled Europe, Japan, Southeast Asia, Near East, Orient, India, Egypt. **Taught:** U. of Washington, 1946-80. **Member:** American Institute of Architects. **Commissions:** Seattle Public Library; Renton Center, Renton, Wash.; Lloyd Center, Portland, Ore.; St. Marks Cathedral, Seattle; Century 21, Seattle World's Fair, 1962 (US Commemorative Medal); Northgate Shopping Center, Seattle; J.W. Robinson Department Store, Anaheim, Calif.; Pacific First Federal Savings and Loan Association, Tacoma,

Wash.; Bon Marche Dept. Store, Tacoma, Wash.; Fresno (Calif.) Civic Mall; Commerce Tower, Kansas City, Mo. (sunken garden); University YMCA, Seattle; Lake City Library, Seattle; U. of Washington (Phi Mu fountain); Washington Cathedral, Washington, D.C.; UCLA School of Public Health; Jefferson Plaza, Indianapolis, 1971; Safeco Plaza, Seattle, 1973; The Pennsylvania State U., 1974; Expo '74, Spokane, US Commemorative Medal, 1974; Northwest Medical Center, Bellingham, 1976; City Hall Plaza, Aberdeen, Washington, 1977; North Kitsap H.S., Silverdale, Washington, 1979; Tsutsujigaoka Park, Sendai, Japan, 1981; Ohkura Park, Setagaya, Tokyo, 1982; Government Center, Toledo, Ohio, 1983; Governor's Mansion, Olympia, Wash., 1983. **Film:** *Three Northwest Artists: Roethke, Anderson, Tsutakawa*, 1976, 45 min. **Awards:** Washington State, Governor's Award of Commendation, 1967; Order of Rising Sun, Japan, 1981; Hon. DFA, Seattle U., 1986. **Address:** 3116 South Irving Street, Seattle, WA 98144. **Dealer:** Foster-White Gallery, Seattle. **One-man Exhibitions:** (first) Studio Gallery, Seattle, 1947; U. of Washington, 1950, 54; Press Club, Spokane, Wash., 1953; Zoe Dusanne Gallery, Seattle, 1953, 58; U. of Puget Sound, 1955, 64; Tacoma; Seattle/AM, 1957; Foster-White Gallery, Seattle, 1977, 78, 84, 86; U. of Washington, 1984; Seattle/AM, 1985. **Retrospective:** Whitman College (with Morris Graves), 1978. **Group:** Seattle/AM Annuals, 1933-; Oakland/AM, 1951; Spokane Art Center of Washington State U., 1954-57; III Sao Paulo Biennial, 1955; Vancouver, 1955, 57; SFMA, 1955, 58, 60; Portland, Ore./AM, 1955, 60; Yoseido Gallery, Tokyo, 1956; Santa Barbara/MA, 1959, 60, 61; San Diego, 1960; Los Angeles/County MA, 1960; Denver/AM, 1960, 64; Amerika Haus, East Berlin, International Arts Festival, 1965, 66; Expo '70, Osaka, 1970; NCFA, Art of the Pacific Northwest, 1974; U. of Oregon, Annual, 1968; U. of Washing-

ton, Art of the Thirties, 1972; AAIAL, 1978; Seattle, Northwest Traditions, 1978; Osaka/National, Pacific Northwest Artists and Japan, 1982; Seattle/AM, American Prints of the 1930s and 1940s, 1983. **Collections:** Bellevue, Wash.; Denver/MA; Luther Burbank Park, Mercer Island, Wash.; Memphis/Brooks; Santa Barbara/MA; Seattle/AM; UCLA; U. of Washington. **Bibliography:** *Art of the Pacific Northwest*; Clark and Cowles; *Northwest Traditions*.

TUM SUDEN, RICHARD. b. December 9, 1936, USA. **Studied:** Cooper Union, 1956-57; Wagner College, 1958, BA cum laude; NYU, 1961; Hunter College, 1962, MFA, with R. Motherwell, R. Kippold, W. Baziotes; Haystack Mountain School of Crafts, 1963; Brooklyn Museum School, 1965; Parsons School of Design. Traveled Europe, China, Japan. **Taught:** Cornell U., 1964; Hunter College, 1964, 72; Hull College of Art, England, 1964; New York Institute of Technology, 1967; U. of California, Davis, 1968; C. W. Post College, 1970-72; New School for Social Research, 1972, 73; ASL, 1973; U. of Minnesota, 1974; Parsons School of Design, NYC, 1974-. Traveled Canada, Great Britain. **Awards:** Brooklyn Museum Sculpture Prize, 1959; Yaddo Fellowship, 1964; CAPS, 1976. **Address:** 40 Great Jones Street, NYC 10012. **One-man Exhibitions:** Hilda Carmel Gallery, NYC, 1961; Tibor de Nagy Gallery, NYC, 1963, 64, 67, 68; Cornell U., 1964; French & Co., Inc., NYC, 1971; Nancy Hoffman Gallery, 1973, 74; New School for Social Research, NYC, 1975; Cole & Co., NYC, 1976. **Group:** Chicago/AI, 1965. **Collections:** Chase Manhattan Bank; MOMA; NYU; Rybak.

TUTTLE, RICHARD. b. 1941, Rahway, N.J. **Studied:** Trinity College, Hartford, Conn., 1963; Cooper Union, 1963-64. **Address:** 734 11th Avenue,

Richard Tuttle   *Blue Over*   1986

NYC 10019. **Dealer:** Blum Helman Gallery, NYC. **One-man Exhibitions:** Betty Parsons Gallery, 1965, 67, 68, 70, 72, 74, 78; Galeria Schmela, 1968; Nicholas Wilder Gallery, 1969; Buffalo/Albright, 1970; Galerie Rudolph Zwirner, 1970, 72; Dallas/MFA, 1971; Galerie Lambert, Paris, 1972, 74, 76, 78; Galerie Schlesa, Dusseldorf, 1972; MOMA, 1972; Konrad Fischer Gallery, Dusseldorf, 1973; Kunstraum, Munich, 1973; Weinberg Gallery, San Francisco, 1973; Galerie Annemarie Verna, Zurich, 1973, 79; The Clocktower, NYC, 1973; Galleria Toselli, Milan, 1974; Galleria Marilena Bonomo, Bari, 1974, 79; Cusack Gallery, Houston, 1974, 75; Nigel Greenwood, Inc., Ltd., London, 1974; Parsons-Truman Gallery, NYC, 1975; d'Alessandro Ferranti, Rome, 1975; Hartford/Wadsworth, 1975; Otis Art Institute, Los Angeles, 1976; Brooke Alexander, Inc., NYC, 1976, 79; Northwest Artists Workshop, Portland, Ore., 1976; Fine Arts Building Gallery, NYC, 1976; U. of Western Ontario, 1976; Graeme Murray Gallery, Edinburgh, 1976; Ohio State U., 1977; Ugo Ferranti, Rome, 1977, 78, 79; Kunsthalle, Basel, 1977; Kunstraum, Munich, 1977; Galerie Heiner Friedrich, Munich, 1977; Young-Hoffman Gallery, Chicago, 1978; Brown U., 1978; Daniel Weinberg Gallery, San Francisco, 1978; Francoise Lambert, Milan, 1978; Ghent/Moderne, 1978; Galerie Schmela, Dusseldorf, 1978; Amsterdam/Stedelijk, 1979; Truman Gallery, NYC, 1979; U. of California, Santa Barbara, 1979; Centre d'Arts Plastiques Contemporains, Bordeaux, 1979; Krefeld, 1980; Centre d'Art Contemporain, Geneva, 1980; California Institute of Technology, Pasadena, 1980; Yvon Lambert, Paris, 1981, 84; Galerie Annemarie Verna, Zurich, 1981, 84; Ugo Alessandro Ferranti, Rome, 1982; Nigel Greenwood Ltd. Inc., London, 1982; Betty Parsons Gallery, NYC, 82; Musée des Beaux-Arts de Calais, 1982; Blum Helman Gallery, 1983, 84; Galerie Hubert Winter, Vienna, 1983; Galerie Schmela, Dusseldorf, 1984; Daniel Weinberg Gallery, Los Angeles, 1984; Portland (Ore.) Center for the Visual Arts, 1984; Galeriet Kungsgatan, Lund, 1984; Marilena Bonomo Gallery, Bari, Italy, 1985; Galleria Toselli, Milan, 1985; Paris/Moderne, 1986. **Retrospective:** WMAA, 1975. **Group:** American Abstract Artists, 1968; Des Moines, Painting, Out from the Wall, 1968; Detroit/Institute, Other Ideas, 1969; Berne, When Attitudes Become Form, 1969; WMAA, Anti-Illusion: Procedures/Materials, 1969; Corcoran, 1969; Bennington College, Paintings without Supports, 1971; Utica, 1972; Documenta V, Kassel, 1972; Stockholm/National, Young American Artists, 1973; MOMA, Printed, Folded, Cut and Torn, 1974; Baltimore/MA, 14 Artists, 1975; Princeton U., Line as Language; Six Artists Draw, 1974; A.F.A., Recent Drawings, 1977; Cincinnati/Contemporary, Bochner, Le Va, Rockburne, Tuttle, 1975; U. of North Carolina, Works on Paper, 1975; MOMA, Drawing Now, 1976; Amherst College, Critical Perspectives in American Art, 1976; Venice Biennial, 1976; Documenta, Kassel, 1977; Yale U., Long, Hewitt, Tuttle, 1977; Amsterdam/Stedelijk, Door Belldhouwers gemaakt, 1978; Amsterdam/Stedelijk, '60-'80: Attitudes, Concepts, Images, 1982; Documenta VII, Kassel, 1982; Ars 83, Helsinki, 1983. **Collections:** Amsterdam/Stedelijk; Buffalo/Albright; Cologne; Cologne/Ludwig; Corcoran; Essen; Krefeld/Kaiser Wilhelm; MOMA; National Gallery of Canada; Oberlin College; Ottawa/National; Paris/Beaubourg; St. Louis/City; Seattle/AM; U. of Texas; WMAA; Zurich. **Bibliography:** *Art Now 74; Contemporanea;* De Wilde 2; Honisch and Jensen, eds.; Kren; *List of Drawing Material of Richard Tuttle; Options and Alternatives;* Pincus-Witten; *When Attitudes Become Form.*

TWARDOWICZ, STANLEY. b. July 8, 1917, Detroit, Mich. **Studied:** Skowhegan School, 1946-47, with Henry Poor. Traveled Mexico, Europe, Canada. **Taught:** The Ohio State U., 1946-51; Hofstra U., 1954, 66-86. **Awards:** Guggenheim Foundation Fellowship, 1956. **Address:** 57 Main Street, Northport, NY 11768; 133 Crooked Hill Road, Huntington, NY 11743. **Dealer:** Soghor, Leonard & Assoc., NYC. **One-man Exhibitions:** (first) Contemporary Arts Gallery, NYC, 1949, also 1951, 53, 56; The Peridot Gallery, 1958-61, 1963-65, 67, 68, 70; Dwan Gallery, 1959, 61; Columbus, 1963. **Retrospective:** Huntington, N.Y./Heckscher, 1974. **Group:** PAFA, 1950; SRGM, 1954; Chicago/AI, 1954, 55; WMAA, 1954, 55, 57, 64; Carnegie, 1955; Sao Paulo, 1960; U. of Nebraska, 1960; MOMA, The New American Painting and Sculpture, 1969. **Collections:** Columbus; Fisk U.; Harvard U.; Hirshhorn; Huntington, N.Y./Heckscher; Los Angeles/County MA; MOMA; U. of Massachusetts; Milwaukee; NYU; Newark Museum; U. of North Carolina; St. Joseph/Albrecht; Vassar College; Youngstown/Butler.

TWOMBLY, CY. b. April 25, 1928, Lexington, Va. **Studied:** Boston Museum School; ASL; Black Mountain College, with Franz Kline, Robert Motherwell. Resided Rome, 1957-. **Address:** 149 via Monserrato, Rome, Italy. **Dealer:** Leo Castelli, Inc., NYC; Sperone Westwater Inc., NYC; Hirschl & Adler Modern, NYC. **One-man Exhibitions:** The Kootz Gallery, NYC, 1951; The Stable Gallery, 1953, 55, 57; Galleria del Cavallino, Venice, 1958; Gallerie d'Arte del Naviglio, Milan, 1958, 60; La Tartaruga, Rome, 1958, 60, 63; Galerie 22, Dusseldorf, 1960; Leo Castelli, Inc., 1960, 64, 66, 67, 68, 72, 74, 76; Galerie J. Paris, 1961; Galerie Rudolf Zwirner, Essen, 1961, Cologne, 1963, 69; Notizie Gallery, Turin, 1962; Galleria del Leone, Venice, 1962; Brussels/Royaux, 1962, 65; Galerie Anne Abels, Cologne, 1963; Galerie Jacques Benador, Geneva, 1963, 75; Galerie Bonnier, Lausanne, 1963; Galerie Handschin, Basel, 1964; Galerie Friedrich & Dahlem, Munich, 1964; Amsterdam/Stedelijk, 1966; Milwaukee, 1968; Nicholas Wilder Gallery, 1969; Galerie Hans R. Neuendorf, Cologne, 1970; Stockholm/SFK, 1970; Galerie Bonnier, Geneva, 1970; Gian Enzo Sperone, Turin, 1971, 73; Yvon Lambert, Paris, 1971, 77, 80, 82; Galleria dell'Ariete, 1971; Galerie Mollenhoff, Cologne, 1971; Dunkelman Gallery, Toronto, 1972; Janie C. Lee Gallery, Houston, 1972; F. H. Mayor Gallery, London, 1973; Berne, 1973; Galerie Oppenheim, Brussels, 1973, 74; Galerie Heiner Friedrich, Munich, 1974; Modern Art Agency, Naples, 1975; Galerie Art in Progress, Munich, 1975; ICA, U. of Pennsylvania, 1975; SFMA, 1975; Galleria Bertesca, Genoa, 1975; Galerie Art in Progress, Dusseldorf, 1976, Paris/Moderne, 1976; Galerie Jacques Brosser, Paris, 1976; Gian Enzo Sperone, Rome, 1976, 84; School of Visual Arts, NYC, 1977; Galerie Klewan, Munich, 1978; Heiner Friedrich, Inc., NYC, 1978; Lucio Amelio Gallery, Naples, 1979; Galleriet, Lund, 1979; Galerie Karsten Greve, Cologne, 1979, 80, 82, 84; Southern Methodist U., 1980; Richard Hines Gallery, Seattle, 1980; PAC, Milan, 1980; Castelli Graphics, NYC, 1981; Sperone Westwater Fischer Inc., NYC, 1982; The Mayor Gallery, London, 1982, 84; Stephen Mazoh & Co., NYC, 1983; Lucio Amelio Gallery, Naples, 84; Hirschl & Adler Modern, 1984, 86; Ulysses Gallery, Vienna, 1984; Bordeaux/Contemporain, 1984. **Retrospectives:** WMAA, 1979; Newport Harbor, circ., 1981; Santa Barbara (Calif.) Contemporary Arts Center, 1984; Kunsthalle, Baden-Baden, 1984. **Group:** Gutai 9, Osaka, 1958; Festival of Two Worlds, Spoleto, 1961; Premio Lissone, 1961; Premio Marzotto, 1962; Amsterdam/Stedelijk, Art and Writing, 1963; Salon du Mai, Paris, 1963; L'Aquila, Aspetti dell'Arte Contemporanea, 1963; SRGM, 1964; MOMA, 1966; NYU, 1967; WMAA Annual, 1967; Indianapolis/Herron, 1969; WMAA Biennials, 1969, 73; Indianapolis, 1969; Dublin/Municipal (ROSC), 1971; WMAA, The Structure of Color, 1971; Dusseldorf/Kunsthalle, Surrealität Bildrealitat, 1924-1974, 1974; MOMA, Drawing Now, 1976; SRGM, Twentieth Century American Drawings, 1976; Royal Academy, London, A New Spirit in Painting, 1981; SRMG, The New York School: Four Decades, 1982; Documenta VII, Kassel, 1982; Galeria Politi, Milan, Transavantgarde International, 1982; Internationale Kunstausstellung Berlin, 1982; Pall Mall Canada Ltd., American Accents, circ., 1983; Ars 83, Helsinki, 1983; Amsterdam/Stedelijk, La Grande Parade, 1984. **Collections:** Cologne; Darmstadt/Hessisches; First National City Bank, Houston; MOMA; Milwaukee; RISD; Rome/Nazionale; WMAA. **Bibliography:** Calas, N. and E.; *Contemporanea;* De Wilde 1; Downes, ed.; Honisch and Jensen, eds.; Joachimides and Rosenthal; *Kunst um 1970; Metro;* Murken-Altrogge; Restany 2; Tomkins 2.

TWORKOV, JACK. b. August 15, 1900, Biala, Poland; **d.** September 4, 1982, Provincetown, Mass. To USA, 1913; citizen, 1928. **Studied:** Columbia U., 1920-23; NAD, 1923-25, with Ivan Olinsky, C. W. Hawthorne; privately with Ross Moffett, 1924-25; ASL,

Jack Tworkov   *Q3-82-OP#10*   1981

1925-26, with Guy Du Bois, Boardman Robinson. **Taught:** Fieldston School, NYC, 1931; Queens College, 1948-55; American U., 1948-51; Black Mountain College, summer, 1952; Pratt Institute, 1955-58; Yale U., 1963-69; American Academy, Rome, 1972; Dartmouth College, 1973; Columbia U., 1973; Royal College of Art, London, 1974. Federal A.P.: Easel painting, 1935-41. **Member:** Century Association; AAIAL. **Awards:** Corcoran, William Al Clark Prize and Corcoran Gold Medal, 1963; Guggenheim Foundation Fellowship, 1970; Hon. DFA, Maryland Institute, 1971; Honorary Doctor of Humane Letters, Columbia U., 1972; Skowhegan School Painting Award, 1973; Hon. DFA, RISD, 1979. **One-man Exhibitions:** (first) ACA Gallery, 1940; Charles Egan Gallery, 1947, 49, 52, 54; Baltimore/MA, 1948; U. of Mississippi, 1954; Walker, 1957; The Stable Gallery, 1957, 58, 59; B. C. Holland Gallery, 1960, 63; Leo Caselli, Inc., 1961, 63; Tulane U., 1961; Yale U., 1963; Gertrude Kasle Gallery, 1966, 67, 69, 71, 73; WMAA, 1971; Toledo/MA, 1971; Dartmouth College, 1973; Portland (Ore.) Center for the Visual Arts, 1974; Reed College, 1974; Denver/AM, 1974; Jack Glenn Gallery, Corona del Mar, 1974, 76; Harcus Krakow Rosen Sonnabend, 1974; Nancy Hoffman Gallery, 1974, 75, 77, 82, 83, 85; Ohio State U., 1975; Youngstown State U., 1975; Cincinnati/Contemporary, 1975; New Gallery, Cleveland, 1975; Washburn U., 1976; Jack Glenn Gallery, 1976; John Berggruen Gallery, San Francisco, 1976; Dobrick Gallery, Chicago, 1977; U. of California, Santa Barbara, 1977; Baum-Silverman Gallery, Los Angeles, 1979; RISD, 1980; Middlebury College, 1981; SRGM, 1982; AAIAL, 1983; Provincetown (Mass.) Art Association, 1983; Adams Middleton Gallery, Houston, 1985; PAFA, circ., 1986. **Retrospectives:** WMAA, 1964; Third Eye Center, Glasgow, circ., 1979. **Group:** PAFA, 1929; MOMA, The New American Painting, circ., Europe, 1958-59; Docu-menta II, Kassel, 1959; Walker, 60 American Painters, 1960; Carnegie, 1961; SRGM, Abstract Expressionists and Imagists, 1961; U. of Illinois, 1961; SRGM/USIA, American Vanguard, circ., Europe, 1961-62; MOMA, Abstract American Drawings and Watercolors, circ., Latin America, 1961-63; Seattle World's Fair, 1962; ART:USA:Now, circ., 1962-67; WMAA Annual, 1963; Corcoran, 1963; MOMA, The New American Painting and Sculpture, 1969; VMFA, 12 American Painters, 1974; Santa Barbara/MA, Five Americans, 1974; Indianapolis, 1974; U. of Illinois, 1974; ASL, 100 Years, NYC, 1975; Fort Wayne, Hue and Far Cry of Color, 1976; Hirshhorn, The Golden Door: Artist Immigrants of America, 1876-1976, 1976; Milwaukee, From Foreign Shores, 1976; Rice U., Drawing Today in New York, circ., 1977; Chicago/AI, Drawings of the 70's, 1977; Montclair/AM, Drawing the Line, 1978; Philadelphia College of Art, Seventies Painting, 1978; Creighton U., A Century of Master Drawings, 1978; Pomona College, Black and White Are Colors, 1979; Brooklyn Museum, American Drawings in Black and White: 1970-1979, 1980; WMAA Biennial, 1981. **Collections:** AAAL; Allentown/AM; Amerada-Hess Corp., NYC; American U.; Baltimore/Albright; Brooklyn Museum; Buffalo/Albright; U. of California, Santa Barbara; Chase Manhattan Bank, NYC; Cleveland/MA; Dartmouth College; Denison U.; Detroit/Institute; Fort Wayne; Hartford/Wadsworth; Honolulu Academy; Indianapolis; Kent State U.; Little Rock/MFA; MMA; MOMA; McCrory Corp., NYC; NCFA; National Gallery; New Paltz/SUNY; Owens-Corning Fiberglas Corp.; Phillips; Prudential Insurance Co. of America, Newark; RISD; Rockefeller Institute; SRGM; Santa Barbara/MA; Storm King Art Center; Toledo/MA; U. of Texas, Austin; Union Carbide Corp.; WGMA; WMAA; Walker; U. of Wisconsin; Yale U. **Bibliography:** *Black and White Are*

Colors; Downes, ed.; *From Foreign Shores;* Goodrich and Baur 1; Hess, T.B., 1; Hunter 1, 6; Hunter, ed.; *Metro;* Nordness, ed.; Plous; Pousette-Dart, ed.; Read 2; Rodman 3; Rose, B., 1; Sandler 1; Tomkins 2. Archives.

U

URRY, STEVEN. b. September 5, 1939, Chicago, Ill. **Studied:** U. of Chicago, 1957-59. Chicago/AI, 1957-59; California College of Arts and Crafts, 1960-61; SFAI, 1962-63. **Taught:** Chicago/AI, 1968; Cranbrook, 1970; U. of Kentucky, 1971, 72; Carnegie-Mellon U., 1975. **Commissions:** Loyola U., 1969; Popeil Bros., Inc., 1971; Shire National Corp., 1975; Carnegie-Mellon U., 1975; R. Lavin & Sons, 1976; Nebraska Bicentennial Interstate 80 Sculpture, 1976. **Awards:** U. of Illinois, **P.P.,** 1966; National Endowment for the Arts Award, 1966; Chicago/AI, Linde Prize, 1967; Chicago/AI, Emilie L. Wild Prize, 1967. **Address:** 64 Wooster Street, NYC 10012. **Dealer:** The Zabriskie Gallery. **One-man Exhibitions:** Kendall College, Evanston, Ill., 1966; Dell Gallery, Chicago, 1966; The U. of Chicago, 1967, 68; Royal Marks Gallery, 1967; De Paul U., Chicago, 1968; Chicago/AI, 1969; The Zabriskie Gallery, NYC, 1969, 72, 76; Phyllis Kind Gallery, Chicago, 1972, 74; Hakeley Art Museum, Muskegon, Mich., 1977; Grand Rapids, 1977. **Group:** SFAI, 1962; Illinois Institute of Technology, Chicago, 1965; U. of Illinois, 1966, 74; Chicago/AI, 1967, 70; U. of Nebraska, 1970; Grand Rapids, Off the Pedestal, 1974; Stamford, Conn., American Salon des Refuses, 1976. **Collections:** Chicago/AI; Carnegie; Envair Corp.; Hakeley Art Museum, Muskegon, Mich.; U. of Illinois; K-Mart Corp.; Kendall College; NCFA; Loyala U.; Palm Springs Desert Museum; Playboy Enterprises, Inc.; Standard Oil Co.; U. of Wisconsin.

V

VALENTINE, DeWAIN. b. August 27, 1936, Fort Collins, Colorado. **Studied:** U. of Colorado, BFA, 1958; MFA, 1960; Yale U. Summer School, Norfolk, Conn. 1958. **Taught:** U. of Colorado, 1958-61, 64-65; U. of California, Los Angeles, 1965-67. **Member:** Los Angeles/MOCA, Board of Trustees. **Award:** Guggenheim Foundation Fellowship, 1980; National Endowment for the Arts, 1981. **Address:** 69 Market Street, Venice, CA 90291. **One-man Exhibitions:** U. of Colorado, 1958, 60; The Gallery, Denver, 1964; Douglas Gallery, Vancouver, 1968; ACE Gallery, Los Angeles, 1968; U. of California, Santa Barbara, 1968; U. of Washington, Seattle, 1969; U. of British Columbia, 1969; Galerie Bischofberger, Zurich, 1969; Pasadena/AM, 1970; Galerie Denise Rene, NYC, 1973; Walter Kelly Gallery, Chicago, 1973; San Jose/Museum of Art, 1974; Edward Thorp Gallery, Santa Barbara, 1974; Betty Gold, Los Angeles, 1974; La Jolla, 1975; Long Beach/MA, 1975; California State U., Northridge, 1975; Santa Barbara/MA, 1977; Los Angeles/MA, 1979; U. of California, Irvine, 1979; Thomas Babeor Gallery, La Jolla, 1982; Laumeier Sculpture Park, 1982; Madison Art Center, 1983; Honolulu Academy, 1985. **Group:** WMAA Annuals, 1966, 68, 70; Los Angeles/County MA, American Sculpture of the Sixties, 1967; Portland, Ore./AM, West Coast Now, 1968; HemisFair, '68, San Antonio, Tex., 1968; Museum of Contemporary Crafts, NYC, Plastic as Plastic, 1968; Jewish Museum, NYC, A Plastic Presence, 1969; Seattle/AM, American Art, Third Quarter Century, 1973; Chicago/AI, 1974; ICA, Los Angeles, One Hundred Plus, 1977; U. of Hartford, Conn., Southern California Drawings, 1980; U. of California, Irvine, Structural Imagery, 1980, San Diego, Sculpture in California, 1975-1980, 1980; Laguna Beach Museum of Art, Southern California Artists, 1981; U. of Southern Caifornia, California Sculpture Show, circ., 1984. **Collections:** Atlantic Richfield Co., Washington, D.C.; Avco Finance Corp.; Bradley U.; Chicago/AI; Colorado State U.; U. of Colorado; Denver/AM; Fourth Financial Corp., Wichita; Omaha/Joslyn; La Jolla; Los Angeles Times; Los Angeles/County MA; Milwaukee; U. of New Mexico; Newport Beach; Palm Springs Desert Museum; Pasadena/AM; Ridgefield/Aldrich; Roswell; San Diego; Stanford U.; Vancouver; WMAA; Xerox Corp., Rochester, N.Y. **Bibliography:** *California Sculpture Show.*

VALERIO, JAMES. b. December 2, 1938, Chicago, Ill. **Studied:** Wright Jr. College, 1959-62; School of the Art Institute of Chicago, 1962-66, BFA, 1968, MFA. **Taught:** School of the Art Institute of Chicago, 1966-68; Rock Valley College, 1968-70; UCLA, 1970-79; Cornell U., 1979-82; Northwestern U., 1985-. **Awards:** School of the Art Institute of Chicago, Anne Louise Raymond Foreign Travelling Fellowship, 1968; National Endowment for the Arts, 1985. **Address:** 1308 Gregory, Wilmette, Ill. 60091. **Dealer:** Allan Frumkin Gallery, NYC. **One-man Exhibitions:** (first) Gerard John Hayes Gallery, Los Angeles, 1971, 72, 75; Tucson, 1973; Michael Walls Gallery, NYC, 1974; John Berggruen Gallery, 1977;

James Valerio   *Spring Mambo*   1986

Frumkin-Struve Gallery, Chicago, 1981, 84; Wilmington, 1983; Allan Frumkin Gallery, 1983. **Group:** Chicago/AI, Chicago & Vicinity Show, 1969; Indianapolis, 1971; Long Beach/MA, American Portraits-Old and New, 1971; Documenta V, Kassel, 1973; Lincoln, Mass./De Cordova, The Super-Realist Vision, 1973; SFMA, Painting and Sculpture in California, 1976; ICA, Los Angeles, 100+, Current Directions in Southern California Art, 1977; Albuquerque Museum, Reflections of Realism, 1979; U. of Rochester, Uncommon Visions, 1979; Tulsa/Philbrook, Realism/Photorealism, 1980; Newport Harbor, Inside Out: Self Beyond Likeness, 1981; PAFA, Contemporary American Realism Since 1960, 1981; San Antonio/MA, Real, Really Real, Super Real, circ., 1981; Laguna Beach Museum of Art, The Real Thing: Southern California Realist Painting, 1982; U. of California, Santa Barbara, A Heritage Renewed: Representational Drawing Today, 1983; Houston/Contemporary, American Still Life, 1945-1983, circ., 1983; IEF, Twentieth Century American Drawing: The Figure in Context, circ., 1984; Isetan Museum of Art, Tokyo, American Realism: The Precise Image, 1985. **Collections:** Albuquerque Museum; Iowa State U.; Long Beach/MA; MMA; PAFA; SRGM; U. of Virginia. **Bibliography:** Arthur 3; Arthur 4.

VAN BUREN, RICHARD. b. 1937, Syracuse, N.Y. **Studied:** San Francisco State College; U. of Mexico; Mexico

City College. **Taught:** NYU; School of Visual Arts. **Address:** 155 Wooster Street, NYC 10012. **Dealer:** Paula Cooper Gallery. **One-man Exhibitions:** New Mission Gallery, San Francisco, 1961; SFMA, 1962; Dilexi Gallery, San Francisco, 1964; Bykert Gallery, 1967, 68, 69; Bennington College, 1970; Ithaca College (three-man), 1970; Janie C. Lee Gallery, Dallas (two-man), 1971; Paula Cooper Gallery, 1972, 75, 77; Greene Street, NYC, 1973; The Texas Gallery, 1974; Rice U., 1974; City U. of New York, 1975. **Group:** SFMA, Bay Area Artists, 1964; Jewish Museum, Primary Structure Sculptures, 1966; ICA, U. of Pennsylvania, A Romantic Minimalism, 1967; U. of Illinois, 1967; Ridgefield/Aldrich, Cool Art: 1967, 1968; WMAA, 1968, 70; Milwaukee, A Plastic Presence, circ., 1969; Finch College, NYC, Art in Process, 1969; Chicago/AI, 1969, 72; Foundation Maeght, 1970; Akron/AI, Watercolors and Drawings by Young Americans, 1970; Walker, Works for New Spaces, 1971; Milwaukee, Directions 3: Eight Artists, 1971; Buffalo/Albright, Kid Stuff, 1971; Harvard U., New American Graphic Art, 1973; Cincinnati/Contemporary, Options 73/70, 1973; Indianapolis, 1974; VMFA, Works on Paper, 1974. **Collections:** MOMA; Walker. **Bibliography:** *Art Now 74.*

VANDER SLUIS, GEORGE. b. December 18, 1915, Cleveland, Ohio. **Studied:** Cleveland Institute of Art, 1934-39; Colorado Springs Fine Arts Center, 1939-40, with Boardman Robinson. US Army, 1942-45. Traveled Europe, USA. **Taught:** Colorado Springs Fine Arts Center, 1940-42, 1945-47; Syracuse U., 1957. Federal A.P.: Mural Painting, 1939. Designed 9¢ and 11¢ US postage stamps in 1971. **Commissions:** US Post Office, Rifle, Colo., 1941, and Riverton, Wyo., 1942; Syracuse U., 1955; J. C. George Company, Syracuse, N.Y., 1947. **Awards:** Fulbright Fellowship (Italy), 1951-52; New York State Council on the Arts, 1966. **Ad-**

dress: 4132 Onondaga Boulevard, Camillus, NY 13031. **One-man Exhibitions:** (first) Salt Lake Art Center, Salt Lake City, Utah, 1942; Columbia U., 1943; Colorado Springs/FA, 1945; Southern Methodist U., 1946; U. of Nebraska, 1947; Hood College, 1948; Galleria d'Arte Contemporanea, Florence, Italy, 1952; Syracuse U., 1955, 74; Syracuse/Everson, 1956, 61, 71, 77; Alfred U., 1957; Colgate U., 1957; U. of Rochester, 1959, 69; J. Seligmann & Co., 1959; Cleveland Institute of Art, 1962; Royal Marks Gallery, 1962, 63, 64; Utica, 1963; The Krasner Gallery, 1968, 69, 71; Lubin House, NYC, 1978; Hanover Gallery, Syracuse, 1979. **Group:** Cleveland/MA, The May Show, 1937, 38, 40, 41; Smithsonian, American Watercolors, 1941; Chicago/AI Annual, 1941; San Francisco Art Association Annuals, 1941, 42; MMA, Artists for Victory, 1942; Pepsi-Cola Co., Paintings of the Year, 1946, 47; Corcoran, 1947, 57; Utica Annuals, 1948-70; PAFA, 1953; WMAA, 1954; WMAA, Fulbright Artists, 1958; U. of Illinois, 1961; The White House, Washington, D.C., 1966-69; Museum of Contemporary Crafts, The Door, 1968; New York State Fair, Enviro-Vision, circ., 1972. **Collections:** Arnot; Brookings Institute; Cleveland/MA; Colgate U.; Colorado Springs/FA; General Electric Corp.; Hamline U.; Kalamazoo/Institute; Kansas City/Nelson; New Britain; U. of Rochester; St. Lawrence U.; Southern Methodist U.; Syracuse/Everson; Syracuse U.; Utica.

VENEZIA, MICHAEL. b. July 23, 1935, Brooklyn, N.Y. **Studied:** Buffalo/SUNY, BS, 1963, with Peter Busa; U. of Michigan, MFA, 1968; ASL, 1954. Traveled England. **Taught:** U. of Michigan, Ann Arbor, 1967-68; U. of Rochester, 1968; Guildford College, Surrey, 1967-68; London College of Printing, 1967-68. Designed sets and projections for *Brechtsongs*, London, 1966. **Awards:** CAPS, 1974; L. C. Tiffany Grant, 1980; National Endowment for the Arts, 1981. **Address:** 20 North Moore Street, NYC 10013. **Dealer:** Margarete Roeder Gallery, NYC. **One-man Exhibitions:** (first) Bykert Gallery, NYC, 1942, 73; Heiner Friedrich Gallery, NYC, 1976; Nina Freudenheim, Buffalo, 1976; Sperone Westwater Fischer, Inc., NYC, 1977, 79. **Retrospectives:** Detroit/Institute, 1980; U. of Rochester, 1986. **Group:** MOMA, Works on Paper, 1974; U. of North Carolina, Drawing about Drawing Today, 1979; U. of Rochester, Contemporary Drawings on Watercolors, 1980. **Collections:** Best Products, Richmond, Va.; Canberra/National; Detroit/Institute; Hartford/Wadsworth; U. of Michigan; MOMA; National Gallery of Canada, Ottawa; Potsdam/SUNY; U. of Rochester; Whitney Communications, NYC.

VICENTE, ESTEBAN. b. January 20, 1904, Segovia, Spain. **Studied:** Real Academia de Bellas Artes de San Fernando, Madrid, BA. Resided Paris, 1927-32. To USA, 1936. **Taught:** U. of California, Los Angeles and Berkeley, 1954-55; Queens College; Black Mountain College; High Field School, Falmouth, Mass.; NYU; Yale U.; and in Puerto Rico; Princeton U., Artist-in-Residence, 1965, 69, 70, 71; New York Studio School, Paris, 1965-79; Honolulu Academy, 1969; American U., 1973; Columbia U., 1974. **Member:** Century Association; NAD. **Awards:** Ford Foundation, 1961, 62; Tamarind Fellowship, 1962; AAAL, 1971; Hon. DFA, Parsons School, 1984. **Address:** Main Street, Bridgehampton, NY 11932; 1 West 67th Street, NYC 10023. **Dealer:** Gruenebaum Gallery, NYC. **One-man Exhibitions:** Kleemann Gallery, NYC, 1937; The Peridot Gallery, 1950, 51; Allan Frumkin Gallery, Chicago, 1953; Charles Egan Gallery, 1955; Rose Fried Gallery, 1957, 58; Leo Castelli, Inc., 1958; U. of Minnesota, 1959; Holland-Goldowsky Gallery, Chicago, 1960; Andre Emmerich Gallery, NYC, 1960, 62, 64, 65, 69, 72, 75; Primus-Stuart Gallery, Los Angeles, 1961; New Arts Gallery, Houston, 1962; B.C. Holland Gallery, 1963; Dayton/AI, 1963; St. John's Gallery, Annapolis, Md., 1963; Des Moines, 1967; Princeton U., 1967, 71; Cranbrook, 1968; Honolulu Academy, 1969; Benson Gallery, 1969, 72; Guild Hall, 1970; J.L. Hudson Art Gallery, Detroit, 1972; Gruenebaum Gallery, NYC, 1979, 81, 84, 86; Yares Gallery, 1979; Hoshour Gallery, 1979; Light Gallery, Southampton, N.Y., 1979; Fischbach Gallery, NYC, 1977. **Group:** International Biennial Exchange of Paintings, Tokyo; Corcoran; The Kootz Gallery, NYC, New Talent, 1950; Ninth Street Exhibition, NYC, 1951; Carnegie, 1958, 59, 61; WMAA Annuals, 1958, 59, 61, 62, 65, 67, 70; ICA, Boston, 100 Works on Paper, circ., Europe, 1959; Columbus, Contemporary American Painting, 1960; Walker, 60 American Painters, 1960; Chicago/AI, 1960, 66; MOMA, The Art of Assemblage, circ., 1961; SRGM, Abstract Expressionists and Imagists, 1961; SRGM/USIA, American Vanguard, circ., Europe, 1961-62; Seattle World's Fair, 1962; Hartford/Wadsworth, Continuity and Change, 1962; Sao Paulo, 1963; New York World's Fair, 1964-65; Black Mountain College, 1966; MOMA, The New American Painting and Sculpture, 1969; NAD, 1982. **Collections:** Baltimore/MA; Brandeis U.; U. of California, Berkeley; Chase Manhattan Bank; Chicago/AI;   Ciba-Geigy   Corp.; Dallas/MFA; Dartmouth College; Hartford/Wadsworth; Honolulu Academy; Iowa State U.; Kansas City/Nelson; Los Angeles/County MA; MMA; MOMA; NCFA; NYU; Newark Museum; U. of North Carolina; Princeton U.; Reynolds Metals Co.; U. of Rochester; SFMA; Shuttleworth Carton Co.; The Singer Company, Inc.; Tate; Trenton/State; Union Carbide Corp.; Vanderbilt U.; WGMA; WMAA; Worcester/AM; Yale U. **Bibliography:** Hess, T.B., 1; Hunter 6; Janis and Blesh 1; Sandler 1; Seitz 3. Archives.

VICKREY, ROBERT R. b. August 20, 1926, NYC. **Studied:** Yale U., 1950, BA, BFA; Wesleyan U.; Art Students League, NYC. **Commissions:** 77 *Time* covers. Subject of film, *Robert Vickrey, Lyrical Realist,* 28 minutes, produced by Fairfield U. Made short films 1947-57. **Awards:** NAD, Joseph S. Isidor Gold Medal, 1970; MAD, S.J. Wallace Truman Prize; American Watercolor Society, Silver Medal, 1976. **Address:** Crystal Lake Drive, Orleans, Mass. 02653. **Dealer:** ACA Gallery, NYC. **One-man Exhibitions:** (first) Creative Gallery, NYC, 1952; Midtown Galleries, NYC, biannually 1953-78; Hirschl & Adler Galleries, 1979; Gallery Nicholas, Palm Beach, Fla., 1981; Harmon Gallery, Naples, Fla., 1981; Harmon Meed Gallery, Naples, Fla., 1982-86; Munson Gallery, Chatham, Mass., 1976, 77, 78, 79, 80; ACA Galleries, 1980; Midwest Museum of American Art, Elkhart, Ind., 1985; Frances Aaronsen Gallery, Atlanta, 1985. **Retrospectives:** U. of Arizona, 1973; Fairfield U., circ., 1982. **Group:** WMAA annuals, 1951, 52, 53, 54, 55, 56, 57, 63; U. of Illinois, 1953, 55, 59; WMAA, 35 Americans, 1957; Youngstown/Butler, 1960, 61, 82; WMAA, Sixty Years of American Art, 1963; WMAA, The Theatre Collects, 1963; U. of Rochester, In Focus: A Look at Realism in Art, 1964; Purchase/SUNY, American Drawings and Watercolors, 1976; Norfolk/Chrysler, American Figure Painting, 1980; San Antonio/MA, Real, Really Real, Super Real, circ., 1981. **Collections:** Atlanta U.; Brooklyn Museum; Chattanooga/Hunter; Colorado Springs/FA; Corcoran; Cornell U.; Florida Southern College; High Museum; Indianapolis; U. of Kansas; MMA; Memphis/Brooks; Michigan State U.; NAD; NMAA; NPG; New Britain/American; New Orleans Museum; Newark Museum; Norfolk/Chrysler; Oklahoma; Omaha/Joslyn; Princeton U.; Purchase/SUNY; Randolph-Macon College; Rio de Janeiro; Rutgers U.; San Diego; Syracuse U.; Trenton/State; Utica; VMFA; WMAA; Youngstown/Butler.

VON SCHLEGELL, DAVID. b. May 25, 1920, St. Louis, Mo. **Studied:** U. of Michigan, 1940-42; ASL, with William Von Schlegell (his father) and Yasuo Kuniyoshi, 1945-48. US Air Force, 1943-44. **Taught:** Privately, 1950-55; U. of California, 1968; School of Visual Arts, NYC, 1969-70; Yale U., 1971-. **Commissions:** Sculpture, Miami Lakes, Fla., 1974; State Park, Duluth, Minn., 1974; GSA, 1975; City of Baltimore, 1977; NASA, at Clark U., 1978; Arabian Royal Navy Headquarters Bldg., Saudi Arabia, 1978; Indiana U., 1979; Yeatmen's Cove Sculpture Project, Cincinnati, 1979; Tulsa International Airport, 1980. **Awards:** Rhode Island Arts Festival, First Prize, 1962; Carnegie, **P.P.,** 1967; National Council on the Arts, $5,000 Award, 1968; Guggenheim Foundation Fellowship, 1974; Skowhegan School Medal for Sculpture, 1978. **Address:** 115 New Quarry Road, Guilford, Ct. 06437. **One-man Exhibitions:** (first) The Swetzoff Gallery, Boston, 1955, also 1961; Poindexter Gallery, 1960; Stanhope Gallery, Boston, 1964; U. of New Hampshire, 1964; NYU (three-man), 1966; Ogunquit, 1965; Royal Marks Gallery, 1966-67; Ward-Nasse Gallery, Boston, 1968; Obelisk Gallery, 1968; Reese Paley Gallery, NYC, 1970, 71; The Pace Gallery, NYC, 1974-77; ICA, Boston, 1976. **Retrospective:** Brandeis U., 1968. **Group:** WMAA Annuals, 1960-68; ICA, Boston, 1963; Hartford/Wadsworth, 1963; WMAA, Contemporary American Sculpture, Selection I, 1966; Jewish Museum, Primary Structures, 1966; Los Angeles/County MA, American Sculpture of the Sixties, 1967; Carnegie, 1967; Walker, Works on New Space, 1971; Middelheim Park, Antwerp, XI Sculpture Biennial, 1971; U. of Washington, 1971. **Collections:** Andover/Phillips; U. of California, Santa Barbara; Carnegie; Cornell U.; Hirshhorn; Lannan Foundation; Lincoln, Mass./De Cordova; MIT; U. of Massachusetts; Ogunquit; Ridgefield/ Aldrich; RISD; South Mall, Albany; Storm King Art Center; WMAA; Yale U. **Bibliography:** Calas, N. and E.; Davies; Tuchman 1.

VON WEIGAND, CHARMION. b. March 4, 1896, Chicago, Ill. **d.** June 9, 1985, NYC. **Studied:** Barnard College; Columbia U.; NYU; self-taught in art. Traveled Europe, Mexico. Subject of film *The Circle of Charmion von Weigand.* **Member:** American Abstract Artists (president, 1952-53). **Awards:** Cranbrook, Religious Art Exhibition, First Prize, 1969. **One-man Exhibitions:** Rose Fried Gallery, 1942, 48, 56; Saidenberg Gallery, 1952; John Heller, NYC, 1956; Zoe Dusanne Gallery, Seattle, 1958; La Cittadella d'Arte Internazionale e d'Avanguardia, Ascona, Switzerland, 1959; The Howard Wise Gallery, NYC, 1961; U. of Texas, 1969; Birmingham, Ala./MA, 1970; Galleria Fiamma Vigo, Rome and Venice, 1973; Annely Juda Fine Art, London, 1974; Noah Goldowsky Gallery, NYC, 1975; Andre Zarre Gallery, NYC, 1975; Marilyn Pearl Gallery, NYC, 1978, 81, 85; Buffalo/Albright, Plus by Minus, 1968; Chicago/Contemporary, Post-Mondrian Abstraction in America, 1973; Springfield, Mass./MFA, Three American Purists, 1975; Paris/ Beaubourg, Paris-New York, 1977; Newark Museum, Geometric Abstraction and Related Works, 1978; Yale U., Mondrian and New-plasticism in America, 1979; AAIAL, 1980; MOMA, Contrasts of Form: Geometric Abstract Art 1910-1980, 1985. **Collections:** Buffalo/Albright; Carnegie; Ciba-Geigy Corp.; Cincinnati/AM; Cleveland/MA; Container Corp. of America; Cornell U.; Hirshhorn; Indiana U.; MOMA; McCrory Corporation; Milwaukee; Montclair/AM; Mount Holyoke College; NYU; Newark Museum; New York Hospital; U. of North Carolina; U. of Notre Dame; SRGM; Seattle/AM; Springfield, Mass./MFA; U. of Texas;

WMAA. **Bibliography:** Janis and Blesh 1; MacAgy 2; Rickey; Seitz 3; Seuphor 1. Archives.

VON WICHT, JOHN. b. February 3, 1888, Holstein, Germany; **d.** January 22, 1970, Brooklyn, N.Y. **Studied:** Private art school of the Grand Duke of Hesse, 1909-10, BA; School of Fine and Applied Arts, Berlin, 1912. Traveled Europe. To USA, 1923; citizen, 1936. **Taught:** ASL, 1951-52; John Herron Art Institute, 1953. **Member:** American Abstract Artists; Audubon Artists; Federation of Modern Painters and Sculptors; International Institute of Arts and Letters; SAGA. Federal A.P.: Mural painting. **Commissions:** Pan American Airways Terminal, Miami, Fla.; McGill U.; New York World's Fair, 1939; Pennsylvania Railroad Station, Trenton, N.J. **Awards:** Brooklyn Museum, First Prize, 1948, 49, **P.P.,** 1951, 64; SAGA, Mrs. A.W. Erickson Prize, 1953; The Print Club, Philadelphia, William H. Walker Memorial Prize, 1957; Audubon Artists, Gold Medal of Honor, 1958; Ford Foundation, **P.P.,** 1960; SAGA, **P.P.,** 1967-68. **One-man Exhibitions:** (first in USA) Architects Building, NYC, 1936; 608 Fifth Avenue, NYC, 1939; Artists' Gallery, NYC, 1944; Kleemann Gallery, NYC, 1946, 47; UCLA, 1947; Passedoit Gallery, NYC, 1950, 51, 52, 54, 56, 57, 58; Indianapolis/Herron, 1953; Esther Robles Gallery, 1959; Pasadena/AM, 1959; Liege, 1959; The Bertha Schaefer Gallery, 1960, 61, 62, 64, 66; Galerie Neufville, Paris, 1962; Grippi Gallery, 1966; Martin Diamond Fine Arts, NYC, 1984. **Retrospective:** Santa Barbara/MA, 1959. **Group:** California Palace, 1964; Brooklyn Museum; Audubon Artists; MMA; WMAA Annuals; Federation of Modern Painters and Sculptors; Corcoran; PAFA; SRGM; Carnegie; NAD; Chicago/AI. **Collections:** Baltimore/MA; Boston/MFA; Brandeis U.; Brooklyn Museum; Chase Manhattan Bank; Cincinnati/AM; Jewish Museum; S.C. Johnson & Son, Inc.;

Library of Congress; Liege; Lincoln, Mass./De Cordova; MMA; MOMA; Madrid/Nacional; NCFA; PMA; Paris/Moderne; Norfolk/Chrysler; Stockholm/National; Union Carbide Corp.; WMAA; Yale U. **Bibliography:** Baur 7; Nordness, ed.; Pousette-Dart, ed. Archives.

VOULKOS, PETER. b. January 29, 1924, Bozeman, Mont. **Studied:** Montana State College, BS; California College of Arts and Crafts, MFA. Traveled Italy, Japan. **Taught:** Archie Bray Foundation, Helena, Mont.; Black Mountain College; Los Angeles County Art Institute; Montana State U.; U. of California, Berkeley, 1959-85; Greenwich House Pottery, NYC; Teachers College, Columbia U. *Voulkos and Company*, 16mm film produced by Clyde Smith, 1972. **Awards:** RAC, First Prize; National Decorative Art Show, Wichita, Kans., First Prize; Portland, Ore./AM, Northwest Craft Show, First Prize; Pacific Coast Ceramic Show, First Prize; Denver/AM, **P.P.;** Cranbrook, **P.P.;** Smithsonian, **P.P.;** Los Angeles/County Fair, **P.P.;** Pasadena/AM, **P.P.;** Ford Foundation, **P.P.;** International Ceramic Exhibition, Ostend, Belgium, Silver Medal, 1959; International Ceramic Exhibition, Cannes, France, Gold Medal; I Paris Biennial 1959; Rodin Museum Prize in Sculpture; SFMA, Ford Foundation, **P.P.;** L.H.D. (Hon.), Montana State U., 1968; Brandeis U., Creative Arts Award, 1982; Hon. DFA, SFAI, 1982; American Craft Council, Gold Medal, 1986; Guggenheim Foundation Fellowship, 1984; San Francisco Art Commission, Award of Honor, 1981. **Address:** 1306 3rd Street, Berkeley, CA 94710 **Dealers:** Braunstein Gallery, San Francisco; Charles Cowles Gallery, NYC; Exhibit A Gallery, Chicago; Leedy-Voulkos Gallery, Kansas City, Mo. **One-man Exhibitions:** Gump's Gallery; U. of Florida; Historical Society of Montana; Felix Landau Gallery; Chicago/AI; Bonniers, Inc., NYC.; Fresno

Peter Voulkos   *Untitled*   1982

State College; Scripps College; U. of Southern California; Pasadena/AM; David Stuart Gallery, 1967; Los Angeles/County MA; Hansen Gallery, San Francisco; Quay Gallery, 1968, 74, SFMA, 1972; Kansas City, 1975; Detroit/Institute, 1976; Exhibit A, Chicago, 1979; Braunstein Quay Gallery, San Francisco, 1975, 78; Charles Cowles Gallery, 1981, 83; Exhibit A Gallery, 1981, 84; Thomas Segal Gallery, Boston, 1981; Braunstein Gallery, 1982, 84, 86; Morgan Gallery, Kansas City, Mo., 1983; Magnolia Editions, Oakland, Calif., 1984; Leedy-Voulkos Gallery, 1986; Point View Gallery, Tokyo, 1983. **Retrospective:** SFMA, circ., 1978. **Group:** MMA; Scripps College; Syracuse/Everson, National Ceramic Exhibition; U. of Tennessee; Brussels World's Fair, 1958; de Young; Seattle World's Fair, 1962; Stanford U.; Denver/AM; Smithsonian; Los Angeles/County MA; Battersea Park,

London, International Sculpture Exhibition, 1963; Los Angeles State College, 1964; U. of California, Irvine, 1966; WMAA, 1970; WMAA, 200 Years of American Sculpture, 1976; Houston/Contemporary, 1978; WMAA, Ceramic Sculpture: Six Artists, 1981; Los Angeles/County MA, Art in Los Angeles, 1981; Kansas City/Nelson, Ceramic Echoes, 1983; Los Angeles Municipal Art Gallery, Art in Clay, 1984. **Collections:** Arizona State U.; Baltimore/MA; Archie Bray Foundation; Boston/MFA; City of Fresno; Corcoran; Cranbrook; Des Moines; Denver/AM; U. of Florida; Fresno State College; Highland Park (Ill.) Public Library; Honolulu Academy; U. of Illinois; State U. of Iowa; Iowa State Teachers College; Japanese Craft Museum; Kansas City/Nelson; La Jolla; Los Angeles County Fair Association; Los Angeles/County MA; Minnesota/MA; MOMA; Montana State College; Museum of Contemporary Crafts; Oakland/AM; PMA; Pasadena/AM; Phoenix; Portland, Ore./AM; SFMA; Sacramento/Crocker; St. Louis/City; Santa Barbara/MA; Seattle/AM; Smithsonian; Syracuse/Everson; Tokyo Folk Art Museum; UCLA; U. of Utah; WMAA; Wichita/AM; U. of Wisconsin. **Bibliography:** Read 3; *Report*; Selz, P., 2; Trier 1; Tuchman 1.

VYTLACIL, VACLAV. b. November 1, 1892, NYC; **d.** January 5, 1984, NYC.

Studied: Chicago Art Institute School, 1908-12; ASL, 1912-14; Hofmann School, Munich, 1922-26. Traveled extensively; resided Europe 16 years. **Taught:** Minneapolis Institute School, 1918-22; U. of California, Berkeley, summers, 1927-28; ASL, 1928-69; California College of Arts and Crafts, summers, 1936, 37; Colorado Springs Fine Arts Center, summers, 1947, 48, 49; Chicago Art Institute School, 1954; U. of Georgia, 1968. **Member:** Federation of Modern Painters and Sculptors; American Abstract Artists. Federal A.P.: Organized an art school in Harlem, NYC. **Awards:** Chicago/AI, William R. French Memorial Gold Medal. **One-man Exhibitions:** (first) Feigl Gallery, NYC, 1942; Phillips; U. of Rochester; Baltimore/MA; Minneapolis Institute School; The Krasner Gallery; Southern Vermont Art Center, Manchester; U. of Notre Dame, 1975; Martin Diamond Gallery, NYC, 1979, 81. **Retrospective:** Montclair/AM, 1975. **Group:** American Abstract Artists Annuals; Federation of Modern Painters and Sculptors Annuals; Chicago/AI; Carnegie; PAFA; WMAA; Corcoran; MMA. **Collections:** ASL; Colorado Springs/FA; Dalton School; U. of Georgia; Hartford/Wadsworth; MMA; Montclair/AM; PAFA; Phillips; U. of Rochester; WMAA. **Bibliography:** Baur 7; Blesh 1; Cheney; Janis, S.; Lane and Larsen; Marter, Tarbell, and Wechsler; Pousette-Dart, ed.; Toher, ed. Archives.

WALD, SYLVIA. b. October 30, 1915, Philadelphia. Pa. **Studied:** Moore Institute of Art, Science and Industry, Philadelphia, 1931-35. Traveled Europe, Central America, Greece, Spain, India, Nepal, Kashmir, Japan, Korea. Federal A.P.: Teacher. **Awards:** MOMA, **P.P.,** 1941; Library of Congress, Pennell **P.P.,** 1944; National Serigraph Society, NYC, First Prize, 1948; Brooklyn Museum, **P.P.,** 1951, 54; Pratt Institute, International Miniature Competition, 1967; The Print Club, Philadelphia, 1969. **m.** Po Kim. **Address:** 417 Lafayette St., NYC 10003. **Dealer:** Marden Fine Arts, NYC. **One-man Exhibitions:** (first) ACA Gallery, 1939; Kent State College, 1945; U. of Louisville, 1945, 49; National Serigraph Society, NYC, 1946; Grand Central Moderns, NYC, 1957; Devorah Sherman Gallery, 1960; Briarcliff (N.Y.) Public Library, 1966; New School for Social Research, 1967; Book Gallery, White Plains, N.Y., 1968; Benson Gallery, Bridgehampton, N.Y., 1977; Amerika Haus, Munich, 1979; Knoll International, Munich, 1979; Aaron Berman, NYC, 1981. **Group:** WMAA; National Sculpture Society, 1940; City of Philadelphia, Sculpture International, 1940; Chicago/AI, Directions in American Painting, 1941; Brooklyn Museum, Print Biennials, MOMA, 1941, 53, 56; Library of Congress, 1943, 52, 58; WMAA Annuals, 1948, 55; PAFA Annuals, 1950, 53, 54, 57; International Print Exhibition, Salzburg and Vienna, 1952; II Sao Paulo Biennial, 1953; Smithsonian, Curators' Choice—1942-52, circ., USA, 1954; MOMA, 50 Years of American Art, circ., Europe, 1955; Brooklyn Museum, 10 Years of American Prints, 1947-56, 1956; Bordighera, 1957; PCA, American Prints Today, circ., 1959-62; New York Cultural Center, Women Choose Women, 1973; MOMA, American Prints: 1913-1963, 1974-75. **Collections:** Aetna Oil Co.; American Association of University Women; Ball State U.; Bibliotheque Nationale; Brandeis U.; Brooklyn Museum; Howard U.; State U. of Iowa; Library of Congress; Louisville/Speed; U. of Louisville; MOMA; NYPL; National Gallery; U. of Nebraska; Ohio U.; U. of Oklahoma; PMA; Princeton U.; Raleigh/NCMA; Rutgers U.; SRGM; Toronto; Utica; Victoria and Albert Museum; WMAA; Walker; Worcester/AM. **Bibliography:** Peterdi. Archives.

WALDMAN, PAUL. b. August 1, 1936, Erie, Pa. **Studied:** Brooklyn Museum School; Pratt Institute. **Taught:** New York Community College, 1963-64; Brooklyn Museum School, 1963-67; The Ohio State U., 1966; U. of California, Davis, 1966; School of Visual Arts, NYC, 1966-. **Awards:** Ford Foundation, Artist-in-Residence, 1965. **Address:** 38 West 26th Street, NYC. 10010. **Dealer:** Leo Castelli, Inc., NYC. **One-man Exhibitions:** (first) Allan Stone Gallery, 1963, 65; St. Joseph/Albrecht, 1966; Leo Castelli, Inc., NYC, 1973, 75, 78, 81, 84; Blum Helman Gallery Inc., NYC, 1978; Kunsthalle Tranegarden, Copenhagen, 1981; Norbyllands Kunstmuseum, Aalborg, 1981. **Group:** Barnard College, Young Americans, 1962; Louis Alexander Gallery, NYC, Recent American Drawings, 1962; WGMA, 1963, 64; Brandeis U., Recent American Drawings, 1964, Hartford/Wadsworth, Figures, 1964; U. of Colorado, Survey of World Painting and Sculpture, 1964; Brooklyn Museum, Print Biennials; Finch College, 1966, 67 (circ.), 68; Smithsonian, circ., Germany, 1967; WMAA Annual, 1967; Finch College, NYC, The Dominant Female, 1968; Hirshhorn, Inaugural Exhibition, 1974; Philadelphia College of Art, Private Notation, Artists' Sketchbooks, 1976; NYC, Precious, 1985; U. of North Carolina, Art on Paper, 1985. **Collections:** Achenbach Foundation; Brandeis U.; Brooklyn Museum; U. of California; Colby College; Colgate U.; Cornell U.; Darmouth College; Denver/AM; Des Moines; Fairleigh Dickinson U.; Harvard U.; Hirshhorn; John Hopkins U.; Houston/MFA; J. Turner Jones, Inc.; Kansas City/Nelson; La Jolla; Los Angeles/County MA; MIT; MOMA; U. of Massachusetts; Mount Holyoke College; NYU; Newark Museum; Oberlin College; Pasadena/AM; RISD; U. of Rochester; Russell Sage College; Rutgers U.; The Singer Company, Inc.; Smithsonian; SRGM; Stony Brook/SUNY; Storm King Art Center; Toledo/MA; Washington U.; Yale U.

WALKOWITZ, ABRAHAM. b. March 28, 1878, Tyumen, Russia; **d.** January 18, 1965. **Studied:** NAD; Academie Julian, Paris, with Jean Paul Laurens. Traveled Europe extensively. **Taught:** Educational Alliance, NYC. **Awards:** AAAL, Marjorie Peabody Waite Award, 1962. **One-man Exhibitions:** "291," NYC, 1912; The Downtown Gallery, 1930; Park Gallery, NYC, 1937; Brooklyn Museum, 1939; Newark Museum, 1941; NYPL, 1942; Schacht Gallery, NYC, 1944; Chinese Gallery, NYC, 1946; Charles Egan Gallery, 1947; Jewish Museum, 1949; Hartford/Wadsworth, 1950; ACA Gallery, 1955; The Zabriskie Gallery, 1959, 64, 66, 68, 69, 70, 73, 74; Danenberg Gallery, 1971. **Retrospectives:** Utah, 1974; Purchase/SUNY, 1982. **Group:** NAD, 1904; WMAA; The Armory Show, 1913; Anderson Galleries, NYC, Forum Exhibition, 1916. **Collections:** Andover/Phillips; Boston/MFA; Brooklyn Museum; Columbus; Kalamazoo/Institute; Library of Congress; MMA; MOMA; Newark Museum; Phillips; WMAA. **Bibliography:** Avant-Garde Painting and Sculpture in America 1910-25; Baur 7; Biddle 4; Blesh 1; Brown 2; Cahill and Barr, eds.; Cheney; Frank, ed.; Goodrich and Baur 1; Haftman; Hartmann; Hunter 5; Janis, S.; Levin 2; McCoubrey 1; McCurdy, ed.; Mellquist; Richardson, E.P.; Rose, B., 4; **Walkowitz 1, 2;** Wright 1. Archives.

WARHOL, ANDY. b. August 6, 1928; McKeesport, Pa.; **d.** February 22, 1987, NYC. **Studied:** Carnegie, BFA, 1945-49. Illustrator for *Glamour* magazine, 1949-50; commercial artist, 1950-57; produced and directed films with Paul Morrissey; Executive producer, "Andy Warhol's TV," 1980-87. **Award:** Art Directors Club Medal, 1957. Publisher of Andy Warhol's *Interview.* **One-man Exhibitions:** Ferus Gallery, Los Angeles, 1962, 63; The Stable Gallery, 1962, 64; Ileana Sonnabend Gallery, Paris, 1964, 65, 67, 74; Leo Castelli, Inc., NYC, 1964, 66, 77, 82; Morris International Gallery, Toronto, 1965; Galleria Sperone, Turin, 1965; Galleria Rubbers, Buenos Aires, 1965; ICA, U. of Pennsylvania, 1965; Eva de Buren Gallery, Stockholm, 1965; ICA, Boston, 1966; Galerie Hans R. Neuendorf, Hamburg, 1966; Galerie Rudolf Zwirner, 1967; Stockholm/National, 1968; Rowan Gallery, London, 1968; Leo Castelli, Inc./David Whitney Gallery, 1969; Chicago/Contemporary, 1970; Eindhoven, 1970; Paris/Moderne, 1970; Tate, 1971; WMAA, 1971; Gotham Book Mart, NYC, 1971; Modern Art Agency, Naples, 1972; Walker, 1972; New Gallery, Cleveland, 1973; Musée Galliera, Paris, 1973; Jared Sable Gallery, Toronto, 1974; F. H. Mayor Gallery, London, 1974, 76; Margo Leavin Gallery, 1975; Hugo Gallery, NYC, 1952; Bodley Gallery, NYC, 1956, 57, 58, 59, 62; Bal-

Andy Warhol *Self Portrait* 1979

timore/MA, 1975; Greenberg Gallery, St. Louis, 1975; Max Protetch Gallery, Washington, D.C., 1975; Dusseldorf/Kunsthalle, 1976; Freeman-Anacker, New Orleans, 1976; Arno Schefler Gallery, NYC, 1976; Coe Kerr Gallery, NYC (two-man), 1976, 77; Pyramid Art Galleries, Ltd., Washington, D.C., 1977; Sable-Castelli Gallery, Ltd., Toronto, 1977; ACE, Los Angeles, 1977; ACE, Venice, Calif., 1977, 78; Seattle/AM, 1977; Optica, Montreal, 1977; Galerie Heiner Friedrich, Cologne, 1977; Musée d'art et d'histoire, Geneva, 1978; Texas Gallery, Houston, 1978; SMU, 1978; ICA, London, 1978; Humlebaek/Louisiana, 1978; Heiner Friedrich, Inc., NYC, 1979; Massimo Valsecchi Gallery, Milan, 1979; ACE Gallery, Vancouver, 1979; Hartford/Wadsworth, 1979; Lucio Amelio Gallery, Naples, Italy, 1980; Amsterdam/Stedelijk, 1980, 81; Galerie Bischofberger, Zurich, 1980, 83, 84; Centre d'Art Contemporain, Geneva, 1980; Gray Gaultney Gallery, NYC, 1980; Richard Hines Gallery, Seattle, 1980; Lisson Gallery, London, 1980; Jewish Museum, 1980; Palomar College, 1980; Portland (Ore.) Center for the Visual Arts, 1980; Galerie Daniel Templon, Paris, 1980, 82; Virginia Commonwealth U., 1980; Thomas Babeor Gallery, La Jolla, 1981; Ronald Feldman Gallery, NYC, 1981; Thomas Segal Gallery, Boston, 1981; Galerie Watari, Tokyo, 1981; Castelli-Goodman-Solomon, East Hampton, N.Y., 1982; Dover Museum, England, 1982; Galerie Kammer, Hamburg, 1982; Modernism Gallery, San Francisco, 1982; Galerie des Ponchettes, Nice, France, 1982; Galeria Vijande, Madrid, 1982; American Museum of Natural History, NYC, 1983; Fraenkel Gallery, San Francisco, 1983; Gloria Luria Gallery, Bay Harbor Islands, Fla., 1983; Govinda Gallery, Washington, D.C., 1983, 85; Ridgefield/Aldrich, 1983; Galerie Borjeson, Malmo, 1984; Delahunty Gallery, Dallas, 1984; Marisa del Re Gallery, NYC, 1985; Linda Farris Gallery, Seattle, 1985; Museo e Galleria Nazionale di Capodimonte, Naples, Italy, 1985; Old Westbury/SUNY, 1985; Vanguard Gallery, Philadelphia, 1985. **Retrospectives:** Stuttgart, Kunstverein, circ., 1976; Zurich, 1978; WMAA, 1979; Hannover/K-G, circ., 1981. **Group:** SRGM, Six Painters and the Object, circ., 1963; WGMA, The Popular Image, 1963; Kansas City/Nelson, 1963; Oakland/AM, Pop Art USA, 1963; ICA, London, The Popular Image, 1963; Stockholm/National, American Pop Art, 1964; Salon du Mai, Paris, 1964; U. of Rochester, 1964; Worcester/AM, 1965; Palais des Beaux-Arts, Brussels, 1965; Hamburger Kunstkabinett, 1965; SRGM, 1966; RISD, Recent Still Life, 1966; Flint/Institute, I Flint Invitational, 1966; Expo '67, Montreal, 1967; Detroit/Institute, Color, Image and Form, 1967; IX Sao Paulo Biennial, 1967; MOMA, The 1960's, 1967; Carnegie, 1967; Eindhoven, 1967; Palazzo Grassi, Venice, 1967; WMAA Annual, 1968; Jewish Museum, 1968; Documenta IV, Kassel, 1968; Milwaukee, Directions I: Options, circ., 1968; Finch College, NYC, 1968; Jewish Museum, Superlimited: Books, Boxes and Things, 1969; Ars 69, Helsinki, 1969; Indianapolis, 1969; U. of California, Irvine, New

York: The Second Breakthrough, 1959-1964, 1969; Hayward Gallery, London, Pop Art, 1969; MMA, New York Painting and Sculpture, 1940-1970, 1969; Denver/AM, Report on the Sixties, 1969; Pasadena/AM, Painting in New York: 1944-1969, 1969; WMAA, 1969, 73; Expo '70, Osaka, 1970; Indianapolis, 1970; Kunsthalle, Nurnberg, The Thing as Object, 1970; Cincinnati/Contemporary, Monumental Art, 1970; Buffalo/Albright, Kid Stuff, 1971; Dusseldorf/Kunsthalle, Prospect, '71, 1971; ICA, U. of Pennsylvania, Grids, 1972; High Museum, The Modern Image, 1972; Detroit/Institute, Art in Space, 1973; Parcheggio di Villa Borghese, Rome, Contemporanea, 1974; Seattle/AM, American Art—Third Quarter Century, 1974; Chicago/AI, Idea and Image in Recent Art, 1974, WMAA, American Pop Art, 1974; Lincoln Center, NYC, The Florists Transworld Delivery Collection, 1974; MOMA, Drawings Now, 1976; High Museum, The New Image, 1976; SRGM, 20th Century American Drawing, 1976; Dallas/MFA, American Art Since 1945, 1976; Venice Biennial, 1976; Cambridge U., Jubilation, 1977; Minnesota/MA, American Drawing 1927-1977, 1977; WMAA, Art about Art, 1978; Buffalo/Albright, American Painting of the 1970s, circ., 1978; Pomona College, Black and White Are Colors, 1979; Milwaukee, Emergence and Progression, circ., 1979; Brooklyn Museum, American Drawings in Black and White: 1970-1979, 1980; Norfolk/Chrysler, American Figurative Painting, 1950-1980, 1980; Akron/AM, The Image in American Painting and Sculpture, 1950-1980, 1981; Royal Academy, London, An New Spirit in Painting, 1981; Documenta VII, Kassel, 1982; Houston/Contemporary, The Americans: The Collage, 1982; Internationale Kunstausstellung Berlin, 1982; Houston/Contemporary, American Still Life, 1945-1983, 1983; Krefeld/Haus Lange, Sweet Dreams Baby!: American Pop Graphics, 1983; WMAA, Blam!, 1984; Paris/Beaubourg, Livres d'Ar-

tistes, 1985. **Collections:** Brandeis U.; Buffalo/Albright; Canberra/National; Chicago/AI; Cologne; Des Moines; Detroit/Institute; Hirshhorn; Kansas City/Nelson; Los Angeles/County MA; MOMA; MMA; Pasadena/AM; Stockholm/National; Tate; Toronto; WGMA; WMAA; Walker. **Bibliography:** Alloway 1, 4; *Art Now 74*; Battcock, ed.; Becker and Vostell; *Black and White Are Colors*; Danto; De Wilde 2; Haskell 5; Honisch and Jensen, eds.; Calas, N. and E.; *Contemporanea*; Coplans 3; **Coplans, Mekas, and Tomkins; Crone;** Davis, D.; Dienst 1; Finch; Green; Hunter, ed.; Joachimides and Rosenthal; Johnson, Ellen H.; **Koch, S.;** Kosloff 3; *Kunst um 1970*; Lippard 5; Lucie-Smith; Murken-Altrogge; *Report*; Rose, B., 1; Rublowsky; Russell and Gablik; Sandler 1; Sager, Tomkins and Time-Life Books; Tomkins 2; **Warhol; Warhol et al, eds.;** Whitney, ed., Weller.

WASHINGTON, JAMES W., JR. b. November 10, 1909, Gloster, Miss. Studied painting privately with Mark Tobey in Seattle. Changed from painting to sculpture in 1956. Traveled Mexico, Europe, Middle East. Federal A.P.: Teacher (Vicksburg, Miss.). **Taught:** Baptist Academy, Vicksburg, Miss., 1938; Western Washington College, 1968; Director, Baptists Training Union, Mt. Zion Baptist Church, Seattle, 1947-51. **Commissions:** Island Park School, Mercer Island, Seattle, Wash. (sculpture); First National Bank of Seattle, 1968; World Trade Center, Seattle; Odessa Brown Clinic, Seattle, 1981; Seattle Sheraton Hotel, 1982; Washington State Capitol Museum, Olympia, 1983. **Awards:** SFMA, **P.P.,** 1956; Oakland/AM, **P.P.,** 1957; Seattle World's Fair, 1962, Second Prize; Hon. DFA, Graduate Theological Union, 1975. **Address:** 1816 26th Avenue, Seattle, WA 98122. **Dealer:** Foster-White Gallery, Seattle. **One-man Exhibitions:** Feingarten Gallery, Los Angeles, 1958; Haydon Calhoun Gallery,

Dallas, 1960, 61; Nordness Galleries, 1962; Gordon Woodside Gallery, 1963, 64, 65; Richard White Gallery, Seattle, 1968; St. Mary's College (Ind.), 1969; Foster-White Gallery, Seattle, 1972, 74, 76, 78, 85; (first) US Army Base, Auburn, Wash., 1954; San Diego, American Baptist Sculpture, 1977. **Retrospective:** Frey Museum, 1980. **Group:** Santa Barbara/MA, 1959; Otis Art Institute, 1963; Seattle World's Fair, 1962; Expo '70, Osaka, 1970; Seattle Urban League, 1978. **Collections:** Oakland/AM; SFMA; Seattle/AM. **Bibliography:** *Art of the Pacific Northwest;* Dover.

WATTS, ROBERT M. b. June 14, 1923, Burlington, Iowa. **Studied:** U. of Louisville, 1944, B. Mech. Eng.; Columbia U., 1951, AM; ASL, with Bernard Klonis, John McPherson, Ethel Katz, Morris Kantor, William Zorach. US Naval Reserve, 1941-46. Traveled Mexico, Europe, Caribbean. **Taught:** Institute of Applied Arts and Sciences, Brooklyn, 1951-52; Rutgers U., 1952-84; Douglass College, 1953-. Changed from painting to sculpture, 1956; changed to light-sound-motion sculpture, 1957; first Events and Happenings, 1958. Designed costumes for James Waring Dance Co. Films: *Cascade,* 1962, *G.W. & Sons,* 1963, *89 Movies,* 1965; *Alice,* 1958. **Awards:** Rutgers U. Research Fund Grant, 1961, 62, 63; Carnegie Corporation Grant, 1965. **Address:** R.D. 3, Bangor, PA 18013. **One-man Exhibitions:** Douglass College Art Gallery, 1953, 57; U. of Alabama, 1957; Delacorte Gallery, NYC, 1958 (welded sculpture); Grand Central Moderns, NYC, 1960, 61; Smolin Gallery, NYC, 1960 (Magic Kazoo), 1963; The Kornblee Gallery, 1963; Galerie Rolf Ricke, 1966, 67; Galleria Christian Stein, Turin, 1967; SFAI, 1969; Apple Gallery, NYC, 1971; Galleria Bertesca, Milan, 1973; Galerie Baecker, 1973; Multipla, 1974, 75; Francesco Conz, Verona, Italy, 1982. **Group Exhibitions, Events, Happenings:** Newark Mu-

seum, New Jersey Artists, 1955; Montclair/AM, New Jersey State Annual, 1955, 56; American Abstract Artists, 1957; Martha Jackson Gallery, New Media—New Forms, II, 1961; Amsterdam/Stedelijk, Art in Motion, circ., Europe, 1961-62; MOMA, The Art of Assemblage, circ., 1961; Fluxus International Festival, NYC, 1962-63; WGMA, The Popular Image, 1963; Smolin Gallery, NYC, Yam Festival, A Series of Events, 1963 III Paris Biennial, Two Inches (event), 1963; Buffalo/Albright, Mixed Media and Pop Art, 1963; Dwan Gallery, Boxes, 1964; Douglass College, 1964; MOMA, The Machine, 1968; MOMA, Photography into Sculpture, 1970; Cologne/Kunstverein, Happening & Fluxus, 1970; MOMA, Information 1971; Documenta V, Kassel, 1972; Akademie der Kunst, Berlin, SoHo, 1976; Cranbrook, Fluxus Etc., 1981; WMAA, Blam!, 1984. **Bibliography:** Atkinson; *Contemporanea;* Gerdts; *Happening & Fluxus;* Hulten; Kozloff 3; *Kunst um 1970;* Lippard 5; *Report;* Ruhe; Seitz 3.

WAYNE, JUNE. b. March 7, 1918, Chicago, Ill. Self-taught in art. Traveled Europe extensively. Federal A.P.: Easel painting. **Member:** Artists Equity; Society of Washington Printmakers; The Print Club, Philadelphia; SAGA, Founder and director of Tamarind Lithography Workshop, Inc. (1959-75), funded by the Program in Humanities and the Arts of the Ford Foundation. Visiting Committee of the School of Visual and Environmental Studies, Harvard U., 1972-76. **Awards:** Los Angeles County Fair, **P.P.,** 1950; Los Angeles/County MA, **P.P.,** 1951; Library of Congress, Pennell **P.P.,** 1953; The Print Club, Philadelphia, **P.P.,** 1958; Pasadena/AM, **P.P.,** 1958, 59; SAGA, Edna Pennypacker Stauffer Memorial Prize, 1963; and others; Academy of Motion Pictures Arts and Sciences Nomination, documentary category, 1974; *The Golden Eagle* (film);

AEA/AFEA, Recognition Award, 1978; Hon. DFA, International College, London, 1976; National Endowment for the Arts, 1980; YMCA, Silver Achievement Award, 1983. Advisor: Board of Directors, California Confederation of the Arts, 1975-. **Address:** 1108 North Tamarind Avenue, Los Angeles, Calif. 90038. **Dealer:** A.A.A. Gallery, NYC. **One-man Exhibitions:** (first) Boulevard Gallery, Chicago, 1935; Mexico City/Nacional, 1936; SFMA, 1950; Santa Barbara/MA, 1950, 53, 58; Pasadena/AM, 1952; Chicago/AI, 1952; The Contemporaries, NYC, 1953; de Young, 1956; California Palace; Achenbach Foundation, 1958; Los Angeles/County MA, 1959; Long Beach/MA, 1959; Philadelphia Art Alliance, 1959; U. of New Mexico, 1968; U. of Iowa, 1970; Grunwald Graphic Arts Foundation, Los Angeles, 1971; Gimpel & Weitzenhoffer, 1972; Los Angeles Municipal Art, 1973; Van Doren Gallery, San Francisco, 1974, 76; Muchenthaler Cultural Center, Fullerton, Calif., 1974; La Demeure, Paris, 1975, 76; Artemisia, Chicago, 1975; U. of Wisconsin, Oshkosh, 1975; U. of Southern Colorado, 1976; Adams State College, 1976; French American Institute, Rennes, 1976; Brest, Musée Municipal, 1977; Rubicon Gallery, Los Altos, 1977; Cypress College, 1977; Les Premontres, Nancy, France, 1977; Palm Springs Desert Museum, 1977; Claremont College, 1978; Arizona State U., 1979; Corvallis Art Center, 1979; American Library, Brussels, 1978; Foundation Pescatore, Luxembourg, 1979; Maison de la Culture Andre Malraux, Reims, 1979; Musee de Chartres, 1979; Lyons, Musee, 1979; Occidental College, Los Angeles, 1980; Charleston Heights Art Center, Las Vegas, 1981; San Diego, 1981; Anita Seipp Gallery, Palo Alto, Calif., 1981; West Hills Community College, Coalinga, Calif., 1981; U. of Alabama, 1982; Des Moines, 1982; Jewish Museum, 1982; North Denton U., 1982; Sacramento/Crocker, 1982; Sunset Cultural Center, Carmel, Calif., 1982; Tobey C. Moss Gallery, Los Angeles, 1983, 85; Pomona College, 1983; San Jose Institute of Contemporary Art, 1983; Armstrong Gallery, NYC, 1984; A.A.A. Gallery, 1985; Galerie des Femmes, Paris, 1985; Print Club of Philadelphia, 1985. **Retrospectives:** FAR Gallery, 1969; Cincinnati/AM, 1969. **Group:** Library of Congress; Brooklyn Museum; Seattle/AM; PAFA; U. of Illinois; Los Angeles/County MA; MMA; SAGA Annuals; MOMA, circ. (graphics); MOMA, Young American Printmakers, 1953; California State Fair; San Diego; Denver/AM; WMAA Annuals; Sao Paulo, 1955; Smithsonian; Achenbach Foundation; PCA, American Prints Today, circ., 1959-62; Paris/Moderne; The Japan Print Association, Tokyo, 1961; Smithsonian, 1964; CSCS, Fullerton, 1964; SFAI, 1965; Cincinnati/AM, 1968; and many others. **Collections:** Achenbach Foundation; Bibliotheque Nationale; Bibliotheque Royale de Belgique; UCLA; U. of California, Santa Barbara; Chicago/AI; Cincinnati/AM; Columbia, S.C./MA; De Pauw U.; Fort Worth; Grunwald Foundation; Iowa State U.; La Jolla; Lehigh U.; Library of Congress; Long Beach/MA; Los Angeles/County MA; MOMA; U. of Minnesota; NYPL; National Gallery; Newberry Library; U. of New Mexico; Northwestern U.; Oberlin College; PMA; Pasadena/AM; The Print Club, Philadelphia; San Diego; San Jose State College; Santa Barbara/MA; Smithsonian; Walker. **Bibliography:** *Art: A Woman's Sensibility*; Rodman 1, 3. Archives.

WEBER, IDELLE. b. March 12, 1932, Chicago, Ill. **Studied:** Scripps College; UCLA, BA; Chouinard Art Institute, with Millard Sheets; Otis Art Institute; with Else Palmer Paynes and Theodore Lukits in Los Angeles; ASL, with Theodore Stamos; Brooklyn Museum, with Reuben Tam. Traveled England, Southern France, Italy, Spain, Greece. **Taught:** UCLA, 1955; NYU, 1976-80. **Member:** Women's Caucus for Art;

Idelle Weber   *The Saugerties Vase I*   1986

trustee of the Museum of Holography. **Address:** 429 West Broadway, NYC 10012. **Dealer:** Ruth Siegel Gallery, NYC. **One-man Exhibitions:** (first) Bertha Schaefer Gallery, NYC, 1963, 64; Hundred Acres Gallery Ltd., NYC, 1973, 75, 77; Chatham College, 1979; OK Harris Works of Art, NYC, 1979, 82; Ruth Siegel Gallery, 1984, 85; Arts Club of Chicago, 1986. **Group:** SRGM, American Drawings, 1964; Worcester/AM, New Realism, 1965; Hartford/Wadsworth, New/Photo Realism, 1974; Wichita State U., The New Realism; Rip-Off or Reality?, 1975; San Antonio/McNay, American Artists, 76: A Celebration, 1976; Smithsonian, America as Art, 1976; St. Petersburg, Fla., Photo Realism, 1978; U. of Connecticut, Photo Realism, 1979; San Antonio/MA, Real, Really Real, Super Real, circ., 1981; IEF, 20th Century American Drawings: The Figure in Context, circ., 1984; SFMA, American Realism (Janss), circ., 1985; Indianapolis, 1986. **Collections:** Buffalo/Albright; MMA; NCFA; NYPL; Rochester U.; San Antonio/McNay; VMFA; Worcester.

WEBER, MAX. b. April 18, 1881, Byalestok, Russia; **d.** October, 1961, Great Neck, N.Y. To USA, 1891. **Studied:** Pratt Institute, 1898-1900, with Arthur Dow; Academie Julian, Paris, 1905-06, with Jean Paul Laurens; Academie de la Grande Chaumiere; Academie Colarossi, Paris, 1906-07. Traveled Europe extensively. **Taught:** Lynchburg, Va. public schools, 1901-03; U. of Virginia (summer); State Normal School, Duluth, Minn., 1903-05; helped organize a class under Henri Matisee, Paris, 1907-08; White School of Photography, NYC, 1914-18; ASL, 1920-21, 1925-27; U. of Minnesota, 1931. **Member:** Society of Independent Artists, NYC (Director, 1918-19); American Artists Congress (National Chairman, 1937, Hon. National Chairman, 1938-40). **Awards:** Chicago/AI, Potter Palmer Gold Medal, 1928; PAFA, Joseph E. Temple Gold Medal, 1941; Corcoran, Third William A. Clark Prize, 1941; Chicago/AI, Ada S. Garrett Prize, 1941; Pepsi-Cola, Second Prize, 1945, 1946, ($500), 1947 ($750); Carnegie, Fourth Prize, 1946; La Tausca Competition, First Prize, 1946. **One-man Exhibitions:** (first) Haas Gallery, NYC, 1909; Photo-Secession, NYC, 1911; Murray Hill Gallery, NYC, 1912; Ehrich Galleries, NYC, 1915; Jones Gallery, Baltimore, 1915; Montross Gallery, NYC, 1915, 23; J. B. Neumann Gallery, NYC, 1924, 25, 27, 30, 35, 37; The Downtown Gallery, 1928, 57, 58; Dayton/AI, 1938; A.A.A. Gallery, NYC, 1941, 70; Baltimore/MA, 1942; P. Rosenberg and Co., 1942, 43, 45, 46, 47; Carnegie, 1943; Santa Barbara/MA, 1947; WMAA, 1949; Walker, 1949; California Palace, 1949; Jewish Museum, 1956; Weyhe Gallery, 1956; Brandeis U., 1957; Pomona College, Stieglitz Circle, 1958; Pratt Institute, 1959; B'nai B'rith Gallery, Washington, D.C., 1961; U. of California, Santa Barbara, 1968; Danenberg Gallery, 1969, 70, 71, 72; Graham Gallery, 1970; Pratt Manhattan Center, NYC, 1971; Long Beach/MA, 1971; Alpha Gallery, 1974; Medici II Gallery, Bay Harbor Island, Fla. 1974; The Forum Gallery, 1975, 79,

81, 82. **Retrospectives:** Danenberg Gallery, 1969; Newark Museum, 1913, 59; Galerie Bernheim-Jeune, Paris, 1924; MOMA, 1930; P. Rosenberg and Co., 1944; A.F.A., circ., 1953; AAAL, Memorial, 1962; Jewish Museum, 1983. **Group:** MOMA, Paintings by 19 Living Americans, 1929; Corcoran; Chicago/AI; MOMA; WMAA; Akademie der Kunst, Berlin, American Art 1920-1940, 1980; IEF, Twentieth Century American Drawings, circ., 1984. **Collections:** Andover/Phillips; Arizona State College; Baltimore/MA; Bezalel Museum; Brandeis U.; Britannica; Brooklyn Museum; Buffalo/ Albright; California Palace; Carnegie; Chicago/AI; Cleveland/MA; Columbus; Cranbrook; Dartmouth College; Des Moines; Detroit/Institute; Fort Worth; Hartford/Wadsworth; Harvard U.; Howard U.; State U. of Iowa; Jewish Theological Seminary; Kansas City/Nelson; La Jolla; Los Angeles/County MA; MMA; MOMA; U. of Nebraska; Newark Museum; U. of North Carolina; PMA; Phillips; Sara Roby Foundation; San Antonio/ McNay; San Diego; Santa Barbara/ MA; Seattle/AM; Tel Aviv; Utica; Vassar College; WMAA; Walker; West Palm Beach/Norton; Wichita/AM; Youngstown/Butler.   **Bibliography:** American Artists Congress, Inc.; *Arthur Dove: The Years of Collage;* Ashton 5; *Avant-Garde Painting & Sculpture in America 1910-25;* Barker 1; Baur 7; Bazin; Biddle 4; Blesh; Brown 2; Bulliet 1; **Cahill;** Cahill and Barr, ed.; Cassou; Cheney; Christensen; Eliot; Flanagan; Flexner; Frost; *From Foreign Shores;* Genauer; **Goodrich 9;** Goodrich and Baur 1; Haftman; Hartmann; Hess, T.B., 1; Hunter 6; *Index of 20th Century Artists;* Janis, S.; Kootz 1, 2; Lee and Burchwood; Levin 2; McCoubrey 1; McCurdy, ed.; Marter, Tarbell, and Wechsler; Mellquist; Mendelowitz; Munsterberg; Newmeyer; Pagano; Pearson 1, 2; Phillips 1, 2; Poore; Pousette-Dart, ed.; Read 2; Richardson, E.P.; Ringel, ed.; Ritchie 1; Rose, B., 1; Rosenblum 1; Sachs, Smith, S.C.K.;

Schwartz 2; Soby 5; Story; Sutton; **Weber 1, 2;** Wight 2. Archives.

WEEKS, JAMES. b. December 1, 1922, Oakland, Calif. **Studied:** San Francisco Art Institute, 1940-42, with David Park; Nebraska State Teachers College, 1943; Hartwell School of Design, 1946-47; Escuela de Pintura y Excultura, Mexico City, 1951. US Army Air Force, 1942-45. **Taught:** San Francisco Art Institute, 1947-50, 1958, 64; Hartwell School of Design, 1948-50; California College of Arts and Crafts, 1958-59; UCLA, 1967-70; Tanglewood Summer Art Program, 1970-72; Brandeis U., 1973; Boston U., 1970-. **Commission:** US Department of the Interior, Bicentennial Program, 1975. **Awards:** Abraham Rosenberg Foundation Fellowship, 1952; Howard U., 1961; California Palace, 1961, 62; National Endowment for the Arts, grant, 1978; AAIAL, **P.P.,** 1980. **Address:** 11 Notre Dame Road, Bedford, MA 01330. **Dealers:** Hirschl & Adler Modern, NYC; Charles Campbell Gallery, San Francisco. **One-man Exhibitions:** (first) Lucien Labaudt Gallery, San Francisco, 1951; California Palace, 1953; Gallery 6, San Francisco, 1955; The East-West Gallery, San Francisco, 1958; Poindexter Gallery, NYC, 1960, 61, 63, 74; Felix Landau Gallery, 1963, 65, 66, 67, 70; Sunne Savage Gallery, Boston, 1976, 80; Charles Campbell, San Francisco, 1977, 81; Brandeis U., 1978; Hirschl & Adler Modern, 1985. **Retrospective:** SFMA, 1965; Boston U., 1971; Brandeis U., circ., 1978. **Group:** Los Angeles/County MA, 1957; Birmingham, Ala./MA, Figure Painting, 1961; Corcoran Biennial, 1961; California Palace, 1961, 62; Houston/MFA, 1961, 62; Yale U., 1962; St. Louis Artists' Guild, 1962; State U. of Iowa, Five Decades of the Figure, 1962; Chicago/AI, 1963; La Jolla, 1963; Skowhegan School, 1969; Carnegie, 1966; U. of Illinois, 1968; Scripps College, Figurative Painting, 1968; Expo '70, Osaka, 1970; Oakland/AM, A Period of Exploration,

James Weeks *Towards the Japanese Gardens* 1983–84

1973; US Department of the Interior, America 1976, circ., 1976, Brown U., Recent Landscape Painting, 1979; AAAIL, 1980; PAFA, Perspectives on Contemporary American Realism, 1982; U. of California, Davis, Directions in Bay Area Painting, 1983; SFMA, American Realism (Janss), 1985. **Collections:** A.F.A.; Boston/MFA; Boston Public Library; Brandeis U.; Capitol Records, Los Angeles; Corcoran; First National Bank of Seattle; Howard U.; Lytton Savings and Loan Association; New England Mutual Life Insurance Co., Boston; Norfolk/Chrysler; Oakland; Ringling; SFMA; US Department of the Interior. **Bibliography:** America 1976; Arthur 2; McChesney.

WEINBERG, ELBERT. b. May 27, 1928, Hartford, Conn. **Studied:** Hartford Art School, 1946-48 (certificate), with Henry Kreis; RISD, 1948-51, BFA with Waldemar Raemisch and Gilbert Franklin; Yale U., with Waldemar Raemisch 1953-55, MFA. **Taught:** RISD, Yale U.; Cooper Union; Union College. **Commissions:** Atlanta, Ga. (copper eagle for a facade); Alavath Achim Synagogue, Atlanta, Ga.; 405 Park Avenue, NYC (terra cotta mural); Jewish Museum, 1959 (sculpture for the garden); Brandeis U.; Colgate U.; Jewish Community Center, White Plains, N.Y.; Washington, (D.C.) Hebrew Congregation; Jewish Theological Seminary; Congregation Emanuel, Providence, R.I., 1978; Freedom Plaza, Wilmington, Del., 1980; Jewish Community Center, West Hartford, Ct., 1982; Embarcadero Center, San Francisco, 1982. **Awards:** Prix de Rome, 1951-53; ICA, London/Tate, International Unknown Political Prisoner Competition, Hon. Men. 1953; *Progressive Architecture* magazine, 1954; Yale U., Silver Medal for Achievement in the Arts, 1959; Guggenheim Foundation Fellowship, 1960. **Address:** % Dealer. **Dealer:** Grace Borgenicht Gallery, Inc. **One-man Exhibitions:** Providence (R.I.) Art Club, 1951, 54; Grace Borgenicht Gallery, Inc., NYC, 1957-66, 1969, 70, 75, 82; Menges Museum, Berkeley, 1974; Alpha Gallery, Boston, 1966, 69, 81; Schenectady, 1977. **Group:** WMAA, 1935, 36, 57, Annuals, 1957, 58, 60, 64, 65; Andover/Phillips, 1954; Silvermine Guild, 1954; Jewish Museum, 1954; ICA, Boston, 1957; Hartford/Wadsworth, Connecticut Artists, 1957; AAAL, 1958; A.F.A./USIA, Religious Art, circ., Europe, 1958-59; U. of Nebraska, 1958, 59, 61; Carnegie, 1958, 61; MOMA, Recent Sculpture USA, 1959; Chicago/AI, 1959, 61; Utica, 1960; Boston Arts Festival, 1961; PAFA 1961; Smithsonian, 1961. **Collections:** Andover/Phillips; Boston/MFA; Brandeis U.; Brooklyn Museum; Colgate U.; Dartmouth College; 405 Park Avenue, NYC; Harcourt Brace Jovanovich, NYC; Hartford/Wadsworth; Jewish Museum; MOMA; RISD; Storm King Art Center; WMAA; Yale U. **Bibliography:** Chaet; Rodman 3.

WEINER, LAWRENCE. b. February 10, 1942, NYC. **Studied:** Hunter College. **Address:** 13 Bleecker Street, NYC 10012. **Dealer:** Leo Castelli Inc., NYC; Marian Goodman Gallery, NYC. **One-man Exhibitions:** (first) Mill Valley, Calif., 1960; Siegelaub Gallery, NYC, 1964, 65, 68; Art & Project, Amsterdam, 1969, 70, 72, 73, 84, 85; Konrad Fischer Gallery, Dusseldorf, 1969, 70, 72, 75, 81, 85; Nova Scotia College of Art and Design, 1969, 70, 72, 79, 83, 85; Gian Enzo Sperone, Turin, 1969, 70, 72, 73; Wide White Space Gallery, Antwerp, 1969, 70, 72, 73, 77; Galerie Folker Skulima, Berlin, 1970; Yvon Lambert, Paris, 1970, 71, 72, 74, 77; Leo Castelli Inc., 1971, 72, 73, 74, 76, 79, 80, 81; California Institute of the Arts, Los Angeles, 1972; Munster, 1972; Galleria Toselli, Milan, 1972, 73, 74; Jack Wendler Gallery, London, 1972, 73; Kabinett fur Aktuele Kunst, Bremerhaven, 1973, 75, 81; Modern Art Agency, Naples, 1973; Monchengladbach, 1973; Project Inc., Cambridge, Mass., 1973; Sperone Fischer Galleria, Rome, 1973; Claire S. Copley Gallery, Los Angeles, 1974, 77; Cusack Gallery, Houston, 1974; Gentofte Kommunes Kunstbibliotek, Hellerup, Denmark, 1974; Rolf Preisig Gallery, Basel, 1974, 75, 78; Max Protetch Gallery, Washington, D.C., 1974; Artists Space, NYC, 1976; Basel/Kunsthalle, 1976; Eindhoven, 1976, 79, 80; ICA, London, 1976; The Kitchen, NYC, 1976, 77; P.S. 1, Long Island City, 1976, 77; Rudiger Schöttle, Munich, 1976, 78, 79; Robert Self Gallery, Newcastle-upon-Tyne, 1976; CEAC, Toronto, 1977; Centre d'Art Contemporain, Geneva, 1977, 80; Contemporary Art Society, Sydney, 1977; Laguna Gloria, 1977; Robert Self Gallery, London, 1977; U. of Chicago, 1978; InK, Zurich, 1978; Galeria Foksal, Warsaw, 1979; Françoise Lambert, Milan, 1979; Saman Gallery, Genoa, 1979; Galeria Akumulatory, Poznan, Poland, 1980; Chicago/Contemporary, 1980; Anthony d'Offay Gallery, London, 1980, 85; David Bellman Gallery, Toronto, 1981, 84; Berne, 1983; GEWAD, Ghent, 1983; Galeria Media, Newchatel, 1983; Galerie Micheline Swaczer, Antwerp, 1983; U. of Cincinnati, 1984; ELAC, Lyon, 1984; Ohio State U., 1984; Galerie Daniel Templon, Paris, 1984, 85; A.I.A. Gallery, London, 1985; City Thoughts, Amsterdam, 1985; Le Coin du Miroir, Dijon, 1985; Fruitmarket Gallery, Edinburgh, 1985; Musée St. Pierre, 1985; Old Westbury/SUNY, 1985; Orchard Gallery, Derry, North Ireland, 1985; Paris/Moderne, 1985; Pier Art Center, Stremness, Orkeny, Scotland, 1985. **Group:** Berne, When Attitudes Become Form, 1969; Dusseldorf/Kunsthalle, Prospect '69, 1969; Seattle/AM, 557, 087, 1969; Jewish Museum, Software, 1970; Arnhem, Sonsbeek '71, 1971; Humlebaek/Louisiana, American Art, 1950-1970, 1971; SRGM, Guggenheim International, 1981; Basel, Konzept Kunst, 1972; Documenta V, Kassel, 1972; XXXVI Venice Biennial, 1972; Lenbachhaus, Munich, Bilder-Objekte-Filme-Konzepte, 1973; Chicago/AI, Idea and Image in Recent Art, 1974; Dusseldorf/Kunsthalle, Prospect '74, 1974; Chicago/AI, 72nd American Exhibition, 1976; MOMA, Drawing Now, 1976; Chicago/Contemporary, A View of a Decade, 1977; Museum Bochum, Words, 1979; Chicago/Contemporary, Options 3, 1980; Hayward Gallery, London, Pier and Ocean, 1980; Amsterdam/Stedelijk, Artists Books, 1981; Cologne/Stadt, Westkunst, 1981; Purchase/SUNY, Soundings, 1981; Amsterdam/Stedelijk, '60 '80-Attitudes/Concepts/Images, 1982; New Museum, Language, Drama Source & Vision, 1983; P.S. 1., Long Island City, About Place, 1986. **Collections:** Amsterdam/Stedelijk; The Art Gallery of Ontario; British Museum; Canberra/National; Chicago/AI; Eindhoven; Ghent/Contemporary; The Hague; MOMA; Monchengladbach; Musée St. Pierre; Nova Scotia College of Art & Design; Paris/Beaubourg; Rijksmuseum Kröller-Müller; Rotterdam; Toronto; Toulon. **Bibliography:** De Wilde 2.

WELLIVER, NEIL. b. July 22, 1929, Millville, Pa. **Studied:** Philadelphia Museum School, 1948-52, BFA; Yale U., with Josef Albers, James Brooks, Burgoyne Diller, Conrad Marca-Relli, 1953-54, MFA. Traveled Southeast Asia, Europe. **Taught:** Cooper Union, 1953-57; Yale U., 1955-65; Swarthmore College, 1966; U. of Pennsylvania, 1966-83. **Commissions:** Painted murals for the architect Paul Randolph. **Awards:** NAD, Samuel F. B. Morse Fellowship, 1962. **Address:** RD 2, Lincolnville, ME 04849. **Dealer:** Marlborough Gallery, Inc., NYC. **One-man Exhibitions:** (first) Alexandra Grotto, Philadelphia, 1954; Boris Mirski Gallery, Boston, 1949; The Stable Gallery, 1962-65; Swarthmore College, 1966; Tibor de Nagy Gallery, NYC, 1968-69, 1970; McLeaf Gallery, Philadelphia, 1969; John Bernard Myers Gallery, NYC, 1970, 71; Parker Street 470 Gallery, Boston, 1970; U. of Rhode Island, 1974; Fischbach Gallery, NYC, 1974, 76, 79, 80, 81; Bates College, 1976; Munson Gallery, New Haven, 1977; Brooke Alexander, NYC, 1978; Florida International U., 1981; College of the Mainland, 1981; Marlborough Gallery, Inc., NYC, 1983, 85; Marlborough Fine Art Ltd., Tokyo, 1986; Southern Methodist U., 1983; Marlborough Fine Art Ltd., London, 1984; The Knight Gallery, Charlotte, N.C., 1984. **Retrospective:** Currier, circ., 1984. **Group:** PAFA Annual, 1962; A.F.A., Wit and Whimsy in 20th Century Art, circ., 1962-63; Baltimore/MA, 1963; Swarthmore College, Two Generations of American Art, 1964; WMAA Annuals; U. of Illinois, 1964; Vassar College, 1968; PAFA, 1968; A.F.A., Painterly Realism, 1970; NIAL, 1971; 1971; Boston U., The American Landscape, 1972; U. of North Carolina, Works on Paper, 1972; WMAA Annuals, 1972, 73; U. of Nebraska, 1973; Queens Museum, New Images, 1974; Oklahoma, Contemporary American Landscape Painting, 1974; Tokyo, 1st Biennial of Figurative Painting, 1975; Lincoln, Mass./De Cordova, Candid

Painting: American Genre 1950-1975, 1975; US Department of the Interior, America 1976, circ., 1976; U. of Missouri, American Painterly Realists, 1977; PAFA, 8 Contemporary American Realists, 1977; Youngstown/Butler, Annual, 1977; William and Mary College, American Realism, 1978; Youngstown/Butler, Mid-Year Show, 1979; Danforth Museum, Aspects of the 70's, 1980; San Antonio/MA, Real, Really Real, Super Real, 1981; PAFA, Contemporary American Realism Since 1960, 1981; Utica, Appreciation of Realism, 1982; Lincoln, Mass./De Cordova, Henry Thoreau as a Source for Artistic Inspiration, 1984; Fort Lauderdale, An American Renaissance: Painting and Sculpture Since 1940, 1986. **Collections:** Amerada-Hess Corp., NYC; AT&T; Baltimore/MA; Bank of New York; Boston/MFA; Bowdoin College; Brandeis U.; Brooklyn Museum; Cameron Iron Works, Houston; Chase Manhattan Bank; Colby College; Commerce Bank of Kansas City; Currier; Des Moines; Federal Reserve Bank, Boston; Hirshhorn; Houston/MFA; IBM; J. Henry Schroeder Banking Corp., NYC; Kansas City/Nelson; La Salle College; Lehman Brothers, NYC; Little Rock; Madison Art Center; MMA; MOMA; New England Life Insurance Co., Boston; NYU; U. of North Carolina; PAFA; PMA; Prudential Insurance Corp. of America, Newark; Philadelphia Free Library; Raleigh; SFMA; Smith College; Springfield, Mo./AM; Security Pacific Corp.; Los Angeles/County MA; SFMA; Trenton State; Utah; Vassar College; Westinghouse Electric Corp., Pittsburgh; WMAA; Youngstown/Butler. **Bibliography:** *America 1976*; Arthur 2, 4; Goodyear 1, 2; Strand ed.

WELLS, LYNTON. b. October 21, 1940, Baltimore, Md. **Studied:** RISD, 1962, BFA; Cranbrook, 1965, MFA. Resided Rome, 1961-62. **Taught:** Yale U., 1974; School of Visual Arts, NYC,

1976-. **Awards:** CAPS, 1975, 77; National Endowment for the Arts, grant, 1976. **Address:** 307 West Broadway, NYC 10013; Twin Lakes Road, Salisbury, Conn. 06068. **Dealer:** Ruth Siegel Gallery, NYC. **One-man Exhibitions:** (first) Cranbrook, 1969, 72; Newark College of Engineering, 1969; Syracuse/Everson, 1971; Cunningham-Ward Gallery, NYC, 1973, 74; Jared Sable Gallery, Toronto, 1974, 75, 76; Andre Emmerich Gallery, NYC, 1975, 77; Claire S. Copley Gallery, Los Angeles, 1976; Galerie Andre Emmerich, Zurich, 1976; Sable-Castelli Gallery Ltd. Toronto, 1977, 78, 79, 80; Nina Freudenheim Gallery, Buffalo, 1977; Grapestake Gallery, San Francisco, 1977; Droll/Kolbert Gallery, NYC, 1978; U. of Wisconsin, Eau Claire, 1979; Tortue Gallery, Los Angeles, 1979; Holly Solomon Gallery, NYC, 1980, 82, 83; Sable-Castelli Gallery Ltd., Toronto, 1982, 83, 84; Lawrence Oliver Gallery, Philadelphia, 1983, 85. **Retrospective:** Princeton U., 1979. **Group:** MOMA, Photography into Sculpture, 1970; Walker, Figures/Environments, 1970-71; Vassar College, New American Abstract Painting, 1972; WMAA Biennial, 1973; Cincinnati/Contemporary, Options, 73/30, 1973; Rutgers U., Photographic Process as Medium, 1976; Cornell U., Photo/Synthesis, 1976; C.W. Post College, An Exploration of Photography, 1836-1976, 1976; Indianapolis, 1976; Santa Barbara/MA, Attitudes: Photography in the 1970s, 1979; Florida International U., Other Media, 1980. **Collections:** Arnot; Buffalo/Albright; Cincinnati/AM; Cornell U.; Dallas/MFA; Indianapolis; MOMA; U. of New Mexico; Princeton U.; U. of Sydney; Vassar College; U. of Virginia; VMFA; Walker.

WESLEY, JOHN. b. November 25, 1928, Los Angeles, Calif. Traveled USA, Europe. **Taught:** School of Visual Arts, NYC, 1970-73. **Address:** 52 Barrow Street, NYC 10014. **One-man Exhibitions:** The Elkon Gallery, 1963, 64, 65, 67, 69, 71, 72, 73, 74, 76, 78, 79, 80, 82, 83; Galerie Rudolf Zwirner, 1973; Carl Solway Gallery, Cincinnati, 1974; U. of Rochester, 1974; Galerie Onnasch, Berlin, 1982, 83; Carl Solway Gallery, Cincinnati, 1984. **Group:** Washington (D.C.) Gallery of Modern Art, Popular Image, 1965; Brussels/Beaux-Arts, Nouveau Realisme, 1967; A.F.A., The Figure International, 1967-68; WMAA, 1968, 69; Indianapolis, 1969; Documenta V, Kassel, 1972: Indianapolis, 1976; Long Island City, Another Aspect of Pop Art, 1978; WMAA, Art about Art, 1978. **Collections:** Brandeis U.; Chase Manhattan Bank, Minneapolis; Buffalo/Albright; Hirshhorn; U. of Kentucky; MOMA; Newport Harbor; Pecos Art Museum; Portland, Ore./AM; U. of Rochester; U. of Texas. **Bibliography:** Honisch and Jensen, eds.; Schwartz 2.

WESSELMANN, TOM. b. February 23, 1931, Cincinnati, Ohio. **Studied:** Hiram College, 1949-51; U. of Cincinnati, BA (psychology), 1951-52; Art Academy of Cincinnati, 1954-56; Cooper Union, with Nicholas Marsicano, 1956-59. US Army 1952-54. **Address:** 115 East 9th Street, NYC 10002. **Dealers:** Sidney Janis Gallery. **One-man Exhibitions:** (first) Tanager Gallery, NYC, 1961; Green Gallery, NYC, 1962, 64, 65; Ileana Sonnabend Gallery, Paris, 1966; Sidney Janis Gallery, NYC, 1966, 68, 70, 72, 74, 76, 79, 80, 82, 83, 85; Galleria Sperone, Turin, 1967; Dayton's Gallery 12, Minneapolis, circ., 1968; Newport Harbor, circ., 1970; Jack Glenn Gallery, Corona del Mar, 1971; Rosa Esman Gallery, 1972; Galerie Aronowitsch, Stockholm, 1972; Multiples Inc., Los Angeles, 1973; California State U., Long Beach, circ., 1974; Galerie des 4 Mouvements, Paris, 1974; Boston, 1978; ICA, Boston, 1978; Serge De Bloe Gallery, Brussels, 1979; Ehrlich Gallery, NYC, 1979; Hokin Gallery, Miami, 1981, 85; Margo Leavin Gallery, 1982; Carl Solway Gallery, Cincinnati, 1982; Delahunty Gallery, Dallas, 1983;

Tom Wesselmann *Amy in the Bedroom* 1986

Galerie Esperanza, Montreal, 1984; Sander Gallery, NYC, 1983; Modernism, San Francisco, 1984; Jeffrey Hoffeld & Co., 1985. **Group:** Sidney Janis Gallery, The New Realists, 1962; MOMA, Recent Painting USA: The Figure, circ., 1962-63; Dwan Gallery, 1962, 64; Ileana Sonnabend Gallery, Paris, 1963; Buffalo/Albright, Mixed Media and Pop Art, 1963; WGMA and ICA, London, The Popular Image, 1963; Amsterdam/Stedelijk, American Pop Art, 1964; Stockholm/National, 1964; Chicago/AI, 1964; Carnegie, 1964, 67; Milwaukee, 1965; Palais des Beaux-Arts, Brussels, 1965; WMAA, Young America, 1965; WMAA, Annuals, 1965, 68, 72, 73; MOMA, Art in the Mirror, 1966; Toronto, 1966; WMAA, Art of the U.S. 1670-1966, 1966; RISD, Recent Still Life, 1966; IX Sao Paulo Biennial, 1967; Expo '67, Montreal, 1967; Trenton/State, Focus on Light, 1967; Documenta IV, Kassel, 1968; WMAA, Artists under 40, 1968; Vancouver, circ., 1969; Cincinnati/Contemporary, Monumen-tal Art, 1970; Mathildenhole, Darmstadt, III Internationale der Zeichnung, 1970; ICA, U. of Pennsylvania, Highway, 1970; Roko Gallery, Homage to Tanager: 1952-62, 1971; Dublin/Municipal, International Quadriennial (ROSC), 1971; Hofstra U., Art around the Automobile, 1971; Chicago/AI, 1972, 74; WMAA, American Drawings, 1963-1973, 1973; Turin/Civico, La Fotografia e l'Arte, 1973; New School for Social Research, Erotic Art, 1973; Yale U., American Drawing: 1970-1973, 1973; WMAA, American Pop Art, 1974; Corcoran Biennial, 1975; New York Cultural Center, Three Centuries of the American Nude, 1975; Philadelphia College of Art, Private Notations: Artists' Sketchbooks II 1976; de Young, The Great American Foot Show, 1976; Sydney/AG; Illusions of Reality, 1976; Williamstown/Clark, The Dada/Surrealist Heritage, 1977; WMAA, Art about Art, 1978; Brooklyn Museum, American Drawings in Black and White,

1970-1979, 1980; Youngstown/Butler, 1982; Houston/Contemporary, American Still Life, 1945-1983, 1983; Osaka/National, Modern Nude Paintings, 1880-1983, 1983. **Collections:** Aachen/Suermondt; Brandeis U.; Buffalo/Albright; Cincinnati/AM; Cologne; Dallas/MFA;   Darmstadt/Hessisches; Hirshhorn; U. of Kansas; Kansas City, Mo./Atkins;   Krefeld/K-W;   MOMA; Minneapolis/Institute; U. of Nebraska; Oslo; PMA; Princeton U.; Rice U.; U. of Texas;   Walker;   Washington   U.; WMAA; Worcester/AM. **Bibliography:** Alloway 1, 4; Battcock; ed.; Bihalji-Merin; *Black and White Are Colors*; Calas, N. and E.; *Celebrate Ohio*; Davis, D.; Dienst 1; Haskell 5; Honisch and Jensen, eds.; Hunter, ed.; *Kunst um 1970*; Lippard 5; Murken-Altrogge;   Rose,   B.,   1; Rublowsky; Russell and Gablik; Sager; Weller.

WESTERMANN, H.C. b. December 11, 1922, Los Angeles, Calif. **d.** November 3, 1981, Danbury, Conn. **Studied:** Chicago Art Institute School, 1947-54, with Paul Wieghardt. US Marine Corps, World War II. Traveled the Orient. **Member:** Artists Equity. **Awards:** Chicago/AI, Campana Prize, 1964; National Council on the Arts, 1967; Tamarind Fellowship, 1968; Sao Paulo Biennial Prize, 1973; Chicago/AI, The Mr. & Mrs. Frank G. Logan Medal, 1974. **One-man Exhibitions:** Allan Frumkin Gallery, Chicago, 1957, also 1962, 67, 71, NYC, 1961, 63, 65, 67, 68, 70, 71, 73, 74, 76; Dilexi Gallery, Los Angeles, 1962, San Francisco, 1963; Kansas City/Nelson, 1966; U. of California, Berkeley, 1971; Moore College of Art, Philadelphia, 1972; Galerie Rudolf Zwirner, 1972; Galerie Hans R. Neuendorf, Hamburg, 1973; Galerie Thomas Borgmann, Cologne, 1973; James Corcoran Galleries, Los Angeles, 1974; National College of Education, Wilmette, 1954; Rockford College, 1956; John Berggruen Gallery, 1977, 84; U. of Rhode Island, 1977; Xavier Fourcade, Inc., 1981; Morgan Gallery, Shawnee Mission, Mo., 1982; Akron/AM, 1982. **Retrospectives:** Los Angeles/County MA,   1968;   Chicago/Contemporary, 1969; WMAA, circ., 1978; Serpentine Gallery,   London,   1981.   **Group:** Houston/MFA;   Hartford/Wadsworth; A.F.A.; MOMA, New Images of Man, 1959; MOMA, The Art of Assemblage, circ., 1961; U. of Illinois, 1961; Tate,

H.C. Westermann   *Death Ship Out of San Pedro, Adrift*   1980

Gulbenkian International, 1964; The Hague, New Realism, 1964; Chicago/AI, 1964, 67, and Exhibition Momentum; WMAA, 1964, 68; Worcester/AM, 1965; RISD, 1965; Walker, 1966; The Ohio State U., 1966; Los Angeles/County MA, 1967; Carnegie, 1967; Documenta IV, Kassel, 1968; ICA, U. of Pennsylvania, The Spirit of the Comics, 1969; WMAA, Human Concern/Personal Torment, 1969; La Jolla, Continuing Art, 1971; SRGM, 10 Independents, 1972; Chicago/Contemporary, Chicago Imagist Art, 1972; New York Cultural Center, 3D into 2D, 1973; WMAA, American Drawings: 1963-73, 1973; Sao Paulo Biennials, 1973, 74, 79; Chicago/AI, 1974; NCFA, Made in Chicago, 1974; Portland, Ore./Art, Masterworks in Wood: The Twentieth Century, 1975; NCFA, Sculpture: American Directions 1945-1975; WMAA, 200 Years of American Sculpture, 1976; U. of Massachusetts, Critical Perspectives in American Art, 1976; Venice Biennial, 1976; Chicago Art Institute School, Visions, 1976; WMAA Biennials, 1977, 79; School of Visual Arts, NYC, The Intimate Gesture, 1979; Sao Paulo Biennial, 1979; Brooklyn Museum, American Drawings in Black and White, 1970-1979, 1980; Sunderland Arts Centre, Who Chicago?, 1980; Milwaukee, American Prints 1960-1980, 1982; WMAA, Block Prints, 1982; Sunderland (Eng.) Arts Centre, Drawing in Air, 1983; Ecole des Beaux-Arts, Paris, American Drawing: 1930-1980, 1985. **Collections:** Chicago/AI; Des Moines; Hartford/Wadsworth; Indiana U.; Los Angeles/County MA; Pasadena/AM; WMAA; Walker; Wichita/AM. **Bibliography:** Adrian; Atkinson; Friedman and van der Marck; Haskell 3; Janis and Blesh; **Kozloff 1;** Lippard 5; Read 3; Rose, B., 1; Schulze; Seitz 3; Tuchman 1; Weller; *Who Chicago?*. Archives.

WHARTON, MARGARET A. b. August 4, 1943, Portsmouth, Va. **Studied:** U. of Maryland, 1965, BS; School of the

Margaret Wharton *Chastity* 1985

Art Institute of Chicago, 1975, MFA, with Ray Yoskida, James Zanzi, Richard Keane. Traveled USA, England. **Taught:** School of the Art Institute of Chicago, 1979. **Awards:** Chicago/AI, The Mr. & Mrs. Frank G. Logan Medal, 1974; National Endowment for the Arts, 1980; Awards in the Visual Arts, 1984. **Address:** 1334 Pinehurst, Glenview, Ill. 60025. **Dealer:** Phyllis Kind Gallery, NYC and Chicago. **One-man Exhibitions:** (first) Phyllis Kind Gallery, Chicago, 1975, 80, 85, NYC, 1977, 78, 79, 81, 83; Chicago/Contemporary, circ., 1981. **Group:** School of the Art Institute of Chicago, Visions, 1976; U. of Illinois, 1976; ICA, U. of Pennsylvania, Improbable Furniture, 1977; John Michael Kohler Arts Center, Sheboygan, Wisc., American Chairs, 1978; Cincinnati/Contemporary, Chicago/Chicago, 1980; Indianapolis, 1980; Sunderland (Engl.) Arts Centre, Drawing in Air, 1983; Sacramento/Crocker, Contemporary American Wood Sculpture, 1984. **Collections:** Chicago/Contemporary;

Madison Art Center; Seattle/AM; WMAA.

WHITMAN, ROBERT. b. 1935, NYC. **Studied:** Rutgers U., 1957; Columbia U. **Address:** % Dealer. **Dealer:** Dia Art Foundation, Inc., 393 West Broadway, NYC 10012. **One-man Exhibitions:** (first) Hansa Gallery, NYC, 1959; Reuben Gallery, NYC, 1959; The Pace Gallery, 1967; Chicago/Contemporary, 1968; Jewish Museum, 1968; MOMA, 1973; Bykert Gallery, 1974; Galleria l'Attico, Rome, 1974. **Happenings:** Since 1960, more than 15 theater pieces, incl. *Prune Flat, The American Moon, The Night Time Sky.* **Cinema Pieces:** *Cinema, Shower,* and others. **Group:** Reuben Gallery, NYC, 1959; Martha Jackson Gallery, New Media— New Forms, I & II 1960, 61, also 1962; Nine Great Jones Street, NYC (two-man, with Walter de Maria), 1963; SRGM, 1965; Finch College, 1967; Walker, 1968; Newark College of Engineering, 1968; Walker, 6 Artists—6 Exhibitions, 1968; Newark College of Engineering, Light as Art, 1968; Kansas City/Nelson, Magic Theater, 1968; Expo '70, Osaka, 1970; Los Angeles/County MA, Art & Technology, 1971; MOMA, Projects: Robert Whitman, 1973; Amsterdam/Stedelijk, '60-'80: Attitudes/Concepts/Images, 1982; WMAA, Blam!, 1984. **Collections:** Chicago/Contemporary; Jewish Museum. **Bibliography:** *Art Now 74;* Becker and Vostell; *Contemporanea;* Davis, D.; De Wilde, 2; *Figures/Environments;* Hansen; *Happening & Fluxus;* Haskell 5; Hunter, ed.; Kaprow; Kirby; Lippard 5; *Report;* Sontag; Tomkins 2.

WIESENFELD, PAUL. b. April, 1942, Los Angeles. **Studied:** Chouinard Art Institute, Los Angeles, 1945-59; UCLA, 1960-61; Yale U., 1962; Kunstakademie, Munich, 1964-66; Indiana U., 1966-68. **Taught:** Buffalo/SUNY, 1969-73.

Paul Wiesenfeld   *Still Life with Oranges* 1974

Awards: Yale U., scholarship; Tiffany Foundation, grant, 1963; Fulbright Grant, 1964; German Government Grant, 1969; NAD, 1st Julius Hallgarten Prize, 1972; National Endowment for the Arts, 1976. **Address:** % Dealer. **Dealer:** Robert Schoelkopf Gallery, NYC. **One-man Exhibitions:** Indiana U., 1968; Galerie Harman, Munich, 1969; Robert Schoelkopf Gallery, NYC, 1973, 76, 81; Buffalo/Albright, 1973; Aachen/Ludwig, 1976; Lenbachhaus, Munich, 1980; Louisville/Speed (two-man), 1984. **Group:** WMAA, 22 Realists, 1970; Yale U., 7 Realists, 1974; PAFA, Contemporary American Realism Since 1960, 1981; Houston/Contemporary, American Still Life, 1945-1983, 1983; SFMA, American Realism (Janss), circ., 1985. **Collections:** Aachen/Ludwig; Lehman Bros.; Munich/S-G; VMFA; WMAA.

WILDE, JOHN. b. December 12, 1919, Milwaukee, Wisc. **Studied:** U. of Wisconsin, 1947, MA. **Taught:** U. of Wisconsin, Madison, 1948-82, Alfred Sessler Distinguished Professor Emeritus. **Awards:** PAFA, Lambert **P.P.,** 1957; NAD, Childe Hassam **P.P.** 1961, 81. **Address:** RFD #1, Evansville, WI 53536. **Dealers:** Schmidt-Bingham Gal-

John Wilde   *Myself Lecturing on the Divine Physiognomy of Rock*   1983

lery, NYC; Perimeter Gallery, Chicago; Marilyn Pink Gallery, Los Angeles; Charles Campbell Gallery, San Francisco. **One-man Exhibitions:** (first) U. of Wisconsin, 1942; David Porter Gallery, Washington, D.C., 1944; Kalamazoo/Institute, 1945; Layton School of Art, 1947; Milwaukee, 1948, 59; Pennsylvania College for Women, 1949; Hewitt Gallery, NYC, 1950, 53, 55; Bresler Galleries Inc., Milwaukee, 1949, 51, 53, 55, 58, 61, 63; Newman Brown, Chicago, 1953; Robert Isaacson Gallery, NYC, 1959, 61; Columbia, S.C./MA, 1960; Lane Gallery, Los Angeles, 1960; U. of Wisconsin, Milwaukee, 1960; Durlacher Brothers, NYC, 1963; The Banfer Gallery, 1968; Northern Illinois U., 1969; Veldman Galleries, 1971, 73; Nordness Galleries, 1971; Frank Oehlschlaeger Gallery, Chicago, 1974; Bradley Galleries, Milwaukee, 1979; Haslem Fine Arts, Inc., Washington, D.C. 1980; Milwaukee, 1982; David Findlay Jr. Gallery, NYC, 1984; Bradley Galleries, Milwaukee, 1985; Schmidt-Bingham Gallery, 1986. **Retrospectives:** Milwaukee, 1967; U. of Wisconsin, Madison, 1984. **Group:** Chicago/AI, 1940, 41, 42, 51, 52, 54, Abstract and Surrealist Art, 1948; PAFA, 1941, 46, 50, 52, 53, 58, 59, 60, 62; Walker, 1947, 49, 51, 62; Reality and Fantasy, 1954; U. of Illinois, 1948, 52, 55, 57, 58, 61, 63; A.F.A., American Watercolors, 1949; MMA, 1950, 52, Americans under 35, 1954; WMAA, 1950, 52, 53, 55, 56, 58, 60, 62, 70; Corcoran, 1953; Youngstown/Butler, 1953, 55, 57, 60; Denver/AM, 1955, 56; Hallmark Art Award, 1955, 58; MOMA, Recent Drawings USA, 1956; Carnegie, 1958; Detroit/Institute, 1959; ART:USA:Now, circ., 1962-67; NAD, 1968; St. Joseph/Albrecht, Drawing—America; 1973, 1973; A.F.A., American Master Drawings and Watercolors, 1976; San Diego American Drawings

Invitational, 1977; U. of Nebraska, Things Seen, 1978; WMAA, 20th Century Drawings from the Permanent Collection, 1975; NPG, Distinguished American Portrait Drawings, 1980; Rutgers U., Realism & Realities, 1982; West Palm Beach/Norton, The Fine Line, 1985. **Collections:** Carnegie; Chicago/AI; De Beers Collection; Detroit/Institute; Hartford/Wadsworth; Kalamazoo/Institute; Little Rock/MFA; Marquette U.; Milwaukee; Milwaukee Journal; Minnesota/MA; NCFA; U. of Nebraska; Neenah/Bergstrom; U. of North Carolina; PAFA; Rahr-West Museum; Sara Roby Foundation; St. Joseph/Albrecht; Santa Barbara/MA; Stony Brook; SUNY; U. of Vermont; U. of Wisconsin; WMAA; Walker; Washington Federal Bank, Miami; U. of Wisconsin; Worcester/AM; Yale U.; Youngstown/Butler.   **Bibliography: John Wilde: Drawings 1940-84;** Lindy; Nordness, ed.; Wilde. Archives.

WILEY, WILLIAM T. b. October 21, 1937, Bedford, Ind. **Studied:** California School of Fine Arts, 1956-60, BFA. **Taught:** U. of California, Davis, 1962-ca. 1968. **Awards:** CSFA, Painting Award, 1959, Fletcher Award, 1960; SFMA, First Prize, 1960; Oakland/AM, cash award, 1961; Chicago/AI, First Prize and Guest of Honor Award, 1961; Los Angeles/County MA, sculpture prize, 1962; San Francisco/MA, Nealie Sullivan Award, 1968; Chicago/AI, William H. Bartels Prize, 1976; Australian Arts Council, travel grant, 1980. **Address:** Box 661, Forest Knolls, Calif. 94933. **Dealer:** Allan Frumkin Gallery, NYC; Fuller Goldeen, San Francisco. **One-man Exhibitions:** RAC, 1960; Staempfli Gallery, 1960, 62, 64; The Lanyon Gallery, 1965; Allan Frumkin Gallery, NYC, 1968, 70, 73, 76, 79, 81, 83, 86, Chicago 1969, 74, 79; Hansen-Fuller Gallery, San Francisco, 1969, 71, 72, 75, 78, 80, 83; SFAI, 1969; Eugenia Butler, 1969; Studio Marconi, Milan,

William T. Wiley   *For Guitar Players Forsoothe Sayers*   1985

1971; James Manolides Gallery, Seattle, 1972; Margo Leavin Gallery, 1972, 75, 76; Eindhoven, 1973; U. of Utah, 1974; U. of Texas, Austin (three-man), 1975; MOMA, 1976; Galerie Paul Fachetti, Paris, 1977; Landfall Press Gallery, Chicago, 1978, 80; Delahunty Gallery, Dallas, 1978; Galleria Odyssia, Rome, 1972; Galerie Richard Froncke, Ghent, 1972; Morgan Gallery, Shawnee Mission, 1978; Illinois State U., 1980; San Jose/MA, 1980; Cornish Institute, Seattle, 1980; Glen Hanson Gallery, Minneapolis, 1980; Realities Gallery, Brisbane, 1980; Emily Carr College, Vancouver, 1981; Florida State U., 1981; Santa Barbara Contemporary Arts Forum, 1982; Birmingham, 1983; Newport Beach, 1984; L. A. Louver Gallery, Venice, Calif., 1984; Frumkin/Struve Gallery, Chicago, 1985; Moore College of Art, Philadelphia, 1986. **Retrospectives:** U. of California; Walker, circ., 1979; Baltimore/MA, 1979. **Group:** SFMA, 1959, 60; RAC, 1959, 60; San Francisco Art Festival, 1960; WMAA, Young America, 1960; Chicago/AI, 1961; U. of Illinois, 1961; U. of Nebraska, 1961; California Palace, 1961;

WMAA, Fifty California Artists, 1962; Los Angeles/County MA, American Sculpture of the Sixties, 1967; U. of California, Berkeley, Funk, 1967; WMAA Annual, 1967; Moore College of Art, Philadelphia, Beyond Literalism, 1968; Tampa Bay Art Center, Forty California Sculptors, 1968; Chicago/Contemporary, Violence in Recent American Art, 1968; Indianapolis, 1969; Berne, When Attitudes Become Form, 1969; MOMA, New Media; New Methods, circ., 1969; Eindhoven, Kompas IV, 1969-70; Foundation Maeght, 1970; Omaha/Joslyn, Looking West, 1970; SFAI, Centennial Exhibition I, 1970; Sacramento/Crocker, Sacramento Sampler I, 1972; Documenta V, Kassel, 1972; Venice Biennial, 1972; Ringling, After Surrealism, 1972; WMAA, 1973; WMAA, Extraordinary Realities, 1973; U. of Illinois, 1974; WMAA, Annual, 1974; Dusseldorf, Kunsthalle, Surrealitat-Bildrealitat: Words and Images, 1975; WMAA, 200 Years of American Sculpture, 1976; SFMA, Painting and Sculpture in California, 1976; Minnesota/MA, American Drawings, 1927-1977, 1977; U. of Texas, Austin, New in the Seventies, 1977; San Diego, American Drawing Invitational, 1977; The Hague, Recent Art from San Francisco, 1977; Houston/Contemporary, American Narrative/Story Art, 1977; ICA, Boston, Narration, 1978; Buffalo/Albright, American Painting of the 1970s, 1978; Rijeka, 6th International, Drawings, 1978; Denver/AM, Biennial, 1979; Brooklyn Museum, American Drawings in Black and White, 1970-1979, 1980; XXXIX Venice Biennial, 1980; Purchase/SUNY, Soundings, 1981; Akron/AM, The Image in American Painting and Sculpture, 1981; U. of Santa Clara, Northern California Art of the Sixties, 1982; Oakland Museum, 100 Years of California Sculpture, 1982; Houston/Contemporary, The Americans: The Collage, 1982; SFMA, 20 American Artists, 1982; WMAA Biennial, 1983; Palm Springs Desert Museum, Return of the Narrative, 1984; MOMA, International Survey of Paint-

ing and Sculpture, 1984; Hirshhorn, Content, 1984. **Collections:** Akron/AM; Brooklyn Museum; U. of California, Berkeley; Carnegie; Chicago/AI; Dallas/MFA; Denver/AM; Des Moines; Eindhoven; Fort Worth; Hirshhorn; U. of Illinois; Illinois Bell Telephone Company; Indiana U.; U. of Kansas; Los Angeles/County/MA; U. of Massachusetts; MOMA; U. of Miami; Minneapolis/Institute; Oakland/AM; NMAA; Oakland Museum; Oberlin College; PMA; Palm Springs; SFMA; WMAA; Walker. **Bibliography:** Art Now 74; Lippard, ed.; Report; Richardson, B., 2; Selz, P. 2; The State of California Painting; Tuchman 1; When Attitudes Become Form; Drawings: The Pluralist Decade; New in the Seventies.

WILFRED, THOMAS (Richard Edgar Løvstrøm). b. June 18, 1889. Naestved, Denmark; **d.** August 15, 1968, West Nyack, N.Y. **Studied:** Sorbonne. Traveled Europe, USA. **Awards:** Hon. Ph.D., Philadelphia College of Art, 1968. **Group:** MOMA, Fifteen Americans, circ., 1952; Stockholm/National, Art in Motion, 1961; Eindhoven, Kunst-Licht-Kunst, 1966; Walker and Milwaukee, Light Motion Space, 1967; Trenton/State, Focus on Light, 1967; The Howard Wise Gallery, Lights in Orbit, 1967; and Festival of Lights, 1968; Worcester/AM, Light and Motion, 1968. **Collections:** Clairol, Inc.; Cleveland/MA; Honolulu Academy; MMA; MOMA; Omaha/Joslyn. **Bibliography:** Davis, D.; Rickey; Rubin 1.

WILKE, ULFERT S. b. July 14, 1907, Bad Toelz, Germany. **Studied:** Arts and Crafts School, Brunswick, 1924-25; privately with Willy Jaeckel, 1923; Academie de la Grande Chaumiere, 1927-28; Academie Ranson, Paris, 1927-28; Harvard U. Graduate School, 1940-41; State U. of Iowa, 1946-47, MA. Traveled Europe extensively, Japan. US citizen, 1943. US Army, 1942-45. **Taught:** Kalamazoo College, 1940-42;

Springfield (Ill.) Art Association, 1946-47; State U. of Iowa, 1947-48; U. of Louisville, 1948-55, 1958-59, 1961-62; U. of Georgia, 1955, 56; Rutgers U., 1962-67. Director, Museum of Art, State U. of Iowa, 1968-75. **Commissions:** Mural for Prudential Insurance Company Building, Merillville, Ind., 1978; Rockwell International, Cedar Rapids, Iowa, 1980; Deere & Co., Moline, Ill., 1973. **Awards:** Albrecht Durer Prize, 1928; New Orleans/Delgado, First Prize, 1928; US Army Arts Contest, Gold Medal 1945; Louisville Art Center Annual Exhibition, First Prize, Painting, 1951; Georgia Museum of Art, **P.P.,** 1956; Guggenheim Foundation Fellowship, 1959, 60; AAIAL, prize 1978. **Address:** R.R. #3, Solon, IA 52333; winters: Box 409. Anahola, Kauai, HI 96703. **One-man Exhibitions:** (first) a gallery in Germany, 1927; Brunswick Castle, 1929; Anton Ullrich Museum, Brunswick, 1933; Westermann Gallery, NYC, 1939; Harvard U., 1940; Denver/AM, 1943; Springfield (Ill.) Art Association, 1946; Decatur, 1947; Kalamazoo/Institute, 1947; Muhlenberg College, 1947; Memphis Academy of Arts, 1948; U. of Louisville, 1948; Santa Barbara/MA, 1949; Sweet Briar College, 1949; U. of Nebraska, 1949; The Little Gallery, Louisville, 1950, 53; Kunstverein Hannover, 1952; Kraushaar Galleries, 1958, 60; Tulane U., 1958; Yamada Gallery, Kyoto, 1958; de Young, 1959; Dallas/MFA, 1960; American Academy, Rome, 1960; Primus-Stuart Gallery, Los Angeles, 1961; Rutgers U., 1963; Kalamazoo/Institute, 1964 (two-man, with George Rickey); The Howard Wise Gallery, 1965 (three-man); Design Center of Berea, Cleveland, 1970; Des Moines, 1970; SFMA, 1971; Omaha/Joslyn, 1971; Columbus, 1971; Percival Galleries, Des Moines, 1972, 78; Jodi Scully Gallery, Los Angeles, 75, 1972; Poindexter Gallery, 1973; Waterloo, 1974; MacNider Museum, 1974; Makler Gallery, Los Angeles, 1978; James Willis Gallery, San Francisco, 1978; U. of Iowa, 1975; E.F. Gurewitsch Gallery, NYC (two-

man), 1976; Arts Club of Chicago, 1977; Waterloo Art Association, 1978; Galerie Querschnitt, Brunswick, Germany, 1978; James Willis Gallery, San Francisco, 1978; Mekler Gallery, Los Angeles, 1979; Honolulu Academy, 1981; Cedar Rapids, 1982. **Retrospective:** U. of Iowa, circ., 1983. **Group:** Academy of Fine Arts, Berlin, 1929, 31; *Life* magazine, War Art, circ., USA, 1942; Chicago/AI, 1943-47; MMA, 1952; SRGM, Younger American Painters, 1954; Brooklyn Museum, 1955, 56, 57, 58, 61; Smithsonian, Italy Rediscovered, circ., USA, 1955-56; MOMA, Lettering by Hand, 1962; M. Knoedler & Co. Art across America, circ., 1965-67; International Biennial Exhibition of Paintings, Tokyo. **Collections:** Aetna Oil Co.; Brandeis U.; Brunswick; Buffalo/Albright; Carnegie; Chase Manhattan Bank; Citizens Fidelity Bank; Louisville; Columbia U.; Cooper Union; Dayton/AI; Decatur; U. of Georgia; Hartford/Wadsworth; Honolulu Academy; U. of Illinois; State U. of Iowa; Kultusministerium; Louisville State U.; Mills College; Minneapolis/Institute; NYU; U. of Notre Dame; Nurnberg; Omaha-Joslyn; PMA; Phoenix; Pratt Institute; SFMA; Seagram Collection; Stanford U. **Bibliography:** Lippard 3; **Nordland 5; Seldjs and Wilke; Wilke.** Archives.

WILLENBECHER, JOHN. b. May 5, 1936, Macungie, Pa. **Studied:** Brown U. (with William Jordy, George Downing), BA, 1958; NYU (with Craig Hugh Smyth), 1958-61. Traveled Europe. **Taught:** Philadelphia College of Art, 1972-73; U. of Wisconsin, Milwaukee, 1981. Designed decor for Andre de Groat and Dancers, Brushes of Conduct, 1979; presented outdoor sculpture performance, Artpark, 1978. **Awards:** MacDowell Colony Grant, 1974; National Endowment for the Arts, grant, 1977; MacDowell Colony Fellowship, 1974, 80. **Address:** 145 West Broadway, NYC 10013. **One-man Exhibitions:** (first) Feigen-Herbert Gallery, NYC, 1963; Feigen-Palmer Gallery, Los Angeles, 1964; Richard Feigen Gallery, Chicago, 1964, 68, NYC, 1965, 67; A.M. Sachs Gallery, 1973, 75; Syracuse/Everson, 1975; Brown U., 1975; Arts Club of Chicago, 1976; Hamilton Gallery of Contemporary Art, NYC, 1977 (two-man), 1979; Wright State U. 1977; U. of Massachusetts, 1977; Dartmouth College, 1977; U. of Rhode Island, 1978. **Retrospective:** Purchase/SUNY, 1979. **Group:** Buffalo/Albright, Mixed Media and Pop Art, 1963; ICA, U. of Pennsylvania, Current Art, 1965; RISD, 1965; WMAA, Young America, 1965; Eindhoven, Kunst-Licht-Kunst, 1966; U. of Illinois, 1967; WMAA Annual, 1968; Brooklyn Museum Print Exhibition, 1970; Indianapolis, 1970; Finch College, NYC, Projected Art, 1971; Rice U., Gray is the Color, 1974; U. of North Carolina, Works on Paper, 1974; AAAL, 1974; Purchase/SUNY, Images of Power, Sources of Energy, 1975; U. of California, Santa Barbara, Contemporary Tableau/Construction, 1977; Taft/Museum, Galaxies, 1978; Queens Museum, Private Myths: Unearthings of Contemporary Art, 1978. **Collections:** Alberta College of Art; AT&T, NYC; Austin; Brown U.; Boise-Cascade Corp.; Buffalo/Albright; Champion Paper, Inc.; Chase Manhattan Bank; Chicago/AI; Cornell U.; Hirshhorn; U. of Massachusetts; MMA; Paris/Beaubourg; PMA; U. of Pennsylvania; Purchase/SUNY; RISD; Ridgefield/Aldrich; SRGM; Syracuse/Everson; U. of Texas; 3M Company; WMAA. **Bibliography:** *John Willenbecher.*

WILLIAMS, NEIL. b. August 19, 1934, Bluff, Utah. **Studied:** California School of Fine Arts, 1959, BFA. Traveled Europe, Southwest USA. **Taught:** School of Visual Arts, NYC, 1974-; Syracuse U., 1977; Metro State College, Denver, 1975. **Awards:** National Council on the Arts Award, 1966; Guggenheim Foundation Fellowship, 1968; Athena Foundation Grant, 1983; Gottlieb Founda-

tion, grant, 1984; Scull Foundation, grant, 1985. **Address:** Box 114, Sagaponack, NY 11962. **One-man Exhibitions:** City Lights Book Store, San Francisco, 1959; Green Gallery, NYC, 1964; Dwan Gallery, Los Angeles, 1966; LoGiudice Gallery, NYC, 1971; Walter Kelly Gallery, 1973; Metro State College, Denver, 1975; Galeria Luisa Strina, Sao Paulo, 1982. **Group:** San Francisco Art Association, 1958; RAC, 1959; SRGM, 1964, also Systemic Painting, 1966; WMAA, Young America, 1965; Oberlin College, 1965; Amsterdam/Stedelijk, New Shapes of Color, 1966; Southern Illinois U., 1967; Southern Illinois U., Decade Seven, 1967; Carnegie, 1967; WMAA, 1967, 72; Des Moines, Painting, Out from the Wall, 1968; Vassar College, Current Minimal Paintings, 1969; WMAA Biennial, 1972. **Collections:** Hartford/Wadsworth; MIT; U. of North Carolina; RAC; WMAA. **Bibliography:** Alloway 3; Johnson, Ellen H.

WILLIAMS, WILLIAM T. b. July 17, 1942, Cross Creek, N.C. **Studied:** City U. of New York; New York City Community College, AAS, 1960-62; Skowhegan School of Painting and Sculpture, 1965; Pratt Institute, BFA, 1962-66; Yale U. MFA, 1966-68. **Taught:** Pratt Institute, Brooklyn, 1970; School of Visual Arts, NYC, 1970; Brooklyn College, 1971-. **Awards:** National Endowment for the Arts, grant, 1965, 70; CAPS, 1975; Director pro tem., Skowhegan School of Painting and Sculpture, 1979. **Address:** 654 Broadway, NYC 10012. **One-man Exhibitions:** Reese Palley Gallery, NYC, 1971; Fisk U., 1975; Carlton Gallery, NYC, 1976; Illinois State U., 1976; Miami Dade Community College, 1977; U. of Wisconsin, Menomonie, 1979; U. of Wisconsin, Madison, 1980. **Group:** Studio Museum, NYC, X to the Fourth Power, 1969; WMAA Biennial, 1969; Foundation Maeght, St. Paul de Vence, L'Art vivant aux Etats-Unis, 1970; WMAA, Structure of Color, 1971; Rice

U., The Deluxe Show, 1971; U. of Utah, Drawings by New York Artists, circ., 1972; Hartford/Wadsworth, Extensions, 1974; Fisk U., Amistad II: Afro American Art, 1975; National Museum, Lagos, Second World Black and African Festival of Art and Sculpture, 1977; Studio Museum, NYC, Another Generation, 1979; P.S.1, Long Island City, Afro-American Abstraction, 1980. **Collections:** Chase Manhattan Bank, NYC; Colby College; Cornell U.; Fisk U.; Hartford/Wadsworth; MOMA; Morgan State U.; Schomberg Center for Research in Black Culture, NYC; Syracuse/Everson; WMAA; Yale U.

Thornton Willis *Split End* 1984

WILLIS, THORNTON. b. May 25, 1936, Pensacola, Fla. **Studied:** Auburn U., with David Brisson; U. of Southern Mississippi, 1962, BS; with W. Lock, V. Merrifield; U. of Alabama, 1966, MFA; with Anita Granata, Melville Price. US Marines, 1954-57. Traveled Scandinavia. **Taught:** U. of Southern Mississippi, Wagner College. **Awards:** Guggenheim Foundation Fellowship, 1978; National Endowment for the Arts, 1980. **m.** Vared Lieb. **Address:** 85 Mercer Street, NYC 10012. **Dealer:** Oscarsson Siegeltuch & Co., NYC. **One-man Exhibitions:** (first) Henri Gallery, Washington, D.C., 1968; Paley & Lowe Gallery, NYC, 1970; 55 Mercer Street Gallery, NYC, 1971; Galerie Simone Stern, New Orleans, 1972; Galerie Nordenhake, Malmo, 1980, 83; Oscarsson Hood Gallery, NYC, 1980, 82, 84; Marianne Deson Gallery, Chicago, 1981; Eason Gallery, Santa Fe, 1982; Nina Freudenheim, Buffalo, 1982; Galerie Gonet, Lausanne, 1982; Gloria Luria Gallery, Bay Harbor Islands, Fla., 1985. **Group:** NYU, American Painting: The Eighties, 1979; Cornell U., Painting Up Front, 1981; MOMA, New Art II: Surfaces/Textures, 1981; MOMA, International Survey of Recent Painting and Sculpture, 1984. **Collections:** Buffalo/Albright; Carnegie-Mellon U.; Cornell U.; MOMA; Musée des Beaux Arts, Chaux-de-Fonds, Switzerland;

New Orleans Museum; Phillips; U. of Rochester; U. of Sydney; WMAA.

WILMARTH, CHRISTOPHER. b. June 11, 1943, Sonoma, Calif. **Studied:** Cooper Union, 1960-62, 1964, 65, BFA. Traveled Europe, Peru, Romania. **Taught:** Cooper Union 1969-80; Yale U.; 1971-72; Columbia U., 1976-78. **Awards:** National Endowment for the Arts, 1968; Guggenheim Foundation Fellowship, 1970, 83; Chicago/AI, Norman Wait Harris Award, 1972; Brown U., Howard Foundation Fellowship, 1972; National Endowment for the Arts, grant 1977, 80; American Institute of Graphic Arts, certificate of excellence, 1983; Connecticut Art Directors Club, first place, 1985. **Address:** P.O. Box 281, Red Hook Station, Brooklyn, N.Y. 11213. **Dealer:** Hirschl & Adler Modern, NYC. **One-man Exhibitions:** (first) The Graham Gallery, 1968; Paula Cooper Gallery, 1971, 72; Galleria dell'Ariete, 1973; Janie C. Lee Gallery, Dallas and Houston, 1974; Weinberg Gallery, San Francisco, 1974; Rosa Esman Gallery, 1974; Hartford/Wadsworth, 1974, 77; St. Louis/City, 1975; Galerie Aronowitsch, Stockholm, 1975; Daniel Weinberg Gallery, San Francisco, 1978; Studio for the

Christopher Wilmarth *Delancey
Backs* 1983–86

First Amendment, NYC, 1978; NYU, 1978; Seattle/AM 1979; Andre Emmerich Gallery, NYC, 1978; Studio for the First Amendment, NYC, 1980, 82; Hirschl & Adler Modern, 1984, 86. **Group:** WMAA, 1966, 68, 70, 73; Park Place Gallery, NYC, 1966; Foundation Maeght, 1970; Chicago/AI, 1972; MOMA, 1972, 74; MMA, 1974; Hayward Gallery, London, 1975; WMAA 20 Years of American Sculpture, 1976; PMA, Eight Artists, 1978; WMAA Biennial, 1979; Buffalo/Albright, Eight Sculptors, 1979; MOMA, Contemporary Sculpture, 1979; WMAA Biennial, 1979; Carnegie, International, 1983. **Collections:** Buffalo/Albright; Carnegie; Chicago/AI; Dallas/MFA; Denver/AM; Des Moines; Hartford/Wadsworth; Harvard U.; MMA; MOMA; NYU; Phoenix; Rice U.; PMA; Princeton

U.; RISD; Seattle/AM; SFMA; St. Louis/City; Toledo/MA; WMAA; Walker; Wichita/AM; Woodward Foundation; Yale U. **Bibliography:** *Christopher Wilmarth: Layers.*

WILSON, JANE. b. April 29, 1924, Seymour, Iowa. **Studied:** State U. of Iowa, with Stuart Edie, James Lechay, Mauricio Lasansky, 1945, BA, PBK, 1947, MA (painting). Traveled Mexico, USA extensively, Europe. **Taught:** State U. of Iowa, 1947-49; Parsons School of Design, NYC, 1971-; Columbia U., 1975-; Cooper Union, 1977-78; U. of Iowa, 1974; Pratt Institute, 1967-69; and privately. **Member:** NAD. **Awards:** Ingram Merrill Foundation Grant, 1963; L.C. Tiffany Grant, 1967; NAD, Ranger Fund, **P.P.,** 1977; AAIAL, Childe Hassam Purchase Fund, **P.P.,** 1972, 73, 81; AAIAL, Award in Art, 1981. **Address:** 317 West 83rd Street, NYC 10024. **Dealer:** Fischbach Gallery, NYC. **One-man Exhibitions:** St. John's College, Annapolis, Md., 1951; Hansa Gallery, NYC, 1953, 55, 57; Esther Stuttman Gallery, NYC, 1958, 59; Tibor de Nagy Gallery, 1960-66; Gump's Gallery, 1963; Esther Baer Gallery, 1963, 64; The Graham Gallery, NYC, 1968, 69, 71, 73, 75; Fischbach Gallery, NYC, 1978, 81, 84, 85; Port Washington Public Library, 1979; Sordoni Art Gallery, Wilkes Barre, 1979; Bowling Green, U., 1971; Benson Gallery, East Hampton, N.Y. 1974; Westark Community College, 1976; Port Washington Public Library, 1979; Utica, 1980; Cornell U., 1982. **Group:** Chicago/AI, 1946; The Stable Gallery Annuals, 1951, 52; MOMA, New Talent, circ., 1957-59; WMAA Annual, 1962; A.F.A., circ., 1963; MIT; Corcoran; New York World's Fair, 1964-65; Huntington, N.Y./Heckscher, The New Landscape, 1970; New York Cultural Center, The Realist Revival, 1972; Queens Museum, New Images, 1974; William and Mary College, American Realists, 1978; Hirshhorn, The Fifties: Aspects of Painting in New

York, 1980; NAD, Next to Nature, 1981; Houston/Contemporary, American Still Life, 1945-1983, 1983. **Collections:** Allied Bank, Dallas; Carnegie Corp., NYC; Chase Manhattan Bank; Chemical Bank; Cincinnati/AM; The Commerce Bank of Kansas City; Corcoran; Guild Hall; Hartford/Wadsworth; Hirshhorn; Indianapolis/Herron; Kalamazoo/Institute; MMA; MOMA; NYU; National Bank of Commerce, Dallas; Rockefeller Institute; The Singer Company, Inc.; Oneonta/SUNY; PAFA; Parker Pen Co., NYC; Southampton/ Parrish; Uris Buildings Corp.; Vassar College; WMAA.

WIRSUM, KARL. b. September 27, 1939, Chicago, Ill. **Studied:** Chicago Art Institute School, 1961, BFA, 1966. **Address:** 1936 W. Bradley, Chicago, IL 60613. **Dealer:** Phyllis Kind Gallery, Chicago and NYC. **One-man Exhibitions:** Dell Gallery, Chicago, 1967; St. Xavier College, 1970; Wabash Transit Gallery, Chicago, 1971; Phyllis Kind Gallery, Chicago, 1974, 76, 78, 84; Phyllis Kind Gallery, NYC, 1977, 79; 86; Chicago/Contemporary, 1980. **Group:** Hyde Park Art Center, Chicago, The Hairy Who, 1966, 67, 68; WMAA Biennial, 1968; Chicago/Contemporary, Paintings to Be Read, Poetry to Be Seen, 1968; Chicago/Contemporary, Don Baum Sez, "Chicago Needs Famous Artists," 1969; ICA, U. of Pennsylvania, Spirit of the Comics, 1969; WMAA, Human Concern/Personal Torment, 1970; Chicago/Contemorary, Chicago Imagist Art, 1972; Ottawa/Ontario, What They're Up to in Chicago, 1972; Sao Paulo, XII Biennial, 1973; Chicago/AI, Former Famous Alumni, 1976; Sacramento/Crocker, The Chicago Connection, 1977; U. of North Carolina, Some Recent Art from Chicago, 1980. **Collections:** WMAA, Chicago/AI; Museum des 20. Jahrhunderts, Vienna; Kalamazoo/Institute; AT&T; Ball State U. **Bibliography:** Adrian; *The Chicago Connection; Who Chicago?*.

Karl Wirsum   *Martian Arts Made with Pre-War Rubber*   1984

WITKIN, ISAAC. b. May 10, 1936, Johannesburg, South Africa. **Studied:** St. Martin's School, London, 1957-60, with Anthony Caro; assistant to Henry Moore, 1962-63. **Taught:** Maidstone College of Art, Kent, England, 1963; St.

Isaac Witkin   *Waife's Anchor*   1985

Martin's School of Art, 1963-65; Ravensbourne School of Art, 1964-65; Bennington College, 1965; Parsons School of Design, NYC, 1975-. To England, 1956; USA citizen, 1975. **Address:** 1 Fifth Avenue, NYC 10003. **Dealer:** Hirschl & Adler Modern, NYC. **One-man Exhibitions:** Rowan Gallery, London, 1963; Robert Elkon Gallery, NYC, 1965, 67, 69, 71, 73; Waddington Gallery, London, 1966, 68; Bridgeport U., 1970; Marlborough Gallery, NYC, 1975, 76, 78; Keene/Thorne, 1977; Tanglewood Music Festival, 1977; Hamilton Gallery of Contemporary Art, NYC, 1979; Dag Hammerskjold Plaza, NYC, 1981; McIntosh/Drysdale Gallery, Washington, D.C., 1982; Mattingly Baker Gallery, Dallas, 1982; Hirschl & Adler Modern, 1985. **Retrospective:** Bennington College, 1971. **Group:** Whitechapel Art Gallery, London, The New Generation, 1965; Smith College, Inside Outside, 1965; Jewish Museum, NYC, Primary Structures, 1965; Paris/Biennale, 1965; Sonsbeek, Holland, Open Air Sculpture, 1966; Amsterdam/Stedelijk, Nine English Sculptors; Hayward Gallery, London, Sculpture of the 60's, 1970; Storm King Art Center, Indoor Sculpture, Outdoors, 1973; Hayward Gallery, London, Condition of Sculpture, 1975; Hirshhorn, The Golden Door, 1976; AAAL, 1977; Indianapolis, 1978; Carnegie, International, 1983; Williams College, Six in Bronze, circ., 1984; Newark Museum, American Bronze Sculpture 1850 to the Present, 1984; Sonoma State U., Works in Bronze, A Modern Survey, circ., 1984. **Collections:** American Republic Insurance Co.; Carnegie; Chase Manhattan Bank; Columbus; Federal Reserve Bank, Washington, D.C.; Hirshhorn; U. of Illinois; Milwaukee; MIT; NMAA; SFMA; Storm King Art Center; U. of Sydney; Tate Gallery; Vassar College; Wichita; Wilmington; Worcester/AM.

WITKIN, JEROME. b. September 13, 1939, Brooklyn, N.Y. **Studied:** High School of Music and Art, NYC, 1953-57; Cooper Union, 1957-60, with Nicholas Marsicano; Berlin Academy, 1961; U. of Pennsylvania, 1968-70, MFA. Traveled Europe. Resided Italy, 1960-62; Manchester, England, 1966-68. **Taught:** Maryland Institute; Moore College of Art, Philadelphia; American College, Switzerland; Syracuse U. **Member:** NAD. **Awards:** Guggenheim Foundation Fellowship, 1963; Pulitzer Fellowship, 1960. **Address:** 1138 Lancaster Avenue, Syracuse, N.Y. 13210. **Dealer:** Sherry French Gallery, NYC. **One-man Exhibitions:** (first) Morris Gallery, NYC, 1962; Lake Erie College, 1971; Kraushaar Galleries, NYC, 1973, 76, 82; Cortland/SUNY, 1977; Lake Placid Center for the Arts, 1978; Pennsylvania State U., 1978; U. of New Hampshire, 1981; Oswego/SUNY, 1981; Syracuse Stage, 1984; Sherry French Gallery, 1985. **Retrospectives:** The Pennsylvania State U., circ., 1983; Community College of the Finger Lakes, 1985. **Group:** Yale U., American Drawing: 1970-1973, 1973; Lincoln, Mass./DeCordova, Candid Painting: American Genre 1950-75, 1975; San Antonio/MA, Real, Really Real, Super Real, circ., 1981; Utica, An Appreciation of Realism, 1982; NAD, 1985. **Collections:** Ball State U.; Canton Art Institute; Cleveland/MA; Cortland/SUNY; Exeter; Hirshhorn; La Salle College; Little Rock/MFA; MMA; U. of Maine; Miami-Dade College; Minnesota/MA; NAD; U. of New Hampshire; The Pennsylvania State U.; Rhode Island College; Syracuse/Everson; Syracuse U.; Uffizi Gallery; Youngstown/Butler.

WOELFFER, EMERSON. b. July 27, 1914, Chicago, Ill. **Studied:** Chicago/AI School, with Francis Chapin, Boris Anisfeld, 1935-37, BA. US Air Force, 1939-42. Traveled USA, Mexico and Europe extensively. **Taught:** New Bauhaus, Chicago, 1941-49; Black Mountain College, 1949; Chouinard Art Institute, 1959; Colorado Springs Fine

Jerome Witkin   *Tit for Tat*   1983–84

Arts Center; Southern Illinois U., 1962; California Institute of the Arts, Valencia, 1969-73; Honolulu Academy, 1970; Otis Art Institute, 1974-; Parsons School of Design, Paris, summer, 1980. Federal A.P.: Easel painting and project assistant. **Awards:** SFMA, Hon. Men., 1948; Chicago/AI, Pauline Palmer Prize, 1948; Tamarind Fellowship, 1961, 70; US State Department Grant (Turkey), 1965; Guggenheim Foundation Fellowship, 1967-68; PAFA, Raymond A. Speiser Memorial Prize, 1968; Los Angeles All-City show, **P.P.,** 1968; Tamarind Institute, grant, 1983; Pollock-Krasner Foundation, grant, 1985. **Address:** 475 Dustin Drive, Los Angeles, CA 90065. **Dealer:** Gruenebaum Gallery, NYC. **One-man Exhibitions:** Bennington College, 1938; 740 Gallery, Chicago, 1946; Black Mountain College, 1949; Chicago/AI, 1951; Margaret Brown Gallery, Boston, 1951; Artists Gallery, NYC, 1951, 54; Paul Kantor Gallery, Beverly Hills, Calif., 1956, 60; Poindexter Gallery, 1959, 61, 75; Primus-Stuart Gallery, Los Angeles, 1961; La Jolla, 1962; Quay Gallery, 1968; David Stuart Gallery, 1969; Jodi Scully Gallery, 1972, 73; Phillips, 1974; Gruenebaum Gallery, NYC, 1979, 82, 84. **Retrospective:** Pasadena/AM, 1962. **Group:** WMAA, 1947, 49, Six American Painters; Salon des Realites Nouvelles, Paris, 1948; ICA, Boston, 1950; MIT, Four Americans, 1952; Corcoran, 1952; Carnegie, 1952, 54, 55, 58; Houston/MFA; 1957; SRGM, 1962; WMAA, Fifty California Artists, 1962-63; Los Angeles/County MA, Post

Painterly Abstraction, 1964; PAFA, 1968; Chicago/AI, 100 Artists—100 Years, 1979. **Collections:** Avco Corp.; ARCO (Atlantic Richfield Corp.), Los Angeles; California State U., Los Angeles; U. of California, Berkeley; Amon Carter Museum; Chicago/AI; Colorado Springs/FA; Dresdener Bank; Fort Worth; Honolulu Academy; U. of Illinois; U. of Iowa; La Jolla; Los Angeles/County MA; MOMA; New Orleans/Delgado; Pasadena/AM; Raleigh/NCMA; UCLA; WGMA; WMAA. **Bibliography:** Archives.

WOFFORD, PHILIP. b. August 14, 1935, Van Buren, Ark. **Studied:** U. of Arkansas, 1957, BA; U. of California, 1958. **Taught:** NYU, 1964-68; Ben-

nington College, 1969-. **Awards:** Oakland Museum Bronze Medal, 1958; Woodrow Wilson Foundation Fellowship, 1957; National Endowment for the Arts, grant, 1974; CAPS, 1977. **Address:** RD #2, Hoosick Falls, NY 12090. **Dealer:** Nancy Hoffman Gallery, NYC. **One-man Exhibitions:** Green Gallery, NYC, 1962; Allan Stone Gallery, 1964; David Whitney Gallery, NYC, 1970, 71; Andre Emmerich Gallery, NYC, 1972, 74, 76; Little Rock/MFA, 1973; Corcoran, 1972; Yale U., 1973; Pyramid Gallery, Washington, D.C., 1974; Windham College, 1974; Bennington College, 1975; Berenson Gallery, Bay Harbor Islands, 1976; Max Hutchinson Gallery, Houston, 1978; Osuna Gallery, Washington, D.C., 1979; Nancy Hoffman Gallery,

Philip Wofford   *Child's Prayer Wheel*   1985

NYC, 1979, 81, 83, 86; Carnegie, 1982. **Group:** SFMA, 1958; Oakland/AM, 1958; Yale U., Young New York Painters, 1964; WMAA, 1969, 72, 73; WMAA, Lyrical Abstraction, 1971; Corcoran, The Way of Color, 1973; U. of Illinois, 1974; U. of Vermont, Landscape Images, 1976; MOMA, New Art II: Surfaces/Textures, 1981. **Collections:** Brooklyn Museum; Carnegie; Canberra/National; Corcoran; Corning Fiberglas Corp.; Northside Parklane National Bank, St. Louis; RISD; Ridgefield/Aldrich; WMAA.

WOLFE, JAMES MARTIN. b. April 28, 1944, NYC. Autodidact. **Taught:** School of Visual Arts, NYC, 1979; Virginia Polytechnic and State U., 1978; Boston Museum School, 1980. **Awards:** National Endowment for the Arts, 1974; Augustus Saint Gaudens Prize, 1984. **Address:** 736 Broadway, NYC 10003. **Dealer:** Andre Emmerich Gallery, NYC. **One-man Exhibitions:** (first) Andre Emmerich Gallery, 1973, 75, 76, 85, 86; Meredith Long Contemporary Art, NYC, 1978, 79; Osuna Gallery, Washington, D.C., 1980; Virginia Polytechnic Institute and State U., 1981; Stephen Rosenberg Gallery, NYC, 1982, 83. **Group:** Phillips, Contemporary Sculpture, 1972; Dartmouth College, New England Sculpture, 1973; Cleveland/MA, Contemporary American Artists, 1974; Newport, R. I., Monumenta, 1974; Indianapolis, 1977; Houston/MFA, A Century of Modern Sculpture, 1882-1982, 1983; St. Lawrence U., Pre-Postmodern: Good in the Art of Our Time, 1985. **Collections:** Boston/MFA; Edmonton Art Gallery; Exeter; Harvard U.; Hirshhorn; Michigan State U.; Storm King Art Center; Syracuse U.; WMAA.

WONNER, PAUL JOHN. b. April 24, 1920, Tucson, Ariz. **Studied:** California College of Arts and Crafts, 1937-41, BA; ASL, 1947; U. of California,

Paul Wonner *The Five Senses* 1984

Berkeley, 1950-53, MA, 1955, MLS. US Army, 1941-45. Traveled Europe. **Taught:** U. of California, Berkeley, 1952-53, Los Angeles, 1962-63; Otis Art Institute, 1965-68; College of Creative Studies, 1968-71; Art Center, Los Angeles, 1973; California State U., Long Beach, 1975, 81-; U. of California, Davis, 1975-76; U. of Hawaii, 1978. **Commission:** San Francisco, Moscone Center, mural, 1981-82. **Address:** 468 Jersey Street, San Francisco, CA 94994. **Dealers:** John Berggruen Gallery; Hirschl & Adler Modern, NYC. **One-man Exhibitions:** (first) de Young, 1955; San Francisco Art Association, 1956; Felix Landau Gallery, 1959, 60, 62, 63, 64, 68, 71; Santa Barbara/MA, 1960, California Palace, 1961; Poindexter Gallery, 1962, 64, 71; Esther Baer Gallery, 1964 (two-man, with William T. Brown); San Antonio/McNay, 1965; Waddington Gallery, London, 1965; The Landau-Alan Gallery, NYC, 1967; Charles Campbell Gallery, 1972; Jodi Scully Gallery, 1973; John Berggruen Gallery, San Francisco, 1978, 81; California State U., Long Beach, 1981; James Corcoran Gallery, Los Angeles, 1979, 80; Hirschl & Adler Modern, 1983. **Group:** SRGM, Younger American Painters, 1954; III Sao Paulo Biennial, 1955; Walker, Vanguard, 1955;

Oakland/AM, Contemporary Bay Area Figure Painting, 1957; Festival of Two Worlds, Spoleto, 1958; Carnegie, 1958, 64; ART:USA:59; NYC, 1959; WMAA Annuals, 1959, 67; U. of Illinois, 1961, 63; Chicago/AI Annuals, 1961, 64; VMFA, American Painting 1962; MOMA, Recent Painting USA: The Figure, circ., 1962-63; Denver/AM, 1964; Carnegie, International, 1964; WMAA Annual, 1967; U. of Oklahoma, East Coast—West Coast Paintings, 1968; Omaha/Joslyn, Looking West, circ., 1970; La Jolla, Continuing Art, 1971; in the West, 1972; Eindhoven, Relativerend Realisme, 1972; U. of Illinois, 74; SFMA, California Painting and Sculpture: The Modern Era, 1976. **Collections:** Chattanooga/Hunter; Hirshhorn; Lytton Savings and Loan Association; MMA; MOMA; Minneapolis/Institute; NCFA; U. of Nebraska; U. of North Carolina; Oakland/AM; Reader's Digest; SFMA; SRGM. **Bibliography:** Arthur 3; Nordness ed.; *The State of California Painting.*

WOOD, GRANT. b. February 13, 1891, Anamosa, Iowa; **d.** February 12, 1942, Iowa City, Iowa. **Studied:** State U. of Iowa; Minneapolis School of Design; Academie Julian, Paris. US Army, 1918-19. Traveled Germany, France. **Taught:** Rosedale, Iowa, 1911-12; Jackson, Iowa, 1919-23; Chicago Art Institute School, 1916; State U. of Iowa, 1934-42. **Member:** NAD; National Society of Mural Painters. Federal A.P.: Director, Iowa Division, 1934. **Commissions:** Cedar Rapids (Iowa) Memorial Building, 1926-28 (stained glass window). **Awards:** Iowa State Fair, First Prize, 1929, 30, 31, 32; Carnegie, 1934; Hon. Ph.D., U. of Wisconsin; Hon. MA, Wesleyan U.; Hon. DFA, Lawrence College; Hon. DFA, Northwestern U. **One-man Exhibitions:** Ferargil Galleries, NYC, 1935; Lakeside Press Gallery, Chicago, 1935; Hudson D. Walker Gallery, NYC, 1936. **Retrospectives:** U. of Kansas, 1959; Davenport/Municipal, 1966; Cedar Rapids/

AA, 1969; Minneapolis/Institute, circ., 1983. **Group:** Chicago/AI, 1930; Carnegie, 1934; Iowa State Fair; WMAA. **Collections:** Abbott Laboratories; Cedar Rapids/AA; Chicago/AI; Dubuque/AA; MMA; U. of Nebraska; Omaha/Joslyn; Terre Haute/Swope; WMAA. **Bibliography:** Baigell 1; Barr 3; Baur 7; Bazin; Beam; Beaton 1; Biddle 4; Blanchard; Blesh 1; Boswell 1; Brown; Canaday; Cheney; Christensen; **Corn;** Craven, T. 1; Eliot; Finkelstein; Flanagan; **Garwood;** Gaunt; Goodrich and Baur 1; Haftman; Hall; Hunter 6; *Index of 20th Century Artists;* Kent, R., ed.; Kootz 2; Kouvenhoven; Lee and Burchwood; McCurdy, ed.; Mellquist; Mendelowitz; Newmeyer; Pagano; Pearson 1; Reese; Richardson, E.P.; **Rinard and Pyle;** Rose, B., 1; Wight. Archives.

WYETH, ANDREW. b. July 21, 1917, Chadds Ford, Pa. **Studied:** with N. C. Wyeth. **Member:** NAD; Audubon Artists; NIAL; AAAL. **Awards:** AAAL, Medal of Merit, 1947; Hon. DFA, Harvard U., 1955; Hon. DFA, Colby College, 1955; Hon. DFA, Dickinson College, 1958; Hon. DFA, Swarthmore College, 1958; Freedom Medal, 1963; Hon. DFA, Princeton U.; Hon. DFA, Tufts U.; Hon. DFA, Franklin and Marshall College; Hon. DFA, Northeastern U.; Hon. DFA, Amherst College; Hon. DFA, Bowdoin College; Hon. DFA, U. of Pennsylvania; Hon. DFA, U. of Delaware; Hon. DFA, La Salle U. **Address:** Chadds Ford, PA 19317; Cushing, Me. **Dealer:** Coe Kerr Gallery. **One-man Exhibitions:** Currier, 1951; Doll and Richards, Boston, 1938, 40, 42, 44, 46; Macbeth Gallery, NYC, 1938, 39, 48; Rockland/Farnsworth, 1951, 63; de Young, 1956, 73; Santa Barbara/MA, 1956; Wilmington, 1957; M. Knoedler & Co., NYC, 1958; MIT, 1960; Buffalo/Albright, 1962; Pierpont Morgan Library, 1963; Corcoran, 1963; Harvard U., 1963; Southampton/Parrish, 1966; PAFA, 1966; WMAA, 1966; Chicago/AI,

1966; Baltimore/MA, 1966; Brandywine Museum, Chadds Ford, Pa., 1971; National Gallery, 1987. **Retrospective:** Tokyo/Modern, circ., 1974; MMA, 1976. **Group:** Houston/MFA; MOMA; PMA; Wilmington; PAFA, 1938, 39, 41-45, 49-52, 58, 63; WMAA, 1946, 48, 51, 52, 53, 56 57, 59, 63, 64; Carnegie, 1947-50, 52, 55, 58, 61, 64; U. of Illinois, 1948, 49, 63, 65, 69; A.F.A., 1954; Brussels World's Fair, 1958; Tate, 1963. **Collections:** Andover/ Phillips; Boston/MFA; California Palace; Chicago/AI; Colby College; Currier; Dallas/MFA; Hartford/Wadsworth; Houston/MFA; MOMA; McDonnell & Co. Inc.; Montclair/AM; National Gallery; U. of Nebraska; New London; Omaha/Joslyn; Oslo/National; PMA; Rockford/Farnsworth; Utica; Wilmington; Winston-Salem; Public Library. **Bibliography:** *Andrew Wyeth* (two-titles); Barker 1; Baur 7; Canaday; *8 American Masters of Watercolor*; Eliot; Flanagan; Gaunt; Hoving; Hunter 6; McCurdy, ed.; Mendelowitz; Nordness, ed.; O'Doherty; **Pitz;** Pousette-Dart, ed.; Richardson, E.P.; Rodman 1, 3; Rose, B., 1; Sachs; Watson, E.W., 1; Wyeth, B.J.

WYETH, JAMES. b. July 6, 1946, Wilmington, Del. Delaware Air National Guard, 1966-71. Subject of TV documentary, *A Portrait of Jamie Wyeth,* produced by Nebraska Educational Television, 1975. **Address:** Lookout Farm, 701 Smith Bridge Road, Wilmington, Del. 19807; and Monhegan Island, Me. **Dealer:** Coe Kerr Gallery, NYC. **One-man Exhibitions:** (first) M. Knoedler Gallery, NYC, 1966; Coe Kerr Gallery, NYC, 1974, (two-man) 76; 77; Hotel de Paris, Monte Carlo, 1980. **Retrospective:** Omaha/Joslyn, 1975; PAFA, circ., 1980. **Group:** Brandywine River Museum, The Wyeth Family, 1971; PAFA, Contemporary American Realism Since 1960, circ., 1981; Anchorage, circ. 1983. **Collections:** Birmingham, Ala./MA; Brandywine River Museum; Greenville; Joslyn/Omaha; MOMA; NPG; Rockland/Farnsworth; Wilmington.

X

XCERON, JEAN. **b.** February 24, 1890, Isari, Greece; **d.** March 29, 1967, NYC. To USA, 1904. **Studied:** The Corcoran School of Art, 1910-16, with George Lohr, Abraham Rattner. Resided Paris, 1927-37. Art reviewer for American newspapers from Paris, 1930-34. **Member:** American Abstract Artists; Federation of Modern Painters and Sculptors. Federal A.P.: Christian Science Chapel, Rikers Island, NYC, 1941-42 (murals). **Commissions:** U. of Georgia, 1947. **Awards:** U. of Illinois, **P.P.,** 1951. **One-man Exhibitions:** (first) Galerie de France, Paris, 1931 (sponsored by Cahiers d'Art); Galerie Percier, Paris, 1933; Galerie Pierre, Paris, 1934; Garland Gallery, NYC, 1935; Karl Nierendorf Gallery, NYC, 1938; Bennington College, 1944; Sidney Janis Gallery, 1950; Rose Fried Gallery, 1955, 57, 60, 61, 62, 63, 64; The Peridot Gallery, NYC, 1971; Andre Zarre Gallery, NYC, 1975, 77, 80; Kouros Gallery, NYC, 1984. **Retrospectives:** Jean Xceron, circ. seven museums in the Southwest and West Coast, 1948-49; SRGM, 1952. **Group:** Independent Artists, NYC, 1921-24; Salon des Surindependents, Paris, 1931-35; New York World's Fair, 1939; Golden Gate International Exposition, San Francisco, 1939; SRGM, 1939-52, 1954, 55, 56, 58, 62; American Abstract Artists, 1941-44, 1951-57; Carnegie, 1942, 43, 44, 44, 46, 47, 48, 49, 50; Federation of Modern Painters and Sculptors, 1945, 46, 48, 49, 50, 51, 53, 54, 55, 56; California Palace; WMAA Annuals, 1946, 49, 52, 56; Salon des Realites Nouvelles, Paris, annually, 1947-52; U. of Illinois, 1948, 49, 50, 52, 55, 57; Houston/MFA, The Sphere of Mondrian, 1957; MOMA, circ., Latin America, 1963-64. **Collections:** Andover/Phillips; Brandeis U.; Carnegie U. of Georgia; U. of Illinois; Karlsruhe; MOMA; NYU; U. of New Mexico; Phillips; Pittsfield/Berkshire; SRGM; Smith College; WMAA: Washington U.; Wellesley College. **Bibliography:** Bethers; Blanchard; Hess, T.B., 1; Hunter, ed.; Janis and Blesh 1; Kootz 2; Lane and Larsen; Pousette-Dart, ed.; Rickey; Rose B., 1. Archives.

Y

YEKTAI, MANOUCHER. b. December 22, 1921, Teheran, Iran. **Studied:** with Amedee Ozenfant and Robert Hale, 1945; Academie des Beaux-Arts, Paris, 1946, with Andre Lhote. **Address:** 225 West 86th Street, NYC 10024. **Dealer:** Alex Rosenberg Gallery, NYC. **One-man Exhibitions:** Grace Borgenicht Gallery, Inc., 1952-54; A.A.A. Gallery, NYC, 1956; Poindexter Gallery, 1957, 59, 60, 62; Galerie Anderson-Mayer, Paris, 1963; Galerie Semiha Huber, Zurich, 1963; Picadilly Gallery, 1963, 66, 72, 73; Felix Landau Gallery, 1963; Gertrude Kasle Gallery, 1965, 66, 67, 68, 70; Feingarten Gallery, Chicago; Robert Elkon Gallery; Gump's Gallery; Alex Rosenberg Gallery, 1982, 84; Gump's Gallery, San Francisco, 1964, 65; Benson Gallery, East Hampton, N.Y., 1967, 72. **Group:** Salon des Comparaisons, Paris; Walker, 60 American Painters, 1960; Carnegie, 1961; USIA, Paris, 1961; MOMA, Recent Painting, USA: The Figure, circ., 1962-63; Chicago/AI, Directions in American Painting, 1963; Paris/Moderne, 1963. **Collections:** Baltimore/MA; Charleston/Carolina; MOMA; Syracuse/Everson; Union Carbide Corp.

YOSHIDA, RAY. b. October 3, 1930, Kapaa, Kauai, Hawaii. **Studied:** U. of Hawaii, BA, 1951; Chicago Art Institute School, BAE, 1953; Syracuse U., MFA, 1958. US Army, 1954-56. Traveled Europe, Mexico, the Orient, South America. **Taught:** Syracuse U., 1956-57; Rochester Institute of Technology, 1957-58; Rockford College, 1959-61; Washington U., 1965; Chicago Art Institute School, 1965-80. **Awards:** Frank G. Locan Medal, 1971. **Address:** 1944 N. Wood Street, Chicago, IL 60622. **Dealer:** Phyllis Kind Gallery, NYC, Chicago. **One-man Exhibitions:** Phyllis Kind Gallery, Chicago, 1975, 77, 81, 82; Syracuse U., 1957; Rockford College, 1960; N.A.M.E. Gallery, Chicago, 1984. **Group:** Chicago/Contemporary, Don Baum Sez "Chicago Needs Famous Artists," 1969; ICA, U. of Pennsylvania, Spirit of the Comics, 1969; SFAI, Surplus Slop from the Windy City, 1970; Chicago/Contemporary, Imagist Art, 1972; Ottawa/National, What They're Up to in Chicago, 1972; Sao Paulo, Biennial, 1974; NCFA, Made in Chicago, 1974; Chicago/AI, Famous Alumni, 1976; Sacramento/Crocker, The Chicago Connection, circ., 1976; Chicago/AI, 100 Artists, 100 Years, 1979; U. of North Carolina, Some Recent Art from Chicago, 1980; Sunderland (Eng.) Arts Centre, Who Chicago?, circ., 1980; Kansas City/AI, Chicago Imagists, 1982; WMAA (Downtown) The Comic Art Show, 1983. **Collections:** AT&T NYC; Ball State U.; Chicago/AI; Chicago/Contemporary; Museum des 20. Jahrhunderts, Vienna; NMAA; Northern Ill. U.; South Bend Art Center; Springfield, Ill./State; Syracuse/Everson. **Bibliography:** Adrian; *The Chicago Connection; Who Chicago?*.

YOUNGERMAN, JACK. b. March 25, 1926, Webster Groves, Mo. **Studied:** U. of North Carolina (US Navy Training Program), 1944-46; U. of Missouri, 1947, BA; Academie des Beaux-Arts, Paris, 1947-48. Traveled Europe, Near East; resided Europe, 1947-54. De-

Ray Yoshida   *Mindless Mimic*   1985

signed stage sets for *Histoire de Vasco*, produced by Jean-Louis Barrault, Paris, 1956, and *Deathwatch*, by Jean Genet, NYC, 1958. **Commissios:** Federal Court Building, Portland, Ore., 1975; PPG Industries/Howard Heinz Foundation, 1977. **Awards:** *Art in America* Magazine, New Talent, 1959; National Endowment for the Arts, grant, 1972; Guggenheim Foundation Fellowship, 1976. **Address:** 130 West 4th Street, NYC 10012. **One-man Exhibitions:** Galerie Arnaud, 1951; Gres Gallery, Washington, D.C., 1957 (two-man); Betty Parsons Gallery, 1957, 60, 61, 64, 65, 67, 68; Galleria dell'Ariete, 1962; Galerie Lawrence, Paris, 1962, 65; Everett Ellin Gallery, Los Angeles, 1963; Worcester/AM, 1965; MIT, 1966; Galerie Maeght, 1966; Phillips, 1968; The Pace Gallery, NYC, 1971, 72, 73, 75, J. L. Hudson Art Gallery, Detroit, 1971; The Berenson Gallery, 1972; Portland (Ore.) Center for the Visual Arts, 1972; Seattle/AM, 1972; Arts Club of Chicago, 1973; Galerie Denise Rene, Paris, 1973; Fendrick Gallery, 1974; Kingpitcher Gallery, Pittsburgh, 1974; Fendrick Gallery, Washington, D.C., 1974; Southampton/Parrish, 1976; Tampa Bay Museum, 1977; Truman Gallery, NYC, 1978; Washburn Gallery, Inc., NYC, 1981, 82, 84, 85; Central Park, NYC, 1981; N.Y. Institute of Technology, Old Westbury, 1981; Stony Brook/SUNY, Alex Rosenberg Gallery, NYC, 1983; Heath Gallery, Atlanta, 1984. **Retrospective:** SRGM, 1986. **Group:** Galerie Maeght, Les Mains Eblories, 1950; Galerie Denise Rene, Paris, 1952; Carnegie, 1958, 61, 67, 71; MOMA, Sixteen Americans, circ., 1959; Corcoran, 1959, 62; Kimura Gallery, Tokyo, American Painters, 1960; SRGM, Abstract Expressionists and Imagists, 1961; Chicago/AI, 1961,

Jack Youngerman *Untitled* 1986

62; MOMA, Recent American Painting and Sculpture, circ., USA and Canada, 1961-62; Seattle World's Fair, 1962; International Biennial Exhibition of Paintings, Tokyo; SRGM, American Drawings, 1964; WMAA, A Decade of American Drawings, 1965; SRGM, Systemic Painting, 1966; Rotterdam, 1966; WMAA Annual, 1967; Utica, American Prints Today, 1968; Indianapolis, 1969; Jewish Museum, Superlimited; Books, Boxes, and Things, 1969; Foundation Maeght, L'Art Vivant, 1970; Carnegie, International, 1971; U. of North Carolina, Art on Paper, 1973; U. of Texas, Austin, Abstract Expressionists and Imagists, 1976; Montgomery, Ala., Art Inc., 1979; Museo de Arte Moderno, Bogota, 25 Anos Despues, 1970; California State U., Northbridge, Americans in Paris; the 50s, 1979; Hirshhorn, The Fifties: Aspects of Painting in New York, 1980; Haus der Kunst, Munich, Amerikanische Malerie, 1930-1980, 1981; National Gallery and Yale U., Washington, D.C., The Folding Image, 1984. **Collections:** Baltimore/MA; Buf-falo/Albright; U. of California, Berkeley; Carnegie; Chase Manhattan Bank; Chicago/AI; Columbus; Corcoran; Equitable Life Assurance Society; Hartford/Wadsworth; Hirshhorn; Houston/MFA; Milwaukee; MOMA; NCFA; Phillips; Reynolds Metals Co.; SRGM; VMFA; WMAA; Wichita/AM; Worcester/AM; Yale U. **Bibliography:** Alloway 3; Battcock, ed.; Nordness, ed.; Rickey; Rose, B., 1; Sandler; Weller. Archives.

YUNKERS, ADJA. b. July 15, 1900, Riga, Latvia. **d.** December 24, 1983, NYC. **Studied:** art in Leningrad, Berlin, Paris, and London. Traveled the world extensively; resided Paris 14 years, Stockholm during World War II. Edited and published art magazines *ARS* and *Creation* in Sweden, 1942-45. To USA, 1947; became a citizen. **Taught:** New School for Social Research, 1947-54; U. of New Mexico, summers, 1948, 49; Cooper Union, 1956-67; Honolulu Academy, 1964; U. of California, Berkeley, 1966; U. of Colorado, 1967; Columbia U., 1974; Bard College, 1969-78. **Commissions:** Syracuse U., 1966; Stony Brook/SUNY, 1967. **Awards:** Guggenheim Foundation Fellowship, 1949-50; renewed 1954-55; Ford Foundation, 1959; Chicago/AI, Norman Wait Harris Medal, 1961; Tamarind Fellowship, 1961. **One-man Exhibitions:** (first) Maria Kunde Gallery, Hamburg, 1921 or 1922; Galerie Per, Oslo; Tokanten (Gallery), Copenhagen, 1947-54; Kleemann Gallery, NYC; Corcoran; Smithsonian; Chicago/AI; Pasadena/AM; Colorado Springs/FA; Grace Borgenicht Gallery, Inc., 1954, 55; Galerie Paul Facchetti; Gallerie Schneider, Rome; Salon des Realites Nouvelles, Paris, 1955; Zwemmer Gallery, London, 1957-59; Los Angeles/County MA; Rose Fried Gallery; The Howard Wise Gallery, Cleveland; Andre Emmerich Gallery, NYC; Honolulu Academy, 1964-65; The Zabriskie Gallery, NYC, 1974, 75; Nielsen Gallery, Boston, 1981; Allrich Gallery, San Francisco, 1982; C.D.S. Gallery, NYC, 1982; Fine Arts Museum of Long Island, 1984. **Retrospectives:** Baltimore/MA; U. of Utah; Mexico City/Nacional, 1975; Albion College, circ., 1982. **Group:** MOMA, The New American Painting and Sculpture, 1969. **Collections:** Arts Council of Great Britain; Atlanta/AA; Baltimore/MA; Basel; Bibliotheque Nationale; Bibliotheque Royale de Belgique; Boston/MFA; Brandeis U.; Brooklyn Museum; UCLA; Carnegie; Cleveland/MA; Colorado Springs/FA; Corcoran; Florence (Italy)/Modern; Hamburg; Harvard U.; Johannesburg/Municipal; Library of Congress; Lima, Peru; Louisville/Speed; MMA; MOMA; Memphis/Brooks; Minneapolis/Institute; Minnesota/MA; NCFA; NYPL; National Gallery; Oslo/National; PMA; The Print Club, Philadelphia; Rijksmuseum Amsterdam; SRGM; Sao Paulo; Springfield, Mass./MFA; Stockholm/National; Trenton State; U. of Utah; Victoria and Albert Museum; WMAA; Walker; Wellesley College; Worcester/AM. **Bibliography:** Goodrich and Baur 1; *From Foreign Shores;* Nordness, ed.; Read 2. Archives.

Z

ZACHARIAS, ATHOS. b. June 17, 1927, Marlborough, Mass. **Studied:** RISD, 1952, BFA; ASL, with Yasuo Kuniyoshi, summer, 1952; Cranbrook Academy of Art, with Zoltan Sepeshy, 1953, MFA. Traveled Europe, eastern USA. **Taught:** Brown U., 1953-55; Parsons School of Design, 1963-65; Long Island U., summer, 1967; Wagner College, 1969-. **Commissions:** Fram Corporation, 1963 (painting of explorer ship *Fram*). **Awards:** Scholarship to RISD, 1950; Longview Foundation Grant, 1962; Guild Hall, First and Second Prizes; Long Island U., **P.P.,** 1968; MacDowell Colony Fellowship, 1969. **Address:** 463 West Street, NYC 10014. **One-man Exhibitions:** (first) Brown U., 1954; Great Jones Gallery, NYC, 1960; Joachim Gallery, Chicago, 1961; Gallery Mayer, NYC, 1961; Bob Keene, Southampton, N.Y., 1961-64; Louis Alexander Gallery, NYC, 1962, 63; Guild Hall, 1965; Benson Gallery, Bridgehampton, NYC, 1962, 63; Guild Hall, 1965; Benson Gallery, Bridgehampton, N.Y. 1967, 78; Westbeth Gallery, NYC, 1970, 71; Landmark Gallery, Inc., NYC, 1973; Glassboro State College, 1976; James Yu Gallery, NYC, 1977; Fred Dorfman Gallery, NYC, 1978; Guild Hall, East Hampton, 1980; Loonam Gallery, Bridgehampton, N.Y., 1981; Loft Gallery, Southampton, N.Y., 1981; Bologna-Landi Gallery, East Hampton, N.Y., 1982; Adagio Gallery, East Hampton, N.Y., 1983, 84. **Group:** Boston Arts Festival, 1954; ART: USA: 59, NYC, 1959; Raleigh/NCMA, 1959; Pan-Pacific Exhibition, circ., Japan, 1961; Tenth Street Days, NYC, 1978; Guild Hall, Objects by Artists, 1984; NAD, 1986. **Collections:** Best Products, Richmond, Va.; E.F. Hutton & Company, NYC; Kalamazoo/Institute; McCrory Corp., NYC; U. of North Carolina; Phoenix; RISD; Westinghouse.

ZAJAC, JACK. b. December 13, 1929, Youngstown, Ohio. **Studied:** Scripps College, 1949-53, with Millard Sheets, Henry McFee, Sueo Serisawa. Traveled the world extensively. Resided Rome, 1954-74. Changed from painting to sculpture, 1955. **Taught:** Pomona College, 1959; Dartmouth College, 1970. **Commissions:** Reynolds Metals Co., 1968. **Awards:** California State Scholarship, 1950; Youngstown/Butler, Second Prize, 1950; Pasadena/AM, **P.P.,** 1951; Los Angeles/County MA, **P.P.,** 1953, 58; Prix de Rome, 1954, 56, 57; AAAL, 1958; Guggenheim Foundation Fellowship, 1959; Limited Editions Club, $2,500 Prize for Etching, 1959; Sarasota Art Association, Prize for Sculpture, 1959; Grace Cathedral, San Francisco, Art in Religion, First Prize, 1960; National Religious Art Exhibition, Birmingham, Mich., 1962; NAD, Ellin P. Speyer Prize for Sculpture, 1983. **Address:** 1316 West Cliff Drive, Santa Cruz, Calif. 95060. **Dealer:** Stephen Wirtz Gallery, San Francisco. **One-man Exhibitions:** (first) Pasadena/AM, 1951; Felix Landau Gallery, 1951, 53, 54, 56, 58, 60, 62, 63, 66, 68, 70; Santa Barbara/MA, 1953; Scripps College, 1955; Galleria Schneider, Rome, 1955; John Young Gallery, Honolulu, 1956; Il Segno Rome, 1957; The Downtown Gallery, 1960; Devorah Sherman Gallery, 1960; Roland, Browse and Delbanco, London, 1960; Gallery Marcus, Laguna Beach, Calif., 1961; The

Landau-Alan Gallery, NYC, 1966, 68; Alpha Gallery, 1969; Fairweather-Hardin Gallery, 1970; The Forum Gallery, 1971, 74, 78, 83; La Margherita Gallery, Rome, 1972; Galleria d'Arte l'Obelisco, 1973; Jodi Scully Gallery, 1973; San Diego, 1975; Santa Barbara/MA, 1978; Mekler Gallery, Los Angeles, 1983; Stephen Wirtz Gallery, 1984. **Retrospectives:** Newport Harbor, 1965; California Institute of Technology, Pasadena, 1969; Temple U., Rome, 1969; Dartmouth College, 1970; El Paso Museum of Art, 1984. **Group:** Santa Barbara/MA, 1959; WMAA Annual, 1959; Chicago/AI, Annual, 1959; MOMA, Recent Sculpture USA, 1959; Los Angeles/County MA, 1959, 60; Claude Bernard, Paris, Aspects of American Sculpture, 1960; Smithsonian, Drwings by Sculptors, circ., USA, 1961-63; SRGM, The Joseph H. Hirshhorn Collection, 1962; WMAA, American Painters Today, circ., 1962; VMFA, American Painting, 1962; WMAA, Fifty California Artists, 1962-63; MOMA, Recent Painting USA: The figure, circ., 1962-63; Carnegie International, 1965; U. of Illinois, 1965; Biennale de Roma, 1968; Laguna Beach Museum of Art, 1979. **Collections:** California Federal Savings and Loan Association; Gibraltar Savings & Loan Association; Hirshhorn; Home Savings and Loan Association; Kansas City/Nelson; Los Angeles/County MA; Lytton Savings and Loan Association; MOMA; Milwaukee; U. of Nebraska; PAFA; Pasadena/AM; Santa Barbara/MA; Stanford U.; State of California; Syracuse U.; Utica; Walker. **Bibliography: Seldis and Wilke;** Weller.

ZAKANITCH, ROBERT S. b. May 24, 1935, Elizabeth, N.J. **Taught:** U. of California, San Diego, 1974; Chicago Art Institute School, 1976. **m.** Patsy Norvell. **Address:** 78 Greene Street, NYC 10012. **Dealer:** Robert Miller Gallery, Inc., NYC. **One-man Exhibitions:** Henri Gallery, Alexandria, Va., 1965; Stable Gallery, NYC, 1968; Reese Palley Gallery, NYC, 1970, 71; Holly Solomon Gallery, NYC, 1977; Galerie Liatowitsch, Basel, 1978; Robert Miller Gallery, NYC, 1978, 79, 80, 81, 84, 85; Galerie Rudolf Zwirner, Cologne, 1979; Galerie Bischofberger, Zurich, 1980; Galerie Daniel Templon, Paris, 1980, 82; Akira Ikeda Gallery, Nagoya, Japan, 1981; The Greenberg Gallery, St. Louis, Mo., 1981; ICA, U. of Pennsylvania, 1981; Mayor Gallery, London, 1981; McIntosh-Drysdale Gallery, Washington, D.C., 1981; Asher/Faure, Los Angeles, 1982, 85; Harcus Krakow Gallery, Boston, 1982; Michael H. Lord Gallery, Milwaukee, 1982; Makler Gallery, Philadelphia, 1982; Fondation de Château de Jau, France, 1983; Galerie 151, Palm Beach, 1983; McIntosh-Drysdale Gallery, Houston, 1983; Delahunty Gallery, Dallas, 1984; Harcus Gallery, Boston, 1984; Heladner Gallery, Palm Beach, 1985. **Group:** WMAA Annual, 1968; U. of Illinois, 1969; U. of Rochester, Aspects of Current Painting, 1971; WMAA, Structure of Color, 1971; Indianapolis, 1972; Vassar College, New American Abstract Painting, 1972; Corcoran, Biennial, 1973; P.S. 1, Long Island City, Pattern Painting, 1977; Rice U., Pattern and Decoration, 1978; Dayton/AI, Pattern Plus, 1979; The New Museum, NYC, The 1970s, 1979; ICA, U. of Pennsylvania, The Decorative Impulse, 1979; Mannheim/Kunstverein, Dekor, 1980; ICA, U. of Pennsylvania, Drawings: The Pluralist Decade, 1980; Indianapolis, 1980; XXXIX Venice Biennial, 1980; Wesleyan U. of Illinois, Pattern Painters, 1980; WMAA Biennial, 1981; Galeria Civica, Modena, Transavanguardia, 1982; Bonn, Back to the USA, circ., 1983; MOMA, International Survey of Recent Painting and Sculptures, 1984; Municipal Museum of Art, Kitakyushu, Painting Now: The Restoration of Painterly Figuration, 1984; Columbus, American Art Now!, 1985. **Collections:** Aachen/Ludwig; Blue Cross-Blue Shield, Chicago; Hartford/Wadsworth; High Museum; Hirshhorn, Milwaukee; Musée de

Strasbourg; Phoenix; PMA; Princeton U.; Ridgefield/Aldrich; VMFA; Vassar College; WMAA. **Bibliography:** *Back to the USA; Drawings: The Pluralist Decade;* Hiromoto; Murken-Altrogge. Archives.

ZAMMITT, NORMAN. b. February 3, 1931, Toronto, Canada. US Air Force, 1951-56. US Citizen, 1956. **Studied:** Pasadena City College AA, 1950-51, 1956-57; Otis Art Institute, MFA, 1957-61. **Taught:** School of Fine Arts, Los Angeles, 1962-63; Occidental College, 1963; U. of New Mexico, 1963-64; CSCS, Fullerton, 1964-66; California Institute of the Arts, Los Angeles, 1967; U. of Southern California, 1968-69; UCLA, 1971-72. **Awards:** Pasadena City College, Ruth Estes Bissiri Memorial Scholarship, 1957; Otis Art Institute, four-year scholarship, 1957-61, 50th Anniversary Sculpture Exhibition, **P.P.,** 1968; Tamarind Fellowship; Guggenheim Foundation Fellowship, 1968; Long Beach/MA. **Address:** 233 N. Wilson Avenue, Pasadena, CA 91106. **One-man Exhibitions:** Felix Landau Gallery, 1962, 63, 69; Robert Schoelkopf Gallery, 1963; The Landau-Alan Gallery, NYC, 1967, 68; Santa Barbara/MA, 1968; Los Angeles/County MA, 1977; Corcoran, 1978. **Group:** Los Angeles/County MA, 1961, 64, American Sculpture of the Sixties, 1967; Pasadena/AM, 1962; U. of St. Thomas (Tex.), 1965; MOMA, 1965; U. of Illinois, 1967; Hansen Gallery, San Francisco, 1967; Lytton Art Center, Los Angeles, 1967. **Collections:** Library of Congress; MOMA; Ridgefield/Aldrich. **Bibliography:** Davis, D.; Tuchman 1.

ZOGBAUM, WILFRID. b. September 10, 1915, Newport, RI; **d.** January 7, 1965, NYC. **Studied:** Yale U., 1933-34; with John Sloan, NYC, 1934-35; Hoffmann School, NYC and Provincetown, 1935-37 (class monitor). US Army, 1941-46. Traveled Europe, the Orient, West Indies, USA. Began sculpture, 1954. **Taught:** U. of Califor-

nia, Berkeley, 1957, 1961-63; U. of Minnesota, 1958; Pratt Institute, 1960-61; Southern Illinois U., 1961. **Member:** American Welding Society; Sculptors Guild. **Awards:** S. R. Guggenheim Fellowship for Painting, 1937; U. of California Institute for Creative Work in the Arts, 1963. **One-man Exhibitions:** (first) Alexander Iolas Gallery, 1952 (paintings); The Stable Gallery, 1954, 58; Walker, 1958; Staempfli Gallery, 1960; Obelisk Gallery, Washington, D.C. 1962; Dilexi Gallery, San Francisco, 1962; U. of California, Berkeley, 1962; Grace Borgenicht Gallery Inc., 1963; Everett Ellin Gallery, Los Angeles, 1963; Hansen-Fuller Gallery, San Francisco, 1969; SFMA, 1973; Zabriskie Gallery, NYC, 1979. **Group:** American Abstract Artists, 1935-41; Oakland/AM, 1957; U. of Nebraska, 1961; Baltimore/MA, 1961; MOMA, Modern American Drawings, circ., Europe, 1961-62; Seattle World's Fair, 1962; WMAA Annuals; Chicago/AI, 1962; Carnegie, 1962; Turin/Civico, 1962. **Collections:** Brooklyn Museum; U. of California; Hirshhorn; International Institute for Aesthetic Research; New School for Social Research; SFMA; WMAA. **Bibliography:** Hunter, ed.; Tuchman 1. Archives.

ZORACH, MARGUERITE. b. September 25, 1887, Santa Rosa, Calif.; **d.** June 27, 1968, Brooklyn, N.Y. **Studied:** in Paris, 1906-10. Traveled Europe, Mexico, Central America, and around the world, 1911-12. **Taught:** Provincetown, 1913-18; Columbia U., intermittently during the 1940s. **Commissions** (murals): US Post Offices, Peterborough, N.H., and Ripley, Tenn. **Awards:** Chicago/AI, The Mr. & Mrs. Frank G. Logan Medal, 1920; Golden Gate International Exposition, San Francisco, 1939, Silver Medal; Hon. Ph.D., Bates College. **m.** William Zorach. **One-man Exhibitions:** (first) The Daniel Gallery, NYC, 1915, also 1917; Montross Gallery, NYC, 1921; Joseph Brummer Gallery, NYC, 1930;

The Downtown Gallery, 1935, 38; M. Knoedler & Co., NYC, 1944; Kraushaar Galleries, 1953, 57, 62, 68, 74. **Retrospective:** NCFA, 1973. **Group:** Salon d'Automne, Paris, 1910; The Armory Show, 1913; WMAA; MOMA. **Collections:** Colby College; Louisville/Speed; MMA; MOMA; Massillon Museum; Newark Museum; WMAA. **Bibliography:** *Avant-Garde Painting & Sculpture in America, 1910-25*; Biddle 4; Brown 2; Cheney; Goodrich and Baur 1; Hunter 6; Marter, Tarbell, and Wechsler; Richardson, E.P.; Ringel, ed.; **Tarbell;** Wright 1. Archives.

ZORACH, WILLIAM. b. February 28, 1887, Eurburg, Lithuania; **d.** November 15, 1966, Bath, Me. To USA, 1891. **Studied:** Cleveland Institute of Art, 1902-05; NAD, 1908-10; and in Paris, 1910-11. **Taught:** ASL, 1929-66; The Des Moines Art Center, 1954. **Member:** NIAL (vice-President, 1955-57); Sculptors Guild. **Commissions:** Radio City Music Hall, NYC, 1932; US Post Office, Benjamin Franklin Station, Washington, D.C., 1937; New York World's Fair, 1939; Mayo Clinic, Rochester, Minn., 1954; Municipal Court Building, NYC, 1958; R.S. Reynolds Memorial Award, 1960 (a sculpture). **Awards:** Chicago/AI, The Mr. & Mrs. Frank G. Logan Medal, 1931, 32; Architectural League of New York, Hon. Men., 1939; Bates College, Citation, 1958; Hon. MA, Bowdoin College, 1958; NIAL, Gold Medal for Sculpture, 1961; PAFA, George D. Widener Memorial Gold Medal, 1962. **m.** Marguerite Zorach. **One-man Exhibitions:** Taylor Galleries, Cleveland, 1912; The Daniel Gallery, NYC, 1915, 16, 18; O'Brien's Gallery, Chicago, 1916; Dayton/AI, 1922; U. of Rochester, 1924; Kraushaar Galleries, 1924, 26, 48; Arts and Crafts Club, New Orleans, 1927; Eastman-Bolton Co., NYC, 1929; The Downtown Gallery, 1931, 32, 33, 36, 43, 44, 47, 51, 55, 67; Passedoit Gallery, NYC, 1937; Ansel Adams Gallery, San Francisco, 1941; Boston Museum School, 1941;

Dallas/MFA, 1945; California Palace, 1946; San Diego, 1946; Pasadena/AM, 1946; Ten Thirty Gallery, Cleveland, 1948; Coleman Gallery, NYC, 1949; New Paltz/SUNY, 1950; Clearwater/Gulf Coast, 1952; Des Moines, 1954; San Antonio/McNay, 1956; Bowdoin College, 1958; Philadelphia Art Alliance, 1961; Coe College, 1961; Queens College, 1961; Brooklyn Museum, 1968; Danenberg Gallery, 1970; The Zabriskie Gallery, 1974, 81. **Retrospectives:** ASL, 1950, 69; WMAA, circ., 1959. **Group:** Salon d'Automne, Paris, 1910; The Armory Show, 1913; Society of Independent Artists, NYC, 1914-16; Anderson Galleries, NYC, Forum Exhibition, 1916; PAFA, New Tendencies, 1918; A Century of Progress, Chicago, 1933-34; American Painting and Sculpture, Moscow, 1959; PAFA; MOMA; WMAA; Corcoran; Chicago/AI. **Collections:** AAAL; Andover/Phillips; Arizona State College; Baltimore/MA; Bezalel Museum; Buffalo/Albright; Chicago/AI; Cleveland/MA; Colby College; Columbia U.; Columbus; Corcoran; Dallas/MFA; Des Moines; Dubuque/AA; Fairleigh Dickinson U.; Fort Worth; IBM; Los Angeles/County MA; MMA; MOMA; U. of Nebraska; Newark Museum; New Britain; Oberlin College; Ogunquit; PMA; The Pennsylvania State U.; Phillips; Pittsfield/Berkshire; Sara Roby Foundation; tion; Shelburne; Syracuse U.; Tel Aviv; Terre Haute/Swope; Utica; VMFA; WMAA; West Palm Beach/Norton; Wichita/AM; Wilmington. **Bibliography:** *Avant-Garde Painting & Sculpture in America, 1910-25*; Baur 7; Beam; Biddle 4; Blesh 1; Brown 2; Brumme; Bryant, L.; Cahill and Barr, eds.; Cheney; Craven, W.; Flanagan; *From Foreign Shores*; Gertz; Goodrich and Baur 1; Hall; Halpert; **Hoopes;** Hunter 6; *Index of 20th Century Artists*; Jewell 2; Lee and Burchwood; Marter, Tarbell, and Wechsler; McCurdy, ed.; Mellquist; Mendelowitz; Myers 2; Neuhaus; Parkes; Pearson 2; Phillips 2; Richardson, E.P.; Ringel, ed.; Ritchie 3; Rose, B., 1;

Seuphor 3; Weller; Wheeler; **Wingert;** Wright 1; **Zorach 1, 2.** Archives.

ZOX, LARRY. b. May 31, 1936, Des Moines, Iowa. **Studied:** U. of Oklahoma, with Amelio Amero, Eugene Bavinger; Drake U., with Karl Mattern; The Des Moines Art Center, with George Grosz, Louis Bouche, Will Barnet. Traveled USA, Mexico, and Canada extensively. **Taught:** Cornell U., Artist-in-Residence, 1961; U. of North Carolina, Artist-in-Residence, 1967; School of Visual Arts, NYC, 1967-68, 1969-70; Juniata College, Artist-in-Residence, 1968; Dartmouth College, Artist-in-Residence, 1969; Yale U., 1972; Kent State U., 1974. **Awards:** Guggenheim Foundation Fellowship, 1967; National Council on the Arts Award, 1969; National Endowment for the Arts, Grant, 1969. **Address:** 238 Park Avenue South, NYC 10003. **Dealer:** Andre Emmerich Gallery, NYC. **One-man Exhibitions:** (first) The American Gallery, NYC, 1962; The Kornblee Gallery, 1964, 66, 68, 69, 70, 71; J. L. Hudson Art Gallery, Detroit, 1967; Galerie Rolf Ricke, 1968; Colgate U., 1968; Dartmouth College, 1969; Janie C. Lee Gallery, Dallas, 1970, 74, Houston, 1974; Akron/AI, 1971; Des Moines, 1971, 74; WMAA, 1973; Andre Emmerich Gallery, NYC, 1973, 75, 76; WMAA, 1973; Galerie Daniel Templon, Paris, 1975; Medici-Berenson Gallery, Bay Harbor Islands, 1978. **Group:** Des Moines, 1955, 56; Gallery of Modern Art, NYC, 1965; WMAA, Young America, 1965, Annuals, 1965-66, 1967-68, 1969, 70, 73; Chicago/AI, 1965; Boston/MFA, 1966; SRGM, Systemic Painting, 1966; Expo '67, Montreal, 1967; New Delhi, First World Triennial, 1968; Kent State U., 1968; Worcester/AM, The Direct Image, 1969; The Edmonton Gallery, New Abstract Sculpture, 1977. **Collections:** American Republic Insurance Co.; Columbia Broadcasting System; Cornell U.; Dallas/MFA; Dartmouth College; Des Moines; Des Moines Register & Tribune; Hirshhorn; Houston/MFA; Indianapolis; MOMA; National Bank of Des Moines; Oberlin College; South Mall, Albany; Tate; WMAA. **Bibliography:** Alloway 3; Battcock, ed.; Hunter, ed.; **Monte;** Rose, B., 1.

Bibliography

I. = Illustrated; **B.** = Bibliography; **D.** = Diagrams; **G.** = Glossary;
P. = Plans; **C.** = Chronologies; **A.** = Appendices.
In cases of more than one entry for the same author, the numeral immediately following the author's name is keyed to the Bibliography section of the Artists' entries. A supplemental list of Books of General Interest follows the main bibliography.

Abstraction création 1931–1936. Münster: Westfälisches Landesmuseum, 1978. Foreword by Peter Berghaus. Preface by Jacques Lassaigne. Essay by Gladys C. Fabre. I.B.D.C. (German and French text.) *Documentation and major survey of this art movement.*

ADAMS, PHILIP RHYS. 1. *Painter of Vision: Walt Kuhn.* Tucson: University of Arizona Art Gallery, 1966. Foreword by William B. Steadman. I. *Major retrospective catalogue.*

____, 2. Walt Kuhn. *Cincinnati: The Cincinnati Art Museum, 1960. I. Monograph.*

ADRIAN, DENNIS. *Sight Out of Mind: Essays and Criticism on Art.* Ann Arbor, MI: UMI Research Press, 1985. *Collected essays. The most intelligent post-World War II Chicago criticism.*

ADRIANI, GOETZ; KOEPPLIN, DIETER; and ROSE, BARBARA. *Zeichnungen von Claes Oldenburg.* Tubingen: Kunsthalle Tubingen, 1975. I.B.C. (German text). *A major exhibition and study of the drawings.*

AGEE, WILLIAM C. 1. *Marca-Relli.* New York: The Whitney Museum of American Art, 1967. I.B. *Retrospective catalogue.*

____, 2. *Ralston Crawford.* Pasadena, CA: Twelve Trees Press, 1983. I.B.C. *Excellent introduction to the art and life, includes Crawford statements.*

AGEE, WILLIAM C., and ROSE, BARBARA. *Patrick Henry Bruce: American Modernist.* New York: The Museum of Modern Art, 1979, I.C. *A catalogue raisonné. Documents the life and work of the painter.*

ALBERS, JOSEF. 1. *Day and Night.* Los Angeles: Tamarind Lithography Workshop, Inc., 1964. *Boxed folio of 10 lithographs (ed. 20).*

____, 2. *Despite Straight Lines.* New Haven, Conn.: Yale University Press, 1961. I.B. *Captions by Albers; analysis of his graphic constructions, by François Bucher. (German edition, Trotz der Geraden. Berne: Benteli, 1961).*

____, 3. *Homage to the Square. Ten Works by Josef Albers.* New Haven, Conn.: Ives-Sillman, 1962. Preface by Richard Lippold. *Ten color silkscreens in folio.*

____, 4. *Interaction of Color.* New Haven, Conn., and London: Yale University Press, 1963. I. *More than 200 color studies, with commentaries.*

____, 5. *Poems and Drawings.* New Haven, Conn.: Readymade Press, 1958. I. *(German and English text.)*

____, 6. *Poems and Drawings* (2nd ed., rev. and enlarged). New York: George Wittenborn, Inc., 1961. I. *(Bilingual text.)*

____, 7. *Zeichnungen—Drawings.* New York: George Wittenborn, Inc.; Berne: Spiral Press, 1956. (Text by Max Bill in German and English.) *Twelve b/w plates loose in folio.*

Albert Bloch: 1882–1961. Utica, N.Y.: Munson-William-Proctor Institute, 1974. I. *Exhibition catalogue.*

Alexander Archipenko. A Memorial Exhibition. Los Angeles: University of California, 1967. Foreword by Katherine Kuh. Archipenko Collection: Frances Archipenko. Life and Work:

Frederick S. Wight. The Drawings and Prints: Donald H. Karshan. I.B. *Well-documented retrospective catalogue.*

Alexander Calder. Berlin: Akademie der Kunste, 1967. Preface by William Sandberg. I.B. (German text.) *Retrospective catalogue.*

Alexander Calder. New York: A Studio Book/Viking Press, 1971. Introduction by H. Harvard Arnason. Photographs and design by Ugo Mulas. I.B. *Photo survey of Calder, his works, and his milieu.*

Alexander Liberman: Painting and Sculpture 1950–1970. Washington, D.C.: Corcoran Gallery of Art, 1970. Introduction by James Pilgrim. I.B.C. *Retrospective catalogue.*

ALFIERI, BRUNO. *Gyorgy Kepes,* Ivrey, Italy: Centro Culturale Olivetti, 1958. I.B. *Monograph.*

Alfred Jensen. Bern: Kunsthalle Bern, 1973. I.B. (German and English text.) *Retrospective catalogue.*

Al Held. San Francisco: San Francisco Museum of Art, 1968. I.B. *One-man exhibition catalogue.*

ALLEN, CLARENCE CANNING, ed. *Are You Fed Up with Modern Art?* Tulsa, Okla.: The Rainbow Press, 1957. I. *Popular reaction against the new art.*

ALLEN, VIRGINIA. *Jim Dine Designs for "A Midsummer Night's Dream."* New York: The Museum of Modern Art, 1967. I. *Costume designs for the play.*

ALLOWAY, LAWRENCE. 1. *American Pop Art.* New York: Collier Books, 1974. I.B. *Exhibition survey of pop art.*

____, 2. *Samaras: Selected Works 1960–1966.* New York: The Pace Gallery, 1966. I.B. *Includes a statement by the artist.*

____, 3. *Systemic Painting.* New York: The Solomon R. Guggenheim Museum, 1966. I.B. *Catalogue including artists' statements.*

____, 4. *Topics in American Art since 1945.* New York: W. W. Norton & Co., Inc., 1975. I. *Collected reviews and articles written in the sixties and early seventies.*

____, 5. *William Baziotes.* New York: The Solomon R. Guggenheim Museum, 1965. I.B. *Retrospective catalogue.*

ALVARD, J. *Mark Tobey.* Paris: Musée des Arts Décoratifs, Palais du Louvre, 1961. I.B. (French and English text.) *Retrospective catalogue.*

America 1976. Washington, D.C.: The Hereward Lester Cooke Foundation, 1976. Foreword by Thomas S. Kleppe. Painting America First: Robert Rosenblum. Inclusive Painting: Neil Welliver. Pyrography: John Ashbery. On the United States Considered as a Landscape: Richard Howard. I. *US Department of the Interior commissions realist artists.*

AMERICAN ABSTRACT ARTISTS, ed. *American Abstract Artists.* New York: American Abstract Artists, 1946. I. *Documents members and activities.*

AMERICAN ARTISTS CONGRESS, INC. *America Today, a Book of 100 Prints.* New York: Equinox Cooperative Press, 1936. I.

AMERICAN ARTISTS GROUP, INC. 1. *Handbook of the American Artists Group.* New York: American Artists Group Inc., 1935. I.B. *Members and organizational information.*

____, 2. *Missouri, Heart of the Nation.* New York: American Artists Group, Inc., 1947. I.B. *Midwest art of the 1930s and 1940s.*

____, 3. *Original Etchings, Lithographs and Woodcuts by American Artists.* New York: American Artists Group, Inc., 1936. I.

Amerikanischer Fotorealismus. Stuttgart: Wurttembergischer Kunstverein, 1972. Introduction by Uwe M. Schneede. I.C. (German text.) *Survey exhibition, including artists' statements.*

AMMANN, JEAN-CHRISTOPHE. *Richard Artschwager.* Basel: Kunsthalle Basel, 1985. (German and English text; French laid in.) B. *Retrospective catalogue.*

AMMANN, JEAN-CHRISTOPHE, and BUSSMANN, G. *Man Ray: Inventionen und Interpretationen.* Frankfurt:

Frankfurter Kunstverein, 1979. *Retrospective catalogue: various essays; includes artists' statement.*

ARCHIPENKO, ALEXANDER. 1. *Archipenko, 50 Creative Years.* New York: Tekhne, 1960. I.B. *Autobiography.*

____, 2.*Archipentura.* New York: Anderson Galleries, 1928. B. *Exhibition catalogue.*

Arman: Selected Works 1958–1974. La Jolla: La Jolla Museum of Contemporary Art, 1974. Introduction by Jan van der Marck. I.B. *Retrospective catalogue.*

ARMITAGE, MERLE. *Rockwell Kent.* New York: Alfred A. Knopf, 1932. I.B. *Monograph.*

ARMSTRONG, RICHARD. *William Brice.* Los Angeles: Museum of Contemporary Art, 1986. B. *Exhibition catalogue.*

ARMSTRONG, RICHARD, and MARSHALL, RICHARD. *Five Painters in New York.* New York: Whitney Museum of American Art, 1984. B.C.I. *Exhibition catalogue. Decorative art and recent abstraction.*

ARNASON, H. HARVARD. 1. *Marca-Reli.* New York: Harry N. Abrams Inc., 1962. I. *Monograph.*

____, 2. *Philip Guston.* New York: The Solomon R. Guggenheim Museum, 1962. I.B. *Exhibition catalogue.*

____, 3. *Stuart Davis.* Minneapolis: The Walker Art Center, 1957. I. *Exhibition catalogue.*

____, 4. *Stuart Davis, Memorial Exhibition.* Washington, D.C.: National Collection of Fine Arts, 1965. I.B. *Major retrospective catalogue.*

____, 5. *Theodore Roszak.* Minneapolis: The Walker Art Center, 1956. I.B. *Exhibition catalogue.*

ARP, HANS. *Onze Peintres.* Zurich: Editions Girsberger, 1949. (French and German text.) I.

Art as a Muscular Principle. South Hadley, Mass.: Mount Holyoke College, 1975. I.B. *A study of ten artists and San Francisco, 1950–1965.*

Art: A Woman's Sensibility. Valencia, Calif: California Institute of the Arts, 1975. Introduction by Deena Metzger. I. *Exhibition catalogue; includes artists' statements.*

Arthur Dove: The Years of Collage. College Park, MD.: University of Maryland Art Gallery, 1967. I.B. *Major study of the collages of Dove.*

ARTHUR JOHN. 1. *Realism/Photorealism.* Tulsa: Philbrook Art Center, 1980. Foreword by Jesse G. Wright, Jr. I.C. *An examination and defense of this school of recent painting.*

____, 2. *Realist Drawings & Watercolors: Contemporary American Works on Paper.* Boston: New York Graphic Society, 1980. I. *Brief examination of various modes of realism.*

____, 3. *American Realism: The Precise Image.* Tokyo: The Isetan Museum of Art, 1985. B.C.I. (Japanese and English texts.) *Mostly photorealism.*

____, 4. *Realists at Work.* New York: Watson-Guptil Publications, n.d. I. *How to do it interviews.*

Art Now 74: A Celebration of the American Arts. Washington, D.C.: Artrend Foundation, 1974. Foreword by Jocelyn Kress. Introduction by Henry T. Hopkins and Maurice Tuchman. I. *Catalogue of performances and exhibition objects: includes artists' statements.*

Art of the Pacific Northwest: From the 1930s to the Present. Washington, D.C.: National Collection of Fine Arts, 1974. Foreword by Adelyn D. Breeskin. Introduction by Joshua C. Taylor. Essays by Rachel Griffin and Martha Kingsbury. I.B. *Important survey exhibition and catalogue.*

ASHBERY, JOHN, and MOFFETT, KENWORTH. *Fairfield Porter: Realist Painter in an Age of Abstraction.* Boston: Museum of Fine Arts, 1982. B.C. *Retrospective catalogue; includes other essays, an interview, and 5 poems by the painter.*

ASHTON, DORE. 1. *The Mosaics of Jeanne Reynal.* New York: George Wittenborn, Inc., 1964. I. *Monograph.*

____, 2. *Philip Guston.* New York: Grove Press, Inc., 1960. I.B. *Monograph.*

____, 3. *A Reading of Modern Art.*

Cleveland and London: The Press of Case Western Reserve University, 1969. I. *Criticisms of recent modern art and literature.*

___, 4. *Richard Lindner.* New York: Harry N. Abrams Inc., 1970. I. *Monograph.*

___, 5. *The Unknown Shore.* Boston: Little, Brown and Co., 1962. I. *Collected essays mostly reprinted from Art and Architecture magazine.*

___, 6. *Yes, But . . . A Critical Study of Philip Guston.* New York: The Viking Press, 1976. I.B.C. *An evaluation of the artist's work.*

ASHTON, DORE, ed. *A Joseph Cornell Album.* New York: Viking Press, 1974. I. *Collected writings by and about Cornell.*

ATKINSON, TRACY. *Directions I: Options 1968.* Milwaukee: Milwaukee Art Center, 1968. Preface by Lawrence Alloway. I. *Catalogue of "people involved in art" with statements by artists.*

AULT, LOUISE. *Artist in Woodstock. George Ault: The Independent Years.* Philadelphia: Dorrance & Co., 1978. *A brief life of the artist.*

Avant-Garde Painting and Sculpture in America: 1910–1925. Wilmington: Delaware Art Museum, 1975. Preface and acknowledgments by William Innes Homer. Foreword by Charles T. Wyrick, Jr. I.B.C. *Useful essays by various authors on modern tendencies in American art.*

AXOM, RICHARD H. *The Prints of Frank Stella: A Catalogue Raisonné.* New York: Hudson Hills Press, 1983. B.C.G. Foreword by Evan M. Maurer. *Exhibition and works catalogue for the years 1967–82.*

Back to the USA. Cologne: Rheinland-Verlag, 1983. B.I. (German text.) *Exhibition catalogue; survey of pattern and decoration, neo-expressionism, and other recent tendencies.*

BAIGELL, MATTHEW. 1. *The American Scene: American Paintings.* New York: Praeger Publishers (American Art

and Artists of the 1930s), 1974. I.B. *Superficial survey.*

___, 2. *Thomas Hart Benton.* New York: Harry N. Abrams Inc., 1974. I.B.C. *Heavily illustrated monograph.*

BALDES, ALTON PARKER. *Six Maryland Artists.* Baltimore: Balboa Publishers, 1955. I.

BALDINGER, WALLACE. S., in collaboration with Harry B. Green. *The Visual Arts.* New York: Holt, Rinehart and Winston, Inc., 1960. I.B. *Includes chapters on the visual arts.*

BALLO, FERDINANDO, ed. *Grosz.* Milan: Rosa e Balio Editori, 1956. I. (German and Italian text.) *Critical essays.*

BARKER, VIRGIL. 1. *From Realism to Reality in Recent American Painting.* Lincoln: University of Nebraska Press, 1959. I. *Essays on the rise of abstract and nonfigurative painting.*

___, 2. *Henry Lee McFee.* New York: The Whitney Museum of American Art (American Artists Series), 1931. I. *Monograph.*

BARNES, ALBERT C. *The Art in Painting.* Merion, Pa.: The Barnes Foundation Press, 1925. I. *Dr. Barnes's theories.*

BARO, GENE. *Paul Feeley,* New York: The Solomon R. Guggenheim Museum, 1968. I.B. *Retrospective catalogue.*

BARR, ALFRED, H., Jr. 1. *Cubism and Abstract Art.* New York: The Museum of Modern Art, 1936. I.B. *Essays on Cubism and its evolution.*

___, 2. *Edward Hopper.* New York: The Museum of Modern Art, 1933. I.B. *Exhibition catalogue.*

___, 3. *What Is Modern Painting?* New York: The Museum of Modern Art, 1956. I. *Popular introduction to modern art.*

BARTLETT, JENNIFER. *In the Garden.* New York: Harry N. Abrams, Inc., 1982. Introduction by John Russell. *Folio of drawings with no text by the artist.*

BASKIN, LEONARD. *Leonard Baskin.* Brunswick, Me.: Bowdoin College, 1962. I.B. *Exhibition catalogue.*

BATES, KENNETH. *Brackman, His Art and Teaching.* Noank, Conn.: Noank Publishing Studio, 1951. I. *Monograph.*

BATTCOCK, GREGORY, ed. *Minimal Art: A Critical Anthology.* New York: E.P. Dutton, 1968. I. *Critical essays reprinted from periodicals and exhibition catalogues.*

BAUDSON, PIERRE. *Steinberg: Zeichnungen und Collagen.* Hamburg: Hamburger Kunsthalle, 1968. Foreword by Helmut R. Leppien. I.B. (German text.) *Retrospective catalogue including an interview with the artist.*

BAUR, JOHN I.H. 1. *Charles Burchfield.* New York: The Whitney Museum of American Art, 1956. I.B. *Retrospective catalogue.*

_____, 2. *George Grosz.* New York: The Whitney Museum of American Art, 1954. I.B. *Retrospective catalogue.*

_____, 3. *Joseph Stella.* New York: The Whitney Museum of American Art, 1963. I.B. *Retrospective catalogue.*

_____, 4. *Loren MacIver—Rice Pereira.* New York: The Whitney Museum of American Art, 1953. I.B. *Exhibition catalogue.*

_____, 5. *Nature in Abstraction.* New York: The Macmillan Company, for The Whitney Museum of American Art, 1958. I.B. *Nature considered as catalyst for abstraction.*

_____, 6. *Philip Evergood.* New York: Frederick A. Praeger, for The Whitney Museum of American Art, 1960. I.B. *Monograph.*

_____, 7. *Revolution and Tradition in Modern American Art.* Cambridge, Mass.: Harvard University Press, 1959. I. *Important essays on conservative and advance guard art.*

BAYER, HERBERT. 1. *Book of Drawings.* Chicago: Paul Theobald and Co., 1961. I.B.

_____, 2. *Herbert Bayer: Painter, Designer, Architect.* New York: Reinhold Publishing Co., 1967. I.B.D.P. *Autobiographical monograph.*

BAZALGETTE, LEON. *George Grosz.* Paris: Les Ecrivains Reunis, 1927. I.B. (French text.) *Monograph.*

BAZIN, GERMAIN. *History of Modern Painting.* New York: Hyperion Press, Harper and Brothers, 1951. I.B. *Includes recent American artists of international reputation.*

BEAM, PHILIP C. *The Language of Art.* New York: The Ronald Press, 1958. I.B. *Essays on interpretation.*

BECKER, JURGEN, and VOSTELL, WOLF. *Happenings, Fluxus, Pop, Nouveau Realism.* Reinbeckbei Hamburg: Rowohlt Verlag GMBH, 1965. I. *International survey.*

BEEKMAN, AARON. *The Functional Line in Painting.* New York: Thomas Yoseloff Inc., 1957. I.

BEEREN, WIM. *Roy Lichtenstein.* Amsterdam: Stedelijk Museum, 1967. I.B. (Dutch and English text.) *Major retrospective catalogue includes interview of the artist by John Coplans.*

BEGGS, THOMAS M. *Paul Manship.* Washington, D.C.: Smithsonian Institution, 1958. I. *Exhibition catalogue.*

BENSON, E.M. *John Marin, The Man and His Work.* Washington, D.C.: American Federation of Arts, 1935. *Monograph.*

BENTON, THOMAS HART. 1. *An American in Art.* Lawrence: University of Kansas, 1969. I. *Autobiography.*

_____, 2. *An Artist in America.* New York: Robert M. McBride and Co., 1937. I. *Autobiography.*

_____, 3. *Thomas Hart Benton.* New York: American Artists Group Inc., 1945. I. *Autobiographical monograph.*

_____, 4. *Thomas Hart Benton.* Lawrence: University of Kansas, 1958. I. *Exhibition catalogue.*

BERMAN, EUGENE. *Imaginary Promenades in Italy.* New York: Pantheon Books, 1956. I. *Illustrated essays.*

Bernard Reder. Tel Aviv: The Tel Aviv Museum of Art, 1963. I.B. *Retrospective catalogue including statements by the artist.*

BETHERS, RAY. *How Paintings Happen.* New York: W.W. Norton and Co., 1951. I. *Artists at work.*

BIDDLE, GEORGE. 1. *An American Artist's Story.* Boston: Little, Brown and Co., 1939. I. *Autobiography*.

____, 2. *Ninety-Three Drawings*, Colorado Springs: Colorado Springs Fine Arts Center, 1937. I. *Essays on Boardman Robinson's drawings*.

____, 3. *Tahitian Journal*. St. Paul: University of Minnesota, 1968. I. *Travel book*.

____, 4. *The Yes and No of Contemporary Art*. Cambridge, Mass.: Harvard University Press, 1957. I. *An artist comments on the contemporary scene*.

BIEDERMAN, CHARLES. 1. *Art as the Evolution of Visual Knowledge*. Red Wing, Minn.: Privately published, 1948. I.B. *History, aesthetics, and theory*.

____, 2. *Letters on the New Art*. Red Wing, Minn.: Privately published, 1951. *Essays*.

____, 3. *The New Cezanne*. Red Wing, Minn.: Art History, 1955. I.B. *Homage to Cezanne and theories of subsequent developments*.

____, 4. *Search for New Arts*. Red Wing, MN: Art History, 1979. B.I. *Critical essays*.

BIHALJI-MERIN, OTO. *Adventures of Modern Art*. New York: Harry N. Abrams Inc., 1966. I.B. *Sets postwar Americans in the world art scene*.

BIRCHMAN, WILLIS. *Faces and Facts*. New York: Privately published, 1937. 1. *Short biographies with photographs*.

BIRD, PAUL. *Fifty paintings by Walt Kuhn*. New York: Studio Publications, 1940. 1. *Monograph*.

BIRNBAUM, MARTIN. *Introductions*. New York: Frederic Fairchild Sherman, 1919. *New talent in 1919*.

BITTNER, HUBERT. *George Grosz*. New York: A Golden Griffin Book, Arts, Inc., 1959. I. *Monograph*.

Black and White Are Colors: Paintings of the 1950s–1970s. Claremont, Calif.: Pomona College, 1979. Foreword by David W. Steadman. Essay by David S. Rubin. I. *A psychological-aesthetic investigation of the problems*.

BLANCH, ARNOLD. 1. *Arnold Blanch*. New York: American Artists Group Inc., 1945. I. *Autobiographical monograph*.

____, 2. *Methods and Techniques for Gouache Painting*. New York: American Artists Group Inc., 1946. I.

____, 3. *Painting for Enjoyment*. New York: Tudor Publishing Co., 1947. I.

BLANCHARD, FRANCES BRADSHAW. *Retreat from Likeness in the Theory of Painting*. New York: Columbia University Press, 1949. I.B. *From art as illustration to the object as art*.

BLESH, RUDI. 1. *Modern Art, USA. Men—Rebellion—Conquest 1900–1956*. New York: Alfred A. Knopf, 1956. I. *Popular study of American art from 1900 to 1956*.

____, 2. *Stuart Davis*. New York: Grove Press Inc., 1960. I. *Monograph*.

BORN, WOLFGANG. *American Landscape Painting, an Interpretation*. New Haven, Conn.: Yale University Press, 1948. I.

BOSWELL, PEYTON, Jr. 1. *Modern American Painting*. New York: Dodd, Mead and Co., 1939. I. *Painting in the first 40 years of the twentieth century*.

____, 2. *Varnum Poor*. New York: Hyperion Press, Harper and Brothers, 1941. I.B. *Monograph*.

BOSWELL, PEYTON, Jr., ed. *An Appreciation of the Work of Frederic Taubes*. New York: Art Design Monographs, 1939. I. *Monographs*.

BOURDON, DAVID. *Christo*. New York: Harry N. Abrams Inc., 1971. I.B.C. *Considerable biographical data included in this critical study*.

BOURGEADE, PIERRE. *Bonsoir, Man Ray*. Paris: Pierre Belfond, 1972. *An interview, in French*.

BREEKSIN, A.D. 1. *Franz Kline*. Washington, D.C.: Washington Gallery of Modern Art, 1962. I. *Retrospective catalogue*.

____, 2. *Ilya Bolotowsky*. New York: The Solomon R. Guggenheim Museum, 1974. I.B. *Retrospective catalogue; includes artist's statements*.

BRETON, ANDRE. 1. *Le Surrealisme et*

la peinture. Paris: N.F.R., Gallimard, 1928. I. *The Surrealist movement in art.*

———, 2. *Le Surrealisme et la peinture.* New York: Brentano's 1945. I. *Revised and expanded edition of the above entry.*

———, 3. *Le Surrealisme en 1947.* Paris: Editions Maeght, 1947.

———, 4. *Yves Tanguy.* New York: Pierre Matisse Editions, 1946. I. (French and English text.) *Monograph.*

BRION, MARCEL. 1. *Art abstrait.* Paris: Editions Albin Michel, 1956. I. (French text.) *Development of abstract art in the twentieth century.*

———, 2. *Modern Painting: From Impressionism to Abstract Art.* London: Thames and Hudson, 1958. I.

BROOK, ALEXANDER. *Alexander Brook.* New York: American Artists Group Inc., 1945. I. *Autobiographical monograph.*

BROOKS, VAN WYCK. *John Sloan, a Painter's Life.* New York: E.P. Dutton, 1955. I. *Biography.*

BROWN, JULIA, ed. *Michael Heizer: Sculpture in Reverse.* Los Angeles: Museum of Contemporary Art, 1984. B.C. *Retrospective catalogue with interviews and documentation.*

BROWN, MILTON W. 1. *American Painting: From the Armory Show to the Depression.* Princeton, N.J.: Princeton University Press, 1955. I.B.

———, 2. *The Modern Spirit. American Painting 1908–1935.* London: Arts Council of Great Britain, 1977. Foreword by Joanna Drew. I.B. *Major study of American art of this period seen in Britain.*

Bruce Conner Drawings: 1955–1972. San Francisco: San Francisco Museum of Art, 1974. Preface by Ian McKibbin White. Introduction by Thomas H. Garver. I. *Retrospective catalogue of drawings.*

BRUCE, EDWARD, and WATSON, FORBES. *Art in Federal Buildings.* Washington, D.C.: Art in Federal Buildings, Inc., 1936. I.P.

Bruce Nauman. London: Whitechapel Art Gallery, 1986. Essays by Joan Simon and J.C. Ammann. B. *Exhibition catalogue.*

BRUMME, C. LUDWIG. *Contemporary American Sculpture.* New York: Crown Publishers Inc., 1948. I.B.

BRYANT, EDWARD. *Nell Blaine.* Southampton, N.Y.: Parrish Art Museum, 1974. I.B.C. *Retrospective exhibition catalogue.*

BRYANT, LORINDA M. *American Pictures and Their Painters.* New York: John Lane Co., 1917. I.

BULLIET, C.J. 1. *Apples and Madonnas.* Chicago: Pascal Covici, Inc., 1927. I. *Critical essays on American artists.*

———, 2. *The Significant Moderns and Their Pictures.* New York: Covici-Friede, Publishers, 1936. I.

BUNCE, LOUIS. *Louis Bunce.* Portland, Ore.: Portland Art Museum, 1955. I. *Exhibition catalogue.*

BURCHFIELD, CHARLES. 1. *Charles Burchfield.* Buffalo: Buffalo Fine Arts Academy, Albright Art Gallery, 1944. I. *Exhibition catalogue.*

———, 2. *Charles Burchfield.* New York: American Artists Group Inc., 1945. I. *Autobiographical monograph.*

———, 3. *Eugene Speicher.* Buffalo: Albright Art Gallery, 1950. I. *Exhibition catalogue.*

BURROUGHS, ALAN. *Kenneth Hayes Miller.* New York: The Whitney Museum of American Art (American Artists Series), 1931. I.B. *Exhibition catalogue.*

BUSH, MARTIN H. 1. *Ben Shahn: The Passion of Sacco and Vanzetti.* Syracuse: Syracuse University, 1968. I.B. *A history of the development of the mural.*

———, 2. *Doris Caesar.* Syracuse, N.Y.: Syracuse University, 1970. Introduction by Marya Zaturenska. I.B. *Appreciation with some biographical data.*

BUSH, MARTIN H., and MOFFETT, KENWORTH. *Goodnough.* Wichita: Wichita Art Museum, 1973. I.B.C. *Retrospective catalogue.*

BYWATERS, JERRY. 1. *Andrew*

Dasburg. Dallas: Dallas Museum of Fine Arts, 1957. I. *Exhibition catalogue.*

_____, 2. *Andre Dasburg.* New York: American Federation of Arts, 1959. I. *Retrospective catalogue.*

CABANNE, PIERRE. *Dialogues with Marcel Duchamp.* Translated by Ron Padgett. New York: Viking Press (The Documents of 20th-Century Art), 1971. Preface by Salvador Dali. Introduction by Robert Motherwell. Appreciation by Jasper Johns. I.B.C. *Talking with Marcel, with an eye on history.*

CAGE, JOHN. *The Drawings of Morris Graves, with Comments by the Artist.* Boston: For the Drawing Society, Inc., by the New York Graphic Society Ltd., 1974. Preface by David Daniels. I.C. *Survey of drawings.*

CAHILL, HOLGER. *Max Weber.* New York: The Downtown Gallery, 1930. I. *Monograph.*

CAHILL, HOLGER, and BARR, ALFRED, H., Jr., eds. *Art in America, a Complete Survey.* New York: Reynal and Hitchcock, 1935. I.B. *Considers architecture, fine arts, folk art, etc.*

CALAS, NICOLAS. *Bloodflames, 1947.* New York: Hugo Galleries, 1947. I. *Essays on the advance guard in New York in the 1940s.*

CALAS, NICOLAS and ELENA. *Icons and Images of the Sixties.* New York: E.P. Dutton, 1971. I. *Collected essays.*

CALDER, ALEXANDER. 1. *Calder: An autobiography with pictures.* New York: Pantheon Books, 1966. Foreword by Robert Osborn. I. *Folksy presentation of Calder's life.*

_____, 2. *Three Young Rats.* New York: The Museum of Modern Art, 1946, 2nd ed. I. *A children's story.*

CALDER, ALEXANDER, and LIEDL, CHARLES. *Animal Sketching.* Pelham, N.Y.: Bridgeman Publishers, Inc., 1941, 6th ed. I.

California Sculpture Show. Los Angeles: University of Southern California, 1984. (English, Spanish, French, and German texts.) Foreword by Henry T. Hopkins. B. *Multiple texts in a brief examination of recent sculpture.*

CAMPOS, JULES. *Jose de Creeft.* New York: Erich S. Herrmann, Publisher, 1945. I. *Monographs.*

CANADAY, JOHN. *Mainstreams of Modern Art.* New York: Simon and Schuster, 1959. I. *Popular history of art.*

CARANDENTE, GIOVANNI. *Calder.* Milan: Electra Editrice, 1983. (Italian text.) B. *Retrospective catalogue of over 450 items 1906–1976.*

Carl Andre Sculpture: 1958–1974. Bern: Kunsthalle Bern, 1975. Foreword by Johannes Gachnang. Introduction by Carl Andre. I.B.C.

Carl Holty Memorial Exhibition. New York: Andrew Crispo Gallery, 1974. Introduction by Andrew J. Crispo. I.B.C. *Catalogue includes encomiums by friends.*

CARMEAN, E.A., Jr., and RATHBONE, ELIZA E., with HESS, THOMAS B. *American Art at Mid-Century: The Subjects of the Artist.* Washington, D.C.: National Gallery of Art, 1978. Foreword by J. Carter Brown. I. *A review of the major post-World War II figures.*

Carol Summers. Woodcuts 1950–1967. San Francisco: San Francisco Museum of Art, 1967. Preface by Anneliese Hoyer. I. *Retrospective catalogue; includes statements by the artist.*

CASSOU, JEAN. *Gateway to the 20th Century.* New York: McGraw-Hill Book Co., Inc., 1962. I. *Development of nineteenth-century art and indications of its twentieth-century ramifications.*

CATHCART, LINDA L. *Milton Resnick Paintings 1945–1985.* Houston: Contemporary Arts Museum, 1985. B. *Retrospective catalogue.*

CELANT, GERMANO. *Arte Povera.* New York: Praeger Publishers, 1969. I. *Catalogues artists' statements and illustrations of their works: earthworks, actual art, concept art.*

Celebrate Ohio. Akron: Akron Art Institute, 1971. Foreword by Orrel

Thompson. Introduced by Alfred Radloff. I.C. *Exhibition catalogue.*

CHAET, BERNARD. *Artists at Work.* Cambridge, Mass.: Webb Books Inc., 1960. I. *Interviews with artists.*

Charles Biederman: The Structurist Relief 1935–1964. Minneapolis: The Walker Art Center, 1965. Introduction by Jan van der Marck. I.B.G.C. *Retrospective catalogue.*

Charles Demuth: The Mechanical Encrusted on the Living. Santa Barbara: University of California Press, 1971. Introduction by Phyllis Plous. I.B.C. *A bad centennial retrospective catalogue.*

Charles Sheeler. Washington, D.C.: National Collection of Fine Arts, 1968. I.B. *Essays by Martin Friedman, Bartlett Hayes, Charles Millard; major retrospective catalogue.*

CHENEY, MARTHA CHANDLER. *Modern Art in America.* New York: Whittlesey House, McGraw-Hill Book Co., Inc., 1939. I.

The Chicago Connection. Sacramento: E.B. Crocker Art Gallery, 1976. Foreword by Wilma Beaty Cox. Introduction by Roger D. Clisby. I.B.C. *Survey exhibition of artists mostly born after the late 1930s.*

CHIPP, HERSCHEL B. *Theories of Modern Art.* Berkeley and Los Angeles: University of California Press, 1968. I.B. *Artists' statements.*

CHRISTENSEN, ERWIN O. *The History of Western Art.* New York: New American Library, 1959. I.

CHRIST-JANER, ALBERT. *Boardman Robinson.* Chicago: The University of Chicago Press, 1946. I.B. *Monograph.*

Christopher Wilmarth: Layers. Works from 1962–1984. New York: Hirschl & Adler Modern, 1984. Preface by Dore Ashton. B.C.I. *Exhibition catalogue.*

Cityscape 1919–39. Urban Themes in American, German, and British Art. London: Arts Council of Great Britain, 1977. Preface by Joanna Drew. Essays by Ian Jeffrey and David Mellor. I. *A study of the city and its inhabitants through the art produced therein.*

CLARK, SARAH, and COWLES, CHARLES. *Northwest Tradition.* Seattle: Seattle Art Museum, 1978. Introduction by Sarah Clark. Foreword by Willis F. Woods. B.C. *An essay by Martha Kingsbury examines modern art in the Northwest.*

CLEARWATER, BONNIE. *Mark Rothko: Works on Paper.* New York: Hudson Hills Press, 1984. Introduction by Dore Ashton. B.C. *Drawings and paintings on paper.*

Clyfford Still. Foreword by Katherine Kuh. Buffalo: The Buffalo Fine Arts Academy, 1966. I. *Exhibition catalogue; includes statements by the artist.*

COATES, ROBERT M. *Walter Quirt.* New York: American Federation of Arts, 1959. I. *Retrospective catalogue.*

COKE, VAN DEREN. 1. *Nordfeldt, the Painter.* Albuquerque: The University of New Mexico Press, 1972. Foreword by Sheldon Cheney. I.B.C. *Exhibition catalogue.*

_____, 2. *Taos and Santa Fe. The Artistic Environment. 1882–1942.* Albuquerque: University of New Mexico Press, 1963. I.

CONE, JANE HARRISON. 1. *David Smith.* Cambridge, Mass.: Fogg Art Museum, 1966. I.B. *Exhibition catalogue; includes statements by the artist.*

_____, 2. *Walter Darby Bannard.* Baltimore: The Baltimore Museum of Art, 1972. Foreword by Tom Le Freudenheim. I.B. *Retrospective catalogue; includes artist's statements.*

Contemporanea. Rome: Incontri Internazionali d'Arte, 1973. Introduction by Graziella Lonardi. I.B. (Italian and English text.) *Comprehensive international avant-garde exhibition: art, cinema, theatre, photography, books, visual poetry, etc.*

COPLANS, JOHN. 1. *Ellsworth Kelly.* New York: Harry N. Abrams Inc., 1973. I.B.C. *Picturebook monograph.*

_____, 2. *Roy Lichtenstein.* Pasadena: The Pasadena Art Museum, 1967. I.B. *Includes an interview with the artist.*

_____, 3. *Serial Imagery.* Pasadena: The Pasadena Art Museum, 1968. I.B. *Includes statements by some artists.*

COPLANS, JOHN, ed. *Roy Lichtenstein.* New York: Praeger Publishers (Documentary Monographs in Modern Art), 1972. I.B. *Collected essays about the artist; monograph; biographical notes.*

COPLANS, JOHN, with contributions by JONAS MEKAS and CALVIN TOMKINS. *Andy Warhol.* Greenwich, Conn.: New York Graphic Society Ltd., 1970. I.B. *Monographic study; filmography.*

CORN, WANDA M. *Grant Wood: The Regionalist Vision.* New Haven, CT: Yale University Press, 1983. B.C. *Retrospective catalogue.*

Correspondance, an Exhibition of the Letters of Ray Johnson. Raleigh, N.C.: North Carolina Museum of Art, 1976. Foreword by Moussa M. Domit. Introduction by William S. Wilson. I. *Mail art from the New York Correspondance School.*

CORTISSOZ, ROYAL. 1. *American Artists.* New York: Charles Scribner's Sons, 1923. *Essays on noted artists of the late nineteenth and early twentieth century.*

_____, 2. *Guy Pene Du Bois.* New York: The Whitney Museum of American Art (American Artists Series), 1931. I.B. *Monograph.*

CRAVEN, THOMAS. 1. *Modern Art, The Men, The Movements, The Meaning.* New York: Simon and Schuster, 1934. I. *Essays on twentieth-century American figurative artists.*

_____, 2. *The Story of Painting: From Cave Pictures to Modern Art.* New York: Simon and Schuster, 1943. I. *Popular history of art.*

_____, 3. *Thomas Hart Benton.* New York: Associated American Artists, 1939. I. *Monograph.*

CRAVEN, WAYNE. *Sculpture in America.* New York: Thomas Y. Crowell Co., 1968. I.B. *Historical survey of traditional sculpture.*

CRESPELLE, J.-P. *Montparnasse vivant.* Paris, Hachette, 1962. I. *The panorama of Montparnasse life.*

CRICHTON, MICHAEL. *Jasper Johns.* New York: Harry N. Abrams Inc.,

Publishers, in association with The Whitney Museum of American Art, 1977. Foreword by Joseph F. Cullman, 3rd, and Tom Armstrong. I.B. *Exhibition catalogue.*

CRONE, RAINER. *Andy Warhol.* New York: Praeger Publishers, 1970. I.B. *Critical essays and catalogue of works; filmography.*

CROYDON, MICHAEL. *Ivan Albright.* New York: Abbeville Press, n.d. Foreword by Jean Dubuffet. B.C. *Monograph including artist's poetry and statements.*

CUMMINGS, PAUL. 1. *Artists in Their Own Words.* New York: St. Martin's Press, Inc., 1979. I. *Interviews.*

_____, 2. *David Smith: The Drawings.* New York: Whitney Museum of American Art, 1979. Foreword by Tom Armstrong. *Retrospective catalogue.*

_____, 3. *Walter Murch.* Geneva: Galerie Jan Krugier, 1976. I.C. *Exhibition catalogue.*

CUMMINGS, PAUL, MERKERT, JÖRN, and STULLIG, CLAIRE. *Willem de Kooning: Drawings, Paintings, Sculpture.* New York: Whitney Museum of American Art, 1983. (German and English texts.) Foreword by Tom Armstrong. B.C.I. *Major retrospective catalogue.*

CURRY, JOHN STEUART. 1. *John Steuart Curry.* New York: American Artists Group Inc., 1945. I. *Autobiographical monograph.*

_____, 2. *John Steuart Curry.* Syracuse, N.Y.: Joe and Emily Lowe Art Center, Syracuse University, 1956. I. *Exhibition catalogue.*

_____, 3. *John Steuart Curry.* Lawrence: University of Kansas, 1957. I. *Exhibition catalogue.*

Dan Flavin. Cologne: Kunsthalle Koln, 1973. I.B. (German and English text.) *Artist's statement.*

DANTO, ARTHUR C. *The State of the Art.* New York: Prentice-Hall Press, 1987. I. *Collected essays from the popular column in* The Nation.

DAUBLER, THEODOR, and GOLL, IWAN. *Archipenko-Album*. Potsdam: Gustav Kiepenheuen Verlag, 1921. I. (German text.) *Monograph.*

David Simpson 1957–1967. San Francisco: San Francisco Museum of Art, 1967. Preface by John Humphrey. I.B. *Retrospective catalogue; includes statements by the artist.*

David Smith: The Prints. New York: Pace Editions, 1987. B.C. *Catalogue raisonné by Alexandra Schwartz with essay by Paul Cummings.*

DAVIDSON, MORRIS. 1. *An Approach to Modern Painting*. New York: Coward-McCann, Inc., 1948. I. *Appreciation of modern art.*

___, 2. *Understanding Modern Art*. New York: Coward-McCann, Inc., 1931. I. *Appreciation and understanding of modern concepts in art.*

DAVIES, HUGH MARLAIS. *Artist & Fabricator*. Amherst: University of Massachusetts, 1975. I. *Modern technology and commissioned sculpture; includes artists' statements.*

DAVIS, DOUGLAS. *Art and the Future*. New York: Praeger Publishers, 1973. I.B.D.G. *An effusion of the collaboration of art and science.*

DAVIS, STUART. *Stuart Davis*. New York: American Artists Group Inc., 1945. I. *Autobiographical monograph.*

DAWSON, FIELDING. *An Emotional Memoir of Franz Kline*. New York: Pantheon Books, 1967. I. *A personal memoir.*

DAY, HOLLIDAY T. *Shape of Space: The Sculpture of George Sugarman*. Omaha, NE: Joslyn Art Museum, 1981. Texts by Irving Sandler and Brad Davis. B.C. *Retrospective catalogue.*

DE CREEFT, JOSE. *Jose de Creeft*. Athens: University of Georgia Press (American Sculptors Series), 1950. I. *Autobiographical monograph.*

DEHN, ADOLF. *Watercolor Painting*. New York: Studio Publications, 1945. I.

DE KOONING, WILLEM. *De Kooning: Drawings*. New York: Walker & Co., 1967. I. *Two dozen charcoal drawings with a statement by the artist.*

DEVREE, CHARLOTTE. *Jose de Creeft*. New York: American Federation of Arts and The Ford Foundation, 1960. I. *Retrospective catalogue.*

DE VRIES, GERD, ed. *Uber Kunst/On Art*. Cologne: Verlag M. DuMont Schauberg, 1974. I.B. (German and English text.) *Artists writings on art after 1965; exhibition lists.*

DE WILDE, EDY. 1. *La Grande Parade: Highlights in Painting after 1940*. Amsterdam: Stedelijk Museum, 1984. (Dutch and English texts.) *A panorama of painting from 1940 to the present.*

___, 2. *'60–'80: Attitudes/Concepts/Images*. Amsterdam: Stedelijk Museum, 1982. (Dutch and English texts.) B.C.I. *Multiple brief essays and artist statements.*

D'HARNONCOURT, ANNE, and McSHINE, KYNASTON, eds. *Marcel Duchamp*. New York: The Museum of Modern Art and the Philadelphia Museum of Art, 1973. Preface by Richard E. Oldenburg and Evan H. Turner. Introduction by Anne d'Harnoncourt. I.C.B. *Retrospective exhibition catalogue.*

DIAMONSTEIN, BARBARALEE. *Inside New York's Art World*. New York: Rizzoli International Publications, Inc., 1979. I. *Transcribed from video interviews at the New School. Popular; occasional insights.*

DIENST, ROLF GUNTER. 1. *Pop-Art*. Wiesbaden: Limes Verlag, 1965. I.B. (German text.) *Pop art in Europe and the USA.*

___, 2. *Richard Lindner*. New York: Harry N. Abrams Inc., 1970. I. *Critical study of the oeuvre.*

DIJKSTRA, BRAM, ed. *A Recognizable Image: William Carlos Williams on Art and Artists*. New York: New Directions, 1978. I. *Collected essays by the poet on visual art.*

DOCHTERMAN, LILLIAN. *The Quest of Charles Sheeler*. Iowa City: State University of Iowa, 1963. I. *Biography.*

DORIVAL, BERNARD. *Twentieth Cen-*

tury Painters. New York: Universe Books, Inc.; Paris: Editions Pierre Tisne, 1958. I.B. *Painting in Europe and America.*

DORNER, ALEXANDER. *The Way Beyond Art*. New York: New York University Press, 1958. I. *Development of art and its influence in the museums.*

DOTY, ROBERT. *Will Barnett*. New York: Harry N. Abrams, Inc., 1984. B.C. *Monograph.*

DOTY, ROBERT, ed. *Jane Freilicher: Paintings*. New York: Taplinger Publishing Co., Inc., 1986. B. *Retrospective catalogue including multiple short essays.*

DOVER, CEDRIC. *American Negro Art.* Greenwich, Conn.: New York Graphic Society, 1965. I.B. *Illustrated history.*

DOWNES, RACKSTRAW, ed. *Fairfield Porter: Art in Its Own Terms*. New York: Taplinger Publishing Co., 1979. I. *Collected critical writings by the artist-writer.*

The Drawings of Charles E. Burchfield. Cleveland: Print Club of Cleveland and The Cleveland Museum of Art, 1953. I. *Exhibition catalogue. (See also Jones, ed.).*

Drawings: The Pluralist Decade. Philadelphia: Institute of Contemporary Art, University of Pennsylvania, 1980. Introduction by Janet Kardon. I.C. *39th Venice Biennale, US Pavilion, exhibition catalogue: exploratory essays by several critics.*

DREIER, KATHERINE S. 1. *Burliuk*. New York: The Societe Anonyme, Inc., 1944. I. *Monograph.*

____, 2. *Western Art and the New Era, an Introduction to Modern Art*. New York: Brentano's, 1923. I. *Early polemic on abstract and nonfigurative art.*

DU BOIS, GUY PENE. 1. *Artists Say the Silliest Things*. New York: American Artists Group Inc., 1940. I. *Autobiography.*

____, 2. *Edward Hopper*. New York: The Whitney Museum of American Art (American Artists Series), 1931. I.B. *Monograph.*

____, 3. *Ernest Lawson*. New York: The Whitney Museum of American Art (American Artists Series), 1932. I.B. *Monograph.*

____, 4. *John Sloan*. New York: The Whitney Museum of American Art (American Artists Series), 1931. I.B. *Monograph.*

____, 5. *Wiliam Glackens*. New York: The Whitney Museum of American Art (American Artists Series), 1931. I.B. *Monograph.*

____, 6. *William Glackens*. New York: The Whitney Museum of American Art, 1939. *Exhibition catalogue.*

DUCHAMP, MARCEL. 1. *Marcel Duchamp*. Pasadena: The Pasadena Art Museum, 1963. I.B. *Exhibition catalogue.*

____, 2. *Marchand du Sel*. Paris: Le Terrain Vague, 1958. I.B. *Essays.*

Edward Kienholz. Dusseldorf: Stadtische Kunsthalle Dusseldorf, 1970. Introduction by Jurgen Harten. I.B.C. *Retrospective catalogue.*

Edward Kienholz: 11 + 11 Tableaux. Stockholm: Modern Museet, 1971. Introduction by K.G.P. Hulten. I.B. *Exhibition catalogue.*

8 American Masters of Watercolor. Los Angeles: County Museum of Art, 1968. Preface by Larry Curry. I.B. *Documented survey.*

ELDERFIELD, JOHN. *Morris Louis.* New York: The Museum of Modern Art, 1986. Includes notes on methods, materials, and conservation problems. B.C.I. *Retrospective catalogue.*

ELIOT, ALEXANDER. *Three Hundred Years of American Painting*. New York: Time Inc., 1957. I.B. *Popular history of American art.*

ELLIOTT, JAMES. "Stuart Davis." *Bulletin of the Los Angeles County Museum of Art*, Vol. XIV, No. 3, 1962. I. *Entire issue devoted to this essay.*

ELSEN, ALBERT. 1. *Paul Jenkins*. New York: Harry N. Abrams Inc., 1973. I.B.C. *A major monograph.*

____, 2. *Purposes of Art*. New York: Holt

Rinehart and Winston, Inc., 1962. I.B. *Elucidation of the art process.*

_____, 3. *Seymour Lipton.* New York: Harry N. Abrams Inc., 1969. I. *Monograph.*

ELY, CATHARINE BEACH. *The Modern Tendency in American Painting.* New York: Frederic Fairchild Sherman, 1925. I.

ETTING, EMLEN. *Drawing the Ballet.* New York: Studio Publications, 1944. I.

Eva Hesse: A Memorial Exhibition. New York: The Solomon R. Guggenheim Museum, 1972. I.B.C. *Retrospective exhibition catalogue; includes essays by Robert Pincus-Witten, Eva Hesse, Linda Shearer.*

EVANS, MYFANWY, ed. *The Painter's Object.* London: Gerald Howe Ltd., 1937. I. *Critical essays.*

FARNHAM, EMILY. *Charles Demuth: Behind a Laughing Mask.* Norman, Okla.: University of Oklahoma Press, 1971. I.B.C. *A poor book that fails profoundly.*

FARRELL, JAMES T. *The Paintings of Will Barnet.* New York: Press Eight, 1950. I. *Monograph.*

FAITH, CREEKMORE, ed. *The Lithographs of Thomas Hart Benton.* Austin and London: University of Texas Press, 1969. I. *Catalogue of the prints; includes comments by the artist.*

Fay Lansner. Swarthmore: Ava Books, 1976. Conversation with Irving H. Sandler. Introduction by Barbara Guest. I.B.C. *Illustrated essay.*

FEININGER, T. LUX. *Lyonel Feininger: At the Edge of the World.* New York: Frederick A. Praeger, 1968. I. *Essay on the development of imagery and ideas.*

FERN, ALAN. *Leonard Baskin.* Annotated by Leonard Baskin. Washington, D.C.: Smithsonian Institution Press, 1971. I.B.C. *Exhibition catalogue, filmography.*

FIERENS, PAUL. *Sculpteurs d'aujourd' hui.* Paris: Editions de Chroniques de Jour, 1933. I. (French text.)

Figures/Environments. Minneapolis: The Walker Art Center, 1970. Introduction by Martin Friedman. I.C. *Exhibition catalogue.*

FINCH, CHRISTOPHER. *Pop Art: Object and Image.* New York: Studio Vista/Dutton Pictureback, 1968. I. *Well-illustrated popular assessment of international pop art.*

FINKELSTEIN, SIDNEY. *Realism in Art.* New York: International Publishers, 1954.

FLANAGAN, GEORGE A. *Understanding and Enjoying Modern Art.* New York: Thomas Y. Crowell Co., 1962. I.B.

FLEXNER, JAMES THOMAS. *A Short History of American Painting.* Boston: Houghton Mifflin Co., 1950. I.B. *Authoritative history of American painting.*

FLOCKHART, LOLITA L.W. *Art and Artists in New Jersey.* Somerville, N.J.: C.P. Hoagland Co., 1938. I.

FORD, CHARLES HENRI. *Poems for Painters.* New York: View Editions, 1945. I. *Poems illustrated by surrealist artists.*

Forerunners of American Abstraction. Pittsburgh: Museum of Art, Carnegie Institute, 1971. Foreword by Leon Anthony Arkus. Introduction by Herdis Bull Teilman. I.B. *Survey exhibition with biographical sketches.*

FOSTER, JOSEPH K. *Raphael Soyer, Drawings and Watercolors.* New York: Crown Publishers Inc., 1968. I. *A selection of 52 watercolors and 72 drawings.*

FRANK, WALDO, ed. *America and Alfred Stieglitz.* Garden City, N.Y.: Doubleday, Doran and Co., Inc., 1934. I. *A history of Alfred Stieglitz and his influence.*

FRASCONI, ANTONIO. *Against the Grain: The Woodcuts of Antonio Frasconi.* New York: Macmillan Publishing Co. Inc., 1974. Introduction by Nat Hentoff. Appreciation by Charles Parkhurst. I.D. *Thirty-five years of his woodcuts reviewed; includes section on his methods.*

Frederick Kiesler Architekt: 1890–1965.

Vienna: Galerie Nachst St. Stephen, 1975. Introduction by Friedrich St. Florian. I.D.P. *Retrospective catalogue; includes artist's statements.*

FREUNDLICH, AUGUST L. *William Gropper: Retrospective.* Los Angeles: Ward Ritchie Press, 1968. I.B. *Retrospective catalogue including statements by the artist.*

FRIED, MICHAEL. 1. *Morris Louis.* Boston: Museum of Fine Arts, 1967. I.B. *Major retrospective catalogue including essay by Clement Greenberg.*

____, 2. *Morris Louis.* New York: Harry N. Abrams Inc., 1970. I. *Monograph.*

FRIEDMAN, B.H. 1. *Alfonso Ossorio.* New York: Harry N. Abrams Inc., 1971. I.B.C. *Picturebook monograph.*

____, 2. *Jackson Pollock: Energy Made Visible.* New York: McGraw-Hill Book Co., 1972. I.B. *A biographical study of the painter.*

FRIEDMAN, B.H., ed. *School of New York: Some Younger Artists.* New York: Grove Press, Inc., 1959. I. *Younger artists of promise in the 1950s.*

FRIEDMAN, MARTIN. 1. *Adolph Gottlieb.* Minneapolis: The Walker Art Center, 1963. I.B. *Exhibition catalogue.*

____, 2. *14 Sculptors: The Industrial Edge.* Minneapolis: The Walker Art Center, 1969. I.B. *Exhibition catalogue with essays by Barbara Rose, Christopher Finch, and Martin Friedman.*

____, 3. *Nevelson Wood Sculpture.* New York: E.P. Dutton, n.d. I.B.C. *Exhibition catalogue.*

FRIEDMAN, MARTIN, and VAN DER MARCK, JAN. *Eight Sculptors: The Ambiguous Image.* Minneapolis: The Walker Art Center, 1966. I.B.C. *Exhibition catalogue.*

Fritz Glarner. Bern: Kunsthalle Bern, 1972. Foreword by Max Bill. I.B. *Retrospective catalogue.*

From Foreign Shores. Milwaukee: Milwaukee Art Center, 1976. Introduction by I. Michael Danoff. I. *Bicentennial survey of emigrant artists from colonial times to the present.*

FROST, ROSAMOND. *Contemporary Art: The March of Art from Cezanne Until Now.* New York: Crown Publishers Inc., 1942. I.B.

FRY, EDWARD. *David Smith.* New York: The Solomon R. Guggenheim Museum, 1969. I.B. *Retrospective catalogue.*

FRY, EDWARD, and KUSPIT, DONALD. *Robert Morris: Works of the Eighties.* Newport Beach, CA: Newport Harbor Art Museum, 1986. B.C.I. *Exhibition catalogue includes multiple brief essays.*

Fundamentele Schilderkunst/Fundamental Painting. Amsterdam: Stedelijk Museum, 1975. Essay by Rini Dippel. Preface by E. de Wilde. I.B.C. *International minimalist painting.*

GABLIK, SUZI. *Progress in Art.* New York: Rizzoli International Publications Inc., 1977. I.B. *A proposed aesthetic for an abstract nonfigurative art.*

GABO, NAUM. *Of Divers Arts.* London: Faber and Faber, Ltd., 1962. I. *Critical essays.*

GALLATIN, A.E. 1. *American Watercolourists.* New York: E. P. Dutton, 1922. I.

____, 2. *Certain Contemporaries: A Set of Notes in Art Criticism.* New York: John Lane Co., 1916.

____, 3. *Gallatin Inconography.* n.p.: Privately published, 1934. I. *Genealogy through portraits.*

____, 4. *Gaston Lachaise.* New York: E.P. Dutton, 1924. I. *Critical essay.*

____, 5. *John Sloan.* New York: E.P. Dutton, 1925. I. *Critical essay.*

____, 6. *Paintings by Gallatin.* New York: Wittenborn, Schultz, Inc., 1948. I.B.

____, 7. *Paul Manship.* New York: John Lane Co., 1917. I.B. *Critical essay.*

____, 8. *Whistler, Notes and Footnotes.* New York: The Collector and Art Critic Co., 1907. I. *Critical essays.*

GARVER, THOMAS H. 1. *George Tooker.* San Francisco: California Palace of the Legion of Honor, 1974. I.B.C. *Retrospective catalogue*

____, 2. *George Tooker.* New York: Clarkson Potter, Inc., Publishers, 1985. B.C. *Monograph with checklist of artist's paintings and prints.*

GARWOOD, DARRELL. *Artist in Iowa.* New York: W. W. Norton and Co., 1944. *Biography.*

GASCOYNE, DAVID. *A Short Survey of Surrealism.* London: Cobden-Sanderson, 1935. I. *Essays and documentation.*

GAUGH, HARRY F. *de Kooning.* New York: Abbeville Press, 1983. B.C. *Eccentric monograph but includes artist's statements.*

GAUNT, WILLIAM. *The Observer's Book of Modern Art from Impressionism to the Present Day.* London: Frederick Warne and Co. Ltd., 1964. I.G.

GENAUER, EMILY. *Best of Art.* Garden City, N.Y.: Doubleday and Co. Inc., 1948. I. *Painting during the 1940s.*

Gene Davis. San Francisco: San Francisco Museum of Art, 1968. Preface by Gerald Nordland. I.B. *One-man exhibition.*

Gene Davis: Drawings. New York: The Arts Publisher Inc., 1982. Introduction by Gene Boro. I. *Monograph on 30 years of drawings.*

George Grosz: Dessins et Aquarelles. Paris: Galerie Claude Bernard, 1966. Preface by Edouard Roditi. I. *Exhibition catalogue.*

George Rickey. Los Angeles: University of California, Los Angeles, 1971. An interview by Frederick S. Wight. I.B.D.C. *Exhibition catalogue.*

GEORGE, WALDEMAR. 1. *Les Artistes juifs et l'ecole de Paris.* Algiers: Editions du Congres Juif Mondial, 1959. I. (French text.)

_____, 2. *John D. Graham.* Paris: Editions Le Triangle, n.d. I. *Critical essay.*

GERDTS, WILLIAM H., Jr. *Painting and Sculpture in New Jersey.* Princeton, N.J.: D. Van Nostrand, 1964. Foreword by Richard J. Hughes. I.B.D. *The first art history of New Jersey.*

GERSTNER, KARL Kalte Kunst. Switzerland: Verlag Arthur Niggli, 1957. I. (German text). *Hard-edge paintings and sculpture.*

GERTZ, ULRICH. *Contemporary Plastic Art.* Berlin: Rembrandt/Verlag, GMBH, 1955. I. (German and English text.) *Postwar painting in Europe, including American influence.*

GESKE, NORMAN A. *The Figurative Tradition in Recent American Art.* Washington, D.C.: National Collection of Fine Arts, 1968. *Catalogue for the 34th International Biennial, Venice.*

GETLEIN, FRANK. 1. *Chaim Gross.* New York: Harry N. Abrams Inc., 1974. I.B.C. *Illustrated monograph.*

_____, 2. *Jack Levine.* New York: Harry N. Abrams Inc., n.d. I. *Monograph.*

_____, 3. *Peter Blume.* New York: Kennedy Galleries, 1968. I. *Exhibition catalogue.*

GETLEIN, FRANK and DOROTHY. *Christianity in Art.* Milwaukee: The Bruce Publishing Co., 1959. I.B.

GETTINGS, FRANK. *Drawings 1974-1984.* Washington, DC: Smithsonian Institution Press, 1984. Foreword by Abram Lerner. B.I.P. *International Survey Exhibition.*

GIEDION-WELCKER, CAROLA. 1. *Contemporary Sculpture: An Evolution in Volume and Space.* Documents of Modern Art, Vol. 12. New York: George Wittenborn, Inc., 1955. I.B.

_____, 2. *Modern Plastic Art: Elements of Reality, Volume and Disintegration.* Zurich: Dr. H. Girsberger, 1937. I.B. *Twentieth-century sculpture.*

GLACKENS, IRA. *William Glackens and the Ashcan Group: The Emergence of Realism in American Art.* New York: Crown Publishers Inc., 1957. I.

GLENN, CONSTANCE W. *Jim Dine: Drawings.* New York: Harry N. Abrams Inc., 1985. B.I. *Monograph includes interviews and artist's statements.*

GLIMCHER, ARNOLD B. *Louise Nevelson.* New York: Praeger Publishers, 1972. I.C. *Monograph.*

GOLDMAN, JUDITH. 1. *American Prints: Process and Proofs.* New York: Whitney Museum of American Art, 1981. Foreword by Tom Armstrong. Includes glossary of printing terminology. B.I. *Historical survey empha-*

sizing 14 contemporary artists.

——, 2. *James Rosenquist.* New York: Viking Press, 1985. B.C.I. *Major biographical and art study.*

GOLDWATER, MARGE, SMITH, ROBERTA, and TOMKINS, CALVIN. *Jennifer Bartlett.* New York: Abbeville Press, 1985. B.C. *Retrospective catalogue.*

GOLDWATER, ROBERT, and TREVES, MARCO, eds. *Artists on Art. From the XIV to the XX Century.* New York: Pantheon Books, 1945. I.

GOMRINGER, EUGEN. *Josef Albers.* New York: George Wittenborn, Inc., 1968. I.B. *Essays on all the aspects of Albers's work, with comments by the artist.*

GOODRICH, LLOYD. 1. *American Watercolors and Winslow Homer.* New York: The Walker Art Center, for American Artists Group Inc., 1945. I.

——, 2. *The Drawings of Edwin Dickinson.* New Haven, Conn.: Yale University Press, 1963. I.

——, 3. *Edward Hopper.* New York: Penguin Books, 1949. I. *Monograph.*

——, 4. *Edward Hopper.* New York: The Whitney Museum of American Art, 1956. I.B. *Exhibition catalogue.*

——, 5. *Edwin Dickinson.* New York: The Whitney Museum of American Art, 1965. I.B. *Retrospective catalogue.*

——, 6. *H. E. Schnakenberg.* New York: The Whitney Museum of American Art (American Artists Series), 1931. I.B. *Monograph.*

——, 7. *John Sloan.* New York: The Whitney Museum of American Art, 1952. I.B. *Exhibition catalogue.*

——, 8. *Kuniyoshi.* New York: The Whitney Museum of American Art, 1948. I. *Exhibition catalogue.*

——, 9. *Max Weber.* New York: The Whitney Museum of American Art, 1949. I. *Exhibition catalogue.*

——, 10. *Raphael Soyer.* New York: The Whitney Museum of American Art, 1967. I.B. *Retrospective catalogue.*

——, 11. *Reginald Marsh.* New York: The Whitney Museum of American Art, 1955. I. *Exhibition catalogue.*

GOODRICH, LLOYD, and BAUR, JOHN I.H. 1. *American Art of Our Century.* New York: The Whitney Museum of American Art, 1961. I. *Development of American Art illustrated through the collection of the WMAA.*

——, 2. *Four American Expressionists.* New York: The Whitney Museum of American Art, 1949. I. *Exhibition catalogue: Doris Caesar, Chaim Gross, Karl Knaths, Abraham Rattner.*

GOODRICH, LLOYD, and IMGIZUMI, ATSUO. *Kuniyoshi.* Tokyo: National Museum of Modern Art, 1954. I. (Japanese and English text.) *Retrospective catalogue.*

GOODRICH, LLOYD, and MANDEL, PATRICIA FITZG. *John Heliker.* New York: The Whitney Museum of American Art, 1968. I.B. *Retrospective catalogue.*

GOODYEAR, FRANK H., Jr. 1. *8 Contemporary Realists.* Philadelphia: Pennsylvania Academy of the Fine Arts, 1977. Preface by Richard J. Boyle. Acknowledgments by Frank H. Goodyear, Jr. I. *An exploration of realism, its definitions and uses.*

——, 2. *Welliver.* New York: Rizzoli, 1985. Introduction by John Ashbery. *An appreciation.*

GOOSSEN, E.C. 1. *The Art of the Real USA 1948–1968.* New York: The Museum of Modern Art, 1968. I.B. *A proposal that some art is more "real" than other art.*

——, 2. *Ellsworth Kelly.* New York: The Museum of Modern Art, 1973. I.B.A. *Retrospective monograph.*

——, 3. *Helen Frankenthaler.* New York: The Whitney Museum of American Art, 1969. I.B. *Retrospective catalogue.*

——, 4. *Stuart Davis.* New York: George Braziller, Inc., 1959. I.B. *Monograph.*

——, 5. *Three American Sculptors.* New York: Grove Press Inc., 1959. I. *Monograph: Herbert Ferber, David Hare, Ibram Lassaw.*

GORDON, JOHN. 1. *Franz Kline.* New York: The Whitney Museum of American Art, 1968. I.B.C. *Retrospective catalogue.*

___, 2. *Isamu Noguchi*. New York: The Whitney Museum of American Art, 1968. I.B.C. *Retrospective catalogue.*

___, 3. *Karl Schrag*. New York: American Federation of Arts and The Ford Foundation, 1960. I. *Retrospective catalogue.*

___, 4. *Louise Nevelson*. New York: The Whitney Museum of American Art, 1967. I.B. *Retrospective catalogue.*

Gordon Onslow-Ford: Retrospective Exhibition. Oakland, CA: Oakland Museum, 1980. Introduction by Harvey L. Jones. Foreword by Herschel B. Chipp. C. *Includes artist's statements.*

Graham, Gorky, Smith & Davis in the Thirties. Providence: Brown University, 1977. Foreword by William H. Jordy. Introduction by Ellen Lawrence. I.B.C. *Examines interplay and evolution of these artists' work in one decade.*

GRAHAM, JOHN D. *System and Dialectics of Art.* New York: Delphic Studios, 1937. *Critical essays.*

The Great Decade of American Abstraction: Modernist Art 1960 to 1970. Houston: The Museum of Fine Arts, 1974. Foreword by R. A. Carmean, Jr. Introduction by Philippe de Montebello. I.B. *Exhibition catalogue; reprints, critical essays, and essays on the conservation of color-field paintings.*

GREEN, SAMUEL ADAMS. *Andy Warhol.* Philadelphia: Institute of Contemporary Art, 1965. I. *Exhibition catalogue.*

GREENBERG, CLEMENT. 1. *Art and Culture.* Boston: Beacon Press, 1961. *Critical essays.*

___, 2. *Hofmann.* Paris: The Pocket Museum, Editions George Fall, 1961. I. *Monograph.*

GREENGOOD, LILLIAN. *Great Artists of America.* New York: Thomas Y. Crowell Co., 1963. I.B. *Popular biographical essays.*

GROSS, CHAIM. *Fantasy Drawings.* New York: Beechhurst Press (A Bittner Art Book), 1956. I. *Drawings.*

GROSSER, MAURICE. 1. *The Painter's Eye.* New York: Rinehart and Co., Inc., 1951. I. *Essays on divers topics.*

___, 2. *Painting in Public.* New York: Alfred A. Knopf, 1948. *Autobiographical.*

GROSZ, GEORGE. 1. *George Grosz.* Berlin: Akadmie der Kunste, 1962. I. *Retrospective catalogue.*

___, 2. *George Grosz Drawings.* New York: H. Bittner and Co., 1944. I. *Drawings.*

___, 3. *Die Gezeichneten.* Berlin: Malik Verlag, 1930. I. (German text.) *Drawings.*

___, 4. *A Little Yes and a Big No. The Autobiography of George Grosz.* New York: The Dial Press, 1946. I.

___, 5. *Der Spiesser-Spiegel.* Dresden: Carl Reisser Verlag, 1925. I. (German text.) *Drawings.*

GUEST, BARBARA, and FRIEDMAN, B.H. *Goodnough.* Paris: The Pocket Museum, Editions George Fall, 1962. I. *Monograph.*

GUGGENHEIM, PEGGY, ed. *Art of This Century.* New York: Art of This Century, 1942. I. *Documents her New York gallery.*

GUTMAN, WALTER, K. *Raphael Soyer, Paintings and Drawings.* New York: Shorewood Publishing Co., Inc., 1960. I. *Monograph.*

HAAS, IRVIN. *A Treasury of Great Prints.* New York: Thomas Yoseloff Inc., 1959. I.

HAENLEIN, CARL. *New York Now.* Hannover: Kestner-Gesellschaft Hannover, 1982. (German text.) B.C. *Survey of the newest art of the early 1980s.*

HAFTMAN, WERNER. *Paintings in the Twentieth Century.* New York: Frederick A. Praeger, 1960. 2 vols. I. *A major history of twentieth-century art.*

HAHN, OTTO. *Arman.* Paris: Fernand Hazan Editeur, 1972. I.B. (French text.) *Appreciation with biographical information.*

HALE, ROBERT BEVERLY. *Waldo Peirce.* New York: American Artists Group Inc., 1945. I. *Monograph.*

HALL, W.S. *Eyes on America.* New

York: Studio Publications, 1939. I. *Figurative painting in America.*

HALPERT, EDITH GREGOR. *The Downtown Gallery.* New York: The Downtown Gallery, 1943. I. *Documents members of the gallery.*

HAMILTON, GEORGE H. *Josef Albers.* New Haven, Conn.: Yale University Art Gallery, 1956. I. *Exhibition catalogue.*

HAMILTON, RICHARD. *The Bride Stripped Bare by her Bachelors, Even.* New York: George Wittenborn, Inc., 1960. *Documentary essay on Marcel Duchamp.*

HANSEN, AL. *A Primer of Happenings and Time/Space Art.* New York: Something Else Press Inc., 1965. I. *People places events and Hansen in happenings and time/space.*

Happening & Fluxus. Cologne: Kolnischer Kunstverein. I.B.D.P.C. *The major documentary resource on happening, fluxus, events, non-art, 1959–1970.*

HARRISON, HELEN A. *Larry Rivers.* New York: Harper & Row, Publishers, 1984. B.C. *Monograph.*

HARTLEY, MARSDEN. *Adventures in the Arts.* New York: Boni and Liveright, Inc., 1921. *Autobiography.*

HARTMANN, SADIKICHI. *A History of American Art.* Boston: L.C. Page and Co., 1932, rev. ed., 2 vols. I. *Important history of American art.*

HASKELL, BARBARA. 1. *Arthur Dove.* San Francisco: San Francisco Museum of Art, 1974. I.B.C. *Retrospective catalogue.*

___, 2. *Claes Oldenburg: Object into Monument.* Pasadena: The Pasadena Art Museum, 1971. I.B.C. *Exhibition catalogue with comments on individual pieces by the artist.*

___, 3. *H.C.W.* New York: The Whitney Museum of American Art. Introduction by Tom Armstrong. I.B.C. *Retrospective catalogue of H. C. Westermann.*

___, 4. *Marsden Hartley.* New York: The Whitney Museum of American Art in association with NYU Press, 1980. Forewords by Tom Armstrong

and A. James Speyer. I.B.C. *Retrospective exhibition catalogue.*

___, 5. *Blam! The Explosion of Pop, Minimalism, and Performance 1958–1964.* New York: Whitney Museum of American Art, 1984. Foreword by Tom Armstrong. B.C.I. *A miscellaneous view of vanguard art of the times. Includes an essay on independent cinema by John G. Hanhardt.*

___, 6. *Milton Avery.* New York: Whitney Museum of American Art, 1982. Foreword by Tom Armstrong. B.C.I. *Retrospective catalogue.*

HAYTER, S.W. 1. *About Prints.* London: Oxford University Press, 1962. I.B. *Print appreciation and techniques.*

___, 2. *New Ways of Gravure.* New York: Pantheon Books, 1949. I.D. *Printmaking techniques.*

HEADLEY, DIANE UPRIGHT. *The Drawings of Morris Louis.* Washington, D.C.: National Collection of Fine Arts, 1979. Foreword by Joshua C. Taylor. I. *Exhibition and catalogue raisonné.*

HELM, MacKINELY. *John Marin.* New York: Pellegrini and Cudahy, 1948. I. *Monograph.*

HELM, MacKINLEY, and WIGHT, FREDERICK S. *John Marin.* Boston: Institute of Modern Art, 1947. I. *Exhibition catalogue.*

HENNING, EDWARD. B. *Paths of Abstract Art.* Cleveland: The Cleveland Museum of Art, 1960. I. *Twentieth-century development of abstract art.*

HESS, HANS. *Lyonel Feininger.* London: Thames and Hudson, 1961. I.B. *Catalogue raisonné.*

HESS, THOMAS B. 1. *Abstract Painting: Background and American Phase.* New York: Viking Press, 1951. I. *Important documentation of abstract painting in America.*

___, 2. *Barnett Newman.* New York: Walker & Co., 1969. I.B. *Monograph.*

___, 3. *Barnett Newman.* New York: The Museum of Modern Art, 1971. I.B. *Retrospective monograph.*

___, 4. *Willem de Kooning.* New York: The Museum of Modern Art, 1968.

I.B. *Retrospective monograph; includes statements by the artist.*

___, 5. *Willem de Kooning: Drawings.* Greenwich, Conn.: New York Graphic Society Ltd., 1972. I.B.C. *Essays on his drawings.*

HICKEY, DAVE, and PLAGENS, PETER. *The Works of Edward Ruscha.* New York: Hudson Hills Press, 1982. Introduction by Anne Livet. Foreword by Henry T. Hopkins. B.C.I. *Retrospective catalogue.*

HILDEBRANDT, HANS. *Alexander Archipenko.* Berlin: Ukrainske Slowo Publishers Ltd., 1923. I. (Ukrainian and English text.) *Monograph.*

HILL, ANTHONY, ed. *D.A.T.A.—Directions in Art, Theory and Aesthetics.* London: Faber and Faber, Ltd., 1968. I.B. *Collected statements by neoplastic and kinetic artists, including Charles Biederman.*

HIROMOTO, NOBUYUKI. *Painting Now.* Kyushu, Japan: Kitakyushu Municipal Museum of Art, 1984. Foreword by Kazuaki Mitsuiki. (Japanese and English texts.) B.

HIRSCH, RICHARD. *Charles Sheeler.* Allentown, Pa.: Allentown Art Museum, 1961. I. *Exhibition catalogue.*

HOBBS, ROBERT CARLETON, and LEVIN, GAIL. *Abstract Expressionism: The Formative Years.* Ithaca: Herbert F. Johnson Museum of Art, 1978. Introduction by Thomas W. Leavitt and Tom Armstrong. I. *A singular account of the evolution of this theory.*

HOFMANN, HANS. *Search for the Real.* Andover, Mass.: Addison Gallery of American Art, 1948. I. *Hofmann's theory of painting.*

HOLME, BRYAN. 1. *Master Drawing in Line.* New York: Studio Publications, 1948. I.

___, 2. *Master Drawings.* New York: Studio Publications, 1943. I.

HOLT, NANCY, ed. *The Writings of Robert Smithson: Essays with Illustrations.* New York: New York University Press, 1979. Introduction by Philip Leider. I. *Biographical note. The collected writings and interviews.*

HONIG, EDWIN. *Mauricio Lasansky— The Nazi Drawings.* Iowa City: Mauricio Lasansky Foundation, 1966. I. *Exhibition catalogue.*

HONISCH, DIETER, and JENSEN, JENS CHRISTIAN, eds. *Amerikanische Kunst von 1945 bis heute. Kunst der USA in europaischen Sammlungen.* Koln: DuMont Buchverlag, 1976. I.D. (German text.) *Collected essays in this major study on the exhibition of, collecting of, and critical efforts concerning American art. Works in public collections and lists of influential exhibitions.*

HONNEF, KLAUS. *Concept Art.* Cologne: Phaidon Verlag, 1971. I.B.D.C. (German text.) *Critical essay including artists' statements and documentation.*

HOOPES, DONELSON F. *William Zorach.* New York: Brooklyn Museum, 1968. I. *Retrospective of the paintings, drawings, and watercolors.*

HOPE, HENRY R. *The Sculpture of Jacques Lipchitz.* New York: The Museum of Modern Art, 1954. I.B. *Exhibition catalogue.*

HOPPER, EDWARD. *Edward Hopper.* New York: American Artists Group, Inc., 1945. I. *Autobiographical monograph.*

HOPPS, WALTER. *Frank Lobdell.* Pasadena: The Pasadena Art Museum, 1966. I. *Retrospective catalogue.*

HOVING, THOMAS. *Two Worlds of Andrew Wyeth: A Conversation with Andrew Wyeth.* Boston: Houghton Mifflin Co., 1978. I. *A lengthy interview.*

HOWARD, CHARLES. *Charles Howard.* San Francisco: California Palace of The Legion of Honor, 1946. I.B. *Exhibition catalogue.*

Howard Kanovitz. Duisburg: Wilhelm-Lehmbruck-Museum, 1974. I.B.C. (German and English text.) *Ten-year retrospective including artist's statements.*

HUBER, CARLO. *Cy Twombly. Bilder 1953-1972.* Bern: Kunsthalle Bern, 1973. Foreword by Carlo Huber and Michael Pelzet. I.C. (German text.) *Exhibition catalogue.*

HULTEN, K.G. PONTUS. *The Machine.* New York: The Museum of Modern Art, 1968. I.B. *Art and the mechanical age.*

HUMPHREY, JOHN. *Roy De Forest: Retrospective.* San Francisco: San Francisco Museum of Art, 1974. I.B.C. *Catalogue including artist's statements.*

HUNTER, SAM. 1. *Art since 1945.* New York: Harry N. Abrams Inc., 1958. I.B. *Comprehensive study of world art since 1945.*

____, 2. *Hans Hofmann.* New York: Harry N. Abrams Inc., 1962. I.B. *Monograph.*

____, 3. *James Brooks.* New York: The Whitney Museum of American Art, 1963. I.B. *Retrospective catalogue.*

____, 4. *James Metcalf.* Chicago: William and Noma Copley Foundation, n.d. I. *Monograph.*

____, 5. *Larry Rivers.* New York: Harry N. Abrams Inc., 1970. I. *Monograph.*

____, 6. *Modern American Painting and Sculpture.* New York: Dell Publishing Co., 1959. I. *Concise history of American art since 1900; includes biographies.*

____, 7. *Philip Guston.* New York: Jewish Museum 1966. I.B. *Major retrospective catalogue, including a dialogue with Harold Rosenberg.*

____, 8. *Rosenthal: Sculpture.* New York: M. Knoedler & Co., n.d. I. *Exhibition catalogue, including dialogue with the artist.*

HUNTER, SAM, ed. 1. *The Dada/Surrealist Heritage.* Williamstown: Sterling and Francine Clark Art Institute, 1977. I.B. *Williams College student exhibition of fine quality.*

____, 2. *New York Around the World: Painting and Sculpture.* New York: Harry N. Abrams Inc., 1966. I. *16 essays on the most modern art since 1945, updated to 1966.*

HUYGHE, RENE. *Histoire de l'art contemporain. La Peinture.* Paris: Librairie Felix Alcan, 1936. I.B. *(French text.)*

Index of 20th Century Artists. New York: The College Art Association,

1933–37, 4 vols. B. *Comprehensive reference on American artists of the 1920s and 1930s.*

IRWIN, ROBERT. *Robert Irwin.* New York: The Whitney Museum of American Art, 1977. I.B.D.P. *Exhibition catalogue.*

Isabel Bishop. Tucson: University of Arizona Museum of Art, 1974. Foreword by Sheldon Reich. Introduction by Martin H. Bush. B. *Retrospective catalogue.*

Isamu Noguchi. Tokyo: Minami Gallery, 1973. I.D.C. *(English and Japanese text.) Exhibition catalogue: includes artist's statements.*

JACKMAN, RILLA EVELYN. *American Arts.* Chicago: Rand McNally and Co., 1928. I.B. *Popular essays on the arts.*

Jackson Pollock. Paris: Centre Georges Pompidou, 1982. *(French text.)* B.C.I. *Numerous short essays in a poorly printed retrospective catalogue.*

JACOBSON, J.Z., ed. *Art of Today: Chicago 1933.* Chicago: L. M. Stein, 1932. I.

JAKOVSKI, ANATOLE. *Arp, Calder, Helion, Miro, Pevsner, Seligmann.* Paris: Chez J. Povolozky, 1933. I. *(French text.)*

JANIS, HARRIET, and BLESH, RUDI. 1. *Collage. Personalities—Concepts—Techniques.* Philadelphia and New York: Chilton Co., 1962. I.G. *Documents development of collage in the world.*

____, 2. *de Kooning.* New York: Grove Press Inc., 1960. I. *Monograph.*

JANIS, SIDNEY. *Abstract and Surrealist Art in America.* New York: Reynal and Hitchcock, 1944. I. *Essays on the two schools of art in the 1940s.*

Jan Matulka. 1890–1972. Washington, D.C.: Smithsonian Institution Press, 1980. Foreword by Joshua C. Taylor. Acknowledgments. Introduction by Patterson Sims and Merry A. Fresta. Essays by Patterson Sims, Merry A. Fresta, Dorothy Dehner, Janet A. Flint. I.B.C. *Retrospective catalogue; includes a checklist of prints.*

JENKINS, PAUL and ESTHER, eds. *Observations of Michael Tapie.* New York: George Wittenborn, Inc., 1956. I.A. *Collection of the critic's commentaries.*

JENKINS, PAUL with JENKINS, SUZANNE DONNELLY. *Anatomy of a Cloud.* New York: Harry N. Abrams, Inc., 1983. B.C. *Autobiography in words and pictures.*

Jeremy Anderson. San Francisco: San Francisco Museum of Art, 1966. Preface by Gerald Nordland. I.B. *Retrospective catalogue.*

JEWELL, EDWARD ALDEN. 1. *Alexander Brook.* New York: The Whitney Museum of American Art (American Artists Series), 1931. I.B. *Monograph.*

____, 2. *. . . America.* New York: Alfred A. Knopf, 1930. I. *Critical essays.*

____, 3. *Have We an American Art?* New York and Toronto: Longmans, Green and Co., 1939. *Critical essays.*

JOACHIMIDES, CHRISTOS M. and ROSENTHAL, NORMAN, eds. *Zeit Geist.* New York: George Braziller, Inc., 1983. B. *Seven essays accompany this review of international angst art.*

Joan Mitchell: My Five Years in the Country. Syracuse: Everson Museum of Art, 1972. Introduction by James Harithas. I.B.C. *Exhibition catalogue.*

John Altoon. San Francisco: San Francisco Museum of Art, 1967. Preface by Gerald Nordland. I.B. *Retrospective catalogue.*

John McLaughlin. La Jolla: La Jolla Museum of Contemporary Art, 1973. Foreword by Jay Belloli. Introduction by John McLaughlin. I.B.C. *Retrospective catalogue.*

John Wilde: Drawings 1940–1984. Madison, WI: Elvehjem Museum of Art, 1984. Appreciation by James Watrous. Foreword by Carlton Overland. *Retrospective catalogue of 435 drawings.*

John Willenbecher. Allentown: Allentown Art Museum, 1978. Foreword by Richard N. Gregg. Introduction by Jean-Louis Bourgeois. I.B. *Retrospective catalogue including artist's statements.*

JOHNSON, ELLEN H. *Modern Art and the Object.* New York: Harper & Row, Publishers (Icon Editions), 1976. I. Index. *Collected essays on modern art.*

JOHNSON, UNA E. 1. *Gabor Peterdi.* New York: Brooklyn Museum, 1959. I. *Exhibition catalogue.*

____, 2. *Isabel Bishop.* New York: Brooklyn Museum, 1964. I.B. *The prints and drawings of Miss Bishop with two essays by the artists.*

____, 3. *Paul Cadmus.* New York: Brooklyn Museum, 1968. I.B. *Catalogue of an exhibition of prints and drawings.*

Jonathan Borofsky: Dreams 1973–1981. London: Institute of Contemporary Art, 1981. B. *Multiple texts and artist's statements on note-taking.*

JONES, DAN BURNE. *The Prints of Rockwell Kent.* Chicago: The University of Chicago Press, 1975. Foreword by Carl Zigrosser. I.B. *Catalogue raisonné.*

JONES, EDITH H., ed. *The Drawings of Charles Burchfield.* New York: Frederick A. Praeger, 1968. I. *A pictorial survey. (See also under "Drawings . . ." for Cleveland volume.)*

JORDAN, JIM M. and GOLDWATER, ROBERT. *The Paintings of Arshile Gorky: A Critical Catalogue.* New York: New York University Press, 1980. *Catalogue of paintings.*

Jose De Rivera: Retrospective Exhibition 1930–1971. La Jolla: La Jolla Museum of Contemporary Art, 1972. Introduction by Thomas B. Tibbs. I.C. *Includes catalogue raisonné of 191 works.*

Joseph Goto. Providence: Rhode Island School of Design, 1971. Foreword by Stephen E. Ostrow. Introduction by William H. Jordy. I.C. *Exhibition catalogue.*

Joseph Hirsch. Athens, Ga.: Georgia Museum of Art, 1970. Foreword by William D. Paul, Jr. Introduction by Frank Getlein. I.C.B. *Exhibition catalogue.*

JOYNER, BROOKS. *The Drawings of Arshile Gorky.* College Park, Md.: University of Maryland, 1969. Preface by George Levitine. Foreword by William H. Gerdts. I.B. *Major essay on the drawings.*

JUIN, HUBERT. *Seize peintres de la jeune ecole de Paris.* Paris: Le Musée de Poche, 1956. I.

KALLEM, H. M. *Maurice Sterne.* New York: The Museum of Modern Art, 1933. I.B. *Exhibition catalogue.*

KAPROW, ALLAN. *Assemblage, Environments and Happenings.* New York: Harry N. Abrams Inc., 1965. I. *Scripts. A major illustrated and documented book.*

KARFIOL, BERNARD. *Bernard Karfiol.* New York: American Artists Group Inc., 1945. I. *Autobiographical monograph.*

KARDON, JANET. 1. *Siah Armajani.* Philadelphia: U. of Pennsylvania, 1985. B.C. *Retrospective catalogue.*

____, 2. *David Salle.* Philadelphia: University of Pennsylvania, 1986. Essay by Lisa Phillips. B.C. *Retrospective catalogue.*

KARSHAN, DONALD. 1. *Archipenko: The Sculpture and Graphic Art.* Tubingen: Ernst Wasmuth Verlag, 1974. I.B.C. *Catalogue raisonné.*

____, 2. *Archipenko: Sculpture, Drawings, and Prints, 1908–1963.* Danville, OH: Centre College, 1985. Foreword by Richard L. Morrill. C.I. *Reviews and catalogues the author's collection.*

KASS, RAY. *Morris Graves: Visions of the Inner Eye.* New York: George Braziller, Inc., 1983. Introduction by Theodore F. Wolff. Foreword by Laughlin Phillips. B.C.I. *Retrospective catalogue with multiple essays.*

KATZ, LESLIE. *William Glackens in Retrospect.* St. Louis: The City Art Museum, 1966. I.B. *Major retrospective catalogue.*

Keith Haring. Bordeaux, France: C.A.P.C., Musée d'art contemporain, 1986. (French text.) C.B. *Includes numerous brief essays.*

KELDER, DIANE, ed. *Stuart Davis.* Documentary Monographs in Modern Art. New York: Praeger Publishers, 1971. I.B.C. *Collected writing of and about the artist. Monograph.*

KENT, NORMAN. *Drawings by American Artists.* New York: Watson-Guptill Publishing Co. Inc., 1947. I.

KENT, ROCKWELL. 1. *It's Me O Lord.* New York: Dodd, Mead and Co., 1955. I. *Autobiography.*

____, 2. *Rockwell Kent.* New York: American Artists Group Inc., 1945. I. *Autobiographical monograph.*

____, 3. *Rockwellkentiana.* New York: Harcourt, Brace and Co., 1945. I. *Autobiographical monograph.*

KENT, ROCKWELL, ed. *World Famous Paintings.* New York: Wise and Co., 1939. I. *Paintings of all ages.*

KEPES, GYORGY. 1. *Language of Vision.* Chicago: Paul Theobold and Co., 1944. I. *An aesthetic of seeing.*

____, 2. *The New Landscape in Art and Science.* Chicago: Paul Theobald and Co., 1956. I. *Convolutions of science and art.*

KEPES, GYORGY, ed. *The Visual Arts Today.* Middletown, Conn.: Wesleyan University Press, 1960. I.B. *Essays on architecture, fine arts, graphics, typography, etc.*

KIRBY, MICHAEL. *Happenings.* New York: E.P. Dutton, 1965. I. *A history with scripts of the happenings.*

KIRSTEIN, LINCOLN. 1. *Elie Nadelman.* New York: The Eakins Press, 1973. I.B. *Catalogue raisonné: monograph including artist's statements and writings.*

____, 2. *Elie Nadelman Drawings.* New York: H. Bittner and Co., 1949. I. *Drawings.*

____, 3. *Pavel Tchelitchew.* New York: Gallery of Modern Art, 1964. I.B. *Retrospective catalogue.*

____, 4. *The Sculpture of Elie Nadelman.* New York: The Museum of Modern Art, 1948. *Retrospective catalogue.*

____, 5. *Paul Cadmus.* New York: Imago Imprint Inc., 1984. B.C. *Essays and catalogue of paintings.*

KIRSTEIN, LINCOLN, ed. *Pavel Tchelitchew Drawings.* New York: H. Bittner and Co., 1947. I. *Drawings.*

KLIGMAN, RUTH. *Love Affair: A Memoir of Jackson Pollock.* New York: William Morrow & Co. Inc., 1974.

KOCH, JOHN. *John Koch in New York.* New York: Museum of the City of New York, 1963. I.B. *Retrospective catalogue.*

KOCH, STEPHEN. *Stargazer: Andy Warhol's World and His Films.* New York: Praeger Publishers, 1973. I. *Filmography.*

KOOTZ, SAMUEL M. 1. *Modern American Painters.* n.p.: Brewer and Warren Inc., 1930. I. *Survey of painting in the 1930s.*

____, 2. *New Frontiers in American Painting.* New York: Hastings House, 1943. I. *Surveys the advance guard in painting.*

KOSTELANETZ, RICHARD, ed. *Moholy-Nagy.* Documentary Monographs in Modern Art. New York: Praeger Publishers, 1970. I.B.D.C. *Edited essays by and about the artist. Monograph.*

KOUVENHOVEN, JOHN A. *Made in America: The Arts in Modern Civilization.* Garden City, N.Y.: Doubleday and Co. Inc., 1948. I.B. *Critical essays on American culture.*

KOZLOFF, MAX. 1. *H.C. Westermann.* Los Angeles: County Museum of Art, 1968. I.B. *Retrospective catalogue.*

____, 2. *Jasper Johns.* New York: Harry N. Abrams Inc., 1967. I.B. *Well-illustrated monograph.*

____, 3. *Renderings.* New York: Simon and Schuster, 1968. I. *Collected critical essays on modern art.*

KRAMER, HILTON. 1. *David Smith.* Los Angeles: County Museum of Art, 1965. I.B. *Includes statements by the artist.*

____, 2. *Milton Avery: Paintings, 1930–1960.* New York: Thomas Yoseloff Inc., 1962. I. *Monograph.*

____, 3. *The Sculpture of Gaston Lachaise.* New York: The Eakins Press, 1967. I.B. *Well-illustrated monograph.*

KRAUSS, ROSALIND E. 1. *Jules Olitski—Recent Painting.* Philadelphia: Institute of Contemporary Art, 1968. I.B. *Exhibition catalogue.*

____, 2. *Passages in Modern Sculpture.* New York City: The Viking Press, 1977. I.B. *Observations on sculptured objects from Rodin to the late twentieth century.*

____, 3. *The Originality of the Avant-Garde and Other Modernist Myths.* Cambridge, MA: MIT Press, 1985. I. *Collected thoughts on art as seen through recent French philosophy.*

KREN, ALFRED. *Drawing Distinctions: American Drawings of the Seventies.* Munich: Prestel-Verlag, 1981. (Separate German and English editions.) B.C.I. *Several miscellaneous essays examine this decade of drawing.*

KRIEGER, REGINE TESSIER. *Kay Sage.* Ithaca: Herbert F. Johnson Museum of Art, 1977. Foreword by Thomas W. Leavitt. I.B.C. *Retrospective catalogue; quotes from the artist's writings.*

KROLL, LEON. 1. *Leon Kroll.* Cleveland: Print Club of Cleveland and The Cleveland Museum of Art, 1945. I. *Exhibition catalogue.*

____, 2. *Leon Kroll.* New York: American Artists Group Inc., 1946. I. *Autobiographical monograph.*

KUH, KATHARINE. 1. *Art Has Many Faces—The Nature of Art Presented Visually.* New York: Harper and Brothers, 1951. I.

____, 2. *The Artist's Voice: Talks with Seventeen Artists.* New York: Harper and Row, 1962. I.

____, 3. *Break-up: The Core of Modern Art.* Greenwich, Conn.: New York Graphic Society, 1965. I.

KUHN, WALT. 1. *The Story of The Armory Show.* n.p.: Privately published, 1938.

____, 2. *Walt Kuhn.* Cincinnati: The Cincinnati Art Museum, 1960. I. *Exhibition catalogue.*

KUNIYOSHI, YASUO. *Yasuo Kuniyoshi.* New York: American Artists Group Inc., 1945. I. *Autobiographical monograph.*

Kunst um 1970: Art Around 1970. Aachen: Neue Galerie der Stadt Aachen, 1972. Foreword by Wolfgang Becker, I.B. (German and En-

glish text). *Mostly American art from the Peter Ludwig collection.*

KUSPIT, DONALD. *Leon Golub: Existential/Activist Painter.* New Brunswick, NJ: Rutgers University Press, 1985. B.C. *Monograph.*

KYROU, ADO. *Le Surrealisme au Cinema.* Paris: Le Terrain Vague, 1963. I.

LADER, MELVIN P. *Arshile Gorky.* New York: Abbeville Press, 1985. B.C.I. *Popular introduction to the artist.*

LANDON, EDWARD. *Picture Framing.* New York: American Artists Group Inc., 1945. I.

LANE, JAMES W. *Masters in Modern Art.* Boston: Chapman and Grimes, 1936. I.

LANE, JOHN R. *Stuart Davis: Art and Art Theory.* Brooklyn: The Brooklyn Museum, 1978. Foreword by Michael Botwinick. I.B.C.A. *A major study of this artist's work.*

LANE, JOHN R., and LARSEN, SUSAN C. *Abstract Painting and Sculpture in America 1922–1944.* Pittsburgh, PA: Carnegie Institute, 1983. B.I. *Numerous brief essays examine the rise of abstraction in this important survey.*

LANGSNER, JULES. *Man Ray.* Los Angeles: County Museum of Art, 1966. I.B. *Major exhibition catalogue including essays by the artist.*

LANGUI, EMILE. *Fifty Years of Modern Art.* New York: Frederick A. Praeger, 1959. I. *Critical historical survey.*

LARSON, PHILIP. *Burgoyne Diller.* Minneapolis: The Walker Art Center, 1971. I.B. *Retrospective exhibition.*

LARSON, PHILIP, and SCHJELDAHL, PETER. *De Kooning: Drawings/Sculptures.* New York: E.P. Dutton, 1974. Acknowledgements by Martin Friedman. I.B.C. *Exhibition catalogue.*

LEACH, FREDERICK D. *Paul Howard Manship: An Intimate View.* St. Paul: Minnesota Museum of Art, 1973.

Prologue by Malcolm E. Lein. I.B. *Major retrospective catalogue; quotes from the artist.*

LEBEL, ROBERT. *Marcel Duchamp.* New York: Grove Press Inc., 1959. I.B. *Monograph.*

LEE, KATHRYN DEAN and BURCHWOOD, KATHARINE TYLER. *Art Then and Now.* New York: Appleton-Century-Crofts Inc., 1949. I. *A popular history.*

LEEPA, ALLEN. *The Challenge of Modern Art.* New York: Thomas Yoseloff Inc., 1957. I. *Problems presented by abstract and nonfigurative art.*

LEVIN, GAIL. 1. *Edward Hopper, the Art and the Artist.* New York: W. W. Norton & Co. in association with The Whitney Museum of American Art, 1980. Foreword by Tom Armstrong. I.B.C. *Exhibition catalogue.*

_____, 2. *Synchromism and American Color Abstraction 1910–1925.* New York: George Braziller, 1978. I.B.C.A. *Chronicles the evolution of Synchromism.*

LEVY, JULIEN. 1. *Arshile Gorky.* New York: Harry N. Abrams Inc., 1966. I.B. *Well-illustrated monograph.*

_____, 2. *Eugene Berman.* New York: American Studio Books, 1947. I. *Monograph.*

LICHT, FRED. *Sculpture, 19th and 20th Centuries.* Greenwich, Conn.: New York Graphic Society, 1967. I. *Well-illustrated introduction to modern sculpture.*

LICHT, JENNIFER. *Eight Contemporary Artists.* New York: The Museum of Modern Art, 1974. I.B.D.C. *Small exhibition catalogue including artists' statements.*

LINDMAN, JOAN. *Fairfield Porter: A Catalogue Raisonné of His Prints.* Westbury, NY: Highland House Publishers Inc., 1981. B.C.

LINDY, CHRISTINE. *Superrealist Painting and Sculpture.* New York: William Morrow and Co., Inc., 1980. B.I. *Exhibition chronology 1966–1978. Examines the post-1960 confrontation between the photograph and realist painting.*

LIPCHITZ, JACQUES, with AR-NASON, H.H. *My Life in Sculpture.* New York: Viking Press (Documents of Twentieth Century Art), 1972. I. *Biography.*

LIPMAN, JEAN, with WOLFE, RUTH, editorial director. *Calder's Universe.* New York: (A Studio Book) The Viking Press in cooperation with The Whitney Museum of American Art, 1976. I.B.C. *Documents with joyfulness the artist's life, work, and friends.*

LIPPARD, LUCY R. 1. *Ad Reinhardt.* New York: Jewish Museum, 1967. Preface by Sam Hunter. I.B.D. *Major retrospective catalogue.*

_____, 2. *Changing: Essays in Art Criticism.* New York: E.P. Dutton, 1971. Foreword by Gregory Battcock. I. *Collected essays, written mostly in the mid 1960s.*

_____, 3. *From the Center: Feminist Essays on Women's Art.* New York: E.P. Dutton, 1976. I. Biography. *Collected essays on this topic.*

_____, 4. *The Graphic Work of Philip Evergood.* Selected drawings and complete prints. New York: Crown Publishers Inc., 1966. Foreword by Abram Lerner. Poem by James Michener. I. *Catalogue raisonné of prints augmented with selected drawings.*

_____, 5. *Minimal Art.* The Hague: Haags Gemeentemuseum, 1968. Preface by E. Develing. I.B. (Dutch and English text.) *Important early minimal exhibition catalogue with artists' statements.*

_____, 6. *Pop Art.* New York: Frederick A. Praeger, 1966. I. *Early international survey of Pop, with contributions by Lawrence Alloway, Nancy Marmer, Nicolas Calas.*

_____, 7. *Ad Reinhardt.* New York: Harry N. Abrams, Inc., 1981. B.C. *Monograph.*

LIPPARD, LUCY R., ed. *Six Years: The Dematerialization of the Art Object from 1966 to 1972: a cross-reference book of information on some esthetic boundaries: consisting of a bibliography into which are inserted a fragmented text, art* works, documents, interviews, and symposia, arranged chronologically and focused on so-called conceptual or information or idea art with mentions of such vaguely designated areas as minimal, anti-form, systems, earth or process art, occurring now in the Americas, Europe, England, Australia, and Asia (with occasional political overtones). New York: Praeger Publishers, 1973. Annotated by Lucy R. Lippard. I.B. *See title for description.*

LISLE, LAURIE. *Portrait of an Artist: A Biography of Georgia O'Keeffe.* New York: Seaview Books, 1980. B. *A well-researched popular essay.*

List of Drawing Material of Richard Tuttle and Appendices. Zurich: Gianfranco and Annemarie Verna and others, 1979. Foreword by Gianfranco Verna. I.C.A. *Catalogues 347 drawings; includes artist's statements.*

LIVINGSTON, JANE, and TUCKER, MARCIA. *Bruce Nauman: Work from 1965–1972.* Los Angeles: Los Angeles County Museum of Art, 1972. I.B.C. *Exhibition catalogue with critical essays.*

LOMBARDO, JOSEF VINCENT. *Chaim Gross.* New York: Dalton House Inc., 1949. I.B. *Monograph.*

LORAN, ERLE. 1. *Cezanne's Composition.* Berkeley: University of California Press, 1947. I.

_____, 2. *Recent Gifts and Loans of Paintings by Hans Hofmann.* Berkeley: University of California Press, 1964. I.

Lorser Feitelson and Helen Lundeberg: A Retrospective Exhibition. San Francisco: San Francisco Museum of Modern Art, 1980. B.C.I. *Catalogue with essays by Diane Degasis Moran.*

Louise Nevelson: Atmospheres and Environments. New York: Clarkson N. Potter, Inc., Publisher, in association with The Whitney Museum of American Art, 1980. Introduction by Edward Albee. Preface and Acknowledgements by Tom Armstrong. Essays by Richard Marshall and Louise Wilson. I.B.C. *Exhibition catalogue.*

LOWRY, BATES. *The Visual Experience:*

An Introduction to Art. Englewood Cliffs, N.J.: Prentice-Hall Inc.; New York: Harry N. Abrams Inc., 1961. I. *Methods for extending the visual experience.*

LUCIE-SMITH, EDWARD. *Art in the Seventies.* Ithaca: A Phaidon Book, Cornell University Press, 1980. I.B. *The 1970s, concentrating on the vanguard and the bizarre of the vanguard.*

LUNDE, KARL. *Isabel Bishop.* New York: Harry N. Abrams Inc., 1975. I.B.C. *Well-illustrated monograph.*

LYNTON, NORBERT. *The Modern World.* New York: McGraw-Hill Book Co., Inc., 1965. I.B.G. *Introduction to modernism in the arts.*

MacAGY, DOUGLAS. 1. *James Boynton.* New York: Barone Gallery, Inc., 1959. I. *Monograph.*

_____, 2. *Plus by Minus: Today's Half-Century.* Buffalo: Albright-Knox Art Gallery, 1968. I.D.P. *Major survey of the development of "cool" art.*

MAN RAY. 1. *Alphabet for Adults.* Beverly Hills, Calif.: Copley Gallery, 1948. I.

_____, 2. *Man Ray.* Pasadena, Calif.: Pasadena Art Institute, 1944. I. *Exhibition catalogue.*

_____, 3. *Ogetti d'Affezione.* Turin: Giulio Einavdi, 1970. I. (Italian text.) *Catalogue of work.*

_____, 4. *Self Portrait.* Boston: Little, Brown and Co., 1963. I. *Autobiography.*

Man Ray. Rome: Galleria Il Collezionista d'Arte Contemporanea, 1973. Introduction by Murizo Fagiolo. I.C. (Italian text.) *Retrospective catalogue.*

Mark Tobey. Basel: Editions Beyeler, 1971. Introduction by John Russell. I.C. *Exhibition catalogue including essays by John Cage, Naum Gabo, and Lyonel Feininger, and artist's statements.*

MARLLING, KARL ANN. *Thom Benton and his Drawings.* Columbia: University of Missouri Press, 1981. B. *Popular monographic study of his drawings.*

MARSH, REGINALD. *Anatomy for Artists.* New York: American Artists Group Inc., 1945. I.

MARSHALL, RICHARD. *New Image Painting.* New York: The Whitney Museum of American Art, 1978. I.B.C. *A Return to anecdotal literary figure painting; includes artists' statements.*

MARTER, JOAN M., TARBELL, ROBERTA K., and WECHSLER, JEFFREY. *Vanguard American Sculpture 1919–1939.* New Brunswick: Rutgers University Art Gallery, 1979. Introduction by Phillip Dennis Cate. I. *A major study of this tendency.*

MARTIN, HENRY. *Arman or Four and Twenty Blackbirds Baked in a Pie or Why Settle for Less When You Can Settle for More.* New York: Harry N. Abrams Inc., 1969. I.B. *A critical study of his art.*

MARTIN, J.L., NICHOLSON, B., and GABO, N., eds. *Circle.* London: Faber and Faber Ltd., 1937. I.B. *Essays on purist art.*

MATHER, FRANK JEWETT, Jr. 1. *The American Spirit in Art.* New Haven, Conn.: Yale University Press, 1927. I. *Historical survey with commentary.*

_____, 2. *Eugene Speicher.* New York: The Whitney Museum of American Art (American Artists Series), 1931. I.B. *Monograph.*

Mauricio Lasansky. Iowa City: University of Iowa Museum of Art, 1976. Acknowledgements by Jan K. Muhlert. Text by Joanna Moser, J. Michael Danoff, and Jan K. Muhlert. I.B.C. *Retrospective of prints and drawings.*

MAYERSON, CHARLOTTE LEON, ed. *Shadow and Light.* New York: Harcourt Brace & World, Inc., 1964. I. *Biography of Maurice Sterne, edited from the artist's own writings.*

McBRIDE, HENRY. *John Marin.* New York: The Museum of Modern Art, 1936. I.B. *Exhibition catalogue.*

McCAUSLAND, ELIZABETH. *Marsden Hartley.* Minneapolis: University of Minnesota Press, 1952. I. *Biography.*

McCHESNEY, MARY FULLER. *A*

Period of Exploration: San Francisco 1945–1950. Oakland: The Oakland Museum, 1973. Introduction by Terry N. St. John. I.A. *An excellent study and survey of five years' activity surrounding the California School of Fine Arts, San Francisco: biographies.*

McCOUBREY, JOHN W. 1. *American Tradition in Painting.* New York: George Braziller, Inc., 1963. I.B. *Postulates an American tradition.*

_____, 2. *Robert Indiana.* Philadelphia: Institute of Contemporary Art, University of Pennsylvania, 1968. I.B. *Retrospective catalogue including artist's statements.*

McCOY, GARNETT, ed. *David Smith.* Documentary Monographs in Modern Art. New York: Praeger Publishers, 1973. I.B.C. *Collected writing of the artist. Monograph.*

McCURDY, CHARLES, ed. *Modern Art . . . A Pictorial Anthology.* New York: The Macmillan Company, 1958. I.B.

McShine, KYNASTON, ed. *Joseph Cornell.* New York: The Museum of Modern Art, 1980. I.B. *Retrospective catalogue; includes essays by Dawn Ades, Carter Ratcliff, P. Adams Sitney, and Lynda Roscoe Hartigan.*

MEDFORD, RICHARD C. *Guy Pene Du Bois.* Hagerstown, Md.: Washington County Museum of Fine Arts, 1940. I. *Exhibition catalogue.*

MEDINA, JOSE RAMON. *Marisol.* Caracas: Ediciones Armitano, 1968. I. (Spanish text.) *Picture book of the sculpture.*

MEHRING, WALTER. *George Grosz. Thrifty Drawings and Watercolors.* New York: Erich S. Herrmann, 1944. I. *Monograph.*

MELLQUIST, JEROME. *The Emergence of an American Art.* New York: Charles Scribner's Sons, 1942.

Mel Ramos: Watercolors. Berkeley: Lancaster-Miller Publishers, 1979. Foreword by Mel Ramos. I.B.C. *Watercolors from the series "A Salute to Art History."*

MENDELOWITZ, DANIEL M. *A History of American Art.* New York: Holt, Rinehart and Winston, Inc., 1961. I.

MERKERT, JÖRN, ed. *David Smith: Sculpture and Drawings.* Munich: Prestel-Verlag, 1986. (Editions in English and German exist.) B.C.D. *Major retrospective catalogue with essays by various writers; selected writings by the artist.*

MESSER, THOMAS M. *Jan Muller.* New York: The Solomon R. Guggenheim Museum, 1962. I. *Retrospective catalogue.*

METRO International Directory of Contemporary Art. Milan: Metro, 1964. I.B. (English and Italian text.)

MEYER, URSULA. *Conceptual Art.* New York: E.P. Dutton, 1972. *Collected exegeses of concept art.*

MICHAELSON, KATHERINE J. and GURALNIK, NEHAMA. *Alexander Archipenko: A Centennial Tribute.* Washington, DC: National Gallery of Art, 1986. B.C. *Retrospective catalogue.*

MILLER, DOROTHY C., ed. 1. *Americans 1942. 18 Artists from 9 States.* New York: The Museum of Modern Art, 1942. I. *Documented exhibition catalogue.*

_____, 2. *14 Americans.* New York: The Museum of Modern Art, 1946. I.B. *Documented exhibition catalogue.*

_____, 3. *The Sculpture of John B. Flanagan.* New York: The Museum of Modern Art, 1942. I. *Retrospective catalogue.*

MILLER, KENNETH HAYES. *Kenneth Hayes Miller.* New York: Arts Students League, 1953. I. *Exhibition catalogue.*

MILLER, LYNN F. and SWENSON, SULLY S. *Lives and Works: Talks with Women Artists.* Metuchen, NJ: The Scarecrow Press, 1981. I. *Brief interviews.*

MILLIER, ARTHUR. 1. *Henry Lee McFee.* Claremont, Calif.: Scripps College, 1950. I. *Exhibition catalogue.*

_____, 2. *Millard Sheets.* Los Angeles: Dalzell Hatfield Gallery, 1935. I. *Monograph.*

Miriam Schapiro: The Shrine, The Computer, and The Dollhouse. La Jolla: Mandeville Art Gallery, 1975. Introduction by Linda Nochlin. I.B.

Documentary exhibition catalogue including interview and essays.

MOAK, PETER. *The Robert Laurent Memorial Exhibition.* Durham: University of New Hampshire, 1972. Foreword by Melvin J. Zabarsky. Essay by Henry Hope. I.B. *Retrospective exhibition catalogue.*

MOCSANYI, PAUL. *Karl Knaths.* Washington, D.C.: The Phillips Gallery, 1957. I.B. *Exhibition catalogue.*

MOFFETT, KENWORTH. *Jules Olitski.* Boston: Museum of Fine Arts, 1973. I.B. *Retrospective catalogue.*

MOHOLY-NAGY, LAZLO. 1. *A New Vision and Abstract of an Artist.* 4th rev. ed. New York: George Wittenborn, Inc., 1947. Preface by Walter Gropius. I.B. *A primer of modern design.*

____, 2. *Painting, Photography, Film.* Cambridge, Mass.: MIT Press, 1969. I. *English-language reprint of this famous book.*

MOHOLY-NAGY, SIBYL. 1. *Experiment in Totality.* New York: Harper and Brothers, 1950. I. *Biography: Lazlo Moholy-Nagy.*

____, 2. *Lazlo Moholy-Nagy.* Chicago: Museum of Contemporary Art, 1969. I.B. *Retrospective catalogue.*

MONTE, JAMES. *Larry Zox.* New York: The Whitney Museum of American Art, 1973. I.B.C. *Exhibition catalogue.*

MONTE, JAMES, and TUCKER, MARCIA. *Anti-illusion: Procedures/Materials.* New York: The Whitney Museum of American Art, 1969. I.B. *Survey of the anti-illusion expression.*

Monumenta. Newport, R.I.: Monumenta Newport Inc., 1974. Introduction by Sam Hunter. I. *Catalogue of an outdoor exhibition, including interviews and statements by the artists.*

MORGAN, ANN LEE. *Arthur Dove: Life and Works, with a Catalogue Raisonné.* Newark: University of Delaware Press, 1984. Foreword by Roxane Berry. B.I. *Exhibition chronology. Greatly flawed attempt at a works catalogue and biographical study.*

MORRIS, G.I.K. *American Abstract Artists.* New York: Ram Press, 1946. I.B. *Documentation of members.*

MORSE, JOHN D., ed. *Ben Shahn.* Documentary Monographs in Modern Art. New York: Praeger Publishers, 1972. I.B.C. *Collected writings of the artist. Monograph.*

MOSER, JOANN. 1. *Atelier 17: A 50th Anniversary Retrospective Exhibition.* Madison, Wis.: Elvehjem Art Center, 1977. Foreword by Eric S. McCready. I.B. *A history of Stanley William Hayter, his teaching and art, and the artists.*

____, 2. *The Graphic Art of Emil Ganso.* Iowa City: University of Iowa Museum of Art, 1980. I.C. *A study of the prints.*

MOTHERWELL, ROBERT. 1. *The Dada Painters and Poets.* New York: Wittenborn, Schultz, Inc., 1951. Documents of Modern Art, Vol. 8. I.B. *A documented history of this group.*

____, 2. *Robert Motherwell.* Northampton, Mass.: Smith College, 1962. I. *Exhibition catalogue.*

MOTHERWELL, ROBERT, ed. *Possibilities, No. 1.* New York: Wittenborn, Schultz, Inc., 1947. I. *An occasional review concerned with all the arts.*

MOTHERWELL, ROBERT, and REINHARDT, AD, eds. *Modern Artists in America.* New York: Wittenborn, Schultz, Inc., 1951. I.B. *The European and American advance guard in the 1940s.*

MULAS, UGO, and ARNASON, H.H. *Calder.* New York: A Studio Book/Viking Press, 1971. I.B. *Picture book with comments by Calder.*

MULLER, GREGOIRE. *The New Avant-garde.* New York: Praeger Publishers, 1972. I.D. *Photographs by Gianfranco Gorgoni documenting artists and works.*

MUNSTERBERG, HUGO. *Twentieth Century Painting.* New York: Philosophical Library, 1951. I. *Critical essays.*

MURDOCK, ROBERT M. 1. *Modular Paintings.* Buffalo: Albright-Knox Art

Gallery, 1970. Foreword by Gordon M. Smith. I.C. *Exhibition catalogue.*

_____, 2. *Nassos Daphnis.* Buffalo: Albright-Knox Art Gallery, 1969. Foreword by Gordon M. Smith. I.B.C. *Retrospective catalogue.*

MURKEN-ALTROGGE, CHRISTA. *Von Expresionismus bis zum Soul and Body Art.* Cologne: DuMont Buchverlag, 1985. B.G. (German text.) *Persistant figuration related to abstraction.*

MURRELL, WILLIAM. 1. *Charles Demuth.* New York: The Whitney Museum of American Art (American Artists Series), 1931. I. *Monograph.*

_____, 2. *Elie Nadelman.* Woodstock, N.Y.: William M. Fischer, 1923. I. *Monograph.*

MURTHA, EDWIN. *Paul Manship.* New York: The MacMillan Company, 1957. I. *Monograph.*

MYERS, BERNARD. 1. *Fifty Great Artists.* New York: Bantam Books, 1953. I.B. *Historical essays.*

_____, 2. *Understanding the Arts.* New York: Henry Holt and Co., 1958. I. *Art appreciation.*

MYERS, JANE, ed. *Stuart Davis.* Fort Worth, Texas: Amon Carter Museum of Western Art, 1986. Foreword by Jan K. Muhlert. B.D.I. *Catalogue raisonné of the prints includes quotes from the artist's writings.*

NAIFEH, STEVEN, with **SMITH, GREGORY WHITE.** *Gene Davis.* New York: The Arts Publisher Inc., 1982. B.I. *Monograph.*

Nancy Graves. La Jolla: La Jolla Museum of Contemporary Art, 1973. Introduction by Jay Belloli. I.B.C. *Exhibition catalogue including artist's statements.*

Nancy Graves: Sculpture/Drawings/Films 1969–1971. Aachen: Neue Galerie im Alten Kurhaus, 1971. Introduction by Phyllis Tuchman. I.C. *Exhibition catalogue.*

NARODNY, IVAN. *American Artists.* New York: Roerich Museum Press,

1930. B. *Figurative painting before 1930.*

NASH, STEVEN A. and **MERKERT, JÖRN,** eds. *Naum Gabo.* Munich: Prestel-Verlag, 1986. B.C. (German text.) *Retrospective and works catalogue.*

Nathan Oliveira: A Survey Exhibition 1957–1983. San Francisco: San Francisco Museum of Modern Art, 1984. B.C. Essays by Thomas H. Garver and George W. Neubert. Foreword by Henry T. Hopkins. *Retrospective catalogue.*

NEFF, TERRY ANN R., ed. *In the Mind's Eye: Dada and Surrealism.* New York: Abbeville Press, 1986. I. Foreword by I. Michael Danoff. *Collected essays by several authors. Catalogue to the 1984 Chicago exhibition: Dada and Surrealism in Chicago Collections.*

NELSON, JUNE KOMPASS. *Harry Bertoia, Sculptor.* Detroit: Wayne State University Press, 1970. I.B.C. *Exhibition catalogue: the essay contains some biographical data.*

NEMSER, CINDY. *Art Talk.* New York: Charles Scribner's Sons, 1975. I.B.C. *Conversations with 12 women artists.*

NESS, JUNE L., ed. *Lyonel Feininger.* New York: Praeger Publishers (Documentary Monographs in Modern Art), 1974. I.B.C. *Collected writings of and about the artist. Monograph.*

NEUHAUS, EUGENE. *The History and Ideals of American Art.* Stanford, Calif.: Stanford University Press, 1931. I.B. *Critical essays.*

NEUMEYER, ALFRED. *The Search for Meaning in Modern Art.* Englewood Cliffs, N.J.: Prentice-Hall Inc. 1964. I. *Essays on the understanding of art.*

New in the Seventies. Austin: The University of Texas, 1977. Foreword by Donald B. Goodall. Introduction by Fred Seabolt. I.C. Some photos of artists. *Survey exhibition: figuration and abstraction.*

NEWMEYER, SARAH. *Enjoying Modern Art.* New York: Reinhold Publishing Co., 1955. I. *Popular essays on art appreciation.*

NEWTON, ERIC. 1. *The Arts of Man.* Greenwich, Conn.: New York Graphic Society, 1960. I. *Critical essays.*

_____, 2. *In My View.* London: Longmans, Green and Co., 1950. *Critical essays.*

NOCHLIN, LINDA. *Philip Pearlstein.* Athens, Ga.: Georgia Museum of Art. Preface by William D. Paul, Jr. I.B.C. *Exhibition catalogue.*

NOGUCHI, ISAMU. 1. *A Sculptor's World.* New York: Harper and Row, 1968. Preface by R. Buckminster Fuller. I. *Autobiography.*

_____, 2. *The Sculpture of Spaces.* New York: The Whitney Museum of American Art, 1980. Foreword by Tom Armstrong, I.C. *Exhibition catalogue concerned with sculpture, realized and unrealized projects, and theater sets.*

NORDLAND, GERALD. 1. *Gaston Lachaise.* Los Angeles: County Museum of Art, 1963. I.B. *Retrospective catalogue.*

_____, 2. *Gaston Lachaise: The Man and His Work.* New York: George Braziller, Inc., 1974. I.B. *Monograph including artist's writings.*

_____, 3. *Jeremy Anderson.* San Francisco: San Francisco Museum of Art, 1966. I.B. *Retrospective catalogue.*

_____, 4. *Paul Jenkins: Retrospective.* Houston: Museum of Fine Arts, 1971. I.B.C. *Essay is brief sketch of the artist's life.*

_____, 5. *Ulfert Wilke: A Retrospective.* Salt Lake City: Utah Museum of Fine Arts, 1983. B.C. *Well-documented retrospective catalogue.*

NORDMARK, OLLE. *Fresco Painting.* New York: American Artists Group Inc., 1947. I.

NORDNESS, LEE, ed. *Art:USA:Now.* Lucerne: C. J. Bucher, 1962, 2 vols. I.B. *A collection catalogue with biographies and critical essays.*

NORMAN, DOROTHY, ed. *The Selected Writings of John Marin.* New York: Pellegrini and Cudahy, 1949. I. *Letters.*

Norman Lewis: A Retrospective. New York: The Graduate School and University Center of the City University of New York, 1976. Foreword by Milton W. Brown. Text by Thomas Lawson. I.B.C.

Northwest Traditions. Seattle: Seattle Art Museum, 1978. Foreword by Willis F. Woods. Essay by Martha Kingsbury. Organized by Charles Cowles and Sarah Clark. I.B.C. *Biographies. The Twentieth century, emphasizing the decades of the 1930s, '40s, '50s, '60s.*

O'DOHERTY, BRIAN. *American Masters: The Voice and the Myth.* Photographed by Hans Namuth. New York: A Ridge Press Book/Random House, n.d. I.B. *Essays incorporating extracts from interviews.*

O'HARA, FRANK. 1. *Art Chronicles: 1954–1966.* New York: George Braziller, Inc., 1975. I.B. *Collected essays.*

_____, 2.*David Smith.* London: Tate Gallery, 1966. I.B. *Retrospective catalogue.*

_____, 3. *Franz Kline.* London: Whitechapel Art Gallery, 1964. I. *Exhibition catalogue.*

_____, 4. *Jackson Pollock.* New York: George Braziller, Inc., 1959. I.B. *Monograph.*

_____, 5. *Nakian.* New York: The Museum of Modern Art, 1966. I.B. *Retrospective catalogue.*

OLDENBURG, CLAES. 1. *Log May 1974—August 1976.* Stuttgart: Edition Hansjörg Mayer, 1976. 2. vols. in slipcase. I.B.C. *Press clips and photos of the artist at work.*

_____, 2. *Notes in Hand.* New York: E.P. Dutton, 1971. I.B. *Miniature version of his sketchbooks.*

_____, 3. *Proposals for Monuments and Buildings.* Chicago: Follett Publishing Co., 1969. I. *New concepts for decorating the landscape.*

_____, 4. *Raw Notes.* Halifax: Nova Scotia College of Art and Design, 1973. I. *Documents and scripts for Stars, Moveyhouse, Massage, The Typewriter: annotated.*

Oldenburg: Six Themes. Minneapolis: The Walker Art Center, 1975. Introduction by Martin Friedman. I.B.C. *Exhibitions catalogue, including statements by the artist.*

OLSON, RUTH, and CHANIN, ABRAHAM. *Gabo-Pevsner.* New York: The Museum of Modern Art, 1948. I.B. *Exhibition catalogue.*

O'NEAL, BARBARA. *E. Lawson.* Ottawa: National Gallery of Canada, 1967. I.B. (French and English text.) *Retrospective catalogue.*

O'NEILL, JOHN P., ed. *Clyfford Still.* New York: The Metropolitan Museum of Art, 1979. Foreword by Philippe de Montebello. Essay by Katharine Kuh, and writings of the artist. I.B.C. *Exhibition catalogue.*

ONSLOW-FORD, GORDON. *Towards a New Subject in Painting.* San Francisco: San Francisco Museum of Art, 1948. I. *The artist's theory of painting.*

Options and Alternatives: Some Directions in Recent Art. New Haven: Yale University Art Gallery, 1973. Preface by Alan Shestack. "Toward a Definition" by Anne Coffin Hanson. "Notes on the Anatomy of an Exhibition" by Klaus Kertess. "Intellectual Cinema; A Reconsideration" by Annette Michelson. I.B.D. *Survey of new media and materials.*

Oscar Bluemner: American Colorist. Cambridge, Mass.: Fogg Art Museum, 1967. I.B. *Retrospective catalogue.*

PAALEN, WOLFGANG. *Form and Sense. Problems of Contemporary Art No. 1.* New York: Wittenborn and Co., 1945. I. *Essays in aesthetics.*

PACH, WALTER. 1. *Ananias or the False Artist.* New York: Harper and Brothers, 1928. I. *Critical essays.*

____, 2. *The Masters of Modern Art.* New York: B.W. Huebsch, Inc., 1926. I.B. *American and European art before 1926.*

____, 3. *Queer Thing, Painting.* New York: Harper and Brothers, 1938. I. *Autobiography.*

PAGANO, GRACE. *Contemporary American Painting. The Encyclopedia Britannica Collection.* New York: Duell, Sloan and Pearce, 1945. I.

PALMER, WILLIAM C. *William C. Palmer.* Utica, N.Y.: Munson-Williams-Proctor Institute, 1956. I. *Exhibition catalogue.*

PARKES, KINETON. *The Art of Carved Sculpture.* New York: Charles Scribner's Sons, 1931, 2 vols. I.B.

PASSLOFF, PATRICIA. *The 30's. Painting in New York.* New York: Poindexter Gallery, 1963. I.

Paul Manship: Changing Taste in America. St. Paul: Minnesota Museum of Art, 1985. B. *Multiple essays re-examining the accomplishments of the sculptor.*

PEARSON, RALPH M. 1. *Experiencing American Pictures.* New York: Harper and Brothers, 1943. I. *Appreciation of modern art.*

____, 2. *The Modern Renaissance in American Art.* New York: Harper and Brothers, 1954. I. *Development of modern art in America.*

PEIRCE, WALDO. *Waldo Peirce.* New York: American Artists Group Inc., 1945. I. *Autobiographical monograph.*

PENROSE, ROLAND. *Man Ray.* Boston: New York Graphic Society Ltd., 1975. I.B. *Appreciation and biographical sketch.*

PERLMAN, BENNARD B. *The Immortal Eight.* New York: Exposition Press, 1962.

PETERDI, GABOR. *Printmaking: Methods Old and New.* New York: The Macmillan Company, 1959. I.

PHILLIPS, DUNCAN. 1. *The Artist Sees Differently.* New York: E. Weyhe, 1931. I. *Critical essays.*

____, 2. *A Collection in the Making.* New York: E. Weyhe, 1926. I. *Development of the Phillips collection in Washington, D.C.*

PHILLIPS, LISA. *The Third Dimension: Sculpture of the New York School.* New York: Whitney Museum of American Art, 1984. Foreword by Tom Armstrong. *Survey show re-examining the influence of nature-inspired abstraction.*

PINCUS-WITTEN, ROBERT. 1. *Postminimalism.* New York: Out of London Press, Inc., 1977. I. *Collected essays on recent American art, written between 1966 and 1976.*

____, 2. *Entries (Maximalism)*. New York: Out of London Press, 1983. I. *Collected essays.*

PITTMAN, HOBSON. *Hobson Pittman.* Raleigh: North Carolina Museum of Art, 1963. I.B. *Retrospective catalogue.*

PITZ, HENRY C. *The Brandywine Tradition.* Boston: Houghton Mifflin Co., 1969. I.B. *Popular biographies of many recent painters, including Andrew Wyeth.*

PLOUS, PHYLLIS. *5 American Painters: Recent Work.* Santa Barbara, 1974. I.B. *Exhibition catalogue.*

Poets & Painters. Denver: Denver Art Museum, 1979. Foreword by Dianne Perry Vanderlip. Introduction by David Shapiro. I.B. *Urban artists' views accompanied by poems. Exhibition catalogue.*

POMEROY, RALPH. *Stamos.* New York: Harry N. Abrams Inc., 1974. I.B.C. *Monograph.*

PONENTE, NELLO. *Modern Painting: Contemporary Trends.* Geneva: Skira, 1960. I.B.

POOR, HENRY VARNUM. 1. *An Artist Sees Alaska.* New York: Viking Press, 1945. I.

____, 2. *A Book of Pottery, from Mud into Immortality.* Englewood Cliffs, N.J.: Prentice-Hall Inc., 1958. I.B. *Autobiographical*

POORE, HENRY R. *Modern Art: Why, What and How?* New York: G.P. Putnam's, 1931. I. *Investigation into the reasons for modern art.*

PORTER, FAIRCHILD. *Thomas Eakins.* New York: George Braziller, Inc., 1959. I.B. *Monograph.*

POTTER, JEFFREY. *To a Violent Grave: An Oral Biography of Jackson Pollock.* New York: G.P. Putnam's Sons, 1985. B.I. *Conversational memories elicited from friends, relatives, and others.*

POUSETTE-DART, NATHANIEL, ed. *American Painting Today.* New York: Hastings House, 1956. I. *Pictorial documentation of American painting in the mid 1950s.*

PRINT CLUB OF CLEVELAND. *The Work of Rudy Pozzatti.* Cleveland: The Cleveland Museum of Art, 1955. I. *Exhibition catalogue.*

PRINT COUNCIL OF AMERICA. *Prints.* New York: Holt, Rinehart and Winston, Inc., 1962. I.

RAGON, MICHEL. 1. *L'Aventure de l'art abstrait.* Paris: Robert Laffont, 1956. I.B. (French text.) *Development of abstract art.*

____, 2. *Expression et non-figuration.* Paris: Editions de la Revue Neuf, 1951. I. (French text.) *Expressionism and the development of non-figurative art.*

RAMSEN, E.H. 1. *An Introduction to Modern Art.* London: Oxford University Press, 1940. I.

____, 2. *Sculpture: Theme and Variations Toward a Contemporary Aesthetic.* London: Lund Humphries, 1953. I.B.

RAND, HARRY. 1. *Seymour Lipton: Aspects of Sculpture.* Washington, D.C.: National Collection of Fine Arts, 1979. Foreword by Joshua C. Taylor. I.B. *Illustrates the working methods from drawing to maquette to sculpture.*

____, 2. *Arshile Gorky: The Implications of Symbols.* Montclair, NJ: Allanheld & Schram, 1981. B.I. *A bizarre interpretation of the artist's accomplishments.*

Raymond Duchamp-Villon/Marcel Duchamp. Paris: Musee National d'Art Moderne, 1967. I.B. (French text.) *Major exhibition of the brothers.*

RAYNAL, MAURICE. 1. *A. Archipenko.* Rome: Valori Plastici, 1923. I. (French text.) *Monograph.*

____, 2. *Jacques Lipchitz.* Paris: Edition Jeanne Bucher, 1947. I. (French text.) *Monograph.*

____, 3. *Modern Painting.* Geneva: Skira 1953. I.B. *Survey of modern painting.*

____, 4. *Peinture moderne.* Geneva: Skira, 1953. I.B. (French text.)

READ, HERBERT. 1. *The Art of Sculpture.* Bollingen Series XXV, No. 3. New York: Pantheon Books, 1956. I. *Documented critical essays on connoisseurship of sculpture.*

____, 2. *A Concise History of Modern*

Painting. New York: Frederick A. Praeger, 1959. I.B.

____, 3. *A Concise History of Modern Sculpture.* New York: Frederick A. Praeger, 1964. I.B. *Essay source book.*

____, 4. *The Quest and the Quarry.* Rome: Rome-New York Art Foundation Inc., 1961. I. *Critical essays.*

____, 5. *Surrealism.* New York: Harcourt, Brace and Co., 1939. I. *Essays on Surrealism.*

____, 6. *The Tenth Muse.* London: Routledge and Kegan Paul, 1957. I. *Critical essays.*

READ, HERBERT, and MARTIN, LESLIE. *Gabo.* London: Lund Humphries, 1957. I.B. *Monograph.*

Recent Figure Sculpture. Cambridge, Mass.: Fogg Art Museum and Harvard University, 1972. Preface by Daniel Robbins. Introduction by Jeanne L. Wasserman. I.B. *Small survey exhibition.*

REESE, ALBERT. *American Prize Prints of the 20th Century.* New York: American Artists Group Inc., 1949. I.

A Report on the Art and Technology Program of the Los Angeles County Museum: 1967–1971. Los Angeles: Los Angeles County Museum of Art, 1971. Introduction by Maurice Tuchman. Essay: Thoughts on Art and Technology, by Jane Livingston. I.D.P. *Documents an amalgam of art, science, and business.*

RESTANY, PIERRE. 1. *J. F. Koenig.* Paris: Galerie Arnaud, 1960. I. (French and English text.) *Monograph.*

____, 2. *Lyrisme et abstraction.* Milan: Edizioni Apollinairi, 1960. I. *(French text.) Exposition of a lyrical theory in painting leading toward abstraction.*

RIBEMONT-DESSAIGNES, G. *Man Ray.* Paris: Librairie Gallimard, 1924. I. *Monograph.*

RICH, DANIEL CATTON. 1. *Georgia O'Keeffe.* Chicago: The Art Institute of Chicago, 1943. I. *Retrospective catalogue.*

____, 2. *Georgia O'Keeffe.* Worcester, Mass.: The Worcester Art Museum, 1960. *Retrospective catalogue.*

Richard Diebenkorn: Paintings and Drawings, 1943–1976. Buffalo: Albright-Knox Art Gallery, 1976. Foreword by Robert T. Buck, Jr. Acknowledgments by Linda L. Cathcart. Essays by Robert T. Buck, Jr., Linda L. Cathcart, Gerald Nordland, and Maurice Tuchman. *Retrospective Catalogue.*

Richard Haas: An Architecture of Illusion. New York: Rizzoli, 1981. Preface by Paul Goldberger. *On trompe l'oeil mural painting.*

RICHARDSON, BRENDA. 1. *Barnett Newman: The Complete Drawings, 1944–1969.* Baltimore: The Baltimore Museum of Art, 1979. I.B. *Exhibition and catalogue raisonné.*

____, 2. *Joan Brown.* Berkeley: University of California, Berkeley, 1974. I.B. *Retrospective catalogue.*

____, 3. *William T. Wiley.* Berkeley: University of California, Berkeley, 1971. I.B. *Retrospective catalogue.*

RICHARDSON, E.P. *Painting in America, the Story of 450 Years.* New York: Thomas Y. Crowell Co., 1956. I.B. *Important history of American painting.*

RICHTER, HANS. *Dada Profile.* Zurich: Verlag Die Arche, 1961. I. *(German text.) Snapshot introductory essays on the Dadaists.*

RICKEY, GEORGE. *Constructivism: Origins and Evolution.* New York: George Braziller, Inc., 1967. I.B.D. *Biographies. History of this movement.*

RINARD, PARK, and PYLE, ARNOLD. *Grant Wood.* Chicago: Lakeside Press Galleries, 1935. I. *Exhibition catalogue.*

RINGEL, FRED J., ed. *America as Americans See It.* New York: The Literary Guild, 1932. I. *Anthology of the writings of various Americans on American culture.*

RITCHIE, ANDREW CARNDUFF. 1. *Abstract Painting and Sculpture in America.* New York: The Museum of Modern Art, 1951. I.B. *Documented exhibition catalogue.*

____, 2. *Charles Demuth.* New York: The Museum of Modern Art, 1950. I.B. *Retrospective catalogue.*

_____, 3. *Sculpture of the Twentieth Century*. New York: The Museum of Modern Art, 1952. I.B.

RIVERS, LARRY, with BRIGHTMAN, CAROL. *Drawings and Digressions.* New York: Clarkson N. Potter, Inc., Publishers, 1979. Foreword by John Ashbery. *Biographical sketches, travelogues, and salty art talk illustrated by the artist's drawings.*

ROBBINS, DANIEL. *Walter Murch.* Providence: Rhode Island School of Design, 1966. I.B. *Retrospective catalogue.*

Robert Barnes. Madison, WI: Madison Art Center, 1985. Introduction by Dennis Adrian. B. *Retrospective catalogue.*

Robert Beauchamp: An American Expressionist. Syracuse, NY: Everson Museum of Art, 1984. B.C.I. *Retrospective exhibition with a brief essay by April Kingsley and a self-interview by the artist.*

Robert Rauschenberg. Washington, D.C.: National Collection of Fine Arts, 1976. Foreword by Joshua C. Taylor. Acknowledgments by Walter Hopps. Essay by Lawrence Alloway. I.B.C. *Retrospective exhibition and documentation of projects.*

Robert Ryman. Amsterdam: Stedelijk Museum, 1974. I.B.C. *Retrospective catalogue.*

ROBERTS, COLETTE. *Mark Tobey.* New York: Grove Press Inc., 1959. I. *Monograph.*

ROBERTSON, BRYAN. 1. *Charles Howard.* London: Whitechapel Art Gallery, 1956. I. *Retrospective catalogue.*

_____, 2. *Jackson Pollock.* New York: Harry N. Abrams Inc., 1960. I.B. *Monograph.*

RODMAN, SELDEN. 1. *Conversations with Artists.* New York: Capricorn Books, 1961. I.

_____, 2. *The Eye of Man.* New York: Devin-Adair, 1955. I. *Polemic devised toward figuration.*

_____, 3. *The Insiders.* Baton Rouge: Louisiana State University Press, 1960. I. *A thesis for figurative artists.*

ROSE, BARBARA. 1. *American Art since 1900, a Critical History.* New York: Frederick A. Praeger, 1967. I.B.

_____, 2. *Claes Oldenburg.* New York: The Museum of Modern Art, 1969. I.B. *Retrospective catalogue.*

_____, 3. *Frankenthaler.* New York: Harry N. Abrams Inc., 1971. I.B. *Monograph.*

_____, 4. *Readings in American Art since 1900.* New York: Frederick A. Praeger, 1968. I.B. *Collected essays by and about artists and their work.*

ROSE, BARBARA, ed. *Art as Art: The Selected Writings of Ad Reinhardt.* Documents of Twentieth-Century Art. New York: The Viking Press, 1975. I.B. *Anthology of the painter's writings.*

ROSE, BERNICE. *Jackson Pollock: Works on Paper.* New York: The Museum of Modern Art, 1969. I. *A study of the drawings.*

ROSENBERG, HAROLD. 1. *Arshile Gorky, The Man, The Time, The Idea.* New York: Horizon Press, Inc., 1962. I.B. *Monograph.*

_____, 2. *De Kooning.* New York: Harry N. Abrams Inc., 1974. I.B.C. *Monograph.*

_____, 3. *Saul Steinberg.* New York: Alfred A. Knopf in association with The Whitney Museum of American Art, 1978. Foreword by Paul H. Eliker and Tom Armstrong. I.B.C. *Major retrospective catalogue.*

ROSENBLUM, ROBERT. 1. *Cubism and Twentieth Century Art.* New York: Harry N. Abrams Inc., 1961. I.B. *Chronicles Cubism and its influence.*

_____, 2. *Modern Painting and the Northern Romantic Tradition: Friedrich to Rothko.* New York: Harper and Row Publishers Inc., 1975. I.B. *Essays on the dark side of romantic painting.*

ROSENTHAL, MARK. *Neil Jenney: Paintings and Sculpture 1967–1980.* Berkeley, CA: University Art Museum, 1981. Foreword by James Elliott and Jean-Christophe Ammann. B.I. *Retrospective catalogue.*

ROSENTHAL, MARK, and MARSHALL, RICHARD. *Jonathan Borofsky.* Philadelphia: Philadelphia

Museum of Art, 1984. B.C.I. *Includes artist's texts and statements.*

ROTERS, EBERHARD. *Painters of the Bauhaus.* New York: Frederick A. Praeger, 1969. I.B. *A history of the master teachers.*

ROTHSCHILD, LEON. *Style in Art.* New York: Thomas Yoseloff Inc., 1960. I. *Critical essays.*

ROTHSCHILD, LINCOLN. *To Keep Art Alive: The Effort of Kenneth Hays Miller, American Painter.* Philadelphia: The Art Alliance Press, 1974. I.B. *Monograph.*

ROURKE, CONSTANCE. *Charles Sheeler, Artist in the American Tradition.* New York: Harcourt, Brace and Co., 1938. I. *Biography.*

ROWELL, MARGIT. *Qu est ce que la sculpture moderne?* Paris: Centre Pompidou, 1986. Preface by Dominique Bozo. B. Index. *Includes essays by several critics.*

RUBIN, LAWRENCE. *Frank Stella: Paintings 1958–1965.* New York: Steward Tabori & Chang, Publishers, 1986. Introduction by Robert Rosenblum. B. *Catalogue raisonné.*

RUBIN, WILLIAM S. 1. *Dada, Surrealism, and Their Heritage.* New York: The Museum of Modern Art, 1968. I.B. Chronology. *Catalogue of controversial MOMA exhibition.*

____, 2. *Frank Stella.* New York: The Museum of Modern Art, 1970. I.B.C. *A major retrospective catalogue.*

RUBLOWSKY, JOHN. *Pop Art.* New York: Basic Books, 1965. I. *Pop art, its artists, dealers, collectors, and activities.*

RUHÉ, HARRY. *Fluxus, the Most Radical and Experimental Art Movement of the Sixties.* Amsterdam: 'A,' 1979. I.B.C. *Biographies. Major document on this international manifestation.*

RUSSELL, JOHN, and GABLIK, SUZI. *Pop Art Redefined.* New York: Frederick A. Praeger, 1969. I. *Includes statements by other critics.*

SACHS, PAUL J. *Modern Prints and Drawings.* New York: Alfred A. Knopf, 1954. I.B.

SAGER, PETER. *Neue Formen des Real-*ismus. Cologne: Verlag M. DuMont Schauberg, 1973. I.B.C. (German text.) *First international survey of various forms of new realist painting and sculpture; list of international group exhibitions; artists' statements.*

ST. JOHN, BRUCE. *John Sloan.* American Art and Artists. New York: Praeger Publishers, 1971. I.B.C. *Appreciation and life of the artist.*

ST. JOHN, BRUCE, ed. *John Sloan's New York Scene.* With an introduction by Helen Farr Sloan. New York: Harper and Row, 1964. I. *Edited from diaries, notes, and correspondence of the artist dating from 1906 to 1913.*

SALVINI, ROBERTO. *Guida all'arte moderna.* Florence: L'arco, 1949. I.B. (Italian text.)

SAMARAS, LUCAS. 1. *Samaras Album. Autointerview Autobiography Autopolaroid.* New York: The Whitney Museum of American Art and Pace Editions Inc., 1971. I. *The complete autoexposé of Samaras.*

____, 2. *Crude Delights.* New York: Pace Gallery Publications, 1980. *Rude imaginative tales.*

Sam Francis. Paintings 1947–1972. Buffalo: Albright-Knox Art Gallery, 1972. I.B.C. *A major retrospective catalogue; contains essays by Franz Meyer; Wieland Schmied; Robert T. Buck, Jr.*

SANDLER, IRVING. *The New York School: The Painters and Sculptors of the Fifties.* New York: Harper & Row, Publishers, 1978. I.B.A. *Review of the decade 1950–1960.*

____, 2. *The Triumph of American Painting: A History of Abstract Expressionism.* New York: Praeger Publishers, 1970. I.B.C. *A history of the mid-20th-century period.*

SASOWSKY, NORMAN. *Reginald Marsh. Etchings, Engravings, Lithographs.* New York: Frederick A. Praeger, 1956. I. *Catalogue raisonné.*

SAWYER, KENNETH. *The Paintings of Paul Jenkins.* Paris: Editions Two Cities, 1961. I. *Monograph.*

SCHEYER, ERNST. *Lyonel Feininger, Caricature and Fantasy.* Detroit: Wayne State University Press, 1964. I.B. *Documentary monograph drawn from letters and notes of the artist, showing development from cartoonist to painter.*

SCHMECKEBIER, LAURENCE E. 1. *Boris Margo.* Syracuse: School of Art, Syracuse University, 1968. I.B. *Exhibition catalogue, including a catalogue raisonné of the artist's prints.*

———, 2. *John Steuart Curry's Pageant of America.* New York: American Artists Group Inc., 1943. I. *Biography.*

SCHNEIDER, PIERRE. *Louvre Dialogues.* Translated from the French by Patricia Southgate. New York: Atheneum, 1971. I. *Interviews he made while walking through the Louvre.*

SCHULZE, FRANZ. *Fantastic Images: Chicago Art since 1945.* Chicago: Follett Publishing Co., 1972. I. *Eccentric figurative art from 1945 to 1972.*

SCHWABACHER, ETHEL K. *Arshile Gorky.* New York: The Whitney Museum of American Art, 1957. I.B. *Biography.*

SCHWARTZ, SANFORD. 1. *Myron Stout.* New York: The Whitney Museum of American Art, 1980. Introduction by B. H. Friedman. I.B.C. *Retrospective exhibition catalogue including artist's statements.*

———, 2. *The Art Presence.* New York: Horizon Press, 1982. Index. I. *Collected essays, some rewritten.*

SCHWARZ, ARTURO. 1. *The Complete Works of Marcel Duchamp.* New York: Harry N. Abrams Inc., 1969. I.B. *Biographical, critical catalogue raisonné: the major source book.*

———, 2. *Marcel Duchamp: Notes and Projects for the Large Glass.* New York: Harry N. Abrams Inc., 1969. I. *Facsimile reproduction of the notes for this work.*

SCOTT, DAVID W. *The Art of Stanton Macdonald-Wright.* Washington, D.C.: National Collection of Fine Arts, 1967. I.B. *Includes "A Treatise on Color" and selected writings of the artist. Retrospective catalogue.*

Sculpture and Drawings by Michael Lekakis. Dayton: Dayton Art Institute, 1968. Introduction by Priscilla Colt. I.C. *Appreciation.*

Sculpture of the Western Hemisphere. New York: International Business Machines Corp. 1942. I. *Catalogue of IBM sculpture collection.*

SEITZ, WILLIAM C. 1. *Abstract Expressionist Painting in America.* Cambridge, MA: Harvard University Press, 1983. Foreword by Robert Motherwell. Introduction by Dore Ashton. C.I. *Remains the most sensitive and understanding study of this movement.*

———, 2. *Arshile Gorky.* NewYork: The Museum of Modern Art, 1962. Foreword by Julien Levy. I.B. *Retrospective catalogue.*

———, 3. *The Art of Assemblage.* New York: The Museum of Modern Art, 1961. I.B. *Documented exhibition catalogue.*

———, 4. *Hans Hofmann.* New York: The Museum of Modern Art, 1963. I.B. *Exhibition catalogue.*

———, 5. *Mark Tobey.* New York: The Museum of Modern Art, 1962. I.B. *Retrospective catalogue.*

SELDIS, HENRY J. *Rico Lebrun.* Los Angeles: County Museum of Art, 1967. I.B. *Retrospective catalogue with major documentation: notes on "Genesis" by Peter Selz.*

SELDIS, HENRY J., and WILKE, ULFERT. *The Sculpture of Jack Zajac.* Los Angeles: Gallard Press, 1960. I.B. *Monograph.*

SELIGMANN, HERBERT J., ed. *Letters of John Marin.* New York: An American Place, 1931.

SELIGMANN, KURT. *The Mirror of Magic.* New York: Pantheon Books, 1948. I. *This artist was an authority on magic: his art reflects its influence.*

SELZ, JEAN. *Modern Sculpture.* New York: George Braziller, Inc., 1963. I.B. *Origins of modern sculpture from 1850 to 1920.*

SELZ, PETER. 1. *Directions in Kinetic Sculpture.* Berkeley: University of California, 1966. Preface by George Rickey. I.B. *International survey exhibition catalogue including artists' statements.*

———, 2. *Funk.* Berkeley: University of

California, 1967. I.G. *Includes statements by artists.*

____, 3. *German Expressionist Painting.* Berkeley: University of California Press, 1957. I.B. *Major work documenting the development of German Expressionism and its influence.*

____, 4. *Mark Rothko.* New York: The Museum of Modern Art, 1961. I.B. *Retrospective catalogue.*

SEUPHOR, MICHEL. 1. *Abstract Painting. 50 Years of Accomplishment, from Kandinsky to the Present.* New York: Dell Publishing Co., 1964. I.

____, 2. *L'Art abstrait.* Paris: Editions Maeght, 1949. I.B. (French text.)

____, 3. *The Sculpture of This Century.* Dictionary of Modern Sculpture. London: A. Zwemmer, Ltd., 1959. I.B.

7 *Decades.* Andover, Mass.: Addison Gallery of American Art, Phillips Academy, 1969. Foreword by Bartlett H. Hayes, Jr. I.C. *Exhibition catalogue, including artists' statements.*

SEYMOUR, CHARLES, Jr. *Tradition and Experiment in Modern Sculpture.* Washington, D.C.: The American University Press, 1949. I.

SHAHN, BEN. 1. *The Biography of Painting.* New York: Paragraphic Books, 1966. I. *A testament of the artist.*

____, 2. *The Shape of Content.* Cambridge, Mass.: Harvard University Press, 1957. I. *Critical essay.*

SHAHN, BERNARDA BRYSON. *Ben Shahn.* New York: Harry N. Abrams Inc., 1972. I.B.C. *Picture catalogue of works and biographical sketch.*

SHAPIRO, DAVID. *Jasper Johns: Drawings 1954–1984.* New York: Harry N. Abrams, Inc., 1984. Exhibition history. B.I. *Drawing encomiums.*

SHAPIRO, DAVID, ed. *Social Realism: Art as a Weapon.* New York: Frederick Ungar Publishing Co., 1973. I.B. *A study of the social implications of figurative art in the 1930s and 1940s.*

SHEARER, LINDA. *Brice Marden.* New York: The Solomon R. Guggenheim Museum, 1975. I.B. *A ten-year survey.*

SIEGFRIED, JOAN C. *Bruce Conner.* Philadelphia: Institute of Contemporary Art, 1967. Preface by Stephen S. Prokopoff. I. *Retrospective catalogue.*

SIMS, PATTERSON, and PULITZER, EMILY RAUH. *Ellsworth Kelly: Sculpture.* New York: Whitney Museum of American Art, 1982. Foreword by Tom Armstrong. B.C.I. *Exhibition catalogue including catalogue raisonné.*

SLOAN, HELEN FARR. *The Life and Times of John Sloan.* Wilmington, Del.: Wilmington Society of the Fine Arts, 1961. I.

SLOAN, HELEN FARR, ed. *American Art Nouveau: The Poster Period of John Sloan.* Lock Haven, Pa.: Privately published by Hammermill Paper Co., n.d. I. *New material on an unknown period of the artist's work.*

SLOAN, JOHN. 1. *The Art of John Sloan.* Brunswick, Me.: Walker Art Museum, Bowdoin College, 1962. *Exhibition catalogue.*

____, 2. *The Gist of Art.* New York: American Artists Group Inc., 1939. I. *The artist's theory of painting.*

____, 3. *John Sloan.* Andover, Mass.: Addison Gallery of American Art, Phillips Academy, 1938. I.B. *Exhibition catalogue.*

____, 4. *John Sloan.* New York: American Artists Group Inc., 1945. I. *Autobiographical monograph.*

____, 5. *John Sloan. Paintings and Prints.* Hanover, N.H.: Dartmouth College, 1946. I. *Exhibition catalogue.*

SLUSSER, JEAN PAUL. *Bernard Karfiol.* New York: The Whitney Museum of American Art (American Artists Series), 1931. I.B. *Monograph.*

SMITH, ANDRE. *Concerning the Education of a Print Collector.* New York: Harlow, Keppel and Co., 1941. I.

SMITH, BERNARD. *Moses Soyer.* New York: ACA Gallery, 1944. I. *Monograph.*

SMITH, BRYDEN. *Donald Judd.* Ottawa: National Gallery of Canada, 1975. I.B.C. *Retrospective catalogue and catalogue raisonné, 1960–1974.*

SMITH, DAVID. *David Smith.* New York: Holt, Rinehart and Winston, Inc., 1968. I. *Writings and photographs.*

SMITH, S.C. KAINES. *An Outline of Modern Painting.* London: The Medici Society, 1932. I. *Early documentation of twentieth-century art.*

SOBY, JAMES THRALL. 1. *After Picasso.* Hartford, Conn.: Edwin Valentine Mitchell; New York: Dodd, Mead and Co., 1935. I. *Critical essays.*

____, 2. *Ben Shahn.* New York: The Museum of Modern Art. West Drayton, England: Penguin Books, 1947. I. *Monograph.*

____, 3. *Ben Shahn.* New York: George Braziller Inc., 1963. I.B. *Monograph.*

____, 4. *Ben Shahn, His Graphic Work.* New York: George Braziller, Inc., 1957. I.B. *Monograph.*

____, 5. *Contemporary Painters.* New York: The Museum of Modern Art, 1948. I. *Documented exhibition catalogue.*

____, 6. *Modern Art and the New Past.* Norman: University of Oklahoma Press, 1957. *Critical essays and documentation.*

____, 7. *Tchelitchew.* New York: The Museum of Modern Art, 1942. I.B. *Exhibition catalogue.*

____, 8. *Yves Tanguy.* New York: The Museum of Modern Art, 1955. I.B. *Exhibition catalogue.*

Sol LeWitt. New York: The Museum of Modern Art, 1978. Introduction by Alicia Legg. Essays by Robert Rosenblum, Lucy R. Lippard, Bernice Rose. I.B.D. *Retrospective catalogue including artist's writings.*

SONTAG, SUSAN. *Against Interpretation.* New York: Dell Publishing Co., 1966. *Assorted collected essays.*

SOYER, MOSES. *Painting the Human Figure.* New York: Watson-Guptill Publishing Co., Inc., 1964. I. *How-to-paint book.*

SOYER, RAPHAEL. 1. *Homage to Thomas Eakins, etc.* Rebecca L. Soyer, ed. South Brunswick, N.J.: Thomas Yoseloff, Inc., 1965. I. *Travelogue and art-world personalities.*

____, 2. *A Painter's Pilgrimage.* New York: Crown Publishers Inc., 1962. I. *A European travelogue.*

____, 3. *Raphael Soyer.* New York: American Artists Group Inc., 1946. I. *Autobiographical monograph.*

SPEICHER, EUGENE. *Eugene Speicher.* New York: American Artists Group Inc., 1945. I. *Autobiographical monograph.*

STABER, MARGIT. *Fritz Glarner.* Zurich: ABC Verlag, 1976. (English and German text.) I.B.C. *Biography. The monograph and catalogue raisonné.*

The State of California Painting. New Plymouth, N.Z.: Govett-Brewster Art Gallery, 1972. Foreword by Robert H. Ballard. Introduction by Michael Walls. I.C. *Exhibition catalogue.*

STRAND, MARK, ed. *Art of the Real: Nine American Figurative Painters.* New York: Clarkson N. Potter, Inc., Publishers, 1983. Foreword by Robert Hughes. B.C. *Text from edited interviews. Portrait photos by Timothy Greenfield-Sanders.*

STEINBERG, LEO. *Jasper Johns.* New York: George Wittenborn, Inc., 1964. I.B. *Monograph.*

STEINBERG, SAUL. 1. *The Art of Living.* New York: Harper and Brothers, 1945. I. *Cartoons.*

____, 2. *The Passport.* New York: Harper and Brothers, 1945. I. *Cartoons.*

____, 3. *Steinberg Dessins.* Paris: N.R.F., Gallimard, 1955. I. *Cartoons.*

STORY, ALA. *First comprehensive retrospective exhibition in the West of Max Weber.* Santa Barbara: University of California, 1968. I.B. *Major retrospective catalogue.*

STRACHAN, W.J. *Towards Sculpture.* London: Thames and Hudson, 1976. I.B. *Biographies. From the classical tradition to Oldenburg: drawings, maquettes, and realized works.*

Stuart Edie. Iowa City: The University of Iowa Museum of Art, 1979. Foreword by Jan K. Muhlert. Introduction by Judy Cizek. I.C. *Retrospective catalogue.*

SUTTON, DENYS. *American Painting.* London: Avalon Press, 1948. I. *Mid-twentieth-century painting.*

SWEENEY, JAMES JOHNSON. 1. *Alexander Calder.* New York: The Museum of Modern Art, 1951. I.B. *Exhibition catalogue.*

___, 2. *Jacques Villon, Raymond Duchamp-Villon, Marcel Duchamp.* New York: The Solomon R. Guggenheim Museum, 1957. I.B. *Exhibition catalogue.*

___, 3. *Sam Francis.* Houston: Museum of Fine Arts of Houston, 1967. I. *Exhibition catalogue.*

___, 4. *Stuart Davis.* New York: The Museum of Modern Art, 1945. I.B. *Exhibition catalogue.*

SWEET, FREDERICK, A. *Ivan Albright.* Chicago: The Art Institute of Chicago, 1964. I. *Retrospective catalogue.*

SYLVESTER, JULIE. *John Chamberlain: A Catalogue Raisonne of the Sculpture 1954–1985.* New York: Hudson Hills Press, 1986. B.C. *Includes an essay by Klaus Kertess.*

TAFT, LORADO. *Modern Tendencies in Sculpture.* Chicago: The University of Chicago Press, 1921. I.

TAKIGUCHI, SHUZO. *Noguchi.* Tokyo: Bijutsu Shippan-Sha, 1953. I. *Monograph.*

TANGUY, YVES. *Un Recueil de Ses Ouevres/A Summary of His Work.* New York: Pierre Matisse, 1943. I.B. (French and English text.) *Catalogue raisonné.*

TAPIE, MICHEL. 1. *Un Arte autre.* Paris: Gabriel Giraud et Fils, 1952. I. (French text.) *Polemic thesis for advance-guard painting.*

___, 2. *Ossorio.* Turin: Edizioni d'Arte Fratelli Pozzo, 1961. I. (English and French text.) *Monograph.*

TARBELL, ROBERTA K. *Marguerite Zorach: The Early Years, 1908–1920.* Washington, D.C.: National Collection of Fine Arts, 1973. Foreword by Joshua C. Taylor, I.B.C. *Exhibition catalogue and detailed study of the artist's early life.*

TASHJIAN, DICKRAN. *Skyscraper Primitives.* Middletown, Conn.: Wesleyan University Press, 1975. I.B. *Observations on dadamerica.*

TAUBES, FREDERIC. 1. *Anatomy of Genius.* New York: Dodd, Mead and Co., 1948. I. *Critical essay.*

___, 2. *The Art and Techniques of Portrait Painting.* New York: Dodd, Mead and Co., 1957. I.

___, 3. *Better Frames for Your Pictures.* New York: Studio Publications, 1952. I.

___, 4. *Frederic Taubes.* New York: American Artists Group Inc., 1946. I.B. *Autobiographical monograph.*

___, 5. *The Mastery of Oil Painting.* New York: Studio Publications, 1953. I. *Technique.*

___, 6. *Modern Art, Sweet or Sour?* New York: Watson-Guptill Publishing Co. Inc., 1958. I. *Critical essays.*

___, 7. *The Painter's Question and Answer Book.* New York: Watson-Guptill Publishing Co. Inc., 1948. I. *Technique.*

___, 8. *Paintings and Essays on Art.* New York: Dodd, Mead and Co., 1950. I.

___, 9. *Pen and Ink Drawing, Art and Technique.* New York: Watson-Guptill Publishing Co. Inc., 1958. I.

___, 10. *Pictorical Composition and the Art of Drawing.* New York: Dodd, Mead and Co., 1949. I.

___, 11. *Studio Secrets.* New York: Watson-Guptill Publishing Co. Inc., 1943. I. *Technique.*

___, 12. *The Technique of Oil Painting.* New York: Dodd, Mead and Co., 1941. I.

___, 13. *You Don't Know What You Like.* New York: Dodd, Mead and Co., 1947. I. *Critical essays.*

TAVOLATO, ITALO. *George Grosz.* Rome: Valori Plastici, 1924. I. (French text.) *Monograph.*

TERENZIO, STEPHANIE. *The Painter and The Printer: Robert Motherwell's Graphics, 1943–1980.* New York: The American Federation of Arts, 1980. Introduction includes a note by the artist on collaboration. I.B. *Biographical sketch. Catalogue raisonné by Dorothy C. Belknap.*

THOMAS, EDWARD B. *Mark Tobey.* Seattle: Seattle Art Museum, 1959. I. *Exhibition catalogue.*

Three Realists: Close, Estes, Raffael. Worcester, Mass.: The Worcester Art Museum, 1974. Foreword by Leon Shulman. I.B. *Exhibition catalogue.*

TILLIM, SIDNEY. *Richard Lindner.* Chicago: William and Noma Copley Foundation, n.d. I. *Monograph.*

TOBEY, MARK. *Mark Tobey.* New York: The Whitney Museum of American Art, 1951. I. *Exhibition catalogue.*

TOHER, JENNIFER, ed. *Beyond the Plane: American Construction 1930–1965.* Trenton: New Jersey State Museum, 1983. Introduction by Joan Marter. B. *Numerous brief essays examine the topic.*

TOMKINS, CALVIN. 1. *The Bride and the Bachelors.* New York: Viking Press, 1965. I. *Essays on the avant-garde.*

____, 2. *Off the Wall: Robert Rauschenberg and the Art World of Our Time.* Garden City: Doubleday & Co., Inc., 1980. I.C. *Extracts from "Profiles" in the New Yorker.*

TOMKINS, CALVIN, and the Editors of TIME-LIFE BOOKS. *The World of Marcel Duchamp.* New York: Time Inc., 1966. I.B.

Tony Smith: Painting and Sculpture. Baltimore: University of Maryland Art Gallery, 1974. Foreword by Eleanor Green. I. *Exhibition catalogue.*

Transparency, Reflection, Light, Space: Four Artists. Los Angeles: UCLA Art Galleries, 1971. Foreword by Frederick S. Wight. I.B.C. *Exhibition catalogue: interviews and artists' statements.*

TRIER, EDUARD. 1. *Form and Space: Sculpture in the 20th Century.* New York: Frederick A. Praeger, 1968. I.B. *Survey by concept.*

____, 2. *Moderne Plastik von August Rodin bis Marino Marini.* Frankfurt am Main: Buchergilde Gutenberg, 1955. I.B. (German text.) *Short illustrated history of twentieth-century sculpture.*

TSUJIMOTO, KAREN. *Wayne Thiebaud.* Seattle: U. of Washington Press, 1985. Exhibition history. Foreword by Henry T. Hopkins. B.C.I. *Retrospective catalogue.*

TUCHMAN, MAURICE. 1. *American Sculpture of the Sixties.* Los Angeles: County Museum of Art, 1967. I.B.G. *Major survey exhibition catalogue includes essays by 10 critics and statements by the artists.*

____, 2. *Edward Kienholz.* Los Angeles: County Museum of Art, 1966. I.B. *Retrospective catalogue.*

____, 3. *The Spiritual in Art: Abstract Painting 1890–1985.* Los Angeles: Los Angeles County Museum of Art, 1986. B.C.D. *Numerous essays by artists and scholars comprise this vast and unsparing confection of ocultism.*

TUCHMAN, MAURICE, ed. *New York School. The First Generation: Paintings of the 1940s and 1950s.* Los Angeles: County Museum of Art, 1965. I.B. *Major exhibition catalogue with statements by artists and critics.*

TUCKER, MARCIA. *Al Held.* New York: The Whitney Museum of American Art, 1974. I.B.C. *Retrospective catalogue.*

TYLER, KENNETH E. *Josef Albers: White Line Squares.* Los Angeles: Gemini G.E.L., 1966. I.B. *Graphics exhibition catalogue includes artist's statements.*

TYLER, PARKER. 1. *The Divine Comedy of Pavel Tchelitchew.* New York: Fleet Publishing Co., 1967. I.B. *Biography.*

____, 2. *Marca-Relli.* Paris: The Pocket Museum, Editions George Fall, 1960. I. *Monograph.*

USA West Coast. Hamburg: Kunstverein in Hamburg, 1972. Foreword by Helmut Heissenbuttel. Essay by Helene Winer. I.C. (German and English text.) *Exhibition catalogue.*

VALENTINE, W.R. 1. *Letters of John B. Flanagan.* New York: Curt Valentine, 1942.

____, 2. *Origins of Modern Sculpture.* New York: Wittenborn and Co., 1946. I.

VAN BORK, BERT. *Jacques Lipchitz: The*

Artist at Work. With a critical evaluation by Dr. Alfred Werner. New York: Crown Publishers Inc., 1966. I. *Well-illustrated popular essay about the artist at work.*

VAN BRUGGEN, COOSJE, and OLDENBURG, CLAES. *Claes Oldenburg: Large-Scale Projects, 1977–1980.* New York: Rizzoli International Publications, Inc. Includes essay on his monuments by R. H. Fuchs. I.D.P. Biographies. *Documentation on ten projects.*

VARGA, MARGIT. *Waldo Peirce.* New York: Hyperion Press, Harper and Brothers, 1941. I. *Monograph.*

VERKAUF, WILLY, ed. *Dada: Monograph of a Movement.* New York: Wittenborn and Co., 1957. I.B. *Documented monograph.*

VITRY, PAUL. *Paul Manship.* Paris: Editions de la Gazette des Beaux Arts, 1927. I. *Monograph.*

WALDBERG, PATRICK. 1. *Bernard Pfriem.* Chicago: William and Noma Copley Foundation, 1961. I. (French and English text.) *Monograph.*

_____, 2. *Main et merveilles.* Paris: Mercure de France, 1961. I. *Essays on Surrealism.*

_____, 3. *Surrealisms.* Geneva: Skira, 1962. I.B. *Documentation and essays on Surrealism.*

_____, 4. *Surrealism.* New York: McGraw-Hill Co., Inc., 1965. I.B. Chronology. *A short history of Surrealism.*

WALDMAN, DIANE. 1. *Carl Andre.* New York: The Solomon R. Guggenheim Museum, 1970. I.B. *A ten-year survey of Andre's work.*

_____, 2. *Chryssa: Selected Works 1955–1967.* New York: The Pace Gallery, 1968. I.B. *Well-illustrated exhibition catalogue.*

_____, 3. *Joseph Cornell.* New York: The Solomon R. Guggenheim Museum, 1967. I.B. *Retrospective catalogue.*

_____, 4. *Kenneth Noland: A Retrospective.* New York: The Solomon R. Guggenheim Museum, 1977. Preface and acknowledgments by Thomas

M. Messer. I.B.C. *Retrospective catalogue.*

_____, 5. *Mark Rothko, 1903–1970: A Retrospective.* New York: Harry N. Abrams Inc./The Solomon R. Guggenheim Museum, 1978. Acknowledgments and preface by Thomas M. Messer. Includes "The Aquamarine Sunrise: A Memory of Rothko," by Bernard Malamud. I.B.C. *Comprehensive retrospective.*

_____, 6. *Robert Mangold.* New York: The Solomon R. Guggenheim Museum, 1971. I.B. *Exhibition catalogue.*

_____, 7. *Arshile Gorky, 1904–1948. A Retrospective.* New York: Harry N. Abrams, Inc., 1981. Preface by Thomas M. Messer. B.C.I. *Major retrospective catalogue.*

WALKOWITZ, ABRAHAM. 1. *A Demonstration of Objective, Abstract and Non-Objective Art.* Giraud, Kans.: Haldeman: Julius Press, 1945. I. *The artist's theories, illustrated.*

_____, 2. *100 Drawings.* New York: B. W. Huebsch, Inc., 1925. I.

WARHOL, ANDY. *The Philosophy of Andy Warhol.* New York: Harcourt Brace Jovanovich, 1975. *Artist's statements.*

WARHOL, ANDY; KONIG, KASPER; HULTEN, PONTUS; and GRANTH, OLLE, eds. *Andy Warhol.* Stockholm: Moderna Museet, 1968. I. *Pictorial history of the development of the artist, his work, and friends, including comments by the artist.*

WARHOL, ANDY, and HACKETT, PAT. *POPism: The Warhol '60s.* New York: Harcourt Brace Jovanovich, 1980. I. *Gossip or history: choose!*

WATSON, ERNEST, W. 1. *Color and Method in Painting.* New York: Watson-Guptill Publishing Co. Inc., 1942. I. *Studies of various artists' use of color.*

_____, 2. *Twenty Painters and How They Work.* New York: Watson-Guptill Publishing Co. Inc., 1950. I.

WATSON, FORBES. *William Glackens.* New York: Duffield and Co., 1923. I. *Monograph.*

WEBER, NICHOLAS FOX. 1. *The Drawings of Josef Albers.* New Haven,

CT: Yale University Press, 1984. I. *Survey of the drawings.*

____, 2. *Josef Albers: His Art and His Influence.* Montclair, NJ: Montclair Art Museum, 1981. C. *A review of the artist and his students.*

WEBER, MAX. 1. *Essays on Art.* n.p.: Privately published, 1916.

____, 2. *Max Weber.* New York: American Artists Group Inc., 1945. I. *Autobiographical monograph.*

WEITEMEIER, HANNAH. *Moholy-Nagy.* Eindhoven, Holland: Stedelijk van Abbe-Museum, 1967. I. (Dutch and English text.) *Retrospective catalogue including statements by the artists.*

WELL, HENRY W., ed. *Selected Poems by Marsden Hartley.* New York: Viking Press, 1945. I.

WELLER, ALLEN S. *The Joys and Sorrows of Recent American Art.* Urbana: University of Illinois Press, 1968. I.

"What Abstract Art Means to Me." *Bulletin of the Museum of Modern Art,* Vol. XVIII, No. 3, Spring 1951. I. *Statements by leading artists.*

WHEELER, MONROE. *Painters and Sculptors of Modern America.* New York: Thomas Y. Crowell Co., 1942. I.

When Attitudes Become Form: Works/Concepts/ Processes/Situations/ Information. Bern: Kunsthalle Bern, 1969. Foreword by Harold Szeemann. Introduction by John A. Murphy. I.B.C. (English, French, and German text.) *Major international exhibition of abovementioned tendencies.*

WHITNEY, DAVID, ed. *Andy Warhol: Portraits of the 70s.* New York: Random House, in Association with The Whitney Museum of American Art, 1979. Foreword by Tom Armstrong. Essay by Robert Rosenblum. I. *Exhibition catalogue and picture book of commissioned portraits.*

Who Chicago? Sunderland, England: Sunderland Arts Centre, 1980. Preface by Tony Knipe. Introduction by Victor Musgrave. B.I. *Essays by Dennis Adrian, Russell Bowman, and Roger Brown examining 14 Chicago School artists.*

WIGHT, FREDERICK, S. 1. *Hans Hofmann.* New York: The Whitney Museum of American Art, 1957. I. *Exhibition catalogue.*

____, 2. *Milestones of American Painting in Our Century.* New York: Chanticleer Press, 1949. I. *Historical view of American painting.*

____, 3. *Milton Avery.* Baltimore: Baltimore Museum of Art, 1952. I. *Exhibition catalogue.*

____, 4. *Nathan Oliveira.* Los Angeles: University of California, 1963. I. *Monograph.*

WIGHT, FREDERICK S.; BAUR, JOHN I.H.; and PHILLIPS, DUNCAN. *Morris Graves.* Berkeley: University of California Press, 1956. I.B. *Exhibition catalogue.*

WIGHT, FREDERICK S., and GOODRICH, LLOYD. *Hyman Bloom.* Boston: Institute of Contemporary Art, 1944. I. *Exhibition catalogue.*

WILDE, JOHN. *44 Wilde 1944.* Mt. Horeb, WI: The Perishable Press, 1984. Foreword by Lincoln Kirstein. I. *Drawings and text by the artist from 1944.*

WILENSKI, R.H. *The Modern Movement in Art.* London: Faber and Faber, Ltd., 1955. I. *European and American development of modern art.*

WILKE, ULFERT. *Music to Be Seen.* Louisville, Ky.: Erewhon Press, n.d. I. (English, French, and German text.) *A collection of drawings.*

WILKEN, KAREN. *Frankenthaler: Works on Paper 1949–1984.* New York: George Braziller, 1984. B.C.I. *Retrospective catalogue including artist's statements.*

WILLARD, CHARLOTTE. *Moses Soyer.* Cleveland: World Publishing Co., 1962. I. *Monograph.*

William Baziotes: A Retrospective Exhibition. Newport Beach: Newport Harbor Art Museum, 1978. Introduction by Michael Preble, with essays by Barbara Cavaliere and Mona Hadler. I.B.C. *An important study of the artist and his works.*

WILLIAMS, WILLIAM CARLOS. *Charles Sheeler.* New York: The Museum of Modern Art, 1939. I.B. *Exhibition catalogue.*

WINGERT, PAUL S. *The Sculpture of William Zorach.* New York: Pitman Publishing Co., 1938. I.B. *Monograph.*

WINGLER, HANS M., ed. *Graphic Work from the Bauhaus.* Greenwich, Conn.: New York Graphic Society, 1968. I.B.

WOELFFER, EMERSON. *Emerson Woelffer.* Pasadena: The Pasadena Art Museum, 1962. I. *Exhibition catalogue.*

WOLANI, BARBARA A. *Arthur B. Carles: Painting with Color.* Philadelphia: Pennsylvania Academy of Fine Arts, 1983. B.C. *Retrospective catalogue.*

WOLFF, THEODORE L. *Enrico Donati: The Most Recent Work.* Paris: Prints Etc./Georges Fall, 1984. (English and French texts.) I.C. *Examines the paintings of the 1980s.*

WOOD, JAMES N. *Six Painters.* Buffalo: Albright-Knox Art Gallery, 1971. Foreword by Gordon M. Smith. I.B.C. *Exhibition catalogue.*

Woodstock: An American Art Colony 1902–1977. Poughkeepsie: Vassar College Art Gallery, 1977. Foreword by Peter Morrin. Introduction by Karal Ann Marling. I. *A history of the artists and their activities.*

WRIGHT, WILLARD HUNTINGTON. 1. *The Forum Exhibition of Modern American Painters.* New York: Anderson Galleries, 1916. I.B.

____, 2. *Modern Painting.* New York: Dodd, Mead and Co., 1927. I. *Essays on modern art.*

WYETH, BETSY JAMES. *Christina's World.* Boston: Houghton Mifflin Co., 1982. I. *History of the painting.*

Yves Tanguy: Retrospective 1925–1955. Paris: Centre Georges Pompidou, 1982. (French text.) Preface by Dominique Bozo. Texts by Jean Manuel, Roland Penrose, Robert Lebel, Jose Piene. B.C.I. *Retrospective catalogue.*

ZAIDENBERG, ARTHUR, ed. *The Art of the Artists.* New York: Crown Publishers Inc., 1951. I. *Pictorial documentation of various artists.*

ZERVOS, CHRISTIAN. *Histoire de l'art contemporain.* Paris: Editions Cahiers d'Art, 1938. I.B. *Documented history of contemporary art.*

ZERVOS, CHRISTIAN, and ADAMS, PHILIP R. *Mary Callery.* New York: Wittenborn and Co., 1961. I.B. *Monograph and catalogue raisonné.*

ZIGROSSER, CARL. 1. *The Artist in America.* New York: Alfred A. Knopf, 1942. I. *Critical essays and biographies.*

____, 2. *Mauricio Lasansky.* New York: American Federation of Arts, 1960. I. *Retrospective catalogue.*

ZORACH, WILLIAM. 1. *William Zorach.* New York: American Artists Group Inc., 1945. I. *Autobiographical monograph.*

____, 2. *Zorach Explains Sculpture, What It Is and How It Is Made.* New York: American Artists Group Inc., 1947. I.

Books of General Interest

AGEE, WILLIAM C. *The 1930's; Painting and Sculpture in America.* New York: Frederick A. Praeger, 1968. I.B. *Based on a Whitney Museum exhibition.*

ALBRIGHT, THOMAS. *Art in the San Francisco Bay Area 1945–1980.* Berkeley: University of California Press, 1985. Index. I. *Significant regional history.*

America: Traum und Depression 1920–40. 1980. I.B. Biographies (German text.) *A major survey of art, architecture, books, magazines, movies, posters, and photography in over 1,000 objects.*

AMERICAN ABSTRACT ARTISTS, ed. *The World of Abstract Art.* New York: George Wittenborn and Co., 1957. I. *Documentation of the group and its members.*

ARMSTRONG, TOM; CRAVEN, WAYNE; FEDER, NORMAN; HASKELL, BARBARA; KRAUSS, ROSALIND E.; ROBBINS, DANIEL; TUCKER, MARCIA. *200 Years of American Sculpture.* Boston: David R. Godine, Publisher, in association with The Whitney Museum of American Art, 1976. Foreword by Tom Armstrong. Introduction by David Rockefeller. I.B. *Major survey exhibition.*

ARNASON, H. HARVARD. *American Abstract Expressionists and Imagists.* New York: The Solomon R. Guggenheim Museum, 1961. B. *Documented exhibition catalogue.*

____. *History of Modern Art.* New York: Harry N. Abrams Inc., 1968. I.B. *The world of modern art, up to date.*

ARONSON, CHIL. *Artistes americains modernes de Paris.* Paris: Editions Le Triangle, 1932. I. (French text.)

ASHTON, DORE. *Modern American Sculpture.* New York: Harry N. Abrams Inc., 1968. I. *Well-illustrated survey book.*

____. *The New York School: A Cultural Reckoning.* New York: Viking Press, 1973. I.B. *Sociophilosophic observations on mid-20th-century New York art and culture.*

BARR, ALFRED H., Jr., ed. *Masters of Modern Art.* New York: The Museum of Modern Art, 1955. I.B. *Major anthology of modern art.*

BATTCOCK, GREGORY, ed. *Idea Art.* New York: E.P. Dutton, 1973. I. *Reprints magazine pieces on concept art.*

____. *The New Art, a critical anthology.* New York: E.P. Dutton, 1966. I. *Reprints of selected vital essays from periodicals and museum catalogues, with a preface by the editor.*

____. *Super Realism.* New York: E.P. Dutton, 1975. I. *The initial critical anthology.*

____. *Why Art.* New York: E.P. Dutton & Co., Inc., 1977. I. *General essays on the 1960s and 1970s.*

BAZIN, GERMAIN. *The History of World Sculpture.* Greenwich, Conn.: New York Graphic Society, 1968.

BERMAN, GRETA, and WECHSLER, JEFFREY. *Realism and Realities: The Other Side of American Painting 1940–1960.* New Brunswick, NJ: Rutgers University Art Gallery, 1982. *Exhibition catalogue examines diverse approaches to "realism."*

BELMONT, I.J. *The Modern Dilemma in Art.* New York: Harbinger House, 1944. I. *Critical evaluation of increasing abstractionism.*

BETHERS, RAY. *Art Always Changes.* New York: Hastings House, 1958. I. *Critical essays.*

BROWN, MILTON W. *The Story of the Armory Show.* New York: The Joseph H. Hirshhorn Foundation, 1963. I.B. *Documented history of the famous exhibition.*

BURNHAM, JACK. *Beyond Modern*

Sculpture. New York: George Braziller, Inc., 1968. I.B. *Survey of recent modern sculpture.*

CAHILL, HOLGER. *New Horizons in American Art.* New York: The Museum of Modern Art, 1936. I. *Exhibition catalogue related to Federal Art Project.*

CALAS, NICOLAS. *Art in the Age of Risk and Other Essays.* New York: E.P. Dutton, 1968. Introduction by Gregory Battcock. I. *A collection of essays from periodicals.*

CANADAY, JOHN. *Culture Gulch: Notes on Art and Its Public in the 1960s.* New York: Farrar, Straus and Giroux, 1969. I. *Essays garnered from the New York Times.*

CHENEY, SHELDON. *A Primer of Modern Art.* New York: Boni and Liveright, 1924. I.

____. *Sculpture of the World.* New York: Viking Press, 1968. I.B. *Valuable survey of the sculpture of all time.*

____. *The Story of Modern Art.* New York: Viking Press, 1958. I. *Popular history of modern art.*

CIRLOT, JUAN-EDUARDO. *Del Expresionismo a la Abstraccion.* Barcelona: Editorial Seix Barral, S.A., 1955. I. (Spanish text.) *Development of nonfigurative art.*

CRANE, AIMEE, ed. *Portrait of America.* New York: Hyperion Press, Harper and Brothers, 1945. I. *Critical essays.*

CUMMINGS, PAUL. *American Drawings: The 20th Century.* New York: The Viking Press, 1976. I.B. Index. *Survey of 120 artists.*

DAVIDSON, ABRAHAM A. *Early American Modernist Painting 1910–1935.* New York: Harper & Row, Publishers, 1981. B.I. *Text-book approach to the modernist development emphasizing minor characters.*

DAVIDSON, MARSHALL B. *Life in America.* Boston: Houghton Mifflin Co., 1951, 2 vols. *Critical essays and documentation.*

DAVIS, DOUGLAS. *Artculture: Essays on the Post-Modern.* (Icon Editions.) New York: Harper & Row, Publishers, 1977. Introduction by Irving Sandler. I. *On politics, business, publicity, and art.*

DUBERMAN, MARTIN. *Black Mountain: An Exploration in Community.* New York: E.P. Dutton & Co., 1972. *Controversial history of this vanguard school.*

DUFFUS, R.L. *The American Renaissance.* New York: Alfred A. Knopf, 1928. *Critical discussion of American culture.*

FAULKNER, RAY; ZIEGFELD, EDWIN; and HILL, GEROLD. *Art Today. An Introduction to the Fine and Functional Arts.* New York: Henry Holt and Co., 1941.

FELDMAN, EDMUND BURKE. *Art as Image and Idea.* Englewood Cliffs, N.J.: Prentice-Hall Inc., 1967. I.B. *The great themes of all time in art.*

GARDNER, ALBERT TEN EYCK. *History of Water Color Painting in America.* New York: Reinhold Publishing Co., 1966. I. *Popular survey of watercolor painting from the late eighteenth century to the present time.*

GELDZAHLER, HENRY. *American Painting in the 20th Century.* New York: The Metropolitan Museum of Art, 1965. I.B. *A survey based mainly on the Museum's collection.*

GOODALL, DONALD B. *Partial Bibliography of American Abstract-Expressive Painting, 1943–58.* Los Angeles: University of Southern California, Department of Fine Arts, 1958. *Periodicals and a few books.*

GOODRICH, LLOYD. *Three Centuries of American Art.* New York: Frederick A. Praeger, 1966. I. *Survey book based on a Whitney Museum exhibition.*

____. *The Whitney Studio Club and American Art: 1900–1932.* New York: The Whitney Museum of American Art, 1975. I. *Reviews the Club's history and the founding of the Museum.*

GOODYEAR, FRANK H. Jr. *Contemporary American Realism Since 1960.* Boston: New York Graphic Society, 1981. B. *Exhibition catalogue reviews artists who examine the visual world.*

GOWANS, ALAN. *The Restless Art: A History of Painters and Painting, 1760–1960.* Philadelphia: J.B. Lippincott, 1966. I.B. *History developed by major artists and major works.*

GREGG, FREDERICK JAMES. *For and Against.* New York: Association of American Painters and Sculptors Inc., 1913. *Anthology of commentary on the Armory Show of 1913.*

GRUSKIN, ALAN D. *Painting in the USA.* Garden City, N.Y.: Doubleday and Co., 1946. I. *Survey of American painting in the 1940s.*

GUGGENHEIMER, RICHARD. *Sight and Insight, a Prediction of New Perceptions in Art.* New York: Harper and Brothers, 1945. *Critical discussion.*

HARSHE, ROBERT B. *A Reader's Guide to Modern Art.* San Francisco: The Wahlgreen Co., 1914. *Bibliography.*

HENNING, EDWARD B. *50 Years of Modern Art 1916–1966.* Cleveland: The Cleveland Museum of Art, 1966. I.B. *Extensive survey exhibition.*

HENRI, ADRIAN. *Total Art: Environments, Happenings, and Performance.* New York: Praeger Publishers, 1974. I.B.C.A. *International survey.*

HESS, THOMAS B., and BAKER, ELIZABETH C., eds. *Art and Sexual Politics.* New York: Collier Books, 1973. I. *Essays on women's role in the creative arts.*

HOOPES, DONELSON F. *American Watercolor Painting.* New York. Watson-Guptill Publishers, 1977. I.B. *Biographies. Popular introduction from the nineteenth century to the late twentieth century.*

HUNTER, SAM. *American Art of the 20th Century.* New York: Harry N. Abrams Inc., 1972 (?) I.B. *An Up-to-date survey.*

HUNTER, SAM, ed. *An American Renaissance: Painting and Sculpture Since 1940.* New York: Abbeville Press, 1986. Preface by George Bolge. Foreword by James D. Robinson III. B.I. *A greatly flawed review of the times.*

INGA-PIN, LUCIAN. *Performances: Happenings, Actions, Events, Activities, Installations.* Padova: Mastrogiacomo Editore, 1978. I.B. (Italian text, English supplement.) *Includes artists' statements.*

KARPEL, BERNARD, ed. *Arts in America: A Bibliography.* Washington, D.C.: Smithsonian Institution, 1979. B. 4 vols., indexed. *A massive research resource for most of the visual arts.*

KEAVENEY, SYDNEY STAN. *American Painting: A Guide to Information Sources.* Detroit: Gale Research Co., 1974.

KEPPEL, FREDERICK P., and DUFFUS, R.I. *The Arts in American Life.* New York: McGraw-Hill Book Co., Inc., 1933. *Survey of the arts and their development in America.*

KRAMER, HILTON. *The Age of the Avant-Garde: An Art Chronicle of 1956–1972.* New York: Farrar, Straus and Giroux, 1973. I. *Collected essays.*

KULTERMANN, UDO. *Art and Life.* Translated by John William Gabriel. New York: Praeger Publishers, 1971. I. *Investigations into happenings, events, environments; underground film, television, theater; intermedia, concept art.*

____. *The New Painting.* New York: Frederick A. Praeger Publishers, 1969. I.B.C. *International critical survey of art of the 1960s.*

Kunst der letzten 30 jahre. Vienna, Austria: Museum fur Moderner Kunst, 1979. B.I. *International review with essays by several authors.*

LASSALLE, HELENE. *Art Americain.* Paris: Musee National d'Art Moderne, 1981. (French text.) Preface by Pontus Hulten. B. *American art in this museum's collection; includes art-ists' statements and biographies.*

LIPPARD, LUCY. *955,000.* Vancouver, Canada: Vancouver Art Gallery, 1970. I.D.P. *An informative deck of 4 × 6 inch cards in a brown paper envelope.*

LOZOWICK, LOUIS. *100 Contemporary American Jewish Painters and Sculptors.* New York: YKUF Art Section, 1947. I. *Includes statements by the artists.*

LUCAS, E. LOUISE. *Art books, a basic bibliography on the fine arts.* Greenwich, Conn.: New York Graphic Society, 1968. B.

LUCIE-SMITH, EDWARD. *American Art Now.* New York: William Morrow & Co., Inc., 1985. Index. *A journalistic snapshot of recent art; includes artists' biographies.*

MARTIN, ALVIN. *American Realism: Twentieth-Century Drawings and Watercolors from the Glenn C. Janss Collection.* New York: Harry N. Abrams, Inc., 1986. Introduction by Glenn C. Janss. Foreword by Henry T. Hopkins. B.I. *Realism, mostly since 1960.*

McDARRAH, FRED W. *The Artist's World in Pictures.* New York: E.P. Dutton, 1961. I. *Major pictorial documentation of the art scene in the 1950s.*

McMAHON, A. PHILIP. *The Meaning of Art.* New York: W.W. Norton and Co., 1930. B.

____. *Preface to an American Philosophy of Art.* Chicago: The University of Chicago Press, 1945. B.

MORRIS, LLOYD R. *Incredible New York: 1850–1950.* New York: Random House, 1951. I. *Social history.*

MYERS, BERNARD S. *Modern Art in the Making.* New York: McGraw Hill Book Co., Inc., 1959. I.B. *Historical development of modern art.*

MYERS, BERNARD S., ed. *Encyclopaedia of Painting. Painters and Painting of the World from Prehistoric Times to the Present Day.* New York: Crown Publishers Inc., 1955. I.

MYERS, JOHN BERNARD. *Tracking the Marvelous: A Life in the New York Art World.* New York: Random House, 1983. I. *Autobiography which reveals nearly all.*

NAYLOR, GILLIAN. *The Bauhaus.* New York: Studio Vista/Dutton Picturebacks, 1968. I. *Popular introduction to the Bauhaus program.*

NEUHAUS, EUGENE. *The Appreciation of Art.* Boston: Ginn and Co., 1924. I.

____. *Painters, Pictures, and the People.* San Francisco: Philopolis Press, 1918. I.

New York—Downtown Manhattan: SoHo. Berlin: Akademie der Kunste, 1976. Werner Duttmann. (German and English text.) I. *Documents SoHo history and recent art activities and individuals.*

NORMAN, DOROTHY. *Alfred Stieglitz. Introduction to an American Seer.* New York: Duell, Sloan and Pearce, 1960. I. *Appreciation, with his famous photographs.*

O'DOHERTY, BRIAN. *Object and Idea: An Art Critic's Journal 1961–1967.* New York: Simon and Schuster, 1967. *Collection of published essays.*

OERI, GEORGINE. *Man and His Images.* New York: Viking Press, 1968. I. *A way of seeing art.*

One Hundred Prints by 100 Artists of the Art Students League of New York: 1875–1975. New York: The Art Students League, 1975. Foreword by Judith Goldman. I. *Centennial print exhibition catalogue; biographies.*

One Hundredth Anniversary Exhibition of Paintings and Sculpture by 100 Artists Associated with the Art Students League of New York. New York: The Art Students League, 1975. Foreword by Lawrence Campbell. I. *Exhibition catalogue including short history of the League; biographies and appreciations.*

PACH, WALTER. *Modern Art in America.* New York: C. W. Kraushaar Art Galleries, 1928. I. *Concise discussion of modern art and its development.*

PARK, ESTHER AILEEN. *Mural Painters in America: A Biographical Index.* Pittsburg: Kansas State Teachers College, 1949.

PARKER, R.A. *First Papers of Surrealism.* New York: Coordinating Council of French Relief Societies Inc., 1942. *Documented exhibition catalogue.*

PLAGENS, PETER. *Sunshine Muse: Contemporary Art on the West Coast.* New York: Praeger Publishers, 1974. I.B. *Survey of 20th-century West Coast art, mostly post-World War II.*

Provincetown Painters 1890–1970. Syracuse: Everson Museum of Art, 1977. Foreword by Ronald A. Kuchta. "History of the Provincetown Art Colony," by Dorothy Gees Seckler. I.B.A. *Exhibition catalogue records by means of documents and art the history of this community and its artists.*

PUMA, FERNANDO. *Modern Art Looks Ahead.* New York: The Beechhurst Press, 1947. I. *Popular essays on art.*

REID, B.L. *The Man From New York: John Quinn and His Friends.* New York: Oxford University Press, 1968. I.B. *Biography of the master patron of the early twentieth century.*

RICH, DANIEL CATTON, ed. *Essays and Criticism of Henry McBride.* New York: Athenaeum Publishers, 1975. Prefatory essay by Lincoln Kirstein. I. Index. *The collected writings of this critic.*

RICHARDSON, E.P. *A Short History of Painting in America, the Story of 450 Years.* New York: Thomas Y. Crowell Co., 1963. I. *A basic history of American painting.*

____. *Twentieth Century Painting.* Detroit: Detroit Institute of Arts, 1947, 4th ed. I.B. *Concise essays.*

RICHMAN, ROBERT, ed. *The Arts of*

Mid-Century. New York: Horizon Press, Inc., 1954.

RITTERBUSH, PHILLIP C. *The Art of Organic Forms.* Washington, D.C.: Smithsonian Institution Press, 1969. I.B. *A science, art, and nature concept.*

ROBBINS, DANIEL. *The Neuberger Collection.* Preface by Roy R. Neuberger. Providence: Rhode Island School of Design, 1968. I. *Documented catalogue of a major modern collection.*

ROSE, BARBARA, and KALLIL, SUSIE. *Fresh Paint: The Houston School.* Austin, Texas: Texas Monthly Press, 1985. B.C.I. *History of Houston painting from 1900 to the present includes artists' statements and biographies.*

ROSENBERG, HAROLD. *Artworks and Packages.* New York: Horizon Press, Inc., 1969. I. *Essays, some of which first appeared in the* New Yorker.

____. *The De-definition of Art: Action Art to Pop to Earthworks.* New York: Horizon Press, 1972. I. *Collected essays, mostly from the* New Yorker.

____. *Discovering the Present.* Chicago: The University of Chicago Press, 1973. *Collected essays on art, culture, and politics.*

SAYLOR, OLIVER M. *Revolution in the Arts.* New York: Brentano's, 1930. *Critical essays.*

SCHNIER, JACQUES. *Sculpture in Modern America.* Berkeley: University of California Press, 1948. I.B.

SEWCALL, JOHN IVES. *A History of Western Art.* New York: Holt, Rinehart and Winston, Inc., 1961. I.

SMITH, RALPH C. *A Biographical Index of American Artists.* Baltimore: The Williams and Wilkins Co., 1930. B.

STEBBINS, THEODORE E. Jr., with the assistance of John Caldwell and Carol Troyen. *American Master Drawings and Watercolors.* New York: Harper & Row Publishers, in association with The Drawing Society. 1976. Foreword by David Daniels. I.B. Index. *The only major survey of* *works on paper from the late seventeenth century to 1976.*

SWEENEY, JAMES JOHNSON. *Vision and Image.* New York: Simon and Schuster, 1968. B. *Concise commentary on our present-day culture.*

TASHJIAN, DICKRAN. *William Carlos Williams and the American Scene, 1920–1940.* New York: The Whitney Museum of American Art, 1978. I.B. *Appraisal of Dr. Williams's cultural interests and achievements and association with visual artists, utilizing literary documents and many works from the Whitney collection.*

WALLIS, BRIAN. *Art after Modernism: Rethinking Representation.* New York: The New Museum of Contemporary Art, 1984. Foreword by Marcia Tucker. Introduction by Brian Wallis. B.I. *Poorly printed adventures about socio-political art writing.*

WATSON, FORBES. *American Painting Today.* Washington, D.C.: American Federation of Arts, 1939. I.

Concerned with the period before World War II.

WESCHER, HERTA. *Die Collage.* Cologne: M. DuMont, 1968. I.B. (German text.) *The major history of collage.*

WESTON, NEVILLE. *Kaleidoscope of Modern Art.* London: Geo. C. Harrap & Co. Ltd., 1968. I.B. *Popular introduction to international modern art.*

WICKES, GEORGE. *Americans in Paris: 1903–1939.* Paris Review Editions. Garden City, New York: Doubleday & Co., Inc., 1969. I.B. *A history of Americans in the art world abroad.*

WILMERDING, JOHN. *A History of American Marine Painting.* Salem, Mass.: The Peabody Museum, 1968. I.B. *The major work on American marine painting.*

WOLFE, TOM. *The Painted Word.* New York: Farrar, Strauss & Giroux, 1975. I. *Common opinions on high culture by a cartoonist and journalist.*

YOUNG, A.R., ed. *Art Bibliography.* New York: Teachers College of Columbia University, 1941. *A bibliography for the educator.*